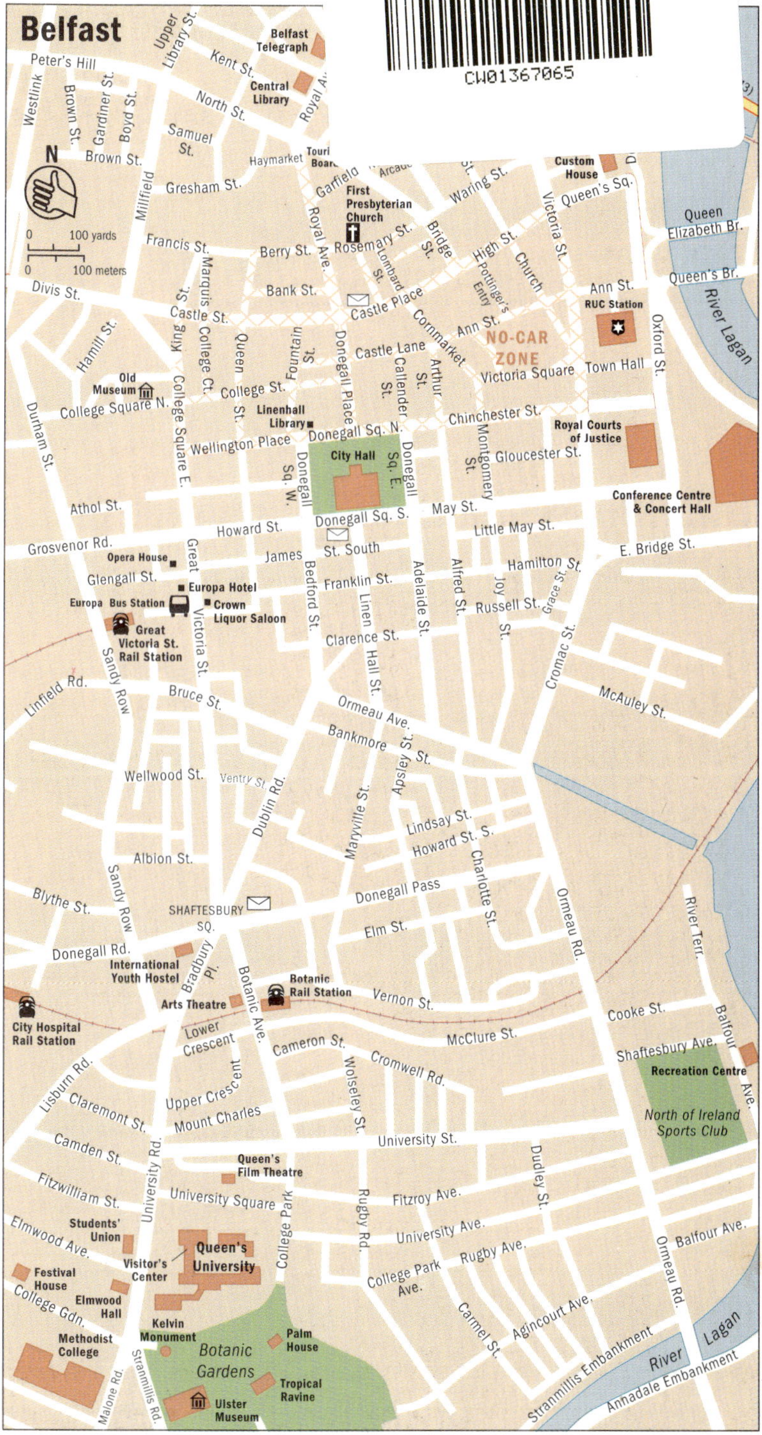
Belfast
N
0 100 yards
0 100 meters
Peter's Hill
Upper Library St.
Kent St.
Belfast Telegraph
Central Library
North St.
Royal Ave.
Westlink
Brown St.
Gardiner St.
Boyd St.
Samuel St.
Brown St.
Haymarket
Millfield
Gresham St.
Garfield
First Presbyterian Church
Waring St.
Custom House
Queen's Sq.
Victoria St.
Queen Elizabeth Br.
Queen's Br.
River Lagan
Francis St.
Berry St.
Rosemary St.
Bridge St.
High St.
Church
Lombard St.
Pottinger's Entry
Ann St.
RUC Station
Oxford St.
Divis St.
Bank St.
Castle Place
Cornmarket
Ann St.
Marquis
King St.
Castle St.
College Ct.
Queen St.
Fountain St.
Donegall Place
Castle Lane
Callender St.
Arthur St.
NO-CAR ZONE
Victoria Square
Town Hall
Hamill St.
Old Museum
College Square N.
College St.
Linenhall Library
College Square E.
Chinchester St.
Royal Courts of Justice
Durham St.
Wellington Place
Donegall Sq. N.
City Hall
Donegall Sq. W.
Donegall Sq. E.
Montgomery St.
Gloucester St.
Athol St.
May St.
Conference Centre & Concert Hall
Howard St.
Donegall Sq. S.
Little May St.
Grosvenor Rd.
Opera House
James St. South
Hamilton St.
E. Bridge St.
Great Victoria St.
Glengall St.
Europa Hotel
Franklin St.
Bedford St.
Linen Hall St.
Adelaide St.
Alfred St.
Joy St.
Grace St.
Europa Bus Station
Crown Liquor Saloon
Russell St.
Great Victoria St. Rail Station
Clarence St.
Cromac St.
Linfield Rd.
Sandy Row
Bruce St.
McAuley St.
Ormeau Ave.
Bankmore St.
Wellwood St.
Ventry St.
Dublin Rd.
Apsley St.
Maryville St.
Lindsay St.
Howard St. S.
Albion St.
Charlotte St.
Ormeau Rd.
Blythe St.
Sandy Row
Donegall Pass
SHAFTESBURY SQ.
Elm St.
River Terr.
Donegall Rd.
International Youth Hostel
Bradbury Pl.
Botanic Ave.
Botanic Rail Station
Vernon St.
City Hospital Rail Station
Arts Theatre
Lower Crescent
Cameron St.
McClure St.
Cooke St.
Balfour Ave.
Shaftesbury Ave.
Recreation Centre
Lisburn Rd.
Cromwell Rd.
Wolseley St.
Upper Crescent
North of Ireland Sports Club
Claremont St.
Mount Charles
University Rd.
University St.
Camden St.
Queen's Film Theatre
Dudley St.
Fitzwilliam St.
University Square
Rugby Rd.
Fitzroy Ave.
College Park
University Ave.
Students' Union
Elmwood Ave.
Queen's University
Visitor's Center
Balfour Ave.
Festival House
Rugby Ave.
College Park Ave.
Ormeau Rd.
College Gdn.
Elmwood Hall
Kelvin Monument
Carmel St.
Agincourt Ave.
Methodist College
Palm House
Botanic Gardens
Tropical Ravine
Stranmillis Embankment
River Lagan
Annadale Embankment
Malone Rd.
Stranmillis Rd.
Ulster Museum

Dublin

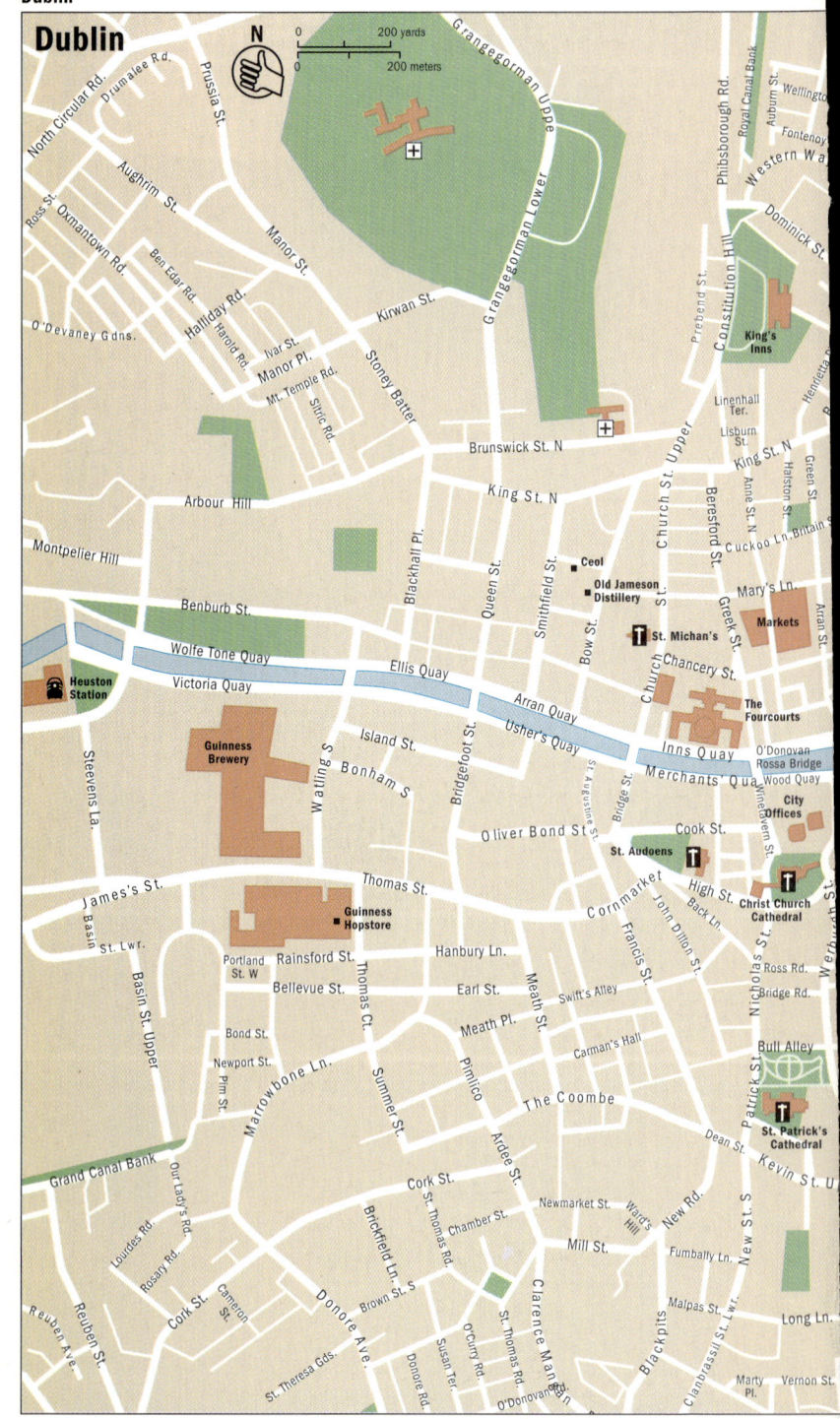

Dublin

Cork and Galway

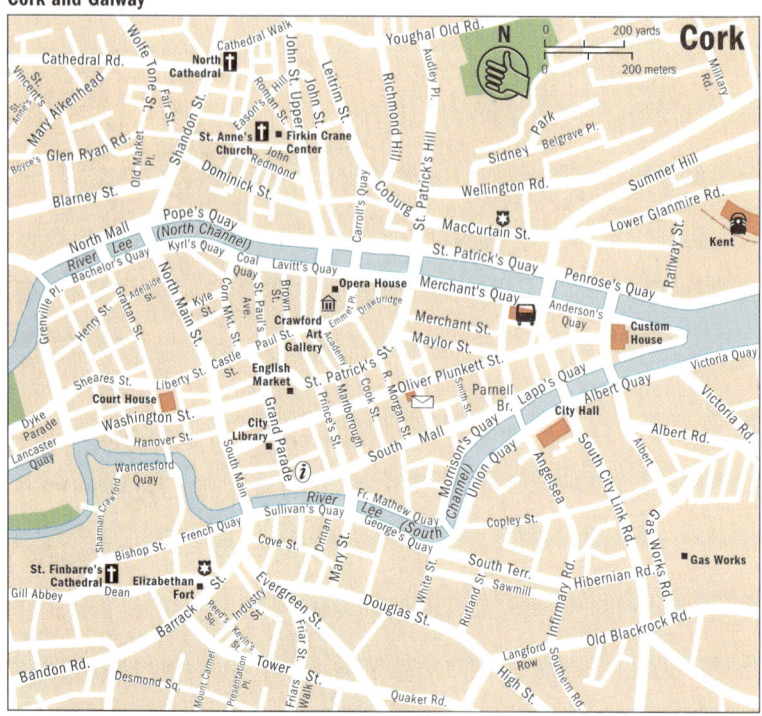

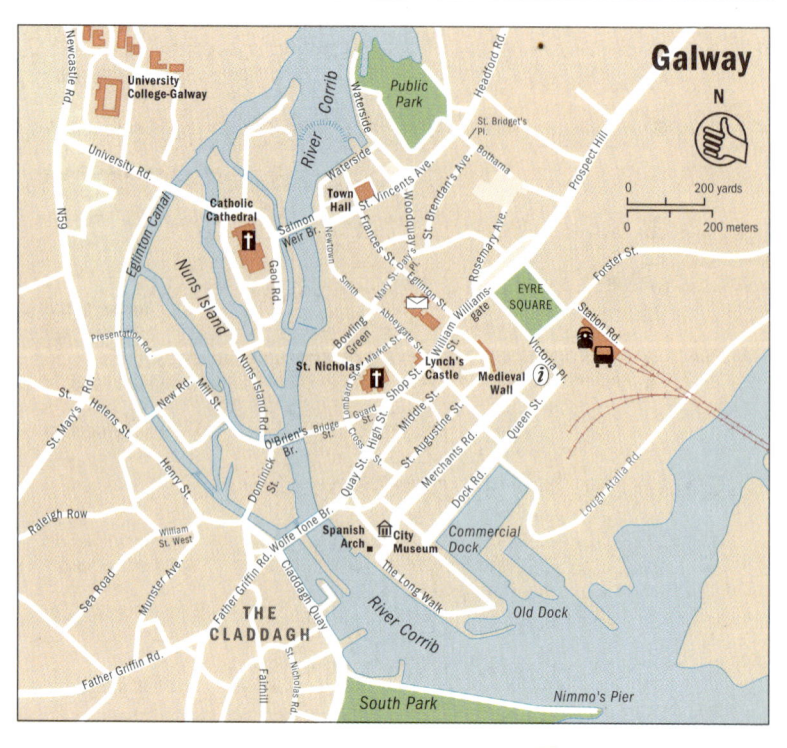

◪ Let's Go writers travel on your budget.

"Guides that penetrate the veneer of the holiday brochures and mine the grit of real life."
—*The Economist*

"The writers seem to have experienced every rooster-packed bus and lunar-surfaced mattress about which they write."
—*The New York Times*

"All the dirt, dirt cheap."
—*People*

◪ Great for independent travelers.

"The guides are aimed not only at young budget travelers but at the independent traveler; a sort of streetwise cookbook for traveling alone."
—*The New York Times*

"Flush with candor and irreverence, chock full of budget travel advice."
—*The Des Moines Register*

"An indispensible resource, *Let's Go*'s practical information can be used by every traveler."
—*The Chattanooga Free Press*

◪ Let's Go is completely revised each year.

"Only *Let's Go* has the zeal to annually update every title on its list."
—*The Boston Globe*

"Unbeatable: good sightseeing advice; up-to-date info on restaurants, hotels, and inns; a commitment to money-saving travel; and a wry style that brightens nearly every page."
—*The Washington Post*

◪ All the important information you need.

"*Let's Go* authors provide a comedic element while still providing concise information and thorough coverage of the country. Anything you need to know about budget traveling is detailed in this book."
—*The Chicago Sun-Times*

"Value-packed, unbeatable, accurate, and comprehensive."
—*Los Angeles Times*

Let's Go Publications

Let's Go: Alaska & the Pacific Northwest 2001
Let's Go: Australia 2001
Let's Go: Austria & Switzerland 2001
Let's Go: Boston 2001 **New Title!**
Let's Go: Britain & Ireland 2001
Let's Go: California 2001
Let's Go: Central America 2001
Let's Go: China 2001
Let's Go: Eastern Europe 2001
Let's Go: Europe 2001
Let's Go: France 2001
Let's Go: Germany 2001
Let's Go: Greece 2001
Let's Go: India & Nepal 2001
Let's Go: Ireland 2001
Let's Go: Israel 2001
Let's Go: Italy 2001
Let's Go: London 2001
Let's Go: Mexico 2001
Let's Go: Middle East 2001
Let's Go: New York City 2001
Let's Go: New Zealand 2001
Let's Go: Paris 2001
Let's Go: Peru, Bolivia & Ecuador 2001 **New Title!**
Let's Go: Rome 2001
Let's Go: San Francisco 2001 **New Title!**
Let's Go: South Africa 2001
Let's Go: Southeast Asia 2001
Let's Go: Spain & Portugal 2001
Let's Go: Turkey 2001
Let's Go: USA 2001
Let's Go: Washington, D.C. 2001
Let's Go: Western Europe 2001 **New Title!**

Let's Go *Map Guides*

Amsterdam
Berlin
Boston
Chicago
Florence
Hong Kong
London
Los Angeles
Madrid
New Orleans
New York City
Paris
Prague
Rome
San Francisco
Seattle
Sydney
Washington, D.C.

Coming Soon: *Dublin* and *Venice*

Let's Go

IRELAND
2001

Maja Groft editor
Derek (Teddy) Wayne associate editor
Daisy Stanton map editor

researcher-writers
Mandy Davis
Sarah C. Haskins
Kalen Ingram
Ian T. McClure

Macmillan

HELPING LET'S GO If you want to share your discoveries, suggestions, or corrections, please drop us a line. We read every piece of correspondence, whether a postcard, a 10-page email, or a coconut. Please note that mail received after May 2001 may be too late for the 2002 book, but will be kept for future editions. **Address mail to:**

> **Let's Go: Ireland**
> **67 Mount Auburn Street**
> **Cambridge, MA 02138**
> **USA**

Visit Let's Go at **http://www.letsgo.com,** or send email to:

> **feedback@letsgo.com**
> **Subject: "Let's Go: Ireland"**

In addition to the invaluable travel advice our readers share with us, many are kind enough to offer their services as researchers or editors. Unfortunately, our charter enables us to employ only currently enrolled Harvard students.

Published in Great Britain 2001 by Macmillan, an imprint of Macmillan Publishers Ltd, 25 Eccleston Place, London, SW1W 9NF, Basingstoke and Oxford.
Associated companies throughout the world
www.macmillan.com

Maps by David Lindroth copyright © 2001, 2000, 1999, 1998, 1997, 1996, 1995, 1994, 1993, 1992, 1991, 1990, 1989, 1988 by St. Martin's Press.

Published in the United States of America by St. Martin's Press.

Let's Go: Ireland. Copyright © 2001 by Let's Go, Inc. All rights reserved. Printed in the United States of America. No part of this book may be used or reproduced in any manner whatsoever without written permission except in the case of brief quotations embodied in critical articles or reviews. For information, address St. Martin's Press, 175 Fifth Avenue, New York, NY 10010, USA.

ISBN: 0-333-90130-4
First edition
10 9 8 7 6 5 4 3 2 1

Let's Go: Ireland is written by Let's Go Publications, 67 Mount Auburn Street, Cambridge, MA 02138, USA.

Let's Go® and the thumb logo are trademarks of Let's Go, Inc.
Printed in the USA on recycled paper with biodegradable soy ink.

ADVERTISING DISCLAIMER All advertisements appearing in Let's Go publications are sold by an independent agency not affiliated with the editorial production of the guides. Advertisers are never given preferential treatment, and the guides are researched, written, and published independent of advertising. Advertisements do not imply endorsement of products or services by Let's Go, and Let's Go does not vouch for the accuracy of information provided in advertisements.
  If you are interested in purchasing advertising space in a Let's Go publication, contact: Let's Go Advertising Sales, 67 Mount Auburn St., Cambridge, MA 02138, USA.

CONTENTS

DISCOVER IRELAND 1
THINGS TO DO 2
SUGGESTED ITINERARIES 5
LIFE AND TIMES 7
HISTORY 7
LITERARY TRADITIONS 22
MUSIC 29
POPULAR MEDIA 32
FOOD AND DRINK 34
2001 HOLIDAYS AND FESTIVALS 37
ESSENTIALS 40
DOCUMENTS AND FORMALITIES 40
MONEY 44
SAFETY AND SECURITY 49
GETTING THERE 55
ONCE THERE 60
ADDITIONAL INFORMATION 75
COUNTY DUBLIN 82
DUBLIN 84
DUBLIN'S SUBURBS 123
Howth 124
Dún Laoghaire And Vicinity 127
EASTERN IRELAND 133
COUNTY WICKLOW 133
WICKLOW COAST 133
Wicklow Town 135
WICKLOW MOUNTAINS 138
Glendalough 138
The Wicklow Way 141
WESTERN WICKLOW 143
COUNTY KILDARE 144
Maynooth 144
Kildare 145
COUNTY MEATH 147
Boyne Valley 148
Brú Na Bóinne: Newgrange, Knowth, and Dowth 148
Hill Of Tara 149
Beyond The Valley Of The Boyne 151
LOUTH, MONAGHAN, AND CAVAN 153
Drogheda 153
Dundalk 156
COOLEY PENINSULA 157
Monaghan 159
WESTMEATH, OFFALY, LAOIS, AND LONGFORD 161
Mullingar 161
Near Mullingar 162
Athlone 163
SOUTHEAST IRELAND 170
KILKENNY AND CARLOW 170
Kilkenny 170
Carlow 177
COUNTY TIPPERARY 178

Clonmel (Cluain Meala) 182
The East Munster Way 184
WEXFORD AND WATERFORD 187
Enniscorthy 188
Wexford 190
Rosslare Harbour 194
THE HOOK PENINSULA 198
WATERFORD HARBOUR 200
Dungarvan 203
Waterford 205
SOUTHWEST IRELAND 211
COUNTY CORK 211
Cork 213
Youghal 227
WEST CORK 228
The Inland Route 229
Coastal Route 230
Kinsale 230
Clonakilty 232
Skibbereen 234
The Mizen Head Peninsula 238
BEARA PENINSULA 240
Bantry 241
Castletownbere 244
Northern Beara Peninsula 246
COUNTY KERRY 247
Kenmare 248
Killarney 250
KILLARNEY NATIONAL PARK 254
RING OF KERRY 257
DINGLE PENINSULA 265
Dingle 265
North Dingle 270
Tralee 271
WESTERN IRELAND 277
LIMERICK AND CLARE 277
LIMERICK CITY 277
LOUGH DERG 284
Ennis 286
CLARE COAST 289
CLIFFS OF MOHER 295
Doolin 296
THE BURREN 298
ARAN ISLANDS 303
Inishmore (Inis Mór) 305
COUNTY GALWAY 312
COUNTY GALWAY 313
GALWAY 313
LOUGH CORRIB 322
Oughterard 322
CONNEMARA 323
Clifden (An Clochán) 324
Clifden To Westport 328
COUNTY MAYO 330
Cong 330
Westport 332
ACHILL ISLAND 336

CONTENTS

Mullet Peninsula 338
Ballina 339
Near Ballina 341

NORTHWEST IRELAND 344
COUNTY SLIGO 344
Sligo 344
ROSCOMMON AND LEITRIM 353
Carrick-on-shannon 353
Boyle 355
COUNTY DONEGAL 357
Donegal Town 360
SLIEVE LEAGUE PENINSULA 364
THE DONEGAL GAELTACHT 372
The Rosses 372
Gweedore (Gaoth Dobhair) 376
Glenveagh National Park 379
FANAD PENINSULA 382
Letterkenny (Leitir Ceannan) 384
INISHOWEN PENINSULA 386
West Inishowen 389
North Inishowen 390
East Inishowen 392

NORTHERN IRELAND 395
ESSENTIALS 395
HISTORY AND POLITICS 397
BELFAST 406

DOWN AND ARMAGH 427
Bangor 427
Ards Peninsula 431
LECALE 434
Downpatrick 435
Newcastle And The Mournes 438
ARMAGH 443
ANTRIM AND DERRY 447
Larne 447
Glens Of Antrim 448
Cushendall 450
Near Cushendall 452
CAUSEWAY COAST 453
Ballycastle 455
Giant's Causeway 459
Portrush 460
DERRY (LONDONDERRY) 465
FERMANAGH 475
Enniskillen 475
TYRONE 478
Omagh 479
Near Omagh 481

LONDON 483

APPENDIX 494

INDEX 501

MAPS

Map Of Chapter Divisions VII
Ireland: Republic Of Ireland And Northern Ireland X-XI
Trails, Mountains, And Parks In Ireland / Historical Sights In Ireland XII-XIII
Dublin Environs 83
Dublin Overview 86-87
Central Dublin 88-89
Dublin Pub Crawl 104
Eastern Ireland 132
East Coast: Near Dublin 134
Midlands And Boglands 140
Southeast Ireland 171
Kilkenny 172
Southeast Coast 187
Wexford 190
Waterford 206
Southwest Ireland 212
Cork 214-215
County Cork And South Kerry 224
County Kerry 248
Killarney Town 251
Killarney National Park 255
Dingle 266

Tralee 272
Western Ireland 278
Limerick 279
County Clare 290
Aran Islands 304
Counties Galway, Mayo, And Sligo 310-311
Galway 312
Northwest Ireland 345
Sligo 346
Lake Districts 350
County Donnegal 356
Inishowen Peninsula 387
Northern Ireland 396
Belfast 408-409
Belfast Pub Crawl 416
County Down And County Armagh 428
Newcastle 439
Armagh 443
The Causeway Coast 454
Portrush 461
Derry 466
Counties Tyrone & Fermanaugh 474
Central London 484-485

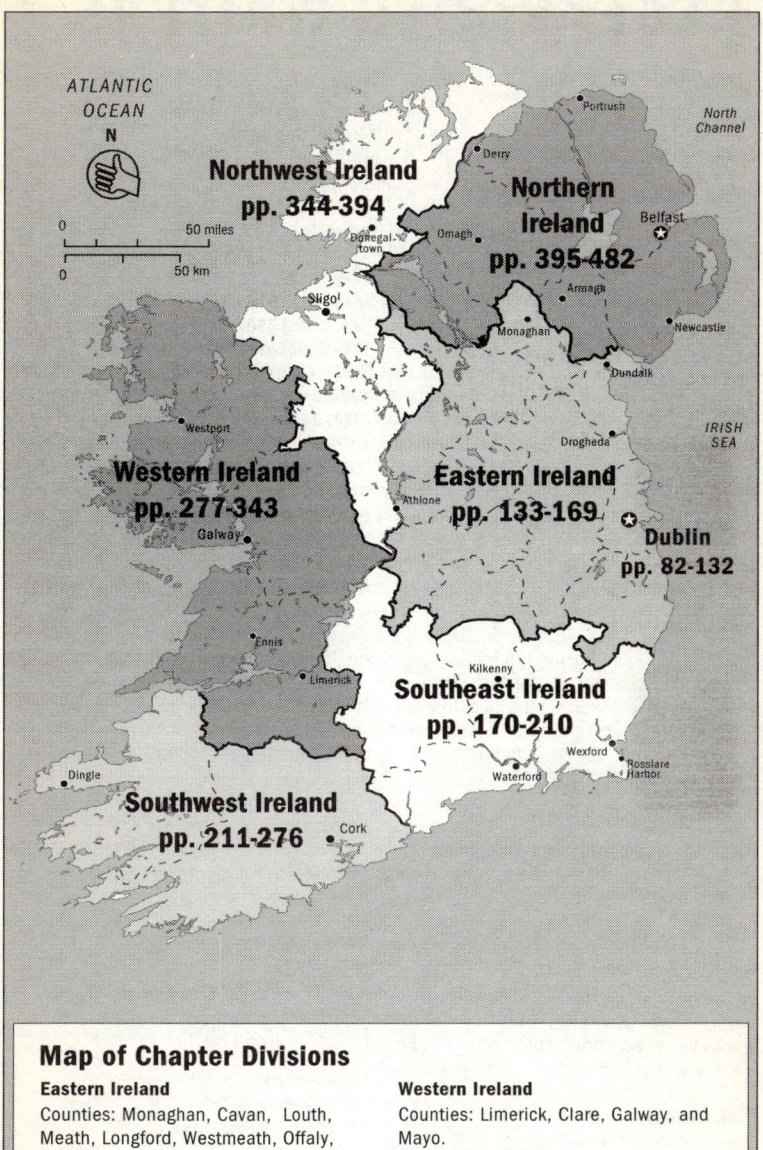

Map of Chapter Divisions

Eastern Ireland
Counties: Monaghan, Cavan, Louth, Meath, Longford, Westmeath, Offaly, Laois, Kildare, and Wicklow.

Southeast Ireland
Counties: Tipperary, Kilkenny, Carlow, Wexford, and Waterford.

Southwest Ireland
Counties: Cork and Kerry.

Western Ireland
Counties: Limerick, Clare, Galway, and Mayo.

Northwest Ireland
Counties: Roscommon, Leitrim, Sligo and Donegal.

Northern Ireland
Counties: Derry, Antrim, Tyrone, Fermanagh, Armagh, and Down.

RESEARCHER-WRITERS

Mandy Davis *Counties Armagh, Cavan, Clare, Fermanagh, Galway, Leitrim, Mayo, Monaghan, Roscommon, Sligo, Tyrone*

Mandy scrolled her findings of Ireland into our book with a sensual pen: butterflies, flowers, sweaters, islands, and finer points of Irish seaweed were all subjects of her loving admiration. A fierce outdoorswoman with a discriminating eye, Mandy hooked fish in rural *loughs*, braved left-handed traffic, and conquered the grisly frontier of contemporary Irish fiction. An eye for beauty, walks, and ways accompanied every batch of calm and collected copy that we received. Many a good meal you enjoy in western Ireland at *Let's Go*'s recommendation is probably due to Mandy's culinary enthusiasm and panache.

Sarah C. Haskins *Counties Carlow, Dublin, Kildare, Kilkenny, Longford, Meath, Waterford, Westmeath, Wexford, Wicklow*

Sarah debunked Viking myths and de-mystified Victorian bunks. Improvising her way through Dublin and beyond, her historical and hysterical copy passed witty judgment on everything from Drogheda to drag shows. She located Ireland's best surfing, and even inverted hemispheres by studying Australia in preparation for the Olympics. Then, to top off her stellar research, she socked it to us. It's no wonder the conjunction of her first and last names spells out "ah-ha"—she certainly made us exclaim this, as both awestruck response and through fits of giggling.

Kalen Ingram *Counties Cork, Kerry, Limerick, Tipperary, Waterford*

Canadian and candid Kalen motored through her itinerary, taking no days off and no prisoners. She applied her field hockey skills to learning the nuances of road bowling as she charmed old locals and young tourists alike. Her Cashel Rock-solid copy, fact-checked to the last detail, was tailored to this sporty gal's preferences for the outdoors and small towns. All she requested from us was a magazine or two for fuel, and she was jetting off, "discovering" out-of-the-way gems such as Sixmilebridge. As cool as she was fast, Kalen tackled everything that came her way, from tourist office skirmishes to sheep family reunions.

Ian T. McClure *Counties Antrim, Derry, Donegal, Down, Louth*

Ian is a young man with a big heart. A veteran of *Let's Go: South Africa 2000*, he agreed to join team Ireland for a last contribution to budget travel before trotting off to medical school to assist the world in still greater measure. Ian traversed the isolated reaches of the northern island, survived the dark night of rural Irish transportation difficulties, and unfailingly sent home copy that enlightened us as might a rosy Irish dawn. He did not shy from delving into tricky politics, and traded beers with any who wished to converse about "The Troubles," the weather, or any subject of the day. On top of his colloquial appeal, Ian was a map mercenary, reworking our cartography from Larne to Slieve League. *Buíochas*, Ian.

John Reuland *Editor, London*

Whitney Bryant London
Daryl Sng London
Tobie Whitman London

ACKNOWLEDGMENTS

TEAM IRELAND THANKS: Our plucky researchers, whom we are proud to call our own. Esti, who managed us like a pro and was never afraid to swallow her pride with a "stet." Daisy, who was fresh on the scene with chic maps to make Magellan jealous. The production team of wizards and tinkers. John for swinging London—freedom *and* responsibility, very cool. Our podmates, who kept the badinage up like Molière. The triumvirate of Kaya, Kate, and Anne, for smoothly captaining the S.S. *Let's Go*. All previous editors and researchers for the book. Everyone to the right. Food. Words. Music.

MAJA THANKS: T. Wayne for his delightful and steadfast presence on the ramparts. H.B. for all the sandwiches *avec salmon*. I thank the prehistoric bears who no longer inhabit Ireland. I thank my beloved parents, the parents of Mike Seid, Carl for being out of the country, mysterious Minna, and many people on Vancouver Island North. *Vive les* Irish and *les* Canadians (and the Danish). I also thank Cadbury and my lovely grandmother, Elna. I wish Pia and Stor Mitra a snappy journey to Ireland soon.

TEDDY THANKS: I would like to thank the Academy. The Academy consists of Maja (25 years, 1 per lifetime, £priceless), with whom I have bled on the tracks numerous times; my family, of whom Greg will get the biggest kick out of seeing his name in print; Nate; Clara; Andrew; and Jesse. Person X for emotional aid Y in troubling times of Z. I have space to scrawl an anti-corporate message right now for thousands to read, but I will later regret my action as a gesture of self-aggrandizement under the guise of altruism. So I'll finish with a joke: What do you call an Irishman who sells lawn chairs? Paddy O'Furniture. (No O'Ffense intended.)

Editor
Maja Groff
Associate Editor
Derek (Teddy) Wayne
Managing Editor
Esti Iturralde
Map Editor
Daisy Stanton

Publishing Director
Kaya Stone
Editor-in-Chief
Kate McCarthy
Production Manager
Melissa Rudolph
Cartography Manager
John Fiore
Editorial Managers
Alice Farmer, Ankur Ghosh,
Aarup Kubal, Anup Kubal
Financial Manager
Bede Sheppard
Low-Season Manager
Melissa Gibson
Marketing & Publicity Managers
Olivia L. Cowley, Esti Iturralde
New Media Manager
Jonathan Dawid
Personnel Manager
Nicholas Grossman
Photo Editor
Dara Cho
Production Associates
Sanjay Mavinkurve, Nicholas Murphy, Rosa Rosalez
Matthew Daniels, Rachel Mason, Dan Williams
Office Coordinators
Sarah Jacoby, Chris Russell

Director of Advertising Sales
Cindy Rodriguez
Associate Sales Executives
Adam Grant, Rebecca Rendell

President
Andrew M. Murphy
General Manager
Robert B. Rombauer
Assistant General Manager
Anne E. Chisholm

The Counties of the Republic and Northern Ireland

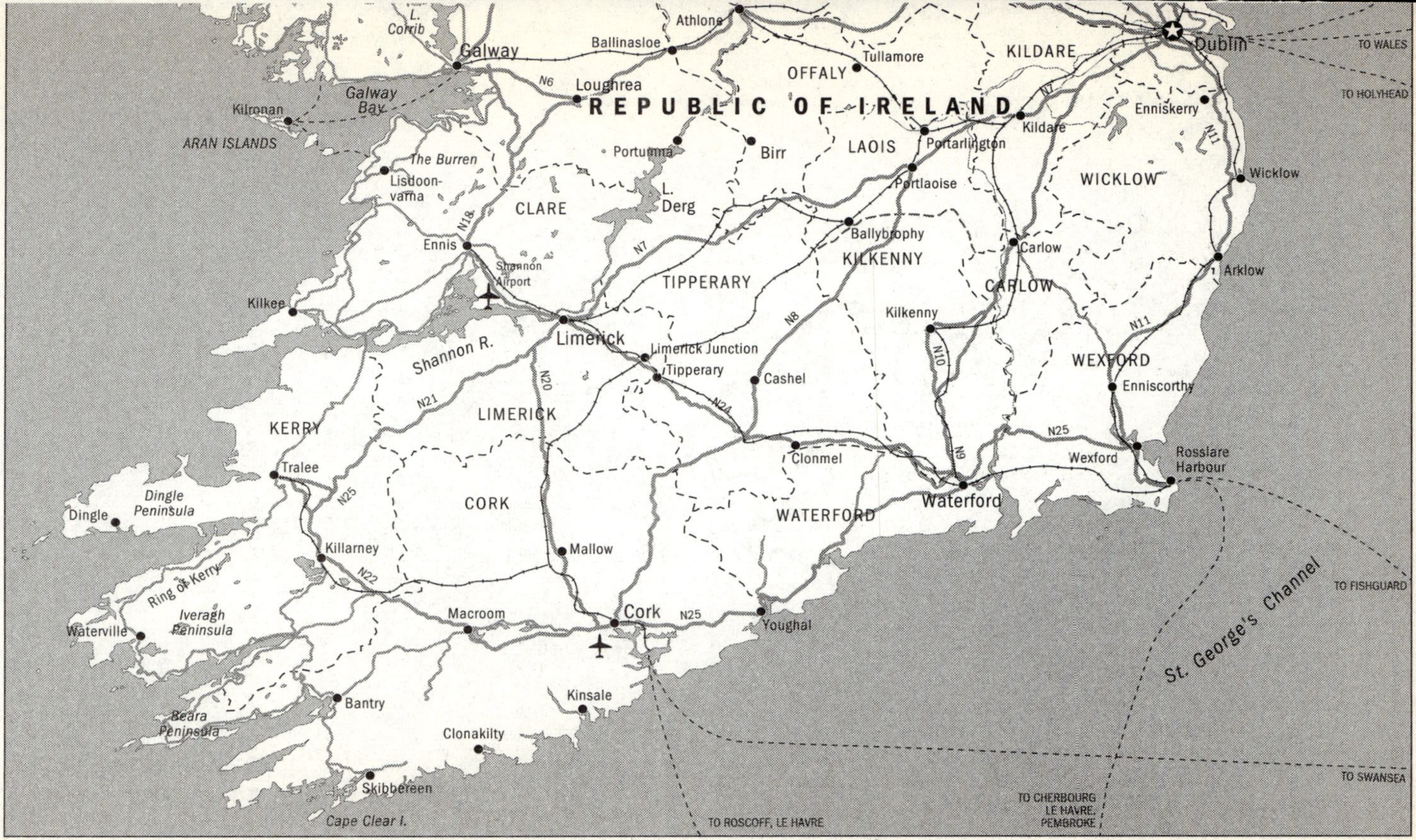
REPUBLIC OF IRELAND
Dublin
TO WALES
TO HOLYHEAD
Athlone
L. Corrib
Galway
Ballinasloe
Tullamore
KILDARE
OFFALY
N6
Loughrea
Galway Bay
Kilronan
ARAN ISLANDS
Enniskerry
N11
N7
Kildare
Portarlington
LAOIS
Portumna
Birr
The Burren
Lisdoonvarna
Portlaoise
WICKLOW
Wicklow
CLARE
L. Derg
N18
Ballybrophy
Ennis
N7
Carlow
Shannon Airport
KILKENNY
Arklow
TIPPERARY
CARLOW
Kilkee
Limerick
Kilkenny
Shannon R.
Limerick Junction
N8
N11
Tipperary
Cashel
WEXFORD
N20
N10
Enniscorthy
N21
N24
KERRY
LIMERICK
N25
Tralee
Clonmel
N9
Wexford
Rosslare Harbour
Dingle Peninsula
Dingle
CORK
N25
Waterford
WATERFORD
Killarney
Mallow
Ring of Kerry
N22
TO FISHGUARD
Iveragh Peninsula
Macroom
Cork
N25
Youghal
Waterville
St. George's Channel
Kinsale
Bantry
Beara Peninsula
Clonakilty
TO SWANSEA
Skibbereen
TO CHERBOURG LE HAVRE, PEMBROKE
Cape Clear I.
TO ROSCOFF, LE HAVRE

Trails, Mountains, and Parks in Ireland

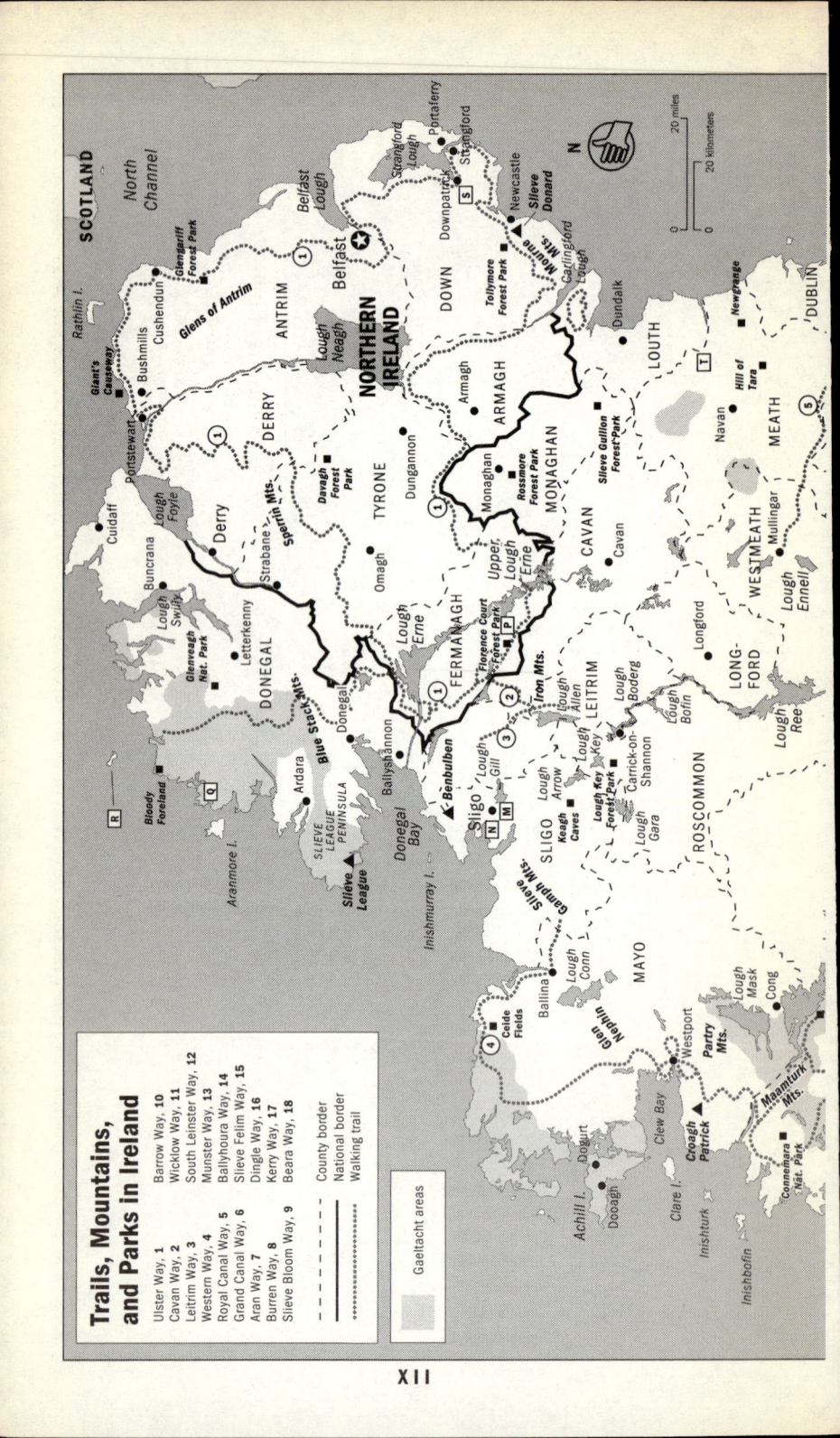

Ulster Way, **1**
Cavan Way, **2**
Leitrim Way, **3**
Western Way, **4**
Royal Canal Way, **5**
Grand Canal Way, **6**
Aran Way, **7**
Burren Way, **8**
Slieve Bloom Way, **9**
Barrow Way, **10**
Wicklow Way, **11**
South Leinster Way, **12**
Munster Way, **13**
Ballyhoura Way, **14**
Slieve Felim Way, **15**
Dingle Way, **16**
Kerry Way, **17**
Beara Way, **18**

– – – County border
–··–··– National border
············ Walking trail

Gaeltacht areas

XII

Historical Sights in Ireland

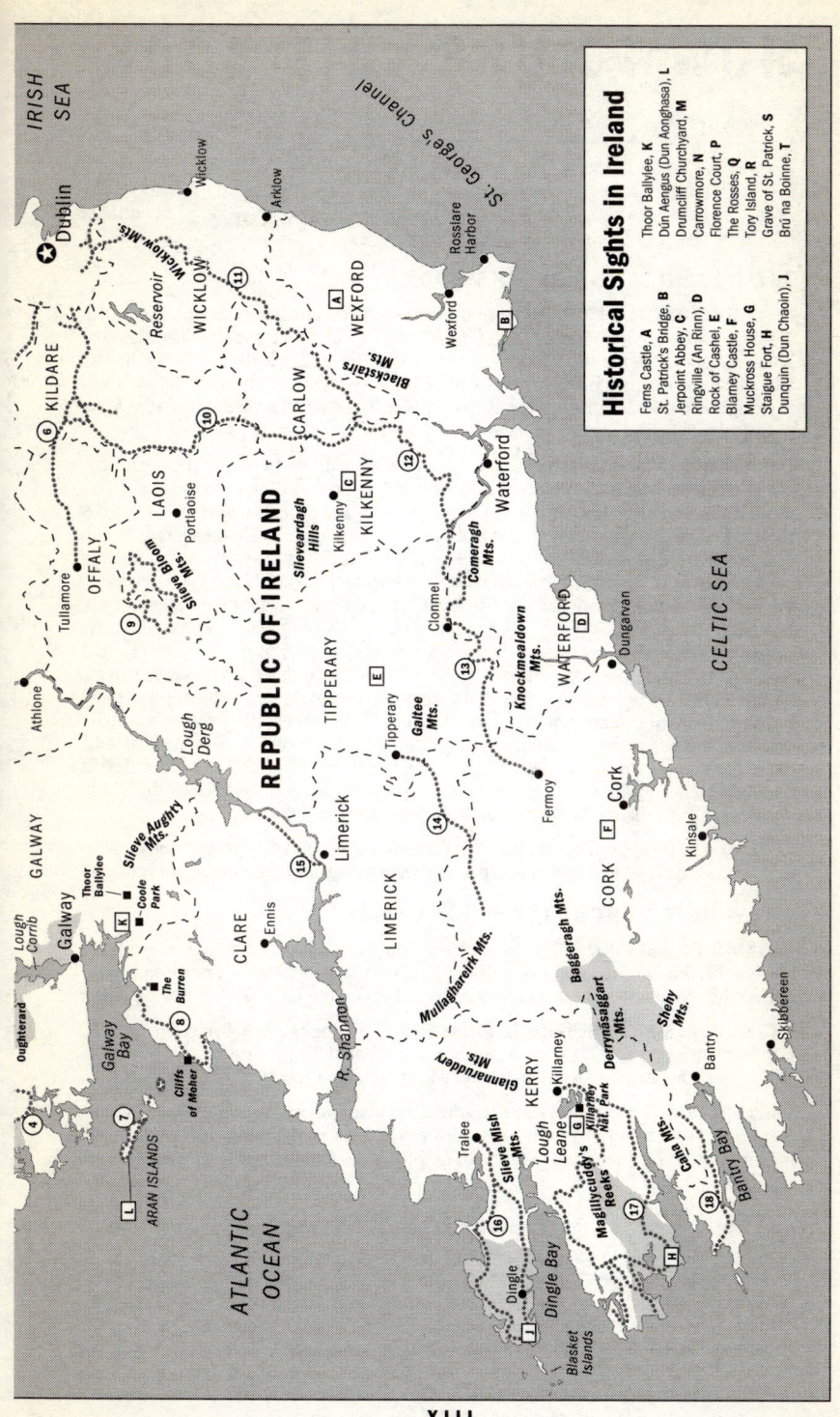

Ferns Castle, **A**
St. Patrick's Bridge, **B**
Jerpoint Abbey, **C**
Ringville (An Rinn), **D**
Rock of Cashel, **E**
Blarney Castle, **F**
Muckross House, **G**
Staigue Fort, **H**
Dunquin (Dun Chaoin), **J**
Thoor Ballylee, **K**
Dún Aengus (Dun Aonghasa), **L**
Drumcliff Churchyard, **M**
Carrowmore, **N**
Florence Court, **P**
The Rosses, **Q**
Toy Island, **R**
Grave of St. Patrick, **S**
Brú na Bóinne, **T**

XIII

HOW TO USE THIS BOOK

Call me Ireland—that is, *Let's Go: Ireland 2001*. Some years ago—never mind how long precisely—having little or no money in my budget traveler's purse, and nothing particular to interest me on shore, I thought I would sail about a little and see the watery part of the world. Whenever I find myself growing grim about the mouth; whenever it is a damp, drizzly November in my soul—then, I account it high time to get to Ireland as soon as I can.

THE ORGANIZATION OF THIS BOOK

INTRODUCTORY MATERIAL. The first chapter, **Discover Ireland,** of this book provides you with an overview of travel in Ireland, including **Suggested Itineraries** that give you an idea of what you shouldn't miss and how long it will take to see it. The **Life and Times** chapter provides you with a general introduction to the tangled history and trad-filled culture of the Emerald Isle. The **Essentials** section outlines the practical information you will need to prepare for and execute your trip.

THE "MEAT". A word on how this tome is organized: We begin with Co. Dublin, then sweep around the country in a clockwise fashion, ending for a stopover section all the way over in London, England. We also list potential **daytrips** or nearby towns, but feel free to connect the dots any way you please. The **black tabs** in the margins will help you navigate between chapters quickly and easily. At the start of each chapter, we provide a list of **Regional Highlights** that should help you prioritize your travels. **Getting There and Getting Around** details transportation by plane, train, bus, ferry, bike, car, and hitchhiking, although *Let's Go* never recommends the last of these (a phrase you will come to know and love). For each major town, a **map** lists accommodations, eateries, pubs, and sights. In these and smaller towns, an **Orientation** section lays out a verbal map of the city and relative locations of key points. **Practical Information** provides hard data on necessities such as tourist offices, financial services, emergency contacts, and Internet access. **Accommodations, Food,** and **Pubs** listings aid you in your search for a bed, bite, or beer. **Sights** and **Entertainment** name the places we recommend you visit, the hiking and biking you tackle, the music you absorb, and the festivals you debauch.

APPENDIX. The appendix contains useful **conversions,** a handy **phrasebook** of Irish and Irish-English words and slang, **political terminology** and, of course, **pubspeak.**

A FEW NOTES ABOUT LET'S GO FORMAT

RANKING ESTABLISHMENTS. In each section (accommodations, food, etc.), we list establishments in order from best to worst. Our absolute favorites are so denoted by the highest honor given out by Let's Go, the Let's Go thumbs-up (☛).

PHONE CODES AND TELEPHONE NUMBERS. The **phone code** for each region, city, or town appears opposite the name of that region, city, or town, and is denoted by the ☎ icon. **Phone numbers** in text are also preceded by the ☎ icon.

GRAYBOXES AND WHITEBOXES. Grayboxes provide an appropriate blend of cultural insight and humorous interjection. **Whiteboxes** provide important practical information, such as warnings (▲) and helpful hints and further resources (♥).

A NOTE TO OUR READERS The information for this book was gathered by *Let's Go* researchers from May through August of 2000. Each listing is based on one researcher's opinion, formed during his or her visit at a particular time. Those traveling at other times may have different experiences since prices, dates, hours, and conditions are always subject to change. You are urged to check the facts presented in this book beforehand to avoid inconvenience and surprises.

DISCOVER IRELAND

To Ireland, I.
—Shakespeare, *Macbeth*.

Literary imaginations have immortalized Ireland's natural scenery since the ancient times of Celtic bards. Travelers who come to Ireland with this poetic imagery in mind won't be disappointed: this largely agricultural and sparsely populated island has experienced little physical change over thousands of centuries. Wind-swept scenery wraps around the coast, and small mountain chains punctuate interior expanses of bogland. Pockets of civilization dot the landscape, ranging in size from one-street villages to small market towns to a handful of cities. Dublin and Belfast have flowered into cosmopolitan urban centers, seeding sophistication into their immediate surroundings. While some fear that the encroachment of international influences means the end of native folkways, the survival of traditional music, dance, storytelling, and pub culture in both rural and urban areas proves otherwise. The Irish language lives on in small, secluded areas known as *gaeltachta*, as well as on road signs, in national publications, and in a growing body of modern literary works. For international visitors, today's Ireland promises an old-world welcome along with the edge of urban counter-cultures.

Although the chapters in *Let's Go: Ireland* do not mirror these divisions, it's useful to know that Ireland is traditionally divided into four provinces: **Leinster,** the east and southeast; **Munster,** the southwest; **Connacht,** the province west of the river Shannon; and **Ulster,** the north. Six of Ulster's nine counties make up Northern Ireland, part of the United Kingdom. Under the 1998 Northern Ireland Peace Agreement, residents of Northern Ireland may choose whether to individually identify as Irish or British, but word choice can still be sticky. "Ireland" can mean the whole island or the Republic of Ireland, depending on who's listening. "Ulster" is a term used almost exclusively by Protestants in Northern Ireland. It's best to refer to "Northern Ireland" or "the North" and "the Republic" or "the South." "Southern Ireland" is not a viable term.

FACTS AND FIGURES

- **Capitals:** Dublin and Belfast.
- **Populations:** 3,619,480 people live in the Republic. 1,642,000 people live in Northern Ireland.
- **Population Distribution:** More than 35% of the population lives within 60 mi. of Dublin.
- **Population Under 25:** 41.2%.
- **Population Under 15:** 23.7%.
- **Land Area:** 70,280 sq. km.
- **Land Use:** Arable land 13%, permanent pastures 68%, forests 5%.
- **Natural Resources:** Zinc, lead, natural gas, barite, copper, gypsum, limestone, dolomite, peat, silver.
- **Daily Caloric Intake:** 3638 calories.
- **Yearly Beer Consumption Per Capita:** 123 liters (5th highest in world).

WHEN TO GO

Traveling during the low or off season (mid-Sept. to May) has its benefits: airfares and accommodations are less expensive, and you won't have to fend off flocks of fellow tourists. The flip side is that many attractions, hostels, bed and breakfasts (B&Bs), and tourist offices close in winter, and in some rural areas of western Ireland, local transportation drops off significantly or shuts down altogether. Winter daylight hours also shut down, as the sun sets at around 5pm.

The infamous rainy Irish weather is subject to frequent changes but relatively constant temperatures. The southeastern coasts are the driest and sunniest, while western Ireland is wetter and cloudier. May and June are the sunniest months, particularly in the south and southeast, and July and August are the warmest. December and January have the worst weather of the year: wet, cold, and cloudy. Take heart and remember that many a cloudy Irish morning has cleared by noon.

Avg. Temp. (lo/hi), Precipitation	January			April			July			October		
	°C	°F	mm	°C	°F	mm	°C	°F	mm	°C	°F	mm
Dublin	2/7	37/46	63	5/11	41/52	48	12/18	54/66	66	7/12	46/55	73
Cork	3/7	38/46	124	4/11	40/52	66	11/18	53/65	68	7/12	46/65	106
Belfast	4/7	40/45	83	6/10	44/51	51	13/17	56/63	79	8/11	47/52	85
London	2/7	36/45	60	5/12	41/55	43	13/22	56/72	45	7/14	46/58	78

THINGS TO DO

Ireland's small area is well-stocked with activities to suit the whims of hikers, bikers, surfers, divers, aesthetes, poets, birdwatchers, musicians, drinkers, and come what may. The following is a brief summary of popular activities, destinations, and cultural phenomena. For more specific regional attractions, see the **Highlights of the Region** section at the beginning of each chapter.

NATURAL WONDERS AND WANDERS

The west coast is spread with a gorgeous and dense concentration of natural wonders, including the limestone moonscape of **The Burren** (p. 298) and the **Cliffs of Moher** (p. 295), which soar 700 ft. above the sea. The tranquil, gorgeous **Beara Peninsula** (p. 240) and its 125 mi. **Beara Way** don't know the meaning of tour buses. **Killarney National Park** (p. 254) is a hiker's, biker's, and climber's paradise, and makes a good gateway to the heavily touristed, but still beautiful, **Ring of Kerry** (p. 257). In remote Co. Donegal, the **Slieve League** mountain-pass is fronted by the highest sea cliffs in Europe. Donegal's **Glenveagh National Park** (p. 379) contains salt-and-peppered **Mount Errigal**, close to the bewitching **Poison Glen** (p. 376). The bizarre honeycomb columns of **Giant's Causeway** (p. 459) spill out from the Antrim Coast, a long strip of rocky crags and white beaches. Several developed paths allow hikers to spend any number of days exploring Ireland's various mountain chains: the **Wicklow Way** passes through the **Wicklow Mountains** (p. 138) in Dublin's backyard, the **Ulster Way** treks through the **Sperrin Mountains** (p. 481), and the **Dingle Way** (p. 265) courses along the bumps of one of the island's prettiest stretches.

STONES, BONES, AND REGAL THRONES

The ancient peoples of Ireland took to rocks and underground chambers, resulting in structures that have withstood millennia. In Co. Meath, the 5000-year-old passage-grave at **Newgrange** (p. 144) is an architectural feat that stumps present-day engineers. The nearby **Hill of Tara** (p. 149) has been the symbolic throne of sorts for Irish bigwigs from pre-Christian rulers to St. Patrick to 19th-century nationalists. On the west coast, the **Poulnebrane Dolmen** (p. 299) marks a group grave site with a 25-ton capstone atop two standing rocks. On the limestone **Rock of Cashel** (p. 179), a mish-mash of early Christian structures pop up across the skyline, including a medieval cathedral and a Celtic cross. **Glendalough** (p. 138) is the picturesque home of St. Kevin's 6th-century monastery and 100 ft. round tower.

LITERARY LANDMARKS

Ireland's natural beauty and urban grime have inspired many centuries of superb literary output. Dublin (p. 84) has endured the caustic wit of **Jonathan Swift, Oscar Wilde, George Bernard Shaw, James Joyce, Sean O'Casey, Samuel Beckett, Brendan**

Behan, Flann O'Brien, and **Roddy Doyle,** to name but a few. **W.B. Yeats** scattered his poetic settings throughout the island, but he chose Co. Sligo for his grave site (p. 352). **John Millington Synge** found literary greatness by depicting the domestic squabbles of Aran Islanders (p. 303). **Seamus Heaney** has compared the bogland's fossilized remains of pre-Christian sacrifices to The Troubles of present-day Northern Ireland. In Belfast (p. 406), **Brian Moore** and **Paul Muldoon** illustrate the everyday life of individuals in a city that receives world recognition only for its extraordinary events. **Brian Friel's** plays bring to life the wilds and folkways of Co. Donegal (p. 357). Limerick (p. 277) has had a successful face-lift since the poverty-stricken days described by **Frank McCourt** in his childhood memoirs. Ireland's ancient **mythology** is the most pervasive of all its literary forms; virtually every nook and cranny on the island is accountable to fairies, giants, gods, and even the occasional leprechaun.

ISLANDS

Ireland's island geography has helped it preserve unique traditional customs that separate it from the rest of Europe; its satellite islands play the same role in relation to the mainland. The people of the **Aran Islands** (p. 303) still live much like the rest of Ireland did at the turn of the century: they speak Irish, eke out their living fishing in *curraghs*, ancient cloth covered rowboats, and have numerous quirky superstitions, including one that prevents fishermen from learning to swim. Off the Dingle Peninsula, the now depopulated **Blasket Islands** (p. 269) were once the home of several impoverished memoirists who prophesied "after us there will be no more." Today the island provides little talk but great walks around exquisite natural scenery and haunting village ruins. **Tory Island's** (p. 378) counter-culture is undoubtedly Ireland's strangest: this island of 160 individuals elects its own king, sponsors its own school of painters, remembers having descended from pirates and *poitín* smugglers, and refers to the mainland as "the country."

BREWERIES AND DISTILLERIES

The Irish claim that stout is good for you, and whiskey is the "water of life"; it follows that the island's breweries and distilleries are its holy wells. The **Guinness Hopstore** (p. 114) provides only a handful of clues about how to concoct the dark stuff. **Smithwicks** stores its blonder brew in a former monastery in Kilkenny (p. 170). Dublin's **Jameson Distillery** (p. 117) makes a slightly sweeter version of whiskey than that stored in barrels at **Bushmills Distillery** (p. 460) in Co. Antrim.

FESTIVALS: HE-GOATS AND ROSES

Ireland celebrates its warmer months with festivals galore—virtually every small village finds reason to gather its sheep for show, pull pints, and tune its fiddles. See **Festivals and Holidays,** p. 37, for a complete 2001 festivals listing. In mid-July, the **Galway Arts Festival** (p. 322) hosts theater, trad, rock, and film during two weeks of vigorous revelry, second in fun only to the island-wide frenzy of **St. Patrick's Day** (March 17th). Mid-May brings Armagh's **Apple Blossom Festival** (p. 446). James Joyce enthusiasts take part in an 18-hour ramble through Dublin's streets every year on June 16, **Bloomsday** (p. 120). Early August brings all types of musicians, artists, and merrymakers to Waterford's **Spraoi** festival (p. 210). He-goats compete for the title of alpha-male in Killorglin's **Puck Fair** (p. 258) in mid-August. The **Connemara Pony Show** (p. 324) brings its colts to Clifden in late August. Around the same time, every set in Ireland tunes in to the nationally televised **Rose of Tralee Festival and Pageant** (p. 271). Cape Clear Island spins yarns at the **International Storytelling Festival** (p. 237), also in late August. Many return home happy from the **Lisdoonvarna Matchmaking Festival** (p. 298) in early September. Fat ladies sing at the **Wexford Festival Opera** (p. 193) in late October, while skinny trombones wail at the **Guinness Cork Jazz Festival** (p. 223). Ireland's largest arts festival, the **Belfast Festival at Queen's** (p. 426), is a city-wide three-week winter pot-luck of cultural treats.

4 ■ THINGS TO DO

🔖 LET'S GO PICKS

BEST PUBS: The **Stag's Head**, Dublin, serves good pints and better food to a mixed crowd in elegant Victorian surroundings (p. 103). In Belfast, everyone who's anyone heads to **Lavery's Gin Palace** (p. 417). **An Droichead Beag** keeps Dingle tipsy and toe-tapping with constant trad sessions (p. 267).

BEST MUSIC: Dublin's young virtuosos play at **Cobblestone's**, in Smithfield (p. 119). In Westport, **Matt Molloy's** has Ireland's musicians stopping by at all hours (p. 334). **McGrory's**, in Culdaff, boasts big name trad groups as well as local songsters (p. 391). **Dolan's**, in Limerick, plays for a raucous crowd (p. 282). **Roisín Dubh**, in Galway, promotes top-rung rock and rising new artists (p. 318).

BEST VIEWS: Admire as Yeats did the mile-high cliff views from **Drumcliff** towards **Ben Bulben** (p. 352). Hike to **Pedlars Lake**, Connor Pass, for the waterfall and views stretching across the Dingle Peninsula (p. 270). The sheer **Bunglass** cliffs near the Slieve League terrify and tantalize (p. 366).

BEST ODDBALL COLLECTIONS: **The Irish National Stud**, Kildare, is an unforgettable equine experience (p. 146). The bizarre little collection in Sneem's **sculpture park** includes an homage to pro-wrestling (p. 264). **Fox's Lane Folk Museum** in Youghal has razor-sharp exhibits on shaving and sewing (p. 228). The **Ceim Hill Museum** in Union Hall has dinosaur dung and revolutionary rifles (p. 234).

BEST WATER-SPORTS: Carve waves at the **Tramore Bay Surf Center**, or slide down them in the nearby water park (p. 203). Snorkelers see U-boat and galleon wrecks, or surface for waterskiing and boating in **Baltimore** (p. 236). **Lahinch** has all the beach fare you can handle (p. 294).

BEST LEGENDARY LANDSCAPES: The spurge is poisonous, so gaze but don't graze at the **Poison Glen**, Donegal (p. 376). Take in the lake views at **Glendalough**, which St. Kevin preferred to women (p. 138). **Navan Fort**, near Armagh, is home to twins, men with childbirth pangs, and a fascinating archaeological site (p. 446).

BEST PLACES TO STAY: The **Shiplake Mountain Hostel**, Dunmanway, is a culinary treat (p. 229). **Maria's Schoolhouse**, Union Hall, has the best and the brightest of everything (p. 233). Relax at cushy, beachfront **Downhill Hostel** (p. 464). Live like the Earl of Cork at **Ballintaggart Hostel** in Dingle, but watch out for his wife (p. 266). Step through the cultured doors of **The Green Gate** B&B in Ardara (p. 369). Get spoiled in Georgian splendor at **The Saddler's House** in Derry (p. 469). Abandon technology and relax inside gas-lamp-lit **Flax Mill Hostel** in the Sperrin Mountains (p. 482).

BEST LITERARY HIDEOUTS: Escape the *fatwa* in the safety of Howth's **lighthouse**, just as Salman Rushdie did (p. 125). James Joyce holed up in the **Martello tower** in Sandycove that now bears his name, then used it in *Ulysses* (p. 128). Claim the throne of literary genius at **Synge's Chair** on Inishmaan in the Aran Islands (p. 308). Dubliners pause poetically beside Patrick Kavanagh's memorial bench by the **Grand Canal** (p. 112).

BEST CRITTERS: ★ Knocknarea's **bilingual sheep** win for the fourth year in a row (p. 351). The Fota Island **lemurs** follow behind (p. 227), as does the one and only **king's cow** of Tory Island (p. 378). See what 19th-century house cats looked like in Dublin's **Natural History Museum** (p. 111). And who could resist the ice cream-producing **goats** of Cape Clear Island (p. 238)?

SUGGESTED ITINERARIES

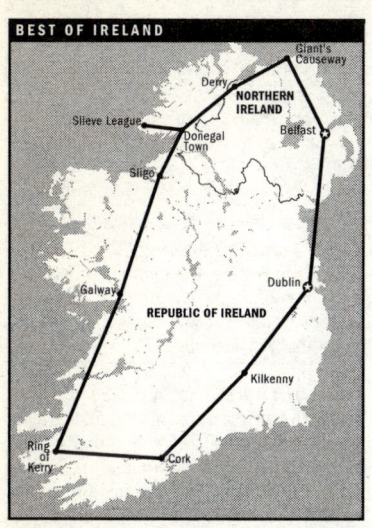

THE BEST OF IRELAND (3½ WEEKS) Land in **Dublin** (p. 84) and spend several days exploring this thousand-year-old city that's a bastion of literary history and, these days, the stomping-ground of international hipsters. Take the train up to **Belfast** (p. 406). Belfast's complex history is spectacularly illustrated in the murals that decorate its sectarian neighborhoods. Catch the bus to **Giant's Causeway** (p. 459), a strange formation of octagonal rocks that some call the earth's eighth natural wonder. Before you head back into the Republic, stop in at **Derry** (p. 465). A city that wears its strife-ridden past on its sleeve, Derry provides a hopeful forecast for the possibility of reconciliation among Northern communities. Ride the bus to **Donegal Town** (p. 360), spend a night at the pub, and head out the next morning to climb **Slieve League** (p. 364) and view the tallest sea-cliffs in Europe. Use **Sligo** (p. 344), once the beloved home of W.B. Yeats, as a nighttime hub and daytrip to **Drumcliff** and majestic **Ben Bulben** (p. 352). From there, head to **Galway** (p. 313), an artsy student town that draws the best musicians on the island to its pubs. Catch up on sleep on the ride to the **Ring of Kerry** (p. 257). This peninsula contains picture-postcard villages and **Killarney National Park** (p. 254), an area with exquisite mountains, lakes, and wildlife. Return to civilization in the relaxed city of **Cork** (p. 213). On your way back to Dublin, take a detour to medieval **Kilkenny** (p. 170), where a former monastery is now the Smithwick's brewery, Ireland's oldest.

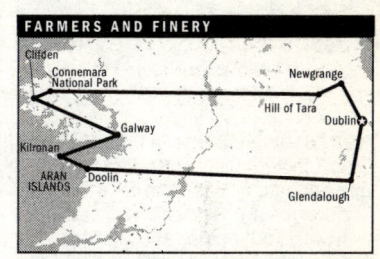

IRELAND'S FARMERS AND FINERY (3 WEEKS) Get a taste of both urban and rural Ireland. Arrive in **Dublin** (p. 84), hit the National museums by day, spend the evening on a literary pub crawl, and finish off the night in Temple Bar, one of the trendiest spots in Europe. From Dublin, take a daytrip to **Newgrange** (p. 148), a neolithic burial site with some dandy engineering behind it; nearby **Hill of Tara** (p. 149) was the seat of Irish rulers from pre-Christian times to just several hundred years ago. Go cross-country to **Connemara National Park** (p. 328). Connemara is an Irish-speaking peninsula with **Clifden** (p. 324) as its accommodating capital. Wind along Connemara's breathtaking coastal road to **Galway** (p. 313). This friendly city plays spokesperson for rural Ireland's traditional music and crafts, entertaining thousands of international visitors in its small pedestrianized streets. Take the boat from Galway to the **Aran Islands** (p. 303) and check out ancient ring forts and recently knit Aran sweaters. Return via **Doolin** (p. 296). This superbly musical village sits beside the **Burren** (p. 298), a rocky bed of ancient fossils and unique vegetation. South of Doolin, waves smash pathetically against the looming **Cliffs of Moher** (p. 295). Return to Dublin via the **Wicklow Mountains** (p. 138). The Wicklow Way offers several days of hiking through "The Garden of Ireland."

6 ■ SUGGESTED ITINERARIES

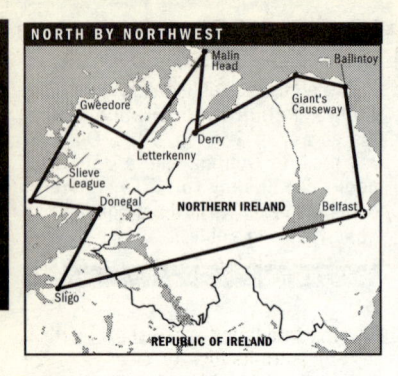

NORTH BY NORTHWEST (3 WEEKS)
Step off the plane in **Belfast** (p. 406) and hop into a Black Cab for a fascinating tour of the Golden Mile, sectarian murals, and the peace wall of this famous but little understood city. Take the Antrim Coaster bus north along the waterfront past the glorious **Glens of Antrim** (p. 448). Farther along the coast, Ballintoy village lies beside the **Carrick-a-rede Rope Bridge** (p. 458), a fishermen's construction that provides thrills for landlubbers. The volcanic spillage of **Giant's Causeway** (p. 459) is the stuff of Irish legend and most any tour of the North. From there, head to **Derry** (p. 465), a medieval city that competes with Dublin for historic importance. It's just a hop and a skip across the border to Co. Donegal, the most remote and untouched area on the island. Head up the Inishowen Peninsula to reach **Malin Head** (p. 391), the northernmost point on the island. Back inland, **Letterkenny** (p. 384) serves as a transportation hub to the rest of the county. To the west lies the mountainous **Glenveagh National Park** (p. 379) and the Irish-speaking area of **Gweedore** (p. 376), a source of brilliant Irish traditional music. Continue on to the **Slieve League Peninsula** (p. 364), where soaring sea cliffs are a bus ride away from the conveniences of **Donegal Town** (p. 360). Before heading back to Belfast, tour Yeats Country around **Sligo** (p. 344).

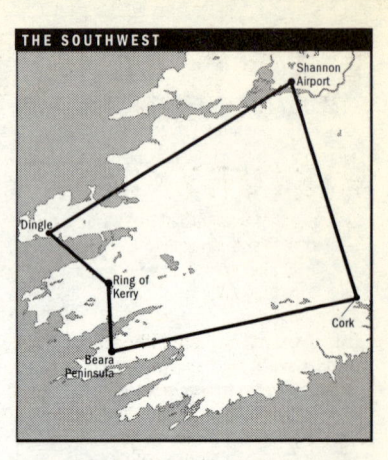

THE SOUTHWEST (2 WEEKS) Land at **Shannon Airport,** stay overnight in **Sixmilebridge** (p. 285), and make your way to the **Dingle Peninsula** (p. 265), where mountains, beaches, and Irish-speakers abound. Make sure to hit the isolated *gaeltacht* on the **Blasket Islands** (p. 269). Next, circle the **Ring of Kerry** (p. 257), southeast of Dingle. Home to magnificent **Killarney National Park** (p. 254), this highly touristed peninsula provides access to the mostly bypassed **Valentia Island** (p. 260) and **Skellig Rocks** (p. 261). Don't miss a third finger of land—the **Beara Peninsula** (p. 240), the most remote and, arguably, most splendid of the three. Stop in to **Cork City** (p. 213) on the way back to the airport to reacclimatize to a busier pace of life and enjoy a final pint.

LIFE AND TIMES

HISTORY

Books about Ireland that begin with its history have a tendency to remain unread. The misunderstandings are so many.
—attributed to Frank O'Connor (1903-1966), writer and IRA fighter in the Irish Civil War.

Travel on this ancient Hibernian island with its overwhelming sense of past will be more rewarding for those who take some time to learn its history. *Let's Go* here provides you with a taste of the complex and controversial historic web that has woven the landscape, intellectual and concrete, of modern Ireland. Your travels on the Emerald Isle may begin to feel like one great and confounding jigsaw puzzle that is—in fact—none other than Man's eternal effort to understand his past. And while this quest shouldn't distract one from seizing the Guinness of the day, we at *Let's Go* have a bit of advice: don't fight it, read on… embrace history.

ANCIENT IRELAND (TO 350 AD)

What little knowledge historians have of ancient Irish culture they have ascertained from the fragile and spotty remains of its stone structures, landscaping, and metalware. Ireland's first settlers came from Britain in about 7000 BC. These Neolithic mound-builders founded an agrarian civilization. They left behind various structures that may be identified today on the Irish landscape. **Dolmens**, arrangements of enormous stones to create table-like forms, were probably created as shrines (see **Poulnabrane Dolmen**, p. 300). **Passage graves** are ornamented, underground stone hallways and chambers containing corpses and cinerary urns (see **Newgrange**, p. 148). **Stone circles** are rings of pint-sized gravestones most likely marking spots of religious importance, including passage graves.

Bronze blazed into Ireland circa 2000 BC; over the next 700 years, the agrarian society restructured itself to form a warrior aristocracy. In the first two centuries of the **Bronze Age** (900-700 BC), known as the Irish Golden Age, Irish culture flowered, due in part to the central position held by warrior nobles in Atlantic trade routes between Gibraltar and Sweden. During this period, the past era's stone structures evolved to create new types: **ring forts** (see **Dún Aengus**, p. 307), which are protective walls that circled encampments and villages; **souterrains**, or underground hideouts for storing loot and escaping from marauders; and **clochans**, which are mortarless beehive-shaped stone huts. Remains of these structures are scattered across Ireland and many of its islands.

Although there is much speculation that some groups arrived as early as 2000 BC, the **Celts** began their main migration to Ireland from central Europe around 600 BC and kept coming for the next 600 years. Probably initially named by the Greeks as *Keltoi* or "hidden people" (because of their reluctance to write down their great stores of scholarship and knowledge), the Celts settled Ireland as the western-most extremity of a pan-European migration that stretched east to

circa 7000 BC
Ireland's first settlers—neolithic agrarian mound-builders—arrive from Britain. Ireland is one of the last areas in Europe to be colonized by human populations.

circa 3000 BC
Mound-builders construct first Megalithic tombs. Hill of Tara, known in both myth and history as the traditional seat of the High Kings of Ireland, is established.

2000 BC-1300 BC
Bronze age comes to Ireland: society is restructured into a warrior aristocracy.

900 BC-700 BC
Ancient Irish Golden Age.

700 BC- AD 0
The Celts migrate from central Europe.

AD 254-277
The Uliad Kingdom enters decline.

circa AD 379
More southern (Co. Meath) Uí Néill clan gains prominence.

AD 350
The first Christians arrive in Ireland.

AD 432
Traditional date of St. Patrick's arrival in Ireland.

Asia Minor. The Romans were too busy conquering Germanic tribes on the continent and in England to ever make it to Ireland. The Celts prospered on the peaceful isle, speaking Old Irish, a hybrid tongue comprised of Celtic and indigenous pre-Celtic languages, and living in small farming communities organized under regional chieftains. In the new power structure, chieftains ruled over territories called *tuath*, while provincial kings ruled over several *tuatha*. The **Uliad of Ulster**, a northern kingdom of chariot warriors and the famous chieftains, dominated the La Tène culture from their capital near Armagh (Navan, near Armagh, p. 446). These kings organized raids on Britain, established settlements in Scotland and Wales, and inspired the mythic heroism prominent in the *Tain* and other Irish epics (see **Legends and Folktales,** p. 23).

EARLY CHRISTIANS AND VIKINGS (350-1200)

Ireland was Christianized in a piecemeal fashion by a series of hopeful missionaries, beginning most famously with **St. Patrick** in the 5th century. According to legend, St. Patrick was born in Scotland and kidnapped as a boy into Irish slavery, from which he escaped to return home. He later returned to Ireland at the command of a prophetic vision, but without the church's sanction, most likely landing in southeast Co. Down (see **Saul,** p. 437) and proselytizing to the northwestern parts of the island.

Missionaries and monks entering Ireland after the 5th century brought a new culture along with them. They recorded what they found in Latin, including a description of a system of writing already present on the island. They found this script on **ogham stones,** large obelisks engraved with a non-Latin script of dots and slashes that marked property. These monuments recorded the name of a man and his father, and are still present in the Burren (see p. 298), at the Hill of Tara (see p. 149), and at Bruna Boinne in Co. Meath (see p. 148). Missionaries also introduced a new architectural style to Ireland that included the Viking-inspired **round tower.** These towers were built as fortifications against invaders; their sturdy form survives by the dozens today. A few now charge admission, but most are just sitting in fields and forests, in various states of disrepair. **High crosses,** or Celtic crosses, are a hybridization of Christian and Celtic aesthetics: their form combined the cross with a circle to win the devotion of the native sun-worshipping pagans. These stone crucifixes can be large enough to dwarf a person and have elaborate carvings on their sides, sometimes illustrating Bible stories or legends of saints.

As barbarians overran the continent, safety-seeking monks began arriving in Ireland in mass numbers. The enormous **monastic cities** of the 6th to 8th centuries earned Ireland its reputation as the "land of saints and scholars." Within their bases in Armagh (see p. 446), Glendalough (see p. 138), Derry (see p. 465), Kells (see p. 151), Clonmacnoise (see p. 165), and elsewhere, the monastics of the Early Irish Church recorded the old epics, wrote long religious and legal poems in Old Irish and Latin, and illuminated gospels. The 7th-century **Book of Durrow,** the earliest surviving illuminated manuscript, and the early 9th-century **Book of Kells,** are now exhibited at Trinity College (see

p. 109). Irish missionaries converted (and reconverted) much of Europe to Christianity, although the Early Irish Church remained decidedly independent of Rome. Instead, monastic cities allied themselves with up-and-coming chieftains; Armagh, an important religious center, owed its prominence in part to the **Uí Néill** (O'Neill) clan, whose jurisdiction gradually spread from Meath to central Ulster.

The golden age of Irish scholasticism was interrupted by Viking invasions in the 9th and 10th centuries. Their raidings were most frequent along the southern coast, where they founded permanent settlements at Limerick, Waterford, and Dublin. They built Ireland's first castles, allied themselves with the equally fierce chieftains, and left the southeast littered with Viking-derived place names.

In the first decade of the new millennium, strife broke out among the chieftains: High King **Brian Boru** and his warlike **Dal Cais** clan of Clare challenged the Uí Néill clan for control of Ireland with the capture of Armagh in 1002. In the following years, the clans of Ireland fought ferociously among themselves. The Dal Cais won a heroic victory against the Vikings in the epic **Battle of Clontarf**, fought near Dublin in 1014, in which Brian Boru was lost. Ireland was then divided between chieftains **Rory O'Connor** and **Dermot MacMurrough**, who continued fighting for the crown of High King. Dermot made the mistake of seeking the assistance of English Norman nobles in reconquering Leinster. Richard de Clare, known popularly as **Strongbow**, was all too willing to help. Strongbow and his Anglo-Normans arrived in 1169 and cut a bloody swath through south Leinster. Strongbow married Dermot's daughter **Aoife** after Dermot's death in 1171 and seemed ready to proclaim an independent Norman kingdom in Ireland. Instead, he affirmed his loyalty to King Henry II and generously offered to govern Leinster (eastern and southeastern Ireland) on England's behalf.

FEUDALISM (1200-1607)

Thus began English hold over Irish land. The following feudal period saw constant power struggles between Gaelic and Norman-descended English lords. Norman strongholds, concentrated in Leinster, had more towns, including the **Pale**, a fortified domain around Dublin, as well as more trade, while Gaelic Connacht and Ulster remained agrarian. Yet, the two sides were hardly divided culturally: old English and Irish fiefdoms built similar castles, ate similar foods, appreciated the same poets, and hired the same mercenaries. Overseas, the crown fretted over this cultural cross-pollination, and in 1366, it sponsored the notorious **Statutes of Kilkenny**. These decrees banned English colonists (dubbed "more Irish than the Irish themselves") from speaking Irish, wearing Irish styles of dress, or marrying native Irish, and forbade the Irish from entering walled cities (like Derry). The harsh statutes had little effect, especially in the face of the Gaelic lords' increased success in reclaiming their territorial inheritance. Feudal skirmishes and economic decline plagued the English lords until the rise of the "Geraldine Earls," two branches of the FitzGerald family who fought for control of south Leinster. The victors, the **Earls of Kildare**, ruled Ireland fairly unhindered from 1470 to 1534, to such an extent that the English crown grew fearful of their indepen-

---

AD 500-700
Huge monastic cities flourish.

circa AD 600
monks craft Book of Durrow.

AD 795
Full-scale Viking invasions begin.

early AD 800s
Book of Kells illuminated.

1000-1100
Irish chieftains fight amongst themselves.

1002
Dal Cais clan of Co. Clare captures Armagh.

1014
Battle of Clontarf: Vikings trounced once and for all.

1171
Irish Chieftain Strongbow allies himself with English crown.

1172
Pope decrees that Henry II of England is feudal lord of Ireland.

1176
Strongbow dies.

1185
Important Anglo-Irish dynasties established by Prince (later King) John on Irish land.

LIFE AND TIMES

1366
Statutes of Kilkenny passed by English rulers. Intermarriage is forbidden between Irish and English.

1470-1534
Anglo-Irish Earls of Kildare bring relative stability to Irish politics.

1494
The English crown attempts to limit the Earls' power through Poynings' Law.

1537
With the Irish Supremacy Act, English King Henry VIII makes Ireland property of the English crown under the Protestant Church of Ireland.

1579
Catholic-minded FitzGerald uprising against the English.

1595-1601
Hugh O'Neill leads open rebellion against English rule.

1601
The Spanish Armada sits passive in Kinsale Harbour.

1607
Flight of the Earls. Irish land is systematically parceled out to Protestants.

dence. In 1494, **Poynings' Law** limited their authority, and that of subsequent leaders, by declaring that the Irish Parliament could convene only with the consent of England and that any laws passed must meet the approval of the Crown.

The English Crown increased its control over Ireland throughout the next century. When Henry VIII broke with the Catholic Church to create the Church of England, a newly convened Dublin Parliament passed the 1537 **Irish Supremacy Act,** which declared Henry head of the Protestant **Church of Ireland** and effectively made the island property of the Crown. The Church of Ireland held a privileged position over Irish Catholicism, even though the English neither articulated any substantive difference between the two religious outlooks nor attempted to convert the Irish masses. The lords of Ireland, however, both English and Gaelic, wished to remain loyal both to Catholicism and to the Crown—a nearly impossible order to fill. Bold **Thomas FitzGerald** of Kildare sent a missive to Henry VIII stating this position. In response, Henry denied his aristocratic title. A retaliatory FitzGerald uprising in Munster in 1579 planted in English heads the idea that Irish land had to be directly controlled by Protestants if it were to be considered safe and loyal. In defiance of the crown, **Hugh O'Neill,** an Ulster earl, raised an army of thousands in open rebellion in the late 1590s. Gaelic lords supported him, but the Old English lords were divided. The King of Spain promised naval assistance; his Armada arrived in Kinsale Harbour in 1601 but sat inactive as armies from England demolished O'Neill's forces. Their power broken, O'Neill and the rest of the major Gaelic lords soared out of Ireland in 1607 in what came to be known as the **Flight of the Earls.** They promised to return with assistance from the forces of Catholic rulers on the continent, but never achieved this aim. The English took control of the land, and parceled it out to Protestants.

PLANTATION AND CROMWELL (1607-1688)

The English project of dispossessing Catholics of their land and "planting" Ireland with Protestants was most successful in Ulster. Scottish Presbyterian tenants and laborers (themselves displaced by the English) joined the expected mix of adventurers, ne'er-do-wells, and ex-soldiers. The project in the North became known as the **Ulster Plantation.** King Charles's representative in Ireland, Lord Wentworth, pursued a policy with few supporters outside England that closed off the South to the Scots and continued confiscating more land than there were Protestant takers. The now landless Irish revolted in Ulster in 1641 under a loose group of Gaelic-Irish leaders. **Owen Roe O'Neill,** of the next O'Neill generation, returned from the Continent to lead the insurrection; the uprising even received the backing of the Catholic Church. The rebels advanced south, and in 1642 formed the **Confederation of Kilkenny,** an uneasy alliance of the Church and Irish and Old English lords. Some English lords considered themselves to be rebelling against a treasonous viceroy, while still remaining loyal to the King; thus, the concurrent English Civil War complicated their already tangled interests. Negotiations between the Confederation and

King Charles ended with **Oliver Cromwell's** victory in England and his arrival in Ireland at the head of a Puritan army.

Cromwell's army destroyed anything they did not occupy, and then some. Catholics were massacred and whole towns razed as the Confederation dwindled away. Entire tracts of land were confiscated and handed out to soldiers and Protestant adventurers. The native Irish landowners had the options of going "to Hell or to Connacht," the desolate and infertile region in Ireland's west. Some of the richest landowners found (paid for) ways to stay, while smaller farmers were displaced. By 1660, the vast majority of Irish land was owned, maintained, and policed by Protestant immigrants. After Cromwellian forces were deposed in the Restoration, Charles II passed the 1665 **Act of Explanation;** it required the Protestant newcomers to relinquish one-third of their land to the "innocent papists." In actuality, Catholics received scant compensation.

THE PROTESTANT ASCENDANCY (1688-1801)

Thirty years after the English Civil War, English political disruption again resulted in Irish bloodshed. Catholic **James II**, driven from England by the "Glorious Revolution" of 1688, came to Ireland with his army, intending to gather military support to reclaim his throne. Jacobites (James's supporters) and Williamites (supporters of new Protestant King William III) fought each other in battles that had far-reaching political and symbolic consequences throughout Ireland. The battle between the two kings has since been mythologized to represent the subjugation of Irish Catholics under their Protestant superiors. In 1689, James attempted to take the northern city of Derry, where a young band of **Apprentice Boys** closed the gates at his approach. The ensuing **Seige of Derry** lasted 105 days. The Apprentice Boys have since becomes Loyalist icons (see p. 465). The war between William and James ended on July 12, 1690 at the **Battle of the Boyne,** with James's defeat and exile. The battle is still celebrated by many Northern Protestants in marches that take place on July 12, Orange Day (named for William of Orange). The war's end delivered the **Treaty of Limerick,** which ambiguously promised Catholics undelivered civil rights. Instead, the **Penal Laws,** enacted at the turn of the 18th century, further limited Catholics economically and banned the public practice of their religion at a time when Catholics comprised 90 percent of the island's population.

The newly secure Anglo-Irish elite built their own culture in Dublin and the Pale with garden parties, gossip, and architecture second only to London. The term **"Ascendancy"** was coined to describe a social elite whose distinction depended upon Anglicanism. Within this exclusive social structure, such thinkers as **Bishop George Berkeley** and **Edmund Burke** rose to prominence. **Trinity College** flourished as the quintessential institution of the Ascendancy. Despite their cultural ties, many of these aristocrats felt little political allegiance to England. **Jonathan Swift** (see p. 25) campaigned against dependency upon England, tirelessly pamphleteering on behalf of both the Protestant Church and the rights of the Irish people. Swift was an early proponent of the Irish Par-

1641
Landless Irish revolt in Ulster.

1642
Confederation of Kilkenny: an alliance is formed between the Church, Irish Lords, and English Earls.

1649
Cromwell arrives in Ireland.

1654-1655
Cromwell's policy of Plantation implemented. Nearly half of indigenous Irish massacred under his invasions.

1665
Act of Explanation passed under English Restorers: Catholics receive some meagre compensation for losses.

1689
Deposed English King James II flees to Ireland.

1689
The Seige of Derry: the loyalist Apprentice Boys close the gates to James.

1690
Battle of the Boyne: Catholic James is defeated.

1695
Penal Laws restricting Catholic education, arms-bearing, and horse-owning rights are passed. Catholic clergy banished.

12 ■ HISTORY

LIFE AND TIMES

1710
Berkeley publishes his *Treatise concerning the Principles of Human Knowledge,* in which he outlines his theory of idealism.

1713
Jonathan Swift becomes Dean of St. Patrick's Cathedral in Dublin.

1744
Edmund Burke, the son of a Protestant Dublin solicitor and a Roman Catholic mother, enters Trinity College.

NOTES TOWARDS A TRINITY COLLEGE CHRONOLOGY

Throughout the late 16th century, the English toyed with the idea of an Irish university. In 1592, a small group of Dubliners took education into their own hands and obtained a charter from Queen Elizabeth to found Trinity College. The city granted the new foundation the lands and run-down buildings of a monastery just southeast of the city walls. The late 17th century brought turmoil to its hallowed halls: the Provost fled in 1641, the college had to pawn its plate in 1643, and all fellows and students were expelled in order to turn the college into barracks for James II's soldiers in 1689. Trinity was up and running again by the beginning of the 18th century, with the construction of the library underway. Trinity, the university of the Protestant Ascendancy, met few disturbances save the small number of boisterous Jacobites who unsuccessfully tried to introduce radical politics into this burgeoning intellectual aristocracy. In 1793, Trinity admitted its first Roman Catholic students (even though the Catholic Church declared attendance a cardinal sin). In the late 19th century, the tumultuous political climate finally seeped into the college grounds. The government made numerous attempts to incorporate Trinity into a federated university with several other Irish academic institutions; the college vehemently and successfully opposed such threats to its independence. It began admitting women in 1904, and they comprised 16% of the student population only 10 years later. World War I and the creation of the Republic left Trinity without resources or strength in a divided Ireland, while newer universities in the UK quickly gained prestige. With the help of a long-needed annual state grant, finally secured in 1947, Trinity has continued to prosper through its fourth century. (For more on Trinity, see **Dublin,** p. 109.)

liamentary patriots, men who advocated an Anglo-Irish state free from the authority of the English Parliament, yet owing allegiance to the King and excluding Catholics. Meanwhile, displaced peasants filled Dublin's poorer quarters, creating the horrific slums that led Swift to write "A Modest Proposal" (see **Literature 1600-1880,** p. 25).

Away from the Pale and Ulster, the Catholic merchant class continued to grow in cites like Galway and Tralee. Early in the 18th century, Catholics practiced their religion furtively, using large, hidden, flat rocks—appropriately dubbed **Mass rocks**—when altars were unavailable. Denied official education, Gaelic-Irish teens learned literature and religion in **hedge schools,** hidden assemblies with teachers who were often fugitive priests. The hedge schools became a symbol of the dispossessed Irish in the 18th century. Landlords were typically Anglo-Irish Protestants and their tenants Gaelic-Irish Catholics—a cultural divide that made brutal rents and eviction policies easier for landlords to adopt. Meanwhile, secret agrarian societies, like the **Defenders,** formed to defend peasant land.

REBELLION, UNION, REACTION (1775-1848)

The American and French Revolutions inspired notions of independence in small political organizations such as the **United Irishmen,** which began as a radical Protestant Ulster debating society. (Despite the flagrant abuse of Irish Catholics, the major rebels against the English at this time were Protestants.) When war between England and Napoleon's France seemed likely, the United Irishmen were outlawed. They managed to reorganize themselves as a secret society. Their Protestant leader, **Theobald Wolfe Tone,** hoped that a general uprising would create an independent, non-sectarian Ireland. He made the significant first step of admitting Catholics among the ranks of the United Irishmen. A bloody uprising of peasants and priests erupted in May 1798. The rebels made their last stand at **Vinegar Hill,** near Enniscorthy in Co. Wexford (see p. 188); they fell in the thousands. A month into the battle, French troops arrived and managed to hold territory there for about a month before meeting utter destruction. French soldiers were held as prisoners of war and shipped home; Irish soldiers were executed. The Battle of Vinegar Hill became embedded in the Nationalist imagination as an episode of unrestrained English brutality.

Any hopes England had held of making Irish society less volatile by relaxing anti-Catholic laws were canceled by the rebels' actions in Co. Wexford. The British abolished Irish "self-government" altogether. The 1801 **Act of Union** dissolved the Dublin Parliament and created "The United Kingdom of Great Britain and Ireland;" the Church of Ireland was subsumed by the "United Church of England and Ireland." Wolfe Tone committed suicide in captivity, while other United Irishmen escaped to France, building a secret network that would eventually link up with the Fenians (see **The Famine,** below).

Dublin's mad gaiety vanished. The Anglo-Irish gentry collapsed as agrarian violence escalated. English and Continental visitors to Ireland were aghast at its rural poverty. Meanwhile, the Napoleonic Wars raged in Europe, and many feared that Napoleon would set his sights on discontented Ireland. Paranoid generals constructed short, thick, cylindrical structures named **Martello towers** along the Irish coast for the assault that never came. The British copied the form of these towers from examples they saw on Cape Mortella in Corsica. (The British, apparently, felt free to improve on the name.)

Union meant Irish representatives now held seats in the British Parliament. Electoral reforms of the 1810s and 20s lowered the property qualifications for voting, allowing many Catholic farmers to vote. They elected Catholic **Daniel O'Connell** to Parliament in 1829, essentially forcing Westminster to repeal the remaining anti-Catholic laws that would have barred him from taking his seat. O'Connell acquired the nickname "The Liberator," and his efforts within Parliament allotted money to improve Irish living conditions, health care, and trade. When unsympathetic Tories took power, O'Connell convened huge rallies in Ireland, showing popular support for repealing the Act of Union. Romantic Nationalism, imported from Germany and Italy, pervaded the intellectual air, and some felt O'Connell had not gone far enough. "Young Ireland" poets and journalists, led

Early 1700s
Catholics practice their religion in hiding on Mass rocks. Catholic youngsters educated in underground "hedge schools."

1775, 1789
The American and French Revolutions foment Irish unrest.

1789
The Vinegar Hill uprising in Co. Wexford is the last stand for Irish patriots; the French join Irish rebels against the English. The English are victorious.

1801
British dissolve the Irish Parliament and create "the United Kingdom of Great Britain and Ireland" in the Act of Union.

1835
French political philosopher Alexis de Tocqueville visits Ireland, memoirs of which he publishes in his work, *Journey to England and Ireland.*

1829
Irish Catholic Daniel O'Connell elected to British Parliament; Catholic Emancipation Act allows Catholics to sit in Parliament.

by John Mitchel (whom Yeats quoted: "Send war in our time, O Lord"), saw violence as the necessary means to independence. They tried to revolt in 1848, but much of Ireland was starving and their efforts went unnoticed.

From this political enthusiasm arose unprecedented social reform. The 1830s brought the passage of the **Irish Poor Law Act,** which established workhouses to provide in-kind services for impoverished citizens. In 1836, the police force was centralized and professionalized under the title **Royal Irish Constabulary,** which later became the model for the British Empire's colonial police forces.

THE FAMINE (1845-1870)

In the first half of the 19th century, the potato was embraced for providing more nutrients per acre than any other crop, ideal for the rapidly-growing Irish population. This reliance had devastating effects when the potato, along with most other crops, fell victim to fungal disease between 1845 and 1847. The **Great Famine,** which was far harsher than any small blight or crop failure of the early 19th century, lasted roughly from 1847-1851. In that short period of time, an estimated two to three million people died. Another million emigrated to Liverpool, London, Australia, and America. Depopulation in Connacht, in the west, was particularly severe.

While the Irish were eating grass, the British shipped thousands of pounds of grain from the island. British authorities often forcibly exchanged what few decent potatoes peasants could find with inedible grain. Catholic peasants who accepted British soup in exchange for their conversion to Protestantism earned the disdainful title "Soupers," a slur that stuck with families for decades. In future decades, Nationalists interpreted British insensitivity to the starvation of the Irish masses as ethnic cleansing. In analyzing the Famine, most contemporary English economists took an uninvolved, economic perspective of the Famine, explaining that it was the result of a standard (Malthusian) law of population growth. **Isaac Butt,** founder of the Irish Home Rule Party (see **Parnell's Cultural Nationalism,** below) argued that it was hypocritical of the British to claim political unity while refusing to provide economic aid.

After the famine, the societal structure of surviving Irish peasants completely reorganized itself, and the Irish language had suffered a near-fatal blow. The bottom layer of truly penniless farmers had been eliminated, men married late, and eldest sons inherited whole farms, while unskilled younger sons often left Ireland. The depopulation of the island continued after the 1840s as **emigration** became an Irish way of life. The **Encumbered Estates Act** began the 50-year process of removing the landlord class—a process which was continued by a series of Land Acts and the Congested Districts Board, which converted Ireland, with the exception of Dublin and northeast Ulster, into a nation of conservative, culturally uniform, Catholic smallholders. Rural standards of living improved with the extension of railroads into a system farther-reaching than today's.

British injustice fueled the formation of more angry, young nationalist groups. In 1858, James Stephens, who had previously worked with the Young Ireland movement, founded the Irish Republican Brotherhood (IRB), commonly known as the

---

LIFE AND TIMES

1831
National system of elementary education implemented and Irish Poor Law Act passed under the O'Connell-Whig parliament.

1836
Royal Irish Constabulary established.

1841
Population of Ireland over 8 million.

1845-1847
Potato and most other crops fall prey to a fungal disease.

1847-1851
The Great Famine: 2 to 3 million people die, 1 million emigrate elsewhere. Emigrés usually composed of young, able-bodied men and women of working age. The Irish rural society becomes distinguished by bachelor farms, deserted villages, and late marriages. The Irish language suffers.

Fenians (a name for Ireland's ancient population, now often confused with "fíann," the name of a body of warriors said to have been the defenders of Ireland in the time of Finn and other legendary Irish kings). The Fenians was a secret society aimed at the violent removal of the British. In 1867, Fenian violence made William Gladstone, among others, notice the Irish discontent, and a year later he became Britain's Prime Minister under the slogan "Justice for Ireland." Gladstone's justice consisted of diminishing the minority Protestant Church of Ireland and battling for land reform. Combining agrarian thinkers, Fenians, and Charles Stewart Parnell, the **Land League** of the 1870s pushed for reforms with O'Connell-style mass meetings.

PARNELL'S CULTURAL NATIONALISM (1870-1914)

In 1870, Member of Parliament Isaac Butt (see **the Famine**, above) founded the **Irish Home Rule Party**. Its several dozen members adopted obstructionist tactics: making long, dull speeches, introducing endless amendments, and generally trying to keep the rest of Parliament angry, bored, and ineffective until they saw fit to grant Ireland autonomy. Home Ruler **Charles Stewart Parnell** was a charismatic Protestant aristocrat with an American mother and a hatred for everything English. Backed by Parnell's invigorated Irish party, Gladstone introduced a **Home Rule Bill**, which was defeated. Parnell found redemption in the public eye when letters linking him to the **Phoenix Park Murders**, an infamous Fenian crime, turned out to be forgeries. In 1890, however, allegations that Parnell was having an extra-marital affair were proven true; the scandal split all of Ireland into Parnellites and anti-Parnellites. The moral divide also ran through the Home Rulers, leaving their political ideals to fall by the wayside.

While the parliamentary movement split, civil society grew ambitious. The **Irish Women's Suffrage Federation** was established in 1911, following the lead of the British and American suffragettes. Marxist **James Connolly** led strikes in Belfast. In Dublin, **James Larkin** spearheaded an enormous general strike in 1913, a short-term defeat that nevertheless established large trade unions in Ireland. Conservatives, attempting to "kill Home Rule by kindness," also pushed for social reform. Most important of their efforts was the **Wyndham Land Purchase Act** of 1903, which provided huge incentives for landlords to sell their estates to the government so that ownership might be transferred to the tenants.

Meanwhile, various groups tried to revive what they took to be essential "Gaelic" culture, unpolluted by foreign influence. The **Gaelic Athletic Association** (see **Sports**, p. 33) worked to replace English sports with hurling, camogie, and Gaelic football. The **Gaelic League** (see **The Irish Language**, p. 22) spread the use of the Irish language. A side effect of these organizations' work was that the word "Gaelic" became synonymous with "Catholic." In addition, cultural developments rapidly merged with political movements. The Fenians actively involved themselves in the Gaelic cultural organizations as an opportunity to disseminate their ideas. Arthur Griffith, who advocated Irish abstention from British politics, began a tiny movement and lit-

1849
Encumbered Estates Act facilitates the sale of land.

1849-1899
Process of removal of Irish landlord class enacted.

1858
Irish Republican Brotherhood (IRB), also known as the Fenians, founded, with aims set to remove British by way of force.

1867
The Fenians revolt.

1868
William Gladstone elected as British Prime Minister; continues land reform.

1870
Isaac Butt founds the Irish Home Rule Party and seeks to disrupt parliamentary procedure.

1880
Gladstone and Parnell's Home Rule Bill is defeated.

1884
The Gaelic Athletic Association founded.

1890
Parnell scandal divides the Home Rule contingent.

1893
Gaelic League founded to reinvigorate the Irish language.

1905
Arthur Griffith forms Sinn Féin.

1911
Women's Suffrage movement established.

1910-1913
Protestants commence mass rallies in Northern Ireland to protest Home Rule.

1913
Great Dublin general strike led by trade unionist James Larkin.

1913
The Nationalist and revolutionary Irish Volunteers founded. The Unionist Ulster Volunteers established in Northern Ireland.

1914
Home Rule Bill passed with an amendment excluding Ulster. 770,000 Irishmen enlist to fight with the Allies in WWI.

1915-1916
The Irish Volunteers and the Fenians prepare for the Easter Rising.

tle-read newspaper, both of which went by the name **Sinn Féin** (SHIN FAYN), meaning "Ourselves Alone." As the Home Rule movement grew, so did resistance to it. Between 1910 and 1913, thousands of Northern Protestants opposing Home Rule joined mass rallies, signed a covenant, and organized into a quasi-militia named the **Ulster Volunteer Force (UVF).** Nationalists led by **Eoin MacNeill** in Dublin responded in 1913 by creating the **Irish Volunteers,** which the Fenians correctly saw as a potentially revolutionary force.

THE EASTER RISING (1914-1918)

In the summer of 1914, Irish Home Rule seemed imminent and Ulster ready to go up in flames, but neither happened—World War I did. British Prime Minister Henry Asquith passed a **Home Rule Bill** on the condition that the Irish Volunteer and Home Rule parties would recruit Irishmen for the British army. Asquith followed with a Suspensory Act, which delayed home rule until peace returned to Ulster; meanwhile, 170,000 Irish Volunteers and 600,000 other Irishmen enlisted on the Allied side. An 11,000-member armed guard, the remnants of the Volunteers, remained in Ireland. They were officially led by MacNeill, who knew nothing of the revolt that the Fenians were planning. If an architect can be ascribed to the ensuing mayhem, it was poet and schoolteacher **Padraig Pearse,** who won his co-conspirators over to an ideology of "blood sacrifice." Pearse believed that if a small cache of committed men died publicly and violently as martyrs for Ireland, then the island's entire population would join in the struggle for independence.

The Volunteers conducted a series of unarmed maneuvers and parades throughout 1915 and 1916. The government at Dublin Castle was convinced of their harmlessness. Fenian leaders were meanwhile planning to receive a shipment of German arms for use in a nationwide revolt on **Easter Sunday, 1916.** The arms arrived a day too early and were never picked up. The British captured and hanged **Roger Casement,** the man who was to meet the shipment. Fenian leaders, however, continued planning their rebellion and mustering support from the Volunteers. They told MacNeill about the arms shipments, and provided "evidence" of Dublin Castle's intention to suppress the Volunteers. Fearing the destruction of the Volunteers, MacNeill gave orders for mobilization on Easter Sunday. On Saturday, he learned that the Castle order had been forged and the arms had been captured. He then inserted in the Sunday papers a plea ordering all Volunteers *not* to mobilize.

MacNeill and most Fenian leaders had been thinking in terms of military success, which at that point was clearly impossible, but Pearse's followers wanted martyrdom. On Sunday, the Pearse group met and decided to have the uprising on the following Monday, April 24, in Dublin. Pearse, James Connolly, and about one thousand others seized the **General Post Office** on O'Connell St. (see p. 116), read aloud a "Proclamation of the Republic of Ireland," and held out through five days of fighting in downtown Dublin. Dubliners initially saw the Easter rebels as criminals, since their only tangible accomplishment was massive property damage.

The harsh reaction of the British martial-law administration to "Easter Sunday" turned popular opinion on its head. Over ten days in May, fifteen "ringleaders" received the death sentence, among them Pearse, Pearse's brother (executed primarily for being Pearse's brother), and James Connolly, who was shot while tied to a chair because his wounds prevented him from standing. **Éamon de Valera** was spared because the British wrongly thought him an American citizen. **Kilmainham Gaol,** the site of the executions, became a shrine of martyrdom. By June, Pearse's prophecy proved true: the public had grown sympathetic to the martyrs and increasingly anti-British. In 1917, the Volunteers reorganized under master spy and Fenian bigwig **Michael Collins**. The Sinn Féin party, falsely associated with the Rising, became the political voice of military Nationalism. Collins brought the Volunteers to Sinn Féin, and de Valera became the party president. When, in 1918, the British tried to introduce a military draft in Ireland, the public turned overwhelmingly to Sinn Féin, repudiating the nonviolence of the Home Rule party.

INDEPENDENCE AND CIVIL WAR (1919-1922)

Extremist Irish Volunteers became known as the **Irish Republican Army (IRA),** which functioned as the military arm of the Sinn Féin government. The new government fought the **War of Independence** against the British, who reinforced their police with **Black and Tans**—demobilized soldiers whose nickname referred to their patched-together uniforms. Both the IRA's guerrillas and the Black and Tans were notorious for committing atrocities. In 1920, British Prime Minister Lloyd George, supported by US President Woodrow Wilson, passed the **Government of Ireland Act,** which divided the island into Northern Ireland and Southern Ireland, two partially self-governing areas within the UK. After the general elections for Parliament, Lloyd George felt compelled to open negotiations with de Valera, a nearly impossible feat when both sides refused to recognize the other's legality. Finally, hurried negotiations produced the **Anglo-Irish Treaty,** which created a 26-county Irish Free State while recognizing British rule over the northern counties. The treaty also imposed on Irish officials a tortuous oath of allegiance to the King of England, but not to the British government. Lloyd George pushed the treaty forward by threatening war if it were rejected.

Sinn Féin, the IRA, and the population each split on whether to accept the treaty. Collins said yes; de Valera said no. When the representative parliament voted yes, de Valera resigned from the presidency, and Arthur Griffith assumed the position. The capable Collins government began the business of setting up a nation, with treasury, tax collection, a foreign ministry, and an unarmed police force called the *Garda Siochana* (GUARD-a SHEE-a-khahn). A portion of the IRA, led by **General Rory O'Connor,** opposed the treaty; this faction was also thought to be behind the assassination of Sir Henry Wilson, the newly appointed military advisor to the government of Northern Ireland. O'Connor's Republicans occupied the Four Courts in Dublin, took a pro-treaty Army general hostage, and were attacked by the forces of Collins's government. Two years of **civil war** followed, tearing up the countryside and dividing the population. The pro-treaty government won, but Griffith died

1916
Easter Risings. Its leaders are executed and become public martyrs for the cause of Irish Independence.

1917
The Irish Volunteers reorganize under Fenian Michael Collins.

1918
The Irish public turns to Sinn Féin to resist British plans for Irish conscription.

1919
The Anglo-Irish War begins.

1920
The first Black and Tans recruited. Government of Ireland Act is passed to divide Northern Ireland from Southern Ireland.

1921
The Anglo-Irish Treaty is signed to produce the 26-county Free State of Ireland. The British retain control of Northern Ireland.

LIFE AND TIMES

1922
Arthur Griffith is elected Irish President and begins to establish the infrastructure of an independent nation.

1922-1923
The Irish Civil War is fought between supporters and dissenters of the Anglo-Irish treaty.

Dec. 1922
A first constitution is framed for the Irish Free State.

1923
Valera's government squelches Republican insurgents and ends armed resistance to the Irish State.

1923-1932
Cosgrave rules, granting women's suffrage (1923) and bringing electric power to the Irish west.

1927
Valera breaks with Sinn Féin to establish the Fianna Fáil party.

1932-1948
Valera and Fianna Fáil rule Ireland, siding with Catholic small farmers.

1936
The IRA is outlawed.

1937
The permanent Irish Constitution is ratified.

suddenly from the strain of the struggle, and Collins was assassinated before the end of 1922. The dwindling minority of anti-treaty IRA officers went into hiding. The disillusioned Sinn Féin denied the legitimacy of the free state government and resisted referring to the Republic by its official name of Éire, calling it instead "the 26-county state" or "the Dublin Government."

THE DE VALERA ERA (1922-1960)

The new 26-county Irish Free State emerged from civil war having lost its most prominent leaders and needing to protect those ministers who remained. The Anglo-Irish Treaty required the newly elected Dáil to frame a constitution by December 6, 1922. With time running out, **W.T. Cosgrave** was elected prime minister and passed a preliminary constitution in haste. Under the guidance of **Éamon de Valera,** the government ended armed resistance by May 1923, imprisoned Republican insurgents, and executed 77 of them. Cosgrave and his party **Cumann na nGaedheal** (which evolved into today's **Fine Gael** party) headed the first stable Free State administration until 1932. His government restored civil order, granted suffrage to women in 1923, and brought **electrical power** to much of the West by damming the Shannon River. In the first elections of the newly-formed Republic, the anti-treaty voters supported abstentionist Sinn Féin (see p. 15). Then, in 1927, de Valera broke with Sinn Féin and the IRA and founded his own political party, **Fianna Fáil,** in order to participate in government and oppose the treaty nonviolently. Fianna Fáil won the 1932 election, and de Valera held power for much of the next 20 years. In line with de Valera's vision of Ireland as a nation of Catholic small farmers, Fianna Fáil broke up the remaining large landholdings and imposed high tariffs, producing a trade war with Britain that battered the Irish economy until 1938. Meanwhile, IRA hard-liners trickled out of jails in the early 30s, resumed violence, and saw their party outlawed in 1936.

"In the name of the most Holy Trinity," de Valera and the voters approved the permanent Irish Constitution in 1937. It declares the state's name to be Éire and establishes the country's legislative structure, which consists of two chambers, both with five-year terms. The **Dáil** (DAHL), the powerful lower house, is composed of 166 seats directly elected in proportional representation. The less important upper house, the **Seanad** (SHA-nud), has 60 members who are chosen by electoral colleges. The **Taoiseach** (TEE-shuch; Prime Minister) and **Tánaiste** (tah-NESH-tuh; Deputy Prime Minister) lead a Cabinet, while the **President** is the ceremonial head of state, elected to a seven-year term. The constitution originally contained a "special position" clause concerning the **Catholic Church** in Ireland, but the clause was deleted by a constitutional amendment in 1972.

Ireland maintained neutrality during WWII, despite German air raids on Dublin and pressure from US President Franklin Roosevelt. Despite their neutral status, many Irish citizens identified with the Allies, and around 50,000 served in the British army. **The Emergency,** as the war was known, meant strict rationing of basic foodstuffs and severe censorship of newspapers and letters. While the young government lacked the monetary and military strength to have a large effect on the war, Éire's brand of neutrality effectively assisted the Allies. For example, downed American or British airmen were shipped north to Belfast, while downed German pilots were detained in P.O.W. camps. When the Germans firebombed Belfast in 1941 for its involvement in the war, Dublin's fire brigade came to the city's rescue. De Valera, in an exaggerated show of neutrality, was the world's only head of government to deliver official condolences to the German ambassador on the death of Hitler.

A Fine Gael government under **John Costello** in 1948 had the honor of officially proclaiming "the Republic of Ireland" and ending supposed British Commonwealth membership. Britain recognized the Republic in 1949, but declared that the UK would maintain control over Ulster until the Parliament of Northern Ireland consented to join the Republic.

The last de Valera government, in office from 1951 to 1959, and its successor, under **Sean Lemass,** finally boosted the Irish economy by ditching protectionism in favor of attempts to attract foreign investment. In place of verbal and military skirmishes over constitutional issues, which had dominated the 20s, Irish politics became a contest between two ideologically similar parties. Fianna Fáil and Fine Gael vied against each other to provide local benefits and constituent services.

RECENT HISTORY (1960-2000)

By reaching out, Ireland has kept its young people from leaving. In the 1960s, increased contact with the rest of the world meant slowed emigration and accelerated economic growth, resulting in increased national confidence. In 1967, the government introduced free secondary education, including state grants for privately owned schools; in 1968, it introduced free university education for those below a certain income level. Tourism became a major industry; Bord Fáilte has expanded tremendously to create a major source of employment. In 1969, the "Troubles in the North" disturbed citizens but the Republic's political and economic trends remained stable. While politicians still expressed nationalist sentiments, few people cast votes based on Northern events (see p. 397).

Ireland entered the European Economic Community, now the **European Union** (**EU**), in 1973. EU membership and an increased number of international visitors helped introduce the process of secularization in Ireland. **Garret FitzGerald** revamped the Fine Gael party under a secular banner; during the late 70s and early 80s, he and **Charlie Haughey,** a Fianna Fáil leader, alternated as Taoiseach. Flip-flopping between parties produced a bewildering set of economic programs and initiatives, which were periodically interrupted by internal corruption. EU membership and funds continued to be crucial to Ireland's economy, helping to pull it out of mid-80s recession. Greater involvement in the Continent's culture and economy offered Ireland an alternative to dependence on the United Kingdom. In 1985, FitzGerald signed the **Anglo-Irish agreement,** which granted Éire an official, though not legal, role in Northern negotiations.

In 1990, the Republic broke progressive social and political ground when it elected its first female president, **Mary Robinson.** Social reform made further gains when the small, leftist **Labor Party** enjoyed enormous and unexpected success in the 1992

1939
Britain enters WWII; Ireland maintains an Allied-friendly neutrality throughout the war.

1948
An intermittently Fine Gael government declares the Republic of Ireland and ends Irish membership in the British Commonwealth.

1949
Britain recognizes the Republic and states that it will maintain control over Northern Ireland until its people consent to join the Republic.

1955
The Republic is admitted to the United Nations.

1958
The first program for economic expansion is initiated in the Republic.

1966
Anglo-Irish Free Trade Agreement is signed.

1967
Free secondary education is introduced.

LIFE AND TIMES

1969 "Troubles" and clashes intensify in Northern Ireland. Protestants launch siege of Catholic Bogside neighborhood in Derry.

1973 Ireland enters the European Economic Community. Secularization of Irish society marches forward.

1985 The Republic gains an official place in Northern Ireland negotiations.

1990 Mary Robinson is elected as the first female president of Ireland.

1994 Peace-minded president Reynolds is forced to step down over Church scandals. The Catholic Church is no longer beyond reproach.

1997 Fianna Fáil wins elections with the youngest Prime Minister ever at its head.

1998 Peace talks produce the Northern Ireland Peace Agreement. Voters all over the island ratify the agreement.

1999-2000 London revokes direct rule and hands power back to Northern Ireland.

elections. In September of 1993, a coalition between the Labor Party and Fianna Fáil was elected. The new Taoiseach, **Albert Reynolds,** declared that his top priority was to stop violence in Northern Ireland. In August 1994 he announced the nearly miraculous cease-fire agreement with Sinn Féin and the IRA.

Reynolds was forced to resign in December 1994, following a scandal involving his appointee for President of the High Court, Attorney General **Harry Whelehan.** Whelehan had been heavily criticized for his lack of action in a case involving a pedophile priest, **Father Brendan Smyth.** Other scandals in the Church indicated that the conservative government had been protecting priests from legal charges of sexual misconduct and abuse, and that the Church was no longer beyond reproach in Ireland. During the week following Whelehan's appointment, Fine Gael, led by **John Bruton,** introduced a no-confidence motion against the government. After Reynold's resignation, the Labour Party formed a coalition with Fine Gael, with Bruton as Taoiseach.

In June 1997, Fianna Fáil won the general election, making **Bertie Ahern,** the 45-year-old party leader, the youngest Taoiseach in the history of the state. Ahern joined the peace talks that produced the **Northern Ireland Peace Agreement** in April of 1998 (see p. 397). On May 22, 1998, in the first island-wide election since 1918, an overwhelming 94% of voters in the Republic voted for the enactment of the Agreement. Among other things, the historic Agreement created a North-South Ministerial Council, a cross-border authority focusing on such issues as education, transportation, urban planning, environmental protection, tourism, and EU programs. In December 1999, London revoked its direct rule and handed power back to Northern Ireland, but continual conflicts with the IRA over disarmament prevented any development until June. (For the recent status of direct rule, see p. 402.)

FURTHER READING ON IRISH HISTORY

For more intensive reading on Irish history, Mark Tierney's *Modern Ireland* is a clear and comprehensive narrative covering the period from 1850 to 1968; *The Oxford History of Ireland* is a good source on earlier periods; Thomas Cahill's *How the Irish Saved Civilization* is an eye-opening account of monastic Ireland; and Peter Harbison's *Pre-Christian Ireland* is a photo-enhanced introduction to ancient Irish archaeology and culture. For a history of Northern Ireland since Republican independence, see **Northern Ireland,** p. 397. Locals will do their best to fill you in on what you can't learn ahead of time.

CURRENT ISSUES

Eighty-one years of Republican independence has created a modern civic society with a flowering culture that infuses modernity with centuries-old practices. Strong regional distinctions and accents combine with a gaping urban-rural divide to enliven the national character. The social role of government, along with its unique relation to the church, are complicated by the increasing secularization of this traditionally pious society. Poverty and unemployment have historically been widespread,

CURRENT ISSUES ■ 21

but the Republic's membership in the European Union has proven enormously beneficial to its economic infrastructure and development; in recent years, the media has dubbed Ireland the "Celtic Tiger." In the face of change, the lifestyle of the Irish goes unspoiled, continuing to center itself around music, sports, a laid-back attitude, and the pub.

WOMEN. The Republic's progressive liberal movement gained ground in 1990 with the election of President Mary Robinson. A forward-looking activist, Robinson worked vigorously to elevate her office above the purely ceremonial role it traditionally played. With the greater involvement of women in public life, the women's movement has emerged from its position as a subsidiary of general political activism.

DIVORCE. In November 1995, the closest vote in Irish history—50.3% to 49.7%—legalized divorce. The Divorce Bill allows divorce if spouses have lived apart for four years with "no reasonable prospect of a reconciliation."

SEXUAL ORIENTATION. Equally encouraging to progressives and disturbing to the Catholic Church is the **gay and lesbian rights** movement, which is slowly gaining legal ground. In 1980, the first legal challenge to laws against homosexuality was brought before the High Court. Lawyer Mary Robinson (later to be President) represented David Norris, a gay lecturer at Trinity College, in his challenge of the tacit discriminatory laws. Their challenge lost in both the High and Supreme Court of Ireland. In 1988, Norris won an appeal to the European Court of Human Rights in Strasbourg, and Ireland was required to change its laws. In June 1993, the age of consent between gay men was set at age 17. A large and relatively open gay scene has developed in Dublin, and colleges are becoming more aware of gay issues. A pamphlet offering advice to third-level students about "coming out" at college was recently distributed nationwide, and many campuses support gay student groups. The recent public "coming out" by the lead singer of Boyzone, one of Ireland's favorite pop groups, is sure to increase awareness and acceptance of gay lifestyles.

ABORTION. Irish policies on abortion have changed little over the decades. In 1983, voters approved a constitutional amendment securing "the right to life of the unborn." In February of 1992, the High Court horrified much of the public by ruling that a 14-year-old girl (called X in court papers), who said she had been raped, could not leave the country to obtain an abortion. In November 1992, voters passed a measure allowing the "right to information;" in May 1995, the High Court made it legal for centers to give advice on where to go abroad. Voters, however, still reject motions to legalize abortion. Current President **Mary McAleese**, a law professor and the first Northern resident to hold her office, was elected in 1997, claiming that she would rather resign from the presidency than sign into law a bill liberalizing abortion policies.

ECONOMY. Ireland's economy is booming, in large part due to increased foreign investment over the past decade. Relatively few regulations and huge incentives have drawn foreign investors, strengthening the currency and boosting Ireland's economy at one of Europe's fastest rates. Industry has been expanding at an unprecedented pace and tourism remains one of the most profitable portions of the Republic's economy. Unemployment is comparatively low. After the fiscally fantastic years of 1996 and 1997, EU funding appeared so successful that the organization drastically reduced the quantity of its aid to Ireland. In 1998, however, the inflation rate reached 3.2%, a three year high, placing it well above that of the rest of the EU. There is some concern about economic overheating and the effects of converting to the **euro** (see p. 47), the new EU currency that came into non-cash existence in 1999. The transition will be tempered by dual (euro and punt) currency, price listing, and exchange rates until January 1, 2002.

According to a report completed in 1999, the unemployment rate should be reduced to three percent by the year 2005. This is indicative of a drastic change in

Ireland's pattern of emigration. Since the time of the Famine, emigration had become a way of life for young Irish seeking work. The year of 1999 was the first in recent history in which the rate of immigration to Ireland surpassed the rate of emigration away from the island. The Republic has opened its borders to thousands of refugees, who are greatly aided by the Church and economic upswing.

As more young Irish spend time abroad and more international travelers spend time in Ireland, the culture's conservatism slowly cracks. The short-term result is a growing generation gap and disparity between rural and urban areas. The majority of the Republic remains safe and sober, but Dubliners endure the problems of all large cities, including crime and drugs. While the Irish are eager to dispel the picturesque stereotype of the "land of saints and scholars" (and poverty and drunkenness), they hope to retain the safety afforded by their religious and family-oriented past.

LITERARY TRADITIONS

THE IRISH LANGUAGE

Irish is the corpse that sits up and talks back.
—Nuala Ní Dhomhnaill

The Irish constitution declares Irish to be the national language of the Republic. Yet, only 86,000 individuals compose the exclusively Irish speaking community, or **gaeltacht** (GAYL-tacht). The larger *gaeltacht* is composed of small settlements scattered about the most remote regions of the island. The most prominent *gaeltacht* are located in Connemara in Co. Galway (see p. 323), in patches of Co. Donegal (see p. 376), on the Dingle Peninsula (see p. 265), on Cape Clear Island (see p. 237), and in the Aran Islands (see p. 303). These geographically disparate communities are further divided by three different dialects: Donegal Irish, Connemara Irish, and Munster Irish in the South. Donegal's Irish, like its traditional music, retains traces of past contact with Scotland and Scottish Gaelic. The transformation of Ireland into an English-speaking island began in the 17th century, with the arrival of the English merchant and professional class. Everyone in contemporary Ireland speaks English, but the purest form of Celtic culture survives in the *gaeltacht*'s centuries-old traditions such as storytelling and singing. The oldest vernacular literature and the largest collection of folklore in Europe are in Irish.

ANCIENT ROOTS. Irish is a Celtic language that shares its Indo-European origin with Scottish Gaelic and Manx, and more distantly with Breton, Welsh, and Cornish. The Irish language is called *Gaeilge* by its speakers; the English word "Gaelic" refers to the Scottish language. The Celtic language arrived in Ireland in about the third century BC. The earliest written records of Irish remain on **ogham** stones (see p. 8), in a script composed of variously angled strokes. The Latin alphabet took over soon after, and Irish scholastic writing flourished between AD 600 and 900, when monastic scholarship flowered. This blessed bliss was interrupted by the Viking raids in the 8th century. Even so, the Viking settlers learned to speak Irish. In 1600, there were as many speakers of Irish worldwide as of English. The Anglophones, however, had more money and better armies; over the next 250 years, Irish speakers had to learn English to conduct business, and their children grew up speaking only English. Irish became the language of the disenfranchised. In the mid-19th century, the British introduced systematic schooling in rural areas and required that pupils receive their education in English. The Famine hit Irish-speaking areas hardest, and the number of Irish speakers continued to decline.

THE GAELIC REVIVAL. Irish re-entered the lives of the privileged classes with the advent of the Gaelic Revival. In 1893, Douglas Hyde (who later became the first president of Éire) founded the **Gaelic League** in order to inspire enthusiasm for Irish among people who didn't grow up speaking it. Writers who were bilingual from birth enjoyed Douglas Hyde's famous mispronunciations, while native English-speakers excitedly took up his cause. W.B. Yeats and Lady Gregory count among Hyde's admirers; they founded the Abbey Theatre in Dublin for the promotion of Irish playwrights. The League aimed to spread the everyday use of Irish as part of a project to de-Anglicize the island, just as the Gaelic Athletic Association aimed to overpower English sports.

The revolutionaries of 1916 and the political leaders of the 20s were almost without exception excited about reinvigorating the Irish language, and they tried to use the government to strengthen it: the civil service exam included an Irish test, and Irish became a compulsory subject in school. Preoccupied with economic development, the people and governments of the postwar Republic resented these policies. Today, several civil service positions still require a language examination, but a leaving certificate in Irish is no longer needed to attend university. As Irish has lost its compulsory stigma, it has grown in popularity with native English speakers. The last 15 years have seen a renewed interest in all things Celtic and more controversy over the fate of Irish. Adults who hated Irish in their youth regret having let it atrophy and now attend classes. All schoolchildren are still required to take extensive Irish courses, and many parents are sending their children to *gaelscoileanna* (GAYL-kol-AH-nuh), Irish immersion schools located in the *gaeltacht*. The modern Irish literature community, which produces dozens of novels, poetry collections, and essays every year, has finally begun to influence the Irish language curriculum, once filled only with antiquated traditional novels.

A CONTEMPORARY EMBRACE. Late 20th-century authors have returned to writing in Irish. **Michael Hartnett** writes solely in Irish, while **Nuala ní Dhomhnaill** composes poetry in Irish, although her public readings are generally bilingual. In contrast to the archaic subject matter non-speakers associate with the Irish language, her work brings refrigerators, feminism, and smart bombs into proximity with the *banshee*. The younger poet **Biddy Jenkinson** refuses to authorize any translation of her work into English, although it has been translated into French. The preeminent Irish-language novel is **Maírtín Ó Cadhain's** *Cré na Cille* (Churchyard Clay), a dialogue among corpses in a graveyard. Seamus Heaney is best known for his poems in English, but much of his scholarly work involves translating poems from Irish. Heaney and others have thus revived interest in the works of itinerant poets of past centuries, such as the masterful **Rafferty.**

The government continues its efforts to preserve, if not promote, modern Irish. A Connemara-based Irish radio station and a new Irish language television station, *Telifís na Gaelige* (T na G [TEE NUH JEE] to locals), expand Irish-hearing opportunities. While most Irish do not want to see their language die, some see the appropriation of money to Irish programs as excessive.

Peruse the **Glossary** (p. 494) for a list of Irish words and phrases.

LEGENDS AND FOLKTALES

> The old literature of Ireland... has been the chief illumination of my imagination all my life.
> —W.B. Yeats (from a speech to the Irish Senate, 1923)

In early Irish society, language was equal to action. What the bard (directly from the Irish *baird*) sang about battles, valor, and lineage was the only record a chieftain had by which to make decisions. Poetry and politics of the Druidic tradition were so intertwined that the *fili*, trained poets, and *breitheamh* (BREH-huv), judges of the Brehon Laws, were often the same people. The poet-patron relationship was symbiotic—the poet sang long praise poems about his lord in return for food and shelter.

ÉIRE'S EMBELLISHED PAST. Scholars have been arguing for decades about the conflation of fact and fiction in Ireland's epic mythology. The vast repertoire includes romances, war stories, revenge tales, and many instances of cattle raid-

24 ■ LITERARY TRADITIONS

> **LIFE AND TIMES**
>
> **MEN IN LABOR** According to legend, there was a young woman by the name of Macha who took up with a very wealthy, but lonely, landlord in Ulster. She cooked, swept, kept him clothed, and soon became pregnant with his child. One day they went to a local fair. The landlord grew boastful and bragged that his wife could outrun the king's chariot. The crowd insisted that she prove herself despite the woman's pleas that she be pardoned from the race since she was with child. She found no sympathy, and as she began to run, she cursed the whole of Ulster. Remarkably, she tied with the chariot in spite of her condition, but upon crossing the finish line, she let out a terrible scream as she gave birth to twins. The nearby area was named *Emain Macha* ("the twins of Macha") after her children. The men who had heard her scream, as well as nine generations of their families, were cursed by the otherworldly Macha with the pangs of childbirth in their most desperate times. That is how Queen Macha cursed Ulster, how the men of Ulster came to have labor pains for five nights and four days, and why these men were unable to protect their famous bull from Queen Medbh in the Cattle Raid of Cooley (see **The Famous Bull**, p. 24).

ing. (Cattle was the ancient Celtic men's most marketable commodity—slaves and women were valued in cows.) Long sagas were passed down orally through many generations. They survive today in written form thanks to the scholastic diligence of medieval monks; manuscripts compiled bits and pieces of different narrative versions. The less fortunate aspect of the monks' work is that they sometimes altered details to propagate Christianity. Despite the many hands through which these tales fell, they still provide essential clues to reconstructing Ireland's ancient past. They reveal much about the lifestyles of its chiefly culture, as well as the rituals that are evidenced by today's archeological remains.

The long, famous **Book of Invasions** (*Leabhar Gabhála*; LOWR GA-vah-lah) is a record of the pre-Christian cultures and armies that have invaded Ireland, from Noah's daughter Cesair up to the Celts. These tales locate the Irish peoples' ancestry in the Greek islands, where Nemed, a Scythian, became lost at sea after pursuing a mysterious tower of gold that rose out of the waves. After a year and a half of wandering, he and his ships landed safely in Ireland, until the next wave of settlers arrived... and the next, and the next, including the **Fir Bolg**, meaning "bag men." They were soon defeated by the **Túatha de Danann** (TOO-uh DAY dah-NAN), invaders from northern lands. The Túatha were a god-like race associated with light, but prone to human foibles. The Tuatha de Danann battled the evil, dark, and ugly **Formorian** race, but eventually met their equal in the **Milesians,** the forefathers of the Celts. The Milesians drove the Túatha de Danann into the ground, where they were reduced to what are known simply as *fairies*. Many people in Ireland today still believe that fairies emerge occasionally to aid or fight with mortals and seduce (or abduct) mortal beauties. When the Túatha de Danann retreated to the other world, the Celts acquired some of their ways and skills.

THE POWER OF WIT AND THE FAMOUS BULL. Poets living in the chieftains' households invented the art of verse satire. These poets had the power to curse and to lay a *geis*, a magical compulsion or prohibition. Several "cycles," or collections, of tales narrate the life stories of a set of heroes and villains. The most extensive is the **Ulster Cycle,** which includes the adventures of King Conchobar, or Conor, of Ulster and his clan, the **Ulaid,** and his archenemy, his ex-wife Queen Medbh of Connacht. Ulster's champion is **Cúchulainn** (COO-khull-yun), the king's nephew and an athlete extraordinare known as the "Hound of Ulster," whose adventures begin at the age of five. The Amazonian warrior Scathach taught him the arts of war and how to wield the Gae Bolga, the sun-god's destructive spear. The central tale of the Ulster Cycle is the **Táin bo Cuailnge** (Cattle Raid of Cooley), in which Queen Medbh (MAVE) decides first to borrow, and then to steal, the most famous bull in the country, the Donn of Cooley. She assembles an army to capture the bull and invades Ulster when all the Ulster warriors are disabled by the curse of Queen Macha (see p. 24). Only the 17-year-old Cúchulainn is immune, and he single-handedly defeats Medbh's soldiers over a season-long period. The cycle also includes the story of Deirdre, Queen of Sorrow, who King Conor courted, coveted, and cursed to make Ireland's version of the Helen of Troy story.

VOICE CEDES TO PEN. Toward the end of the first millennium, the oral tradition of the bards ceded some ground to the monastic penchant for writing it all down. The monastic settlements of pre-Norman Ireland compiled enormous annals of myth, legend, and history. An established pagan tradition and the introduction of Christianity created a tension in Irish literature between recalling old bardic forms and incorporating a new world-view. Resentment of the church's high-handedness is apparent in **Sweeney Astray,** the story of a pagan king turned into a bird by a monk's curse. The relevance of the tale to the continued interference of the church in Irish literary imagination is evidenced by Seamus Heaney's translation of the poem in the 1980s.

Literati have periodically compiled Ireland's **folktales.** These tales include otherworldly creatures like **banshees,** which are still believed to forecast an imminent death when they are heard wailing outside the house of an ailing individual, and descendants of the Túatha de Danann (the **faeries**). **Leprechauns** are a late, degenerate conflagration of Ireland's mythic creatures, mainly embraced by foreign cultures. For more myths and tales, try *Folktales of Ireland,* edited by Sean O'Sullivan; W.B. Yeats's *Fairy Folk Tales of Ireland* and *A Treasury of Irish Myth, Legend, and Folklore;* or *Irish Myths and Legends* by Yeats and Lady Augusta Gregory.

1600-1880: YET MORE WIT AND RESISTANCE

After the English succinctly dispossessed the local Irish chieftains in the Battle of Kinsale in 1601 (see p. 9), most Irish writers predicted the imminent collapse of Irish language and culture. The new English lords sought to maintain their power by forcing the native Irish tenants to speak English and convert to the Church of Ireland. As the bards of the Irish courts lost their high status, they carried on their work among the peasant classes, so that Ireland developed a vernacular literary culture. The majority of the works written in Irish at this time lament the state of Ireland as a land under cultural attack; a common theme in poetry of the time is the metaphor of Ireland as a captive woman. Perhaps the most famous of these poems is "Roisin Dubh," which describes Ireland as a beautiful dark woman, or "black rose."

By the 17th century, wit and satire began to characterize this period of emerging modern Irish literature. In long-colonized Dublin, **Jonathan Swift** (1667-1745), long-time Dean of St. Patrick's Cathedral, wrote some of the most sophisticated, misanthropic, and marvelous satire in the English language. Like writers throughout the island, Swift felt compelled to write about the sad condition of starving, Irish peasants. Besides his masterpiece *Gulliver's Travels,* Swift wrote political pamphlets and essays decrying English cruelty to the native Irish, while defending the Protestant Church of Ireland. "A Modest Proposal" (1729) suggests that the overpopulated and hungry native Irish sell their children as food.

Through original writings and frequent translations, three main attitudes towards poetry and language evolved in Ireland. Rapidly following Swift, Dublin-born nationalist **Thomas Moore** (1779-1852) blurred the lines between satire and poetry. His *Irish Melodies* (1807-1834), a collection of 130 poems, includes the enduring "Oft in the Stilly Night." Though their audience was the London aristocracy, Moore believed his ballads, set to his own music, advanced the Irish cause, a sentiment confirmed by his heroic popularity with the nationalist crowd. Moore moved on to less sentimental work with his narrative poem *Lalla Rookh* (1817) and his later political satire. This was more in line with the militant stance adopted by writers for *The Nation,* a Dublin-based periodical, which propounded outright rebellion against all things English to preserve Irish purity.

THE JOKER IS WILDE

"I summed up all systems in a phrase, and all existence in an epigram." Oscar Wilde wrote this in an 1897 letter to his lover Lord Alfred "Bosie" Douglas from jail while serving his two-year sentence for sodomy. Most of Wilde's wit is immortalized in ink, but perhaps more remarkable was his ability to come up with spontaneous quips. He was a dinner party favorite, unleashing caustic quips in his deep, rhythmic voice for the Victorian society he so often mocked. Though one of the aesthete's preferred activities was to lounge on his couch for hours in deep contemplation, where he undoubtedly coined many of his witticisms for later use, he was never at a loss for words, even under duress. During his 1895 trial, the lawyer for the Marquess of Queensbury (Douglas's irate father, against whom Wilde originally pressed charges for libel, but who turned the evidence against the writer) read what he deemed an immoral verse from one of Wilde's essays, taunting "And I suppose you wrote that also, Mr. Wilde?" The irrepressible Oscar replied, "Ah, no, Mr. Carson, *Shakespeare* wrote that." He continued to delight the court until the gravity of the case became too overwhelming. But for a man who boldly announced on arrival at the New York Custom House, "I have nothing to declare except my genius," even life-and-death matters were not exempt from his nimble tongue. On his Parisian deathbed, he is reported to have said, "My wallpaper and I are fighting a duel to the death. One or the other of us has to go."

In the mid-19th century, the Famine hit, and folk-culture fell by the wayside in the face of destitution; while the peasants starved, the Industrial Revolution passed by Ireland. Cosmopolitan Dublin managed to breed talent, but talented young writers moved on from Trinity to London to make their names. **Oscar Wilde** (1856-1900) moved to London and set up as a cultivated aesthete to write one novel and many sparklingly witty plays, including *The Importance of Being Earnest* (1895). His work critiqued society and propriety while fetishizing it; he personally challenged Irish clichés and Victorian determinism by perfecting a pithy style whose absurd truths still stand today. Prolific playwright **George Bernard Shaw** (1856-1950) was also born in Dublin but moved to London in 1876, where he became an active socialist. *John Bull's Other Island* (1904) depicts the increasing hardships of the Irish peasant laborer. Shaw himself identified much of his writing as Irish, in form if not always in content: "When I say I am an Irishman I mean that my language is the English of Swift and not the unspeakable drivel of the mid-19th-century newspapers." Shaw won the Nobel Prize for Literature in 1925 for a body of work that includes *Arms and the Man* (1932), *Candida* (1905), *Man and Superman* (1931), and *Pygmalion* (1938).

THE IRISH LITERARY REVIVAL: 1880 TO THE WAR YEARS

Towards the end of the 19th century, a portion of Ireland's crop of young writers no longer turned to London to cultivate their talent. Rather, a vigorous and enduring effort known today as the **Irish Literary Revival** took over the scene. Members of this movement turned to Irish culture, from its ancient mythology to contemporary folktales, for inspiration. Writers such as W.B. Yeats, Lady Gregory, and A.E. (George Russel) overturned the assumption that the indigenous culture was less sophisticated than that of England. The task of literature was now to discover the real Ireland, whether Gaelic or Anglicized (or both). Interest in the Irish language suddenly revived. The memoirs of Irish speakers were discovered and embraced. The most famous of them is *Peig*, the autobiography of **Peig Sayers**; it is a mournful book about a girl growing up on the Blaskets (see p. 269) that is still read in schools today. This memoir, and others like it, led readers to mourn the decline of Gaelic culture and language. (See also **The Irish Language**, p. 22.)

YEATS AND LADY GREGORY LEAD THE CHARGE. The Irish Literary Revival was hardly a nostalgic movement; it recognized the Anglo-Irish perspective as a practical reality, so that many authors continued to write in English, the most commonly understood language on the island by that time. Yeats and Lady Gregory recorded and published mythology and folktales in English. Lady Augusta Gregory (1852-1932) wrote 40 plays and a number of translations, poems, and essays. She began her career by collecting the folktales and legends of Galway's poor residents and later discovered her own skill as a writer of dialogue, creating mainly comedic plays with a staunch nationalism. The revival also looked to ancient mythology and fairytales to find personal meaning, a strain that is exhibited in the works of the mystic George Russel, who went by the pseudonym A.E. The early poems of William Butler Yeats (1865-1939) create a dreamily rural Ireland of loss and legend. His early work, from *Crossways* (1889) to *In the Seven Woods* (1904), won Yeats worldwide fame thanks to the appeal of his mystic vision of picturesque Ireland. Yeat's vision changed remarkably after he realized the role of the Gaelic Revival in promoting the nationalism that led to the violence of the Irish Civil War. "Easter 1916" describes the sudden transformation that the Easter rebels brought to the Irish national self-image: "All changed, changed utterly / A terrible beauty is born." Yeats later bought and renovated a stone tower, **Thoor Ballylee** (see p. 302), in which he lived with his family in isolation. The tower became a part of the idiosyncratic symbolism that appears in the last two decades of his poems, from *The Tower* (1928) to the posthumous *Last Poems* (1939). In 1923, he became the first Irishman to win the Nobel Prize.

In 1904, Yeats and Lady Gregory founded the **Abbey Theater** in Dublin (see p. 119), in order to "build up a Celtic and Irish school of dramatic literature." But conflict almost immediately arose between various contributors. Was this new body of drama to be written in verse or prose, in the realistic or the fantastic and heroic mode? In theory, the plays would be written in Irish, but in practice they needed to be written in English. A sort of compromise was found in the work of **John Millington Synge** (1871-1909), whose English plays were perfectly Irish in essence. A multi-faceted man who "wished to be at once Shakespeare, Beethoven, and Darwin," he spent much of his early years traveling and living in Paris. During one of his many stays in Ireland, Synge met Yeats, who advised that he look for inspiration on the Aran Islands. This advice, which Synge followed in 1898, led him to write *The Aran Islands*, a documentary of life on the islands (see p. 303). His experiences also gave him the subject matter for writing his black comedy *The Playboy of the Western World* (1907), which destroys the pastoral myth about Irish peasantry and portrays a rural society divided into classes. The play's first production instigated riots. **Sean O'Casey** (1880-1964) also caused rioting at the Abbey with the premier in 1926 of *The Plough and Star*, which depicted the Easter Rebellion without mythologizing its leaders. In general, however, his plays were well received by Dublin's middle class, as they were the first portrayals of gritty urban life in their fair city; examples of his work are *Juno and the Paycock* (1924) and *The Shadow of a Gunman* (1923).

After the heroism of the Civil War and Republicanism, Ireland had suddenly become conservative. In this atmosphere, the **Irish Ireland** movement, provincial and Catholic in its beliefs, brought about the **Censorship of Publications Act** in 1929. This act severely restricted the development of Irish literature. In the journal which he edited, the poet A.E. fought against such repression. He envisioned a broad cultural synthesis that would include various cultures and religions, not just those that Ireland's new government accepted.

MODERNISM: JOYCE AND BECKETT

Many authors still found Ireland too small and insular an island to suit their literary aspirations. The most famous of Ireland's expatriates is **James Joyce** (1882-1941); his novels are recognized as some of the seminal works of Modernism. Joyce was born and educated in Dublin, but he left Ireland forever in 1904, because of the following sentiment: "How sick, sick, sick, I am of Dublin! It is the city of failure, of rancour and of unhappiness. I long to be out of it." All the same, Joyce's writing never did leave Ireland, as his novels and stories exclusively describe the lives of Dubliners, and obsessively detail the city's geography and establishments. Joyce's most accesible writing is the collection of short stories titled *Dubliners* (1914). His first novel, *A Portrait of the Artist as a Young Man* (1914), uses the protagonist Stephen Daedalus to describe Joyce's own youth in Dublin, and his decision to leave his country, religion, and family behind him. Stephen Daedalus reappears in *Ulysses*, Joyce's revolutionary novel of 1922. *Ulysses* chronicles one day in the life of Leopold Bloom, a middle-class Jewish man wandering around a stagnating Dublin. The novel's structure follows that of Homer's *Odyssey*—hence the title. It was first published in serial form in a small American magazine in 1918 and banned for obscenity by a US Court in 1920. In 1922, Paris-based Shakespeare and Co. published the first full edition. In his last book, *Finnegans Wake* (1939), Joyce falls into a reverie of allusion, puns, and onomatopoeia that defy all attempts at light reading, but sound fantastic.

Samuel Beckett (1906-89) served as Joyce's personal assistant in his twenties, admiring him so much that he's said to have modeled his personal costume after Joyce. Like Joyce, Beckett fled to Paris to pursue his writing career; unlike Joyce, he left most of vernacular Ireland behind him. He wrote most of his work in French between the years 1946 and 1950. His three novels *(Molloy, Malone Dies,* and *The Unnameable)*, world-famous plays *(Waiting for Godot, Endgame)*, and bleak prose poems convey a deathly pessimism about language, society, and life. Beckett won the Nobel Prize in 1969, but did not accept it on the grounds that Joyce had never received it.

POEMS, PLAYS, AND PLOTS IN THE 20TH CENTURY

Censorship remained an overwhelming force through most of this century, banning writers from Edna O'Brien to F. Scott Fitzgerald. Should a citizen's complaint prove a book to be indecent, obscene, or advocating unnatural forms of birth control, the censorship board would outlaw the book indefinitely. Even classic Irish language works came under scrutiny, although *Ulysses* escaped attack in the Republic despite being banned in the US.

After the 1940s, Irish poetry was once again commanding wide-spread appreciation. Living in the backwash of the Revival and the Civil War, these new Irish poets questioned their cultural inheritance, finding a new version of Ireland that was a parody of the old one. **Patrick Kavanaugh** (1906-67) debunked a mythical Ireland in such poems as "The Great Hunger" (1945), which was banned for its obscenities, prompting the Irish police to visit Kavanaugh's house and seize the manuscript. The works of both **Thomas Kinsella** and **John Montague** display a keen awareness of the history of Irish poetry with a sensitivity to mid-nineteenth-century civil strife. **Derek Mahon** tried to focus on the common elements that people of all cultures share. Although some poets are directly political and almost propagandistic, much of contemporary poetry is intensely private. Most poets treat the political issue from a distant, everyday perspective. Contemporary poet **Frank Ornsby** writes poetry devoid of political conflict that celebrates the rituals of domestic life. **Eavan Boland** is one of the few modern Irish writers who has attempted to capture the experience of middle-class Irish women and reached public recognition.

The dirt of Dublin continues to provide fodder for generations of writers beyond O'Casey and Joyce. Notorious wit, playwright, poet, and terrorist **Brendan Behan** created semi-autobiographical works about delinquent life, such as his play *The Quare Fellow* (1954). The mild-mannered schoolteacher **Roddy Doyle** wrote the well-known Barrytown Trilogy about family good times in down-and-out Dublin (see **Film**, p. 32), as well as the acclaimed *The Woman Who Walked Into Doors* (1996). Doyle won the Booker Prize in 1994 for *Paddy Clarke Ha Ha Ha.*

Poetry and the novel are the dominant strains of Irish literature in this century, but other types of authorship have also produced fine results. Native playwrights include politically conscious **Frank McGuinness** and **Brian Friel.** Friel's *Dancing at Lughnasa* (1990) was a Broadway hit. **Conor McPherson's** *The Weir* won the 1998 Olivier Award for "Best New Play," and captivated sold-out Broadway audiences with comic and poignant tales told in a rural Irish pub. Important critics and essayists include **Conor Cruise O'Brien,** a former diplomat who writes about most everything—history, literature, culture, politics; **Denis Donoghue,** whose *We Irish* is a vigorous, skeptical lit-crit grab-bag; and the provocative **Declan Kiberd,** whose Ireland is a postcolonial society more like India than like England.

A pair of brothers who grew up in Limerick and emigrated to New York have recently achieved international best-seller stardom. **Frank McCourt** won the Pulitzer Prize for his 1996 memoir about his poverty stricken childhood, *Angela's Ashes* (1996). His brother **Malachy McCourt** recently published his equally popular memoir, *A Monk Swimming* (1999).

MODERN WRITERS IN NORTHERN IRELAND

The literature of Northern Ireland describes two culturally divided groups, Catholics and Protestants. Many Northern writers attempt to create works of relevance to members of both communities. Protestant poet **Louis MacNeice** (1907-63) infused his lyric poems with a Modernist concern for struggle and social upheaval, but he took no part in the sectarian politics. His *Valediction* masterfully attacks an idealized Ireland. Novelist **Brian Moore's** *The Emperor of Ice Cream* (1965) is a coming-of-age story set in wartime Belfast. Born in rural Co. Derry, **Seamus Heaney** won the Nobel Prize for Literature in 1995 and is the most prominent living Irish poet. His subject matter ranges from bogs to bombings to archaeological remains. While his tone is often highly lyrical and his focus is on rural themes, Heaney writes in an anti-pastoral mode. His fourth book, *North* (1975), tackles the Troubles head-on. He was part of the **Field Day Movement,** led by Derry poet and critic **Seamus Deane,** which produced what was billed as the definitive anthology of Irish writing, although it has recently come under heavy fire for its relative lack of women writers. One of Heaney's contemporaries, **Paul Muldoon,** occupies himself more with self-skepticism and an ear for weird rhymes rather than politics.

MUSIC

TRADITIONAL FOLK MUSIC AND DANCE

> It is the cultivation of instrumental music I consider the proficiency of this people to be worthy of commendation; and in this their skill is, beyond all comparison, beyond that of any nation I have ever seen.
> —Giraldus Cambrensis, c.1146-1223: *The History and Topography of Ireland*

Irish traditional music is alive and kicking. Commonly called "trad," it is the centuries-old array of dance rhythms, cyclic melodies, and embellishments that has been passed down through generations of musicians. These tunes can be written down, but that's not their primary means of transmission. Indeed, a traditional musician's training consists largely of listening to and innovating from the work of others. Any music session in a pub will sample from a variety of types, including reels, jigs, hornpipes, and slow airs. These are the skeletons around which the players in a trad session build the music. The same tune will produce a different result every session.

Irish traditional music may be heard in two ways: recordings and impromptu evening pub sessions. Best-selling recording artists include **Altan, De Danann,** and the **Chieftains.** Other excellent groups that are available on compact disks are the **Bothy Band** and **Planxty** of the 1970s, and, more recently, **Nomos, Solas, Dervish,** and

Deanta. These bands have brought Irish music into international prominence, starting with the early recordings of the Chieftains and their mentor **Sean O'Rioda**, who, in the 1950s, fostered the resurrection of trad from near extinction to a national art form. While recording bands perform regularly at concerts, most traditional musicians are accustomed to playing before smaller, more intimate audiences of locals at a pub. A session takes place when independent musicians gather at the pub to play together; as such, sessions are an excellent way to witness the real, amorphous identity of Irish traditional tunes. *Let's Go* lists many pubs with regular trad sessions, but you'll find the best music by asking local trad enthusiasts. Pubs in Counties Clare, Kerry, Galway, Sligo, and Donegal are especially strong. If you want a guarantee that you'll hear lots of traditional music, find a **fleadh** (FLAH), a musical festival at which musicians' officially scheduled sessions often spill over into nearby pubs. **Comhaltas Ceoltóirí Éireann**, the national traditional music association, organizes *fleadhs*. Write or call them at 32 Belgrave Sq., Monkstown, Co. Dublin (☎ (01) 280 0495; www.mayo-ireland.ie/CCE.htm).

A DIFFERENT MUSIC. The techniques of trad have little in common with those of European classical music; it's often said that training in one is an impediment to playing the other. The instruments with which Irish trad music is most frequently played are the fiddle, the wooden flute, the button accordion or smaller concertina, the tin whistle, and the *uilleann* pipes (elbow pipes). These pipes appear similar to the Scottish bagpipes, but are played significantly differently: the bellows are held under the arm and pumped thus. The resulting sound is far more melodic than the Scottish instrument, resembling a sweet fiddle rather than an accompaniment for war. The unwieldy harp, Ireland's national symbol, is rarely encountered in live trad music now, but is frequently heard in recordings. The *bodhrán* (BAU-ron), a hand-held drum, wasn't seen as a legitimate instrument until the 60s, when **Sean Ó Riada** introduced it in an effort to drive rock and jazz drumming out. Today, the *bodhrán* has skillful specialists. It is played either with both ends of a stick or with the bare hand. Less common percussion instruments include the spoons and the bones, which are played by clicking two sheep ribs together. Irish music has benefited from the recent introduction of instruments from other cultures, so that a session might feature anything from a guitar or banjo to a jew's harp or digereedoo.

VOCAL STRAINS. Purists get in heated arguments about what constitutes "traditional" singing. A style of unaccompanied vocals called *sean-nós* ("old-time") is definitely the oldest form on the island. This style of nasal singing descends from keening, an ancient practice of wailing lamentation. It requires the vocalist to sing each verse of a song differently, by peppering the tune with syllabic embellishments and tonal variations. More common than *sean-nos* is folk singing, which refers to guitar- or mandolin-accompanied ballads. Sessions in pubs typically alternate between fast-paced traditional instrumental music and folk songs. Ireland's favorite traditional songsters include **Dominick Behan**, **The Dubliners**, **Christy Moore**, and **Sean Tyrell**. The Irish also appreciate international crooners, so that sessions will likely feature a Joni Mitchell tune.

IT'S NOT ALL FLASHY RIVERDANCE. For the atonal, traditional dance provides a means of participating in Irish culture. Indeed, hard-shoe dancing involves creating a percussion accompaniment by pounding the floor with foot-loose fury. Individual **step-dancing** and group **set-dancing** are centuries-old practices, but the spontaneous and innovative streak in each is fading fast. Today, traditional dancing follows the regimentation of formal competitions, where traditional dancers compete according to rote standards of perfection. *Céilís*, at which attendants participate in traditional Irish set-dancing, still take place in most Irish towns. The world-sweeping spectacles of *Riverdance* and *Lord of the Dance* offer loose interpretations of Irish dance, breathing (entirely) new life into the form.

IRISH ROCK, PUNK, AND POP

Music is one of Ireland's national resources, meaning that most everyone has some sort of audible talent. Concurrently, the Irish have a wide-ranging musical appreciation. Along with their vastly successful exportation of trad, the Irish have developed a taste for outside forms of music, and often times adapt them. This cross-pollination produces musicians who draw on traditional and eclectic elements. The first commercially successful artist to do so was **John McCormack** of Athlone, one of the finest tenors of the early 20th century. While he was known internationally for opera, he endeared audiences to the Irish folk songs he invariably included in his recitals.

Bridging the gap between traditional folk ballads and contemporary Ireland to great popular acclaim is **Christy Moore,** who has been called the Bob Dylan of Ireland. The ballads and anthems that Moore made popular now form something of a pub sing-along canon—hardly a late-night session goes by without someone's moving rendition of "Ride On," "City of Chicago," or the lament "Irish Ways and Irish Laws." His younger brother **Luka Bloom** takes a few steps further along the road to pop sensibility, but still sings the confessionals of a proud young Irishman. **Horslips** became hugely popular in the 70s by trying to merge trad and rock forms, but wound up shuffling uneasily between the two. **Van Morrison's** early inspirations included American soul and blues, which he submerged into Celtic "soul." The London-based **Pogues** also felt the desire to fuse rock and trad, to far different effect. Their lead singer Shane MacGowan named the Dubliners' Luke Kelly and Jimi Hendrix as his idols. In albums such as *Rum, Sodomy, and the Lash,* they whipped out reel and jigs of drunken, punk-damaged revelry, accompanied by MacGowan's poetic descriptions of Irish emigrant sorrows and the horrors of sectarian violence.

Another outlet for trad in modernity is the synthesizer. **Enya** used Irish lyricism and electronics to create a style of pervasive tunes you hear before Aer Lingus in-flight movies. The rest of her immediate family makes up the members of Clannad, who sound much like Enya, with the infusion of several wooden and winded instruments. More recently, the **Afro-Celt Sound System** have achieved popular and critical success with their fusion of traditional Celtic and African sounds with manic rhythms of drum and bass.

Irish musicians have dabbled in practically every genre of pure-bred rock. In the 70s, **Thin Lizzy** produced early heavy metal laced with a sensitivity to Irish literary greatness. Around the same time, the worldwide punk rock explosion spawned brilliance in Belfast, where **Stiff Little Fingers** spat forth three years of excellent anthems. Throughout the North, punk became an outlet for the youth culture trying to escape the conflicts and bigotries of its parents. The most successful of these groups were Derry's **Undertones,** which eventually evolved into the garage rock of That Petrol Emotion. Punk was also creating a ruckus down in late 70s Dublin. The **Boomtown Rats** sold well and made a star of their frontman Bob Geldoff, who went on to found Live Aid. Slightly afterwards, the **Virgin Prunes** did their best to live up to their name, which is Dublinese for "freak" or "outcast." Their lead singer **Gavin Friday** continues to create cabaret-style alternative rock. In the 90s, punk's grunge legacy has made waves in both Northern Ireland and the Republic. **Ash** heralded a 90s revival of the Belfast punk aesthetic; their album *1977* reached number one on the UK charts. The eternally on-hiatus **My Bloody Valentine** weaved shimmering distortions to land them in the outskirts of grunge.

Ireland's musicians have also set their sights on mainstream super-stardom, and achieved that goal often enough. **U2** is Ireland's biggest rock export. From the adrenaline-soaked promise of the 1980 *Boy,* the band slowly ascended into the rock stratosphere, culminating in world-wide fame with *The Joshua Tree* (1987). The band found new vitality in *Achtung Baby* (1991) and *Pop* (1997), and while fans wondered if the band had sold out or was only pretending to, the music spoke for itself. **Sinéad O'Connor** stood her own as an independent female rockstar with attitude long before the lauded American phenomenon of the late 1990s. The lowercase **cranberries** and the sibling-based **Coors** have cornered the international soft rock market. The boy-group **Boyzone** has recently conquered the UK charts and the hearts of millions of pre-adolescent girls; similar black magic is practiced on the opposite sex by their sisters in the girl-group **B*witched**.

POPULAR MEDIA

FILM: THE GREEN SCREEN

The deceivingly luscious green soil that devastated the lives of the native Irish for so many centuries is finally turning a profit thanks to Ireland's burgeoning movie industry. The island's expanses of green, its picturesque villages, and comparatively low labor costs are a filmmaker's dream. Hollywood discovered Ireland in John Wayne's 1952 film **The Quiet Man,** giving an international audience of millions their first view of the island's beauty, albeit through a stereotypical lens Irish film has long struggled to change. Aside from the garish green of Hollywood technicolor vision, art-filmmakers have also found Ireland. Robert Flaherty created cinematic Realism in his classic documentary about coastal fishermen, **Man of Aran** (1934). Alfred Hitchcock filmed Sean O'Casey's **Juno and the Paycock** with the Abbey Theatre Players in 1930. American director John Huston, who eventually made Ireland his home, made numerous films there; his last work **The Dead** (1987) is the film version of James Joyce's story from *Dubliners*.

FROM INDIE FILM TO HOLLYWOOD. In the last ten-odd years, the Irish government has begun to encourage a truly Irish film industry. An excellent art cinema has opened in Temple Bar in Dublin, and there's an office two blocks away to encourage budding moviemakers. These recent efforts have resulted in a less idealistic but, most times, equally loving vision of Ireland. **Jim Sheridan** helped kick off the Irish cinematic renaissance with his universally acclaimed adaptation of Christy Brown's autobiography, **My Left Foot** (1991). More recently, Sheridan has worked with actor Daniel Day Lewis in two films that take a humanitarian approach to the lives of Catholics and Protestants during the Troubles, with **In the Name of the Father** (1993) and **The Boxer** (1997). Based on the novels of the Barrytown Trilogy by Roddy Doyle, **The Commitments** (1991), **The Snapper** (1993), and **The Van** (1996) follow a family from the depressed North Side of Dublin as its members variously form a soul band, have a kid, and get off the dole by running a chipper. Another Dublin saga, **The General** (1998; see p. 143), by the English director John Boorman, describes the true rise and fall of one of the most notorious criminals in recent Irish history. Dublin-native **Neil Jordan** has become a much sought-after director thanks to the success of **The Crying Game** (1992), **Michael Collins** (1996), and **The Butcher Boy** (1998). The Ireland of fairytales is captured with exquisite cinematography in **The Secret of Roan Inish** (1995) and **Into the West** (1993). The darkly comic **I Went Down** (1997) demonstrated the growing overseas popularity of Irish independent film. In 1999, the appeal of Irish scenery and accents was attested to by the profitable production of two highly Irish sounding and looking films by non-Irish filmmakers: Hollywood produced a film version of Donegal playwright Brien Friel's **Dancing at Lunasa**, and the government of the Isle of Man sponsored **Waking Ned Devine,** which describes the antics of a village of rustic eccentrics.

NATIVE FESTIVALS. The **Galway Film Fleadh** is Ireland's version of Cannes, appropriately reduced in scale but still featuring a week's worth of quality films. The **Dublin Film Festival** runs for a week in the middle of April. The month-long **Dublin Lesbian and Gay Film Festival** occupies all of August. Dublin also hosts the **Junior Dublin Film Festival** during the last week of November and the first week of December, showing the world's best children's films. In Northern Ireland, the **Foyle Film Festival** takes place in Derry during the last week in April.

NEWSPAPERS AND OTHER MEDIA

The Republic and Northern Ireland together support eight national **dailies** with a combined circulation of around 1.5 million. The largest of these papers in the Republic are the *Irish Times* and the *Irish Independent* (www.ireland.com and www.independent.ie). The *Times* takes a liberal voice, and is renowned worldwide for its excellent coverage of international affairs. The *Independent* is more internally focused, and often times maintains a chatty writing style. *The Herald* is an evening daily that hovers somewhere in the middle. Neither the *Times* nor the *Independent* comes out with a Sunday paper, but their readership is generally satisfied with an Irish version of *The London Times*. The best-selling paper in the North is the *Belfast Telegraph* (www.belfasttelegraph.co.uk). The sectarian community is represented by two mainstream newspapers: Unionists read the *Belfast Newsletter*, while Nationalists turn to the *Irish News*. **Tabloids** like the *Daily Mirror*, the *Irish Sun*, the *Irish Star*, and the *Sporting News* offer low-level coverage with an emphasis on stars, scandals, and sports, and the occasional topless picture. A large number of regional papers offer more in-depth local news; the largest is the *The Cork Examiner*. British papers are sold throughout the Republic and Northern Ireland.

BBC brought radio to the Irish island when it established a station in Belfast in 1924; two years later, the Irish Free State started the radio station 2RN in Dublin. Television struck when BBC began TV broadcasts from Belfast in 1953. Ulster Television, the island's first independent channel, was established in 1959. In 1961, the Republic's national radio service made its first television broadcast, renaming itself **Radio Telefís Éireann (RTE).** Most of the island now has cable service with access to the BBC and other independent British channels, the most popular of which is Rupert Murdoch's SKY Television. The Irish government's most recent developments include the start of Irish language radio and TV stations, called Telifis na Gaelige (see **The Irish Language,** p. 22). These efforts aim at combatting the contribution of modern media forms to the deterioration of the Irish language.

Computers have infected Ireland—viruses, email chain-letters, and all. Most of the major international manufacturers are represented, and local companies make personalized computers (some, such as the **Celtic®computer,** are even proud of their heritage). Software is a huge industry in Ireland, the world's second largest exporter of the stuff. While email has yet to overrun the Trinity campus, access is becoming easier to find in cafes and hostels. The tourism industry is also becoming Internet commerce savvy; many towns and accommodations have their own websites and email accounts.

SPORTS

The Irish take enormous pride in their two native sports: hurling and Gaelic football. For many Irish, these games are the reason that spring changes into summer. Many a day would be wasted trying to find a farmer, business executive, or sheep unaware of his or her county's progress. Regional divisions are most obvious in county allegiances. Take notice of the hysteria of any Irish sporting event, when hordes of fans bedecked in their county colors bring bedlam to Irish city streets. Attending a pub the day of that county's game will leave you happy, deaf, drunk, and counting down the days to the next round.

FOUNDING BODIES. Most traditional Irish sports are modern developments of contests fought between whole clans or parishes across expanses of countryside. In 1884, the **Gaelic Athletic Association (GAA)** was founded to establish official rules and regulations for hurling, Gaelic football, and other ancient Irish recreations. A secondary function of their efforts was to promote a non-British identity on the island. The organization's first patron was Archbishop Croke of Cashel and Emly; his name later came to adorn Croke Park in Dublin, Ireland's biggest Gaelic games stadium. The GAA divided the island on a club-county-province level, in which the club teams organized mostly according to parish lines. Arranged according to the four provinces Connacht, Munster, Leinster, and Ulster, all 32 counties of the island compete in the knockout rounds of the two sports' "All Ireland" Championships, but only two make it to the finals in September. Despite the fervent nationalism of its beginnings, the GAA has always included the Northern Ireland teams in these leagues. Sectarian politics plague today's GAA, leaving its fate uncertain.

HOW IT'S PLAYED IN THE OLD COUNTRY. According to the GAA, "played well, **Gaelic football** is a fast, skillful game striking to the eye. Played badly, it is an unimpressive spectacle of dragging and pulling!" Gaelic football seems like a cross between soccer and rugby, although it predates both of them. The ball is shorter and fatter than a rugby ball. Players may run holding the ball for no more than four paces, after which they must bounce, kick, or punch it in any direction. At each end of the field is a set of goalposts, and below the crossbar there is a net resembling a soccer net. One point is scored for putting the goal over the crossbar between the posts, three for netting it. The game is played by both men and women in teams of 15 for two 30-minute periods. Charging is within the rules.

MUSCLE OVER DISTANCE. As fans like to say, if football is a game, then **hurling** is an art. This fast and dangerous-looking game was first played in the 13th century. Perhaps best imagined as a blend of lacrosse and field hockey, the game is named after the stick with which it is played, the *caman* or "hurley." The hurley—like a hockey stick with a shorter and wider blade—is used to hit the ball along the ground or overhead. Players may also kick the ball, or hit it with the flat of their hands. The ball, or *sliothar*, is leather-covered and can be caught for hitting, or carried along on the stick. Teams of 15 players each try to score a point by hitting the ball over the eight-foot-high crossbar of the goalposts. A goal is worth three points and is scored by hitting the ball under the crossbar. The female version of hurling is called camogie, and permits only twelve team members but considerably more protective-wear.

FOOTBALL AND OTHERS. Imported to Ireland in 1878, **football** (or soccer, to Americans) enjoys an equally fanatical, if less patriotic, following as hurling and gaelic football. The Irish dream of international stardom in this sport, and came closer to achieving it when they reached the quarter finals of the 1994 World Cup. The Irish are also fiercely devoted to the football clubs of England. Rugby achieves a strong fan base in both the Republic and Northern Ireland. Horse racing maintains a devoted following in the Republic, thanks to Co. Kildare's well-appreciated place as a breeding ground for champion racehorses. Watersports like **surfing** and **sailing** are popular hobbies, particularly along the Western and Northwestern coasts.

FOOD AND DRINK

SOLIDS

Food in Ireland can be fairly expensive, especially in restaurants. The basics—and that's what you'll get—are simple and filling. The restaurant business is a fairly recent phenomenon in Ireland: up until the economy took off about 20 years ago, only a few restaurants graced the streets of even Dublin. Today, eateries clutter the streets of Ireland's mini-metropolises, many of which specialize in international fares. The rural byways of the island still remain limited in their culinary offerings. A quick and greasy staple everywhere are "chippers" (fish and chips shops) and "take-aways" (take-outs). At chippers, "fish" is a whitefish, usually cod, and chips are served with salt and vinegar; ketchup sometimes costs extra. Fried food delicacies include chips with gravy, potato cakes (flat pancakes made of potato flakes), or the infamous spiceburger (a fried patty of spiced breadcrumbs). Most pubs serve food as well as drink, and **pub grub** is a good option for a substantial and inexpensive meal. Typical pub grub includes Irish stew (meat, potatoes, carrots, and onions), burgers, soup, and sandwiches.

Most Irish meals are based on a simple formula: meat, potatoes, and greens. Preparation usually involves frying or boiling. *Colcannon* (a potato, onion, and cabbage dish), "ploughman's lunch," and Irish stew are Irish specialties. Loud and long will the Irish bards sing the praises of the Clonakilty man who first concocted **black pudding**. This delicacy was invented during a shortage and makes the most of the bits of the pig not usually eaten. Black pudding is, as one local butcher put it, "some pork, a good deal of blood, and grains and things—all wrapped up in a tube." White pudding is a similar dish that uses milk instead of blood. **Irish breakfasts**, often served all day and a given at any B&B, include eggs, sausage, white or black pudding, porridge, rashers (a more thickly sliced version of American bacon), a fried tomato, brown bread, and toast.

The culinary merit of the Irish resides in their bread. Most famous is **soda bread**, a heavy white bread sweetened by raisins, and especially yummy when fried. Most common are **brown bread** and **batch loaves**. Brown bread is thick and grainy, while batch loaves are square-shaped white bread ideal for sandwiches. Another indigenous bread is **barm brack;** perfect for holidays, it is a spicy mixture of dried fruits and molasses mixed to a lead-like density. Sandwiches are often served on a **bap**, a round, white bun. All of these breads are excellent in combination with locally produced cheeses, which make up a small industry in the Southwest.

Seafood can be a real bargain in smaller towns; mussels and oysters are delectable when marinated in Guinness. In addition to the widespread fried fish, smoked mackerel is splendid year-round, and Atlantic salmon is freshest around July.

> ## TURLOUGH'S IRISH SODA BREAD
>
> **Dry Ingredients**
> 2½ cups coarse brown flour
> 1 cup white flour
> ¼ cup rolled oats
> ¼ cup bran
> 2 tsp. baking soda (NO clumps!)
>
> **Wet Ingredients**
> ¼ cup vinegar
> 2 cups milk
> 1 Guinness beer
>
> **Directions:**
> Preheat oven to 400°F. Mix dry ingredients well (the baking soda needs to be well-distributed). Add wet ingredients, except Guinness, and mix through to the bottom. Pour mixture into a greased, regular-sized bread-pan. Open Guinness and enjoy your reward as you wait 40 minutes for your bread to bake!

Regional specialties include **crubeen** (tasty pigs' feet) in Cork, **coddle** (boiled sausages and bacon with potatoes) in Dublin, and **blaa** (sausage rolls) in Waterford. Wexford berries in the Southeast are luscious May through July. **Tea** accompanies most meals; it has come to signify more than just that which quenches thirst or politely washes down unwanted cabbage. If the Irish drink Guinness for strength, they drink tea for everything else.

In the North, an Irish Breakfast is called an **Ulster Fry.** Aside from that, food in the North is much the same as that in the Republic. Throughout the island, breakfast is the first meal of the day, followed by "dinner" at midday, and then an evening "tea" accompanied by a light meal fare.

LIQUIDS: PUBS AND PINTS

> I was blue mouldy for the want of that pint. Declare to God I could hear it hit the pit of my stomach with a click.
> —James Joyce, *Ulysses* (1922)

A study released in the summer of 1998 found that Irish students spend roughly $80 a month on drinks, which is no wonder considering the centrality of pubs in Irish culture. More so in the Republic than in the North, the pub is, in a sense, the living room of the Irish household. Locals of all ages from every social milieu head to the public house for conversation, food, singing and dancing, and **craic** (crack), an Irish word meaning "a good time." Although the clientele of the average public house is predominantly male, women feel comfortable here, especially on the weekends in urban areas, when students swarm the town. People aren't normally looking for much other than communal talk and drink. In the evening, some pubs host traditional music. Local and traveling musicians toting fiddles, guitars, *bodhráns* (a shallow, one-sided drum), and tin whistles drop in about 9:30pm to start impromptu sessions (see **Music**, p. 29). In rural pubs, there's also a chance that a *seanachaí* (SHAN-ukh-ee), a roving storyteller, might demand an audience.

Pubs in the Republic are generally open Monday through Saturday from 10:30am to 11:30pm (11pm in winter) and Sunday from 12:30 to 2pm and 4 to 11pm (closed 2-4pm due to the Holy hour). Pubs are now able to obtain late-hours licenses that allow them to stay open until midnight-2am. These later hours are becoming increasingly common in Dublin. Some pubs, especially ones catering to a clientele of fishermen, have been granted special "early" licenses, which allow them to open at 7:30am and require an act of Parliament to revoke. Pubs almost never charge a cover price or require a drink minimum. Pubs in the North tend to be open Monday through Saturday from 11:30am to 11pm (or recently until 1 or 2am on the weekends since the Troubles have calmed) and Sunday from 12:30 to 2:30pm and 7 to 10pm. Some pubs close for a few hours on weekday afternoons as well, particularly in rural areas. Pub lunches are usually served Monday to Saturday, 12:30 to 2:30pm, while soup, soda bread, and sandwiches are served all day. Children are often not allowed in pubs after 7pm. The legal drinking age in Ireland and Northern Ireland is 18.

Beer wins a landslide victory as the drink of choice in Irish pubs. Cocktails are an oddity found mainly in American-style bars and discos, and most pubs stock only a few bottles of wine. Beer comes in two basic varieties, **lagers** (blond, fizzy brews served cold, a bit weaker than ales or stouts) and **ales** (slightly darker, more bitter, and sometimes served a bit warmer than lagers). **Stout**, a type of ale, is thick, dark-ruby colored, and made from roasted barley to impart an almost meaty flavor. Guinness stout inspires a reverence otherwise reserved for the Holy Trinity. Known variously as "the dark stuff," "the blonde in the black skirt," or simply "I'll have a pint, please," it's a rich, dark brew with a head thick enough to stand a match in. It's also far better in Ireland than anywhere else. For a sweeter taste, try it with blackcurrant or cider. **Murphy's** is a similar, slightly creamier stout brewed in Cork. Cork also produces **Beamish**, a tasty "economy" stout. Stout takes a while to pour properly (usually 3-4min.); it should be drunk in slow measure as well, and never before it settles. **Smithwicks** is a hoppy, English-style bitter commonly perceived as an old man's drink. Two more popular domestic lagers are **Kilkenny** and **Harp**. You may be surprised by the many pubs serving Budweiser or Heineken here and by the number of young people quaffing such imported lagers. In general, the indigenous brews are far worthier. Beer is served in imperial **pint glasses** (about 20oz.) or half-pints (called a "glass"). Ordering a beer by name will bring you a full pint, so be loud and clear if you can only stay for a half (or just take the pint and drink faster). A pint of Guinness usually costs between IR£2-3 in the Republic and about £2 in Northern Ireland, with prices rising steeply in urban settings.

Irish whiskey, which Queen Elizabeth once claimed was her only true Irish friend, is sweeter than its Scotch counterpart, spelled "whisky" (see p. 226). Irish monks invented whiskey, calling it *uisce beatha*, meaning "water of life." In Ireland, whiskey is served in larger measures than you might be used to. **Jameson** is popular everywhere. Dubliners are partial to **Powers and Sons**. **Bushmills**, distilled near Portstewart, is the favorite in the North. Drinkers in Cork enjoy **Paddy's**. **Irish coffee** is sweetened with brown sugar and whipped cream and laced with whiskey. It's been more popular with the tourists than the natives ever since its alleged invention at Shannon Airport by a desperate bartender looking to appease cranky travelers on a layover. (Others place the drink's origin in San Francisco.) **Hot whiskey** (spiced up with lemon, cloves, and brown sugar) can provide a cozy buzz. In the west, you may hear some locals praise "mountain dew," a euphemism for *poitín* (put-CHEEN), an illegal distillation sometimes given to cows in labor that ranges in strength from 115 to 140 proof. *Poitín* makes after-hour appearances in pubs throughout the island, but be warned that *poitín* is a highly toxic substance. While most alcoholic drinks are based on ethanol, *poitín* uses lethal methanol.

2001 HOLIDAYS AND FESTIVALS

DATE	CITY OR REGION	FESTIVAL
	SPRING	
*April 13		Good Friday
*April 16		Easter Monday
Late April	Galway	Poetry and Literature Festival (Cúirt)
Early May	Creggan	Bealtaine Festival
Early May	Dungarvan	Féile na nDéise
Early May	Cork	Choral Festival
Early May	Glengarriff	Caha Walking Festival
*May 7	Republic of Ireland and U.K.	May Day, Bank holiday
Mid-May	Killarney	Killarney Races
Mid-May	Armagh	Apple Blossom Festival
*May 28	United Kingdom	Bank holiday
Late May to Early June	Sligo	Arts Festival
*June 4	Republic of Ireland	Bank holiday
Early June	Armagh	Comhietas Collton Traditional Music Festival
Early June	Carlow	Éigse
Early June	Ardara	Weaver's Fair
Mid-June	Bangor	The Bangor and North Down Festival
Mid-June	Ballycastle	Fleadh Amhrán agus Rince
Mid-June	Inisheer	St. Kevin's Mass and Festival
Mid-June	Oughterard	Currach racing Championships
June 16	Dublin	Bloomsday
	SUMMER	
4th Weekend in June	Galway	Galway Hooker Festival and Traditional Boat Regatta
Late June	The Curragh	Irish Derby
Late June	Cork	Sense of Cork Festival
Late June	Portaferry	Galway Hookers' Regatta
Late June	Athlone	Athlone Festival
Late June	Bantry	West Cork Chamber Music Festival
Late June to Early July	Donegal Town	International Arts Festival
Early July	Glencolmcille	Glencolmcille Folk Festival
Early July	Duncannon	Duncannon Festival
Early July	Killarney	Killarney Regatta
Early July	Galway	Galway Film Fleadh
Early July	Glenarm	Glenarm Festival
Early July	Milltown Malbay	Willy Clancy Summer School
Early July	Ramelton	Lennon Festival
*July 12	Northern Ireland	Orange Day
July 15	Ballina, Co. Mayo	Heritage Day
Mid-July	Galway	Galway Arts Festival
Mid-July	Kilmore Quay	Seafood Festival

38 ■ 2001 HOLIDAYS AND FESTIVALS

Mid-July	Youghal	Youghal Carnival
Mid-July	Cobh	Seisiún Gis Cuan Festival
Mid-July	Castlegregory	Summer Festival
Mid-July	Drogheda	Samba Festival
Mid-July	Dungarvan	Motorsport Weekend
Mid-July	Killarney	Killarney Races
Mid-July	Ballina	Ballina Street Festival
Mid-July	Boyle	Gala festival
Mid-July	Cushendall	Guinness Relay
July 24	Ardmore	Pattern Day (St. Declan's Festival)
Late July	Sligo	Irish National Sheepdog Trials
Late July	Galway	Galway Races
Late July	Rostrevor	Fiddler's Green Festival
Late July	Boyle	Arts Festival
Late July	Burtonpoint	Burtonpoint Festival
Late July	Skibbereen	Welcome Home Week
Late July	Wicklow	Regatta Festival
Late July to Early August	Sligo	Yeats International Summer School
Late July to Early August	Youghal	Youghal Premier Busking Festival
Late July to Early August	Dungloe	Mary from Dungloe International Festival
Mid-Summer	Cong	Midsummer Ball, John Wayne/Maureen O'Hara Look-Alike Contest
*August 6	Republic of Ireland	Bank holiday
Early August	Belturbet	Festival of the Erne
Early August	Youghal	Busking Festival
Early August	Castletownbere	Festival of the Sea
Early August	Achill Island	Scoil Acla
Early August	Cahersiveen	Celtic Music Festival
Early August	Clonmany	Clonmany Festival
Early August	Kilkenny	Arts Week
Early August	Waterford	Spraoi
Early August	Kilcar	International Sea Angling Festival, Street Festival
Early August	Kinsale	Kinsale Regatta
Early August	Glencolmcille	Fiddle Festival
Early August	Dingle	Dingle Races
August 10-12	Killorglin	Puck Fair
August 15	Malin Head	Sports Day
Mid-August	Dingle	Dingle Regatta
Mid-August	Bantry	Bantry Bay Regatta
Mid-August	Armagh	Ulster Road Bowls Finals
Mid-August	Milltown Malbay	International "Darlin' Girl from Clare" Festival
Mid-August	Warrenpoint	Maiden of the Mournes Festival
Mid-August	Cobh	Cobh People's Regatta
August 21	Knock	Feast of Our Lady of Knock
Late August	Boyle	Quatrocentennial Celebration
Late August	Clifden	Connemara Pony Show
Late August	Clonmel	Fleadh Ceoil na hÉireann
Late August	Tralee	Rose of Tralee International Festival
Late August	Ballycastle	Oul' Lammas Fair

2001 HOLIDAYS AND FESTIVALS

Late August	Carlingford	Medieval Oyster Fair
Late August	Mullet Peninsula	Feille Iorras
Late August	Ballycastle, Co. Antrim	Ould Lammas Fair
Late August	Cape Clear	International Storytelling Festival
*August 27	U.K.	Summer Bank holiday
Early September	Monaghan	Jazz and Blues Festival
September	Dublin	All-Ireland Hurling and Football Finals
September	Cork	Folk Festival
September	Lisdoonvarna	Lisdoonvarna Matchmaking Festival
September 12	Glenties	Harvest Fair
AUTUMN		
Mid-September	Passage East	Mussel Festival
Late September	Westport	Arts Festival
Late September	Clifden	Arts Week
Late September	Galway	International Oyster Festival
Late September	Waterford	Waterford Festival of Light Opera
Early October	Cork	International Film Festival
Early October	Kildare	Irish National Yearling Sales
Early October	Dublin	Dublin Theatre Festival
Early October	Glenties	Fiddler's Weekend
Mid-October	Bundoran	Bundoran Music Festival
Mid-October	Armagh	Arts Festival
Mid-October	Cork	Guinness Jazz Festival
Mid-October	Kinsale	Kinsale Gourmet Festival
Mid-October	Wexford	Wexford Opera Festival
*October 29	Republic of Ireland	Bank holiday
Late October to Early November	Athlone	John McCormack Golden Voice Competition
November	Belfast	Belfast Festival at Queen's
WINTER		
*December 25		Christmas Day
*December 26		St. Stephen's Day/Boxing Day
*January 1		New Year's Day
Valentine's Day weekend	Dungarvan	Dungarvan Jazz Festival
Late February	Dublin	Dublin Film Festival
Mid-March	Killarney	Guinness Roaring 1920s Festival
*March 17	Republic of Ireland and Northern Ireland	St. Patrick's Day

ESSENTIALS

DOCUMENTS AND FORMALITIES

EMBASSIES AND CONSULATES

IRISH EMBASSIES AND CONSULATES IN...
For addresses of Irish embassies in countries not listed here, check the Worldwide Embassies and Consulates Search Engine at http://consulate.travel.com.hk.

Australia: 20 Arkana St., Yarralumla ACT 2600 (☎ (02) 62 73 30 22; fax 62 73 37 41).

Canada: 130 Albert St., Ste. 1105, Ottawa, ON, K1P 5G4 (☎ (613) 233 62 81; fax 233 58 35; email emb.ireland@sympatico.ca).

New Zealand: Consulate General, Dingwall Bldg., 6th Fl., 18 Shortland St., P.O. Box 279, Auckland 1 (☎ (09) 302 28 67).

South Africa: Tubach Centre, 1234 Church St., 0083 Colbyn, Pretoria (☎ (012) 342 50 62; fax 342 47 52).

UK: 17 Grosvenor Pl., London SW1X 7HR (☎ (020) 72 35 21 71; fax 72 45 69 61).

US: Irish Embassy, 2234 Massachusetts Ave. NW, Washington, D.C. 20008 (☎ (202) 462 3939; fax 232 5993). Consulates: 345 Park Ave., 17th floor, New York, NY 10154 (☎ (212) 319 2555); Rm. 911, 400 N. Michigan Ave., Chicago, IL 60611 (☎ (312) 337 1868); 44 Montgomery St., #3830, San Francisco, CA 94104 (☎ (415) 392 4214); 535 Boylston St., Boston, MA 02116 (☎ (617) 267 9330).

UK EMBASSIES AND CONSULATES IN...
For embassies in countries not listed here, check the Foreign and Commonwealth Office website at www.fco.gov.uk/directory/posts.asp (☎ (020) 7238 4503).

Australia: British High Commission, Commonwealth Ave., Yarralumla, Canberra, ACT 2600 (☎ (02) 6270 6666; fax (02) 6273 3236; www.uk.emb.gov.au).

Canada: British High Commission, 80 Elgin St., Ottawa, ON, K1P 5K7 (☎ 613 237 1530; www.britain-in-canada.org). British Consulate-General, 777 Bay St., Suite 2800, Toronto, ON, M5G 2G2 (☎ 416-593-1290; www.uk-canada-trade.org).

France: British Embassy, 35 Rue du Faubourg St. Honoré, 75383 Paris CEDEX 08 (☎ (331) 44 51 31 00; www.amb-grandebretagne.fr).

Ireland: British Embassy, 29 Merrion Rd., Ballsbridge, Dublin 4 (☎ (01) 205 3700; www.britishembassy.ie).

New Zealand: British High Commission, 44 Hill St., Thorndon, Wellington 1 (☎ (64) (4) 472 6049; www.brithighcomm.org.nz).

South Africa: British High Commission, 91 Parliament St., Cape Town 8001 (☎ (27) (21) 461 7220); also at 255 Hill St., Arcadia 0083, Pretoria (☎ (012) 483 1200).

US: British Embassy, 3100 Massachusetts Ave. NW, Washington, D.C. 20008 (☎ (202) 588-6500; www.britainusa.com/bis/embassy/embassy.stm).

FOREIGN EMBASSIES AND CONSULATES IN IRELAND

Australia: Fitzwilton House, Wilton Terr., Dublin 2 (☎ (01) 676 1517; fax 668 5266).

Canada: The Republic, Canadian Embassy, Canada House, 65 St. Stephen's Green, Dublin 2 (☎ (01) 478 1988; fax 478 1285). **UK,** Canadian High Commission,

McDonald House, 1 Grosvenor Sq., London W1X 0AB (☎ (020) 7258 6600; fax 258 6506).

France: 36 Ailesbury Rd., Dublin 4 (☎ (01) 260 1666; fax 283 0178). Contact Maison de la France (www.maison-de-la-france.fr) for more information.

New Zealand: The Republic, Consulate General, 37 Leeson Park, Dublin 6 (☎ (01) 660 4233; fax 660 4228). **UK,** New Zealand Embassy, New Zealand House, 80 Haymarket, London SW1 4TQ (☎ (020) 7930 8422).

South Africa: The Republic, South Africa Embassy, Alexandra House, Earlsford Terr., Dublin 2 (☎ (01) 661 5553; fax 661 5590). **UK,** South African High Commission, South Africa House, Trafalgar Sq., London WC2N 5DP (☎ (020) 7930 4488; fax 7451 930 1510).

United Kingdom: See **UK Embassies and Consulates,** above.

United States: The Republic, American Embassy, 42 Elgin Rd., Ballsbridge, Dublin 4 (☎ (01) 668 7122; fax 668 9946). **Northern Ireland,** Consulate General, Queen's House, 14 Queen St., Belfast BT1 6EQ (☎ (01232) 328239; fax 248482).

> **ENTRANCE REQUIREMENTS.**
> **Passport** (see below). Required for citizens of Australia, Canada, New Zealand, South Africa, the EU, and the US.
> **Visa** (p. 42). Not required for short-term travel from EU, Commonwealth, and North American countries.
> **Inoculations.** No inoculations are required for visiting Ireland.
> **Work Permit** (p. 42). Required for all foreigners planning to work in Ireland.
> **Driving Permit** (p. 62). Required for all those planning to drive.

PASSPORTS

REQUIREMENTS. Citizens of Australia, Canada, New Zealand, South Africa, the EU, and the US need valid passports to enter Ireland and to re-enter their own country. Citizens of the UK do not need a passport, but may want to bring it. Ireland does not allow entrance if the holder's passport expires in under six months; returning home with an expired passport is illegal and may result in a fine.

PHOTOCOPIES. It is a good idea to photocopy the page of your passport that contains your photograph, passport number, and other identifying information, along with other important documents such as visas, travel insurance policies, airplane tickets, and traveler's check serial numbers, in case you lose anything. Carry one set of copies in a safe place apart from the originals and leave another set at home. Consulates also recommend that you carry an expired passport or an official copy of your birth certificate in a part of your baggage separate from other documents.

LOST PASSPORTS. If you lose your passport, immediately notify the local police and the nearest embassy or consulate of your home government. To expedite its replacement, you will need to know all information previously recorded and show identification and proof of citizenship. In some cases, a replacement may take weeks to process, and it may be valid only for a limited time. Any visas stamped in your old passport will be irretrievably lost. In an emergency, ask for immediate temporary traveling papers that permit you to re-enter your home country. Your passport is a public document belonging to your nation's government. You may have to surrender it to a foreign government official, but if you don't get it back in a reasonable amount of time, inform the nearest mission of your home country.

NEW PASSPORTS. All applications for new passports or renewals should be filed several weeks or months in advance of your planned departure date. Most passport offices do offer emergency passport services for an extra charge. Citizens residing abroad who need a passport or renewal should contact their nearest embassy or consulate. Otherwise, contact your passport agency or post office.

VISAS AND WORK PERMITS

Citizens of most countries, including Australia, Canada, EU countries, New Zealand, South Africa, the UK, and the US, do not need visas to visit Ireland. If in doubt, or if your home country is not one of these, check with your embassy.

Admission as a visitor does not include the right to work, which is authorized only by a work permit, and entering Ireland to study requires a special visa. For more information, see **Alternatives to Tourism**, p. 79.

OTHER IDENTIFICATION

When you travel, always carry two or more forms of identification on your person, including at least one photo ID. A passport combined with a driver's license or birth certificate usually serves as adequate proof of your identity and citizenship. Many establishments, especially banks, require several IDs before cashing traveler's checks. Never carry all your forms of ID together, however; you risk being left entirely without ID or funds in case of theft or loss. It is useful to carry extra passport-size photos to affix to the various IDs or railpasses you may acquire.

> **ONE EUROPE.** With the Maastricht Treaty of 1993, the European Union came into existence. Since then, the EU has extended from its original six member-states to 15 today: Austria, Belgium, Denmark, Finland, France, Germany, Greece, Ireland, Italy, Luxembourg, the Netherlands, Portugal, Spain, Sweden, and the UK (these do **not** include the Channel Islands or the Canary Islands).
> On May 1, 1999, the Treaty of Amsterdam came into effect, incorporating the Schengen Convention (which had previously abolished internal border checks for all EU citizens between many but not all EU countries) into the EU institutional framework. With the exception of Denmark, Ireland, and the UK, visa and immigration policies are now harmonized throughout the EU, simplifying border crossings for both EU and non-EU citizens enormously. Nationals of EU member-states need only a European Identity Card to pass between Schengen countries; most non-EU nationals (including citizens of Australia, Canada, the Republic of Ireland, New Zealand, the US, and the UK) need only a passport.
> Citizens of EU member states also have right of residence and employment throughout the Union, though some regulations do apply (see **Visas and Work Permits,** p. 42). There are **no customs** at internal EU borders (travelers arriving in one EU country from another by air should take the **blue channel** when going through customs), and travelers are free to transport whatever legal substances they like across the Union provided they can demonstrate that it is for personal (i.e., non-commercial) use. Correspondingly, on June 30, 1999, **duty-free was abolished** for travel between EU member states. Those arriving from outside the EU will still have a duty-free allowance.

STUDENT AND TEACHER IDENTIFICATION. The **International Student Identity Card (ISIC)** is the most widely accepted form of student identification. Flashing this card in Ireland can procure you discounts for sights, theaters, museums, accommodations, meals, train, ferry, bus, and airplane transportation, and other services. Present the card wherever you go, and ask about discounts even when none are advertised. The international identification cards are preferable to institution-specific cards because the tourism personnel in Ireland are taught to recognize the former. For US cardholders traveling in Ireland, the ISIC also provides insurance benefits (see **Insurance**, p. 53). In addition, cardholders have access to a toll-free 24-hour ISIC helpline whose multilingual staff can provide assistance in medical, legal, and financial emergencies overseas (☎ (800) 626-2427 in the US and Canada; elsewhere call collect (181) 666 90 25).

Many student travel agencies (p. 55) around the world issue ISICs; ISICs are also issued on the web (www.counciltravel.com/idcards/index.htm). When you apply for the card, request a copy of the *International Student Identity Card Handbook*, which lists some of the available discounts worldwide. You can also write to Council for a copy. The card is valid from September of one year to December of the following year (or December of one year to March of the year after in the Southern hemisphere) and costs AUS$15, CDN$15, or US$22. Applicants must be at least 12 years old and degree-seeking students of a secondary or post-secondary school. Because of the proliferation of phony ISICs, many airlines and some other services require additional proof of student identity, such as your school ID card. The **International Teacher Identity Card (ITIC)** offers the same insurance coverage, and similar but limited discounts. The fee is AUS$13, UK£5, or US$22. For more information on these cards, contact the **International Student Travel Confederation (ISTC)**, Herengracht 479, 1017 BS Amsterdam, Netherlands (from abroad, call 31 20 421 28 00; email istcinfo@istc.org; www.istc.org).

The **TravelSave stamp**, available for £8 at any **usit** (see p. 55) in Ireland, is an addition to your ISIC card, which cuts fares almost in half on national rail and will let you break your journey to visit at any stop on the way to your final destination (valid for one month). It also provides 15% discounts on bus fares (except on fares less than £1) and on various ferry routes from Britain to the continent (see p. 59).

YOUTH IDENTIFICATION. The International Student Travel Confederation also issues a discount card to travelers who are 25 years old or younger but not students. Known as the **International Youth Travel Card (IYTC**; formerly the GO25 Card), this one-year card offers many of the same benefits as the ISIC, and most organizations that sell the ISIC also sell the IYTC. A brochure that lists discounts is free when you purchase the card. To apply, you will need either a passport, valid driver's license, or copy of a birth certificate, and a passport-sized photo with your name printed on the back. The fee is US$22.

TOURIST BOARDS

Almost every town in Ireland possesses a tourist office. Their offerings, however, range from the useful (free local maps, pamphlets on regional history, transportation schedules, and accommodation booking services) to the propagandistic and partial (many tourist boards, especially in the Republic, will only list accommodations that have paid them a fee). The natural tourist boards are excellent resources from which to receive info on national hikes, parks, and walking ways by mail.

Irish Tourist Board (Bord Fáilte): Head Office: Baggot St. Bridge, **Dublin** 2. (☎ (1850) 230 330 in Ireland; (020) 7493 3201 from the UK; (353) (01) 666 1258 from elsewhere); www.ireland.travel.ie. **Australia:** Level 5, 36 Carrington St., Sydney NSW 2000 (☎ (02) 9299 6177; fax 9299 6323). **Canada:** 2 Bloor St. W., Toronto, ON, M4W3E2 (☎ (416) 925 6368; fax 961 2175). **US:** 345 Park Ave., New York, NY 10154 (☎ (800) 223 6470 or (212) 418 0800; fax 371 9052). **New Zealand:** Dingwall Building, 87 Queen St., Auckland (☎ (00649) 379 3708; fax 302 2420). **South Africa:** Everite House, 20 De Korte St., Braamfontein, Johannesburg (☎ (002711) 339 4865; fax 339 2474). **UK:** 150 New Bond St., London W1Y 0AQ (☎ (020) 7493 3201; fax 7493 9065).

Northern Ireland Tourist Board: Head Office: 59 North St., **Belfast**, BT1 1NB, Northern Ireland (☎ (01232) 246609; fax 240960; www.ni-tourism.com). **Dublin:** 16 Nassau St., Dublin 2 (☎ (01) 679 1977; CallSave (1850) 230230; fax (01) 677 1587). **Canada:** 2 Bloor St. W., Toronto, ON, M4W3E2 (☎ (416) 925 6368; fax 925 6033). **UK:** British Travel Centre, 12 Lower Regent St., London SW1Y 4PQ (☎ (020) 7839 8417). From elsewhere overseas, contact any British Tourist Office. Tourist boards should have free brochures as well as *Where to Stay in Northern Ireland 2000*, a list of all B&Bs and campgrounds (UK£4). **US:** #701, New York, NY 10176 (☎ (800) 326 0036 or (212) 922 0101; fax 922 0099).

WEBSITES. The brand-new **Intercelt** site (www.intercelt.com) has listings for tourism based on the Irish language and culture—from language-learning to traditional music festivals. **Ireland's National Tourism Database** (www.touch.ie) has extensive information on hostels, camping, car rentals, and more, accessible by county and region. Also includes some information on Northern Ireland. **Official Guide to Northern Ireland** (www.interknowledge.com/northern-ireland) provides information on sights, accommodations, transportation, and other travel tips for Northern Ireland, arranged by city and county. **City.Net Ireland** (www.city.net/countries/ireland) provides links of interest to travelers.

CUSTOMS

ENTERING IRELAND. Upon entering Ireland, you must declare certain items from abroad and pay a duty on the value of those articles that exceed the allowance established by Irish customs service.

LEAVING IRELAND. If you're leaving for a non-EU country, you can claim back any **Value Added Tax** paid (see p. 49). Keeping receipts for purchases made abroad will help establish values when you return. Upon returning home, you must declare all articles acquired abroad and pay a duty on the value of articles that exceed the allowance established by your country's customs service. Goods and gifts purchased at duty-free shops abroad are not exempt from duty or sales tax at your point of return; you must declare these items as well. For more specific information on customs requirements, contact the following information centers in: **Australia** (☎ 1 300 363; www.customs.gov.au); **Canada** (☎ (613) 993-0534 or 24hr. automated service (800) 461-9999; www.revcan.ca); **Ireland** (☎ (01) 878 8811; www.revenue.ie/customs.htm); **New Zealand** (☎ (04) 473 6099; www.customs.govt.nz); **South Africa** (☎ 012 314 99 11; www.gov.za); **United Kingdom** (☎ (020) 8910 3744; www.hmce.gov.uk); **United States** (☎ (202) 354-1000; www.customs.gov).

EUROPEAN UNION MEMBERS. See **One Europe**, p. 42.

MONEY

If you stay in hostels and prepare your own food, expect to spend anywhere from US$18-30 per person per day. **Hostel accommodations** start at about £8-10 per night for a single bed while the cost for a basic sit-down **meal** begins around £6. Transport and beer will increase your daily budget significantly.

CURRENCY AND EXCHANGE

Carrying cash with you, even in a money belt, can be risky but necessary; personal checks from home are usually not accepted, traveler's checks may not be accepted in a few locations, and the smaller businesses of Ireland tend not to accept credit cards. Legal tender in the Republic of Ireland is the **Irish pound** (or **"punt"**), denoted £. It comes in the same denominations as the **British pound** (which is called **"sterling"** in Ireland) but has been worth a bit less recently. British small change is no longer accepted in the Republic of Ireland. The Irish punt is difficult to convert abroad. Legal tender in Northern Ireland is the **British pound**. Northern Ireland has its own bank notes, which are identical in value to English, Scottish, or Manx notes of the same denominations. Although all of these notes are accepted in Northern Ireland, Northern Ireland bank notes are not accepted across the water. UK coins now come in denominations of 1p, 2p, 5p, 10p, 20p, 50p, and £1. An old "shilling" coin is worth 5p, a "florin" 10p. Residents of both nations refer to pounds as **"quid,"** as in "ten quid" (never "quids").

Banks are closed on Saturday, Sunday, and on all public and bank holidays (for a complete list of holidays, see p. 37). The majority of Irish towns have 24-hour **ATMs.** Banks in Ireland are usually open Monday to Friday 9am to 4pm; in Northern

Ireland Monday to Friday 9:30am to 4:30pm. In both the Republic and the North, some close for lunch and many close early or late one day per week.

The currency chart below is based on published exchange rates from **August 2000**. For UK exchange rates, applicable to Northern Ireland, see p. 396.

THE IRISH POUND	IR£1 =
US$1 = £0.87	= US$1.15
CDN$1 = £0.58	= CDN$1.71
UK£1 = £1.31	= UK£0.76
AUS$1 = £0.51	= AUS$1.96
NZ$1 = £0.40	= NZ$2.53
SAR1 = £0.12	= SAR8.04
EUR€1 = £0.79	= EUR€1.27

As a general rule, it's cheaper to convert money in Ireland. It's good to bring enough foreign currency to last for the first 24-72 hour of a trip to avoid being penniless after banking hours or on a holiday. Watch out for commission rates and check newspapers for the standard rate of exchange. Banks generally have the best rates. A good rule of thumb is to go only to banks or bureaux de change that have at most a 5% margin between their buy and sell prices. Since you lose money with each transaction, convert in large sums. Also, using an ATM card or a credit card (see p. 47) will often get you the best possible rates.

If you use traveler's checks or bills, carry some in small denominations (US$50 or less), especially for times when you are forced to exchange money at disadvantageous rates. However, it is good to carry a range of denominations since charges may be levied per check cashed.

TRAVELER'S CHECKS

Traveler's checks are one of the safest and least troublesome means of carrying funds, since they can be replaced if stolen, and nearly every town in Ireland has facilities to cash them (and hostels and B&Bs often accept them). Agencies and banks sell them, usually for face value plus a small percentage commission. (Members of the American Automobile Association, and some banks and credit unions, can get American Express checks commission-free). **American Express** and **Visa** are the most widely recognized. If you're ordering checks, do so well in advance, especially if you are requesting large sums.

Each agency provides refunds if your checks are lost or stolen, and many provide additional services, such as toll-free refund hotlines in the countries you're visiting, emergency message services, and stolen credit card assistance. In order to collect a **refund for lost or stolen checks**, keep your check receipts separate from your checks and store them in a safe place or with a traveling companion. Record check numbers when you cash them, leave a list of check numbers with someone at home, and ask for a list of refund centers when you buy your checks. Never countersign your checks until you are ready to cash them, and always bring your passport with you when you plan to use the checks.

American Express: Call 800 251 902 in Australia; in New Zealand 0800 441 068; in the UK (0800) 521 313; in the US and Canada 800-221-7282. Elsewhere, call US collect 1-801-964-6665; www.aexp.com. The hotline number in Ireland is (800) 626 000. The Dublin office can be reached at (3531) 679 9000 or (3531) 605 7709. Checks can be purchased for a small fee (1-4%) at American Express Travel Service Offices, banks, and American Automobile Association offices. AAA members (see p. 62) can buy the checks commission-free. American Express offices cash their checks commission-free (except where prohibited by national governments), but often at slightly worse rates than banks.

46 ■ MONEY

ESSENTIALS

Money From Home In Minutes.

If you're stuck for cash on your travels, don't panic. Millions of people trust Western Union to transfer money in minutes to 176 countries and over 78,000 locations worldwide. Our record of safety and reliability is second to none. For more information, call Western Union: USA 1-800-325-6000, Canada 1-800-235-0000. Wherever you are, you're never far from home.

www.westernunion.com

WESTERN UNION | MONEY TRANSFER®

The fastest way to send money worldwide.

> **THE PUNT AND THE EURO.** On Jan. 1, 1999, 11 countries of the EU (and in June 2000, Greece), including Ireland, officially adopted the **euro (€)** as their common currency, irrevocably fixing exchange rates between the 12 national currencies. Euro notes and coins will not be issued until Jan. 1, 2002, and until that time the euro will exist only in electronic transactions and traveler's checks. On June 1, 2002, the Irish pound will be entirely withdrawn from circulation and the euro will become the only legal currency in Ireland. *Let's Go* lists all prices in Irish pounds, as these will still be most relevant in 2001.
>
> Bureaux de change are obliged to exchange euro-zone currencies at the official rate with no commission, though they may still charge a nominal service fee. Euro-denominated traveler's checks may be used throughout the euro-zone, and can also be exchanged commission-free throughout the **12 euro nations** (Austria, Belgium, Finland, France, Germany, Greece, Ireland, Italy, Luxembourg, the Netherlands, Portugal, and Spain). Updated information on the euro can be found on the EU's website at www.europa.eu.int. Up-to-date exchange rate information can be found at http://finance.yahoo.com/m3?u.

- **Citicorp:** Call (800) 645-6556 in the US and Canada; in Europe, the Middle East, or Africa, call the London office at 44 (020) 7508 7007; from elsewhere, call US collect 1 (813) 623-1709. Traveler's checks, including for the punt. Commission 1-2%. Guaranteed hand-delivery of checks when a refund location isn't convenient. Call 24hr.
- **Visa:** Call (800) 227-6811 in the US; in the UK (0800) 895 078; from elsewhere, call 44 1733 318 950 and reverse the charges. Any of the above numbers can tell you the location of their nearest office.

CREDIT CARDS

Credit cards are generally accepted in urban and larger Irish establishments, but the small businesses, B&Bs, and hostels usually do not accept them. Major credit cards—**MasterCard** and **Visa** most often—can be used to extract cash advances in Irish pounds from associated banks and teller machines throughout Ireland. Credit card companies get the wholesale exchange rate, which is generally 5% better than the retail rate used by banks and other currency exchange establishments. **American Express** cards also work in some ATMs, as well as at AmEx offices and major airports. Credit cards often offer an array of other services, from insurance to emergency assistance. Check with your company to find out what is covered.

CREDIT CARD COMPANIES. Visa (US ☎ (800) 336-8472) and **MasterCard** (US ☎ (800) 307-7309) are issued in cooperation with individual banks and some other organizations. If you lose your VISA, call 1 (800) 558 002 in Ireland. **American Express** (US ☎ (800) 843-2273) has an annual fee of up to US$55, depending on the card. Cardholder services include the option of cashing personal checks at AmEx offices, a 24-hour hotline with medical and legal assistance in emergencies (☎ (800) 554-2639 in US and Canada; from Ireland call the British number at 00 44 29 2066 5555; from elsewhere call US collect 1 (202) 554-2639), and the American Express Travel Service. Benefits include assistance in changing airline, hotel, and car rental reservations, baggage loss and flight insurance, sending mailgrams and international cables, and holding your mail at one of the more than 1700 AmEx offices around the world. **Diner's Club** (US ☎ (800) 234-6377; elsewhere, call the US collect (303) 799-1504) is another popular option, but it may be less accepted in smaller towns. The **Discover** card may not be readily accepted in Ireland.

CASH CARDS (ATM CARDS)

Cash cards—popularly called **ATM** (Automated Teller Machine) cards—are widespread in Ireland, though some small towns still do without. Depending on the system that your home bank uses, you can probably access your own personal bank

> **PLEASE, SIR, MAY I HAVE SOME MORE?** All automatic teller machines require a 4-digit Personal Identification Number (PIN), which credit cards in the United States do not always carry. You must ask your credit card company to assign you one before you leave. Without a PIN, you will be unable to withdraw cash with your credit card abroad. There are no letters on the keypads of European ATMs, so work out your PIN numerically: ABC correspond to 2; DEF to 3; GHI to 4; JKL to 5; MNO to 6; PRS to 7; TUV to 8; and WXY to 9. If you punch the wrong code into an ATM 3 times it will eat your card. If you lose your card, call for help at the above numbers.

account whenever you need money; if the first machine you try doesn't work, try another. (**Ulster Bank Limited** and **AIB Bank** accept Cirrus transactions.) ATMs get the same wholesale exchange rate as credit cards. Despite these perks, do some research before relying too heavily on automation. Your bank may charge an additional fee and there is often a limit on the amount of money you can withdraw per day (usually about US$500, depending on the type of card and account).

The two major international money networks are **Cirrus** (US ☎ (800) 4-CIRRUS (424-7787) and **PLUS** (US ☎ (800) 843-7587 for the "Voice Response Unit Locator"). To locate ATMs around the world, use www.visa.com/pd/atm or www.mastercard.com/atm.

GETTING MONEY FROM HOME

AMERICAN EXPRESS. Cardholders can withdraw cash from their checking accounts at any of AmEx's major offices and many of its representatives' offices, up to US$1000 every 21 days (no service charge, no interest). AmEx also offers Express Cash at any of their ATMs in Ireland. Express Cash withdrawals are automatically debited from the Cardmember's checking account or line of credit. There is a 2% transaction fee for each cash withdrawal, with a US$2.50 minimum/$20 maximum. To enroll in Express Cash, Cardmembers may call (800) CASH-NOW (227 4669) in the US; outside the US call collect 1 (336) 668-5041. The AmEx national number in Ireland is (800) 626 000.

WESTERN UNION. Travelers from the US, Canada, and the UK can wire money abroad through Western Union's international money transfer services. In the US, call 800 325 6000; in the UK, call (0800) 833 833; in Canada, call (800) 235 0000; in Ireland, call (800) 395 395. The rates for sending cash are generally US$10-11 cheaper than with a credit card, and the money is usually available at the place you're sending it to within an hour.

US STATE DEPARTMENT (US CITIZENS ONLY). In emergencies, US citizens can have money sent via the State Department. For US$15, they will forward money within hours to the nearest consular office, which will disburse it according to instructions. The office serves only Americans in the direst of straits abroad; non-American travelers should contact their embassies (see p. 40) for information on wiring cash. Check with the State Department or the nearest US embassy or consulate for the quickest way to have the money sent. Contact the Overseas Citizens Service, American Citizens Services, Consular Affairs, Room 4811, US Department of State, Washington, D.C. 20520 (☎ (202) 647-5225; nights, Sundays, and holidays 647-4000; fax (on demand only) 647-3000; http://travel.state.gov).

TIPPING AND BARGAINING

Some restaurants in Ireland figure a service charge into the bill; some even calculate it into the cost of the dishes themselves. The menu often indicates whether or not service is included (ask if you're not sure). For those restaurants that do not include a tip in the bill, more common in cities, customers should leave 10-15%.

The exact amount should truly depend upon the quality of the service. Tipping is less common for other services, especially in rural areas, but is always very welcome. Porters, parking lot attendants, waitstaff, and hairdressers are usually tipped. Cab drivers are usually tipped 10%. Hotel housekeepers will welcome a gratuity, but owners of establishments, including B&Bs, may be insulted by a tip. Likewise, barmen at older or rural pubs may be offended if you leave them a gratuity, while in cities or at bars with a younger clientele a tip may be expected (watch and learn from other customers).

VALUE ADDED TAX

Both Ireland and Northern Ireland charge **Value Added Tax (VAT)**, a national sales tax on most goods and some services. In Ireland, the VAT ranges from 0% on food and children's clothing to 17% in restaurants to 21% on large consumer items. The VAT is usually included in listed prices. The British rate, applicable to Northern Ireland, is 17.5% on many services (such as hairdressers, hotels, restaurants, and car rental agencies) and on all goods (except books, medicine, and food). Prices stated in *Let's Go* include VAT. **Refunds** are available only to non-EU citizens and only for goods taken out of the country, not services. In Ireland, VAT refunds are available on goods purchased in stores displaying a "Cashback" sticker (ask if you don't see one). Ask for a voucher with your purchase, which you must fill out and present at the Cashback service desk in Dublin or Shannon airports. Purchases greater than £200 must be approved at the customs desk first. Your money can also be refunded by mail, which takes six to eight weeks.

Visitors to Northern Ireland can get a **VAT refund** on goods taken out of the country through the **Retail Export Scheme.** Look for signs like "Tax Free Shopping" or "Tax Free for Tourists" and ask the shopkeeper about minimum purchases (usually £50-100) as well as for the appropriate form. Keep purchases in carry-on luggage so a customs officer can inspect the goods and validate refund forms. To receive a refund, mail the stamped forms back to the store in the envelope provided. Refunds can take up to three months to be processed. In order to use this scheme, you must export the goods within three months of purchase.

SAFETY AND SECURITY

> The **national emergency number** in Ireland for police, ambulance, fire, and (in appropriate areas) mountain rescue services is **999**. The **112** EU-wide number will also work.

Ireland's friendliness makes for a relatively safe country with a low rate of violent civilian crime, but with some incidence of petty crime from **muggers** and **pickpockets** (see **Financial Security,** below). Tourists are particularly vulnerable to crime because they often carry large amounts of cash and walk in known touristed areas. Try to blend in as much as possible. The camera-toter is a more obvious target than the low-profile traveler. Wearing a backpack on both shoulders, a worn-in white baseball cap, or a fanny pack can immediately mark you as a foreigner. Certain areas of larger cities are particularly dangerous at night—don't walk alone, don't wear revealing clothing, and don't carry valuables. Check with the reception at hostels or hotels for more information on dangerous areas. You may want to carry a **whistle** to scare off attackers or attract attention. If you're by yourself, be sure that someone at home knows your itinerary. In the **countryside,** take care walking along roads without sidewalks during the day and don't do so at night. Walk on the right so that you can see the traffic coming toward you.

TERRORISM. Terrorist groups in Northern Ireland have attacked cities throughout the North over the past several decades. Obviously, it is difficult to predict where or when these attacks will occur. (See **Safety and Security,** p. 397, in the

50 ■ SAFETY AND SECURITY

Northern Ireland chapter for more information.) Most Irish terrorist organizations set out to cause maximum monetary damage but minimum casualty. Though the recent peace talks and the IRA's promise to put its weapons "beyond use" should reduce terrorist acts, dissident splinter groups are still at large. The government asks the population to stay alert—if you see **unattended packages** on public transport, notify the driver or a guard immediately. The following government offices provide travel information and advisories over the phone or on their websites: **Australian Department of Foreign Affairs and Trade** (☎ (02) 6261 1111; www.dfat.gov.au); **Canadian Department of Foreign Affairs and International Trade (DFAIT)** (☎ (800) 267-8376 or (613) 944-4000 from Ottawa; www.dfait-maeci.gc.ca); **United Kingdom Foreign and Commonwealth Office** (☎ (020) 7238 4503; www.fco.gov.uk); and the **United States Department of State** (☎ (202) 647-5225; http://travel.state.gov). Check for updates on the Irish terrorist situation at www.state.gov.

SAFETY ON THE ROAD. The main concern for most drivers is getting used to driving on the left-hand side of the road (and especially making right turns), which holds for both the Republic and Northern Ireland. If you are using a car, learn local driving signals and wear a seatbelt. Children under 40 lbs. should ride only in a specially designed carseat, available for a small fee from most car rental agencies. Study route maps before you hit the road; some roads have poor (or nonexistent) shoulders, few gas stations, and roaming animals. In many regions, road conditions necessitate driving more slowly and more cautiously than you would at home. For long drives in desolate areas invest in a cellular phone and a roadside assistance program. Be sure to park your vehicle in a garage or well-traveled area, and use a steering wheel locking device in larger cities. **Sleeping in your car** is a dangerous (and often illegal) way to get your rest. (See also **By Car,** p. 62.)

If you're **cycling**, wear reflective clothing, drink plenty of water (even if you're not thirsty), and ride on the same side as the traffic. Learn the international signals for turns, and use them. Know how to fix a modern derailleur-equipped chain mount and change a tire, and practice on your own bike; a few simple tools and a good bike manual will be invaluable. Exercise caution when biking at night and on heavily trafficked roads.

Let's Go does not recommend **hitchhiking** under any circumstances, particularly for women (see also **By Thumb,** p. 66).

SELF-DEFENSE. There is no sure-fire set of precautions that will protect you from all of the situations you might encounter when you travel. A good self-defense course will give you more concrete ways to react to different types of aggression. **Impact, Prepare, and Model Mugging** can refer you to local self-defense courses in the United States (☎ (800) 345 5425) and Vancouver, Canada (☎ (604) 878 3838). Workshops (2-3 hrs.) start at US$50, and full courses run US$350-500. Both women and men are welcome.

DRUGS AND ALCOHOL. A meek "I didn't know it was illegal" will not suffice. Remember that you are subject to the laws of the country in which you travel, not to those of your home country. Minor marijuana possession generally results in a fine or warning, but harder substances are treated with severity. If you carry **prescription drugs** while you travel, it is vital to have a copy of the prescription and a note from a doctor, readily accessible at country borders. The drinking age is 18 throughout Ireland.

FINANCIAL SECURITY

PROTECTING YOUR VALUABLES. To prevent easy theft, don't keep all your valuables in one place. Keep **photocopies** of important documents in case they are lost or filched. Carry one copy separate from the documents and leave another copy at home. Label every piece of luggage both inside and out. **Don't put a wallet with money in your back pocket** when in touristed or busy areas. Never count your money in public and carry as little as possible. If you carry a purse, buy a sturdy one with

Spend less, EXPLORE MORE!

- LOW STUDENT AIRFARES
- EURAIL PASSES
- BUS PASSES
- STUDY ABROAD

800.272.9676

www.studentuniverse.com

Why wait in line when you can go online?
Low student airfares the easy way.
Go ahead... put your feet up and
plan your trip.

student universe.com
IT'S YOUR WORLD. EXPLORE IT

Council *Travel*

America's Student Travel Leader for over 50 years

"Happiness is not a destination. It is a method of life"
-Burton Hills

Visit us at your nearest office or online @
www.counciltravel.com

Or call: **1-800-2COUNCIL**

ISIC *It's your world at a discount!*

*Accepted at over 17,000 locations worldwide.
Great benefits at home and abroad!*

a secure clasp, and carry it crosswise on the side, away from the street with the clasp against you. Secure packs with small combination padlocks which slip through the two zippers. A **money belt** is the best way to carry cash; you can buy one at most camping supply stores. A **neck pouch** is equally safe, although far less accessible. Refrain from pulling out your neck pouch in public; if you must, be discreet. Avoid keeping anything precious in a fanny pack (even if it's worn on your stomach): your valuables will be highly visible and easy to steal. Keep some money separate from the rest to use in an emergency or in case of theft.

CON ARTISTS AND PICKPOCKETS. Among the more colorful denizens of large cities are **con artists**. Con artists and hustlers often work in groups, and children are among the most effective. Be especially suspicious in unexpected situations. Do not respond or make eye contact, walk quickly away, and keep a solid grip on your belongings. Contact the police if a hustler is particularly aggressive. In city crowds and especially on public transportation, **pickpockets** are amazingly deft at their craft. Also, be alert in public telephone booths. If you must say your calling card number, do so very quietly; if you punch it in, make sure no one can look over your shoulder.

ACCOMMODATIONS AND TRANSPORTATION. Never leave your belongings unattended; crime can occur in even the most demure-looking hostel or hotel. If you feel unsafe, look for places with either a curfew or a night attendant. *Let's Go* lists locker availability in hostels and train stations, but you'll need your own **padlock**. Lockers are useful if you don't want to lug everything with you, but don't store valuables in them. Most hotels also provide lock boxes free or for a minimal fee. Count any cash or checks before storing them in a hostel's safe.

Be particularly careful on **buses**, carry your backpack in front of you where you can see it, don't check baggage on trains, and don't trust anyone to "watch your bag for a second."

If you travel by **car**, try not to leave valuable possessions—such as radios or luggage—in it while you are away. If your tape deck or radio is removable, hide it in the trunk or take it with you. If it isn't, at least conceal it under something else. Similarly, hide baggage in the trunk—although savvy thieves can tell if a car is heavily loaded by the way it sits on its tires.

HEALTH

Common sense is the simplest prescription for good health while you travel. Travelers complain most often about their feet and their gut, so take precautionary measures: drink fluids to prevent dehydration and constipation, wear sturdy, broken-in shoes and clean socks, and use talcum powder to keep your feet dry.

BEFORE YOU GO

PACKING. Preparation can help minimize the likelihood of contracting a disease and maximize the chances of receiving effective health care in the event of an emergency. For minor health problems, bring a compact **first-aid kit** (see p. 54). In your **passport,** write the names of any people you wish to be contacted in case of a medical emergency, and also list any **allergies** or medical conditions you would want doctors to be aware of. Allergy sufferers might want to obtain a full supply of any necessary medication before the trip. Matching a prescription to a foreign equivalent is not always easy, safe, or possible. Carry up-to-date, legible prescriptions or a statement from your doctor stating the medication's trade name, manufacturer, chemical name, and dosage. While traveling, be sure to keep all medication with you in your carry-on luggage.

MEDICAL ASSISTANCE ON THE ROAD

In the event of sudden illness or an accident, dial **999**, the general **emergency** number for the Republic of Ireland and Northern Ireland. It's a free call from any pay phone to an operator who will connect you to the local police, hospital, or fire brigade. EU citizens receive health care; others must have medical insurance or be prepared to pay; hospitals are plentiful and listed in **Practical Information** sections.

If your regular **insurance** policy does not cover travel abroad, you may wish to purchase additional coverage. With the exception of Medicare, most major US health insurance plans cover members' medical emergencies during trips abroad; check with your insurance carrier to be sure. (For more information, see p. 53).

PREVENTING DISEASE

INSECT- AND TICK-BORNE DISEASES. Be aware of insects—particularly mosquitoes, fleas, and lice—in wet or forested areas in Ireland (particularly in the northwest and near boglands). **Mosquitoes** are most active from dusk to dawn; use insect repellents such as DEET, wear long pants, long sleeves, and shoes with socks, and buy a mosquito net. Natural repellents can be useful supplements: taking vitamin B-12 pills regularly can eventually make you smelly to insects, as can garlic pills. Calamine lotion or topical cortisones (like Cortaid) may stop insect bites from itching, as can a bath with a half-cup of baking soda or oatmeal.

Ticks can be particularly dangerous in rural and forested regions. If you find a tick attached to your skin, grasp the tick's head parts with tweezers as close to your skin as possible and apply slow, steady traction. Do not try to remove ticks by burning them. **Lyme disease,** carried by ticks, is a bacterial infection marked by a circular bull's-eye rash of two inches or more that appears around the bite. Antibiotics are effective if administered early. Left untreated, the disease can cause problems in joints, the heart, and the nervous system.

FOOD- AND WATER-BORNE DISEASES. Prevention is the best cure: be sure that everything you eat is cooked properly and that the water you drink is clean. **Parasites** hide in unsafe water and food. Symptoms of parasitic infection include swollen glands or lymph nodes, fever, digestive problems, and anemia. Tap water in Ireland is generally safe. River, streams, and lakes, however, may carry bacteria, and water from them should always be purified to avoid **giardia.** To purify your own water, bring it to a rolling boil or treat it with **iodine tablets,** available at any camping goods store. As in all parts of the world, raw shellfish, unpasteurized milk, and sauces containing raw eggs may also have harmful bacteria. Always wash your hands before eating, or bring a quick-drying purifying liquid hand cleaner like Purell. Your bowels will thank you.

AIDS, HIV, AND STDS. Acquired Immune Deficiency Syndrome (AIDS) is a growing problem around the world. In Ireland, approximately 35,000 adults are HIV-positive. For more information on AIDS, call the **National AIDS Helpline** (☎ (0800) 568 7123; open 24hr.). Council's brochure *Travel Safe: AIDS and International Travel*, is available at all Council Travel offices and at their website (www.ciee.org/study/safety/travelsafe.htm).

Sexually transmitted diseases (STDs) such as gonorrhea, chlamydia, genital warts, syphilis, and herpes are easier to catch than HIV, and some can be just as deadly. **Hepatitis B and C** are also serious sexually transmitted diseases. Warning signs for STDs include swelling, sores, bumps, or blisters on sex organs, rectum, or mouth; burning and pain during urination and bowel movements; itching around sex organs; swelling or redness in the throat; and flu-like symptoms with fever, chills, and aches. If these symptoms develop, see a doctor immediately. Health professionals recommend the use of **latex condoms,** theoretically available over-the-counter in Ireland but often not sold by pharmacies on "moral grounds." Consider bringing some from home; the quality may be lower in Ireland. When having sex, condoms may protect you from certain STDs, but oral or even tactile contact can lead to transmission. The **Centers for Disease Control and Prevention (CDC;** US ☎ (800) 342-2437; www.cdc.gov) can provide more information.

INSURANCE ■ 53

WOMEN'S HEALTH. Women traveling in unsanitary conditions are vulnerable to **urinary tract** and **bladder infections,** common and severely uncomfortable bacterial diseases that cause a burning sensation and painful and sometimes frequent urination. To avoid these infections, drink plenty of vitamin C-rich juice and plenty of clean water. Untreated, these infections can lead to kidney infections, sterility, and even death. If symptoms persist, see a doctor.

Reliable contraceptive devices may be difficult to find, especially in rural areas. Women on the birth-control pill should bring enough to allow for possible loss or extended stays. Bring a prescription, since forms of the Pill vary a good deal. Women who use a diaphragm should bring enough contraceptive jelly.

Abortion is illegal in Ireland. Women who need an abortion while abroad should contact the **International Planned Parenthood Federation,** European Regional Office, Regent's College Inner Circle, Regent's Park, London NW1 4NS (☎ 44 (020) 7487 7900; fax 7487 7950), for more information.

INSURANCE

Travel insurance generally covers four basic areas: medical/health problems, property loss, trip cancellation/interruption, and emergency evacuation.

Medical insurance (especially university policies) often covers costs incurred abroad; check with your provider. **Medicare does not cover foreign travel.** Canadians are protected by their home province's health insurance plan for up to 90 days after leaving the country; check with the provincial Ministry of Health or Health Plan Headquarters for details. Australians traveling in the UK are entitled to many of the services that they would receive at home as part of the Reciprocal Health Care Agreement. **Homeowner's insurance** (or your family's coverage) often covers theft during travel and loss of travel documents (passport, plane ticket, railpass, etc.) up to US$500.

ISIC and **ITIC** provide basic insurance benefits, including US$100 per day of in-hospital sickness for a maximum of 60 days, US$3000 of accident-related medical reimbursement, and US$25,000 for emergency medical transport (see **Identification,** p. 42). Cardholders have access to a toll-free 24-hour helpline whose multilingual staff can provide assistance in medical, legal, and financial emergencies overseas (☎ (877) 370-4742, elsewhere call US collect +1 (713) 342-4104. **American Express** (☎ (800) 528 4800) grants most cardholders automatic car rental insurance (collision and theft, but not liability).

Prices for travel insurance purchased separately generally run about US$50 per week for full coverage, while trip cancellation/interruption may be purchased separately at a rate of about US$5.50 per US$100 of coverage.

INSURANCE PROVIDERS. Council and **STA** (see p. 57 for complete listings) offer a range of plans to supplement your basic insurance coverage. Other private insurance providers in the **US and Canada** include: **Access America** (☎ (800) 284 8300); **Berkely Group/Carefree Travel Insurance** (☎ (800) 323 3149; www.berkely.com); **Globalcare Travel Insurance** (☎ (800) 821 2488; www.globalcare-cocco.com); and **Travel Assistance International** (☎ (800) 821 2828; www.worldwide-assistance.com). Providers in the **UK** include **Campus Travel** (☎ (01865) 258 000) and **Columbus Travel Insurance** (☎ (020) 7375 0011). In **Australia** try **CIC Insurance** (☎ 9202 8000).

PACKING

Pack light: Lay out only what you absolutely need, then take half the clothes and twice the money. The less you have, the less you have to lose (or store, or carry on your back). Any extra space left will be useful for any souvenirs or items you might pick up along the way. If you plan to do a lot of hiking, also see **Outdoors,** p. 70.

LUGGAGE. If you plan to cover most of your itinerary by foot, a sturdy **frame backpack** is unbeatable. (For the basics on buying a pack, see p. 71.) Toting a **suitcase** or **trunk** is fine if you plan to live in one or two cities and explore from there, but a very bad idea if you're going to be moving around a lot. In addition to your main piece of luggage, a **daypack** (a small backpack or courier bag) is a must.

CLOTHING. No matter when you're traveling, and especially in Ireland, it's always a good idea to bring a **warm jacket** or wool sweater, a **rain jacket**, sturdy walking shoes or **hiking boots**, and **thick socks**. **Flip-flops** or waterproof sandals are crucial for grubby hostel showers. You may also want to add one outfit beyond the jeans and t-shirt uniform and a nicer pair of shoes if you plan to explore the nightlife.

SLEEPSACK. Some hostels require that you either provide your own linen or rent sheets from them. Save cash by making your own sleepsack: fold a full-size sheet in half the long way, then sew it closed along the long side and one of the short sides.

CONVERTERS AND ADAPTERS. In Ireland, electricity is 220 volts AC, enough to fry any 110V North American appliance. 220/240V electrical appliances don't like 110V current, either. Americans and Canadians should buy an adapter (which changes the shape of the plug) and a converter (which changes the voltage; US$20). Don't make the mistake of using only an adapter (unless appliance instructions explicitly state otherwise). New Zealanders and South Africans (who both use 220V at home) as well as Australians (who use 240/250V) won't need a converter, but will need a set of adapters to use anything electrical.

TOILETRIES. Toothbrushes, towels, cold-water soap, talcum powder (to keep feet dry), deodorant, razors, tampons, and condoms are often available, but may be difficult to find, so bring extras. **Contact lenses**, on the other hand, may be expensive and difficult to find, so bring enough extra pairs and **solution** for your entire trip. Also bring glasses and your prescription in case you need emergency replacements.

SUNCARE. Bring sunscreen, a hat, and sunglasses, even if traveling to rainy areas.

FIRST-AID KIT. For a basic first-aid kit, pack bandages, aspirin or other painkiller, antibiotic cream, a thermometer, a Swiss Army knife, tweezers, moleskin, decongestant, motion-sickness remedy, diarrhea or upset-stomach medication (Pepto Bismol or Immodium), an antihistamine, sunscreen, insect repellent, burn ointment, and a syringe for emergencies (get an explanatory letter from your doctor).

FILM. Film in Ireland costs about US$5 for a roll of 24 color exposures, so consider bringing along enough film for your entire trip and developing it at home. Despite disclaimers, airport security X-rays *can* fog film, so buy a lead-lined pouch at a camera store or ask security to hand-inspect it. Always pack it in your carry-on luggage, since higher-intensity X-rays are used on checked luggage.

VIDEOTAPES. Ireland uses the PAL system for videotapes, unlike the NTSC system used in Canada and the US or the SECAM one in France. So unless you find tapes specially marked "NTSC" or "SECAM," don't purchase any tapes.

OTHER USEFUL ITEMS. For safety purposes, you should bring a **money belt** and small **padlock** to lock your pack and personal items in hostel lockers. Basic equipment (plastic water bottle, compass, waterproof matches, pocketknife) may also prove useful. Quick repairs of torn garments can be done on the road with a needle and thread; also consider bringing electrical tape for patching tears. Doing your **laundry** by hand (where it is allowed) is both cheaper and more convenient than doing it at a laundromat—bring detergent and string for a makeshift clothesline. Other things you're liable to forget: an umbrella; sealable **plastic bags** (for damp clothes, soap, food, shampoo, and other spillables); an **alarm clock**; safety pins; rubber bands; a flashlight; **earplugs** for noisy hostel dorms; garbage bags; and a small **calculator** for currency conversion.

IMPORTANT DOCUMENTS. Don't forget your passport, traveler's checks, ATM and/or credit cards, and adequate ID (see p. 42). Also check that you have any of the following that might apply to you: hosteling membership card (see p. 67); driver's license (see p. 63); travel insurance forms; rail and/or bus pass (see p. 61).

GETTING THERE
BY PLANE

When it comes to airfare, a little effort can save you a bundle. If your plans are flexible enough to deal with the restrictions, courier fares are the cheapest. Tickets bought from consolidators and standby seating are also good deals, but last-minute specials, airfare wars, and charter flights often beat these fares. The key is to hunt around, to be flexible, and to persistently ask about discounts. Finding a cheap airfare will be easier if you understand the airlines' systems. Call every toll-free number and don't be afraid to ask about discounts; if you don't ask, it's unlikely they'll be volunteered. Have knowledgeable travel agents guide you; an agent whose clients fly mostly to Nassau or Miami will not be the best person to hunt down a bargain flight to Dublin.

Students and others under 26 should never pay full price for a ticket. Seniors can also get great deals; many airlines offer senior traveler clubs or airline passes with few restrictions and discounts for their companions as well. Sunday newspapers often have travel sections that list bargain fares.

DETAILS AND TIPS
Airplanes fly between Dublin, Shannon, Cork, Kerry, Galway, Knock, Sligo, and Waterford (in Ireland); Belfast and Derry (in Northern Ireland); Gatwick, Stansted, Heathrow, Luton, Manchester, Birmingham, Liverpool, and Glasgow airports; and Ronaldsway on the Isle of Man.

- **Timing:** Airfares to Ireland peak between early June and late August, and holidays are also expensive periods in which to travel. Midweek (M-Th morning) round-trip flights run US$40-50 cheaper than weekend flights, but the latter are generally less crowded and more likely to permit frequent-flier upgrades. Return-date flexibility is usually not an option for the budget traveler; traveling with an "open return" ticket can be pricier than fixing a return date when buying the ticket and paying later to change it.
- **Route:** Round-trip flights are by far the cheapest; "open-jaw" (arriving in and departing from different cities) and round-the-world, or RTW, flights are pricier but reasonable alternatives. Patching one-way flights together is the least economical way to travel. Flights between capital cities or regional hubs will offer the most competitive fares.
- **Destinations:** Since Ireland is mostly smaller cities, you might find it cheaper to take the plane to London and ferry across the Irish Sea (see p. 59). Major Irish destinations are Shannon, Dublin, Cork, and Belfast. Shannon is often cheaper for transatlantic flights, as many stop there anyway en route to other airports (until recently, airlines were required by law to do so); Cork and Belfast tend to be the most expensive destinations.
- **Boarding:** Whenever flying internationally, pick up tickets for international flights well in advance of the departure date, and confirm by phone within 72 hours of departure. Most airlines require that passengers arrive at the airport at least 2 hours before departure. One carry-on item and 2 pieces of checked baggage is the norm for non-courier flights. Consult the airline for weight allowances.
- **Fares:** Budget round-trip tickets during the summer to Dublin from: **New York:** around US$600/$350 (summer/off-season); **Los Angeles:** US$850/$600; **London:** US$150/$50; **South Africa:** US$700/$500; **Australia:** US$1500/$1200; **New Zealand:** US$2000/$1300. Flying into Shannon airport is occasionally cheaper.

BUDGET AND STUDENT TRAVEL AGENCIES

A knowledgeable agent specializing in flights to Ireland can make your life easy and help you save, too, but agents may not spend the time to find you the lowest possible fare—they get paid on commission. Students and under-26ers holding **ISIC and IYTC cards** (see **Identification**, p. 42), respectively, qualify for big discounts from student travel agencies. Most flights from budget agencies are on major airlines, but in peak season some may sell seats on less reliable chartered aircraft.

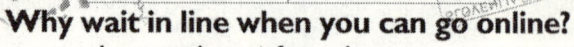

usit world (www.usitworld.com). Over 50 **usit campus** branches in the UK (www.usitcampus.co.uk), including **London** (☎ (0870) 240 1010); **Manchester** (☎ (0161) 273 1721); and **Edinburgh** (☎ (0131) 668 3303). Nearly 20 **usit** offices in Ireland, including **Dublin** (☎ (01) 602 1600; www.usitnow.ie), and **Belfast** (☎ (02890) 327 111; www.usitnow.com). Offices also in Athens, Auckland, Brussels, Frankfurt, Johannesburg, Lisbon, Luxembourg, Madrid, Paris, Sofia, and Warsaw.

Council Travel (www.counciltravel.com). US offices include: **Atlanta**, GA (☎ (404) 377-9997); **Boston**, MA (☎ (617) 266-1926); **Chicago**, IL (☎ (312) 951-0585); **Los Angeles**, CA (☎ (310) 208-3551); **New York**, NY (☎ (212) 254-2525); **San Francisco**, CA (☎ (415) 566-6222); **Seattle**, WA (☎ (206) 329-4567); **Washington, D.C.** (☎ (202) 337-6464). For US cities not listed, call (800) 2-COUNCIL (226-8624). In the UK, **London** (☎ (020) 7437 7767).

CTS Travel, 44 Goodge St., **London** W1 (☎ (020) 7636 0031; email ctsinfo@ctstravel.com.uk).

STA Travel (☎ (800) 777-0112; www.sta-travel.com). A student and youth travel organization with over 150 offices worldwide. Ticket booking, travel insurance, railpasses, and more. US offices include: **Boston**, MA (☎ (617) 266-6014); **Chicago**, IL (☎ (312) 786-9050); **Los Angeles**, CA (☎ (323) 934-8722); **New York**, NY (☎ (212) 627-3111); **Seattle**, WA (☎ (206) 633-5000); **Washington, D.C.** (☎ (202) 887-0912); **San Francisco**, CA (☎ (415) 391-8407). In the UK, **London** (☎ (020) 7436 7779 for North American travel). In New Zealand, **Auckland** (☎ (09) 309 0458). In Australia, **Melbourne** (☎ (03) 9349 4344).

Travel CUTS (Canadian Universities Travel Services Limited), 187 College St., **Toronto**, ON M5T 1P7 (☎ (416) 979-2406; fax 979-8167; www.travelcuts.com). 40 offices across Canada. Also in the UK, 295-A Regent St., **London** W1R 7YA (☎ (020) 7255 1944).

COMMERCIAL AIRLINES

The commercial airlines' lowest regular offer is the **APEX** (Advance Purchase Excursion) fare, which provides confirmed reservations and allows "open-jaw" tickets. Generally, reservations must be made 7 to 21 days in advance, with 7- to 14-day minimum and up to 90-day maximum-stay limits, and hefty cancellation and change penalties (fees rise in summer). Book peak-season APEX fares early, since by May you will have a hard time getting the departure date you want.

Although APEX fares are probably not the cheapest possible fares, they will give you a sense of the average commercial price, from which to measure other bargains. Specials advertised in newspapers may be cheaper but have more restrictions and fewer available seats. A popular carrier to Ireland is its national airline, **Aer Lingus** (☎ (800) 474 7424; www.aerlingus.ie), which has direct flights to the US and constant flights to London and Paris. **Ryanair** (☎ (01) 609 7900; www.ryanair.ie) is a smaller airline that offers a "lowest-fare guarantee"; check

> **SHE'S GOT AN E-TICKET TO RIDE.** The Web is a great place to look for travel bargains—it's fast, it's convenient, and you can spend as long as you like exploring options without driving your travel agent insane.
>
> Many airline sites offer special last-minute deals on the Web. Other sites do the legwork and compile the deals for you—try www.bestfares.com, www.onetravel.com, www.lowestfare.com, and www.travelzoo.com.
>
> **STA** (www.sta-travel.com) and **Council** (www.counciltravel.com) provide quotes on student tickets, while **Expedia** (msn.expedia.com) and **Travelocity** (www.travelocity.com) offer full travel services. **Priceline** (www.priceline.com) allows you to specify a price, and obligates you to buy any ticket that meets or beats it; be prepared for antisocial hours and odd routes. **Skyauction** (www.skyauction.com) allows you to bid on both last-minute and advance-purchase tickets.
>
> Just one last note—to protect yourself, make sure that the site uses a secure server before handing over any credit card details. Happy hunting!

the website for details. If another airline doesn't fly directly to one of the airports in Ireland, it can almost certainly get you to London. For connections to Ireland from London, see **Flights from Britain,** below.

FLIGHTS FROM BRITAIN

Flying to London and connecting to Ireland is often easiest and cheapest. Aer Lingus (see p. 57) and several other carriers offer service on these routes. **British Midland Airways** (in the UK (0870) 607 0555; in the Republic (01) 283 0700); www.britishmidland.com) flies about seven times per day to London Heathrow. **British Airways** (in the UK ☎ (0345) 222111; in the Republic (800) 626747; in the US ☎ (800) AIRWAYS or 247 9297; www.british-airways.com) flies about five times per day Monday through Friday, Saturday and Sunday six per day. Prices range from UK£70-150 round-trip but can drop from time to time. Call and inquire about specials. **Ryanair** (in the UK ☎ (0870) 333 1250; in the Republic (01) 609 7800) connects Kerry, Cork, and Knock to London and nine other destinations in England and Scotland. Flights from London to Dublin or Belfast generally take 1¼ hours.

OTHER CHEAP ALTERNATIVES

TICKET CONSOLIDATORS. Ticket consolidators, or **"bucket shops,"** buy unsold tickets in bulk from commercial airlines and sell them at discounted rates. The best place to look is in the Sunday travel section of any major newspaper, where many bucket shops place tiny ads. Call quickly, as availability is typically extremely limited. Not all bucket shops are reliable, so insist on a receipt that gives full details of restrictions, refunds, and tickets, and pay by credit card (in spite of the 2-5% fee) so you can stop payment if you never receive your tickets. For more info, see www.travel-library.com/air-travel/consolidators.html.

For destinations worldwide, try **Travel Avenue** (☎ (800) 333-3335; www.travelavenue.com), which will search for cheap flights through other consolidators for a fee. Other consolidators worth trying are **Interworld** (☎ (305) 443-4929); **Pennsylvania Travel** (☎ (800) 331-0947); **Rebel** (☎ (800) 227-3235; www.rebeltours.com); **Cheap Tickets** (☎ (800) 377-1000; www.cheaptickets.com); and **Travac** (☎ (800) 872-8800; www.travac.com). Yet more consolidators on the web include the **Internet Travel Network** (www.itn.com); **SurplusTravel.com** (www.surplustravel.com); **Travel Information Services** (www.tiss.com); **TravelHUB** (www.travelhub.com); and **The Travel Site** (www.thetravelsite.com). Keep in mind that these are just suggestions to get you started in your research; *Let's Go* does not endorse any of these agencies. As always, be cautious, and research companies before you hand over your credit card number.

CONSOLIDATORS IN THE UK, AUSTRALIA, AND NEW ZEALAND. In London, the **Air Travel Advisory Bureau** (☎ (020) 7636 5000; www.atab.co.uk) can provide names of reliable consolidators and discount flight specialists. From Australia and New Zealand, look for consolidator ads in the travel section of the *Sydney Morning Herald* and other papers.

CHARTER FLIGHTS. Charters are flights contracted by a tour operator to fly extra loads of passengers during peak season. Charters are often considerably cheaper than flights on scheduled airlines, some operate nonstop, and restrictions on minimum advance-purchase and minimum stay are more lenient. However, charter flights fly less frequently than major airlines, make refunds particularly difficult, and are almost always fully booked. Schedules and itineraries may also change or be cancelled at the last moment (without a full refund), and check-in, boarding, and baggage claim are often much slower. As always, pay with a credit card if you can, and consider traveler's insurance against trip interruption.

Discount clubs and **fare brokers** offer members savings on last-minute charter and tour deals. Study their contracts closely. **Travelers Advantage,** Stamford, CT (☎ 800-548-1116; www.travelersadvantage.com; US$60 annual fee includes discounts, newsletters, and cheap flight directories) specializes in European tour packages.

STANDBY FLIGHTS. To travel standby, you will need considerable flexibility in the dates and cities of your arrival and departure. Companies that specialize in standby flights don't sell tickets but rather the promise that you will get to your destination (or near your destination) within a certain window of time (anywhere from 1-5 days). You may only receive a monetary refund if all available flights which depart within your date-range from the specified region are full, but future travel credit is always available.

Carefully read agreements with any company offering standby flights, as tricky fine print can leave you in the lurch. It is difficult to receive refunds, and clients' vouchers will not be honored when an airline fails to receive payment in time.

One established company in the US is **Airhitch**, in **New York,** NY (☎ (800) 326 2009; www.airhitch.org) and **Los Angeles,** CA (☎ (310) 726-5000). In Europe, the flagship office is in **Paris** (☎ 0147 00 16 30) and the other one is in **Amsterdam** (☎ (020) 626 32 20). Flights to Europe cost US$159 each way when departing from the Northeast, US$239 from the West Coast or Northwest, US$209 from the Midwest, and US$189 from the Southeast. Travel within the USA and Europe is also possible, with rates ranging from US$79-$139.

AIR COURIER FLIGHTS. Couriers help transport cargo on international flights by guaranteeing delivery of the baggage claim slips from the company to a representative overseas. Generally, couriers must travel light (carry-ons only) and deal with complex restrictions on their flight. You will probably never see the cargo you are transporting—the company handles it all—and airport officials know that couriers are not responsible for the baggage checked for them. Most flights are round-trip only with short fixed-length stays (usually one week) and a limit of a single ticket per issue. Most of these flights also operate only out of the biggest cities, like New York. Generally, you must be over 21, have a valid passport, and procure your own visa, if necessary. Groups such as the **Air Courier Association** (☎ (800) 282-1202; www.aircourier.org) and the **International Association of Air Travel Couriers** (☎ (561) 582 8320; www.courier.org) provide their members with lists of opportunities and courier brokers worldwide for an annual fee.

BY FERRY

Ferries are popular and usually a more economical, albeit considerably more time-consuming, form of transportation than airplanes. Almost all sailings in June, July, and August are "controlled sailings," which means that you must book the crossing ahead of time (a few days in advance is usually sufficient). Low season on ferry prices runs March to May and October to December; mid-season is June to mid-July and September; high season is mid-July to August.

Fares vary tremendously depending on time of year, time of day, and type of boat. Traveling mid-week and during the night promises the cheapest fares. Adult single tickets usually range from £20 to £35, and a world of discount rates is out there waiting to be explored. Some people tag along with car drivers who are allowed four free passengers. Students, seniors, families, and youth traveling alone should almost never pay full fare. Children under 5 almost always travel free, and bikes can usually be brought on for no extra charge. **An Óige (HI) members** receive up to a 20% discount on fares from Irish Ferries and Stena Sealink. **ISIC cardholders** with the **TravelSave Stamp** (available at Irish **usit** offices; see p. 55) receive a 15% discount from Irish Ferries and an average 17% discount (variable among four routes) on Stena Line ferries. Ferry passengers from the Republic are taxed an additional IR£5 when travelling from England to Éire.

BRITAIN AND FRANCE TO IRELAND

Assorted bus and train tickets that include ferry connections between Britain and Ireland are also available as package deals through ferry companies, travel agents, and usit offices. Contact Bus Éireann for information (see **By Bus,** p. 61).

- **Irish Ferries** sails from Holyhead, North Wales, to Dublin (3½hr.) and from Pembroke, Wales, to Rosslare Harbour (4hr.). Also sails from Cherbourg and Roscoff, France to Cork and Rosslare Harbour (about 22hr.); **Eurailpasses** grant passage on ferries from France. For specific schedules and fares contact them at: 2-4 Merrion Row, **Dublin** 2 (reservations ☎ (01) 638 3333); St. Patrick's Bridge, **Cork** (☎ (021) 551 995); **Rosslare Harbour** (☎ (053) 33158); **Holyhead, Wales** (☎ (0990) 329 129); and **Pembroke, Wales** (☎ (0990) 329 543). Their after-hours information line in Ireland is (01) 661 0715 and their website is www.irishferries.ie.
- **Stena Line** ferries go from Holyhead, North Wales, to Dún Laoghaire (3½hr. on the Superferry); from Fishguard, South Wales, and Pembroke, Wales to Rosslare Harbour (3½-3¾hr.); and from Stranraer, Scotland, to Belfast (90min. on the Stena Line, 3hr. on the SeaCat). Offers package deals that include train service from London. Contact them at: Charter House, Park St., Ashford, Kent TN24 8EX, England (☎ (0990) 707 070; fax (01233) 202 241); **Dún Laoghaire Travel Centre** (☎ (01) 204 7777); **Rosslare Harbour** (☎ (053) 33115); Tourist Office, **Cork** (☎ (021) 272 965); Tourist Office, Arthurs Quay, **Limerick** (☎ (061) 316 259). For 24hr. recorded information, contact **Ferry Check** (☎ (01) 204 7799).
- **Cork-Swansea Ferries** sails between Swansea, South Wales, and Cork (10hr.). Contact them at 52 South Mall, Cork (☎ (021) 271166).
- **Hoverspeed SeaCat** sails from Stranraer to Belfast (1hr.), and the **SuperSeaCat Ferry** sails from Liverpool, England to Dublin (4hr.). These SeaCat trips are faster than ferries but considerably pricier. For information and bookings, contact them at UK ☎ (0990) 523 523 or in the Republic ☎ (1800) 551 743.

BY BUS

Bus Éireann (the Irish national bus company) reaches Britain and even the continent by working in conjunction with ferry services and the bus company **Eurolines** (UK ☎ (01582) 404 511; www.eurolines.com). To get to Ireland from Britain, there are connecting services from Bristol and London to Cork, Waterford, Tralee, Killarney, Ennis, and Limerick, and from Cardiff and Birmingham to Cork, Waterford, Ennis, and Limerick. Prices range from IR£10 to £25. Tickets can be booked through usit, any Bus Éireann office, Irish Ferries, Stena Line, or any Eurolines (or National Express office in Britain (☎ (0990) 808 080). Inconvenient arrival and departure times mean you won't be sleeping very well. The immense Eurolines network connects with many European destinations. London to Dublin UK£18, return £34; London to Paris UK£33, return £47 (prices for first ferry in the morning; more expensive for later ferries and after July 1; Dublin route more expensive for travelers over 26). Contact the Bus Éireann General Inquiries desk in Dublin (☎ (01) 836 6111) or a travel agent.

ONCE THERE

GETTING AROUND

Fares on all modes of transportation are either "single" (one-way) or "return" (round-trip). "Period returns" require you to return within a specific number of days; "day return" means you must return on the same day. Unless stated otherwise, *Let's Go* always lists single fares. Round-trip fares on trains and buses are rarely more than 30% above the one-way fare.

Roads between Irish cities and towns have official letters and numbers ("N" and "R" in the Republic; "M," "A," and "B" in the North), but most locals refer to them by destination ("Kerry Rd.," "Tralee Rd."). Signs and printed directions sometimes give only the numbered and lettered designations, sometimes only the destination. Most signs are in English and Irish; destination signs in outlying *gaeltachta* are most often only in Irish. Old black-and-white road signs give distances in miles; new green and white signs are in kilometers. Speed limit signs are in miles.

BY BUS

Buses in the Republic of Ireland reach many more destinations and are less expensive than trains. Bus drivers are often very accommodating in where they will pick you up and drop you off. The national bus company, **Bus Éireann** (www.buseireann.ie), operates both long-distance Expressway buses, which link larger cities, and Local buses, which serve the countryside and smaller towns. Find timetables for bus services by visiting local bus stations, or Bus Éireann's website. The invaluable bus timetable book (£1) is hugely difficult to obtain for personal ownership, although it should be available for purchase at Busáras Station in Dublin as well as the occasional tourist office. A myriad of **private bus services** are faster and cheaper than Bus Éireann. *Let's Go* lists these private companies in areas they service. Most of these services link Dublin to one or two towns in the west. In Donegal, private bus providers take the place of Bus Éireann's nearly nonexistent local service. Expressway buses allow passengers to store luggage in the bus's undercarriage, or carry hand-luggage on board. Bicycles may be stored for a £5 fee in the undercarriage, provided there's room.

 Return (or round-trip) tickets are always a great value. For students, purchasing a TravelSave stamp along with your ISIC affords huge discounts on bus travel (see p. 42). Bus Éireann's discount **Rambler** tickets aren't usually worth buying; individual tickets often provide better value. The Rambler ticket offers unlimited bus travel within Ireland for three of eight consecutive days (£28; child £14), eight of 15 consecutive days (£68; child £34), or 15 of 30 consecutive days (£98; child £49). A combined **Irish Explorer Rail/Bus** ticket allows unlimited travel eight of 15 consecutive days on rail and bus lines (£100; child £50). Purchase these tickets from Bus Éireann at their main bus station on Store St. in Dublin (☎ (01) 836 6111), or at their Travel Centres in Cork (☎ (021) 508188), Waterford (☎ (051) 879000), Galway (☎ (091) 562000), Limerick (☎ (061) 313333), and other transportation hubs.

 Ulsterbus, Laganside, Belfast (☎ (01232) 333000; www.ulsterbus.co.uk), the North's version of Bus Éireann, runs extensive and reliable routes throughout Northern Ireland, where there are no private bus services. Coverage expands in summer, when several buses run a purely coastal route, and full- and half-day tours leave for key tourist spots from Belfast. Pick up a regional timetable free at any station. Again, the bus discount passes won't save you much money: a **Freedom of Northern Ireland** bus and rail pass offers unlimited travel for one day (UK£10), or several consecutive days (3-day pass £25; 7-day pass £38).

 The **Irish Rover** pass covers both Bus Éireann and Ulsterbus services. It sounds ideal for visitors intending to travel in both the Republic and Northern Ireland, but unless you're planning to spend lots of time on the bus, its true value is debatable (unlimited travel for 3 of 8 days £36, child £18; for 8 of 15 days £85, child £43; for 15 of 30 £130, child £65). The **Emerald Card** offers unlimited travel on Ulsterbus; Northern Ireland Railways; Bus Éireann Expressway, Local, and City services in Dublin, Cork, Limerick, Galway, and Waterford; and intercity, DART, and suburban rail Iarnród Éireann services. The card works for eight out of 15 consecutive days (£115, child £58) or 15 out of 30 consecutive days (£200, child £100).

BUS TOURS. Though some may find that they limit a traveler's independence, bus tours can often free you from agonizing over the minutiae of your trip while exposing you to a knowledgeable tour leader. Tours cost around £20 per day, with longer tours costing less per day. **Tír na nÓg Tours** (☎ (01) 836 4684; www.tirnanogtours.com) offers three- to 10-day tours which include breakfast, hostels, and entrance to sights. **Paddywagon** (☎ (0800) 783 4191; www.paddywagontours.com) has three- and six-day packages, also with breakfast, hostels, and sights. The **Stray Travel Network** in London (☎ (020) 7373 7737; www.straytravel.com) provides three- and six-day tours of Ireland but does not make your sleeping and eating arrangements (except for first night's accommodations) so you can choose where to spend your money.

BY TRAIN

Iarnród Éireann (Irish Rail), is useful only for travel to urban areas, from which you'll need to find another form of transportation to reach Ireland's picturesque villages and wilds. Trains from Dublin's Heuston Station chug towards Cork, Tralee, Limerick, Ennis, Galway, Westport, Ballina, and Waterford; others leave from Dublin's Connolly Station to head for Belfast (express), Sligo, Wexford and Rosslare (express). Trains also make connections between these various cities. For schedule information, pick up an InterCity Rail Travellers Guide (50p), available at most train stations. The **TravelSave** stamp, available for £8 at any **usit** agency if you have an ISIC card, cuts fares by 30-50% on national rail. (It also provides 15% discounts on bus fares above £1.) A **Faircard** (£5) can get anyone age 16 to 26 up to 50% off the price of any InterCity trip. Those over 26 can get the less potent **Weekender card** (£8; up to a third off, valid F-Tu only). Both are valid through the end of the year. The **Rambler** rail ticket allows unlimited train travel on five days within a 15-day travel period (£67). For combined bus-and-train travel passes, see **By Bus,** p. 61. Information is available from Irish Rail information office, 35 Lower Abbey St., Dublin (☎ (01) 836 3333; www.irishrail.ie). Unlike bus tickets, train tickets sometimes allow travelers to break a journey into stages yet still pay the price of a single-phase trip. Bikes may be carried on most trains for a fee of £2-6, depending on weight; check at the station for the restrictions of specific trains.

While the **Eurailpass** is not accepted in Northern Ireland, it *is* accepted on trains (but not buses) in The Republic. A range of youth and family passes are also available, but Eurailpasses are generally cost-effective only if you plan to travel to the Continent as well. The BritRail pass does not cover travel in Northern Ireland, but the month-long **BritRail+Ireland** works in both the North and the Republic with rail options and round-trip ferry service between Britain and Ireland (US$408-770). Great value resides in the youth passes for individuals under the age of 26. You'll find it easiest to buy a Eurailpass before you arrive in Europe; contact Council Travel, Travel CUTS (see p. 55), or any of many other travel agents. The **Rail Europe Group** (☎ (800) 438 7245; www.raileurope.com), also sells point-to-point tickets.

Northern Ireland Railways (☎ (01232) 899411; www.nirailways.co.uk) is not extensive but covers the northeastern coastal region well. The major line connects Dublin to Belfast. When it reaches Belfast, this line splits, with one branch ending at Bangor and one at Larne. There is also rail service from Belfast and Lisburn west to Derry and Portrush, stopping at three towns between Antrim and the coast. British Rail passes are not valid here, but Northern Ireland Railways offers its own discounts. A valid **Northern Ireland Travelsave** stamp (UK£6, affixed to back of ISIC) will get you 50% off all trains and 15% discounts on bus fares over UK£1 within Northern Ireland. The **Freedom of Northern Ireland** ticket allows unlimited travel by train and Ulsterbus and can be purchased for seven consecutive days (UK£38), three consecutive days (£25), or a single day (£10).

BY CAR

The advantages of car travel speak for themselves. Disadvantages include high gasoline prices (£0.60-0.90 per liter), the unfamiliar laws and habits associated with driving in foreign lands, and, for Americans and most other nationalities, the fact that in Ireland, as in Britain, **you drive on the left.** Be particularly cautious at roundabouts (rotary interchanges)—give way to traffic from the right. Irish drivers speed along narrow, twisting, pot-holed, poorly lit back roads. You will need to drive rather slowly and cautiously, especially at night. Be alert for trucks and huge tour buses that whiz along even winding roads, and be vigilant for drunk-drivers at night. The **Association for Safe International Road Travel (ASIRT)** can provide more specific information about road conditions (☎ (301) 983-5252; www.asirt.org). ASIRT considers road travel (by car or bus) to be relatively safe in Ireland.

Irish law requires drivers and passengers to wear **seat belts**—these laws are enforced. In Ireland, children under 12 are not allowed to sit in the front seat of a car. Children under 40 lbs. should ride only in a specially designed carseat, which can be obtained for a small fee from most car rental agencies.

In the Republic, roads numbered below N50 are "primary routes," which connect all the major towns; roads numbered N50 and above are "secondary routes," not as well trafficked but still well signposted. Regional "R-roads" are rarely referred to by number. Instead, the road takes the name of its destination. The general speed limit is 55 mph (90km per hr.) on the open road and either 30 mph (50km per hr.) or 40 mph (65km per hr.) in town. There are no major highways.

Northern Ireland possesses exactly two major highways (M-roads or motorways) connecting Belfast with the rest of the province. The M-roads are supplemented by a web of "A-roads" and "B-roads." Speed limits are 60 mph (97km per hr.) on single carriageways (non-divided highways), 70 mph (113km per hr.) on motorways (highways) and dual carriageways (divided highways), and usually 30 mph (48km per hr.) in urban areas. Speed limits are always marked at the beginning of town areas. Upon leaving, you'll see a circular sign with a slash through it, signaling the end of the speed restriction. Speed limits aren't rabidly enforced; remember, though, that many of these roads are sinuous and single-track—use common sense. (See **Safety on the Road,** p. 50 for more on driving.)

CAR RENTALS. Renting (hiring) an automobile is the least expensive option if you plan to drive for a month or less, but the initial cost of renting a car and the price of gas will astound you in Ireland. People under 21 cannot rent, and those under 23 (or even 25) often encounter difficulties. Major rental companies include Alamo, Avis, Budget Rent-A-Car, Murrays Europcar, Hertz, Kenning, McCausland, and Swan National. Prices range from IR$100 to IR$300 (plus VAT) per week with insurance and unlimited mileage. For insurance reasons, most companies require renters to be over 23 and under 70. Some plans require sizable deposits unless you're paying by credit card. Make sure you understand the insurance agreement before you rent; some require you to pay for damages that you may not have caused. Automatics are around 40% more expensive to rent than manuals (stickshifts). Rental agencies convenient to major airports are **Budget Rent-A-Car,** 151 Lower Drumcondra Rd., Dublin 9 (☎ (01) 837 9611; $45 per day) and **Thrifty** (☎ (061) 472 649) at the Shannon Airport ($35 per day).

INTERNATIONAL DRIVING PERMIT (IDP). If you plan to drive a car while in Ireland for longer than a three-month period, you must have an International Driving Permit (IDP). If you intend to drive for longer than one year, you'll need to get an Irish driver's license.

Your IDP, valid for one year, must be issued in your own country before you depart; AAA affiliates cannot issue IDPs valid in their own country. You must be 18 to receive an IDP. A valid driver's license from your home country must always accompany the IDP. An application for an IDP usually needs to include one or two photos, a current local license, an additional form of identification, and a fee.

Australia: Contact your local Royal Automobile Club (RAC) or the National Royal Motorist Association (NRMA) if in NSW or the ACT (☎ (08) 9421 4444; www.rac.com.au/travel). Permits AUS$15.

Canada: Contact any Canadian Automobile Association (CAA) branch office or write to CAA, 1145 Hunt Club Rd., #200, K1V 0Y3 (☎ (613) 247-0117; www.caa.ca/CAAInternet/travelservices/internationaldocumentation/idptravel.htm). Permits CDN$10.

Ireland: Contact the nearest Automobile Association (AA) office or write to the UK address below. Permits IR£4. The Irish Automobile Association, 23 Suffolk St., Rockhill, Blackrock, Co. Dublin (☎ (01) 677 9481), honors most foreign automobile memberships (24hr. breakdown and road service ☎ (800) 667 788; toll-free in Ireland).

New Zealand: Contact your local Automobile Association (AA) or their main office at Auckland Central, 99 Albert St. (☎ (9) 377 4660; www.nzaa.co.nz). Permits NZ$8.

South Africa: Contact the Travel Services Department of the Automobile Association of South Africa at P.O. Box 596, 2000 Johannesburg (☎ (11) 799 1400; fax 799 1410; http://aasa.co.za). Permits SAR28.50.

UK: To visit your local AA Shop, contact the AA Headquarters (☎ (0990) 44 88 66), or write to: The Automobile Association, International Documents, Fanum House, Erskine, Renfrewshire PA8 6BW. To find the location nearest you that issues the IDP, call (0990) 50 06 00 or (0990) 44 88 66. For more info, see www.theaa.co.uk/motoringandtravel/idp/index.asp. Permits UK£4.

US: Visit any American Automobile Association (AAA) office or write to AAA Florida, Travel Related Services, 1000 AAA Drive (mail stop 100), Heathrow, FL 32746 (☎ (407) 444-7000; fax 444-7380). You don't have to be a member to buy an IDP. Permits US$10. AAA Travel Related Services (☎ (800) 222-4357) provides road maps, travel guides, emergency road services, travel services, and auto insurance.

CAR INSURANCE. Most credit cards cover standard insurance. If you rent, lease, or borrow a car, you will need a **green card**, or International Insurance Certificate, to prove that you have liability insurance. Obtain it through the car rental agency; most include coverage in their prices. If you lease a car, you can obtain a green card from the dealer. Some travel agents offer the card; it may also be available at border crossings. Verify whether your auto insurance applies abroad; even if it does, you will still need a green card to certify this to foreign officials. If you have a collision abroad, the accident will show up on your domestic records if you report it to your insurance company. Rental agencies may require you to purchase theft insurance in countries that they consider to have a high risk of auto theft. Ask your rental agency about Ireland.

BY MOPED AND MOTORCYCLE

Motorized bikes don't use much gas, can be put on trains and ferries, and are a good compromise between the high cost of car travel and the limited range of bicycles. However, they're uncomfortable for long distances, dangerous in the rain, and unpredictable on rough roads and gravel. Always wear a helmet, and never ride with a backpack. If you've never been on a moped before, the winding Wicklow Mountains are not the place to start.

BY BICYCLE

Many insist that cycling is *the* way to see Ireland and Northern Ireland. Much of the Island's countryside is well suited for pedaling by daylight, as many roads are not heavily traveled. Single-digit N roads in the Republic, and M roads in the North, are more busily trafficked; try to avoid these. Begin your trip in the south or west to take advantage of prevailing winds. (See also **Safety On the Road,** p. 50.)

Many airlines will count your bike as your second free piece of luggage, and a few charge extra. The additional fee runs about US$60-110 each way. Bikes must be packed in a cardboard box with the pedals and front wheel detached; airlines sell bike boxes at the airport (US$10). Most ferries let you take your bike for free or for a nominal fee. You can always ship your bike on trains, but the cost varies.

Riding a bike with a frame pack strapped on it or your back is about as safe as pedaling blindfolded over a sheet of ice; panniers are essential. The first thing to buy, however, is a suitable **bike helmet** (US$25-50). U-shaped Citadel or Kryptonite **locks** are expensive (starting at US$30), but the companies insure their locks against theft of your bike for one to two years. For mail order equipment, **Bike Nashbar** (☎ 800-627-4227; www.nashbar.com) beats all competitors' offers and ships anywhere in the US or Canada.

Bikes can go on some trains but not all: inquire at the information desk. You'll have better luck getting your bike on a bus if you depart from a terminal, not a wayside stop. Bikes are allowed on Bus Éireann at the driver's discretion (if the bus isn't crowded) for a fee of £3-5, but this fee isn't always enforced; the fee for taking a bike on the train is between £2-6, depending on the weight of the bike. It's a pain to bring a bike on an airplane, and each airline has different rules. *Let's Go* lists bike shops and bike rental establishments wherever we can find them. The cash deposit may often be waived if you pay for the rental with a credit card.

Irish Cycle Hire (☎ (041) 984 1067; email irch@iol.ie), has offices in Drogheda, Dublin, Cork, Killarney, Dingle, Galway, Westport, Ennis, and Donegal. The Drogheda office, which is the office to contact with any questions, is open daily from 9am to 5:30pm. All charge IR£7 per day, £35 per week, with £30 deposit. Bikes come with lock, pump, and repair kit. One-way rental (renting in one location and dropping off in another) is possible for IR£10.

Rent-A-Bike, 58 Lower Gardiner St., Dublin (☎ (01) 872 5399), rents 21-speed cross-country and mountain bikes for IR£40 per week, plus IR£40 deposit. Used bikes, which you can sell back up to four months later for half price, are sometimes available in September or October at the Dublin shop. All bookings should be made through the head office in Dublin.

Raleigh Rent-A-Bike rents for IR£10 per day, £40 per week, plus £50 deposit. The shops will equip you with locks, patch kits, and pumps, and for longer journeys, pannier bags (IR£7-10 per week). Their One-Way Rental plan allows you to rent a bike at one shop and drop it off at another for a flat charge of IR£15. Reservations should be made through the main office at 8 Botanic Road, Galssnevin, Dublin 9 (☎/fax (01) 873 3622; www.trackbikes.com). You might also contact **Raleigh Ireland Limited** (☎ (01) 626 1333) in Dublin.

Many small local dealers and hostels also rent bikes. Rates are usually IR£5 to £9 per day and £25 to £45 per week; bike quality varies. Tourist offices can direct you to bike rental establishments and distribute leaflets on local biking routes, as well as providing the extensive *Cycle Touring Ireland* (£7). If you plan to do much long-distance riding, you might also check a travel bookstore for other Irish cycling guides. Mountaineers Books (☎ (800) 553 4453; mountaineersbooks.org) sells *Ireland by Bike: 21 Tours* for US$15 (plus US$3 shipping). Adequate **maps** are a necessity; Ordnance Survey maps (£4.50) or Bartholomew maps are available in most bookstores in Ireland and the UK, and in good ones in the US.

BY FOOT

Ireland's mountains, fields, and heather-covered hills make walking and hiking an arduous joy. The **Wicklow Way,** a popular trail through mountainous Co. Wicklow, has hostels designed for hikers within a day's walk of each other. The best hill-walking maps are the *Ordnance Survey* series (IR£4.50 each; available in bookstores). Other remarkable trails include the **Burren Way** (p. 298), the **Western Way** (p. 323), and the **Fore Trail** (p. 162). There are a multitude of other trails all over the island; consult Bord Fáilte (see p. 43) for more information and free pamphlets. *Let's Go* lists many of these longer hikes in the **Sights** sections of town listings, as well as including a plethora of shorter strolls in virtually every Irish town.

The **Ulster Way** encircles Northern Ireland with 560 mi. of marked trails. Less industrious trekkers are accommodated by frequent subdivisions. For the booklet The *Ulster Way* (free), contact the **Sports Council for Northern Ireland,** House of Sport, Upper Malone Rd., Belfast BT9 5LA (☎ (028) 9038 1222). If you're planning a hike through the Mourne Mountains, contact the **Mourne Heritage Center,** 87 Central Promenade, Newcastle, Co. Down BT33 0HH (☎ (028) 4372 4059).

WALKING FESTIVALS. Many counties host walking festivals throughout the year, particularly in May and June. The Wicklow Mountains have festivals on bank holidays in both April and October; contact Wicklow Co. Tourism (☎ (0404) 66058; wctr@iol.ie). The Slieve Bloom Mountains also has a festival on the May bank holiday (☎ (0509) 37247). Most other festivals are shorter, less expansive, and have variable dates; consult www.walking.travel.ie for a comprehensive list.

WALKING TOURS. For those looking to avoid some of the pitfalls of hiking, **guided tours** may be the solution. Though expensive (upwards of £60 per day), an area expert will guide hiking greenhorns over the green hills as a bus transports their luggage, meals are served, and accommodations await. Less expensive and more independent, **self-guided tours** include the luggage transport and accommodations but usually do away with meals (and, of course, the guide). For a list of tours, see www.kerna.ie/wci/walking or www.walking.travel.ie. **Tír na nÓg Tours** (57 Lower Gardiner St., Dublin 1; ☎ (01) 836 684), is a reputable and acclaimed choice.

BY THUMB

No one should hitch without careful consideration of the risks involved. Not everyone can be an airplane pilot, but almost any bozo or lunatic can drive a car. Hitching means entrusting your life to a random person who happens to stop beside you on the road and risking theft, assault, sexual harassment, and unsafe driving. Hitching in Ireland has a glowing reputation, but the risks remain the same. Locals in Northern Ireland do not recommend hitching there; many caution against hitching in the Co. Dublin and Eastern Ireland regions, and in the Irish Midlands. In spite of these disadvantages, some find the gains are many. Favorable hitching experiences allow you to meet local people and get where you're going, especially in the rural areas of Ireland where public transportation is less reliable. While we don't endorse hitchhiking, we'll tell you some ways to make it safer and how to do it right.

> ❗ *Let's Go* strongly urges you to consider seriously the risks before you choose to hitch. We do not recommend hitching as a safe means of transportation, and none of the information presented here is intended to do so.

The decision to pick up a hitcher can be a difficult one for a driver, so a smart hitcher will do everything possible to make it easier. Successful hitchers travel light and stack their belongings in a compact but visible cluster. Most Europeans signal with an open hand, rather than a thumb; many write their destination on a sign in large, bold letters and draw a smiley-face under it. Drivers prefer hitchers who are neat and wholesome-looking. No one stops for anyone wearing sunglasses. Where you stand is vital. Experienced hitchers stand where drivers can stop, have time to look over potential passengers as they approach, and return to the road without causing an accident. Hitching on hills or curves is hazardous and largely unsuccessful; traffic circles and access roads to highways are better. If you are hitching a **long distance** or to a remote spot with an intervening town between your present and desired location, you would do well to make your sign for the intervening town rather than your final destination. Shorter lifts are easier to pick up because it's easier for the driver and because more cars will be going to the nearby spot than to the distant one. Always ask for a "lift" and not a "ride"; you would do better to save the latter term for a visit to a Hibernian brothel.

In the Practical Information section of many cities, we list the bus lines that take travelers to strategic points for further hitching. You can get a sense of the amount of traffic a road sees by its letter and number: in the Republic, single-digit N-roads (A-roads in the North) are as close as Ireland gets to highways, double-digit N-roads see some intercity traffic, R-roads (B-roads in the North) generally only carry local traffic but are easy hitches, and non-lettered roads are a **hitcher's purgatory**. In Northern Ireland, hitching (or even standing) on motorways (M-roads) is illegal: you may only thumb at the entrance ramps—*in front* of the nifty blue-and-white superhighway pictograph (a bridge over a road).

Safety issues are always imperative, even for those who are not hitching alone. If you're a woman traveling alone, don't hitch. A man and a woman are a safer combination, two men will have a harder time, and three will go nowhere. Hitchhiking at night can be particularly dangerous. Safety-minded hitchers avoid getting in the back of a two-door car and never let go of their backpacks. They will not get into a car that they can't get out of again in a hurry. If they ever feel threatened, they insist on being let off, regardless of where they are. Acting as if they are going to open the car door or vomit on the upholstery usually gets a driver to stop.

ACCOMMODATIONS

Bord Fáilte (bored FAHL-tshah; meaning "welcome board") is the Republic of Ireland's tourism authority. Actually a government department (and a fairly important one), its system for approving accommodations involves a more-or-less frequent inspection and a fee. Approved accommodations get to use Bord Fáilte's national booking system and display its icon, a green shamrock on a white field. Be aware that Bord Fáilte meets at the end of the year and decides how much prices should increase in the Republic of Ireland. As our prices were researched in the summer of 2000, they may have increased since publication. Approved campgrounds and bed and breakfasts are listed with prices in the *Caravan and Camping Ireland* and *Bed and Breakfast Ireland* guides, respectively, available from any Bord Fáilte office. Bord Fáilte's standards are very specific and, in some cases, far higher than what hostelers and other budget travelers expect or require. Unapproved accommodations can be a better value than their approved neighbors, though some unapproved places are, of course, real dumps. Most official tourist offices in Ireland will refer *only* to approved accommodations; some offices won't even tell you how to get to an unapproved hostel, B&B, or campground. Most tourist offices will book a room for a £1-3 fee, plus a 10% deposit. **Credit card reservations** can be made through Dublin Tourism (☎ (1800) 6686 6866). Approval by the **Northern Ireland Tourist Board** is legally required of all accommodations in the North. Their tourist offices can therefore provide you with all the contact information you'll need to find a night's lodging.

HOSTELS

> **A HOSTELER'S BILL OF RIGHTS.** There are certain standard features that we do not include in our hostel listings. Unless we state otherwise, you can expect that every hostel has: no lockout, no curfew, a kitchen, free hot showers, some system of secure luggage storage, and no key deposit.

For those looking to make friends and for a unique experience minus the expense, hostels are the place. Hostels are generally dorm-style accommodations, often in single-sex large rooms with bunk beds, although some hostels do offer private rooms for families and couples. They sometimes have storage space for your use, bike rentals, and laundry facilities. There can be drawbacks: a few hostels close for daytime "lock-out" hours, have a curfew, don't accept reservations, or impose a maximum stay. In Ireland, a bed in a hostel will usually fall in the range £7.50-12 (light breakfast often included, or £1-3). In Ireland more than anywhere else, senior travelers and families are invariably welcome. Some hostels are strikingly beautiful (a few are even housed in castles), but others are little more than run-down barracks. You can expect every Irish hostel to provide blankets, although you may have to pay extra for sheets (see **Packing**, p. 53). Hostels listed are chosen based on location, price, quality, and facilities. Be warned that because of an influx of refugees to Ireland over the last year, **a number of (mostly independent) hostels are closing to tourists** and are instead accepting government contracts to house these asylum-seekers. Be aware of this circumstance, and try to call ahead to independent hostels to ensure that they still open for business.

For the various services and lower rates offered at member hostels, hostelling associations, especially **Hostelling International (HI)**, can definitely be worth joining (regional addresses listed below). A membership in any national HI affiliate allows you to stay in HI hostels in any country. HI's umbrella organization's web page (www.iyhf.org) lists the web addresses and phone numbers of all national associations and can be a great place to begin researching hosteling in a specific region. Hosteling membership is rarely necessary in Ireland, although there are sometimes member discounts. For non-members, an overnight fee plus one-sixth of the annual membership charge buys one stamp; a card with six stamps is proof of full

> **TIPS ON IRISH SHOWERS.** While outside ample liquid often falls from the Irish heavens, getting a little moisture on your weary body inside many hostels may prove a challenge. Here are a few tips to get the liquid **HOT** and flowing at the end of the day: A) Many hostels heat their shower-water electrically; you must pull a cord or push a button (sometimes red, sometimes outside the bathroom door or positioned high on the wall) to ensure that you do not take a cold shower without a good reason. B) Many hostel showers require that you push a button inside the stall at regular intervals (every 10-30 seconds) to keep the water flowing; the trick is to establish an easy rhythm of "push-and-scrub, push-and-scrub." C) Whenever in doubt, ask at the hostel's desk how to master the use of their subtle shower; instead of berating your hosts with unclean language, you may just end up showering them with praise.

HI membership. In Ireland, **An Óige** (an OYJ), the **HI** affiliate, operates 34 hostels countrywide (61 Mountjoy St., Dublin 7; ☎ (01) 830 4555; www.irelandyha.org; one-year membership IR£10, under 18 IR£4, families IR£20). Many An Óige hostels are in remote areas or small villages and were designed mostly to serve hikers, long-distance bicyclists, anglers, and others who want to see nature rather than meet people. The North's HI affiliate is **HINI** (Hostelling International Northern Ireland; formerly known as **YHANI**). It operates only eight hostels, all comfortable (22-32 Donegall Rd., Belfast BT12 5JN, Northern Ireland; ☎ (01232) 32 47 33; www.hini.org.uk; one-year membership UK£7, under 18 UK£3). Some HI hostels operate only from March to November, April to October, or May to September.

A number of hostels in Ireland belong to the **Independent Holiday Hostels (IHH)**. The 150 IHH hostels usually have no lockout or curfew, accept all ages, require no membership card, and have a comfortable atmosphere that generally feels less institutional than that at An Óige hostels; all are Bord Fáilte-approved. Pick up a free booklet with complete descriptions of each at any IHH hostel. Contact the IHH office at 57 Lower Gardiner St., Dublin (☎ (01) 836 4700).

Also, if you have Internet access, check out the **Internet Guide to Hostelling** (www.hostels.com), which includes hostels from around the world in addition to oodles of information about hostelling and backpacking worldwide. Another comprehensive hosteling website includes www.eurotrip.com/accommodation.

HOSTEL RESERVATIONS. Reservations for over 300 **Hostelling International (HI)** hostels may be made via the International Booking Network (IBN), a computerized system that allows you make reservations months in advance for a nominal fee. Because An Óige and HINI are both affiliated with HI, many of their hostels accept reservations via the IBN at the following numbers for a nominal fee: ☎ (02) 9261 1111 from Australia; 800-663-5777 from Canada; (01629) 581 418 from the UK; (01) 301 766 from Ireland; (09) 379 4224 from New Zealand; 800-909-4776 from the US; or on the web at www.hiayh.org/ushostel/reserva/ibn3.htm. Reservations for a growing number of hostels and transportation services can be made on www.hostelireland.com. You may also make credit card bookings over the phone; contact An Óige or HINI. In summer, it is often necessary to reserve at least two days in advance at many hostels.

REGIONAL HI OFFICES. To join H.I. contact one of the following organizations:

- **Australian Youth Hostels Association (AYHA)**, 422 Kent St., Sydney NSW 2000 (☎ (02) 9261 1111; fax 9261 1969; www.yha.org.au). AUS$49, under 18 AUS$14.50.
- **Hostelling International-Canada (HI-C)** (☎ (800) 663-5777 or (613) 237-7884; email info@hostellingintl.ca; www.hostellingintl.ca). CDN$25, under 18 CDN$7.
- **Youth Hostels Association of New Zealand (YHANZ)** (☎ (03) 379 9970; fax 365 4476; email info@yha.org.nz; www.yha.org.nz). NZ$40, ages 15-17 NZ$12, under 15 free.

Hostels Association of South Africa, 3rd fl. 73 St. George's St. Mall, P.O. Box 4402, Cape Town 8000 (☎ (021) 424 2511; fax 424 4119; email info@hisa.org.za; www.hisa.org.za). SAR50, under 18 SAR25, lifetime SAR250.

Scottish Youth Hostels Association (SYHA), 7 Glebe Crescent, Stirling FK8 2JA (☎ (01786) 89 14 00; fax 89 13 33; www.syha.org.uk). UK£6, under 18 UK£2.50.

Youth Hostels Association (England and Wales) Ltd. (☎ (01727) 85 52 15; fax 84 41 26; www.yha.org.uk). UK£12, under 18 UK£6, families UK£24.

Hostelling International-American Youth Hostels (HI-AYH) (☎ (202) 783-6161 ext. 136; fax 783-6171; email hiayhserv@hiayh.org; www.hiayh.org). US$25, under 18 free.

BED AND BREAKFASTS

For a cozy alternative to impersonal hotel rooms at rates that can be competitive to private rooms at hostels, B&Bs (private homes with rooms available to travelers) range from the acceptable to the sublime. Hosts will sometimes go out of their way to be accommodating by accepting travelers with pets, giving personalized tours, or offering home-cooked meals. "Full Irish breakfasts"—eggs, bacon, bread, sometimes black or white pudding, fried vegetables, cereal, orange juice, and coffee or tea—often fill tummies until dinner. Singles run about £15-25, doubles £24-40. On the other hand, many B&Bs do not provide phones or private bathrooms. But by and large, Irish B&Bs are a plentiful and excellent way to meet locals who might give you insight into the land through which you are traveling.

B&Bs displaying a shamrock are officially approved by Bord Fáilte. For accommodations in Northern Ireland, check the Northern Ireland Tourist Board's annual *Where to Stay in Northern Ireland* (UK£4), available at most tourist offices. For **further reading,** consult *The Complete Guide to Bed and Breakfasts, Inns and Guesthouses in the US, Canada, and Worldwide,* by Pamela Lanier (Ten Speed Press; US$17).

UNIVERSITY DORMS

Many colleges and universities open their residence halls to travelers when school is not in session—some do so even during term-time. These dorms are often in student areas (and thus proximate to bookstores, nightlife, cafes, transportation, and so on), include kitchen facilities, and are usually very clean. Getting a room may take a couple of phone calls and require advanced planning, but rates tend to be low (especially if you book for six or more people), and many offer free local calls. For appropriate cities, including Dublin, Galway, and Belfast, *Let's Go* lists among the accommodations colleges which rent dorm rooms. (Cork and Limerick are also big university towns with student housing available in summer.) For **further reading,** consult *Campus Lodging Guide (18th Ed.;* B&J Publications; US$15).

GOING GREEN

ECEAT (the European Centre for Eco Agro Tourism)-**International** publishes a *Green Holiday Guide to Ireland,* where it lists hostels, B&Bs, campgrounds, and guest houses that are either organic farms or otherwise "environmentally friendly" places to stay. All ECEAT-listed accommodations are in beautiful, wild areas, and frequently lie beside protected parkland. Contact ECEAT-International at P.O. Box 10899, 1001 EW, Amsterdam (☎ (31) 206 681030; www.pz.nl/eceat), for a guide. For more about work exchanges on Irish organic farms see **Work,** p. 80.

HOME EXCHANGE

Home exchange offers the traveler various types of homes (houses, apartments, condominiums, villas, even castles in some cases), plus the opportunity to live like a native and to cut down on accommodation fees. For more information, contact **HomeExchange.Com** (☎ (805) 898-9660; www.homeexchange.com), **Intervac International Home Exchange** (☎ (353) (41) 983 0930; www.intervac.com), or **The Invented City: International Home Exchange** (US ☎ (800) 788-CITY, elsewhere call US (415) 252-1141; www.invented-city.com), or surf www.aitec.edu.au/~bwechner/Documents/Travel/Lists/HomeExchangeClubs.html.

CAMPING AND THE OUTDOORS

Camping brings you closest to the land, the water, the insects, and continued financial solvency. Ireland is well endowed with sites and not at all endowed with snakes. Most campsites are open from April to October, although some stay open year-round. Youth hostels often have camping facilities (the charge is usually half the hostel charge), which is fortunate for many backpackers as many campsites are designed for people with caravans (RVs) rather than people with tents. Sites cost £3-10, depending on the level of luxury. You can legally set up camp only in specifically marked areas unless you get permission from the person on whose land you plan to squat. It is legal to cross private land by **public rights of way;** any other use of private land without permission is considered trespassing. Remember, **bogs catch fire** extremely easily.

Camping in State Forests and National Parks is not allowed in Ireland, nor is camping on public land if there is an official campsite in the area. It is also illegal to light fires within 2km of these forests and parks. Designated caravan and camping parks provide all the accoutrements of bourgeois civilization: toilets, running water, showers, garbage cans, and sometimes shops, kitchens, laundry facilities, restaurants, and game rooms. In addition, many have several caravans for hire at the site. **Northern Ireland** treats its campers royally; there are well-equipped campsites throughout, and spectacular parks often house equally mouth-watering sites.

USEFUL PUBLICATIONS AND WEB RESOURCES. A variety of publishing companies offer hiking guidebooks to meet the educational needs of novice or expert. For information about camping, hiking, and biking, call the publishers listed below to receive a free catalogue.

- **Sierra Club Books,** 85 Second St., 2nd fl., San Francisco, CA 94105, USA (☎ (415) 977-5704; www.sierraclub.org/books). Books include *Wild Ireland* ($16).
- **The Mountaineers Books,** 1001 SW Klickitat Way, #201, Seattle, WA 98134, USA (☎ (800) 553-4453 or (206) 223-6303; www.mountaineersbooks.org). Over 400 titles on hiking, biking, mountaineering, natural history, and conservation.
- **Automobile Association,** A.A. Publishing. Orders and enquiries to TBS Frating Distribution Centre, Colchester, Essex, CO7 7DW, UK (☎ (01206) 25 56 78; www.theaa.co.uk). Publishes *Camping and Caravanning: Britain & Ireland* (UK£8).

CAMPING AND HIKING EQUIPMENT

Good camping equipment is both sturdy and light. Camping equipment is generally more expensive in Australia, New Zealand, and Europe than in North America.

- **Sleeping Bag:** Most good sleeping bags are rated by "season," or the lowest outdoor temperature at which they will keep you warm ("summer" means 30-40°F at night and "four-season" or "winter" often means below 0°F). Sleeping bags are made either of down (warmer and lighter, but more expensive, and miserable when wet) or of synthetic material (heavier, more durable, and warmer when wet). Prices range from US$80-210 for a summer synthetic to US$250-300 for a good down winter bag. Sleeping bag pads, including foam pads (US$10-20) and air mattresses (US$15-50) cushion your back and neck and insulate you from the ground. Bring a "stuff sack" or plastic bag to store your sleeping bag and keep it dry.
- **Tent:** The best tents are free-standing, with their own frames and suspension systems; they set up quickly and only require staking in high winds. Low-profile dome tents are the best all-around. When pitched their internal space is almost entirely usable, which means little unnecessary bulk. Tent sizes can be somewhat misleading: two people *can* fit in a two-person tent, but will find life more pleasant in a four-person. If you're traveling by car, go for the bigger tent, but if you're hiking, stick with a smaller tent that weighs no more than 5-6 lbs. (2-3kg). Good two-person tents start at US$90, four-person tents at US$300. Seal the seams of your tent with waterproofer, and make sure it has a rain fly. Other tent accessories include a battery-operated lantern, a plastic groundcloth, and a nylon tarp.

Backpack: If you intend to do a lot of hiking, you should have a frame backpack. **Internal-frame packs** mold better to your back, keep a lower center of gravity, and can flex adequately to allow you to hike difficult trails that require a lot of bending and maneuvering. **External-frame packs** are more comfortable for long hikes over even terrain since they keep the weight higher and distribute it more evenly. Whichever you choose, make sure your pack has a strong, padded hip belt, which transfers the weight from the shoulders to the legs. Any serious backpacking requires a pack of at least 4000 cubic inches (16,000cc). Allow an additional 500 cubic inches for your sleeping bag in internal-frame packs. Sturdy backpacks cost anywhere from US$125-420. This is one area where it doesn't pay to economize—cheaper packs may be less comfortable, and the straps are more likely to fray or rip or may fall apart altogether.

Boots: Be sure to wear hiking boots with good ankle support which are appropriate for the terrain you plan to hike. Your boots should fit snugly and comfortably over one or two wool socks and a thin liner sock. Breaking in boots properly before setting out requires wearing them for several weeks. Bring "moleskin" for blisters.

Other Necessities: Raingear in two pieces, a top and pants, is far superior to a poncho. Synthetics, like polypropylene tops, socks, and long underwear, along with a pile jacket, will keep you warm even when wet. When camping in autumn, winter, or spring, bring along a "space blanket," which helps you to retain your body heat and doubles as a groundcloth (US$5-15). Plastic canteens or water bottles keep water cooler than metal ones do, and are virtually shatter- and leak-proof. Large, collapsible water sacks will significantly improve your lot in primitive campgrounds and weigh practically nothing when empty, though they are bulky and heavy when full. Bring **water-purification tablets,** or shell out money for a portable water-purification system, for when you can't boil water. Though most campgrounds provide campfire sites, you may want to bring a small metal grate or grill of your own. For those places that forbid fires or the gathering of firewood, you'll need a camp stove. The classic Coleman stove starts at about US$40. You will need to purchase a fuel bottle and fill it with propanel. A first aid kit, swiss army knife, insect repellent, calamine lotion, and waterproof matches or a lighter are other essential camping items.

The mail-order/online companies listed below offer lower prices than many retail stores, but a visit to a local camping or outdoors store will give you a good sense of items' look and weight.

- **Campmor** (US ☎ (888) 226-7667; elsewhere call US +1 (201) 825-8300; www.campmor.com).
- **Discount Camping** (Australia ☎ (08) 8262 3399; www.discountcamping.com.au).
- **Eastern Mountain Sports (EMS),** 327 Jaffrey Rd., Peterborough, NH 03458, USA (☎ (888) 463-6367 or (603) 924-7231; www.shopems.com).
- **Mountain Designs** (Australia ☎ (07) 3252 8894; www.mountaindesign.com.au).
- **Recreational Equipment, Inc. (REI),** Sumner, WA 98352, USA (☎ (800) 426-4840 or (253) 891-2500; www.rei.com).
- **YHA Adventure Shop,** 14 Southampton St., London, WC2E 7HA, UK (☎ (020) 7836 8541). The main branch of one of Britain's largest outdoor equipment suppliers.

CAMPERS AND RVS. Renting an RV, called a caravan in Ireland, will always be more expensive than tenting or hosteling, but the costs compare favorably with the price of staying in hotels and renting a car (see **Car Rentals,** p. 63), and the convenience of bringing along your own bedroom, bathroom, and kitchen makes it an attractive option, especially for older travelers and families with children.

Rates vary widely by region, season (July and August are the most expensive months), and type of RV. It always pays to contact several different companies to compare vehicles and prices. For **further reading,** consult *Camping Your Way through Europe*, by Carol Mickelsen (Affordable Press; US$15); *Exploring Europe by RV*, by Dennis and Tina Jaffe (Globe Pequot; US$15); *Great Outdoor Recreation Pages (*www.gorp.com).

WILDERNESS SAFETY

Stay warm, stay dry, and stay hydrated. The vast majority of life-threatening wilderness situations result from a breach of this simple dictum. On any hike, however brief, you should pack enough equipment to keep you alive should disaster befall. Let someone know when and where you are going hiking, either a friend, your hostel, a park ranger, or a local hiking organization. This includes raingear, hat and mittens, a first-aid kit, a reflector, a whistle, high energy food, and extra water. Dress in warm layers of synthetic materials designed for the outdoors, or wool. Pile fleece jackets and Gore-Tex raingear are excellent choices. Never rely on cotton for warmth. This "death cloth" will be absolutely useless should it get wet. Make sure to check all equipment for any defects before setting out, and see **Camping and Hiking Equipment,** above, for more information. Be knowledgeable of outdoor ailments such as hypothermia, giardia, rabies, and insects bites, as well as basic medical concerns and first-aid.

> **ENVIRONMENTALLY RESPONSIBLE TOURISM.** The idea behind responsible tourism is to leave no trace of human presence behind. A campstove is the safer (and more efficient) way to cook than using vegetation, but if you must make a fire, keep it small and use only dead branches or brush rather than cutting vegetation. Make sure your campsite is at least 150 ft. (50m) from water supplies or bodies of water. If there are no toilet facilities, bury human waste (but not paper) at least 4 in. (10cm) deep and above the high-water line, and 150 ft. or more from any water supplies and campsites. Always pack your trash in a plastic bag and carry it with you until you reach the next trash can.

KEEPING IN TOUCH

MAIL

SENDING MAIL TO AND RECEIVING MAIL IN IRELAND. An Post is Ireland's national postal service (www.anpost.ie). **Airmail** letters under 1 oz. between North America and Ireland take six to nine days and cost US$0.90 or CDN$0.95. Allow at least five to seven days from Australia (postage AUS$1.80 for up to 20 grams) and two to three from Britain (postage 32p for up to 25g). Envelopes should be marked "air mail" or "par avion" to avoid having letters sent by sea. There are several ways to arrange pick-up of letters sent to you by friends and relatives while you are abroad.

General Delivery: Mail can be sent to Ireland through **Poste Restante** (the international phrase for General Delivery) to almost any city or town with a post office. Address *Poste Restante* letters to (for example): "Gregory WAYNE, Poste Restante, Enniscorthy, Co. Wexford, Ireland." The mail will go to a special desk in the central post office, unless you specify a post office by street address or postal code. As a rule, it is best to use the largest post office in the area since mail may be sent there regardless of what is written on the envelope. When picking up your mail, bring a form of photo ID, preferably a passport. There is generally no surcharge; if there is a charge, it generally does not exceed the cost of domestic postage. If the clerks insist that there is nothing for you, have them check under your first name as well. *Let's Go* lists post offices in the Practical Information section for each city and most towns.

American Express: AmEx's travel offices throughout the world will act as a mail service for cardholders if you contact them in advance. Under this free **Client Letter Service,** they will hold mail for up to 30 days and forward upon request. Address the letter in the same way shown above. Some offices will offer these services to non-cardholders (especially those who have purchased AmEx Travelers Cheques), but you must call ahead to make sure. Check the Practical Information section of the countries you plan to visit; Let's Go lists AmEx office locations for most large cities. A complete list is available free from AmEx (☎ (800) 528 4800).

If regular airmail is too slow, **Federal Express** (☎ 13 26 10 in Australia; Ireland ☎ 800 535 800; New Zealand ☎ 0800 733 339; South Africa ☎ 021 551 7610; UK ☎ 0800 123 800; the US and Canada ☎ 800-463-3339; for other countries, call the US ☎ for international operator 800-247-4747) can get a letter from New York to Dublin in two days for a whopping US$25.50; rates among non-US locations are prohibitively expensive (London to Dublin, for example, costs upwards of US$40). By **US Express Mail,** a letter from New York would arrive in Dublin within four days and would cost US$5. From Australia, **EMS** can get a letter to Ireland in three to four working days for AUS$27.

Surface mail is by far the cheapest and slowest way to send mail. It takes one to three months to cross the Atlantic and two to four months to cross the Pacific—appropriate for sending large quantities of items you won't need to see for a while.

SENDING MAIL FROM IRELAND. Airmail from Ireland to the US averages five to six days; to Europe it averages three to four days. To Australia, NZ, or South Africa, it will take one to two weeks. Times are less predictable from small towns.

To send a postcard or letter (up to 25g) to a destination within Europe or to any other international destination via airmail costs 45p. Add IR£2 for Swiftpost International. Domestically, postcards and letters require 32p.

TELEPHONES

> **CALLING IRELAND FROM HOME.**
> To call Ireland direct from home, dial:
> 1. The international access code of your home country. International access codes include: **Australia** 0011; **NZ** 00; **South Africa** 09; **UK** 00; **US** 011.
> 2. The country code of the region you're calling. Country codes include: 353 to reach the **Republic of Ireland**; 44 to reach **Northern Ireland** and **Britain**; 048 to reach **Northern Ireland** from the Republic.
> 3. The city code. City codes are usually listed with a 0 at their start (for example, Dublin's city code is 01). This zero is dropped when dialing. Let's Go lists telephone codes opposite each city header (marked by a ☎ icon), except when covering rural areas where more than one telephone code may apply—here we list the area code before the number. The city code is 028 throughout the north.
> 4. The local number. Regional telephone codes range from two to five digits, and local telephone numbers range from five to seven digits.

CALLING HOME FROM IRELAND

A **calling card** purchased in your home country from your home telephone company can be your best bet. Wherever possible, use a calling card for international phone calls, as the long-distance rates for national phone services are often exorbitant. To obtain a calling card from your national telecommunications service before you leave home, contact the appropriate company below. For a complete list of collect and calling card service numbers of the providers below to dial while in Ireland or Northern Ireland, consult the **Inside Back Cover** of this guide.

US: AT&T (☎ (888) 288-4685), **Sprint** (☎ (800) 877-4646), or **MCI** (☎ (800) 444-4141).
Australia: Telstra Australia Direct (☎ 13 22 00).
Canada: Bell Canada **Canada Direct** (☎ (800) 565-4708).
New Zealand: Telecom New Zealand (☎ (0800) 00 00 00).
South Africa: Telkom South Africa (☎ 09 03).
UK: British Telecom **BT Direct** (☎ (800) 34 51 44).

Where available, prepaid Irish phone cards and occasionally major credit cards can be used for direct international calls. **Swiftcall** phone cards or other prepaid Irish phone cards (available at post offices and newsagents) can score you great rates after 9pm, Irish time—often as low as 20-30p per minute.

If you do dial direct, dial 00 (the international access code in both the Republic and Northern Ireland), and then dial the country code and number of your home. **Country codes** include: Australia 61; New Zealand 64; South Africa 27; UK 44; US and Canada 1. Alternatively, you can access an Irish international operator at 114. Note that to call the North from the Republic, you dial 048 plus the number. Phone rates tend to be highest in the morning, lower in the evening, and lowest on Sunday and late at night. International calls from the Republic are cheapest during **economy periods.** The low-rate period to North America is Monday through Friday 10pm to 8am and Saturday and Sunday all day; to EU countries it's Monday through Friday 6pm to 8am and Saturday and Sunday all day; to Australia and New Zealand call Monday through Friday 2 to 8pm and midnight to 8am, and Saturday and Sunday all day. There are no economy rates to the rest of the world.

The expensive alternative to dialing direct or using a calling card is using an international operator to place a **collect call.** An English-speaking operator from your home nation can be reached by dialing the appropriate service provider listed above (their numbers are listed on the **Inside Back Cover** of this guide), and they will typically place a collect call even if you don't possess one of their phone cards.

> **CALLING HOME FROM THE REPUBLIC OF IRELAND.**
> **Operator (not available from card phones):** 10.
> **Directory inquiries (for the Republic and the North):** 1190.
> **International directory inquiries:** 1197 **(Britain),** 1198 **(International).**
> **Telecom Éireann information number:** (1800) 330 330.
> **International operator:** 114.
> **International access code:** 00.

CALLING WITHIN IRELAND

The simplest way to call within the country is to use a coin-operated phone. Using Irish pay phones can be tricky. Public phones come in two varieties: **coin phones** and **card phones.** Public coin phones will give you back unused coins (but not fractions of coins; don't insert a £1 coin for a 20p call) but private pay phones (called "one-armed bandits") in hostels and restaurants do not—once you plunk in your change, kiss it good-bye. In any pay phone, do not insert money until asked to, or until the call goes through. The frightening pip-pip noise that the phone makes as you wait for it to start ringing is normal and can last up to 10 seconds. Local calls cost 20p on public phones; "one-armed bandits" can charge 30p or whatever they please. Local calls are not unlimited—one unit pays for four minutes.

The smart option for non-local calls is buying a **prepaid phone card,** which carries a certain amount of phone time depending on the card's denomination. The time is measured in minutes or talk units (e.g. one unit/one minute), and the card usually has a toll-free access telephone number and a personal identification number (PIN). Most cards contain the pin on the card itself. To make a phone call, you dial the access number, enter your PIN, and at the voice prompt, enter the phone number of the party you're trying to reach. A computer tells you how much time or how many units you have left on your card. Phone rates tend to be highest in the morning, lower in the evening, and lowest on Sunday and late at night. News agents sell phone cards in denominations of £2, £5, £10, or £20. For calls direct-dialed to the US during the cheapest hours, a £10 Swiftcall Card can last 25 minutes. Card phones have a digital display that ticks off the perilous plunge your units are taking. When the unit number starts flashing, you may push the eject button on the card phone; you can then pull out your expired calling card and replace it with a fresh one. If you try to wait until your card's units fall to zero, you'll be disconnected. Eject your card early and use the remaining unit or two for a local call.

> **CALLING WITHIN AND FROM NORTHERN IRELAND AND LONDON.**
> **Operator:** 100.
> **Directory inquiries:** 192.
> **International operator:** 155.
> **International directory assistance:** 153.
> **International access code:** 00.

Pay phones in Northern Ireland initially charge 10p for local calls; most calls cost 20p. A series of harsh beeps warns you to insert more money when your time is up. The digital display ticks off your credit in 1p increments so you can watch your pence in suspense. Only unused coins are returned. You may use all remaining credit on a second call by pressing the "follow on call" button (often marked "FC"). Phones don't accept 1p, 2p, or 5p coins. The dial tone is a continuous purring sound; a repeated double-purr means the line is ringing. Northern **British Telecom Phonecards,** in denominations of £2, £5, £10, and £20, are sold at post offices and newsstands, and are accepted at most public phones. The £5 and higher denominations provide extra credit.

Reduced rates for most international calls from the UK apply Monday through Friday 8pm to 8am, and weekends all day. Rates are highest Monday through Friday 3 to 5pm. The low-rate period to Australia and New Zealand is daily midnight to 7am and 2:30 to 7:30pm. Rates to the Republic of Ireland go down Monday through Friday 6pm to 8am and weekends.

EMAIL AND INTERNET

Let's Go lists and indexes **Internet access,** which is steadily increasing in Ireland. **Electronic mail (email)** is an attractive option for staying in touch. For information on internet accessibility world-wide, contact cyber-star.com, cybercaptive.com, netcafeguide.com, which list a host of connections to sites supplying further internet information on any country.

Internet access is available in Irish cities in privately owned cafes, hostels, and often in libraries. One hour of access costs £3-5 (an ISIC card may win you a discount), but a library membership in the Republic (IR£2) gives you unlimited access to libraries and their Internet. Other free, web-based email providers include Hotmail (www.hotmail.com), RocketMail (www.rocketmail.com), Yahoo! Mail (www.yahoo.com) and, in Ireland, Ireland.com. Many free email providers are funded by advertising and some may require subscribers to fill out a questionnaire. Almost every internet search engine has an affiliated free email service.

ADDITIONAL INFORMATION

SPECIFIC CONCERNS

WOMEN TRAVELERS

Women exploring on their own inevitably face some additional safety concerns, but it's easy to be adventurous without taking undue risks. In general, Ireland is an extremely safe place to travel. If you are concerned, you might consider staying in hostels which offer single rooms that lock from the inside or that offer rooms for women only. Communal showers in some hostels are safer than others; check them before settling in. Stick to centrally located accommodations and avoid solitary late-night treks or metro rides. When traveling, always carry extra money for a phone call, bus, or taxi. Look as if you know where you're going (even when you don't) and consider approaching older women or couples for directions if you're lost or feel uncomfortable. **Hitching** is never safe for lone women, or even for two women traveling together, although some women report Ireland as the safest country in Europe to hitch.

Cities in Ireland are safe by city standards; however, harassment may be more common in urban areas, and especially in pubs, where the men may have Irish faces, but "Roman" hands—some men assume that if a woman is not Irish, then she must be on birth control and therefore has no reason to reject their advances. Your best answer to verbal harassment is no answer at all; feigned deafness, sitting motionless and staring straight ahead at nothing in particular will do a world of good that reactions usually don't achieve. Wearing a conspicuous **wedding band** may help prevent unwanted overtures. Some travelers report that mentioning or carrying pictures of a "husband" or "children" is extremely useful to help document marriage status. The extremely persistent can sometimes be dissuaded by a firm, loud, and very public "Go away!"

Don't hesitate to seek out a police officer or a passerby if you are being harassed. *Let's Go: Ireland* lists emergency numbers (including rape crisis lines) in the Practical Information listings of most cities. Memorize the emergency numbers in the places you visit. Carry a whistle or an airhorn on your keychain, and don't hesitate to use it in an emergency. An IMPACT Model Mugging self-defense course will not only prepare you for a potential attack, but will also raise your level of awareness of your surroundings as well as your confidence (see **Self Defense**, p. 50). Women also face some specific health concerns when traveling (see **Women's Health**, p. 53).

For **further reading**, consult *A Journey of One's Own: Uncommon Advice for the Independent Woman Traveler*, Thalia Zepatos. Eighth Mountain Press (US$17); or *A Foxy Old Woman's Guide to Traveling Alone*, Jay Ben-Lesser. Crossing Press (US$11).

TRAVELING ALONE

A number of organizations supply information for savvy, independent-type, solo travelers, others find travel companions for those who shirk at solitary adventure, and some do both. Two of the latter are listed here.

Connecting: Solo Traveler Network, P.O. Box 29088, 1996 W. Broadway, Vancouver, BC V6J 5C2, Canada (☎ (604) 737-7791; email info@cstn.org; www.cstn.org). Bi-monthly newsletter features going solo tips, single-friendly tips and travel companion ads. Annual directory lists holiday suppliers that avoid single supplement charges. Advice and lodging exchanges facilitated between members. Membership US$25-35.

Travel Companion Exchange, P.O. Box 833, Amityville, NY 11701 (☎ (631) 454 0880 or 800-392-1256; www.whytravelalone.com). Publishes the pamphlet *Foiling Pickpockets & Bag Snatchers* (US$4.70) and *Travel Companions*, a bi-monthly newsletter for single travelers seeking a travel partner (subscription US$48).

OLDER TRAVELERS

Senior citizens are eligible for a wide range of discounts on transportation, museums, theaters (midweek), concerts, restaurants, and accommodations. If you don't see a senior citizen price listed, ask, and you may be delightfully surprised. **Age and Opportunity** (☎ (01) 837 0570); ageandop@indigo.ie) promotes the participation of the elderly in all aspects—from cultural to physical—of Irish society.

Agencies for senior group travel are growing in enrollment and popularity. These are only a few:

ElderTreks, 597 Markham St., Toronto, ON, Canada, M6G 2L7 (☎ 800-741-7956 or (416) 588-5000; fax 588-9839; email passages@inforamp.net; www.eldertreks.com).

Elderhostel, 75 Federal St., Boston, MA 02110-1941 (☎ (617) 426-7788 or (877) 426-8056; email registration@elderhostel.org; www.elderhostel.org). Programs at colleges, universities, and other learning centers in Ireland on varied subjects lasting 1-4 weeks. Must be 55 or over (spouse can be of any age).

The Mature Traveler, P.O. Box 50400, Reno, NV 89513 (☎ (775) 786-7419 or 800-460-6676). Has soft-adventure tours for seniors. Subscription US$30.

Walking the World, P.O. Box 1186, Fort Collins, CO 80522 (☎ (970) 498-0500; fax 498-9100; email walktworld@aol.com; www.walkingtheworld.com), sends trips to Ireland.

For **further reading,** consult *No Problem! Worldwise Tips for Mature Adventurers,* by Janice Kenyon (Orca Book Publishers; US$16); *A Senior's Guide to Healthy Travel,* Donald L. Sullivan (Career Press; US$15); or *Unbelievably Good Deals and Great Adventures That You Absolutely Can't Get Unless You're Over 50,* Joan Rattner Heilman (Contemporary Books; US$13).

BISEXUAL, GAY, AND LESBIAN TRAVELERS

Ireland is more tolerant of homosexuality than one might expect. As is true elsewhere, people in rural areas may not be as accepting as those in cities, whose attitudes have noticeably changed since the decriminalization of homosexuality in the Republic in 1993. Dublin now supports a gay community, with growing student societies at Trinity and UCD, a gay youth group that has doubled its size over the last five years, and a growing array of pubs and clubs. Belfast and, to a lesser degree, Cork and Galway also have increasingly open gay scenes. *Gay Community News* covers mostly Irish gay-related news, and its listings page covers most gay locales in all of Ireland. *Let's Go: Ireland* has gay pub and nightlife listings as well as phone numbers for gay information in Dublin, Belfast, Cork, and elsewhere (see the **Practical Information** sections). Clubs tend to be frequented by both sexes but with a larger male contingent. Below are a few resources for the BGL traveler:

Ireland's Pink Pages (http://indigo.ie/~outhouse/). Ireland's web-based BGL directory. Regional info, including the Republic and the North. Helpful links.

Gay's the Word, 66 Marchmont St., London WC1N 1AB (☎ (020) 7278 7654; www.gaystheword.co.uk). The largest gay and lesbian bookshop in the UK, with both fiction and non-fiction titles. Mail-order service available.

International Gay and Lesbian Travel Association, 4331 N. Federal Hwy., Suite 304, Fort Lauderdale, FL 33308 (☎ (954) 776-2626 or 800-448-8550; www.iglta.com). An organization of over 1350 companies serving gay and lesbian travelers worldwide. Call for lists of travel agents, accommodations, and events.

For **further reading,** consult *Spartacus International Gay Guide,* by Bruno Gmünder Verlag (US$33); *Ferrari Guides' Gay Travel A to Z, Ferrari Guides' Men's Travel in Your Pocket, Ferrari Guides' Women's Travel in Your Pocket,* and *Ferrari Guides' Inn Places* (Ferrari Guides; for more information, ☎ 800-962-2912 or www.q-net.com; US$14-16); or *The Gay Vacation Guide: The Best Trips and How to Plan Them,* Mark Chesnut (Citadel Press; US$15).

TRAVELERS WITH DISABILITIES

Ireland is not particularly wheelchair accessible. Ramps, wide doors, and accessible bathrooms are less common than in the US, even in cities such as Dublin. *Let's Go: Ireland* lists and indexes **wheelchair-accessible hostels.** Guide dogs are always conveyed free, but both the UK and Ireland impose a six-month quarantine on all animals entering the country and require that the owner obtain an import license. Write to the British Tourist Authority or Bord Fáilte for free access guides.

Those with disabilities should inform airlines and hotels of their disabilities when making arrangements for travel; some time may be needed to prepare special accommodations. Advance booking is strongly recommended; if you notify a bus company of your plans ahead of time, they will have staff ready to assist you. Call ahead to restaurants, hotels, parks, and other facilities to find out about the existence of ramps, the widths of doors, the dimensions of elevators, etc. Rail is probably the most convenient form of travel for disabled travelers in Ireland. Not all train stations are wheelchair accessible.

The following organizations provide information or publications that might be of assistance:

DTour (www.iol.ie/infograf/dtour) is a web-based visitors' guide to Ireland for people with disabilities. Index of accommodation and transportation facilities, with links to other resources in Ireland.

Access Department, The National Rehabilitation Board, 25 Clyde Rd., Dublin 4. Offers a county-by-county fact sheet about accommodations facilities.

Mobility International USA (MIUSA) (☎ (541) 343-1284 voice and TDD; fax 343-6812; email info@miusa.org; www.miusa.org). Sells *A World of Options: A Guide to International Educational Exchange, Community Service, and Travel for Persons with Disabilities* (US$35).

The following organizations arrange **tours** or trips for disabled travelers:

Directions Unlimited, 123 Green Ln., Bedford Hills, NY 10507, USA (☎ (914) 241-1700 or (800) 533-5343; www.travel-cruises.com). Specializes in arranging individual and group vacations, tours, and cruises for the physically disabled.

The Guided Tour Inc., 7900 Old York Rd., #114B, Elkins Park, PA 19027, USA (☎ (800) 783-5841 or (215) 782-1370; www.guidedtour.com). Organizes travel programs for persons with developmental and physical challenges around Ireland.

For **further reading,** consult *Resource Directory for the Disabled*, by Richard Neil Shrout (Facts on file; US$45), or *Wheelchair Through Europe*, by Annie Mackin (Graphic Language Press; ☎ (760) 944 9594; email niteowl@cts.com; US$13). *Global Access* (www.geocities.com/Paris/1502/disabilitylinks.html) has links for disabled travelers in Ireland.

MINORITY TRAVELERS

The majority of Ireland's 5 million people are white and Christian (largely Catholic in the Republic, mixed Catholic and Protestant in the North). While a growing Malaysian, Indian, and Pakistani population resides mainly in and around Dublin, on the whole, the Irish have never had to address racial diversity on a large scale. (Recent influxes of non-European immigrants drawn by Ireland's present economic boom my change this, however.) Darker-skinned travelers may be the subjects of unusual attention, especially in rural areas, but comments or stares are more likely to be motivated by curiosity than ill will. Ireland has a Jewish community of 1800 people, concentrated in Dublin, that experiences little anti-Semitism.

TRAVELERS WITH CHILDREN

Family vacations often require that you slow your pace, and always that you plan ahead. When deciding where to stay, remember the special needs of young children; call ahead to hostels and B&Bs to make sure they are child-friendly. If you rent a car, make sure the rental company provides a car seat for younger children. Consider using a papoose-style device to carry a baby on walking trips. Be sure that your child carries some sort of ID in case of an emergency or he or she gets lost, and arrange a reunion spot in case of separation when sight-seeing.

Virtually all museums and tourist attractions also have a children's rate. Children under two generally fly for 10% of the adult airfare on international flights (this does not necessarily include a seat). International fares are usually discounted 25% for children from two to 11.

For **further reading,** consult *Take Your Kids to Europe*, by Cynthia W. Harriman (Globe Pequot; US$17); *How to take Great Trips with Your Kids*, by Sanford and Jane Portnoy (Harvard Common Press; US $10); *Adventuring with Children: An Inspirational Guide to World Travel and the Outdoors*, by Nan Jeffrey (Avalon House Publishing; $15).

DIETARY CONCERNS

Let's Go lists restaurants with vegetarian options when we find them. You're not likely to find much pub grub without meat, but in almost every town at least one restaurant will have something for vegetarians. Vegans will have more of a challenge and may frequently need to cook for themselves. For more information about vegetarian travel, contact the **North American Vegetarian Society** (☎ (518) 568-7970; www.cyberveg.org/navs/), which publishes *Transformative Adventures*, a guide to vacations and retreats (US$15).

For **further reading,** consult *The Vegan Travel Guide: UK and Southern Ireland* (Book Publishing Co.; US$15) or *Europe on 10 Salads a Day*, by Greg and Mary Jane Edwards (Mustang Pub; US$10).

Travelers who keep **kosher** should contact synagogues in larger cities for information on kosher restaurants; your own synagogue or college Hillel should have access to lists of Jewish institutions across the nation and in other parts of the world. Kosher is not a common term or practice in Ireland; if you are strict in your observance, you will have to prepare your own food on the road. **The Jewish Travel Guide** lists synagogues, kosher restaurants, and Jewish institutions in over 80 countries. Available in the UK (Vallentine-Mitchell Publishers; ☎ (020) 8599 88 66; fax 8599 09 84) or in the US (ISBS; ☎ 800-944-6190; US$16).

ALTERNATIVES TO TOURISM

For an extensive listing of "off-the-beaten-track" and specialty travel opportunities, try the **Specialty Travel Index** (☎ (888) 624-4030 or (415) 455-1643; www.spectrav.com; US$6). **Transitions Abroad** (www.transabroad.com) publishes a bimonthly on-line newsletter for work, study, and specialized travel abroad. **Council** sponsors work, volunteer, academic, internship, and professional study abroad programs in Ireland (see **Travel Agencies,** p. 55).

STUDY

It's not difficult to spend a summer, a term, or a year studying in Ireland or Northern Ireland. Each of the major regions in Ireland has a university and smaller, *gaeltacht* communities support Irish language programs. Enrolling as a full-time student is more difficult. The requirements for admission can be hard to meet unless you attended an EU secondary school. American students must pay full fees; EU students go free, so Americans are a welcome source of funds, but places are few, especially in Ireland. The website, www.studyabroad.com has a comprehensive list of programs in Ireland. **Council** sponsors over 40 study abroad programs throughout the world. Contact them for more information (see **Travel Agencies,** p. 55).

UNIVERSITIES. Most American undergraduates enroll in programs sponsored by American universities. However, good local universities can be much cheaper than an American university program, though it may be more difficult to receive academic credit. A few of the many schools that offer study abroad programs are listed below.

Trinity College Dublin: Offers a 1-year program of high-quality undergraduate courses for visiting students. Graduates can also register as one-year students not reading for a degree. Trinity College, Dublin 2, Ireland (☎ (01) 608 1396; email isa.office@tcd.ie).

University College Dublin: Offers a 2-week international summer course on "all aspects of Irish heritage and culture." (International Summer School, UCD, NewmanHouse, 86 St. Stephen's Green, Dublin 2. ☎ (01) 475 2004. www.ucd.ie/summerschool.)

Irish Studies Summer School at usit NOW, 19-21 Aston Quay, Dublin 2, Ireland (☎ (01) 602 1741; www.usitnow.ie) is a seven-week-long program offering courses in Irish culture and history. Contact Irish Studies Summer School in New York (☎ (212) 663 5435; email usitny@aol.com). usit also administrates the summer program **Ireland in Europe,** 2 weeks of courses about Irish civilization.

University College Galway: International Office, Galway, Ireland (☎ (091) 750 304; email intloffice@nuigalway.ie). Offers year and semester opportunities for junior-year students who meet the college's entry requirements. **Summer school** courses offered July-Aug. include Irish Studies, Education, and Creative Writing.

80 ■ ADDITIONAL INFORMATION

Queen's University Belfast: Study Abroad for a semester or year. There is also a new 4-week **Introduction to Northern Ireland** program in January that studies the political, social, and economic questions unique to the North. Contact the International Liaison Office (☎ (028) 9033 5415; email ilo@qub.ac.uk).

American Institute for Foreign Study, College Division, 102 Greenwich Ave., Greenwich, CT 06830 (☎ (800) 727-2437; www.aifs.com). Organizes programs for high school and college study in universities in Ireland. Summer, fall, spring, and year-long programs available. Scholarships available. Contact Dana Maggio at dmaggio@aifs.com.

Experiment in International Living, Summer Programs (☎ 800-345-2929; email eil@worldlearning.org). Founded in 1932, it offers cross-cultural, educational homestays, community service, ecological adventure, and language training in Ireland. Programs are 3-5 weeks long and run from US$1800-5000. Positions as group leaders are available for college graduates with experience working with high school students.

Oideas Gael: Glencolmcille, Co. Donegal, Ireland (☎ (073) 30248; www.OideasGael.com). Offers week-long Irish language and culture courses from Easter until Aug. in various activities including bilingual hillwalking, setdancing, painting, and archaeology.

For **further reading,** consult *Academic Year Abroad* (Institute of International Education Books; US$45); *Vacation Study Abroad.* Institute of International Education Books (US$40); *Peterson's Study Abroad Guide* (Peterson's; US$30).

WORK

Ireland's economic boom means that for the first time in centuries, more people are coming to work in Ireland than leaving it. Even so, unemployment in Ireland is high for an EU country. Travelers are most likely to find work in touristed urban centers such as Dublin, Galway, or Cork. Aside from semi-skilled labor, the recent investments of software companies in Ireland favor computer-savvy types. European Union citizens can work in any EU country, and if your parents were born in an EU country, you may be able to claim dual citizenship with Ireland, or at least the right to a work permit. Commonwealth residents with a parent or grandparent born in the UK do not need a work permit to work in Northern Ireland. Contact your British Consulate or High Commission (see p. 40) for details before you go and the **Department of Employment** (☎ (01) 631 2121; www.entemp.ie) when you arrive. If you do not fit into any of these categories, you must apply for a **work permit** to be considered for paid employment in the Republic or Northern Ireland. The permit takes approximately 4 weeks to process, is valid for between one month and one year, and can be renewed upon expiration. Your prospective employer must obtain this document, usually demonstrating you have skills that locals lack.

If you are a full-time student at a US university, the simplest way to get a job in Ireland is through work permit programs run by **Council** (see p. 55) and its member organizations. For a US$225 application fee, Council can procure three- to six-month work permits and a handbook to help you find work and housing.

For au pair work, **interExchange,** (☎ (212) 924 0446; email interex@earthlink.net), provides information on international work and au pair positions in Ireland. Only nationals of most European countries are eligible as au pairs in Ireland.

For those who would rather tend to crops, membership in **Willing Workers on Organic Farms (WWOOF)** (www.phdcc.com/sites/wwoof; US$20; UK$10) allows you to receive room and board at a variety of organic farms in Ireland in exchange for your help on the farm.

For **further reading,** consult *International Jobs: Where they Are, How to Get Them,* by Eric Koocher (Perseus Books; US$17); *How to Get a Job in Europe,* by Robert Sanborn (Surrey Books; US$22); or *Overseas Summer Jobs 2001, Work Your Way Around the World,* and *Directory of Jobs and Careers Abroad* (Peterson's; US$17-18 each).

VOLUNTEER

Volunteers need no work permit or special visa to take part in organized voluntary work provided the employment lasts fewer than three months and is unpaid. You can sometimes avoid the high application fees charged by the organizations that arrange placement by contacting the individual workcamps directly. For **Further reading,** try *International Directory of Voluntary Work*, Victoria Pybus (Vacation Work Publications; US$16).

- **Service Civil International Voluntary Service (SCI-VS)** (☎/fax (206) 545-6585; www.sci-ivs.org). Arranges placement in workcamps in Ireland for those age 18 and over. Local organizations sponsor groups for physical or social work. Registration fees US$50-250, depending on the camp location.

- **Volunteers for Peace** (☎ (802) 259-2759; www.vfp.org). Arranges placement in 2- to 3-week workcamps in Ireland comprising 10-15 people. Annual *International Workcamp Directory* US$20. Registration fee US$200. Free newsletter.

THE WORLD WIDE WEB

The web provides a wealth of information on Ireland and budget travel. The **Yahoo! UK and Ireland** (uk.yahoo.com) search engine is a good starting point, as is **www.ireland.com,** which links to the Irish Times. **MyTravelGuide** (www.mytravelguide.com) and **Geographia** (www.geographia.com) both provide country overviews and more. **How to See the World** (www.artoftravel.com) is a compendium of great travel tips, from cheap flights to self defense to interacting with local culture. **The Rec. Travel Library** (www.travel-library.com) has a fantastic set of links for general information and personal travelogues. For more local information, take a gander at the on-line cultural magazine www.irelandseye.com. To brush up on your Gaelic, **Cumasc** (www.cumasc.ie) is a magazine written entirely in Irish. (For more Ireland web resources, see **Tourist Office WebSites,** p. 44.)

AND OUR PERSONAL FAVORITE... Let's Go: www.letsgo.com. Our recently revamped website features photos and streaming video, info about our books, a travel forum buzzing with stories and tips, and links that will help you find everything you could ever want to know about Ireland.

COUNTY DUBLIN

Dublin and its suburbs form a single economic and commercial unit, the majority of which can be reached by DART (Dublin Area Rapid Transit), suburban rail, or Dublin buses. On weekends, the city center teems with suburbanites, tourists, and international hipsters out on the prowl. Despite the homogenizing effects of a booming economy and sprawling development, Dublin's suburbs offer a competitive, less polluted alternative to the city, but the mobs they attract preclude any notions of romantic Irish villages. Dublin County entertains and educates with beautiful beaches, literary landmarks, imposing castles, and monastic ruins, but the chief impression of most visitors is that this jet-setting metropolis has flown past the relaxed, agricultural lifestyle of the rest of the island.

HIGHLIGHTS OF COUNTY DUBLIN: PUBS, PENS, AND THE PAST

Explore Ireland's **National Museums** (p. 112), taking in Celtic gold work, a Carravagio, and the skeleton of an ancient Irish Elkhorn.

Window shop on **Grafton Street** (p. 103), then head around the corner to **Temple Bar** (p. 113) for a night of raucous tomfoolery in its pubs and clubs.

The late 16th-century campus of **Trinity College** shelters the **Book of Kells** (p. 109), a four-volume medieval edition of the Gospels with gold illumination.

Follow the footsteps of Joyce from his **Martello Tower** (p. 128) at Dún Laoghaire and along **O'Connell St.** (p. 115), making stops at pubs that hosted such literary giants as Samuel Beckett, Brendan Behan, Bernard Shaw, and Flann O'Brien.

Check out the blond in the black skirt at the **Guinness Hopstore** (p. 114).

Get a glimpse into the rebellion of Easter 1916 at **Kilmainham Gaol** (p. 114).

Escape the city and head to **Howth** (p. 124) for a breath of fresh sea air.

GETTING AROUND THE COUNTY

Rail lines, bus lines (both state-run and private), and the national highway system radiate from Ireland's capital. Major highways **N5** and **N6** lead to **N4**, **N8**, **N9**, and **N10** all feed into **N7**, dumping buses and cars into Dublin's vehicular sphere. Because inter-city transport is so Dublin-centric, you may find it more convenient in the long run to arrange your travel in other parts of the Republic while you're in the capital. Students may wish to get a TravelSave stamp for bus and rail discounts (see **Practical Information**, p. 92); for more information on national and international transportation, see **Essentials**, p. 59.

BY BUS

The lime-green **Dublin Buses** service the entire county extensively. The buses, which come in a variety of shapes and sizes all sporting "db" logos, run from 5am to 11:30pm and comprehensively cover the city and its suburbs: north to **Howth**, **Balbriggan**, and **Malahide**; west to **Rathcoole**, **Maynooth**, and **Celbridge**; and south to **Blessington**, **Enniskerry**, **Dún Laoghaire**, and **Bray**. Buses are cheap ($0.60-1.15; prices rise according to distance traveled), and most frequent between 8am and 6pm (generally every 8-20min., off-hours every 30-45min.). Most bus routes end or begin at the city center, at stops located near Christ Church, the Trinity College facade, St. Stephen's Green, O'Connell St., or Parnell St. Bus stands along the quays post timetables detailing routes around the city center and their termini. The most important pamphlet to pick up for the bustling traveler is the free "Which Ticket Type Are You?" leaflet available at the Dublin bus office. Along with the *Map of Greater Dublin* and the *Dublin Bus Timetable*, this handy guide will clue you into every variety of special ticket and student discount available. All are available from newsagents and the **Dublin Bus Office** at 59 Upper O'Connell St.,

GETTING AROUND THE COUNTY ■ 83

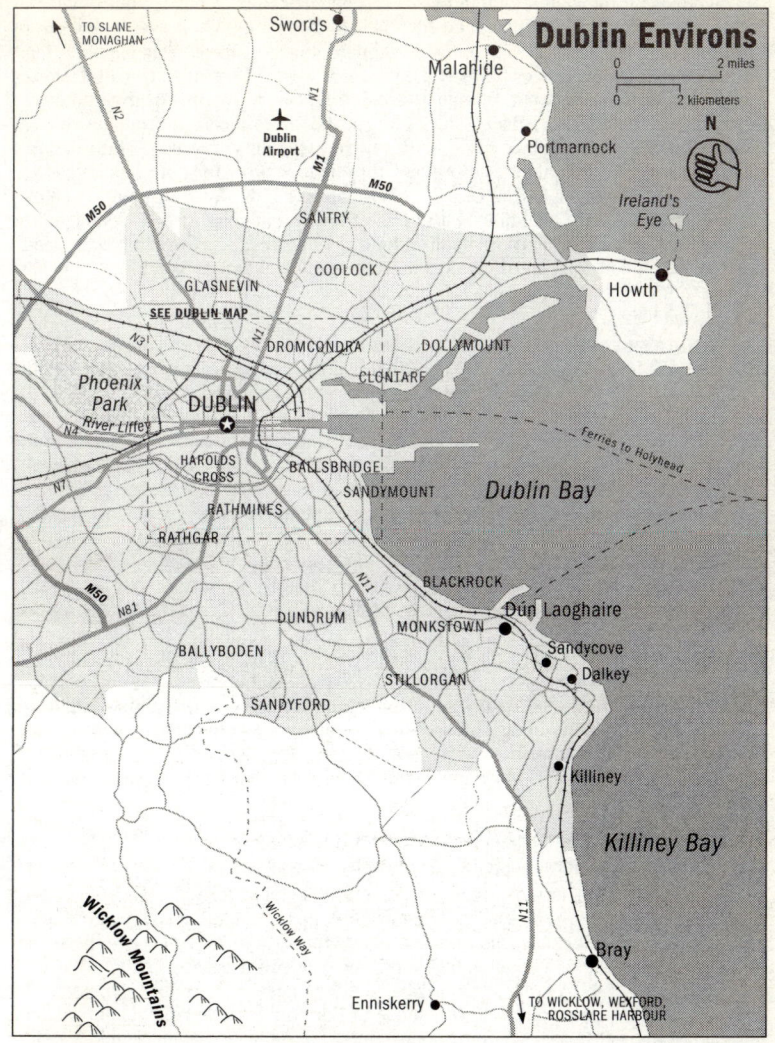

along with free handouts about individual routes (see **Getting There and Around,** p. 85). The Dublin buses run fairly regularly within the city, especially the smaller **City Imp** buses (every 8-15min.). Suburban routes often have an hour between scheduled stops. Dublin Bus runs the **NiteLink** service to the suburbs (Th-Sa nights at 12:30, 1:30, 2:30, and 3:30am; $3; Celbridge/Maynooth $4.50; no passes valid). Tickets for the NiteLink are sold at the Dublin Bus Office, by Nitelink bus drivers, and from a van parked on the corner of Westmoreland and College St. next to the Trinity College entrance. NiteLink leaves for the northern suburbs from D'Olier St., the southern suburbs from College St., and the western suburbs from Westmoreland. The **Airlink** service (#747 and 748) connects **Dublin airport** to the Central Bus Station ($3) and Heuston Station ($3.50), with stops including O'Connell St. (every 10-15min., 6:30am-11:45pm). **Wheelchair-accessible buses** are limited: the only options are the **OmniLink** service (#300), which cruises around Clontarf (60p), and the #3 bus from Whitehall to Sandymount (via O'Connell St.).

Travel passes, nicknamed "Ramblers" and advertised by a bizarre duck with a large proboscis, were not designed for the casual traveler; each pass has a time limit that requires several trips a day to validate its price. **Travel Wide** passes offer unlimited rides for a day or a week. (Day £3.50; week £13, students with Travel-Save stamp £10.) Be warned, though, that a Dublin Bus week runs from Sunday to Saturday inclusive, no matter when you purchase the pass. In other words, a weekly pass bought Friday night will expire after only one day. Dublin Bus months, similarly, are calendar months. Other tickets allow for both bus and sub-urban rail/DART travel. (Adult one-day **short hop** £5.20, weekly £17, monthly £63.) All special tickets are available at the bus office and at roughly 250 newsagents around the city; an ISIC card is required for student rates. Be aware that taller riders may find the limited legroom extremely uncomfortable for long rides.

BY TRAIN

Co. Dublin's suburban rail network reaches a sizable range of outlying areas. The electric **DART** trains run frequently up and down the coast, serving the suburbs on both the north and south sides. The trains put buses to shame in terms of cost and speed, but only reach a limited number of destinations. Fortunately, that number will continue to increase over the next couple years. From **Connolly, Pearse,** and **Tara St.** stations in the city center, the DART shoots all the way south past **Bray** and north to **Howth.** The DART runs every 10-15min. from roughly 6:30am to 11:30pm; a ride costs £0.55-1.10. Tickets are sold in the station and usually must be presented at the end of the trip. The orange trains of the **suburban rail** network continue north to **Malahide, Donabate,** and **Drogheda;** south to **Wicklow** and **Arklow;** and west to **Maynooth** and **Mullingar.** These trains all leave from Connolly Station. All but the westbound lines stop at Tara St. and Pearse Stations as well. Trains to **Kildare** leave from Heuston Station. Trains are frequent every day (roughly 30 per day) except Sundays. Complete DART/suburban rail timetables are available at many stations (50p). **Bicycles** are never permitted on DART trains, sometimes on suburban rail lines (ask first), and usually on mainline trains for a small fee (£6 single, £12 return). Special rail and bus/rail tickets are generally cost-effective only for those with a transport addiction.

DUBLIN ☎01

In a country known for its relaxed pace of life and rural sanctity, Dublin stands out for its international style and boundless energy. The city's offerings have expanded enormously with the booming Irish economy. The Irish who live outside of Dublin worry that it has taken on the characteristics of big cities everywhere: crime, rapid social change, and a weakness for short-lived trends. Yet, while Dublin may seem harsh by Irish standards, it's still as friendly a major city as you'll find. While not cosmopolitan in the sense of London or New York, Dublin is as eclectic as both. It boasts vibrant theater, music, and literary productions. A new generation of pubs need not fight with their elders—there's plenty of business to go around, for now at least. New accommodations, museums, concert venues, and construction projects litter the city.

Ireland is changing at a startling pace, and Dublin, with close to a third of the country's population in its environs, is leading the charge. Fueled by the EU and international and rural immigration, the city's zooming cultural and economic growth has led to the rocket-ship success of Temple Bar as the new nightlife hub. Smithfields, west across the River Liffey, is undergoing development to make it the next cultural center. The gentrification comes with tension and trade-offs. The suburbs are booming, but traffic is as congested as one's head after a night at Temple Bar. The upwardly mobile carry similarly mobile phones, but few young Dubliners can afford to buy a house in their own city. Shimmering with prosperity, Dublin faces the challenge of retaining its distinct identity as a capital city with a devotion to history, an appreciation of culture, and a sense of irony that takes the gleaming tourist trade in stride. Despite all the change, the image of old Ireland persists in the castles, cathedrals, and fine pubs that saturate the city.

The first record of human settlement around Dublin is a map made by the Greek scholar Ptolemy, who called the site Eblana. After years of visiting, the Vikings eventually set up a permanent town, Dubh Linn ("Black Pool"), around the modern College Green. The Viking Thingmote, or hill of assembly, stood there as the administrative center for both Viking powers and the Norman Pale until William III's 1690 victory at the Battle of the Boyne. During the ensuing Protestant Ascendancy (see p. 11), the Irish Parliament House sprang up near the old Viking center. The period's Protestant English culture remains evident today in the architecture of Dublin's tidy Georgian squares.

The capital of Ireland since the late 17th century, Dublin's blend of cultures has occasioned extraordinary intellectual and literary communities. From Swift and Burke to Joyce and Beckett, Dublin has produced so many great writers that nearly every street contains a literary landmark. Pubs continue to shelter much of Dublin's public life and world-renowned music scene. Dublin may not look like the "Emerald Isle" that the tourist brochures promote, but its people still embody the notorious charm and warmth of the Irish.

■ ■ GETTING THERE AND AROUND

For more on national and international transportation, see **Essentials**, p. 59.

Airport: Dublin Airport (☎ 844 4900). **Dublin buses** #41, 41B, and 41C run to Eden Quay in the city center with stops along the way (every 20min., £1.20). The **Airlink shuttle** runs non-stop directly to Busáras Central Bus Station and O'Connell St. (30-40min., every 10-15min., £3) and on to Heuston Station (50min., £3.50), but it's hardly worth the price in comparison to the #41 line. **Airport Express buses** (☎ 844 4265) go to Busáras and O'Connell St. (30min.; every 15-30min.; M-Sa 6:30am-10:50pm, Su 7:10am-11pm; £2.50). **Taxis** to the city center costs roughly £12-15. Wheelchair-accessible cabs may be available; call ahead (see **Taxis**). Beware Dublin traffic, even when planning on catching an express bus.

Trains: Irish Rail, Iarnród Éireann (EER-ann-road AIR-ann) has a travel center at 35 Lower Abbey St. (☎ 836 6222). Its information desks and booking windows at all 3 of the city's major stations may have longer lines. You can purchase a ticket in advance at the center, or buy one at a station 20min. before departure time. The travel center also spews data on DART, suburban trains, international train tickets, and cross-channel ferries. Open M-F 9am-5pm, Sa 9am-1pm. For specific routes, you can also call the 24hr. "talking timetables," which recite schedules of trains to **Belfast** (☎ 855 4477), **Cork** (☎ 855 4400), **Galway/Westport** (☎ 855 4422), **Killarney/Tralee** (☎ 855 4466), **Limerick** (☎ 855 4411), **Sligo** (☎ 855 4455), **Waterford** (☎ 855 4433), and **Wexford/Rosslare** (☎ 855 4488). Bus #90 circuits Connolly, Heuston, and Pearse Stations and Busáras (every 10min., 60p). Connolly and Pearse are also **DART** stations serving the north and south coasts (see **Getting Around the County**, p. 82).

Connolly Station, Amiens St. (☎ 836 3333; night ☎ 703 2358, M-Sa 5:30-9pm and Su 4:30-8:30pm), is north of the Liffey and close to Busáras Bus Station. Buses #20, 20A, and 90 at the station head south of the river, and the DART runs to Tara on the south quay, but it's faster to walk. Trains to **Belfast** (2¼hr.; 8 per day, Su 5 per day; £18), **Wexford** via **Rosslare** (3hr.; 3 per day, Su 2 per day; £11), and **Sligo** (3½hr.; 3 per day, F 4 per day, Su 3 per day; £14.50).

Heuston Station (☎ 703 2132; night ☎ 703 2131, M-Sa 5:30-8pm and 9-10pm, Sa 7:30am-8pm and 9-10pm, Su 8am-10pm) is south of Victoria Quay, well west of the city center, a 25min. walk from Trinity College. Buses #26, 51, and 79 go from Heuston to the city center. Trains to **Limerick** (2¼hr., 9 per day, £16-25), **Galway** (2½hr.; 5 per day, Su 4 per day; £13, F and Su £22), **Waterford** (2½hr.; 4 per day, Su 3 per day; £13), **Cork** (3½hr.; 8 per day, F 11 per day, Su 6 per day; £33.50), and **Tralee** (4½hr.; 6 per day, F 7 per day, Su 4 per day; £34). Eastbound Dublin buses go into the city.

Pearse Station, just east of Trinity College on Pearse St. and Westland Row, receives southbound trains from Connolly Station.

86 ■ DUBLIN OVERVIEW

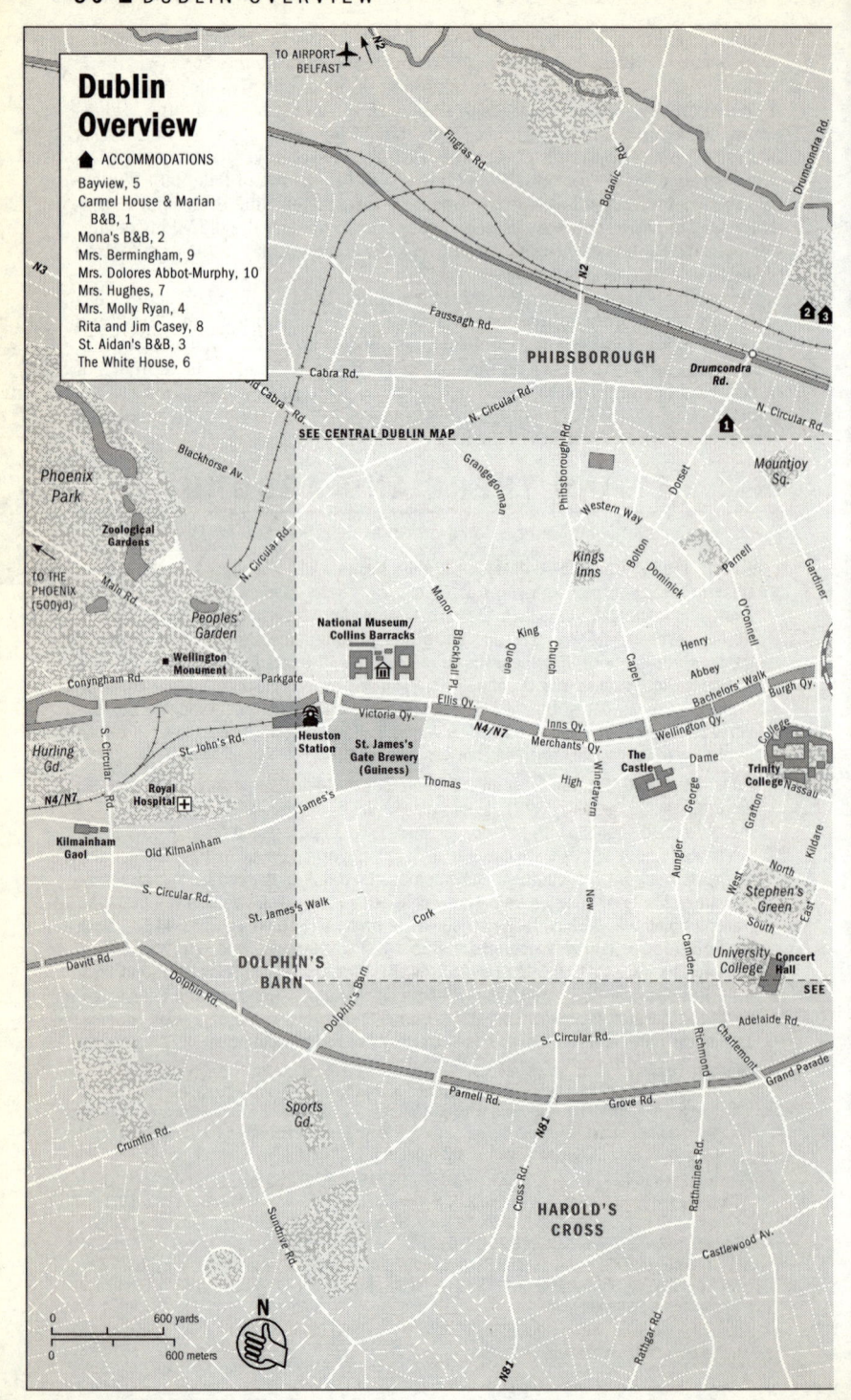

Dublin Overview

ACCOMMODATIONS
Bayview, 5
Carmel House & Marian B&B, 1
Mona's B&B, 2
Mrs. Bermingham, 9
Mrs. Dolores Abbot-Murphy, 10
Mrs. Hughes, 7
Mrs. Molly Ryan, 4
Rita and Jim Casey, 8
St. Aidan's B&B, 3
The White House, 6

DUBLIN OVERVIEW ■ 87

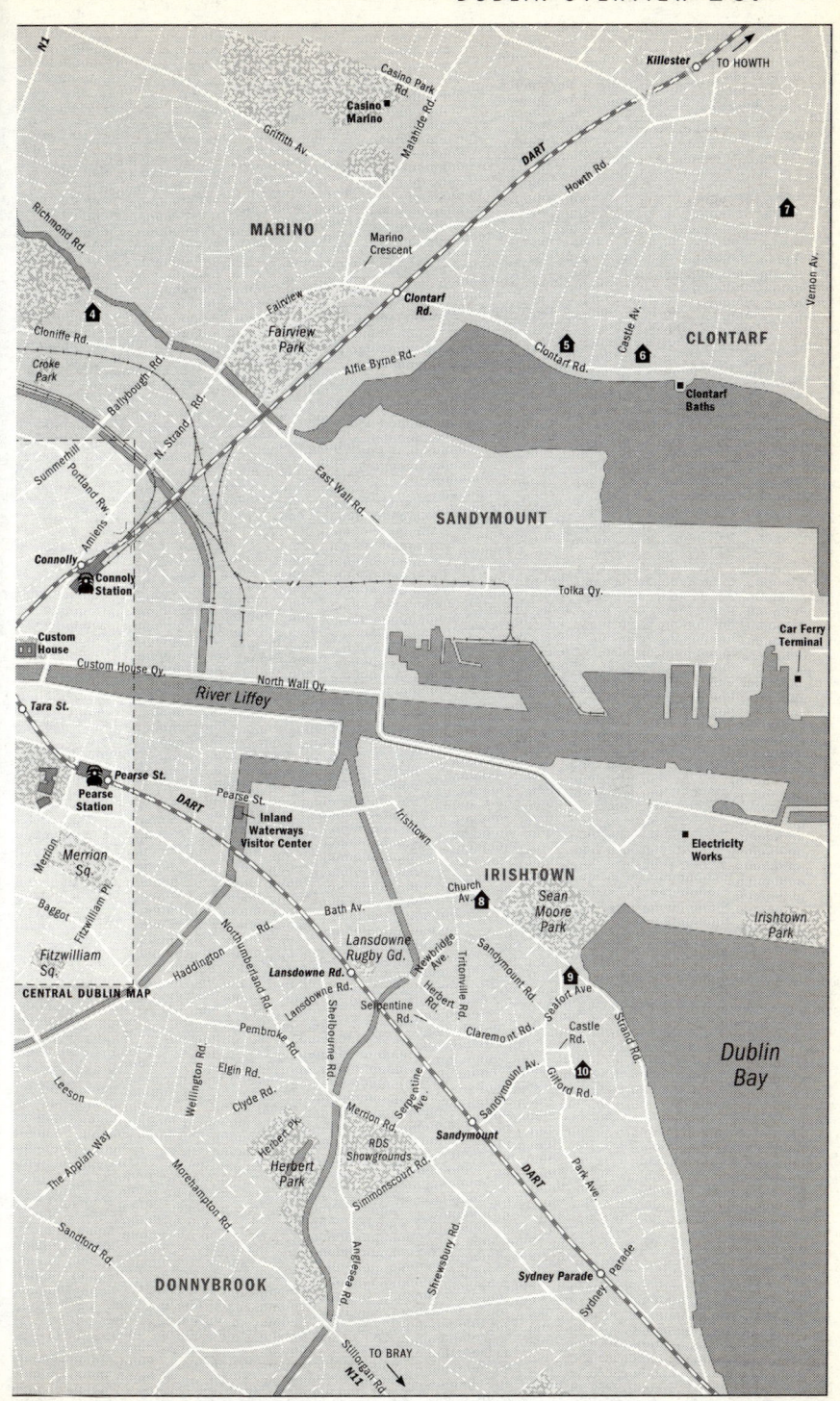

Central Dublin

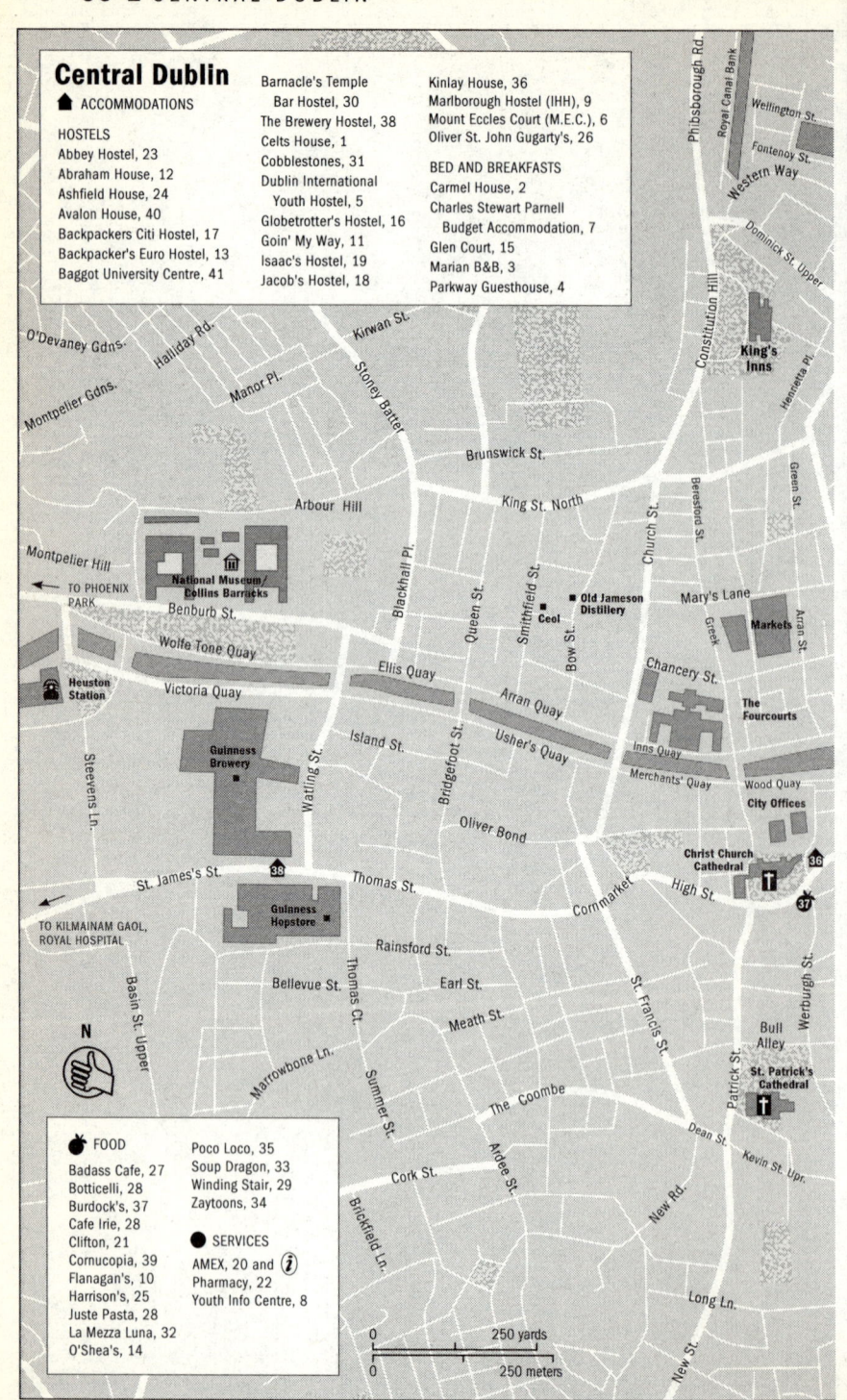

ACCOMMODATIONS

HOSTELS
Abbey Hostel, 23
Abraham House, 12
Ashfield House, 24
Avalon House, 40
Backpackers Citi Hostel, 17
Backpacker's Euro Hostel, 13
Baggot University Centre, 41
Barnacle's Temple Bar Hostel, 30
The Brewery Hostel, 38
Celts House, 1
Cobblestones, 31
Dublin International Youth Hostel, 5
Globetrotter's Hostel, 16
Goin' My Way, 11
Isaac's Hostel, 19
Jacob's Hostel, 18
Kinlay House, 36
Marlborough Hostel (IHH), 9
Mount Eccles Court (M.E.C.), 6
Oliver St. John Gugarty's, 26

BED AND BREAKFASTS
Carmel House, 2
Charles Stewart Parnell Budget Accommodation, 7
Glen Court, 15
Marian B&B, 3
Parkway Guesthouse, 4

FOOD
Badass Cafe, 27
Botticelli, 28
Burdock's, 37
Cafe Irie, 28
Clifton, 21
Cornucopia, 39
Flanagan's, 10
Harrison's, 25
Juste Pasta, 28
La Mezza Luna, 32
O'Shea's, 14
Poco Loco, 35
Soup Dragon, 33
Winding Stair, 29
Zaytoons, 34

SERVICES
AMEX, 20 and ⓘ
Pharmacy, 22
Youth Info Centre, 8

CENTRAL DUBLIN ■ 89

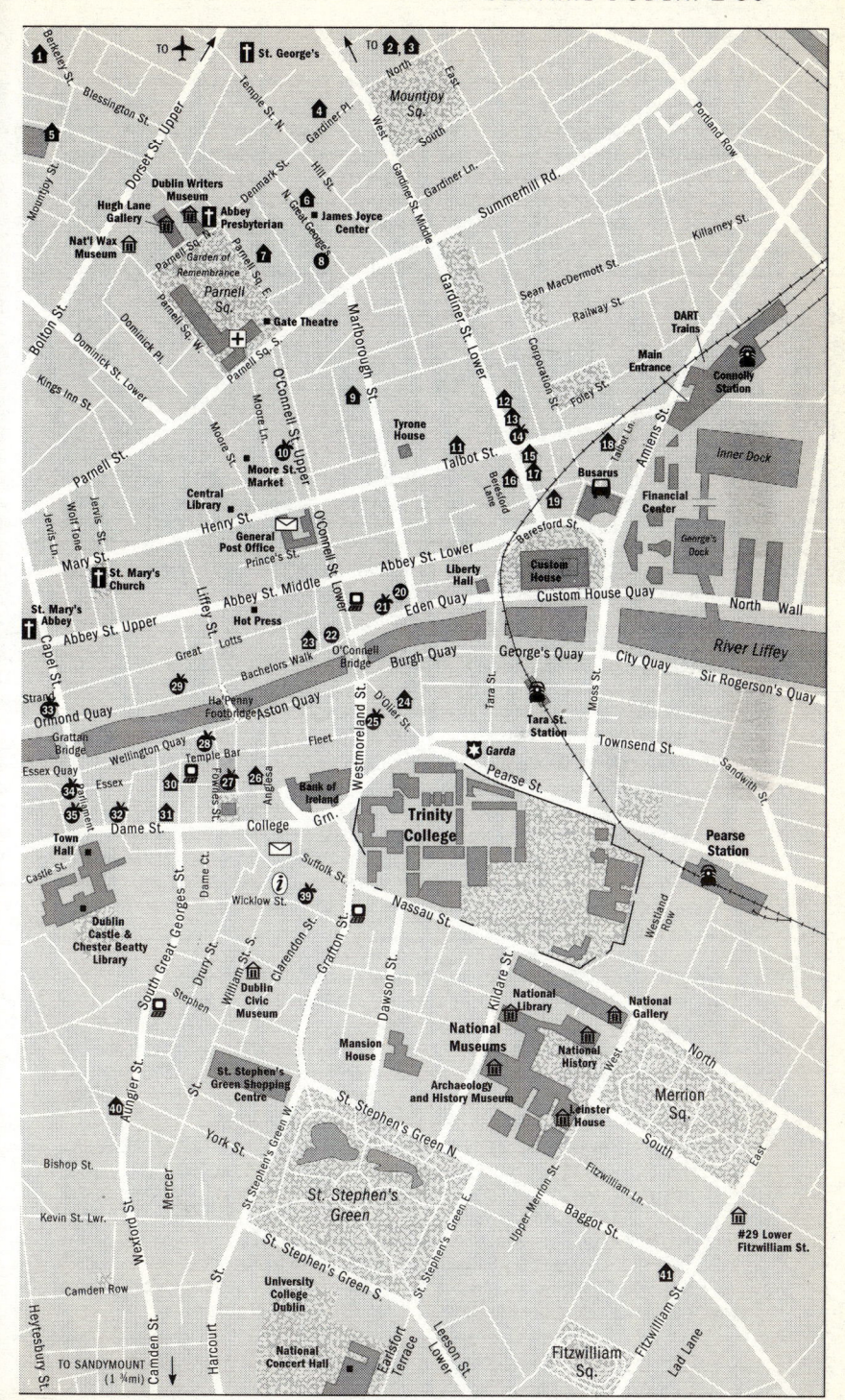

Buses: Info available at the **Dublin Bus Office,** 59 O'Connell St. (☎ 873 4222 or 872 0000); the **Bus Éireann** window is open M-F 9am-5pm, Sa 9am-1pm. Inter-city buses to Dublin arrive at **Busáras Central Bus Station,** Store St. (☎ 836 6111), directly behind the Customs House and next to Connolly Station. Bus Éireann runs to **Waterford** (2¾hr.; 7 per day, Su 5 per day; £7), **Wexford** (2¾hr.; 10 per day, Su 7 per day; £8), **Belfast** (3hr.; 7 per day, Su 4 per day; £10.50), **Rosslare Harbour** (3hr.; 10 per day, Su 7 per day; £10), **Limerick** (3¼hr.; 13 per day, Su 7 per day; £10), **Sligo** (4hr., 3 per day, £9), **Galway** (4hr.; 14 per day, Su 4 per day; £9), **Derry** (4¼hr.; 4 per day, F 5 per day, Su 4 per day; £10.50), **Donegal Town** (4¼hr.; 5 per day, F 6 per day, Su 3 per day; £10), **Shannon Airport** via a shuttle connection every 30min. from Limerick (4½hr., 13 per day, £14), **Cork** (4½hr.; 4 per day, Su 3 per day; £12), **Westport** (5hr.; 3 per day, Su 1 per day; £10), **Tralee** (5½hr.; 8 per day, Su 9 per day; £15), and **Killarney** (6½hr., 5 per day, £15). For more information on inter- and intra-city buses, see **By Bus,** p. 82. Private bus companies have proliferated. If the tourist office is not yet allowed to help you out here, it's possible that **PAMBO** (Private Association of Motor Bus Owners), 32 Lower Abbey St. (☎ 878 8422), can provide the names and numbers of private bus companies serving particular destinations. Open M-F 10am-5pm.

Ferries: Bookings in **Irish Rail office** (see **Trains**). **Irish Ferries** also has an office off St. Stephen's Green on Merrion Row. (☎ 661 0511. Open M-F 9am-5pm, Sa 9:15am-12:45pm.) **Stena Line** ferries arrive from **Holyhead** at the **Dún Laoghaire** ferry terminal (see p. 127; ☎ 204 7777), from which the **DART** shuttles passengers to Connolly Station, Pearse Station, or Tara St. Station in the city center (£1.30). **Buses** #7, 7A, and 8 go from Georges St. in Dún Laoghaire to Eden Quay (£1.30), though the DART is the easier way to see. **Irish Ferries** (24hr. ☎ (1890) 313 131; www.irishferries.ie) arrive from Holyhead at the **Dublin Port** (☎ 607 5665), from which buses #53 and 53A run every hr. to Busáras (80p); to get to the ferryport, **Dublin Bus** also runs connection buses timed to fit the ferry schedule (£2-2.50). **Merchant Ferries** also docks at the Dublin ferryport and runs a route to **Liverpool** (8hr.; 2 per day; £40, car £150-170); booking for Merchant is only available from **Gerry Feeney,** 19 Eden Quay (☎ 819 2999). **The Isle of Man Steam Packet Company** (☎ 44 (1800) 551 743) also docks at Dublin Port, and runs services to its own country.

Local Transportation: Dublin Bus, 59 O'Connell St. (☎ 873 4222 or 872 0000). Open M 8:30am-5:30pm, Tu-F 9am-5:30pm, Sa 9am-1pm. See **By Bus,** p. 82.

Taxis: National Radio Cabs, 40 James St. (☎ 677 2222 or 836 5555). **Blue Cabs** (☎ 676 1111), **ABC** (☎ 285 5444), and **City Group Taxi** (☎ 872 7272) have wheelchair-accessible taxis (call in advance). All 24hr. £2.20 plus 90p per mi.; 80p call-in charge. It's easiest to pick up cabs at numerous taxi stands around the city, including in front of Trinity, and Lower Abbey St. at the bus station, and on Parnell St.

Car Rental: Be warned that Dublin traffic is heavy, and that parking fees are exorbitant and spaces are minimal. **Budget,** 151 Lower Drumcondra Rd. (☎ 837 9611), and at the airport. Summer from £35 per day, £165 per week; winter £30, £140. Ages 23-75. **Argus,** 59 Terenure Rd. East (☎ 490 4444; fax 490 6328). Also in the tourist office on Suffolk St. and the airport. Summer from £45 per day, £230 per week; winter £140 per week. Ages 26-70; seasonable prices by special arrangement for ages 23-26 and 70-74. **Alamo,** Dublin Airport (☎ 844 4086). Summer from £35 per day, £195 per week; winter £30, £175. Ages 21-75; additional insurance cost for ages 21-24. If booked early enough, many rental agencies offer free pick-up or delivery.

Bike Rental: see **By Bicycle,** p. 64. **Raleigh Rent-A-Bike,** Kylemore Rd. (☎ 626 1333). Limited one-way rental system (£10 surcharge). £10 per day; £40 per week; deposit £50. Raleigh dealers close to city center are **MacDonald Cycles,** 38 Wexford St. (☎ 475 2586), and **Cycle Ways,** 185-6 Parnell St. (☎ 873 4748). The cheaper **Irish Cycle Hire** (☎ (041) 41067) runs out of the An Óige youth hostel. £6-7 per day, £30-35 per week; deposit £30. Open daily 9:30am-6pm. **Dublin Bike Tours** (☎ 679 0889), behind the Kinlay House hostel on Lord Edward St., also rents and provides advice on route planning. £10 per day, £40 per week; students £8, £35; ID deposit.

Bike Repair and Storage: Square Wheel Cycleworks, Temple Lane South (☎ 679 0838), off Dame St. Excellent advice on bicycle touring and expert repair; storage 30p per half-day, 60p per day, £2.50 per week. Open M-F 8:30am-6:30pm. **Dublin Bike Tours** (see **Bike Rental**) has a smaller storage space, roughly £5 per week. **Cycle Ways** (see **Bike Rental**), will do same-day repairs.

Hitchhiking: Since Co. Dublin is well served by bus and rail, there is no good reason to hitch, and *Let's Go* does not recommend it. Hitchers coming to Dublin generally ask drivers to drop them off at one of the myriad bus and DART stops outside the city. Those leaving Dublin ride a bus to the city outskirts where the motorways begin. Buses #25, 25A, 66, 66A, 67, and 67A from Middle Abbey St. travel to Lucan Rd., which turns into N4 (to Galway and the West). To find a ride to Cork, Waterford, and Limerick (N7), hitchers usually take bus #51, 51B, 68, or 69 from Fleet St. to Aston Quay to Naas Rd. (pronounced "nace"). N11 (to Wicklow, Wexford, and Rosslare) can be reached by buses #46 and 84 from Eden Quay, or #46A from Fleet St. toward Stillorgan Rd. N3 (to Donegal and Sligo) can be reached on buses #38 from Lower Abbey St. or #39 from Middle Abbey St. to Navan Rd. Buses #33, 41, and 41A from Eden Quay toward Swords send hitchers on their way to N1 (Belfast and Dundalk).

ORIENTATION

The **River Liffey** is the natural divide between Dublin's North and South Sides. The more famous sights, posh stores, excellent restaurants, and Heuston Station are on the **South Side.** The majority of hostels, the bus station, and Connolly Station sprout up on the **North Side.** Over all, Dublin is refreshingly compact, if complicated by the abundance of names each street adopts during its passage though town. Buying a map with a street index is a great idea and time saver. Collins publishes the invaluable *Handy Map of Dublin* ($4.64), available at the tourist office and most book stores. For less handiness but more detail, get the *Ordnance Survey Dublin Street Map* ($4.50); its hefty street index is in a separate booklet. The streets running alongside the Liffey are called **quays** ("keys"); their names change every block. Each bridge over the river also has its own name, and streets change names as they cross. If a street is split into "Upper" and "Lower," then the "Lower" is always the part of the street closer to the mouth of the Liffey.

The core of Dublin is circumscribed by **North** and **South Circular Rd.**, which have their own assortment of name changes. Almost all sights are located within this area, and you can walk from one end to the other in about 40 minutes. **O'Connell St.**, three blocks west of the Busáras Central Bus Station, is the primary link between north and south Dublin. South of the Liffey, O'Connell St. becomes **Westmoreland St.**, passes **Fleet St.** on the right, curves around Trinity College Dublin on the left, and then becomes **Grafton St.** One block south of the Liffey, **Fleet St.** becomes **Temple Bar.** While Temple Bar is the name of a street, it usually applies to the area as a whole, which has ballooned in the last decade with battalions of students and tourists hitting its pubs nightly. During the day, its eclectic array of funky restaurants and assortment of art museums and workshops attract better-behaved crowds. **Dame St.** runs parallel to Temple Bar with Trinity College as its terminus, and defines the southern edge of the district. **Trinity College** functions as the nerve center of Dublin's cultural activity, drawing legions of bookshops and student-oriented pubs into its orbit. The college touches the northern end of **Grafton St.**, where street entertainers and world-class shoppers appreciate each other. Grafton's southern end opens onto **St. Stephen's Green,** a sizable public park.

The North Side bustles with urban grit and hawks merchandise generally cheaper than in the more touristed South Side. **Henry St.** and **Mary St.** comprise a pedestrian shopping zone that intersects with O'Connell just after the **General Post Office (GPO),** two blocks from the Liffey. The North Side has the reputation of being a rougher area, especially after sunset. This reputation may not be wholly deserved, but avoid walking in unfamiliar areas on either side of the Liffey at night, especially if you're alone. It is wise to steer clear of Phoenix Park at night.

◪ PRACTICAL INFORMATION

TOURIST AND FINANCIAL SERVICES

Tourist Information: Main Office, Dublin Tourist Centre, Suffolk St. (☎ (1850) 230 330 in Ireland, ☎ (0171) 493 3201 in the UK, ☎ (066) 979 2083 from outside both; email information@dublintoursim.ie; www.visitdublin.com). From Connolly Train Station, walk left down Amiens St., take a right onto Lower Abbey St., pass Busáras, and continue until you come to O'Connell St. Turn left, cross the bridge, and walk past Trinity College; Suffolk St. will be on your right. The Centre is in a converted church. Accommodation service with £1 booking fee and 10% non-refundable deposit; £2 charge to book outside Dublin. Credit card bookings by phone (☎ (0800) 6686 6866; email reservations@dublintourism.ie). **American Express** maintains a branch office with currency exchange here (☎ 605 7709; open M-Sa 9am to 5pm); there is another at 41 Nassau St. **Bus Éireann** and **Irish Ferries** have representatives to provide info and tickets. Irish Ferries desk open all year M-F 9am-5:30pm. **Argus Rent a Car** (☎ 490 4444; fax 490 6328; email info@argus-rentacar.com; www.argus-rentacar.com) has a desk here (☎ 607 7701; open M-Sa 9am-5pm). A list of car rental agencies is also available from the Bord Fáilte folk. Office open July-Aug. M-Sa 9am-7pm, Su 10:30am-2:30pm; Sept.-June M-Sa 9am-6pm. Reservation desks close 1hr. early. The tourist office can also book tours, concerts, plays, and most anything in Dublin that needs a ticket.

Branch Tourist Offices: Dublin Airport. Open daily 8am-10pm. **Dún Laoghaire Harbour,** Ferry Terminal Building. Open daily 10am-6pm (subject to ferry arrivals). **Tallaght,** The Square. Open M-Sa 9:30am-noon and 12:30-5pm. **Baggot St.** Open M-Sa 9:30am-12:30pm and 1-5pm. **13 Upper O'Connell St.** Open M-Sa 10am-1:30pm and 2-5:30pm. The latter 4 branches are well-stocked and less crowded than the airport and Suffolk St. branches. All telephone inquiries handled by the central office.

Northern Ireland Tourist Board: 16 Nassau St. (☎ 679 1977 or (1850) 230 230). Books accommodations in the North. Open M-F 9am-5:30pm, Sa 10am-5pm.

Temple Bar Information Centre: 18 Eustace St. (☎ (1850) 260 027). Heading away from Trinity College, make a right off Dame St. where it intersects both Eustace and Great Georges St. Information available about Temple Bar's numerous cultural events Open June-Sept. M-F 9:30am-5:30pm.

Community and Youth Information Centre: Sackville Pl. (☎ 878 6844), on Marlborough St. Library with a wealth of resources on careers, culture, outings, travel, hostels (no bookings), camping, roommates, sporting events, counseling, and referrals. Info on youth and special-needs groups. Open M-W 9:30am-1pm and 2-6pm, Th-Sa 9:30am-1pm and 2-5pm.

Budget Travel: usit NOW (Irish student travel agency), 19-21 Aston Quay (☎ 679 8833), near O'Connell Bridge. The place to seek Irish travel discounts. ISIC, HI, and EYC cards; TravelSave stamps £8. Photo booths £4. Big discounts, especially for people under 26 and ISIC cardholders. They will book you into Kinlay House (see **Hostels,** below), a hostel run by usit, for a £1 deposit. **Internet access** £1 per 15min., £2.50 per 45min. with ISIC card. Open M-W and F 9am-6pm, Th 9am-8pm, Sa 10am-5:30pm. **Dust Travel** (☎ 677 5076), located inside Trinity College, also specializes in student travel. Turn left inside the main gate. Open M-F 9:30-10:30am and noon-5pm.

An Óige Head Office (Irish Youth Hostel Association/HI), 61 Mountjoy St. (☎ 830 4555; www.irlandyha.org), at Wellington St. Follow O'Connell St. north, continuing through all its name changes. Mountjoy St. is on the left, about 20min. from O'Connell Bridge. Book and pay for HI hostels here. Also sells package bike and rail tours. The *An Óige Handbook* lists all HI hostels in Ireland and Northern Ireland. Membership £10, under 18 £4. Open M-F 9:30am-5:30pm, Sa 10am-12:30pm.

Embassies: Australia, 2nd fl., Fitzwilton House, Wilton Terr. (☎ 676 1517; fax 678 5185). Open M-Th 8:30am-12:30pm and 1:30-4:30pm, F 9am-noon. **Canada,** 65 St. Stephen's Green South (☎ 478 1988). Open M-F 9am-1pm and 2-4:30pm. **New Zealand** embassy in London: New Zealand House, 80 Haymarket, London SW1Y 4TQ.

From Ireland, ☎ 00 44 (207) 930 8422. **South Africa,** 2nd fl., Alexandra House, Earlsfort Centre (☎ 661 5553; email saembdub@iol.ie). Open M-F 8:30am-5pm. **UK,** 29 Merrion Rd. (☎ 269 5211). Open M-F 9am-5pm. **US,** 42 Elgin Rd., Ballsbridge (☎ 668 8777). Open M-F 8:30am-5pm.

Banks: Bank of Ireland, AIB, and **TSB** branches with **bureaux de change** and **24hr. ATMs** cluster on Lower O'Connell St., Grafton St., and in the Suffolk and Dame St. areas. Most bank branches are open M-F 10am-4pm. Bureaux de change also found in the General Post Office and in the tourist office main branch.

American Express: 41 Nassau St. (☎ 679 9000). Traveler's check refunds. Currency exchange; no commission for AmEx Traveler's Checks. Client mail held. Open M-F 9am-5pm. Smaller branch inside the tourist center on Suffolk St.

LOCAL SERVICES

Luggage Storage: Connolly Station. £2 per item. Open M-Sa 7:40am-9:20pm, Su 9:10am-9:45pm. **Heuston Station.** £1.50, £2.50, or £3.50 per item, depending on size. Open daily 6:30am-10:30pm. **Busáras.** £2.50 per item, backpacks £3. Open M-Sa 8am-7:45pm, Su 10am-5:45pm.

Lost Property: Connolly Station (☎ 703 2363), **Heuston Station** (☎ 703 2102), **Busáras** (☎ 703 2489), and **Dublin Bus** (☎ 703 3055).

Library: Dublin Corporation Central Library, Henry and Moore St. (☎ 873 4333), in the ILAC Centre. Video and listening facilities and a children's library. Telephone directories on shelves for EU countries and on microfilm for US and Canada. Free Internet research (not email). Open M-Th 10am-8pm, F-Sa 10am-5pm.

Women's Resources: Women's Aid helpline (☎ (1800) 341 900) staffed 10am-10pm. Info on legal matters, and support groups. **Dublin Well Woman Centre,** 35 Lower Liffey St. (☎ 872 8051) is a private health center for women; it also runs a **clinic** (☎ 668 3714) at 67 Pembroke Rd.

Gay, Lesbian, and Bisexual Information: See p. 122.

Ticket Agencies: HMV record stores and **TicketMaster** have something of a marriage; head to the HMV on Grafton St., or the HMV ticket desk at the Suffolk St. tourist office. The website, www.ticketmaster.ie, is convenient for credit card payments.

Laundry: The Laundry Shop, 191 Parnell St. (☎ 872 3541). Closest to Busáras and the North Side hostels. Wash and dry £4.20-5. Open M-F 8am-7pm, Sa 9am-6pm. **All-American Launderette,** 40 South Great Georges St. (☎ 677 2779). Wash and dry £5, serviced £5.50. Open M-Sa 8:30am-7pm, Su 10am-6pm.

EMERGENCY AND COMMUNICATIONS

Emergency: ☎ 999; no coins required.

Police (*Garda*): Dublin Metro Headquarters, Harcourt Sq. (☎ 478 5295), Store St. Station (☎ 855 7761), Fitzgibbon St. Station (☎ 836 3113). *Garda* **Confidential Report Line:** ☎ (1800) 666 111.

Counseling and Support: Tourist Victim Support, Harcourt Sq., Harcourt St. (☎ 478 5295, 24hr. helpline ☎ 1800 661 771; email tvss@clubi.ie.) If you are robbed, this organization helps you find accommodations and contacts your Embassy or family; a loss or crime report must first be filed with a police station. Open M-Sa 10am-6pm, Su noon-6pm. **Samaritans,** 112 Marlborough St. (☎ (1850) 609 090 or 872 7700), for the depressed, or suicidal. **Rape Crisis Centre,** 70 Lower Leeson St. (24hr. hotline ☎ (1800) 778 888; office ☎ 661 4911). Office open M-F 8:30am-7pm, Sa 9am-3pm. **Cura,** 30 South Anne St. (☎ 671 0598), Catholic-funded support for women with unplanned pregnancies. **AIDS Helpline** (☎ 872 4277). Open M-F 7-9pm, Sa 3-5pm.

Pharmacy: O'Connell's, 35 Lower O'Connell St. (☎ 873 0427). Convenient to city bus routes. Open M-Sa 8:30am-10pm, Su 10am-10pm. Other branches are scattered around the city center, including Grafton St.

Hospital: St. James's Hospital, James St. (☎ 453 7941). Served by bus #123. **Mater Misericordiae Hospital,** Eccles St. (☎ 830 1122 or 830 8788), off Lower Dorset St.

Served by buses #10, 11, 13, 16, 121, and 122. **Beaumont Hospital,** Beaumont Rd. (☎ 837 7755 or 809 3000). Served by buses #27B, 51A, 101, 103, and 300. The conglomerate **Tallaght Hospital** (☎ 414 2000), farther south, is served by buses #49, 49A, 50, 54A, 65, 65B, 75, 76, 77, 77A, 201, 202.

Post Office: General Post Office (GPO), O'Connell St. (☎ 705 7000). Dublin is the only city in Ireland with postal codes. Even-numbered postal codes are for areas south of the Liffey, odd-numbered are for the north. *Poste Restante* pick-up at the **bureau de change** window. Open M-Sa 8am-8pm, Su 10am-6:30pm; stamps and bureau de change only. **Postal code:** Dublin 1.

Internet Access: Free Internet research (not email) is available at the **central library** (see **Local Services,** above), and you can pay for access at many hostels and some shops. The best deals are roughly £3-4 per hr. Reliable Internet cafes operate on a use first, pay later basis. Several chains abound, the best being **The Internet Exchange,** with branches at 146 Parnell St., the Suffolk St. tourist office, and in the Granary at Temple Bar South, in addition to two others in Temple Bar. Membership entitles the user to very low rates. Open daily 9am-11pm, excepting Tourist Office branch 9am-5pm. **Global Internet Cafe,** 8 Lower O'Connell St. (☎ 878 0295), a block north of the Liffey and on the right. The widest array of services and the best coffee and smoothies. £1.25 per 15min., students £1. Open M-F 8am-11pm, Sa 9am-11pm, Su 10am-10pm. **Central Cybercafe,** 6 Grafton St. (☎ 677 8298). £1.25 per 15min., students £1. **The Planet Cyber Cafe,** 23 South Great Georges St. (☎ 679 0583). Science-fictiony, with tasty nibblies, too. £1.50 per 15min. Open Su-W 10am-10pm, Th-Sa 10am-midnight.

Phones: Telecom Éireann (inquiries ☎ 1904, phonecard refunds ☎ (1850) 337 337). Public pay phones are on almost every corner. Recent privatization of Ireland's phone industry means other companies are erecting pay phones. Pay careful attention to rates for local calls on the varying phones. For more info, see **Keeping in Touch,** p. 72.

Directory Inquiries: ☎ 11810 for all of Ireland. No charge.

ACCOMMODATIONS

Dublin has a handful of marvelous accommodations, but the high demand for lodging keeps lesser places open, too. Reserve as early as possible, particularly around Easter weekend, bank holiday weekends (in either Ireland or England), sporting weekends, St. Patrick's Day, New Year's, and July through August. Private hostel rooms and B&B singles are especially hard to come by. The tourist offices books local accommodations for £1, but they only deal in Bord Fáilte-approved B&Bs and hostels, which aren't necessarily better than unapproved ones but, in the case of hostels, are usually cleaner.

Phoenix Park may tempt the desperate, but camping there is a terrible idea. If the *Garda* or park rangers don't get you to leave, the threat of thieves and drug dealers should. If the accommodations listed below are full, consult Dublin Tourism's annually updated *Dublin Accommodation Guide* (£3), or ask hostel and B&B staff for referrals.

HOSTELS

To deal with the large crowds, Dublin's hostels lean toward the institutional, especially in comparison to their more personable country cousins. The beds south of the river fill up fastest, as they are closest to the city's sights and nightlife; they also tend to be more expensive than their northern counterparts. Dorm prices range from £9 to £17 per night. Always **reserve ahead** in the summer and on weekends throughout the year, especially for private rooms. Call as early as possible, even if it's a few hours before you'll arrive. The hostels in **Dún Laoghaire** (see p. 127), only a DART ride away, are an alternative to city life. All listed hostels have 24-hour reception unless otherwise noted.

Barnacle's Temple Bar House, 19 Temple Ln. (☎ 671 6277; email templeba@barnacles.iol.ie). "The burning hot center of everything." A new, well-kept hostel right in Temple Bar. All rooms with bath and excellent security. Small continental breakfast included. June-Sept. 10-bed dorms £11; 6-bed dorms £13; 4-bed dorms £15; doubles and twins £40; Mar.-May and Oct. about £1 cheaper; Nov.-Feb. £2-3 cheaper.

The Brewery Hostel, 22-23 Thomas St. (☎ 453 8600; fax 453 8616; email breweryh@indigo.ie). Follow Dame St. past Christ Church through its name changes, or take bus #123. Next to Guinness and a 20min. walk to Temple Bar. The only hostel in Dublin to combine excellent facilities with a personable feel. Rooms are a bit snug but the beds are good. The distinct odors of Guinness production waft through the whole neighborhood, which, unfortunately, isn't the safest. If the main hostel is full, the staff may offer you the option of booking a room at their less clean and comfortable "overflow" hostel 8min. away. All rooms with bath. Free carpark. Kitchen and small dining area open 24hr. Continental breakfast included. Free luggage storage. Laundry £3.50. 8- to 10-bed dorms £10-12; 4-bed dorms £15 per person; singles £28; doubles £44.

Litton Lane Hostel, 2-4 Litton Ln. (☎ 872 8389, fax 872 0039; e-mail litton@indigo.ie), off Bachelor's Quay. This former recording studio for the likes of U2, Van Morrison, and Sinead O'Connor is Dublin's newest hostel. The colorful common areas and spacious dorms offset the snug kitchen (which may be only temporary). The staff is professional, yet funny and relaxed. Continental breakfast included. **Internet access.** Luggage storage opened every hr. Key deposit £2. Laundry at Abbey Hostel £5. July-Sept. 10-bed dorms £12.50; 8-bed dorms £13.50; doubles £46; off-season £9.50, £11, £42.

Avalon House (IHH), 55 Aungier St. (☎ 475 0001; fax 475 0303; email info@avalon.ie; www.avalon-house.ie). Turn off Dame St. onto Great Georges St.; the hostel is a 10min. walk down on your right. Temple Bar is within stumbling distance. Large, but not overwhelming, and clean but not spotless, Avalon hums with the energy of the trans-continental traveler. Top-notch security, email access, and an adequate kitchen. Co-ed showers, toilets, and dorms. Dorms provide privacy with a split-level setup. This is your best bet near the city center. Bike rack. Small continental breakfast included. Free luggage storage opened every 2hr., or get a personal luggage cage (£1). Towels £1 with £5 deposit. Non-smoking. Wheelchair accessible. June-Sept. large dorms £12.50; 4-bed dorms with bath £16.50; doubles £36, with bath £40; Mar.-May and Oct. £9.50, £14, £36; Nov.-Feb. £8, £11.50, £28. Singles also available.

Abbey Hostel, 29 Bachelor's Walk, O'Connell Bridge (☎ 878 0700; fax 878 0719; email info@abbey-court.com; www.indigo.ie/~abbeyhos). From O'Connell Bridge, turn left to face this emphatic yellow addition to Dublin's hostel scene. A little pricey, but it's clean, comfy, and well-kept. Great location. **Internet access** £1 per 7min. Continental breakfast included. Cereal 50p. Free luggage storage, or super-security (whether you're staying at the hostel or not) for £2.50. Big dorms June-Sept. £15; 6-bed dorms £16, with bath £17; 4-bed dorms £18; Oct. and Mar.-May £11, £14, £15. Doubles £40-60. Some prices higher on weekends.

Abraham House, 82-3 Gardiner St. Lower (☎ 855 0600; ☎/fax 855 0598; email stay@abraham-house.ie). Respectable, tidy rooms. **Bureau de change. Internet access.** Kitchen open until 10pm. Light breakfast and towels included. Laundry £4. June-Sept. 12-bed dorms £9; 4-bed £15; doubles £40; more for rooms with bath.

Globetrotter's Tourist Hostel (IHH), 46-7 Lower Gardiner St. (☎ 873 5893; fax 878 8787; email gtrotter@indigo.ie; www.iol.ie/globetrotters). A dose of luxury for the weary backpacker. Beds are snug, but there's plenty of room to stow your travel debris. Excellent bathrooms and superb showers—just too few of them. **Internet access.** Hearty, healthy breakfast included. Free luggage storage. Safety deposit boxes £1.50. Towels 50p. July to mid-Sept. dorms £15, mid-Sept. to June £12.

Jacobs Inn, 21-28 Talbot Pl. (☎ 855 5660; fax 855 5664; email jacobs@isaacs.ie). 2 blocks north of the Customs House, Talbot Pl. stretches from the back of the bus station up to Talbot St. Rooms, all with bath, are spacious, clean to the point of sterility, and cheery. Kitchen and TV room are sterile without the cheer. Luggage storage accessible every 30min. Towels £1. Laundry £5. Bed lockout 11am-3pm. **Bureau de change.** Bike storage at Isaacs (see p. 96). Breakfast £2.50. Excellent wheelchair accessible facilities. Apr.-Oct. dorms £11.25; 3-bed dorms £17.50; doubles £43; Nov.-Mar. £2 cheaper per person.

Ashfield House, 19-20 D'Olier St. (☎ 679 7734; fax 679 0852; email ashfield@indigo.ie). Smack in the center of Dublin, this "guest accommodation" offers a variety of bedrooms, and big yellow common areas. The beds are average, and occasionally crowded, but every room has a decent bathroom/shower attached. Good security. Luggage storage. **Bureau de change.** Kitchen open until 10pm. **Internet access.** Laundry £4. Light breakfast included. 6-bed dorms £14; 4-bed £16; triples £18; doubles £28; singles £40. Weekend prices £1-2 higher, Nov.-Apr. all prices £1-2 lower.

Dublin International Youth Hostel (An Óige/HI), 61 Mountjoy St. (☎ 830 4555; fax 830 1600; email anoige@iol.ie; www.irelandyha.org). O'Connell St. changes names 3 times before reaching the left turn onto Mountjoy St. Welcome to the mothership. Under a new captain, this 365-bed convent-turned-hostel has made giant improvements. A keycard system and lockers beef up security. Beds are decent, and rooms and bathrooms are clean for the troops. The beautiful breakfast room is in the body of the old church, and an information center books ahead and vends toiletries. Cafe has cheap meals (£3.50) and packed lunches (£2). Shuttles to Temple Bar. Breakfast included. Luggage storage £1. Towels £1. Self-service laundry £4. Carpark. Wheelchair accessible. June big dorms £11; 6- to 8-bed £12; 4-bed £13.50; doubles £29. July-Aug. £13; £13.50; £14; £30; Oct.-May £1-2 cheaper.

Celts House, 32 Blessington St. (☎ 830 0657; email res@celtshouse.iol.ie). 38 comfy, solid, wooden bunk beds in a brightly-painted atmosphere. The bedrooms are nicer than the bathrooms, and it's all a 15min. walk from the city center. Key deposit £5. Caretaker is sleeping, but available 11pm-9am. **Internet access.** May-Sept. 8-bed dorms £10.50; 6-bed £12; 4-bed £12.50; doubles £36. Sept.-May 8-bed dorms £9.

Mount Eccles Court (M.E.C.), 42 North Great Georges St. (☎ 878 0071; fax 874 6472; email meccles@iol.ie). Walk up O'Connell to Parnell St., turn right, then take the first left. The hostel is ¾ block down on the right. A former convent, this boxy Georgian edifice seems impossibly large inside. Dorms have lots of beds but even more room. En suite rooms have nicer bathrooms. Nice lawn in back, and the street is restfully quiet. Stone walls in the breakfast room add a touch of class. Small continental breakfast included. Free luggage storage and car park available. Towels £1. With bath add £0.50-1. Apr.-Sept. 16-bed dorms £8.50; 12-bed £10.15; 10-bed £11; 6-bed £11.50; 4-bed £13.50; doubles £36. Oct.-Mar. £8; £9; £9; £10; £12.50; £28.

Marlborough Hostel (IHH), 81-82 Marlborough St. (☎ 874 7629; fax 874 5172; email marlboro@internet-ireland.ie), between O'Connell and Gardiner St. Mega-renovations will be complete by 2001. Large rooms, and a nice barbecue patio in back. Bike shed. **Internet access.** Small continental breakfast included. Sheets 50p. Check-out 10:30am. July-Sept. 4- to 10-bed dorms £8.50-10; doubles £30; Oct.-June dorms £7.50-8.50; doubles £26.

Isaacs Hostel, 2-5 Frenchman's Ln. (☎ 855 6215; fax 855 6574; email hostel@issacs.ie), off the lower end of Gardiner St. behind the Customs House. The most basic of a biblical chain that includes plusher Jacob's nearby. Rooms are comfortable enough, but save the begetting for the singles. Heavy timber ceilings and a split log-furnished common area give a rough-hewn feel. Cafe. **Internet access.** Towels £1. Laundry £5. Bed lockout 11am-2:30pm. Dorms £8-9.25; 4-bed dorms £14; singles £20; doubles £34; Nov.-Mar. £1 cheaper per person.

Cobblestones, 29 Eustace St. (☎/fax 677 5614). In the middle of Temple Bar action, this smaller hostel has a friendly staff, and bright rooms, but uncomfortable beds, and no self-catering kitchen. Free towels and small breakfast. Dorms £14-16; doubles £37.

Kinlay House (IHH), 2-12 Lord Edward St. (☎ 679 6644; fax 679 7437; email kindub@usit.ie), the continuation of Dame St. Country boys who came to work in the city once slid down the beautifully carved oak banisters in the lofty entrance hall. Today, tired backpackers trudge upstairs to collapse on institutional beds. You can gaze out at Christ Church Cathedral across the street from the soft couches in the TV room. **Bureau de change. Internet access.** Wake-up calls. Breakfast and hand-towel included. Lockers 50p. Free luggage storage. Laundry £5. 15- to 24-bed dorms £10.50; 20-bed dorms partitioned into 4-bed nooks £11.50, 4- to 6-bed dorms £14.50, with bath £16; singles £22; doubles £34, with bath £36. Oct.-June prices £1-2.50 less.

Oliver St. John Gogarty's Temple Bar Hostel, 18-21 Anglesea St. (☎ 671 1822; fax 671 7637). Joyce once roomed here with the poetic doctor Gogarty. Although legend claims Gogarty ran Joyce off with a gun, perhaps James just found the tiny tower a tad pricey. Everything is clean, but the kitchen is tiny. The location's unbeatable if you're looking to frolic in Temple Bar. £5 key deposit. **Internet access.** Laundry £2. June-Sept. dorms £16; twins £42 per person; triples £51; Mar.-May and Oct. £14, £36, £48; Nov.-Feb. £12-13, £32, £42; weekends always £1 more.

Baggot University Centre, 114 Baggot St. (☎ 661 8860 or 661 6516), by the intersection with Fitzwilliam St. The Baggot is undergoing some serious renovations, but this term-time university housing will reopen in 2001. Sean and Moira Fitzgerald add a personal touch unparalleled in the city. Free coffee, tea, bread, and fruit available at all times. They'll also drive you to and from the ferryport. Carpark and bike storage. Key deposit £2. Free luggage storage. 5- to 8-bed dorms £12-13; doubles £30.

Goin' My Way (Cardijn House), 15 Talbot St. (☎ 878 8484; email goinmyway@esatclear.ie). Cheap, uncomfortable beds in non-smoking rooms. The beds in the coach house are slightly nicer. **Internet access.** Towels and a continental breakfast included. Midnight curfew. 8-bed dorms £9; doubles £28; quads £48.

Backpackers Citi Hostel, 61-62 Lower Gardiner St. (☎ 855 0035). Wiry, squishy beds and beat-up showers seem to value history over hygiene, but they don't take reservations, so if you're in a pinch there's almost always a bed free. The rooms, luckily, are slightly cleaner than the hallways. **Internet access.** Bed lockout 11am-3pm. Dorms Su-Th £8-10; F-Sa £15.

Backpackers Euro Hostel, 80-81 Lower Gardiner St. (☎ 836 4900). Same as its sister Citi Hostel, but the dorms have 12 beds instead of 8 and the bathrooms are even more questionable. Older, rowdy male clientele. Again, no reservations, so you're likely to find a wiry bed here. Bed lockout 11am-5pm. M-F May-Sept. dorms £8, Apr.-Oct. £10; Sa-Su always £15.

Worth considering is university housing, available during the summer months (roughly mid-June to mid/late-Sept.). Don't expect anything fancy, but the prices are only a fraction more expensive than those of hostels. **Dublin City University,** Glasnevin, can be reached on bus #11, 11A, 11B, 13, or 19A from the city center. (☎ 704 5736. Singles with bath around £23, doubles with bath around £34.) Other options are through **usit** (see p. 55), which operates **University College Dublin** dorms in Belfield (☎ 269 7111; take bus #3; £26 single in an apartment of four), and **University of Dublin** dorms in Rathmines (☎ 497 1772; £32 per person).

BED AND BREAKFASTS

A blanket of quality B&Bs covers Dublin and the surrounding suburbs. Those with a green shamrock sign out front are registered, occasionally checked, and approved by Bord Fáilte. B&Bs without the shamrock haven't been inspected but may be cheaper and better located; with a good location, B&Bs often find that Bord Fáilte's advertising is unnecessary. General housing costs have skyrocketed in Dublin, dragging B&B prices along with them. Prices range from £16 at the very lowest to well upwards of £30 per person sharing. On the North Side, B&Bs cluster along **Upper** and **Lower Gardiner St.,** on **Sheriff St.,** and near **Parnell Sq.** Exercise caution when walking through this inner-city area at night. The B&Bs listed below are warm and welcoming standouts in this neighborhood.

Suburban B&Bs are often spare rooms in houses emptied of children. With everything in Dublin so compact, they tend to be close to the city center. **Clonliffe Rd., Sandymount,** and **Clontarf** are no more than a 15-minute bus ride from Eden Quay. Suburban chances for decent B&Bs are greater, especially for those without a reservation. B&Bs in **Howth** (see p. 124) and **Dún Laoghaire** (see p. 127) are just as accessible (by DART) from Dublin. **Maynooth** (see p. 144) and **Malahide** (see p.

126), accessible by suburban rail, are also good places to stay. Aside from the regions covered below, you can find large numbers of B&Bs within the city limits in **Rathgar** (Dublin 6), **Drumcondra** (Dublin 9), **Templeogue** (Dublin 6W), and **Santry Rd.** (Dublin 9, close to the airport). Dublin Tourism's annually updated *Dublin Accommodation Guide* (£3) lists the locations and rates of all approved B&Bs.

NEAR O'CONNELL STREET: PARNELL SQUARE AND GARDINER STREET

The B&Bs in this area can be a budget traveler's hell. Many travelers arrive late at night by bus or train and, knowing no better, are plundered here. Flea-bags abound, tucked between quality guest houses with exorbitant rates. Plan ahead, or choose a suburban B&B. Gardiner St. runs parallel to O'Connell St. and leads to the Custom House; Parnell Sq. sits at the top of Upper Gardiner St. Both Lower and Upper Gardiner St. are within walking distance of Busáras and Connolly; buses #41, 41A, 41B, and 41C from Eden Quay will take you to the farthest reaches of the road.

Parkway Guest House, 5 Gardiner Pl. (☎ 874 0469). Rooms are plain but high-ceilinged and immaculate, and the location just off Gardiner St. is excellent. Run by a mother-and-son team. The son offers discerning advice on the city's restaurants and pubs, and could talk for hours about Irish sports—his hurling scars brand him an authority. Singles £23; doubles £36-40, with shower £44-48.

Charles Stewart Budget Accommodation, 5-6 Parnell Sq. (☎ 878 0350 or 878 1767; fax 878-1367; email cstuart@iol.ie; www.iol.ie/~cstuart). Continue up O'Connell St. past Parnell St. and look on your right. Technically a hostel but much more like a guesthouse. Full Irish breakfast included. Laundry £3. Singles £20; twins £40, with bath £45; doubles £50, with bath £60; triples with bath £84. Rates 10% lower in winter.

Carmel House, 16 Upper Gardiner St. (☎ 874 1639; fax 878 6903). An elegant breakfast room and a generally high comfort factor are fairly priced, given the skyrocketing rates in the area. Rooms £27.50-30 per person.

Marian B&B, 21 Upper Gardiner St. (☎ 874 4129). Brendan and Catherine McElroy provide lovely rooms at a better price than comparable neighborhood accommodations. Singles £20; doubles £38.

Glen Court, 67 Lower Gardiner St. (☎ 836 4022), 1 block west of Busáras, 2 blocks east of O'Connell. A Georgian house that's showing its age. The rooms are tiny. For the location you can't beat the price. Singles £16; doubles £30; triples £42; quads £52.

CLONLIFFE ROAD

This modest, respectable neighborhood has a few empty-nests-turned-B&Bs with friendly proprietors. The neighborhood is an ideal place to stay if you're planning to attend an event at **Croke Park,** or if you want to listen to the concerts there for free. Take bus #51A from Lower Abbey St., or make the 20-minute walk from the city center up O'Connell St., right on Dorset St., across the Royal Canal, and right onto Clonliffe Rd. Buses #41A, 41B, and 41C all serve the area from the airport.

Mona's B&B, 148 Clonliffe Rd. (☎ 837 6723). Firm beds in rooms kept tidy by a proprietress who offers tea and cakes upon arrival. Open May-Oct. Singles £17; doubles £36.

St. Aidan's B&B, 150 Clonliffe Rd. (☎ 837 6750). The neighborhood's first. Good beds, non-smoking rooms, and friendly proprietor create a relaxing atmosphere. Open Apr.-Sept. Singles £17; doubles £34, with bath £40.

Mrs. Molly Ryan, 10 Distillery Rd. (☎ 837 4147), off Clonliffe Rd., on the left if you're coming from the city center. A yellow house attached to #11. The unsinkable Molly Ryan, in her countless years, has never marked the B&B with a sign. Small rooms, small prices. Sometimes she makes breakfast, sometimes she doesn't, but she's honest as they come. Singles £17, £11 without breakfast; doubles £30, less without breakfast.

SANDYMOUNT

Sandymount is a peaceful neighborhood near **Dublin Port**, 1¾ mi. south of city center, and famous for its Joycean associations. Take bus #3 from Clery's on O'Connell St. or the DART to **Lansdowne Rd.** or Sandymount stops (10min.).

- **Rita and Jim Casey,** Villa Jude, 2 Church Ave. (☎ 668 4982), off Beach Rd. Bus #3 to the first stop on Tritonville Rd.; Church Ave. is back a few yards. Call for directions from the Lansdowne Rd. DART stop. Mr. Casey is only the mayor of Sandymount, but this B&B specializes in the royal treatment. Clean rooms and big breakfasts for the best B&B price in Dublin. Not a very quiet street by day. Singles £16; doubles £32.
- **Mrs. Dolores Abbot-Murphy,** 14 Castle Park (☎ 269 8413). Ask the #3 bus driver to drop you off at Sandymount Green; continue past Browne's Deli and take the 1st left. At the end of the road, look right. 5min. walk from Sandymount DART stop. Cheerful rooms look onto a peaceful cul-de-sac with flowers bloomin' everywhere. The dining room adds elegance to every meal. Singles £23; doubles £38, with bath £44.
- **Mrs. Bermingham,** 8 Dromard Terr. (☎ 668 3861), on Dromard Ave. Take the #3 bus. Disembark at the Tesco supermarket and make the next left. Down the street, the road forks. The left fork in the road is Dromard Terrace. Mrs. Bermingham's red brick house is covered with ivy. One room has a lovely bay window over the garden. Soft beds with fluffy comforters. Most rooms without bath. Open Feb.-Nov. Singles £18; doubles £34.

CLONTARF

Clontarf Rd. runs north from the city along Dublin Bay, to the neighborhood that shares its name. The view along it includes coastal grass, the harbor, some industrial smokestacks of the **Dublin Port** facility, and the impressive **Dublin Mountains** in the backdrop. Sea breezes are more pleasant than the harbor traffic; some B&Bs are inland a few blocks and avoid both. Make arrangements ahead of time, since many B&Bs in Clontarf go unmarked. Bus #130 runs from Lower Abbey St. to Clontarf Rd. (15min.).

- **The White House,** 125 Clontarf Rd. (☎ 833 3196). Sink into your bed and look out at pristine rose gardens. Singles £25, off-season £24; doubles £44, with bath £48.
- **Bayview,** 98 Clontarf Rd. (☎ 833 3950). The Barry family provides fresh, airy rooms, with every sort of wallpaper imaginable. Singles £25; doubles £45, with bath £50.
- **Mrs. Geary,** 69 Hampton Ct. (☎ 833 1199). Take bus #130 from Lower Abbey St., and up Vernon Ave. in Clontarf. Ask the bus driver to drop you off at Hampton Court, a walled cul-de-sac. Spacious and relaxing. Open Apr.-Sept. Singles £25; doubles £38, with bath £43.

CAMPING

Most campsites are far from the city center, but camping equipment is available in the heart of the city. **The Great Outdoors,** Chatham St., off the top of Grafton St., has an excellent selection of tents, backpacks, and cookware. (☎ 679 4293. 10% discount for An Óige/HI members. Open M-W and F-Sa 9:30am-5:30pm, Th 9:30am-8pm.) **O'Meara's Camping,** 4-6 Bridgefoot St. (☎ 670 8639), off Thomas St. near the Guinness brewery, sells camping equipment and rents tents. (4-person tent £29 per week. Open Jan.-Sept. M-Sa 10am-6pm, Su 2:30-5:20pm; Oct.-Dec. M-Sa 10am-6pm.) **Phoenix Park** is **not safe** for camping.

- **Camac Valley Tourist Caravan & Camping Park,** Naas Rd., Clondalkin (☎ 464 0644; fax 464 0643; email camacmorriscastle@tinet.ie), near Corkagh Park. Accessible by bus #69 (35min. from city center, £1.10). Food shop and kitchen facilities. Laundry £3.50. Showers 50p. Wheelchair accessible. No dogs. July-Aug. 2 people with tent and car June-Aug. £10, otherwise £9; hikers £5, cyclists £4.
- **Shankill Caravan and Camping Park** (☎ 282 0011; fax 282 0108). The DART and buses #45 and 84 from Eden Quay run to Shankill, as does bus #45A from the Dún

Laoghaire ferryport. Middle-aged tourists in caravans alternate with shrubs and tents. Showers 50p. £4.50-5 per tent plus £1 per adult, 50p per child.

North Beach Caravan and Camping Park (☎/fax 843 7131), in Rush. Bus #33 from Eden Quay (1hr., 23 per day) and the suburban train come here. Peaceful, beach-side location in a quiet town just outside Dublin's sphere of urbanity. Kitchen. Open Mar.-Oct. Electricity £1. Showers 50p. £4 per person, children £2.

LONG-TERM STAYS

Visitors expecting to spend several weeks in Dublin may want to consider a bedsit or sublet. Longer stays are often most economical when sharing the cost of renting a house or apartment with others. Rooms in locations outside the city center, like Marino and Rathmines, fetch about £32-50 per week (ask whether electricity, phone, and water are included). B&Bs sometimes give reduced rates for long-term stays but are very reluctant to do it in the summer. There are a number of sources for finding roommates and possible sublets; Dublin's countless university students are often looking for them, usually for the summer but also on a weekly basis. The most up-to-date, comprehensive postings of vacancies are at **usit,** 19-21 Aston Quay (see **Tourist Services,** p. 92). Supermarket notice boards are another source. **Trinity College** has two spots worth checking out: the notice board near the guard's desk in the Student Union, and by the main gate. Also check out the tourist office's comprehensive *Dublin Accommodation Guide* (£3), and classified ads in the *Irish Independent*, the *Irish Times*, and, most useful, the *Evening Herald*.

If you want someone else to do the legwork, **Dublin Central Reservations,** 3 Sandholes, Castleknock, can arrange for short or long stays in both humble and super-snazzy accommodations, for as low as £150 per week, with no finder's fee. (☎ 820 0394; email bookings@dcr.ie. Open M-F 9am-7pm, Sa 11am-5:30pm.)

■ FOOD

Dublin's many **open-air markets** sell fresh and cheap fixings. Vendors with thick Dublin accents hawk fruit, fresh Irish strawberries, flowers, and smelly fish from their pushcarts. The later in the week, the more lively the market. Actors head to **Moore St. Market** to try to perfect a Dublin guttural accent, and get fresh veggies to boot. (Open M-Sa 7am-5pm.) Moore St. runs between Henry and Parnell St. The **Thomas St. Market,** along the continuation of Dame St., is a calmer alternative for fruit and vegetable shopping. (Open M-Sa 9am-5pm.) On Saturdays, a gourmet open-air market takes place at **Temple Bar** in Meeting House Square. The cheapest **supermarkets** around Dublin are in the **Dunnes Stores** chain, with branches at St. Stephen's Green (☎ 478 0188; open M-W and F-Sa 8:30am-7pm; Th 8:30am-9pm; Su noon-6pm), the ILAC Centre off Henry St., and on North Earl St. off O'Connell. **Quinnsworth** supermarkets, gradually changing names to **Tesco**, are also widespread. The **Runner Bean,** 4 Nassau St., vends whole foods, homemade breads, veggies, fruits, and nuts for the squirrel in you. (☎ 679 4833. Open M-F 7:30am-6pm, Sa 7:30am-3pm.) **Down to Earth,** 73 South Great Georges St., stocks health foods, herbal medicines, and a dozen varieties of granola. (☎ 671 9702. Open M-Sa 8:30am-6:30pm.) Health food is also available around the city at various branches of **Nature's Way;** the biggest is at the St. Stephen's Green shopping center. (☎ 478 0165. Open M-Sa 9am-6pm, Th 9am-8pm.)

TEMPLE BAR

This neighborhood is ready to implode from the proliferation of creative eateries catering to every budget. Temple Bar has more ethnic diversity in its restaurants than the combined counties of Louth, Meath, Wicklow, and Longford (and probably Offaly, too). The **Temple Bar Passport** is a culinary coupon book available to guests at certain accommodations; of the hostels, only Gogarty's Hostel stocks it.

Cafe Irie, 11 Fownes St. (☎ 672 5090), above the colorful Sé Sí Progressive. Probably the best value in Temple Bar. Lip-smackingly good sandwich concoctions under £3. Vegan-friendly. Great coffee. Open M-Sa 9am-8pm, Su noon-5:30pm.

La Mezza Luna, 1 Temple Ln. (☎ 671 2840), corner of Dame St. Celestial food. Roast pepper and chicken crepe £8.50. Daily lunch specials £5; served noon-5pm. Delicious desserts £3.50. Open M-Th noon-11pm, F-Sa noon-11:30pm, Su noon-10:30pm.

Poco Loco, 32 Parliament St. (☎ 679 1950) between Grattan Bridge and City Hall. Good Mexican with a wide variety of choices. Even the appetizers are filling.

Juste Pasta, 12 Fownes St (☎ 670 3110) Next to Cafe Irie. A mighty selection of hearty pasta dishes, for less than £7. Vegetarians will have more than just a good time. Open daily noon-midnight. In winter, 5pm-midnight.

Zaytoons, 14-15 Parliament St. (☎ 677 3595). Persian food served on big platters of warm bread. A good lunch or a healthier way to fill the post-party munchies. Excellent chicken kebab £3.50. Open M-W noon-3am, Th-Sa noon-4am, Su 2pm-3am.

Bad Ass Cafe, Crown Alley (☎ 671 2596), off Temple Bar. Burned down in 1994 but, like phoenixes, Bad Asses rise from the ashes. American food in a gimmicky, touristy atmosphere. Sinead O'Connor once worked here. Lunch £4-7. Medium pizza £5.15-7.75. Student discount with ISIC card. Open daily 11am until "late" (past midnight).

Botticelli, 3 Temple Bar (☎ 672 7289). Don't expect flowers on the tables or a lot of attention from the waitstaff. This bustling Italian joint is all about quality food. Pasta or pizza £6, Moët champagne £45. Open daily 10am-midnight.

GRAFTON STREET AND SOUTH GREAT GEORGES STREET

Cornucopia, 19 Wicklow St. (☎ 677 7583). This vegetarian horn of plenty spills huge portions onto your plate. If you can find a seat, sit down for a rich meal (about £5) or just a snack (about £1.50). Take-away. Open M-W and F-Sa 9am-8pm, Th 9am-9pm.

Wed Wose Cafe, 18 Exchequer St. (☎ 672 7323), off South Great Georges St., near the red brick market. My wove is wike the filling all-day breakfasts in Dubwin's swickest gweasy spoon. Irish breakfast £3. Open M-Sa 8am-5pm, Su 10am-4pm.

Metro Cafe, 43 S. William St. (☎ 679 4515). New wave cafe with a fine coffee selection and homemade breads. Simple but scrumptious. Sandwiches £3.50. Open M-Tu and F 8am-8pm, W 8am-9pm, Th 8am-10pm, Sa 9am-7pm, Su 10am-6pm.

Govinda's, 4 Aungier St. (☎ 475 0309). Fabulous vegetarian fare with a relaxed Buddhist sensibility. The £4.95 dinner special is overwhelming. Open M-Sa 11am-9pm.

Wagamama, South King St. (☎ 478 2152). Satisfy your noodle and Oedipal cravings at this London-based chain. Don't let the fast-food service fool you; the fare is good enough to canoodle over with a loved one. Open M-Sa noon-11pm, Su noon-10pm.

Leo Burdock's, 2 Werburgh St. (☎ 454 0306), uphill from Christ Church Cathedral. Take-away only. Burdock's fish and chips is a religious experience that's a holy ritual for many Dubliners. Fish £3; chips £1.20. Open M-Sa noon-midnight, Su 4pm-midnight.

Harrison's, Westmoreland St. (☎ 679 9373). Romance them cheaply. Lunch specials under £6 or 4-course dinner (5-7pm; M-Th £10, F-Sa £11). Open daily noon-10pm.

NORTH OF THE LIFFEY

Eateries here are less interesting than their counterparts on the South Side. **O'Connell St.** sports blocks of neon fast-food chains, and side streets overflow with fish-and-chips shops and newsagents hawking overpriced groceries.

The Winding Stair Bookshop and Cafe, 40 Lower Ormond Quay (☎ 873 3292), near the Ha'penny Bridge. Cafe overlooking the river shares 2 floors with bookshelves. Contemporary Irish writing, periodicals, and soothing music decrease the pace. Salads around £4; sandwiches £2. Open M-Sa 10:30am-5:30pm, Su 1-6pm.

Flanagan's, 61 O'Connell St. (☎ 873 1388). "A well-regarded establishment whose tourist trade occasionally suffers from being too close to a McDonald's," describes Tom Clancy in *Patriot Games*. Veggie dishes £6; calzone £4.90. Cheaper eats and leopard-print seats at the pizza-pasta joint upstairs. Open daily 8am-11pm.

Soup Dragon, 168 Capel St. (☎ 872-3277). Around a dozen different soups (£3-8.55) each day and healthy juices, fruits, and breads for prices so reasonable, you will dragoon your friends into coming here as the day drags on. Roar. Open daily 8am-5:30pm.

Clifton Court Hotel, Eden Quay (☎ 874 3535). Excellent pub grub served with cigars in a convivial atmosphere. Chef's, vegetarian, and seafood specials daily £6. Food served daily noon-9pm. Trad music nightly 9pm.

O'Shea's Hotel, 19 Talbot St. (☎ 836 5670), at Lower Gardiner St. Good pub grub until 10pm nightly. Very convenient to the north side accommodations that cluster nearby.

THE BEST OF THE REST

Dail Bia, 46 Kildare St. (☎ 670 6079). Dublin's bilingual, all-Irish restaurant. Irish food, fresh and freed from the turgid trappings of the carvery lunch. Delicious scones, cakes, and sandwiches. Many sandwiches under £3. Open M-Sa 7:30am-7pm.

Bewley's Cafes. A Dublin institution. Dark wood paneling, marble table tops, and mirrored walls complete the "oriental" look, apparently. Decadent pastries (£1), but the coffee is variable. Meals are plain but inexpensive. 3 branches: 78 Grafton St., was recently renovated for the worse, but the room for its most famous patron, James Joyce, still charms (☎ 635 5470; open daily 7:30am-11pm, weekends may go later); 12 Westmoreland St. (☎ 677 6761; open M-Sa 7:30am-7:30pm, Su 9:30am-8pm); 13 South Great Georges St. (open M-Sa 7:45am-6pm); and on Mary St., past Henry St. (open M-W 7am-9pm, Th-Sa 7am-2am, Su 10am-10pm).

Beshoff's. Surge to this dream-chipper named after the cook in the montage-laden 1925 Russian film *Battleship Potemkin*. Branches at 6 Lower O'Connell St. (open daily 10am-10pm) and 14 Westmoreland St. (open Su-Th 11am-11pm, F-Sa 11am-3am).

■ PUBS

James Joyce once proposed that a "good puzzle would be to cross Dublin without passing a pub." A local radio station once offered £100 to the first person to solve the puzzle. The winner explained that you could take any route—you'd just have to visit them all on the way. Dublin's pubs come in all shapes, sizes, specialties, and subcultures. Dublin is the place to hear Irish rock and, on occasion, trad. Ask around or check *In Dublin*, *Hot Press*, or *Event Guide* for pub music listings. Normal pub hours in Ireland end at 11:30pm, but the laws that dictate these hours are rapidly changing. An increasing number of Dublin pubs have permits for late hours, at least on some nights; drink prices at these watering holes tend to rise around 11pm, in order to cover the permit's cost (or so they claim). Bars will post their closing time as "late," meaning after midnight and, sometimes, after their legal limit. ID-checking is more enforced in Dublin than in most of Ireland. Carding almost always takes place at the door, rather than at the bar.

Many heated debates stem from the postulate that Guinness tastes slightly different from every tap. In-depth *Let's Go* research continues to fuel the rivalry between two pouring heavyweights. Multiple trips and dozens of tastings have failed to pick out a clear-cut winner. The **Guinness Hop Store** (see p. 114), behemoth of stout production, shares its pedestal with **Mulligan's** (see **Pubs,** p. 105). Honorable mention goes to **The Stag's Head** (see p. 103) and **Brogan's Bar** (see p. 105).

The *Let's Go* **Dublin Pub Crawl** aids in discovering the city and researching the perfect pint. We recommend that you begin your crawl at the gates of Trinity College, then stroll up Grafton St., teeter to Camden St., stumble to South Great Georges St., and triumphantly drag your soused self to Temple Bar. Start early (say, noon).

WHERE HAS ALL THE FLOWING GONE? For years travelers have come to liquid-indulgent Ireland from arid lands, seeking the Holy Pint. Expecting a purity of consumption untainted by inferior brews, our pilgrims are in for a sobering fact: Budweiser is everywhere. The smooth American King sits on tap next to the legendary ales and lagers of Guinness, Smithwicks, Harp, and Murphys. And, shockingly, it's popular. Beer consumption in Ireland's Generation X has developed certain trendy affects. Budweiser and bottled beer, while technically inferior to a strong, healthy pint, are the drink of choice for many young party-goers. They deliver less punch per punt, but their neat appearance and guzzle-ability makes them status symbols. Guinness is, of course, still the brewsky king, but the trend (resulting from international distribution deals between Anheuser-Busch and Guinness) is worrisome. As a dedicated student of Irish culture, there is only one solution: keep your head.

GRAFTON STREET AND VICINITY

Sinnott's, South King St. (☎ 478 4698). Classy crowd of 20-somethings gather in this basement pub with wooden beam rafters. Portrays itself as a pub for readers and writers, but let's be honest, it's for drinkers. Chart music packs the dance floor until 2am.

McDaid's, 3 Harry St. (☎ 679 4395), off Grafton St. across from Anne St. The center of Ireland's literary scene in the 50s. Book-adorned walls pack in a yuppie crowd downstairs and a more sedate set above. W blues; Su blues and jazzier tunes.

Café en Seine, 40 Dawson St. (☎ 677 4369). Built to impress. A chic cafe with dainty pastries in front, while a very long bar undulates through a high-ceilinged hall with a super-nouveau decor. A large crowd of mixed ages packs in, apparently indifferent to the fact that the Seine is not at all nearby. Late bar W-Sa until 2am; Su jazz 1-3:30pm.

M. J. O'Neill's, Suffolk St. (☎ 679 3614), across from the tourist office. The maze of staircases is quiet by day, but a fun, young crowd meets here at night. Sports screen. Late closing Th-F 12:30am, Sa midnight.

Davy Byrne's, 21 Duke St. (☎ 677 5217), off Grafton St. A lively, middle-aged crowd throngs at the pub that Joyce chose as the setting for the Cyclops chapter in Ulysses. The images of Joyce himself on the walls hint at some redecorating since then.

The International Bar, 23 Wicklow St. (☎ 677 9250), on the corner of South William St. Excellent improv comedy M, stand-up W and Th (cover £5). All other nights, and Su afternoon, blues and trad (cover £5).

The Pavilion, Trinity College (☎ 608 1000), head to the far right corner of campus from the main gate. Watch a summer cricket match over Guinness at the Pav. Open all year, daily noon-11pm. You can also join the Trinity students Oct.-May under the vaults of **The Buttery,** in a basement to the left as you enter campus. Open M-F 2-11pm.

HARCOURT AND CAMDEN ST.

The Bleeding Horse, 24 Upper Camden St. (☎ 475 2705). You can't beat it, 'cause it ain't dead yet. All sorts of little nooks for private affairs. Late bar with DJ Th-Sa.

The Odeon, the Old Harcourt Train Station (☎ 478 2088). The Odeon has a columned facade, and the second longest bar in Ireland (after the one at the Galway races). Everything here is gargantuan. The upstairs is cozier (but still huge). DJ on Sa. Late bar Th-Sa.

The Chocolate Bar, Harcourt St. (☎ 478 0225), in the Old Harcourt Railway Station. Dress sharp. Young clubbers drink here until **The Pod,** the attached nightclub, opens (see p. 106). Happy hours on afternoons and Su evenings.

WEXFORD ST. AND SOUTH GREAT GEORGES

■ The Stag's Head, 1 Dame Ct. (☎ 679 3701). The subtle and ancient entrance has a mosaic of a stag's head on the sidewalk. Beautiful Victorian pub with stained glass, mirrors, and yes, a stag's head. The crowd dons everything from t-shirts to tuxes and spills out into the alleys. Excellent grub. Entrees around £5-7; served M-F 12:30-3:30pm and 5:30-7:30pm, Sa 12:30-2:30pm. Late bar Th-F till 12:30am. Closed Su.

104 ■ DUBLIN

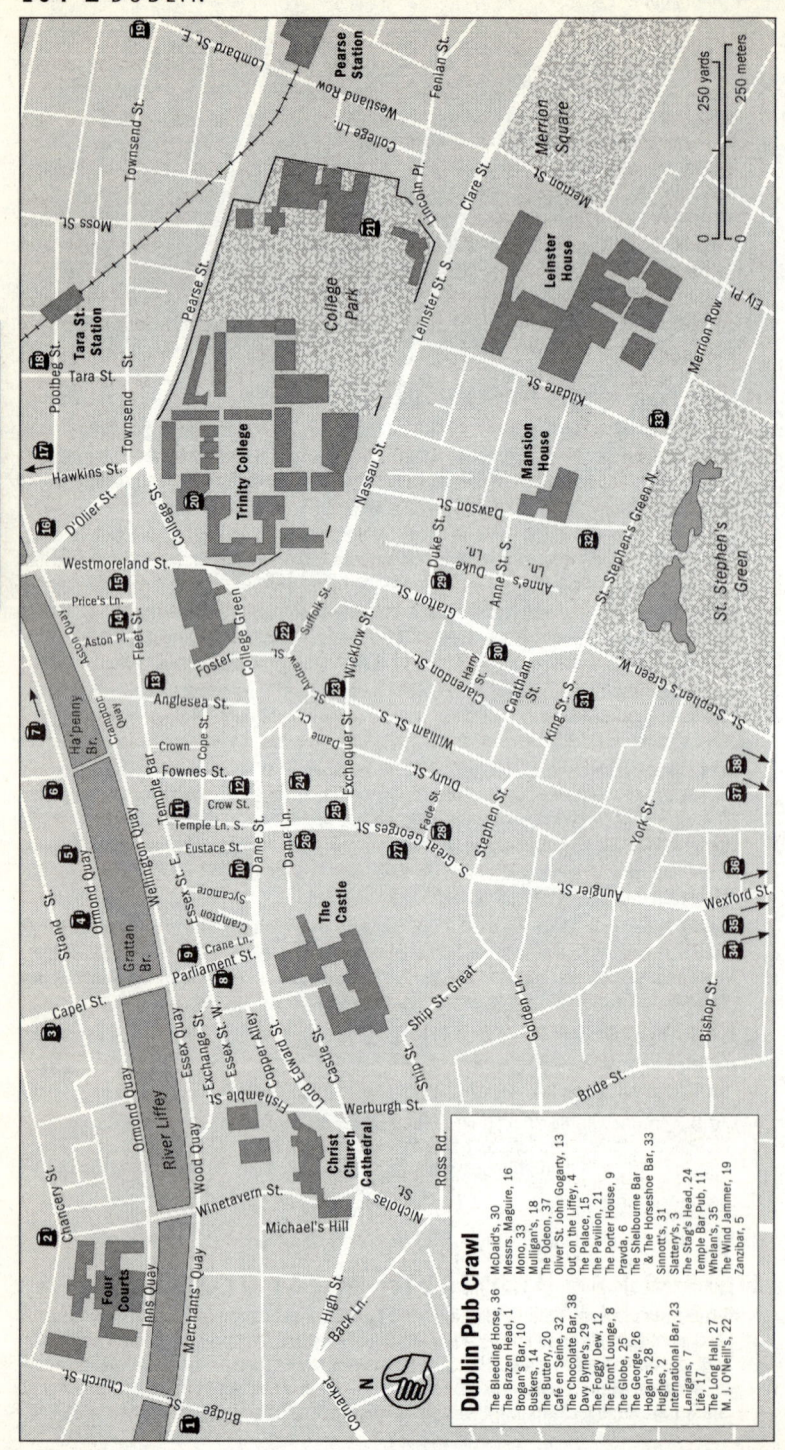

Dublin Pub Crawl

The Bleeding Horse, 36
The Brazen Head, 1
Brogan's Bar, 10
Buskers, 14
The Buttery, 20
Café en Seine, 32
The Chocolate Bar, 38
Davy Byrne's, 29
The Foggy Dew, 12
The Front Lounge, 8
The Globe, 25
The George, 26
Hogan's, 28
Hughes, 2
International Bar, 23
Lanigans, 7
Life, 17
The Long Hall, 27
M. J. O'Neill's, 22
McDaid's, 30
Messrs. Maguire, 16
Mono, 33
Mulligan's, 18
The Odeon, 37
Oliver St. John Gogarty, 13
Out on the Liffey, 4
The Palace, 15
The Pavilion, 21
The Porter House, 9
Pravda, 6
The Shelbourne Bar
 & The Horseshoe Bar, 33
Sinnott's, 31
Slattery's, 3
The Stag's Head, 24
Temple Bar Pub, 11
Whelan's, 35
The Wind Jammer, 19
Zanzibar, 5

Whelan's, 25 Wexford St. (☎ 478 0766). Continue down South Great Georges St. The stage venue in back hosts big-name trad and rock groups. Cover £5-8. Gigs followed Th-Su by pop and dance music. Open Th-Su until 1:30am.

Mono, 26 Wexford St. (☎ 475 8555), next door to Whelan's. A neon club scene. Late bar every night. Occasional theme nights. Cover £5-7.

The Globe, 11 South Great Georges St. (☎ 671 1220). Pretentious clientele? "Wankers," the barman corrects, "not pretentious. Arty-farty wannabe artists." Maybe so, but it's a fine spot for relaxing with a Guinness or frothy cappuccinos. Meet the regular cast of amicable if somewhat freakish characters—if your hair's not dyed, you might want to bleach it. **Rí Rá** nightclub attached (see p. 106).

Hogan's, 35 South Great Georges St. (☎ 677 5904). Heroically attracts a trendy crowd despite its basic name and bizarre decor. Su DJ from 4pm. Late bar Th-Sa until 1:30am.

The Long Hall, South Great St. Georges, across the street from Hogan's. Lots of mirrors for primping, pints for chatting, and an authentic old world feel to please youngsters.

TEMPLE BAR

The Palace, 21 Fleet St. (☎ 677 9290), behind Aston Quay. This classic, neighborly Dublin pub has old-fashioned wood paneling and close quarters; head for the comfy seats in the skylit back room. The favorite of many-a-Dubliner.

The Porter House, 16-18 Parliament St. (☎ 679 8847). The largest selection of world beers in the country, and 8 self-brewed kinds of porter, stout, and ale. Their excellent sampler tray includes a sip of ale brewed with oysters and other oddities (£6). Late bar Th-F to 1:30am, Sa to midnight. Occasional trad, blues, and rock gigs.

The Foggy Dew, Fownes St. (☎ 677 9328). Like a friendly, mellow neighborhood pub, but twice as big. The Foggy Dew makes a great spot for a pint or two without the artsy flash of other Temple Bar pubs. Live rock Su nights.

Oliver St. John Gogarty (☎ 671 1822), at Fleet and Anglesea St. Also see the hostel (p. 97). Lively and convivial atmosphere in a traditional, but touristed, pub. Named for Joyce's nemesis and onetime roommate, who appears in *Ulysses* as Buck Mulligan (see p. 128). Stately, plump trad sessions daily from 2:30pm on. Open M-F until 1:30am, Sa until midnight, Su until 1am.

Messrs. Maguire, Burgh Quay (☎ 670 5777). You'll still find new rooms here after hours inside, especially if you've been quaffing the homemade microbrews. The Weiss stout is a spicy delight. Late bar W-Sa. Trad Su-Tu.

Brogan's Bar, 75 Dame St. (☎ 679 9570). An unassuming little place, largely ignored by tourists in spite of its location. An impressive collection of Guinness paraphernalia.

Buskers, Fleet St. (☎ 677 3333 ext. 2145). Large, industrial bar with a small dance floor in the back. Dance to DJ hits as you swill your pint. Late bar Th-F until 1am.

Temple Bar Pub, Temple Ln. S. Touristy, but one of the very few wheelchair accessible pubs. Music nightly 4-6pm and 8pm-close.

THE BEST OF THE REST

Mulligan's, 8 Poolbeg St. (☎ 677 5582), behind Burgh Quay off Tara St. Upholds its reputation as one of the best pint pourers in Dublin. The crowd consists mainly of middle-aged men. A taste of the typical Irish pub: low-key and nothing fancy. Really.

The Brazen Head, 20 North Bridge St. (☎ 679 5186), off Merchant's Quay. Dublin's oldest pub, established in 1198 as the 1st stop after the bridge on the way into the city. The courtyard is a summer night pickup scene. The United Irishmen met here (see **Rebellion, Reunion, Reaction,** p. 13). Nightly Irish music, F-Sa late bar until 12:30am.

The Shelbourne Bar, the Shelbourne Hotel (☎ 676 6471), at the corner of Kildare St. and St. Stephen's Green North. The best place for cocktails in Dublin; their Bloody Mary is a divine hangover remedy. Also the center of Ireland's media culture—political cartoons decorate the walls, and journalists chat it up. The hotel's other bar, the **Horseshoe Bar,** attracts the bigwig politicians, who gripe about the journalists. Open M-Sa.

Lanigans, Clifton Court Hotel, Eden Quay (☎ 874 3535). Imagine a pub with Irish singers that actually attracts more Dubliners than tourists: this happy pub is it. Live music nightly at 9pm breaks down generational barriers and breaks into Irish dancing M-Th.

Zanzibar, (☎ 878 7212), at the Ha'Penny Bridge. Stylistically similar to "The Return of Jafar." If you can worm your way down the long hall to the dance floor, it's all pop favorites. Quite the hot spot. Late bar past 1am nightly. DJ M-Th from 10pm, F-Sa from 9pm.

Slattery's, 129-31 Capel St. (☎ 872 7971). Trad and pop nightly downstairs. Upstairs rock and blues Th-Su (£3-4 cover).

Hughes, 19 Chancery St. (☎ 872 6540), behind the Four Courts. Attracts the prosecution, the defense, and is loaded with the *Garda* at lunch. A delightful venue for trad (nightly) and set dancing (M, W, and Th around 9:30pm).

The Wind Jammer, Townsend St. (☎ 677 2576), at East Lombard St. For mornings when you need a pint with your mueslix, this "early house" opens at 7:30am every day.

Pravda, (☎ 874 0090), at the north side of the Ha'penny Bridge. The Russian late bar and Russian DJ action lasts until a Russian 1:30am. Actually, there's nothing Russian about the place other than the Cyrillic on the wall murals. This theme bar is trendy, popular, and gay-friendly. Probably Russian-friendly, too.

Life, Lower Abbey St. (☎ 878 1032), next to the Irish Life Mall. The young and the beautiful head here after work to talk about important things, like image. Decently priced menu for lunch. Late bar Th-F until 1:30am, Sa until midnight.

🎵 CLUBLIN

In recent years, clubs have displaced rock venues at pubs as the hippest source of Dublin's nightlife, though the pubs are fighting back with later hours. As a rule, clubs open at 10:30 or 11pm, but the action only starts up after 11:30pm when the pubs close. Clubbing is an expensive way to end the night, since covers run £5-12 and pints are a steep £3—if you're not trendy enough to be drinking a Red Bull and vodka. The last four clubs listed are a bit cheaper, but can't provide a full night's entertainment. **Concessions** provide discounts with varying restrictions. A good place to get them is Stag's Head (see **Pubs,** p. 103) around 11pm, though any nightclub attached to a bar distributes in the home bar. There are a handful of smaller clubs on **Harcourt** and **Leeson St.** that can be fun, if austere. Most clubs close at between 1:30 and 3am, but a few have been known to last until daybreak. To get home after 11:30pm when Dublin Bus stops running, dancing fiends take the **NiteLink bus** (1 per hr., Th-Sa 12:30-3:30am, £2.50), which runs designated routes from the corner of Westmoreland and College St. to Dublin's suburbs. **Taxi** stands are located in front of Trinity, the top of Grafton St. by St. Stephen's Green, and on Abbey St. Lower. Be prepared to wait 30 to 45 minutes on Friday and Saturday nights. For further listings, see **Gay and Lesbian Dublin,** p. 122.

🎵 **The Kitchen,** The Clarence Hotel (☎ 677 6635), Wellington Quay, Temple Bar. The entrance is behind the hotel on Essex St. With 2 bars and a dance floor, this U2-owned club is exceptionally well designed and the coolest spot in town. Half of it is impossible to get into on most nights because it's filled with "VIPs." Dress as a rocker or a model. Cover £8-10, students £3-4 on Tu.

Rí-Rá, 1 Exchequer St. (☎ 677 4835), in the back of the Globe (see **Pubs,** p. 103). Generally good music that steers clear of pop and house extremes. 2 floors, several bars, and more nooks and crannies than a crumpet. Open daily 11pm-2:30am. Cover £6-7.

PoD, 35 Harcourt St. (☎ 478 0225). Spanish-style decor meets hard-core dance music. As trendy as The Kitchen. The truly brave venture upstairs to **The Red Box** (☎ 478 0225), a separate, more intense club with a warehouse atmosphere, brain-crushing music, and an 8-person-deep crowd at the bar to winnow out the weak. Often hosts the big name DJs—cover charges skyrocket. Cover £8-10; Th ladies free before midnight; Th and Sa £5 with ISIC card. Start the evening at the Chocolate Bar or the Odeon, which also share the building (see **Pubs,** p. 103).

Velur, at the Vicar St. theater, (☎ 454 6656). Funk, soul, and a little bit of Austin Powers sound mixed with people who can wear multiple shades of gray, black, and brown. Live bands and DJs. Th-Sa, Cover £6.

Club M, Blooms Hotel, Anglesea St. (☎ 671 5622), Temple Bar. One of Dublin's largest clubs, attracting a crowd of diverse ages and styles, with multiple stairways and a few bars in the back. Pseudo-dance cages by the DJ occasionally host "exotic dancers" who try mightily to inject an aura of debauched celebration. If at first you don't succeed, grind, grind again. Cover around £6.

Velvet, 60 Harcourt St. (☎ 478 3677). A smaller venue, usually blasting house and glam-girly sounds; looks up to the PoD and Kitchen crowd. Open nightly. Cover Th £6, F-Sa £8, W student night £3 or free.

The Funnel, 24 City Quay (☎ 677 5304). A smoky, mixed crowd grooves under the military netting to psychedelic techno, funk, house, and garage. Occasional live acts. Cover hovers around £7, before 11pm £5.

Boomerang, Temple Bar Hotel, Fleet St. (☎ 677 3333). Come back for danceable tunes in a broad dance pit under a low basement ceiling. Open Th-Su until 2:30am. Cover M-Sa £5-8, Su free. Concessions available in Busker's upstairs (see **Pubs,** p. 105).

Republica, Kildare St., in the bottom of the Kildare Hostel. A funny little place that plays charts, is relatively cheap, and has a variety of good drink deals. Cover £4-5.

Club Aquarium (Fibber's), 80-82 Parnell St. (☎ 872 2575). No charts here; mostly indie. Houses Ireland's only metal club. Occasional goth nights. Weekend cover £3-5.

Klub ZaZu, 21-5 Eustace St. (☎ 670 7655). The only 18+ club in Temple Bar, so the crowd's a bit younger here. Cover W-Th £5, F £6, Sa £7.

The Palace Niteclub, Camden St., in the Camden de Luxe Hotel (☎ 478 0808). A meat market for a large, drunk, mostly under-20 crowd. Pop faves blast under a huge barrel-vaulted ceiling. Free every night until 10pm; W students £3, Th-F cover £5, Sa £6. The legal age for consent in Ireland is 17.

The Turk's Head (☎ 679 2606), beneath the bar on Parliament St. A selection of 70s and 80s classics. Open nightly 10:30pm-2am. No cover.

TOURS

SELF-GUIDED WALKING TOURS

Dublin is definitely a walking city. Most major sights lie within a mile of O'Connell Bridge. The tourist office sells *Dublin's Top Visitor Attractions* ($2.50), which lists the main sights, essential info about them, and directions. Several signposted walks wind through the city. The first three walking tours listed are in *Heritage Trails: Signpost Walking Tours of Dublin,* available at the tourist office ($2.50).

THE CULTURAL TRAIL. Starring James Joyce and Sean O'Casey, this route zips past the important sights on the North Side: the Four Courts, the Custom House and King's Inns, the Municipal Gallery, and the Dublin Writers' Museum.

THE OLD CITY TRAIL. This walk begins on College Green and weaves its way through the Liberties and the markets, ending in Temple Bar. Ironically, the Old City trail hits some of the city's newest, most garish exhibits, including Dublinia and the Dublin Viking Adventure.

GEORGIAN HERITAGE TRAIL. This path covers the best-preserved Georgian streets, terraces, and public buildings south of the Liffey, which no visitors to Dublin should deprive themselves the pleasure of viewing.

ULYSSES MAP OF DUBLIN. A tourist office brochure ($1) charts Leopold Bloom's haunts and retraces his heroic actions, beginning with kidneys for breakfast. The entire walk takes 18 hours (including drinking and debauching).

ROCK 'N' STROLL TRAIL. The disturbingly worshipful brochure sold at the tourist office (£2.50) makes a circuit of significant sights in Dublin's recent musical history. It provides the grim details of Sinead O'Connor's waitressing job at the Bad Ass Cafe and U2's Windmill Lane Studios.

GUIDED WALKING TOURS

If you lack the discipline to follow a self-guided walking tour in its entirety, you might consider a guided one. Tours generally last about two hours, but entertaining anecdotes and continuous movement preclude boredom.

HISTORICAL WALKING TOUR. Provides a two-hour crash course in Dublin's history and Irish history, stopping at a variety of Dublin sights. Guides seamlessly move the group from one era to another, and one street to another, simultaneously protecting the tour from ignorance and Dublin's maniac drivers. You won't be bored. *(Meet at Trinity's front gate. ☎ 878 0227; email tours@historicalinsights.ie; www.historicalinsights.ie. May-Sept. M-F 11am and 3pm, Sa-Su 11am, noon, and 3pm; Oct.-Apr. F-Su noon. £6, students £5.)*

TRINITY COLLEGE WALKING TOUR. Moderately irreverent and hugely pretentious, it concentrates on University lore, while glimpsing Dublin's history. Still, all that pretension can get you to the front of the line at the Book of Kells. *(June-Sept. Leaves roughly every 45min. from the info booth inside the front gate. March, April, May, weekends only. ☎ 608 1000. 30min. £6, students £5; includes admission to the Old Library and the Book of Kells.)*

DUBLIN FOOTSTEPS. Treads the beaten path of Irish literary greats past the Georgian architecture that housed them. *(Meet upstairs at the Grafton St. Bewley's. ☎ 496 0641 or 490 9341. 2hr. M, W, F, and Sa 10:30am. £5. Free coffee at the end.)*

1916 REBELLION WALKING TOUR. The creation of the Republic began with the 1916 Rebellion (see **Easter Rising**, p. 16), which took place solely in Dublin. See the scars it left and the state it created. *(Meet at the International Bar, 23 Wicklow St. ☎ 676 2493. 2hr. Mid-May to Aug. Tu-Sa 11:30am. £6, students and seniors £5.)*

AUDIO WALKING TOUR OF DUBLIN. This comprehensive guide will please those who don't ask questions. *(Aston Quay. ☎ 670 5266. Open daily 10am-5pm. Half-day £6, students £4.50; full day £8; deposit required.)*

GUIDED PUB CRAWLS

THE DUBLIN LITERARY PUB CRAWL. The tour traces Dublin's liquid history in reference to its literary history, spewing snatches of history between entrancing monologues. *(Meet at The Duke, 2 Duke St. ☎ 670 5602; email colm@dublinpubcrawl.com; www.dublinpubcrawl.com. Easter-Oct. M-Sa 7:30pm, Su noon and 7:30pm; Nov.-Easter Th-Sa 7:30pm, Su noon and 7:30pm. £6.50, students £5.50. Book at the door or at the Suffolk St. tourist office for 15p extra.)*

MUSICAL PUB CRAWL. An enjoyable jaunt led by two musicians and their instruments, who'll teach you how to differentiate between one session and another by the end. *(Show up a little early upstairs at Oliver St. John Gogarty's, on the corner of Fleet and Anglesea St. ☎ 478 0193; email musical.pub.crawl@officelink.eunet.ie. May-Oct. daily 7:30pm, Nov. and Feb.-Apr. F-Sa 7:30pm. £6, students and seniors £5.)*

GUIDED BICYCLE TOURS

DUBLIN BIKE TOURS. If you want to get more exercise and cover more ground, rent a bike and take a tour. In addition to seeing more sights, the bike tour lets the rider see more of Dublin's neighborhoods and get a feel for the city off the beaten path. *(Meet 15min. early at the front gate of Christ Church. ☎ 679 0899. 3hr. Apr.-Oct. daily 10am and 2pm; Dublin at Dawn Tour Sa 6am. £15 includes bike and insurance, concession £12. Booking ahead is advised.)*

BUS TOURS

Dublin Bus runs a number of tours through and around the city, including the first three listings below. All three depart from the Dublin Bus office, 59 O'Connell St. (☎ 873 4222. Open M-Sa 9am-7pm.)

THE GRAND DUBLIN TOUR. Parades non-stop around all the major sights and every corner of the city. Take photographs from an open-top bus, or a normal double-decker in the rare event of Irish rain. *(3hr. Daily 10:15am and 2:15pm. £10.)*

THE DUBLIN CITY HOP-ON HOP-OFF. This tour lets you thoroughly explore Dublin's major sights, including the Writers Museum, Trinity, and the Guinness Brewery. You can exit and board the bus at your leisure. *(Roughly 1¼hr. Departs Apr.-Sept. daily nearly every 10min. 9:30am-5pm, then every 30min. until 7pm. £7.)*

THE GHOSTBUS TOUR. The "world's only Ghostbus" lets you see the dead and undead aspects of the city. *(2¼hr. Tu-F 7:30pm, and Sa 7, 7:30, and 9:30pm. £12.)*

GUIDE FRIDAY. Hear the perspective of a private bus line, with open-top buses and full hop-on/hop-off privileges, not to mention discounts at a number of sights. *(Trips depart from O'Connell St. ☎ 676 5377. Buses run frequently mid-July to Aug. 9:30am-7:30pm; Oct.-Mar. 9:30am-4:30pm; Sept. and Apr. to mid-July 9:30am-5:30pm. £8, students and seniors £7, children £3.)*

VIKING SPLASH TOURS. Ride on water and land in converted World War II amphibious vehicles. Razz other tours with the Viking Roar, and hear diverse tales of Dublin history from the surprisingly amiable Vikings at the helm. *(1¼hr. Tours depart from Bull Alley St. behind St. Patrick's Cathedral on the hr. ☎ 296 6047 www.vikingsplashtours.com. M-Sa 9am-6:30pm, Su 11am-6:30pm. £9.)*

SIGHTS

SOUTH SIDE

TRINITY COLLEGE AND NEARBY

TRINITY COLLEGE. Ancient walls contain Trinity's sprawling expanse of stone buildings, cobblestone walks, and green grounds. The British built Trinity in 1592 as a Protestant religious seminary that would "civilize the Irish and cure them of Popery" (see **Trinity College Chronology,** p. 12). The college became part of the accepted path that members of the Anglo-Irish elite tread on their way to high government and social positions. The Catholic Jacobites who briefly held Dublin in 1689 used the campus as a barracks and prison (see **The Protestant Ascendancy,** p. 11). Jonathan Swift, Robert Emmett, Thomas Moore, Edmund Burke, Oscar Wilde, and Samuel Beckett are just a few of the famous Irishmen who studied here. Bullet holes from the Easter 1916 uprising scar the stone entrance. Until the 1960s, the Catholic church deemed it a cardinal sin to attend Trinity; once the church lifted the ban, the size of the student body more than tripled. *(Between Westmoreland and Grafton St. in the very center of Dublin, the main entrance fronts the block-long traffic circle now called College Green. Pearse St. runs along the north edge of the college, Nassau St. to its south. ☎ 608 1000. Grounds always open. Free.)*

THE OLD LIBRARY. This 1712 chamber holds an invaluable collection of ancient manuscripts, including the magnificent **Book of Kells.** Around AD 800, four Irish monks squeezed multicolored ink from bugs and plants to illuminate this four-volume edition of the Gospels. Each page holds a dizzyingly intricate latticework of Celtic designs, into which images of animals and Latin text are interwoven. In 1007 the books were unearthed at Kells, where thieves had apparently buried them. For preservation purposes, the display is limited to two volumes, of which one page is turned each month. A new exhibit elegantly details the history of the book's illumination, as well as describing the library's other prize holdings. The **Book of Durrow,**

Ireland's oldest manuscript (see **Early Christians and Vikings**, p. 8), is also on display here periodically. Upstairs, the library's **Long Room** contains "Ireland's oldest harp," the so-called **Brian Ború Harp** (the design model for Irish coins), and one of the few remaining 1916 proclamations of the Republic of Ireland. The room exudes scholarship, and many busts of dead white males. The towering shelves hold thousands of obsolete tomes which are occasionally displayed in mini-exhibits. *(From the main gate, go straight; the library is on the southern side of Library Square. Open June-Sept. M-Sa 9:30am-5pm, Su noon-4:30pm; Oct.-May M-Sa 9:30am-5pm, Su noon-4:30pm. £4.50, students and seniors £4.)*

OTHER SIGHTS WITHIN TRINITY. The Douglas Hyde Gallery, on the south side of campus, exhibits the works of contemporary artists. *(Open M-Sa 10am-5pm. Free.)* During the academic year, Trinity pulses with events, which are listed on bulletin boards under the front arch and by the Nassau St. entrance. Upwards of 50 concerts and plays are posted.

THE PHIL Founded in 1684, Trinity College's University Philosophical Society is the oldest undergraduate student society in the world. With a current membership of 2000 students, "the Phil" counts Jonathan Swift, Oscar Wilde, Bram Stoker, and Samuel Beckett among its alumni. Throughout the past three centuries, the Society has held debates and read papers every Thursday evening at 7:30pm, even through times of trouble. Perhaps its most famous feat began as a humble protest against a young dean with a penchant for Draconian discipline. Three or four students in 1734 threw rocks at the window of the teacher, Edward Ford. He responded by shooting a gun vaguely in their direction. The students, in heightened anger, returned to their own rooms and loaded up on the pistols that—being responsible students—they kept there. In the ensuing shoot-out, Ford was mortally wounded and died within hours. The students were promptly expelled from Trinity, but they avoided incarceration because the judge deemed the event merely a student prank that got out of hand.

BANK OF IRELAND. Staring down Trinity from across College Green is the monolithic Bank of Ireland. Built in 1729, the building originally housed the 18th-century **Irish Parliament,** a body that represented the Anglo-Irish landowning class. Its members envisioned a semi-independent Irish "nation" under the British crown made up of the privileged Protestants of the Pale. After the Act of Union (see p. 13), the British sold the building to the bank on the condition that the bank blot out any material evidence of the parliament. Foreshadowing the present popularity of corporate charity, the two small cannons near the entrance were bought to protect Dublin in case Napoleon invaded Ireland. Enormous curved walls and pillars were erected around the original structure to make the whole thing look more impressive; the bank inside is actually much smaller. Tourists can still visit the former chamber of the **House of Lords,** which contains a huge 1780s chandelier and Maundy Money—special coins once given to the poor on the Thursday before Easter and legal tender only for that day. *(☎ 677 6801. Open M-W and F 10am-4pm, Th 10am-5pm. 45min. guided talks Tu 10:30, 11:30am, and 1:45pm. Free.)*

GRAFTON STREET. The few blocks South of College Green are off-limits to cars and ground zero for shopping tourists and residents alike. Grafton Street's **street performers** range from string octets to jive limboists. Upstairs at the Grafton St. branch of Bewley's is the **Bewley's Museum,** inside the coffee chain's former chocolate factory. Tea-tasting machines, corporate history, and a display on Bewley's Quaker heritage are among the curiosities. *(Open during cafe hours, see p. 102. Free.)*

THE DUBLIN CIVIC MUSEUM. This pint-sized, two-story townhouse holds photos, antiquities, and knick-knacks relating to the whole range of Dublin life, from the accessories of the Vikings to the shoes of Patrick Cotter, the 8½ ft. "giant of Ireland." *(58 South William St. ☎ 679 4260. Open Tu-Sa 10am-6pm, Su 11am-2pm. Free.)*

KILDARE STREET

The block bordered by Kildare St., Merrion St. (the continuation of Nassau St.), and St. Stephen's Green is loaded with national buildings.

THE NATIONAL MUSEUMS

General Information Line for all three museums, ☎ 677 7444. All open Tu-Sa 10am-5pm, Su 2-5pm. All free. The Museum Link bus runs from the adjacent Natural History and Archaeology museums to Collins Barracks roughly once an hour. An all-day pass costs £2, but one-way is 85p.

Dublin's three national museums cover a broad slice of Irish life, history, and scholarship. The new National Museum at Collins Barracks is the farthest out geographically, while the Museum of Natural History is the farthest out conceptually. The National Museum of Archaeology and History is in the middle.

■ **THE NATURAL HISTORY MUSEUM.** A museum within a museum, this creepily fascinating collection of world wildlife displays not so much the natural world as how museums used to interpret their role in it. A skeleton of the ancient Irish Elk, glass cases of stuffed animals, amoebae replicas, and jars of Irish tapeworms are mysteriously compelling. The great cats case houses a Donegal house cat shot in 1885. Use the litter box next time. *(Merrion Square West. Free.)*

THE NATIONAL MUSEUM OF ARCHAEOLOGY AND HISTORY. The largest of Dublin's museums contains a number of beautiful artifacts spanning the last two millennia. The museum contains extraordinary artifacts of ancient Ireland. One room gleams with the **Tara Brooch, Ardagh Hoard** (including the great chalice), and other Celtic gold work. Another section is devoted to the Republic's founding years, and shows off the bloody vest of nationalist hero **James Connolly**. *(Kildare St., adjacent to Leinster House. ☎ 677 7444. Guided tours £1. Call for times.)*

THE NATIONAL MUSEUM OF DECORATIVE ARTS AND HISTORY, COLLINS BARRACKS. The most sophisticated of the three, the baby of the National Museum family gleams with exhibits that range from the traditional to the multi-disciplinary. The Curator's Choice room displays a range of objects in light of their artistic importance, cultural context, and historical significance. *(Benburb St., off Wolfe Tone Quay. Take the Museum Link, or bus 10 from O'Connell. Bus 90 to Heuston Station stops across the street. 1-2 guided tours daily. £1.)*

OTHER SIGHTS

THE NATIONAL GALLERY. A collection of over 2400 canvases includes paintings by Brueghel, Goya, Carravaggio, Vermeer, Rembrandt, and El Greco. Works by 19th-century Irish artists comprise a major part of the collection; of special interest are the works of **Jack Yeats**, the brother of William. Portraits of Lady Gregory, James Joyce, and George Bernard Shaw complete the display. A new Millennium wing housing a Centre for the Study of Irish Art and new gallery space will be completed in 2001. Concerts and art classes enhance the summertime. *(Merrion Square West. ☎ 661 5133; www.nationalgallery.ie. Open M-Sa 10am-5:30pm, Th 10am-8:30pm, Su 2-5pm. Free guided tours Sa 3pm, Su 2:15, 3, and 4pm. Free.)*

LEINSTER HOUSE. The Duke of Leinster built his home on Kildare Street back in 1745, when most of the urban upper-crust lived north of the Liffey. By erecting his house so far south, where land was cheaper, he was able to front it with an enormous lawn. Now Leinster House provides chambers for the **Irish parliament,** or **An tOireachtas** (on tir-OCH-tas). It holds both the **Dáil** (DOIL), which does most of the government work, and the **Seanad** (SHAN-ad), the less-powerful upper house. The Dáil meets, very roughly, from October to Easter (with lots of breaks), Tuesday and Wednesday 3-9pm, and Thursday 10am-3pm. When the Dáil is in session, visitors can view the proceedings by contacting the Captain of the Guard, who conducts some **tours** of the Dáil's galleries. *(☎ 678 9911. Passport necessary for identification. Tours meet every hr. Sa in the adjacent National Gallery.)*

THE NATIONAL LIBRARY. Chronicles Irish history and exhibits literary objects in its entrance room. A genealogical research room can help one trace the thinnest tendrils of their Irish family tree. The reading room is stunning, with an airy, domed ceiling. *(Kildare St., adjacent to Leinster House. ☎ 661 2523. Open M-W 10am-9pm, Th-F 10am-5pm, Sa 10am-1pm. Free. Academic reason required to obtain a library card and entrance to the reading room; usually just "being a student" is enough.)*

ST. STEPHEN'S GREEN AND MERRION SQUARE

ST. STEPHEN'S GREEN. The 22-acre park was a private estate until the Guinness clan bequeathed it to the city. Today the park is a hotbed of activity, crowded with arched bridges, an artificial lake, flower beds, fountains, gazebos, punks, couples, strollers, swans, a waterfall, and a Henry Moore statue. During the summer, all enjoy the outdoor musical and theatrical productions near the old bandstand. *(Kildare, Dawson, and Grafton St. all lead to it. Open M-Sa 8am-dusk, Su 10am-dusk.)*

MERRION SQUARE. The square and adjacent **Fitzwilliam St.** visually stimulate with Georgian buildings fronted by elaborate doorways. W.B. Yeats moved from 18 Fitzwilliam St. to 82 Merrion Sq. Farther south on **Harcourt St.**, playwright George Bernard Shaw and Dracula's creator, Bram Stoker, were once neighbors at #61 and #16, respectively. The Electricity Supply Board tore down a row of the Georgian townhouses to build a monstrous new office. Dubliners had a row over this, so to compensate the ESB now funds **#29 Lower Fitzwilliam St.**, a completely restored Georgian townhouse-turned-living museum that demonstrates the lifestyle of the 18th-century Anglo-Irish elite. *(☎ 702 6165. Open Tu-Sa 10am-5pm, Su 2-5pm. A short audio-visual show leads to a 25min. tour of the house. £2.50, students and seniors £1.)* The prim Georgian townhouses continue up **Dawson St.**, which connects St. Stephen's Green to Trinity College one block west of Leinster House. Dawson street has the honor of providing an address to the **Mansion House**, home of the Lord Mayors of Dublin since 1715. The house's eclectic facade exhibits the styles of several eras. The Irish state declared its independence here in 1919; the Anglo-Irish truce was signed here in 1921.

NEWMAN HOUSE. A fully restored building that was once the seat of **University College Dublin**, the Catholic answer to Trinity (see p. 109). Joyce's years here are chronicled in *Portrait of the Artist as a Young Man*. The poet Gerard Manley Hopkins spent the last years of his life teaching classics at the college. The cursory tour is geared to the architectural and literary. Hello, Newman. *(85-86 St. Stephen's Green South. ☎ 706 7422. Tours on the hour. Open June-Sept. Tu-F noon-5pm, Sa 2-5pm, Su 11am-2pm. £3, students and seniors £2.)*

THE SHAW BIRTHPLACE. Suitable for viewing as either a period piece or a glimpse into the childhood of George Bernard Shaw. Mrs. Shaw held recitals here, sparking little George's interest in music, and kept a lovely Victorian garden, sparking George's interest in landscape painting—until socialism, that is. *(33 Synge St. ☎ 475 0854. Stroll down Camden, make a right on Harrington, and then a left onto Synge. Convenient to buses #16, 19, or 122 from O'Connell St. Open May-Oct. M-Sa 10am-5pm, Su 11am-5pm. £2.60, students and seniors £2.10; joint ticket with Dublin Writers Museum £4.60, or the Writers Museum and the James Joyce Museum £6.50.)* Nearby is the **Grand Canal**, where a statue of the poet **Patrick Kavanagh** sits on his favorite bench by the water.

THE IRISH JEWISH MUSEUM. A restored, former synagogue houses a large collection of artifacts, documents, and photographs chronicling the history of the small Jewish community in Ireland from 1079 (five arrived and were sent away) through later waves of European migration. The most famous Dublin Jew covered is predictably Leopold Bloom, hero of *Ulysses*. *(3-4 Walworth Rd., off Victoria St. South Circular Rd. runs to Victoria St.; from there the museum is signposted. Buses #16, 20, or any others to South Circular Rd. will take you there. ☎ 490 1857. Open May-Sept. Tu, Th, and Su 11am-3:30pm, Oct.-Apr. Su 10:30am-2:30pm. Access at other times is fairly easily arranged.)*

TEMPLE BAR

West of Trinity between Dame St. and the Liffey, the Temple Bar neighborhood wriggles with activity. Narrow cobblestone streets link cheap cafes, hole-in-the-wall theaters, rock venues, and used clothing and record stores. In the early 1980s, the Irish transport authority intended to replace the neighborhood with a seven-acre transportation center and short-term leased the land while acquiring all the necessary property. The artists and nomads who lived around Temple Bar started a brouhaha about being forced into homelessness. In 1985 they circulated petitions and saved their homes and businesses from the transit project. Temple Bar then grew at lightning speed into one of the hottest spots for nightlife in Europe. To steer the growth to ends more cultural than alcoholic, the government-sponsored Temple Bar Properties has since spent over £30 million to build a whole flock of arts-related tourist attractions, with independent ones sprouting up, too.

CULTURAL CENTERS AND GALLERIES. Among Temple Bar's most inviting are: **The Irish Film Centre** (see **Cinema**, p. 120), featuring specialty and art house film (6 Eustace St.; ☎ 679 3477; www.fii.ie); **The Temple Bar Music Centre** (see p. 118), with events and concerts virtually every night (Curved St.; ☎ 670 9202; www.indigo.ie/~tbmusic); **The Ark,** a cultural center aimed at seven- to 14-year-olds (Eustace St.; ☎ 670 7788); Ireland's only **Gallery of Photography** (Meeting House Sq.; ☎ 671 4654; email gallery@irish-photography.com); and the sizeable **Temple Bar Gallery & Studios** (5-9 Temple Bar; ☎ 671 0073; www.paddynet.ie/tbgs).

DAME STREET AND THE CATHEDRALS

DUBLIN CASTLE. Norman King John built the castle in 1204 on top of the first Viking settlement of *Dubh Linn*; more recently, a series of structures from various eras have covered the site, dating mostly from the 18th and 19th centuries and culminating in a rather uninspired 20th-century office complex. For 700 years after its construction, Dublin Castle was the seat of British rule in Ireland. Fifty insurgents died at the castle's walls on Easter Monday, 1916 (see **Easter Rising,** p. 16). Since 1938, the presidents of Ireland have been inaugurated here. The **State Apartments,** once home to English viceroys, now entertain EU representatives and foreign heads of state. Next door, the **Dublin City Hall,** designed as the Royal Exchange in 1779, boasts an intricate inner dome and statues of national heroes like Daniel O'Connell. (*Dame St., at the intersection of Parliament and Castle St.* ☎ *677 7129. State Apartments open M-F 10am-5pm, Sa-Su and holidays 2-5pm, except during official functions. £3, students and seniors £2. Grounds free.*)

CHESTER BEATTY LIBRARY. Honorary Irish citizen Alfred Chester Beatty was an American rags-to-riches mining engineer who amassed an incredibly beautiful collection of Asian art, sacred scriptures, and illustrated texts. Upon his death he donated this collection to Ireland. A new library behind Dublin Castle houses and exhibits this cultural wonderland. An illustrated book by Matisse and a collection of Chinese snuff bottles are just two of the highlights among the eclectic displays. Special exhibits and public lectures further the academic atmosphere. (*Behind Dublin Castle.* ☎ *407 0750; www.cbl.ie. Open Tu-F 10am-5pm, Sa 11am-5pm, Su 1-5pm. Free. Small charge for visiting exhibitions.*)

CHRIST CHURCH CATHEDRAL. Dublin's cathedrals are considered works of art more than centers of worship in the 20th century. Built centuries ago for Catholic worship, they were forced to convert to the Church of Ireland in the 16th century (see p. 9). Sitric Silkenbeard, King of the Dublin Norsemen, built a wooden church on this site around 1038, and Strongbow rebuilt it in stone in 1169. Further additions were made in the following century and in the 1870s. Stained glass sparkles above the raised crypts, one of which supposedly belongs to Strongbow. The cavernous crypt once held shops and drinking houses, but now cobwebs hang down from the ceiling, fragments of ancient pillars lie about like bleached bones, and a mummified cat is caught in the act of chasing a mummified mouse. (*At the end of*

Dame St., uphill and across from the Castle. ☎ 677 8099. Take buses #50 from Eden Quay or 78A from Aston Quay. Open daily 10am-5:30pm except during services. Donation of £2 strongly encouraged, concessions £1.)

DUBLINIA. This recent appendage to **Christ Church Cathedral** recreates medieval Dublin, with life-sized reconstructions. It's informative, if a little underwhelming. Uncharming is the bubonic mannequin in the Black Death display. *(Adjacent to Christ Church Cathedral.* ☎ *679 4611. Open Apr.-Oct. daily 10am-5pm; Sept.-Mar. 11am-4pm. £4, students and children £3, with admission to Christ Church £4.95, £3.50.)*

ST. PATRICK'S CATHEDRAL. The body of the church dates to the 12th century, although Sir Benjamin Guinness remodeled much of the church in 1864. Measuring 300 ft. from stem to stern, it's Ireland's largest cathedral. St. Patrick allegedly baptized converts in the park next door. Artifacts and relics from the Order of St. Patrick are inside. Jonathan Swift spent his last years as Dean of St. Patrick's; his crypt rises above the south nave. *(From Christ Church, Nicholas St. runs south and downhill, becoming Patrick St. Take bus #49, 49A, 50, 54A, 56A, 65, 65B, 77, or 77A from Eden Quay.* ☎ *475 4817. Open Apr.-Sept. M-F 9am-6pm, Oct.-Mar. Sa 9-5. Su closed 11am-12:45pm and 3-4pm. £2, concessions £1.)* Beside the cathedral, **Marsh's Library** is Ireland's oldest public library. A peek inside reveals its elegant wire alcoves, and an extensive collection of early maps. Occasional exhibitions. *(St. Patrick's Close.* ☎ *454 3511. Open M and W-F 10am-12:45pm and 2-5pm, Sa 10:30am-12:45pm. £2, students and seniors £1.)*

ST. AUDOEN'S CHURCH. The Normans founded Dublin's oldest parish church. It's not to be confused with the more modern, Catholic St. Audoen's. Papal Bulls were read aloud here during the Middle Ages. *(High St. Open Sa-Su 2:30-5pm.)* **St. Audoen's Arch,** built in 1215 next to the church and now obscured by a narrow alley, is the only gate that survives from Dublin's medieval **city walls.** During the 16th century, the walls ran from Parliament St. to Dublin Castle, along the castle walls to Little Ship St., along Francis St. to Bridge St., and then along the Liffey.

DUBLIN'S VIKING ADVENTURE. Walk through the Dublin of the 9th and 10th centuries, and talk with Dubliners of that time. For added fun, try to get the actors to break character. *(Essex St. West.* ☎ *679 6040. Take buses #51, 51A, 51B, 79, and 90 from Aston Quay. Open Tu-Sa 10am-4:30pm; closed Nov.-Feb. 1-2pm. Tours depart on the half-hour. £4.95, students and seniors £3.95.)*

GUINNESS BREWERY AND KILMAINHAM

GUINNESS HOPSTORE. Guinness brews its black magic on Crane St. off James St., and perpetuates the legend of the world's best stout at its Hopstore. Farsighted Arthur Guinness signed a 9000-year lease at the original 1759 brewery nearby. The Hopstore has displays on the historical and modern processes of brewing and a short promotional film. At the bar, visitors get one pint of dark and creamy goodness. Some believe this glass to be the best Guinness in Dublin and, as such, the world's best beer. Certainly this pint is the best part of the Hopstore's rather prosaic paean to the product. Appreciate the exhibit on Guinness's infamously clever advertising, and then drink, silly tourist, drink. *(St. James's Gate. From Christ Church Cathedral, follow High St. west, away from downtown, through its name changes—Cornmarket, Thomas, and James. Take bus #51B or 78A from Aston Quay or bus #123 from O'Connell St.* ☎ *408 4800; www.guinness.ie. Open Apr.-Sept. M-Sa 9:30am-5pm, Su 10:30am-4:30pm; Oct.-Mar. M-Sa 9:30am-4pm, Su noon-4pm. £5, students and seniors £4, under 12 £1.)*

KILMAINHAM GAOL. A place of bondage that is also a symbol of freedom. Almost all of the rebels who fought in Ireland's struggle for independence from 1792 to 1921 spent time here. "The cause for which I die has been rebaptized during this past week by the blood of as good men as ever trod God's earth," wrote Sean MacDiarmada in a letter from Kilmainham to his family while he awaited execution for participation in the 1916 Easter Rising (see p. 16). The jail's last occupant was **Éamon de Valera,** the future Éire leader. Today the former prison is a museum that traces the history of penal practices over the last two centuries. Tours wander

DUBLINESE Mastering the Dublin dialect has been a persistent challenge to writers and thespians of the 20th century. James Joyce, Brendan Behan, and Roddy Doyle are just a few ambitious scribes who have tried to capture the nuances of this gritty, witty city. The following is a short introduction to Dubliners' favorite phrases.

Names for Outsiders: The rivalry between Dubliners and their country cousins is fierce. For Dubliners, all counties outside their own blur into one indiscriminate wasteland populated with "culchies," "plonkers," "turf-gobblers," and "muck-savages."

In Times of Difficulty: Dublinese is expeditious in keeping others in line. Idiots are rebuked as "eejits"; in dire situations, they are called "head-the-ball." Total exasperation calls for "shite and onions." When all is restored to order, it's said that "the job's oxo and the ship's name is murphy."

Affectionate Nicknames for Civic Landmarks: Over the past couple decades, the government has graced the city with several public artworks that personify the Irish spirit in the female form. Dubliners have responded with poetic rhetoric. Off Grafton St., the statue of the fetching fishmongress Molly Malone is commonly referred to as "the dish with the fish" and "the tart with the cart." The goddess of the River Liffey sits in a fountain on O'Connell St. and is popularly heralded as the "floozy in the jacuzzi," "Anna Rexia," and even "the whore in the sewer" (pronounced HEW-er).

through the chilly limestone corridors of the prison and end in the haunting atmosphere of Kilmainham's execution yard. *(Inchicore Rd. Take bus #51 from Aston Quay, #51A from Lower Abbey St., or #79 from Aston Quay.* ☎ *453 5984. Open Apr.-Sept. daily 9:30am-5pm; Oct.-Mar. M-F 9:30am-4pm, Su 10am-5pm. Tours every 35min. £3.50, seniors £2.50, students and children £1.50.)*

THE ROYAL HOSPITAL KILMAINHAM. It was built in 1679 as a hospice for retired or disabled soldiers. Today the compound houses the **Irish Museum of Modern Art.** The facade and courtyard copy those of Les Invalides in Paris; the baroque chapel is quite a sight, too. Museum curators took some heat over the avant-garde use of this historic space. Modern Irish artists are intermixed with others as the gallery builds up a permanent collection. The formal gardens let you wander where the soldiers recuperated. *(Military Road.* ☎ *612 9900; email info@modernart.ie. Bus #90 and 91 from Heuston Station, #78A and 79 from the City Center. Museum and building open Tu-Sa 10am-5:30pm, Su noon-5:30pm. Free. Guided tours W and F 2:30pm, Su 12:15pm. Call for events.)*

NORTH SIDE

O'CONNELL ST. AND PARNELL SQUARE

O'CONNELL STREET. Dublin's biggest shopping thoroughfare starts at the Liffey and leads to Parnell Square. At 150 ft., it was once the widest street in Europe, though it's hard to imagine anyone traveling to Madrid in 1749 with a yardstick to compare. In its pre-Joycean heyday, it was known as Sackville St.; later the name was changed in honor of "The Liberator" (see p. 15). The center traffic islands contain monuments to Irish leaders Parnell, O'Connell, and James Larkin, who organized the heroic Dublin general strike of 1913 (see p. 15). **O'Connell's statue** faces the Liffey and O'Connell Bridge; the winged women aren't angels but Winged Victories, although one has a bullet hole from 1916 in a rather inglorious place. At the other end of the street, **Parnell's statue** points towards nearby Mooney's pub while Parnell's famous words "Thus far and no further" are engraved below his feet. A block up O'Connell street, where Cathedral St. intersects on the right, the 1988 statue of a woman lounging in water is officially named the Spirit of the Liffey or **"Anna Livia."** A newer statue of **Molly Malone** of ballad fame, on Grafton St., also has many aliases (for other names, see **Dublinese,** above). One monument you won't see is **Nelson's Pillar,** a freestanding column that remembered Trafalgar and stood outside the GPO for 150 years. The IRA blew it up in 1966 in commemoration of the 50th anniversary of the Easter Rising. Nelson's English head rests safely in the Dublin Civic Museum.

THE GENERAL POST OFFICE. Not just a fine place to send a letter, the Post Office was the nerve center of the 1916 Easter Rising (see p. 16). Patrick Pearse read the Proclamation of Irish Independence from its steps. When British troops closed in, mailbags became barricades. Outside, a number of bullet nicks are visible. *(O'Connell Street. ☎ 705 7000. Open M-Sa 8am-8pm, Su 10am-6:30pm.)*

HUGH LANE MUNICIPAL GALLERY OF MODERN ART. A small but impressive collection hangs in Georgian **Charlemont House.** When American painter Lane offered to donate his collection of French Impressionist paintings to the city, he did so on the condition that the people of Dublin contribute to the gallery's construction. Because his collection and the architect chosen to build the gallery were foreign, Dubliners refused to lend their support; Yeats lamented their provincial attitudes in a string of poems. Lane's death aboard the *Lusitania* in 1915 raised decades of disputes over his will, resolved by a plan to share the collection between the gallery in Dublin and the Tate Gallery in London. *(Parnell Sq. North. ☎ 874 1903; www.hughlane.ie. Buses #3, 10, 11, 13, 16, and 19 all stop near Parnell Sq. Open Tu-Th 9:30am-6pm, F-Sa 9:30am-5pm, Su 11am-5pm. Free, although occasional special exhibits may charge entrance fees.)*

THE DUBLIN WRITERS' MUSEUM. Read your way through placards and placards describing the city's rich literary heritage, or listen to it on an audio headset tour. Rare editions, manuscripts, and memorabilia of Swift, Shaw, Wilde, Yeats, Beckett, Brendan Behan, Patrick Kavanagh, and Sean O'Casey blend with caricatures, paintings, a great bookstore and an incongruous attached Zen Garden. *(18 Parnell Sq. North. ☎ 872 2077. Open June-Aug. M-F 10am-6pm, Sa 10am-5pm, Su 11am-5pm; Sept.-May M-Sa 10am-5pm. £3.10, students and seniors £2.89. Combined ticket with either Shaw birthplace or James Joyce Centre £4.60.)* Adjacent to the museum, the **Irish Writer's Centre,** is the center of Ireland's living writing community, providing a working space for today's aspiring Joyces. Frequent poetry and fiction readings present current writings to the public. The Centre is not a museum, but if you ring the doorbell you can get information about Dublin's literary happenings. *(19 Parnell Sq. North. ☎ 872 1302; www.writerscentre.ie. Open M-F 9am-5pm.)*

JAMES JOYCE CENTRE. This new museum features Joyceana ranging from portraits of individuals who inspired his characters, to the more arcane delights of Joyce's nephew, who runs the place. Feel free to mull over Joyce's works in the library or the tearoom. Call for info on lectures, walking tours, and Bloomsday events. *(35 North Great Georges St. Up Marlborough St., and past Parnell St. ☎ 873 1984; email joycecen@iol.ie. Open M-Sa 9:30am-5pm, Su 12:30-5pm; July-Aug. extra Su hours 11am-5pm. £3, students and seniors £2.)*

HOT PRESS IRISH MUSIC HALL OF FAME. Dublin's sparkling new anthem to its musical wonders found a great location. A headset tour takes you through memorabilia-laden displays on the history of Irish music from bards to the studio, heaping lavish praise on such stars as Van Morrison, U2, and, uh, Boyzone. The concert venue **HQ** (see **Music,** p. 118) is attached. *(57 Middle Abbey St. ☎ 878 3345; www.irishmusichof.com. Open daily 10am-6pm last entry. £6; students, seniors, and children £4.)*

OTHER SIGHTS. Just past Parnell Sq., the **Garden of Remembrance** eulogizes the martyrs who took the General Post Office (see **The Easter Rising,** p. 16). A cross-shaped pool is visually anchored at one end by a statue representing the mythical Children of Lir, who turned from humans into swans. They proclaim, in Irish, their faith in a vision of freedom: "In the winter of bondage we saw a vision. We melted the snows of lethargy and the river of resurrection flowed from it." *(Open until dusk.)* Turn right on Cathedral St., to find the inconspicuous **Dublin Pro-Cathedral,** the city's center of Catholic worship, where tens of thousands once gathered for Daniel O'Connell's memorial service. "Pro" means "provisional"—many Dublin Catholics want Christ Church Cathedral returned (see p. 113). On Granby Row, the **National Wax Museum** has life-size replicas of everyone from Hitler to the Teletubbies, including the Pope (and his Popemobile) and a life-sized rendering of Da

SIGHTS ■ 117

Vinci's "Last Supper." Ill-fitting assemblies are highly amusing. The best montage may be the American Presidents—and the Ayatollah Khomeni. (☎ 872 6340. *Open M-Sa 10am-5:30pm, Su noon-5:30. £3.50, students £2.50, children £2.*)

ALONG THE QUAYS

THE CUSTOM HOUSE. Dublin's greatest architectural triumph, the Custom House was designed and built in the 1780s by James Gandon, who gave up the chance to be St. Petersburg's state architect to settle in Dublin. The building's expanse of Roman and Venetian columns and domes hints at what the city's 18th-century Anglo-Irish wanted Dublin to become. Carved heads along the frieze represent the rivers of Ireland; the Liffey is the only girl in the bunch. (*East of O'Connell St. at Custom House Quay, where Gardiner St. meets the river.* ☎ *878 7660. Visitors Centre open mid-Mar. to Nov. M-F 10am-12:30pm, Sa-Su 2-5pm; Nov. to mid-Mar. W-F 10am-12:30pm, Su 2-5pm.*)

FOUR COURTS. Another of Gandon's works, the building appears monumentally impressive from the front, but the back and sides reveal 20th-century ballast. On April 14, 1922, General Rory O'Connor seized the Four Courts on behalf of the anti-Treaty IRA; two months later, the Free State government of Griffith and Collins attacked the Four Courts garrison, starting the Irish Civil War (see p. 17). The building now houses the highest court in Ireland. (*Inn's Quay, several quays to the west of the Custom House.*)

ST. MICHAN'S CHURCH. The dry atmosphere in the church has preserved the corpses in the vaults, which inspired Bram Stoker's *Dracula*. Of particular interest is a 6½ ft. tall crusader (dead) and the hanged, drawn, and quartered bodies (very dead) of two of the 1798 rebels. (*Church St. Open Mar.-Oct. M-F 10am-12:45pm and 2-4:45pm, Sa 10am-12:45pm; Nov.-Feb. M-F 12:30-3:30pm, Sa 10am-12:45pm. Church of Ireland services Su 10am. £2, students and seniors £1.50, under 16 50p.*)

SMITHFIELD

Dublin is trying to turn this neighborhood by the quays into the next Temple Bar, but with an emphasis on culture rather than nightlife.

OLD JAMESON DISTILLERY. Learn how science, grain, and tradition come together to create the golden fluid called whiskey. A film recounts the rise, fall, and spiritual renaissance of Ireland's favorite spirit; the subsequent tour walks you through the actual creation of the drink. More entertaining and less commercial than the Guinness Brewery tour, the experience ends with a glass of the Irish whiskey of your choice; be quick to volunteer in the beginning and you'll get to sample a whole tray of different whiskeys. Feel the burn. (*Bow St. From O'Connell St., turn onto Henry St. and continue straight as the street dwindles to Mary St., then Mary Ln., then May Ln.; the warehouse is on a cobblestone street on the left.* ☎ *807 2355. Tours daily 9:30am-5:30pm. £3.95, students and seniors £3.*)

CEOL IRISH TRADITIONAL MUSIC CENTRE. Just because the content's traditional doesn't mean the presentation is. Computers and interactive media provide extensive demonstrations of the various instruments, songs, and dances that make up trad as we now know it. A 20-minute 180-degree film concludes the exhibit. Ceol also offers rides on a giant chimney elevator, atop which you'll find panoramic views of Dublin. Quite a few pence, but fun to figure out where you've been. (*Next door to Jameson, at the base of the large chimney between North King St. and Arran Quay.* ☎ *817 3820; email info@ceol.ie; www.ceol.ie. Open M-Sa 10am-6pm, Su 11am-6pm. £5, students and seniors £4, children £3. Chimney open M-Sa 10am-6pm, Su 11am-6pm; £5, £4 student. Combined music and chimney £10, £8.*)

DISTANT SIGHTS

PHOENIX PARK. Europe's largest enclosed public park is most famous for the "Phoenix Park murders" of 1882. The Invincibles, a tiny nationalist splinter group, stabbed the Chief Secretary of Ireland, Lord Cavendish, and his Under-Secretary

200 yd. from the Phoenix Column. A British Unionist journalist forged a series of letters linking Parnell to the murderers (see p. 15). The **Phoenix Column,** a Corinthian column capped with a phoenix rising from flames, is something of a pun—the park's name actually comes from the Irish *Fionn Uísce,* "clean water." The 1760-acre park incorporates the **President's residence** *(Áras an Uachtaraín),* the US Ambassador's residence, cricket pitches, polo grounds, cattle, and grazing red deer. The deer are quite tame and not to be missed; they usually graze in the thickets near Castleknock Gate. The park is usually peaceful during daylight hours but unsafe at night. *(Take bus #10 from O'Connell St. or #25 or 26 from Middle Abbey St. west along the river. Free.)* **Dublin Zoo,** one of the world's oldest zoos and Europe's largest, is in the park. It contains 700 animals and a discovery center that features the **world's biggest egg.** For an urban zoo, the habitats are fairly large and animals tend to move around a bit, except for the lions, who sleep over 20 hours a day. *(Bus #10 from O'Connell St. passes the zoo.* ☎ *677 1425. Open M-Sa 9:30am-6pm, Su 10:30am-6pm. Closes at sunset in winter. £6.30, students £4.80, seniors £3.70, families £18.50-22.)*

CASINO MARINO. It's an architectural gem and house of tricks. You can certainly gambol here, but you can't gamble; it's a casino only in the sense of "small house," built for the Earl of Charlemont in 1758 as a seaside villa. Funeral urns on the roof are chimneys, the columns are hollow and serve as drains, the casino has secret tunnels and trick doors, and the lions standing guard are actually made of stone. *(Off Malahide Rd. Take bus #123 from O'Connell St. or #27 or 42 from the quays by Busáras.* ☎ *833 1618. Open daily June-Sept. 9:30am-6:30pm, May and Oct. 10am-5pm, Nov. W and Su noon-4pm, Feb.-Apr. Th and Su noon-4pm. Admission by guided tour only. £2, seniors £1.50, students and children £1.)*

GAELIC ATHLETIC ASSOCIATION MUSEUM. Those interested in or mystified by the culturally significant world of Irish athletics—hurling, gaelic football, camogie, and handball—will appreciate this establishment at **Croke Park.** The Gaelic Athletic Association presents the rules, history, and heroes of its national sports, with the help of touchscreens and audio-visual shows. *(*☎ *855 8176. Open May-Sept. daily 9:30am-5pm, Oct.-Apr. Tu-Sa 10am-5pm, Su noon-5pm; last admission 4:30pm; admission on game days to ticket holders only. £3, students and seniors £2, under 12 £1.50.)*

INLAND WATERWAYS VISITOR CENTRE. Known as the "box on the docks" in Dublinese, this floating museum yearns to educate those who are ignorant of the significance of the inland waterway. Since the canals don't get no respect, this takes you back to school. *(Take bus #3 to the Grand Canal. Open June-Sept. 9:30am-5:30pm, Oct.-May W-Su 12:30-5pm. Adult £2, student £1.)*

♫ ARTS AND ENTERTAINMENT

Be it poetry or punk you fancy, Dublin is equipped to entertain you. The *Event Guide* (free) is available at the tourist office, Temple Bar restaurants, and the Temple Bar Info center. It comes out every other Friday with ads in the back, fawning reviews in the front, and reasonably complete listings of museums and literary, musical, and theatrical events in between. The glossier *In Dublin* (£1.95) comes out every two weeks with feature articles and listings for music, theater, art exhibitions, comedy shows, clubs, museums, gay venues, and movie theaters. *Events of the Week* is a much smaller, free booklet, and also jammed with ads, but there's good info buried in it. Additionally, hostel staffers are often good, if biased, sources of information.

MUSIC

Dublin's music world attracts performers from all over the country. Pubs are the scene of much of the musical action, since they provide musicians with free beer and a venue. There is often a cover charge of £3-4 on better-known acts. *Hot Press* (£1.50) has the most up-to-date music listings, particularly for rock. Its commentaries on the musical scene are insightful, and its left-leaning editorials give a clear impression of what the Dublin artistic community is thinking. Tower Records on

Wicklow St. has reams of leaflets. Bills posted all over the city also inform of coming attractions. Scheduled concerts tend to start at 9pm, impromptu ones later.

Traditional music (trad) is not a tourist gimmick but a vibrant and important element of the Dublin music scene. Some pubs in the city center have trad sessions nightly, others nearly so: **Hughes', Slattery's, Oliver St. John Gogarty,** and **McDaid's** are all good choices (see **Pubs**, p. 102). The best pub for trad in the entire city is **Cobblestones,** King St. North (☎ 872 1799), in Smithfield. No rock(s) here, but there are live shows every night, plus a trad session in the basement, plus real live spontaneity. Another great small venue for live music, from rock to folk, is **Whelan's,** 25 Wexford St., the continuation of South Great Georges St., with music nightly. (☎ 478 0766. Covers vary.) Big-deal bands frequent the **Baggot Inn,** 143 Baggot St. (☎ 676 1430). U2 played here in the early 80s; some people are still talking about it. **The Temple Bar Music Centre,** Curved St. (☎ 670 9202), has events and concerts virtually every night. The **National Concert Hall,** Earlsfort Terr., provides a venue for classical concerts and performances. July and August bring nightly shows. (☎ 671 1533. Tickets £6-12, students half-price.) A summer lunchtime series makes a nice break from work on occasional Tuesdays and Fridays. (Tickets £3-6.) Programs for the **National Symphony** and smaller local groups are available at classical music stores and the tourist office. Sunday afternoon jazz is a common phenomenon at such places as the **Café en Seine** (see **Pubs**, p. 103). **Isaac Butt** on Store St. and the **Life** bar (see **Pubs,** p. 105) have periodic jazz as well. The new **HQ** venue (☎ 878 3345), in the Hot Press Hall of Fame on Middle Abbey St. (see **Sights,** p. 115), considers itself one of the nicest venues in Europe. Big acts play at the 1600-capacity **Olympia,** 72 Dame St. (☎ 677 7744), and **Vicar St.,** 99 Vicar St., off Thomas St. (☎ 454 6656). Star acts play to huge crowds at **Tivoli Theatre,** 135-138 Francis St. (☎ 454 4472), and the musical monsters play at **Croke Park,** Clonliffe Rd. (☎ 836 3152), and the **R.D.S.** (☎ 668 0866) in Ballsbridge.

THEATER

Dublin's curtains rise on a full range of mainstream productions and experimental theater. Showtime is generally 8pm. Off Dame St. and Temple Bar, smaller theater companies thrive, presenting new plays and innovative interpretations of the classics. Box office hours are usually for phone reservations; box offices stay open until curtain on performance nights.

- **Abbey Theatre,** 26 Lower Abbey St. (☎ 878 7222), was founded by Yeats and his collaborator Lady Gregory in 1904 to promote Irish cultural revival and modernist theater, which turned out to be a bit like promoting corned beef and soy burgers—most people wanted one or the other. J.M. Synge's *Playboy of the Western World* was first performed here in 1907. The production occasioned storms of protest and yet another of Yeats' political poems (see **The Irish Literary Revival,** p. 26). Today the Abbey, like Synge, has become quite respectable as the National Theatre. Tickets £10-17.50, matinees Sa 2:30pm £8; student rate M-Th £8. Box office open M-Sa 10:30am-7pm.

- **Peacock Theatre,** 26 Lower Abbey St. (☎ 878 7222), the more experimental studio theater downstairs from the Abbey. The usual evening shows plus occasional lunchtime plays, concerts, and poetry. Lunch events £8, students £5; theater tickets £8-10, matinee £6. Box office open M-Sa at 7:30pm, 8:15pm curtain; Sa matinees 2:45pm.

- **Gate Theatre,** 1 Cavendish Row (☎ 874 4045), specializes in international period drama. Tickets £13-15; M-Th student discount at curtain with ID £6, subject to availability. Box office open M-Sa 10am-7pm.

- **Project Arts Centre,** 39 East Essex St. (☎ (1850) 260 027). Sets its sights on being avant-garde, and presents every imaginable sort of artistic presentation. Tickets under £10; student concessions available. Box office open daily 11am-10pm. The gallery hosts rotating visual arts exhibitions. Open same time as box office. Free.

- **Gaiety,** South King St. (☎ 677 1717; www.gaietytheater.com), provides space for modern drama, ballet, music, and the Opera Ireland Society. Tickets £10-16. Box office open M-Sa 10am-8pm.

Andrews Lane Theatre, Andrews Ln. (☎ 679 5720), off Dame St. Every sort of drama on two stages; the studio stage is usually more experimental. Main stage tickets £8-13, studio £5-8. Box office open daily 10:30am-7pm.

City Arts Centre, 23-25 Moss St. (☎ 677 0643), parallel to Tara St. off Georges Quay. Avant-garde exploration of political and sexual issues. Tickets £6, students £4. Box office open daily 9:15am-5pm.

Samuel Beckett Theatre, Trinity College (☎ 608 1000). Inside the campus. Hosts anything it happens by, including scores of student shows.

Olympia Theatre, 72 Dame St. (☎ 677-7744) Hosts commercial musical theater events, plus midnight music revues and tributes to the likes of ABBA and other anagrammatic 70s Swedish bands. Tickets £10.50-26.50. Box office open daily 10:30am-6:30pm.

CINEMA

Ireland's well-supported film industry reeled with the arrival of the **Irish Film Centre,** 6 Eustace St., Temple Bar. The IFC mounts tributes and festivals, including a French film festival in October and a gay and lesbian film festival in early August. A variety of classic and European art house films appear throughout the year. You must be a "member" to buy tickets. (☎ 679 3477; email fii@ifc.ie; www.fii.ie. Weekly membership £1; yearly membership £10, students £7.50. Membership must be purchased at least 15min. before start of show; each member can buy only 4 tickets per screening. Matinees £2; 5pm showing £2.50; after 7pm £4, students £3. 18 and older.) **The Screen,** D'Olier St. (☎ 672 5500), also runs artsy reels. First-run movie houses cluster on O'Connell St., the quays, and Middle Abbey St. The **Savoy,** O'Connell St. (☎ 874 6000), and **Virgin,** Parnell St. (☎ 872 8400), offer a wide selection of major releases. If their screens aren't big enough for you, head to the **Sheridan IMAX,** Parnell Center, Parnell St. (☎ 817 4200; www.dublinimax.ie).

SPORTS AND RECREATION

Dubliners aren't as sports-crazy as their country cousins tend to be, but that's not saying much. Sports are still a serious business, especially since most final games take place here. The season for **Gaelic football** and **hurling** (see **Sports,** p. 33) runs from mid-February to November. Action-packed and often brutal, these games are entertaining for any sports-lover. Provincial finals take place in July, national semifinals on Sundays in August (hurling the first week, football the 2nd and 3rd weeks), and All-Ireland Finals in either late August or early September. Games are played in **Croke Park** and on **Phibsborough Rd.** Tickets are theoretically available at the turnstiles, but they tend to sell out quickly; All-Ireland Finals tickets sell out immediately. Your best bet is to hit the Dublin pubs on game day and see who's selling. Home games of the Irish **rugby** team are played in **Lansdowne Road Stadium,** with the peak of the season spanning from February to early April. **Camogie** (women's hurling) finals also occur in September. For sports information, check the Friday papers or contact the **Gaelic Athletic Association** (☎ 836 3232). **Greyhound racing** continues all year. (W, Th, and Sa at 8pm at Shelbourne Park; ☎ 668 3502. M, Tu, and F at 8pm at Harold's Cross; ☎ 497 1081.) **Horse racing** runs and bets at Leopardstown Racetrack, Foxrock, Dublin 18 (☎ 289 2888). At the beginning of August the **Royal Dublin Horse Show** takes place at the RDS in Ballsbridge.

■ FESTIVALS AND EVENTS

The tourist office's annual *Calendar of Events* (£1) offers info on events throughout Ireland, including Dublin's many festivals, antique and craft fairs, flower marts, horse shows, and the like. The biweekly *Events Guide* or *In Dublin* (£1.95) are also good sources.

BLOOMSDAY. Dublin returns to 1904 each year on June 16, the day on which the 18-hour journey of Joyce's *Ulysses* takes place. Festivities are held all week long, starting before the big day and (to a lesser extent) continuing after it. The James

Joyce Cultural Centre (see p. 115) sponsors a reenactment of the funeral and wake, a lunch at Davy Byrne's, and a breakfast with Guinness. (☎ 873 1984.) On the day itself, a Messenger Bike Rally culminates in St. Stephen's Green with drink and food. Many bookstores have readings from *Ulysses*. Some of the better ones are Hodges Figgis and Waterstone's (see **Literary Shopping,** below). If you're in Dublin on Bloomsday, should you join in on the fun? Yes I wrote yes you will Yes.

MUSIC FESTIVALS. The **Festival of Music in Great Irish Houses,** held during the second and third weeks of June, organizes concerts of period music in 18th-century homes across the country, including ones in the city. (☎ 278 1528.) The **Feis Ceoil** music festival goes trad in mid-March. (☎ 676 7365.) The **Dublin International Organ and Choral Festival** lifts every voice in Christ Church Cathedral. (☎ 677 3066 ext. 416; email organs@diocf.iol.ie.) The **Guinness Blues Festival** is a three-day extravaganza in mid-July, getting bigger and broader each year. (☎ 497 0381; www.guinnessbluesfest.com.) Ask at the tourist office about *fleadhs* (FLAHS), traditional day-long music festivals that pop up periodically.

ST. PATRICK'S DAY. The half-week leading up to March 17 occasions a city-wide carnival of concerts, fireworks, street theater, and intoxicated madness. Many pubs offer special promotions, contests, and extended hours. (☎ 676 3205; email info@paddyfest.ie; www.paddyfest.ie.)

THE DUBLIN THEATRE FESTIVAL. This premier cultural event, held the first two weeks of October, is a spree of about 20 works of theater from Ireland and around the world. Tickets may be purchased all year at participating theaters, and, as the festival draws near, at the Festival Booking Office. (47 Nassau St. ☎ 677 8439. Tickets £10-16, student discounts vary by venue.)

THE DUBLIN FILM FESTIVAL. Irish and international movies make up nearly two weeks of screenings, with a panoply of seminars in tow. (*Early to mid-March.* ☎ 679 2937; email dff@iol.ie; www.iol.ie/dff.)

🛍 SHOPPING

Dublin is not really a center for international trade, and consumer goods are generally expensive. Your time may be better spent in pubs and castles. That said, if something is made anywhere in Ireland, you can probably find it in Dublin. Stores are usually open Monday through Saturday from 9am to 6pm, with later hours on Thursdays (until 7-8pm). Tiny shops pop up everywhere along the streets both north and south of the Liffey, but Dublin's major shopping is on **Grafton** and **Henry St.** On pedestrianized Grafton St., well-dressed consumers crowd into boutiques and restaurants, while sidewalk buskers lay down their caps for money. Teens and barely-twenties buy their used clothes and punk discs in the **Temple Bar.** Across the river, **Henry St.** and **Talbot St.** sport shops for those on a tighter budget. On **Moore St.,** street vendors sell fresh produce at very low prices. (M-Sa 7am-5pm.) **Clery's,** Upper O'Connell St., is Dublin's principal department store. (☎ 878 6000. Open M-W and Sa 9am-6:30pm, Th 9am-9pm, F 9am-8pm.)

At the top of Grafton St., **St. Stephen's Green Shopping Centre** mauls shoppers. Two more shopping malls are planted near O'Connell Street: **ILAC,** off Mary St., and the **Jervis Shopping Center,** up by Parnell St. Nearby, Lord Powerscourt's 200-year-old townhouse on Clarendon St. has been converted into the **Powerscourt Townhouse Centre**—a string of chic boutiques carrying Irish crafts. Gen-X shoppers should head to **Georges St. Market Arcade** on South Great Georges St. near Dame St. The arcade includes a number of vintage clothing, jewelry, and used record stalls as well as a fortune-teller. (Open M-Sa 10am-6pm, Th 8am-7pm.)

DUBLIN'S LITERARY SHOPPING

Eason, 80 Middle Abbey St. (☎ 873 3811), off O'Connell St. A floor-space behemoth. Lots of serious tomes and an extensive "Irish interest" section. Wide selection of local and foreign magazines and newspapers. Their bargain shelves are in the cleverly named **Bargain Books,** and reside diagonally across Abbey St. Open M-W and Sa 8:30am-6:45pm, Th 8:30am-8:45pm, F 8:30am-7:45pm, Su 1:45-5:45pm.

Winding Stair Bookstore, 40 Ormond Quay (☎ 873 3292), on the North Side. 3 atmospheric floors of good tunes, great views, and cheap food. New and used books, contemporary Irish literature, and literary periodicals. Open M-Sa 10am-6pm, Su 1-6pm.

Fred Hanna's, 27-29 Nassau St. (☎ 677 1255), across from Trinity College at Dawson St. An intelligent staff answers all questions about contemporary Irish writing. Open M-W and Sa 8:30am-6:45pm, Th 8:30am-8:45pm, F 8:30am-7:45pm, Su 1:45-5:45pm.

Books Upstairs, 36 College Green (☎ 679 6687), across from Trinity Gate. Extensive sections on gay literature and women's studies. The principal distributor for *Gay Community News.* Open M-F 10am-7pm, Sa 10am-6pm, Su 1-6pm.

Hodges Figgis, 56-58 Dawson St. (☎ 677 4754). Part of an English chain, this large bookstore has a good selection for eclectic tastes. Open M-F 9am-7pm, Sa 9am-6:30pm, Su noon-6pm.

Waterstone's, 7 Dawson St. (☎ 679 1415), off Nassau St. 5 floors of well-stacked books and an informed reference staff. Open M-W and F 9am-8pm, Th 9am-8:30pm, Sa 9am-7pm, Su 11am-6pm.

An Siopa Leabhar, 6 Harcourt St. (an SHUP-a LAU-er; ☎ 478 3814). Varied selection of Irish historical and political books, as well as tapes and books on traditional music. Specializes in literature and resources in Irish. Open M-F 9:30am-5:30pm, Sa 10am-1:30pm and 2-4pm.

RECORDS, TAPES, AND CDS

Megastores sit around Grafton St. and the quays.

Claddagh Records, 2 Cecilia St. (☎ 677 0262), Temple Bar, between Temple Ln. and Crow St. Best selection of trad and a variety of music from other countries. Open M-F 10:30am-5:30pm, Sa noon-5:30pm.

Celtic Note, 14-15 Nassau St. (☎ 670 4157). Specializes in traditional Irish music. Open M-W and F-Sa 9:30am-6:30pm, Th 9:30am-8pm, Su 11am-6pm.

Freebird Records, 1 Eden Quay (☎ 873 1250), on the North Side facing the river. Crowded basement has perhaps Dublin's best selection of indie rock. Proprietors can recommend local bands. Open M-W and Sa 10:30am-6pm, Th-F 10:30am-7:30pm.

Comet Records, 5 Cope St. (☎ 671 8592), Temple Bar. Much like Freebird, but smaller and open later. More info on current groups and gigs. Lots of vinyl and indie CDs. Punk, metal, techno, and t-shirts, too. Open M-Sa 10am-6:30pm, Th-F 10am-7:30pm.

Smile, 59 South Great Georges St. (☎ 478 2005). Good selection of American soul and jazz. A wall of used books, some of which expound on rock. Open M-Sa 10am-6pm.

Sound Cellar, 43 Nassau St. (☎ 677 1940). Heavy metal, but also sells some concert tickets. Open M-Sa 9:30am-5:30pm.

GAY, LESBIAN, AND BISEXUAL DUBLIN

Dublin's progressive thinking fosters PRIDE, an annual, week-long festival in July celebrating gay identity. **Gay Community News (GCN),** 6 South William St. (☎ 671 0939 or 671 9076; email gcn@tnet.ie), is free and comes out monthly, offering the most comprehensive and up-to-date information on gay life and nightlife in Dublin. It's available at Books Upstairs (see **Literary Shopping**), Cornucopia, the George, and venues around Temple Bar. *GCN* has extensive listings of support groups and other organizations. *Sceneout* magazine is a periodic supplement to *GCN* that focuses on nightlife and prints classifieds. The "queer" pages of *In Dublin* list pubs, dance clubs, saunas, gay-friendly restaurants, bookshops, hotlines, and organizations. Since gay Dublin seems to be in a particularly constant state of flux, the listings are comprehensive but sometimes outdated. Books Upstairs was Dublin's first bookstore to have a gay literature shelf, and it's still got the best selection. The **Eason** bookstore is another source of gay periodicals.

Gay Switchboard Dublin is a good resource for events and updates, and sponsors a hotline (☎ 872 1055; Su-F 8-10pm). **The National Gay and Lesbian Federation**, Hirschfield Centre, 10 Fownes St. (☎ 671 0939), in Temple Bar, offers counseling on legal concerns. The lesbian community meets at **Lesbians Organizing Together (LOT)**, 5 Capel St. (☎ 872 7770). The drop-in resource center and library is open Tuesdays through Thursdays 10am to 5pm. **Outhouse**, 65 William St. (☎ 670 6377), is a queer community resource center, offering a library, cafe, info, and advice. Outhouse organizes all sorts of social groups, support groups, seminars, and information sessions for gays, lesbians, teenagers, alcoholics, combinations of the above, and everyone else. **Gay Information Ireland** has a website at www.geocities.com/WestHollywood/9105. Tune into local radio for gay community talk shows: **Innuendo** is broadcast on 104.9FM (Tu 2-3pm); 103.8FM has **Out in the Open** (Tu 9-10pm); and **Equality** airs on 101.6FM (Th 4:30pm).

GAY-FRIENDLY BARS AND NIGHTCLUBS

The gay nightclub scene is particularly thriving, with gay venues (usually clubs rented out) just about every night. Keep up-to-date by checking out the various entertainment publications around town. Pubs that haven't advertised as gay or gay-friendly are an assortment of good and bad apples.

- **The George,** 89 South Great Georges St. (☎ 478 2983). This throbbing, purple man o' war is Dublin's first and most prominent gay bar. A mixed-age crowd gathers throughout the day to chat and sip. The attached nightclub opens W-Su. Su night Bingo is accompanied by so much entertainment that sometimes the bingo never happens. Cover £5-7 after 10pm. Look spiffy—no effort, no entry. Frequent theme nights.
- **Out on the Liffey,** 27 Upper Ormond Quay (☎ 872 2480). Ireland's second gay bar; its name plays on the more traditional Inn on the Liffey a few doors down. Comfortably small. The short hike from the city center ensures a more local crowd on most nights. Late bar W until 12:30am, F until 1:30am, and Sa until midnight. F-Su nights filled with music and a variety of live acts and dancing. Cover £2-3.
- **The Front Lounge,** Parliament St. (☎ 670-4112). The velvet seats of this gay-friendly bar are popular with a very mixed, trendy crowd.

WEEKLY GAY ENTERTAINMENT

- **Sundays: Playground** at Republica, Earl of Kildare Hotel, Kildare St. (☎ 679 4388). 11pm-late. Cover £4-5. **Lollipop** at Velvet, 60 Harcourt St, spins the charts. 11pm-late. Cover £4-5.
- **Mondays: Freedom** at ZaZu, 21-5 Eustace St. (☎ 670 7655). It's been around for a while, and draws trendy crowds. 11pm-late, cover £4. **Baby 2k** cries out for attention at Club Mono.
- **Tuesdays: Tag & Shag** at Republica, Earl of Kildare Hotel, Kildare St. (☎ 679 4388). Sometimes just called "Shag"—the name says it all. Cover £3-4.
- **Fridays: HAM,** at the PoD, 35 Harcourt St. (☎ 478 0225), in the Old Harcourt St. Railway Station. One of the oldest, most established, and most widely-known gay nights. Cover £6-8, before 11pm £5. Every other week, HAM is preceded by **Gristle,** a sit-down cabaret. 9-11pm. £5 includes HAM entry.

DUBLIN'S SUBURBS ☎01

Strung along the Irish Sea from Donabate in the north to Bray in the south, Dublin's suburbs offer a calm alternative to the voracious human tide on Grafton Street. Two regions that stand out from the uniform suburban sprawl are the tranquil Howth Peninsula to the north and the cluster of suburbs around the port of Dún Laoghaire south of Dublin Bay. North of Dublin, castles and factories are surrounded by planned housing developments, all clamoring for a view of the rocky shore. The Velvet Strand in Malahide, a plush stretch of rock and water, is Dublin's best beach (see p. 126). Dublin's southern suburbs tend to be tidy and fairly well-off. The coastal yuppie towns from Dún Laoghaire to Killiney form a nearly unbroken chain of snazzy houses and bright surf. The DART, suburban rail, and buses make the region accessible for an afternoon's jaunt.

HOWTH

The affluent peninsula of Howth (rhymes with "both") dangles from the mainland in Edenic isolation, less than 10 mi. from the center of Dublin. Howth offers a brief look-in at many of Ireland's highlights: rolling hills, pubs, a literary landscape, and a castle. The town's sprawl is densest near the harbor, where the fishing industry sometimes makes the air less Edenic. Man-made structures from various millennia pepper the rest of the island, connected by quiet paths around hills of heather and stunning cliffs.

GETTING THERE AND PRACTICAL INFORMATION

The easiest way to reach Howth is by **DART**. Take a northbound train to the end of the line (30min., 6 per hr., £1.15). **Buses** bound for Howth leave from Dublin's Lower Abbey St.: #31 runs every hour to the center of Howth, near the DART station, and #31B adds a loop that climbs Howth Summit. Turn left out of the station to get to the harbor and the **tourist office**, in the Old Courthouse on Harbour Rd. It provides free, xeroxed maps and glossier, more comprehensive map-and-book packs for £4. (☎ 832 0405 Open May-Aug. M-F 11am-1pm, 1:30-5pm.) When the tourist office is closed, head for the hand-drawn map of the peninsula posted at the harbor entrance across from the St. Lawrence Hotel.

There is an **ATM** at the **Bank of Ireland** (☎ 839 0271), on Main St. (Open M-F 10am-4pm, Th 10am-5pm.) Down the street is **C.S. McDermott's Pharmacy**, 5 Main St. (☎ 832 2069. Open M-Sa 9am-6pm, Su 10:30am-1pm.) The **post office** is at 27 Abbey St. (☎ 831 8210).

ACCOMMODATIONS

Howth's expensive B&Bs concentrate around Thormanby Rd., which forks off upper Main St. and heads for the Summit; bus #31B heads up the hill hourly.

Gleann na Smól (☎ 832 2936), on the left at the end of Nashville Rd. off Thormanby Rd. The closest affordable option to the harbor. Firm beds for the weary; MTV and CNN for the post-literate; and a generous supply of books to suit wormier guests. Homemade jams and breads. Singles £25; doubles £38-42. Ask about ISIC discounts.

Hazelwood (☎ 839 1391; www.hazelwood.net), at the end of the cul-de-sac in the Thormanby Woods estate, 1 mi. up Thormanby Rd. Mrs. Rosaleen Hobbs serves breakfast around a single large table for the paying guests. The non-paying ones—foxes, birds, and other wildlife in the backyard—also get their feed. Top-notch beds on the most silent of streets. Bus #31B runs up Thormanby Rd., or call from the DART station for a lift. Singles £30; doubles £42; all rooms with bath.

Highfield (☎ 832 3936), 1 mi. up Thormanby Rd. Highfield's sign is obscured by its hedges; it's on the left as you go up the hill. Inside, tidy, floral-covered bedrooms. Outside, a beautiful view. Singles £35; doubles £42-44; all rooms with bath.

FOOD AND PUBS

Quash your monstrous traveler's appetite with fabulous pizza and sundaes at **Porto Fino's**, on Harbour Rd. (☎ 839 3054. Open M-F 5pm-midnight, Sa-Su noon-midnight.) **Caffe Caira**, at Harbour Rd. and Abbey St., is an above-average chipper. The takeaway window serves the same fare as the restaurant for a fraction of the price. (☎ 832 3699. Burgers or fish £1.50, chips £1.10. Restaurant open daily noon-

9:30pm; take-away open noon-1am.) Hungry shoppers run to **Spar Supermarket,** St. Laurence Rd., off Abbey St. (☎ 832 6496. Open M-Sa 8am-10pm, Su 8am-9pm.) At the tip-top of Howth lies **The Summit.** Climb Thornmaby Rd. all the way up to drinks, an incredible view of North Howth, and the **K2** nightclub F-Su. (☎ 832 4615. Cover £3-7). The **St. Lawrence Hotel** drops trad in the Anchor Bar during the summer months. (☎ 832 2643. Music M-F from 9pm.) For more local flavor, join the fishermen at the **Lighthouse,** Church St., and relax with a pint and frequent trad. (☎ 832 2827. Sessions Su, M, W, and F from about 9pm.)

SIGHTS

Maud Gonne, winner of Yeats' unyielding devotion, described her childhood in Howth in *A Servant of the Queen:* "After I was grown up I have often slept all night in that friendly heather... From deep down in it one looks up at the stars in a wonderful security and falls asleep to wake up only with the call of the sea birds looking for their breakfasts." A three-hour **cliff walk** rings the peninsula and passes heather and thousands of seabird nests. The trail is well tread, but narrow. The best section of the walk is a hike (1hr.) that runs between the harbor and the lighthouse at the southeast tip of the peninsula. At the harbor end, **Puck's Rock** marks the spot where the devil fell when St. Nessan shook a Bible at him. The nearby **lighthouse,** surrounded by tremendous cliffs, housed Salman Rushdie for a night during the height of the *fatwa* against him. To get to the trailhead from town, turn left at the DART and bus station and follow Harbour Rd. around the coast for about 20 minutes. From the lighthouse, hike downhill. Bus #31B from Lower Abbey St. in Dublin makes it to the cliffs; from the bus stop make your way to the lower path, or stay in the parking lot and admire the magnificent view: on a clear day you can see the Mourne Mountains in Northern Ireland.

In town, the relatively intact ruins of 14th-century **St. Mary's Abbey** stand peacefully surrounded by a cemetery at the bend in Church St. Get the key to the courtyard from the caretaker, Mrs. O'Rourke, at 13 Church St.

Several sights cluster in the middle of the peninsula, to the right as you exit the DART station and then left after ¼ mi. at the entrance to the Deer Park Hostel Up this road lies the private **Howth Castle,** an awkwardly charming patchwork of different materials, styles, and degrees of upkeep. At the end of the driveway to the side of the castle, the **National Transport Museum** fills a barn with a dusty graveyard of tired, green buses, trams, and fire engines, with lots of reminders that the way we used public transport says a lot about a culture. You can't even climb on them or toot their horns. (☎ 848 0831. Open June-Aug. M-Sa 10am-5pm, Su 2-5pm; Sept.-May Sa-Su 2-5pm. £1.60, seniors and children 80p.) Farther up the hill, an uncertain path leads around the right side of the Deer Park Hotel to the fabulous **Rhododendron Gardens,** in which Molly remembers romance (and such) at the end of Joyce's *Ulysses.* (Always open. Free. Yes.) At the top of the forested path, you emerge into an astounding floral panorama overlooking Howth and Dublin to the south. No particular path is the correct one. Spare time for exploring (getting lost). The flowers bloom in June and July. Turn right as soon as you enter the gardens (or cut beforehand through the golf course to tee four) to see a collapsed **portal dolmen** (see **Ancient Ireland,** p. 7) with a 90-ton capstone that marks the grave of someone much more important in 2500 BC than now.

AMAZING GRACE Howth Castle is a private residence, belonging to the St. Lawrence family, which has occupied it for four centuries, but you might try knocking if your surname is O'Malley. In 1575, the pirate queen Grace O'Malley (see **Clare Island,** p. 335) paid a social call but was refused entrance on the grounds that the family was eating. Not one to take an insult lightly, Grace abducted the St. Lawrence heir and refused to hand him back until she had word that the gate would always be open to all O'Malleys at mealtimes.

Just offshore, **Ireland's Eye** once provided both religious sanctuary and strategic advantage for monks, whose former presence is notable in the ruins of **St. Nessan's Church,** and one of the coast's many **Martello towers** (see **Rebellion, Union, Reaction,** p. 13). The monks eventually abandoned their island refuge when pirate raids became too frequent. The island's long beach is now primarily a bird haven. **Ireland's Eye Boat Trips** (☎ 831 4200; mobile (087) 267 8211) jets passengers across the water (15min.; every 30min. weather permitting; £5 return, students £3, children £2.50). Their office is on the East Pier, toward the lighthouse.

MALAHIDE

Eight miles north of Dublin, rows of prim and proper shops smugly line the main street in Malahide. The gorgeous parkland around historic **Malahide Castle,** and the gorgeous furnishings inside, help justify the town's pride. The National Gallery has loaned furnishings and portraits from various periods between the 14th and 19th centuries. The dark carved panelling of the oak room and the great hall are magnificent. The tours are slightly bizarre, as a disembodied voice (via audio tape, not ghost) waxes eloquently about the furniture. (☎ 846 2184. Open Apr.-Oct. M-Sa 10am-5pm, Su 11am-6pm; Nov.-Mar. M-F 10am-5pm, Sa-Su 2-5pm. Admission by tour only; no tours 12:45-2pm. £3.15; students and seniors £2.65. Castle and **Fry Model Railway** £4.85, £3.80.) The adjacent **Talbot Botanic Gardens** are abloom and open only from May to September. (Open daily 2-5pm. £2.) If you do get a craving for wintry twigs, though, the 250-acre **park** of the castle desmesne keeps its densely foliated paths open all year. (Open daily June-Aug. 10am-9pm, May and Sept. 10am-8pm, Apr. and Oct. 10am-7pm, Nov.-Jan. 10am-5pm, Feb.-Mar. 10am-6pm. Free.) Next to the castle, you can also choo-choo-choose to see the **Fry Model Railway,** a 2,500 sq. ft. working model with detailed renderings of all your favorite Dublin landmarks. (☎ 846 3779. Open Apr.-Sept. M-Sa 10am-1pm and 2-5pm, Su 2-6pm; Apr.-May and Sept. closed F; Oct.-Mar. Sa-Su 2-5pm. £2.85, seniors and under 18 £2.15. Admission by tour only; tours every 45min.) If you're in town, make sure to hit Malahide's gorgeous **beach;** continue slightly farther towards neighboring Portmarnock for the even softer, more luxurious **Velvet Strand.**

With the expansion of the DART line to Malahide scheduled to finish in late 2000, getting there should become easier than ever. The less frequent suburban rail will continue to swing through town as always, as will buses #42 (from Beresford Place, behind the Custom House), 32A (from Lower Abbey St.), and 230 (from Dublin airport). All forms of transport to Dublin (except the 32A) run at least once an hour, usually more, and cost around £1.15. From the **train/DART station** on Main St. (☎ 845 0422), turn right to reach the nearby castle desmesne, or turn left to reach the equally nearby **Diamond,** the central intersection of town. The friendly folks at the **Citizens Information Centre,** Main St., in the parking lot behind the library, provide free maps and info about Malahide, its sights, its B&Bs, and unexpected pregnancies. (Open M-F 10am-noon and 2:30-4pm.) The library has limited **Internet access** by appointment. (☎ 845 2026. Open M-W 10am-5:15pm, Tu and Th-Sa 2-8:30pm.) Across the street from the library in Malahide Shopping Center, **Malahide Cycles** rents bicycles. (☎ 845 0945. Open M-Sa 10am-6pm. £8 per day, week by negotiation.) Continue straight on Main St. for 10 minutes (it becomes Coast Rd.) to reach the B&Bs of Biscayne, a cul-de-sac development to the right. Betty O'Brien wings conversation at **Pegasus,** 56 Biscayne. (☎ 845 1506. June-Aug. singles £30, doubles £38-40; Mar.-May and Sept.-Oct. singles £25, doubles £36-38.) Its neighbor **Aishling,** 59 Biscayne (☎/fax 845 2292), offers tea facilities, hairdryers, and lots of pink in all rooms. (Open Apr.-Oct. Doubles £36, with bath £38.)

Most of the town restaurants cater to those with heavy purses, but a few reasonable food options exists. The **L&N SuperValu** offers groceries at the shopping center. (☎ 845-0233. Open M-W 8am-8pm, Th-Sa 8am-9pm, Su 9:30am-6pm.) **Kupz,** Main St., across from the DART, has a varied menu of Spanish tapas, freshly-squeezed juices, coffees, and gargantuan bowls of soup for under £5. (☎ 845 6262. Open daily 9am-6pm.) **Smyth's,** on New St., by The Diamond, serves up burgers until 9:45pm and trad afterward. (☎ 845 0960. Burgers £5-6. Trad M-Th.) **Duffy's,** Main St. (☎ 845 0735), serves cheap and delicious sandwiches for under £3.

DÚN LAOGHAIRE AND VICINITY

As Dublin's major out-of-city ferry port, Dún Laoghaire (dun-LEER-ee) is the first peek at Ireland for many tourists. Fortunately, it makes a good spot to begin a ramble along the coast south of Dublin. The surrounding towns, from north to south, are: Blackrock, Monkstown, Dún Laoghaire, Dalkey, and Killiney; all are connected by a series of paths called the "Dún Laoghaire Way," the "Dalkey Way," and so on. Getting from one town to the next is quick and simple if you stay within a few blocks of the sea. For those who don't want to invest the shoe leather, the DART also makes for great (if brief) coastal views between Dalkey and Bray. An entertaining ramble would begin with a ride on bus #59 from the Dún Laoghaire DART station to the top of Killiney Hill and proceed along the path through the park and down into Dalkey. In reverse, one can disembark at the Dalkey Dart and ramble over the hills to Killiney's wonderful beach. Literary buffs may want to investigate the James Joyce Tower, where the artist once stayed as a young man. Summer evenings are the best time to visit, when couples stroll down the waterfront and the whole town turns out for weekly sailboat races.

🛈 PRACTICAL INFORMATION

Reach Dún Laoghaire by **DART** from Dublin (£1.10), or southbound **buses** #7, 7A, 8, or (on a longer, inland route) 46A from Eden Quay. From the ferry port, **Marine Rd.** climbs up to the center of town. **George's St.**, at the top of Marine Rd., holds most of Dún Laoghaire's shops, many right at the intersection in the **Dún Laoghaire Shopping Centre.** (Open M-W and Sa 9am-6pm, Th-F 9am-9pm, Su noon-6pm.) **Patrick St.**, which continues Marine Rd.'s path uphill on the other side of George's St., offers cheap eateries. The **tourist office**, in the ferry terminal, is equipped with copious maps and pamphlets on the whole area up to Dublin. (Open M-Sa 10am-5:30pm.) Exchange money at the ferry terminal's **bureau de change.** (☎ 280 4783. Open M-Sa 9am-5pm, Su 10am-5pm.) The **Bank of Ireland** is at 101 Upper George's St. (☎ 280 0273. Open M-W and F 10am-4pm, Th 10am-5pm. **24hr. ATM.**) **Bike hire** happens at **Mike's Bikes** on Patrick St. **Internet access** is available at the **Dun Laoghaire Youth Info Centre**, in the church on Marina St. (☎ 280 9363; free by appointment; M-F 9:30am-5pm, Sa 10am-4pm) and at **Net House**, 28 Upper George's. (☎ 230 3085. Open M-F 8am-midnight, Su 10am-12am. £6 per hr., students £5.)

🛌 ACCOMMODATIONS

As the port for the Stena ferries and a convenient DART stop on the way to Dublin, Dún Laoghaire is prime breeding ground for B&Bs, only a portion of which are modestly priced. Three hostels are also within walking distance.

Belgrave Hall, 34 Belgrave Sq. (☎ 284 2106; email info@dublinhostel.com; www.dublinhostel.com). From the Seapoint DART station, head left down the coast, then zigzag right, left, right, and left at each intersection to Belgrave Sq. A top-tier hostel that feels old but not run-down: high ceilings, wood and marble floors, and old furniture. Small continental breakfast included. **Internet access.** Laundry £3-6. **Bike rental** £10 per day. Free parking. Summer F-Sa 10-bed dorm £15, Su-Th all rooms £13.

Marina House, 7 Old Dunleary Rd. (☎ 284 1524; mobile 086 233 9283; www.marina-house.com). Head left out of Salthill and Monkstown DART station; it's next to the Purty Kitchen (see **Pubs,** below). Spotlessly new, just rough raw wood and solid, comfy beds. Owners Donagh and Mike will join you for drinks out back at night and then get up early to bake *pain au chocolat* for breakfast. **Internet access.** Non-smoking bedrooms. Dorms summer £12; 4-beds £14; doubles £35; winter dorms £10.

Marleen, 9 Marine Rd. (☎ 280 2456). Fall off the DART or ferry; you're here. Great location, just west of the harbor. 200 years old and a floor to prove it. Friendly owners; TV and tea facilities, and artistic themes in each room. Singles £20; doubles £36.

Avondale, 3 Northumberland Ave. (☎ 280 9628; avondalebandb@eircom.net), next to Dunnes Stores. A crimson carpet and darling cocker spaniel lead guests to big beds. Singles £30 when available; doubles £40.

FOOD, PUBS, AND ENTERTAINMENT

Tesco Supermarket vends downstairs in the Dún Laoghaire shopping center. (☎ 280 8441. Open M-W and Sa 8:30am-7pm, Th-F 8:30am-9pm, Su 11am-6pm.) Fast-food restaurants and inexpensive coffee shops line George's St. **The Red Onion,** 60 Upper George's, is the place to be seen for chic coffee and lunches in the limelight. (☎ 230 0275. Breakfast and lunch 8am-3pm, expensive dinner starts at 6pm.) **Bits and Pizzas,** 15 Patrick St., wins local approval for good value. (☎ 284 2411. Lunch special of pizza, cole slaw, and tea £4.35. Open M-Sa noon-midnight.) **La Strada,** 2-3 Cumberland St. (☎ 280 2333), near the Marina hostel on the continuation of George's St., is worth the journey for reasonably priced Italian dishes.

For the best collection of pubs, head north to Monkstown. If you insist on staying south, have no shame and head to **Farrell's** (☎ 284 6595), upstairs in the Dún Laoghaire Shopping Centre; the panoramic coastal view looks fine through a pint glass. Next door to the Marina Hostel, the **Purty Kitchen** pub opens its loft for a purty little nightclub with poppy music and jazz on Wednesdays. (☎ 280 1257. No cover Th and Su; W and F-Sa £5.) The best *craic* is at the **Cultúrlann na hÉireann,** next door to the Belgrave Hall hostel. The headquarters of Comhaltas Ceoltóirí Eireann, a huge international organization for Irish traditional music, the Cultúrlann houses bona fide, non-tourist oriented trad sessions, as well as *céilí* dancing. It's as much a community center as a pub. (☎ 280 0295. Mid-June to Sept. M-Th sit-down performances 9pm. Tickets £6; year-round F *céilí* £4.50, Sa sessions £2.)

SIGHTS

JAMES JOYCE TOWER. The tower is a fascinating retreat, especially for tourists with a specific interest. James Joyce stayed in the tower for a tense six days in August 1904 as a guest of Oliver St. John Gogarty, a Dublin surgeon, poetic wit, man-about-town, and the first civilian tenant of the tower. Unfortunately, Gogarty's other guest was an excitable Englishman with a severe sleepwalking problem. The Englishman, Samuel Trench, dreamt there was a panther in the tower and fired his pistol into the fireplace. Gogarty mockingly seized the pistol, shouted "Leave him to me!" and fired his own shotgun overhead into a row of saucepans that fell onto Joyce. Not as amused, Joyce left that morning, and later infamized Gogarty in the first chapter of *Ulysses*. The novel is partially set in and around the tower, with Gogarty transformed into Buck Mulligan, Trench into Haines, and Joyce into Stephen Dedalus, who meditates on the "snotgreen" sea from the gun platform at the top of the tower. The two-room museum contains Joyce's death mask, his personal effects, including his guitar, his bookshelves, some of his correspondence (such as love letters to Nora Barnacle), a page of the original manuscript of Finnegan's Wake, and lots of editions of *Ulysses*, including one illustrated by Henri Matisse. One letter to Italo Svevo mentions a briefcase "the color of a nun's belly." Genius! Upstairs, the Round Room reconstructs Joyce's bedroom; even if you haven't read any Joyce (see **Ulysses Pub Primer,** above), you'll enjoy views from the gun platform of "many crests, every ninth, breaking, plashing, from far, from farther out, waves and waves." *(From the Sandycove DART station, go left at either the green house or Eagle House down to the coast, turn right and continue to the Martello tower in Sandycove; or take bus #8 from Burgh Quay in Dublin to Sandycove Ave.* ☎ 872 2077. Open Apr.-Oct. M-Sa 10am-1pm and 2-5pm, Su 2-6pm; Nov.-Mar. by appointment. £2.70, seniors and students £2.20.)

ULYSSES PUB PRIMER

So, you've meant to read *Ulysses* but were intimidated by its 700 pages, thousands of allusions, and dense verbal puzzles. Despite its ranking as greatest book of the 20th century in several polls, very few people have read it in its entirety. *Let's Go*, a far more accessible book, is here with some trivia to help you bluff your way through a literary pub crawl:

The first and last letters of the book are both "s"; other than symmetrizing the novel, the "s" stands for "Stephen" (Dedalus, one of the three main characters), while "P" stands for "Poldy" (nickname of Leopold Bloom, the central figure), and "M" for "Molly" (Poldy's wife). The first words of the novel—"Stately, plump Buck Mulligan"—also incorporate these letters. Taken together, S-M-P stands for subject-middle-predicate, or logical sentence structure. The form (a syllogism) suggests a logical and narrative structure which readers can grasp, but which eludes the central characters.

The final words of Molly's stream-of-consciousness monologue to end the book—"yes I said yes I will Yes" (her memory of her response to Bloom's marriage proposal)—have drawn much critical attention, namely as a "yes" of female affirmation. An interesting theory places the capitalized final "Yes" in the typographical realm; in Molly's thoughts, words are not capitalized, but on the page they are. This counters, to some degree, the female affirmation theory by granting final authorship to Joyce.

Ulysses uses 33,000 different words, and 16,000 are used only once. Shakespeare was known to have used 25,000 different words throughout all his plays.

Since Molly calls Leopold "Poldy," she takes the "Leo" out of him—de-lionizing him. Her first sounds in the novel are "Mn." The word "melon" echoes in Leopold's mind throughout the day. Why? The word recalls Molly's voluptuous figure while it reconfigures "Leo" and "Mn" in a palatable way through anagram. (He also carries around a bar of lemon soap.)

Joyce once said he expected readers to devote nothing less than their entire lives to figuring out his epic. For the less ambitious and less masochistic, this primer Suffices.

FORTY FOOT MEN'S BATHING PLACE. At the foot of the tower lies this infamous aquatic spot, also of Joycean fame. A wholesome crowd with plenty of toddlers splashes in the shallow pool facing the road. But behind a wall, on the rocks below the battery and adjacent to the Martello Tower, men traditionally skinny-dip year-round; apparently, they don't mind that they're a tourist attraction. The pool rarely contains 40 men, and even more rarely 40 ft. men; instead, the name derives from the Fortieth Regiment of British foot soldiers, who made it their semi-private swimming hole. Joyce's host, Oliver St. John Gogarty, once took the plunge here with a reluctant W.B. Yeats in tow. Yeats failed to apply to his epic poems the principles of shrinkage he learned in the cold waters.

NAUTICA. The **harbor** itself is a sight, filled with yachts, boat tours, car ferries, and fishermen. Frequent summer evening boat races draw much of the town. On a clear day, head down to the piers—the setting for Samuel Beckett's *Krapp's Last Tape*—to soak up the sun, or brood with extended alienated pauses. For more organized sightseeing, try the **National Maritime Museum**. The massive lens from the Bailey Lighthouse in Howth rotates majestically in front of a large stained-glass window. Other exhibits include a longboat (like a rowboat, but better) sent by revolutionary France to support the United Irishmen in 1796, and a piece of the first transatlantic cable, laid by a local captain. *(From the ferry port, turn left on Queen's Rd. to the stone steps that lead up to Haigh Terr. The museum is in the Mariners' Church.* ☎ *280 0969. Open May-Sept. Tu-Su 1-5pm; Apr. and Oct. Sa-Su 1-5pm. £1.50, children 80p.)*

KILLINEY. Farther south from Dún Laoghaire, Killiney (kill-EYE-nee), Dublin's poshest suburb, has a gorgeous beach. Pick up the Heritage map of Dún Laoghaire for details on seven area walks that hit Killiney. From the top of **Killiney Hill Park**, the views are breathtaking—that dark smudge on the horizon is called Wales. A commemorative obelisk tops the western summit, with the **wishing steps** nearby.

Walk around each level of the steps from base to top, turn to face Dalkey Island, and make a wish: it's bound to come true. Beware that this process only works if you walk in a clockwise direction; in earlier times, women wishing to acquire the power of witchcraft walked naked in a counter-clockwise direction. The Heritage guide states that "visitors should not do this on Killiney Hill!" *(To reach the twin summits of the park, start on Castle St., take a left onto Dalkey Ave. and climb Dalkey Hill.)* Slip down the path to Torca Rd., where **Shaw's Cottage,** up the road on the left, was home to young George Bernard Shaw (see **1600-1880: Yet More Wit and Resistance,** p. 25). Steps descend from Torca Rd. to coastal Vico Rd., which runs to Dalkey.

BRAY

Despite its official location in Co. Wicklow, Bray functions as suburb of Dublin: cityfolk flock to its beach, and the DART and Dublin bus trundle through the town regularly. Well-tended gardens set against a somewhat over-developed seafront are demonstrative of Bray's compromising position between urban and rural Ireland. Bray's transport to both is extremely handy.

GETTING THERE AND PRACTICAL INFORMATION.
Bray is a 45-minute **DART** ride from Connolly Station (£2.60 return), and buses #45 and #84 arrive from Eden Quay. Bray has good connections to **Enniskerry,** Co. Wicklow: from the Bray DART station, bus #85 runs to Enniskerry (£1), competing with **Alpine Coaches,** which runs to **Enniskerry, Powerscourt Gardens, Powerscourt Waterfall,** and **Glencree.** (☎ 286 2547. May-Sept.; see the tourist office for a schedule.) **St. Kevin's Bus Service** shuttles from the town hall on Main St. to **Glendalough.** (☎ 281 8119. 1hr., 2 per day, £5.) To reach **Main St.** from the DART station, head out either **Quinsborough Rd.** or **Florence Rd.** which run perpendicular to the tracks. The **tourist office** is the first stop south of Dublin that can give you info on Co. Wicklow. (☎ 286 7128. Open June-Sept. M-F 9am-5pm, Sa 10am-4pm, Oct.-May M-F 9:30am-4:30pm, Sa 10am-4pm. Closed for lunch 1-2pm.) The office, which supplies a handy town map (free), shares a building with the Heritage Centre, downhill on Main St. next to the Royal Hotel. **Bray Sports,** 8 Main St., **rents bikes.** (☎ 286 3046. £10 per day, £50 per week; deposit £50. Open M-Sa 9am-6pm.) The **Bray Launderette,** Quinsborough St. (☎ 282 8298) washes up for £4.90 and dries for £1.15. The **Net Stop Cafe** upstairs at 89 Main St., has email and **Internet access** (£5 per hr.) as well as games for £3 per hour. (☎ 205 0003. Open M-Sa 10am-10pm, Su 1-10pm.) The **post office** (☎ 286 2554) posits its position on Main St.

ACCOMMODATIONS, FOOD, AND PUBS.
Seafront **B&Bs** line the strand, but cheaper B&Bs can be found on Meath St., behind the strand, and closer to the town center. Anne and Pat Duffy welcome guests to **Moytura,** Herbert Rd., which is the continuation of Quinsborough Rd. after it crosses Main St. Moytura is just before the fork in the road, on the right. The hosts serve up good food, supreme orange juice, and chats about Irish history. All rooms with bath. (☎ 282 9827. Singles £25; doubles £40.) Mary Wafer provides a good value at **Bayview,** Meath Rd., a small B&B whose three rooms have high ceilings and TVs. (☎ 286 0887. Singles £20-25; doubles £40.) Across the street, **Shoreline** has been splendidly overhauled by new owners. (☎ 286 6063. Doubles £36.)

SuperQuinn shelves groceries on Castle St., the continuation of Main St. downhill and across the bridge from the tourist center. (☎ 286 7779 or 286 1270. Open M-Tu 8:30am-8pm, W-F 8:30am-9pm, Sa 8:30am-7pm.) The surrounding shopping center also houses fruit stands and sandwich shops. At the other end of Main St., the historic **town hall** now houses the cutest little McDonald's you'll ever see. If it's good food, not history, you want, the best meal in town is waiting at **Escape,** Albert Ave., at the intersection with the Strand. Heaping portions of creative vegetarian dishes please any appetite. A new menu appears daily. (☎ 286 6755. Lunches around £4.75, dinners about £8. Open M-Sa 11am-10:30pm, Su noon-8:45pm.) **Pizzas 'n' Cream,** Albert Walk (☎ 286 1606), serves crepes, too (under £6). **The Martello** restaurant, The Strand, serves a nice selection of burgers and salads. (☎ 286 8000.)

Lunch 12:30-3pm, bar food 3-5pm, slightly more expensive dinners until 9pm.) The liveliest pub action takes place along the Strand, on huge patios lined with picnic benches when the weather cooperates. The **Porter House,** the country cousin of Dublin's Temple Bar Porter House (see p. 105), boasts a near endless list of beers and microbrews. (☎ 286 0668. Food served till 9pm. Music W.)

SIGHTS. Bray's history since the Neolithic Age is on display in the small but well-designed **Heritage Centre,** Main St., in the same building as the tourist office. A renovation will add a model railway to the current collection of Bray's historical artifacts. (☎ 286 7128. Same hours as tourist office. Donations requested.) Along the beachfront, grim amusement palaces cater to a dwindling crowd of Dublin beachgoers. Halfway down the strand, the new **Natural Sea Life Centre** marks the dawning of the age of aquariums. New wave music, dark passages, and fish of all sizes make for a mellow time, as long as you don't confuse the touchpools with the manta ray tank. (☎ 286 6939; www.sealife.ie. Open daily 10am-5pm. $5.50, seniors $4.50, students $4, children $3.95. Wheelchair accessible.)

If the neon's bugging you and you need a breath of fresh air, head to the summit of **Bray Head,** which looms high above the south end of the strand. The trailhead begins after a short paved pedestrian walkway begins to curve up the hill. On the right, past the picnicking area, is a set of concrete steps that launches one of several winding trails to the top. The hike up is very steep, and requires some clambering over rocks at the summit. Aim for the cross atop the hill, and you should be overlooking incredible views of the Wicklow Mountains, Bray Bay, and the Kiliney and Dalkey hills in about 30 minutes. For further direction, check out the crude mural of a map on the snack shed of the golf course to the right of the steps. **Raheenacluig,** in the middle of the golf course, is what's left of a 13th-century Augustinian Church.

DAYTRIPS FROM BRAY: POWERSCOURT ESTATE AND WATERFALL.
*To reach the estate, take a **bus** from Bray (#85 stops in Enniskerry's Sq.; the private Alpine line drops visitors off at the garden entrance) or from Dublin directly (#45). The estate is a few hundred yards up the left fork as you face the town clock, and the house and gardens are an additional few hundred yards up from the gatehouse. Beware the bloodthirsty tour buses that speed past. A couple of Alpine buses from Bray head to the waterfall daily, and hikers along the Wicklow Way (see p. 141) pass close by. Otherwise, follow the somewhat cryptic signs from Enniskerry.*

Five miles east of Bray, the grand **Powerscourt Estate** perches by Enniskerry in Co. Wicklow. Built in the 1730s, the house developed into an architectural landmark, designed in part by a man who measured the length of his workday with a bottle of sherry. Unfortunately, the house was gutted by flames in 1974. Work has recently commenced to fix up gradually the lost interior; for now, an exhibition about the house's history is the main attraction of its interior. The terraced **gardens** out back justify their high admission cost. Landscaping of every sort, from formal Italian vistas to Japanese paths, surround the house while the pointed Sugar Loaf mountain admires from the distance. Beasts rest in peace under the headstones of the **pet cemetery** in the back. Taking time for the "long walk" (roughly 1 hr., depending on horticultural voyeurism) about the gardens is worth it to escape the thronging crowds on the tea terrace. (☎ (01) 204 6000; www.powerscourt.ie. Open daily 9:30am-5:30pm. Gardens and house $5.50, seniors and students $4.80; gardens only $4, 3.50. Free if shopping.)

The famed **Powerscourt Waterfall** is 5km outside Enniskerry, Co. Wicklow. The waterfall, Ireland's highest at 398 ft., is most impressive in late spring and after heavy rains. A 40-minute nature walk begins at the base of the waterfall and rambles through quieter, untended woods. Leaflets 50p from the snack shop. (Open summer 9:30am-7pm, winter 10:30am to dusk. $2, students and seniors $1.50.)

132 ■ EASTERN IRELAND

EASTERN IRELAND

Woe to the unfortunate tourists whose exposure to eastern Ireland is limited to what they see out of the window on a bus headed from Dublin to the West. Untouristed Eastern towns are the sources of many a marvel. The monastic city at Clonmacnois and the ruins in Co. Meath, which are older than the pyramids, continue to mystify archaeologists. The mountains of Wicklow offer spectacular views, and tired hikers can head downhill to relax on the beach. The tiny lakeland towns of Co. Monaghan, really a part of the Fermanagh Lake District in the North (see p. 475), harbor the warmest waters in the northern half of Ireland. And where else but Kildare can you find a horse farm run according to the laws of metaphysics or a theme-park based on bogs? Counties Meath, Louth, Wicklow, and Kildare all hold delights fit for daytrips from Dublin.

HIGHLIGHTS OF THE EAST: MOUNTAINS AND MONUMENTS

A vision from God told St. Kevin to build his monastery at **Glendalough** (p. 138), the most blessed spot on the island, with ruins and hikes through the valley.

The **Wicklow Mountains** (p. 138) please hikers with the 76 mi. long **Wicklow Way**, while drivers enjoy the scenic **Mountain Rd.**

Brú na Bóinne (p. 148) is a spread of impressive pre-Christian monuments: **Newgrange, Knowth** and **Dowth,** and the **Hill of Tara.**

COUNTY WICKLOW

Mountainous Co. Wicklow allows wilderness fans to lose themselves on deserted back roads, zoom down seesaw ridges by bicycle, and still be back in Dublin by nightfall. Wild as parts of it are, the whole county is in the capital's backyard. Its major sights are accessible by buses from downtown Dublin, but moving about within the county is often best done by bike or car. The Wicklow Way hiking trail is an excellent reason to forsake urban amenities and rough it for a week.

Co. Wicklow was once rich in gold, but Bronze-age peoples exhausted the source. Later, 9th-century Vikings used present-day Wicklow and Arklow as bases from which to raid Glendalough and other monasteries. Norman invaders in the 1100s followed the same pattern, building defenses on the coast while leaving the mountains to the Gaelic O'Toole and O'Byrne clans. English control was not fully established until the 1798 rebellion, when military roads and barracks were built through the interior so that the British Army could hunt down the remaining guerrillas (see **Rebellion, Union, Reaction,** p. 13). The mountains later produced a mining industry in the southern part of the county. Bray is in Co. Wicklow, but since it's on the DART, *Let's Go* covers it as a suburb of Dublin (see p. 131).

WICKLOW COAST

The uncrowded towns of the Wicklow coast seem a world away from nearby, jet-setting Dublin. As an entry way to the southeast coast, it lacks the heavy-hitting historical sites of the inland route through Glendalough and Kilkenny, but it is also faster by any means of transport. For those interested in catching a glimpse of Dublin, these towns aren't *too* outrageously far to make a cheaper home base.

134 ■ WICKLOW COAST

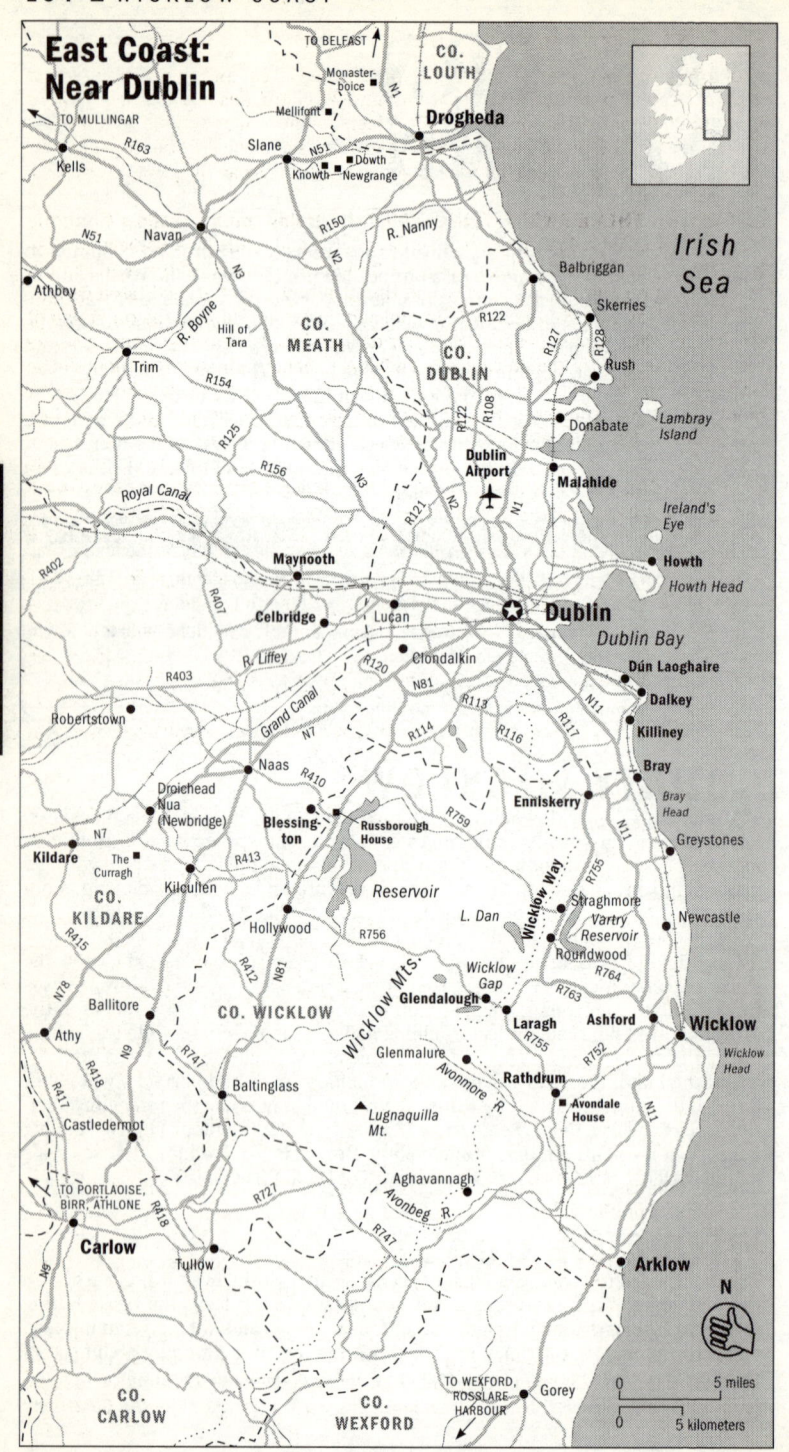

WICKLOW TOWN ☎ 0404

Wicklow Town is touted for both its coastal pleasures and its usefulness as a departure point into the Wicklow Mountains. Wicklow has a wider selection of restaurants than the surrounding area and plenty of accommodations within walking distance of the pubs. Visitors can exhaust the sightseeing in the town proper fairly swiftly, but numerous hikes and cycling excursions can fill a few afternoons.

GETTING THERE AND GETTING AROUND. Trains run to **Dublin's** Connolly Station (1¼hr.; M-Sa 4 per day, Su 3 per day; £7.50) and to **Rosslare Harbour** via **Wexford** (2hr., 3 per day, £15). The station is a 15-minute walk east of town on Church St.; head out on Main St. past the Grand Hotel and turn right at the Statoil garage. **Bus Éireann** leaves for Dublin from the gaol and the Grand Hotel at the other end of Main St. (1½hr.; M-Sa 9 per day, Su 6 per day; £4.50). **Wicklow Tours** runs a somewhat reliable van to **Glendalough** via **Rathdrum**, picking up from the hostel, the Bridge Tavern, and the Grand Hotel. (☎ 67671. June-Aug. 2 per day. £6.) **Wicklow Hiring,** Abbey St., **rents bikes.** (☎ 68149. £6 per day, £42 per week; deposit £30; helmet included. Open M-Sa 8:30am-1pm and 2-5:30pm.)

PRACTICAL INFORMATION. Long, skinny **Abbey St.** snakes past the Grand Hotel to the grassy triangle of **Fitzwilliam Square** (by the tourist office), then continues as **Main St.** to its terminus in **Market Square.** The historic **gaol** sits up the hill from Market St. The **tourist office,** Main St., Fitzwilliam Sq., provides free maps of town and county, and can tell you about the Wicklow Way and other nearby attractions. (☎ 69117. Open June-Sept. M-F 9am-6pm, Sa 9:30am-5:30pm; Oct.-May M-F 9:30am-5:30pm; always closed for lunch 1-2pm.) An **AIB**, with a **24-hour ATM**, is on Main St. (Open M 10am-5pm, Tu-F 10am-4pm.) The **post office** sits on Main St. (☎ 67474. Open M-F 9am-5:30pm, Sa 9:30am-12:50pm and 2:10-5:30pm.)

ACCOMMODATIONS. The lovely ■**Wicklow Bay Hostel,** The Murrough, sports good beds, clean rooms, a friendly atmosphere, and amazing sea views. The owners are full of advice on good hikes, and they know James Bond. From Fitzwilliam Sq., walk toward the river, cross the bridge, and head left until you see the big building called "Marine House." (☎ 69213; fax 66456; email wicklowbayhostel@tinet.ie. Open Feb. to mid-Nov. Dorms £8.50-9; private rooms £10 per person.) Travelers will also be content in almost any of the many B&Bs on Patrick Rd., uphill from Main St. and past the church. It takes a bit of energy to hike the 15min. up to friendly Helen Gorman's **Thomond House,** Upper Patrick Rd., but the splendid panoramic views and superbly comfortable rooms justify it. Call for a pick-up. (☎ 67940. Open Apr.-Oct. Singles £23; doubles £36, with bath £40.) Though directly across from the old gaol, Ann O'Reilly's **The Warrens,** Kilmantin Hill, hasn't copied its design, offering instead mellow, comfy bedrooms with TVs and small baths. (☎ 69899. Singles £21; doubles £34.) **Kilmantin B&B** is next to the gaol, and since it no longer houses the prison guards, its bright, shiny rooms, all with bath and TV, won't remind you of the clink. (☎ 67373. Singles £25; doubles £40.) Several campgrounds are scattered around the area. **Webster's Caravan and Camping Park,** 2½ mi. south of town on the coastal road at Silver Strand (see **Sights**), will let you pitch a tent. (☎ 67615. Open June-Aug. Showers 50p. One-person tent £3.50; two-person £6.) In Redcross, 7 mi. down N11, **River Valley** offers greater luxuries. (☎ 41647. Open Mar.-Sept. Showers 50p. £5 for a tent plus £1 per person.)

FOOD AND PUBS. Main St. is lined with greasy take-aways alongside fresh produce shops. The new **SuperValu**, Wentworth Pl., just off Church St., offers a large selection. (☎ 61888. M-W and Sa 8am-8pm, Th-F 8am-9pm, Su 10am-7pm.) **Tesco's**, out on Dublin Rd., offers an even wider selection of nutriments. (☎ 69250. Open M-W and Sa 8:30am-8pm, Th-F 8:30am-10pm, Su 10am-6pm.) ■**The Bakery Cafe** is nothing less than gourmet, and at lunch, some fabulously filling salads can be had for under £5. (☎ 66770. M-Sa 9am-5pm, Su 11am-5pm.) **The Old Court Inn,**

Market Sq. (☎ 67680), serves a good plate of grub daily until 9pm, specializing, as the entire Wicklow coast does, in fish. Dine with 7½ sweet friends at **La Dolce Vita**, Main St., and enjoy a variety of Italian foods. (☎ 67075. Full breakfast £4, lunch specials with tea or coffee £4.50, unique desserts £1.70-4. Open daily 1-10:30pm.) **Philip Healy's**, Fitzwilliam Sq. (☎ 67380), serves food all day but wins fans as a lively, welcoming hotspot at night. The **Bridge Tavern**, Bridge St. (☎ 67718), reverberates occasionally with music (Th trad) and is known to have informal concertina sessions on summer nights to complement the snooker.

◼ SIGHTS. The premier attraction in town is **Wicklow's Historic Gaol**, up the hill from Market Sq., which you can now inspect without leading a rebellion or stealing a loaf. The newly opened museum fills up nearly 40 cells with tableaux, audio clips, displays, and activities about the gaol, its history, and convict transportation to Australia. If the recorded wails and moans seem a bit overdone, the live actors keep things grounded and entertaining. Blow your nose at an improper time and you might get two days of bread and water. (☎ 61599; www.wicklow.ie/gaol. Open daily Apr.-Sept. 10am-5pm, Mar. and Oct. 10am-4pm. Tours leave every 10min., excepting 1-2pm. £4.20, students and seniors £3.30, children £2.60.) Above the gaol rests the dysfunctional **Family Heritage Center** (☎ 20126), functioning well for genealogy buffs. The first left past Market Sq. leads to **Black Castle**. The Normans built the castle in 1178; the local Irish lords quickly began attacking and finally destroyed it in 1301. Since then, many attacks and changes in ownership have left only a few wind-worn stones, though the promontory on which it was built is a great vantage point above the sea and meadows. The staircase cut into the seaward side of the remains reputedly accesses a tunnel to the nearby convent. At the other end of Main St., the crumbs of a 13th-century **Franciscan Friary** hide behind a small gate and a run-down hut. The Friary was founded at the same time as Black Castle and fell along with it. It was subsequently rebuilt and became a place of retirement for both Normans and native Irish, who considered it neutral ground.

A cliff trail provides smashing views en route to ◪**St. Bride's Head** (a.k.a. Wicklow Head), where St. Patrick landed on Travilahawk Strand in 432. The local population greeted him by knocking the teeth out of one of his companions (Mantan, "the toothless one" or "gubby"), who was later assigned to convert the local residents. Either cut through the golf course from Black Castle or head out the coastal road past the golf club and meet the trailhead in the parking lot on the left. Hiking to St. Bride's Head takes over an hour. On some days, sea lions frolic at the grassy rock. Adventurous walkers can continue to the isolated lighthouse at Wicklow Head (1½hr.). At Market Sq., Main St. becomes Summer Hill and then Dunbur Rd., the coastal road, from which beaches extend south to Arklow. From Wicklow, the closest strips of sun and sand are **Silver Strand** and **Jack's Hole**, though most people head to the larger stretch of **Brittas Bay**, midway between Wicklow and Arklow. Starting in the last week of July, Wicklow hosts its **Regatta Festival**, the oldest such celebration in Ireland. The two-week festival features hard-core skiff racing and, on the lighter side, a race of whimsically homemade barges; join the spectators on the bridge and let loose with eggs and tomatoes! At night, amicable pub rivalries foster singing competitions and general merriment. The **Wicklow Gaol Arts Festival** livens up mid-July nights with plays and concerts for roughly £8-12. (☎ 69117; www.wicklowartsweek.com.) Contact the tourist office for more information.

NEAR WICKLOW: AVONDALE HOUSE AND RATHDRUM ☎ 0404

Avondale House, the birthplace and main residence of political leader **Charles Stewart Parnell**, is now a Parnell museum where restorers have turned the clocks back to the 1850s. The Parnell family study contains framed love letters from Parnell to mistress Kitty O'Shea, and a small pantry off the impressive dining room is bedecked with political cartoons of the day. The 20-minute biographical video is an illuminating glimpse into Parnell's life and his role in the development of Irish independence (see **Parnell's Cultural Nationalism,** p. 15). Whether hungry for independence or a sausage roll, a small cafe downstairs can meet your needs. (☎ 46111. Museum open daily 11am-6pm. Closed on W in winter. £3, students and seniors £2.75.) Flora fanatics and hikers will fawn over several hundred acres of **forest** and parkland that surround the house and spread along the west bank of the Avonmore River. There are three hikes, each approximately one hour in length and always open: the Pine Trail, the Exotic Tree trail, and the River walk.

Avondale House is on the road from Wicklow Town to Avoca, one mile after **Rathdrum** (RAY-th DRO-ma; see below) and before the Meeting of the Waters. From Rathdrum, take Main St. heading toward Avoca and follow the signs. **Buses** arrive in Rathdrum from **Dublin** (2¾hr., M-Sa 2 per day, Su 1 per day), as do **trains** (1hr., M-F 4 per day). Rathdrum is not easily visible from the train station; after you exit the station's driveway, turn left at the *Garda* station. A 200 yd. uphill stroll will bring you to a path on your right that cuts through the Parnell National Memorial Park and up to Main Street. The **tourist office,** in the square at the center of town is helpful, offering pamphlets on other area attractions and hikes. (☎/fax 46262. Open Sept.-May M-F 9:30am-5:30pm; July-Aug. M-F 9:30am-5:30pm, Sa-Su 1-6pm. May be closed between 1-2pm for lunch.) The **post office** (☎ 46211) is concealed within "Smith's Fancy Goods" on the square, and the Bank of Ireland there has a **24-hour ATM.**

The cheapest rooming option is **The Old Presbytery Hostel (IHH),** a fairly luxurious setup in a 200-year-old former monastery, with everything from free laundry services to an exercise room (£4 per use). To find it, continue past the tourist office, turn left after the grocery store, and then right at the top of the hill. (☎ 46930; email thehostel@hotmail.com. Wheelchair accessible. Up to 6-bed dorms £9, Sept.-Apr. £8; doubles £20.) Among the many B&Bs around Rathdrum is the family-run **Woodland B&B,** on the road to Avondale House (☎ 46011. £19 per person.)

Rathdrum now serves primarily as a hub for excursions outside the town, most notably to Avondale House. The **Cartoon Inn** (☎ 46774), on Main St., a pub with wacky cartooned walls, refers to the International Cartoon Festival that Rathdrum held until recently. If you need to kill time until the bus comes, check out the **Woolpack Pub** in the square (☎ 46574. Main courses £4-7). Hollywood groupies might recognize the upstairs as one of the settings for the film *Michael Collins.*

ARKLOW ☎ 0402

When St. Kevin visited Arklow in the 5th century, he blessed the town's fishermen and guaranteed prosperity. The Anglo-Irish gentry bestowed a more tangible blessing in the 18th century by building a modern harbor, and Arklow blossomed into a strapping and well-known port and shipbuilding center. These days, the town is an increasingly popular weekend spot for Dubliners craving a break from the city.

GETTING THERE. Arklow is 40 mi. south of Dublin on N11 (Dublin/Wexford Rd.). **Trains** run to Arklow from **Dublin** on their way to **Rosslare** (M-Sa 4 per day, Su 2 per day). **Bus Éireann** runs local service to Arklow and also passes through on its way to **Rosslare** and **Wexford,** stopping by the bridge and at The Chocolate Shop on Main St. (M-Sa 7-8 per day, Su 6 per day, £6.50).

ORIENTATION AND PRACTICAL INFORMATION. The town spans the mouth of the Avoca River, with a harbor, two beaches, potteries along the quays, and most shops up the hill along Main St. The Arklow **tourist office** lies on the hill, in the kink in Main St., just past the church. (☎ 32484. Open May-Sept. M-F 9am-6pm, Sa 10am-6pm.) The **Bank of Ireland** (☎ 32004) and **AIB** (☎ 32529) on Main St. both have **24-hour ATMs.** Black's Cycle Center, Wexford Rd., is a **bike rental** agency off Main St., to the left of the rotary. (☎ 31898. Open in summer M-Sa 9:30am-6pm, winter hours vary. £10 per day.) Arklow now has **Internet access** at the **Arklow Internet Cafe,** upstairs at 6 Main St. (☎ 086 859 9058. £5 per hour, minimum £1.50.)

ACCOMMODATIONS AND FOOD. The cheapest stay in Arklow is the new **Avonmore House Hostel,** Ferrybank. Turn left off Main St. to Arklow's famous stone bridge with 19 arches. After crossing the longest stone bridge in Ireland, Avonmore will be three blocks ahead on your left. Whether you stay in a six- to eight-bed dorm (£8-9.50) or **camp** on the back lawn (£5), you'll have access to sparkling showers, kitchen, **Internet access,** and cable TV. (☎ 32825. Breakfast £2; £3 key deposit.) Avonmore is a small hostel, but Arklow also has a slew of B&Bs. **Vale View,** Coolgrevaney Rd., has glass-roofed suites on the top floor, great for star-gazing or listening to the patter of raindrops; to find it, continue straight past the roundabout on Main St., which changes names to Coolgrevaney Rd. (☎/fax 32622. £17-19.) If you go left at the roundabout (past the bike shop), and past the hostel on Ferrybank, you'll find a bevy of other B&B options.

Main St. offers a number of cheap eats; try the **Parlour Café** for all-day breakfast (£1-3), the **New Delhi** for a lunchtime sandwich (£1.50), and just about any of the pubs for dinner. The upscale **Kitty's Restaurant** on lower Main St. offers an early-bird dinner special. Though she doesn't serve food, **Mary B** on Lower Main St. (☎ 32788) offers a lounge bar with a smorgasbord of live music on weekend nights in the summer starting at around 9pm. **Maizie Kelly's,** on Coolegrevaney, right after the roundabout, is a relaxed pub that mixes the tourist and local crowds.

SIGHTS. Spread across Arklow's sea coast are several swimmable **beaches,** miles of turf for roaming, and a small **wildlife reserve** at the North Beach. Arklow's North Beach is also close to a swimming pool at the **Arklow Sports and Leisure Center,** where adults can break a sweat and then cool off in the pool for £4-5. (☎ 23328.) To reach North Beach turn right off Ferrybank onto Seaview Ave. Potheads can reenact the love scene in *Ghost* with props from the Arklow and Wicklow Vale **pottery shops** at the end of the south quay, which sell a large selection straight from the kilns, as well as glassware. If you prefer model ships to real ones, head away from the harbor and set sail for the **Arklow Maritime Museum,** on St. Mary's Rd. between the train station and Main St. (☎ 32868. Open M-Sa 10am-1pm and 2-5pm in summer; Oct.-Apr. closed on Sa. £3, students £1.50.) The two-room museum celebrates Arklow's community pride in its maritime history with photos and models of Arklow's ships, medals earned by Arklow's merchant marines in WWI, and a video on the history of the town. Hidden in binders on the window-sill are fabulous narratives of Arklow's sailors rescuing passengers from the Lusitania.

WICKLOW MOUNTAINS

Over 2000 ft. high, covered by heather, and pleated by rivers, the Wicklow summits are home to grazing sheep and a few villagers. Glendalough, a lush, blessed valley draws a steady summertime stream of coach tours from Dublin. Visitors in the know make it a point to see Ireland's largest waterfall, the Powerscourt Waterfall, in Enniskerry (see p. 131). Public transportation is severely limited, so driving is the easiest way to connect the scattered sights and towns. The climbs can be rough for hikers, but their efforts are rewarded by the best-kept trail in Ireland, the Wicklow Way, and hostels catering to their interests. Stop by the tourist offices at Bray, Wicklow Town, Arklow, and Rathdrum for advice and free, colorful maps.

GLENDALOUGH ☎0404

In the 6th century, a vision told St. Kevin to give up his life of ascetic isolation and found a monastery. He offset the austerity of monastic life by choosing one of the most spectacular valleys in Ireland and founded Glendalough (GLEN-da-lock, "glen of two lakes"). During the great age of Irish monasteries—AD 563 to 1152—monastic schools were Ireland's religious and cultural centers, attracting pilgrims from all over Europe to a "land of saints and scholars." Supported by lesser monks who farmed and traded, the privileged brothers inscribed religious texts and collected jewels and relics for the glory of God. Today the valley is known for its monastic ruins, excellent hikes, and swarms of tourists. Glendalough consists of just St. Kevin's habitat, a hostel, and an overpriced hotel and restaurant; for more affordable food, B&Bs, and groceries, travelers should head to Laragh (LAR-a), a village 1 mi. up the road (signposted; 10min. walk from the Wicklow Way; 15 mi. from Powerscourt, 7 mi. from Roundwood). On Sundays, the 2km drive to Laragh can take up to 15 minutes due to traffic.

GETTING THERE. Aside from the countless charter bus tours, most pilgrims to Glendalough come by car, a few hike the Wicklow Way into town, and the rest take buses run by the private **St. Kevin's Bus Service** (☎ (01) 281 8119), or **Wicklow Tours**. The St. Kevin's buses run from St. Stephen's Green West, Dublin (M-Sa at 11:30am and 6pm; Su 11:30am and 7pm; £6, return £10). They also leave from Bray, just past the Town Hall-cum-McDonald's (M-Sa 12:10 and 6:30pm, Su 12:10 and 7:30pm; return £6). Buses return from the glen in the evening (M-F 7:15am and 4:15pm, Sa 9:45am and 4:15pm, Su 9:45am and 5:30pm; 9:45am departure F year-round and daily July-Aug.). **Bus Éireann** (☎ (01) 836 6111 to book) also runs **tours** to Glendalough and through the mountains, with the driver as tour guide (daily Apr.-Oct.; depart Busáras Station in Dublin 10:30am, return by 5:45pm; £17, children £9). **Wicklow Tours** (☎ 67671) runs a fairly reliable van to **Rathdrum** (Avondale) and **Wicklow**. (Departs from Glendalough Hotel daily June-Aug. £4 return.) **Hitching** to Glendalough is fairly easy from Co. Wicklow towns, though from Dublin much of the Glendalough-bound traffic is bus tours. Hitchers starting at the beginning of N11 in southwest Dublin hop to the juncture of N11 with Glendalough's R755. *Let's Go* does not recommend hitchhiking.

PRACTICAL INFORMATION. Various vendors offer tourist information. The Board Fáilte **tourist office,** across from the Glendalough Hotel, provides info about the area and Dublin, and can book accommodations. (☎ 45688. Open mid-June to Sept. Tu 11am-1pm and 2-6pm, W-Su 10am-1pm and 2-6pm.) The **Glendalough Visitor Centre** (see **Sights**) helps out when the tourist office is closed. The **National Park Information Office,** between the two lakes, is the best source for hiking information in the region. (☎ 45425. Open May-Aug. daily 10am-6pm, Apr. and Sept. Sa-Su 10am-6pm. When closed, call the **ranger office,** ☎ 45338 or 45561.) **Bike rental** is available at the Glendaloch hostel. (£5 for under 5 hr.; £10 per day; £35 per week; £30 deposit.) **Laragh IT,** in the parking lot next to Lynham's pub, has **Internet access.** (☎ 45600. £5 per hr.)

ACCOMMODATIONS, FOOD, AND PUBS. The **Glendaloch Hostel (An Óige/HI)** is a five-minute walk up the road past the Glendalough visitors' center. An Óige opened up this new beauty last year after £1.3 million renovations. Prices are high, but with good beds, excellent security, and an in-house cafe, it's the best option in the area. (☎ 45342. Breakfast £2.25, £4.50 full Irish; dinners £6.50; always a vegetarian option. Towels 50p. Laundry £4. **Internet access. Bike rental.** Wheelchair accessible. Dorms £11; doubles £30; £1-2 less per person in off season.) In nearby Laragh, the **Wicklow Way Hostel** offers a less comfortable and less expensive stay. The showers are exposed, but the private rooms are cleaner and more agreeable. The attached cafe serves inexpensive breakfasts. (☎ 45398. Dorms £7.)

B&Bs abound in Laragh. One of the most welcoming is **Gleann Albhe,** next to the post office. Bathrooms, TVs, and tea facilities are found in every room, and you can look out a spectacular bay window while you choose your breakfast option. (☎ 45236. Singles £25; doubles £36-40.) Part of the view is **Oakview B&B,** down the driveway by the Wicklow Heather, where excellent, flowered rooms await. (☎ 45453. Open Mar.-Oct. Singles £24; doubles £32, with bath £38.) Follow signposts to the **Woolen Mills** shop, behind which is a 30-minute hike aptly named the Green Road that drops visitors into the splendor of Glendalough's upper lakes.

The **Wicklow Heather,** 75m up the road toward Glendalough, serves divine concoctions, especially for well-behaved vegetarians. (☎ 45157. Open daily 8:30am-

140 ■ WICKLOW MOUNTAINS

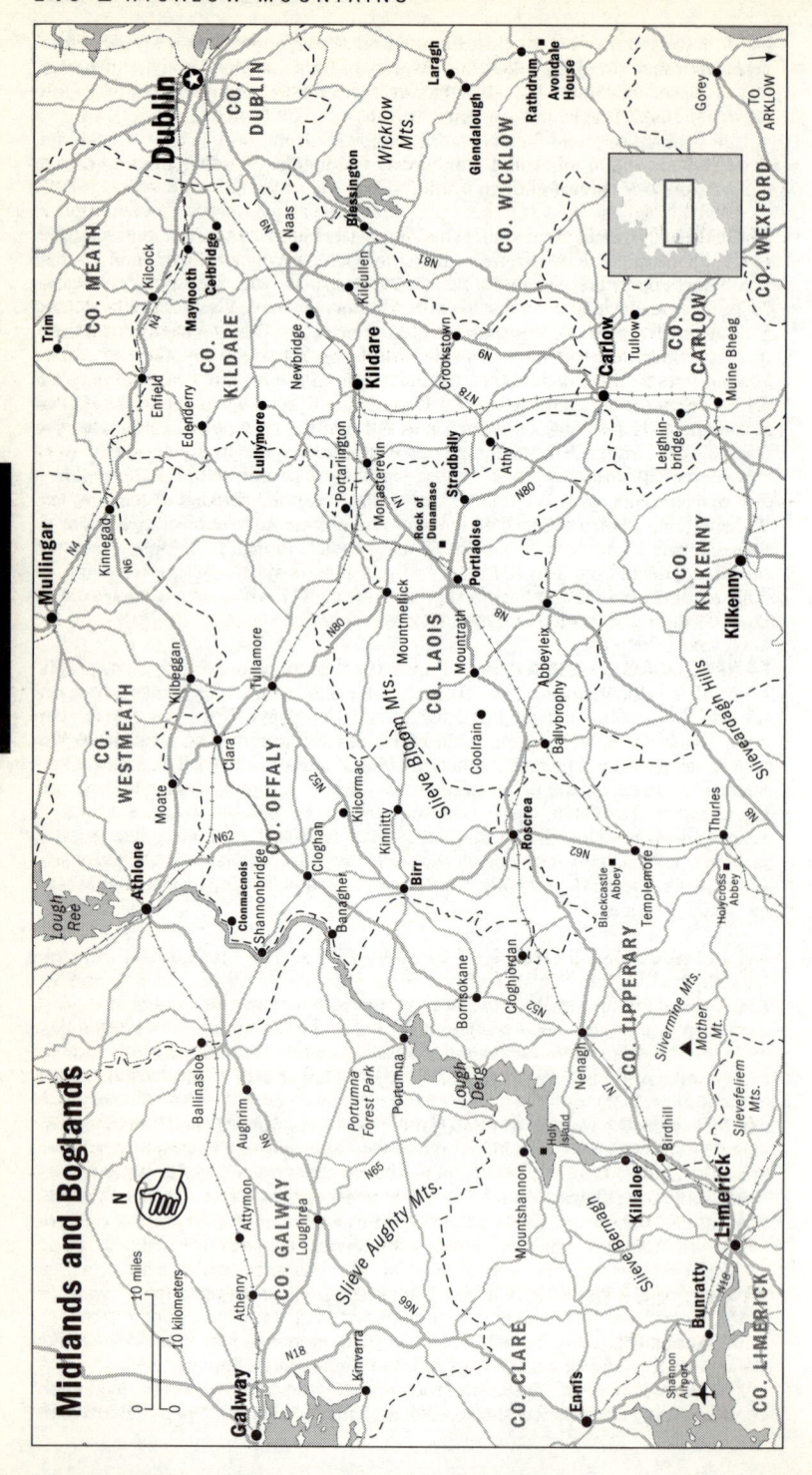

10pm. Breakfast £4.25, most entrees under £8. Baguette sandwiches £4.95.) **Lynaham's** also piles plates high with hot edibles. (☎ 45345. Entrees £7-10. Open daily 12:30-3:30 and 5:30-9pm.) Attached **Lynham's Pub** attracts travelers with its cover bands and rock sessions most weekend nights.

◨ SIGHTS. Glendalough is a single, manifold sight. Smooth glacial valleys embrace the two lakes and the monastic ruins, where the **Visitors Centre** presents everything that's known about them. The admission charge covers an exhibition, a 17-minute audiovisual show on the history of Irish monasteries in general, and a tour of the ruins. (☎ 45324. Center open daily June-Aug. 9am-6:30pm, Sept. to mid-Oct. 9:30am-6pm, mid-Oct. to mid-Mar. 9:30am-5pm, mid-Mar. to May 9:30am-6:30pm. Tours every 30min. on peak days. £2, students and children £1. Wheelchair accessible.) The ruins themselves, next to the hotel, are free and always open.

The present ruins were only a small part of the monastery in its heyday, when wooden huts for low-status laborer monks were plentiful. The centerpiece is **St. Kevin's Tower,** a 100 ft. round tower with a mere 3 ft. foundation, built in the 10th century as a watchtower, belltower, and retreat. The entrance is 12 ft. from the ground: when Vikings approached, the monks would climb the inside of the tower floor by floor, drawing up the ladders behind them. The **Cathedral,** constructed in a combination of Greek and Roman architectural styles, was once the largest in the country. In its shadow is **St. Kevin's Cross,** an unadorned, early high cross. It was carved before the monks had tools to cut holes clean through the stone (see **Early Christians and Vikings,** p. 8). The 11th-century **St. Kevin's Church,** with an intact stone roof, acquired the misnomer "St. Kevin's Kitchen" because of its chimney-like tower. After use as a church for 500 years, it lay derelict until the 19th century, when locals revived its use for a brief period.

The **Upper and Lower Lakes,** across the bridge and to the right, are a rewarding side-trip from the monastic site. Hikers and bikers can cross the bridge at the far side of the monastery and head right on the paved path for 5 minutes to reach the serene **Lower Lake.** Twenty-five minutes farther, the path hits the National Park Information Office (see **Practical Information**) and the magnificent **Upper Lake.** Drivers should continue past the hotel and park in the lot by the Upper Lake. The trail continues along the lakeside, looking across to **St. Kevin's Bed,** the cave where he prayed. Legend says that when St. Kevin prayed, his words ascended in a vortex of flame and light that burned over the Upper Lake's dark waters with such intensity that none but the most righteous monks could witness it without going blind. Farther along the trail are the **burial grounds** of local chieftains.

THE WICKLOW WAY

Founded in 1981, Ireland's oldest marked hiking trail is also its most spectacular. Stretching from Marlay Park at the border of Dublin to Clonegal, Co. Carlow, the 76 mi. Wicklow Way meanders south through Ireland's largest highland expanse. Yellow arrows and signs keep the trail well-marked along various footpaths, dirt roads, and even paved roads that weave over heathered summits and through steep glacial valleys. Civilization is rarely more than 3km away, but appropriate wilderness precautions should still be taken. Bring warm, windproof layers and raingear for the exposed summits, and while the terrain never gets frighteningly rugged, sturdy footwear is still a must (see **Wilderness Safety,** p. 72). Water is best taken from farmhouses (with permission), not streams. Open fires are illegal within a mile of the forest and should be monitored vigilantly.

✦ ▨ ORIENTATION AND PRACTICAL INFORMATION

Most tourist offices in the county sell the invaluable *Wicklow Way Map Guide* (£4.50), which is the best source for information about the trail and its sights. Six days of hiking for seven to eight hours will carry you from one end to the other, though shorter routes proliferate. Numerous side trails around the Way make excellent day hikes; *Wicklow Way Walks* (£5) outlines a number of these loops. The northern 44 mi. of the Way, from Dublin to Aghavannagh, attracts the most people with the best scenery and all of the hostels; An Óige publishes a pamphlet detailing four- to five-hour hostel-to-hostel walks. (Available at An Óige hostels in Co. Wicklow and Dublin.) A trip hitting the highlights of the Way would run from the Powerscourt Waterfall near Enniskerry (see p. 131) to Glendalough (about 20 mi.), passing the stupendous **Lough Dan**, and the even more stupendous **Lough Tay**, with views as far as Wales. For further information about the Way, contact the **National Park Information Office** (☎ (01) 45425) between Glendalough's lakes (see Glendalough, p. 138); if they're closed try the **ranger station** nearby (☎ 45338 or 45561). Forestry lands are governed by **Coillte** (KWEEL-chuh, ☎ (01) 286 7751), though much of the Way is simply on a right-of-way through private lands.

GETTING THERE AND GETTING AROUND

Several bus companies can drop you off at various spots in the mountains. **Dublin Bus** (☎ (01) 873 4222) runs frequently to Marlay Park in **Rathfarnham** (#47B and 48A) and **Enniskerry** (#44, or 85 from **Bray**), and less frequently to **Glencullen** (#44B). **Bus Éireann** (☎ (01) 836 6111) comes somewhat near the Way farther south, with infrequent service from **Busáras** to **Aughrim, Tinahely, Shillelagh**, and **Hackettstown**. **St. Kevin's** (☎ (01) 281 8119) runs two shuttles daily between St. Stephen's Green West (in **Dublin**), **Roundwood**, and **Glendalough** (£6, return £10). To avoid trail erosion, bikes are allowed only on forest tracks and paved sections of the Way, but many off-Way roads are equally stunning. For a particularly scenic route, take R759 to **Sally Gap**, west of the Way near Lough Tay, and then head south on R115 past **Glenmacnass Waterfall** to Glendalough (roughly 15 mi.).

ACCOMMODATIONS

Camping is feasible along the Way but generally requires planning ahead. Many local farmhouses will let you pitch a tent on their land if you ask. National Park lands are fine for short-term, low-impact camping; pitching a tent in state forest plantations is prohibited. An Óige runs a cluster of hostels, most of which lie quite close to the Way; except for the Glendalough Hostel, all bookings are handled through the An Óige head office in Dublin (☎ (01) 830 4555, email anoige@iol.ie). Hostels line the Wicklow Way from north to south in the following order:

- **Glencree (An Óige/HI),** Stone House, Enniskerry (☎ (01) 286 4037). From Enniskerry, 12km out on the Glencree Rd. 3½km off the Way and a bit too remote. Dorms June-Sept. £7, Oct.-May £6.50.

- **Knockree (An Óige/HI),** Lacken House, Enniskerry (☎ (01) 286 4036), on the Way. A reconstructed farmhouse 4 mi. from the village and 2 mi. from Powerscourt Waterfall. From Enniskerry, take the right fork road leading uphill from the village green, take a left at Buttercups Newsagent, and begin a steep walk, following signs for Glencree Dr. Fireplace in the dining area. Sheets £1. Lockout 10am-5pm (unless it's raining). Dorms June-Sept. £7, Oct.-May £6.50.

- **Tiglin (An Óige/HI),** a.k.a. **Devil's Glen,** Ashford (☎ 0404 40259), 5 mi. from the Way by the Tiglin Adventure Centre. From Ashford, follow Roundwood Rd. for 3 mi., then follow the signs for the Tiglin turnoff and R763 on the right; a hilly 8 mi. from Powerscourt. 50 beds in basic, single-sex dorms; mattresses are droopy, but sleepable. Towels 50p. 11pm curfew. June-Sept. £7, Oct.-May £6.

- **Wicklow Way Hostel** (☎ (0404) 45398), beside the Way in Laragh. Dorms £7. See **Glendalough**, p. 138.

- **Glendaloch (An Óige/HI;** ☎ (0404) 45342), a stone's throw from the Way, by the monastic ruins. Dorms £11; doubles £30. See **Glendalough**, p. 138.

- **Glenmalure (An Óige/HI),** Glenmalure. At the end of a dead-end road, 12km south along the Way from Glendalough. On the roads, head from Glendalough to Laragh and take every major right turn. Back-to-nature lodging; not even connected by telephone. June-Sept. £6.50, Oct.-May £5.50.

A number of B&Bs along the Way offer **camping** and pick-up, if you call ahead. The *Wicklow Way Map Guide* comes with a sheet that lists about twenty. The following few will both allow camping and pick-up hikers if necessary. **Coolakay House** is 2½ mi. outside Enniskerry, neighbors the Powerscourt Waterfall, and even has a small cafe. (☎ (01) 286 2423. £23 per person.) In Knockananna, **Hillview B&B**, Tinahely, sits 1 mi. from the Way. (☎ (0508) 71195. Singles £16; doubles £30. **Camping** £3-5 per person.) **Rosbane Farmhouse**, Rosbane, is a seven-minute walk from the Way, near the summit of Garryhoe. (☎ (0402) 38100. £19 per person. **Camping** £4 per tent.) **Orchard House**, Tinahely, is within earshot of the trail. (☎ (0402) 38264. Singles £22-24; doubles £36-40. **Camping** £10 per tent.)

WESTERN WICKLOW

Squatter, lumpier, and less traveled than the rest of the county, western Wicklow offers scenic hikes for misanthropes. You won't find picnicking families from the suburbs here. It's possible to hike through western Wicklow and the Wicklow Way, but turn around if you see a red flag—Communists! Actually, the straight-shooting Irish Army maintains a few shooting ranges in the region. Hiking is safe in areas without flags. To reach **Ballinclea Hostel (An Óige/HI)**, hike 2½km uphill to Donard (well-signposted), and then follow the hostel signs for another 2½km uphill. Clean, simple, and well off the beaten path, Ballinclea offers good access to hikes in the region. (☎ (045) 404 657. Lockout 10am-5:30pm. Open daily Mar.-Nov.; Dec.-Feb. F-Sa. Sheets £1. Dorms £7.) More beds exist in Blessington.

BLESSINGTON   ☎045

Blessington lies beside the reservoir of the Liffy, close to the intersection of the N81 from Dublin and the R410 from Naas. Hikers come to rest here after exploring the western Wicklow Mountains, while cultured types make the daytrip from Dublin to check out the world-class art at Russborough House.

Russborough House spreads its Palladian grandeur 3km south on the N81, toward Baltinglass. Richard Cassells, who also designed Dublin's Leinster House and much of Trinity College, built the house in 1741 for Joseph Leeson, a member of the Anglo-Irish parliament. Russborough now houses an impressive collection of paintings, sculpture, furniture, and baroque plaster-work. In 1986, a Dublin gangster known as "The General" orchestrated the theft of the 17 most valuable paintings, including works by Goya, Vermeer, and Velasquez; all but one have since been recovered. The best pieces are now in the National Gallery in Dublin, but a few excellent ones remain, among them a Rubens. Unfortunately, the tour is little more than a catalog of each room's contents. (☎ 865 239. Open Easter-Apr. and Oct. Su 10:30am-5:30pm, May-Sept. daily 10:30am-5:30pm. Admission by hourly 45min. tours only. £4, seniors and students £3, children £2.)

The easiest way to reach town is by the hourly #65 **bus** from Eden Quay in Dublin (£2.35). **Bus Éireann** also passes through on its Dublin-Waterford route (M-W and Sa 2 per day, Th and Su 3 per day, F 4 per day); only southbound buses will pick up passengers, while northbound buses drop off. Turn to the Blessington **tourist office**, in the town square, for ideas on outdoor pursuits. (☎ 865 850. Open mid-June to Aug. M-Sa 10am-5pm, Su erratically; Sept. to mid-June M-F 10am-2pm.) **Ulster Bank**, Main St. (☎ 865 125), has a **bureau de change** and an **ATM**. **Hillcrest Hire**, Main St., **rents bikes**. (☎ 865 066. £8 per day, £34 per week; £40 deposit.)

Five miles out on the road to Valleymount in an old schoolhouse, **Baltyboys (An Óige/HI)**, known simply as the Blessington Lake Hostel, has excellent views and a warden who will bend over backwards to help you out. (☎ 867 266. Lockout 10am-5pm. Open daily Mar.-Nov., Th-Su. Dec.-Feb. June-Sept. dorms £7.50, Oct.-May £6.50; students £5.50, under 16 £4.50.)

COUNTY KILDARE

The towns immediately west of Dublin in Co. Kildare are still well within the city's orbit; the best sights—Kildare's horses and Lullymore Heritage Park—make easy daytrips. The county is linked to Dublin by more highways: half of Kildare was included in the Pale, the region of English dominance centered around Dublin. From the 13th to the 16th century, the FitzGerald Earls of Kildare controlled all of eastern Ireland. Today, mansions and the big-money Irish Derby evoke Kildare's former prominence, and it remains an international hotspot of the horse world.

MAYNOOTH ☎ 01

A growing Catholic seminary and university makes Maynooth (ma-NOOTH) a town of the erudite and the religious. In 1795, King George III was concerned that priests educated in Revolutionary France would acquire dangerous notions of independence. He granted permission for St. Patrick's College, the first Catholic seminary in Ireland, to open. He later said that opening St. Patrick's "cost me more pain than the loss of the colonies." The Maynooth Seminary was the only site for training Irish Catholic priests during much of the 19th century. Priests are still ordained here, but the 120 clerical students are far outnumbered these days by their 5000 peers in other disciplines.

GETTING THERE. Maynooth is 15 mi. west of Dublin on the M4. Suburban **trains** run from Connolly Station in **Dublin** (20min.; M-Sa 15 per day, Su 3 per day; £1.60). **Bus** #66 runs directly to Maynooth, and #67A gets there via **Celbridge** (both about 1hr.; roughly 2 per hr.; £1.70 from Middle Abbey St. or £1.15 from the quays by Heuston Station). **Hitchers** from Dublin stand on Chapelizod Rd., between Phoenix Park and the Liffey, or even farther west where Chapelizod becomes Lucan Rd. *Let's Go* does not recommend hitchhiking.

PRACTICAL INFORMATION. The **Citizens Information Centre**, upstairs on Main St., before Cassidy's Roost Inn, is a volunteer-staffed center that answers questions about the area and hands out photocopied maps. (☎ 628 5477 or 629 5065. Open M-F 9:30am-4:30pm.) **usit** has a budget travel office on Main St., specializing in student travel and discounts. (☎ 628 9289. Open M-F 9:30am-5:30pm, Sa 10am-1pm.) The **St. Patrick's Visitor Centre** (see **Sights,** below) also provides helpful information about the town and area. The **Cyber X Internet Cafe** provides **Internet access** in the Glenroyal Shopping Center off Celbridge Rd. (☎ 629 1747. Open daily noon-midnight. £5 per hr., students £3.)

ACCOMMODATIONS, FOOD, AND PUBS. St. Patrick's College rents out student apartments during the summer; the fee includes access to the college sports facilities. Loads of options include luxury suites and self-catering apartments. The housing office is under the right arch of Stoyte House, the first building apparent as you enter the old campus. Knock on the unlabeled wooden door on the right. (Contact Bill Tinley ☎ 708 3726; email Guest.Rooms@may.ie. Available mid-June to Sept. Singles £16-18, with breakfast £21.50; doubles from £27, with breakfast £38.) The **Leinster Arms,** Main St., is mainly a pub, but it's also a great B&B value for groups since guests pay a flat £30 per room. Tea, coffee, and TVs in each room. Reserve ahead in summer; some rooms have bath and kitchen. (☎ 628 6323. Food served 10:30am-10pm.) Enjoy light fare and lots of baked goods at **Elite Confectionery,** Main St. (☎ 628 5521. £2-3. Open M-Sa 9am-6pm.)

SIGHTS. The powerful FitzGerald family controlled its vast domain from **Maynooth Castle,** built in 1176. Since being dismantled in 1647, the castle has crumbled, leaving only the ruins of a few block-like towers, which nevertheless cast a stately shadow over the beer can-strewn lot on Main St. Hundreds of birds will take off when you climb the staircase to the roofless Great Hall and become the sole, if temporary, resident of the castle. (Pick up key from Mrs. Bernadette Foy, 10 Parson St., on the road across from the castle. £5 key deposit.) Beside the castle sits **St. Patrick's College,** whose sculpted gardens and austere architecture put students in the right frame of mind to study Catholic dogma. The impressive **College Chapel,** ornamented from top to toe, dates from the late 19th-century Gothic revival and resides in a building designed by A.W. Pugin. Pugin Hall is actually the newest building on **St. Joseph's Square,** despite its aged appearance. In the college's **Bicentennial Garden** behind Pugin Hall, walk the Path of Saints or the Path of Sinners, past Fonts of Faith, Understanding, and Pain, or gaze meditatively at a carving of the Apocalypse in 5000-year-old bog wood. Behind that courtyard, follow the building around to the left to reach a cathedral nave of interwoven trees, leading to a small cemetery that spans centuries. The **Visitor Centre,** in the left arch of the Georgian Stoyte House, the first building visible as you enter the old campus, provides a campus map and Christian paraphernalia displays. Their tours of the college, given on demand, are worth your while. (☎ 708 3576. Open M-F 11am-5pm, Sa-Su 2-6pm. Tours £3, students £2.) The college's **Ecclesiastical Museum** combines Catholic ritualistic props with 19th-century scientific equipment. (Open Tu and Th 2-4pm, Su 2-6pm. £1.)

DAYTRIP FROM MAYNOOTH

CELBRIDGE

Buses #67 and 67A run to Celbridge from Middle Abbey St., Dublin. (£1.70; #67A also stops in between at Maynooth.) The Arrow suburban rail arrives roughly every hr. at the Hazelhatch & Celbridge stop from Dublin's Heuston Station (£6). A shuttle bus runs the large distance between the station and town during peak hours; otherwise it's a £3 taxi.

The *raison d'être* of Celbridge (SELL-bridge) is **Castletown House,** the magnificent home of sometime Speaker of the Irish House of Commons, William Connolly. The richest man in 1720s Ireland, Connolly built himself this magnificent home and touched off a nationwide fad for Palladian architecture. After major refurbishing, the castle opened for public tours last summer and has since been trying to reclaim its sumptuous original furniture from disparate corners of the world. At this point the rooms are pretty bare. What does survive is worth seeing; the print room, with Ireland's only surviving cut-out wall decorations, and the garish Venetian chandeliers in the Long Gallery are particularly fantastic. The tours go heavy on architectural history. (☎ (01) 628 8252. Open Apr.-May Su 1-6pm; June-Sept. M-F 10am-6pm, Sa-Su 1-6pm; Oct. M-F 10am-5pm, Su 1-5pm; Nov. Su 1-5pm. Last tours 1¼hr. before closing. Admission by guided tour only; tours should start on the hour, with more tours during the high season. £3, seniors £2, children and students £1.25.) Instead of donating money to charity, Connolly's widow built an obelisk 2 mi. behind the estate to employ famine-starved locals in 1740. Known as **Connolly's Folly,** its unruly stack of arches was copied and enlarged for the original plans of the Washington Monument. At the other end of Main St., the grounds of **Celbridge Abbey** harken back to a rich girl's enigmatic relationship with Jonathan Swift around 1700. Elegant gardens and walks make for fine picnicking. (☎ 627 5508. Open M-Sa 10am-6pm, Su noon-6pm. £3.50, seniors and children £3.)

KILDARE ☎ 045

Kildare is Ireland's horse-racing mecca. Carefully bred, raised, and raced here, purebloods are the lifeblood of the town. Kildare's past was more influenced by Christianity; it grew up around a church founded here around 480 by St. Brigid. The sacred lass chose a site next to an oak tree that she saw in a vision, giving the town its original name *Cill Dara*, meaning "Church of the Oak." The center of town is a triangular square ("The Square") scarred, unlike its calmer equine periphery, by the unceasing trucking traffic of the N7.

COUNTY KILDARE

GETTING THERE. Kildare saddles the busy, harrowing N7 (Dublin-Limerick) and is well-connected by **train** to **Dublin's** Heuston Station (40min.; M-Th 12 per day, F 14 per day, Su 11 per day; £7.50). Head straight out of the train station for several blocks to reach The Square. **Bus Éireann** hits big, bad **Dublin** (1½hr.; M-F 14 per day, Sa 13 per day, Su 7 per day; £6.50), and if you place your money right you may even land in **Cork** (3½hr.; 3 per day, Su 2 per day; £12) or **Limerick** (2½hr., 14 per day). **Rapid Express Coaches** (☎ (01) 679 1549) offers a cheaper service between Middle Abbey St. (Dublin) and Kildare (4-6 per day, £2.50).

PRACTICAL INFORMATION. The Kildare **tourist office** is temporarily based just off the Square as it remodels, but it still offers basic information. (☎ 522 696. Open June-Sept. M-Sa 10am-1pm and 2-6pm.) The **Bank of Ireland**, The Square, has a **24-hour ATM**. (☎ 521 276. Open M 10am-5pm, Tu-F 10am-4pm.) If you can't ride a horse, **Bikes and Bits** offers **bike rental** on Claregate St. (☎ 521 457. Open M-Sa 9am-6pm. £5 day, £25 week.) The **post office** is on Dublin St., near The Square. (☎ 521349. Open M and W-F 9am-5:30pm, Tu 9:30am-5:30pm, Sa 10am-1pm.)

ACCOMMODATIONS, FOOD, AND PUBS. Accommodations in Kildare are neither handsome nor sleek. A short walk from The Square, **Fremont**, Tully Rd., sets up its rooms in a quasi-rural setting, en route to the Stud Farm and Japanese Gardens. (☎ 521 604. Singles £22; doubles £34.) Five miles out of town, in the middle of nowhere, Julie and Colm Keane run the new **Eagle Hill B&B** on a working sheep farm. As you approach the town southbound, take the left before Kildare and follow the Eagle Hill signs to top-notch beds, showers, and morning meals. Call for pick-up. (☎ 526 097. £20 per person.)

If you're hungry enough to eat a horse, **Kristina's Bistro**, Main St., next to Bikes and Bits, serves large and delectable lunches for £4-5. The "big plate" harnesses a large entree and appetizer for £8.50. (☎ 522 895. Lunch 12:30-2:30pm.) Pubs are plentiful, and most serve food. **The Silken Thomas**, The Square, has locally renowned meals, ranging from sandwiches (£2-3) to bar lunches (lamb with mint sauce £5.25) to pricey entrees. (☎ 522 232. Food served 12:30-10pm.) The pub's name isn't a euphemism, but a reference to "Silken Thomas" FitzGerald, who raised a revolt against the British in Dublin in 1534. **Li'l Flanagan's**, in back of The Silken Thomas, is a small, delightfully scruffy, old-time pub with dark, low ceilings and open peat fires. (☎ 522 232. Trad or rock W-M.) **Nolan's**, The Square (☎ 521 528), is a low-key pub that was once a hardware store. The saws are gone, but Nolan's compensates with trad most nights.

SIGHTS. The 10th-century **Round Tower**, just off The Square, is one of the few in Ireland that visitors can actually enter and climb up; most of the others have no floors inside. (Open M-Sa 10am-1pm and 2-5pm, Su 2-5pm. £2, children £1.) Recently restored **St. Brigid's**, a Church of Ireland cathedral that has weathered over 200 derelict years, lies in the shadow of the tower. The cathedral dates from the 12th and 13th centuries, and sits on the site of a church founded by St. Brigid in AD 480. A small exhibit on Christianity in Ireland lies inside. Brigid was one of the first and only powerful women in the Catholic Church, accidentally ordained as a bishop by the scatter-brained Mel of Ardagh. (Open May-Oct. M-Sa 10am-1pm and 2-5pm, Su 2-5pm.) Next to the church is **St. Brigid's Fire Temple**, a pagan ritual site that Brigid repossessed for Christianity. Only female virgins were allowed to tend the fire, which burned continually for 1000 years. Archbishop George Browne of Dublin ended all of this (by extinguishing the flames, not the virginity).

More exciting is ⚑**The Irish National Stud and Japanese Gardens**, "where strength and beauty live as one." Colonel William Hall-Walker, the mastermind behind the 1900 creation of the Stud, was a little eq-centric. The mystical son of a Scottish brewer, he would cast a foal's horoscope at its birth; if unfavorable, the foal would be sold, regardless of its lineage. These days, the Irish National

Stud farm facilitates the rearing of thoroughbred racehorses. The mating season kicks off, appropriately, on Valentine's Day. The small **Irish Horse Museum** tells the history of the horse with a few displays and the skeleton of Arkle, a quite dead champion. Tours leave every hour to educate the ignorant about the world of stud farms, racing, and euphemisms for sexual intercourse. The tours are straightforward and an excellent introduction to roaming around the farm. **The Japanese Gardens** tell the allegory of the "life of man" through a beautiful, if male-oriented, semi-narrative trail. From the cave of birth to the hill of mourning, visitors experience learning, disappointment, and marriage in the media of caves, hills, and bridges. Hall Walker designed it, and while he was clearly a few leaves short of a bonsai, it makes a worthy game. The newest addition to the Stud grounds is the four-acre **St. Fiachra's Garden,** that opened just last year for the new millennium. St. Fiachra's is a peaceful garden that blandly evokes "monastic spirituality" with quiet lakes, huts, and a pit of Waterford Crystal. (1 mi. from The Square out Tully Rd. and well signposted. ☎ 521 617 or 522 693; email stud@irish-national-stud.ie. Open daily mid-Feb. to mid-Nov. 9:30am-6pm; last admission 5pm. 35min. guided tours of the National Stud leave on the hour beginning at 11am. £6, students and seniors £4.50.)

THE CURRAGH

Entertainment in Kildare is understandably equinocentric. Between Newbridge and Kildare on the M7 lies **The Curragh,** 5000 acres of perhaps the greenest fields in Ireland. Thoroughbred horses graze and train, hoping one day to earn fame and fortune at the **Curragh Racecourse** (☎ (045) 441 205), which hosts the **Irish Derby** (DAR-bee) on the first Sunday in July. The Derby is Ireland's premier sporting and social event, and one of the most prestigious races in the world. Other races are held from late March through October, roughly every third weekend (Sa and Su only). The Irish Rail timetable lists dates, and trains stop at The Curragh on race days. (**Train** £14 from Heuston Station, includes admission. Admission generally £8-10, but up to £35 for the Derby; students and seniors half-price.) **Bus Éireann** also serves the Curragh on race days (leaves 1½hr. before races from **Dublin,** £9). Hit the Curragh as early as 7:30am, and watch scores of horses take their daily training run on one of the five gallops, each 1-1½ mi. long. Driving off-road is acceptable within reason, but horses always have the right of way.

PEATLAND WORLD AND LULLYMORE

The boglanders know to whom to turn in times of need: their friend, peat. Ten miles from Kildare in Lullymore, **Peatland World** explains this phenomenon. Located on a mineral island in the immense Bog of Allen, Peatland World features a museum and natural history gallery. On display are bog-preserved prehistoric artifacts, a model of an Irish cottage with a turf fire, and trophies from turf-cutting competitions. (☎ (045) 860 133. Open Apr.-Oct. M-F 9:30am-5pm, Sa-Su 2-6pm; Nov.-Mar. M-F 9:30am-5pm. £3, students £2.50.) Two miles toward Allentown, the **Lullymore Heritage & Discovery Park** shows what life in the boglands was like from the Mesolithic era to the 1798 rebellion to the Famine. To reach Lullymore from Kildare, take Rathangan Rd. to Rathangan, and then Allentown Rd. from there. (☎ (045) 870 238. Open Apr.-Oct. M-F 9am-5pm, Sa-Su noon-6pm, Nov.-Mar. M-F 9am-4:30pm; other times by appointment. 1½hr. tour. 3 tours per afternoon daily in summer. £3.50, students £3.) Buses drive to **Allenwood,** a few miles north of Lullymore, from **Dublin** (1hr; M-Sa 8 per day, Su 3 per day; £4.40).

COUNTY MEATH

Meath is a hush county, with ancient crypts lurking in its hills. The Hill of Tara was Ireland's political and spiritual center in pre-historic times, and retains its mystery of purpose. In pre-Norman times, Meath was considered Ireland's fifth province.

BOYNE VALLEY

The thinly-populated Boyne Valley safeguards Ireland's greatest archaeological treasures, and is about a one-hour bus ride from Dublin. Massive passage tombs like Newgrange create subtle bumps in the landscape that belie the cavernous underground chambers they cover. They are older than the Pyramids and at least as puzzling: virtually nothing is known about the rituals and design on which they are based. The Celtic High Kings once ruled from atop the Hill of Tara, leaving a wake of mysterious folklore. The Hill's enduring symbolic significance and 360-degree views attract visitors a-plenty, as do the well-preserved Norman fortifications in the town of Trim. According to legend, St. Patrick lit a flame atop the Hill of Slane that brought Christianity to Ireland. Every so often, farmers plow up artifacts from the 1690 Battle of the Boyne (see **Drogheda**, p. 153), which are filed away in a small information center.

BRÚ NA BÓINNE: NEWGRANGE, KNOWTH, AND DOWTH

Along the curves of the river between Slane and Drogheda sprawls Brú na Bóinne (broo na BO-in-yeh, "homestead of the Boyne"). The 10 sq. km landscape swells with no fewer than 40 passage tombs all circa the 4th millennium BC. The Neolithic farming architects' mind-boggling engineering talents constructed Newgrange, Dowth, and Knowth within walking distance of one another in the valley.

One explanation for their existence proposes that improvements in farming gave people some extra time to build structures that would remain intact and even waterproof some 5000 years later. The larger mounds took a good half-century to build, by men with only 30-year lifespans. Hundreds of enormous kerbstones were moved by raw manpower from 10km away (each took 80 men four days), and countless smaller rocks were boated in from 80km away in Wicklow. Passage tombs are hardly limited to the Boyne Valley, but the world's largest and finest tombs are here. Their grandeur is enhanced by their mystery—the residents of and reasons for the tombs remain unknown, despite continued excavations.

The most impressive of the three, for archaeologists if not for visitors, is **Knowth** (rhymes with "mouth"). Evidence exists of a hunter-gatherer settlement on the site (4000 BC), and also of an extraordinary number of more recent dwellers: the Stone Age brainiacs who built the mound you see today; mysterious Bronze Age "beaker people," named for their distinctive urns; Iron Age Celts, whose many burials include two headless men with their gaming dice; and Christians as late as the 12th century. The enormous passage tomb houses an unusual *two* burial chambers, back to back, with separate entrances east and west. Knowth's artistic carvings are the best-preserved, with unexplained spirals and etchings adorning the passage. Long-term excavations, and the demands of preservation, prevent visitors from entering the tomb, but the visitors center tour (see below) offers a peek.

Newgrange regained a fraction of its ancient prominence in the 1960s when a roof box was discovered over the passage entrance. At dawn on the shortest day of the year (Dec. 21), and for two days to either side, 17 minutes of golden sunlight reach straight to the back of the 19m passageway and irradiate the burial chamber. The calendar alignment, while impressive, is quite common in passage tombs; Newgrange is unique in having a separate entrance exclusively for the worshipped golden orb. Because the passage is shorter and a little wider than Knowth, you can actually enter into the cool bowels of the one-acre mound and see two-thirds of all the Neolithic art in Western Europe. Amidst the intricately carved patterns, diamonds, and spirals, you can read graffiti from 18th-century visitors who clearly didn't have the brains of their distant ancestors. The highlight of the tour is a simulation of the golden winter solstice.

Dowth (rhymes with "Knowth") has been closed to the public for several years, because of ongoing excavations. To gain admission, get a Ph.D. in archaeology. To access Knowth and Newgrange, it's necessary to pay admission into the **Brú na Bóinne Visitors Centre,** located near Donore on the south side of the River Boyne, across from the tombs themselves. Do not try to make your way directly to the sites—a guard minds the gate. Instead, head to the visitors center and immediately book a tour. The place is mobbed every day in the summer, and Sundays are manic; from June through August, you'll most likely be turned away if you get there after 2:30pm, since the tours have limited sizes. While you wait for your tour, check out the center's excellent exhibit on how gifted and talented stone-agers lived. A nifty film on the winter solstice runs every 15 minutes. Remember to dress appropriately to visit the passage tombs, as most of the tour takes place outside, and Neolithic tombs lack central heating. (☎ (041) 988 0300. Open Mar.-Apr. 9:30am-5:30pm, May 9am-6:30pm, June to mid-Sept. 9am-7pm, the rest of Sept. 9am-6:30pm, Oct. 9:30am-5:30pm, Nov.-Feb. 9:30am-5pm. Admission to center only £2, seniors £1.50, students and children £1; center and Newgrange tour £4, £3, £2; center and Knowth £3, £2, £1.25; center, Newgrange, and Knowth £7, £5, £3.25. Tours last 1hr. and start every 30min. until 1½hr. before closing. Last admission to center 45min. before closing.) Downstairs, a **tourist office** can give you a free area map. (☎ (041) 980305. Open daily 9am-7pm.)

To reach the center from Drogheda, turn left by the bus station and head straight on the uphill road. It's a pleasant 5 mi. bike ride, and hitchers report successful journeys, despite *Let's Go*'s non-recommendation. **Bus Éireann** (☎ (01) 836 6111) shuttles to the visitors center from **Dublin** (1½hr.; M-F 5 per day, Sa-Su 4 per day; £10 return), stopping at **Drogheda** (10min., £3 return). Several guided bus tours from Dublin include admission to the sights. Bus Éireann covers Newgrange and either Tara/Trim or Mellifont/Monasterboice (Sa-Th, £19). Just down the road from the Newgrange site, **Newgrange Farm** has a coffee shop and a petting zoo for the kids. Willie Redgrave will charm kids and parents alike with his tractor tour of the farm, including a smaller passage tomb, a bit of wildlife, and agitated bulls. (☎ (041) 24119. Open daily Easter-Aug. 10am-6pm; last admission 5pm. 30min. tour leaves Su 3 and 4pm, or whenever there's enough interest. £1.50.)

HILL OF TARA

From prehistoric times until at least the 10th century, Tara was the political and often religious center of Ireland. Three of the 70 sites strewn around the hill have been excavated, leaving archaeologists and tourists with a fistful of questions. They do know that ancient peoples built a Stone Age tomb and an Iron Age fort here. Later it was the seat of the powerful Uí Néill family, when control of Tara theoretically entitled a warlord to be High King. Ownership of the hill was disputed until the 10th century, but the arrival of St. Patrick around AD 400 deposed Tara from its position as the Jerusalem of Ireland. In modern times, the hill's aura persists; Daniel O'Connor gathered "a million" people here for a Home Rule rally in 1843, and a cult destroyed one site a century ago in their fervent search for the Arc of the Covenant. Five thousand years of history have left a strong mark of myth and legend, much of which is refuted by archaeological findings—the interest of the site lies in choosing which side to believe.

The enormous site is about 5 mi. east of Navan on the N3. Take any local (not express) bus from Dublin to **Navan** (1hr.; M-Sa 37 per day, Su 15 per day; £5.50) and ask the driver to let you off at the turnoff, to the left and marked by a small brown sign. The site is about a mile straight uphill. The actual buildings—largely wattle, wood, and earthwork—have long been buried or destroyed; what you'll see are grassy, windswept dunes forming concentric rings. They are always open for exploration, but to make any sense of them you have to hit the **visitors center,** in the old church at the site. The center displays aerial photos of Tara, and shows a good 20-minute slideshow about Tara's history. After the film, your ticket entitles you to an excellent guided tour (35min.) that circles the site. The full site encompasses 100 acres of many smaller mounds and ring forts, though the tour usually covers only the sites at the top of the hill. (☎ (046) 25903. Center open daily early-May to mid-June and mid-Sept. to Oct. 10am-5pm, mid-June to mid-Sept. 9:30am-6:30pm. £1.50, seniors £1, students and children 60p.)

TRIM   ☎046

A flock of enormous, well-preserved Norman castles and abbeys overlook this jewel of a heritage town on the River Boyne. Jaded travelers should treat themselves to this daytrip from Dublin.

GETTING THERE AND ORIENTATION. Bus Éireann stops on Castle St. in front of the castle en route to **Dublin** (1½hr.; M-Sa 8 per day, Su 3 per day; £5). **Castle St.** intersects the central **Market St.**, which has most of the town's shops, then crosses the **River Boyne** under the pseudonym **Bridge St.** and curves uphill on the far side as **High St.** before splitting. The left fork becomes **Haggard St.** and the right side becomes the road to the nearby Newtown ruins.

PRACTICAL INFORMATION. Trim's **tourist office**, Mill St., has a useful map of Trim's sights and meaty information on Meath. (☎ 37111. Open daily 10am-1pm and 2-5pm.) The **Bank of Ireland** surveys Market St. (☎ 31230. Open M 10am-5pm, Tu-F 10am-4pm.) The **post office** (☎ 31268) collects stamps up the street.

ACCOMMODATIONS, FOOD, AND PUBS. The **Bridge House Tourist Hostel**, perched next to the tourist office, on the River Boyne, offers a mixed bag of coed rooms, ranging from cramped to luxurious. The nifty TV lounge is a converted medieval wine cellar. (☎ 31848. Free towels. 4-bed dorms £10; doubles £25; all with bath.) Trim's B&B options are, on the whole, excellent. To reach the sunny and spacious **White Lodge**, call from the bus stop for a pick-up, or cross the bridge and stay to the right at the fork with Haggard St. At the second fork, again stay right, even though a small sign says "cul-de-sac." The lodge is 100 yd. ahead. (Non-smoking. Singles £25, doubles £34-38; £3 cheaper per person without breakfast.) In the heart of town, **Brogan's**, High St., offers top-notch rooms with TV, bath, and telephones. (☎ 31237. Singles £25; doubles £40.)

Get your groceries at **SuperValu**, at the top of Haggard St. (☎ 31505. Open M-W and Sa 8am-7:30pm, Th-F 8am-9pm, Su 8am-6pm.) **The Pastry Kitchen,** Market St., is a greasy spoon that serves a decent meal. (☎ 38902. Sandwiches £1.50. Open M-Sa 7:30am-6pm, Su 10am-2pm.) For lunch, head to **The Abbey Lodge,** Market St., for a huge plate of standard pub fare. (☎ 31285. Meals £4-5. Lunch served 12:30-2:30pm.) The **Emmet Tavern** (☎ 31378), on Emmet St. (left as you face the post office), has boisterous customers. Bring your fiddle to old-fashioned **The Bounty** (☎ 31640), across the street from the hostel.

SIGHTS. **Trim Castle**, first built by Norman invader Hugh de Lacy in 1172, sits majestically in Trim's center, now open to the public with a regal £3 million facelift. The castle served as the center of Trim life during the Middle Ages when Trim was a powerful and populous town with seven monasteries. When Norman power here collapsed, the castle lost nearly all its strategic importance and therefore survived relatively untouched. Now, touched up, tourists can visit the castle grounds and tour the keep. The keep tours cost a little extra, but the renovations inside are extraordinarily well done, and the views from the top temporarily make you King of Meath. If visiting the home of the lusty Hugh de Lacy does not inspire, Mel Gibson also filmed several scenes of *Braveheart* at the castle in 1994. You can take the tour, but you'll never take his freedom. (☎ 38619. Open May-Oct. 10am-6pm. Admission with 35-45 min. guided tour only. Tours every 45min. and limited to 15 people, so sign up upon arrival in Trim. No tour required to wander the grounds. Tour and grounds £2.50, students £1. Grounds only £1, 40p.)

Across the river stands what's left of the 12th-century **Yellow Steeple**, a belltower named for its twilight gleam; the gleam left with the lichen that was removed during restoration. In its shadow, **Talbot's Castle** was adapted from the steeple's original abbey and lived in by Jonathan Swift and the undefeated, jazzy Duke of Wellington at different points. Despite the "private house" sign, the current owner often provides tours of its motley interior upon request. To get there, take the first right after crossing the bridge; a right-of-way through the driveway leads to the Yellow Steeple and the **Sheep Gate,** the only surviving medieval gate of the once walled town. Ten minutes out on Dublin Rd. in the direction opposite the castle, you can hear your own glorious voice bouncing off the ruins of **St. Peter and St. Paul's Cathedral,** across the river from **Echo Gate.** The cathedral grounds contain a tomb with two figures mistakenly called the **Jealous Man and Woman.** The name comes from the sword between them, which conventionally signified not resentment but chastity. Put a pin between the two figures; when the pin rusts (which shouldn't take long in this damp country) your warts should disappear.

For more spicy history, **Trim Visitors Centre,** next to the tourist office on Mill St., educates and frightens with a multimedia presentation and an excellent, dramatic slideshow. Displays describe decapitations, the lecherous behavior of sinewy, hairy Hugh de Lacy, and hideous plague rats—maybe Trim isn't so prim and proper after all. (☎ 37287. Open M-F 10am-5pm, Su 1:30-5pm. Closed for lunch 12:30-1:30pm. Admission for the 35min. shows every 45min. £2.50, students and seniors £1.75.) Green thumbs will enjoy the **Butterstream Gardens,** a 15-minute walk past the SuperValu and left of the off-license. The several serene acres of paths, flowers, and pools are especially beautiful in late June. (☎ 36017. Open daily Apr.-Sept. 11am-6pm. £4, students £2.)

For one week each June (usually the last), the **Scurlogstown Olympiad Town Festival** fills Trim with animal shows, carnival rides, and traditional music concerts.

BEYOND THE VALLEY OF THE BOYNE

KELLS (CEANANNAS MÓR) ☎ 046

Kells is internationally famous thanks to a book that neither began nor ended up there. The monastery at Kells was founded by St. Columcille (colum-SEEL or colum-KEEL; also known as St. Columba) in 559, before he went on to found the more important settlement of Iona on an island west of Scotland. At Iona, the famous *Book of Kells,* an elaborately decorated Latin version of the Gospel, was begun. It came to Kells in some form of development in 804, when the Columbans fled Iona. In 1007, the book was stolen, its gold cover ripped off, and the pages buried in the bog, from which they were rescued two months later. It remained in Kells until 1661, when Cromwell carted it off to Trinity College Dublin, where it is now recovering. Kells is trying to get the book back, which Trinity finds amusing.

Even without the book, Kells boasts some of Ireland's best-preserved monastic ruins, including an oratory, a round tower, and four high crosses. The fifth and largest cross, Market Cross, stood for a millennium with relatively little mishap before it was knocked off its pedestal two years ago by a school bus driver. The discombobulated cross has been moved to Trim.

GETTING THERE AND PRACTICAL INFORMATION. Bus Éireann stops outside the tourist office en route to Dublin (1hr.; M-Sa 2 per hr., Su 12 per day; £6.70). The **tourist office,** housed inconspicuously in the town hall on Headfort Pl., provides free town maps and a handy heritage trail booklet. (☎ 49336. Open M-F 9am-5pm.) **AIB** bank has an **ATM** on John St. (☎ 40610. Open M 10am-5pm, Tu-F 10am-4pm.) The **post office** sits on Farrel St. (☎ 40127. Open M-Sa 9am-5:30pm.)

ACCOMMODATIONS, FOOD, AND PUBS. Kells Hostel sports a big kitchen, a friendly staff, and decent facilities, although the showers leave a bit to be desired. A giant map painted on the common room wall points denizens to sights, restaurants, and pubs. From the center of town, head uphill on Carrick St.; the bus from Dublin will stop across the street from the hostel. Hostelers can use the attached gym for £3. (☎ 49995. Open Mar.-Dec. Laundry £4.50. June to mid-Sept. coed 7-bed dorms £8; private 2- to 4-bed rooms £12 per person; mid-Sept. to Dec. and Mar.-June £7.50, £10.)

B&Bs in town are pricey but excellent. **White Gables**, Headfort Pl., is just down the hill from the tourist office on the left. The rooms are top-notch, the garden is a splendid enclave, and your eggs will be cooked by a former chef. (☎ 40322 or 49672; email kelltic@tinet.ie. Singles £25; doubles £40.)

SuperValu is smack-dab across from the hostel. (Open M-W and Sa 8am-7:30pm, Th-F 8am-9pm, Su 9am-6:30pm.) **Pebbles**, Newmarket St., is the most popular coffee shop in Kells, serving up a light fare. (☎ 49229. Lasagne £1.50, lunch specials around £4. Open M-Sa 8am-5:30pm.) **The Round Tower**, Farrell St., offers a sizeable menu of grub within a wide price range. (☎ 40144. Food served until 9pm.) Get a hell of a meal at **Dante's**, Market St., which serves up pasta and pizza (among other circular allusions) in abundance. (☎ 41630. Lunch £5, dinner around £8. Open noon-3pm and 6-11pm.) **O'Shaughnessy's**, Market St. (☎ 41110), has good pub grub (£4.50) and a variety of live music Friday through Sunday evenings. **The Blackwater Inn**, Farrell St., offers much music. Black water? They must mean Guinness. (☎ 40386. Trad M, rock W and F.) The students drink until they drop at **Chaser's**, Cross St., and enjoy the music and pool table until 1am.

■ SIGHTS. As part of its centuries-long position as a center of Christian learning, the monastery at Kells was a favorite target of rival monasteries. The current structure, with the exception of the 12th-century belltower, dates back only as far as the 1700s. Most sights lie straight up the street from the tourist office. Inside **St. Columba's Church**, there's a replica of the *Book of Kells*, and copies of selected pages enlarged for your viewing pleasure. (☎ 40151. Open M-F 10am-1pm and 2-5pm.) Four large **high crosses** covered with biblical scenes sprinkle the south and west side of the church. The north cross is little more than a stump, but the east cross remains intact and depicts the making of crosses. A 12th-century wall successfully encircled the church until 1997, when the County Council began building a path alongside it that undermined its foundations and caused it to topple. The nearby 100 ft. round tower failed to serve any protective function: its monks were torched, its book and saintly relics were stolen, and the would-be High King Murchadh Mac Flainn was murdered in it in 1076. If you hoist yourself up into its doorway and look in, the pigeons may use your head as a bull's-eye.

Fortune reserved her smile for **St. Columcille's House**, across Church Ln., an awe-inspiring oratory where the *Book of Kells* may have been completed. Pick up the key from Mrs. Carpenter in a beige house at 10 Church Ln., and head 200 yd. uphill to the unmistakable oratory. The place looks almost exactly as it would have in St. Columcille's day, except that the current doorway enters into the basement, which was originally connected by a secret tunnel to the church. In centuries past, the three tiny attic rooms housed large relics and larger families.

ANALYZING INSECURE CASTLES When you're scampering around the half-ruins of Ireland's medieval castles, take a minute to think about the stairs. Even in castles designed to be homesteads, stairs could be a significant form of defense. Most obvious is the occasional absence of them: a number of castles had their doorways on the second (Irish "first") floor, so that access was only possible through a ladder that could be raised. And if attackers made it past the moat, gate, and walls, the staircases inside could still favor the owner. The distances between steps are often awkwardly inconsistent, not from poor construction but rather to trip any strangers running up. And the twists in the spirals are significant, too: some steps curve up to the left—making ascending assaulters attack as southpaws, while defenders descending could fight with the right. In a culture where left-handedness was suppressed as a sign of the devil, fighting right-handed was practically universal. Sometimes, castles were built with stairs curving right, favoring the invader; in such instances, the owner was so often away from his castle that reclaiming it from rogues was expected to be a regular affair.

Two miles down Oldcastle Rd., within the People's Park, is the **Spire of Loyd,** a 150 ft. viewing tower erected by the old Headfort landlords. Constructed as a work project for the poor, its ostensible purpose was to allow the Headfort women to watch the hunt comfortably and safely. (Adults £1.50, children £1.) Next to the spire is the recently restored **Graveyard of the Poor,** where the area's huge pauper population buried its dead in mass graves during the Famine.

LOUTH, MONAGHAN, AND CAVAN

Co. Louth's Cooley Peninsula boasts hills and seacoasts that hold a position of high esteem in the minds of hikers, bikers, and ancient bards. The tiny villages of Co. Cavan and Co. Monaghan make convenient and pleasing rest-stops on journeys to the Northwest. Belturbet in Co. Cavan is covered under the Fermanagh Lake District in Northern Ireland.

DROGHEDA ☎ 041

Drogheda (DRA-hed-a) slopes steeply over the Boyne river. Cheerful pubs on inland streets counter its drab and industrial waterfront. Drogheda's Norman past lingers in the crumbling walls and gates that surround the city. Most sights in Co. Meath are a pleasant bike ride from Drogheda.

GETTING THERE AND GETTING AROUND

Trains: ☎ 983 8749, east of town on the Dublin road. Follow John St. south of the river. To **Dublin** (1hr., express 30min.; M-Sa 20 per day, Su 7 per day; £9) and **Belfast** (2hr.; M-Sa 7 per day, Su 4 per day; £14).

Buses: Station on John St. (☎ 983 5023), at Donore Rd. Inquiries desk and **luggage storage** open M-F 9am-6:15pm, Sa 8:30am-1:30pm. To **Dundalk** (40min.; M-Sa 13 per day, Su 10 per day; £4.40), **Dublin** (50min.; M-F 24 per day, Sa 17 per day, Su 9 per day; £4.80), **Belfast** (2hr.; M-Sa 7 per day, Su 3 per day; £8.60), **Mullingar** (2hr.; M-Th and Sa 1 per day, F 2 per day, Su 1 per day; £5), **Athlone** (2½hr.; M-Th and Sa 1 per day, F 2 per day, Su 1 per day; £9), and **Galway** (4hr.; M-Th and Sa 1 per day, F 2 per day, Su 1 per day; £14).

Bike Rental: Quay Cycles, 11 North Quay (☎ 983 4526). £8 per day, £30 per week; ID deposit. Helmet included. Open M-Sa 9am-6pm.

PRACTICAL INFORMATION

Tourist Offices: (☎ 983 7070), in the bus station. Has a regional and *Drogheda Town Map* (£1). Open M-Sa 9:30am-5:30pm, Su noon-5pm. A superior 2nd office is in Millmount (☎ 984 5684); head to the Martello tower. Open M-F 9:30am-1pm and 2-5pm.

Banks: Numerous banks line West St. **AIB** (☎ 983 6523) and **TSB** (☎ 983 8703) have **ATMs.** Both open M-W and F 9:30am-5pm, Th 9:30am-7pm.

Emergency: ☎ 999; no coins required. **Police** (*Garda*): West Gate (☎ 983 8777).

Hospital: Our Lady of Lourdes, Cross Lanes (☎ 983 7601).

Laundry: FM Laundrette, 13 North Quay (☎ 983 6837). Self-service £4.50. Open M-Sa 9am-6pm.

Post Office: West St. (☎ 983 8157). Open M-Sa 9am-5:30pm; Tu late opening 9:30am.

ACCOMMODATIONS

The **Green Door Hostel,** 47 John St., is the best place to stay in Drogheda. One block up from the bus station, it offers top-notch beds in a friendly atmosphere that more than compensates for the small kitchen and common area. A porch on the Boyne magnetically attracts BBQ and good *craic*. (☎ 983 4422. Laundry £2.

Limited **Internet access.** Bike and car park. June-Sept. 10-bed dorms £10; doubles £32; triples £39; Oct.-May £9, £30 £36.) Drogheda's older hostel/quasi-B&B, **Harpur House (IHO),** William St., is cheap but ranks far behind the Green Door in terms of quality and a smoke-free environment. Follow Shop St. from the bridge up the hill, continue up Peter St. and take a right onto William St.; the hostel is the last house on the right. (☎ 983 2736. Full Irish breakfast £2. 10-bed dorms £7; private rooms £12 per person.) Well-kept and backpacker-friendly, **Abbey View House,** Mill Lane, is making the slow transition to guest house by converting several standard rooms to en suites. From the bus station, head north on the Belfast Rd. (N1) over the bridge and take the first left and the first left again. Sitting pretty on the River Boyne, the house has parking, big rooms with patchwork quilts, and an alleged tunnel to Monasterboice. (☎ 983 1470. Singles £20, with bath £25; doubles £30, £40.) Amiable Denbis Dineen at the **Roseville Lodge B&B,** Georges St., offers motel-like rooms, all with bath. (☎ 983 4046. Singles £21; doubles £35.)

FOOD AND PUBS

An **open-air market** has been held in Bolton Square every Saturday since 1317. **Dunnes Stores** (☎ 983 7063) and the smaller **Tesco** (☎ 983 7209) on West St. have groceries every day. (Both open M-Tu 9am-7pm, W-F 9am-9pm, Sa 8:30am-6:30pm, Su noon-6pm; Tesco open until 7pm on Sa.) **Monk's,** North Quay, is a shiny cafe with decidedly non-austere breakfasts and lunches—if your name is Jerry, you might go for cereal. (☎ 984 3680. Open M-Sa 8:30am-6pm, Su 10:30am-5pm.) The heritage center (see **Sights,** below) is home to tasty **Mollie's Coffee Shop,** with excellent mocha for £1.50. **La Pizzeria,** 38 Peter St., cooks all kinds of Italian specialities. It's also very popular, so make reservations or arrive before 9pm if you want a seat. (☎ 983 4208. Pasta £5.50, pizza around £6. Open M-Tu and Th-Su 6-11pm.) For breakfast or a tasty sandwich creation, heat it up at **Jalepeño** on West St. (Sandwiches £4-5. Open M-Sa 8:30am-6pm.) **Bridie Mac's,** West St., supplies everything from snacks (£3) to full meals (£7) to live music. (☎ 983 0965. Bar food served daily 3-8pm. Music Th-Sa.)

As the largest town in the area, Drogheda has a pretty active nightlife. Dark wood engulfs **Peter Matthews,** 9 Laurence St., better known as **McPhail's,** a very old, very likeable pub. (☎ 983 7371. Live rock, blues, jazz, and Latin Th-Su nights.) **The Weavers,** West St., is renowned for its carvery lunch and dinner grub, but the crowd really comes for cover bands and top 40 DJs on weekends. (☎ 983 2816. No cover.) Sessions in the poster-plastered confines of **Cairbre (Carberry's),** Back Strand, stand out among the town's sparse trad offerings.

When the pubs close, Drogheda keeps on running like a syndicated Hanna-Barbera cartoon. **The Earth,** in back of the Westcourt Hotel on West St., resembles a Flintstones pub, with fossil-embedded walls and bar, rock-themed bathrooms, and not a single straight wall. (☎ 983 0969. Open Th-Su from 11pm. Cover £5; less with concession available at Bridie Mac's.) George and Jane Jetson whizz around the corner to **Number 4,** Stockwell Ln., for the sleekest and trendiest of late bars. (☎ 984 5044. Open past 2am. DJ Th-Su, live bands F. Cover £2-5 Th-Sa.) Leave Pebbles and Elroy at home—Number 4 is 21+, and the Earth is 23+.

SIGHTS

TOURS. Walking Tours of Historical Drogheda provide a good introduction to town. (☎ 984 5684. 1½hr. Tours leave Tu-Sa at 10:20am and 2:20pm from Millmount. £1.50, seniors £1.) Better still is doing the walk on your own under the guidance of either the *Drogheda Heritage Route* pamphlet or the *Local Story* booklet, both available at the Millmount tourist office.

MILLMOUNT MUSEUM AND DROGHEDA HERITAGE CENTRE. The newly reconstructed Martello tower dominates the skyline. Inside, the **Millmount Museum** displays artifacts from the Civil War period (see **Independence and Civil War,** p.

THE SIEGE OF DROGHEDA Cromwell's two-day siege of Drogheda in 1649 was the first time in the town's illustrious history that its walls were breached. Originally twin towns separated by the Boyne, Drogheda was well-entrenched on both sides, and only a retractable drawbridge connected the two halves. So how did a warty man like Cromwell win so quickly? He was a lying, lucky bastard. One of the Drogheda captains had a wooden leg, so Cromwell sparked a rumor that the limb was full of gold. (His troops must not have been too bright, since no one could possibly walk with that sort of weight.) The rumor worked: Cromwell's men tracked down the poor captain faster than you can say "greed," and immediately ripped off his prosthesis. Disappointed that a wooden leg is, in fact, merely wood, they consoled themselves by beating the captain to death with his own limb—no doubt one of the more ignoble deaths in military history. If Cromwell's troops were gullible, though, the Drogheda citizens were just plain clueless. Retreating from Cromwell's bloody charge, once the walls were breached, the Droghedans all crossed from the south side of the river to the north—and forgot to raise the drawbridge behind them. Cromwell proceeded to flame-broil the town, churches and all.

17), antique household appliances, and a geological collection. The museum also offers tours of the recently restored Martello tower that was shelled during the Irish Civil War. The tours are roughly 25 minutes and whiz through Drogheda's copious military history. *(Up the hill from the bus station.* ☎ *983 3097. Open Apr.-Oct. M-Sa 10am-5:30pm, Nov.-Mar. W and Sa-Su 2-5pm. Museum only £2.50, student £2, seniors and children £1.50. Tour only £2, £1.50, £1. Museum and tour £3.50, £2, £2.)* Behind it, on Mary St., the new **Drogheda Heritage Centre** has a mural-timeline that paints the contours of Drogheda history. It also hosts special exhibits, and a 25-minute video presentation straightens out the Battle of the Boyne.

CHURCHES. Drogheda has two **St. Peter's Churches,** both worth visiting. Stare face-to-face with a blackened, shriveled head in the imposing, neo-Gothic St. Peter's Church on West St. Built in the 1880s, St. Peter's safeguards what's left of the martyred saint Oliver Plunkett. A handful of his bones are on display, as is the door of his London prison cell. *(Open daily 8:30am-8:30pm.)* The other St. Peter's Church (Church of Ireland) hoards bad luck up at the top of Peter St. The original timber structure was destroyed in a 1548 storm. Another timber structure replaced it, only to be torched (with refugees inside) by Cromwell in 1649. The present church dates to 1753. Mounted on the wall of the cemetery's back left corner are **cadaver tombs,** with brutally realistic carvings of the half-decayed bodies of a man and woman. Dating from 1520, they are two of only 19 such tombs left in the world. At the end of West St. stand the four-story twin towers of **St. Laurence's Gate,** a 13th-century outer gate that is no less impressive for never having faced a serious attack. At the top of the hill on Peter St., the 14th-century **Magdalen Tower,** covered with tufts of grass, is all that remains of the Dominican Friary that once stood on the spot. Old Abbey, south of West St., collects urban refuse under the few remaining arches of the 5th-century **Abbey of St. Mary d'Urso.**

OTHER SIGHTS. The Battle of the Boyne raged at **Oldbridge,** 3 mi. west of Drogheda on the Slane Rd. In 1690, William of Orange's momentous victory over James II secured for Protestants the English Crown and at least the eastern half of Ireland (see **The Protestant Ascendancy,** p. 11). A small information trailer parks there now, providing historical and genealogical information about the battle. You can climb some steps for a view of the battle site, but there's little to see. *(☎ 984 1644. Open all year M-F 9:30am-5pm, May-Sept. additionally Sa-Su 10am-5pm. £1.)*

During the second week of July, locals swagger through the streets to the Latin rhythms of the **Samba Festival.**

MONASTERBOICE AND MELLIFONT ABBEY

What were once two of the most important monasteries in Ireland stand crumbling 5 mi. north of Drogheda. The grounds of **Monasterboice** (MON-uh-ster-boyce) hold a round tower and some of the most spectacular high crosses in existence. The monastery was one of Ireland's most wealthy from its founding around AD 520 until the Vikings sacked it in 1097. (Always open. Free.) A volunteer information office mans the site, giving out information on the crosses or impromptu tours. (Open July-Aug. M-Sa 10am-6pm.) **Muireadach's Cross,** the first high cross you'll see upon entering, sports an array of Biblical scenes and Celtic designs. On one side, Satan pulls down his side of the Judgment scales and then kicks 14 souls to hell. At a height of nearly 7 yd., the **West Cross** is the tallest High Cross in Ireland.

As the monastery at Monasterboice fell, the Cistercians planted their first foothold for Rome just a few miles away. **Mellifont Abbey** quickly grew from its 1142 founding to become one of Ireland's wealthiest monastic settlements, playing host to a number of tragedies en route. The 1152 Senate of Mellifont weakened the independent Irish monastic system, and sent their traditions of scholarship into decline. Three years later Cistercian Pope Adrian IV issued a bill giving the English King authorization to "correct" Ireland, which served as approval for the Norman invasion of the 1170s. In 1603, the last of the O'Neills, who had once ruled Ulster, surrendered to the English here and then fled Ireland for the Continent (see **Feudalism,** p. 9). The ruins lack grandeur as well as basic substance, since most of the site's stones were plundered between 1727 and 1880 for use in nearby buildings. The romanesque octagon of the **lavabo,** where monks once cleansed themselves of sins and grime, offers a sense of the original structure's impressiveness. A small visitors center offers a good tour of the site that explains the ruins with a Marxist twist. (☎ (041) 982 6459. Open daily May to mid-June 10am-5pm, mid-June to mid-Sept. 9:30am-6:30pm, mid-Sept. to Oct. 10am-5pm. £1.50, seniors £1, students 60p. After hours the site is free.)

Both sets of ruins are well-signposted off the Drogheda-Collon Rd. The best route for cyclists heads 5 mi. north on the wide shoulder of the N1 (Belfast Rd.) until the Dunleer exit; at the bottom of the ramp, turn left and follow the Monasterboice signs. When that road ends, turn right and veer left when you meet the larger Drogheda-Collon Rd. to get to Mellifont and eventually return to Drogheda. The Mellifont visitors center has a free hand-drawn map of the area.

DUNDALK ☎ 042

The home of the Harp brewery, Dundalk is located at the mouth of Dundalk Bay. Recently, the town has made efforts to establish itself in the tourism industry as a source of knowledge about the history and mythology of the Cooley Peninsula. Unfortunately, this mid-sized town suffers from big-city congestion during the day; it has a more long-standing reputation as a nightlife hub for locals throughout the eastern counties.

☞ GETTING THERE. The N1 highway zips south to Dublin and north to Belfast, becoming A1 at the border. The **train station** (☎ 933 5526) is on **Carrickmacross Rd.** From Clanbrassil St., turn right on Park St. then right on Anne St., which becomes Carrickmacross. Trains run to **Belfast** (1hr.; M-Sa 7 per day, Su 4 per day; £9) and **Dublin** (1hr.; M-Th 10 per day, F 11 per day, Sa 12 per day, Su 5 per day; £11). **Buses** stop at the Bus Éireann station (☎ 933 4075) on Long Walk, which is parallel to Clanbrassil, and run to **Belfast** via **Newry** (1½hr.; M-Sa 7 per day, Su 3 per day; £7), and **Dublin** (1½hr.; M-F 16 per day, Sa 13 per day, Su 7 per day; £7).

☞ ORIENTATION AND PRACTICAL INFORMATION. The main street in Dundalk is **Clanbrassil St.,** with **Park St.** as the runner-up. Dundalk's streets change names often; Clanbrassil becomes **Market Square,** then **Earl St.** as it heads south. Earl St. intersects **Park St.,** which becomes **Francis St.,** then **Roden Pl.,** then **Jocelyn St.** if you head left from Earl St. To the right, Earl St. becomes **Dublin St.** The **tourist office,** Jocelyn St., provides the free *Dundalk Town Guide,* which includes maps marked with the city's sights. From the bus stop, take Clanbrassil St. down to Park and turn left to reach Jocelyn St.; the office is on the right after the cathedral. (☎ 933 5484. Open June-mid-Sept. M-F 9:30am-5:30pm, Sa 9:30am-1pm and 2-5:30pm; mid-Sept.-May M-F 9:30am-1pm and 2-5:30pm.) **Banks,** including the **AIB,** and the **Bank of Ireland,** are scattered within a block of each other on Clanbrassil St.; most have **24hr. ATMs. FonaCab,** Francis St. (☎ 937 4777), has 24-hour **taxi** service. Additionally, many taxis stand in the square. The **post office** is on Clanbrassil St. (☎ 933 4444. Open M and W-Sa 9am-5:30pm, Tu 9:30am-5:30pm.)

ACCOMMODATIONS, FOOD, AND PUBS. **Glen Gat House,** 18-19 The Crescent, rests off Anne St. near the train station, around the corner from Dublin St. Its award-winning garden and quality accommodations justify the splurge. (☎ 933 7938; glengat@indigo.ie. £20 with breakfast.) In town, **Oriel House,** 63 Dublin St., is well located and inexpensive. Its dim rooms lack any accoutrement, though the proprietress is lovely. (☎ 933 1347. Singles £12; doubles £20.)

Restaurants and late-night fast food cluster on the main streets in town. The sign hanging in the window of **Deli Lites** on Clanbrassil St. challenges passersby with "Try our delicious sandwiches, no one likes a coward." (☎ 932 9555. "Titanic Sandwich" £1.95. Open M-Sa 9am-6pm.) **Cafe Metz,** Francis St., serves hip meals to hipsters in a very hip joint. (☎ 933 9106. Sandwiches £3.50. Open W-Su 8:30am-10:30pm, Tu until 6pm.)

Only the trepidatious will need guidance in seeking out Dundalk's pub scene, but here are a few picks. The miniature buggy in its front window and the antiques inhabiting its cabinets lend **M. Courtneys,** 43-44 Park St., the air of a converted carriage house. Hitch up here for a night of good *craic* and, perhaps an impromptu session of trad. (☎ 932 6652. Open 4:30pm-late.) The **Windsor Bar,** Dublin St., is convenient to Oriel House and serves particularly tasty pub grub. (☎ 933 8146. Full meals £5.50, sandwiches £2; food served noon-3pm.) **Mr. Ridleys,** 92 Park St., welcomes patrons with live music and a nightclub running almost nightly. (☎ 933 3329. Cover varies.) **Jockey's,** on Anne St., tempts pedestrians with its alluring front, and serves good, cheap pub grub during the day. (☎ 933 4621. Breakfast daily 10am, lunch noon-3:30pm. Trad F 10pm.) Dance an Irish jiggy wit' it at Park Street's **Imperial Hotel,** home of the **Arc Nightclub,** a late-night disco. (☎ 933 2241. Bar open daily 11:30am-11:30pm. Club open Th-Su 10:30pm-2:15am. Cover varies.)

SIGHTS. The gothic **St. Patrick's Cathedral,** Francis St., was modeled after King's College Chapel in Cambridge. (☎ 933 4648. Open daily 7:30am-5pm.) Next to the tourist office, the **County Museum** caters to those with a particular interest in "Louth's industrial legacy"—perfect for that research paper on Louth's tractors. It's real draw, however, is upstairs on two newly opened floors exhibiting the archaeology, mythology, and history of the county. Other gems include reproductions of a prehistoric cave dwelling and modern Irish living room. (☎ 932 6578. Open Tu-Sa 10:30am-5:30pm, Su 2-6pm. £2, students and seniors £1, children 60p.) In the far northwest corner of town off Mount Ave., the 12th-century **Cúchulainn's Castle** supposedly stands on the birthplace of this famous hero of the **Ulster Cycle** of myths (see **Legends and Folktales,** p. 23). The seven-story-high **Seatown Windmill** was once the largest in Ireland, but the wind was taken out of its sails when they were removed in 1885. Beaches beckon from **Blackrock,** 3 mi. south on R172.

COOLEY PENINSULA

The numerous trails in the mountains that surround the Cooley Peninsula are a hiker's paradise, and Carlingford Lough has the warmest waters in the northern half of the island. Several ancient Irish myths are set in this dramatic landscape, among them the epic *Táin bo Cuailnge*, "The Cattle Raid of Cooley" (see **The Power of Wit and the Famous Bull,** p. 24). Remarkably well preserved stone remnants of medieval settlements are scattered throughout the peninsula.

CARLINGFORD ☎ 042

Situated at the foot of Slieve Foy, the highest of the Cooley Mountains, the coastal village of Carlingford has hardly grown in size since it hit its mercantile heyday in the 14th to 16th centuries. Today, its magnificent narrow alleys and tidy buildings house numerous craft shops and closet-sized art galleries. The village, a little pile-up of buildings and ruins, was named "Tidiest Town" by Board Fáilte.

GETTING THERE AND PRACTICAL INFORMATION. Buses (☎ 933 4075) stop along the waterfront on their way to **Newry** (30min., M-Sa 2 per day) and **Dundalk** (50min., M-Sa 5 per day, £3.20). **Teach Eoalais** (CHOCK OAL us), in the Holy Trinity Heritage Centre at the town's edge, offers **tourist information.** (☎ 937 3888.) From the bus stop, walk half a block inland and half a block to the left. (Open mid-June-Aug. daily 9:30am-7pm; Sept.-mid-June M-F 9:30am-5pm.) The **AIB bank** on Newry St. is seldom open, but has a **24-hour ATM.** (☎ 937 3105. Open Tu and Th 10:30am-12:30pm and 1:30-2:30pm.) For **taxi** service call **Gally Cabs** (☎ 937 3777).

ACCOMMODATIONS, FOOD, AND PUBS. At the **Carlingford Adventure Centre and Hostel (IHH),** Tholsel St., the friendly staff leads adventurers down long cement-block corridors to small, dark rooms with wooden bunks. The hostel is often filled with groups of school children; call ahead in May and June. (☎ 937 3100. Open Feb.-Nov., all year for groups. 8-bed dorms £8.50; 4-bed dorms £9.50; bunked doubles £21.) **B&Bs** in Carlingford tend to be posh and expensive. You can dance the *hora* all the way to the **Shalom B&B,** Ghan Rd., sign posted from the waterfront. Outstanding mountain views, a "passion suite," **Internet access,** and the owner's unparalleled hospitality make this B&B Carlingford's nicest place to stay. (☎ 937 3151. Singles £25; doubles £38.) **Murphy House,** Dundalk St., offers small, charming rooms in a converted 18th-century cottage. (☎ 937 3735. Singles £25, available weekdays; doubles £36.) **Viewpoint,** Omeath Rd., just off the waterfront beyond King John's castle, provides motel-style rooms with baths, private entrances, and incredible views of the mountains and the lough. (☎ 73149. £20.)

Carlingford contains a handful of pubs and eateries, whose offerings range from traditional Irish hospitality to supernatural phenomena. Particularly good *craic* is on tap at **PJ Anchor's Bar.** It's barely larger than a breadbox, but tight quarters make for close friendships. During good weather, the backyard provides an alternative location to drink with the locals and devour locally caught oysters (£3.50 for six). Inside, the publicans proudly display the clothes of a leprechaun caught in the nearby hills several years ago. (See **The Leprechaun of Slieve Foy,** below. ☎ 937 3106. Open M-Sa 10:30am-11:30pm, Su 12:30pm-11pm). Down the street, **Carlingford Arms,** Newry St., serves hearty meals. (☎ 937 3418. Entrees around £5. Food served M-Sa 12:30-10pm, Su until 8:30pm. Folk music F-M nights.) Homemade sweets and light lunches are for the taking at **Georgina's Bakehouse,** located atop Castle Hill. (☎ 937 3346. Soup, sandwich, deserts about £2 each. Open daily 10:30am-6pm.)

SIGHTS. The **Holy Trinity Heritage Centre,** Church Yard Rd., is housed in a renovated medieval church squeezed between several recent centuries' worth of buildings. The center's staff educates visitors on the history and local lore of Carlingford from the 9th century to the present. (☎ 937 3454. Open Sa-Su and bank holidays noon-5pm. £1, children 50p.) Nearby, the ruins of the **Dominican Friary** are open for exploration. You can pretend that you're a Dominican friar and Cromwell is oppressing you. Carlingford's three other surviving medieval buildings provide interesting scenery for a stroll through town, but their interiors are closed to visitors. **King John's Castle,** by the waterfront, is the largest and most foreboding of Carlingford's medieval remains. Built in the 1190s and named for King John, who visited briefly in 1210, the castle is now locked as renovations are taking place. **Taaffe's Castle,** toward town along the quay, was built in the 16th century as a merchant house on what was then the waterfront, and it contains classic Norman defensive features. In a tiny alley off Market Square, the turret-laden, 16th-century

> **THE LEPRECHAUN OF SLIEVE FOY** One misty morn about a decade ago, PJ (the late owner of PJ's Anchor Bar) was going about his usual morning work—painting murals over the windows of abandoned houses—when he heard a high-pitched yell. On his way to investigate the source of the noise, he met a school teacher who had also heard the scream. The men's keen ears soon led them to the place where the yell had originated. About halfway up Slieve Foy was a "fairy ring" of trampled grass with bones and a wee leprechaun suit at its center. The men picked up the leprechaun's remains and returned to Carlingford with their amazing discovery in hand. Further investigation determined that the bones were from a sheep. However, as PJ later commented, everyone knows that leprechauns are changelings, and this one had probably turned into a sheep on the men's approach. The story soon reached the ears of national and international reporters, and for a short time afterwards, Carlingford was known worldwide as the town that had seen a leprechaun.

Mint is fenestrated with five ornate limestone windows. At the end of the street, one of the old 15th-century town gates, the **Tholsel** (TAH sehl), makes a narrow passageway for cars entering town. The **Adventure Centre** (see **Accommodations**, above), gives instruction in **canoeing, windsurfing, kayaking, currach building, sailing,** and a new **high ropes** course. (☎ 937 3100. Day trips start at £22.)

For those seeking more group-oriented recreation with spirits and brews, Carlingford hosts several festivals during the year. In late September, a **medieval banqueting weekend** brings parades, costumes, and indigestion, and a weekend-long **folk festival** draws musicians from all over the Republic.

MONAGHAN ☎047

Monaghan (MOH-nah-han; pop. 6000) is a busy, lake-side market town that's encircled by minor, egg-shaped hills called drumlins. Its inland location means most tourists fly by it on their way from Dublin to coasts north and west. While not many look in at Monaghan, it still looks out, and boasts a thriving, eclectic music scene—you're as likely to hear a harmonica in a pub as you are a *bodhrán* or even a saxophone. Surprisingly, the town is relatively tourist-free, but that just means the *craic* is less polluted.

GETTING THERE AND PRACTICAL INFORMATION. The **bus depot** is five minutes north of Market Sq. From the station, walk against traffic up North Rd. to reach the center of town. (☎ 82377. Open M-Sa 8:30am-8pm.) Buses run to **Belfast** (1½hr.; M-Sa 5 per day, Su 2 per day; £6.50) and **Dublin** (2hr.; M-Sa 7 per day, Su 3 per day; £7). From Church Sq., walk up the Market St. hill to find the **tourist office.** (☎ 81122. Open June-Sept. M-Sa 9am-6pm, Su 10am-2pm. Call for winter hours.) **AIB,** the Diamond (open M 10am-5pm, Tu-F 10am-4pm), has an **ATM. Tommy's** (☎ 84205) runs **taxis.** You can **rent bikes** at **Clerkin's** on Park St. (☎ 81113. £5 per day. Open M-W and F-Sa 9am-1pm and 2-6pm.) The **post office** lies just north of Church Sq. on Mill St. (☎ 82131. Open M-Sa 9am-6pm.) **Resolutions,** on Dublin St., which stretches away from the Diamond, is convenient for keeping promises-to-write with its row of **Internet**-enabled computers. (☎ 38156. Open M-F 11am-11pm, Sa 11am-8pm, Su 2-10pm. £4.50 per hr.) To call the **hospital,** ☎ 81811; for the **police** (*Garda*), ☎ 82222.

ACCOMMODATIONS, FOOD, AND PUBS. Monaghan has no hostels, but **Ashleigh House,** 37 Dublin St., has rosy rooms and "whatever you want" for breakfast. (☎ 81227. Doubles £34). Two doors down, **Argus Court,** 32 Dublin St., provides a no-frills B&B upstairs from your basic pub. (☎ 81794. Singles £18; doubles £32.) If all else fails, call Monaghan's **Ancestor Research Centre** (☎ 82304) and stay with a distant relative.

There's a **SuperValu** supermarket on Church Sq. (☎ 81344. Open M-Th 9am-7pm, F 9am-9pm, Sa 9am-6pm.) **Pizza D'Or,** 23 Market St., behind the tourist office, is a town institution. It stays open until after the pubs close, and your *Let's Go* book gets you a £1 discount on a pizza. (☎ 84777. Pizzas from £3.50. Open M-F 5pm-1am, Sa-Su 5pm-3am.) **Tommy's,** around the corner from the Squealing Pig, has burgers and grease. The diner furniture was new in the 50s and hasn't died yet and, yes, they serve pizza. (☎ 81772. 12 in. pies from £3.50. Open M-Sa 10am-8pm.) For classier surroundings at low-brow prices, **Mediterraneo** on Main St. makes decadent pasta and gourmet pizzas. (Pizza from £6.95. Open M-Sa 6-11pm, Su 6-10pm.)

Pubs cluster off Church Sq. and down Dublin St. from the Diamond. **The Squealing Pig,** The Diamond, with its barn-like wooden floor and large-screen TV, gets the vote for the most popular pub in town. (☎ 84562. 21+.) **McKenna's Pub,** Dublin St. (☎ 81616), books mostly blues acts for its upstairs stage. The floor, dating from 1934, is far newer than the tables, which were once distillery barrels. **Patrick Kavanaugh's,** off Church Sq. (☎ 81950), is an intimate old kitchen that was converted into a pub well before anyone can remember. It draws a young crowd with trad Wednesday and Sunday evenings. **Jimmy's** (☎ 81694), an elegant 1950s pub on Mill St. off Church Sq., serves up trad on Thursdays and jazz on Sunday mornings.

◾ SIGHTS. The comprehensive and detailed **St. Louis Heritage Centre,** Market Rd., which traces the St. Louis Order of nuns, occupies a red-brick building in the convent school grounds. (☎ 83529. Open M-Tu and Th-F 10am-noon and 2:30-4:30pm, Sa-Su 2:30-4:30pm. Wheelchair accessible. £1, children 50p.) Past sisters' hairshirts and cutlery are on display, while chaste Barbie dolls model the evolution of nun fashion. In the center of town, the **Monaghan County Museum,** Hill St., across from the tourist office, painstakingly chronicles Co. Monaghan's history. (☎ 82928. Open Tu-Sa 11am-1pm and 2-5pm. Free.) The 14th-century **Cross of Clogher** looks on. The 1895 **St. Macartan's Cathedral,** on the south side of town, is Monaghan's most impressive building and offers panoramic views of the town. The Monaghan pub scene goes into overdrive during the **Jazz and Blues Festival.** (First weekend in Sept. Contact Somhairle McChongaille, ☎ 82928, for details.) Acts from Delta to Dublin land in Monaghan to shake the town to its rafters.

CASTLEBLAYNEY ☎042

Twenty miles southeast of Monaghan on the bus route to Dublin, Castleblayney specializes in fun, games, fishing, and beautiful walks. It has an adventure center, a main street crammed with pubs, and a karaoke bar. Nearby, **Lough Muckno Leisure Park** has 900 acres of forest; **Lough Muckno** ("Lake of the Swimming Pig") is where large numbers of perch, trout, and pike live until caught. The adventure center and hostel are both within the park, on the **Hope Castle** grounds (the same Hope family that once owned the gigantic 45-carat blue Hope Diamond, purchased by a Washington D.C. heiress in 1912 and now living at the Smithsonian). Nowadays, the only jewels to be found are the walks around the ◾**Black Island** and like the yang to its yin, **White Island.**

The **Adventure Centre,** within the castle grounds, offers all manner of land and water sport to the energetic. (Open June-Sept. Tu-F 2-7pm, Sa-Su noon-7pm. **Windsurfing** £20 per 4hr., **tennis** £2 per hr.) If you liked summer camp, you'll love **Castleblayney's Hostel (IHH),** in the same building as the adventure center. (☎ 46256. Open Apr.-Oct. Kitchen not available. Dorms £10, with continental breakfast £12, with full breakfast £15. **Camping** open St. Patrick's Day to mid-Oct. £4 per tent plus £1 per person.) The **White House B&B,** outside the park, has bright rooms and a garden for lounging in the sun. (☎ 46242. Singles £20; doubles £34, with bath £36.)

Pack a picnic at **Spar** supermarket, on the way to the park. (☎ 40137. Open M-Sa 8am-10pm, Su 9am-10pm.) **Barney's,** Main St., fries fast food and is the cheapest of the town's offerings. (☎ 40120. Open M-Sa noon-1am, Su 3pm-1am.) The best desserts are at **Deirdre's Home Bakery** (☎ 49588) two doors down. The town's a wee bit hipper since the **Hale-Bopp Nightclub** opened above **The Comet Bar** in 1998, two decades after space funk imploded. (☎ 49550. Cover £6.) Enlarge your liver with some pints from **Tiny's** (☎ 40510), Main St. Karaoke fever strikes at **The Conabury Inn** (☎ 40047) on most Wednesdays and Saturdays in the summer. During the rest of the week, the place is just your average, smoky pub.

WESTMEATH, OFFALY, LAOIS, AND LONGFORD

These central counties are often passageways rather than destinations. The 19 lakes of Co. Westmeath have earned it the buttery nickname "Land of Lakes and Legends." Farther south in famously soggy Co. Offaly, small towns and the impressive ruins of Clonmacnois civilize the peatland. The Slieve Bloom Mountains, between Mountrath, Kinitty, and Roscrea, are splendid and under-appreciated. Co. Longford is calm and collected, but hardly exciting.

MULLINGAR ☎ 044

Mullingar is planted in the center of Co. Westmeath and serves most travelers as a transportation stop between Dublin and the west coast. Discos at night and the nearby sights during the day might occupy travelers spending the night in town.

GETTING THERE. From the train station, follow the road and turn right onto **Dominick St.,** which runs through the town center and various names (Dominick, **Oliver Plunkett, Pearse,** and **Austin Friars St.**). The station is open 6am-9pm and occasionally charges a minimum of £1 for **luggage storage. Trains** (☎ 48274) chug to **Dublin** (1¼hr.; M-Th 4 per day, F 5 per day, Sa-Su 3 per day; £9) and **Sligo** (2hr.; M-Th and Sa-Su 3 per day, F 4 per day; £11). **Bus Éireann** stops variously at the train station, Kilroy's on Austin Friars St., and the Belvedere Gift Shop on Castle St., on its way to **Athlone** (1hr., 1-2 per day, £5), **Dublin** (1½hr.; M-Sa 6 per day, Su 3 per day; £7), **Sligo** (2½hr., 3 per day, £4.80), and **Galway** (2¾hr., 1-2 per day, £7). **O'Brien's Bus Co.** (☎ 48977) sends buses to **Dublin** (M-Sa 5 per day, Su 3 per day) from in front of the post office on Dominick St.

PRACTICAL INFORMATION. The **tourist office,** in Market Sq. at the corner of Pearse and Mount St., offers a free county guide with an area map and plenty of info about nearby sights and activities. (☎ 48650. Open all year M-F 9am-6pm, plus May-Oct. Sa 10am-1pm and 2-6pm.) Every major bank has a branch, most with **ATMs,** along the main drag; **TSB,** Oliver Plunkett St., has the longest hours. (☎ 42343. Open M-W and F 9:30am-5pm, Th 9:30am-7pm.) Mull over correspondence at the **Wry Mill Internet cafe** on Oliver Plunkett St. (☎ 48635. £4 per hr. Open daily 8am-9pm.) The **post office** is on Dominick St. (☎ 48393. Open M-Sa 9am-5:30pm.)

ACCOMMODATIONS, FOOD, AND PUBS. The **Railway House,** Dominick St., offers decent rooms and a cheery dining space, with TV and tea. (☎ 41142. Singles £25; doubles £40.) The **Newbury Hotel,** Dominick St., offers clean, well-equipped rooms just up from the train station. (☎ 42888. Singles £20, with bath £35; doubles £50.) Across the road, **John Daly's** pub, 2 Oliver Plunkett St., offers a B&B upstairs on Market Sq. (☎ 42724. Singles £25; doubles £40.)

A **Londis** supermarket lends out food for money just up from John Daly's on Oliver Plunkett St. (☎ 40475. Open M-W and Sa 8:30am-6:30pm, Th-F 8:30am-7pm.) The health food store **Nuts n' Grains** nestles in the Town Centre Mall. (☎ 45988. Open M-Sa 9:30am-6pm.) **The Fat Cat Brasserie,** Market Sq., has near purr-fect lunches and cool statues of cats. Heaping pastas and salads for under £5 are practically gourmet. Dinner is more expensive, but there are vegetarian entrees for £6.80. (☎ 49969. Open Tu-Su noon-2:30pm and 6-10pm.) **The Spiced Bean Cafe,** Church St., makes good coffee and fresh lunches. (M-Sa 9am-5:30pm.) **The Wry Mill**

Cafe, Oliver Plunkett St., offers simple, fat sandwiches (£2.50) and entrees (£4-5.50). **The Kitchen Fare Deli,** Mount St. (☎ 41294), is a great place to lunch on delicious specials (£4) and fruit scones. (Open M-Sa 8:30am-6pm.) Candlelit trad sessions draw big crowds on Wednesday nights at **Hughes Corner House** (☎ 48237), on the corner of Pearse and Castle St. **The Final Fence,** Oliver Plunkett St., hosts a nightclub with disco, top 40, and techno on weekend nights. (☎ 48688. Cover £5, concessions available in pubs.)

SIGHTS AND ENTERTAINMENT. Crowned with two spires, the **Cathedral of Christ the King** towers over Mary St. Inside, an **ecclesiastical museum** fills display cases with all sorts of items, from the vestments of St. Oliver Plunkett, Ireland's most recently canonized saint, to a model of the cathedral made from 68,750 matchsticks. (☎ 48338. Museum open Th and Sa-Su 3-4pm or by appointment. £1.) Plays, art exhibits, and summer workshops keep the new **Mullingar Arts Center** on Mount St. busy. (Tickets from £10-12, students and seniors from £8. Box office ☎ 47777; open 9am-10pm.)

The tourist office can provide all the info you need about **fishing** for trout, bream, carp, pike, rudd, and roach on the many nearby lakes, including equipment and boat rentals. The best fishing in town actually takes place in mid-July at the **Mullingar International Bachelor Competition** (☎ 44044), the culmination of a week-long festival supposedly geared toward family-oriented activities.

NEAR MULLINGAR

Heading north of Mullingar, the Fore Trail first follows N4 to Coole, then turns east onto R395, and finally swoops back down to Mullingar on R394 through Fore. The Belvedere Trail, which covers the area south of Mullingar, follows N52 to N6 and then takes Kilbeggan Rd. back to Mullingar. The trails are designed with car drivers in mind, but both are perfectly bikable as well.

THE FORE TRAIL

The first stop on the Fore Trail is the little village of **Multyfarnham,** 6 mi. along the way. At a 15th-century **Franciscan friary,** life-size figures in a peaceful garden depict the stations of the cross. Hiking trails lace the area. Four miles farther, the N4 runs between the town of **Coole** and **Turbotstown House,** a 200-year-old Georgian mansion that's privately owned. (Open May-Sept.) Two miles east on the R395, toward Castlepollard, are the Gothic Revival towers of romantic **Tullynally Castle,** Ireland's largest castle still inhabited by a family. The surrounding 30 acres of gardens include a pond inhabited by black Australian swans. (☎ (044) 61159. Tours of castle Sept. 1-15 and mid-June to mid-August 2:30-6pm. Gardens open daily May-Sept. 2-6pm. Castle and gardens £4.50, children £2.50.)

With a little publicity, the ruins of **Fore** could be the next Glendalough (see p. 138). The most extensive Benedictine ruins in Ireland, Fore is widely known for its seven wonders: water that flows uphill, water that won't boil, a tree that won't burn, a monastery that should have sunk into the bogs, a mill without a source of water to turn its wheel, a stone lifted by prayer alone, and a saint encased in stone. **Fore Abbey** was founded around 630 by St. Fechin and rebuilt 12 times after fires. Additions to the site date from the 11th, 13th, and 15th centuries. **St. Fechin's Church,** in the graveyard, is the oldest standing building. Up the hill, the tiny **Anchorite's Church** housed hermits well into the 17th century; get the key at the Seven Wonders pub nearby. The abbey is on the **Shamrock Experience** tour (☎ (046) 40127), based in Kells (see p. 151).

A smart detour from the Fore Trail heads 8 mi. out Oldcastle Rd. (R335) to the **Loughcrew Cairns** (Slieve na Calliagh, meaning "Witch Hill"). Similar to Newgrange (see p. 148), Loughcrew is a collection of passage tombs dating to 3000 BC; unlike Newgrange, Loughcrew is under-touristed and cheap. The largest of the 30 scattered tombs, the creatively named **Cairn T** features fine carving and the famous **Hag's Chair,** thought to have been used first for a royal seat and much later for a clandestine Christian altar. From May to October, a trailer at the base of the hill allows you to probe the tomb. Bring a flashlight. (☎ (049) 854 2009. £1, seniors 70p, students 40p.) From the trailer, it's a 20-minute hike up to the tomb.

The Fore Trail continues along the R395 to the R394, where it turns south to reach **Collinstown.** Another detour leads out the R395 to **Delvin,** where the ruins of a 12th-century castle mark the onetime western boundary of the British-controlled Pale. Back in Collinstown, the trail carries on to **Crookedwood,** where a well-preserved 14th-century church sits in front of a ring fort. (Key at the nearby house.) The trail continues south and returns to Mullingar.

THE BELVEDERE TRAIL

Four miles south of Mullingar, the 18th-century **Belvedere House and Gardens** pompously promenade along the shore of Lough Ennel. Don't drop-kick your jacket as you enter the door; recently renovated so that you won't find any streaks on the china, the house strives for imperial grandeur, with Roman gods frescoed along the ceiling. Robert Rochford, Lord Belvedere, for whom the house was built, also commissioned the fake "ruins" of a nonexistent abbey in order to obstruct his view of his brother's superior rose garden. The ruin is now called the **Jealous Wall** to his disgrace. (☎ (044) 49060. Open daily July-Aug. 10:30am-7pm; Easter-June and Sept. 10:30am-6:30pm. Oct.-Mar 10:30am-4:30pm, £3.50, students £2.50.)

Turning off the N52 and onto the N6, the trail continues to the small town of **Kilbeggan** at the next major intersection west. **Locke's Distillery,** a former firewater factory, has been converted into a museum. The zany anecdotes about workers' experiences on the job make the tour worthwhile. (☎ (0506) 32134. Open daily Apr.-Oct. 9am-6pm; Nov.-Mar. 10am-4pm. £3.25; students, seniors, and children £2.75.) From Kilbeggan, the trail turns right, heading northeast toward **Lough Ennell,** a major bird sanctuary favored by trout fishermen. To fish, you may need a permit from a local tackle shop. (Pike fishing is free; permit needed for trout. £5 per day.) On the shore of the lough sits **Lilliput House,** sadly life-size, and **Jonathan Swift Park,** with trails, fishing piers, and a good beach for swimming. Swift supposedly conceived *Gulliver's Travels* during a visit to Lough Ennell in the 1720s, and the surrounding area was renamed Lilliput shortly after the book's publication in 1726. The Belvedere Trail returns to Mullingar along the N52.

ATHLONE ☎0902

Set amongst the flatlands of Roscommon and Westmeath, Athlone is the center of everything in the middle of nowhere. Positioned at the intersection of the Shannon River and the Dublin-Galway road, the city is a transportation hub, with cars, truck, trains, and buses charging through town on cross-country trips. The 13th-century Norman castle that dominates the waterfront attests to former Athlone's past strategic importance. Visitors spending the night in Athlone might best spend their day at sights outside of town, either along the scenic Shannon or at the monastic ruins at nearby Clonmacnois.

GETTING THERE. Athlone's **train** and **bus** depot is on **Southern Station Rd.,** which runs parallel to **Church St.** (☎ 73322. Ticket window staffed M-Sa 9am-5:30pm.) **Trains** leave for **Galway** (1¼hr.; 8-9 per day; M-Th and Sa £8, F and Su £11.50), and **Dublin** (1¾hr.; M-Sa 11 per day, Su 9 per day; M-Th and Sa £10, F and Su £14.50). **Buses** shuttle in from **Dublin** on route to **Galway** (14-15 per day, £7), **Kilkenny** (1 per day, £11), **Cork** (1 per day, £13), **Limerick** (M-Sa 3 per day, Su 1 per day; £9.70), and **Killarney** (M-Sa 3 per day, Su 1 per day; £14). A private bus line, **Nestor Buses** (☎ (091) 797 244), also serves the region; for their routes and schedules, call Nestor or stop by the Royal Hotel on Church St.

PRACTICAL INFORMATION. The besieged **tourist office,** in the castle, can only withstand your cannon-balls of questions for so long; ask for the free maps and the *Athlone and District Visitors Guide.* (☎ 94630. Open Easter-Oct. M-Sa

9am-6pm, Su 10am-5pm.) **Bank of Ireland** (☎ 75111) and **AIB** (☎ 72089), on Church St., have **24-hour ATMs.** (Both open M 10am-5pm, Tu-F 10am-4pm.) The **post office** is by the castle on Barrack St. (☎ 83550. Open M and W-Su 9am-5:30pm, Tu 9:30am-5:30pm.) **Internet access** is splendid and cheap at **Interpoint,** Paynes Lane, just past the Dunnes Stores, heading away from the river on Church St. (☎ 78888. Open M-Sa 11am-9:45pm. £4 per hr., students £3.)

ACCOMMODATIONS. The **Lough Ree Lodge** (LOCK-ree), Dublin Rd., is the sole hostel in the area. Walk out Church St. past the shopping center, take the right fork; keep going, over the bridge, until the college. Two buses shuttle between the Esso station near the hostel and the Golden Island shopping mall. The Bus Éireann bus stops at the mall entrance. (75p, every 15-20min., 9am-6pm.) The shuttle bus stops at the road. (50p, roughly every 30min. M-Sa 9am-6pm.) Either bus ride takes roughly five minutes. Located a 25-minute walk from Athlone city center, Lough Ree is a step above other hostels. The biggest dorms have four beds and the singles have TVs, but resist the temptation of passivity—instead, mingle in the superb kitchen. (☎ 76738; email loughreelodge@tiniet.ie. Continental breakfast included. Laundry £2. Singles £14; doubles £24; all with bath. Wheelchair accessible.)

For a more lively locale, look no farther than **The Bastion,** 2 Bastion St., a bed and breakfast that is itself a bastion of cool, right in the middle of the funkier left bank. You'll wish your house was this well-decorated, with art and tapestries adding a chic touch. They may not serve a cooked breakfast, but the cheese, toast, yogurt, and cereal more than compensate. (☎ 94954; email bastion@iol.ie. Singles £22; doubles £36-38.) On the right bank of the Shannon, one can get a cozy room at **Shannon View,** 3 Shannon Villas, a few blocks up Church St. from the church. (☎ 78411. £16 per person.) **The Thatch,** opposite the castle, has palatial rooms and a good deal of noise from the bars below; quieter rooms are pricier. (☎ 94981; email info@thatch_tavern. Singles £25; doubles £38-50.) The closest camping is at **Lough Ree East Caravan and Camping Park,** staked out 3 mi. northeast on N55 (Longford Rd.) by a pleasant inlet on Lough Ree Lake. Follow signs for Lough Ree. (☎ 78561 or 74414. Showers 50p. Laundry £6. Open May-Sept. Tent £3.)

FOOD AND PUBS. Head downstairs at **Dunnes Stores** on Irishtown Rd. for your multiple grocery needs. (☎ 75212. Open M-W and Sa 9am-6:30pm, Th-F 9am-9pm, Su noon-6m.) **The Left Bank Bistro,** Bastion St., has been named one of the 100 best restaurants in Ireland. It lives up to its billing, creating affordable and filling lunches garnished with delicious green salads. Marinated steak sandwich with sauteed potatoes and salad £5.95. (☎ 94446. Lunch 10am-5pm.) **loaves & fishes bistro,** tucked away by the fork in Church St., may not be great at capitalization, but its dishes are miraculously tasty, especially for vegetarians and e.e. cummings-lovers. (☎ (087) 290 9370. Entrees around £4.50. Open July-Sept. M-W 9:30am-6pm, Th-Sa 9:30am-8pm, Su noon-4pm; winter hours 9am-5pm.) The **Bonne Bouche** serves a small variety of dishes that will fill your plate and please your palate. (☎ 72112. Entrees £6. Open roughly 10am-8pm daily.)

To ensure that you're not all athlone, check out one of the musical pubs in town. **Sean's Bar** (☎ 92358), behind the castle on Main St., may be Ireland's oldest inn, but the building stands up to raucous trad and other music seven nights a week. She went through a phase as The Hooker, but now **Gertie Brown's,** the Strand, found her old self and entertains more regulars than ever. (☎ 74848. M trad sessions). The crowd at the **Palace Bar,** Market Sq. (☎ 92229), crosses all generational lines, and enjoys occasional live music. Two clubs vie for late-night attention. At **BoZo's,** in Conlon's on Dublingate St., kids have a clownishly good time boogying to chart music. (£3-5 cover. Open Th-Su 11:15pm-2am.) At **Ginkel's 2000,** the 19-24 crowd spiffs up for the trendy leopard-skin decor. (W-Sa cover around £5.) *The Westmeath Independent* has entertainment listings, as does the alternative *B-Scene* magazine that appears fortnightly and can be grabbed at local cafes.

◼ **SIGHTS.** Athlone's national fame comes from a single, crushing defeat. Williamite forces besieged **Athlone Castle** in 1691. With the help of extra beer rations and 12,000 cannon-balls, they didn't take long to cross the river and sweep up. The defending Jacobites, unskilled soldiers at best, suffered massive casualties; the attackers, in contrast, lost fewer than 100 of their 25,000 strong (see **The Protestant Ascendancy,** p. 11). The castle is now free for all to wander around, providing some grand Shannon views. (Open May-Sept. daily 9:30am-6pm.) Inside, the **Athlone Castle Visitor Centre** tells a 45-minute audio-visual story of the battle, and marches on (without the slightest hint of transition) through Athlone history to tell the tales of the famous tenor John McCormack and the river Shannon. The museum inside the visitor center has gramophones, uniforms from the Civil War, and other oddities. (☎ 92912. Open May-Sept. daily 10am-4:30pm. £2.60, seniors and students £1.80; museum only, half-price.) The two master craftspeople at **Athlone Crystal Factory,** 29-31 Pearse St., invite you to drop in and crystallize your knowledge of crystal-making any time you'd like; covet the final product in the factory shop. (☎ 92867. Open M-Sa 10am-1pm and 2-6pm.) **Viking Tours,** 1-2 Gleeson St., departs from the strand across the river from the castle and sails a replica Viking ship up the Shannon to Lough Ree and, depending on demand, to Clonmacnois. (☎ 73833; mobile (086) 262 1136. 1½-4hr.; 2 or more per day. £6, students and children £4.)

The last week in June brings the **Athlone Festival,** which includes parades, exhibits, and free concerts. Aspiring singers head to Athlone in late autumn for the **John McCormack Golden Voice** opera competition, named for Athlone's most famous tenor (see **Music,** p. 29). Contact the Athlone Chamber of Commerce (☎ 73793).

CLONMACNOIS ☎0905

Isolated 14 mi. southwest of Athlone, the monastic ruins of Clonmacnois (clon-muk-NOYS) watch over the Shannon's boglands. St. Ciaran (KEER-on) founded the monastery in 548; his settlement grew into a city and important scholastic center. Monks wrote the precious **Book of the Dun Cow** at Clonmacnois around 1100, on vellum supposedly from St. Ciaran's cow. The holy cow traveled everywhere with the saint, and miraculously produced enough milk for the whole monastery. More recently, Seamus Heaney's *Seeing Things* retells a vision of manned ships passing through the air above the city in 748, described in the monastery's *Annals.*

Nowadays, the ships stay in the Shannon and the cows speckling the landscape have ordinary udders, but the grandiosity of the site still incites the imagination. The **cathedral** shows evidence of having endured countless attacks in its day; the current structure dates from about 909. One of its doorways is known as the **whispering arch;** even quiet sounds will travel audibly up one side over to the other. Various stories explain the arch: perhaps priests didn't want to get too close to plague-riddled confessors, or perhaps it allowed young lovers to maintain all the proper appearances of prayer while actually having private conversations. The cathedral is the final resting place, after a number of less reliable resting places, of the body of Rory O'Connor, the last High King of Ireland (died 1198). **O'Connor's Church,** built in the 12th century, has Church of Ireland services at 4pm on Sundays in July and August. Peaceful **Nun's Church** is beyond the modern graveyard behind the main site, about a ¼ mi. away down the path. Its finely detailed chancel and doorways are some of the best Romanesque architecture in Ireland.

If you have a car, the easiest way to reach Clonmacnois from Athlone or Birr is to take N62 to Ballynahoun, then follow the signs. Clonmacnois is accessible by bike, but it involves 14 mi. of hilly terrain. Hitchers first get a lift to Ballynahoun on heavily trafficked N62, then get a ride from there to Clonmacnois. *Let's Go* does not recommend hitchhiking, even on envisioned manned ships.

Access to Clonmacnois is through the **visitors' center** with displays that include a 23min. audio-visual show. (☎ 74195. Open mid-Mar.-May and mid-Sept.-Oct. daily 10am-6pm, June to early-Sept. daily 9am-7pm, Nov.-mid-Mar. daily 10am-5pm. £3.50, seniors £2, students £1.50. Wheelchair accessible.) The **tourist office,** at the entrance to the Clonmacnois car park, gives local information and sells various guides to the monastic city. (☎ 74134. Open Mar.-Nov. daily 10am-6pm.) **Paddy Kavanaugh** (☎ (0902) 74839 or (087) 240 7706) runs a minibus tour that hits the monastery, a local pub, the Clonmacnois, and **West Offaly Railway,** a train tour through a peat bog. Paddy accommodates almost all schedules and connects with incoming buses and trains. He will also pick up eager sightseers from their accommodations if called ahead of time. The tour is engaging and offers several "surprises" as Paddy displays his Ireland with heart and charm. (☎ 74114. Runs Apr.-Oct., or by arrangement. £17, students £13.)

Mr. and Mrs. Augustin Claffey's B&B, Shannonbridge Rd., near the ruins, is a restored cottage dating from 1843. Two double beds, a lambskin rug, and a peat fire are complemented by modern, self-catering conveniences. Reservations are recommended. (☎ 74149. £12 per person. No heat, so only open Apr.-Oct.) Another option is **Kajon House,** Shannonbridge Rd., a few hundred yards past the Claffeys. The splendid Mrs. Kate Harte will pick you up in Athlone if you call ahead. She'll also make an inexpensive dinner and greet you with delicious homemade scones. (☎ 74191. Singles £21-23; doubles £34, with bath £38; no extra charge for spunky stuffed animals.) The area's camping is 3 mi. east, at the **Glebe Touring Caravan and Camping Park.** (☎ (0902) 30277. Laundry £3. Open Easter-Oct. Tents £3.)

BIRR   ☎0509

William Petty labelled Birr *"Umbilicus Hiberniae,"* the belly button of Ireland. Who knows why; it's not the center of Ireland—maybe he'd had a pint too many at the pub. The highlight of the town, and well worth a visit, is **Birr Castle,** which developed into a hotbed of scientific discovery in the 19th century. The rest of Birr is pleasant if unremarkable, and makes a good starting point for exploring the **Slieve Bloom Mountains.** The mountains don't actually start until **Kinnitty,** 9 mi. east; if you don't have a car, your best bet is to bike there. Too few cars go by to make hitching practical, and hitchhiking is frowned upon by *Let's Go.*

GETTING THERE. Bus Éireann runs to **Athlone** (50min.; M-Sa 3-5 per day, Su 1 per day; £5), **Cahir** (2hr., 1 per day, £8.80), **Dublin** (2½hr.; M-Sa 4 per day, Su 2 per day; £6-7) and **Limerick** (M-F 4-5 per day, Su 1 per day; £9.20). **Kearns Coaches** offer better fares to **Dublin** (2-3 per day) and **Galway** (1¾hr., every other day); get a schedule at Square News in Emmet Sq.

ORIENTATION AND PRACTICAL INFORMATION. The *umbilicus* of Birr is **Emmet Sq.** Most shops and pubs are in The Square, or south down **O'Connell St.** The areas north and west of The Square down **Emmet St.** and **Green St.** are primarily residential. Buses stop at the post office in The Square. To reach the **tourist office** from Emmet Sq., walk down O'Connell and Main St., then make a right onto Castle St.; the office is on the left, under Malting's Craft Center. (☎ 20110. Open May-Sept. daily 9:30am-1pm and 2-5:30pm.) They have some maps of the Slieve Blooms and can put you in touch with guides. **P.L. Dolan,** Main St., **rents bikes.** (☎ 20006. £7 per day, £30 per week; deposit £40. Open M-W and F-Sa 9:30am-1pm and 2-6:30pm.) The **Bank of Ireland** (☎ 20092) has an **ATM** in Emmet Sq. **Internet access** is available at **The Book Mark,** Connaught St. (☎ 21988. £1.50 per 15min., £6 per hr.)

ACCOMMODATIONS, FOOD, AND PUBS. Kay Kelly's B&B rests atop her toy store on Main St. in a three centuries-old Georgian house that has a fireplace in one of the bathrooms. Kelly's tends to comfortable rooms with a car park and garden out back. (☎ 21128. £17.50 per person, all with bath.) **Spinners Town House,** Castle St., offers a crisp decor and spacious rooms; framed documents from Birr's past sprinkle the walls. In addition, there's a charming bistro downstairs, and breakfast options include scrambled eggs with smoked salmon. (☎ 21673. £25 per person sharing, additional £10 for a single. All rooms with bath.) For a lower price for singles try **Maltings Guest House,** on Castle St. Indulge in loads of amenities and little soaps. (☎ 21345. Singles £30; doubles £50.)

A **Supervalu** lies on O'Connell St. (☎ 20015; open M-Th and Sa 8am-7:30pm, F 8am-8pm, Su 9am-6pm) and a **Londis** heading away from Emmet Sq. in the other direction, stays open until 9pm every day (☎ 21250). Locals will point you to **Kong Lam**, Main St., for a cheap Chinese meal that you can eat in or take out. (☎ 21253. Entrees £5-6. Open Su-Th 5pm-12:30am, F-Sa 5pm-1am.) Spend a few more pence on lunch at the **Coachhouse Lounge** (☎ 20032) in Dooly's Hotel on the square. The liveliest pub is **Whelehan's**, Connaught St. (☎ 21349), owned by three members of the stellar Offaly hurling team.

SIGHTS. You're welcome to tread on the Earl of Rosse's turf at **Birr Castle**, which, unusually, remains his private home. The 120-acre demesne contains babbling brooks and the tallest box hedges in the world, while the 3km of trails are perfect for aimless wandering. For those who like romanticism without all the walking, **Declan Cleer** offers horse-and-carriage rides through the gardens (☎ 21753). The new **Historic Science Centre**, inside, has some good exhibits on the 19th-century residents' pioneering work in photography and astronomy. The Third Earl of Rosse discovered the Whirlpool Nebula with the Leviathan, an immense telescope whose 72 in. mirror was the world's largest for 72 years. The fourth Earl measured the heat of the moon. When the weather cooperates, you can observe the Leviathan in action. (☎ 20336. Castle open daily 9am-6pm. £5, seniors and students £3.50, children £2.50. Leviathan tours daily 3pm. Wheelchair accessible.) During **Birr Vintage Week**, in mid-August, people across the town celebrate their Georgian heritage: they wear vintage clothes, create vintage store windows, drive vintage cars, watch a vintage air show, and drink until the night is old.

SLIEVE BLOOM MOUNTAINS

Though not even 2000 ft. at their highest, the Slieve Bloom Mountains seem to burst from the rolling plains between Birr, Roscrea, Portlaoise, and Tullamore. A combination of boglands (no smoking—it's highly flammable!) and primarily managed forest, the Slieve Blooms are best seen while hiking along the 48 mi. circle of the **Slieve Bloom Way**. The best asset of the Slieve Blooms, contrary to what a tourist office might tell you, is precisely their lack of tourist-oriented activity—there's nothing to do but relax, as well you should. The towns around the mountains are bastions of rural Ireland's highly local, small-town lifestyle.

Transportation is the tricky part. Drivers should have no problem. Some of the best towns for entry to the mountains are **Kinnitty**, to the northwest, and **Mountrath**, to the south; getting from one to the other makes a reasonable driving route. Travelers reliant on public transportation are considerably handicapped. The most important thing is to talk to people; ask how to get places, where to go, and who else to talk to. The **tourist offices** of the surrounding towns are good starting points; the Portlaoise office (☎ (050) 221 178) can provide a very handy list of Co. Laois residents who have recently trained as tourist guides. Noreen Murphy (☎ (050) 32727) is a mountain specialist. Marguerite Sheeran runs the **Slieve Bloom Bike Hire** out of Coolrain, to the south of the mountains, and can provide routes, maps, and multi-day route-planning as needed; what she can't do is flatten the hills. Call to arrange pick-up, if needed, from any nearby town. (☎ (050) 235 277. £7 per day, £30 per week; deposit £40. Raleigh one-way rental available.)

The owners of the **Farren House** hostel (☎ (0502) 34032) can give you a lift out to their place from **Ballacolla**, a town accessible by two buses a day from Portlaoise. The hostel rooms are large and comfy, and the sculptures made of old farm junk in the driveway will force a smile. (Continental breakfast £2.50. Laundry service £3-4. Dorms £9. Wheelchair accessible.)

The *craic* can be mighty in these villages if your timing's right. When the town pubs have trad sessions, it's not to draw tourists. On Thursday nights the **Thatched Village Inn** (☎ (0502) 35277) in Coolrain gets the locals together for some contagiously fun set dancing. If you'd rather have your set dancing outside, in a bog, and on a mountain, the **Fraughan Festival** is the event for you: ten days of music and

ROSCREA

Picturesque Roscrea (ross-CRAY), actually in Co. Tipperary, strikes a pose 10 mi. south of Birr and to the southwest of the Slieve Blooms. On Castle St., a 13th century castle with a fine vaulted ceiling presents the setting for **Damer House**, the best-preserved example of Queen Anne architecture in Ireland. The house rotates exhibits, but the rotation period seems to be a decade or so. An exhibit on the **Monastic Midlands** and a millennium-aged chunk of **Bog Butter** are the primary highlights. A small **tourist office** in Damer House has the useful and free *Roscrea Heritage Walk* map. (Open daily June-Aug. 9:30am-5pm. Last admission 5:45pm.) Across the courtyard, the **Heritage Center** provides access to the castle and tours on the hour. The interesting castle tour has a nifty model of what the complete castle looked like in the 13th century. (☎ (0505) 21850. Open daily from mid-May-Sept. 9:30am-6:30pm; last admission 5:45pm. £2.50, seniors £1.75, students £1.)

Bus Éireann stops at Christy Maher's pub on Castle St., just downhill from the castle. Buses go to and from **Athlone** (1½hr., 1 per day), **Limerick** (1½hr., 13 per day), **Dublin** (2hr., 13 per day), and **Cork** (3hr., 1 per day). **Rapid Express Coaches** (☎ (056) 31106) leave from the Rosemary Quare fountain to follow similar routes at better prices (M-Sa 6 per day, Su 4 per day). **Bank of Ireland** on Castle St. sports a **24-hour ATM**. (☎ (050) 521 877. Open M-W and F 10am-4pm, Th 10am-5pm.) **Internet access** is available at the Roscrea information center, across the street from the Castle. (Open daily either 9am-5pm or 10am-6pm; £3 per 30min., £5 per hr.). The **pharmacy** (☎ 22718) in the shopping center will tend to your medical needs.

Mrs. Fogarty will take good care of you in the elegant rooms of the **White House**, Castle St.; look for a building painted lavender and lime green or enter the restaurant next to the castle. (☎ 21996. £20 per person.) Groceries abound at **Tesco**, Castle St., in the Roscrea Shopping Center. (☎ 22777. Open M-W and Sa 8:30am-7pm, Th-F 8:30am-10pm, Su 10am-6pm.) **Fresh Fields**, Main St., vends fruits and veggies. (☎ 22384. Open M-Sa 9am-6pm.) **Mick Delahunty's**, Main St., offers pub grub and music. (☎ (050) 522 139. Food served 10:30am-9pm. Music Tu and Th.)

PORTLAOISE ☎ 0502

Ask the folks at the tourist office what there is to do in the town of Portlaoise (port-LEESH), and it's a safe bet that they'll direct you exclusively to things outside it. The one worthwhile sight within close range is the **Rock of Dunamase**. Take Stradbally Rd. eastward 4 mi., and follow the sign at the big red church to Athy/Carlow, and the rock is on your left. The truly ancient fortress, recorded by the Greek astronomer Ptolemy, was the definition of impregnability until Cromwellian technology impregnated it with iron balls. Modern visitors can scramble among its ruins and nab great photo opportunities from the meager hill that provides an excellent lookout point for viewing the Slieve Bloom Mountains and beyond.

Lawlor Ave. runs parallel to **Main St.** Lawlor Avenue is a four-lane highway that opens onto several shopping centers, the most prominent of which is **Lyster Square**. Small lanes connect the square with Main St. The **train station** is in a quirky gray house at the curve on Railway St. which is roughly behind Main St. (☎ 21303. Open daily 6:45am-6:30pm.) **Trains** run to **Dublin** and points south (1hr.; 11-13 per day, Su 6 per day; £10.50). **Bus Éireann** stops at Egan's Hostelry on Main St. and on Lawlor Ave. (the highway) on the way to **Dublin** (1½hr., 13 per day, £6). **Rapid Express** (☎ (067) 26266) also serves **Dublin** from Lawlor Ave. (5-6 per day) and **Carlow** twice a day. The **tourist office**, in Lyster Square off Lawlor Ave., provides information on the Slieve Blooms and the Midlands. (☎ 21178. Open July-Aug. M-Sa 9:30am-5:30pm, Sept.-June M-F 10am-1pm and 2-6pm.) **AIB** (☎ 21349) graces Lawlor Ave. with a **24-hour ATM**, as does the **Bank of Ireland**. (☎ 21414. M-W and F 10am-4pm; Th 10am-5pm.) The **Kelton House laundromat** (☎ 62088; wash and dry £5; Open M-Sa 9am-6pm) scrub-a-dubs in the mini-mall across from the public library which provides **Internet access** for free if you purchase a £2 Ireland library card. (☎ 22333.

Open Tu and F 10am-5pm, W-Th 10am-7pm, Sa 10am-1pm). The regional **post office** is inside the shopping court on Lawlor Ave. (☎ 74220. Open M-F 9am-5:30pm, Sa 10am-1pm and 2-5pm.)

Affordable accommodations in town are limited. **Donoghue's B&B,** 1 Kellyville Park, is in a beautifully kept house with flower gardens and a friendly proprietor. (☎ 21353. Singles £25; doubles £36, with bath £40.) **No. 8 Kellyville** at, of all places, 8 Kellyville Park, offers basic, though rather small, B&B accommodations with old fashioned coverlets. (☎ 22774. Private car park. Singles £27.50-35; doubles £44.)

For loony groceries, head to **CrazyPrices,** inside the shopping mall on Lawlor Ave. (☎ 21730. Open M-Tu and Sa 9am-7pm, W-F 9am-9pm.) In addition to plentiful pub grub choices, brilliant coffee and a touch of class flow at the **Cafe Latte** branch in the sparkling and fabulous **Dunamaise Arts Center** (☎ 63355; www.dunamaisetheater.com. Cafe open 8:30am-5:30pm.) The Cafe offers delectable lunches, and the Arts Center is home to a well-designed 250-seat theater.

SOUTHEAST IRELAND

Historically the power base of the Vikings and then the Normans, the influence of the Celts is faintest in southeast Ireland. Town and street names in this region are likely derived from Viking, Norman, and Anglo-Saxon origins. Beaches are the most fruitful of the Southeast's tourist attractions, drawing mostly native Irish admirers to the coastline that runs from Kilmore Quay to tidy Ardmore. Wexford is a charismatic town, packed with historic sites and convenient to many of the Southeast's finest attractions, while Waterford has the resources, nightlife, and grit of a real city. Cashel boasts a superbly preserved cathedral complex. Continue your hunt for raging nightlife south from Dublin through Carlow, Kilkenny, and Waterford; alternatively, the daylight hours are most enjoyably spent exploring the pretty paths through Glendalough, the Wicklow Mountains, Enniscorthy, and Wexford. Continental and British travelers stuff themselves into cars speeding to and from Europe via Rosslare Harbour on the southeastern tip of the island.

HIGHLIGHTS OF THE SOUTHEAST: VIKING VILLAGES

Kilkenny (p. 170) dazzles in its medieval costume, accessorizing with a castle (p. 175) and Jerpoint Abbey's Cistercian ruins (p. 176).

Cashel (p. 179) proudly points the way to nearby natural wonders: the looming Rock of Cashel, the Galty Mountains, and the Mitchelstown Caves.

Follow the 43 mi. East Munster Way through the bumpy **Comeragh** and **Knockmealdown Mountains** (p. 185).

KILKENNY AND CARLOW

Northwest of Wexford and Waterford, and east of the Irish metropolis of Dublin, the counties of Kilkenny and Carlow consist of lightly populated hills and plains characterized by small farming villages and the occasional medieval ruin. Kilkenny City is the bustling exception to the seemingly endless string of provincial towns; it's a popular destination for both international tourists and young Irish on the move. The town of Carlow, though much smaller, buzzes on weekend nights.

KILKENNY ☎056

As the economy of the Celtic Tiger roars, the best-preserved medieval town in Ireland has launched a historical preservation campaign to draw more visitors and net a few more Tidy Town awards. Kilkenny's handsome streets, nine churches, and 80 pubs are all cloaked in the architecture of past eras. Kilkenny storefronts have done away with tacky neon, and now even fast-food joints have hand-painted facades. These efforts are reaping their just reward: the town's population of 25,000 doubles during the high season.

▗ GETTING THERE AND GETTING AROUND

Trains: Kilkenny MacDonagh Station, Dublin Rd. (☎ 22024). Open M-Sa 8am-9:30pm, Su 9am-9pm. Always staffed, although the ticket window is open only around departure times. Kilkenny is on the main **Dublin-Waterford** rail route (M-Sa 4-5 per day, Su 3-4

KILKENNY ■ 171

Southeast Ireland

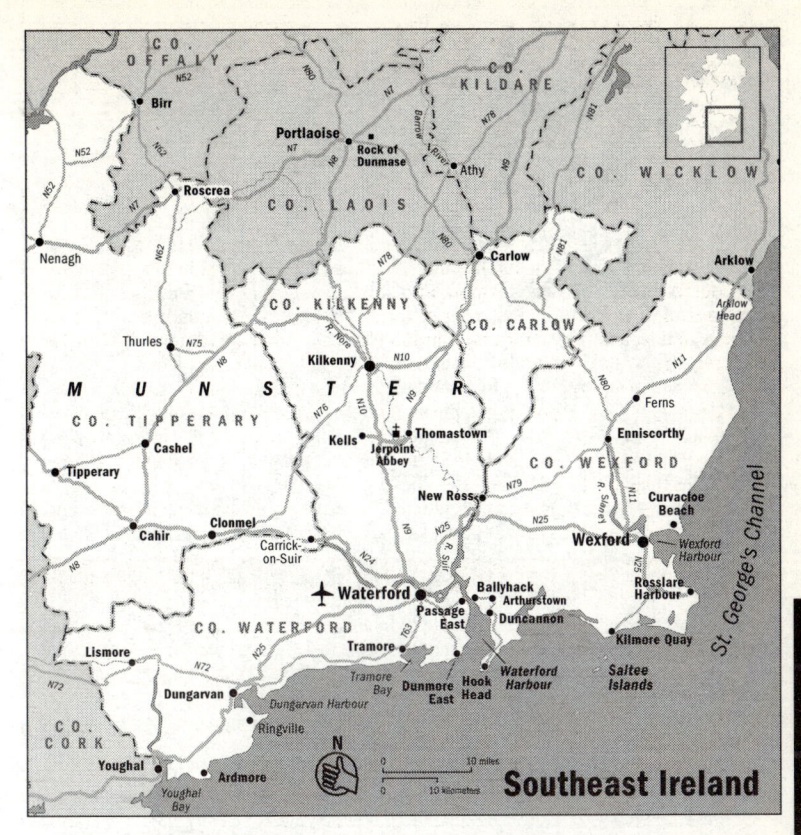

per day). To **Thomastown** (15min., £4.50), **Waterford** (45min., £5), and **Dublin** (2hr., £11). Connections to western Ireland can be made at **Kildare Station**, 1hr. north on the Dublin-Waterford line.

Buses: Kilkenny Station, Dublin Rd. (☎ 64933), and on Patrick St. in the city center. Buses leave for **Clonmel** (1½hr.; 6 per day; £4), **Waterford** (1½hr.; M-Sa 2 per day, Su 1 per day; £5), **Rosslare Harbour** via Waterford (2hr.; M-Sa 5-6 per day, Su 3 per day; £10.50), **Dublin** (2hr.; M-Sa 6 per day, Su 5 per day; £7), **Limerick** via Clonmel (2½hr.; M-Sa 5 per day, Su 1 per day), **Cork** (3hr.; M-Sa 3 per day, Su 2 per day; £10), and **Galway** via Athlone or Clonmel (5hr.; M-Sa 5 per day, Su 3 per day; £17). **Buggy's Coaches** (☎ 41264) run from Kilkenny to **Ballyragget** (30min., M-Sa 2 per day) and to **Castlecomer** (15min., M-Sa 5 per day, £1) with stops at **Dunmore Cave** (20min.) and the An Óige hostel (15min.). **J.J. Kavanagh's Rapid Express** (☎ 31106) has routes in the area with prices that routinely beat Bus Éireann's (**Dublin** M-Sa 5 per day, Su 1 per day).

Taxi: All the companies now have a £4 minimum, plus an additional £1.20 per mile after 3-4 miles. **Kevin Barry** (☎ 63017). **Kilkenny Cabs** (☎ 52000).

Car Rental: Barry Pender, Dublin Rd. (☎ 65777 or 63839), rents to anyone 23+. Compact car £50 per day, £250 per week. Open M-F 9am-5:30pm, Sa 9am-1pm.

Bike Rental: The thriftiest place is **Kilkenny Cycles,** Michael St. (☎ 64374). £7 per day, £35 per week; £50 or passport deposit. Open M-Sa 9am-6pm. Otherwise, try **J.J. Wall Cycle,** Maudlin St. (☎ 21236). £7 per sentimental day, £40 per effusive week. Tearjerking ID deposit. Open M-Sa 9am-6pm.

172 ■ KILKENNY AND CARLOW

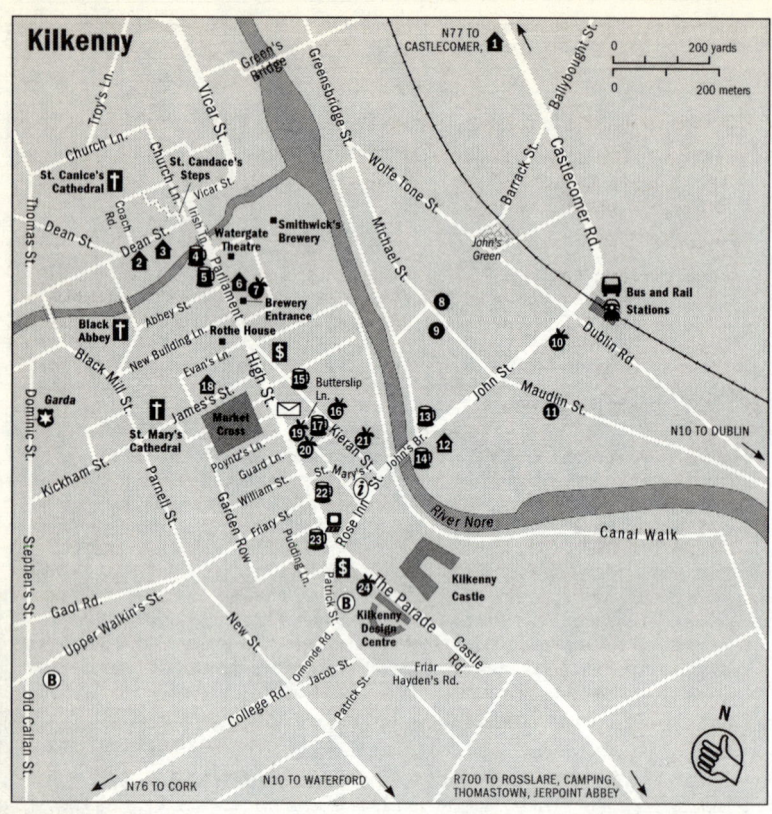

Kilkenny

ACCOMMODATIONS
Bregagh B&B, 3
Daly's B&B, 12
Demsey's B&B, 18
Foulksrath Castle Hostel, 1
Kilkenny B&B, 2
Kilkenny Tourist Hostel (IHH), 6

FOOD
Dunnes Supermarket, 16
Italian Connection, 7
Langton's, 10
Lautrec's, 21
Ml. Dore, 20
Pordylo's, 19
Ristorante Rinuccini, 24

PUBS
Caisleán Uí Cuain, 23
Cleere's, 4
Kytelet's Inn and Nero's, 15
Maggie's, 17
Matt the Miller's, 13
Paris, Texas, 22
The Pump House, 5
Quay's, 14

SERVICES
Brett's Laundrette, 8
J.J. Wall Cycle, 11
Kilkenny Cycles, 9

ORIENTATION AND PRACTICAL INFORMATION

From **MacDonagh Station,** turn left on **John St.** and continue downhill to reach a large intersection with **High St.** and **The Parade,** dominated by the castle on your left. Most activity takes place in the triangle formed by **Rose Inn, High,** and **Kieran St.** Hitchhikers take N10 south to Waterford, Freshford Rd. to N8 toward Cashel, and N10 past the train station toward Dublin. Patience is required of hitchhikers, of whom *Let's Go* does not approve.

Tourist Office: Rose Inn St. (☎ 51500; fax 63955). On the second floor of a 16th-century pauper house. Free town maps. Open Oct.-Mar. M-Sa 9am-5pm, Apr.-Sept. M-Sa 9am-6pm, July-Aug. M-Sa 9am-8pm, May-Sept. also Su 11am-1pm and 2-5pm.

Banks: Bank of Ireland, Parliament St. (☎ 21155), has an **ATM,** while the High St.-Parade intersection has 5 more at 4 banks. All open M 10am-5pm, Tu-F 10am-4pm.

KILKENNY ■ 173

Laundry: Brett's Launderette, Michael St. (☎ 63200). Soap 70p. Wash and dry £5.70. Open M-Sa 8:30am-8pm; last wash 6:30pm. No self-service drying.

Pharmacy: Several on High St. All open M-Sa 9am-6pm; Sunday rotation system.

Emergency: Dial ☎ 999; no coins required. **Police** (*Garda*): Dominic St. (☎ 22222).

Hospital: St. Luke's, Freshford Rd. (☎ 51133). Continue down Parliament St. to St. Canice's Cathedral, then turn right and veer left onto Vicars St., then left again onto Freshford Rd. The hospital is down on the right.

Post Office: High St. (☎ 21891). Open M-Tu, Th-Sa 9am-5:30pm, W 9:30am-5:30pm.

Internet Access: Web Talk, Rose Inn. 2 shops closer to The Parade than the tourist office. £1 per 10min, £5 per hr. (Open M-Sa 10am-9pm, Su 2-8pm.) **Compustore** (☎ 71200), in the Market Cross shopping center off High St. £2 per 15min., £3 per 30min., £5 per hr. Open M-W and Sa 10am-6pm, Th-F 10am-8pm.

ACCOMMODATIONS

B&Bs average £20, but some places will hike prices up to £30 on weekends. Call ahead in summer, especially on weekends. Waterford Rd. and more remote Castlecomer Rd. have the highest concentration of beds.

Foulksrath Castle (An Óige/HI), Jenkinstown (☎ 67674. Leave a message 10am-5pm). 8 mi. north of town on N77 (Durrow Rd.). Turn right off N77 at signs for Connahy; it's ¼ mi. down on the left. Buggy's Buses (☎ 41264) run from The Parade to the hostel M-Sa at midday and 5:30pm and leave the hostel for Kilkenny shortly after 8:25am and around 3pm (20min., £1; call the hostel for exact times). Housed in a 15th-century castle, it's one of the nicest hostels in Ireland. Breakfast for a small fee if you call ahead. Sheets £1. Kitchen open 8am-10pm. Dorms £5.50-7.50.

Kilkenny Tourist Hostel (IHH), 35 Parliament St. (☎ 63541; email kilkennyhostel@tiniet.ie). Directly across from popular pubs and next to the Smithwicks brewery. The brightly colored rooms brim with activity as people bustle about in the kitchen, lounge on couches, and sip Guinness on the front steps. If it's not luxurious, at least it's fun. Great town info posted in front hall, from train schedules to trad sessions to cyclist maps. Non-smoking. Kitchen with microwave open 7am-11pm. Check-out 10:30am. Laundry £3. 6- to 8-bed dorms £7; doubles £20; add £1 May-Sept.; Sept.-June 50p discount to *Let's Go* readers.

Demsey's B&B, 26 James's St. (☎ 21954). A little old house by the Superquinn, off High St. Spacious, well-decorated rooms with TVs, and friendly proprietors. Singles £25; doubles with bath £36-40.

Bregagh House B&B, Dean St. (☎ 22315). Pristine rooms with handsome wood furniture and firm beds. Singles £18-25; doubles with bath £36-44, Nov.-May £34.

Kilkenny B&B, Dean St. (☎ 64040). Basic, clean rooms. A sign warns that the house is guarded by an attack housewife, but don't worry, she's actually rather charming. It's worth a try to charm the prices down; their range can be huge and arbitrary. Weekends especially high. Singles £15-25, doubles £32-50.

Daly's B&B, 82 Johns St. (☎ 62866). Immaculately nondescript rooms. Breakfast £3 per person. Singles £23; doubles £40, reduced prices in the off-season.

Nore Valley Park (☎ 27229 or 27748). 7 mi. south of Kilkenny between Bennetsbridge and Stonyford, signposted from Kilkenny: Take the R700 to Bennetsbridge; just before the actual bridge take the signposted right. How green is your valley. A class act, with hot showers included, a TV room, and a play-area for children. Open Mar.-Oct. Laundry £4.50. 2-person tent £7.50. Backpackers (with no car) slightly cheaper.

Tree Grove Caravan and Camping Park (☎ 70302). 1 mi. past the castle on the New Ross road (R700). Showers included. 2-person tent £6.

174 ■ KILKENNY AND CARLOW

FOOD

Dunnes Supermarket sells housewares and food on Kieran St. (☎ 61655. Open M-Tu and Sa 8:30am-7pm, W-F 8:30am-10pm, Su and bank holidays 10am-6pm.) The mighty **Superquinn,** in the Market Cross shopping center off High St., has a slightly smaller selection. (☎ 52444. Open M-Tu and Sa 9am-7pm, W-F 9am-9pm.) Everything in Kilkenny's restaurants is great except the prices, which all hover in the lower stratosphere. Here are some reasonable options; otherwise, hit the pubs.

Pordylo's, Butterslip Ln. (☎ 70660), between Kieran and High St. Zesty dinners from across the globe, many of which love vegetarians. Some meals under £8. Open nightly 6-11pm. Reservations recommended.

Langton's, 69 John St. (☎ 65123). An eccentric owner has earned a host of awards for his ever-changing pub. Full lunch menu with an Irish twist. Lunch £5, served daily noon-6pm. Sophisticated dinner menu in the double digits, served daily 6-10:30pm.

Ristorante Rinuccini, 1 The Parade. (☎ 61575), opposite the castle. Couples enjoy mood lighting and romantic music while sucking face. Lunch £5-6, served noon-2:30pm; dinner £7-9, served 6-10:30pm; early evening specials 6-7:30pm for £6-7.

Italian Connection, 38 Parliament St. (☎ 64225). Italian food, mahogany, carnations, and still it's not fancy. Lunch specials daily noon-3pm, £5-6. Open daily noon-11pm.

Lautrec's, 9 Kieran St. (☎ 62720). A well-trained chef makes quick, mostly Italian lunches for £5-6. Your belt won't be too loose after dinner, but your wallet may be. Lunch M-F noon-2pm, dinner daily 6-10:30pm.

Ml. Dore, High St. (☎ 63374). Near Kieran St. It's not impossible to find sandwiches for £2 and light entrees for £5-6. Open M-Sa 8am-10pm, Su 9am-9pm.

PUBS

Kilkenny is known as the "oasis of Ireland." Music, from trad to rock, rages on most nights, especially in the summer. U2 is known as the "Oasis of Ireland."

The Pump House, 26 Parliament St. (☎ 63924). Remains a favorite among locals and many hostelers. Loud, conveniently located, and packed. An ultra-hip enclave upstairs makes you wish you packed some Prada. Trad M-Th in the summer, Su rock and blues.

Cleere's, 28 Parliament St. (☎ 62573). Thespians from the theatre across the street converge here during intermission for a pint (and to watch *Monty Python* rather than the game). A black box theater in back hosts vivacious musical and theatrical acts.

Paris, Texas, High St. (☎ 61822). Be as cool as a Parisian and as crowded as cattle in this extremely popular bar, where over-23s shake, shimmy, smoke, and lasso themselves some good times with vim and vigor.

Maggie's, Kieran St. (☎ 62273). Crowds bury themselves in this superb, aged-wine cellar. Trad most nights of the week, rock on summer weekends.

Matt the Miller's, 1 John St. (☎ 61696), at the bridge. Not a Canterbury Tale. Huge, thronged, and magnetic. It'll suck you in and force you to dance to silly Euro pop. M cover £2 for rock music and late bar hours.

Kyteler's Inn, Kieran St. (☎ 21064). The 1324 house of Alice Kyteler, Kilkenny's witch, whose 4 husbands had in common a knack for getting poisoned on their first anniversaries. Nowadays the food and drink are safer, and trad fills the air 2 nights a week. Late night F-Su, fiddle away the evening at **Nero's,** a nightclub that's burning down the house. Cover £5-7. Open 11pm-2am.

Caisleán Uí Cuain (cash-LAWN ee COO-an), 2 High St. (☎ 65406), at The Parade. A local crowd settles in for pints and all types of music on all sorts of nights.

Ryan's (☎ 62881), on Friary St. just off High St. No frills, just a pub with a good crowd and frequent trad.

Quay's, John St. (☎ 70844). Across from Matt the Miller's, with a deliciously aged feel. Music every night. Trad W and F, and Su morning jazz.

SIGHTS

Kilkenny itself is a sight, since the government preserved (or recreated) most of the buildings' medieval good looks. The belle of the ball is 13th-century **Kilkenny Castle,** The Parade. It housed the Earls of Ormonde from the 1300s until 1935. Many rooms have been restored to their former opulence. Ogle the Long Room, reminiscent of a Viking ship, which displays portraits of English bigwigs. The basement houses the **Butler Gallery,** which hangs modern art exhibitions. This level also houses a cafe in the castle's kitchen, home to the castle's ghost. (☎ 21450. Castle and gallery open June-Sept. daily 10am-7pm; Oct.-Mar. Tu-Sa 10:30am-12:45pm and 2-5pm, Su 11am-12:45pm and 2-5pm; Apr.-May daily 10:30am-5:30pm. Castle access by guided tour only. £3.50, students £1.50.) The 52-acre landscaped **park** adjoining the castle provides excellent scenery for an afternoon jaunt. (Open daily 10am-8:30pm. Free.) Across the street, the internationally known **Kilkenny Design Centre** fills the castle's old stables with expensive Irish crafts. (☎ 22118. Open Apr.-Dec. M-Sa 9am-6pm, Su 10am-6pm; Jan.-Mar. M-Sa 9am-6pm.) For the down-and-dirty on Kilkenny's folkloric tradition, and an introduction to other sights in the town, take the **Tynan Walking Tours.** Besides conjuring some animated lore, the tour is the only way to see the old city jail. Tours depart from the tourist office on Rose Inn St. (☎ 65929, mobile (087) 2651745; email tynantours@eircom.net. Tours Mar.-Oct. M-Sa 6 per day, Su 4 per day; Nov.-Feb. Tu-Sa 3 per day. About 1hr. £3, students and seniors £2.50.)

13th-century **St. Canice's Cathedral** sits up the hill off Dean St. The name "Kilkenny" itself is derived from the Irish Cill Chainnigh, "Church of St. Canice." The thin, 100 ft. tower next to the cathedral was somehow built without scaffolding, in pre-Norman times, and still stands on its 3 ft. foundations. £1 and a bit of faith let you climb the series of six steep ladders inside to behold a panoramic view of the town and its surroundings. (☎ 64971. Open Easter-Sept. M-Sa 9am-1pm and 2-6pm, Su 2-6pm; Oct.-Easter M-Sa 10am-1pm and 2-6pm; Su 2-6pm. Donation requested.) The **Black Abbey,** off Abbey St., was founded in 1225 and got its name from the habits of its Dominican friars. Outside, you'll see a row of stone coffins used to contain bodies struck by the Black Death. Inside, a non-period restoration job and heavy silence reign. Nearby you can gaze up at the dark heights of **St. Mary's Cathedral,** constructed during the darkest years of the famine. **Rothe House,** Parliament St., a Tudor merchant house built in 1594, is now a small museum of local archaeological finds and Kilkennian curiosities. (☎ 22893. Open Apr.-Oct. M-Sa 10:30am-5pm, Su 3-5pm; Nov.-Mar. Sa-Su 3-5pm. £2, students £1.50.)

It is rumored that crafty 14th-century monks brewed a light ale in the **St. Francis Abbey** on Parliament St.; the abbey is in ruins but its industry survives in the abbey's yard at the **Smithwicks Brewery.** Commercial use started in 1710, making it the oldest brewery in Ireland (Guinness started up nearly 50 years later). Unfortunately, the company profanes the abbey by brewing Budweiser as well. Show up at 3pm outside the green doors on Parliament St. for a free audio-visual tour and ale tasting. (Tours July-Aug. M-F.)

ENTERTAINMENT

The tourist office can provide a bimonthly guide to the town's happenings, and *The Kilkenny People* (£1) is a good newsstand source for arts and music listings. **The Watergate Theatre,** Parliament St., stages shows year-round. (☎ 61674. Tickets usually £6-7, student discounts available. Booking office open M-F 11am-7pm, Sa 2-6pm, Su 1hr. before curtain.) During the second or third week of August, Kilkenny holds its annual **Arts Festival,** which has a daily program of theater, concerts, recitals, and readings by famous European and Irish artists. (☎ 63663. Event tickets free-£12; student and senior discounts vary by venue. Tickets sold at 92 High St., or by phone.) Kilkenny's population increases by over 10,000 for the **Cat Laughs** (☎ 51254), a festival held on the first weekend of June, featuring international comedy acts. The cat in question is the Kilkenny mascot of nursery rhyme fame:

176 ■ KILKENNY AND CARLOW

There once were two cats from Kilkenny.
Each thought there was one cat too many.
So they fought and they fit,
And they scratched and they bit,
'Til excepting their nails and the tips of their tails
Instead of two cats there weren't any.

DAYTRIPS FROM KILKENNY

THOMASTOWN AND JERPOINT ABBEY

Bus Éireann stops at the Jerpoint Inn in Thomastown between **Waterford** and **Kilkenny** (M-Sa 7 per day, Su 4 per day). The folks at the **Jerpoint Inn** can provide a schedule for the **Rapid Express** (☎ 31106), a private bus service running between Dublin and **Tramore. Trains** run through Thomastown in search of **Dublin** (M-Sa 5 per day; Su 3 per day) and **Waterford** (M-Sa 5per day, Su 4 per day). The train station is a 10-min. walk out of town on **Marshes Rd.**

The eerie Dunmore Caves to the north and Jerpoint Abbey to the south of Kilkenny provide worthy excuses to flee town for an afternoon. Thomastown, a tiny community perched on the Nore River, is the gateway to the impressive **Jerpoint Abbey,** 1½ mi. away. The strict Cistercian order founded Jerpoint in 1160. Cistercians stressed simplicity, but somewhere along the line the Jerpoint monks cut loose by decorating the abbey with beautiful stone carvings of their favorite saints. Eventually nothing could stop them from traveling down the dangerous path of ecclesiastical artistry. Free tours, given on the half-hour, will clue you in to the archaeological detective work that's been done on the stonework and paintings. (☎ 24623. Open daily Apr.-June Tu-Su 10am-1pm and 2-5pm; July-Aug. 9:30am-6:30pm; Sept.-Oct. 10am-1pm and 2-6pm. £2, seniors £1.50, students £1.) In town, at one end of Market St. rests the remains of **Thomastown Church,** built in the early 13th century. Three curiosities lie amongst the church's gravestones: an ancient ogham stone (see **History of the Irish Language,** p. 22), part of a Celtic cross, and a weathered 13th-century effigy.

Withdraw cash at the **ATM** of **Bank of Ireland** (☎ 24213). **Simon Treacy Hardware rents bikes.** (☎ 24291. £6 per day, £40 per week; deposit £20. Open M-Sa 9am-6pm).

The serene **Watergarden,** Ladywell St., serves an amazing lunch. Members of **Camphill Community,** an organization that supports and employs the mentally handicapped, serve primarily vegetarian and organic delectables in a cozy cafe with lovely gardens out back. (☎ 24690. Sandwiches and small entrees £3-4. Open Tu-F 10am-5pm, Su noon-5pm.) **O'Hara's** pub (☎ 24597) has 200-year-old walls and fireplaces, but don't expect to find a full menu.

DUNMORE CAVE

Coaches (☎ 41264) runs a bus between Kilkenny and Castlecomer; the driver will stop 1km from the site on request. From the drop-off point, the route is well signposted. (20min., M-Sa 5 per day, £1). If you're driving, take N78 (Dublin-Castlecomer Rd.) from Kilkenny; the turn-off for the cave is on the right after the split with N77 (Durrow Rd.). ☎ 67726. Open mid-Mar. to mid-Sept. daily 10am-7pm; mid-Sept. to Nov. daily 10am-6pm; Nov.-mid-Mar. Sa-Su and holidays 10am-5pm; last admission 45min. before closing. £3, children free.

On the road to Castlecomer 10km north of Kilkenny lurks the massive Dunmore Cave. Known fondly as "the darkest place in Ireland," the cave is bedecked with fascinating limestone formations. Recently unearthed human bones show that roughly 100 people died underground here in 928, probably while hiding from Viking marauders.

CARLOW ☎ 0503

A small, busy town, Carlow sits on the eastern side of the River Barrow on N9 (Dublin-Waterford). Seamlessly placid today, in past centuries Carlow hosted several of the most gruesome historic battles between Gael and Pale. During the 1798 Rising (see **Rebellion, Union, Reaction,** p. 13), 640 Irish insurgents were ambushed in the streets of Carlow; they were buried across the River Barrow in the gravel pits of Graiguecullen (greg-KULL-en). A part of the gallows from which they were hanged is now displayed in the county museum. For those who'd rather hang out, Carlow's surprisingly good nightlife routinely attracts a crowd from all over.

GETTING THERE. Trains run through Carlow from Heuston Station in **Dublin** on their way to **Waterford** (1¼hr.; M-Sa 5 per day, Su 3 per day; £12). From the train station, it's a 15-minute walk to the center of town; head straight out of the station down **Railway Rd.**, turn left onto **Dublin Rd.**, and make another left at the Court House onto **College St.** The cheapest **buses** to **Dublin** depart from Doyle's by the Shamrock D.I.Y.—you can go to the Custom House for as little as £4 return. Buses leave from the corner of Barrack and Kennedy, in a little bus turnabout next to a veterinarian's. **Bus Éireann** bounces from Carlow to **Waterford** (1¼hr.; M-Sa 7 per day, Su 6 per day; £5), **Dublin** (1¾hr.; M-Sa 7 per day, Su 4 per day; £6), and **Athlone** (2¼hr., 1 per day, £10). **Rapid Express Coaches,** Barrack St. (☎ 43081 or (056) 31106), runs a bus through **Tramore-Waterford-Carlow-Dublin** and back (M-Sa 8-10 per day, Su 7-8 per day); stop by their office to pick up timetables to a variety of Midland destinations.

PRACTICAL INFORMATION. The Carlow **tourist office,** Kennedy Ave., is tucked in the car park by the Dinn Rí, past the Carlow shopping center (Kennedy Ave. is the first left from the bus station) and hands out *A Guide to County Carlow*, which includes a town map. (☎ 31554. Open M-Sa 9:30am-1pm and 2-5:30pm.) **Rent bikes** from **Coleman Cycle,** 19 Dublin St. (☎ 31273. Open M-Sa 8:30am-7pm. £5 per day, £30 per week; deposit £40.) The **post office** mails your post or posts your mail from the corner of Kennedy Ave. and Burrin St. (Open M and W-Sa 9am-5:30pm, Tu 9:30am-5:30pm.) The **AIB** on Turrow St. offers a **24-hour ATM** and a **bureau de change.** (☎ 31758. Open M 10am-5pm, Tu-Sa 10am-4pm.) **Internet access** links up at **Web Talk** in Shamrock Square at the intersection of Barrick and Tullow. (☎ 35747. Open M-Sa 10am-9pm. £1 per 10min., £5 per hr., £3 per hr. with an ISIC card.) For lovers of the imperative, **Communicate Now** connects in the Carlow Shopping Centre between Tullow St. and Kennedy Ave. (☎ 43700. First 20min. £2, each subsequent 10min. £1. Open M-W and Sa 10am-6pm, Th-F 10am-9pm.)

ACCOMMODATIONS. The **Otterholt Riverside Lodge,** a hostel near the banks of the River Barrow, provides sturdy beds in clean, colorful rooms, while the stuffed otter in the hallway of this 200-yr.-old Georgian residence welcomes an eclectic set of guests to Carlow. It's a half-mile from the center of town on Kilkenny Rd.; if you don't feel up to the 10-minute walk, the bus to Kilkenny will stop in front of it upon request. (☎ 30404; fax 31170. Wash and dry clothes for £3. Dorms £8-9; doubles £22-26. **Camping** £4. Sa nights tend to fill up, so reserve ahead.) The **Redsetter Guesthouse,** 14 Dublin St., next to the Royal Hotel in the center of town, offers a little luxury for a little cash in spacious rooms with phones and TVs. (☎ 41848; fax 42937. Singles £18, with bath £22; small doubles £34, larger doubles £42.)

FOOD AND PUBS. Superquinn, in the Carlow Shopping Centre, has groceries that taste good as an Über-market's should. (☎ 30077. Open M-W and Sa 8:30am-7pm, Th-F 8:30am-9pm.) The **SuperValu** on Tullow St. battles it out for grocery domination. (☎ 31263. Open M-W 9am-7pm, Th-F 9am-9pm, Sa 9am-6pm.) Most pubs in town offer basic lunchtime grub until 2pm with a few hot entrees and sides for about £5. **La Napoletana,** 63 Tullow St., serves heaps of pasta at delicious prices. (☎ 40951. Open daily noon-3pm and 5:30-11pm.) **Bradbury's,** 144 Tullow St., offers basic lunchtime entrees for £3.85. (☎ 40366. Open M-Sa 8:30am-6pm.) **Teach Dolmain** (CHOCK DOL-men), 76 Tullow St., sets a good price for a plate that's *teach*-full of award-winning grub; it's a pretty happening pub at night, too. (☎ 31235. Food served daily noon-9pm.)

The hippest spot in town is the **Dinn Rí** (☎ 33111), a super-pub that spans the entire block between Tullow St. and Kennedy Ave. It's been named one of Ireland's best pubs for the past two years, and its two nightclubs combine on Saturday nights to admit 2000. Of the two, **The Foundry** is rumored to be the coolest. (Nightclub open F-Su until 2am. Cover F and Su £5, Sa £7.) Carlow grooves to live rock and tributes at **Scragg's Alley,** Tullow St. (☎42233. Music W, F, and Su.) Saturday and most Friday nights, the music continues upstairs at the **Nexus Nightclub.** (Cover F £5, Sa £6.) **Tully's,** 149 Tullow St. (☎ 31862), has a crowd of beautiful people and occasional live music. **O'Loughlin's,** 53 Dublin St. (☎ 32205), is dark and velvety. There's no music, but a young crowd tries desperately to be bohemian.

SIGHTS. In the middle of a field 4km from Carlow lies the **Brownshill Dolmen,** marking the site of a 4000 BC burial ground. The granite capstone is somewhat large, sort of the way Mama Cass was somewhat large. It is, in fact, the largest of its kind in Europe, tipping the scales at no fewer than 150 tons. How it was lifted, six millennia ago, is a total mystery. Follow Tullow St. through the traffic light, turn right at the first roundabout, left at the second, and cruise forth: the dolmen is 2 mi. away in a field on the right. **The Carlow Museum,** just off Centaur St., looks like somebody's attic. Current plans are to move the assortment of artifacts to the old library on Dublin St. and restore the vacated building to its proper form as a concert hall and stage. (☎ 40730. Open Tu-F 11am-5pm, Sa-Su 2-5pm. £1.50, students 75p.) **Carlow Castle** lurks behind the storefronts on Castle St. Sadly, the castle ruins are closed to the public. The castle's current condition can be blamed on one Dr. Middleton, who intended to convert the castle into an asylum that would require larger windows and thinner walls. To make his modifications, he used the delicate touch of dynamite—explosives are fickle.

The best time to visit Carlow is during the first two weeks of June, when the town hosts **Éigse** (AIG-sha, "gathering"), a 10-day festival of the arts. Artists from all over Ireland come to present visual, musical, and theatrical works; some events require tickets. Check in at the Éigse Festival office for more information (☎ 40491; www.itc-carlow.ie/eigse).

COUNTY TIPPERARY

In south Tipperary, the towns of Clonmel, Cahir, and Cashel are enveloped in a sprawl of medieval ruins and idyllic countryside. North Tipperary is far from the beaten tourist track, and for good reason: the fertile region has more spud farmers than visitors centers. South of the Cahir-Cashel-Tipperary triangle stretch the Comeragh, Galty, and Knockmealdown Mountains. Although Lismore is located in Co. Waterford, it is covered under Co. Tipperary with the Knockmealdowns.

TIPPERARY TOWN   ☎ 062

> Good-bye to Piccadilly/Farewell to Leicester Square.
> It's a long way to Tipperary/And my heart lies there.

This celebrated town is perhaps less exciting for today's travelers than the World War I marching song would imply. In fact, the song was written in 1912 by an Englishman who had never been to Tipperary. "Tipp Town," as it's affectionately known, is primarily a market town for the fertile Golden Vale farming region. Compared with the rolling hills of the surrounding area and the acclaimed **Glen of Aherlow** to the south, Tipp Town doesn't tend to impress. Buses tip onto **Abbey St.** from **Limerick** (M-Sa 7 per day, Su 6 per day). The **tourist office,** James St., just off Main St., is a useful resource for trips into the glen and the nearby mountains. Glen of Aherlow trail maps sell for 50p. (☎ 51457; www.iol.ie/tipp. Open mid-Mar. to Oct.

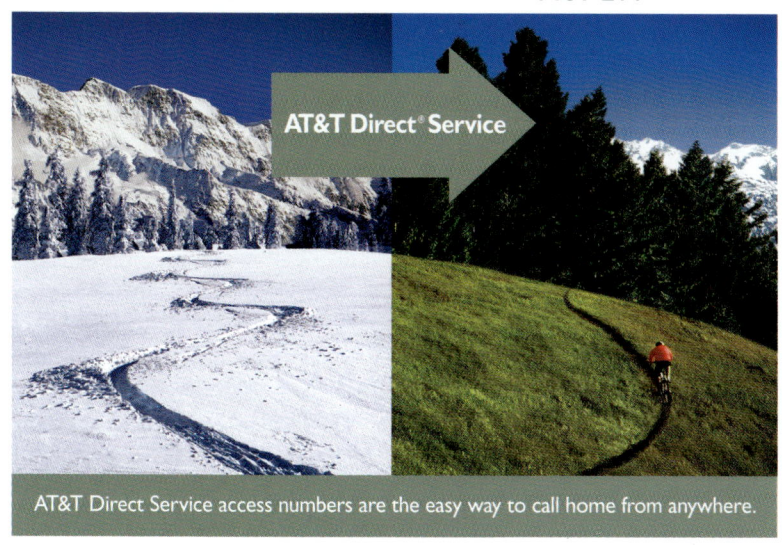

ALPS   ASPEN

AT&T Direct® Service

AT&T Direct Service access numbers are the easy way to call home from anywhere.

Global connection with the AT&T Network | **AT&T direct service**

AT&T

www.att.com/traveler

AT&T Direct® Service

The easy way to call home from anywhere.

AT&T Access Numbers

Austria ● 0800-200-288	France 0800-99-00-11
Belarus ✕ ....8✦800-101	Gambia ● 00111
Belgium ● 0-800-100-10	Germany 0800-2255-288
Bosnia ▲ 00-800-0010	Ghana 0191
Bulgaria ▲ 00-800-0010	Gibraltar 8800
Cyprus ● 080-900-10	Greece ● 00-800-1311
Czech Rep. ▲00-42-000-101	Hungary ● ...06-800-01111
Denmark 8001-0010	Iceland ● 800-9001
Egypt ●(Cairo)✦....510-0200	Ireland ✓......1-800-550-000
Finland ● 0800-110-015	Israel 1-800-94-94-949

AT&T

AT&T Direct® Service

The easy way to call home from anywhere.

AT&T Access Numbers

Austria ● 0800-200-288	France 0800-99-00-11
Belarus ✕ ....8✦800-101	Gambia ● 00111
Belgium ● 0-800-100-10	Germany 0800-2255-288
Bosnia ▲ 00-800-0010	Ghana 0191
Bulgaria ▲ 00-800-0010	Gibraltar 8800
Cyprus ● 080-900-10	Greece ● 00-800-1311
Czech Rep. ▲00-42-000-101	Hungary ● ...06-800-01111
Denmark 8001-0010	Iceland ● 800-9001
Egypt ●(Cairo)✦....510-0200	Ireland ✓......1-800-550-000
Finland ● 0800-110-015	Israel 1-800-94-94-949

AT&T

The best way to keep in touch when you're traveling overseas is with **AT&T Direct® Service**. It's the easy way to call your loved ones back home from just about anywhere in the world. Just cut out the wallet guide below and use it wherever your travels take you.

For a list of AT&T Access Numbers, tear out the attached wallet guide.

AT&T

Italy●	172-1011	Russia (Moscow)▶▲●755-5042
Luxembourg✚	..800-2-0111	(St. Petersbg.)▶▲● ..325-5042
Macedonia●	..99-800-4288	**Slovakia**▲ ..00-42-100-101
Malta	 0800-890-110	**South Africa** ..0800-99-0123
Monaco●	800-90-288	**Spain** 900-99-00-11
Morocco	002-11-0011	**Sweden** 020-799-111
Netherlands●	...0800-022-9111	**Switzerland**● 0800-89-0011
Norway	800-190-11	**Turkey**● 00-800-12277
Poland▲●	..00-800-111-1111	**Ukraine**▲ ....8✦100-11
Portugal▲	800-800-128	U.A. Emirates● 800-121
Romania●.....01-800-4288		**U.K.**............0800-89-0011

FOR EASY CALLING WORLDWIDE
1. Just dial the AT&T Access Number for the country you are calling from.
2. Dial the phone number you're calling.   *3.* Dial your card number.

For access numbers not listed ask any operator for **AT&T Direct®** Service.
In the U.S. call 1-800-331-1140 for a wallet guide listing all worldwide AT&T Access Numbers.
Visit our Web site at: **www.att.com/traveler**
Bold-faced countries permit country-to-country calling outside the U.S.
- ● Public phones require coin or card deposit to place call.
- ▲ May not be available from every phone/payphone.
- ✚ Public phones and select hotels.
- ▶ Await second dial tone.
- ▸ Additional charges apply when calling from outside the city.
- † Outside of Cairo, dial "02" first.
- ✘ Not available from public phones or all areas.
- ✔ Use U.K. access number in N. Ireland.

When placing an international call *from* the U.S., dial 1 800 CALL ATT.

EMEA   © 8/00 AT&T

M-Sa 9:30am-7pm.) An **AIB** is on Main St., along with its rival **Bank of Ireland**. Each offers the convenience of an **ATM**. (Both open M-W and F 10am-4pm, Th 10am-5pm.) The **library** on Davis St. provides free **Internet access** with a £2 card. (Open Tu and F-Sa 10am-1pm and 2-5:30pm, W-Th 2-5:30pm and 6:30-8:30pm.) The **post office** is on Davis St. (Open M-F 9am-5:30pm, Sa 9am-1pm and 2-5:30pm.)

The aptly named **Central House B&B**, 45 Main St., has a welcoming owner and spacious twins and doubles. (☎ 51117. £38.) Other B&Bs are on Emly Rd. about a half-mile west of town off Main St. Tipp features a full-scale **SuperValu** on Main St. (Open M-F 8am-9pm, Sa 8am-7pm, Su 9am-6pm.) For simple bistro fare, you're sure to get lucky at the **Shamrog**, Davis St. (Open M-W 9am-6pm, Th-Sa 9am-8pm.) **The Brown Trout**, Bridge St. (☎ 51912), one block down from Main St., is well-regarded. (Lunch £4.50, dinner £7-11. Open daily 12:30-3pm and 6-9:30pm.) A pool table and music on weekend nights draw young tipplers to **The Underground Tavern**, James St. (☎ 33965), in a converted wine cellar. Tipp's oldest tavern, **Corny's Pub** (☎ 33036), on Davitt St., often hosts trad. The town becomes lively with mid-July's **Pride of Tipperary Festival**, featuring bands, sporting events, and old-fashioned fun.

CASHEL ☎062

The town of Cashel lies halfway between Limerick and Waterford, tucked between a series of mountain ranges on N8. Legend has it that the devil furiously hurled a rock from high above the Tipperary plains when he discovered a church being built in Cashel. The assault failed to thwart the plucky citizens, and today the town sprawls at the foot of the commanding 300 ft. **Rock of Cashel**. With two splendid hostels and a convenient location, Cashel is as fitting a base for the backpacker as it was for the medieval religious orders that scattered the region with ruins.

GETTING THERE. Bus Éireann (☎ 62121) leaves from Bianconi's Bistro on Main St., serving **Cahir** (15min., 4 per day, £2.40), **Cork** (1½hr., 3 per day, £8), **Limerick** (1hr., 4 per day, £8.80), and **Dublin** (3hr., 3 per day, £9). Bus transport to **Waterford** is available via Cahir. Hitching to Cork or Dublin along N8 is a common occurrence, and thumbing west to Tipp and Limerick on N74 is also feasible. *Let's Go* does not recommend this sort of transport.

PRACTICAL INFORMATION. Cashel's **tourist office** shares space with the Heritage Centre in the recently renovated Cashel City Hall on Main St. (☎ 61333. Open July-Aug. M-Sa 9:15am-6pm, Su 11am-5pm, Apr.-June and Sept. M-Sa 9:15am-6pm.) **McInerney's**, Main St., next to SuperValu, **rents bikes**. (☎ 61225. £7 per day, £30 per week. Open M-Tu and Th-Sa 9:30am-6pm.) **AIB**, Main St., has a **bureau de change** and an **ATM**. (Open M-W and F 10am-12:30pm and 1:30-4pm, Th 10am-12:30pm and 1:30-5pm.) The **post office** rocks the Cashel on Main St. (☎ 61418. Open M and W-F 9am-1pm and 2-5:30pm, Tu 9:30am-1pm and 2-5:30pm, Sa 9am-1pm.)

ACCOMMODATIONS. A few hundred yards from the ruins of Hore Abbey lies the stunning **O'Brien's Farm House Hostel**. A five-minute walk from Cashel on Dundrum Rd., the hostel has an incredible view of the Rock and cheerful rooms. (☎ 61003. Serviced laundry £6. 6-bed dorms £9-10; doubles £30. **Camping** £4.50-5.) Back in town, the plush **Cashel Holiday Hostel (IHH)**, 6 John St., just off Main St., has a gorgeous kitchen crowned with a glass pyramid skylight. Spacious bedrooms are named after Irish heroes—there's something thrilling about sleeping in "King Cormac's Room." (☎ 62330; email cashel@iol.ie. Laundry £3.50. Key deposit £3. **Internet access.** 4- to 8-bed dorms £8.50; 4-bed dorms with bath £10; singles £14; doubles £24.) The high quality and high prices of local B&Bs reflect the number of tourists drawn to the Rock. Just steps from the Rock on Dominic St. is **Rockville House**, a fantastic bargain with elegant and fully equipped bedrooms; turn past the tourist office and pass the model village museum. (☎ 61760. Singles £24.50; doubles £34; triples £51.) Three-quarters of a mile up Dualla Rd. lies **Thornbrook House**. All rooms are outfitted with tea and coffee, a TV, and an ever-important hair dryer. (☎ 62388. Singles £19, with bath £21.50; doubles £38, £43.)

180 ■ COUNTY TIPPERARY

FOOD AND PUBS. SuperValu Supermarket, Main St., offers the biggest selection of groceries. (☎ 61555. Open M-Sa 8am-9pm, Su 8am-6pm.) **Centra Supermarket,** Friar St., is open daily 7am-11pm. **The Bake House,** across from the Heritage Centre on Main St., is the town's best spot for coffee and light meals with pseudo-elegant upstairs seating. (☎ 61680. Open M-Sa 8am-7pm, Su 9am-6pm.) Superior pub grub is served up at **O'Sullivan's** on Main St. (☎ 61858. £4.50-5.50; food served M-Sa noon-3pm.) Impale yourself on Mediterranean fare at the **Spearman Restaurant,** on Main St. (☎ 61143. Lunches £6-7, dinner from £8. Open daily 12:30-2:30pm and 6-9pm.) Orange **Pasta Milano,** Lady's Well St., has extensive and affordable cuisine and wines. (☎ 62729. Pasta £7-12, pizza £6-11. Open daily noon-midnight.)

The *craic* is nightly and the atmosphere timeless at **Feehan's,** Main St. (☎ 61929). The bartenders at well-appointed **Dowling's,** 46 Main St., make it their one and only business to pour the best pint in town. Innocuous-looking **Mikey Ryan's,** Main St. (☎ 61431), hides a mighty multilevel beer garden. **Moor Lane Tavern,** Main St. (☎ 62080), excites young locals with cocktails and tunes on the weekends.

SIGHTS. The **Rock of Cashel** (also called **St. Patrick's Rock**) is a huge limestone outcropping topped by medieval buildings. The Rock itself is attached to a number of legends, some historically substantiated, others more dubious. Almost certainly St. Patrick baptized the king of Munster here around AD 450; whether or not he accidentally stabbed the king's feet in the process is debatable. Periodic guided tours are informative if a bit dry; a less erudite but equally awe-inspiring option is to explore the rock's buildings yourself. (Rock open daily mid-June to mid-Sept. 9am-7:30pm, mid-Sept. to mid-Mar. 9:30am-4:30pm, mid-Mar. to mid-June 9:30am-5:30pm. Last admission 45min. before closing. £3.50, students £1.50.) Two-towered **Cormac's Chapel,** consecrated in 1134, holds semi-restored Romanesque paintings, disintegrating stone-carved arches, and a barely visible, ornate sarcophagus once thought to be in the tomb of King Cormac. A highlight of Cashel's illustrious history was the reported burning of the cathedral by the Earl of Kildare in 1495; when Henry VII demanded an explanation, the Earl replied, "I thought the Archbishop was in it." Henry made him Lord Deputy. The 13th-century **Cashel Cathedral** survived the Earl and today's visitors can inspect its vaulted Gothic arches. Next to the cathedral, a 90 ft. **round tower,** built just after 1101, is the oldest part of the Rock. The **museum** (☎ 61437), at the entrance to the castle complex, preserves the 12th-century **St. Patrick's Cross.** A stirringly narrated film on medieval religious structures is shown every hour or so. Down the cow path from the Rock lie the ruins of **Hore Abbey,** built by Cistercian monks who were fond of arches, and presently inhabited by nonchalant sheep. (Always open. Free.)

The small **Heritage Centre,** in the same building as the tourist office on Main St., features permanent exhibitions, including "The Rock: From 4th to 11th Century" and its sequel, "The Rock: 12th-18th Century," as well as temporary exhibitions on such themes as Hore Abbey, Cashel Palace, life in Cashel, and "The Rock: 21st-Century Wrestler Extraordinaire." (☎ 32511. Open May-Sept. daily 9:30am-5:30pm, Oct.-Apr. M-F 9:30am-5:30pm. Free.) The **GPA-Bolton Library,** John St., past the hostel, displays a musty collection of books and silver that formerly belonged to an Anglican archbishop of Cashel, Theophilus Bolton. The collection harbors ecclesiastical texts and rare manuscripts, including a 1550 edition of Machiavelli's *Il Principe,* the first English translation of *Don Quixote,* and what is locally reputed to be the smallest book in the world. (☎ 61944. Open July-Aug. Tu-Su 9:30am-6pm, Sept.-Dec. and Mar.-June M-F 9:30am-5:30pm. £1.50, students and seniors £1.) The **Brú Ború Heritage Centre,** at the base of the Rock, performs Irish traditional music, song, and dance to international acclaim. (☎ 61122. Performances mid-June to mid-Sept. Tu-Sa at 9pm. £8, £27 with dinner.) In the town of **Golden,** 5 mi. west of Cashel on Tipperary Rd., stand the ruins of lovely **Althassel Abbey,** a 12th-century Augustinian priory founded by the Red Earl of Dunster.

CAHIR ☎ 052

Cahir (CARE) maintains a delicate balance of commerce and tourism—a massive concrete grain depot looms over the well-preserved castle that is the town's pride and joy. It's worth an afternoon's visit, but the only hostels are in the surrounding countryside and a long trek to the limited food and pub options in town.

GETTING THERE. Trains leave from the station off Cashel Rd., just past the church, for **Limerick** and **Waterford** (M-Sa 2 per day). **Bus Éireann** runs from the tourist office to **Cashel** (15min., 4 per day, £2.50); **Limerick** via **Tipperary** (1hr.; M-Th and Sa 5 per day, F 6 per day; £7.30), **Waterford** (1¼hr.; M-Th and Sa 6 per day, F 7 per day; £7.70), **Cork** (1½hr., 4 per day, £7), and **Dublin** (3hr., 3 per day, £10). **Hitchers** to Dublin or Cork position themselves on N8, a 20-minute hike from the center of town. Those who hitch to Limerick or Waterford wait just outside of town on N24, which passes through the town square. *Let's Go* does not recommend hitchhiking.

PRACTICAL INFORMATION. The centrally located **tourist office**, Castle St., gives out free town maps but can't provide much advice about the mountains. (☎ 41453. Open daily 9am-6pm.) Backpackers can stow their bags free for a time at the **Crock O' Gold**, across from the tourist office. **AIB**, just up the street from the tourist office, has an **ATM**. (Open M-Tu and Th-F 10am-4pm, W 10am-5pm.) The **post office** is on Church St. (Open M-F 9:30am-1pm and 2-5:30pm, Sa 9:30am-1pm.)

ACCOMMODATIONS, FOOD, AND PUBS. There are two hostels in the countryside relatively close to Cahir. **Lisakyle Hostel (IHH)**, 1 mi. south on Ardfinnan Rd., is the more accessible of the two. If coming from the bus station, walk up the hill and make a right at Cahir House. The exterior is bedecked with flowers, and the rooms are basic but reasonable resting places. Reserve a bed with the hostel's courteous owners at their private residence on Church St., across from the post office; they'll also arrange lifts to the hostel from town. (☎ 41963. Sheets 50p. 6- to 8-bed dorms £7; private rooms £8.50 per person. **Camping** £4.) The **Kilcoran Farm Hostel (IHH)** promises to be an education in rural living—the vocal sheep out back are garrulous hosts. From Cahir, take Cork Rd. for 4 mi., turn left at the Top Petrol Station, and then, after a quarter-mile, veer right at the T-shaped junction. Call for pickup from town. (☎ 41906 or (088) 539 185. Private rooms £10 per person.) One of the closest B&Bs to Cahir is **The Rectory**, Cashel Rd., just beyond the railway tracks, which provides enormous, old-fashioned rooms in a beautiful stately manor. (☎ 41406; email faheyr@tinet.ie. Open Apr.-Oct. Doubles £36-40.) **Tinsley House,** above a small shop in the square, has TV- and bath-equipped rooms, and the proprietor is an encyclopedia of local history. (☎ 41947. Doubles £36.)

The best bet for groceries is **SuperValu Supermarket**, Bridge St., across the bridge from the castle. (☎ 41515. Open M-Th 8am-6pm, F 8am-8pm, Sa 8am-9pm.) **Castle Arms,** Castle St., serves up cheap grub in an atmosphere that could only be called "pub." (☎ 42506. Hot entrees £3.50-4.50.) A local favorite is the **Galtee Inn**, The Square, where lunch is reasonable, though dinners swell in size and price. (☎ 41247. Lunch £5.50; served daily noon-3pm.) Cannons once aimed towards the castle from the site of **J. Morrissey's**, Castle. St., but these days more peaceful invaders reign. Mr. and Mrs. Knight won the pub in a Guinness promotion. **Galtee Inn,** and the **Castle Arms,** Castle St. (☎ 42506), are quieter locales for a civilized drink.

SIGHTS. Cahir is often defined by **Cahir Castle**, one of the larger and better-preserved castles in Ireland. It is exactly what every tourist envisions a castle to be—heavy, lots of battlements, and gray. Built in the 13th century to be all but impregnable to conventional military attack, the castle's defenses were rendered obsolete by the advent of the age of artillery. In 1599, the Earl of Essex forced its surrender by tossing some cannonballs its way, one of which is still visibly stuck in the wall. Note the 11,000-year-old preserved head of the long-extinct Irish Elk; the noble beast's antlers span nearly an entire wall. Climb the towers for an unparalleled view of the tourist office and parking lot. There is a free hour-long tour of the castle. (☎ 41011. Open daily mid-June to mid-Sept. 9am-7:30pm, Apr. to mid-June and mid-Sept. to mid-Oct. 9:30am-5:30pm, mid-Oct. to Mar. 9:30am-4:30pm. Last admission 30min. before closing. £2, seniors £1.50, students £1.)

The broad River Suir that flows into Waterford Harbour is still a mere stream in Cahir. The wildly green **river walk** starts at the tourist office and leads past the 19th-century **Swiss Cottage,** a half-hour walk from town. A charming jumble of architectural styles, the cottage was built so that the occupants of Cahir Castle could fish, hunt, and pretend to be peasants. Gorgeously restored, it is a delight for anyone who fancies building, decorating, and being rich. (☎ 41144. Open May-Sept. daily 10am-6pm, Apr. Tu-Su 10am-1pm and 2-5pm, Mar. and Oct.-Nov. Tu-Su 10am-1pm and 2-4:30pm. Access by 30min. guided tour only. Last admission 45min. before closing. £2, seniors £1.50, students £1.) **Fishing** opportunities line the river walk past the Swiss Cottage. Fishing licenses are required, and can be obtained at the Heritage cornerstone on Church St. (☎ 42730. Open daily 7am-11pm.)

The **Mitchelstown Caves** drip 8 mi. off the Cahir-Cork road in the hamlet of **Burncourt,** about halfway between Cahir and Mitchelstown. A 30-minute tour takes you deep into a series of gooey, rippled subterranean chambers filled with fantastic mineral formations. (☎ 67246. Open daily 10am-6pm; last tour 5:30pm. £3.50.)

NEAR CAHIR: GALTY MOUNTAINS AND GLEN OF AHERLOW

South of Tipperary Town, the river Aherlow cuts a rich and scenic valley. West of Cahir, along the south edge of the glen, the Galty Mountains rise abruptly. This purplish and lake-dotted range boasts **Galtymore,** Ireland's third-highest peak at 3018 ft. The Glen and mountains are idyllic surroundings for a picnic-based daytrip or a full-fledged trek. Serious hikers should invest in sheets 66 and 74 of the *Ordnance Survey,* available at local tourist offices and bookstores in Tipperary and Cahir (£4.20). The Tipp Town tourist office sells a series of trail maps of varying difficulty (50p). The walks wind through the **Glen of Aherlow, Lake Muskry, Lake Borheen, Glencush, Lake Curra,** and **Duntry League Hill. Glenbarra** is also a popular base camp, reached by driving west from Cahir toward Mitchelstown.

The **Glen of Aherlow (Ballydavid Wood) Youth Hostel (An Óige/HI),** 6 mi. northwest of Cahir off Limerick Rd., is a renovated old hunting lodge that makes a good start for cavorting around the Galtees. (☎ (062) 54148. June-Sept. dorms £7, Mar.-May and Oct. £6.) Dedicated hikers sometimes make the 10 mi. trek across the mountains to the **Mountain Lodge (An Óige/HI),** Burncourt, a gas-lit Georgian hunting lodge in the middle of the woods. From Cahir, follow the Mitchelstown Rd. (N8) 8 mi., then turn right at the sign for another 2 mi. on an unpaved path. (☎ (052) 67277. Dorms June-Sept. £7, Mar.-May £5.50.) The **Kilcoran Farm Hostel** (☎ (052) 41906) is a convenient stop on the hike back (see **Cahir,** p. 181). The **campsite** in the Glen of Aherlow, **Ballinacourty House,** is excellent, and the staff provides detailed information on the Glen. (☎ (062) 56230. Open Apr. to mid-Sept. Meals and cooking facilities available. £8 per tent, off-season £7; additional £1 per person.) They also operate a pleasant **B&B** and a pricey restaurant. (Doubles with bath £38.) To reach Ballinacourty House, take R663 off the Cahir-Tipperary road (N24) in Bansha and follow the road for 8 mi. to the signposted turnoff.

CLONMEL (CLUAIN MEALA) ☎052

Clonmel (pop. 17,000) derives its name from the Irish phrase for "the honey meadow." This medieval town on the banks of the River Suir (SURE) sweetens in the fall, when locally produced Bulmer's Cider scents the air with apple notes. As Co. Tipperary's economic hub, Clonmel offers all the comforts of modern life after a day spent exploring the nearby Comeragh Mountains.

CLONMEL (CLUAIN MEALA) ■ 183

GETTING THERE

Trains: Prior Park Rd. (☎ 21982), about 1 mi. north of the town center. Trains chug from here to **Limerick** (50min., M-Sa 2 per day, £9) and **Waterford** on the way to **Rosslare Harbour** (1¼hr., M-Sa 1 per day, £11).

Buses: Bus information is available at **Rafferty Travel,** Gladstone St. (☎ 22622). Open M-Sa 9am-6pm. Buses leave from in front of the train station to **Waterford** (1hr.; M-Sa 6 per day, Su 4 per day; £5.90), **Kilkenny** via **Carrick-on-Suir** (M-Sa 4 per day, Su 3 per day; £3.50), **Limerick** via **Tipperary** (5 per day, £8.80), **Cork** (2hr., 3 per day, £9), **Dublin** (3¼hr., 3 per day, £8), **Rosslare** (3½hr.; M-Sa 3 per day, Su 2 per day; £10), and **Galway** (3¾hr.; M-F 5 per day, Su 3 per day; £12). **Rapid Express** (☎ 29292) runs their own bus to **Dublin** via **Kilkenny** (3hr.; M-Sa 3 per day, Su 2 per day; £5).

ORIENTATION AND PRACTICAL INFORMATION

Clonmel's central street runs parallel to the **Suir River.** From the station, follow **Prior Park Rd.** straight into town. Prior Park Rd. becomes businesslike **Gladstone St.,** which intersects the main drag, known successively as **O'Connell St., Mitchell St., Parnell St.,** and **Irishtown. Sarsfield St.** and **Abbey St.** run off the main street toward the riverside quays.

Tourist Office: Sarsfield St. (☎ 22960), across from the Clonmel Arms Hostel. Pick up the 6 self-guided walking tours of the Knockmealdown Mountains (50p), and the free Heritage Trail map of town. Open July-Aug. M-Sa 9:30am-5:30pm, Sept.-June M-F 9:30am-5pm.

Bank: AIB (☎ 22500) and **Bank of Ireland,** both with **ATMs,** are neighbors on O'Connell St. Both open M 10am-5pm, Tu-F 10am-4pm.

Pharmacy: Joy's, 68 O'Connell St. (☎ 21204), Open M-Sa 9am-6pm.

Emergency: ☎ 999; no coins required. **Police** *(Garda):* Emmet St. (☎ 22222).

Hospital: St. Joseph's/St. Michael's, Western Rd. (☎ 21900).

Post Office: Emmet St. (☎ 21164), parallel to Gladstone St. Open M-Sa 9am-5pm.

Internet Access: Circles, Market St. The snooker club has 2 **Internet** stations, operable for 7½p per min. (☎ 23315. Open daily 11am-11pm.) The **library** also provides free **Internet access** in 30min. slots. (☎ 24545. Open M-Tu 10am-5:30pm, W-Th 10am-8:30pm, F-Sa 10am-5pm.)

ACCOMMODATIONS

Not the most backpacker-friendly town in Ireland, Clonmel caters more to the hotel and B&B crowd. The only hostel, **Powers-the-Pot Hostel and Caravan Park,** Harney's Cross, is well outside of town. To reach the hostel, follow Parnell St. east out of town, turn right at the first traffic light (not N24), cross the Suir, and continue straight for 5½ mi. of arduous mountain road to the signposted turnoff. The 19th-century house is supposedly the highest in Ireland, and holds fluffy beds and a bar/restaurant under a thatched roof. Call before you make the trek to make sure they have a free bed. Owners Niall and Jo can answer all your hillwalking questions and provide maps and guides for the Munster Way. (☎ 23085. Laundry £2. Freezing and smoking facilities for anglers. Open May-Sept. Breakfast £4.50, dinners £7.50-10. Dorms £7; private rooms £8. **Camping** £3.50 per person.)

In Clonmel, the area past Irishtown along the Cahir Rd. is scattered with **B&Bs.** If you're willing to walk a mile or two from town, your options are greater. Closer to downtown, guests watch swans from the windows of their large rooms at the **Riverside House,** on New Quay overlooking the Suir. (☎ 25781. £17.50 per person.)

FOOD

The local outpost of the **Tesco** supermarket empire is on Gladstone St. (☎ 27797. Open M-Tu and Sa 8:30am-7pm, W-F 8:30am-9pm, Su 11am-6pm.) **The Honey Pot**, 14 Abbey St. sells health foods and bulk grains, and hosts an organic vegetable market on Saturday mornings. (☎ 21457. Open M-Sa 9:30am-6pm.)

Niamh's (NEEVS), Mitchell St. (☎ 25698). Specialty coffees, hot lunches, sandwiches, and all-day breakfasts served up in a relaxing deli-style restaurant. Whopping vegetarian pita £3.75. Open M-F 9am-5:45pm, Sa 9am-5pm.

Angela's Restaurant and Coffee Emporium, Abbey St. (☎ 26899), off Mitchell St. Exquisitely fresh and creative vegetarian and meat dishes served on country pine tables. Salads, specials £5-6. Open M-F 9am-5:30pm, Sa 9am-5pm.

O Tuamas Cafe, 5-6 Market Pl. (☎ 27170). A filling meal, hot or cold, for under £6, or mouth-watering desserts. Open M-Th 9am-6pm, F 9am-8pm, Sa 9am-5:30pm.

Catalpa, Sarsfield St. (☎ 26821), next to the tourist office. Italian feasts served in a former bank vault. Popular with the locals. Call ahead for reservations. Pasta £5-7; pizza £4.20-5; meat dishes £7-13. Open Tu-Su 12:30-2:30 and 6:30-11pm.

Tom Skinny's Pizza Parlor, Market St. (☎ 26006). Pizza made fresh right before your eyes. Most pizzas £4-9. Open daily noon-midnight.

PUBS

John Allen's (☎ 29028), next to the church in Irishtown, is surprisingly bright, luring a jolly crowd of all ages with trad every Sunday. Enormous, elaborate **Mulcahy's**, 47 Gladstone, displays a curious combination of decorative themes. (☎ 25054. Trad W nights.) Thursday through Sunday, the pub also hosts **Danno's**, an over-18 disco. (Cover £5-6.) **Barry's**, O'Connell St., counters with a nightclub of their own to amuse you, **Goodfellas**, mobbed by young, grooving clowns Thursday through Sunday. (☎ 25505. Cover £3-6.) Check the *Nationalist* for entertainment listings.

SIGHTS

Clonmel might win the best-signposted tourist-trail award, but certainly not the content or eloquence portions of the pageant. Pick up the Heritage Trail map in the tourist office (free). Stops along the way include the **West Gate** at the west end of O'Connell St., an 1831 reproduction of the medieval gate that separated Irishtown from the more prosperous Anglo-Norman area. The 84 ft. octagonal tower of **Old St. Mary's Church,** Mary St., stands near the remnants of the town wall that failed to keep Cromwell's armies out in 1650. Just inside the door of the **Franciscan Friary,** Abbey St., are the 15th-century tomb effigies of a knight and lady of the Butler family of Cahir. Clonmel's history as a transportation center is remembered at the **Museum of Transport,** in a converted mill off Emmett St., where antique cars are packed in to the ceiling. (☎ 29727. Open June-Sept. M-Sa 10am-6pm, Su 2:30-6:30pm; Oct.-May closed Su. £2.50, students and seniors £1.50.)

The **Tipperary S.R. County Museum,** The Borstan, next to the swimming pool, hosts small traveling exhibitions but focuses on telling the story of the county's history from the Stone Age to modern times. (☎ 25399. Open M-Sa 10am-5pm. Free.) Several walks in the area and nearby Nire Valley are described in the tourist office's glossy leaflets *Clonmel Walk #1* and *#2* (50p each). See **Comeragh Mountains** (below) for day hike info.

THE EAST MUNSTER WAY

The East Munster Way footpath starts in Carrick-on-Suir, hits Clonmel, skirts the Comeragh Mountains, and runs full-force into the Knockmealdowns, ending 43 mi. later in Clogheen. From there, connections can be made through the Druhallow

Way to the Kerry Way. The best maps to use are sheets 74 and 75 of the *1:50,000 Ordnance Survey* series. In addition, the *East Munster Way Map Guide* ($4), available at the tourist office and at Powers-the-Pot Hostel, in Clonmel, provides a written guide and an accurate but less detailed map (as an added bonus, it points out all the pubs along the way). The route contact is the Tipperary Co. Council in Clonmel (☎ (052) 25399), but Powers-the-Pot is the best information center on hiking in the Comeragh and Knockmealdown Mountains. For more wilderness advice, see **Camping and the Outdoors**, p. 70.

COMERAGH MOUNTAINS

The Comeragh "mountains" are more like large hills; not even the highest peaks are very steep. The ground is almost always soft and wet; most of the terrain is manageable in sneakers. *Nire Valley Walk #1 to 12* (50p each, at the Clonmel tourist office and Powers-the-Pot Hostel) are excellent waterproof maps illustrating day hikes from Clonmel. For more extensive hikes, begin from **Powers-the-Pot Hostel,** a half-mile off the Munster Way (see **Clonmel,** p. 182). The best map of the Comeraghs is sheet 75 of the *Ordnance Series*. With a map in hand, head east from Powers-the-Pot and follow the ridges south. The land is mostly open and in good weather it's relatively hard to get lost, but make sure that someone knows you're out there. Guided walking is also available; inquire with Niall at Powers-the-Pot (☎ (052) 23085). You might also consider doing the Comeragh Mountains on horseback. (Call **Melody's** in Ballymacarbry, ☎ (052) 36147. $10 per hr.) The technical term for the mountain hollows so common in the mild Comeraghs is "cwms" (KOOMS). Borrowed from the Welsh, it's the only word in the English language without a vowel (not including those sneaky "y" words).

KNOCKMEALDOWN MOUNTAINS

Straddling the Tipperary-Waterford border 12 mi. south of Cahir, the Knockmealdown Mountains are roughly contoured, like the inside of an Aero bar. *Knockmealdown Walks 1 to 4* (50p) are available at local tourist offices, including those in Clonmel and Clogheen. All four start at Clogheen; walks 2 and 4 assume transportation to nearby carparks. As an alternative, many hikers prefer to begin in the town of **Newcastle,** where tiny but locally renowned **Nugent's Pub** stands. For guided **tours,** contact Helen McGrath (☎ (052) 36359). Tours depart at noon on Sundays from the Newcastle Car Park. ($3-5, other days available by request.) Sights to head for include the spectacular **Vee Road** south from Clogheen, which erupts with purple rhododendrons on its way to the **Knockmealdown Gap.** Just before the **Vee,** in the town of **Graigue,** thirsty pilgrims can stop in at **Ryan's Pub,** a charming little thatched building in the middle of a farm yard. At the pass of the Knockmealdown Gap, about two-thirds of the way to the top of the gap, the pines give way to heather and bracken, and a parking lot marks the path up to the top of **Sugarloaf Hill.** The walk takes about an hour and on a clear day it affords a panorama of patchwork fields. From there, you can continue on to the **Knockmealdown Peak** (2609 ft.), the highest in the range. Beautiful (and supposedly bottomless) **Bay Loch,** on the road down to Lismore, is the stuff of legend. The affable and decidedly unofficious **tourist office** in Clogheen, across from the Vee Rd. turnoff, is generous with local maps and lore. (☎ (052) 65258. Open M-Sa 9am-5pm.) Five minutes from the village on Cahir Rd., **Parsons Green,** part garden and part **campsite,** offers river walks, boat rides, and pony rides. (☎ (052) 65290. Kitchen. Laundry $4. $3 per small tent. $2 per person.) The **Kilmorna Farm Hostel** (☎ (058) 54315) in Lismore is a more luxurious, less convenient base for hiking in the range (see **Lismore,** below).

LISMORE ☎ 058

The disproportionate grandeur of Lismore's castle and cathedral reminds visitors that this sleepy little town was once a thriving monastic center. Nestled against the Blackwater River at the end of Vee Rd., Lismore is actually in Co. Waterford, but makes a convenient base for exploring Tipperary's Knockmealdown Mountains.

COUNTY TIPPERARY

GETTING THERE. Bus Éireann stops across from the tourist office and runs to **Waterford** via **Dungarvan** (1¼hr., M and Th 1 per day, Sa 2 per day) and **Cork** (1¼hr., F 1 per day). The best way to get to Lismore is by foot or bike on the Vee Rd. or along the Blackwater River. Hitching to Dungarvan is common, but not recommended by *Let's Go*. To get to Cork, hitchers first ride east to Fermoy, then head south on N8.

PRACTICAL INFORMATION. Lismore's extremely helpful **tourist office** shares the old courthouse building with the **heritage centre.** (☎ 54975. Open June-Aug. M-Sa 9:30am-5:30pm, Su noon-5:30pm; Apr.-May and Sept.-Oct. M-Sa 9:30am-5:30pm.) Free **Internet access** is available with a £2 card at the **library** on Main St. (Open M-F 11:30am-1pm and 2-5:30pm.) The **post office** is located on East Main St. (☎ 54220. Open M-F 9am-1pm and 2-5:30pm, Sa 9am-1pm.)

ACCOMMODATIONS, FOOD, AND PUBS. One mile from Lismore, barnyard sounds fill the rooms at the **Kilmorna Farm Hostel.** From town, walk up Chapel St. to the left of the Interpretive Centre, take the first left at the Catholic church, and follow the signs (or call for a lift). The 18th-century coach house is completed by gingham curtains and beds built by a local craftsman. The working farm supports cows, chickens, horses, six dogs, and a TV. (☎ 54315. Continental breakfast £4. Laundry £4. 3- to 6-bed dorms £8; doubles £19.) Basic hardwood dorms are tucked above the bar at the **Red House Inn** across from the Interpretive Centre on Main St. (☎ 54248. £16 per person.)

The quality of food in Lismore is not compromised by the lack of quantity. **SuperSave** has groceries on East Main St. (☎ 54122. Open M-W 9am-6pm, Th 9am-7:30pm, F 9am-8pm, Sa 9:30am-8:30pm.) **Eamonn's Place,** East Main St., serves tasty Irish meals in their gorgeous beer garden. (☎ 54025. Lunch entrees from £5, served M-F 12:30-2:30pm; dinners £7-8, served M-Su 6-9pm.) **Madden's Bar,** East Main St. (☎ 54148), serves surprisingly refined lunches at reasonable prices (£4-6) and many a pint in their renovated pub. The **Red House Inn** (☎ (058) 54248) has periodic bursts of trad on weekend nights.

SIGHTS. Swathed in foliage and looming grandly over the Blackwater River, **Lismore Castle** is stunning. Once a medieval fort and bishop's residence, the castle was extensively remodeled in the 19th century with great imagination but little historical insight. In 1814, the Lismore Crozier and the *Book of Lismore*, priceless artifacts thought to have been lost forever, were found hidden in the castle walls. The castle was once the home of Sir Walter Raleigh, and also the birthplace of 17th-century scientist Robert Boyle (of PV=nRT fame). The castle is privately owned by the English Duke of Devonshire, who sometimes takes in guests for an estimated £7000 per week. Admire the castle from the bridge over the Blackwater River, because its **gardens** are not worth their admission fee. (☎ 54424. Open mid-Apr. to Sept. daily 1:45-4:45pm. £3, under 16 £1.50.) The bridge is also the starting point for the peaceful **Lady Louisa's Walk** along the tree-lined Blackwater.

Locals whisper that a secret passage connects the castle to **St. Carthage's Cathedral,** Deanery Hill. Outside the cathedral, a large number of tombs are sealed with stone slabs in the ancient graveyard. The graves are a relic of Lismore's past as a center for body-snatching; the slabs ensured that stiffs wouldn't be stolen. The cathedral did better at retaining historical markers: a collection of 9th- and 10th-century engraved commemorative stones are set into one wall of the cathedral.

Lismore's **Heritage Centre,** in the town square, includes a 30-minute video presentation and a cursory exhibit highlighting the 1000-year-old *Book of Lismore*. (☎ 54975. Open June-Aug. M-Sa 9:30am-5:30pm, Su noon-5:30pm; Apr.-May and Sept.-Oct. M-Sa 9:30am-5:30pm, Su noon-5:30pm. £3, students £2.50.) The center also runs guided tours of town (£3) and sells self-guided tour booklets (£1). Those seeking to vary their Guinness diet should stop in at the **West Waterford Vineyards,** 5 mi. from Lismore off Dungarvan Rd. The Vineyard produces a dry white wine in addition to seasonal fruit wines like pear and strawberry, and will send you on your way armed with any local information you wish. (☎ 54283. Open daily 10am-8pm; call ahead for wine tastings.) Two miles from Lismore is a car park for the locally beloved **Towerswalk.** From the castle, cross the bridge back and make a left. The towers and entrance gate to a grand castle were begun by Keily-Ussher, a mid-19th-century local landlord. Today there is a woodsy walk to "the Folly" (1hr.).

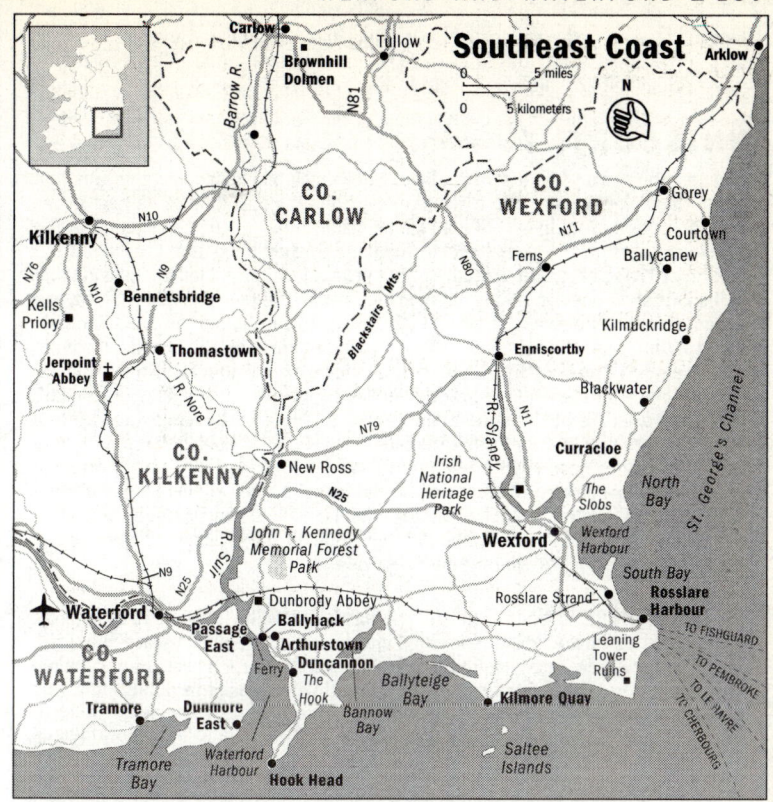

WEXFORD AND WATERFORD

Geography makes Co. Wexford's oceanfront the entrance to Ireland for many visitors coming from France, Wales, or England. Ireland's invaders—from Vikings to Normans, Christians to modern backpackers—have begun their island-conquering here. Naturally, with so many people passing through, Wexford has been particularly prone to foreign influences. Away from the salty pubs and crowded streets of Wexford town, thin beaches stretch from dismal, highly-trafficked Rosslare Harbour and pop up again at the county's southwest edge, along idyllic Waterford Harbour and Tramore. Co. Waterford is dedicated to the production of industrial and agricultural goods. Waterford City is the commercial and cultural core of the Southeast, where thriving crystal and other sootier industries create an urban environment that is worlds apart from the sheep-speckled fields of the inner county. New Ross, with its fine hostels and urban amenities, is a good base for exploring the Southeast.

Slí Charman (SHLEE KAR-man), usually referred to as "An Slí," is a pathway that runs 135 mi. along Wexford's coast from the Co. Wicklow border through Wexford and Rosslare to Waterford Harbour. The relatively close Wicklow Way provides more invigorating hikes. Maps of both paths hang at major Bord Fáilte offices in Wexford and Waterford. Major roads in the region are the east-west N25 (Rosslare-Wexford-New Ross-Waterford), the north-south N11 (Wexford-Enniscorthy-Arklow-Dublin), and the N79 from Enniscorthy to New Ross.

ENNISCORTHY ☎ 054

The handsome town of Enniscorthy lies 14 mi. north of Wexford on the hills that straddle the River Slaney. The town is exceptionally conscious of its part in the history of Irish nationalism and also takes pride in its recent resurgence in the public eye: mention the year "'98" to locals, and they'll assume you mean the Rebellion of 1798 against the British. In that year, a local priest led an uprising that held the British at bay for 12 days at nearby Vinegar Hill (see **Rebellion, Union, and Reaction,** p. 13). "Ninety-eight" might also refer to the leg of the 1998 Tour de France that honored the rebels of 1798 by swinging through hilly Enniscorthy. In the 20th century, Enniscorthy was one of the only towns to join Dublin's 1916 Easter Rising, and the last to surrender (see **The Easter Rising,** p. 16). In the years between the assaults of the British and bicycles, Enniscorthy has evolved into a treasure for the Irish history buff. Large amounts of recent construction have produced a sparkling new 1798 museum and a new hostel. An eclectic museum housed in a 13th-century Norman castle captures the complementary range of sites. While a history lesson on Ireland's political conflicts may be a sobering experience, Enniscorthy's 20 or so pubs greatly diminish the chances of that—especially during one of the town's summer festivals.

GETTING THERE. The N11 motorway passes straight through Enniscorthy, heading north toward Arklow, Wicklow, and Dublin and south toward Wexford. **Trains** connect Enniscorthy to **Rosslare** (50min., £7) in one direction and **Dublin** (2¼hr., £10) in the other (3 per day each direction). **Buses** stop outside the Bus Stop Shop on **Templeshannon Quay,** between the two bridges and across the river from the squares, then run south to **Wexford** (M-Sa 8 per day, Su 6, £4) and **Waterford** (3 per day, £7.50), and north through **Ferns** (10min.) to **Dublin** (M-Sa 6-7 per day, Su 5 per day, £7).

ORIENTATION AND PRACTICAL INFORMATION. From the railway station, cross the river at the **Slaney Dr. bridge,** then take a left to reach **Abbey Square,** one of the main shopping areas, or keep heading uphill to hit bustling **Market Square.** The moderately informed **tourist office** is in the castle off Castle Hill. (☎ 34699. Open M-Sa 10am-6pm, Su 2-5:30pm; winter hours are shorter.) Use the info-center to get a map of the town and other handouts; for intensive advice, fabulous **Maura Flannery** in the souvenir shop across the street is your woman (☎ 36800 or (086) 816 2301; fax 36628). Several banks offer **24-hour ATMs,** among them **AIB** (☎ 33163; open M 10am-5pm, Tu-F 10am-4pm) and the **Irish Permanent Bank,** Market Sq. (☎ 35700; open M-Tu and Th-F 9:30am-5pm, W 10:15am-5pm). **Kenny for Bikes,** on the river at Slaney St., will rent bikes. (☎ 33255 or (087) 232 1137; email kennysfb@iol.ie. £8 per day, £40 per week, with discounts on extended rentals.) For taxis call ☎ 37222, 33975, 36666, or 37888. One **post office** (☎ 33226) is by the Abbey Sq. roundabout, and another is across the street from the cathedral (☎ 33980).

ACCOMMODATIONS, FOOD, AND PUBS. Platform 1, Railway Sq., is a shimmering new hostel right by the train station with a hidden, but helpful, staff. Platform 1 is spacious and secure, with a billiard table and Internet access. (☎ 37766; email plat@indigo.ie. Wheelchair accessible. Dorm £8; twin £30; quad £45, off-season prices may be lower.) B&B options are numerous, and some of the best easily justify a 15-minute walk (or £2 taxi) from Main St. At **Adelmar,** Summerhill, Mrs. Agnes Barry's hospitality and delightful company do the trick. Turn right past Murphy's Hotel then left on Bohreen Hill and follow the signs. (☎ 33668. Open

June-Sept. £15 per person.) Just off Market Square is **P. J. Murphy's B&B,** 9 Main St.—not to be confused with Murphy's Hotel. The B&B is just across the street from the hotel, directly above Murphy's Pub. (Obviously, an industrious branch of Murphys settled in Enniscorthy.) The rooms are comfy and cozy and the guest room is full of plump cushions. (☎ 33522. £17-18 per person.) Ten minutes out of town, **The Summerhill B&B** sports cheerful dishware and brightly colored sheets and pillows. Follow Duffry St. past the cathedral. A signpost marks the turn. Take a right, walk past St. Aidan's school and turn the corner. Summerhill will be on your left. (☎ 34219, fax 38109. £20 per person. Singles may be unavailable in busy seasons.) To find **Don Carr House,** walk past Summerhill and make a sharp right at the first intersection onto Bohreen Hill. The house has a homey feel and a sumptuous sunroom. (☎ 33458. £18-20.)

Food is plentiful at various pubs or at the **L&N SuperValu,** in the shopping center on Mill Park Rd. off Abbey Sq. (☎ 34541. Open M-Tu and Sa 8am-8pm, W 8am-9pm, Th-F 8am-10pm, Su 8-6.) Twice-awarded Wexford County "pub of the year," **The Antique Tavern,** 14 Slaney St. (☎ 33428), is crammed with Enniscorthy artifacts and worldwide antiques, all brought in by devoted patrons of the 200-year-old pub. Vegetarians or those seeking home-baked goodies should head to **The Baked Potato,** 18 Rafter St., for cheap, hot food. (☎ 34085. Open M-Sa 8am-6pm.) The baked goods are especially tasty across the street at **Karen's Kitchen,** 11 Rafter St., where hot scones and tea are a cheap and filling start to a morning. (☎ 36488. Bakery items around £1; most entrees £2.50-4.50. Open M-Sa 9am-6pm.) **Cafe del Mar,** across the street from the Castle, brews good coffee and healthy, inexpensive eats. (☎ 38531. Salads and sandwiches £1-3.) Pubs are alive and well in Enniscorthy. **Rackards,** 23 Rafter St. (☎ 33747), with a little more room and weekly trad sessions, is among the hippest spots in town. A zesty lunch is served here from noon to 3pm. **Shenanigan's** is the mischievous newcomer in Market Square. Munch on the good grub and check out the multiple mosaics. To complement its tomfoolery and ballyhoo, Shenanigan's offers Internet access. (£1 for 8min. Late bar Th-Su and disco on Th-F.)

◼ SIGHTS. The new **National 1798 Visitor Centre,** a five-minute walk away from town on Mill Park Rd., is an impressive multimedia barrage that thoughtfully examines the revolution of 1798 and the battle of Vinegar Hill. One room presents the conflict as a chess problem with larger-than-life pieces; there's also a 14-minute film with all the battle stabbing you could want. The visually sharp exhibits drive home the magnitude of 20,000 patriotic deaths. If you're up for a 4km walk (or drive), head across the river to the summit of **Vinegar Hill** itself; the battle site gives a fantastic view of the town below. For a more intimate perspective, unofficial town historian Maura Flannery's **Walking Tour of Enniscorthy** can't be beat. The one-hour tour reveals the dirty little secrets of the town's prestigious past. Find out about the time in 1649 that Enniscorthy women got Cromwell's soldiers drunk and killed them, or how John P. Holland, a native son, invented the submarine—kind of the way Da Vinci did. (Information available at the tourist office; see **Practical Information,** above. Call one day ahead to reserve a tour in English or French. 5-person tours preferred, so check to see if tours are already scheduled. £3, children £1.50; ask for senior discounts; mention *Let's Go* for further savings.)

The tourist office is inside the Norman castle, but the **Wexford County Museum** fills the bulk of the building. (☎ 35926. Open M-Sa 10am-6pm, Su 2-6pm; shorter hours in the off-season. £3, seniors and students £2, children 50p.) The museum chronicles Co. Wexford's collective stream-of-consciousness, providing a unique take on your customary historical narrative. The museum has rooms that include the original letters and belongings of the principle players of the 1798 and 1916 rebellions. Initially a 13-object display in 1960, curators have stuffed the castle from dungeon to eaves with odd bits such as ship figureheads and a collection of international police patches.

Wexford

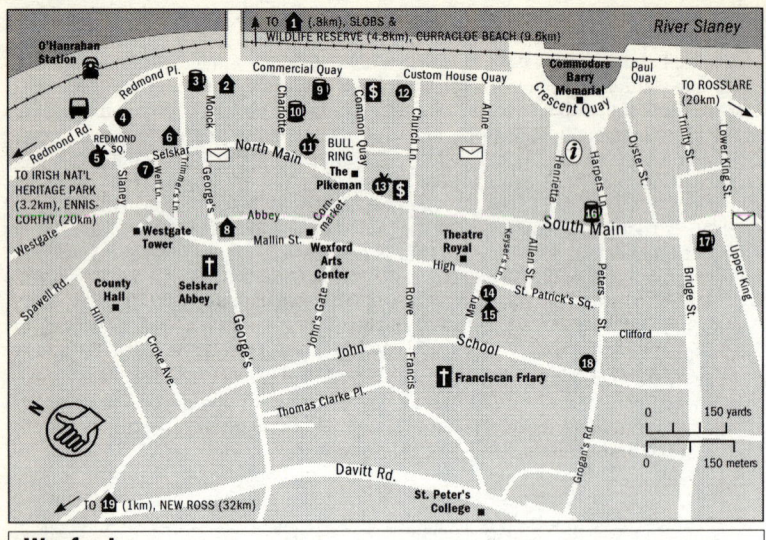

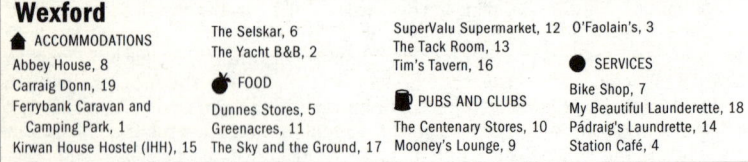

ACCOMMODATIONS			
Abbey House, 8	The Selskar, 6	SuperValu Supermarket, 12	O'Faolain's, 3
Carraig Donn, 19	The Yacht B&B, 2	The Tack Room, 13	SERVICES
Ferrybank Caravan and	FOOD	Tim's Tavern, 16	Bike Shop, 7
Camping Park, 1	Dunnes Stores, 5	PUBS AND CLUBS	My Beautiful Launderette, 18
Kirwan House Hostel (IHH), 15	Greenacres, 11	The Centenary Stores, 10	Pádraig's Laundrette, 14
	The Sky and the Ground, 17	Mooney's Lounge, 9	Station Café, 4

St. Aiden's Cathedral, Cathedral St., uphill from Murphy's Hotel, was started in 1843 under the close supervision of architect Augustus Pugin, who littered his Gothic Revival creations across the whole of Ireland. Its location on an incline required St. Aiden's to take on an unusually long and narrow form. Stained-glass windows of 28 different religious figures light up the airy cathedral. In Market Sq., a statue commemorates **Father Murphy,** who led the town in rebellion in 1798. The priest had been something of a Loyalist before an angry mob threatened to burn down his church. He promptly put himself at the head of the United Irishmen and led the pikemen of Enniscorthy into many battles.

If you're around in late June, check out the annual **Strawberry Fair.** Ten days of festivities and fructose mean you can paint the town red. Pubs host theater performances that draw literati, while music plays on well past sunset. The **Blues Festival** in mid-September features three days of entertainment by locally and internationally renowned musicians. Contact Maura Flannery (see **Practical Information,** above) for information.

WEXFORD ☎ 053

Gaels, Vikings, and Normans all worked together—well, against each other—to create the winding, narrow streets of modern Wexford. The sidewalks are so small that cars along Main St. (technically but not practically closed to traffic) must yield to the flocks of mothers pushing baby carriages down its middle. The town's main attraction for visitors is undoubtedly its quality pubs and restaurants. These fill the stone passageways built in the 12th century when the Normans conquered the Viking settlement of Waesfjord. Conquest after bloody conquest has left the town with an interesting tale to tell—as the Heritage Centre puts it, the "ability to recover from trauma" is central to Wexford's existence. The prominent Bull Ring and surrounding Norman ruins remain visual reminders of the history that features the likes of Henry II and Oliver Cromwell. The Twin Churches punctuate the skyline of the huddled harbor city.

GETTING THERE AND GETTING AROUND

Trains: O'Hanranhan (North) Station, Redmond Sq. (☎ 22522), a 5min. walk along the quays from Crescent Quay. If the booking office is closed, you can buy tickets on the train. Information available from 7am until last departure. Trains hustle to **Rosslare Harbour** (30min., 3 daily, £2) and to Connolly Station in **Dublin** (2¾hr., 3 daily, £11, Friday £14.50).

Buses: They stop at the train station. If the station office is closed, hit the Station Cafe (☎ 24056) across the street for info. Buses run to **Rosslare Harbour** (20min., M-Sa 10 per day, Su 9 per day, £2.65) and to **Dublin** (2½hr., M 8 per day, Tu-Sa 7 per day, Su 4 per day, £10). Buses to and from **Limerick** (4 daily) connect with Irish Ferries and Stena-Sealink sailings. From mid-July to Aug., buses run directly to **Galway** (6hr.) and other western points via **Waterford** (1hr.) and **Limerick** (3½hr.).

Taxi: Walsh Cabs (☎ 41449; mobile (088) 567 489); Noel Ryan (☎ 24056). A list of additional taxi companies is posted in the train station.

Bike Rental: The cheapest rentals are from the **Bike Shop,** 9 Selskar St. (☎ 22514; email gordon@iol.ie), £8 per day, £30 per week; £50 deposit, but will accept a credit card swipe; £12 extra to drop off elsewhere in the country. Open M-Sa 9am-6pm. **Hayes Cycle Shop,** 108 South Main St. (☎ 22462), leases Raleigh touring bikes for £10 per day, £40 per week; £50 or ID deposit. One-way rentals can be arranged. Open M-Sa 9am-6pm; bikes available by arrangement on Su.

Hitchhiking: The odds of getting a ride are highest around noon or 5-7pm. Hitchhikers to Dublin (via N11) should stand by the Wexford Bridge off the quays; those bound for Rosslare want to head south along the quays to Trinity St., just past the Talbot Hostel. Hitchers heading to Cork, New Ross, or Waterford should continue down Westgate and turn left onto Hill St. then right onto Upper John St. (N25). N11 and N25 merge near the city, so savvy hitchers make a point of specifying either the Dublin Rd. (N11) or the Waterford Rd. (N25). *Let's Go* does not recommend hitchhiking.

ORIENTATION AND PRACTICAL INFORMATION

Most of the town's action takes place one block inland and uphill, along the twists and turns of **Main St.** A plaza called the **Bullring** is near the center of town, a few short blocks from where North Main St. changes to South. Another plaza, **Redmond Square,** sits at the north end of the quays, near the train and bus station. The two steeples that define the town's skyline are less prominent to viewers within its narrow streets, but other towers help as landmarks, including the **Franciscan Friary** perched at the top of the hill.

Tourist Office: Crescent Quay (☎ 23111). Scars on the windowsills attest to the centuries of sailors who have sharpened their knives on them. The free, ad-packed *Wexford: Front Door to Ireland* and *Welcome to Wexford* include maps. Open Apr.-Oct. M-Sa 9am-6pm; July-Aug. M-Sa 9am-6pm, Su 11am-5pm; Nov.-Mar. M-F 9:30am-5:30pm.

Banks: 24hr. ATMs are available at, among other places: **AIB,** South Main St. (☎ 22444; open M 10am-5pm, Tu-F 10am-4pm); the **Bank of Ireland** at the Bullring (☎ 23022; open M 10am-5pm, Tu-F 10am-4pm); and **TSB,** 73-75 Main St. (☎ 41922; open M-W and F 9:30am-5pm, Th 9:30am-7pm).

Laundry: My Beautiful Launderette, St. Peter's Sq. (☎ 24317), up Peters St. from South Main St. Full- or self-service; pickup and delivery available. Wash up to 10 lb. £6.50, self-service £5, dry 10 lb. £6. Open M-Sa 9:30am-6pm. **Pádraig's Launderette,** 4 Mary St. (☎ 24677), next to the hostel. No self-service drying available. Wash £2.50, 40p per 5min. of drying. Open M-F 9:30am-6pm, Sa 9am-9pm.

Internet Access: Wexford Library (☎ 053 2163) offers free **Internet access.** Call ahead to reserve a 1hr. slot at speedy computers.

Pharmacy: A gaggle of pharmacies along Main St. rotate Sunday, late, and lunchtime hours. All open M-Sa 9am-1pm and 2-6pm.

Emergency: Dial ☎ 999; no coins required. **Police** *(Garda):* Roches Rd. (☎ 22333).

Hospital: Wexford General Hospital, New Town Rd. (☎ 42233), on N25/N11.

Post Office: Anne St. (☎ 22123). Open M and W-Sa 9am-5:30pm, Tu 9:30am-5:30pm. Smaller offices on South Main St. (☎ 45177) and at Main and Monck St.

ACCOMMODATIONS

If the hostels and B&Bs listed are full, ask the proprietors for recommendations or look along N25 in either direction (Rosslare Rd. or New Town Rd.). If you're planning to be in town during the opera festival (see **Entertainment,** p. 193), book as far in advance as possible; some rooms are reserved a year ahead of time.

Kirwan House Hostel (IHH), 3 Mary St. (☎ 21208; email kirwanhostel@tinet.ie). Short of communal space, but not communal cheer. Kirwan is a refurbished 200-year-old house right in the heart of town with some slants and creaks in its wooden floors. Kirwan also owns a house at 12 Mary St. with excellent singles and doubles. Launderette next door. Internet access. Dorms £7.50-8.50; doubles £38-44.

Abbey House, 34 Abbey St. (☎ 24408), flaunts a fantastic location and comfy quarters. Definitely call ahead, as the owner is often out. Accepts Visa, Access. Singles £20; doubles with bath and TV £32.

The Selskar (☎ 23349), corner of North Main and Selskar St. No frills but a great location. The Selskar recently completed an annex housing spacious rooms. Other options include renting the apartment-style accommodations (two bedrooms, sitting room, kitchen) over the pub for an extended stay. Call ahead or ask at the bar downstairs. Accepts Visa, MC, Access. Singles £25; doubles £40.

The Yacht B&B, 2 Monck St. (☎ 22338). Above the Yacht Pub, overlooking the River Slaney. Reservations encouraged. Accepts Visa, Access. Singles £20; doubles £30.

Carraig Donn, New Town Ct. (☎ 42046), off New Town Rd. (Waterford Rd.) just before the hospital. Call from town for pick-up, or trek 15min. along Main St., and over the hill. Large rooms, though brightly dated. Wheelchair accessible. Singles £17; doubles £32.

Ferrybank Caravan and Camping Park, (☎ 44378). On the eastern edge of town. Cross the bridge and continue straight to the camping site. Striking ocean view, clean area. Showers 75p. Laundry £1.50. Open Easter-Oct. 10% off in Apr.-May and Sept-Oct. £5 per 1-person tent; £7 per 2-person tent.

FOOD

The **Dunnes Store,** Redmond Sq., has everything from food to clothes to lampshades. (☎ 45688. Open M-Tu and Sa 9am-7pm, W-F 9am-9pm, Su 9am-6pm.) **L&N SuperValu,** Custom House Quay (☎ 22290; open M-Tu and Sa 9am-6pm, W-F 9am-9pm), is a large supermarket. In general, restaurant prices increase after 6pm, but there's definitely good grub to be found before then.

The Sky and the Ground, 112 S. Main St. (☎ 21273). Until about 6pm, scaled-down versions of the pricier fare served by the late-night upstairs restaurant **Heavens Above.** Lunch is so good they occasionally sell out the entire menu. Most main courses in the pub £5-7. Music Su-Th, usually trad.

Greenacres, 56 N. Main St. (☎ 21788), is the place to be for gourmet grocery, with a gem of a cafe in back. It's a special find for vegetarians, too. Cafe open M-Sa 9am-5:30pm.

Gusto's, (☎ 24336) 106 S. Main St. Gusto's is to be relished. The small cafe-like appearance belies the high-quality breakfasts, sandwiches and soups inside. The panini are a warm treat for £3-4. Breakfast is £2.50-4. Open 8:30am-6pm M-Sa.

The Tack Room, 38 N. Main St. (☎ 21669), right by the Bullring. Nothing too fancy, but it's done well and will stick to your ribs. Entrees around £5. Food served until 8:30pm. Don't sit down on the tack after 6pm, when prices swell. At night, metamorphoses into a mellow pub. Open until 11:30pm M-W, all other nights 12:30am.

PUBS AND CLUBS

Wexford's pubs run the gamut from traditional to trendy, oftentimes combining the two under one roof. Music, whether it be acoustic or electronic, is a staple.

Mooney's Lounge, Commercial Quay (☎ 21128), by the bridge. Newly expanded into the building next door (though only connected by the kitchen), the two halves of Mooney's comprise *the* late-night hot spot in Wexford. All sorts of live music Th-Su, in one half or the other. The crowd looks young for 21+, but the bouncers are not decorations. Separate entrances for the lounge and concert areas. Occasional cover charge for larger gigs.

The Centenary Stores, Charlotte St. (☎ 24424). A classy crowd of twenty-somethings flocks to the Stores, a pub and dance club within a former warehouse. Excellent trad Su mornings as well as M and W nights. Blues and folk on Tu nights. A DJ spins techno and top 40 on a black-lit dance floor Th-Su 11pm-2am. Nightclub cover £5.

O'Faolain's (oh FWAY lans), 11 Monck St. (☎ 23787). A bar for all generations, with live music almost every night. A nightclub spins F-Su nights, with DJ, dance floor, and 60s-80s music. Nightclub cover £5; £3 if you're chillin' in the pub before 11pm. Pub open M-Th until 11:30pm; nightclub open until 1:30am.

SIGHTS

The historical society (☎ 22311) runs free evening **walking tours** upon request. Tours depend on weather and interest—it's best to call after 5pm for availability. *Welcome to Wexford* (free at the tourist office) details a 45-minute self-guided walking tour. The remains of the Norman **city wall** run the length of High St. **Westgate Tower,** near the intersection of Abbey and Slaney St., is the only one of the wall's six original gates that still stands. The tower gate now holds the **Westgate Heritage Centre,** where an excellent 27-minute audio-visual show recounts the history of Wexford; you'll walk out thinking Wexford's the most important place in Ireland. (☎ 46506. Open M-F 10am-4pm. £1.50, children 50p.) Next door, the peaceful ruins of **Selskar Abbey**—site of Henry II's extended penance for his role in Thomas Becket's murder—act as a flower-bed for glorious weeds. (Enter through the wicket gate to the left of the Centre. Same hours as the Centre. Free.)

An open area between North and South Main St. marks the Bull Ring. Bull baiting was inaugurated in 1621 by the town's butcher guild as a promotional device. The mayor got the hide while the poor got the meat. **The Pikeman,** a statue of a stalwart peasant fearlessly brandishing his homemade weaponry, commemorates the 1798 uprising (see **Rebellion, Union, Reaction,** p. 13). Facing the sea stands the statue of Commodore John Barry, Wexford-born founder of the US Navy. The **Friary Church** (☎ 22758) in the Franciscan Friary, School St., houses the "Little Saint" in the back corner of the nave. This wax effigy of young St. Adjutor shows the bloody gash inflicted by the martyr's Roman father. Franciscan monks have lived in town since 1230—keep a lookout for peaceful fellows in brown robes.

ENTERTAINMENT

Many of the pubs in town offer music nightly. For more detailed information, check *The Wexford People* (85p in newsstands, or leaf through it in a pub), which lists events for all of Co. Wexford. The funky **Wexford Arts Centre,** Cornmarket, presents free visual arts and crafts exhibitions; evening performances of music, dance, and drama also take place in the center throughout the year (generally £5-6). On Wednesday nights between June and August, take part in an open trad session, or pay £2 to watch. (☎ 23764. Centre open M-Sa 10am-6pm.) The **Theatre Royal**, High St., produces performances throughout the year, culminating in the internationally acclaimed **Wexford Festival Opera** (www.wexfordopera.com), held annually in late October and early November. For these festivities, three obscure but deserving operas are rescued from the artistic attic and performed in an intimate setting. (☎ 22400; box office ☎ 22144. Box office open May-Sept. M-F 9:30am-5:30pm and during performances; Oct. daily 9:30am-11pm. Opera tickets £42-52, available from early June.) A **fringe festival** fills afternoons and late nights with cheaper options, from about £5.

IRISH NATIONAL HERITAGE PARK AND THE SLOBS ☎053

Wexford worked hard to get its **Slobs**, and they're a sight to see. "Slob" is the term for the cultivated mudflats to the north and south of Wexford Harbour. Originally watery bays in Wexford harbor, the slobs were filled to create more land for agriculture. Today, 420 of these acres are reserved for the **Wexford Wildfowl Reserve**, a renowned safe haven for rare birds from around the world. Ten thousand of Greenland's white-fronted geese (one-third of the world population) descend on the Slobs from October to April, cohabiting with other rare geese, some from as far away as Siberia and Iceland. Resident Irish birds arrive in the summer to mate along the channels. The **Reserve Centre** will help visitors spot specific species and remains open during the construction of a new wing. The Reserve is on the North Slob, 2 mi. north of Wexford town. Take Castlebridge/Gorey Rd. to well-signposted Ardcavan Ln. (a £3.50 cab ride), or hike through the Ferrybank caravan park and along the increasingly sandy beach for 40 minutes. (Open daily mid-Apr.-Sept. 9am-6pm, Oct.-Apr. 10am-5pm). If you keep hiking along the coast, you'll reach **Curracloe Beach,** 6 mi. north of town, where Steven Spielberg filmed the D-Day landings in *Saving Private Ryan*. Curracloe makes a fabulous cycling or walking day trip, and the broad beach is lined with fantastic dune bluffs that rival the steeples on the other side of the Slaney. To get to Curracloe by bicycle, follow Castlebridge/Gorey Rd. past the turnoff for the Slobs to a signposted right turn for Curracloe Town. After your right turn, cycle past many fields of sheep, and at Curracloe Town, turn right again at the post office and general store. (Requires moderate physical fitness. 35min. from the bridge).

The **Irish National Heritage Park** lets you stroll through 9000 years of Irish history in just a few hours. From a Stone Age campsite to an early Norman tower, check out replicas of houses, tombs, and fortifications that archaeologists have discovered across Ireland. The park is 3 mi. outside Wexford, on the N11; some cab companies offer a discount rate of £3.50. (☎ (053) 20733; www.inhp.com. Open daily 9:30am-6:30pm. £5, students £4. Restaurant open 12:30-5:30pm, entrees around £6. The main trail is wheelchair accessible.)

ROSSLARE HARBOUR ☎053

Rosslare Harbour is a decidedly pragmatic seaside village from which the ferries to France and Wales depart; it is not to be confused with Rosslare Strand, the town between Rosslare Harbour and Wexford on N25. Rosslare Harbour's primary purpose is to receive or bid farewell to Ireland's visitors and voyagers. Unlike other ports, it is not host to international intrigue, spies, and casinos, and has very few pubs and restaurants. There are, however, several quality B&Bs, which run daily from Rosslare Harbour to Britain and every other day to France. To get from the ferry port to the town, climb either the ramp or the steps up the cliff.

GETTING THERE AND GETTING AROUND

Trains: The train office (☎ 33114 or 33592) is open daily 6am-10pm. Trains run from the ferry port to **Wexford** (20min., 3 per day, £2), **Waterford** (1¼hr., same line as Limerick, £6), **Limerick** (2½hr., M-F 2 per day, Sa-Su 1 per day, £12.50), and **Dublin** (3hr., 3 per day, £11).

Buses: Buses run out of the same office as the trains (☎ 33592) and stop in front of J. Pitt's Convenience Store by the ferry port in Kilrane, as well as the Catholic church in Rosslare Harbour. They run to **Wexford** (20min., M 14 per day, Tu-Sa 13 per day, Su 10 per day, £2.65), **Waterford** (M-Sa 4 per day, Su 3 per day, £9.20), **Dublin** (3hr., M 10 per day, Tu-Sa 9 per day, Su 7 per day, £10), **Cork** (M-Sa 4 per day, Su 3 per day, £13.50), **Killarney** (£16), **Tralee** (M-Sa 3 per day, Su 2 per day, £17), **Limerick** (M-Sa 3 per day, Su 3 per day, £13.50), and **Galway** via **Waterford** (2 per day, £17).

Ferries: The terminal is open daily 6:30am-9:30pm. **Stena Line** (☎ 33115, recorded info ☎ 33330) and **Irish Ferries** (☎ 33158; fax 33544; www.irishferries.com) serve the ferry port, which also houses a **bureau de change**. Open daily 7am-10pm. For info on ferries from Rosslare Harbour to England and France, see **By Ferry**, p. 59. **Trains** and **buses** often connect with the ferries. Bus Éireann (☎ (051) 879 000) and Irish Rail (☎ 33114) have desks in the terminal.

Car Rental: An office in the ferry terminal offers **Eurocar** (☎ 33634 or 22712), **Hertz** (☎ 33238), and **Budget** (☎ 33318) rentals; competitive prices hover around £40 a day (includes £10.50 per day for insurance) and £198 for a week. Only Eurocar rents to drivers under 23; drivers aged 21-22 must pay £10 extra per day.

Taxis: To get to B&Bs outside of town, call **Dermot O'Hagan** (☎ 33777), or **Jimmy Ferguson** (☎ 33355).

Hitchhiking: Rides are hard to come by, as neither locals weighed down by tourists nor families in overstuffed cars are likely to stop. *Let's Go* does not recommend hitchhiking.

PRACTICAL INFORMATION

The mediocre Rosslare-Kilrane **tourist office** is 1 mi. from the harbor on Wexford Rd. in Kilrane, and is used best as a souvenir source. (☎ 33622 or 33232. Open daily 10:30am-8pm.) If you need help in the ferry terminal, head to the port authority desk (☎ 33114). Exchange currency at the **Bank of Ireland**, on Kilrane Rd. past the supermarket. (☎ 33304. Open M-F 10am-1:30pm and 2:30-4pm; **ATM**.) **Emergency:** Dial ☎ 999, no coins required. The **post office**, in the SuperValu supermarket, has a **bureau de change**. (☎ 33201. Open M-F 9am-1pm and 2-5:30pm, Sa 9am-1pm.)

ACCOMMODATIONS

The nature and function of Rosslare Harbour makes accommodations here convenient but inevitably mercenary. Exhausted ferry passengers take what they can get in town hostels, while good area B&Bs and accommodations in Wexford and Kilmore Quay are overlooked. B&Bs swamp N25 just outside of Rosslare Harbour. There is a noticeable difference between approved and non-approved B&Bs on N25; in Rosslare, more than anywhere in Ireland, take the Bord Fáilte shamrock as a measure of quality.

- **Mrs. O'Leary's Farmhouse**, Killilane (☎ 33134), off N25 in Kilrane, a 15min. drive from town. Set on a glorious 100-acre farm, Mrs. O'Leary's place is a holiday unto itself. A grassy lane leads past dunes of wildflowers to a secluded beach. Call for pickup from town. £16.50 per person, with bath £18.50.

- **Clifford House**, Michael Delaney (☎ 33226; email cliffordhouse@circom.net), Barryville. Turn left at the top of the cliff and head for the last house down. Clifford's keeps bright, comfortable rooms in a convenient location on a hush cul-de-sac. As you sip your tea, watch the ferries arrive and depart. If your punts are burning a hole in your pocket, try the upscale **Clifford House Restaurant**. Visa, MC. Singles £25, double £40.

- **Marianella B&B** (☎ 33139), off N25 across from the pharmacy. Sue Carty's house lacks a great view and is a hike, but she welcomes you with tea and cookies. Access, MC, Visa. Spacious family room available. Singles £18; doubles £32-36.

Oldcourt House B&B (☎ 33895) Next to Clifford House. Pristine quarters, a bright dining room, and a variety of sleeping arrangements. Access, MC, Visa. £19 per person.

Rosslare Harbour Youth Hostel (An Óige/HI), Goulding St. (☎ 33399; fax 33626). Take a right at the top of the cliff, then head left around the far corner of the Hotel Rosslare; the hostel is past the supermarket to the left. Try for one of the more spacious quads. Hopes to add Internet access, luggage storage, and bike rental by 2001. Lockout 10am-5pm. 6- to 7-bed dorms £8; June-Aug. quads £40, Sept-Apr. £36.

FOOD

The restaurants in Rosslare Harbour tend to be expensive. The **SuperValu** supermarket has a substantial selection; it's to your right on your way to the hostel. (☎ 33107. Open M-F 8am-7pm, Sa 8am-6pm, Su 9am-1pm.) The **Portholes** matches meals with a mini-maritime museum. I shall call him..."mini-(mariti)me." (☎ 33110. Entrees £6-9; served noon-2:30pm and 6-9pm.)

KILMORE QUAY AND THE SALTEE ISLANDS ☎053

Thirteen miles southwest of Rosslare Harbour on Forlorn Point, the small fishing village of Kilmore Quay charms visitors with its beautiful beaches, thatched roofs, and whitewashed seaside cottages. This is the place to come for getting away from it all, and for a variety of sea-themed activities.

ORIENTATION AND PRACTICAL INFORMATION. Two streets diverge from the harbour: **Wexford Rd.** and the **"Back Rd."** A small beach lies to the left of Kilmore's harbor, and the 7mi. **Ballyteigue Beach** is also nearby. Information is available at the **Stella Maris Community Centre** on Wexford Rd., which also has private showers (£1.50), a game room, and the wonderful **Bird's Rock** coffee shop with huge meals for about £3.50. (☎ 29922. Centre open M-Sa 9am-10pm, Su 9am-9pm. Bird's Rock open M-F 8:30am-2pm, F-Su 8:30am-2pm.) The village berths its **Maritime Museum** in the lightship *Guillemot*, once anchored near the harbor, now cemented into it. Climb into the ship's hold and view artifacts from Irish naval histories, marine accessories, and learn the tragic stories of local shipwrecks. Wall speakers trigger short audio explanations of the room's contents in French, German, or English at the press of a button. (☎ 29555. Open June-Aug. daily noon-6pm; May and Sept. Sa-Su noon-6pm. £2, students, seniors, and children £1.) By 2001, a Millennium Memorial Hiking Trail along Forlorn Point to commemorate the lost sailors of Kilmore Quay and Wexford County will be completed. In July, The **Kilmore Seafood Festival** runs for 10 days in mid-July with loads of seafood, music, and games.

GETTING THERE AND GETTING AROUND. To reach Kilmore Quay from Rosslare Harbour, take Wexford Rd. to Tagoat and turn left; from Wexford, take Rosslare Rd., turn right on the R739 near Piercetown, and continue 4 mi. to town. **Bus Éireann** runs between Wexford and Kilmore Quay (M-Sa per day, £4 return). **Doyle's Hackney & Bus Hire** (☎ 29624; mobile (087) 472 959) runs a shuttle into Wexford leaving at 11am and returning at 2pm (Tu, Th, F). Doyle is also available for 24-hour hackney service. (A hackney is similar to a taxi.) **Bike rental** is available at **Kilmore Quay Bike Hire** (☎ 29781), out of the Quay House guest-house on Wexford Rd. past the post office. (£8 per day, £35 per week. £50 deposit.) The **post office** does its business (☎ 29641; open M-F 9am-1pm and 1-5:30pm) in **Murphy's food store** (☎ 29641; open daily 8am-7pm) on Wexford Rd.

ACCOMMODATIONS AND FOOD. Thrifty lodging is available at the **Kilturk Independent Hostel,** 1½ mi. from town on Wexford Rd., between Kilmore Quay and Kilmore Town), where chic rustic decor warms up an old schoolhouse. The buses between Wexford and Kilmore Quay will stop at the hostel by request, or call for a pickup. (☎ 29883. Free self-service laundry. Dorms £7.50; private rooms £9.) Tourists can also treat themselves at one of the town's many fine B&Bs. **The Haven,** 100 yd. down from the first right after the post office, has a water view, several kinds of tea and coffee, and an elegant and friendly proprietor, Betty Walsh. (☎ 29979. Doubles £30-32.) May Bates's pink and pleasant **Harborview B&B** has a lush lawn, very safe showers and, on clear days, a good view of the Saltee Islands and the harbor. She is right in the middle of town, off New Ross Rd., across from the Silver Fox restaurant. Mrs. Deirdre Brady's **Castle View** has bright surroundings right on Wexford Rd. and is within a stone's throw of an anomalous castle that was plopped down here in the 15th century. I don't think we're in Kansas anymore. (☎ 29765. Singles £18; doubles £32.) For the freshest seafood, reel in a meal at the **Silver Fox,** across from the Maritime Museum (☎ 29888; open M-Sa 12:30-9:30pm, Su 12:30-9pm; lunch specials 12:30-2:30pm).

SIGHTS. Kilmore Quay sends boat trips out to the two **Saltee Islands,** formerly pagan pilgrimage sites and now Ireland's largest bird sanctuary, with a winged population nearing 50,000. These islands are the home of puffins, razorbills, and grey seals, but are owned by the absentee landlord Prince Michael Salteens. A narrow ridge of rock is thought to have connected the smaller island to the mainland in ancient times. This land bridge, called **St. Patrick's Causeway,** was used for driving cattle to the island for pasture. At low tide, the beginning of St. Patrick's land bridge is visible. Hike to it on the road to Kilmore town (turn right at the signpost, roughly 1 mi. from town) or scramble over rocks and tide-pools on the beach (turn left, 20min. away from the harbor). Weather permitting, boats leave the mainland each morning, stranding you for picnics and ornithology. **Declan Bates** (☎ 29684; mobile (087) 252 9736) makes the half-hour trip daily at around 11am and returns at 4:30pm (£12). **Dick Hayes** (☎ 29704; mobile (087) 254 9111) will bring you aboard for deep sea angling and reef-fishing; call ahead to arrange a time and ask about renting equipment.

NEW ROSS ☎021

New Ross is an ideal rest stop on a tour of Ireland's southeast corner. Waterford, the Hook, Wexford, and Kilkenny all lie within easy reach. The town also has a tidy list of sights, most involving the Irish exodus and beloved great-grandson John F. Kennedy. The Dunbrody, a coffin ship replica from the Famine era, is a must-see.

ORIENTATION AND PRACTICAL INFORMATION. Most of New Ross's activity takes place on the strip of waterfront known simply as **The Quay.** Other major thoroughfares are **Mary St.,** which extends uphill from the bridge, and **South St.,** which runs parallel to The Quay one block inland (and changes its name to **North St.** once it crosses Mary St.). New Ross is on the N25 (to Wexford and Waterford) and the N30 (to Enniscorthy). Hitchers can find plenty of rides on either, especially in the morning and late afternoon. *Let's Go* does not recommend hitching at any time of day. **Bus Éireann** runs from The Mariners Inn, The Quay, to **Waterford** (25min., M-F 9 per day, Sa 8 per day, Su 5 per day, £3), **Rosslare Harbour** (1hr., M-Sa 6 per day, Su 4 per day, £7), and **Dublin** (3hr., M-Sa 3 per day, Su 4 per day, £7). **Budget,** located on The Quay in the Campus gas station a few blocks from the tourist office, will **rent cars** to anyone 23 or older. (☎ 421 550. £45 per day, £185 per week.) The New Ross **tourist office,** on The Quay, just down the street from the SuperValu, offers useful maps in the free *New Ross Town and Area Guide* and *A Guide to New Ross.* (☎ 421 857; www.newrosschamber.ie. Open May-Sept. M-Sa 9am-1pm and 2-5pm, Su 12-4pm.) Banks with **24-hour ATMs** abound: the **Bank of Ireland,** The Quay (☎ 421 267), is just steps away from the bus stop and tourist office; the **AIB** (☎ 421 319; M 10am-5pm, Tu-F 10am-4pm) and **TSB** (☎ 422 060; M-F 9:30-5pm, Th 9:30-7pm) are across from each other on South St. The **post office** delivers on Charles St., just off the Quay. (☎ 421 261. Open M-Sa 9am-5:30pm.)

ACCOMMODATIONS, FOOD, AND PUBS. Mac Murrough Farm Hostel is a good enough reason to be in (well, near) New Ross. Follow Mary St. uphill to its end, turn left, then take the first right on to Ring Road. Pass the cross and take a left at the supermarket, then a right at the Statoil Station; the remaining mile to the hostel is well-marked with signs. Call for pick-up. Perhaps Bob Dylan ain't gonna work on Mac Murrough's Farm no more, but the delightfully down-to-earth owners make this the place to stay. The sheep give a rowdy greeting, and with a dog named Floozie, you can't go wrong. (☎ 421 383; email machostel@eircom.net. From £8 for a dorm.) For a bed in town and a bigger dent in your wallet, **Riversdale House,** William St., is the nicest of the B&Bs. Follow South St. all the way to William St., then turn left up the hill. Friendly owners take pride in the commanding view of town from their snazzy rooms. (☎ 422 515. Singles £29; doubles £38.) **Inishross House,** 96 Mary St., is closer still and a good deal cheaper, though the ancient house and furnishings feel a little stale. (☎ 21335. Singles £19; doubles £32.) The tourist office can provide a list of other B&Bs, if these are booked.

L&N SuperValu, The Quay, is a generic grocer that keeps existentialist hours. (☎ 421 392. Open M-F 8am-6pm, closing time extends 1hr. each day after M; Sa 8am-7:30pm, Su 9am-6pm.) Bright and airy **John V's,** 5 The Quay, will serve you a hefty portion of pub grub at reasonable cost. Eat outside in nice weather. (☎ 425 188. Lunch around £5, served daily noon-2:30pm; dinner £6-8, served daily 5-9pm.) **Cafe Kaos** brings a dose of Malaysian spice to New Ross and has vegetarian dishes for £3.50. (Open Tu-Sa 5-11pm, Su 5-11:30pm.) Enjoy a meal in sightseeing transit on board **The Galley** (☎ 421 723), which runs daily restaurant cruises from New Ross into Waterford Harbour. Choose your meal: lunch (2hr.; 12:30pm; £14, £7 for cruise only), tea (2hr.; 3pm; £7, £6 for cruise only), or dinner (2-3hr.; 6 or 7pm; £22-26, £11 for cruise only).

SIGHTS. New Ross's sights are as modest as the town itself, but a flashier profile may lie in the town's future upon the completion of **Dunbrody,** an exact replica of a New Ross ship that carried thousands of famine-struck emigrants to North America in the mid-19th century. Visitors can explore the Dunbrody's massive hull and take a captivating 20-minute tour that uses the Dunbrody's oaken keel to frame the history of the famine. In 1847 the original Dunbrody sailed to America with 313 immigrants on board. Upon completion its 420-ton replica will sail to Boston, and then return to New Ross to serve as a floating museum. (Open July-Aug. 10am-7pm, Oct.-Mar. noon-5pm. Adults £3, students and seniors £1.50.) For landlubbers, there's **St. Mary's Church,** off Mary St., built by Strongbow's grandson in the early 13th century. Mrs. Culleton, four doors down at 6 Church St., can provide the key and a booklet detailing the significance of the stone structures inside the building. Protestant masses are still held in a new annex on Sundays. Seven mi. south of New Ross on the R783 Ballyhack Rd., the **John F. Kennedy Arboretum** blooms with life—nearly 6000 species of it. Stroll around 623 gorgeous acres dedicated to Ireland's favorite US President, and learn that the lineage of Camelot traces back to Co. Wexford. A small cafe doubles as a gift shop. (☎ 388 171. Open daily May-Aug. 10am-8pm; Apr. and Sept. 10am-6:30pm; Oct.-Mar. 10am-5pm. Last admission 45min. before closing. £2, seniors £1.50, children £1.)

THE HOOK PENINSULA

Southeast of New Ross, the Hook is a peaceful peninsula noted for its historic abbeys, forts, and lighthouses. Sunny coastlines draw deep-sea anglers to Waterford Harbour and Tramore Bay, while the pubs on the oceanfront keep the midnight oil burning until long past midnight. Unfortunately, public transportation does not reach this burgeoning vacation region, so itinerant travelers are dependent on cars or bikes to explore. The peninsula may be approached by an inland route from New Ross (see p. 197), or by crossing the Waterford Harbour on the Ballyhack-Passage East ferry (see p. 200). Interesting scenery makes for challeng-

ON THE ROAD TO BALLYHACK: DUNBRODY ABBEY

ing bike rides. The Hook is perhaps best explored with a car; hitching short rides is generally quite easy, although *Let's Go* does not recommend hitchhiking. Don't rely on tourist offices; you can plan ahead by checking out www.thehook-wexford.com or emailing hookinfo@iol.ie.

ON THE ROAD TO BALLYHACK: DUNBRODY ABBEY

Two miles north of Ballyhack on New Ross Rd. is Dunbrody Abbey, a magnificent ruin dating back to the late 12th-century Cistercian monastic order. Almost wholly intact, you may wander through little rooms with such freedom that you might even play a short game of medieval hide-and-seek. Get the key and brochures across the road at the visitors center that sits among the ruins of a castle once associated with the abbey. The center features a doll-house replica of what the castle would have looked like fully furnished and intact. An impressive hedge-row maze, planted in 1992, began with 2 ft. high yew trees which confounded only Lilliputians. They're now about 5½ ft. tall, and are expected to reach 15 ft. (☎ 388 603. Centre open July-Aug. 10am-7pm; May-June and Sept. 10am-6pm. Abbey admission £1.50, children £1. Maze and castle admission £1.50, children £1.)

BALLYHACK

Ten miles south of New Ross, Ballyhack shows its cross-channel neighbor, Passage East, a profile dominated by 15th-century **Ballyhack Castle**. Although the Castle does not strike fear into the hearts of current invaders, it was built in by Strongbow's heir, William Marshall, to protect his precious port at New Ross. To do the job right, Marshall hired the Crusading Order of the Knights Hospitallers, an order known for their valor in battle and compassion when tending to the sick. The displays within the castle are fairly mundane, but the castle itself is a wonderful mix of ruin and museum. Tours haul visitors inside the castle tower and take special delight in displaying the ghastly methods of self-defense employed by these "charitable" knights. The 500-year-old intact wicker ceilings will give you new faith in your patio furniture. (☎ 389 468. Open mid-June-Sept. daily 9:30am-6:30pm. £1, students 40p.)

If you're hungry, either go for broke at one of the high-end restaurants, or head to **Byrne's**, a small food store and pub right by Ballyhack's ferry port. The pub offers only sandwiches (under £2), but the store can supply you with more. (☎ 389 107. Store open M-Sa 9:30am-9:30pm, Su noon-2pm and 4-7pm.)

ARTHURSTOWN

For accommodations in the hook, head to nearby **Arthurstown**. Take a right from the landing area of the Ballyhack ferry port and follow the Slí Charman (SHLEE KAR-man) coastal path. The village lies 1km up this trail. **Arthurstown** has a pub and opulent views of water, water everywhere, but nary a bite to eat, so get your grub back at Ballyhack. The first left coming from Ballyhack is the driveway to the **Arthurstown Youth Hostel (An Óige/HI)**, housed in a building that was built to the uncompromising specifications of the English coast guard two centuries ago. The weathered interior disguises a decent arrangement of dorms and a fantastic kitchen with broad pine tables, candles, and an upbeat communal air. (☎ 389 441. Lockout 10:30am-5pm, but the new manager leaves the kitchen open. Dorms £7; doubles £18; quads £36.) To feel like the King of the Hook, treat yourself to **Glendine House B&B**, a large Georgian manor up Duncannon Hill. It's hard to miss: look for the horses on the front lawn. The rooms are huge and beautifully decorated—you'll be tempted to move in. (☎ 389 258; fax; 389 677; email glendinehouse@tinet.ie. **Internet access.** Singles £35; doubles £50.) The small **Country House** cafe, in Glendine House, serves up fresh snacks and sandwiches for those who need energy for the journey ahead. (Open M-Sa 11am-6pm. Entrees £4.50.)

DUNCANNON

South of Arthurstown, the scenic Hook Head Peninsula truly begins after Duncannon village (dun-CAN-on). The area's popularity as a weekend vacation spot is astronomical, but during the week this rolling landscape loses the bedlam, making for pleasant jaunts around the bizarre assortment of medieval ruins and new bungalows that clutters the landscape. The peninsula's circuit is best covered by car, but brave bikers can handle it if they've planned ahead. The nearest bike rental is in Waterford (see p. 205). From Arthurstown, head east on Duncannon Rd. and keep an eye out for the sharp right turn with a sign for "Duncannon." The town lies 1 mi. down that road.

Duncannon Fort holds down the cliffs at the edge of the village. The fort has long failed to meet public expectations. From the moment it was built in the 1580s, people complained that it was too easy to conquer by land. In the 17th century, it surrendered to both Cromwell and William of Orange. Tours are given by request. A small cafe provides shelter from the wind and an assortment of hot and cold eats for around £4. (☎ 389 454 or 389 188. Open daily June-mid-Sept. 10am-5:30pm., mid-May to Oct. daily 10am-5:30pm. £2, seniors £1.50.)

Geared toward families, the **Duncannon Festival,** the first week in July, offers a variety of food and activities. Call Eileen Roche (☎ 389 188) for details. The **Strand Stores,** also in Duncannon, sells groceries. (☎ 389 216. Open daily 9am-10pm.) Across the street, the **Strand Tavern** serves some bar food in front of a tranquil ocean view. (☎ 389 109. Some entrees £5-8; bar food 12:30-6:30pm.)

Stuck halfway between Duncannon and the tip of the peninsula at **Hook Head, Templetown** is home to the **Templar's Inn** (☎ (051) 397 162). This excellent pub serves gargantuan portions from noon to 9pm, but the knightly fare is served with kingly prices. At night, the cheery pub attracts errant adventurers long past its official closing time of 11:30pm.

AT THE TIP: HOOK HEAD

This tiny hamlet possesses the peninsula's biggest (literally) attraction. Six kilometers down the road from Templetown, a scary sign warns "GREAT CARE MUST BE TAKEN NEAR THE WATERS EDGE ALONG THE CLIFFS FREAK WAVES SLIPPERY ROCKS." The **Hook Lighthouse,** a stout medieval tower founded by St. Dubhan, is the oldest operating beacon in the British Isles. Tours run up its hundred-odd 13th-century steps and look out on panoramic views of the peninsula and neighboring Waterford Harbour. While scaling the steps, visitors are treated to a hearty dose of history and lighthouse lore. The top of the lighthouse is a recent addition—that is, they only date back to 1800. A small cafe greets the famished keepers of the harbour with a smart selection of salads, sandwiches and desserts. (☎ 397 055; fax 397 056; email thehook@eircom.net. Open daily 9:30am-5:30pm. Guided tours on the half hour. £3.50, students and seniors £2.50.) On the eastern side of the peninsula is Ireland's own **Tintern Abbey,** founded in the 13th century and 3 mi. from the Ballycullane stop on the Waterford-Rosslare train line. Call the tourist office in nearby **Fethard** for more info on the abbey and on the entire Hook region. (☎ 397 502. Open Sept.-June M-F 9:30am-5:30pm; July-Aug. M-F 9:30am-5:30pm, Sa-Su 11am-3pm. Wander freely; tours £1.50.)

WATERFORD HARBOUR ☎051

East of Waterford City, Waterford Harbour straddles the Waterford-Wexford county line. It is here that Oliver Cromwell coined the phrase "by hook or by crook": he had plotted to take Waterford City from either Hook Head or the opposite side of the harbor at Crooke. Both sides of the harbor are host to historic ruins, fishing villages, and stunning ocean views. In most of the region, travelers should expect peace and quiet, not convenience. To cross the harbor, either drive for 37 mi. up and around through New Ross or take the **Passage East Car Ferry** (☎

382 480 or 382 488) between Ballyhack and Passage East. (Continuous sailings Apr.-Sept. M-Sa 7am-10pm, Su and holidays 9:30am-10pm; Oct.-Mar. M-Sa 7am-8pm, Su and holidays 9:30am-8pm. Pedestrians £1, £1.50 return; cyclists £2, £2.50 return; car £4.50, £6.50 return.) Unless you're looking for complete rest and relaxation, the town of **Passage East** is best passed through. The journey to Passage East from Waterford and then around the Hook is home to spectacular views, but be warned that there's no place to rent a bike in the harbor area other than Waterford (see p. 205). The roads outside of Waterford are hilly and windy, and a long bike journey will test the stamina of even the most ferocious cyclist. From Wexford, follow signs for Ballyhack to reach the ferry.

DUNMORE EAST ☎ 051

Vacationing Irish families have made the small town of Dunmore East their summertime mecca. If the weather's good, be careful not to squish one of the small children swarming on the wee beaches. When you're not looking out for kids underfoot, look out to sea—the calm harbor, stunning cliffs, and distant Hook compose a spectacular view. In general, the summer is busy while the winter months are desolate.

The town is spread along two areas, the strand and **Dock Rd.**, which leads up the hill and to the docks. There's **no ATM** in Dunmore, but any of the small groceries along Dock Rd. should have a **bureau de change**, including **Dingley's** (☎ 383 372; open 8am-9pm). The **Suirway** bus service (☎ 382 209; 24hr. timetable ☎ 382 422) runs the 9½ mi. from Waterford to Dunmore East (30min., M-Sa 3-4 per day, £1.80). Wait for it outside the Bay Cafe, or just flag it down anywhere on its route.

Church Villa is an immaculate B&B with bright rooms, plus a sunny owner to match. Open all year. (☎ 383 390. Singles £22; doubles £40.) At the **Carraig Liath B&B**, Dock Rd., a garden patio overlooking the harbor complements the spotless rooms. (☎ 383 273; email beatltd@esatclear.ie. Open Apr.-Oct. Doubles £40-44.) **Springfield B&B**, up the road from the beach with a signposted left turn, has airy bedrooms along with a solarium that houses dining, tea, and reading. (☎ 383 448; email springfieldbb@esatclear.ie. Open Mar.-Nov. Singles on request £23-25; doubles £40.) Past the Anchor, on the hill from the Dunmore East beach, lies **Qually's Caravan and Camping Park**, where the assorted Qually's will let you squeeze a tent among its trailers. (☎ 383 001. Showers 50p. £8-10.)

Groceries are plentiful at **Londis Supermarket**, Dock Rd. (Open M-F 9am-8:30pm, Sa-Su 9am-10pm; shorter hours in off-season.) The **Bay Cafe**, also on Dock Rd., serves homemade food for sit-down or take-away meals. (☎ 383 900. Sandwiches £1.50, entrees £4-5.50. Open daily 9am-6pm). **The Melting Pot Cafe and Craft shop** simmers with tempting smells. Indulge in their many tasty entrees, like pan-fried cod in herb butter for £6.50. Most entrees £4. (☎ 383 271. Open M, W-Th and Su 11am-5pm, F-Sa 11am-4pm and 7-9:30pm.) In the evenings, Dunmore citizens gather at the **Anchor** (☎ 383 133) to enjoy live music.

Swimming is good at Dunmore's **beaches**, especially at several points where trails descend to isolated coves below, offering more seclusion. Kittiwakes (small gulls) throng the coastline, building their nests in cliff faces unusually close to human habitation. On the cliffs of **Badger's Cove**, especially, you'll see hundreds of them. Less fowled cliffs are accessible by the dirt road past Dock Rd.; the waves crashing into the rocks here are mesmerizing. To leave shore, head to the docks, where the **Dunmore East Adventure Centre** will teach you to **snorkel, surf, kayak, canoe, rock-climb**, and a variety of other activities. Bring a towel and swimsuit; they provide the equipment. Space fills quickly, so call ahead to reserve a spot. (☎ 383 783. Open year-round. July-Aug. £15 per half-day; Sept.-June £14.)

TRAMORE ☎ 051

Trá Mhór means "big beach" in Gaelic; those crazy Celts had an eye for the obvious. Tramore (Tra-MORE) draws an enormous number of tourists to its smooth 3 mi. strand. In the summer, the beach and boardwalk bustle with bathers and music. Despite tacky amusements that can be found at seaside resorts the world over, Tramore retains its small-town character. The cliffs that rise above the beach offer great places to stay and amazing ocean views.

GETTING THERE. Many buses connect Tramore to Waterford, 30 minutes away. **Bus Éireann** runs both local and express routes, stopping at the station and at various other points around town (at least 1 per hr., £4). The Tramore-Waterford-Dublin route runs at least six times a day. **Rapid Express Coaches** (☎ 872 142) also sends buses from the station every two hours to Dublin and other points north.

ORIENTATION AND PRACTICAL INFORMATION. Tramore can be a maze to get around, since few streets keep their names for more than a block and undulating hills confound even the most magnetic nose. The bus station is on **Waterford Rd.** (technically **Turkey Rd.**), a block from the intersection of **Strand St.** (which becomes **Main St.** and then **Summer Hill**) and **Gallwey's Hill** (which joins **Church Rd.** up the cliff). The **tourist office** moves all over town, and was last seen across the street from the bus station. (☎ 381 572. Open June to mid-Sept. M-Sa 10am-1pm and 2-6pm.) An **AIB** (☎ 381 216) is around the corner on Strand St., and the **Bank of Ireland** (☎ 386 611) lies farther up; both have **24-hour ATMs. Pedal Power Cycles,** on Market St. just off Main St., **rents bikes,** but the town is so darn hilly that you'll want to head straight for the somewhat easier countryside. (☎ 381 252. Open 9:30am-5:30pm. £10 per day, £50 per week; £10 deposit required.)

ACCOMMODATIONS. The **Cliff,** Church St., owned by the YWCA, probably has the best view in Tramore. More a guest house than a hostel, the Cliff provides bed, breakfast, and, for a little extra, an evening meal. The YWCA still welcomes construction workers, hip-wiggling policemen, and other singing entourages. (☎ 381 363. Singles £13-18; doubles £40-48.) Tramore is bursting with B&Bs, with the cheapest along Waterford Rd. and the best along Church Rd. **Ard More House,** Doneraile Dr., looks over rooftops and a pretty garden to the water. Head up Church Rd. and take your first left. (☎ 381 716. Open Apr.-Sept. Singles £18; doubles £39.) **Venezia,** Church Road Grove, sign posted off Church Rd., is immaculate and glossy, with top-notch beds. (☎ 381 412; email veneziahouse@tramore.waterford.net. Singles £23-25; doubles £38.) Turn sharply right at the top of Gallwey's Hill to find **Turret House,** Church Rd. Huge rooms with huger windows, some with ocean views and bath, make the climb worthwhile. (☎ 386 342. Singles £30; doubles £36-40.) **Clonleen B&B,** Love Lane, lives up to its street name with romantic doubles and a pair of friendly dogs. (☎ 381 264; email clonleen@iol.ie. Open Mar.-Oct. Occasional singles £25; doubles £38.) If you can live without the ocean view, **Church Villa,** Church Rd., fills its windows with church spires and a cemetery. The rooms are small and clean. (☎ 381 547. £15, with bath £18.) 1½ mi. out Dungarvan Coast Rd., between the golf course and the Metal Man monument to shipwreck victims, the family-style **Newtown Caravan and Camping Park** is the best of several nearby campsites, with sparkling bathrooms. (☎ 381 979. Showers 50p. Open Easter-Sept. Tents £3.50-10 per person, depending on the season and your method of transport.)

FOOD, PUBS, AND ENTERTAINMENT. Up Main St., an **L&N SuperValu** awaits your wandering taste buds. (☎ 386 036. Open M-W 8am-8pm, F 8am-9pm, Sa 8am-8:30pm, Su 10am-8pm.) Greasy grub is ubiquitous in sea towns. For a variety of different tastes, look away from the frying fish. **An Chistin,** newly opened on Main St., serves tasty sandwiches (£2), coffees, and entrees (£4-4.50) to carnivores and vegetarians alike. (☎ 391 416. Open daily 9:30am-7pm, July-Aug. 9am-9pm.) **Apple Brown Betty** is on the beach, next to the Surf Center, with the best, inexpensive beach fare. (Giant crepes £1.80-2. Open 11am-6pm.) **The Sea Horse,** Strand St., has great pub grub, fancy coffee, and a friendly atmosphere. (☎ 386 091. Entrees £5; food served noon-9pm.) As for watering holes, locals love to be hip and abbreviate their faves. The three floors of **The Victoria House ("The Vic"),** Queens St. (☎ 390 338), get younger, louder, and more crowded as you descend. The younger crowd also packs **The Hibernian ("Hi B")**, or, as the late bar is dubbed, **The Cellar** (☎ 386 396), at the intersection of Gallwey's Hill and Strand St. After the nightly live music at the bar ends, everyone hops to the **Hi B disco** next door, where chart music blasts for a packed floor. (Disco W-Su. £5 cover. Doors close at 1am.) Most locals meet in the plush, tamer environs of **O'Neill's** (☎ 381 088) on Summer Hill.

Surfing? In Ireland? Yes—the Emerald Isle boasts some of the best surf in Europe and the **Tramore Bay Surf Center** provides the tops in daytime and evening tide fun. A friendly staff rents surfboards, bodyboards, wet-suits and other surfing accessories that make you look cool out of the water, even if you swim like an Irish Setter in it. To remedy aqua agonies, they also offer individual and group lessons that can help you become the Irish Big Kahuna, or at least tell that to the people at the pub. (☎ 391 297. Hire fees from £3-10. 2½hr. lessons £14, students £12, group rates from £7. Call ahead for bookings.) The promenade on the waterfront provides all sorts of entertainment, such as the **Splashworld** indoor water park, an assortment of rides, specialized pools, and screaming children. (☎ 390 176. Open Mar.-Oct. daily 11am-8pm; Nov.-Feb. M-F noon-8pm, Sa-Su 11am-6pm. £6, students £4.) Just outside of town, the cliffs are more spectacular. The tourist office can provide a list of historic and scenic walks. For the best, follow the red-figure icons along the **Doneraile Walk,** a path stemming off Church Rd. that enchants hikers away from Tramore until only cliffs, ocean, and clouds remain visible. About a mile out, you can dive and swim in **Guillamene Cove**. Ignore the "Men Only" sign; a smaller one underneath explains that it's been "retained merely as a relic of the past." *Let's Go* does not recommend foolish dives or other acts of machismo.

DUNGARVAN ☎ 058

Filled with fishermen and market-goers, Dungarvan is more endearing than most transportation hubs. There isn't too much to see, but ocean winds and a vibrant pub scene make the town a pleasant stop-over for travelers on the south coast.

GETTING THERE AND GETTING AROUND. Main St., also called **O'Connell St.**, runs through the central square; **Emmet St.**, or **Mitchell St.**, runs parallel to Main St. one block uphill and is home to the hostel and a number of B&Bs. The road to Cork veers off Emmet St. at the Garda station. **Buses** (☎ (051) 79000) run from Davitt's Quay east to **Waterford** (1hr., 11 per day, £5), west to **Cork** (M-Sa 9 per day, Su 7 per day; £7), and north to **Lismore** (M and Th-F 1 per day). From **Waterford** buses run through to **Dublin** and **Rosslare**. The best villages in West Waterford are inaccessible by bus; bike rental is available at **O'Mahoney's Cycles,** across the bridge and past the traffic lights in Abbeyside, a 10-minute walk from The Square. (☎ 43346. £5 per day. Call ahead.)

ORIENTATION AND PRACTICAL INFORMATION. The helpful **tourist office** on The Square has free maps and keeps music listings for area pubs. (☎ 41741. Open June-Aug. M-Sa 9am-9pm, Su noon-5pm; Sept.-May M-Sa 9am-6pm.) **Bank of Ireland,** The Square, has a **24-hour ATM** that accepts all major cash networks, as does **AIB,** on Meagher St. (Both open M 10am-5pm, Tu-F 10am-4pm.) Free **Internet access** is available with a £2 card at the **library** on Davitt's Quay. (☎ 41231. Open Tu-Sa 10am-5pm, W-Th 6-8pm.) The **post office** sits on Bridge St., just outside The Square. (☎ 41210. Open M-F 9am-5:30pm, Sa 9am-3pm.)

ACCOMMODATIONS, FOOD, AND PUBS. The **Dungarvan Holiday Hostel (IHH),** Youghal Rd., just off Emmet St., opposite the *Garda* Station, is housed in a former Christian Brothers Friary, and still hasn't shaken off the cold monastic feel. (☎ 44340. Wheelchair accessible. **Bike rental** £6 per day. 8- to 10-bed dorms £7.50; private rooms £8.50 per person.) On Mitchell St. across from St. Mary's Church, **Santa Antoni** and its gregarious owner offer bright rooms. (☎ 42923. Singles £13; doubles £26; £2-3 less without breakfast.) Two doors down the road, **Amron** (☎ 43337) nearly bursts with the energetic hospitality of its proprietress, who lets small but pleasant doubles and twins (£15, with bath £16), and fluffy beds in the skylit loft (£10-12).

The immense **SuperValu** is on Main St. (☎ 92150. Open M-W 9am-7pm, Th and Sa 9am-8pm, F 9am-9pm, Su 10am-6pm.) Laid-back **Ormond's Cafe**, The Square, a few doors down from the tourist office, serves outstanding desserts, and meals to precede them, in its stone-walled, skylit cafe. (☎ 41153. Sandwiches £2-3, hot meals £4-6. Open M-Sa 8am-6pm.) Settle into bizarre wood furniture for finely prepared meals, desserts, and coffee at **Interlude**, in Davitt's Quay next to the castle. (☎ 45898. Sandwiches £3.50, dinners £6-12. Open Tu-W 10:30am-9pm, Th-Sa 10:30am-9:30pm, Su 10:30am-7:30pm.)

The *Events and Activities Guide*, available free at the tourist office, has a pub music directory. The **Gows**, 13 Main St., is probably the best pub in town, even though their sign is upside-down. (☎ 41149. Trad 4-5 nights a week.) **Davitt's Pub**, Davitt's Quay, is huge and usually packed. (☎ 44900. Disco Th-Su 11:30pm-3am. Cover £5-6. Occasional live acts.) **The Lady Belle** (☎ 44222) on The Square, has peerless maritime decor. The regulars at **The Enterprise** (☎ 41327), across The Square, sometimes work themselves into a trad frenzy. In true seaside form, Dungarvan has an **Anchor Bar** (☎ 41249), on Davitt's Quay, where rock and trad bands perform on weekends. Small but sprightly **Bridie Dee's**, 18 Mary St. (☎ 44588), has trad from Thursday to Sunday night.

⏲ SIGHTS. The tourist office offers **walking tours** of medieval and Georgian Dungarvan. (1hr., £1.50.) They also arrange two-hour bus tours to Lismore and Mahon Falls (£5), and give out free Tourist Trail maps, highlighting Dungarvan's seven or eight sights. **King John's Castle**, presiding over Davitt's Quay, fell into disrepair at the beginning of the 14th century. The IRA didn't help matters much when they set the place on fire in 1922. It's not open to the public, but the Office of Public Works has its hands on it, so it's bound to end up a heritage center some day.

There's not much else to see in Dungarvan itself, but the deep-sea **fishing** is excellent. The nearby waters have a reputation for sharks. Capt. John Tynan leads expeditions on "The Avoca." (£30 with rod and tackle; inquire at The Enterprise, ☎ 24657.) The "Chaser V" can also be chartered at a similar price (☎ 41358). **Baumann's Jewellers**, 6 St. Mary St. (☎ 41395), dispenses tackle, licenses, and a wealth of inside information.

Dungarvan is home to several annual festivals. **Féile na nDéise** (FAY-la nah ne-DAY-sya, "Local area festival") packs The Square with free concerts during the first weekend in May. The **Motorsport Weekend** pulls in vintage and race car enthusiasts in mid-July.

ARDMORE ☎ 024

Devotees of beaches and St. Declan flock to Ardmore in equal measure. The monk christianized the town in the 4th century; ruins back the town's claim to be the oldest Christian settlement in Ireland. Pilgrims come to town on July 24 for the Feast of St. Declan, but droves of more casual tourists bask in the mild waters off the sandy beach and jagged cliffs throughout the summer.

🖃🕿 GETTING THERE AND PRACTICAL INFORMATION. Buses run to **Cork** (1½hr.; M-Sa 3 per day, Su 1 per day; £7.30), and **Waterford** via **Dungarvan** (2hr.; M-Th and Sa 2 per day, F 3 per day; £7.70). The **tourist office**, in the carpark by the beach, is housed in what appears to be a demonic sandcastle. The office dispenses information about the local beaches as well as an excellent leaflet outlining a **walking tour** of town. (☎ 94444. Open M-Sa June-Aug. 11am-1pm and 2-5pm.) Ardmore is a 3 mi. detour off Cork-Waterford Rd. (N25). **Hitching** from the junction can be slow, and is not recommended by *Let's Go*. The **post office** is located on Main St. (Open M-F 9am-1pm and 2-5:30pm.)

ACCOMMODATIONS, FOOD, AND PUBS. A hop, skip, and a jump away from the beach are the simple comforts of the **Ardmore Beach Hostel,** Main St., including back-patio beach access. (☎ 94501. Dorms June-Aug. £9, Sept.-May £8; private rooms £12.50 per person.) **Byron Lodge,** Middle Rd., has literary aspirations and rooms with sunny alcoves. From Main St., take the street that runs uphill at the town's thatched cottage. Georgian items vie with more recent additions for furnishing supremacy. (☎ 94157. Open Easter-Sept. Singles with bath £23.50; doubles £32, £36 with bath.) Beach-front **camping** at **Healy's** (☎ 94181) usually requires a reservation months ahead.

Ardmore's food offerings are not extensive but tasty nonetheless. **Quinn's Foodstore** is in the town center. (☎ 94250. Open daily 8am-9pm.) The local favorite is **Cup and Saucer,** Main St., which has a delightful flower garden out back for sunny days. (☎ 94501. Open daily 10am-8pm.) Vast **Paddy Mac's,** Main St. (☎ 94166), has pub grub on reserve, and a variety of music near-nightly. **Keever's Bar,** Main St. (☎ 94141), is another favorite of the older Ardmore crowd.

SIGHTS. The all-encompassing must-do in Ardmore is the **cliffwalk,** a windy 3 mi. path with great views of the ocean and stops at all of Ardmore's historic sites. The free map and guide pamphlet are available at the tourist office and the hostel. At one end of the walk is the **cathedral,** built piecemeal between 800 and 1400, on the site of St. Declan's monastery. He is said to be buried here, and the faithful avow that soil from the saint's grave cures diseases. The cathedral houses two **ogham stones** in addition to its own carvings (see **Ancient Ireland,** p. 7). The cathedral and its graveyard are marked by a 97 ft. high **round tower,** whose door is a monk-protecting 12 ft. above the ground. **St. Declan's Stone** is perched at the water's edge, on the right from Main St. along the shore. The stone allegedly floated from Wales after the saint's visit there. Devotees sometimes wedge themselves underneath the stone on "Pattern Day," the saint's feast. Down past the Cliff House hotel at the other end of the cliffwalk is **St. Declan's Well,** which contains water that is said to cure all afflictions. Despite an abundance of old Coast Guard stations on the cliff, the shore has seen the end of many vessels. Ardmore is one end of the 56 mi. **St. Declan's Way,** which runs up to Cahir in Co. Tipperary.

WATERFORD
☎ 051

Huge metal silos and harbor cranes greet the first-time visitor to Waterford. Fortunately, behind this industrial facade lies a city with 10 centuries of history. The grandson of the Viking Ivor the Boneless founded Vadrafjord around AD 914 to harbor his longships, making it the oldest city in Ireland. Long considered mere brutes, the Vikings have recently gained recognition as suave contributors to the development of this mercantile hub, along with the Angles and Normans that followed (see **Early Christians and Vikings,** p. 8). Traces of the Viking settlement persist in Waterford's streets, despite the massive freighters that have since replaced the longships. Scores of pubs and shops make Waterford an indulgent break from touring the small towns that sleep over the rest of the county.

GETTING THERE AND GETTING AROUND

Airport: ☎ 875 589. Served by **British Airways.** Follow The Quay, turn right at Reginald's Tower, then left at the sign. 20min. from town. No city buses head that way, so take a taxi if you aren't driving.

Trains: Plunkett Station, across the bridge from The Quay. For information, call M-F 9am-6pm (☎ 317 889; 24hr. recorded timetable ☎ 876 243). Train station staffed M-Sa 9am-6pm, Su at departure times. JFK's ancestors grew up in Waterford, and the city is still well-connected. Trains chug to **Kilkenny** (40min.; M 5 per day, T-Sa 4 per day, Su 3 per day; £5), **Rosslare Harbour** (1hr., M-Sa 2 per day, £6), **Limerick** (2¼hr., M-Sa 2 per day, £10), and **Dublin** (2½hr.; M and F 5 per day, T-Sa 4 per day, Su 3 per day; £13, F £15).

206 ■ WATERFORD HARBOUR

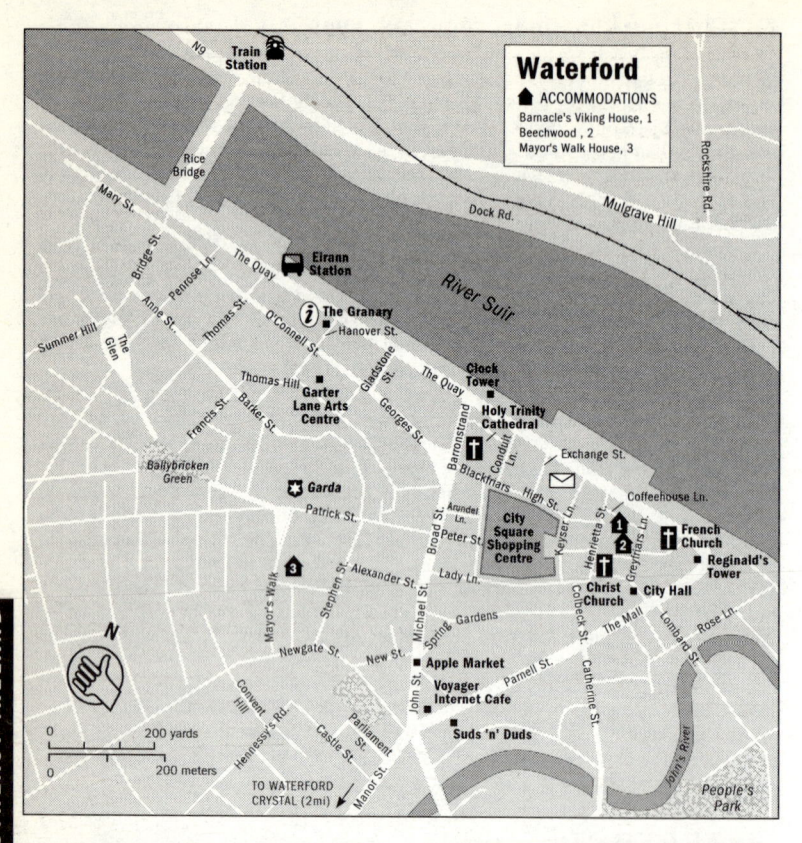

Buses: ☎ 879 000. The shiny new station is on the Quay, across the street from the tourist office. Office open M-Sa 8:15am-6pm. To **Kilkenny** (1hr.; M-Sa 2 per day, Su 1 per day; £5), **Rosslare Harbour** (1¼hr.; 4 per day, Su 3 per day; £9.20), **Limerick** (2½hr.; 5 per day, F 7 per day, Su 6 per day; £10.50), **Cork** (2½hr.; M-Sa 9 per day, Tu-Th 8 per day, F 9 per day, Su 6 per day; £10), **Dublin** (2¾hr.; M-Sa 7 per day, Su 4 per day; £7), and **Galway** (4¾hr.; M-Sa 8 per day, Su 5 per day; £13.50).

Local Transportation: City buses leave from the Clock Tower on The Quay. 75p for trips within the city, mostly around Cork Rd. The **City Imp** minibuses (75p) also cruise the town. Check the tourist office for details.

Bike Rental: Wright's Cycles, 19-20 Henrietta St. (☎ 874 411), for Raleigh rentals. £12 per day, £10 per day after; £52 per week; deposit £50. Open Tu-F 9:30am-6pm, Sa 9:30am-5:30pm, closed daily 1-2pm.

Taxis: A piece of cake to find, 24hr. a day. Either go to the **cab stand** on Broad St., or think of a catchy name and dial it: **7 Cabs** (☎ 877 777); **Five-O Cabs** (☎ 850 000).

Car Rental: Enterprise (☎ 304 804) will rent to anyone 25 or older. £35 per day.

Hitching: The rare hitchers place themselves on the main routes, away from the tangled city center. To reach N24 (Cahir, Limerick), N10 (Kilkenny, Dublin), or N25 (New Ross, Wexford, Rosslare), they head over the bridge toward the train station. For the N25 to Cork, they continue down Parnell St.; others take a city bus out to the Waterford Crystal Factory before they stick out a thumb. *Let's Go* does not recommend hitching.

WATERFORD ■ 207

ORIENTATION AND PRACTICAL INFORMATION

Waterford sits on the ruins of the triangular Viking city. The Vikings must have had a knack for urban planning, because the area between the **Quay, Parnell/Mall St.,** and **Barronstrand St.** is still hopping, even without the longboats. Cars were recently barred from the city center, creating a teeming city square between Barronstrand, Georges, and High St.

Budget Travel: usit, 36-37 Georges St. (☎ 872601; fax 871 723). Near the corner of Gladstone St., 1 block west of the city center. ISICs, **Travelsave** stamps, student deals for daily flights and bus/ferry packages from Waterford to London (see **Getting There,** p. 55). Open M-F 9:30am-5:30pm, Sa 11am-4pm.

Banks: 24hr. ATMs abound all along major roads. On the Quay, they're at **AIB** (☎ 874 824), by the clock tower; and the **Bank of Ireland** (☎ 872 074). Both are open M 10am-5pm, Tu-F 10am-4pm.

Luggage Storage: Plunkett Station. £1 per item. Open M-Sa 7:15am-9pm. Bus Éireann station. £1 in the candy shop.

Laundry: Duds 'n Suds, 6 Parnell St. (☎ 841 168 or 858 790). Self wash and dry £4.20. Service available. Open M-Sa 7:30am-9pm.

Emergency: Dial ☎ 999; no coins required. **Police** (*Garda*): Patrick St. (☎ 874 888).

Counseling and Support: Samaritans, 16 Beau St. (☎ 872 114). 24hr. listening service. **Rape Crisis Centre** (☎ 873 362). Call M-F 9-11:30am, plus Tu 2-4pm and Th 8:30-10pm. **Youth Information Centre:** 130 The Quay (☎ 877 328; email wyic@io.ie). Information on work, travel, health, and on a variety of support groups (including gay and lesbian support groups). Photocopy, fax service, and **Internet access.** Open to all, M-F 9:30am-5:30pm.

Hospital: Waterford Regional Hospital (☎ 873 321). Follow The Quay east to the Tower Hotel; turn left, then follow signs straight ahead to the hospital.

Pharmacy: Gallagher's Pharmacy. Barronstrand St. An oasis of pharmaceutical care in the city centre. (☎ 78103. Open M-Sa 8:15-10pm; Su 10am-7pm)

Post Office: The Quay (☎ 874 321), the largest of several. Open M and W-F 9am-5:30pm, Tu 9:30am-5:30pm, Sa 9am-1pm.

Internet Access: Voyager Internet Cafe, Parnell Court, Parnell St. (☎ 843 843). At the intersection of Parnell and John St., in a dreary, graffitied shopping center. Just computers. £1.50 per 15min, 10p a minute thereafter. Open M-Sa 11am-9pm, Su 3-9pm.

ACCOMMODATIONS

Most B&Bs in the city are nothing special; those outside town on the Cork Rd. are better; the hostels are best of all.

Barnacle's Viking House (IHH), Coffee House Ln., Greyfriars, The Quay (☎ 853 827; email viking@barnacles.iol.ie). Follow The Quay east past the Clock Tower and post office; the hostel is the mango-colored building between Greyfriars Lane and Henrietta Street. Take a right at Henrietta and then take an immediate left. Spacious quarters; even 12-bed dorms can feel private. Large comfy common room, top-notch security, and a small breakfast to top it off. Laundry service £4 per load. Luggage storage 50p per day. Lounge and kitchen accessible 6am-midnight. Wheelchair accessible. Dorms £7.50-9; 6-bed with bath £10-11; 4-person £11-13, with bath £12.50-14; double £28-30, with bath £29-31.

Mayor's Walk House, 12 Mayor's Walk (☎ 855 427). A 15min. prestigious walk from the train station. Quiet rooms at a simple price. The Ryders offer advice, biscuits, and a bottomless pot of tea. Open Feb.-Nov. Singles £16; doubles £30.

Beechwood, 7 Cathedral Sq. (☎ 876 677). From the Quay, go up Henrietta St. Mrs. Ryan invites you into her charming home, located on a silent pedestrian street. Look out the window at Christ Church Cathedral. Doubles £32.

FOOD

Despite an overwhelming presence of fast food chains, Waterford has some bona fide restaurants with fair prices. You might want to try Waterford's contribution to Irish cuisine, the *blaa* ("blah"), a floury white sausage roll of Huguenot origins. Besides the *blaa*, Waterford gave the world the modern process of bacon curing. To satisfy your pork cravings, and pick up some cheap groceries while you're at it, visit **Dunnes Stores** in the City Square Mall. (☎ 853 100. Open M-W 9am-7pm, Th-F 9am-9pm, Sa 9am-6pm, and Su noon-6pm.) **Treacy's**, on The Quay near the Granville Hotel, has a large selection for a late-night grocery, and even a small deli. (Open daily 9am-11pm.)

Cafe Luna, 53 John St. (☎ 834 539). A late-night cafe that serves pastas, salads, and sandwiches with a creative twist on tastes. Sun-dried tomato pesto and garlic bread £4.90. Most entrees £3-5. Open M-W until 12:15am, Th-Su until 3:30am.

Haricot's Wholefood Restaurant, 11 O'Connell St. (☎ 841 299). Vegetarians and the carnivores live in harmony with Haricot's tasty, innovative dishes; if the harmony doesn't incite conversation, they can reach for the stack of newspapers. Most entrees £5-7. Open M-F 9:30am-8pm, Sa 9:30am-6pm.

Gino's, John St. (☎ 879 513), at the Apple Market. A busy family restaurant serves pizza made right before your eyes. Reservations recommended on F-Sa nights, or call in an order to go. Individual pizza £2.70 plus 55p per topping. Veggie pizzas £4.30. Open daily until 10:45pm (for seating) or 11pm (for take-out).

Cafe Sui Sios, 54 High St. (☎ 841 063). The Gaelic phrase "Sui Sios" translates to "Take a seat." Good advice in this intimate cafe, with large portions, coffee, and fine desserts. Open M-Th 8:30am-6pm, F 8:30am-8pm. Summer hours until 8pm daily.

Sizzlers, on The Quay toward Reginald's Tower (☎ 852 100). Always open, always popular. The best greasy spoon you can find (entrees £2-6), but no salad bar.

The Reginald, 2-3 The Mall (☎ 855 087). Feel secure in the Reginald as you eat with your back to a section of the Norman wall that defended Waterford in the 14th century. This bar, restaurant, and "Knight Club" serves rich, delicious food in a classy environment. Dinner's expensive, but lunch is reasonable. The house specialty is Steak and Guinness Pie, £6.95 Carvery lunch daily noon-3pm, bar menu 3-7pm, dinner 6-10:30pm.

PUBS AND CLUBS

The Quays are loaded with pubs; even more reside on the corner of John and Parnell St. A number run discos on weekend nights, so there's always somewhere open late. All pubs close at 12:30am, late bars afterwards.

T&H Doolan's, George's St. (☎ 841 504). In a fantastic building, Doolan's has been serving crowds for 300 years now. Especially popular with out-of-towners. Trad nightly.

The Gingerbread Man, Arundel Lane (☎ 875 041). More authentic trad sessions jam at the front tables and the good time spills over to the back of this small bar. Good grub 12pm-6pm. Brie and sun-dried tomatoes and pesto £3.95.

Geoff's, 9 John St. (☎ 874 787). Most locals will tell you that Geoff's is the place to see and be seen. Bring a cell phone and a slightly cliquish group of buddies while slurping your pint and laughing a bit too loudly.

The Woodman, at Parnell and John St. (☎ 858 130). Late bar hours on M and W keep the downstairs busy with a mixture of drinkers. Ruby's Nightclub spins a variety of music and opens both floors for people to mill around on Tu and Th-Su nights.

The Junction, at Parnell and John St. (☎ 844 842). With the Rhythm Room next door, a billiard table, and a faux-train car to snuggle in, pubbers are always scattered throughout its mega-space. Late bar M, Tu.

Muldoon's, John St. (☎ 873 693). Merlin's dance club next door casts a late night spell on Muldoon's, the ESPN version of a drinking hole. Practically empty before 11:30, since that's when the free snacks begin.

Mullane's, 15 Newgate St. (☎ 873 854), off New St. It's necessary to go a bit out of your way to come across sessions this hard-core. A sprinkling of the young, a dash of tourists, and older regulars result in the perfect mix. Call ahead for session times; the pub is almost empty when there isn't one.

SIGHTS

You can cover all of Waterford's sights in a day, but only if you move as swiftly as a Viking and plan ahead like a Norman invader. The private Suirway (SHURE-way) bus company endeavors to help you achieve that task by running the **Crystal City Explorer,** a hop-on hop-off shuttle that stops at the Waterford Crystal Factory, the Waterford Treasures Museum, and The Reginald Tower. The steep £9.50 shuttle ticket covers the price of admission to all three sights. During the season the pass is valid for only one day. (☎ 382 209; www.suirway.com; timetables available at tourist office.) **The Waterford Crystal Factory,** 2 mi. from the city centre out on N25 (Cork Rd.), is a finely-hewed stone in the rough. Witness master craftsmen transform molten goo into sparkling crystal. Admire the finished products, and their astronomical prices, in the gallery. (☎ 373 311 or 332 500. 1hr. tours every 15min., audio-visual shows on demand. Wheelchair accessible. Apr.-Oct. showroom open 8:30am-6pm, tours daily; Nov.-Mar. showroom open 9am-5pm, call ahead to check on tour times; Jan.-Feb. showroom only 9am-5pm. Tours £3.50, students £2.) Catch the **City Imp** (a red-and-yellow minibus) along Parnell St. and request a stop at the factory (10-15min., runs every 15-20min., 70p) or take city bus #1 (Kilbarry-Ballybeg), which leaves across from the Clock Tower every 30 min. and passes the factory on a slightly more circuitous route (75p).

In the same building as the tourist office, the exhibit of **Waterford Treasures** at the Granary recently replaced the old heritage center. Thanks to a little help from the EU, this £4.5 million project lets you go at your own pace through a sleek presentation of the city's history. A programmable audio-visual handset lets you explore in detail the aspects of this elaborate history that interest you the most. The artifacts, such as the town's written charters, make quite an impressive show; the glitzier exhibits, like the Viking boat simulation with mechanically rocking seats, are worth skipping. (☎ 304 500; www.waterfordtreasures.com. Open daily June-Aug. 9:30am-9pm, Sept.-May 10am-5pm. £3, students and seniors £2.50.)

Reginald's Tower, at the end of The Quay, has guarded the entrance to the city since the 12th century. (☎ 304 220. Tours on demand. Open daily 10am-6pm June-Aug. 9:30am-6:30pm, Sept.-May 9:30am-6pm, last tour 5:15pm. £1.50, seniors £1, students 60p.) Its virtually impenetrable 10 ft. thick Viking walls have housed a prison, a mint, and the wedding reception of Strongbow and Aoife (see **Early Christians and Vikings,** p. 8) The tiny models of Waterford illustrate the contributions Vikings, Normans, and English kings have made to Waterford's growth.

The **Walking Tour of Historic Waterford** sorts out the city's mongrel heritage by touring a variety of the visible ruins, including part of the original Viking walls. These one-hour tours depart from the Granville Hotel on the Quay and the Granary museum at a quarter to the hour. (☎ 873 711 or 851 043. Mar.-Oct. daily at noon and 2pm. £3.) Many of Waterford's more recent monumental buildings were the brainchildren of 18th century architect John Roberts. The **Theatre Royal** and **City Hall,** both on The Mall, are his secular masterpieces. He also designed both the Roman Catholic **Holy Trinity Cathedral** on Barronstrand St., and the Church of Ireland **Christ Church Cathedral** in Cathedral Square (up Henrietta St. from the Quay), making Waterford the only European city to have Catholics and Protestants worship in buildings united by a common architect. Christ Church Cathedral has the cadaver-motif tomb of Bishop Rice, complete with vermin chewing on his corpse.

ENTERTAINMENT

The tourist office can provide an annual list of major events in town, and any of the local newspapers, including the free *Waterford Today*, should have more specific entertainment listings. Keep your eyes peeled for posters as well. The **Waterford Show** at City Hall is an entertaining performance of Irish music, stories, and dance. A ticket costs £8, but that also gets you glasses of Baileys or wine. (☎ 358 397 or 875 788; mobile (087) 681 7191. May-Sept. Tu, Th, and Sa at 9pm. July-Aug. also W at 9pm. Safest to call for reservations or make them at the tourist office.) The **Garter Lane Arts Centre,** 22a O'Connell St., supports all different forms of art in its old Georgian building. Visual exhibits constantly grace the walls and are usually free—musical concerts cost £10 at most—and dance and theater grace its stage year round. (☎ 855 038. Open M-Sa 10am-6pm. Box office open M-Sa 10am-6pm and until 9pm on performance nights. Student and senior prices available.) Waterford's largest festival is the **Spraoi** (SPREE; ☎ 841 808; www.spraoi.com), on the early August bank holiday weekend. A celebration of life in general, the Spraoi attracts bands from around the globe and culminates in a sizeable parade.

SOUTHWEST IRELAND

With a contradictory and dramatic landscape that ranges from lush lakes and mountains to stark, ocean-battered cliffs, it's no wonder Southwest Ireland has produced some of the country's greatest storytellers. The environment is matched by an equally engrossing history. Outlaws and rebels once lurked in hidden coves and glens now frequented by visitors and ruled over by publicans. The grand architecture of Cork City (pop. 150,000) contrasts the area's frantic pace of rebuilding and growth with the ancient rhythm of nearby rural villages. There are good reasons why tourist buses chug to majestic Killarney and the Ring of Kerry. No place in Ireland has as many multilingual signs as Killarney, all of them screaming "buy me." Indeed, the land in west Cork is steadily being bought by investors and the occasional movie star. If the tourist mayhem is too much for you, simply retreat to the placid stretches along the Dingle Peninsula and Cork's southern coast.

HIGHLIGHTS OF THE SOUTHWEST: HEAPS OF RINGS AND SHEEP

Run the **Ring of Kerry** circuit (p. 257), taking in exquisite mountains, lakes, forests, and 850 red deer in glacier-carved **Killarney National Park** (p. 254).

Trek out to the tip of the peninsula and catch a boat to the ancient ruins on **Valentia Island** (p. 260) and a mountaintop monastery on the **Skellig Rocks** (p. 261).

Wave at Fungi the Dolphin from the beach at **Dingle** (p. 265), then explore the ogham stone-peppered coastline of this Irish-speaking peninsula by bike.

Forsake civilization and embrace the wild on a hike through the Miskish Mountains or cycle the 125 mi. Beara Way on the **Beara Peninsula** (p. 240).

Check out a hurling game at the Blackrock stadium and then head to one of **Cork's** pubs to discuss the results and listen to top-notch trad (p. 213).

COUNTY CORK

Historically, eastern Cork's superb harbors along the southern coast of Ireland made it a prosperous trading center. Its distance from Dublin and the Pale gave the English less leverage over it. Perhaps as a result, Cork was a center of patriotic activity during the 19th and early 20th centuries. Headquarters of the "Munster Republic" controlled by the anti-Treaty forces during the Civil War, the county produced patriot Michael Collins, as well as the man who assassinated him in 1922 (see **Independence and Civil War,** p. 17). The energies of today's Cork City are directed toward industry and culture, while the sea towns of Kinsale and Cobh gaily entertain tall ships and stooped backpackers. West Cork, the southwestern third of the county, was once the "badlands" of Ireland; its ruggedness and isolation rendered it lawless and largely uninhabitable. Ex-hippies and antiquated fishermen have replaced the outlaws; they do their best to make the villages ultra-hospitable to tourists. Roaringwater Bay and wave-whipped Mizen Head mark Ireland's land's end. The lonely beauty here is a stately solitude unmarred by the tourist-approved shamrocks planted elsewhere in Ireland. Ireland's rich archaeological history is particularly visible and accessible in Cork, with Celtic ring forts, mysterious stone circles, and long-ruined abbeys dotting the sheep-speckled hills.

212 ■ COUNTY CORK

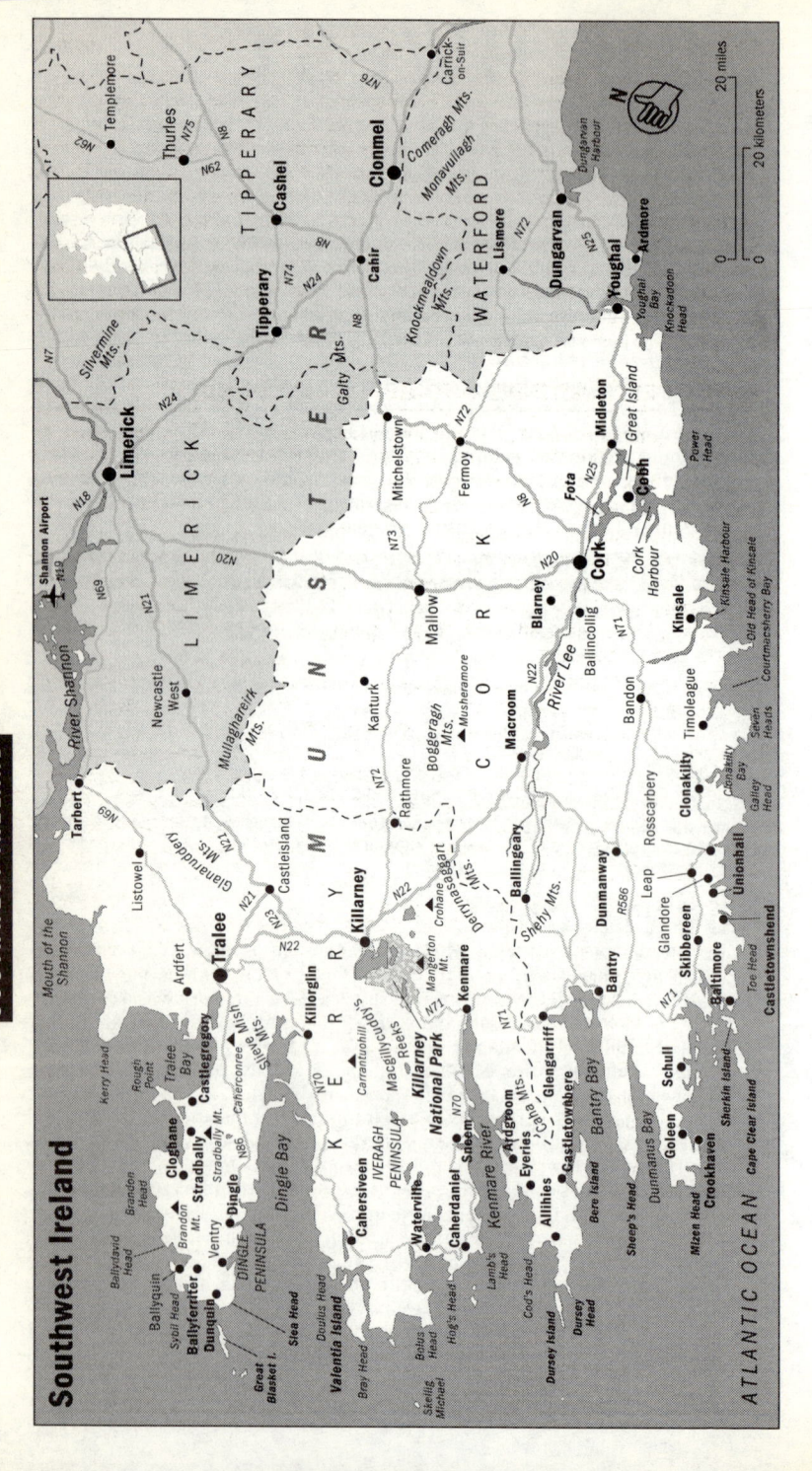

CORK
☎ 021

As Ireland's second-largest city, Cork (pop. 150,000) is the center of the southwest's sports, music, and arts. Strolls along the pub-lined streets and river quays reveal grand and grimy architecture, as well as more recent commercial and industrial development, evidence of Cork's history of ruin and reconstruction. Indeed, what older charms industry has not blackened, the English have blighted. The old city burned down in 1622, Cromwell expelled half its citizens in the 1640s, the English Duke of Marlborough laid siege to Cork in 1690, and the city was torched again in 1920 during the Irish War of Independence. Wise visitors will more politely exploit the city's resources and use Cork as a place to eat, drink, shop, and sleep while exploring the exquisite scenery of the surrounding countryside. Within the city limits, time is best filled by taking in the vibrant street scene, or meandering across the pastoral campus of University College Cork.

GETTING THERE AND GETTING AROUND

Airport: Cork Airport (☎ 431 3131), 5 mi. south of Cork on Kinsale Rd. **Aer Lingus** (☎ 432 7155), **British Airways** (☎ 1 (800) 626 747), and **Ryanair** (☎ (01) 609 7800) connect Cork to Dublin, various English cities, and Paris. A taxi (£7-8) or bus (16-18 per day, £2.50) will deliver you from the airport to the bus station on Parnell Place.

Trains: Kent Station, Lower Glanmire Rd. (☎ 450 6766; www.irishrail.ie), across the river from the city center in the northeast part of town. Open M-Sa 7am-8:30pm, Su 7am-8pm. Train connections to **Limerick** (1½hr., M-Sa 7 per day, Su 4 per day, £14), **Killarney** (2hr., M-Sa 7 per day, Su 4 per day, £14), **Tralee** (2½hr., M-Sa 3 per day, Su 3 per day, £18), and **Dublin** (3hr., M-Sa 7 per day, Su 5 per day, £33.50). Best prices with advance booking.

Buses: Parnell Pl. (☎ 450 8188), 2 blocks east of Patrick's Bridge on Merchants' Quay. Inquiries desk open daily 9am-5pm. Bus Éireann goes to all major cities: **Bantry** (2hr., M-Sa 3 per day, Su 2 per day, £9.40); **Killarney** (2hr., M-Sa 8 per day, Su 6 per day, £9.40); **Limerick** (2hr., M-Sa 6 per day, Su 5 per day, £9.60); **Rosslare Harbour** (4hr., M-Sa 2 per day, Su 2 per day, £13.50); **Tralee** (2½hr., M-Sa 8 per day, Su 6 per day, £10); **Waterford** (2¼hr., M-Sa 8 per day, Sun 6 per day, £10); **Galway** (4hr., M-Sa 5 per day, Su 5 per day, £12.50); **Dublin** (4½hr., M-Sa 4 per day, Su 4 per day, £13); **Sligo** (7hr., 3 per day, £17); **Belfast** (7½hr., M-Sa 4 per day, Su 2 per day, £20); and **Donegal Town** (9hr., 1 per day, £18.50).

Ferries: Ringaskiddy Terminal (☎ 427 5061), 8 mi. south of the city, shoves one ferry off for Roscoff, France weekly (from £63). Call **Brittany Ferries** (☎ 427 7801) or stop by their office on Grande Parade next to the tourist office. The terminal is a 30min. bus ride from the bus station in Cork (£3). Buses leave 1¼hr. prior to ferry departure. The ferry to Swansea, England, runs daily. (☎ 427 1166; £44-64, prices increase slightly June-Aug.) For other ferries to England contact **Irish Ferries** (☎ 455 1995 or 1890 313 131) at the corner of McCurtain St. and St. Patrick's bridge. For 24hr. ferry information, call ☎ (01) 661 0715. See **By Ferry,** p. 59.

Local Transportation: City **buses** criss-cross the city and its suburbs. From downtown, catch the buses (and their schedules) at the bus station on Merchant's Quay or on St. Patrick St., across from the Father Matthew statue. Downtown buses run every 10-30min. from 7:30am-11:15pm M-Sa, with reduced service Su 10am-11:15pm. Fares from 70p. The main bus station at Parnell Pl. offers free timetables (☎ 450 8188).

Car Rental: Great Island Car Rentals, 47 McCurtain St. (☎ 481 1609). £40 per day, £115 for 3 days, £160 per week for subcompact standard. Min. age 23. **Budget Rent-a-Car,** Tourist Office, Grand Parade (☎ 427 4755). £33 per day, £99 for 3 days, £195 per week. Min. age 23.

Bike Rental: The Bike Shop, 68 Shandon St. (☎ 430 4144) rents bikes for £7 per day, £30 per week. The Raleigh Rent-a-Bike program at **Cycle Scene,** 396 Blarney St. (☎ 430 1183) rents bikes that can be returned at the other Raleigh locations across Ireland. £10 per day, £40 per week. £50 deposit.

214 ■ CORK

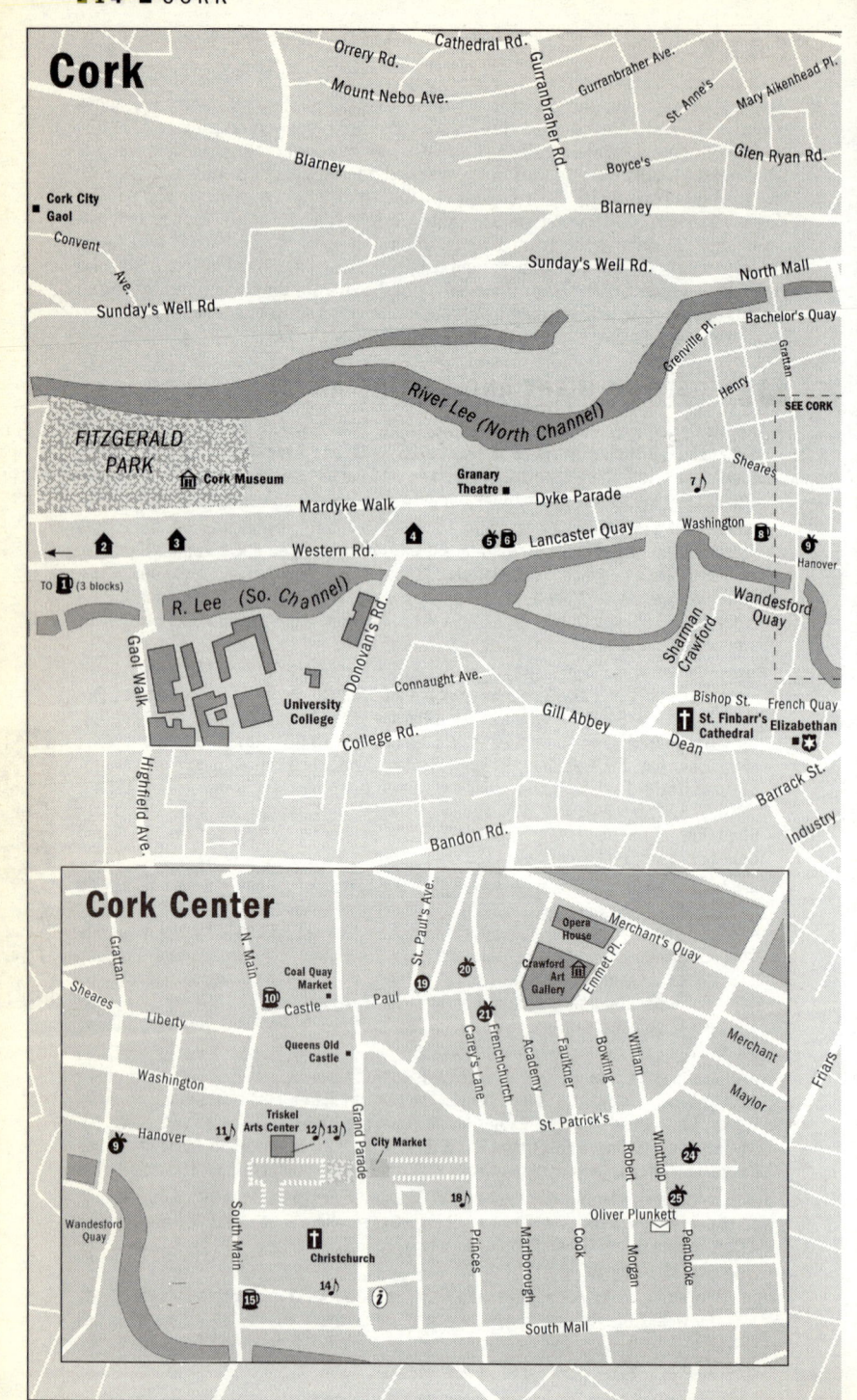

Cork

- Cork City Gaol
- Convent Ave.
- Sunday's Well Rd.
- Orrery Rd.
- Cathedral Rd.
- Mount Nebo Ave.
- Gurranbraher Rd.
- Gurranbraher Ave.
- St. Anne's
- Mary Aikenhead Pl.
- Blarney
- Boyce's
- Glen Ryan Rd.
- Blarney
- Sunday's Well Rd.
- North Mall
- Bachelor's Quay
- Grenville Pl.
- Henry
- Grattan
- SEE CORK
- River Lee (North Channel)
- Sheares
- FITZGERALD PARK
- Cork Museum
- Granary Theatre
- Mardyke Walk
- Dyke Parade
- Washington
- Western Rd.
- Lancaster Quay
- Hanover
- TO (3 blocks)
- R. Lee (So. Channel)
- Donovan's Rd.
- Sharman Crawford
- Wandesford Quay
- Gaol Walk
- University College
- Connaught Ave.
- Gill Abbey
- Bishop St.
- French Quay
- St. Finbarr's Cathedral
- Elizabethan
- Highfield Ave.
- College Rd.
- Dean
- Barrack St.
- Bandon Rd.
- Industry

Cork Center

- Grattan
- Sheares
- N. Main
- Liberty
- Coal Quay Market
- Castle
- St. Paul's Ave.
- Paul
- Opera House
- Merchant's Quay
- Crawford Art Gallery
- Emmet Pl.
- Queens Old Castle
- Carey's Lane
- Frenchchurch
- Academy
- Faulkner
- Bowling
- William
- Merchant
- Maylor
- Friars
- Washington
- Hanover
- Triskel Arts Center
- Grand Parade
- City Market
- St. Patrick's
- Winthrop
- Robert
- Wandesford Quay
- South Main
- Christchurch
- Princes
- Marlborough
- Cook
- Morgan
- Oliver Plunkett
- Pembroke
- South Mall

CORK ■ 215

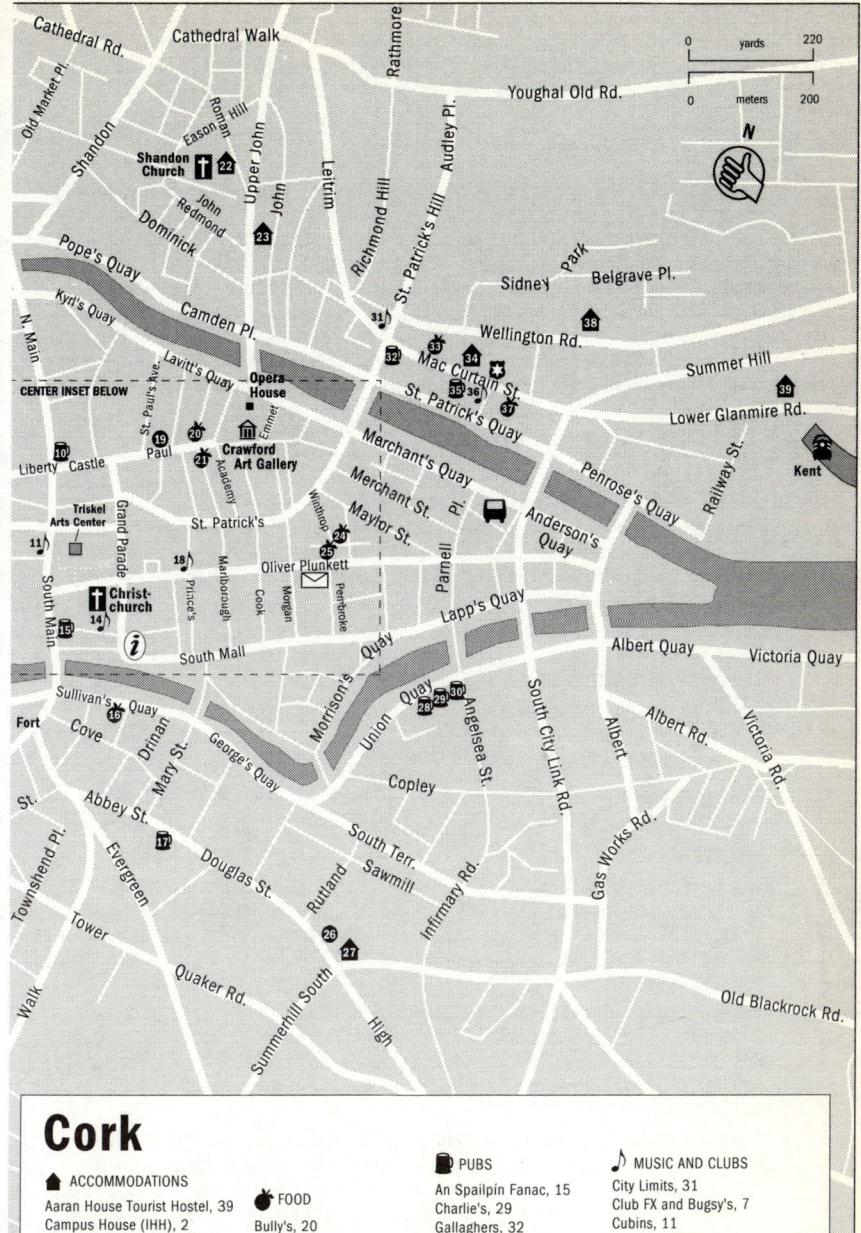

Cork

ACCOMMODATIONS
Aaran House Tourist Hostel, 39
Campus House (IHH), 2
Cork International Hostel (HI), 3
Garnish House, 4
Isaac's (IHH), 34
Kelly's Holiday Hostel, 27
Kinlay House (IHH), 22
Roman House, 23
Sheila's Budget Accommodation Centre (IHH), 38

FOOD
Bully's, 20
Cafe Paradiso, 5
The Delhi Palace, 9
The Gingerbread House, 21
Gino's, 25
Quay Co-op, 16
Scoozi, 24
Tony's Fine Foods, 37
Up Town Grill, 33

PUBS
An Spailpín Fanac, 15
Charlie's, 29
Gallaghers, 32
John Rearden and Son, 8
Loafer's, 17
The Lobby, 30
McGanns, 28
Rosie O'Grady's, 10
The Shelbourne, 35
The Thirsty Scholar, 6
The Western Star, 1

MUSIC AND CLUBS
City Limits, 31
Club FX and Bugsy's, 7
Cubins, 11
Everyman Palace, 36
Gorbys, 18
The Other Place, 14
Sir Henry's, 12
The Yumi Yuki Club, 13

SERVICES
Duds 'n Suds Laundromat, 26
Tesco Supermarket, 19

Hitching: Hitchhikers headed for West Cork and County Kerry walk down Western Rd. past both the An Óige hostel and the dog track to the Crow's Nest Pub, or take bus #8. Those hoping to hitch a ride to Dublin or Waterford may want to stand on the hill next to the train station on the Lower Glanmire Rd. *Let's Go* does not recommend hitching.

ORIENTATION

Downtown Cork is the tip of an arrow-shaped island in the **River Lee.** Many central north-south streets were once Venice-style canals, but in the 1700s, Cork discovered pavement. The river still runs through the present-day city: the center lies on the island, the southern side is filled with quiet avenues, and the sight-saturated **Shandon** district dominates the north side. Downtown action concentrates on **Oliver Plunkett St., Saint Patrick St., Paul St.,** and the north-south streets that connect them. Heading west from the Grand Parade, **Washington St.** becomes **Western Rd.** and then the N22 to Killarney; to the north of the Lee, **McCurtain St.** flows east into **Lower Glanmire Rd.,** which becomes N8 and N25. Cork is pedestrian-friendly.

PRACTICAL INFORMATION

TOURIST AND FINANCIAL SERVICES

Tourist Office: Tourist House, Grand Parade (☎ 427 3251) near the corner of South Mall and Grand Parade downtown, across from the National Monument, offers a Cork city guide and map (£1.50), booking, and car rentals. Open M-Sa 9:15am-5:30pm.

Budget Travel Office: usit, Oliver Plunkett St., around the corner from the tourist office (☎ 427 0900). This helpful travel office sells **TravelSave** stamps that reduce student fares on Irish buses, Rambler tickets, and Eurotrain tickets. Open M-F 9:30am-5:30pm, Sa 10am-2pm. **SAYIT,** Grand Parade (☎ 427 9188), specializes in similar offerings.

Banks: TSB, 4-5 Princes St. (☎ 427 5221). Open M-W and F 9:30am-5pm, Th 9:30am-7pm. **Bank of Ireland,** 70 Patrick St. (☎ 427 7177). Open M 10am-5pm, Tu-F 10am-4pm. Most banks in Cork have **24hr. ATMs.**

LOCAL SERVICES

Luggage Storage: Lockers £1 at the **train station.** Storage at the **bus station** £1.50 per item, 80p each additional day. Open M-F 8:35am-6:15pm, Sa 9:30am-6:15pm.

Bookstores: Waterstone's, 69 Patrick St. (☎ 427 6522). Monstrously huge. Open M-Th 9am-8pm, F 9am-9pm, Sa 9am-7pm, Su noon-7pm. **Mercier Bookstore,** 18 Academy St. (☎ 427 5040), off Patrick St. Specializes in Irish interest books. Open M-Sa 9am-5:30pm. **Cork Bookshop,** Carey Lane (☎ 427 1346) off Patrick St. Easily browsable selection. Open M-F 9am-6pm.

Camping Supplies: Outside World and the Tent Shop, Parnell Pl. (☎ 427 8833), next to the bus station. Extensive stock of camping supplies, including boots and clothing. Open M-F 9:30am-5:30pm. Backpacks and other gear are available for purchase, along with free advice, at **Hillwalking** (☎ 427 1643), also next to the bus station on Summerhill. Open M-Sa 9am-5:30pm.

Bisexual, Gay, and Lesbian Information: The Other Place, 8 South Main St. (☎ 427 8470), is a resource center for gay and lesbian concerns in Cork. Open Tu-Sa 10am-5:30pm. Hosts a gay bar (see **Clubs**). **The Other Side Bookshop** (☎ 427 8470), upstairs, sells new and used gay and lesbian publications. Open Tu-Sa 10am-5:30pm. **Gay Information Cork** (☎ 427 1087) opens a telephone help-line W 7-9pm and Sa 3-5pm. Lesbian line Th 8-10pm. Contact The Other Place for information on events.

Laundry: Duds 'n Suds, Douglas St. (☎ 431 4799), around the corner from Kelly's Hostel. Provides dry-cleaning services, TV, and even a small snack bar. Wash £1.50, dry £1.80. Open M-F 8am-9pm, Sa 8am-8pm. **Clifton Launderette,** Western Rd. (☎ 425 1886), by the University. Large load, full service £5.20. Open M and F 9:30am-8pm, Tu-Th and Sa 9:30am-6:30pm.

CORK ■ 217

EMERGENCY AND COMMUNICATIONS

Emergency: Dial 999; no coins required. **Police** (*Garda*): Anglesea St. (☎ 452 2000).

Crisis and Support: Rape Crisis Centre, 5 Camden Pl. (☎ (800) 449 6496). 24hr. counseling. **AIDS Hotline,** Cork AIDS Alliance, 16 Peter St. (☎ 427 6676). Open M-F 10am-5pm. **Samaritans** (☎ 427 1323 or (800) 460 9090) offers a 24hr. support line for depression.

Hospital: Mercy Hospital, Grenville Pl. (☎ 427 1971). £20 fee for access to emergency room. **Cork Regional Hospital,** Wilton St. (☎ 454 6400), on bus #8.

Pharmacies: Regional Late Night Pharmacy, Wilton Rd. (☎ 434 4575), opposite the Regional Hospital on bus #8. Open M-F 9am-10pm, Sa-Su 10am-10pm. **Phelan's Late Night,** 9 Patrick St. (☎ 427 2511). Open M-Sa 9am-10pm, Su 10am-10pm. **Boots,** 71 Patrick St. (☎ 427 0977). Open M-Th and Sa 9am-5:30pm, F 9am-8pm.

Post Office: Oliver Plunkett St. (☎ 427 2000) at the corner of Pembrooke St. Open M-Sa 9am-5:30pm.

Internet Access: Favourite, 122 Patrick St. (☎ 427 2646), at the top of Patrick St. near Merchant Quay. Internet access in stalls at the rear of the store. £1 per 10min. Open daily 9am-10:30pm. **The Victoria Sporting Club** (☎ 450 3344) on St. Patrick's Quay. One stall in the cafe at the front. £1 per 10min. Open daily 10am-midnight.

ACCOMMODATIONS

Cork's seven hostels range from drearily adequate to wonderfully welcoming. B&Bs are clustered along Western Rd. near University College. The other concentration of accommodations is in the slightly more central area along McCurtain St. and Lower Glanmire Rd., near the bus and train stations.

HOSTELS

Sheila's Budget Accommodation Centre (IHH), 4 Belgrave Pl. (☎ 450 5562), by the intersection of Wellington Rd. and York St. The staff's smiling faces welcome guests to a large, perk-filled and comfortable hostel. Centrally located, Sheila's offers a big kitchen and summertime barbecues in a secluded backyard. **Internet access** £1 per 10 min., video rental £1, sauna £1.50 for 40 min. The 24hr. reception desk doubles as a general store and offers breakfast (£1.50). All rooms non-smoking. Rooms available with bath. Free luggage storage. Sheets 50p. Key deposit £5. Check-out 10:30am. **Bike rental** £6. 6-bed dorms £7; 4-bed dorms £8.50; doubles £21.

Cork International Hostel (An Óige/HI), 1-2 Redclyffe, Western Rd. (☎ 454 3289), a 15min. walk from the Grand Parade. Bus #8 stops across the street if you ask the driver to let you off there. Immaculate and spacious bunk rooms with high ceilings in a stately brick Victorian townhouse. Reduced prices for youths under 18. All rooms with bath. Continental breakfast £2. Check-in 8am-midnight. **Bike rental** £5 per day, £30 per week. 10-bed dorms £8-£9.50; 6-bed dorms £12.50-14.50; 4-bed dorms £10.50-12; doubles £25. Rates seasonal.

Kinlay House (IHH), Bob and Joan Walk (☎ 450 6927; email kincork@usit.ie), down the alley to the right of Shandon Church. Located in less-than-posh but convenient Shandon, Kinlay House is large and clean, if motel-like. Each of the modern rooms has a locker and wash basin. Video library and game room. 10% discount with ISIC. Continental breakfast included. Laundry £3.60. Internet access £1.50 per 15min. 50p key deposit. Free parking. 10- to 14-bed dorms £8; singles £15; doubles £25.

Isaac's (IHH), 48 McCurtain St. (☎ 450 8388; www.ibi.ie/isaacs). From the bus stop, cross the nearby bridge and take the second left onto McCurtain St. This hugely modern institution is located near the bus and train stations. Cafe open for breakfast and lunch. Continental breakfast £2.25, Irish £3.25. 24hr. reception. Dorm lockout 11am-3pm. 14- to 16-bed dorms £7.95; 6- to 10-bed dorms £8.95, 4-bed dorms £9.25.

Aaran House Tourist Hostel, Lower Glanmire Rd. (☎ 455 1566). From the train station, turn right and walk 75 yd.; a bright painted sign marks the hostel on the left. A casual

SOUTHWEST IRELAND

atmosphere adds to the convenient location. Continental breakfast included. 8-bed dorms £7.50. 4-bed dorms £8, with shower and toilet £8.50; 2-bed dorms £9.50.

Kelly's Holiday Hostel, 25 Summerhill South (☎ 431 5612; kellyshostel@hotmail.com). From the bus station, go down Parnell Pl. which turns into Anglesea and then Infirmary Rd., turn right on Old Blackrock Road and look for the sign with a weary Garfield. This hostel sits far from Cork's major attractions, but it still draws plenty of occupants. Each room is named after a famous Irish poet, and hand-inscribed poems share the walls with intricate decorations. Lockers in every room, but you'll need your own padlock. Cable TV and videos. Free coffee and tea. No smoking. Laundry £3.50. 7- to 8-bed rooms £7.50-£8; doubles with shower £24-£30; triples with shower £27-£30.

BED AND BREAKFASTS

Garnish House, Western Rd. (☎ 427 5111). Prepare to be pampered. Gorgeous rooms, fluffy comforters, fruit, and flowers. Fresh tea and scones when you arrive. All rooms come with telephone, hair dryer, color TV, and full bath. The breakfast menu features 30 choices. Family room available. Free laundry service. Singles from £25; doubles from £40, with jacuzzi from £50.

Roman House, St. John's Terrace, Upper John St. (☎ 450 3606, rhbb@ircom.net). Cross the North Channel by the Opera House, make a left on John Redmond St., and then bear right onto Upper John St. Cork's only B&B catering specifically to gay and lesbian travelers, Roman House is decorated decadently. Vegetarian breakfast option. Washbasins, TVs, oversized armchairs, and tea and coffee-making facilities in every room. Singles from £20; doubles £36.

FOOD

Don't explore Cork's city center on an empty stomach; delicious restaurants and cafes abound. Particularly appealing are the lanes connecting Patrick St., Paul St., and Oliver Plunkett St. The **English Market,** accessible from Grand Parade, Patrick St., and Prince St., displays a wide variety of meats, fish, cheeses, and fruits. Pastries soar to the heavens in the second-floor **Farmgate Cafe.** (Market and cafe open M-Sa 9am-5pm.) Cork's historic role as a meat-shipping center meant that Corkonians often got stuck eating leftovers: feet, snouts, and other delectable goodies. Cork's local specialties include *crubeen* (pig's feet), *drisheen* (blood sausage; its texture is a hybrid of liver and Jell-O), and Clonakilty black pudding (an intriguing mixture of blood, grain, and spice). For the less carnivorous, there's a scone around every corner, and many restaurants have vegetarian options. **Tesco,** Paul St., is the biggest grocery store in town. (☎ 427 0791. Open M-W and Sa 8:30am-8pm, Th-F 8:30am-10pm.)

Scoozi, in the alley just off Winthrop Ave. (☎ 427 5077). Follow the tomato signs to this expansive, brick-and-wood-lined establishment. It's the perfect spot for enjoying burgers, pizza, grilled chicken, and pasta with wild abandon amongst crowds. Pesto chicken breast on a bun with fries and coleslaw £6.85. Open M-Sa 9am-11pm, Su noon-10pm.

The Gingerbread House, Paul St. (☎ 429 6411). Huge windows, cool jazz, and heavenly breads, pastries, and quiche all made fresh on the premises. Lunch menu includes soups, sandwiches and pizza. Eat in or take out. Open M-W, Sa 8:15am-7pm, Th-F 8:15am-9pm, Su 8:15am-6pm.

Quay Co-op, 24 Sullivan's Quay (☎ 431 7660). A cow's delight: nary a creature was sacrificed for the scrumptious vegetarian dishes served in this classy establishment. Excellent soups and desserts. Daily specials around £5. Veggie burger £4. Open M-Sa 9am-9pm. The store downstairs caters to all organic and vegan needs. Store open M-Sa 9am-6:15pm.

Cafe Paradiso, 16 Lancaster Quay (☎ 427 7939). This vegetarian restaurant offers a quick meal in a comfortable modern setting. Lunch menu £6-8, dinner £11-13. Open Tu-Sa 10:30am-10:30pm.

Gino's, 7 Winthrop St. (☎ 427 4485), between Patrick and Oliver Plunkett St. Primo pizza draws crowds. Lunch special includes pizza and Cork's best ice cream for £4.50. Open M-Sa noon-11pm, Su 1-11pm.

Bully's, 40 Paul St. (☎ 427 3555). An extensive menu from seafood to omelettes to burgers and pasta in a small pub atmosphere. Dinner meals £7-13. Also serves breakfast. Open daily 8:30am-11pm.

Up Town Grill, McCurtain St. (☎ 450 2120). She hasn't been living in her white-bread world. Come for the full hearty Irish breakfast served daily 10am-12:15pm. Includes egg, bacon, sausage, toast, juice and tea or coffee for £3.40. Also serves burgers and other grill items. Open M-Sa 10am-12am, Su 10am-11:30pm.

Tony's Fine Foods, McCurtain St. (☎ 450 4644). Popular with the locals and recommended by neighboring hostels, this small restaurant serves just about everything. Breakfast is available all day as are their burgers, pizza and various grill items. Open M-F 8am-6pm, Sa 8am-9pm, Su 9am-6pm.

The Delhi Palace, 6 Washington St. (☎ 427 6227). Consume like a maharajah. Vegetarian dishes from £7, meat dishes from £8. Dinner daily 5:30pm-midnight.

■ PUBS

Cork's pubs have all the variety of music and atmosphere you'd expect to find in Ireland's second-largest city. Along Oliver Plunkett St., Union Quay, and South Main St., there are more pubs than you can shake a stick at. Cork is the proud home of **Murphy's,** a thick, creamy stout that some say, especially in Cork, tastes as good as Guinness. The cheaper stout, **Beamish,** is also brewed here. Nearly all pubs stop serving at 11:30pm.

The Lobby, 1 Union Quay (☎ 431 9307). Arguably the most famous venue in Cork, the Lobby has given some of Ireland's biggest folk acts their start. Live music nightly at 9:30pm, from trad to acid jazz. Two floors overlook the river. Occasional cover £4.

An Spailpín Fanac (uhn spal-PEEN FAW-nuhk), 28 South Main St. (☎ 427 7949), across from the Beamish brewery. One of Cork's more popular pubs and as old as they get—it opened in 1790. The name means "the wandering potato picker," but the largely tourist crowd is less likely to stray. Live trad complements the decor most nights. Pub grub (Irish stew £3.75) served M-F noon-3pm.

Gallaghers, McCurtain St. A traditional pub conveniently located to welcome tourists, especially on "Backpacker Nights" (M-Tu), when a three-pint pitcher sells for £6. Also featuring an array of filling pub grub. Most meals around £4.50.

The Western Star, Western Rd. (☎ 454 3047). About a 25min. walk from the town center, this largely student bar rocks with the chart toppers nightly. If you're staying nearby in summer, enjoy the outdoors bar on the patio by the Lee River. Free barbecue F-Sa.

Rosie O'Grady's, N. Main St. (☎ 427 8253). Brace yourself. A wild, swelling crowd and pulsing trad render the Rosie's experience one of Cork's liveliest. Largely a student crowd in the winter. Live trad Su, M, W. Lunch served M-F noon-3pm.

McGanns, 3 Union Quay (☎ 496 4275). Newly renovated, this large Quay pub packs them in with their nightly live trad upstairs, with a calmer scene in the lower level.

John Rearden and Son, Washington St. (☎ 427 1969). Popular with a lively late-twenties local crowd in its pseudo-medieval interior. Open until 2am Th-Su. Over 23yrs. only.

The Thirsty Scholar, Western Rd. (☎ 427 6209). Steps from campus, this intimate student-crowded pub has live summer trad sessions.

The Shelbourne, 16-17 McCurtain St. (☎ 450 9615). Popular with the neighboring hostels, this large bar brings in the crowds with live trad M from 9pm. Pub grub available during the day from noon-2:30pm.

Charlie's, Union Quay (☎ 496 5272). Art by local student artists decks the walls of the smallest of the Quay pubs. Gaggles of locals and tourists pack in for live trad nightly in the summer, and 3-4 sessions per week during the rest of the year.

Loafer's, 26 Douglas St. (☎ 431 1612). Cork's gay and lesbian pub fills up nightly with all age groups. Lively conversation and live bands contribute to this cozy spot.

MUSIC AND CLUBS

Cork fosters a prolific number of aspiring young bands, but the turnover rate is high—what is hip one week can be passé the next. To keep on top of the scene, check out *List Cork*, a free bi-weekly schedule of music available at local stores. The **Lobby** (see **Pubs**) and **Nancy Spain's,** 48 Barrack St. (☎ 431 4452), are consistently sound choices for live music. **Fred Zepplins** on Parliament St., and **An Phoenix** (see **Pubs**) host alternative, punk, and indie bands. (Call for live music schedule. Cover £3-8.) Cork is also full of trendy nightclubs that suck up the sloshed and swaying student population once the pubs have closed. Before you fork over your £3-5 cover charge, remember that clubs close at 2am.

Gorbys, Oliver Plunkett St. (☎ 427 0074). Track lighting illuminates young groovers. The £2-5 cover allows access to the lower dance floor and the retro-flavored upstairs.

Sir Henry's, South Main St. (☎ 427 4391). Arguably the most popular dance club in Cork, and also the most intense. Prepare to wedge yourself between sweaty, semi-conscious bodies on the 3 dance floors. Cover £2-11.

City Limits, Coburg St. (☎ 450 1206). A pleasant, mixed-age crowd. DJs spin anything from the 60s to the 90s Th and Su 11pm-2am. Known for its comedy nights F-Sa 9pm. Cover £3-5.

The Yumi Yuki Club, Tobin St. (☎ 427 5777). Located above the Triskel Arts Center. Restaurant by light, nightclub by dark, this Pan-Asian-themed club offers an alternative to the raucous parties nearby. Come for the sushi and stay for the DJ. Open 10am-1am, food served noon-midnight. Occasional £3 cover.

Club FX and **Bugsy's,** Gravel Ln. (☎ 427 1120). From Washington St., make a right on Little Hangover St. and then a left onto Gravel Ln. Club FX features two levels with plenty of pulsating lights, while Bugsy's sports a Mediterranean decorative scheme and a young and rowdy crowd. Open W-Su 11pm-2am. Cover £3-5.

Cubins, Hanover St. (☎ 427 9250). The wall-paintings of Cork's newest club insist ancient Roman is where it's at. Even a cover charge hovering around £5 and a long wait in line can't cramp the style of local patrons breaking down to 90s dance hits.

Everyman Palace, 15 McCurtain St. (☎ 450 3077). Theatre also houses a late-night blues and jazz club over weekends. Open F-Su 10pm-2am as well as show nights.

The Other Place, in a lane off South Main St. (☎ 427 8470). Cork's gay and lesbian disco rocks F and Sa 11:30pm-2am. Dance floor and a bar/cafe upstairs. Highly appreciated by Cork's gay population, especially the younger set, on weekend nights. The first Friday of the month is ladies' night. Cover £4.

SIGHTS

Cork's sights are loosely divided into several districts: the Old City, the South Bank, the Shandon neighborhood, and the university. All can be reached by foot, which is perhaps the best choice in this pedestrian-friendly city. For guidance, pick up *The Cork Area City Guide* at the tourist office (£1.50).

THE OLD CITY

Cork's major sights are located in the oldest part of the city which sits on the island created by the passage of the River Lee through the center of town.

TRISKEL ARTS CENTRE. The small but dynamic Triskel Arts Centre maintains two small galleries with rotating contemporary exhibits. It also organizes a wide variety of cultural events, including music, film, literature, theater, and the visual arts. *(Tobin St. ☎ 427 2022; triskel@iol.ie. Open M-Sa 10am-5:30pm.)*

KEYSER HILL. On a nice day, you can get a decent view of Cork (and much too good a view of Beamish Brewery) from Keyser Hill. At the top of the stairs leading up the hill is **Elizabethan Fort,** a star-shaped, ivy-covered remnant of English rule in Cork. In true Cork fashion, the fort has been destroyed three times since its completion in 1603, most recently by anti-treaty IRA forces in 1922. In these peaceful times, the fort houses the *Garda* station. To access the fort's strategically valuable view, climb the stairs just inside the main gate. *(Follow South Main St. away from Washington St., cross the South Gate Bridge, and turn right onto Proby's Quay and then left onto Keyser Hill. Always open. Free.)*

ST. FINBARR'S CATHEDRAL. Looming over Proby's Quay, the cathedral is a testament to the Victorian love of Gothic bombast. St. Finbarr allegedly founded his "School of Cork" here in 606, but no trace of the early foundation remains. The present cathedral was built between 1735 and 1870. *(Bishop St. ☎ 496 3387. Open Apr.-Sept. M-Sa, 10am-5:30pm, Oct.-Mar. 10am-5pm. £2 donation requested.)*

CHRIST CHURCH. In the center of the city, the church is an emblem of the persistence of Catholicism in Cork; it has been burned to the ground three times since its 1270 consecration but was rebuilt promptly each time, most recently in 1729. Surrounding the church is an eclectic collection of sculptures, making the church grounds a pleasant resting spot on a stroll through the city. The church now maintains the Cork City Archives, which are closed to tourists. *(Off the Grand Parade just north of Bishop Lucey Park. Walk down the Christ Church Lane, keeping the park on your left, to emerge on South Main St. To the right is the steeple-less Christ Church. Always open. Free.)*

SHANDON AND EMMET PLACE

On the other side of the Lee, North Main St. becomes Shandon St., heart of the Shandon neighborhood. Shandon lacks affluence, but has plenty of pride.

ST. ANN'S CHURCH. Commonly called Shandon Church, the now barely visible red-and-white (sandstone and limestone) strips on the steeple, Shandon Tower, inspired the "Rebel" flag, still ubiquitous throughout Cork; the salmon on top of the church spire represents the River Lee. Like most of Cork, the original church was ravaged by 17th-century pyromaniacal English armies; construction of the current church began in 1722. Four clocks grace the four sides of Shandon's tower. Notoriously out of sync with each other, the clocks have been held responsible for many an Irishman's tardy arrival at work and have earned the church its endearing nickname, "the four-faced liar." Admission to the tower favors the nonclaustrophobic with the option of climbing up the tower's extremely narrow passage to reach a spectacular view. Shandon church is the source of the "Happy Birthday" tunes you'll hear resonating throughout the city in church bells. Sheet music enables visitors to try their best Quasimodo impression; the sequence 8-5-2-1-1-1-8 emerges as the huge victor. *(Walk up Shandon St., take a right down unmarked Church St., and go straight. ☎ 450 5906. Open in summer M-Sa 9:30am-5:30pm. £5 adults, students and seniors £4, group rates available.)*

OTHER SIGHTS. Crawford Municipal Art Gallery is housed within an elegant 18th-century customs house, the gallery specializes in the paintings of Irish masters like James Barry and Jack Yeats, along with contemporary work by aspiring artists of all nationalities. Adjacent is the monstrous, cement Opera House, erected 20 years ago after the older, more elegant opera house went down in flames. *(Emmet Place. Over the hill from Shandon Church and across the north fork of the Lee. ☎ 427 3377. Gallery open M-Sa 10am-5pm. Free.)* **Cork Butter Museum** comes closer than one might think to making Cork's commerce history and preserved butter interesting. *(Church St. ☎ 430 0600. Open M-Sa 10am-5pm. £2.50, students and seniors £2.)* At the **Shandon Craft Centre,** potters, basket-weavers, and other artisans ply their trade and sell their wares. *(Church St. Across from the church.)*

WESTERN CORK

Cork's other major sights are on the western edge of the city. From Grand Parade, walk down Washington St., which soon becomes Western Rd.

CORK CITY GAOL. If time's tight in Cork, go directly to the Cork City Gaol. The museum is a reconstruction of the gaol as it appeared in the 1800s. Visitors are equipped with audio-cassette tours that bring to life the squabbles of the plastic prisoners and guards that fill the gaol's cells. Descriptions of Cork's social history accompany tidbits about miserable punishments, like the "human treadmill" used to grind grain. The tour culminates with a film that presents views of the gaol from both sides of the law. *(Sunday's Well Rd. From Fitzgerald Park, cross the white footbridge at the western end of the park, turn right onto Sunday's Well Rd., and follow the signs.* ☎ *430 5022. Open daily Mar.-Oct. 9:30am-6pm, Nov.-Feb. 10am-5pm. Last admission one hour before closing. £4.50, students and seniors £3. Admission includes audio-tape tour.)* The same building houses the **Radio Museum,** which chronicles the history of radio in Ireland and the world. A shortwave station allows visitors to listen in on static-clouded broadcasts. *(Open daily Mar.-Oct. 9:30am-6pm, Nov.-Feb. 10am-5pm. £3.50, students and seniors £2.50. Combined admission to Gaol, £1 reduction.)*

UNIVERSITY COLLEGE CORK (UCC). Built in 1845, the campus is a collection of gothic buildings, manicured lawns, and sculpture-speckled grounds, all of which make for a fine, secluded afternoon walk or picnic along the Lee. One of the newer buildings, **Boole Library,** celebrates the mathematician George Boole, the mastermind behind Boolean logic. Sir Arthur Conan Doyle used Boole as the model for his character Prof. James Moriarty, Sherlock Holmes's nemesis. *(Main gate on Western Rd.* ☎ *490 300. Always open. Free.)*

CORK PUBLIC MUSEUM. Enclosed within the splendid floral surroundings of **Fitzgerald Park,** the museum's astoundingly esoteric exhibits feature such varied goodies as 17th- and 18th-century toothbrushes and the 1907 costume worn by James Dwyer, chief sheriff of Cork. *(Across the street from UCC on Western Rd.* ☎ *427 0679. Open M-F 11am-1pm, 2:15-5pm, Su 3-5pm. M-Sa free; Su £1. Family £2.)*

🎵 ENTERTAINMENT

The always lively streets of Cork make finding entertainment easy. If you tire of drinking, take advantage of Cork's music venues, dance clubs, theaters, and sports arenas, or just explore the innumerable cafes and bookshops.

THEATER AND FILM

Everyman Palace, McCurtain St. Theatre stages big-name musicals, plays, operas, and concerts. (☎ 450 1673. Tickets £8-18. Box office open M-F 9am-5:30pm, Sa 10am-5:30pm, until 7pm on show dates.) The **Opera House,** Emmet Pl., next to the river, presents an extensive program of dance and performance art. (☎ 427 0022. Ticket prices vary depending on the show. Open M-Sa 9am-5:30pm.) The **Granary,** Mardyke Quay (☎ 490 4275), stages performances of new scripts by local and visiting theater companies. **Triskel Arts Centre,** Tobin St. (☎ 427 2022), simmers with avant-garde theater and performance art and hosts regular concert and film series. **The Firken Crane Center,** Shandon Court, houses two theatres dedicated to developing local dance talent. Performance dates vary throughout the year. (☎ 450 7487. Tickets from £7. Call for details.) For Hollywood celluloid and the occasional Irish or art-house flick, head to the **Capitol Cineplex** at Grand Parade and Washington St. (☎ 427 2216. £4.50; students tickets before 6pm £3.50; matinees £3.)

SPORTS

Cork is sporting-mad. Its soccer, hurling, and Gaelic football teams are perennial contenders for national titles (see **Sports,** p. 33). **Hurling** and **Gaelic football** take place every Sunday afternoon at 3pm from June to September; for additional details, call the GAA (☎ 439 5368) or consult *The Cork Examiner.* Be cautious when venturing into the streets on soccer game days (especially during championships), where screaming, jubilant fans will either bowl you down or, better, force you to take part in the revelry. Tickets to big games are £13-15 and scarce, but Saturday, Sunday, and Wednesday evening matches are cheap (£1-4) or free. You can buy tickets to these local games at the **Pairc Uí Chaoimh** (park EE KWEEV), the Gaelic Athletic Association stadium. To get there, take the #2 bus to Blackrock, and ask the driver to let you off at the stadium. Indoor athletes might head to **The Leisureplex**, 1 McCurtain St. (☎ 450 5155), where 24-hour pool, bowling, video games, and laser tag offer an escape from the Irish rain.

FESTIVALS

See big-name musicians for free in local pubs and hotels during the three-day **Guinness Cork Jazz Festival** (☎ 427 8979) in October. Anyone in town during that weekend needs to book well ahead at hostels. Also popular is the week-long **International Film Festival** (☎ 427 1711), in early October at the Opera House and the Triskel Arts Centre. Documentaries and shorts vie for prizes. In April, the **International Cork Choral Festival** (☎ 430 8308) fills City Hall, churches, and outdoor venues with singing groups from across the globe in both a competitive and non-competitive capacity. **The Irish Gay and Lesbian Film Festival** is in mid-October (call The Other Place for details; see **Music and Clubs** above).

■ DAYTRIPS FROM CORK

Love, tragedy, and free drinks await you just outside Cork City. A kiss is no longer just a kiss at the Blarney Stone, the ultimate Irish tourist attraction. Sweet, sweet Jameson is distilled in Midleton, where visitors learn themselves why Queen Elizabeth once called Irish whiskey her one true Irish friend.

BLARNEY (AN BHLARNA)

Bus Éireann runs buses from **Cork** to **Blarney** M-F 15 per day, Sa 16 per day, Su 10 per day, £3 return. From June 1 to Sept. 4, they also offer an **Open Top Tour**, which leaves from the Cork bus station through the city and on to Blarney Castle, where it stops for sight-seeing and shopping, then heads back to Cork. 3 hr.; buses leave M-F at 10:30am and 2:45pm; £6. Advance booking recommended.

Whether you're in the mood to admire the idyllic Irish countryside or simply dying to stand in a damp castle passageway, ■**Blarney Castle**, with its **Blarney Stone**, is the quintessential tourist spot. The prevailing myth of the stone's origin holds that it is a chip of the Scottish Stone of Scone that was presented to the King of Munster in gratitude for support during a rebellion in 1314. Today it stands as just another slab of limestone among so many others in the castle wall. Still, with everyone else doing it, you might just find yourself bending over backwards to kiss the stone in hopes of acquiring the legendary eloquence bestowed on those who smooch it. The term "blarney" refers to the supposedly Irish talent of stretching, or even obstructing, the truth. Queen Elizabeth I allegedly coined it during her long and tiring negotiations over control of the castle. The owner, Cormac McCarthy, Earl of Blarney, followed the rules of 16th-century diplomacy, writing grandiose letters in praise of the Queen, but he never relinquished the land. Ruffling her royal feathers, the Queen was heard to say, "This is all blarney—he never says what he means!" The Irish consider the whole thing a bunch of blarney; they're more concerned with the sanitary implications of so many people kissing the same rock. Unless stone-smooching is highlighted in your itinerary, roll over to the castle itself, built in 1446. A word of warning to those who suffer from claustrophobia: the castle is explored through steep, narrow, spiralling staircases, and the lineups can make you feel like Rapunzel (i.e., it takes a while to get out of the castle). Other attractions within the castle grounds include the **Rock Close**, an extensive and impressive rock-and-plant garden created by the Druids to mark their sacred grounds. In contrast to the ever-crowded castle, the Rock Close and its surrounding garden and woodland walks are usually unpopulated. The limestone cave and dungeons,

224 ■ COUNTY CORK

found directly next to the castle, are inviting for those who enjoy the dark and dank—remember to bring a flashlight. *Blarney Castle info* ☎ *385 252. Open June-Aug. 9am-7pm, Su 9:30am-5:30pm; Sept. M-Sa 9am-6:30pm, Su 9:30am-sundown; Oct.-Apr. M-Sa 9am-6pm, Su 9:30am-sundown; May M-Sa 9am-6:30pm, Su 9:30am-5:30pm. Last admission is 30min. before closing. To avoid the crowds, come early in the morning. £3.50, seniors and students £2.50, children £1.*

Within the town of Blarney, one can wander among the various shops lining the main road, the largest of which is **Blarney Woolen Mills,** a one-stop Irish tourist shop sheepishly offering more than you could ever want or need. (☎ 385 280. Open M-F 9am-7pm, Sa 9am-6:30pm, Su 9am-6pm.)

Look for a light and quick meal along the main road at a variety of small restaurants. **The Blarney Stone** cooks up Irish specialties in a comfortable dining room. (☎ 385 482. Lunch £4-8, Dinner £7-14. Open M-Su 10:30am-9:30pm.) **The Lemon Tree Restaurant** serves soups, sandwiches and seafood in a more modern setting. (☎ 385 116. Meals £3-12. Open M-Su 8am-4pm, 6-9:30pm.) **Scally's Coffee Dock,** located above the Super Valu, has a wide variety of snacks and light meals starting at £2. (☎ 385 571. Open M-Sa 9am-5:30pm.) In the evening, check out **Muskerry Arms** (☎ 385 066), with nightly live music and pub grub starting at 9:30pm and £5.

Seeing the castle, its grounds, and the shops in Blarney should only take half a day, so there is no reason, practical or otherwise, to stay overnight. Should you fall madly in love with the Blarney Stone after giving it a wet-lickery one, you can rent functional beds at the **Blarney Tourist Hostel,** 2 mi. from town on the Killarney Rd. (☎ 385 580 or 381 430. Dorms £7.) Closer to town but more expensive, the **Rosemount B&B** offers comfortable beds just up the hilly lane from the bus stop. (☎ 438 5584. £15-17.) **Blarney Camping and Caravan Park** is located on Stoneview Rd. near Blarney Castle. (☎ 385 167. Tents £6, £2 per person. Free showers.)

MIDLETON

Whisk away to Midleton with a short drive or bus ride from Cork (30 min., M-F 18 per day, Sa 13 per day, Su 4 per day, £3.80) or Cobh on the main Cork-Waterford highway (N25).

Midleton beckons pilgrims in search of the "water of life" (a literal translation of the Irish word for "whiskey") to the **Jameson Heritage Centre.** The center rolls visitors through a one-hour tour that details the craft and history of whiskey production and includes a glass of the potent stuff at the end—for demonstration, of course. After all, "the story of whiskey is the story of Ireland." ☎ 613 594. Open Mar.-Oct. daily 10am-6pm, tours every 30min.-45 min., last tour 4:30pm; Nov.-Feb. 2 tours M-F 12pm and 3pm, Sa-Su 2pm and 4pm. £3.95; students and seniors £3.50; children £1.50. The highlight of Midleton (aside from the whiskey, of course) is its hostel, **An Stór (IHH).** From Main St., turn onto Connolly St. and then take your first left. The hostel's name means "the treasure" in Irish and that 'tis with a large comfortable TV room and kitchen. Bright, clean, and covered with blooming window boxes, the hostel teaches its guests some elementary Irish that is most popular with ornithologists by naming its rooms after indigenous bird species. Fortunately, they are also listed in English so that you can find your room if you have a drop too much at the Heritage tour. The friendly proprietors can advise you on pubs and eateries as well as on local attractions ranging from castle visits to scenic bike rides. (☎ 633 106. Laundry £3. Dorms £8; doubles £22.) If the folks at An Stór don't give you your fill of Midleton, the **tourist office** (☎ 613 702) is near the entrance to the Jameson Heritage Center. **La Trattoria,** 48 Main St. has a lengthy menu of solid meals from £4.50, and a short wine list. (☎ 631 341. Open daily 9am-10pm.) Hearty Irish food to help soak up the whiskey can be found at the pricey but popular **Finin's,** 75 Main St. (☎ 631 878. Open M-Sa 10:30am-11pm.) Head to **The Meeting Place** and the adjoining **Rory Gallagher's Bar,** Connolly St., for a pint and excellent live music on most nights. Tuesday is Irish Folk Club night (☎ 631 928. Occasional £2.50 cover). **The Town Hall Bar,** inside Walis and Sons at 74 Main St., is another excellent live music venue in the summer on Sunday nights. (☎ 633 185. Open M-Sa 10:30am-11:30pm, Su 12pm-2pm, 4pm-11:30pm).

KNOW YOUR WHISKEY Anyone who drinks his or her whiskey as it's meant to be drunk—"neat," or straight—can tell you that there's a huge difference between Irish whiskeys (Bushmills, Jameson, Power and Son, and the like), Scotch whiskys (spelled without an e), and American whiskeys. But what makes an Irish whiskey *Irish*? The basic ingredients in whiskey—water, barley (which becomes malt once processed), and heat from a fuel source—are always the same. It's the quality of these ingredients, the way in which they're combined, and the means of storage that gives each product its distinctive flavor. The different types of whiskey derive from slight differences in this production process. American whiskey is distilled once and is often stored in oak, bourbon is made only in Kentucky, scotch uses peat-smoked barley, and Irish whiskey is triple distilled. After this basic breakdown, individual distilleries will claim that their further variations on the theme make their product the best of its class. The best way to understand the distinctions between brands is to taste the various labels in close succession to one another. Line up those shot glasses, sniff and then taste each one (roll the whiskey in your mouth like a real pro), and have a sip of water between each brand.

NEAR CORK: COBH AND FOTA ISLAND ☎ 021

Little more than a slumbering harbor village today, Cobh (KOVE) was Ireland's main transatlantic port until the 1960s. For many of the emigrants who left between 1848 and 1950, the steep hillside and multi-colored houses were their final glimpse of Ireland. In keeping with Irish tradition, Cobh has some sad stories to tell. Cobh was the *Titanic's* last port of call four days before the "unsinkable" ship went down. Later, when the Germans torpedoed the *Lusitania* during World War I, most survivors and some of the dead were taken back to Cobh in lifeboats. There is a Lusitania Memorial in Casement Square; a cemetery outside of town contains a mass grave of 150 of the fallen.

GETTING THERE AND PRACTICAL INFORMATION. The **tourist office** occupies the restored site of the Royal Cork Yacht Club, built in 1854 reputedly as the world's first yacht club. Located on the water up the hill from the train station, the office gives out free maps, guides, and advice. (☎ 813 301; www.cobhharbourchamber.ie. Open M-F 9:30am-5:30pm, Sa-Su 11:30am-5:30pm.) Cobh is best reached by **rail** from **Cork** (25min., M-Sa 19 per day, Su 8 per day, £2.90 return).

ACCOMMODATIONS AND FOOD. Should you decide to anchor in Cobh, join the family at **Beechmont House Tourist Hostel.** Their home sits at the top of a steep climb up Bond St. (☎ 812 177. 2- to 8-bed dorms £8. Breakfast included. Call ahead.) Pubs, restaurants, and B&Bs face Cobh's harbor from Beach St. **The River Room**, on West Beach, grills "ciabattas," large sandwiches on tasty bread (£3.25), and lunchtime quiche. (☎ 813 293. Open daily 9am-6pm.) **The Queenstown Restaurant** will offer you a sandwich (£2.95), pastries, or a daily special while you mull over the town's disasters in the pretty entrance hall to the Queenstown Story Heritage Center. (☎ 813 591. Open daily 9:30am-5pm.) New to the Cobh waterfront is **The Titanic Queenstown,** a seafood bistro and bar. The restaurant is an exact replica of the cafe *Parisienne* and the first-class smoke-room of the doomed ship. The James Cameron-like mastermind behind this project is lottery-winner Vincent Keaney, who bought the building and the pier from which the *Titanic* set sail with his newfound loot (or perhaps he found that gigantic diamond). Alternatively, purchase a picnic at **SuperValu** supermarket on West Beach and eat it at John F. Kennedy Park on the waterfront. (☎ 811 586. Open M-W 9am-6pm, Th-F 9am-9pm.) Cobh holds its own in the pub count. The DJs and rock acts at the **Voyager** pack in a young horde nightly and the new restaurant above, an expansion on the pub, promises to be just as popular. (☎ 814 161. M-Tu 4-11:30pm, W-Sa noon-11:30pm, Su noon-2pm, 4-11pm.) **The Ship's Bell** (☎ 811 122) attracts a more seasoned, local crowd for pub grub and live trad on weeknights.

👁 📖 SIGHTS AND ENTERTAINMENT.
In remembrance of its eminent but tragic history, Cobh recently established a museum called ◪**The Queenstown Story,** adjacent to the Cobh railway station. The museum's flashy multimedia exhibits trace the port's history, with sections devoted to emigration, the *Lusitania*, the *Titanic*, and the peak of transatlantic travel. In June 1995, in an incident freighted with irony, the Cork-Cobh train ran into the museum, hurtling through two walls and the ceiling—not an auspicious start in this accident-prone town. (☎ 813 591. Open daily 10am-6pm, last admission 5pm. $3.50, students $3.) **St. Colman's Cathedral** towers over Cobh. Its ornate Gothic spire dominates the town's architectural landscape. The spire is closed to visitors, who will have to content themselves with the view of the harbor from the hill. Completed in 1915, the cathedral boasts the largest carillon, or harmonized bell system, in Ireland, consisting of 47 bells weighing over 7700 pounds. (Open daily 7am-8pm. Free.)

Visitors interested in creating their own ocean adventure can contact **International Sailing.** Based on East Beach, dinghy, windsurfing, and power boat lessons are available (from $28). Canoes can be rented ($4 per 1hr.), along with dinghies and power boats; the latter two require accompaniment by a guide. (☎ 811 237. Open M-Th 9:30am-9pm, F-Sa 9:30am-6pm, Su 10:30am-5:30pm.) Those who prefer to learn the past before they repeat it can take a guided walking tour on the **Titanic Trail,** or scream "I'm king of the world!" atop a guided minibus tour on the same trail. (☎ 815 211 for information. Walking tour 1¼hr., daily at 11am from the Commodore Hotel, May-Sept.; $3.50. Minibus tour 1hr., daily at 3pm from the WatersEdge Hotel, May-Sept.; $4.95.) The middle of August to the beginning of September brings the **Cobh People's Regatta,** when a cruise liner convoy, including the QE2, sails into the harbor while the landlocked swab the dance floor to live music outdoors.

🗺 DAYTRIP FROM COVE: FOTA ISLAND.
Fota is an intermediate stop on the train from Cork to Cobh; if you buy a ticket from Cork to Cobh or vice versa, you can get off at Fota and re-board for free.

Ten minutes from Cobh by rail lies Fota Island, where penguins, peacocks, cheetahs, and giraffes roam, largely free of cages, in the **Fota Wildlife Park.** This may well be the closest you'll ever come to a ring-tailed lemur. The park has as many species as acres—70—with animals from South America, Africa, Asia, and Australia. (☎ 812 678. Open Apr.-Oct. M-Sa 10am-6pm, Su 11am-6pm. Last admission 5pm. $4.80, students and children $2.70.) The **Fota Arboretum,** a kilometer from the station but adjacent to the park, cares for plants and trees as exotic as the beasts next door. (Gates close at 5:30pm. Free.)

YOUGHAL
☎ 024

Thirty miles east of Cork on N25, beach-blessed Youghal (YAWL, or "Y'all" for US Southerners) can be a stopover on the way to Waterford and points east. The movie *Moby Dick* with Gregory Peck was filmed here in 1954. A popular, tacky beach and the narrow streets of what claims to have once been "Europe's leading walled port" keep Youghal interesting even after its 15 minnows of fame.

🚌 GETTING THERE.
Buses stop in front of the public toilets on Main St., across from Dempsey's Bar, and travel to **Cork** (50min.; M-Sa 11 per day, Su 7 per day; $5.50) and **Waterford** via **Dungarvan** (1½-2hr.; M-Sa 11 per day, Su 6 per day; $8.80). **Hitching** to Cork or Waterford along N25 is possible but discouraged by *Let's Go.*

🛈 PRACTICAL INFORMATION.
The helpful **tourist office,** Market Sq., on the waterfront behind the clocktower, distributes a useful "tourist trail" booklet (free) and can steer you to trad sessions in town. (☎ 20170. Open July-Aug. M-F 9am-7pm, Sa 9:30am-5:30pm, Su 11am-5pm; June and Sept. M-F 9am-5:30pm, Sa-Su 11am-5pm; Oct.-May M-F 9am-5:30pm.) The **library** on Church St., off Main St., provides free **Internet access** with a $2 membership to Cork County libraries. (Open Tu-Sa 10am-1pm and 2-5:30pm.)

ACCOMMODATIONS, FOOD, AND PUBS. The **Stella Maris** hostel has a simple, sterile feel and a few rooms with a view. (☎ 91820. Sheets £1. Key deposit £5. 6- to 12-bed dorms £8; doubles and twins with bath £20.) Majestic **Avonmore House,** on South Abbey, has fully-equipped rooms kept tidy by a professional staff. (☎ 92617. Singles £25; doubles and twins £36-50.)

Youghal may have more chip fryers per capita than any other town in Co. Cork; luckily, it also has a few less grease-oriented establishments. Should these not tempt the taste buds, head to **SuperValu** in the town center on Main St. (☎ 92150. Open M-W 9am-7pm, Th and Sa 9am-8pm, F 9am-9pm, Su 10am-6pm.) The **Coffee Pot,** 77 North Main St., is extremely popular among locals, serving pastries, soup, and light meals. (☎ 92523. Entrees £4-6. Open M-F 9:30am-7:30pm, Sa 9:30am-6pm, Su 10:30am-7pm.) The **Tower Restaurant,** at the base of its namesake, grills up omelettes and baguettes at lunchtime (£3-5), and more extensive meals, including vegetarian options, at dinner. (☎ 91869. Dinners around £7.50. Open Tu-W 9:30am-3:30pm, Th-Sa 9:30am-3:30pm and 6:30-10pm, Su 1-5pm.)

Traditional crannies fill with music twice weekly at the popular **Nook Pub** (☎ 92225). Young'uns flock to **The Clock Tavern,** South Main St. (☎ 93052), where the dark recesses are filled with the sounds of frequent rock acts, particularly on weekends. A more sedate atmosphere prevails at the **Central Star** (☎ 92419), North Main St., dedicated to darts and hurling discussions. Tourists have a whale of a time at **Moby Dick's** (☎ 92099), across from the tourist office, filled with nautical murals, weekend trad, and some guy named Herman.

SIGHTS. Enjoyably informative historical **walking tours** of Youghal leave from the tourist office. (☎ 20170 or 92447. 1½hr. June-Aug. daily 11am. £3.) The huge **Clockgate,** built in 1777, straddles narrow, crowded Main St. Visible from the site are the old city walls, built on the hill sometime between the 13th and 17th centuries. The tower served as a prison and low-budget gallows (prisoners were hanged from the windows). On Church St., **St. Mary's Church** and **Myrtle Grove** stand side-by-side. St. Mary's Church is possibly the oldest operating church in Ireland; parts of it remain from the original Danish-built church constructed in 1020. One corner of the church holds the elaborate grave of Robert Boyle, first Earl of Cork. **Myrtle Grove** was the residence of Sir Walter Raleigh when he served as mayor here in 1588-89. Though privately owned and closed to the public, you can gawk or groan, according to your taste, at the window where Raleigh's buddy Edmund Spencer is said to have finished his hefty epic poem *The Faerie Queen.* For an encapsulated version of Youghal's history since the 9th century, drop by the tourist office's **Heritage Centre.** (Same phone and hours as the tourist office. £1.) The center focuses on Youghal's history as a seaport; Cromwell left Ireland from the harbor after he'd finished making a mess of things throughout the country. Across the street from the tourist office and up a little alley, the **Fox's Lane Folk Museum** is the place to investigate the savagely interesting history of razor blades and sewing machines. (Open Tu-Sa 10am-1pm and 2-6pm. Last admission 5:30pm. £2.)

On the first weekend in August, the streets of Youghal fill with music, theater, and food for the annual **Busking Festival.**

WEST CORK

From Cork City, there are two routes to Skibbereen and West Cork: an inland route and a coastal route through Kinsale. Two major **bus routes** begin in Cork City and serve the West Cork region. A coastal bus runs from Cork to **Skibbereen,** stopping in **Bandon, Clonakilty,** and **Rosscarbery** (M-F and Su 3 per day, Sa 2 per day). An inland bus travels from Cork to **Bantry,** stopping in **Bandon** and **Dunmanway** (M-Sa 3 per day, Su 2 per day). **Hitchers** are reported to have few problems in these parts. *Let's Go* does not recommend hitching.

THE INLAND ROUTE

Cyclists and drivers wishing to save time or avoid crowds should consider one of the inland routes from Cork to Skibbereen, Bantry, the Beara, or Killarney. Popular routes are Cork-Macroom-Killarney, Cork-Macroom-Ballingeary-Bantry/Glengarriff, and Cork-Dunmanway-Bantry/Skibbereen. The rocky face of the Shehy Mountains is forested with some of Ireland's best-preserved wilds. The attraction of the area is its abundance of interesting walks and bike rides.

DUNMANWAY AND BALLINGEARY ☎ 023

South of Macroom on R587, **Dunmanway** is a hidden treasure, one of the few Irish towns that prizes tradition over tourism. **Bus Éireann** voyages to Dunmanway from **Cork** (3 per day, Su 2 per day, £6.30) and from Dunmanway to **Glengarriff** via **Bantry** (3 per day, Su 2 per day). Buses stop in Dunmanway in front of Crowley's Pharmacy and depart from in front of the jeweler's on The Square. The best place to stay, and one of the best reasons to come to Dunmanway, is the **Shiplake Mountain Hostel (IHH)**, located in the hills 3 mi. from town. Visitors are welcome to call for a ride from Dunmanway, or follow Castle St. (next to Gatsby's Nightclub) out of town toward Coolkelure and then turn right at the hostel sign. Shiplake is an ideal base for hikers and bikers looking to explore the area's lakes, castles, and countryside. The proprietors have heaps of information and contagious enthusiasm for this spectacular area. They **rent bicycles** (£7 per day) and cook what is perhaps the best hostel food in Ireland. A caravan of cozy, refurbished, and private gypsy trailers overlooking the mountains accommodates couples, families, and dorm-dwellers. (☎ 45750. Kitchen and whole-food groceries available. Vegetarian meals and healthy breakfasts £1.50-7.50, laundry £4.50. Dorms £7.50-8; caravan £8.50-9 per person. **Camping** £4 per person.) Dunmanway's 8500 people support 23 pubs. The **Shamrock** (☎ 45142), owned and operated by a sixth-generation O'Donovan dating from 1750, has a traditional atmosphere and occasional music. They have recently expanded their business to include a restaurant upstairs where a true Irish meal can be enjoyed in a true Irish home. **An Toísin**, Main St. (☎ 45824), fills the square with diverse music on weekend nights. **The Arch Bar** (☎ 45155) packs in the football-watching crowd. **Gatsby's** (☎ 55275), the night club two doors down, attracts the young and funky. Dunmanway townsfolk also show up in droves for two quirky festivals. The **Agricultural Show** holds a variety of competitions, from longest carrot to cutest baby, at the end of June and the beginning of July. During the bank holiday weekend in August, the **Ballabouidhe Horse Fair** races equines and other animals.

Over the mountains to the northwest of Dunmanway on R584, quiet **Ballingeary** is the failing heart of one of West Cork's declining *gaeltachts*, and holds the entrance to the **Gougane Barra Forest**. (Admission £1 for hikers and bikers, £3 for cars.) From the road through the forest, visitors can see the River Lee's pure source streams flow together. A church marking the site of St. Finbarre's monastery lies at the base of the mountains, next to a lake. Sweeping views reward those willing to climb the wooded trails to the ridgeline.

> **BOWL MOVEMENT** If you're driving anywhere in West Cork, watch out for an iron sphere the size of a tennis ball hurtling toward you. Road bowling, or "bowls," is a long-standing tradition in this area (County Armagh in the North is the only other home to the game). The 28oz. ball is "lofted" along the road by the competitors. The player who covers a set distance, usually around 4km, with the fewest throws is the winner. Ireland's irregular hills and bends require great skill to negotiate, but masters are rewarded by the faithful who show up to watch—and by ensuing wagers that can snowball to £8000. So next time you come across a rowdy group of bowlers, pull up, join in on the fun, and prepare to be bowled over—ironically speaking, that is!

COASTAL ROUTE

From Kinsale, southerly R600 stands watch over farming valleys before skirting the coast on the way to Clonakilty. From Cork, N71 stretches its tough asphalt skin all the way to Clonakilty via Bandon. Past Clonakilty, the population begins to thin out. Inland, mountains rise, rocky ridges replace smooth hills, and sunset-laden shoals proliferate as Ireland's southern coast starts to look like its western one. Crossroads along N71 link mellow tourist towns and hardworking fishing villages. "Blow-ins," expatriates from America and Northern Europe, have settled in the area by the hundreds, replacing the area's dwindling Irish population. These kick-back expats appreciate the leisurely pace and extraordinary scenery of the southwest but have shaped its culture to their own tastes.

The islands in the stretch of ocean between Baltimore and Schull may be the wildest, remotest human habitations in all of southern Ireland. High cliffs plunge into the sea, creating a parcel of local shipwrecking tales. The O'Driscoll clan of pirates informally ruled the bay for centuries, sallying into the Atlantic for raids, off-loading brandy from Spanish galleons, then speeding home through secret channels between the islands.

KINSALE ☎ 021

Upscale Kinsale (Cionn tSáile) is mobbed with people and money every summer, when its population temporarily quintuples. Visitors come to swim, fish, and eat at any of Kinsale's 12 famed and expensive "Good Food Circle" restaurants. Luckily, Kinsale's best attractions—its pubs, forts, and pretty seaside location—can be enjoyed on a budget. Kinsale's pleasant present hardly suggests the grimmer role the town has played in history. In the 1601 **Battle of Kinsale,** Elizabethan English armies destroyed the native Irish followers of Ulster chieftain Hugh O'Neill, while O'Neill's blockaded allies from Spain watched the action from ships stationed nearby (see **Feudalism,** p. 9). For almost two centuries after the English victory, Kinsale was legally closed to the Gaelic Irish. In 1688, the freshly deposed King James II of England, trying to gather Catholic Irish support for a Jacobite invasion of Scotland, entered Ireland at this very spot. The attention of the outside world turned here again in 1915, when the *Lusitania* was torpedoed and sank just off the Old Head of Kinsale.

GETTING THERE AND PRACTICAL INFORMATION. Kinsale is a 30-minute drive southwest of Cork on R600. The city lies at the base of a U-shaped inlet. Facing the water, **Charles Fort** and the **Scilly Walk** (pronounced "silly") are to the left; the piers, **Compass Hill,** and **James Fort** are to the right; the town center is behind you. **Buses** to and from **Cork** stop at the Esso station on the Pier (40 min.; M-F 9 per day, Sa 10 per day, Su 3 per day; £3.80 return). The **tourist office,** Emmet Pl. (☎ 772 234), in the black-and-red building on the waterfront, gives out free maps. (Open Mar.-Nov. daily 9am-6pm.) **Bank of Ireland,** Pearse St., has a **24-hour ATM.** (☎ 772 521. Open M 10am-5pm, Tu-F 10am-4pm.) **Rent bikes** (£8 per day, £2 per hr.; £20 deposit with ID) and fishing poles (£8 per day, tackle included, £15 with bike) at **The Hire Shop** on Main St. (☎ 774 884. Open M-Sa 8:30am-6pm.)

ACCOMMODATIONS. Although Kinsale's hotels and plush B&Bs cater to an affluent tourist crowd, there are two hostels nearby. The **Castlepark Marina Centre (IHH)** sits across the harbor, a 40-minute walk from town. From the bus depot, walk along the pier away from town for 10 minutes, turn left to cross large Duggan Bridge, and then take another left just past the bridge; follow this road back toward the harbor. **Ferries** leave the Trident Marina for the hostel June through August (typically on the hour, call the hostel for a schedule, £1). This stone-fronted building stands just below the James Fort and offers marvelous views of Kinsale. Rooms are large, airy, and bright. Some have beach access and bay windows that open out onto the harbor. (☎ 774 959. Open mid-Mar. to Dec. Laundry

£5. Safe-deposit box 50p. Dorms £9, off season £8; doubles £20. Wheelchair accessible.) The hostel's **restaurant** features a gourmet menu (salmon with lime and tarragon crème fraîche £9.25). Closer to town, **Dempsey's Hostel (IHH)**, Cork Rd., is a two-minute walk from town on Cork Rd., next to the Texaco station. The bus into town will stop in front of the hostel if you ask. It's made up of pleasant rooms and an industrial kitchen. (☎ 772 124. Sheets £1. Shower 50p. Check-in by 5pm. Dorms £6; doubles £16. **Camping** £3.) **O'Donovan's B&B**, Guardwell Rd., has comfortable and reasonably priced accommodations. (☎ 772 428. £18-£20 per person.) There's **camping** outside of town at **Garrettstown House Holiday Park**, 6 mi. west of Kinsale on R600 in Ballinspittle. (☎ 778156. Open May-Sept. 2-person tent with car £8.)

FOOD AND PUBS. Kinsale is Ireland's gourmet food capital—locals claim it's the only town in Ireland with more restaurants than pubs. The **Good Food Circle** has 12 restaurants that uphold both Kinsale's well-deserved culinary reputation and its notoriety for tourist-scalping expense. The budget-conscious fill their baskets at the **SuperValu** on Pearse St. (☎ 772 843. Open M-Sa 8:30am-9pm, Su 10am-9pm.) **Jim Edwards** sizzles steak, seafood, and chicken for a fair price. (☎ 772 541. Entrees £7-13.) **Cafe Palermo**, Pearse St., serves delicious Italian food, fresh salads, and rich desserts. (☎ 774 143. Lunch about £5. Open daily 10:30am-5pm.) **1601**, Pearse St., cooks up high-quality pub grub. (☎ 772 529. Soup £2.50, burgers £6.25.)

On a weekend night, a stroll through Kinsale's small maze of streets will magically lead you to great trad. **1601** fiddles four nights a week. Harder to hear from a distance, but worth stepping into, **The Spaniard** (☎ 772 436) rules over the Kinsale pub scene from the hill on the Scilly Peninsula (follow the signs to Charles Fort for ¼ mi.). It has stone walls, dark wood paneling, low-beamed ceilings, a bar the length of the Shannon, and trad several nights a week. Downhill from The Spaniard and farther on the Scilly Walk, **The Spinnaker** (☎ 772 098) presides over the harbor with a nautical theme and a variety of music, including American rock for the expats. Those who make the hike to Charles Fort are rewarded at the inviting **Bulman Bar** (☎ 772 131), a picturesque spot for downing a pint of Ireland's own black gold. Just remember you'll have to take the long Sobriety Walk back to town.

SIGHTS. The half-hour trek up **Compass Hill**, south of Main St., rewards with a view of the town and its watery surroundings. More impressive is the view from **Charles Fort**, a classic 17th-century star-shaped fort that remained a British naval base until 1921. The fort's battlements and buildings, overlooking the water, are an inviting and nearly limitless chance to climb and explore. Reach Charles Fort by following **Scilly Walk** (30min.), a sylvan path along the coast at the end of Pearse St. (☎ 772 263. Sack the fort mid-June to mid-Sept. daily 9am-6pm; mid-Apr. to mid-June and mid-Sept. to mid-Oct. M-Sa 9am-5pm, Su 9:30am-5:30pm. £2, students and children £1. Guided tours on request.) Across the harbor from Charles Fort, the ruins of star-shaped **James Fort** delight casual explorers with secret passageways and panoramic views of Kinsale. To reach the fort, follow the pier away from town, cross the Duggan bridge, then turn left. After exploring the ruins and the rolling heath, descend to Castlepark's hidden arc of beach behind the hostel. (Always open. Free.)

Desmond Castle, Cork St., a 15th-century custom house, served as an arsenal during the 100-day Spanish occupation in 1601, and a naval prison during the 18th century. Inside the castle, drink in the **International Museum of Wine**. The chronicle of Kinsale's history as wine port will have your head reeling, as will accompanying exhibits on destitute French and American prisoners. (Open Apr.-Sept. daily 10am-5pm. £2, students £1.50.)

In 1915, the British ocean liner *Lusitania* sank off the Old Head of Kinsale, a promontory south of the town; over 1000 civilians died. A German torpedo was to blame, and the resulting furor helped propel the United States into World War I. Hearings on the *Lusitania* case took place in the Kinsale Courthouse, Market Sq. The courthouse now contains a regional museum which attracts many tourists. In town, up the hill from Market Square, the restored west tower of the 12th-century

Church of St. Multose, patron saint of Kinsale, is worth "peaking" your head into. Its ancient graveyard bewitches visitors, though nearby construction projects can upset the tranquility of both visitors and residents. (☎ 772 220. Church open until dusk. Graveyard always open. Free.)

If forts and museums aren't adventure enough, the **Kinsale Outdoor Education Centre** (☎ 772 896) rents windsurfing equipment, kayaks, and dinghies. Full-day deep-sea fishing trips and scuba diving excursions can be arranged at **Castlepark Marina.** (☎ 774 959. Boats from £10 per hr., £50 per day, rod rental £5 per day.)

CLONAKILTY ☎023

Once a linen-making town with a workforce of over 10,000 people, Clonakilty ("Clon," pop. 5000) lies between Bandon and Skibbereen on N71. Henry Ford was born nearby, but residents take more pride in the 1890 birth of military leader, spy, and organizational genius **Michael Collins.** During the Civil War Collins returned to his home, incorrectly believing "they surely won't kill me in my own country." He was ambushed and killed 25 mi. from town (see **Independence and Civil War,** p. 17). The area is peppered with monuments to national heroes who met bitter ends. Most visitors, however, are more interested in relaxation than revolution, so they head to the nearby **Inchydoney Beach.** Come nightfall, Clonakilty's streets reverberate with vibrant pubs and live music. During the second week of July, Clon hosts the **Black and White (Pudding) Festival,** when prizes are given out for best recipe and most pudding consumed—not for the faint of heart, or stomach (see **Food,** p. 34).

■? GETTING THERE AND PRACTICAL INFORMATION. The main area of Clonakilty begins at the tourist office on Ashe St. and continues along the road, eventually turning into Pearse St. and finally Western Rd. The axe-wielding statuesque rebel Tadgh an Astna serves as a central point. Pearse St. runs inland and turns into Western Rd. To the rear of the statue Rossa St. passes the Wheel of Fortune Water Pump and runs into Connelly. Astna St. and Wolfe Tone St. angle off the statue towards the harbor, making a triangle with Clark St.

Buses from **Skibbereen** (3 per day, £4.30) and **Cork** (3 per day, £5.90) stop in front of Lehane's Supermarket on Pearse St. The new **tourist office,** Wolfe Tone St., hands out maps and advice. (☎ 33226. Open Mar.-Nov. M-Sa 9:15am-6:30pm.) **AIB** and **Bank of Ireland** cash in on Pearse St.; both have an **ATM.** The **post office** addresses town from a Gothic building on Patrick St. (Open M-F 9am-5:30pm, Sa 10am-4pm). You can walk the 3 mi. to Inchydoney or **rent a bike** at **MTM Cycles** on Ashe St. (☎ 33584. £8 per day, £35 per week.)

♠ ACCOMMODATIONS. The immaculate **Old Brewery Hostel,** Emmet Sq., also known as the Clonakilty Hostel, quietly supports a super kitchen and comfortable new beds. Coming from Lehane's, head down Pearse St., make a left at the Roman Catholic church, then a right at the park in Emmet Sq. (☎ 33525. **Rents bikes** £7 per day. Wheelchair accessible. 6-bed dorms £7; 4-bed dorms £8; doubles £20.) Just east of town is Mrs. McMahon's **Nordav,** 70 Western Rd., a right turn after the museum. Set back from the road behind a well-groomed lawn and splendid rose gardens, this family style B&B features gloriously huge three-room suites and smaller, but still lovely, double rooms. (☎ 33655. £20-25 per person.) **Desert House Camping Park** is connected to a dairy farm, a half-mile southeast of town on Ring Road. (☎ 33331. Showers 50p. Open May-Sept. £7 per family tent, 50p per person; £5 per small tent.)

[*]■ FOOD AND PUBS. Clonakilty is famous (or infamous) for its style of **black pudding,** a sausage-like concoction made from beef, blood, and grains (see **Food and Drink,** p. 34). For those eager to try it, or the white variety (made with pork and no blood) head to the award winning butcher at **Twomey's.** (☎ 33365. Open M-Sa 9am-6pm.) It is also available at most local restaurants, usually for breakfast. Luckily, Clonakilty offers other culinary options. ⬛**The Druid's Table,** 12 Ashe St., is a tasteful and tasty gem that serves breakfast all day, as well as a variety of seafood, sandwiches, and salad dishes. (☎ 33310. Meals from £3. Open M-W 10am-4pm and 5:30-11pm, Th-Sa 10am-4pm and 5-11pm, Su noon-3pm and 5-11pm.) **An Susan,** 41 Wolfe Tone St. has won numerous awards for its seafood and steak offerings. (☎ 33498. Meals from £7.50. Open daily 6:30-9:30pm.) **Fionnuala's Little Italian Restaurant,** 30 Ashe St., has commendable food and a wide variety of wines in an old Irish house. (☎ 34355. Meals from £5.50. Open daily 6-10pm.) **Betty Brosnan,** 58 Pearse St., specializes in homemade baked goods, lasagna, and sandwiches. (☎ 34011. £2-5. Open daily 9am-6pm. Serves pizza only 6-9:30pm.) Brown-bag it at **Lehane's Supermarket** on Pearse St. (☎ 33359. Open M-Th 8am-6:30pm, F 8am-9pm, Sa 8am-7pm, Su 9am-1:30pm.)

There's music aplenty in Clonakilty. The hugely popular **De Barra's** on Pearse St., has folk and trad nightly all year. Though the pub is enormous (3 rooms, 2 bars, and a beer garden), you'll be feeling claustrophobic by 8:30pm. (☎ 33381. Occasional £3 cover.). Four nights a week, trad bounces off the walls of **O'Brien's,** Connolly St. (☎ 35570), and into its beer garden. Around the corner from De Barra's, **Shanley's,** 11 Connolly St. (☎ 33790), juggles folk, rock, and the occasional nationally known star. Nightly music, pool, and darts keep **Bernie's Bar,** Rossa St. (☎ 33567), filled with an athletic crowd from wall to poster-covered wall.

■ SIGHTS. To fill the hours before the pubs pick up, join the locals and birds at **Inchydoney Beach,** billed as one of the nicest beaches east of Malibu. On Inchydoney Rd., you'll pass the **West Cork Model Railway Village,** where the towns of Kinsale, Bandon, and Clonakilty, all along the former West Cork Railway, are replicated in miniature circa 1940. (☎ 33224. Open daily Feb.-Oct. 11am-5pm, Sa-Su 1-5pm. £3, students £2.) Back in town, the **West Cork Museum,** Western Rd., displays an early 20th-century beer pouring machine, the christening shawl of patriot O'Donovan Rossa, and other assorted historical Clon minutiae. (Open May-Oct. M-Sa 10am-6:30pm. £1.50, students 50p.) Tours of various sites relating to the life and death of **Michael Collins** can be arranged through the tourist office or Timothy Crowley (☎ 46107). The **Lios na gCon Ring Fort,** 2 mi. east, has been "fully restored" based on excavators' clues to its 10th-century form. It is the only ring fort in all of Ireland reconstructed in its original site.

UNION HALL AND CASTLETOWNSHEND   ☎ 028

In the land that lies between Clonakilty and Skibbereen, pastures and rolling hills give way to forests as the landscape gets too rocky for farming. Sleepy towns dot the hills, each with a few rows of pastel houses, a couple of B&Bs, and at least a few pubs. Just across the water from the picturesque but unexciting hamlet of Glandore sits the fishing village of **Union Hall,** once a hangout for **Jonathan Swift** and family. Now it's home to the legendary **Maria's Schoolhouse (IHH).** Formerly the Union Hall National School, Maria's hostel has been resplendently redecorated and refitted with a cathedral ceiling and an enormous window in the huge common room, big skylights in the dorm, and a healthy breakfast spread. This hostel is reason enough for a detour en route to Skibbereen. (☎ 33002. Hot breakfast £5, continental £3; occasional 3-course dinner with the off-chance of musical accompaniment £15. Laundry £4. **Bike rental** £7 per day. **Canoeing** lessons £15 per 2hr. Wheelchair accessible. Dorms £8, doubles £25-40.) Maria's also houses **Atlantic Sea Kayaking,** which offers a variety of kayaking lessons and expeditions. (☎ 33002. 2hr. lesson £15, 3hr. £25, 6hr. £35.) To get to Maria's, turn right in the center of Union Hall, left at the church, then take the first right and continue on for half a mile, or call Maria for a lift. Back in town, **Dinty's Bar** serves up huge portions of seafood-geared grub. (☎ 33373. Dinners from £6; food served 12:30-2:30pm and 6-9pm.) **Casey's Bar** provides a waterside-patio beer garden on which to enjoy your fresh seafood or less expensive pub grub. (☎ 33590. Food served daily noon-8:30pm.) **Mahoney's** (☎ 33610) jovial atmosphere and billiard tables draw a young crowd. **Nolan's Bar** (☎ 33758) supplies a few bites and spirited trad on Wednesday and Friday nights.

Pterodactyl teeth, dinosaur droppings, stone age calendars, and rifles from the Easter Rising draw scholars from across the world to the **Ceim Hill Museum**, about 3 mi. outside town. From Maria's Schoolhouse, head right, keeping the lake to your left. The steep road up Ceim Hill is to the right, past a set of farm buildings. The museum's proprietress, who is possibly more interesting than most of her exhibited items, found many of these prehistoric artifacts in her backyard. (☎ 36280. Open daily 10am-7pm. £2.)

Travelers passing along the Skibbereen Road toward Union Hall may want to pause in the shady seaside groves of **Rennin Forest**. Further on, signs point out **Castletownshend**, the point of hasty escape for many defeated rebels after the **Battle of Kinsale**. Visitors with time to pause in this hamlet by the sea can pop into **Mary Ann's Bar and Restaurant** for cream- and seafood-oriented pub grub. (☎ 36146. Food served noon-2:30pm and 6-9pm.) **Knockdrum Fort,** just west of town, is a typical example of what becomes of an Iron Age Celtic fort over the centuries.

SKIBBEREEN ☎028

The biggest town in West Cork, Skibbereen (or "Skib," as it's known among locals; pop. 2100) is a convenient stop for travelers roaming through the more gorgeous wilds of Co. Cork. When Algerian pirates sacked Baltimore in 1631, the survivors moved inland, establishing Skibbereen as a sizable settlement. The town suffered particularly during the Famine; a popular post-Famine folk ballad litanizes the "cruel reasons" that led many residents to "leave old Skibbereen." Recently, however, the town has seen happier days, evolving into a market town for Cork's farmers. Friday is the best day to visit, when farmers tote in plants, fresh produce, and pies for sale on Bridge St. (early afternoon). Or treat yourself to a new heifer at the cattle market on Wednesdays (11am-4pm), also on Bridge St. Many stores in Skibbereen close on Thursday at around noon to recover between busy market days.

GETTING THERE AND PRACTICAL INFORMATION. Skibbereen is L-shaped, with **North St.** standing as the base and **Main St.** and **Bridge St.** comprising the height (Main St. turns into Bridge St. at the small bridge). The clock tower, post office, and stately "Maid of Erin" statue are at the elbow. Hitchers typically stay on N71 to go east or west but switch to R595 to go south. *Let's Go* does not recommend hitchhiking. **Buses** stop in front of Calahane's Bar, Bridge St. and run to **Baltimore** (M-F 5 per day, June-Sept. Sa 4 per day; £2.10), **Cork** (3 per day, £8.80), **Clonakilty** (3 per day, £4.40), and **Killarney** (2 per day, £11). The **tourist office** is housed in the Town Hall, North St. (☎ 21766. Open June M-F 9am-6pm, July-Aug. 9am-7pm, Sept.-May 9:15am-5:30pm.) **AIB**, 9 Bridge St., and **Bank of Ireland**, Market St. (☎ 21388 and ☎ 21700. Both open M-Tu and Th-F 10am-4pm and W 10am-5pm.) **Roycroft Stores**, Ilen St. off Bridge St. **rents bikes.** (☎ 21235. £8.50-10 per day, includes helmet; deposit £40. Raleigh's One-Way Rent-A-Bike program; call for details. Open M-Sa 9:15am-6pm.) Scrub those duds at **Hourihane's Launderette**, Ilen St., behind the Busy Bee. (☎ 21476. £3.50 per load. Open daily 10am-10pm.) **Internet access** is available at the library across from the Arts Center on North St. A £2 membership fee gives you unlimited access to all the libraries and their Internet in County Cork. The **post office** can be found on Market St. (Open M-Sa 9am-5:30pm.)

ACCOMMODATIONS. **Russagh Mill Hostel and Adventure Center (IHH)** grinds to a halt about 2 mi. out of town on Castletownshend Rd. This renovated 200-year-old mill regularly hosts hikers and rock climbers, along with a few hostelers on the side. (☎ 22451. Check-out 10:30am. Dorms £8; private rooms £12 per person.) The proprietress of **Bridge House**, Bridge St., could be a set designer for Victorian period films. Bridge House is a visual experience, with lavish canopy beds in ornate satin-laced rooms, and Cork's biggest bathtub. (☎ 21273. £18-20.) **Ivanhoe** on North St., has a more simple decor but all rooms come with big beds, bathrooms, and TV. (☎ 21749. Singles £20; doubles June-Aug. £36, Sept.-May £30.) The

Hideaway Campground, Castletownshend St., is the popular choice for campers and caravaners. (☎ 22254. Showers 50p. Kitchen facilities available. 2-person tent £8.)

🍴 FOOD AND PUBS.
Along Main and North St. a handful of inviting options exist in the cluster of cafes. Skib's **SuperValu** supermarket struts its stuff on Main St. where it also houses a small cafe. (☎ 21400. Open M-Sa 9am-6:30pm). At **The Wine Vaults,** Bridge St., delicious and inexpensive pizzas, sandwiches, and salads transcend the term "pub grub." (☎ 23112. Food served daily noon-9pm.) Wake up well with **The Stove's,** Main St., scones and hearty breakfasts. Drop by later for Irish specialties. (☎ 22500. Meals £4-5. Open M-Sa Sept.-June 8am-6pm, July-Aug. 8am-8pm.) At **Kalbo's Bistro,** 48 North St., cool jazz and innovative meals go hand in hand. The desserts are a must. (☎ 21515. Lunch £4.50-6.50, dinner from £7. Open M-Sa 11:30am-4:30pm and 6:30-9:30pm, Su noon-2:30pm and 6:30-9:30pm.) **Bernard's,** on Main St., behind O'Brien's Off License, serves above-average pub grub and baked goods in a large, beautiful bar/restaurant. (☎ 21772. Meals £7-10. Open daily 9am-11:30pm. Food served 11:30am-7pm.) The **Blues Bistro,** housed inside Eldon Hotel on Bridge St., claims that Michael Collins ate his last meal here. Supposing things haven't changed since 1922, he had a good variety to choose from, including vegetarian options. (☎ 22000. Meals £6-13. Open daily 8am-9pm.)

Find live blues and folk and a young crowd at the **Wine Vaults** (see above), where locals and tourists mingle jovially. The most comfortable digs are at **Bernard's,** all the better to converse in. **Seán Óg's,** Market St. (☎ 21573), hosts contemporary folk and blues several nights a week, a Tuesday night trad session, and an outdoor beer garden nightly. **Kearney's Well,** 52-53 North St. (☎ 21350), attracts lively locals, while the **Cellar Bar,** Main St. (☎ 23355), has boisterous chatter to accompany the clatter of billiards. On Fridays and Saturdays, the Cellar opens up Skibbereen's only disco, **Curley's Nite Club.** (Disco 11pm-2am. Cover £5.)

👁 SIGHTS.
The **West Cork Arts Centre,** North St., across from the town library, shows changing exhibits of Irish art and a permanent collection of Cork crafts. (☎ 22090. Gallery open M-Sa 10am-6pm. Free.) Get wired into the local arts scene with a free copy of *Art Beat,* a guide to the arts in Cork, available at the Centre. Pick up a copy of the **Skibbereen Trail** map for £1 and take a self-guided tour of the town's major sights. Included on this tour is the **Abbeystrewery Cemetery,** where between 8000 and 10,000 Famine victims are buried. The **gardens** at **Liss Ard Experience,** down Castletownshend Rd. toward the hostel, promise to "induce new perceptions of light and sky." Created as a unique attempt at conservation, the nonprofit organization's 50 acres include a waterfall garden, a wildflower meadow (with over 100 species of butterflies), and the surreal "Irish sky garden," designed by American artist James Turrell. (☎ 22368. Open May-Sept. M-F 9am-6pm, Su noon-6pm. £3, students £2.) Three-and-a-half miles west of town on the Baltimore Rd., the well-maintained **Creagh Gardens** contrast with their woodland setting. (☎ 22121. Open daily 10am-6pm. £3, children £1.50.) During the end of July, Skibbereen celebrates **Welcome Home Week,** featuring street entertainment and bands.

BALTIMORE ☎028

Once a seaside base for pirates, the tiny fishing village of Baltimore (pop. 200) now caters to tourists serving as the center for aquatic sport and as a point of departure for **Sherkin Island** and **Cape Clear Island.** The watery graves offshore hold scores of **shipwrecks,** making Baltimore a diver's hunting grounds. On land, the stone remains of **Dún na Sead,** "The Fort of the Jewels," one of nine 16th-century O'Driscoll castles stand in the center of town. Even today, your best bet at stopping a man in the street is to shout, "Mr. O'Driscoll!" O'Driscoll family members from near and far congregate here every June to elect a chieftain and to stage a family gathering, complete with live music, jammed pubs, and inebriation. Artists and tourists come here with equal enthusiasm to enjoy bright, dramatic seascapes.

236 ■ WEST CORK

GETTING THERE AND PRACTICAL INFORMATION. Baltimore's main road runs about 1½ mi. through town and out to the **Beacon,** a lighthouse atop a magnificent cliff with views over the ocean and across to **Sherkin Island.** The post office window has a full schedule of the **buses** running to and from Skibbereen (M-Sa 3-4 per day). Information about **ferry service** is available from the ferry offices at the Sherkin Islands (☎ 20125) and **Cape Clear Island** (☎ 39119). The small **tourist office** (☎ 20441), halfway up the steps from the ferry depot, is non-Bord Fáilte and keeps sporadic hours. Next door, **Islands Craft** dispenses helpful information on Sherkin and Cape Clear, including ferry schedules and historical accounts of the islands. All crafts in the shop are handmade on one of the islands. (☎ 20347. Open July-Aug. M-Sa 11am-5:30pm, Su 12:30-5:30pm.) The **post office** is inside the small general store above the craft shop. (Open M-F 9am-5:30pm, Sa 9am-1pm.)

ACCOMMODATIONS, FOOD, AND PUBS. A visit to Baltimore requires a stay at **Rolf's Hostel (IHH),** Skibbereen Rd. A delightful German family runs this 300-year-old complex of stone farmhouses a 10-minute walk up the turnoff immediately before the village. Comfortable pine beds (brass in the private rooms) and a dining room with stunning views and delicious food are hard to resist. (☎ 20289. **Internet access** £1 per 8min. Laundry £4. **Bike rental** £7 per day. Dorms £7-8; 4-bed dorms £9; doubles £25; triples £37.50. **Camping** £3.50 per person.) Rolf's also runs **Cafe Art,** where guests can choose from an extensive, if expensive, menu. (Main courses £9-11.50.) **Baltimore Holiday Hostel** is run by the Diving & Watersports Center but welcomes any guest looking for quality budget accommodation. This brand-new hostel includes a fully equipped kitchen, a sauna (£3.50 per hr.), and a restaurant, laundromat, and general store next door. To reach the hostel turn right at the post office and continue for half a mile. (☎ 20300. 8-bed dorms £10). Enjoy an international culinary experience at the reasonably priced **Le Bistro,** next door to Baltimore Holiday Hostel. Vegetarian options as well as breakfast, lunch, and dinner meals range £2-16. (☎ 20644. Open daily 8am-9pm.) The **Lifeboat Restaurant,** in the post office building, serves cheap soup, sandwiches, quiche, and pastries, in a glass room on the harbor's edge. (☎ 20143. Entrees £3-5. Open daily 10am-5:30pm.) Stock up on food for the islands at welcoming **Cotter's,** on the main road facing the harbor. (☎ 20106. Open M-Sa 9:30am-8pm, Su 10:30am-8pm.) All of Baltimore's pubs offer food. **Declan McCarthy's,** just above the pier, is the liveliest pub, with (often big-name) trad and folk bands three to four nights a week in summer. (☎ 20159. Occasional cover £5-10.) The comfortable stools and tables outside **Bushe's Bar** (☎ 20125) are prime spots for scoping out the harbor. **La Jolie Brise** has basic pizza, pasta, and grill items at a decent price (☎ 20600. £4.50-9. Serves breakfast all day. Open daily 8:30am-11pm.) Just around the corner, the **Algiers Inn** lures tourists into its comfortable interior. (☎ 20145. Food served M-Sa 5:30-9:30pm.)

SIGHTS. Much to the woe of landlubbers, many of Baltimore's best sights are under water. Wrecks of U-boats and galleons await the amphibious. To arrange dives or rentals, contact the **Baltimore Diving & Watersports Centre,** located in the Baltimore Holiday Hostel. (☎ 20300. 1hr. snorkel dive, including equipment £12; course and dive for the inexperienced £30.) **Atlantic Boating Service** (☎ 22734), located at the end of the pier, offers waterskiing (starting at £30 per 30min.) and boat rental (summer £15 per hr., off-season £10 per hr.). Explorers equipped with bicycles or cars head east to circle **Lough Ine** (EYEN, sometimes spelled Hyne), Northern Europe's only saltwater lake, where clear rapids change direction with the tide. The lough, originally a freshwater lake, was inundated when sea levels rose after the last Ice Age. It is now a stomping ground for marine biologists, who search out the dozens of sub-tropical species it shelters. Trails thread through the woods around the lake, with the steeper climbs affording incredible views.

NEAR BALTIMORE: SHERKIN ISLAND

Just 10 minutes away by ferry from Baltimore, Sherkin Island (pop. 100) offers sandy, cliff-enclosed beaches, wind-swept heath, an over-abundance of cows, and

CAPE CLEAR ISLAND (OILEÁN CHLÉIRE) ■ 237

absence of people. **Ferries** come from **Baltimore** (in summer 8 per day, in winter 3 per day; £4 return). Ferry schedules are posted outside the Island Craft office in Baltimore (see above), and Vincent O'Driscoll (☎ 20125) can provide information. Ferries also run from **Schull** (1hr.; July-Aug. 3 per day, June and Sept. 2 per day; £6 return). For information, call Kieran Molloy (☎ 28138).

Spending the night on Sherkin Island is a tranquil treat at **Cuinne House** (KWEENA) where every spacious, wood-floored room offers an ocean view. To reach the B&B, take the road behind the Jolly Roger. (☎ 20384. Evening meals £12. £17-19 per person.) **Murphy's Hotel** (☎ 20116), close to the ferry landing and next to Dún-na-Long ruins, gives you plenty of culinary options as it is home to **Murphy's Bar** (food served daily 12:30-7pm) and the **Islander Restaurant** (☎ 20116. Open June-Sept. daily 6-9:30pm). The hotel also **rents bikes** for £7 per day. The amiable **Jolly Roger** (☎ 20379) across the street has sessions nearly every night in summer, and quite dependable pub grub until late. The **Abbey**, on the main road, is the only food store on the island and stocks only the basics. (☎ 20181. Open in summer M-Sa 9am-6pm, Su noon-6pm.)

The first thing you'll encounter off the ferry, are the ruins of a 15th-century **Franciscan abbey** founded by Fineen O'Driscoll. Vengeful troops from Waterford sacked the abbey in 1537 to get back at the O'Driscolls for stealing Waterford's wine. Unimpressive **Dún-na-Long Castle** ("fort of the ships"), also built by the buccaneer clan and sacked in the same raid, lies in ruins north of the abbey behind Murphy's Bar. (Castle always open. Free.) Stay straight on the main road from the ferry dock and you'll pass the blue-green **Kinnish Harbour** and Sherkin's yellow one-room schoolhouse, where the island educates its children. The beaches on Sherkin are sandy, gradually sloped, and great for swimming. **Trabawn Strand, Cow Strand,** and the long **Silver Strand** are all on the west side of the island (follow the main road and sign posts). **Horseshoe Harbour**, with its defunct **lighthouse**, offers some particularly breathtaking views.

CAPE CLEAR ISLAND (OILEÁN CHLÉIRE)

The rugged landscape seen from the bumpy ferry docking at Cape Clear Island seems incapable of providing for its sparse population of 150 individuals. But the island swells in capacity every summer with the arriving secondary school students who come here to brush up on their Irish. The main industry of this wild and beautiful island, however, is still farming; the landscape of patchwork fields separated by low stone walls hasn't changed much since the Spanish galleons stopped calling here hundreds of years ago. The density of the hills in the terrain invites only the most enduring of bike riders.

🚍 **GETTING THERE. Ferries** run to and from **Baltimore** (June and Sept. 2 per day; July-Aug. M-Sa 3 per day, Su 4 per day; Oct.-Apr. M-Th and Sa-Su 1 per day, F 2 per day; May M-F 2 per day, Sa-Su 1 per day; £9 return). Call Capt. Conchúr O'Driscoll (☎ 39135) for more information. Ferries to and from the island from **Schull** leave daily in June at 5:30pm and in July and August at 10am, 2:30pm, and 4:30pm.

🛈 **PRACTICAL INFORMATION.** Life is leisurely and hours are approximate; the island's stores and pubs keep flexible hours, and B&Bs rise and decline according to the residents' inclination to host guests. For an updated version of opening hours and general island information, head to the **Co-op office** (☎ 39119), where they hand out free maps, or check the bulletin board at the end of the pier.

🏠 **ACCOMMODATIONS. Cléire Lasmuigh (An Óige/HI)**, the Cape Clear Island Adventure Centre and Hostel, is about a 10-minute walk from the pier (keep to the left on the main road). The hostel often fills up with Irish students in the summer, so those eager to enjoy its comfy dorms and harbor views should call ahead. (☎ 39198. June-Sept. £8, Oct.-May £7.) The **Roaringwater Bay Centre** runs **sea kayaking** and **diving** trips out of the hostel, luring armies of adventurers to the picturesque stone building. (☎ 39198. Kayaking from £40, diving from £25.) The proprietors of

Ciarán Danny Mike's (see **Food and Pubs**) run the hospitable **Cluain Mara B&B** (☎ 39153) in the house adjacent to their pub. (£15-16; self-catering apartment across the road £25.) Further along the road, up the steep hill past the hostel, **Ard Na Ganthe** has spacious doubles, family rooms and a filling breakfast buffet (☎ 39160. £16 per person). **Cuas an Uisce campsite**, on the south harbor, is a five-minute walk from the harbor: go up the main road, turn right at Ciaran Danny Mike's then bear left. Campers get a glorious view of the hostel across the lovely bay. (☎ 39136. Open June-Sept. Showers 50p. Tent rental £10. £2.70 per person.)

FOOD AND PUBS. The one grocery store, **An Siopa Beag** (☎ 39099), stocks the essentials in a white building a few hundred yards down the pier to the left. The same building also houses a small coffee shop that has take-away pizzas at night (open June-Aug. M-Sa 9:30am-1:30pm, 2:30-6pm; Sept.-May 9:30am-4pm). The island **craft shop** sells everything from used books to warm sweaters, and gives out information for free. (Open Sept.-June daily 9:30am-1:30pm; July 2:30-6pm; Aug. 7:30am-8:30pm.) Food options on Cape Clear are limited, but you can expand your own horizons at **Ciarán Danny Mike's** (☎ 39172), the southern-most pub in Ireland. **The Night Jar** (☎ 39012) vends various vegetarian victuals, verily.

What the Cape Clear pub scene lacks in variety it makes up for in stamina. The island has no resident authorities to regulate after-hours drinking, so the fun usually lasts until 4am or later. The island supports two pubs. **The Night Jar's** (☎ 39102) boisterous atmosphere compensates for its bare interior. The spontaneous should bring their ukuleles to **Ciarán Danny Mike's** for good spirits, song, and billiards.

SIGHTS. About a 25-minute walk up a steep hill from the pier is the island's **Heritage Centre**, half a room containing everything from an O'Driscoll family tree to a deck chair from the equally ubiquitous *Lusitania*. Since over half of the exhibits are in Irish, it's a quick trip for the Irish-challenged. (Open daily June-Aug. 2-5:30pm. £1.80, students £1, under 18 50p.) On the road to the center, **Cleire Goats** (☎ 39126) is home to the best bred goats in Ireland, if not the world. For 75p you can test the owner's claim that goat's milk ice cream is richer than the cow kind. Cleire Goats also runs half-day to one-week goat-keeping courses that promise to blend "theory and practice." A right turn past the heritage center leads to the **windmills** that until recently generated three-quarters of the island's electricity. From the island's many hills, you can gaze out at the ruins of an O'Driscoll castle (near the North Harbour) and the old lighthouse (to the south, beyond the hostel). Neither building, or what remains of them, can be explored, however, for both are private property. Offshore 3 mi. to the east is **Fasnet Lighthouse**. Cape Clear also shelters gulls, stormy petrels, cormorants, and ornithologists. The **bird observatory**, the white farmhouse on North Harbour, is one of the most important in Europe. Get a hefty dose of island lore at Cape Clear's annual **International Storytelling Festival** in early September, featuring puppet workshops, music sessions, and a weekend's worth of memorable tales. (☎ 39157. £6 per event, £24 for the festival.)

THE MIZEN HEAD PENINSULA ☎028

If you've made the mistake of skipping Cape Clear Island, you'll have to take the land route to Schull, Crookhaven, and Mizen Head. Whatever route you choose, you'll end up at the windswept, beach-laden, and gloriously unspoiled southwest tip of Ireland.

SCHULL

A seaside hamlet 45 minutes by ferry from Cape Clear and 4 mi. west of Ballydehob on R592, Schull (SKULL) is the last glimpse of culture and commerce on the peninsula. With its one busy street, a great hostel, and excellent eateries, it's the best base for exploring the Mizen Head Peninsula. Be warned that many travelers are wise to Schull's charms; holiday cottages and B&Bs draw droves of vacationers during the summer months.

SCHULL ■ 239

GETTING THERE AND PRACTICAL INFORMATION. Buses to **Cork** (M-Sa 2 per day, Su 1 per day; £13 return) and **Goleen** (M-Sa 2 per day, Su 1 per day) stop in front of the AIB building on Main St. From June to September, there is also bus service between Schull and **Killarney** (1 per day). Check the schedule posted in the window of the library on Main St., and at the Bunratty Inn, the local Bus Éireann agent. **Ferries** connect Schull to **Cape Clear** and **Sherkin** (June and Sept. 1 per day, July-Aug. 3 per day, £9 return) and to **Baltimore** (June-mid-Sept. 3 per day, £6 return). Contact Capt. O'Driscoll (☎ 39135) for more information. Although many of Schull's attractions are aquatic, terrestrial types and folk singers can **rent bikes** at **Freewheelin'**, Cotter's Yard, off Main St. (☎ 28889. Open M-Sa 10am-11pm. £8 per day, £45 per week.) Pick up the prosaic and lengthy *Schull Guide* (£1.50), which has particularly good suggestions for walks and bike rides in the area, in any store. Either sing on a street corner or get cash at the **24hr. ATM** at **AIB** on Upper Main St. (☎ 28132. Open M-F 10am-12:30pm and 1:30-4pm.) The **post office,** Main St. (☎ 28110), shares shutters with a photography shop.

ACCOMMODATIONS, FOOD, PUBS. Schull's appeal for budget travelers is immeasurably enhanced by the presence of the ▣**Schull Backpackers' Lodge (IHH),** Colla Rd. From the Pier head right towards town, then bear left at the fork, and turn left at the church; the way is well-marked. The wooden lodge is bright and immaculate, with fluffy comforters, and tons of information on local walks and rides. (☎ 28681. Laundry £3.50. **Bike rental** £8 per day, £40 per week. High-season dorms £8; doubles £24-26.) **Adele's B&B,** Main St., above the restaurant by the same name, warms you up with small fireplaces and dark wooden floors. (☎ 28459. From £17.50 per person, includes continental breakfast.) Three miles from town on the way to Goleen, **Jenny's Farmhouse** offers a quiet place to crash. (☎ 28205. £10, with breakfast £12-14. Call for possible pick-up from Schull.)

Schull is known for its upscale shopping and eateries. The town is a treat for scone and brown bread connoisseurs. **Adele's Restaurant** bakes decadent cakes and pastries, and dishes up tasty soups, salads, and sandwiches in a proper tea room. She opens again in the evening for scrumptious, if pricey, Italian meals. (☎ 28459. Dinner £8-10. Open May-Oct. Lunch and tea Tu-Su 9:30am-6pm, dinner Th-Su 6-10pm.) Not to be outdone, the octagonally-talented **Courtyard** down the street bakes eight types of bread (85p-£1) and sells a variety of gourmet wholefoods, soups, and sandwiches. (☎ 28390. Store open M-Sa 9am-6pm, July-Aug. 9am-7pm. Fish, pasta, and meat dinners served daily 6:30-9:30pm.) On Mondays, Fridays, and some Sundays the adjacent **pub** features trad, jazz, and blues. The **Bunratty Inn,** up the hill on Main St., prepares, as proclaimed on a sign outside, some of West Cork's finest pub fare. (☎ 28341. Meals from £6. Food served M-Sa noon-8pm.) Have your choice of pub grub or pricier restaurant meals at **The Waterside Inn,** while enjoying their live music. (☎ 28203. Open daily summer noon-10pm; winter weekends only.). The Bunratty Inn and **An Tigín** (☎ 28830) both host live folk and rock one night a week during the summer. **The Galley Inn** (☎ 28733) has rollicking tunes twice a week and during some long weekends. Before leaving, stock up for Mizen forays at one of Schull's **grocery stores** on Main St.: **Spar Market** (☎ 28236; open July-Sept. daily 7am-9pm, Oct.-June M-Sa 7am-8pm, Su 8am-8pm) or smaller **Hegarty's Centra** across the street (☎ 28520. Open daily 7:30am-10:30pm.)

ACTIVITIES. Schull is a great spot from which to explore the **walking** and **biking** trails that snake along the water and up the nearby hills. Inquire at the Backpacker's Lodge for maps and information. The Republic's only planetarium, the **Schull Planetarium,** Colla Rd., offers extraterrestrial diversions for rainy days. (☎ 28552. 54min. star shows at 4 or 8pm; £3.50) A calm harbor and numerous shipwrecks make Schull a diver's paradise. The **Watersports Centre** on the pier **rents dinghies, sailboards, wet-suits,** and **scuba tanks.** (☎ 28554. Open M-Sa 9:30am-8:30pm. Dinghies £25 per half-day, windsurfing £10 per half-day.)

CROOKHAVEN AND MIZEN HEAD

The Mizen becomes more scenic and less populated the farther west one goes from Schull. The peninsula continues to lose its native population, with reinforcements coming in the form of European house-buyers. Accordingly, the Mizen is mobbed during peak-season weekends, as water-worshippers pack sandy beaches. The most reliable transit is **Betty's Bus Hire**, which will take you on a tour of the Mizen via the scenic coast road. The tour includes bits of local history and runs to the **Mizen Vision** (see below). Call Betty for her schedule. She will make a non-scheduled run for groups of 5 or more. (☎ 28410. £5.) **Bus Éireann** only goes as far as **Goleen** (2 per day; inquire in Schull or Ballydehob for schedule). **Hitching**, which is not recommended by *Let's Go*, is convenient in the peak-season, with hitchers often perching at the crossroads on Goleen Rd. outside of town. Confident **cyclists** can make a daytrip to Mizen Head (36mi. return from Schull).

The block-long town of **Goleen** seems to move at half-pace with only half-charm. Just up the hill from town is **The Ewe** (☎ 35492), a surprising and wonderfully eccentric "art retreat." For £2, visitors can stroll the eclectically decorated garden, and may be enticed to stay for a week-long pottery class (from £125, including spacious accommodation). Recluses wishing to stay the night can treat themselves to **Heron's Cove B&B**, down the hill from Goleen on the water. (☎ 35225. £19.50-25.) The **restaurant** downstairs serves excellent seafood, although catching the fish out back yourself would be a good deal cheaper (sandwiches £4).

Slightly longer than the main road, and tremendously worthwhile, the coast road winds to Barley Cove Beach and Mizen Head. Tiny **Crookhaven** (pop. 37), a 1 mi. detour off this road, is perched at the end of its own peninsula. You can meet half of the population at work in **O'Sullivan's**, which serves sandwiches, soups, desserts, and cold pints on the water's edge (☎ 35319. Food served daily noon-8:30pm), and the **Crookhaven Inn**, which provides similar fare in a lovely outdoor cafe overlooking the bay. (☎ 35309. Sandwiches £1.70, meals £5-7. Food served daily noon-8pm.) **Barley Cove Caravan Park**, 1½ mi. from Crookhaven, offers camping on the edge of the wind-swept peninsula. Includes tennis and pitch-and-putt facilities. (☎ 35302. £9 per tent. Mini-market, take-away, and laundry. Open Easter-Sept. **Bike rental** £5 per half-day, £9 per day; deposit £40.) Campers have a short walk to the warm, shallow waters of **Barley Cove Beach**, a sandy retreat for those bathers not ready to brave the frigid sea.

Three miles past Barley Cove, Ireland ends at spectacular **Mizen Head**, whose cliffs rise to 700 ft. **Mizen Head Lighthouse**, built in 1909, was recently automated and electrified, and the buildings nearby were turned into a small museum, the **Mizen Vision**. To get to the museum, you'll have to cross a suspension bridge only slightly less harrowing than the rendering of a shipwreck that is its centerpiece. The museum also assembles lighthouse paraphernalia and illuminates the solitary lives of lighthouse keepers. Its small, very windy viewing platform is the most southwesterly point in Ireland. (☎ 35115. Open daily June-Sept. 10am-6pm; Apr.-May and Oct. 10:30am-5pm; Nov.-Mar. Sa-Su 11am-4pm. £3, students £2.25.)

BEARA PENINSULA

The wild and majestic scenery of the Beara is combined with a profound sense of tranquility. Fortunately, the hordes of tourists circling the nearby Ring of Kerry usually skip the Beara altogether. For unspoiled scenery and solitude the Beara is superb; if you're looking for pubs, people, and other signs of civilization, you might be happier on the Iveragh or Dingle Peninsulas. The spectacular **Caha** and **Slieve Miskish Mountains** march down the center of the peninsula, separating the Beara's rocky southern coast from its lush northern coast. West Beara remains remote—travelers traverse treacherous single-track roads along the stark Atlantic coastline, picking their way past mountains, rocky outcrops, and the occasional herd of sheep. The dearth of cars west of Glengarriff makes **cycling** the 125 mi. **Beara Way** a joy (weather permitting), but for **hitchhikers**, the town marks the point at which they'll find themselves admiring static views for longer than their sanity can bear. *Let's Go* can neither admire nor bear hitchhikers.

BANTRY ☎ 027

According to the *Book of Invasions*, Ireland's first human inhabitants landed just a mile from Bantry (see **Legends and Folktales**, p. 23). Invading Bantry quickly became a fad, with English settlers arriving in the bay and driving the Irish out in the 17th century. Wolfe Tone and a band of Irish patriots tried to return the favor with the help of an ill-fated French Armada in 1796. Today's invaders come in the form of tourists eager to sample Bantry's elegance and relive its history, or to start off on a trek to the more remote areas westward.

GETTING THERE AND GETTING AROUND. Buses stop outside of Julie's Takeaway in Wolfe Tone Sq., several doors from the tourist office toward the pier. **Bus Éireann** heads to **Glengarriff** (M-Sa 3 per day, Su 2 per day; £2.25), and **Cork** and **Bandon** (M-Sa 3 per day, Su 2 per day; £8.80). June-Sept. only, buses go to **Skibbereen** (2 per day), **Killarney** via **Kenmare** (2 per day), and **Schull** (1 per day). **Berehaven Bus Service** (☎ 70007) stops here before and after **Cork**. **Rent bikes** from **Kramer's** on Glengarriff Rd., Newtown. (☎ 50278. £8 per day, £40 per week; deposit credit card, license, or passport. Open M-Sa 9am-6pm. Low-season closed W.)

ORIENTATION AND PRACTICAL INFORMATION. Bantry sits at the east end of **Bantry Bay**. If your back is to the water, the road leading out of **Wolf Tone Square** to the right is **New St.**, which becomes **Bridge St. Williams St.** branches off New St. to the right. **Barrack St.** intersects New St. a bit farther up. **Sheep's Head** stretches due west and the Beara Peninsula is northwest. Cars, cyclists, and hitchers stay on N71 to get in or out of town. *Let's Go* does not recommend hitchhiking. The **tourist office** in Wolfe Tone Sq. has a **bureau de change** and maps of Bantry and Sheep's Head for sale. (☎ 50229. Open July-Aug. M-Sa 9:30am-7pm, Su 10am-6pm, Sept.-June M-Sa 9:30am-6pm.) A Sheep's Head information kit (£4.95), including a map and well-illustrated book, is sold at the **Craft Shop** on Glengarriff Rd. (☎ 50003. Open M-Sa 9:30am-6pm.) **AIB**, Wolfe Tone Sq. has an **ATM**, unlike **Bank of Ireland**, Wolf Tone Sq. (☎ 50008 and ☎ 51377. Both open M-W and F 10am-4pm, Th 10am-5pm.) **Coen's Pharmacy** dispenses cures on Wolfe Tone Sq. (☎ 50531. Open M-Tu and Th-Sa 9:30am-1pm and 2-6pm, W 9:30am-1pm.) Find the **police** (*Garda*), Wolfe Tone Sq. (☎ 50045), and **St. Joseph's Bantry Hospital**, on Dromlcigh (☎ 50133), ¼ mi. past the library. The **library**, located on Bridge St., has **Internet access**. (☎ 50460. Open Tu-W and F-Sa 10am-1pm and 2:30pm-6pm, Th 10am-6pm.) The **post office** is at 2 William St. (☎ 50050. Open M and W-Sa 9am-5:30pm, Tu 9:30am-5:30pm.)

ACCOMMODATIONS. Bantry Independent Hostel (IHH), Bishop Lucey Pl., not to be confused with the "small independent hostel" on the square, is the more comfortable and relaxed of Bantry's two hostels. Head away from town on Glengarriff Rd. (Marino St.), take the left fork, and walk a quarter mile up the slight hill. It has decent bunks, a pretty common room, and a secluded setting. (☎ 51050. Laundry £4. Open mid-Mar.-Oct. 6-bed dorms £8; private rooms £10 per person.) **Harbour View Hostel**, Harbour View, to the left of the fire station along the water, provides drearily basic, cramped accommodations. (☎ 51140. Dorms £7; private rooms £7.50 per person). Four miles from town in Ballylickey, the **Eagle Point Camping and Caravan Park**, Glengarriff Rd., has a private beach and tennis courts, a TV room, and free showers. (☎ 50630. Laundry £3. Open May-Sept. £4 per person.)

FOOD AND PUBS. SuperValu supermarket is on New St. (Open M-Th 8:30am-7pm, F 8:30am-9pm, Sa 8:30am-6:30pm.) **Organico**, Glengarriff Rd. (☎ 51391), stocks health food. Bantry has a number of inexpensive restaurants. **O'Siochain**, Bridge St., serves well-prepared food in a comfy, kitschy coffeehouse. (☎ 51339. Sandwiches £1.50, pizza and entrees from £5. Open daily 9am-10pm.) Vegetarians need not apply at **Peter's Steak House** on New St. (☎ 50025. Most entrees £5-12. Open daily 10am-11pm.) Large and tasty portions of pizza and pasta can be had inexpensively at the **Brick Oven** in Wolfe Tone Sq. (☎ 52500. Open M-Sa 11:30am-12:30am, Su 2pm-12:30am.)

Filling grub and rollicking good times can be found in Bantry's pubs. Aside from being an exceedingly popular pub, **The Snug,** Wolf Tone Sq. (☎ 50057), also serves up grub at great prices (burgers $4-6) and occasional bursts of trad and folk. As any good seaside town should, Bantry sports its **Anchor Bar,** New St. (☎ 50012). Drop yours next to their miniature lighthouse and listen to folk or rock on Thursdays. **The Schooner,** off New St. (☎ 52115), carries a cargo of mixed music on weekends. Lonely Yankees should stop by the **Kilgoban Pub** (☎ 50649) on the way to the hostel—it was won by an American couple in the Guinness "Win your own pub in Ireland" contest.

SIGHTS. Bantry's biggest tourist attraction is **Bantry House,** a Georgian manor with an imposing garden overlooking Bantry Bay. The long and shaded driveway to the house is a 10-minute walk from town on Cork Rd. The ornate interior is decorated with impressive art and furnishings, which matches the elaborate grounds. The former seat of the four Earls of Bantry, the house was transformed into a hospital during Ireland's Civil War and again during the Emergency (neutral Éire's term for World War II; see **The de Valera Era,** p. 18). The current residents are the somewhat less wealthy descendants of the Earls. (☎ 50047. Open mid-Mar. to Oct. daily 9am-6pm. House and garden $6, students $4. Garden $2.)

The same earls, however, had a bit of scrambling to do when Irish rebel **Theodore Wolfe Tone** successfully borrowed a bit of France's anti-English sentiment for his own anti-English insurrection (see **Rebellion, Union, Reaction,** p. 13). Wolfe Tone's idea and campaign, as well as the 1970s discovery of one Armada ship that had been scuttled in the harbor, is thoroughly documented in the museum of the **1796 Bantry French Armada Exhibition Centre.** Enjoy the irony of its location next to Bantry House, the home of Richard White, who mobilized British resistance to Wolfe Tone's invasion. (☎ 51796. Open Mar.-Nov. daily 10am-6pm. $3, students $1.75.) **Sea trips** circumnavigate the harbor or drop you at **Whiddy Island,** a blend of quiet beaches and crude oil depositories that attracts birds and their watchers. (☎ 50310. Trips depart July-Sept. daily 10am-7pm. every hr. $4 return.)

Bantry is home to the **West Cork Chamber Music Festival** (☎ 61576) during the last week of June and the beginning of July, as well as a fringe festival for young musicians and literary readings and workshops. The heart of the festival is the **RTE Vanburgh String Quartet,** who are joined by scores of other international performers.

SHEEP'S HEAD

Largely ignored by tourists passing through Skibbereen, Bantry, and Glengarriff, narrow Sheep's Head makes a pleasant daytrip by bike or on foot (20 mi. from Bantry to the edge). The **Sheep's Head Way** across the middle of the peninsula affords great mountain views. The **Craft Shop** in Bantry has a book and map detailing the walk (see above). Hitchers may find it difficult to get a ride to or from the peninsula, since it's the least populated part of West Cork. **Cyclists** head west along the cove-filled southern shore and return by the barren and windswept northern road, while **hikers** explore the spine of hills down the middle. Sheep's Head itself is marked by its lighthouse and spectacular, untouristed cliff top vistas. If you're lucky, you might see the tide change in Bantry Bay, where incoming breakers meet the outgoing tide to create a mini-maelstrom. I shall call it "mini-maelstrom." For a snack on the way out, try the **Tin Pub** in **Ahakista,** on the southern road; the corrugated iron "shack" serves gratifying sandwiches.

GLENGARRIFF AND GARINISH ISLAND ☎027

Glengarriff is a choice gateway to the Beara Peninsula, with a handful of cozy pubs and restaurants. A short ferry ride away, unorthodox gardens on Garinish Island contrast with the familiarly Irish scenery on the mainland. Glengarriff's popularity as a tourist portal results in a town with more Aran sweaters than natives.

GETTING THERE AND GETTING AROUND. Buses stop in front of Casey's Hotel on Main St. **Bus Éireann** runs to Glengarriff from **Castletownbere** ($2.25,

Call the USA

"feel free to call"

1-800-COLLECT

When in Ireland
Dial: 1-800-COLLECT (265 5328)

When in N. Ireland, UK & Europe
Dial: 00-800-COLLECT USA (265 5328 872)

Member of **Dublin Tourism**

Australia	0011	800 265 5328 872
Finland	990	800 265 5328 872
Hong Kong	001	800 265 5328 872
Israel	014	800 265 5328 872
Japan	0061	800 265 5328 872
New Zealand	0011	800 265 5328 872

Call the USA

"feel free to call"

1 800 COLLECT

1-800-COLLECT

When in Ireland
Dial: 1-800-COLLECT (265 5328)

When in N. Ireland, UK & Europe
Dial: 00-800-COLLECT USA (265 5328 872)

Member of **Dublin Tourism**

Australia	0011	800 265 5328 872
Finland	990	800 265 5328 872
Hong Kong	001	800 265 5328 872
Israel	014	800 265 5328 872
Japan	0061	800 265 5328 872
New Zealand	0011	800 265 5328 872

Bantry (25min.; M-Sa 3-5 per day, Su 2-3 per day; £2.25), and **Skibbereen** (1½hr., 2 per day). From June to mid-September one Bus Éireann route runs along a string of gems twice a day: **Kenmare** (45min.), **Killarney** (1¾hr.), and **Tralee** (3hr.). **Berehaven Bus Service** (☎ 70007) serves **Cork** (2¾hr.; M-Sa 3 per day, Su 2 per day; £7) and **Bantry** (M 2 per day, Tu and Th-Sa 1 per day; £3). **Rent bikes** from **Jem Creations** on Main St. For £15 you can drop the bike off in an another town and they will pick it up. (☎ 63113. Open M-Sa 9:30am-7pm. £8 per day, £40 per week.).

▶ PRACTICAL INFORMATION. Glengarriff is graced with two friendly **tourist offices.** The Bord Fáilte office is on Bantry Rd. next to the Eccles Hotel, and has more hiking maps than a forest has trees. (☎ 63084. Open June-Sept. M-Sa 9:30am-1pm and 2:15-5:45pm.) The other large, privately run office is next to the public bathrooms and offers typical shamrock schlock. (Open daily 9am-6pm.) There is **no bank** in Glengarriff so stock up on cash before you get there. The **post office** (☎ 63001) is inside O'Shea's Market on Main St.

▶ ACCOMMODATIONS, FOOD, AND PUBS. The best place to stay in Glengarriff is the very friendly ◾**Murphy's Village Hostel,** in the middle of the village on Main St. Munch one of Mrs. Murphy's banana chocolate-chip muffins while perusing readily available maps and information in the cafe downstairs as a great start to your Beara trek. (☎ 63555. Laundry £4.50. **Internet access** £1.50 per 15min. Dorms £7.50-8; private rooms £11 per person.) The **Hummingbird Rest** (☎ 63195), a 10-minute walk from town along Kenmare Rd., has slightly crowded dorms (£6) and the best **camping** (£3) in town. In the center of town, behind the craftshop, **Maureen's B&B**, Main St., offers comfortable rooms. (☎ 63201. From £14.) Two **campsites** are neighbors on Castletownbere Rd. 1½ mi. from town: **Dowling's** and **O'Shea's** (☎ 63154 and ☎ 63140. Both £6-8 per tent. Open mid-Mar.-Oct.) Cook your own meal with groceries from **O'Shea's Market** on Main St. (☎ 63001. Open M-Sa 8:30am-9pm, Su 9am-7pm.) Otherwise, the best place for homebaked treats would be the cafe housed within Murphy's hostel (see above). **Johnny Barry's** (☎ 63315) and **The Blue Loo** (☎ 63167), also on Main St., serve standard pub grub. Johnny Barry's has live folk and cover bands Monday through Saturday; the Blue Loo covers a wide musical spectrum most nights of the week during the summer.

▶ HIKING. Glengarriff's best feature is its proximity to the lush **Glengarriff National Nature Reserve and Ancient Oak Forest,** where trails allow you to hike through giant rhododendrons and moss-strewn evergreens. Walking trail areas range from pebbled paths for curious, scone-snarfing pedestrians to rugged climbs for serious, granola-munching hikers. *Walking Around Glengarriff,* available at hostels in town and at the tourist office, outlines several walks in the park; more detailed maps are available for those with a good pair of boots and a yearning for thrills from hills. A popular walk that rewards with a panoramic view of the water, mountains, and forest is the path leading to **Lady Bantry's Lookout.** Glengarriff is also a good starting point for the Beara Way walking path (see p. 240).

▶ GARINISH ISLAND. The town's popularity, however, really comes from **Garinish Island,** a small island in Glengarriff Harbour. Garinish was a rocky outcrop inhabited by gorse bushes until 1900, when financier Annan Bryce dreamed up a fairyland for his family; a million hours of labor and countless boatloads of topsoil later, he had his garden and mansion. The Bryce family bequeathed their blooming island to the Irish people in 1953. Three companies along the main Glengarriff Rd. run **ferries** to the island (£4-5 return); you'll likely catch a glimpse of seals during the eight-minute journey. (☎ 63040. Open July-Aug. M-Sa 9:30am-6:30pm, Su 11am-7pm; Apr.-June and Sept. M-Sa 10am-6:30pm, Su 1-7pm; Mar. and Oct. M-Sa 10am-4:30pm, Su 1-5pm. Last landing 1hr. before closing. £2.50, students £1.) Bountiful lakes, rivers, and inlets around Glengarriff treat fishermen well. Try to wrap your tongue around the name of **Lake Eekenohoolikeaghaun** while you wait for a nibble on your line. Upper and Lower Lough Avaul are also well-stocked with brown and rainbow trout, but you need a fishing permit to catch them. **Barley Lake,** nearby rivers, and the ocean do not require permits. For more details, pick up the free *Fishing in Glengarriff.* (Call the regional Fisheries Board, ☎ (026) 41222; or ask around at the piers.)

The breathtaking **Healy Pass** branches north off R572 near Adrigole; it's a narrow, winding road that takes you through the green and rocky **Caha Mountains** to **Lauragh** (see **Eyeries and Ardgroom,** p. 247). The top of Healy marks the border between Cork and Kerry. On the south side of the pass, along the Castletownbere Rd. in Adrigole, the spacious new dorms in the ☎**Hungry Hill Hostel** make an ideal base for outdoor exploration. (☎ 60228. **Bike rental** £5 per day. **Internet access** £2 per 10min. Dorms £10; family rooms £25-35. **Camping** £4 per person.). Adventurers can tackle the 2245 ft. **Hungry Hill** where, on rainy days, a mountaintop lake overflows to create Ireland's tallest waterfall.

CASTLETOWNBERE ☎027

A stroll along the waterfront shipyards of Castletownbere, one of Ireland's largest fishing ports, is an informal education in marine biology. The largest town on the Beara Peninsula grows even busier during the summer when long-distance cyclists speed through it, leaving rows of peaceful fishing boats in their wake. In winter, the boats get busy plucking the fruits of the sea. Castletownbere is a gateway to the silent coastal villages further along the peninsula and on Beara Island. This reluctant hub has energetic downtown pubs and flavorful restaurants to revitalize weary trekkers on their way to and from the Beara.

☎🕐 GETTING THERE AND PRACTICAL INFORMATION. Bus Éireann offers service to **Cork** (3hr., 9-11 per day, £14), and summer service between Castletownbere and **Killarney** via **Kenmare** (M-Sa 1 per day, £8.80). **Berehaven Bus Service** (☎ 70007) leaves from the parking lot next to O'Donoghue's and heads to **Bantry** (1½hr., £4) via **Glengarriff** (M 2 per day, Tu-Sa 1 per day; Glengarriff 45min., £2.70) and to **Cork** (3hr., Th only, £8). Two **minibus** services leave **Cork** for Castletownbere (M-Sa 6pm, Su 8pm) and will take groups on tours of the Beara; phone **Harrington's** (☎ 74003) or **O'Sullivan's** (☎ 74168) for mandatory reservations (Cork £8, £14 return; tours £18-25). The closet-sized **tourist office,** behind O'Donoghue's by the harbor, gives away heaps of maps. (☎ 70054. Open June-Sept. M-F 10:30am-5pm.) The **AIB,** Main St., has an **ATM.** (☎ 70015. Open M 10am-12:30pm and 1:30-5pm, Tu-F 10am-12:30pm and 1:30-4pm.) **Bike rental** is possible but not promised during summer months at **Spar,** Main St. (☎ 70057; £7 per day, deposit £20; open M-Sa 8am-10pm, Su 9am-10pm) and **SuperValu,** Main St. (☎ 70020. £7 per day.)

🏠🍴🍺 ACCOMMODATIONS, FOOD, AND PUBS. The only hostel in town is the **Harbour Lodge,** on Main St. behind the church. Fully equipped with a kitchen, TV room, sauna, gym facilities, and laundry. (☎ 71043. Sauna £3. Laundry £3. Dorm £10.) Two miles west of town on Allihies Rd., just past the fork to Dunboy Castle, the **Beara Hostel** has decent rooms and hands out "welcome cakes" upon arrival, but be warned that the rural and not too scenic location may involve more of an outdoorsy experience than you bargained for. (☎ 70184. Bike rental £7 per day, £35 per week; passport deposit. Dorms £7; private rooms £8.50 per person, with bath £9.50. **Camping** £4 per person.) Six miles west on the road to Allihies from Castletownbere is the euphoria-inducing **Garranes Farmhouse Hostel (IHH).** A taxi from Castletownbere costs £7. The sea views from this intimate cottage are worth the trek, but some travelers report the water as not fully potable—you might want to bring some bottled H$_2$O. Phone ahead to confirm that all the space hasn't been absorbed by the Buddhist center (see below) next door. (☎ 73147. Laundry £4. Dorms £7.50; doubles £18.) **Castletown House,** Main St., above the Old Bank Seafood Restaurant, offers lovely rooms and lots of advice. Be sure to show the friendly owner your *Let's Go* guide. (☎ 70252. £15, with bath £17.)

CASTLETOWNBERE ■ 245

SuperValu, Main St., sells the largest selection of groceries. (☎ 70020. Open M-Sa 8am-9pm, Su 9am-9pm.) Seafood spawns in almost all of Castletownbere's restaurants. One exception is **The Old Bakery,** Main St., which serves piping-hot pizzas and an extensive menu of top-quality curries, sandwiches, and pasta (£4-6) in a building that was, once upon a time, a new bakery. It is now a great spot to sit on a rainy day. (☎ 70901. Open daily 9am-9pm.) **Jack Patrick's,** Main St., gets meat fresh from the butcher next door, and so do customers at affordable prices. (☎ 70319. Entrees around £4.25. Open M-Sa 11am-9pm, Su 12:30-9pm.) Seafood lovers should head to **The Lobster Bar,** Main St. (☎ 70031), with homemade bread, potato salad, and seafood platters large enough for two (£12.50), especially if they're Woody Allen and Diane Keaton, circa 1977. For the less gourmet, the **Cronin's Hideaway,** Main St., serves reasonably priced food fast and fresh. (☎ 70386. Entrees £3-7.50. Open M-Tu 12:30-3pm, W-Sa 5pm-12:30am, Su 12:30pm-12:30am.) **MacCarthy's,** Main St., the most popular pub in town and a well-stocked grocery, serves food all day. (☎ 70014. Sandwiches under £2. Trad and ballads on the weekends.) **O'Donoghue's** pub, Main St. (☎ 70007), on The Square, lures a sporty crowd with its big-screen TV and sunny (or starry) tables outside. Occasional music on summer weekends. Trad on summer Fridays keeps feet tapping at **Twoney's Ivy Bar,** Main St. (☎ 70114).

SIGHTS. Castletownbere's seat at the foot of hefty **Hungry Hill** (2245ft.) makes it a fine launch pad for daytrips up the mountain. (Inquire at the tourist office; see **Hungry Hill Hostel,** p. 244.) In addition, the huge harbor is perfect for watersports. **Beara Watersports** (☎ 70692) rents **dinghies, kayaks,** and **canoes.** Call for bookings. Two miles southwest of Castletownbere on the Allihies Rd., a donation of your choice buys you admission to the two separate ruins of **Dunboy Castle.** Cows graze the grounds of the enormous, crumbling Gothic-style halls of its 19th-century mansion. A quarter-mile past the mansion, the ruins of the 14th-century fortress **O'Sullivan Bere** lie in far worse shape. The original owner accidentally blew up the fort in 1594, and English armies ruthlessly finished the job eight years later. The road that runs past the castle becomes a shady trail that passes a number of sheltered coves. If you take the small detour off the road to Allihies (stay right at the fork), you will come across three interesting historical sites. The first is a **stone circle** at Derrintaggart West with 12 of the 15 stones still standing. These stone circles correspond with the rising or setting sun. Approximately 1½km further along the road, you'll find a raised **ring fort** at Teernahillane, 30m in diameter and 2m high. Just beyond that is a small **wedge grave.** Six miles west of town, the **Dzogchen Buddhist Centre** (☎ 73032) is perched on the same cliff top as the Garranes Hostel. The view from the meditation room is inspiration itself. A very respected Tibetan Buddhist teaching site, the center offers a daily program with meditation and compassion exercises.

DAYTRIPS FROM CASTLETOWNBERE

BERE ISLAND

*The spectacular ferry ride to this fishing community makes a quiet daytrip. Two **ferries** chug to Bere Island. **Murphy's Ferry Service** (☎ 75014) leaves from the pontoon 3 mi. east of Castletownbere off the Glengarriff Rd., but lands you much closer to the island's "center," at **Rerrin Village** (June-Aug. 7 per day, Sept.-May 3 per day; £4 return). The other company, **Bere Island Ferry** (☎ 75009), leaves from the center of Castletownbere but drops you inconveniently on the western end of the island (June 21-Sept. 7 per day, Su 5 per day; £3). Off-season return times can be uncertain; you may want to discuss your plans with the skipper.*

The friendliest people, the trashiest cars, and the best view of the Beara await you on Bere Island. Run-down cars get transported here from the mainland, where no police means no restrictions. Beware that the absence of John Q. Law on the island may translate to some drunk driving. Bere Island used to be a British naval base; forts and military remnants are still scattered around the island. The Irish

Army now uses the island for training. Across the harbor from Rerrin, the masts of a fishing ship protrude from the sea like giant iron toothpicks. The ship mysteriously burned in 1982 after her owner ran out of money to pay the crew.

The only place to stay on the island is **The Admiral's House hostel/B&B,** located in a historic home in Rerrin village, a five-minute walk down the dead end lane from Kitty Murphy's. (☎ 75213 or 75064. 6-bed dorms with bath £13.50 per person.) **Kitty Murphy's Cafe** (☎ 75004), next to the Murphy ferry landing or a 4 mi. walk from the Bere Island ferry, is a little cafe that serves the only affordable food on the island. Gaze at the maps or chat with a local at **Desmond O'Sullivan's** pub next door.

DURSEY ISLAND

The best scenery on the Beara is on Dursey Island, reached by Ireland's only cable car (☎ (027) 73017). The cables begin 5 mi. out from Allihies, off Castletownbere Rd., and stretch across the water. Inside the car, a small copy of the 91st Psalm adorns the wall, and you may find yourself calling upon "the Lord your defender" as you dangle above the Atlantic. Car runs based on demand M-Sa 9-10:30am, 2:30-4:30pm, and 7-7:30pm; Su hours vary depending on which church has mass that morning; £2.50 return.

The 10-minute aerial trip is the most exciting aspect of Dursey. Walks around the island expose you to a stark combination of sea, sky, land, and sheep. The English army laid waste to Dursey Fort in 1602 after raiding the unarmed garrison and callously tossing soldiers over the cliffs to their doom. A trip to the western tip provides a stunning view over sea cliffs and a chance to observe the island's much-vaunted migrant bird flocks. Food and rest for the Dursey-bound is dispensed at the **Windy Point House.** Located near the base of the cable car, Windy Point provides a full midday menu, comfortable accommodations, and sweeping views of Dursey Sound. (☎ (027) 73017. Food served 11am-6pm. B&B £17 with bath.) Otherwise, **camping** is legal. The island's seven residents could use the company.

NORTHERN BEARA PENINSULA

Past Castletownbere, the Beara Peninsula stretches out into the Atlantic, extending through craggy knolls, cliff-lined coasts, and desolate villages. A striking dearth of trees makes apparent the harshness of life on the peninsula. The stark isolation of this part of the Ring of Kerry is both an attraction and a frustration for hitchers, who report success only during the mid-afternoon beach traffic in July and August; *Let's Go* does not recommend hitchhiking. Despite some steep hills and barren stretches, biking is the way to go.

ALLIHIES

Set between the **Slieve Mts.** and the sea, abandoned cottages nearly outnumber inhabitants in Allihies. Fenced-off mine shafts, empty buildings, and a carved-up hillside testify to the once booming copper-mining industry in the area. Even **Ballydonegan Strand** is a by-product of the mines: the sand is the ground-up extracts of the mountains. More pristine and secluded are the white sands of **Garinish Strand,** which lies a few miles down the road toward **Dursey** (follow the signs to the right at the fork). At the turnoff to Dursey, look for the largest **wedge tomb** on the Beara peninsula, consisting of two sidestones capped by a single stone. The road to the Dursey cable car, off the Castletownbere Rd., passes by **Lehanmore Ring Fort,** still an impressive remnant, though its crumbling walls can barely keep the cows out these days. Some might call Allihies desolate, while others delight in the sunset at its metallic beaches.

Those planning to stay can find a warm welcome and warmer showers at **The Village Hostel (IHH),** Main St., next to the very red O'Neill's pub. (☎ (027) 73107. Laundry £3.50. Open May-Oct. Dorms £8; private rooms £9 per person.) A mile south of the village (and well-marked by signs) lies the **Allihies Youth Hostel (An Óige/HI),** which, despite remarkable views, makes for a good place to work on your memoirs. (☎ (027) 73014. Dorms £7, under 18 £5.50. Sheets £1. Open June-Sept.) **Anthony's** is well equipped for **camping,** with showers and scenery. Take the road towards the beach, turn right at the beach, and look for signs that say "Campground." (☎ (027) 73002. £6 per tent.) **O'Sullivan's** can fill your shopping bag or picnic basket and **rents bikes.** (☎ (027) 73004. £7 per day. Open daily 9am-9pm.) Allihies's four pubs cater mostly to locals. Usually one pub—seemingly chosen by tacit consensus among the villagers—is lively each night. **O'Neill's** is a safe bet, usually hosting trad and ballads on Wednesdays. It's also the best bet for a prepared meal. (☎ (027) 73008. Sandwiches £1.50-5; hot food £5-8; evening menu from £7.) **The Lighthouse** is a popular spot on Fridays, as are the **Oak Bar** and **O'Sullivans.** All have occasional trad sessions.

EYERIES AND ARDGROOM

Cross some of the most barren land in Ireland to reach the colorful hamlet of Eyeries. Once there, loafers can rest at the beach, while those intent on heading farther afield should examine several mysterious ancient sites. The pamphlet *Eyeries and Ardgroom on the Ring of Beara,* available at the hostel and several stores in the area, can direct you to **Ballycrovane,** where the tallest *ogham* stone in Ireland stands (see **Early Christians and Vikings,** p. 8). This 17 ft. stone is on private property, but is well signposted; the landowners collect £1 from each visitor. Further on in Kilcatherine sits the **Hag of Beara,** a bizarre rock formation that legend holds is the petrified remains of an ancient woman. It's hard to see, but some say that the outline of an old woman's or hag's face is on one side. Nearby, off the Allihies Rd., lie the ruins of Kilcatherine church dating to the 1700s with its unusual stone carving of a cat's head on the entrance door. Also look for the **Mass Rock,** which was used as an altar by Catholics during periods of repression (see **The Protestant Ascendancy,** p. 11). Three miles outside of Eyeries on the main road to Allihies is the **Urhan Hostel,** housed in an old schoolhouse along with the post office and a general store. Clean, spacious, with **The Urhan Inn Pub** (☎ 74088) next door, and gorgeous ocean views, this remote hostel meets all your needs. (☎ (027) 74005 or 74036. Dorms £7.50.) Five minutes east of the village, the **Ard Na Mara Hostel** makes the best base for explorations. Ocean views combine with a friendly staff to make for a soothing stay. (☎ (027) 74271. Dorms £7.50, private rooms £9. **Camping** £3.50). Heading east past Eyeries, you pass through **Ardgroom** (a-GROOM), a small village with a good pub. **The Holly Bar** (☎ (027) 74433) hosts live trad on most Tuesdays, Fridays, and Sundays in July and August, and serves up a mean bowl of seafood chowder (£3.50).

The only other thing to see on the northern side of the Beara (except for more mountains, more forests, and more sea) are the **Derreen Gardens,** half a mile north of **Lauragh** (LAH-rog) on the coast road, where you can lose yourself in the mossy tunnels that run through evergreens and massive rhododendrons. These rhododendrons, taller than most buildings in Ireland and ambitious growers, originally occupied almost the entire garden. (☎ (064) 83103. Open Apr.-Sept. daily 10am-6pm. £3.) The **Glanmore Lake Youth Hostel (An Oíge/HI)** makes a good base for hiking or fishing in the little-explored mountains near Lauragh. Relax from your day of hiking or biking in front of the cozy fireplace in this remote hostel, housed in a stately former schoolhouse with great mountain views. Follow signs from town; it is located 3 mi. off the main road through Lauragh. (☎ (064) 83181. Breakfast available. Open Apr. to mid-Oct. Dorms £7.)

COUNTY KERRY

The wee villages, mountainous landscape, and dramatic seacoast of Co. Kerry fit the bill of what many tourists expect to see in Ireland. Residents know that as the hot breath of the Celtic Tiger roars throughout the rest of the island, their idyllic countryside is becoming a thing of the past. While Kerry's economy relies on tourism, the county hangs on to its cultural isolation. In the rural metropolis of Dingle, townspeople talk of things being brought in from the outside—usually meaning Tralee, only 30 mi. away. Fortunately, importing bus loads of foreign vacationers has hardly polluted the Irish language and folk ways long since abandoned elsewhere in Ireland.

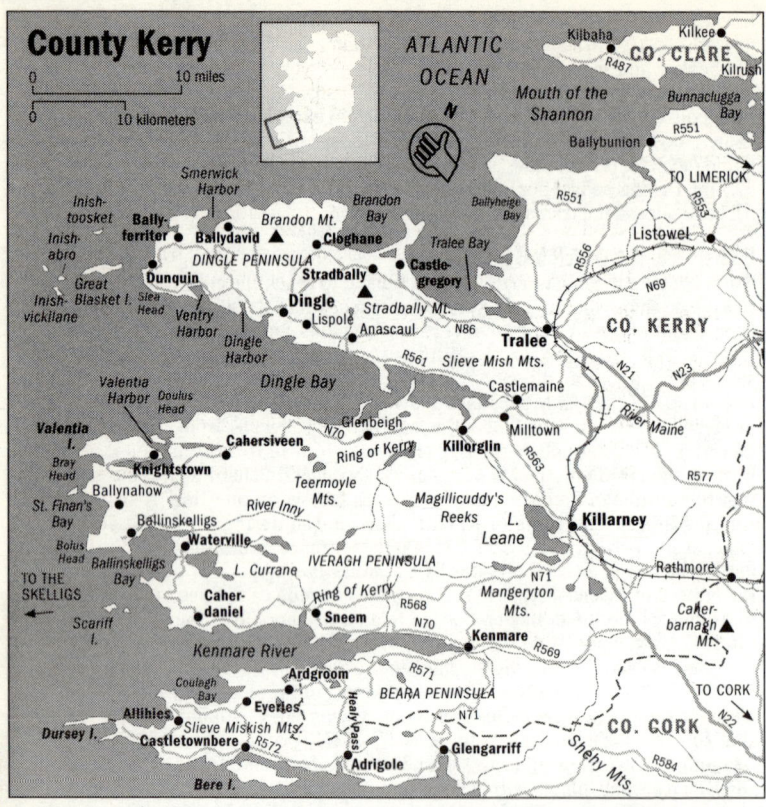

The Iveragh Peninsula, commonly equated with the Ring of Kerry road, has the mountainous Killarney National Park at its base and the Skellig Islands far off its western shore. Noxious tour buses often hog the roads, but the views are incomparable. The Dingle Peninsula is rapidly growing in popularity, but skinny roads help preserve the ancient sights and traditional feel of Slea Head, the West Dingle *gaeltacht*, and the Blasket Islands. Urban Tralee serves as a transportation center to more rural regions to the south and west. Summer bus transport is readily available to most areas of the country, though public transportation dries up, particularly along coastal routes, in the off-season.

KENMARE ☎064

A bridge between the Ring of Kerry and Beara, Kenmare has a continuous stream of visitors. Everything to be seen in an Irish town is here, from colorful houses to misty mountain views. Tourists fresh off the bus can dilute Kenmare's appeal, but services and pleasant surroundings overshadow the sweater stalls and postcard stands.

GETTING THERE AND GETTING AROUND

Buses: Leave from Brennan's Pub on **Main St.** for **Sneem** (35min., June-Sept. M-Sa 2 per day) and **Killarney** (1hr., M-Sa 3 per day, Su 2 per day), where connections to **Cork** and **Tralee** can be made.

Bike Rental: Finnegan's (☎ 41083), on the corner of Henry and Shelbourne St. £8 per day, £40 per week. Open M-Sa 9:30am-6:30pm.

ORIENTATION AND PRACTICAL INFORMATION

Kenmare's streets form a triangle: **Henry St.** is the lively base, while **Main** and **Shelbourne St.** connect on either side. The intersection of Henry and Main St. forms **The Square,** which contains a small park and the tourist office. Main St. then becomes N71 heading towards **Moll's Gap** and **Killarney;** N70 to **Sneem** and the **Ring of Kerry** also branches off this road. From Kenmare, cunning travelers take N70 west (not N71 north) to do the Ring clockwise and avoid tour bus traffic.

Tourist Office: The Square (☎ 41233). Open M-Sa Apr.-June 9am-1pm, 2-5:30pm; daily July-Oct. 9am-6pm.

Bank: AIB, 9 Main St. (☎ 41010). Open M-Tu and Th-F 10am-4pm, W 10am-5pm. **ATM** takes all major cards.

Laundry: O'Sheas, Main St. (☎ 41394). Wash and dry from £5. Open M-F 8:30am-6pm, Sa 9:30am-6pm.

Pharmacy: Sheahan's, Main St. (☎ 41354). Open M-Sa 9am-6pm. **Brosnan's,** Henry St. (☎ 41318). Open M-Sa 9:30am-6:30pm, Su 12:30-1:15pm.

Emergency: ☎ 999; no coins required. **Police** (*Garda*): Shelbourne St. (☎ 41177).

Hospital: Old Killarney Rd. (☎ 41088). Follow Henry St. past The Square.

Post Office: Henry St. (☎ 41490), at the corner of Shelbourne St. Open M-F 9am-1pm and 2-5:30pm, Sa 9am-1pm.

Internet: Bean and Leaf, Rock St. (☎ 40026), off Main St. £1.50 for 15min. Fantastic coffee, cakes, and pastries also available. Open Mar.-Nov. Tu-Sa 10am-6pm.

ACCOMMODATIONS

Kenmare satisfies its steady stream of visitors with convenient, if less than gorgeous, accommodations.

Fáilte Hostel (IHH), corner of Henry and Shelbourne St. (☎ 42333). Cleanliness and perfect location, plus TV room and large kitchen facilities. 1am curfew. Dorms £8.

Keal Na Gower House B&B, The Square (☎ 41202). Sleep comfortably in this small B&B within earshot of a brook. One room has a bathtub; the other 2 have brook views. Doubles and twins £36.

The Coachman B&B, Henry St. (☎ 41311). Decent twin and triple rooms above the bar. Internet £1 per 8min. £12-15 per person, £20 with bath.

Ring of Kerry Caravan and Camping Park, Sneem Rd. (☎ 41648), 3 mi. west of Kenmare. Overlooks mountains and a bay. Equipped with a kitchen, TV room, and small shop. Open May-Sept. £4 per person.

FOOD AND PUBS

Good food is plentiful but pricey in Kenmare. Smaller cafes are good for a scone or a snack, while pubs offer cheap lunches. **SuperValu** is on Main St. (☎ 41307. Open M-Th 8am-8pm, F 8am-9pm, Sa 8am-7pm, Su 9am-5pm.) **The Pantry,** Henry St., sells health food and organic produce. (☎ 42233. Open M-Sa 9:30am-6pm.)

An Leath Phingin, 35 Main St. (☎ 41559). Italian masterpieces served up on 2 floors of an old stone townhouse. Homemade pasta and home-smoked salmon. Features meat cooked over an oakwood fire. Most pizzas £6.95-7.50. Open Th-Tu 6-10pm.

The New Delight, 18 Main St. (☎ 42350). All the veggies you couldn't find in Ireland, a few at unbeatable prices. Just don't ask for meat or a cola. Open June-Nov. High season M-Sa 10am-8pm, low season M-Sa 10am-5pm.

The Coachman's Inn, Henry St. (☎ 41311). This popular wood-paneled pub/restaurant serves affordable meals during the day (from £4) and slightly more expensive grub at night (from £9). Food served noon-9pm. Music twice a week in summer at 9:30pm.

Cafe Indigo, The Square (☎ 42356). Art deco interior and funky blue lighting make this a snazzy refuge. Grilled and marinated tiger prawn skewer £8.50. Food served daily 7-10:30pm. M-F and Su late bar open until 1am.

Mickey Ned's, Henry St. (☎ 41591). Lunch-time crowds come for sandwiches (from £1.60) and ice cream (cones 85p). Open M-Sa 9am-5:30pm.

Kenmare's pubs attract a hefty contingent of tourists. Native Guinness guzzlers, however, hear too much good music to quibble over "Kiss me, I'm a leprechaun" hats. **Ó Donnabháin's,** Henry St. (☎ 42106), is a favorite among locals, with a pleasant beer garden out back. Huge **Murty's,** New Rd. (☎ 41453), just off Henry St., features live bands (W and F-Sa) and disco (Th and Su). **Brennan's,** Main St. (☎ 41011), serves pub grub and weekly live music during the summer. Smart tourists mob nightly music performances at **The Square Pint. Crowley's,** Henry St. (☎ 41472), asks: "With frequent trad sessions, why bother with interior decorating?"

👁 SIGHTS

There are plenty of good hikes in the country around Kenmare, but few sights in the town itself. The ancient **stone circle,** a two-minute walk down Market St. from The Square, is the largest of its kind in southwest Ireland (55 ft. diameter), but it ain't no Stonehenge. (Always open. £1.) The stone circle is one stop on Kenmare's **tourist trail** (maps at the tourist office), a well-marked route that leads visitors over historic bridges and past a small tower known as **Hutchin's Folly.** The new **Kenmare Heritage Centre,** in the same building as the tourist office, has a model of the stone circle and historical exhibits, as well as puzzling attempts to connect the town to Margaret Thatcher and Confederate general P.G.T. Beauregard. (Same hours as the tourist office. Cassette self-tour £2, students £1.50.) The **Kenmare Lace Centre** has demonstrations of the Kenmare lace-making technique, invented in 1862 by Kenmare nuns and once on the cutting edge of lace. Local artisans are currently resurrecting the craft. (Open M-Sa 10am-1pm and 2-5:30pm. Free.)

Seafari Cruises explores Kenmare Bay and its colonies of otters, seals, and whales. (☎ 83171. 3 per day. £10, students £8.) The cruises depart from the pier; follow Glengarriff Rd. and turn right just before the bridge. **Kenmare Bay Sea Sports,** based at the Dromquinna Manor Hotel, 3 mi. from town on the Sneem Rd., launches **kayaking, waterskiing, windsurfing,** and **tube rides.** (☎ 42255. £6-12 per hr.)

KILLARNEY ☎064

With something for everyone, Killarney seems to have just about everything at once. Only a short walk away from some of Ireland's most extraordinary scenery, Killarney's economy celebrates tourism. You'll find all you need in town, plus lots of trinkets to weigh down your pack, but all that fades to dust in the face of the glorious national park outside of town.

🚂 GETTING THERE AND GETTING AROUND

Trains: Killarney Station (☎ 31067, recorded info ☎ (066) 26555), off East Avenue Rd. near the intersection with Park Rd. Open M-Sa 7:30am-10pm, Su 30min. before train departures. Trains run to **Cork** (2hr., 5 per day, £9.50); **Limerick** (3hr.; M-Sa 4 per day, Su 3 per day; £15), and **Dublin** (3½hr., 4 per day, £33.50).

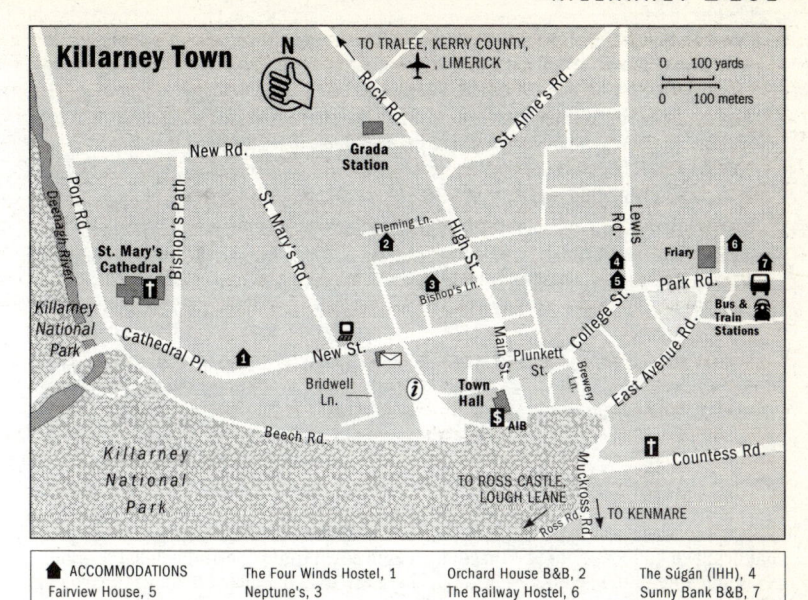

KILLARNEY ■ 251

Killarney Town

[Map of Killarney Town showing streets and landmarks including St. Mary's Cathedral, Killarney National Park, Grada Station, Friary, Town Hall, Bus & Train Stations, with roads labeled Port Rd., Deenagh River, New Rd., Rock Rd., St. Anne's Rd., St. Mary's Rd., Bishop's Path, Cathedral Pl., Fleming Ln., Bishop's Ln., High St., Main St., New St., Bridwell Ln., Plunkett St., College St., Brewery Ln., Park Rd., Lewis Rd., East Avenue Rd., Beech Rd., Muckross Rd., Countess Rd., Ross Rd. — directions to Tralee, Kerry County, Limerick; to Ross Castle, Lough Leane; to Kenmare]

♦ ACCOMMODATIONS
Fairview House, 5
The Four Winds Hostel, 1
Neptune's, 3
Orchard House B&B, 2
The Railway Hostel, 6
The Súgán (IHH), 4
Sunny Bank B&B, 7

Buses: Park Rd. (☎ 30011), connected to the outlet mall on the east end. Open M-Sa 8:30am-5pm. Buses rumble to **Cork** (2hr., 3-7 per day, £9.40), **Dingle** (2hr., 4-6 per day, £9.20), **Limerick** (2hr., 5-6 per day, £9.80), **Shannon** (3hr., 5-6 per day, £11), **Dublin** (6hr., 4-5 per day, £15), **Galway** (7hr., 2-3 per day, £13.50), and **Sligo** (7½hr., 3-4 per day, £18). Buses leave daily June-Sept. for the **Ring of Kerry Circuit,** with stops in **Killorglin, Glenbeigh, Kells, Cahersiveen, Waterville, Caherdaniel, Sneem,** and **Moll's Gap.** £8 if booked from a hostel; £12 return with 1-night stop for students. **Bus Éireann** also runs a no-frills Ring of Kerry circuit in the summer (2 per day; see **Ring of Kerry,** p. 257). The June to mid-Sept. **Dingle/Slea Head** tour (M-Sa 2 per day) stops in **Inch, Anascaul, Dingle, Ventry, Slea Head, Dunquin,** and **Ballyferriter** (£9.70).

Bike Rental: O'Sullivans, Bishop's Ln. (☎ 31282), next to Neptune's Hostel. Free panniers, locks, and park maps. Open daily 8:30am-6:30pm. £7 per day, £35 per week. **Killarney Rent-a-Bike** (☎ 32578), with locations at the An Súgán hostel and Market Cross, Main St. Free maps, locks, and panniers. £7 per day, £35 per week.

ORIENTATION AND PRACTICAL INFORMATION

Killarney packs into three crowded major streets. **Main St.,** in the center of town, begins at the Town Hall, then becomes **High St. New St.** and **Plunkett St.** both intersect Main St. and head in opposite directions. New St. heads west toward Killorglin. Plunkett St. becomes **College St.** and then **Park Rd.** on its way east to the bus and train stations. **East Avenue Rd.** connects the train station back to town hall before becoming Muckross Rd. on its way to the Muckross Estate and Kenmare.

Tourist Office: Beech St. (☎ 31633), off New St. Exceptionally helpful and deservedly popular. Open July-Aug. M-Sa 9am-8pm, Su 10am-1pm and 2:15-6pm; June and Sept. M-Sa 9am-6pm, Su 10am-1pm, 2:15-6pm; Oct.-May M-Sa 9:15am-5:30pm.

Banks: AIB, Main St. (☎ 31047), next to the town hall on Main St. Open M-Tu and Th-F 10am-4pm, W 10am-5pm. **TSB,** 23-24 New St. (☎ 33666). Open M-W and F 9:30am-5pm, Th 9:30am-7pm. Both have **ATMs.**

SOUTHWEST IRELAND

American Express: East Avenue Rd. (☎ 35722). Moneygrams, traveler's checks, card and traveler's check replacement, and client mail service. Open May-Sept. M-F 8am-7:30pm, Sa 9am-6pm; Su in July and Aug. 9am-7pm; Feb.-Apr. M-F 9am-5pm.

Laundry: J. Gleeson's Launderette (☎ 33877), next to Spar Market on Brewery Lane off College St. £5 per load. Open M-W and Sa 9am-6pm, Th-F 9am-8pm.

Pharmacy: Sewell's Pharmacy (☎ 31027), corner of Main and New St. Open Sept.-June M-Sa 9:30am-6:30pm; July-Aug. M-Sa 9:30am-9:30pm.

Emergency: Dial 999; no coins required. **Police** (*Garda*)**:** New Rd. (☎ 31222).

Hospital: District Hospital, St. Margaret's Rd. (☎ 31076). Follow High St. 1 mi. from the town center. Nearest emergency facilities are in Tralee.

Post Office: New St. (☎ 31288). Open M and W-Sa 9am-5:30pm, Tu 9:30am-5:30pm, Sa 9am-1pm.

Internet Access: PC Assist (☎ 37288), at the corner of High St. and New Rd. (not New St.). Open M-Sa 9am-6pm. £1.50 per 15min., £5 per hr. **Cafe Internet,** 18 New St., next to Country Kitchen. Open M-Th 9:30am-8pm, F 9:30am-7pm, Sa 10am-7pm. £1.50 per 15min.; 30min. of access with sandwich and drink £5.

ACCOMMODATIONS

With every other house a B&B, it's easy to find cushy digs in Killarney, though you may want to call ahead to the three hostels in town during the summer. Camping is not allowed in the National Park, but there are excellent campgrounds nearby.

IN TOWN

The Súgán (IHH), Lewis Rd. (☎ 33104), 2min. from the bus or train station. Make a left onto College St.; Lewis Rd. is the 1st right. Somewhat cramped quarters are well compensated for by the exuberant management, and impromptu storytelling and music around the fire-lit stone common room. Small, ship-like bunk rooms blur the distinction between intimacy and claustrophobia. 4- to 8-bed dorms £9.

Neptune's (IHH), Bishop's Ln. (☎ 35255), the first walkway off New St. on the right. Immense and clean with good showers, smaller rooms, but numerous amenities. The staff is friendly and professional. Breakfast £1.50-3.50. Free luggage storage; £5 locker deposit. Laundry £5. **Internet access** £2 per 15min. **Tour booking:** Dingle tour £12, Ring of Kerry £8. 8-bed dorms £7.50-8; 6-bed dorms £8-8.50; 3- to 4-bed dorms £9-9.50; doubles £20; 10% ISIC discount.

The Railway Hostel (IHH), Park Rd. (☎ 35299), the first lane on your right as you head towards town from the bus station. Big building with skylights, modern kitchen, and pool table. Friendly staffers tread on hardwood floors at this recently renovated hostel. **Internet access** £1 per 8 min. 3am curfew. 4- to 8-bed dorms £8.50-9; doubles £25.

The Four Winds Hostel, 43 New St. (☎ 33094). Slightly old, rustic and run-down building, with plenty of common room space and a fireplace. Dorm £7; private rooms £10.

Orchard House B&B, Fleming's Ln. (☎ 31879), off High St. Make yourself at home in the center of town. This friendly and immaculate place is hard to beat. All rooms come with TV, tea, coffee, and hair dryer. Singles £18; doubles £34-36.

Sunny Bank B&B (☎ 34109). A 5min. walk from the town center on Park Rd. directly across from the bus station. Cheerful and downright luxurious with bath and TV in all rooms. Specially modified showers with serious water pressure. Twins and doubles June-Sept. £20; Oct.-May £17-18.

Fairview House, College St. (☎ 34164), next to An Súgán. Treat yourself right with a fluffy bed and TV in this spotless B&B. £17-22.50 per person.

OUTSIDE TOWN

Peacock Farms Hostel (IHH; ☎ 33557). Take Muckross Rd. out of town and turn left just before the Muckross post office. Take that road 2 mi. and follow the signposts—if you think you're nearly there, you haven't gone far enough. A less taxing alternative is to call for a ride from the bus station. Overlooking Lough Guitane and surrounded by Killarney's slopes, this hostel is home to a friendly family of peacocks and a collection of homing pigeons. Skylights, hand-painted showers, and comfy rooms. 2 free daily buses to town at 9:30am and 6:30pm. Open Apr.-Oct. Wheelchair accessible. 8-bed dorms £7; twins £18.

Aghadoe Hostel (An Óige/HI; ☎ 31240). In Aghadoe, 3 mi. west of town on the Killorglin Rd. Call for free van ride to and from bus and train stations. Well-equipped hostel in a stone mansion surrounded by forests and a mountain view. Occasional music, barbecues, and talks on local history. Continental breakfast £2.50; evening meals £5. Laundry £4. **Internet access** £1 per 10min. Reception 7:30am-midnight. **Bike rental** £6 per day. Dorms July-Aug. £9.50; June and Sept. £8.50; Oct.-May £7.50. Singles July-Aug. £12, Sept.-June £10.

Black Valley Hostel (An Óige/HI; ☎ 34712), 14 mi. from town on Gap of Dunloe Rd. This spare but spotless hostel, one of the last places in Ireland to receive electricity, is conveniently located on the Kerry Way. Buy food in town or eat at the hostel. Sheets £1. Midnight curfew. Dorms £7.50, off-season £6.50.

Fossa Caravan and Camping Park (☎ 31497), 3½ mi. west of town on the Killorglin Rd. Kitchen, laundromat, tennis courts, shop, and restaurant. Showers 50p. Wash £2, dry 50p per 20min. Open mid-Apr. to Oct. **Bike rental** £7. July-Aug. £4 per person, mid-Apr.-June and Sept. £3.50.

Flesk Caravan and Camping (☎ 31704), 1 mi. from town on Muckross Rd. by Texaco. Laundry £3.50. Showers 50p. Electricity £1.75. Open Mar.-Oct. £4.50-4.75 per person.

FOOD

Food in Killarney is affordable at lunchtime, but prices skyrocket in the evening. **Tesco,** in an arcade off New St., is the town's largest grocer. (Open M-W and Sa 8am-8pm, Th-F 8am-10pm, Su 10am-6pm.) A number of fast-food joints and takeaways stay open until 2-3am nightly to satisfy the post-Guinness munchies.

The Stonechat, Fleming Ln. (☎ 34295). A small stone cottage just far enough from High St. for a quiet meal. Specializes in vegetarian meals, with chicken and fish dishes also available. Lunches from £4, dinner from £8. Open 11:30am-3pm and 5:30pm-10pm.

Celtic Cauldron, 27 Plunkett St. (☎ 36821). The best bet for the adventurous. Feast on traditionally prepared foods of the ancient Celts, then wash it all down with a tall glass of mead. Bacon, seaweed, and cockle crepe made in the medieval Welsh style £5.75. Open daily mid-Mar. to Nov. 6-10pm.

Cyrano's, Innishfallen Center (☎ 35853). Lower level of the plaza between Main St. and Car Park. Cyrano's knows variety, including tasty vegetarian meals. Sate that silver tongue with a dangerous dessert and a cappuccino. Open M-Sa 9:30am-6pm.

Teo's, 13 New St. (☎ 36344). The taste and feel of the Mediterranean in the heart of Shamrock country. Vegetarian options. Meals £7-13. Open daily noon-10:30pm.

The Country Kitchen, 17 New St. (☎ 33778). Glorious home-baked goods combined with hot meals and plenty for vegetarians. The desserts, however, are what draw the crowds. Main dishes £3.50-5. Open July-Aug. M-Sa 8am-8pm, Sept.-June 9am-6:30pm.

Ma Reilly's, 20 New St. (☎ 39220). Hot Irish stew and other hot treats in a popular little joint. Meals £4.50-7. Open daily July-Aug. 9am-10pm, Sept.-June 9am-6pm.

Mac's, 6 Main St. (☎ 35213). Filling fried breakfasts and cheap lunches £1.50-4.50. Killarney's best selection of ice cream as well. Open M-F 9:30am-6pm, Sa 9:30am-9:30pm, Su noon-9:30pm.

PUBS AND CLUBS

Battalions of jig-seeking tourists have influenced Killarney's pubs, making your drinking narrow and noisy. Trad is a staple of the summer nights.

O'Connor's Traditional Pub, 7 High St. (☎ 31115). Tourists and locals mingle in this upbeat, comfortable pub. Trad M and Th.

Courtney's Bar, Plunkett St. (☎ 32688). Locals and a few well-informed tourists (pat yourself on the back), come here for occasional unplanned trad sessions but mainly for the good company and good beer.

Buckley's Bar, College St. (☎ 31037). Tranquil trad fans gather under the skylight for nightly sessions during July and Aug.

Fáilte Bar, College St. (☎ 33404). A large, relaxed crowd gathers at this dark and woody pub. Disco beats F-Sa are relieved in the summers by trad on Su.

Several **nightclubs** simmer from 10:30pm until 1:30-2am. Most charge £3-5 cover, but often offer discounts before 11pm. Most popular and heterogeneous is **The Grand,** (☎ 31159), on High St., with trad on a nightly basis until 1:30am. Arrive before 10:30 and you won't have to pay the £4 cover. **The Crypt,** College St., next to the Killarney Towers Hotel, looks gothic but attracts neatly dressed trendy types. (☎ 31038. Mixed dance music nightly; 23+.) **Alchemy,** next to Danny Mann's, attempts to funkify a young crowd with three bars and a thumping dance floor. (☎ 31640. Varied music and frequent theme nights.) Check the *Killarney Advertiser* (free) and the *Kingdom* (70p) for town and county events.

SIGHTS AND ENTERTAINMENT

Congested with bureaux de change, souvenir shops, and disoriented foreigners, Killarney town's charm is elusive at best. Divine glory, on the other hand, awaits in the National Park just beyond city limits. The neo-Gothic **St. Mary's Cathedral** on New St., with three huge altars, seats 1400 in its rough limestone structure. (Always open. Free.) You're in luck if you hit town during one of Killarney's festivals; locals take them quite seriously and come out en masse. In mid-March, Killarney hosts the **Guinness Roaring 1920s Festival,** for which pubs, restaurants, and hostels bust out in jazz, barbershop singing, and flapper regalia. In mid-May and mid-July, horses gallop in the **Killarney Races** at the racecourse on Ross Rd. (Tickets available at gate, £3-5.) The **Killarney Regatta,** the oldest regatta in Ireland, draws rowers and spectators to Lough Leane in early to mid-July. (Tickets £5.) For the 4th of July weekend, Killarney celebrates American Independence day Irish style with the **Irish-American Music Festival.** The Killarney area has excellent salmon and trout **fishing,** especially in late summer and September. Unhindered trout fishing is allowed in nearly all of Killarney's lakes, but fishing in rivers and Barfinnihy Lake requires a permit. (Permits £3 per day.) Contact **O'Neill's Fishing Shop,** Plunkett St. (☎ 31970) for details. **Hiking and Biking Outdoor Centre,** 12 College St. (☎ 35153) rents rods for £6 per day.

KILLARNEY NATIONAL PARK

Ice Age glaciers sliced up the Killarney region, scooping out a series of lakes and glens and scattering silk-smooth rocks and precarious boulders. The resulting landscape is a dazzling marvel to hike, bike, or climb. The 37 sq. mi. park, stretching west and south of Killarney toward Kenmare, incorporates a string of forested mountains and the famous **Lakes of Killarney:** huge **Lough Leane (Lower Lake),** medium-sized **Middle (Muckross) Lake,** and small **Upper Lake,** 2 mi. southwest and connected by a canal. An indigenous herd of 850 elusive red deer roams the glens that surround the lakes.

Kenmare Rd. curves along the southeastern shores of the lakes between park sites but misses some woodland paths. With many more tourists than Irish driving these sections, hitching can be difficult. *Let's Go* does not recommend hitchhiking. Biking is a great way to explore, and **bike rentals** are readily available in town (see **Practical Information,** p. 250). Walkers can't travel as far in a day, but they have more freedom to climb off-road trails. Unfortunately for both bikers and hikers, many tourists admire

KILLARNEY NATIONAL PARK ■ 255

Killarney National Park

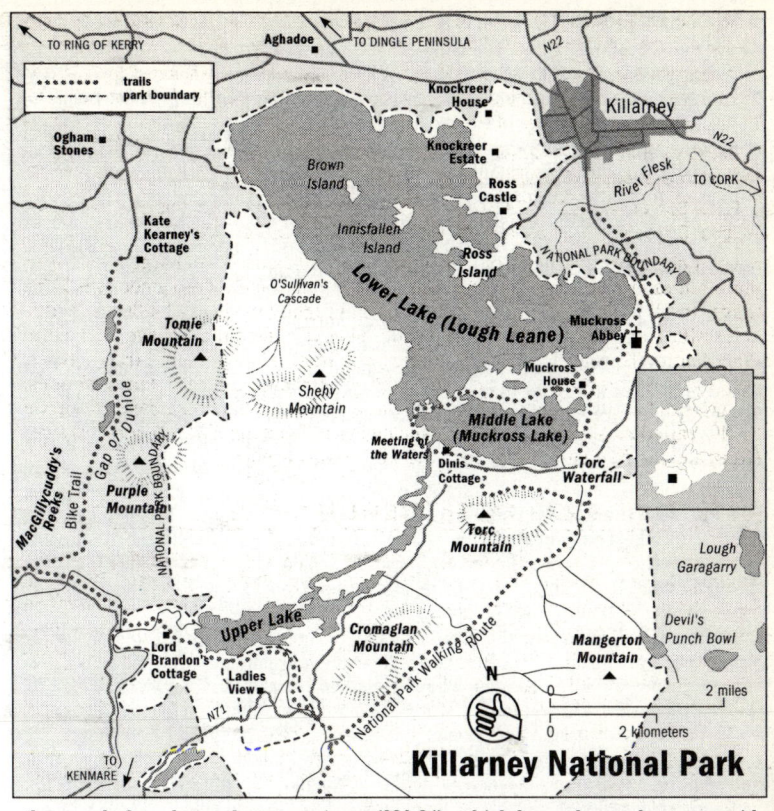

the woods from horse-drawn carriages ($20-24), which leave the roads strewn with *cac capall* (Irish for the substance whose smell may be your constant companion). The park's size demands a map, available at the Killarney tourist office or the **Information Centre** behind Muckross House. (☎ 31440. Open daily July-Sept. 9am-7pm.)

The most frequented destinations are the **Ross Castle** and **Lough Leane** area, **Muckross House** on Middle Lake, and the **Gap of Dunloe** just west of the park area, bordered on the southwest by **Macgillycuddy's Reeks**, Ireland's highest mountain range (most of the peaks are under 3000 ft.). The Gap of Dunloe is a full-day excursion. The others can be managed in several hours, or stretched out over a full day, depending on your mode of transport. Hikers and bikers should take the necessary precautions and watch out for traffic as well (see **Camping**, p. 70).

The best way to see almost all of the park in one day is to bike to the Gap of Dunloe (see **Gap of Dunloe**, p. 257). If the idea of a 14 mi. bike excursion fills you with trepidation, there are several short, well-marked, and well-paved walking trails closer to the Killarney side of the park. The park is also a perfect starting point for those who plan to walk the 129 mi. **Kerry Way**—essentially the Ring of Kerry on foot. Do not attempt the Kerry Way from October to March, when rains make the uneven terrain dangerous. The **Old Kenmare Road,** the first (or last) leg of the walk, passes through the spectacular Torc and Mangerton Mountains and can be managed in one day. From Killarney, follow the Kenmare Rd. 4 mi. and turn left just beyond the main entrance to Muckross House—the path leaves from the carpark on this side road. The Killarney tourist office sells a *Kerry Way* guide, with topographic maps of the Way. The excellent 1:50,000 Ordnance Survey maps (unfortunately, far from waterproof) of the Iveragh include minor roads, trails, and archaeological points of interest ($4.75).

ROSS CASTLE AND LOUGH LEANE

From town, **Knockreer Estate** is a short walk down New St. past the Cathedral. The original mansion housed Catholic Earls of Kenmare and, later, the Grosvenor family of long *National Geographic* fame. The current building, dating only from the 1950s, is unimpressive and not open to the public, but nearby nature trails afford great views of the hills, mountains, and roaming deer. You can drive or walk out to **Ross Castle,** a right on Ross Rd. off Muckross Rd. 2 mi. from Killarney, but the numerous footpaths from Knockreer are more scenic (15min. walk). The castle, built by the O'Donaghue chieftains in the 14th century, was the last in Munster to fall to Cromwell's army (see **Feudalism,** p. 9). In the last two decades, the castle has been completely renovated and refurbished in 15th-century style. Tales of a dreary castle life may be soothing to haggard travelers. (☎ 35851. Admission by guided tour only. Open daily June-Aug. 9am-6:30pm; May and Sept. 10am-6pm; mid-Mar. to Apr. and Oct. 10am-5pm. Last admission 45min. before closing. £3, students £1.25.) Past the castle, paths lead to the wooded and secluded **Ross Island**—not an island at all, but a lobster-claw shaped peninsula that stretches out into Lough Leane. Green colored pools testify to thousands of years of copper mining.

The view of Lough Leane and its mountains from Ross Island is magnificent, but the best way to see the area is from the water. Two **waterbus services,** Pride of the Lakes (☎ 32638) and Lily of Killarney (☎ 31068), leave from behind the castle for lake cruises (5-6 per day in summer, £5). You can hire rowboats by the castle (£2 per hr.), or take a **motorboat trip** (☎ 34351) to Innisfallen Island (£3), the Meeting of the Waters through Lough Leane and Muckross Lake (£5), or the Gap of Dunloe through Lough Leane, Muckross Lake, and Upper Lake (£7.50, £10 return). Bringing your bike by boat to the Gap saves time.

On Innisfallen Island sit the stoic remains of **Innisfallen Abbey,** founded by St. Finian the Leper around AD 600. The abbey was eventually transformed into a university during the Middle Ages. The *Annals of Innisfallen,* now entombed at Oxford, recount world and Irish history. The annals were written in Irish and Latin by 39 monastic scribes and supposedly finished in 1326. At the abbey's center is a yew tree; yew and oak groves were sacred to the Druids, so abbeys were often built among and around them. The separate Augustinian abbey is so ruined it's barely recognizable.

MUCKROSS AND THE MEETING OF THE WATERS

The remains of **Muckross Abbey,** built in 1448, lie 3 mi. south of Killarney on Kenmare Rd. Cromwell tried to burn it down, but enough still stands to demonstrate the grace of the part-Norman, part-Gothic cloisters. The abbey's grounds contain a modern graveyard filled with expired locals and lively tourists. (Always open. Free.) From the abbey, signs direct you to **Muckross House,** a massive 19th-century manor whose garden blooms brilliantly in early summer. The grand and proper house, completed in 1843, reeks of aristocracy and commands a regal view of the lakes and mountains. Its elaborate furnishings and decorations include justifiably angry-looking deer mounted on the walls. Upon first visiting Muckross House, the philosopher George Berkeley proclaimed: "Another Louis XIV may make another Versailles, but only the hand of the Deity can make another Muckross." (☎ 31440. Open daily July-Aug. 9am-7pm; Sept.-June 9am-6pm. House and farms each £3.80, students £1.60; joint tickets £5.50, students £2.75.) Outside the house lie the **Muckross Traditional Farms,** a living history museum designed to recreate rural life in early 20th-century Kerry. Whip up traditional Kerry dishes or crafts in the farm's classes or just lounge on the expansive lawns.

A path leads along the water from Muckross House towards the 60 ft. drop of **Torc Waterfall.** Well worth braving piles of horse manure, the waterfall is also a starting point for several short trails along **Ford Mountain.** Walks along the moss-jacketed trees afford some of Killarney's best views. In the opposite direction from Muckross House, it's a 2 mi. stroll to the **Meeting of the Waters;** walk straight down the front lawn and follow the signs. The paved path is nice, while the dirt trail through the **Yew Woods** is more secluded and not accessible to bikes. **The Meeting of the Waters** is a quiet sight where channels connecting Upper Lough introduce themselves to Middle Lough, which then gives a watery handshake to Lower Lough. The weary, however, will be more happy at meeting a cold drink and sandwich at **Dinis Cottage**. (☎ 31954. Open mid-May-Sept. daily 10:30am-6pm.)

There's no direct route from the Muckross sights to Ross Castle; those wishing to do both in one day have to go back through Killarney, for a total trip of 10 mi.

GAP OF DUNLOE

A pilgrimage to the Gap of Dunloe guarantees misty mountain vistas and significant caloric expenditure. There are plenty of organized trips to the Gap that can be booked from the Killarney tourist office. These trips, designed to be combination walking tour and boat trip, shuttle visitors to the foot of the Gap, effectively cutting the 7 mi. from Killarney. (Around £13.) Foresighted travelers will pack a lunch, though a warm meal or a cold pint may be hard to resist. After walking over the Gap and down to **Lord Brandon's Cottage,** trippers pause for a bite (sandwiches £2-3.50) and meet a boat, which takes them across the lake to **Ross Castle**. (Open June-Sept. daily 9am-6pm.) A bus returns them to Killarney. Walking the Gap in this direction, however, is a trek up the long side of the mountain. It is far better, and potentially less expensive, to attack the Gap by bike from the opposite direction. Bring your bike on the **motorboat** trip to the head of the Gap from Ross Castle (£7, book ahead at the tourist office, bikes permitted on board). From Lord Brandon's Cottage on the Gap, turn left over the stone bridge and continue for about 2 mi. to the hostel and church. A right turn up a road with hairpin turns will bring you to the top of the Gap a breathtaking 1½ mi. later. Beyond is a well-deserved 7 mi. downhill coast through the park's most magical scenery.

At the foot of the Gap, you'll pass **Kate Kearney's Cottage**. Kearney was an independent mountain-dwelling woman famous for brewing and serving a near-poisonous *poitín*. Now her former home is a pub and restaurant that sucks in droves of tourists. (☎ 44116. Open daily 9am-11pm; restaurant open until 9pm. Occasional live trad.) The 8 mi. ride back to Killarney passes the entirely ruined **Dunloe Castle,** an Anglo-Norman stronghold demolished by Cromwell's armies. Bear right after Kate's, turn left on the road to Fossa, and turn right on Killorglin Rd. There is also a set of *ogham* stones from about AD 300 (see **History of the Irish Language**, p. 22).

RING OF KERRY

The Southwest's most celebrated peninsula holds picturesque villages, fabled ancient forts, religious monuments, and rough romantic scenery often perceived as representative of Ireland itself. The majestic views of the Iveragh Peninsula rarely disappoint the droves of tourists who cruise through the region in private buses with tour guides. Greater rewards await travelers who take the time to explore the rugged landscape on foot or by bike. A lucky few spend weeks on the peninsula soaking up the sea spray and grand views that tour buses can't access.

The term "Ring of Kerry" is generally used to describe the entire Iveragh Peninsula, but it more correctly refers to a set of roads: N71 from Kenmare to Killarney, R562 from Killarney to Killorglin, and the long loop of N70 west and back to Kenmare. If you don't like the prepackaged private bus tours based out of Killarney, **Bus Éireann** runs a regular summer circuit through all the major towns on the Ring (2 per day), allowing you to get off anywhere and anytime you like. Riders have the option of paying the round-trip fare, getting off the first bus at a suitable spot, and then using the same ticket on a later bus, as long as it's all done in one day. Buses travel around the Ring counterclockwise, from Killarney to Killorglin, west along Dingle Bay, east along Kenmare River, and north from Kenmare back to Killarney. In summer, other buses also travel clockwise from Waterville back to Killarney (2 per day). Bikers may find themselves jammed between buses and cliffs on the narrow roads, though traffic can often be avoided by doing the Ring clockwise. Additionally, cycling clockwise faces views, rather than leaving them behind. A new bike route, which avoids nearly 70% of the main roads and has better views, is signposted. Elevation maps are available. Drivers are forced to choose between lurching behind large tour buses or meeting them face-to-face on narrow roads.

The Ring of Kerry traditionally commences in Killorglin. If you are traveling clockwise around the Ring on N70, stop at the **Quarry in Kells** (☎ 77601), a restaurant, craft shop, and convenience store with magnificent views. The shop is particularly inviting to haggard bikers cycling against hurricane-like winds. (Open Easter-Oct. daily 10am-5:30pm.)

KILLORGLIN ☎066

Killorglin sits placidly beside the river Laune in the shadow of Iveragh's mountain spine, 13 mi. west of Killarney. Tourists pass through on their way to more spectacular scenery further west. Killorglin makes up for what it lacks in sights with festivities dedicated to he-goats. In mid-August, the streets fill up for the riotous **Puck Fair,** a celebration of the crowning of a particularly virile goat as King Puck. Pubs stay open until 3am, then close for an hour or so to allow publicans to rest their pint-pulling arms. Be forewarned that the town's hostel and B&Bs often book up as early as a year in advance of the revelry. During the rest of the year, residents entertain the Ring crowd. Sights are generally a few miles from town and best reached by car or bike.

GETTING THERE AND PRACTICAL INFORMATION. Killorglin's **Main St.** runs uphill from the water and widens to form **The Square.** At the top of The Square to the right, **Upper Bridge St.** climbs to the tourist office at the intersection of **Iveragh Rd.** The Ring of Kerry **bus** stops in Killorglin just past the tourist office and goes to **Cahersiveen** (50min., £5), **Waterville** (1¼hr., £5.90), and **Sneem** (3hr.) June-Sept. 2 per day. The eastbound Cahersiveen bus goes more directly to **Killarney** (July-Aug. M-Sa 2-4 per day, Sept.-June M-Sa 1 per day). The spiffy, octagonal **tourist office** hands out much information. (☎ 976 1451. Open May-Sept. M-F 9:30am-5:30pm, Sa 9am-6pm, Su 10am-3pm.) **AIB** is at the corner of Main St. and New Line Rd. (☎ 976 1134. Open M and W-F 10am-4pm, Tu 10am-5pm. **ATM.**) **O'Shea's** on Main St. **rents bikes.** (☎ 976 1919. £7.50 per day, £40 per week. Open M-Sa 9am-6pm.) Clean up at **Starlite Cleaners,** Langford St., to the left from the top of The Square. (☎ 976 1296. £6 per load. Open M-Tu and Th-Sa 9:30am-6pm, W 9:30am-1pm.) Get free **Internet access** with a £2 card at the **library** on Iveragh Rd. beside the tourist office. (Open Tu-Sa 10:30am-1:30pm and 2:30-5:30pm.) The **post office** is on Iveragh Rd. (☎ 976 1101. Open M-F 9am-1pm and 2-5:30pm, Sa 9am-1pm.)

ACCOMMODATIONS, FOOD, AND PUBS. Laune Valley Farm Hostel **(IHH),** 1½ mi. from town off Tralee Rd., is bright and bucolic and hosts a local population of cows, chickens, dogs, and ducks—save your table scraps. Fresh milk and eggs from the farm are for sale. (☎ 976 1488. Wheelchair accessible. 8-bed dorms £8; doubles £20, with bath £25. **Camping** £3 per person.) **Orglan House,** a three-minute walk from town on Killarney Rd., has grand views from immaculate rooms and relieves you from brown bread delirium with its delicious, individually tailored breakfasts. (☎ 976 1540. £17-19 per person.) Pleasant **Laune Bridge House** is a few doors down from Orglan. (☎ 976 1161. £18-25 per person.) Tent up at **West's Caravan and Camping Park,** 1 mi. east of town on Killarney Rd. (☎ 976 1240. Showers 50p. Laundry £4. Open Easter-late Oct. July 9-Aug. 20 £3.50, Aug. 21-July 8 £3.)

Fortify yourself at **Bunker's,** a red-faced restaurant and take-away across from the tourist office. (☎ 976 1381. Open daily 9:30am-11pm.) Their regal purple pub lies next door, where occasional live music plays. Across from the tourist office, the **Far East** fries up elegant Chinese meals. (☎ 976 2588. Meals £7.50-9.50; take-away £5-6. Open daily 4:30pm-12:30am.) Budget food comes at the expense of ambiance at the **Starlite Diner,** The Square. Take your food upstairs for a more dignified dining experience. (☎ 976 1296. Burgers £3.50; all-day breakfast £4. Open daily 9:30am-11pm.) Young locals meet their Guinness needs at **Old Forge**, Main St., a lively stone pub. (☎ 976 1231. Trad M-W, occasional disco nights.) An older, more subdued crowd watches football at the **Laune Bar**, Lower Main St., on the water. The Laune Rangers football club began here in 1888. (☎ 976 1158. Th night trad.) DJs and cocktails lure a young mob to **The Shamrock**, Main St. (☎ 976 2277).

SIGHTS. Killorglin hides its only major sight in **The Basement Museum**, down Mill Rd. past the church. The museum's exhibits focus on the Puck Fair and circus visits. (☎ 976 1353. Sporadic hours, call ahead.) Five miles from town off Killarney Rd. sits the 16th-century **Ballymalis Castle** on the banks of the Laune in view of Macgillycuddy's Reeks. **Cromane Beach** lies 4 mi. west of town; follow New Line Rd., which branches off Main St. south of The Square. **Cappanalea Outdoor Education Centre**, 7 mi. southwest of Killorglin off the Ring of Kerry Rd., offers **canoeing, rock-climbing, windsurfing, sailing, hill walking,** and **fishing**. (☎ 976 9244. Open daily 10am-5pm. Book a few days in advance. £10 per half-day, £18.50 per day.)

CAHERSIVEEN ☎066

Best known in Ireland as the birthplace of patriot Daniel O'Connell (see **Rebellion, Reunion, Reaction,** p. 13), even those immune to history lessons will enjoy Cahersiveen's (CARS-veen) coastal location. Its two hostels are excellent bases for exploring the nearby beach and historical sites, or for longer excursions to Valentia Island or the Skelligs. This relaxed stop on the Ring still has no shortage of nightlife—Cahersiveen has 30 pubs, and once had 52 to its name.

GETTING THERE AND PRACTICAL INFORMATION. The Ring of Kerry **bus** stops in front of Banks Store on Main St. (June-Sept. 2 per day) and continues on to **Waterville** (25min., £2.70), **Caherdaniel** (1½hr., £3.10), **Sneem** (2hr., £6.30), and **Killarney** (2½hr., £9). One route heads directly east to **Killarney** (M-Sa 1-2 per day). Cahersiveen's **tourist office** is in former barracks on the road to Ballycarbery Castle. (☎ 947 2589. Open May to mid-Sept. M-F 10am-1pm, 2:15-6pm.) The **Old Oratory** craftshop, on Main St., is another source of information. (☎ 947 2996. Open June-Sept. M-Sa 10am-7pm; July-Aug. also open Su 11am-4pm.) Main St. is home to an **AIB** with an **ATM**. (☎ 947 2022. Open M 10am-5pm, Tu-F 10am-3pm.) **Casey's**, Main St., **rents bikes.** (☎ 947 2474. £7 per day, £35 per week; helmet and lock included. Open daily 9am-6pm.) **Internet access** is free (with a £2 card) at the **library** on Main St. (Open Tu-Sa 10:30am-1:30pm, 2:30-5pm.) The **post office** is a final stop on Main St. (☎ 947 2010. Open M-F 9:30am-1pm and 2-5:30pm, Sa 9:30am-1pm.)

ACCOMMODATIONS, FOOD, AND PUBS. The **Sive Hostel (IHH)**, 15 East End, Main St., has a welcoming and well-informed staff, comfortable beds, and a third-floor balcony that overlooks the castle across the river. (☎ 947 2717. Sheets 50p. Wash and dry £4. 4- to 8-bed dorms £8; doubles £20-25. **Camping** £5 per person.) Behind its charming bay window and flowerpot facade, **Mortimer's Hostel**, Main St., competes with the Sive in friendliness. Mortimer's features a large, comfortable common room and a great garden. (☎ 947 2338. Dorms £7.) Mortimer himself is unsurpassed in local knowledge. He also runs the **Mannix Point Caravan and Camping Park**, located at the west end of town. One of the best campsites in the country, the site adjoins a waterfront nature reserve and faces across the water toward the romantic ruins of Ballycarbery Castle. Mannix Point's common area comes complete with a turf fire. (☎ 947 2806. Open mid-Mar. to mid-Oct. Kitchen. Free showers. £4 per person.)

You'll find the juiciest steaks at **QC's Chargrill Bar & Restaurant**, Main St. The colorful, modern restaurant also specializes in seafood and is home to **Ireland's first indoor barbecue**, imported from Spain. (☎ 947 2244. Lunch £5-9, dinner £12-16. Open daily 11:45am-midnight.) The casual **Cupan Éile**, Main St., meets all sandwich needs (£1.60-3.50) and cooks a filling breakfast. (☎ 947 3200. £3.75-4, vegetarian option.) Seek out hearty pub grub at **The Town House,** Main St., with most meals £5-9. (☎ 947 2531. Open M-Sa 12:30-8:30pm, Su 12:30-8:30pm.)

Cahersiveen's long Main St. still has several pubs of the early 20th century variety: these establishments are both watering holes and the proprietor's "main" business, whether it be general store, blacksmith, leather shop, or farm goods retail. The **Anchor Bar** (☎ 947 2049), toward the west end of Main St., sells Guinness alongside fishing tackle. Don't come before 10pm, and when you do, take your drink into the kitchen for friendly conversation. **The Shebeen** (☎ 947 2361) has trad nearly every night in the summer. Modernity has hit **Fertha Bar** (☎ 947 2023) as trendy rock bands frequently appear on weekends. Locals speak lovingly of **Sceilig Rock** (☎ 947 2305), where pop and trad take turns shaking the wooden floor. **Mike Murt's** (☎ 947 2396) brims with Irish character. Prepare to tell your life story to the entire pint-clutching ensemble. For heavenly mischief, head to **The Harp Nightclub,** Main St. (☎ 947 2436. Open F-Sa and some Su in summer until 3am. Cover £4.)

SIGHTS. **O'Connell's Church** in town is the only one in Ireland named for a layperson. "The Liberator" and other aspects of Irish history are celebrated at the **Old Barracks Heritage Centre,** in the tourist office. (☎ 947 2589. Open May to mid-Sept. M-Sa 10am-6pm, Su 1-6pm. £3, students £2.50.) Though the center's exhibits are well-presented, the appearance of the building will hold your interest longer. Its bizarre architecture inspired a local rumor that confused officials had accidentally built a colonial outpost, while a proper barracks was erected somewhere in India. Across the bridge past the barracks, a wealth of fortifications huddle together. Turn left past the bridge, then left off the Main Rd. to reach the ruins of the 15th-century **Ballycarbery Castle,** once held by O'Connell's ancestors. Two hundred yards past the castle turnoff, two of Ireland's best-preserved stone forts spread over a small stretch of land. You can walk atop the 10 ft.-thick walls of **Cahergall Fort,** or visit the small stone dwellings of **Leacanabuaile Fort.** A few minutes' walk beyond the second fort is **Cuas Crom Beach,** known as a great swimming spot in the area. If you continue on past the turnoff to Cuas Crom and take the next left, you'll arrive at **White Strand Beach,** another popular swimming area. The first weekend in August, Cahersiveen hosts the **Celtic Music Weekend,** featuring street entertainment, fireworks, pub sessions, and numerous free concerts.

VALENTIA ISLAND

Shady country roads thread across Valentia Island, linking beehive huts, ogham stones, and small ruins. The island's stupendous views of the mountainous mainland are reason enough to come to Ireland. Bridge and ferry connections to the mainland are at opposite ends of the island; regardless of which route you choose, be sure to bring along your bike. The first transatlantic telegraph cable connected Valentia to Newfoundland.

GETTING THERE AND PRACTICAL INFORMATION. The comically short **car ferry** trip departs from **Reenard Point,** 3 mi. west of Cahersiveen off the Ring of Kerry Rd. Passing cars make the walk to the Point slightly difficult; a taxi from Cahersiveen runs about £4. The ferry drops you off at **Knightstown,** the island's population center. (Ferries depart every 10min. daily 8:15am-7:30pm. Cars £5 return, pedestrians £1.50, cyclists £3.) The bridge connecting Valentia to the mainland starts at **Portmagee,** 10 mi. west of Cahersiveen. To get to Portmagee, go south from Cahersiveen or north from Waterville (a longer trip), then west on R565. Hitching to Portmagee is difficult and not recommended per *Let's Go*. Enthusiastic bikers can follow the "loop" (Waterville to Ballinskelligs, Portmagee to Knightstown to Cahersiveen). Serious site-seekers can get free maps from the Cahersiveen **tourist office.**

ACCOMMODATIONS AND FOOD. Should you choose to spend the night on Valentia, the island's best budget accommodations can be found at **Coombe Bank House.** Follow the main road and turn right just before the Pitch & Putt. This

YOUR IRISH ANCESTORS

Your grandparents might not have come from Clonakilty, but if you go back far enough, you've probably got an Irish relative. In 1992 Swiss geologist Ivan Stossel discovered a track of small footprints on the rocky shore of Valentia Island. After analyzing layers of volcanic ash in the groove-like prints, scientists concluded that they were made 385 million years ago, making them the oldest fossilized footprints in the Northern Hemisphere. The prints are believed to be those of a "Devonian tetrapod," a four-legged creature that predates the dinosaurs. The prints are currently unmarked and unprotected, although the government is taking steps to preserve this and other important archaeological sites. For now, locals can direct you to the obscure prints.

---

hostel and B&B occupies a grand stone house with a fine interior. (☎ 947 6111. Free laundry. Dorms £8, continental breakfast £2; B&B £18-20.) One-and-a-half miles down the main road from Knightstown lies tiny **Chapeltown,** home to the **Ring Lyne Hostel,** which has basic double and triple rooms above a pub. (☎ 947 6103. £8.50-10 per person.) The large **Royal Pier Hostel (IHH)** in Knightstown once hosted Queen Victoria; with comfy beds, it still maintains some grandeur. (☎ 947 6144. Wash and dry £8. 8-bed dorms £8.50; singles £10; doubles £20; B&B £20.) A few blocks up the hill from the pier, **Altazamuth House** has basic, pretty rooms and a sunny breakfast room. (☎ 947 6300. £17-18 per person.) **Spring Acre,** across from the pier, has bedrooms with great bathrooms and waterfront views. (☎ 947 6141. £18.) **Boston's,** on the main road out of Knightstown, has quality pub grub. (☎ 947 6140. Seafood salads £5.50, sandwiches £3.50-4.95; food served daily 11am-9pm.)

SIGHTS. The road from town to the **old slate quarry** offers some of Valentia's best views across Dingle Bay. Slate from the massive quarry roofed the Paris Opera House and the British Parliament; the hollowed-out cliffside now houses a "sacred grotto." At the opposite end of the island, you can hike up to the ruins of a Napoleonic lookout tower with views to the Skelligs at **Bray Head.** On the way there from Knightstown, you'll pass the turnoff for **Glanleam Subtropical Gardens,** which feature such luminaries as the 50 ft. tall Chilean Fire Bush. (☎ 947 6176. Open daily mid-Sept. to May 11am-5pm. £2.50, students £2.)

THE SKELLIG ROCKS

The Skellig Rocks are a stunning mass of natural rubble about 8 mi. off the shore of the Iveragh Peninsula. As your boat bounces by **Little Skellig,** the rock pinnacles appear to be snow-capped; increased proximity reveals that the peaks are actually covered with 22,000 crooning, nest-wetting gannets. Boats dock at the larger **Skellig Michael.** Climb the vertigo-inducing 650 steps past puffins, kittiwakes, gannets, and petrels to reach a **monastery.** Sixth-century Christian monks carved out an austere community along the craggy faces of the 714 ft. high rock. Their beehive-like dwellings are still intact and fascinatingly explained by guides from the Irish heritage service, though the dark interiors and stark surroundings speak for themselves of the monks' spiritual lives. There is no toilet or shelter on the rock, but you're welcome to picnic on the steep faces that George Bernard Shaw declared "not after the fashion of this world."

The fantastic and stomach-churning **ferry voyage** takes 45 to 90 minutes, depending on conditions, point of departure, and boat. Both hostels and the campsite in Cahersiveen will arrange trips that include a ride to the dock for £20. Joe Roddy (☎ 947 4268) and Sean Feehan (☎ 947 9182) depart from **Ballinskelligs** (£20), and Michael O'Sullivan (☎ 947 4255) and Mr. Casey (☎ 947 2437) leave from **Portmagee** (£20). Seanie Murphy picks up passengers in Reenard and Portmagee (☎ 947 6214). Roddy and O'Sullivan will give you a lift from **Waterville,** and Casey will pick you up from your hostel in **Cahersiveen.** The boats run mid-March to October, depending on the weather; phone ahead for reservations and to confirm that the boats are operating. They usually leave between 9:30am and noon and land for at least two hours on the island. The grass-roofed **Skellig Experience** visitors center is just across the Portmagee Bridge on Valentia Island. Videos and models engulf visitors in virtual Skellig, and for an extra (steep) charge you can sail from the center to the islands themselves, although the boats do not dock. The video is a relaxing diversion, provided you ignore the dramatic rhetorical questions. (☎ 947 6306. Open daily Apr.-Sept. 9:30am-6pm. £3, with cruise £15; students £2.70, £13.50.)

WATERVILLE ☎066

The main strip of Waterville is wedged between the waters of Lough Cussane and crashing Atlantic waves. Lined with hotels built for wealthy English vacationers—Charlie Chaplin among them—Waterville's tourist traffic comes mostly from tour bus groups discharged for a seaside lunch before rumbling on to more sensational destinations. The meditative traveler is left to quietly walk along the shore.

GETTING THERE AND PRACTICAL INFORMATION. The Ring of Kerry **bus** stops in Waterville in front of the Bay View Hotel on Main St. (June-Sept. 2 per day), with service to **Caherdaniel** (20min., £2.20), **Sneem** (50min., £4.30), and **Killarney** (2hr., £8.60). **Bus Éireann** travels to **Cahersiveen** once per day. The **tourist office** soaks up sea spray across from the Butler Arms Hotel on the beach. (☎ 947 4646. Open June-Sept. daily 9am-6pm.) The **post office** is located across from the tourist office. (☎ 947 4147. Open M-F 9am-5:30pm, Sa 9am-1pm.)

ACCOMMODATIONS, FOOD, AND PUBS. Firm mattress fanatics will rejoice in the unyielding beds at **Peter's Place** (☎ 947 4608). The oceanside location and brown bread more than compensate for the cramped quarters. Peter himself is an energetic and friendly host, as well as a savvy sheep-shearing expert. (Sept.-May 6-bed dorms £7.50, June-Aug. £8. **Camping** £3.50.) A mile out of town on the Cahersiveen road, campers get an ocean view at **Waterville Caravan and Camping Park**. (☎ 947 4191. Showers 50p. Tents £7-8.50.) If you're tracking down more luxurious accommodations, aim for **The Huntsman** next to the tourist office, with pleasant rooms above a pub. (☎ 947 4124. Twins £36-44.)

An Corcán, across from the Butler Arms Hotel, feeds the weary affordable meals. (☎ 947 4711. Breakfast £3-5, lunch and dinner entrees £4-10. Open daily 8am-9:30pm.) Up the hill from the tourist office, the **Beach Cove Cafe** offers take-away cuisine. This quasi-fast-food joint nearly overlooks your wallet. (☎ 947 4733. Entrees £2-4. Open M-Th 10am-10pm, F-Su 9:30am-1am.) The **Lobster Bar and Restaurant**, Main St., is worth a visit just to see the icon outside—a giant lobster clutching a Guinness—but stay for the food. (☎ 947 4629. Seafood-sprinkled pub grub around £5.) The Lobster stays lively into the evening, with a pool table, trad four nights a week and a disco on Saturday nights. Gaelic football legend Mick O'Dwyer lends his name to **O'Dwyer's: The Villa Restaurant & Pub** at the Strand Hotel down the road. Mick also runs the **Piper 2000** nightclub in the back of his pub. (Open W and Sa-Su. Cover £4.) **The Bay View Hotel** (☎ 947 4122) throws down a Friday night disco (cover £4); either of its two bars is good for drinking. **The Fishermen's Bar** (☎ 947 4144) poured pints for Charlie Chaplin.

SIGHTS. Lough Currane's waters lie about 2 mi. inland from town; follow the lake road with the ocean to your right and turn left, or just head inland along smaller roads. Locals claim that a submerged castle can be seen in times of low water, but visitors are more likely to see the ruins of a monastery on Church Island. **Waterville Boats** (☎ 947 2455), based at the Lobster Bar, rents motorboats (£25 per day) and fishing gear (rods £5 per day).

The Irish-speaking hamlet of **Ballinskelligs** between Waterville and Bolus Head isn't worth a special trip, but if you're there to catch a Skellig-bound boat, check out the ruins of **Ballinskelligs Monastery**, near the pier. It was here that the monks moved from their lofty heights after 11th-century storms made journeys to the island increasingly treacherous. The quiet **Prior House Youth Hostel (An Óige/HI)** overlooks the bay and offers basic hostel accommodations. (☎ 947 9229. Dorms £7. Open Apr.-Oct.) Two miles south of Ballinskelligs, **Bolus Head** affords great views of the Skelligs and bay on clear days.

CAHERDANIEL ☎066

There's delightfully little in the village of Caherdaniel to attract the Ring's droves of travel coaches, but the hamlet (two pubs, a grocer, a restaurant, and a take-away) has the advantage of proximity to one of Ireland's best beaches and one of the region's finest hostels. Derrynane Strand, 2 mi. of gorgeous beach ringed by sparkling dunes, is 1½ mi. from Caherdaniel in Derrynane National Park.

GETTING THERE AND PRACTICAL INFORMATION. The **bus** stops in Caherdaniel twice a day at the junction of the Ring of Kerry Rd. and Main St., picking up passengers for **Sneem** (30min., June-Sept. 2 per day, £2.90) and **Killarney** (1½hr., June-Sept. 2 per day, £7.30). The **tourist office** is 1 mi. east of town at the Wave Crest Camping Park. (Open May-Sept. daily 8am-10pm.) Information is also dispensed at **Mathius Adams Junk Shop** in the town center. (☎ 947 5167. Open daily 10am-5pm.)

ACCOMMODATIONS, FOOD, AND PUBS. Guests have the run of the house at **The Travellers' Rest Hostel.** A relaxed sitting room with a fireplace and small dorms make the house look and feel more like a B&B. (☎ 947 5175. Continental breakfast £3. 4- to 6-bed dorms £8.50; doubles £20.) The **Caherdaniel Village Hostel,** across the street from Skellig Aquatics, resides in the first English police building to be deserted in the Civil War (see p. 17). The hostel offers basic comforts and a sky-lit common room. The managers can also arrange climbing trips and diving holidays; see Skellig Aquatics listing for rates. (☎ 947 5277. Open Mar.-Nov. 8-bed dorms £8.) A mile west of town on the Ring of Kerry road is the seven-bed **Carrigbeg Hostel,** which features views of the surrounding hills and bay; call for pick-up from Caherdaniel. (☎ 947 5229. Laundry £3.50. 3-bed dorms £7.50-8.50; doubles £17-18.) Campers lodge 1 mi. east of town on the Ring of Kerry road at **Wave Crest Camping Park,** overlooking the beach. The well-stocked shop (open 8am-10pm) and self-service laundry (£4 per load) are handy. (☎ 947 5188. Showers 50p. Open mid-Mar. to Oct. and off-season by arrangement. £3.25 per person.)

The **Courthouse Cafe,** which serves the most affordable food in town, has both sit-down and take-away menus. (☎ 947 5005. Sandwiches under £2. Open daily 5-11:30pm.) **Freddy's Bar** (☎ 947 5400) sells groceries and serves pints to locals. The **Blind Piper** (☎ 947 5126) is a popular local meeting place with outdoor tables by a stream. Occasional folk and trad drown out the bubbling water.

SIGHTS. Derrynane House, sign-posted just up from the beach, was the residence of Irish patriot Daniel "The Liberator" O'Connell, who won Catholic representation in Parliament in 1829 (see **Rebellion, Union, Reaction,** p. 13). Inside the house, you can check out the dueling pistol that O'Connell used to kill challenger John d'Esterre, as well as the black glove he wore to church for years afterwards to mourn his victim. The half-hour film on O'Connell presents an engrossing and refreshingly textured image of the acerbic barrister. A few trails lead from the house through dunes and gardens. A stylized picture of the house, alongside a portrait of its most famous resident, is on the £20 note. (☎ 947 5113. Open May-Sept. M-Sa 9am-6pm, Su 11am-7pm; Apr. and Oct. Tu-Su 1-5pm; Nov.-Mar. Sa-Su 1-5pm. Last admission 45min. before closing. £2, students and children £1.)

If you're up to 6 mi. of uphill hiking or pedaling, the pre-Christian **Staigue Fort,** west of town, will make you feel tall and powerful. The largest stone fort in Ireland, Staigue Fort stands high on a hill overlooking the sea, and protects you from Pictish invaders. Skip the **heritage center** devoted to the fort, which runs the danger of being an over-hyped tourist attraction. (☎ 947 5288. Fort always open. Free. Heritage center open Easter-Oct. daily 10am-10pm. £2, students £1.50.)

For a close look at undersea life, contact **Skellig Aquatics** (☎ 947 5277; half-day dive £30). **Derrynane Sea Sports** handles the watersporting in this area. (☎ 947 5266. **Sailing** £15 per hr., **windsurfing** £8 per hr., **waterskiing** £12 per hr.)

SNEEM ☎ 064

Tourists make Sneem their first or last stop along the Ring, and the town is prepared to receive them. Canned Irish music rolls out of the Irish music shop on the South Square, amongst the clutter of postcard stands. Two public squares and a unique sculpture collection make Sneem a browser's paradise.

GETTING THERE AND PRACTICAL INFORMATION. The Ring of Kerry **bus** travels to **Killarney** via **Kenmare** (1hr., June-Sept. 2 per day, £5.50). Sneem's **tourist information center** is housed in the Joli Coeur Shop near the bus stop. (☎ 45270. Open daily mid-Mar. to Nov. 10:30am-5:30pm.) Helpful advice is also dispensed at the **post office** a few doors down. (☎ 45110. Open M-F 9am-1pm, 2-5:30pm, Sa 9am-1pm.) Bike rental is available at **M. Burns' Bike Hire**, on The North Sq. (☎ 45140. £7 per day, £40 per week. Open M-Sa 9:30am-7pm.) Excellent.

ACCOMMODATIONS, FOOD, AND PUBS. The **Harbour View Hostel**, a quarter-mile from town on Kenmare Rd., used to be a motel and still looks like one, with ranch-style units in a gravel lot. The dorms are crowded and are walk-throughs. (☎ 45276. Sheets 50p. Laundry £5. 4-bed dorms £8; singles £15; doubles or twins £20. Camping £5.) Sneem's oldest and arguably nicest B&B is **The Bank House**, North Sq. The friendly owners giggle with enthusiasm for the region. (☎ 45226; www.sneem.com/bankhouse.html. Open Mar.-Nov. £17-19 per person.) **Old Convent House**, Pier Rd., a right off The South Sq. just after Erin Co. Knitwear, is an old stone house with equally gorgeous mountain and water views. (☎ 45181. Laundry £4. £20 per person.) Near the town center, **Goosey Island Campsite** is ideal for sculpture park exploration and also budget accommodation. (☎ 45577. Showers 50p. **Internet access** £5 per hr. Open Apr. to mid-Oct. £4 per person. Bunks £7.)

You may want to change out of your sweaty clothes for **The Sacre Coeur**, North Square. Elegant steak, seafood and chicken dishes come for £6-13. (☎ 45186. Open Easter-Oct. M-Sa 5:30-9:30pm, Su 12:30-2:30pm.) Run through and to the **Riverain Restaurant** for vegetarian meals and a view of the river. (☎ 45245. Lunches £2-6, most evening meals £7-9. Open daily May-Aug. 12:30-4 and 5-9:30pm.) Massive pub meals are served at **The Blue Bull** (☎ 45382), by the post office. Stick around for ballad sessions on Friday or Saturday nights. On the north side of town, **The Village Kitchen** serves seafood and sandwiches in a comfortable cafe setting. (☎ 45281. Sandwiches under £2; entrees £5-6.50. Open 9:30am-6pm.) Gallop down to the **Hungry Knight** for cheap fish and chips or a game of pool with young Sneemers. (☎ 45237. Open June-Sept. M-Sa 11am-3:30am.) At the **Fisherman's Knot** (☎ 45224), across the bridge on Caherdaniel Rd., locals tap their toes to trad a few nights a week. **O'Shea's**, North Square, reverberates with frequent, old-fashioned sessions.

SIGHTS. When Charles de Gaulle visited Sneem in 1969, the town was so honored that its people erected a monument to commemorate the event: a bronze sculpture of de Gaulle's head mounted on a boulder of local stone. Thus, a tradition was born. Today, Sneem's **sculpture park** celebrates the late President Cearbhaill O'Dalaigh, the Egyptian Goddess Isis, wrestling champ "Crusher" Casey, and the terribly strange set of cave buildings on the banks of the river. It's difficult to decide whether the sculptures or their collective name—"The Way the Fairies Went"—is more bizarre. Pick up the *Sneem Guide* in the tourist office for an abbreviated tour (25p). Jackie O'Shea runs **deep-sea angling** trips from Rossdohan Pier, 5 mi. from town on the Kenmore Rd. (☎ 45369. From £25.)

DINGLE PENINSULA ☎ 066

For decades, the Dingle Peninsula was the under-touristed counterpart to the Ring of Kerry. Word has finally gotten out, and the Killarney and Ring of Kerry tourist blitz has recently begun to encroach upon this scenic, Irish-speaking peninsula. Slieve Mish and the flat farming country of East Dingle are not as convenient for backpackers as Dingle Town, the charming, if increasingly pricey, regional center.

Spectacular cliffs and sweeping beaches rim the Dingle Peninsula, which still remains more congested with ancient sites than tour buses. The films *Ryan's Daughter* and *Far and Away* have taken advantage of these vistas, much to the delight of the natives. A *gaeltacht* to the west of Dingle Town preserves the heritage that local storytellers have kept alive for centuries. Locating a grocery store among Irish signs may be a challenge, but Guinness signs still mark the pubs. Dingle's *bohareens* (side roads) are best explored by bike: the entire western circuit, from Dingle out to Slea Head, up to Ballydavid, and back, is only a daytrip, while the mountainous northern regions are more arduous excursions. The Cloghane/Brandon area in the north remains most free of foreigners; Slea Head, Dunquin, and the Blasket Islands are the most other-worldly spots. Maps available in area tourist offices describe The Dingle Way, a 95 mi. walking trail that circles the peninsula. A Dingle Peninsula website offers more details (www.dingle-peninsula.ie).

While Dingle Town is well-connected to Killarney and Tralee, public transport within the peninsula is scarce. Buses to towns in South Dingle run daily in July and August, but only two or three times a week during the rest of the year. There is no direct bus service to villages north of Dingle Town. For detailed bus information, call the Tralee station (☎ 23566). Summertime hitchers can often get a lift through the Connor Pass, though *Let's Go* vividly disdains hitchhiking in all four seasons.

DINGLE ☎ 066

Though the *craic* in Dingle is still home-grown, increasing armadas of tourists cloy the docks, pubs, and smart pubs of this bayside town. Visitors are indulged with music sessions, fantastic hostels, and the gregarious dolphin, Fungi, who charms the whole town from his permanent residence in Dingle Bay. After scouring the deserted parts of the peninsula for vistas and *ogham* stones, you can return to town in the evening for music and quality time with your publican.

GETTING THERE AND GETTING AROUND

Buses: Buses stop on Ring Rd. by the harbor, behind Garvey's SuperValu. Bus information is available from the Tralee bus station (☎ 712 3566). **Bus Éireann** runs to **Ballydavid** (Tu and F 3 per day, £3.15 return), **Dunquin** and **Ballyferriter** (summer M and Th 4 per day, Tu-W and F-Sa 2 per day; £2.30) and **Tralee** (1¼hr.; June-Sept. 6 per day, Su 3 per day; Oct.-May 6 per day, Su 4 per day; £5.90). June-Sept. additional buses tour the south of the peninsula from Dingle (M-Sa 2 per day).

Bike Rental: Paddy's Bike Shop, Dykegate St. (☎ 915 2311), rents the best bikes in town. £6 per day, £30 per week. Open daily 9am-7pm.

ORIENTATION AND PRACTICAL INFORMATION

Dingle dangles in the middle of the southern coast of Dingle Peninsula. R559 heads east to Killarney and Tralee, and west to Ventry, Dunquin, and Slea Head. A narrow road running north through the Connor Pass leads to Stradbally and Castlegregory. The streets of downtown Dingle approximate a grid pattern. **Strand St.** runs next to the harbor along the marina; **Main St.** is its parallel counterpart further uphill. **The Mall, Dykegate St.,** and **Green St.** connect the two, running perpendicular to the water. On the eastern edge of town, Strand St., The Mall, and **Tralee Rd.** converge in a roundabout.

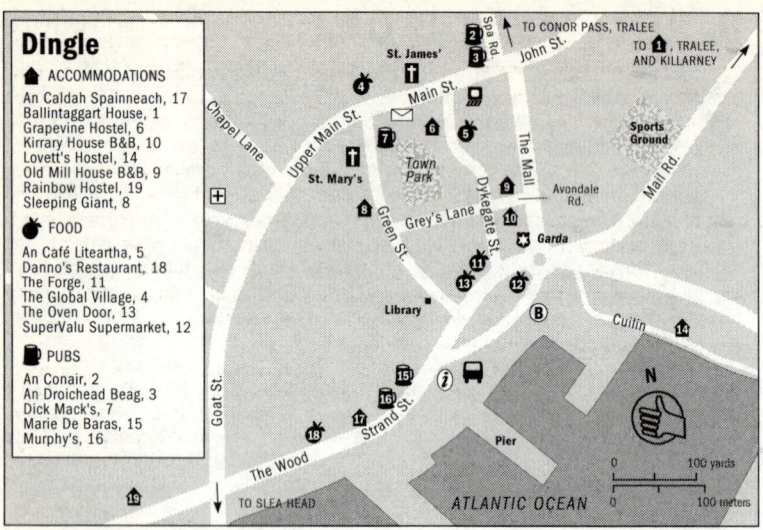

266 ■ DINGLE PENINSULA

Dingle

♦ ACCOMMODATIONS
An Caldah Spainneach, 17
Ballintaggart House, 1
Grapevine Hostel, 6
Kirrary House B&B, 10
Lovett's Hostel, 14
Old Mill House B&B, 9
Rainbow Hostel, 19
Sleeping Giant, 8

🍎 FOOD
An Café Liteartha, 5
Danno's Restaurant, 18
The Forge, 11
The Global Village, 4
The Oven Door, 13
SuperValu Supermarket, 12

🍺 PUBS
An Conair, 2
An Droichead Beag, 3
Dick Mack's, 7
Marie De Baras, 15
Murphy's, 16

Tourist Office: Strand St. (☎ 915 1188). You'll be vying for attention with scores of confused tourists. Open June-Aug. M-Sa 9am-6pm, Su 10am-6pm; Sept.-Oct. and mid-Mar. to May M-Sa 9am-5pm.

Banks: AIB, Main St. (☎ 915 1400). Open M 10am-12:30pm and 1:30-5pm, Tu-F 10am-12:30pm and 1:30-4pm. **Bank of Ireland,** Main St. (☎ 915 1100). Same hours. Both have multi-card tolerant **ATMs.**

Camping Equipment: The Mountain Man, Strand St. (☎ 915 2400). Open daily July-Aug. 9am-9pm, Sept.-June 9am-6pm. No tent rental. Offers 2½hr. bus tours to Connor Pass and Slea Head (£8), and a shuttle to the Blasket ferry (£7), in addition to the very informative *Guide to the Dingle Peninsula*, which includes a walking map (£5).

Laundry: Níolann an Daingin, Green St. (☎ 915 1837), behind El Toro. Wash and dry from £6. Open M-Sa 9am-1pm, 2-5:30pm.

Pharmacy: O'Keefe's Pharmacy Ltd. (☎ 915 1310). Open M-W and F-Sa 9:30am-6pm, Th 9:30am-1pm, Su 9:30am-12:30pm.

Emergency: ☎ 999; no coins required. **Police** *(Garda)*: The Holy Ground (☎ 915 1522).

Post Office: Upper Main St. (☎ 915 1661). Just the place for mailing Fungi postcards. Open M-F 9am-1pm and 2-5:30pm, Sa 9am-1pm.

Internet Access: Dingleweb, Main St. (☎ 915 2478). £1.50 per 15min., £5 per hr. Cheaper rates before noon. Open M-Sa 10am-9pm, Su 2-7pm.

🏠 ACCOMMODATIONS

There are great hostels in Dingle, although some are a long walk from town. Many hostel owners vie for your business as the buses empty. B&Bs along Dykegate and Strand St. and hostels in town tend to fill up fast in the summer; call ahead.

Ballintaggart Hostel (IHH; ☎ 915 1454), a 25min. walk east of town on Tralee Rd. Ballintaggart is set in the grand stone mansion where the Earl of Cork strangled his wife after a poisoning attempt went awry. Her ghost supposedly haunts the enormous bunk rooms, enclosed cobblestone courtyard, and elegant, fire-heated common rooms. Free shuttle to town. Laundry service £4.50. **Bike rental** £7 per day. 8-12-bed dorms £8; 4-bed £10; doubles £30; off-season £1-2 cheaper. **Camping** £4 per person.

Rainbow Hostel (☎ 915 1044; email info@net-rainbow.com; www.net-rainbow.com). Take Strand St. west out of town; 15min. by foot, 3min. by car. Bear right and inland at the corner of Dunquin Rd. The interior decor is interesting, while the beds, bathrooms and kitchens are all clean and spacious. Free lifts to and from town in the rainbow-mobile. **Camping** £4. Laundry £4. **Internet access** £5 per hr. **Bike rental** £6 per day. 6-bed dorms £8; doubles £20.

Grapevine Hostel, Dykegate St. (☎ 915 1434), off Main St. Smack in the middle of town and just a short stagger from Dingle's finest pubs. The friendly folks at the Grapevine welcome you to close but comfy bunk rooms and through the musical common room with cushy chairs. Laundry £4. 4-bed dorms £9.50-10.50; 8-bed dorms £8.50-9.50.

Sleeping Giant, Green St. (☎ 915 2666). Small, well-located house has soft beds and fluffy comforters at decent prices. 4-bed dorms £8; single £14; double £26.

Lovett's Hostel, Cooleen Rd. (☎ 915 1903). Turn opposite the Esso Station past the roundabout, right on the bay. You gotta like this small hostel that perches on the outskirts of town, away from most of the bustle. Dorms £7-8; doubles £18-19; triples £24.

An Caladh Spáinneach (un KULL-uh SPINE-uck; the Spanish Pier), Strand St. (☎ 915 2160). No frills, but reasonable beds and a great waterfront location. Dorms £7-8; doubles £20. Open June-Oct.

Old Mill House, Avondale Rd. (☎ 915 1120; verhoul@iol.ie; www.iol.ie/~verhoul). Off Dykegate St. The comfortable pine beds in this bright house are outdone only by its vivacious owner. You can save a few pounds by passing on breakfast, but the amazing crepes are well worth it. All rooms with bathroom, TV, and hair dryer. Coffee and tea on arrival. Singles £15-22; doubles and triples from £16 per person.

Kirrary House, Avondale Rd. (☎ 915 1606), across from Old Mill House. With good cheer and pride, Mrs. Collins puts guests up in her delightful rooms. Book your archaeological tours here with *Sciuird* Tours, offered by Mr. Collins (see **Sights,** p. 268). **Bike rental** £6 per day. Doubles £40; all rooms with bath.

FOOD

Dingle is home to all sorts of eateries, from gourmet seafood restaurants to doughnut stands. **SuperValu supermarket,** The Holy Ground, stocks a SuperSelection of groceries and juicy tabloids. (☎ 915 1397. Open M-Sa 8am-9pm, Su 9am-6pm.) **An Grianán,** Dykegate St., near the Grapevine Hostel, has crunchy wholefoods and organic vegetables. (☎ 915 1090. Open M-F 9:30am-6pm, Sa 10am-6pm.)

The Oven Door, The Holy Ground (☎ 915 1056), across from SuperValu. Crispy pizzas (£4-7), spectacular sundaes (£3.50), and incredible cakes draw droves to this wood and stone cafe. Open Mar.-Christmas daily 9am-10:30pm.

The Forge, The Holy Ground (☎ 915 2590). This large green-and-red family restaurant serves lunches from £5, and pricier but delightful dinners. Open Mar.-Oct. M, W-Su noon-2:30pm and 6-9:30pm.

Danno's, Strand St. (☎ 915 1855). The railroad theme may send some folks chugging away, but this popular pub can't be beat for hearty burgers and cold pints. Burgers £6-7, other entrees £5-9. Food served M-Sa noon-2:30pm and 6-9pm.

The Global Village, Main St. (☎ 915 2325). Fantastic variety of meals from around the world, including several vegetarian options. Swap travel stories with the owner, who collected many of the recipes himself. Lunch £4-6, most dinners £8-11. Open mid-Mar. to Oct. M-Sa 9:30am-10pm, Su 9am-10pm.

An Café Liteartha, Dykegate St. (☎ 915 2204), across the street from the Grapevine. This cafe and bookstore was one of the first Irish-language cafes in the Republic, and many an Irish *cómbra* can still be heard. Don't bring your full appetite. Open M-F 10am-5:30pm, Sa-Su 11am-5:30pm. Bookstore open until 6pm.

PUBS

Dingle has 52 pubs for 1500 people. Many pubs are beginning to cater to tourists, but the town still produces copious *craic*.

An Droichead Beag (The Small Bridge), Lower Main St. (☎ 915 1723). The most popular pub in town unleashes the best trad around—401 sessions a year. Come early or you'll be left to swim your way to the bar through the packed house.

O'Flaherty's Pub, The Holy Ground (☎ 915 1913), a few doors up from the traffic circle. Trad masters have the pub filled by 9pm.

Murphy's, Strand St. (☎ 915 1450). Nightly ballads boom out of this classic, crowded pub by the marina.

An Conair, off Main St. on Spa Rd. (☎ 915 2011). Lusty Irish singing resonates through the beer garden several nights a week. M night set dancing. Trad W-F starting at 9:30pm, Su 5-7pm.

Marie De Baras, Strand St. (☎ 915 1215), draws a mixed age and largely tourist crowd to hear great folk and trad with a modern twist.

Dick Mack's, Green St. (☎ 915 1960), opposite the church. At "Dick Mack's Bar, Boot Store, and Leather Shop," the proprietor leaps between the bar and his leather-tooling bench. Shoeboxes and whiskey bottles line the walls. Though heavily touristed, the strong local following frequently bursts into song.

SIGHTS

Fungi the Dolphin swam into Dingle Bay one day in 1983 with his mother, and the pair immediately became local celebrities. Dolphins had visited the bay before, but Fungi took to it like a fish to water, cavorting with sailors and swimmers, flirting with TV cameras, and jumping in and out of the water for applause. Mom has gone on to the great tuna can in the sky, but egomaniacal Fungi remains fond of humans. Wetsuited tourists incessantly swarm around him. **Boat trips** to see the dolphin leave from the pier constantly in summer. (Most around £7, free if Fungi is a no-show.) A free alternative is to watch the antics from the shore east of town. To get there, walk two minutes down Tralee Rd., turn right at the Skellig Hotel, and then follow the beach away from town for about 10 minutes. The small beach on the other side of a stone tower is often crowded with Fungi-seekers. Anti-dolphinites can be lured along by the promise of great views on the walk. The best times to see him are 8-10am and 6-8pm. You can rent a **wetsuit** from **Flannery's,** just east of town off Tralee Rd. (☎ 915 1967. £14 per 2hr., £22 overnight.) **Dingle Marine Eco-Tours** (☎ (086) 285 8802) give a broader view of the bay life and cruises past Dunbeg Fort as well. **Deep-sea angling** trips leave daily in the summer. (☎ 915 9947. £20, equipment included.) Perhaps the closest look at sea creatures is available at **Dingle Ocean World,** Strand St. The aquarium is a great option for a rainy day. Observe swimming fish in an underwater tunnel, and pet and prod skates and rays in the touch tank. (☎ 915 2111. Open daily July-Aug. 9am-9:30pm; Apr.-July and Aug.-Sept. 10am-6pm; Oct.-Mar. 10am-5pm. £5, students £4.)

The information office at the Mountain Man sells *The Easy Guide to the Dingle Peninsula* (£5), which details walking tours, cycling tours, and local history, and includes a map. **Sciúird Archaeology tours** take you from the pier on a three-hour whirlwind bus tour of the area's ancient spots. (☎ 915 1606. 2 per day. £8. Book ahead.) Summer festivals periodically bring the carnival to town. There are two **Slea Head Tours,** a two-hour minibus trip highlighting the wonderful scenery of the peninsula and a few of the historic sites. **DJ Tours** (☎ (087) 260 6500 or (087) 250 4767) offers one tour per day with a pick-up at the pier opposite Ocean World. **Moran's Tours** (☎ 915 1155) has at least two tours daily (10am and 2pm) with a pick-up at the Esso station on Strand St. (Both tours £8. Book ahead.) The **Dingle Regatta** hauls in the salty mariners on the third Sunday in August. In early September, the **Dingle Music Festival** lures big-name trad groups and other performers from across the musical spectrum (☎ 915 2477; www.iol.ie/~dingmus).

SLEA HEAD AND DUNQUIN

Glorious **Slea Head** impresses with jagged cliffs and plunging waves. Green hills, interrupted by rough stone walls and occasional sheep, suddenly break off into the foam-flecked sea. *Ryan's Daughter* and parts of *Far and Away* were filmed in these parts, indicative of the scenery's tendency toward the highly dramatic. By far the best way to see Slea Head and Dunquin in a day or less is to bike along the predominantly flat **Slea Head Drive.**

Past Dingle Town toward Slea Head sits the village of **Ventry** (Ceann Trá), home to a sandy beach and the hillside bric-a-brac of **Rahinnane Castle.** While the small ruin is hardly worth a peep, the ■**Celtic and Prehistoric Museum,** farther down the road, is a must-see. The laid-back proprietor will take you on a tour of his astounding collection, ranging from 300-million-year-old sea worm fossils, to Iron Age tools and jewelry, to an electric sheep. Their newest exhibit is a 50,000-year-old woolly mammoth found off the coast of Holland in 1999. The museum's cafe pours cups of coffee (£1) at tables overlooking marshes and the sea. (☎ 915 9841; www.kerryweb.ie. Museum and cafe open daily Apr.-Oct. 10am-5pm, for other months call ahead. £3, children £2.) The Slea Head Drive continues past several Iron Age and early Christian stones and ruins. **Dunbeg Fort** (£1, students 80p) and the less impressive **Fahan Group** (£1) of oratories (beehive-shaped stone huts built by early monks) cluster on hillsides over the cliffs, and are visible for free from the road. Slea Head looks out onto the glorious Blasket Islands. Try to pick out the **Sleeping Giant** from the group of scattered islands. Outstanding exhibits are contained within the ■**Blasket Centre,** just outside of Dunquin on the road to Ballyferriter. Writings and photographs of the Great Blasket authors recreate the lost era of the islands. The museum also shows a sleepy 20 minute film on the islanders and presents exhibits on the past richness and current status of the Irish language. (☎ 915 6444. Open daily July-Aug. 10am-7pm, Easter-June and Sept.-Nov. 10am-6pm. Last admission 45min. before closing. £2.50, students £1.)

Within sight of the castle is the brand-new **Ballybeag Hostel.** The hostel sits on an inland turn just past the beach. Huge beds, soothing sitting rooms, and regular shuttle buses into downtown Dingle make it an ideal shelter for explorers of both Slea Head and Dingle. (☎ 915 9876; email balybeag@iol.ie. **Bike rental** £2.50-5 per day. Laundry £4. 4-bed dorms May-Oct. £9, off-season £7.50.) There's plenty of space on the Head to camp, but in the high season you'll have some neighbors. North of Slea Head, the scattered settlement of **Dunquin** (Dún Chaoin) offers stone houses, a pub, and Irish speakers, but no grocery store. Stock up in Dingle or in Ballyferriter if you're going to stay here or on Great Blasket. **Kruger's,** purportedly the westernmost pub in Europe, features pub grub, spontaneous music sessions, and fantastic views. (☎ 915 6127. Entrees £6-8.) Its adjacent **B&B** has comfortable rooms. (£17 per person.) Along the road to Ballyferriter, **An Óige Hostel (HI)** provides adequate bunk rooms and a window-walled dining room that looks out onto the sea. (☎ 915 6121. Showers closed 9am-5:30pm. Reception 9-10am, 5-10pm. Lockout 10:15am-5pm. Midnight curfew. Breakfast £2. Sheets £1. June-Sept. 8- to 10-bed dorms £7; 4- to 6-bed dorms £8; twins £19; Oct.-May £6, £7, £17.)

BLASKET ISLANDS (NA BLASCAODAÍ)

Six islands comprise the Blaskets: Beginish, Tearaght, Inishnabro, Inishvickillane, Inishtooskert, and Great Blasket. Evacuated in 1953, Great Blasket Island was once inhabited by proud but impoverished villagers, poet-fishermen, and memoirists. At the beginning of the 20th century, the Blaskets were idealized as the bastion of unadulterated Irish culture, and scholar George Thompson compared the isolated *gaeltacht* culture to Homeric Greece. Mainlanders sponsored Blasket storytellers in publishing their autobiographies. The resulting memoirs bemoaned the decline of the *gaeltacht* culture; among them are Maurice O'Sullivan's *Twenty Years A-Growing,* Thomas O'Crohan's *The Islander,* and Peig Sayers's *Peig.* The titles are obscure outside Ireland, but until recently, were required reading for Irish secondary school students. One author reluctantly warned that "after us, there will be no more." Mists, seals, and occasional fishing boats may continue to pass the Blaskets, but the unique way of life that once took place there is extinct.

Days on Great Blasket allow for uninterrupted rumination. Wander through the mist down to the white strand, follow the grass paths along the island's 4 mi. length, explore the silent stone skeletons of former houses clustered in the village, and observe the puffins and seals that populate the island. The isolated Blaskets have no public litter system; kindly pack out all garbage packed in. Also be warned of steep cliff-sides that should be approached with caution; hiking or sturdy walking shoes should be worn at all times to navigate the rocky island terrain.

Keep in mind that if the weather is bad, the boats don't run; people have been stuck here for three weeks during gales. **Boats** for the Blaskets depart from Dunquin. (☎ (066) 915 6422. Weather permitting, daily Apr.-Oct. every 30min. 10am-3pm, £12 return.) A shuttle runs from Dingle to the Blasket ferry and back (2 per day, £6; ask at the Mountain Man for details). **Blasket Island Ferries** also runs two- to three-hour **cruises** that circle the islands without landing (2 per day, £20).

The only accommodations available on the island are at the **Blasket Island Hostel.** Come prepared for Spartan conditions and a kitchen with only a gas stove. (☎ (086) 848 6687 or (086) 852 2321. Open May-Sept. 3- to 6-bed dorms £10.) **Campers** can look forward to an island campsite planned for summer 2001. If you plan to stay, stock up on supplies in Dingle or Ballyferriter—there's no hot water, electricity, or food on the island, other than munchies in the small **cafe** (open irregularly 10am-6pm) near the old village.

BALLYFERRITER (BAILE AN FHEIRTÉARAIGH)

Ballyferriter is West Dingle's closest approximation to a town center. The surrounding settlement is an unpolluted *gaeltacht*—even the Guinness signs are in Irish. The **Chorca Dhuibhne Museum,** in the center of town, brims with photos and text relating to the area's wildlife, archaeology, and folklore. (☎ 915 6100. Open daily 9:30am-6pm. £1.50, students £1.) The museum is a noble attempt to make the area's history accessible, and a good starting point for visiting nearby ancient sites. From the hostel at Ballyferriter, follow the signs to the Iron Age **Dún An Óir** (Fort of Gold), where, in 1580, the English massacred over 600 Spanish, Italian, and Irish soldiers who participated in a rebellion against Queen Elizabeth. From the main road, sign-posted roads branch to **Riasc,** a puzzling monastic site with an engraved standing slab. Heading eastward, **Gallarus Oratory** (☎ 915 5333) is a well-marked detour on the road back to Dingle Town. The small, carefully crafted church is a masterpiece of 8th-century stonework. The adjacent **visitors center** presents a 15-minute video tour of Dingle's ancient places. (Oratory always open and free. Visitors center open daily Apr. to mid-Oct. 9:30am-8pm. £1.50, students £1.)

Five minutes outside town on Dunquin Rd., the very simple **An Cat Dubh** (Black Cat Hostel) crosses your path in a tacky but friendly sort of way. Don't worry—black cats are a sign of good luck in Ireland. (☎ 915 6286. Open May-Sept. Dorms £7. Camping £3 per person.) The B&B next door, **An Spéice,** provides quiet rest. (☎ 915 6254. £15-17.) Many visitors land in Ballyferriter and head straight for **Tigh Pheig** (Peig's Pub), Main St., where voices discuss life all day long. Frequent evening trad sessions in the summer and two pool tables keep the locals coming, as do the appetizing meals. (☎ 915 6433. Daily specials £5.50.) Across the street, **Tigh Uí Mhurchú** (Murphy's; ☎ 915 6224) competes for the lunchtime rush, and pours pints to the rhythm of nightly music. The largest grocery in town is **O Shúilleaghán Market.** (☎ 915 6157. Open daily May-Sept. 9am-9pm, winter 9am-8pm.)

NORTH DINGLE

Both hikers and beach loafers can get their fix on the peninsula's northern shore. Jaw-dropping views from the mountains motivate casual hikers to make the daytrip from Dingle Town. While the seaside villages hold little of enduring interest, they're all pleasant places to get a meal, a pint, or a night's rest.

From Dingle Town, a winding cliff-side road runs north by way of the 1500 ft. **Connor Pass.** Buses won't fit on the narrow road, but cars can squeeze through, and bikers and walkers are sustained by valley views on the 3 mi. of mild incline. As the road crests the **Brandon Ridge,** your labors are rewarded with one of Ireland's best views. On a clear day, visitors can gaze awe-struck at lakes thousands of feet below, and see as far as Valentia Island off the south coast across the peninsula to the Maharee Islands to the north. As the road twists downhill, a small waterfall and a few picnic tables mark the base of **Pedlars Lake.** Be careful on the slippery slope that leads up to the lake, named in honor of a traveling tradesman who lost his wares (and his life) to brigands nearby. These days one is more likely to encounter a geologist than a bandit—the glacier-sliced lakes and boulder-pocked landscape present evidence of the Ice Age.

Beyond the lake, the road heads downhill to the coast. Signs point out the westward fork to **Cloghane.** The quiet hamlet is a good starting point for hikes up the 3127 ft. **Mt. Brandon.** The devout head up the "Saint's Road" to the summit each July 25, in honor of St. Brendan, who allegedly carved the trail. Back in Cloghane, the spacious ■**Tigh Tomsi Hostel** offers clean and comfortable beds with a lively pub next door. (☎ 713 8299. Sheets £1. Laundry £4. Dorms £8.)

Back toward Tralee in **Stradbally,** the friendly **Connor Pass Hostel (IHH)** has a few small but welcoming beds. (☎ 713 9179. Open mid-Mar. to Nov. Dorms £8.50.) The hostel makes a good base for hikes in the **Slieve Mish Mountains** to the east. The 2713 ft. ascent to **Cáherconree** culminates with views of the peninsula, the ocean, and the Shannon Estuary. Stradbally is also an excellent place from which to embark on the **Loch a'Duín** nature and archaeology walk. Stock up on those carbs at **Tomásin's Pub,** across the street from the hostel. (☎ 713 9179. Warm lunch £3.50-7, served noon-4:30pm; dinners £7-11, served 6-9pm.) A trip to Stradbally is incomplete without walking the quarter-mile to the beach. The strand beyond the dune is especially magnificent at low tide.

Castlegregory, with a tourist office and a grocery store, may make the best home base for exploring north Dingle. From Castlegregory, head north up the sandy **Maharees Peninsula** where you can swim at numerous strands, or rent sailboards from **Focus Windsurfing** (☎ 713 9411; from £5 per hr.). The **Maharees Regatta** hits the waves in early July, and a week or two later Castlegregory's **Summer Festival** wakes up the town a bit. A **bus** to **Tralee** runs on Fridays (£3.80). The **tourist information center** is small but informative. (☎ 713 9422. Open M-F 9:30am-5pm.) **Spar Market** offers edible caloric matter. (☎ 713 9433. Open daily 8:30am-10pm.) The quiet **Lynch's Hostel** is the better of the two hostels in town. (☎ 713 9777. **Bike rental** £6 per day. Dorms £8; doubles £18.) If you're stuck, try **Fitzgerald's Euro-Hostel,** above the pub. (☎ 713 9133. Dorms £7.) In a restored stone cottage, ■**Milesian Restaurant,** Main St., hosts frequent music and poetry readings and an ever-changing menu with vegetarian options. (Dinners £5.95-7.95. Open Easter-Nov. and winter weekends 5-9:30pm.) Across the street, **O'Donnell's Pub** (☎ 713 9560) plays frequent trad in a setting based on Western saloons. **Ned Natterjack's** (☎ 713 9491), named for the rare and quite vocal Natterjack toad that resides in this area, presents various styles of music and a glorious beer garden.

TRALEE ☎ 066

While tourists tend to identify Killarney as the core of Kerry, Tralee (pop. 20,000) is the county's residential and economic capital. Tourists often use Tralee's abundance of quality hostels and pubs as a base to see the Ring of Kerry and the Dingle Peninsula, though multi-million pound projects have added splashy tourist attractions to the cosmopolitan city center. Ireland's second-largest museum, detailing the history of Kerry, stands out, but no tourist development could possibly top Tralee's famed gardens. The annual **Rose of Tralee** festival is a centuries-old pageant that has Irish eyes glued to their TV sets every August.

GETTING THERE AND GETTING AROUND

Airport: Kerry Airport (☎ 64644), off N22 halfway between Tralee and Killarney. **Ryanair** (☎ (01) 609 7999) flies to London.

Trains: Oakpark Rd. (☎ 712 3522). Ticket office open daily with sporadic hours. Trains tie Tralee to **Killarney** (40min.; M-Sa 5 per day, Su 4 per day; £5.50), **Cork** (2½hr.; M-Sa 5 per day, Su 3 per day; £17), **Galway** (3 per day, £33.50), **Dublin** (4hr.; M-Sa 4

272 ■ **DINGLE PENINSULA**

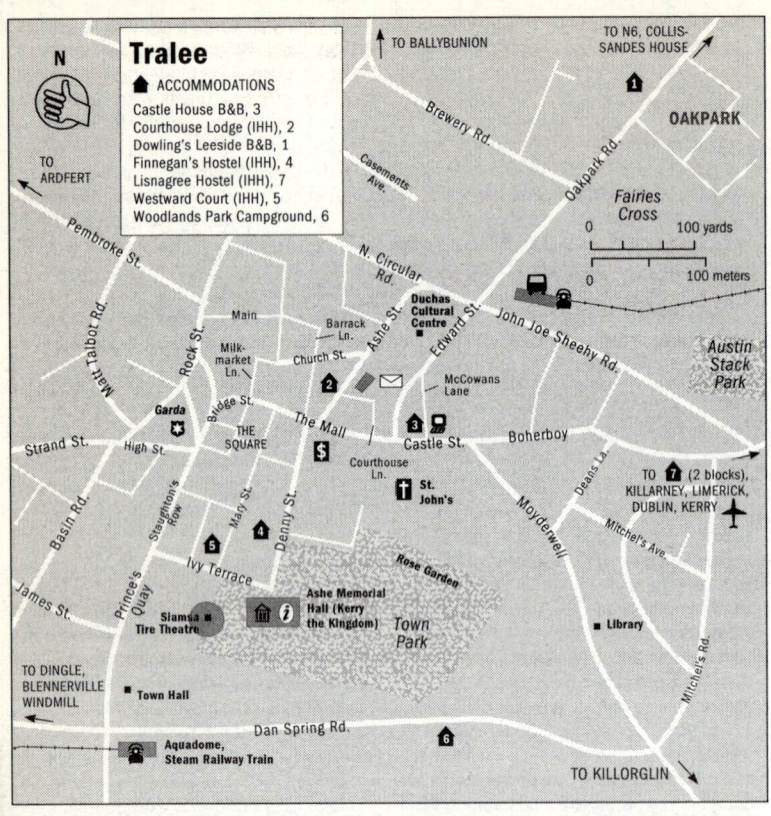

Tralee
ACCOMMODATIONS
Castle House B&B, 3
Courthouse Lodge (IHH), 2
Dowling's Leeside B&B, 1
Finnegan's Hostel (IHH), 4
Lisnagree Hostel (IHH), 7
Westward Court (IHH), 5
Woodlands Park Campground, 6

per day, Su 3 per day; £33.50), **Waterford** (4hr., M-Sa 1 per day, £33.50), and **Rosslare Harbour** (5½hr., M-Sa 2 per day, £33.50).

Buses: Oakpark Rd. (☎ 712 3566). Station open in summer M-Sa 8:30am-6pm, Su 9am-3:30pm; in winter M-Sa 9am-5:15pm. Buses go to **Killarney** (40min.; June-Sept. M-Sa 14 per day, Su 8 per day; Oct.-May M-Sa 5 per day, Su 6 per day; £4.40), **Dingle** (1¼hr.; July-Aug. M-Sa 8 per day, Su 4 per day; Sept.-June M-Sa 4 per day, Su 2 per day; £5.90), **Limerick** (2¼hr.; 7 per day, £9), **Cork** (2½hr.; M-Sa 6 per day, Su 3 per day; £9.70), and **Galway** (M-Sa 6 per day, Su 4 per day; £13).

Taxi: Call-A-Cab (☎ 712 0333). **EuroCabs** (☎ 712 7111). Cabs park at the intersection of Denny St. and The Mall. £1 per mi., less for longer distances.

Bike Rental: O'Halloran, 83 Boherboy (☎ 712 2820). £6 per day; £30 per week; helmet £1 per day. Open M-Sa 9:30am-6pm.

ORIENTATION AND PRACTICAL INFORMATION

Tralee's streets are hopelessly knotted; it's wise to arm yourself with a free map from the tourist office. The main street in town—variously called **The Mall, Castle St.,** and **Boherboy**—holds many stores and restaurants along its roughly east-west path. **Edward St.** connects this main thoroughfare to the train and bus stations. Wide **Denny St.** runs south to the tourist office and park.

Tourist Office: Ashe Memorial Hall (☎ 712 1288), at the end of Denny St. From the station, go into town on Edward St., turn right on Castle St., and then left onto Denny St. The staff provides free maps. Open July-Aug. M-Sa 9am-7pm, Su 9am-6pm; May-June and Oct. M-Sa 9am-6pm; Oct.-Apr. M-F 9am-5pm.

Banks: Bank of Ireland, Castle St. Open M 10am-5pm, Tu-F 10am-4pm. **AIB,** corner of Denny and Castle St. Open M 10am-5pm, Tu-F 10am-4pm. Both have **ATMs.**

Camping Equipment: Landers, Courthouse Ln. (☎ 712 6644), has an extensive selection. No tent rental. Open M-Sa 9am-6pm.

Laundry: Kate's Launderette, Boherboy (☎ 712 7173). Large loads £5-6; 10% student discount. Open M-Sa 8:45am-6pm.

Pharmacy: Kelly's Pharmacy, The Mall (☎ 712 1302). Open M-F 9am-8pm, Sa 9am-6pm.

Emergency: ☎ 999; no coins required. **Police** (*Garda*): High St. (☎ 712 2022).

Counseling and Support: Samaritans (☎ 712 2566), 44 Moyderwell. 24hr. hotline.

Hospital: Tralee County General Hospital, off Killarney Rd. (☎ 712 6222).

Post Office: Edward St. (☎ 712 1013), off Castle St. Open M and W-Sa 9am-5:30pm, Tu 9:30am-5:30pm.

Internet Access: Cyberpost, 26 Upper Castle St. (☎ 718 1284). £2 per 10min., £1 for each additional 20min. Open July-Sept. M-Sa 10am-9pm, Oct.-June 10am-6pm.

ACCOMMODATIONS

Tralee has several scattered but reasonable hostels that can barely contain festival-goers in late August. Rows of pleasant B&Bs line Edward St. as it becomes Oakpark Rd.; others can be found along Princes Quay, close to the Park.

Courthouse Lodge (IHH), 5 Church St. (☎ 712 7199). Off Ashe St. Centrally located but hidden on a quiet street, you'll find a clean bed, shower, kitchen, and TV room with VCR in this new hostel. All rooms come with full bath. Laundry £4. **Internet access** £1 per 10min. 4- to 6-bed dorms £9; singles £17; doubles £24.

Collis-Sandes House (IHH; ☎ 712 8658; www.colsands.com). Near-perfect, but far from town. Follow Oakpark Rd./N69 1 mi. from town, take the first left after Spar Market, and follow signs another ½ mi. to the right, or save yourself and call for pick up. Magnificent high ceilings and Moorish arches lend grandeur to this stone mansion. Free lifts to town and pub-runs. Continental breakfast £1. Laundry £3. Wheelchair accessible. 14-bed dorms £7.50; 8-bed dorms with bathroom £8; 6-bed dorms £8-9.50; 4-bed dorms £8.50; singles £15; doubles £23-25; triples £30-33. **Camping** £4 per person.

Finnegan's Hostel (IHH), 17 Denny St. (☎ 712 7610). At the end of the city's most dignified street, this majestic 19th-century townhouse contains part of the old town castle. Great location and common room, but mattresses could be firmer. Wood-floored bunk rooms are named after Ireland's literary lions. Laundry £3. Dorms £10; doubles £25.

Lisnagree Hostel (IHH), Ballinorig Rd. (☎ 712 7133). On the left fork just after the traffic circle before the Maxol garage (follow Boherboy away from town), 1 mi. from town center and close to the bus/train station. A small, pretty, relaxed hostel perfect for families or couples, but slightly remote for anyone who wants to hit the pubs at night. 4-bed dorms £9.50; singles £15; doubles £20-24.

Westward Court (IHH), Mary St. (☎ 718 0041). Follow Denny St. to the park, then turn right, and right again at the Ivy Terrace Diner. A spotless, uniform series of dorms. All rooms with full bath. Continental breakfast included. Laundry £5. Wheelchair accessible. 3am curfew. 4-bed dorms £12.50; singles £17.50; doubles £32.

Dowling's Leeside, Oakpark Rd. (☎ 712 6475). About ½ mi. from town center on Edward St./Oakpark Rd. Pamper yourself at this cheerful B&B, decorated with Irish pine antique furniture and cushy chairs. The lovely hostess and friendly dog will make you want to move in. All rooms have shower and TV. Singles £19; doubles £34-38.

Castle House, 27 Upper Castle St. (☎ 712 5167). Watch TV and listen to the traffic go by in your well-equipped room. Singles £22-25; doubles £36-40.

Woodlands Park Campground, Dan Spring Rd. (☎ 712 1235), ¼ mi. past the Aquadome. Game room. Showers 50p. Open Mar. 15 to Oct. Tent £4-4.75 without car.

FOOD

True gourmands may be disappointed with the culinary landscape of Tralee, but pub grub and fast food are readily available. If they don't sell it at the massive **Tesco** in The Square, you probably shouldn't be eating it. (☎ 712 2788. Open M-W and Sa 8:30am-8pm, Th-F 8:30am-10pm, Su 10am-6pm.) Across the street, **Seancra**, peddles health food and organic produce. (☎ 712 2644. Open M-W and Sa 9am-6pm, Th 9am-8pm, F 9am-9pm.)

- **Pocott's,** 3 Ashe St. (☎ 712 9500). Quality Irish food, fast and cheap. Their lunches are especially popular (under £5), and small Irish breakfasts are a steal (£2.75). Try the delicious chicken, bacon, and mozzarella baguette (£4.95). Dinner ranges from £4-10. Open July-Sept. 9am-9:30pm, Oct.-June 9am-7pm.
- **Mozart's,** 4 Ashe St. (☎ 712 7977). A range of well-prepared delights, from stuffed baguettes (£2.95-3.95) in the afternoon to stir-fries and steaks in the evening (£6.95-11.95). Open mid-May to Sept. M-Sa 9am-9:30pm; Oct. to mid-May M-Th 9am-7pm, F-Sa 9am-9:30pm.
- **The Skillet,** Barrack Ln. (☎ 712 4561), off The Mall. A traditional decor is matched with stew and other Irish specialties. Lunch runs from £4-7, but dinner is pricier (£7-12). Open M-Sa 9am-10pm, Su noon-10pm.
- **Brat's Place,** 18 Milk Market Ln., a pedestrian walkway off The Mall. Tasty, conscientiously prepared vegetarian food with mostly local and organic ingredients. Soup £2; warm entrees £4.50. Open M-Sa 12:30-2:30pm, later if food lasts.
- **Hob Knobs,** The Square (☎ 712 1846). Low-key cafeteria-style cafe with tasty breakfasts and decent lunches. Most meals £3-5. Open M-Sa 8am-5pm.
- **Roots,** 76 Boherboy (☎ 712 2665). An ever-changing though limited menu of vegetarian food with gargantuan portions (£4-5). Open M-F 11am-3:30pm.
- **Pizza Time,** The Square (☎ 712 6317). No pretense, just high quality food at low prices. Pizza, pasta, and burgers. Open M-Th noon-midnight, F-Sa noon-3am.

PUBS

- **Seán Óg's,** The Square (☎ 712 8822). With its impressive fireplace (hand-built by the owner) and lots of trad, year-old Seán Óg's has already generated a lively following.
- **Abbey Inn,** The Square (☎ 712 3390). Tough crowd comes to hear live rock most weekends. Bono swept here! When U2 played here in the late 70s, the manager made them sweep the floors to pay for their drinks because he thought they were so bad. Meatloaf, however, drank for free. Open Su-F until 1am. Live music Th.
- **Baily's Corner Pub** (☎ 712 3230), at Ashe and The Mall. Kerry's rugby legacy hangs on the walls while real-life players join an older crowd at the bar. Trad Tu night.
- **Paddy Mac's,** The Mall (☎ 712 1572). A Tralee favorite with trad twice a week.
- **McDades,** Upper Castle St. (☎ 712 1877). This immense, polished wood pub attracts a slightly older, touristy crowd.

SIGHTS

Tralee is home to Ireland's second-largest museum, **Kerry the Kingdom,** Ashe Memorial Hall, Denny St. Perennially a contender for museum awards, the Kingdom marshals all the resources of display technology to tell the story of Co. Kerry from 8000 BC to the present. Vivid dioramas and videos of everything from Kerry's castles to her greatest Gaelic football victories keep your attention rapt. "Geraldine Tralee" downstairs takes you through a superbly assembled recreation of medieval city streets, as seen from a small moving cart. You can even sample the old city's stench! (☎ 712 7777. Open Mar.-Oct. daily 10am-6pm; Nov.-Dec. noon-4:30pm. £5.50, students £4.75.)

BY ANY OTHER NAME

If you find yourself in the middle of a spontaneous song-a-thon deep in the heart of southern Ireland's most spirited pubs, *Let's Go* is here to make you feel like one of the locals. The lovely tune *The Rose of Tralee* details the origins of the eponymous pageant. As the story goes, Mary O'Connor was a peasant farmer's girl who worked as a maid in the home of John Mulchinock, a wealthy merchant in Tralee. Mary, nicknamed "Beauty," was just that, with large lustrous eyes. She and Mulchinock's nephew William soon fell in love but had to hide their feelings from William's disapproving family. William would spend hours writing poems and songs for his love, one of which stood the test of time and is still sung today. So when the crowds have downed just enough pints and the songs begin to roll, rise to the occasion and you may just find a rose of your own.

> The pale moon was rising above the green mountain,
> The sun was declining beneath the blue sea;
> When I strayed with my love to the pure crystal mountain,
> That stands in the beautiful vale of Tralee.
> She was lovely and fair as the rose of the summer,
> Yet 'twas not her beauty alone that won me;
> Oh no, 'twas the truth in her eyes ever dawning,
> That made me love Mary, the Rose of Tralee.
>
> The cool shades of evening their mantle was spreading,
> And Mary all smiling was listening to me;
> The moon through the valley her pale rays was shedding,
> When I won the heart of the Rose of Tralee.
> Though lovely and fair as the rose of the summer,
> Yet 'twas not her beauty alone that won me;
> Oh no, 'twas the truth in her eyes ever dawning,
> That made me love Mary, the Rose of Tralee.

Across from the museum, the **Roses of Tralee** bloom each summer in Ireland's second-largest town park. The gardens were designed in 1987 to convert floraphobes into rose-sniffers. The gray carpeting in **St. John's Church**, Castle St., dampens the echo and the Gothic mood, but the stained glass is worth a look. The building on the Prince's Quay traffic circle looks like a cross between a Gothic castle and a space-age solarium, but it's actually Tralee's £4.5-million **Aquadome,** complete with whirlpools, steam room, sauna, and gym. (☎ 712 8899. Open daily 10am-10pm. £6, students £4.)

Just down Dingle Rd., the **Blenneville Windmill and Visitors Centre** is the largest operating windmill in the British Isles. Recalling Blenneville's status as Kerry's main port of emigration during the Famine, a small **museum** focuses on the "coffin ships" that sailed from Ireland during the Famine. (☎ 712 1064. Open Apr.-Oct. daily 10am-6pm. £2.75, students £2.25.) The nearby **Jeanie Johnston Visitor Shipyard** builds in 19th-century style. (☎ 712 9999.) The restored **Tralee & Dingle Railway** runs the 2 mi. between the aquadome and the Blennerville complex. (☎ 712 1064. Trains leave the aquadome every hour on the hour and leave the windmill on the half-hour. July-Aug. 10:30am-5:30pm; May-June and Sept. 11am-5pm; closed on occasional service days. £2.75, students £2.25.)

♪ ENTERTAINMENT

The **Siamsa Tíre Theatre,** next to the museum at the end of Denny St., is Ireland's national folk theater. It mounts brilliant summer programs depicting traditional Irish life through mime, music, and dance. (☎ 712 3055. Productions July-Aug. M-Sa; May-June and Sept. M-Th and Sa. Shows start at 8:30pm. Box office open M-Sa 9am-8:30pm. Tickets £8-12.) The **Dúchas Cultural Centre,** Edward St., produces dance and musical performances. (July-Aug. Tu 8:30pm. Tickets £4.) Less culturally elite entertainment is available in Tralee's two nightclubs. The Brandon Hotel's club **Spirals,** Prince's Quay (☎ 712 3333), dances the disco (W and F-Su), while **The Courthouse** (☎ 712 1877), behind McDades Pub on Upper Castle St., keeps an over-23 crowd groovin'. Both stay open until 1:45am. (Cover £4-5.) For other local goings-on, get a copy of *The Kerryman* (85p) at most newsagents.

Lovely, marriageable Irish lasses from around the world come to town during the last week of August (Aug. 24-28 in 2001) for the nationally beloved **Rose of Tralee Festival.** A maelstrom of entertainment surrounds the main event, a personality competition to earn the coveted title "Rose of Tralee." Rose-hopefuls or spectators can call the Rose Office, in Ashe Memorial Hall (☎ 712 1322).

TARBERT ☎068

A tiny and peaceful seaside spot on the N69, Tarbert is home to an incredible hostel and a convenient ferry service running between Counties Kerry and Clare. The boat ride will save you an 85 mi. coastal drive through Limerick. **Bus Éireann** stops outside the hostel on its way from **Tralee** to **Doolin** and **Galway** (mid-June-Sept. 5hr., M-Sa 3 per day, Su 2 per day; Galway to Tralee £15). During the rest of the year, the nearest stop to Tarbert is in **Kilrush.** Hitchers report mid-afternoon success from Killimer, the ferry port across from Tarbert, to Kilrush (see p. 289). However, *Let's Go* does not recommend hitching. **Shannon Ferry Ltd.** makes the 20-minute ferry trip across the Shannon between the port a mile from Tarbert and Killimer. (☎ (065) 905 3124. June-Aug. every 30min. from both sides, Apr.-Sept. 7:30am-9:30pm and Oct.-Mar. 7am-7:30pm every hr. on the ½hr. from Tarbert and on the hour from Killimer; Su year-round from 9am; £9 per carload, £2 per pedestrian or biker.) A bus leaves from the ferry terminal and goes to Kilrush; check at the hostel for a schedule (M-Sa 2-3 per day, Su 2 per day). Tarbert's **tourist office** (☎ 36500) is in the carefully restored **1831 Bridewell Jail and Courthouse;** walk down the street from the hostel and turn right onto the road toward the ferry. If you're curious about what would have happened to someone who stole 16 cucumber plants during the Great Hunger, wait no more. Make sure to go upstairs—the old newspaper articles upon the wall tell the history of Tarbert. If you pine for more Irish prison history, the tour is surprisingly interesting. (Open Apr.-Oct. daily 10am-6pm. £3, students £2.) Be sure to get cash before you come; the nearest **ATM** is 15 mi. away in Listowel.

The ⌦**Ferry House Hostel** is the three-year-old occupant of a 200-year-old building in the center of town. It is worth a trip to Tarbert just to stay in this hostel; before opening, the friendly owners spent a year traveling and taking detailed notes on the best and worst of the world's hostels. The success of their study is evident in the most comfortable bedding found anywhere, excellent showers, and a cafe (☎ 36555. Sheets £1. Laundry £4. Wheelchair-accessible. Open year-round; cafe open June-Sept. Reception May-Sept. 8am-7pm. Dorms £7; doubles £22-26, off-season doubles £20-24.) Recently revamped **Coolahan's** is the most notable of Tarbert's five pubs, a little establishment with regulars speaking English and Irish at the bar. Drop down to **Anchor's,** on the street perpendicular to the hostel, for a light seafood chowder (£2.75). A few hundred meters from the ferry stands **Tarbert House,** the home of the family of Signeur Leslie of Tarbert since 1690. The recently restored exterior rivals the period pieces and priceless art it protects. (☎ 36198. Open daily 10am-noon and 2-4pm. £2. Tours given by Mrs. Leslie herself.) The hour-long **Tarbert House Woodland Walk** takes ramblers through Leslie's Wood, with views of the River Shannon, Tarbert Old Pier, and Tarbert Bay. The path is marked and begins next to the tourist office, where pamphlets are available.

WESTERN IRELAND

Even Dubliners will tell you that the west is the "most Irish" part of Ireland. Yeats agreed: "For me," he said, "Ireland is Connacht." For less privileged Irish in recent centuries, Connacht mostly meant poor soil and emigration. When Cromwell uprooted the native Irish landowners in Leinster and Munster and resettled them west of the Shannon, the popular phraseology for their plight became "To Hell or Connacht." The potato famine (see p. 14) that plagued the entire island was most devastating in the west—entire villages emigrated or died. Today, every western county has less than half of its 1841 population. Though miserable for farming, the land from Connemara north to Ballina is a boon for hikers, cyclists, and hitchhikers (whom *Let's Go* boos in disapproval), who enjoy the isolation of boggy, rocky, or brilliantly mountainous landscapes. Western Ireland's gorgeous desolation and enclaves of traditional culture are now its biggest attractions.

The city of Galway is a different story: long a successful port, in the 20th century it grew into a boom town for the young. Farther south, the barren moonscape of the Burren, the Cliffs of Moher, and a reputation as the center of the trad music scene attract travelers to Co. Clare. The Shannon River has provided subsistence and tourism to the west for generations. It flows through the city of Limerick, the latest in Ireland's growing list of vibrant, youthful cities.

HIGHLIGHTS OF THE WEST: ISLANDS AND LIMESTONES

The overflowing pubs of **Galway** (p. 313) spawn musical brilliance and copious *craic*.

Glimpse green fields and seaweed-mortared, stone walls on the **Aran Islands** (p. 303), where Iron-Age ring forts and the tarred, cow-skin *curraghs* of today's fishermen float.

See all you can of haunting, wind-smoothed **Connemara** (p. 323): ride in on the **Coast Road** (p. 324); spend a night in the pubs of **Clifden** (p. 324); ferry to **Inishbofin Island** (p. 327) and pass through **Connemara National Park** (p. 328) as you return.

The village of **Doolin** fiddles while the nearby **Cliffs of Moher** (p. 295), **Burren** (p. 298), and **Pounalbrane Dolmen** (p. 300) stun with their natural wonders.

Explore the cliffs and beaches of **Achill Island** (p. 336) to relive the days when Pirate Queen Grace O'Malley controlled the surrounding waters of **Clare Island** (p. 335).

LIMERICK AND CLARE

Limerick City is an urban speck beside the long expanse of weird geology and unique flora that line the Clare Coast. Convenient to Shannon Airport and a host of quintessential Irish attractions, Limerick is attracting tourists like pub patrons to a pint. The economy of Limerick has ridden the tide of the recent EU boom and made the city's historic poverty a fading memory. Geology defines Co. Clare: fine sands glisten on the beaches of Kilkee, skyscraper-high limestone slabs mark the Cliffs of Moher, and 100 sq. mi. of exposed hilly limestone form Ireland's most peculiarly alluring landscape, the Burren.

LIMERICK CITY ☎061

Despite a thriving trade in off-color poems, Limerick City has long suffered from a bad reputation. The Vikings settled around Limerick in 922, presaging a millennium of turbulence. During the English Civil War, Limerick was the last stronghold

Western Ireland

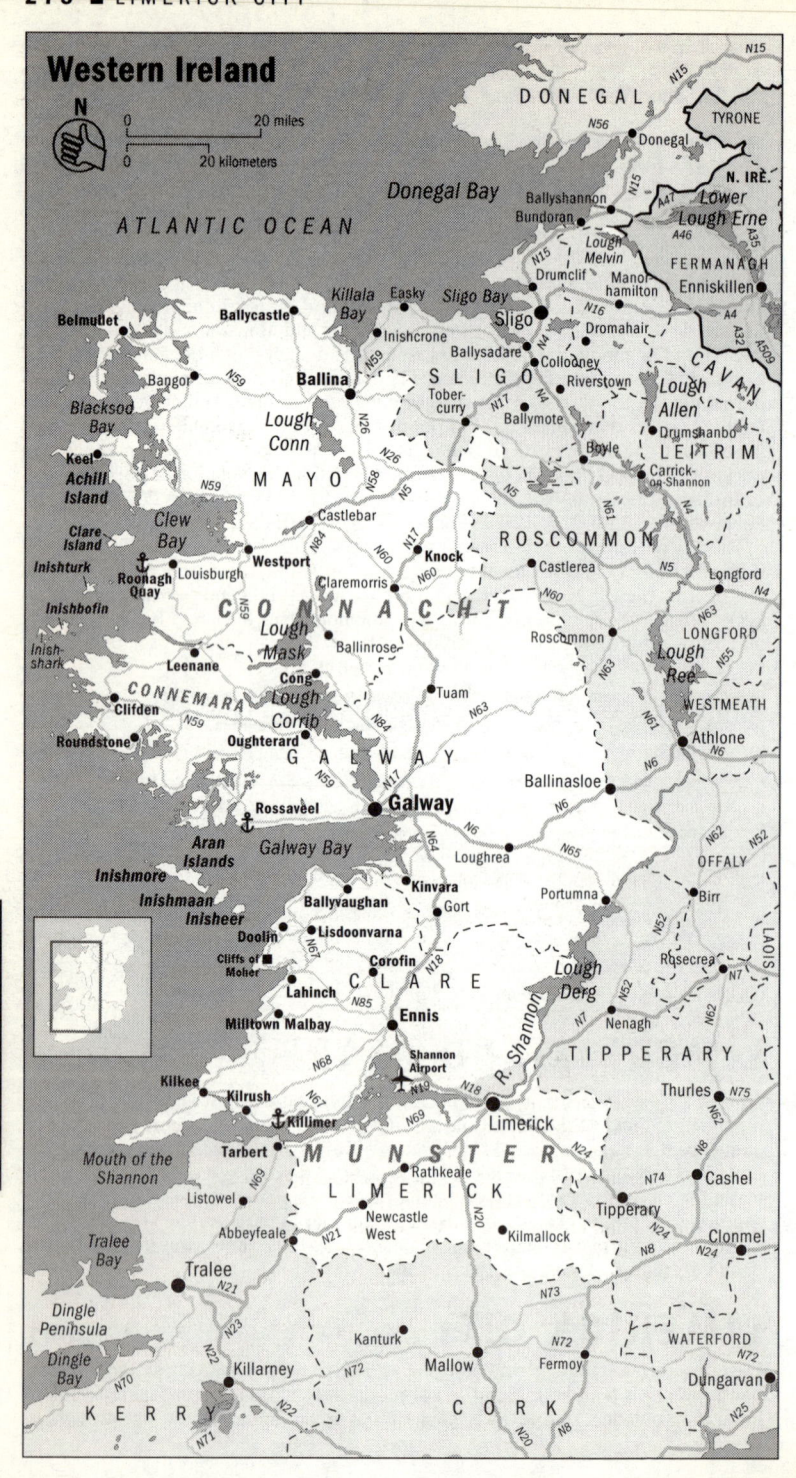

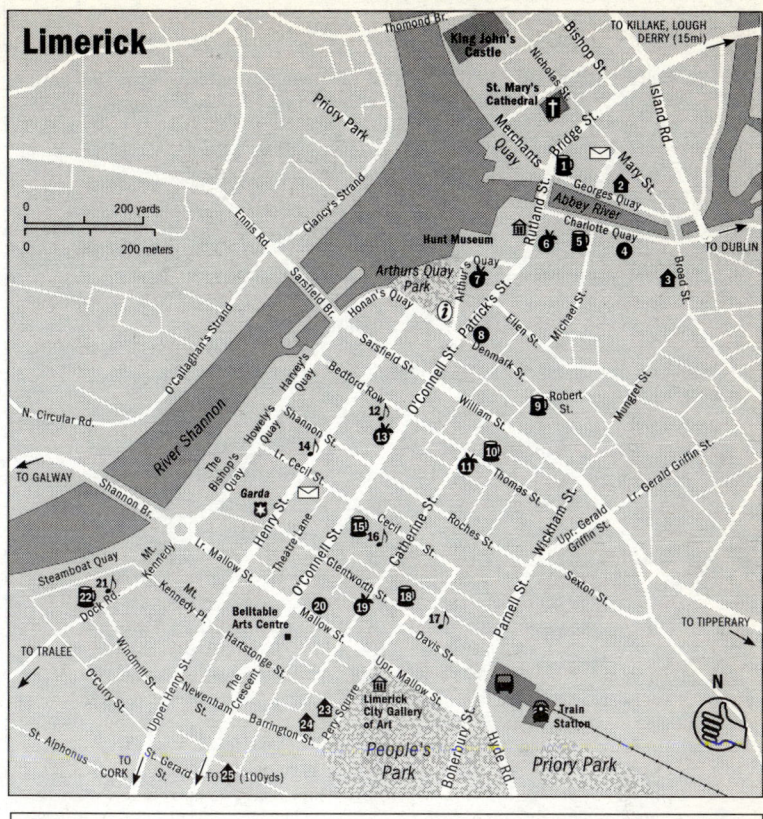

LIMERICK CITY ■ 279

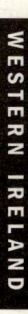

Limerick

ACCOMMODATIONS	
Alexandra House, 25	
An Óige Hostel (HI), 24	
Barrington Hostel (IHH), 2	
Broad St. Hostel, 3	
Finnegan's (IHH), 23	

FOOD AND DRINKS
Cafe Furze Bush, 19
The Green Onion Cafe, 6
Java's Beat Café, 11
Nature's Way and Tesco, 7
O'Grady's Cellar Restaurant, 13

PUBS
Doc's, 5
The Doghouse, 10
Dolan's, 22
The Glen Tavern, 18
Locke Bar 1
Nancy Blake's, 9
Tom Collins, 15

MUSIC AND CLUBS
BPs, 17
The George Hotel, 14
The Globe, 16
The Warehouse, 21
The Works, 12

SERVICES
Charlotte Quay Pharmacy, 4
Emerald Alpine Bike Rental, 8
Laundrette, 20

of Royalist support against Cromwell's army. Three times besieged and conquered, Limerick's citizens thought they had won a measure of peace with the Treaty of Limerick in 1691, agreed upon after the Jacobites were defeated in their last stand against King William's armies. The treaty's vague promise of Catholic protection was soon violated, and the treaty remained a sore point in Anglo-Irish relations for the next 150 years (see **The Protestant Ascendancy**, p. 11).

Though its 18th-century Georgian streets and parks remain regal and elegant, later industrial and commercial developments gave the city a dull and urban feel. During much of the 20th century, hard economic times spawned poverty and crime. What little attention was paid to Limerick seemed to celebrate squalor, as exemplified by the Irish-American author Frank McCourt's internationally successful memoir *Angela's Ashes*. Yet, the mayor of Limerick raised a spirited protest against McCourt's characterization of his city: whether or not outsiders have noticed, today's Limerick is renewed and thriving. A large student population fosters an intense arts scene, adding to a wealth of cultural treasures that have long gone unnoticed. In addition, the Republic's third largest city boasts a top quality museum and a well-preserved 12th-century cathedral.

280 ■ LIMERICK CITY

▐ GETTING THERE AND GETTING AROUND

Trains: Colbert Station (☎ 315 555), off Parnell St. Inquiries desk open M-F 9am-6pm, Sa 9am-5:30pm. Trains from Limerick to **Ennis** (M-Sa 2 per day, £5.70); **Dublin** (2hr.; M-Sa 10 per day, Su 9 per day; £27), **Waterford** (2hr.; M-Sa 2 per day in summer, 1 per day in winter; £13.50), **Cork** (2½hr.; M-Sa 6 per day, Su 5 per day; £14); **Killarney** (2½hr.; M-Sa 4 per day, Su 3 per day; £15), **Tralee** (3hr.; M-Sa 6 per day, Su 3 per day; £16) and **Rosslare** (3½hr., M-Sa 1 per day, £21).

Buses: Colbert Station, just off Parnell St. (☎ 313 333; 24hr. talking timetable ☎ 319 911). Open June-Sept. M-F 8:10am-6pm, Su 9am-6pm; Oct.-May M-Sa 8:10am-6pm, Su 3-7pm. Limerick sends buses to **Ennis** (1hr., 6 per day, £5.50), **Cork** (2hr., 14 per day, £9), **Galway** (2hr., 14 per day, £9), **Tralee** (2hr., 10 per day, £9), **Waterford** (2½hr.; M-Th and Sa-Su 6 per day, F 7 per day; £9.70), **Killarney** (2½hr.; M-Sa 6 per day, Su 3 per day; £9.30), **Dublin** (3hr., 13 per day, £10), **Wexford** and **Rosslare Harbour** with some departures timed to meet the ferries (4hr., 4 per day, £13), and **Sligo** (6hr., 7 per day, £14).

Taxi: Top Cabs, Wickham St. (☎ 417 417). Takes you most places in the city for under £3 and to the airport for about £15.

Bike Rental: Emerald Alpine, 1 Patrick St. (☎ 416 983). £12 per day, £50 per week; deposit £40. £14 for return at other locations. Open M-Sa 9:15am-5:30pm.

✱▐ ORIENTATION AND PRACTICAL INFORMATION

The N7 from Dublin lands drivers at Limerick. The city's streets form a grid pattern, bounded by the **River Shannon** to the west and by the **Abbey River** to the north. Most of the city's activity takes place on a few blocks around **O'Connell St.** (sometimes called **Patrick's St.** or **Rutland St.**). Follow O'Connell St. north and cross the Abbey River to reach **King's Island,** where St. Mary's Cathedral and King John's Castle dominate the landscape. The city itself is easily navigable by foot, but the preponderance of one-way streets makes it a nightmare for drivers. To reach the suburbs, catch a **city bus** (75p) from Boyd's or Penney's on O'Connell St. (M-Sa 7:30am-11pm, 2 per hr.; Su 10:30am-11pm, 1 per hr.) Buses #2 and 8 access the university, while bus #6 follows **Ennis Rd.** A one-week pass ($9) allowing unlimited city bus travel is available at the bus station.

Tourist Office: Arthurs Quay (☎ 317 522), in the space-age glass building. From the station, walk straight down Davis St., turn right on O'Connell St., then left just before Arthurs Quay Mall. Handy city maps (£1), and info on the entire Shannon region. **Bureau de change.** Open July-Aug. M-F 9am-7pm, Sa-Su 9am-6pm; May-June and Sept.-Oct. M-Sa 9:30am-5:30pm; Nov.-Apr. M-F 9:30am-5:30pm, Sa 9:30am-1pm.

Budget Travel Office: usit (☎ 415 064), O'Connell St., across from Ulster Bank. Issues ISICs and **TravelSave** stamps. Open M-F 9:30am-5:30pm, Sa 10am-1pm. Also located at University of Limerick (☎ 332 079).

Luggage Storage: Colbert Station. Lockers £1 per day, 24hr. limit.

Laundry: Laundrette (☎ 312 712), on Mallow St. Full service from £5. Open M-F 9am-6pm, Sa 9am-5pm.

Banks: Bank of Ireland (☎ 415 055), O'Connell St. **AIB** (☎ 414 388), O'Connell St. Both have **ATMs.**

Bookstore: O'Mahoney's, O'Connell St. (☎ 418 155).

Camping Equipment: River Deep, Mountain High, 7 Rutland St. (☎ 400 944), off O'Connell St. Open M-Sa 9:30am-6pm. No tent rental.

Counseling: Samaritans, 20 Barrington Rd. (☎ 412 111), for the lonely or depressed. (Open daily 9am-10pm.)

Pharmacy: Charlotte Quay Pharmacy, Charlotte Quay (☎ 400 722). Open daily 9am-9pm.

Emergency: ☎ 999; no coins required. **Police** (*Garda*): Henry St. (☎ 414 222).

Hospital: Regional (☎ 301 111), follow O'Connell Rd. past the Crescent southward.
Post Office: Main office on Lower Cecil St. (☎ 315 777), just off O'Connell St. Open M and W-Sa 9am-5:30pm, Tu 9:30am-5:30pm.
Internet Access: Webster's, Thomas St. (☎ 312 066). Full web and email access £1 per 10min. Fruit drinks and coffee available. Open M-Sa 9am-9pm, Su 1-9pm.

ACCOMMODATIONS

Limerick has two "real" hostels and several budget accommodation centers geared toward term-time university students. These dorm-like establishments are usually large and in good condition, but are slightly more expensive and less welcoming than most hostels. For those seeking refuge from the bustle of the city, Ennis St. is a B&B bonanza in the price range of £19-22 per person.

An Óige Hostel (HI), 1 Pery Sq. (☎ 314 672). Around the corner from Finnegan's. A pleasant Georgian house, a cheerful staff, and park views help ease the An Óige dreariness. With 2nd- and 3rd-floor dorms and a basement kitchen, this hostel is not for the stair-averse. Sheets £1. Continental breakfast £2. Lockout 10am-2pm. Midnight curfew. June-Sept. 14-bed dorms £8.50, Oct.-May £7.50; £1 less for HI members.

Barrington Hostel (IHH), George's Quay (☎ 415 222). Far from the train and bus station, but very close to sights, restaurants, and pubs. Barrington compensates for its large size by offering relatively private dorms. 2 kitchens and a resplendent garden. Laundry £3-4. 4-bed dorms £7.50; singles £11; doubles with bath £25.

Finnegan's (IHH), 6 Pery Sq. (☎ 310 308). Located in a large brick building overlooking People's Park. From the bus station, cross Parnell St. and head up Daris St. for 1 long block. Take a left on Pery St. and walk 2 blocks to Harstoye St.; the hostel is on the corner. High-ceilinged common rooms and a convenient location, but somewhat crowded. 6- to 22-bed dorms £8-12; private rooms £12 per person.

Broad St. Hostel, Broad St. (☎ 317 222; email broadstreethostel@tinet.ie). Vigilant security and remarkable cleanliness are the main comforts here. Continental breakfast included. Laundry £4. Wheelchair accessible. 4-bed dorms £10.50; singles £15; doubles and twins £34.

Alexandra House, O'Connell St. (☎ 318 472), several blocks south of the Crescent. Victorian, comfortable, and pleasantly decorated. Its proximity to the city center drives prices up. Singles £20; doubles and twins £44-50.

FOOD

Inexpensive and top-notch cafes have sprouted across the city center, presenting culinary alternatives to fast-food chains. Gather groceries at **Tesco** in Arthurs Quay Mall. (☎ 412 399. Open M-W 8:30am-8pm, Th-F 8:30am-10pm, Sa 8:30am-8pm, Su noon-6pm.) **Nature's Way,** also in the mall, has a limited selection of natural foods. (☎ 310 466. Open M, W and Sa 9am-6pm, Th 9am-7pm, F 9am-8pm.)

The Glen Tavern, Lower Glentworth St. (☎ 411 380). Offers the best value for breakfast, lunch or dinner. Prides itself on Irish specialties. Most meals £3-5. Open M-F 8am-9pm.

O'Grady's Cellar Restaurant, O'Connell St. (☎ 418 286). Maroon walls and faux thatch abound in this little subterranean spot. Irish meals are the substance of the menu. Most meals £5-7. Open daily 9:15am-10:30pm.

The Green Onion Cafe, Rutland St. (☎ 400 710). A quality cafe with a modern flair. Lose yourself in their big booths and soothing jazz. Lunch £5-7. After 6pm, dinners skyrocket in price (£10-15). Open M-Sa noon-10pm.

Java's Beat Cafe, 3 Catherine St. (☎ 418 077). Flavored coffees and herbal teas keep a young crowd buzzing through the night. Salads, sandwiches, and bagels served to the strains of cool jazz. Open M-Th 9am-midnight, F-Sa 9am-3am, Su 10:30am-midnight.

Cafe Furze Bush, Catherine St. (☎ 411 733). A new cafe with eclectic sandwiches. Open M-Sa 10am-4pm and 6:30-10pm.

WESTERN IRELAND

PUBS

Limerick's immense student population adds spice to the pub scene, supplying a wide range of music. Trad-seekers can find their nightly dose, though the hunt may present more of a challenge than in other Irish cities. Pick up the tourist office's **Guinness Guide to Irish Music**, which covers the entire Shannon region.

Dolan's, Dock Rd. (☎ 314 483). Worth a Shannon-side walk from the city center to hear some of the best nightly trad played for rambunctious local patrons. The **Warehouse** is part of the building (see **Clubs**, below).

Nancy Blake's, Denmark St. (☎ 416 443). The best of both worlds—an older crowd huddles in the sawdust-floored interior for periodic trad, while boisterous students take in nightly rock in the open-air "outback."

Doc's, Michael St. (☎ 417 266), at the corner of Charlotte's Quay in the Granary. The outdoor beer garden, with palm trees and a waterfall, heals ale-ing young folks. College bands often play in the school year. DJs bust out chart-toppers most weekend nights.

Locke Bar, Georges Quay (☎ 413 733). Join the tourists and locals who drink on the quay-side patio. Inside, owner Richard Costello, former rugby player for Ireland's national team, joins in trad sessions several nights a week.

Tom Collins, Cecil St. (☎ 415 749). A Limerick institution where the affairs of the world should be casually discussed. Don't ask for the eponymous cocktail.

The Doghouse, Thomas St. (☎ 313 177). Howl your troubles away. Blues nearly nightly.

CLUBS

Limerick's insatiable army of students keep dozens of nightclubs thumping from 11:30pm until 2am nightly. Cover charges can be steep ($5-8), but clubs spread concession fliers good for $2-3 discounts throughout the city's pubs.

The Globe, Cecil St. (☎ 313 533). 3 floors of manic clubbery, with suggestive artwork and flashing video screens. Only club members are allowed on the top floor, where the Cranberries and U2 periodically stop by to sip £135 champagne. Cover £5.

The Warehouse (☎ 314 483), behind Dolan's on Dock Rd. Draws big-name bands and rising stars to its snazzy venue. Music Th-Sa. Cover £5-9, higher for well-known acts.

The George Hotel, O'Connell St. (☎ 414 566). Pick a decade: Th for 70s, F for 80s and Sa for modernity. The circular dance floor and balcony are always packed. Cover £6-7.

The Works, Bedford Row (☎ 411 611). Over-23 grinders flood its 2 floors. Smooth, colored lighting lets you see who's got the funk. Cover around £6.

BPs (☎ 418 414), in Baker Place Hotel at the top of Glentworth St. A mixed crowd pulsates between the multi-colored walls. Blasts indie rock and Euro-techno beats Tu-Sa. Cover £3-5. Occasional live bands in the bar upstairs.

SIGHTS

WALKING TOURS. Tours cover either the northern, sight-filled King's Island region, or the more decrepit locations described in Frank McCourt's *Angela's Ashes*. (☎ 318 106. *King's Island tour daily at 11am and 2:30pm; Angela's Ashes tour 2:30pm daily. Both depart from St. Mary's Action Centre, 44 Nicholas St. £4 per walker.*)

KING JOHN'S CASTLE. English King John built a massive castle to protect the conquered city of Limerick, though he never actually visited the edifice. In fact, King John made only one trip to Ireland, during which he supposedly pulled the beards of his subjects for kicks. The visitors' center has vivid exhibits and a video on the castle's gruesome history. The castle's history as a military fortification remains evident outside where the **mangonel** is displayed. Easily recognizable from its use in *Monty Python's Quest for the Holy Grail*, the mangonel was used to catapult pestilent animal corpses into enemy cities and castles. *(Nicholas St. Walk across the Abbey River and take the first left after St. Mary's Cathedral.* ☎ *411 201. Open Mar.-Dec. daily 9:30am-6pm. Last admission 5pm. £4.20, students £3.20.)* The rough exterior of nearby **St. Mary's Cathedral** was built in 1172 on the site of a Viking meeting place. Fold-down seats, built into the wall on the side of the altar, display elaborate carvings that depict the struggle between good and evil. They are called *misericordia*, Latin for "acts of mercy," and used in long services during which sitting was prohibited. *(*☎ *416 238. Open daily 9:15am-5pm.)*

MUSEUMS. The fascinating **Hunt Museum** houses the largest collection of medieval, Stone Age, and Iron Age artifacts outside the national museum in Dublin, as well as what may be one of Leonardo da Vinci's four "Rearing Horses" sculptures. The eclectic collection includes one of the **world's smallest jade monkeys,** a gold crucifix given by Mary Queen of Scots to her executioner, and a coin reputed to be one of the infamous 30 pieces of silver paid to Judas by the Romans. The impressive collection is appreciably enhanced by an excellent guided tour. *(Custom House, Rutland St.* ☎ *312 833. Open M-Sa 10am-5pm, Su 2-5pm. £4.20, seniors and students £3.20.)* **Limerick City Gallery of Art,** Pery Sq., contains a densely packed collection of Irish paintings as well as international exhibits. *(*☎ *310 633. Open M-F 10am-6pm, Sa 10am-5pm. Free.)* Abstract and experimental pieces fill the small **Belltable Arts Centre,** O'Connell St. *(*☎ *319 866. Open M-Sa 9am-7pm. Free.)*

🎵 ENTERTAINMENT

The **Belltable Arts Centre,** 69 O'Connell St. (☎ 319 866; www.commerce.ie/belltable), stages big-name productions year-round. (Box office open M-Sa 9am-5:30pm and prior to performances. Tickets £5-15.) The **Theatre Royal,** Upper Cecil St. (☎ 414 224), hosts the town's largest concerts. The **University Concert Hall,** on the university campus, showcases opera and music. (☎ 331 549. Tickets £6-17.50.) The £1 *Calendar of Events and Entertainment* is available at the tourist office.

🗓 DAYTRIP FROM LIMERICK

ADARE
Buses arrive from Limerick (20min., 7 per day, £3.50) and Tralee (1¾hr., 7 per day).

Adare's well-preserved medieval architecture and meticulous rows of thatched cottages have earned it a reputation as one of the prettiest towns in Ireland. With that distinction come bus-loads of tourists, who patronize the town's pricey restaurants and fancy hotels. While the monastic buildings and castle ruins may be worth a daytrip, there's little to persuade a budget traveler to stay the night. However, many people touring the Shannon region or awaiting flights at the airport prefer to stay here rather than in Limerick.

Walking tours of the town start from the heritage center on request (£5). The tours highlight the four historical sites of the town: the 13th-century **Trinitarian Abbey** on Main St., the 14th-century **Augustinian Priory,** the **Franciscan Friary,** and **Desmond Castle.** The lazy and tired can attempt to see it all in the **Adare Heritage Centre,** in the same building as the tourist office. (☎ 396 666. Open daily 9am-6pm. £3, students and seniors £2.) Nature trails wind through the 600-acre **Curraghchase Forest Park,** 5 mi. from Adare. **Horse trials** and **country fairs** are scheduled in Adare in March, May, and October (☎ 396 770).

The **tourist office** is located on Main St. in the Heritage Center complex. (☎ 396 255. Open June-Oct. M-F 9am-7pm, Sa-Su 9am-6pm; Nov.-Dec. and Mar.-May M-Sa 9am-5pm.) The **AIB,** just off Main St., has an **ATM.** The **library** located next to the heritage center on Main St. has free (with a £2 card) **Internet access.** (Open Tu and F 10am-1pm, 2-5:30, 6:30-8:30pm, W-Th and Sa 10am-1pm and 2-5:30pm.)

Although there is no hostel here, Adare is B&B central. Good choices include the clean, modern rooms at **Riversdale,** Manorcourt, Station Rd. (☎ 396 751; singles

₤20; doubles ₤38), and the friendly **Ardmore** about ¾ mi. outside of town on Tralee/ Killarney Rd. (☎ 396 167. Open Mar.-Oct. Doubles ₤30.) Food is generally expensive. The best budget food option is to stock up at **Centra** on Main St. and picnic in Town Park. (Open M-Sa 8am-7pm, Su 9am-1pm.) **The Blue Door,** a 200-year-old thatched cottage with blooming roses outside, offers reasonable lunches (around ₤5) and pricey dinners. (☎ 396 481. Open M-F 11am-2:30pm and 6:30-9:30pm, Sa noon-4pm and 6:30-9:30pm.) A similar lunchtime value can be found at **The Arches Restaurant,** where a main course and coffee hovers around ₤7. (☎ 396 246. Open M-Sa 11am-9:30pm, Su 11am-3:30pm.) Downtown Adare sports two pubs named "Collin's": **Pat Collin's Bar** (☎ 396 143) next to the post office on Main St., and **Shean Collin's Bar** (☎ 396 400) around the corner, which has one night of trad a week.

LOUGH DERG

Northeast of Limerick, the River Shannon widens into the lake region of Lough Derg. Affluent middle-aged tourists powerboat between the small towns of Killaloe, Mountshannon, and Portumna. Younger and vehicle-free travelers are rarer here than they are in regions to the south and west. Lough Derg's tourist activities provide a good workout, but little sightseeing; there are plenty of fishing, boating, and swimming opportunities, but archaeological attractions are few and far between. The Lough Derg Way walking path starts in Limerick, follows the western bank of the Shannon up to Killaloe, then crosses over to Ballina; it passes Arra Mountain on the way. The Neolithic tombs known as the "Graves of the Leinstermen" mark the refuge of Fintan the White, legendary consort of Cesair, who was the leader of the first invasion of Ireland and the granddaughter of Noah, daughter of Birth, and the name of ancient Rome's national airline.

Commuter **buses** run along Lough Derg Drive to and from **Limerick** (June-Aug. M-F 1 per day, Sept.-May M-F 2 per day), but the thrice-weekly bus (Tu, F, and Sa) will be more conveniently timed for sightseers based in the city. Really lucky hitchhikers may be able to score a lift from Limerick. *Let's Go* does not approve of hitchhikers or their craft.

BUNRATTY

Eight miles northwest of Limerick along Ennis Rd., ■**Bunratty Castle** and ■**Bunratty Folk Park** bring together a jumbled but unforgettable collection of historical attractions from all over Ireland. Bunratty Castle is allegedly Ireland's most complete medieval castle, with superbly restored furniture, tapestries, and stained-glass windows. During summer months, crowds of visitors clog its narrow stairways, making for frustrating tours of the chambers and battlements. (☎ (061) 361 511. Open daily June-Aug. 9am-6:30pm; Sept.-May 9:30am-5:30pm. Last admission 1hr. before closing. ₤6, students ₤4.25.) The castle derives much of its popularity from the medieval feasts that it hosts nightly for deep-pocketed tourists. Local damsels dressed in period costume serve wine and meat to would-be chieftains, accompanied by music. (5-course meal with wine ₤32. Book well in advance.)

The folk park originated in the 60s, when builders at Shannon Airport couldn't bear to destroy a quaint cottage for a new runway. Instead, they moved the cottage to Bunratty. Since then, reconstructions of turn-of-the-century houses and stores from all over Ireland have been added. Peat fires are lit in the cottages each morning by "inhabitants" dressed in period costume. The Bunratty complex also claims one heavily touristed pub. The first proprietress at **Durty Nelly's,** founded in 1620, earned her name by serving Bunratty soldiers more than just beer. **Buses** between **Limerick** and **Shannon Airport** pass Bunratty.

KILLALOE AND BALLINA ☎061

The pleasant hills and lakeside orientation of Killaloe (KILL-a-loo), Co. Clare, 15 mi. outside of Limerick along the Lough Derg Drive and just south of the lake, offer a respite from the throbbing city. Old churches testify to the town's role as a 7th-century religious center, though mushrooming condo developments infringe upon its tranquility. Across a narrow medieval bridge is tiny Ballina, Co. Tipperary.

SIXMILEBRIDGE ■ 285

🛈 PRACTICAL INFORMATION. The **tourist office,** in the former Lock House on the Killaloe side of the bridge, provides free maps of the area and information on several rural walks around Killaloe. (☎ 376 866. Open daily May-Sept. 10am-6pm.) An **ATM**-blessed **AIB** sits on Main St. (☎ 376 115. Open M and W-F 10am-4pm, Tu 10am-5pm.) The **library,** in the same building as the tourist office, provides free **Internet access** with a $2 card. (☎ 376 062. Open M and W 2-6 and 7-8:30pm, Tu and Th-F 11am-1:30pm, 2:30-6:30pm.) The **post office** is farther uphill. (☎ 376 111. Open M-F 9:30am-12:30pm and 1:30-5:30pm, Sa 9:30am-12:30pm.)

🏠🍴🍺 ACCOMMODATIONS, FOOD, AND PUBS. Killaloe is a manageable daytrip from Limerick, but several nice B&Bs near town make it a pleasant stopover. The very hospitable **Kincora House,** Main St., across from Crotty's Pub, is filled with well-maintained antiques and serves a healthy breakfast on request. (☎ 376 149; email kincorahouse@tinet.ie. Doubles and twins $44.) Four miles north of Killaloe is another welcoming B&B, **Shannarra** (☎ 376 548). If you're lucky, friendly Tom and Celine might put on a show for you at the neighboring **Piper's Inn** (☎ 375 544). The best place to stock up for a luau is **McKeogh's** (☎ 376 249), on Main St. in Ballina. (Open M-Th 8am-7:30pm, F-Sa 8am-8pm, Su 8:30am-2pm.) The immensely popular **Crotty's Courtyard Bar** serves up hearty grub on a patio decorated with antique ads. (☎ 376 965. Most meals $5-8; food served noon-3pm and 5-10pm.) Next to the bridge in Ballina, **Molly's** serves pub grub with waterside views. *Al fresco* pints are served if the weather allows. (☎ 376 632. Most meals $4.50-5.50; food served from 12:30-9:30pm.)

📷 SIGHTS. At the base of the town on Royal Parade lies **St. Flannan's Cathedral,** built between 1195 and 1225 and still in use. Inside the cathedral, the **Thorgrim Stone** is inscribed in both Scandinavian characters and the monks' *ogham* script, with a prayer for the conversion of the Viking Thorgrim to Christianity. Market Sq. may have once held the Kincora palace of High King BrianBorú, who lived here from 1002 to 1014. The other candidate for the site ofBorú's palace is the abandoned fort known as **BealBorú,** 1½ mi. out of town toward Mountshannon, now a subtle circular mound in a quiet forest glade. The legends ofBorú continue at the **Heritage Center,** where interactive displays document the days when steamboats chugged across the lake. (Open daily 10am-5:30pm. $1.50, students $1.) The sights of the town can be seen with **Killaloe Historical Walks.** (☎ 376 476. Walks leave daily from the tourist office at 11am, 12:30, 2 and 4pm. Call ahead. $3.) In late July, the **Irish Chamber Orchestra** forms the foundation of the **Killaloe Music Festival** (☎ 202 620). In August, Killaloe celebrates **Féile Brian Ború,** four days of music, watersports, and variousBorú-based activities.

Lough-related activities abound in Killaloe. The **Derg Princess** leaves from across the bridge in **Ballina** for relaxing hour-long cruises. (☎ 376 159. $5 includes admission to the heritage center.) **Whelan's** stations itself across from the tourist office and rents out **motorboats** for fishing or cruising. (☎ 376 159. $10 first hr., $5 per additional hr.) Whelan's also runs their own lake cruises aboard the **Spirit of Killaloe.** ($5 per person.) **Fishing** gear is rented and sold at **T.J.'s** in Ballina. (☎ 376 009. Open M-Sa 8am-11pm, Su 10am-11pm. Rod and reel $8 per day, $30 deposit.) A boat (and a bit of navigational prowess) gives you access to the eminently picnicable **Holy Island.** A couple of miles north of Killaloe, you can indulge in an afternoon of watersports at the **University of Limerick Activity and Sailing Centre.** (☎ 376 622. **Windsurfing** from $8 per hr., **canoeing** from $4 per hr., **sailboats** from $10 per hr.)

SIXMILEBRIDGE ☎ 061

Sitting halfway between Shannon and Limerick, this sleepy town has a spectacular hostel and makes a perfect stop on the way to or from Shannon Airport. The name of the town derives from the old Irish mile, equal to 2230 yards. There are six Irish miles between the town's bridge and Limerick City. Those who spend the day in Sixmilebridge can enjoy several serene outdoor activities. Walkers should head through **Gallows Hill** to **Woodcock Hill,** a site used in the Cromwellian War for hangings. The prisoners were well hanged—they received a tremendous view as well as the condition described by the hill's name (produced by a tightening noose). Fishers can rent a rod and reel from **Riverbank Fish and Tackle,** behind Bridgeside B&B (☎ 369 633; £10 per day). The fish are hungry and active in the nearby **Castle Lake,** approximately 3km north of the town.

Bus Éireann runs to **Shannon Airport** (M-Sa 2 per day, £2.50) and **Limerick** (M-Sa 2 per day, £2.50). A taxi to the airport is around £10. **Bike rental** is available at **Kearney's,** behind the B&B. (☎ 369 633. £7 per day, £25 per week.) The **Credit Union,** on Main St., has a **bureau de change.**

The best reason to make the trek is the **Jamaica Inn** hostel. Bob and Marley, the hostel's two dogs, welcome you to a spotless hostel that has every possible amenity. The owners are great history buffs, multilingual, and go the seventh mile to help out their guests. (☎ 369 220. **Internet** £1 per 8min. Laundry £4. Luggage and bike storage. Open Feb.-Oct. 10-bed dorms £9-10; 4-bed dorms with bath £11-12; singles £15-17; doubles with bath £26-30.) Jamaica Inn also houses the only restaurant in town, serving breakfast, lunch, and dinner. (Open M-Sa 8:30am-6pm, Su 8:30am-3:30pm. £1.50-4, £5, £7.50.) Groceries are available at **John+Seppie Crowe Supermarket.** (☎ 369 215. Open M-Sa 7:30am-9:30pm, Su 8am-8:30pm.) The town's six pubs quench thirst after a hard day's fishing. Great *craic* is had at **The Mill Bar** (☎ 369 145), with music three nights a week, while **Casey's** (☎ 369 215) attracts hurling enthusiasts. **McGregor's** serves pub grub and has trad on weekend nights. (☎ 36909. Food served noon-8pm.)

SHANNON AIRPORT ☎061

Fifteen miles west of Limerick off Ennis Rd. (N18), Shannon Airport (☎ 471 444; **Aer Lingus** info ☎ 471 666) sends jets to North America and Europe. Arriving travelers descend into a blend of cottages, industrial office complexes, and housing developments. There's a small **tourist office** (☎ 471 664) located in the arrival hall along with a **Bus Éireann** ticket office (☎ 474 311). Buses go to **Limerick** (40min.; M-Sa 9 per day, Su 7 per day), **Ennis** (45min.; M-Sa 22 per day, Su 13 per day; £3.50), **Dublin** (4½hr., 5 per day, £10), **Waterford,** and **Tralee. Alamo** is an inexpensive car rental agency (☎ 75061; £22 per day; rates vary by season). **Thrifty** also lets automobiles. (☎ 472 649. £30 per day, £195 per week. 3 day minimum rental. 23 or older. Call ahead.) **Dan Dooley Rent-A-Car** is the only agency that rents to 21- and 22-year-olds. (☎ (062) 53103. Rates vary; as low as £32 per 2-5 days.)

ENNIS ☎065

Ennis (pop. 16,000), a town 20 mi. northwest of Limerick, is known for its safe streets, city-caliber nightlife, and down-home friendliness. The town has doubled in population in the last 10 years due to migrants and industry. Ennis was recently dubbed "Information Age Town" in a contest, and as a prize all families in the town received computers. The town is best experienced on a Saturday, when the pubs and clubs are hopping and a makeshift produce market arises in Market Square. The town is also busy during festival time: the Fleadh Nua Music and Culture festival takes place the last weekend in May. Book early for a room. Its proximity to Shannon Airport and the Burren make Ennis a common stopover for tourists, who can enjoy a day of shopping followed by a night of pub crawling.

■ GETTING THERE

Trains: The station (☎ 684 0444) is a 15min. walk from the town center on Station Rd. Open M-Sa 7am-5pm, Su 15min. before departures. Trains leave for **Dublin** via **Limerick** (M-Sa 2 per day, Su 1 per day, £17).

Buses: The station (☎ 682 4177) is beside the train station. Open M-F 7:15am-5:30pm, Sa 7:15am-4:45pm. To: **Limerick** (40min.; M-Sa 18 per day, Su 6 per day; £5); **Shannon Airport** (40min.; M-F 13 per day, Sa 9 per day, Su 10 per day; £3.50); **Kilkee**

ENNIS ■ 287

(1hr.; M-Sa 2-3 per day, Su 1-2 per day; £6.90); **Doolin** (1hr.; M-Sa 3 per day, Su 1 per day; £5.50); **Galway** (1 hr., 5 per day, £7.70); **Cork** (3hr., 5 per day, £10); and **Dublin** via **Limerick** (4hr., 5 per day, £10). **West Clare** line (7 per day) goes to combinations of **Lisdoonvarna, Ennistymon, Lahinch, Miltown Malbay, Doolin, Kilkee,** and **Kilrush.** The crowded post bus runs from the **post office** (see **Practical Information,** below) to **Liscannor** and **Doolin** (M-Sa 2 per day, £2.50 to Doolin). Arrive early to get a seat.

ORIENTATION AND PRACTICAL INFORMATION

Ennis's layout can be confusing, but the city center is navigable enough that you'll eventually find what you need. The center of town is **O'Connell Square;** to reach it from the bus and train stations, head left down **Station Rd.,** turn right on **O'Connell St.,** and go down a few blocks. You'll know it by the soaring statue of Daniel O'Connell staring down at you from high atop a column. From O'Connell Sq., **Abbey St.** and **Bank St.** lead across the river to the burbs, and **High St.** runs perpendicular to O'Connell St. through the center of town. **Market Place** is between O'Connell and High St. **Westby's Lane** is off O'Connell street, across from **Station Rd.**

Tourist Offices: The brand new **Ennis Tourist Office,** O'Connell Sq. (☎ 28366), answers questions and provides bus and train information. Open June-Sept. daily 9:30am-6:30pm; Apr.-May and Oct. M-Sa 9:30am-5:30pm (closed 1-2pm for lunch); Nov.-Mar. M-F 9:30am-5:30pm (closed 1-2pm for lunch).

Banks: Bank of Ireland, O'Connell Sq. (☎ 682 8615). **AIB,** Bank Pl. (☎ 682 8089). Both have **ATMs** and are open M-Tu and Th-F 10am-4pm, W 10am-5pm.

Bike Rental: Michael Tierney Cycles and Fishing, 17 Abbey St. (☎ 682 9433, after 6pm ☎ 682 1293). Rentals and repair. Tierney helpfully suggests bike routes through the hilly countryside and gives advice on fishing expeditions. Bikes £4 per afternoon, £10 per day, £40 per week; deposit £40 or credit card. Open M-Sa 9:30am-6pm.

Luggage Storage: At the bus station. Lockers 50p. Open M-Sa 7:30am-6:30pm, Su 10am-7:15pm.

Laundry: Parnell's, High St. (☎ 682 9075). Wash and dry £4.90-6. Open M-Sa 9am-6pm. Handy for removing the Guinness stains from your lapels.

Pharmacy: O'Connell Chemist, Abbey St. (☎ 682 0373). Open M-Sa 9am-6:30pm. **Michael McLoughlin,** O'Connell St. (☎ 682 9511), in Dunnes Supermarket. Open M-W 9am-6pm, Th-F 9am-midnight, Sa 9am-6pm.

Counseling and Support: Samaritans (☎ (850) 609 090). 24hr. "Always there at the end of the line."

Emergency: ☎ 999; no coins required. **Police** (*Garda*): ☎ 682 8205.

Internet Access: Devalere Library (☎ 682 1616), down Abbey St., and over the bridge. The library is about two blocks from the bridge, on the left hand side. The public library has 10 terminals for public use—sign in at the desk. Open M, W-Th 10am-5:30pm, Tu, F 10am-8pm, Sa 10am-1pm.

Post Office: Bank Pl. (☎ 682 1054), off O'Connell Sq. Open M-F 9am-5:30pm, Sa 9:30am-2pm.

ACCOMMODATIONS

On the river across Club Bridge from Abbey St., the **Abbey Tourist Hostel** is a 300-year-old labyrinth on Harmony Row. As is the case with most centuries-old buildings, the hostel is a bit drafty. To make up for the drafts, the push-button showers come in one temperature: very, very hot. Generally, however, the hostel is clean, comfortable, and a good place to meet other travelers. It also has a small courtyard with palm trees and a view of the river. (☎ 682 2620. Laundry £3. Dorms £10; doubles £26.) **Mary Conway's Greenlea B&B,** on Station Rd. between the cathedral and the station, has sparklingly clean rooms (three doubles and a single) and cheerful management. (☎ 682 9049. Open Mar.-Oct. Singles £16, doubles £28.) **The**

WESTERN IRELAND

Banner, at the intersection of Old Barrack St. and Market Place, offers clean rooms (mostly doubles) for a reasonable price—all include televisions, bathrooms, and windows that overlook the town. (☎ 682 4224. Breakfast £5. £17 per person.) **Derrynane House,** in O'Connell Sq., will put a roof over your head right in the middle of town. Rooms are clean, cute, and quiet, even with a busy pub and restaurant downstairs. If you're not a carnivore, Derrynane offers a vegetarian alternative to the Irish breakfast prototype. (☎ 682 8464. Singles £20, all with bath.)

FOOD AND PUBS

Meals in Ennis are mostly found in its pubs, but a short supply can be found elsewhere. Enormous **Dunnes Supermarket,** in the mall, O'Connell St., offers inexpensive food and beverages. (☎ 684 0700. Open M-Tu 9am-6:30pm, W-F 9am-9pm, Sa 9am-7pm, Su noon-6pm.) For a quick lunch, **Henry's,** at the end of Westby's Lane, off O'Connell St., offers scrumptious sandwiches and salads. (☎ 682 2848. Emmenthal cheese, olives, and artichoke heart sandwich £2.55.) Their all-natural, homemade ice-cream is the Ennis menace to dieters (one scoop 90p). **Pearl City,** O'Connell St., serves dozens of tasty Chinese dishes. Vegetarian and vegan options available. (☎ 682 1388. Lunch special for under £5. Open M-Th 12:30-2:30pm, 5pm-12:30am, F 12:30-2:30pm, 5pm-1am, Sa 4pm-1:30am, Su 1pm-1am.) **Upper Crust,** off Market Sq., sells high-class helpings for low prices. (☎ 43261. Roast chicken £3.80. Open M-Sa 8am-6pm, Su 8am-2pm.)

With over 60 pubs to its name, there is no shortage of nightlife in Ennis. Most host trad sessions that help Ennis uphold Clare's reputation as a county of musical excellence, especially during festival time. Good pubs line the streets—just listen for the music. *The Clare Champion* has music listings for Ennis, and can be found in just about any shop, pub, or restaurant. **Cruises Pub,** Abbey St., next to the Friary, hosts lively trad in its dimly lit front section, while a high-class restaurant fills its back portion. Its 1658 birth date makes it one of the oldest buildings in Co. Clare, and much of the original interior remains intact. Over the years, Cruises has developed a strong relationship with the county's musicians. Local music stars appear nightly for cozy sessions, and international music star Maura O'Connell once lived upstairs. (☎ 684 1800. Trad nightly and Su afternoons in summer.) **Brandon's Bar,** O'Connell St. (☎ 28133), serves huge plates of spuds, meat, and veggies (entrees £3.50) alongside its pints (trad W-Su). Upstairs is **The Boardwalk,** a hot spot for live trad, world, and indie music. (Cover £3 before midnight, £4 after. Open F-Sa.) On weekends, people pack **The Brewery** (☎ 6844172), 2 Abbey St., to drink pints beneath its celestial ceiling. Ennis has its fair share of dark and woody pubs serving dark and frothy pints, the darkest and woodiest being **The Usual Place,** 5 Market St. (☎ 682 0515).

SIGHTS

Two blocks along Abbey St. away from O'Connell Sq. rest the ruins of the 13th-century **Ennis Friary,** Ennis's pride and joy (after the Clare hurling team, of course). Franciscans used the Friary until the 17th century and the architecture in the Friary ranges from the 13th century to as recent as the 19th century. In 1375 the seminary became one of Ireland's most important pre-Reformation theological schools. In the entrance to the right room, there is a small inset depicting the crucifixion of Christ. Legend has it that Judas's wife, while cooking chicken soup, told her husband, in an attempt to comfort him, that Christ was as likely to rise from the grave as the cock she was cooking was to rise from its pot. The cock also rises, as seen in the lower right corner of the inset. Thirty-minute tours, included in the price, tell a fascinating history of the Friary. (☎ 682 9100. Open mid-May to Sept. daily 9:30am-6:30pm. £1, students 40p.) Across from the Friary, a block of sandstone inscribed with part of Yeats's "Easter 1916" remembers the Easter Rising (see p. 16). **Daniel O'Connell** watches over the town from his square. The original O'Connells were Catholic landowners dispossessed by Cromwell (see **Plantation** and Cromwell, p. 10). In 1828, almost 200 years later, Ennis residents elected Catholic barrister Daniel O'Connell, soon to become "The Liberator," to represent them at Westminster (see p. 13). A 10-minute walk from the town center on Mill Rd. leads to the **Maid of Erin,** a life-sized statue remembering the **"Manchester Martyrs,"** three nationalists hanged in Manchester in 1867 (see also **Kilrush,** p. 289). Saturday is **Market Day** in Market Sq., where all conceivable wares are sold beneath a statue of crafty Daedalus. A 30-minute walk winds along the trout-filled River Fergus; directions (and lists of more animals to watch for) are posted in the parking lot between the river and Abbey St.

COROFIN ☎ 065

Seven lakes and the River Fergus make the village of Corofin lush, but it's only a few miles away from the rocky Burren. There is no longer a hostel in Corofin, so the best bet for a budget traveler without a tent is to stay in Ennis and bike to Corofin for quiet walks beside pastoral scenes. Also, if you have more than a sneaking suspicion that your ancestors emigrated from County Clare, the **Clare Heritage and Genealogical Research Centre,** Church St., can help you trace your roots through birth, marriage, and death certificates. (☎ 603 7955. http://clare.irishroots.net. Open M-F 9am-5:30pm.) A **Heritage Museum** across the street houses artifacts from the potato famine, emigration, and landowner days in a decaying Protestant church. (£2, students £1.50.) A history trail that stays within 2 mi. of the village center leads you to Corofin's sights. Well-preserved 12th-century **St. Tola's Cross** and the battlefield where, in 1318, Conor O'Dea's victory put off English domination for another two centuries. Three miles south of Corofin, **Dysert O'Dea Castle and Archaeology Centre,** housed in a restored 15th-century tower, uncovers the more distant past and explains the archaeological features of the surrounding lands. (☎ 603 7722. Open May-Sept. daily 10am-6pm. £2.50.) The **Dromore National Nature Reserve** and its peaceful, swan-inhabited lakes are about 8 mi. west of Corofin. Follow signs to Ruan Village; the reserve is signposted from there. Guided tours are available, but the trails allow you to ramble. Those eager to try their luck at nabbing one of the fish in Corofin's lakes and rivers can call **Burke's** (☎ 603 7677) and hire boats (£10) with a day's notice.

Buses travel to and from **Ennis** (M-Sa 1 per day, £6) and **Lahinch** (M-Sa 1 per day, £4.20). The **tourist office,** Church St., is in the **Clare Heritage Centre.** (☎ 37955. Open June-Sept. daily 10am-6pm.) The **post office** is on Main St. (Open M-F 9am-1pm and 2-5:30pm, Sa 9am-1pm.) The **Corofin Village Camping Park** on Main St. offers clean, modern facilities including a game room with a pool table for rainy days. (☎ 603 7683. Wheelchair accessible. Laundry £5. Camping £4.50, £11.50 per family; less in off-season.) **Spar Market,** Main St., sells fruits, vegs, and staples. (Open daily 9am-8pm.) The **Corofin Arms** serves up good pub grub at reasonable prices, garnished with occasional trad and folk in the evenings. (☎ 603 7373. Sandwiches with salad and fries £3.95.) The **Teác Celide,** Main St., by the post office, organizes music, song, set dancing, poetry, and tea. (Th evening July-Aug. only. 9pm; £3.)

CLARE COAST

Those traveling between Co. Clare and Co. Kerry may want to take the 20-minute **Tarbert-Killimer car ferry** across the Shannon estuary, avoiding the 85 mi. drive by way of inland Limerick. (☎ (065) 905 3124. £9 per carload, £2 for pedestrians and bikers; see **Tarbert,** p. 276.)

KILRUSH ☎ 065

The route to the Clare Coast from either Tarbert or Limerick passes through Kilrush (pop. 2900), home of the coast's only marina. The town's name means "church of the meadow," derived from the gaelic "Cill Rois." A permanent settlement landed in Kilrush in the 12th century when monks from nearby Scattery Island built a church in a mainland meadow. Seven hundred years later, during the

290 ■ CLARE COAST

Famine, Kilrush tenants banded together to withhold rent from their absentee landlords. Their actions led to the coining of the term "boycott"; the word's namesake is the debt collector who was the first to be refused. In the early 20th century, Kilrush gained fame as the home of the folk musicians, such as Elizabeth Crotty, who rekindled national interest in traditional music. Kilrush hosts a music festival in honor of Mrs. Crotty in mid-August.

▼ PRACTICAL INFORMATION. Bus Éireann stops in Market Sq. on its way to **Ennis** (☎ 682 4177 in Ennis. 1hr.; M-Sa 3-5 per day, Su 2-3 per day; £5.80) and **Kilkee** (20min.; M-Sa 2-4 per day, Su 1-2 per day; £2). The tourist information office, with a **bureau de change,** is across from the **Kilrush Heritage Centre,** Town Hall (☎ 905 1577), on Market Sq. **AIB** on Frances St. has an **ATM.** (☎ 905 1012. Open M 10am-5pm, Tu-F 10am-4pm.) **Bike rental** is available at **Gleesons,** Henry St., the street beside Crotty's, going away from the square, through the Raleigh Rent-A-Bike program. (☎ 905 1127. £8 per day, £35 per week, £50 deposit.) Anthony Malone's **pharmacy,** on the right side of Frances St., the street going towards the pier from the square, has all you need. (☎ 905 2552. Open M-Sa 9am-6pm, Su 11am-1pm.) The **Internet Bureau,** beside the marina, provides access to the web and helpful, knowledgeable management. (☎ 905 1061. £3 per half-hour. Open daily early to late, call for hours.) If it isn't open, try the store next to Katie O'Connor's Holiday Hostel, which has a small **Internet** terminal (£1 for 10min. Open M-Sa 8:30am-9:30pm, Su 9:30am-9:30pm). The **post office** is on Frances St. (☎ 905 1077. Open M-F 9am-5:30pm, Sa 10am-4:30pm.)

▼ ACCOMMODATIONS, FOOD, AND PUBS. Katie O'Connor's Holiday Hostel **(IHH),** on Frances St. next to the AIB, provides clean and comfortable quarters in rooms that date back to 1797. Hostelers enjoy an open hearth. Check in at the store next to the sign for the hostel. (☎ 905 1133. Dorms £8; doubles £19; quads £34.) The **Kilrush Creek Lodge,** in the cyan and red building across from the marina, is a large, clean, group-oriented accommodation next door to an adventure center. (☎ 905 2595. Wheelchair accessible. Laundry £3. Dorms £10 with continental breakfast, £11.50 with a full Irish breakfast; doubles £36.) B&Bs in Kilrush are plentiful and expensive. The **Iveragh House** (☎ 905 1176) on Frances St. boasts beautiful garden views for a reasonable £18-£20 per person.

A **Super Valu** sells groceries at the end of Frances St. (☎ 905 1885. Open M-W, Sat 8:30am-7pm, Th-F 8:30am-9pm, Su 9am-6pm.) The incredible aroma of bread floating across Frances St. to the hostel comes from **Cosidines.** The 150-year-old bakery has been in the same family for five generations; it still uses the same ovens and mixers it did in the 1850s. Another remnant of the bakery's past are the bars on its windows; they kept out the hungry during Famine times, but now the owners welcome local customers by their first names. (☎ 905 1095. Open M-Sa 8am-6pm.) For a quick lunch, the **Quayside** restaurant and coffee shop offers tasty homemade scones, soup, and sandwiches. (☎ 905 1927. £1.85 for a toasted sandwich. Open M-Sa 9:30am-5:45pm.) Of Kilrush's 15 or so pubs, at least one is sure to have music on summer nights. ◪**Crotty's Pub,** Market Sq., is the legendary spot where concertina player Mrs. Crotty helped repopularize trad in the 1950s, as evinced by the inspirational tributes to her inside the pub. (☎ 905 2470. Trad Tu-Th, Sa-Su.) Crotty's also cooks up pub grub and offers a beautifully restored **B&B.** The rooms are spacious and come with fireplaces for toasty evenings (£20 per person).

◨ SIGHTS. At the **Kilrush Heritage Centre,** you can hear the town's memories of the Great Famine on "Kilrush in Landlord Times," a self-guided cassette tour (£2). A permanent exhibition describes Kilrush in the times of Napoleon and the Famine. Audio-visuals disturbingly recreate the scene of an 1888 eviction. In town, a monument facing the Town Hall remembers the Manchester Martyrs of 1867 (see **Ennis,** p. 286). Just outside town on the ferry road, the dirt paths of 420-acre **Kilrush Forest Park** promise adventure, romance, and ultimately a return to town. Kilrush's real attraction, however, lies offshore at **Scattery Island,** the site of a 6th-century

Monastic settlement. St. Senan reputedly once banned women from stepping foot on the island. His words hold little weight today, as co-ed boatloads of tourists visit daily. The island has been uninhabited since the 1970s, leaving behind the rubble of monastic ruins, churchyards, and a circular tower. Boats depart regularly in summer (June-Sept. 4-5 per day, $4.50 return) and irregularly in other seasons. The tourist office books tours, and transportation can be arranged with Gerald Griffins (☎ 905 1327). The island sits in the Shannon estuary, home to Ireland's only known resident population of bottlenose dolphins. The **Scattery Island Ferries** offer an eco-cruise for $9. (☎ 905 1327. Call ahead.) On the mainland, the **Scattery Island Centre,** Merchant's Quay, can tell you more about the island's history and ecology. (☎ 905 2139. Open mid-June to mid-Sept. daily 9:30am-6:30pm. Free.) Get wet at the **Kilrush Creek Adventure Centre** (☎ 905 2855), next to the Kilrush Lodge. The centre allows experts and novices alike to design their own land- or sea-based adventure. **Windsurfing, kayaking, sailing, orienteering,** and a variety of activities are instructed by a fully-certified staff. ($15 for a half-day, includes instruction and equipment. Call ahead.) The **Éigse Mrs. Crotty** ("Rise up, Mrs. Crotty!") festival celebrates the glory of the concertina (see **Music,** p. 29) with lessons, lectures, and non-stop trad for a weekend in mid-August.

KILKEE ☎065

From the first weekend in June to the first weeks of September, Kilkee is an Irish holiday town. Families fill the pastel summer homes spreading toward the headlands and students work in resort jobs, partying until early morning. Bathers fill the swimming holes along the shore and flock to the cliffs. But the crescent-shaped town overlooking a half-circle of soft sand has another side, when the people leave and the population drops from 25,000 to 2300. The crashing waters have cut islands out of craggy cliffs, the seaweed sways in the tide like flowing hair, and the countryside is green and quiet with only an occasional "moo." To skip the crowds, it is best to visit Kilkee right before or, better yet, right after the busy season, when shops are still open but there is room on the beach.

GETTING THERE. Bus Éireann (☎ 682 4177 in Ennis) leaves from Neville's Bar (the sign reads Kett's), around the corner from the tourist office by the central square. Buses head to **Limerick** (2hr., 3-4 per day) via **Ennis** (1hr.), and for **Galway** with an hour-long stop at the **Cliffs of Moher** (4hr., 2-3 per day).

PRACTICAL INFORMATION. The **tourist office** is next to the Stella Maris Hotel in the central square. (☎ 56112. Open daily June-Sept. 10am-6pm.) The **ATM** at the **Bank of Ireland,** O'Curry St., hands out cash. (☎ 56053. Open M 10am-12:30pm and 1:30-5pm, Tu-F 10am-12:30pm and 1:30-4pm.) A **post office** is on Circular Rd. (☎ 56001. Open M-F 9am-5:30pm, Sa 9am-12:30pm.) Across the street is **William's,** a hardware store and pharmacy that also **rents bikes** (☎ 56041; emergency ☎ 905 6141. Open M-Sa 9am-6pm. Bikes $6 per day, $30 per week; deposit $30.)

ACCOMMODATIONS, FOOD, AND PUBS. The family-run **Kilkee Hostel (IHH),** O'Curry St., creates an atmosphere of fellowship among the travelers and itinerant geology students who gather in its large living room. Rooms are sunny, clean, and fill up fast; call ahead. (☎ 56209. Sheets 50p. Laundry $2. Dorms $8.) The **Duggerna B&B,** a 10-minute walk up a winding road out of town, offers views from the top of the cliff. (☎ 905 6152. Open May-Sept. $20 per person with bath.) At **Cunningham's,** a neatly arranged battalion caravans provide a view for canvas-covered campers. Turn left onto the coast road and take the first turn-off behind the pink building. (☎ 905 6430. Open June-Sept. Showers 50p. $4; $18 for a family of 4.)

A **Central Stores supermarket** vends victuals on the corner of O'Curry St. and Circular Rd. (☎ 56249. Open summer M-Th 9am-8:30pm, F-Su 9am-9pm; winter daily 9am-8pm.) **The Pantry,** O'Curry St., is a culinary oasis in a desert of fast food. "Life's too short to drink bad wine," so the Pantry stocks up a large selection, with gourmet offerings to further please your palate. (☎ 56576. Lunches £4-5, dinners £8-10. Open daily June-Sept. 9:30am-noon, 12:30-5pm, and 6:30-9:30pm). In the alley behind the Pantry, the **Country Cooking Shop** makes desserts for the decadent traveler. If you have more than a sneaking suspicion that your ancestors emigrated from County Clare, the **Clare Heritage and Genealogical Research Centre**, Church St., can help you trace your roots through birth, marriage, and death certificates. (☎ 603 7955. http://clare.irishroots.net. Open M-F 9am-5:30pm.) The hum-drum **Heritage Museum** across the street houses artifacts from the potato famine, emigration, and landowner days in a decaying Protestant church. (£2, students £1.50.) A history trail that stays within 2 mi. of the village center leads you to Corofin's sights. Well-preserved 12th-century **St. Tola's Cross** and the battlefield where, in 1318, Conor O'Dea's victory put off English domination for another two centuries. Three miles south of Corofin, **Dysert O'Dea Castle and Archaeology Centre**, housed in a restored 15th-century tower, uncovers the more distant past and explains the archaeological features of the surrounding lands. (☎ 603 7722. Open May-Sept. daily 10am-6pm. £2.50.) The **Dromore National Nature Reserve** and its peaceful, swan-inhabited lakes are about 8 mi. west of Corofin. Follow signs to Ruan Village; the reserve is signposted from there. Guided tours are available, but the trails allow you to ramble. Those eager to try their luck at nabbing one of the fish in Corofin's lakes and rivers can call **Burke's** (☎ 603 7677) and hire boats (£10) with a day's notice. **The Myles Creek Pub**, O'Curry St., is where locals go for lunch (☎ 905 6670. Plate of cabbage and bacon £5, sandwiches £1.75).

After a day spent frolicking, or simply snoring on the beach, you can happily fritter away even more time by drinking your way through the dense strip of pubs along O'Curry St. **Richie's** (☎ 56597) informal setting and friendly staff make it a good place to start. The **Central Bar** (☎ 56103) has plenty of seating, pool tables, and dark red wood to go with the dark pints. The **Old Bistro** (☎ 56898) is a roughhewn gem rebuilt four years ago by a handy Limerick chef and his wife. The upstairs restaurant offers candlelit romance, and the downstairs pub—decorated with choice farm tools—promises good old-fashioned *craic*. Look for acoustic entertainment and the handsome barman Jack. Kilkee has a happening after-hours scene that occasionally sees last call come precariously close to the next first call. If you would rather see the stars and sunrise from the sand, the palatial bar and large stage of the **Strand Bar** (☎ 56177) is a great place to end your crawl. A highheel's throw from the beach, the Strand has live music and dancing on most nights in the summer, from trad and rock to all-out cabaret.

◘ SIGHTS AND ACTIVITIES. The spectacular **Westend Cliff Walk** begins at the end of the road to the left of the seacoast and makes a gentle climb up to the top of the cliffs. If the tide is out, climb out onto the flat rocks in front of the carpark— the three **Pollock Holes** should be exposed. The first and easiest to climb to is traditionally called the Children's Hole, the second, the Women's Hole, and the third, the Men's Hole (where women are now allowed, but men still bath nude). If you don't have a chance to bathe in the ocean, stop by the ◙**Kilkee Thalassotherapy Centre**, across from the bus station. Seaweed baths in a 160-year-old porcelain tub (£12 for 25min.) will make you feel like a mermaid (or merman!). The owner's husband collects seawater at high tide and seaweed at low tide for the baths. The center also offers foot massages (£10 for 30min.) for feet tired after the cliff walk. (☎ 905 6742; email mulcahype@eircom.net. Open year-round except for Feb.; mid-June to mid-Sept. M-Sa 10am-7pm, Su noon-6pm; shorter hours in off-season. Call ahead in the summer.) The **Westend Cliff Walk** intersects with **Loop Head Dr.** after passing the Diamond rocks, where the John Wayne classic *Ryan's Daughter* was filmed. To the right, the photogenic drive runs through small villages, ruined farmhouses, and plenty of pasture to the **Loop Head Lighthouse**, at the very tip of Co. Clare. On the way, it passes through **Carrigaholt**, a village 7 mi. south of Kilkee on the Shannon Estuary. The **Loop Head Dr.** route can be biked—it is about 50km and has steep parts on the way back. To the left, the road leads back to Kilkee. A few blocks away from the town, watch for the turquoise house with a red farm-tool sculpture garden out front. If this sounds like too much walking, the **Kilkee Pony Trekking & Riding Center** will saddle you up and guide you along Kilkee's splendid beach and past some of Ireland's greenest fields. (☎ 906 0071. Morning rides £25.) If underwater is more your style, Kilkee is famous for its **diving.** Jump in at the **Kilkee Diving Centre** (☎ 905 6707), a five-minute walk down the shore road to the right.

MILLTOWN MALBAY ☎065

Barring a superb trad music pub scene on weekends, Milltown Malbay, 20 mi. north of Kilkee on N67, doesn't have much to offer travelers during most of the year. Accommodations are scarce and minimal, the main street has a few pubs, two lanes, and lots of cars turning around at the end of the street when they realize they've missed the turnoff to the Cliffs of Moher. The high point of the year is a large music festival hosted by the **Willie Clancy School of Traditional Music** (☎ 84148). During **Willie Week,** the first Monday in July, thousands of musicians, instrument-makers, fans, tourists, and *craic* addicts will flock here from all corners of the globe to celebrate the famous Irish piper who was born here. Participants pay £50 for the week's lectures, lessons, and recitals, while the musically challenged are given a wide variety of set-dancing classes. Incessant trad sessions in the town's packed pubs are free, but range in quality (beware). Accommodations are booked months in advance, but the notice board at the community center in town can provide some leads. The **Lahinch Hostel** (see below), 10 mi. to the north, is your best bet if there's just no room for you in Milltown. Since it has no hostels and scant transportation, Milltown doesn't get many tourists during the rest of the year. However, **The International Darlin' Girl from Clare Festival,** modeled after the Rose of Tralee Festival (see p. 276), is gathering steam in its 11th year. The pageant, accompanied by open-air *ceilis* (traditional set dances) on the main square, sees the streets filled to the brim with locals and aspiring darlin's each August.

The **Bank of Ireland** is next to O'Friels. (☎ 708 4018. Open M-W and F 10am-12:30pm and 1:30-4pm, Th 10am-12:30pm and 1:30-5pm.) **Byrne's** on Ennis Rd. **rents bikes,** and has a limited supply of camping equipment. (☎ 708 4079. Bikes £7 per day, £35 per week. Open M-Sa 9:30am-6:30pm.) Marie Kelly's **pharmacy** is on Main St. (☎ 708 4440. Open M-Tu and Th-Sa 9am-6pm, W 9am-7pm.)

The affordable **Station House,** at the old railway station, five minutes down the road from Cleary's (see below), is run by darlin' twins. The sprawling building has huge beds, clean rooms, and a good driveway from which to hitch to Lahinch. *Let's Go* does not recommend thumbing it. (☎ 708 4008. Singles £20; doubles £35.) If Station House does not have a room, or if centrality is important, **O'Loughlin's Ocean View B&B,** right in the center of town, has rooms, a staircase built by Willie Clancy himself, and a view of the main street of town. (☎ 708 4249. Summer £18, off-season £15.) **Campers** take refuge above the **Spanish Point Beach** (£5 per tent). **Spar Supermarket & Bakery,** Main St., sells super groceries. (☎ 708 4093. Open M-Sa 9am-9pm, Su 9am-1:30pm.) Its name means "potato skins," but when **An Sceallain,** Main St., fires up the ovens, out come delicious pizzas for £2-7. (☎ 708 4498. Open M and Th 5:30pm-midnight, F-Su 4pm-late.) There is a **Country Market** on Saturday mornings in the **Community Hall** (11am-1pm).

Milltown squeezes 15 pubs into two blocks; Saturday is the night for impromptu sessions. At **Cleary's** (☎ 708 4201), an easy-going, busy bar just off the main street on the Ennistymon Rd., musicians often outnumber listeners. It's locally known as "The Blond's" after a former proprietor. **Clancy's** (☎ 708 4077) also has excellent trad, and the occasional blues session. The sign above **O'Friel's** still says "Lynch's" after all these years; "a local favorite with decent grub" would be more accurate. Willie, of Willie Week fame, once lived here. (☎ 708 4275. Trad weekends.)

LAHINCH ☎065

Surf into Lahinch for fun on the beach. This small holiday spot developed in the 1880s as a haven for the well-to-do, but it now draws surfers, golfers, students, and Irish holiday-goers. Nestled in a corner of a mile-wide strand of smooth sand deposited by the Inagh River, Lahinch is the surfing capital of Ireland (come in the winter for the best waves). Natural wonders aside, those seeking arcades, bars, discos, and people to fill them won't be disappointed in the summer.

Buses (☎ 682 4177) roll in two to three times a day during the summer from **Doolin, Ennis, Galway, Limerick,** and **Cork** to the edge of town near the golf courses. From the bus, walk toward the town and turn right—the main street starts a few blocks down. A **bureau de change** rests at the top of Main St. (☎ 708 1743. Open M-Su 9am-10pm.) The **post office,** Main St., also changes money. (☎ 708 1001. Open M-F 9am-1pm and 2-5:30pm, Sa 9am-1pm.) The new **Lahinch Fáilte** tourist office, at the bottom of Main St., organizes tours and sells ferry and bus tickets. (☎ 708 2082. Open 9:30am-9pm in summer, 9:30am-6pm in the winter. Ask about **bike rentals** and **Internet access.**) An **ATM** is next door. The nearest **bank** is in Ennistymon.

Clean, comfortable bunk rooms, a fun staff, and a waterfront location score a birdie at the **Lahinch Hostel (IHH)**, on Church St. in the town center. (☎ 708 1040. Laundry £2. **Bike rental** £7 per day. Dorms £8-9; doubles £24. Call ahead in the summer.) **The Village Hostel (IHH)**, a 2 mi. bus ride west into Liscannor, features an echoing kitchen, locally mined stone floors, and a laid-back way of life. (☎ 708 1550. Sheets 50p. Dorms £7.50; private rooms £9, with packed lunch and dinner £15. Camping £4 per person.) Although it's a bit of a walk down N67, **Cois Farraige B&B** has beautiful rooms with views of the family's horses and the sea. Ask for an upstairs room. (☎ 708 1580. Open mid-Mar. to mid-Nov. In June-Sept. singles £24; doubles £38. Off-season singles £19; doubles £34.) The **Lahinch Caravan & Camping Park**, also on N67, provides space for camping. (☎ 708 1424. Open Easter-Sept. Reception summer daily 9am-10pm; off-season 9am-5pm. £5 per tent.)

The ✪**Spinnaker Restaurant and Bar,** next to Lahinch Fáilte, offers tasty dinners and lunches. The smoked salmon sandwich, with chive and caper mayonnaise and a salad (£5.95), is refreshing after heavy pub food. (☎ 708 1893. Wheelchair accessible.) At night it draws a twenty-something crowd with its occasional live bands. **Flanasans** (☎ 708 1161), on Main St., has good trad and ballads. At **Kenny's Bar,** Main St. (☎ 708 1433), candles glow from whiskey bottles, and the back patio is a nice spot from which to people-watch. The tasty Irish stew (£5) was once written up in the *New York Times*. The disco ball spins at the **Claremont Hotel** on Main St. (☎ 708 1007. Cover £4. Open F-Su.)

The Surf Shop, along the promenade, rents foam surfboards and wetsuits. (☎ 708 1543. Boards or wetsuits £3 per hr., boots £1 per hr. Open summer 11am-6pm, off-season weekends only.) Arcades, rides, and general **amusements** along the beach provide entertainment during the day or evening. Spot Sammy the Starfish or Harry the Hermit Crab at **Seaworld,** at the far end of the promenade. Tanks filled with fish from the Atlantic give an informative view of local sea life (☎ 708 1900. Open 10am-8pm. £4.50, students £3.65). Or, see the real thing: go fishing with **O'Callaghan Angling.** (☎ 682 1374. Boats run starting the first weekend in June. Evening trips £17.50.) Lahinch is world famous for its **golfing** (☎ 708 1003), but fame costs: one round starts at £45, and reservations should be made three months in advance. The **Cliffs of Moher** are only 15 minutes away by bus, and ferries leave from nearby Liscannor (Lahinch-Doolin bus route) for the Aran Islands (see p. 303).

CLIFFS OF MOHER

The Cliffs of Moher are one of Ireland's most famous sights. The stunning view from the edge leads 700 ft. straight down to the open sea. These cliffs are so high you can actually see gulls whirling below you. On a clear day, the majestic headland affords views of Loop Head, the Kerry Mountains, the Twelve Pins of Connemara, and the Aran Islands. **O'Brien's Tower** sits near the car park; don't fall for its illusion of medieval grandeur—it was built in 1835 as a viewing tower by Cornelius O'Brien, an early tour-promoter. You'll do just as well to stick to the ground view. (Open daily Apr.-Oct. 9am-7:30pm. £2, students 60p.) Most tour groups cluster around the tower, but better views await a bit farther along the coast. Occasionally marked paths wander along the cliffs, but most tourists drop away after the first curve. (Winds occasionally blow a few off every year—stay on the land side of the stone walls. *Let's Go* does not recommend falling off the Cliffs of Moher.)

Three miles south of Doolin, the Cliffs brush against R478; cars pay £1 for use of the parking lot. Bus Éireann clangs by on the summer-only Galway-Cork route (M-Sa, 3 per day). The 26 mi. Burren Way and several trails weave more elusively through raised limestone and beds of wildflowers from Doolin (3hr.) and Liscannor (3½hr.). Hitchhikers report mixed success in finding rides here. *Let's Go* does not recommend hitching. The **tourist office**, beside the parking lot, houses a **bureau de change**. A tea shop in the same building rejuvenates wind-blown travelers. (☎ (065) 81171. Open daily Apr.-Oct. 9:30am-5:30pm.) **Aran Ferries** operates a fantastic cruise that leaves from the pier in nearby Liscannor and sails along directly under the cliffs (☎ 81368. 55min., 1 per day, £10).

DOOLIN ☎065

Something of a national shrine to Irish traditional music, the little village of Doolin draws thousands of visitors every year to its three pubs for nights of lively traditional music. Come to Doolin for music, scenery, and food. Walk 15 minutes up Fisher St. to see crashing waves, or a few minutes out of town for rolling hills criss-crossed with stone walls. Several Doolin restaurants have also won the coveted Bridgestone award for the best food in Ireland and have received world wide critical acclaim. Most of Doolin's 200 or so permanent residents run its four hostels, countless B&Bs, and pubs. The remaining residents farm the land and, in their spare time, wonder how so many backpackers end up in their small corner of the world. But not even bus-loads of tourists and raucous trad can dent the pervasive sense of peace in what is essentially a sleepy little town.

GETTING THERE AND GETTING AROUND

Buses run from the Doolin Hostel and the Campsite (see **Accommodations**, below), and advance tickets can be purchased at the hostel. Route #15 runs to **Kilkee**, or to **Dublin** via **Ennis** and **Limerick** (M-Sa 1 per day in off-season, summer 2 per day; Su 1 per day). Route #50 runs to the **Cliffs of Moher** (15min.), and to **Galway** (1½hr.) via multiple other **Burren** destinations (summer M-Sa 5 per day, Su 2 per day; off-season M-Sa 1 per day). The 8 mi. paved and bicycle-friendly segment of the **Burren Way** links Doolin to the **Cliffs of Moher**. The steep climb along the road from Doolin to the Cliffs lets bicyclists coast the whole way back, reserving energy for another night of foot-stomping fun at the pubs. The **Doolin Bike Store**, outside the Aille River Hostel, **rents bikes** (☎ 707 4282. £7 per day; open M-Su 9am-8pm). Pedestrians will find the route an exhausting but manageable half-day trip. Boats leave the town's pier for the **Aran Islands**, but boats from Galway and Rossaveal are cheaper under almost any circumstances (see **Galway**, p. 313).

ORIENTATION AND PRACTICAL INFORMATION

Doolin is made up of two villages about a mile apart from each other. Close to the shore is the **Lower Village** with **Fisher St.** running through it. Fisher St. traverses a stretch of farmland on its way to the **Upper Village**, where it turns into **Roadford**. A traveling **bank** comes to Lower Village every Thursday from 11am to 2pm, but there's a permanent **bureau de change** at the **post office**, across from the Rainbow Hostel. The nearest **ATM** is in Ennistymon, 5 mi. to the southeast. The **post office** operates from the Upper Village. (☎ 74209. Open M-F 9am-1pm and 2-5:30pm, Sa 9am-1pm.)

ACCOMMODATIONS

Tourists pack Doolin in the summer, so book ahead for hostels. B&Bs are common, but those along the main road tend to be expensive.

- **Aille River Hostel (IHH;** ☎ 707 4260), halfway between the villages, in a cute cottage by the river. Small, relaxed hostel with groovy ambiance and clean, well-maintained rooms. Local musicians often stop by the Aille to warm up before gigs in the pubs. Free laundry. No phone. Internet access £4 per hour for guests and £6 per hour for strangers. Open mid-Mar. to mid-Nov. Dorms July-Aug. £8, Sept.-May £7.50; doubles and triples £8 per person. **Camping** £4.
- **Flanaghan's Village Hostel (IHH;** ☎ 707 4564), a 5min. walk up the road from the Upper Village. This brand-new and still-expanding hostel offers forth spacious sunny rooms, mammoth leather couches, and a back garden with farm animals. Laundry £5. Dorms £7.50; doubles £17-20.
- **Rainbow Hostel (IHH;** ☎ 707 4415), Upper Village. Just a few steps from those pubs of legend, McGann's and McDermott's. Small, with pastel rooms and a casual atmosphere; bed and breakfast next door run by the same people. Free 1½hr. guided walking tours of the Burren for hostelers. Laundry £3. Dorms £7.50; doubles £17.
- **Doolin Hostel (IHH;** ☎ 707 4006), Lower Village. Geared towards large groups, the Doolin is a rambling old hostel with clean, comfortable rooms. Run by "Paddy," as he is affectionately known to visitors, the hostel offers more than the average budget accommodation: a shop, a **bureau de change,** tennis courts and rackets, and bus ticket sales. Buses stop outside the door daily. Reception 7:30am-9pm. Laundry £2. Dorms £7.50, June-Sept. £8; doubles £20, June-Sept. £21.
- **Westwind B&B** (☎ 707 4227), Upper Village, behind McGann's, in the same driveway as the Lazy Lobster. The rooms are sunny and immaculately clean. The breakfasts please, with great french toast. Quentin Tarantino stayed here in '95, but nobody really noticed because Co. Clare had just won the All-Ireland Hurling Championship. The owners give helpful advice to spelunkers and other Burren explorers. £13-15 per person.
- **Doolin Cottage** (☎ 707 4762), 1 door down from the Aille. The friendly, young proprietor keeps her rooms spotless and brightly decorated. The full breakfast menu is hearty with vegetarian-friendly choices. Open Mar.-Nov. Doubles £26-30.
- **Campsite** (☎ 707 4458), near the harbor, has a kitchen, laundry facilities, a view of the Cliffs of Moher, and no apparent name. Showers 50p. Laundry £3. £4 per tent plus £1.50 per person.

FOOD AND PUBS

Doolin's few restaurants are pushing pricey, but all three pubs serve up excellent grub at moderate prices. The **Doolin Deli,** near O'Connor's in the Lower Village, packs overstuffed sandwiches (£1.30) and stocks groceries. (☎ 707 4633. Open June-Sept. M-Sa 8:30am-9pm, Su 9:30am-9pm.) In the Upper Village, the **Lazy Lobster** tickles taste buds with classic and Asian-inspired seafood dishes. (About £20 for a 3-course meal; crab cakes with chillies and coriander £13.50. Open 6:30-10pm.) Or muscle your way into McGann's (☎ 707 4133) for a plate of fresh wild mussels (£5.50). **Bruach na hAille** has a working antique phonograph player and delicious, creative home-grown dishes. The three-course early-bird special is a budget-friendly luxury with huge portions and gourmet flavor. (☎ 707 4120. £10 early-bird special until 7:30pm. Open daily St. Patrick's day-Oct. 6-9:30pm.)

If Doolin looks like a ghost-town at first glance, have no fear: the people are all in the pubs. The pint-pouring threesome keep the camera-clicking tourists and local crowds loyal with their musical brilliance. Both O'Connor's and McGann's have won awards for the best trad music in Ireland. The underdog and unofficial favorite of many a local is **McDermott's** (☎ 707 4328). Most summer standing-room-only sessions start at 9:30pm nightly, and on the weekends in winter. **McGann's** (☎ 707 4133), Upper Village, has music nightly at 9pm in the summer, on winter weekends at 9pm. **O'Connor's** (☎ 707 4168), Lower Village, is the busiest and most-touristed of the three, with drink and song nightly and Sunday afternoons all year.

THE BURREN

If there were wild orchids, cantankerous cows, and B&Bs on the moon, it would probably look a lot like the Burren. The area comprises nearly 100 sq. mi. and almost one third of Co. Clare's coastline. The lunar beauty of the Burren includes jagged gray hills resembling skyscrapers turned to rubble, hidden depressions that open up into a labyrinth of caves, 28 of Ireland's 33 species of butterflies, and Mediterranean and Alpine wildflowers growing side by side. As Oliver Cromwell complained, "There is not wood enough to hang a man, nor water enough to drown him in, nor earth enough to bury him in." He shouldn't have worried, though; there are more than enough rocks to bash a man, and plenty of cliffs to throw him off.

The best way to see the Burren is to walk or cycle it, but be warned that the dramatic landscape makes for exhausting climbs and thrilling descents. Check your brakes *before* you set out. Tim Robinson's meticulous maps ($5) detail the Burren Way, a 26 mi. hiking trail from Liscannor to Ballyvaughan and *The Burren Rambler* maps ($2) are also extremely detailed. Sarah Poyntz's *A Burren Journal* gives a sense of what it is like to live in the Burren today. All of the surrounding tourist offices (at Kilfenora, Ennis, Corofin, the Cliffs of Moher, or Kinvara) are bound to stock these maps, books, and any other Burren info that you may need.

Bus service in the Burren is as confused as the geography. Bus Éireann (☎ (065) 682 4177) connects **Galway** to towns in and near the Burren a few times a day during summer but infrequently during winter. Every summer weekday (June-Oct.) some of those buses continue to **Killimer** and the **Shannon Car Ferry** to **Killarney** and **Cork**. Bus stops are the Doolin Hostel in **Doolin** (p. 299), Burke's Garage in **Lisdoonvarna** (p. 298), Linnane's in **Ballyvaughan** (p. 300), and Winkles in **Kinvara** (p. 301). Other infrequent but year-round buses run from some individual Burren towns to **Ennis**. Full-day bus tours from **Galway** are another popular way to see the Burren (see p. 298). Hitching requires patience. *Let's Go* does not recommend hitchhiking.

LISDOONVARNA ☎ 065

The locals call it "Lis-doon," but for everyone else in Ireland, its name is synonymous with its **Match Making Festival**. The month-long September *craic*-and-snogging fest has drawn the likes of Jackson Browne and Van Morrison to its all-day music stages. Amidst the hullabaloo, farm boys and girls of all ages—their crops safely harvested, but with wild oats yet to sow—gather together to pick their mates. Local celebrity and professional matchmaker Willie Daley from Ennistymon presides over the event. No one is really saying how successful the festival is in making matches that last longer than a six-pint hangover, but as one Lisdoon local puts it, "Everything works if you want it to." Lisdoonvarna's natural groundwater, on the other hand, could be considerably kinder on the kidneys and the heart than the liquids found in its pubs. In the 1700s, Lisdoon saw carriage upon carriage of therapy-seekers rolling in to try the curative wonders of sulphur, iron, magnesia, and copper. You can still give it a whirl at the **Spa Wells Health Centre**, Sulfur Hill Rd., at the bottom of the hill south of town. If you can't stay for a bath, at least savor their aromatic sulfur water. (☎ 707 4023. 30p per glass; sulphur bath $18, full massage $18, sauna $5. Open June-Sept. M-F 10am-6pm, Sa 10am-2pm, water pumps until 6pm.)

Buses travel 4 mi. to **Doolin**, and on to **Lahinch** daily from the main square during summer (1-3 per day). A post bus leaves for **Kilfenora** (M-F 8:15am). Rent a **bike** at the Esso filling station. (☎ 707 4028. Open M-Sa 9am-7pm, Su 10am-6pm. $7 a day, $35 a week; deposit $40 or an ID.) There are no hostels in Lisdoonvarna, but to find a decent, cheap-ish ($15-16) B&B, close your eyes, point your finger, spin around until confused, open your eyes, et voilà! Dermot of ✦**Dooley's Caherleigh House**, right up the hill from the Spa, makes every guest feel pampered with tea and cookies, crackling fires, and superb breakfasts. His rooms are huge and decadently pink. Bring him objects of yellow and he will be pleased. (☎ 707 4543. $18 per person.) Or you can dream of that special someone under the foot-high comforters at

Mrs. O'Connor's Roncalli House. It's a seven-minute walk from the town center, just keep walking past the Esso station and the smokehouse; it is just past the next filling station. (☎ 707 4115. Singles £16, doubles £25; all with bath.)

The **Roadside Tavern,** Doolin Rd., is dimly lit and decorated with shellacked postcards from around the world. Ghostly old photos of sessions past form a backdrop to their living version. (☎ 707 4494. Trad Mar.-Sept. nightly at 9:30pm, Oct.-Feb. Sa only.) The smoked trout salad (£5.90), from the smokehouse next door, is enough for two. (Food served daily noon-8:45pm.) The **Smokehouse** next door is your one-stop-shop for the salmon of knowledge (£3), more trout of truth, or the eel of eternity. (☎ 707 4432. Open M-Su 9am-7pm.)

KILFENORA ☎065

The village of Kilfenora lies 5 mi. southeast of Lisdoonvarna on R478; its Burren Heritage Center and several grocers make it an ideal departure point for trekkers and bicyclists (that is, if you already have a bike; there are no rental agencies in town) heading into the Burren. Visitors are wise not to overlook Kilfenora's several non-geological sights: seven high crosses, numerous wedge tombs, and a castle. Kilfenora also has its store of trad musicians, making it a less advertised participant in the Clare coast's brilliant music scene.

The **Burren Interpretive Centre** presents a lecture on the natural history of the region and shows an excellent film on Burren biology. (☎ 88030. Open daily June-Sept. 9am-5pm; Mar.-May and Oct. 9am-5pm. Lecture and film £2.50, students £2.) Next to the Burren Centre, Church of Ireland services are still held in the nave of the **Kilfenora Cathedral.** (1st and 3rd Su of the month, 9:45am.) The rest of the Cathedral and its graveyard stand open to the sky. Although the structure itself dates from 1190, the site has held churches since the 6th century. (Tours July-Aug. £2.50, students £2. Ask at the tourist office.) West of the church is the elaborate 12th-century **Doorty Cross,** one of the "seven crosses of Kilfenora." Although time and erosion have taken their toll, carved scenes of three bishops and Christ's entry into Jerusalem are still identifiable. Odd birds and menacing heads cover its sides.

The **post office** is across from the grocery store on Main St. (☎ 708 8001. Open M-F 9am-1pm and 2-5:30pm, Sa 10am-1pm.) **Bridgid and Tony's B&B,** at the top of the intersection, has clean and airy rooms, hearty breakfasts, and smart kids. (☎ 708 8148. £14 per person.) In the yellow house across the street from the Burren Centre, **Ms. Mary Murphy,** Main St., greets arriving guests with tea and coffee. Rooms are basic, but include bath. You'll get the full fry in the morning. (☎ 708 8040. Open Feb.-Oct. Singles £17; doubles £30.)

Kilfenora has only three pubs, but enough music and dancing to make you miss your bus in the morning. **Vaughan's** (☎ 88004) offers set dancing in the adjacent thatched cottage on Thursday and Sunday nights, trad sessions on Friday, and open-air dancing on Sunday afternoons. The superb seafood chowder is filled with fish and shellfish. (£3, served 7-9pm.) Kitty Linnane and her *ceili* band of '54 put Kilfenora on the musical map; **Linnane's** still hosts trad sessions although they vary in quality. (☎ 88157. Sessions nightly in summer, weekends in off-season, year-round W supersession.) At **Nagle's** (☎ 708 813), the crimson-plush upholstery and woodwork offer comfy spots to sit for a young, well-dressed crowd.

CARRON ☎065

A pub, a hostel, and a mile-wide, 5 yd. deep puddle in the midst of a limestone landscape is the sum total of Carron. Sure enough, it's dimensions constitute a mind-boggling figure; this is Europe's largest disappearing lake. Four miles northwest of Carron is the **Poulnabrane Dolmen,** a well-known, photogenic group of Irish rocks. About 5000 years ago, over 25 people were put to rest with their pots and jewels under the five-ton capstone, only to be dug up by curious archaeologists in 1989. Two miles east of Carron, Ireland's only **perfumery** creates scents from the Burren's moss and lichens, and inspired by the orchids, spring gentian, and others; the wildflowers are now protected and can no longer be distilled for their scents. The 20-

> **FLIES, BEES, AND BUTTERFLIES—OH MY!**
> With over 300 species of flowers scattered across its rugged landscape, the Burren is a botanist's paradise. Spring starts with the spring gentian, a five-petaled, blue, solitary flower. In the disappearing lakes, or turlough, the rare turlough violet blooms, which is not to be confused with the common dog violet (the latter is slightly more purple). Wild strawberries grow across the Burren and the Aran Islands, as does its pungent friend, Babington's leek—a tall, sleek vegetable with a purple flower and a distinctive garlic scent. Of course, the orchids are what many people come for; the early purple orchid in spring, the common fragrant orchid, and the Fly, the Bee, the Frog, and the Butterfly (if you squint they do look a bit like their namesakes) in the summer. Primrose are common, and the fields are yellow with bird's-foot trefoil and wild iris throughout the warmest months. Watch for snails, slugs, and lizards winding through the foliage. *Wild Plants of the Burren and the Aran Islands* by Charles Nelson is a good investment.

minute meditative slide show fades from stunningly beautiful slide to slide, accompanied by relaxing music. (☎ 89102. Open Mar.-June and Sept.-Oct. 9:30am-5pm, July-Aug. 9am-7pm.)

The village lies off a small road connecting Bellharbor to Killnaboy; to get there, **drive** (8min.) or **hike** (1½hr.) south from Bellharbor. It's also possible to **bike** from Kilfenora, but the climbs on the small roads are exhausting. Hitching odds approach nil, which is how much *Let's Go* recommends this form of transport.

A single magnificent hostel overlooks the giant lough. **Clare's Rock Hostel** houses half the town's population. It opened in 1998 and has comfortable dorms with bath, tasteful decor, and cheerful management. (☎ 89129. Open May-Oct. Reception 8:30am-noon and 6-10:30pm. Laundry £5. Dorms £8; singles £10; doubles £22; triples £30; quads £36; family rooms £39.) Just across the way, Carron's pub **Croide Na Boirne** offers gorgeous views, a crackling fire, and goat burgers. (☎ 89109. Mint-embalmed kid burger £3.95. Food served Apr.-Dec. noon-9:30pm.)

BALLYVAUGHAN ☎065

Along the jagged edge of Galway Bay, 8 mi. west of Kinvara on N67, the Burren's desolation is suddenly interrupted by the little oasis of Ballyvaughan. Its harbor shimmers by day, while its pubs shimmy nightly with lively trad sessions. The town center is just minutes from caves and castles, making it a frequent stop-over for spelunkers and archaeology fiends.

A mile out of Ballyvaughan on N67 is the turn-off for **Newtown Castle and Trail**, where you can find the restored 16th-century home of the O'Loghlens, the princes of the Burren. Another hour-long guided tour covers about a half-mile of beautiful hillside terrain, discusses the geology of the Burren, and visits a Victorian folly "gazebo" (a miniature children's castle), as well as an 18th-century military waterworks system. (☎ 77216. Open Easter-early Oct. daily 10am-6pm. Castle or trail tour £2, both £3.50.) Newtown Castle is right beside the **Burren College of Art,** which offers year-round and summer courses. Several weekend workshops are offered in the summer, focusing on painting the Burren landscape, or learning more about the botany of the area. (Call ☎ 707 7200; email admin@burrencollege.ie for information.) Prehistoric bears once inhabited the two million-year-old **Aillwee Cave** (EYEL-wee), 2 mi. south of Ballyvaughan and almost 1 mi. into the mountain. Caves are the same temperature year-round, so bears felt their way into the cave and scratched out cozy beds. Anyone scared of the dark should avoid the tour, as should experienced spelunkers. (☎ 707 7036. Open daily July-Aug. 10am-6:30pm; mid-Mar. to June and Sept.-early Nov. 10am-5:30pm. £4.25, students £3.50.) Those itching to do serious **spelunking** should contact the University of Galway's caving club or the Burren Outdoor Education Centre (☎708 066) in Bellharbor.

Buses stop in front of Linnane's Pub on Main St. **Bike rental** and **laundry** services are found at **Connoles**, up the road toward N67. (☎ 707 7061. Open M-Sa 9am-6pm. Bikes £8 per day, £30 per week; deposit £20 and ID. Laundry £6.)

There's no hostel directly in Ballyvaughan, but the **Bridge Hostel** is an 8 mi. bus ride west to Fanore. Isolated in the fingers of the Burren, the Bridge pampers visitors with open peat fires and home-cooked meals. (☎ 76134. Open Mar.-Oct. **Bike rental** £5 per day. Breakfast £3, dinner £4. Wash £2. Dorms £7; doubles £32. **Camping** £4 per person.) In town, **Seaside Oceanville**, next door to Monk's on the pier, has gorgeous views and is only a short distance from the pub. (☎ 707 7051. Open Mar.-Oct. £19 per person; singles rarely available.) **Gentian Villa B&B** has clean, comfortable rooms and friendly chat on the Main Rd. towards Kinvara. (☎ 707 7042. Open Easter-Oct. £17 with bath.) **O'Briens B&B**, above the pub and restaurant on Main St., has pleasing rooms, a magic fireplace, and a breakfast buffet. (☎ 707 7003. Singles £25; doubles £49, £33 off-season.)

Spar sells various food stuffs. (☎ 77077. Open M-Sa 8:30am-8pm, Su 9:30am-5:30pm.) At **An Féar Gorta** ("the hungry grass") tea, tasty little cakes, and a garden setting enchant. You can read *The Legend of the Hag of Loughrask* while you wait for your food. (☎ 77023. Sandwiches from £4. Open June-Sept. M-Sa 11am-5:30pm.) The sunny little **Tea Junction Cafe** has sandwiches and veggie entrees, but tempts you to ruin your appetite with their famous rhubarb pie. (☎ 77289. Hummus £3.75. Open daily 9am-6pm.) **Monk's Pub** was recently sold to a new owner, but the location by the sea hasn't changed—have mussels outside on a sunny day. The tourists crowd around the huge stone fireplace for the trad and ballad sessions, while locals gravitate toward the bar. (☎ 707 7059. Fish cakes with salad £6.95. Music three nights a week in summer, nightly off-season.) Back in town, **Greene's** (☎ 707 7147) is a small, card-playing locals' pub with an older crowd that knows where the Guinness runs best. Huge helpings of their daily special (about £5) are hot from noon to midnight. Go early if you value your elbow room.

KINVARA ☎091

Despite the lines of cars that plow right through it every day on their way from Galway to the Burren, Kinvara (pop. 2300 and growing) is a fairly well-kept secret. This fishing village has an excellent music scene, a vibrant artistic community, and a well-preserved medieval castle.

✉ TRANSPORTATION AND PRACTICAL INFORMATION.
Bus Éireann connects Kinvara to **Galway** (£3.80) and **Doolin** (June-Sept. M-Sa 4 per day, Su 2 per day; £5.50). Would-be poets on their way to Yeats's summer homes (see **Coole Park and Thoor Ballylee**, p. 302) can rent bikes at McMahon's, just up the street from the hostel on the Ballyvaughan Rd. (☎ 637 577. £5 per day, £35 per week; ID deposit.) **Kinvara Pharmacy**, Main St., soothes your blisters. (☎ 637 397. Open M-Sa 9:30am-6pm.) The **post office** sends postcards. (☎ 637 101. Open M-F 9am-1pm and 2-5:30pm, Sa 9am-1pm.)

⌂ ACCOMMODATIONS.
Johnston's Hostel (IHH), Main St., uphill from the Quay, is a relaxing, if fortuitous, retreat. Cupid seems to have pitched a tent on the roof: the owner, his sisters, and over a dozen others have met their mates here, as did many others back when the gigantic common room was a dance hall. (☎ 37164. Open July-Sept. Sheets £1. Showers 50p. Laundry £4. Dorms £7.50. **Camping** £4.50.) Right in town, the fabulous **Fallon's B&B** is an excellent abode above Spar market. It's run with the help of their seven fantastic kids. (☎ 637 483. £20 per person sharing.) The gardens of Mary Walsh's **Cois Cuain B&B**, on the Quay, inspire a cheery interior. (☎ 637 119. Open Apr.-Nov. £19 per person sharing.)

⌘ FOOD AND PUBS.
The **Londis Supermarket** does its grocery thing on the main road. (☎ 637 250. Open M-Sa 9am-9pm, Su 9am-8pm.) **Rosaleen's** (☎ 637 503) stuffs you up with divine sandwiches, all-day breakfast, and delicious desserts.

For pub grub with a creative flair, **Keogh's** is a good choice. The dinner menu, served until 9:30pm, is a bit pricey, but daily specials suit a low budget. (Chicken breast $5.95.) The whimsical **Cafe on the Quay** whips up sandwiches and seafood right by the water. (☎ 637 654. Pita with veggies $5.95. Open daily 9am-7pm.)

Kinvara has many more pubs of note than most towns twice its size. Across the street from the hostel is **Tully's** (☎ 637 146), where a grocery and bar keep company in smoky surroundings; US license plates, of all things, provide the atmosphere for the best impromptu trad sessions in Kinvara. **Winkle's** (☎ 637 137) has music and set dancing Wednesday through Saturday nights. Dizzyingly huge amounts of liquor line the wall at **Greene's** (☎ 637 110). The nighttime view of the bay from the candle-lit **Pierhead** is enough to set your heart aflutter. If that doesn't work, perhaps the lively trad will. (☎ 638 188. Music Tu, Th, and Sa.) **Ould Plaid Shawls** (☎ 637 400) has a puzzling name considering the youth of its clientele; they enjoy occasional spontaneous trad sessions, and championship darts (mostly for men) Tuesday at 10:30pm ($2 to play). Pots, pans, and pictures of Kinvara's yesteryear hang on **Connolly's** (☎ 637 131) walls, while a wall of flowers obscures the entrance. The small, intimate interior will nurture your relationship with your pint.

SIGHTS. Dunguaire Castle, 10 minutes from town on Galway Rd., is really a tower house—a popular type of dwelling for country gentlemen of the 16th century. The narrow, winding staircase weaves its way to the windy battlements, which provide an expansive view of the town, sea, and countryside. Locals claim that Kinvara is one of the most beautiful parts of Ireland; the view could prove them right, especially on misty days. (☎ 637 108. Open daily May-Sept., 9:30am-5pm. $2.75, students $1.90.) **Medieval banquets**—at royal prices ($30 per person)—are held at 5:30 and 8:45pm, at which lords and ladies sup as they are entertained with music and a literary pageant. The first weekend in May, the town loses its marbles at the **Cuckoo Fleadh,** which brings over 200 musicians into town. The **Cruinniu Na Mbad Festival** (Gathering of the Boats) draws Galway hookers to Kinvara for a racy weekend in August.

DOORUS PENINSULA ☎091

Alongside Kinvara, the Doorus Peninsula reaches out into Galway Bay. The house that Yeats and Lady Augusta Gregory inhabited while planning the Abbey Theatre (see p. 119) and collaborating on plays is now the isolated **Doorus House Hostel (An Óige/HI;** ☎ 637 512). Originally the country seat of an expatriate French aristocrat, this well-appointed hostel sits gracefully among old oak trees and peers out into the great expanse of a tidal estuary. The hammock out back puts worries to rest. (Reception 5-10:30pm. Sheets $1. June-Sept. dorms $7.50, Oct.-May $5.50.)

For those not enamored of nature, it's probably best to stay in Kinvara, but for families with cars, hikers, and bikers, Doorus is righteous. Three castles, several holy wells, a handful of ring forts, a cave, winged critters, panoramic views, and boggy islands await the rambler; most are detailed in *Kinvara: A Rambler's Map and Guide*, available in town for $2. A 10 mi. round trip west from the hostel to the **Aughinish Peninsula** offers views of the Burren across the bay. The more convenient blue-flag **Traught Strand** is just a five-minute walk from the hostel. **Campers** can pitch a tent in the field nearby and wake to the slosh of surf. After a hike, the **Traveller's Inn** pub and grocery at Knockgarra, in the middle of the peninsula, is a great place to relax over a pint. (☎ 637 116. Open daily 9am-10pm.) The Galway-Doolin **bus** does not pass through Doorus but will stop on request at the turn-off on Ballyvaughan Rd. (June-Sept. M-Sa 4 per day, Su 2 per day; Oct.-May M-Sa 1 per day). From there the hostel is 2 mi. (follow the signs toward the beach). Catching a hitch, like the chance that *Let's Go* will recommend hitchhiking, is unlikely.

COOLE PARK AND THOOR BALLYLEE

W. B. Yeats eulogized his two retreats that lie about 20 mi. south of Galway near **Gort,** where N18 meets N66. Coole Park is now a ruin and national park; Thoor Ballylee has been restored to appear as it did when Yeats lived there. Neither is accessible by bus; biking from Kinvara is the best option, but be warned—high winds can make biking a long, long struggle.

On the turn-off onto the main highway (N18) on the road from Kinvara, the **Kilartan Gregory Museum** greets visitors in a large stone house. The building was the National School where Lady Gregory started one of the first branches of the Gaelic League. A reproduction of a traditional Irish schoolroom charms with actual posters and books from the turn of the century. The rest of the small museum is chockfull of facts and fascinating documents relating to the life of this influential playwright. (☎ (091) 631 069. Open daily June-Aug. 10am-6pm, Sept.-May Su 1-5pm.)

The **Coole Park** nature reserve was once the estate of Lady Augusta Gregory, a friend and collaborator of Yeats (see **The Irish Literary Revival,** p. 26). To Yeats, the estate represented the aristocratic order that crass industrialists and wars of the 1920s were destroying: "ancestral trees/ Or gardens rich in memory glorified/ Marriages, alliances and families/ And every bride's ambition satisfied." Although the house was destroyed in the 1922 Civil War (see **Independence and Civil War,** p. 17), the yew walk and garden survived. In the picnic area, the famous "autograph tree," a great copper beech, bears the initials of some important Irish figures: George Bernard Shaw, Sean O'Casey, Douglas Hyde (first president of Ireland), and Yeats himself. Look for the cow beside the signature of Jack B. Yeats's (W.B.'s artist-brother). The **Coole Park Visitors Centre** eschews talk of Yeats in favor of local rocks, trees, and wildlife. (☎ (091) 631 804. Open mid-Apr. to mid-June Tu-Su 10am-5pm; mid-June to Aug. daily 9:30am-6:30pm; Sept. 10am-5pm. Last admission 45min. before closing. £2, students £1.) A mile from the garden, **Coole Lake** is where Yeats watched "nine-and-fifty swans... all suddenly mount/ And scatter wheeling in great broken rings/ Upon their clamorous wings." Whooper and Mute Swans still gather here in winter, cows lumber down to the beach in summer. There are two trails around the park, the Seven Woods Trail and the shorter Family Trail. Both are well-marked with informative stations and great for a ramble or bike ride.

Three miles north of Coole Park, a road turns off Galway Rd. and runs a mile farther to **Thoor Ballylee,** a tower built in the 13th and 14th centuries. In 1916, Yeats bought it for £35, renovated it, and lived here with his family off and on from 1922 to 1928. While he was cloistered here writing "Meditations in Time of Civil War," Republican forces blew up the bridge by the tower. In Yeats's account, they "forbade us to leave the house, but were otherwise polite, even saying at last 'Goodnight, thank you.'" A film on Yeats's life plays at the **Visitors Centre,** where a coffee shop sells cakes and toasties. (☎ (091) 631 436. Open Easter-Sept. daily 10am-6pm. £3, students £2.50.)

ARAN ISLANDS ☎ 099

The three Aran Islands (Oileáin Árann)—Inishmore, Inishmaan, and Inisheer—rest in Galway Bay 15 mi. southwest of Galway City. Sections of the islands are covered with slabs of limestone that resemble the stark landscape of the Burren in Co. Clare (see p. 298). The green fields that compose the rest of the islands' surface are the result of centuries' worth of farmers piling acres of stones into the walls that create a maze across the island. Their masonry is based on a mixture of thin seaweed, soil, sand, and manure. The harshness of this secluded existence resulted in the survival of only a tiny population on the islands today. Yet the Arans have been inhabited for thousands of centuries. Iron Age peoples appreciated the isolation and built awe-inspiring ring-forts on the edges of precipices to ensure it. Early Christians flocked to the trio seeking spiritual seclusion; the ruins of their ancient churches and monasteries now litter the island. During medieval times, clans fought for control of the Arans. Elizabeth I set up a garrison here. Their position at the mouth of the Galway Bay gave the islands periodic military and commercial importance, but fishing and farming have lasted as the islanders' primary occupations.

Aran Islands

SIGHTS
- Bed of Diarmuid and Brainne, 12
- Black Fort, 6
- Cill Cheannannach, 14
- Cill na Seacht nInion, 20
- Cnoc Raithní, 17
- Dún Aengus, 3
- Dún Chonchúir, 10
- Dún Eoghanachta, 1
- Dún Fearbhaí, 15
- Dún Formna, 19
- Heritage Centre, 5
- Knitwear Factory, 21
- Plassy Wreck, 11
- Puffing Holes, 8
- Seven Churches, 2
- St. Kevin's Church, 18
- Synge's Chair, 9
- Teampall I Chiaraín, 4
- Temple Benan, 7
- Tobar Éinne, 16
- Trá Leitreach, 13

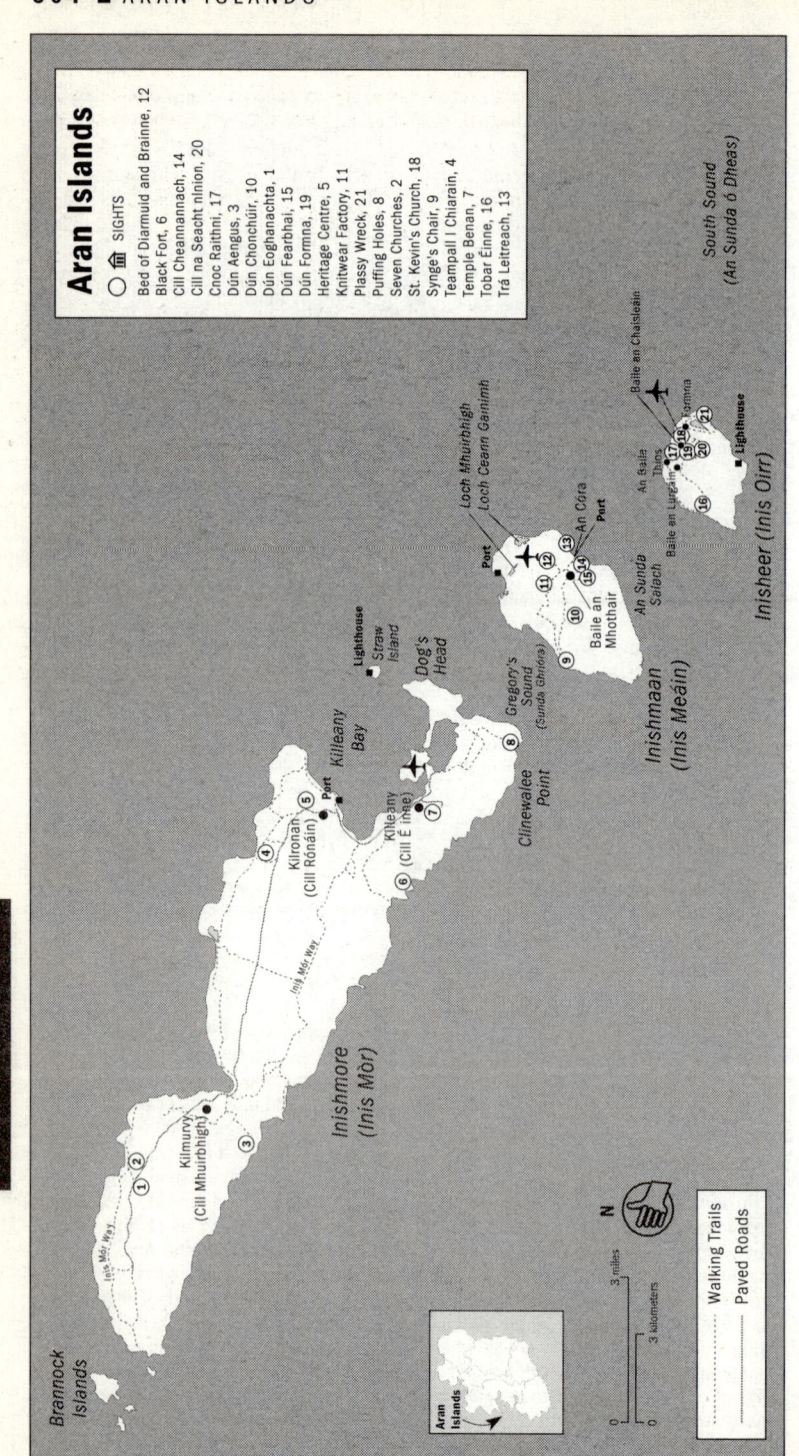

The islands' cultural isolation has drawn artistic attention since the start of the century. In 1894, Dublin-born writer John M. Synge asked W.B. Yeats for creative criticism. Yeats told him to go to the Arans, learn Irish, and write plays about the islanders. Synge followed his advice, and received international attention (see **The Irish Literary Revival**, p. 26). In the 1930s, Robert Flaherty's groundbreaking film *Man of Aran* added to the islands' fame (see **The Green Screen**, p. 32).

During July and August, crowds of curious visitors surround every monument and fill every pub on Inishmore. The stretches of land between the sights, however, remain deserted. Visitors are rarer on Inishmaan and Inisheer, the two smaller islands, but their numbers are rising as the inter-island ferries become more frequent. The scenery remains breathtaking, regardless of the number of people who see it. The lifestyle also remains traditional—locals still make *curraghs* (small boats made from curved wicker rods tied with string and covered with cowskin and black tar). Some retain local styles of dress, footwear, and fishing, and almost all speak Irish.

GETTING THERE

Three ferry companies—**Island Ferries, O'Brien Shipping/Doolin Ferries,** and **Liscannor Ferries**—operate boats to the Aran Islands. They reach the islands from four points of departure: **Rossaveal** several miles west of Galway (30min. to Inishmore), **Doolin** (30min. to Inisheer), **Liscannor** (30min. to Inisheer), and **Galway** (1½hr. to Inishmore). Ferries serving Inishmore are reliable and leave daily. Even in the summer, ferries to the smaller islands are less certain. There is no charge to bring bicycles on board. If the ferry leaves from Rossaveal, the company making the trip will provide a shuttle bus from Galway City to Rossaveal, usually for £3. Flying with **Aer Árann** is double the cost, double the fun, and a fraction of the time.

- **Island Ferries** (☎ (091) 561 767, after hours, 72273), is based in the Galway Tourist Office. The Aran Sea Bird serves all 3 islands year-round from Rossaveal (35min., £15 return). A bus connects the tourist office in Galway with the ferry port (departs 1½hr. before sailing time, £4 return). The Sea Sprinter connects Inishmore with Inisheer via Inishmaan (£10 return per island). They also offer a package deal: the bus from Galway, return ferry to Inishmore, and 1 night's accommodation at the Mainistir House Hostel with breakfast for £21, with B&B instead, £24.

- **O'Brien Shipping/Doolin Ferries** (☎ (065) 74455 in Doolin, ☎ (091) 567 283 in Galway, after hours ☎ (065) 71710). Year-round service connects Doolin and Galway to the Aran Islands. Galway to any island £12 return. Doolin to Inishmore £20 return, to Inishmaan £18 return, and to Inisheer £15 return. ISIC discount £3. Galway-Aran-Doolin £25. All trips from Doolin include inter-island travel; otherwise, inter-island trips £5 return. Cars always £100.

- **Liscannor Aran Ferries** (☎(065) 81368). Ferries depart twice a day from Liscannor and stop at Inishmaan and Inisheer. £17 return.

- **Aer Árann** (☎ (091) 593 034), 19 mi. west of Galway at Inverin, flies to all 3 islands. Reservations are accepted over the phone or in person at the Galway Tourist Office. 10min. to Inishmore. In summer 20-25 per day; in winter 4 per day. £18, £35 return. Bus from Galway tourist office leaves 1hr. before departure (£2.50).

INISHMORE (INIS MÓR)

The archaeological sites of Inishmore (pop. 900), the largest of the Aran Islands, are among the most impressive in Ireland. Of the dozens of ruins, forts, churches, and "minor sites" (holy wells and kelp kilns), the most amazing is the Dún Aengus ring fort, where a small semicircular wall surrounds a sheer 300 ft. drop off the craggy cliffs of the island's southern edge. Inishmore is by far the most touristed of the three islands. Crowds disembark at Kilronan Pier on the center of the island, spread out to lose themselves amid the stone walls and stark cliffs, then coalesce again around major sights. Minivans and "pony traps" traverse the island, encouraging anyone on foot to climb aboard and pay up. Exactly 437 kinds of wildflowers rise from the stony terrain and over 7000 mi. of stone walls divide the land.

GETTING AROUND AND PRACTICAL INFORMATION

Ferries land in **Kilronan**, a cluster of buildings that make up the island's only village, although a cluster of houses and a few restaurants rest below Dun Aengus. **Minibuses** roaming the island can be flagged down for a ride ($5 return to Dún Aengus). The buses also organize 2-hour tours of the island (about $5). Kilronan (Cill Rónáin), above the pier on the north shore, is the only place to buy supplies. The airstrip is on Inishmore's east end, while Kilmurvy and most of the major sites are on the west. The **tourist office** in Kilronan changes money, holds bags during the day (75p), and sells the *Inis Món Way* ($1.50) and several other maps. (☎ 61263. Open Feb.-Nov. daily 10am-6:15pm.) Anyone spending a few days on the Arans should invest in the Richardson map ($5), which meticulously documents virtually every rock on all three islands. **Aran Bicycle Hire** rents bikes (☎ 61132. $5 per day, $21 per week; deposit $9; open Mar.-Nov. daily 9am-5pm), as does **B&M Bicycle Hire**, downstairs from Joe Mac's (☎ 61402. $5 per day, $25 per week; deposit $5; open Mar.-May 9am-5pm, May-Sept. 9am-7pm). Strangely enough, bike theft here is a problem—lock it up, or don't ever leave it. **Internet access** is available at the heritage center ($5 per hour). The **post office**, up the hill from the pier, past the Spar Market, has a **bureau de change**. (☎ 61101. Open M-F 9am-5pm, Sa 9am-1pm.)

ACCOMMODATIONS

A free bus to the hostels meets all the ferries at the pier (ask to make sure that you are on the free bus, as several charge a fee).

The Kilronan Hostel (☎ 61255). Huge, sunny, and spotless, with an ocean view from the dining room. Its location is just seconds from the pier and directly upstairs from the *craic* at Joe Mac's pub. Dorms July-Aug. £9, Sept.-June £8.

Mainistir House (IHH; ☎ 61169). It's earned a reputation as a haven for writers, musicians, and yuppies; it is recently showing signs of this loving wear and tear. However, the dinners are fantastic (reserve a place by 6pm), and munching fresh muffins makes mornings manageable. Book ahead, especially during July and Aug. **Bike rental** £5 per day. Laundry £5. Dorms £8.50; singles £15; doubles £22.

An Aharla (☎ 61305). Take the turn-off across from Joe Watt's on the main road; it's the first building on the left. While away the night before an open peat fire. The family home-turned-hostel is a bit worn, but loyal fans are smitten with its ultra laid back atmosphere and quiet location. Dorms £7.

The Artist's Lodge (☎ 61457), across the road from An Aharla. A new hostel with incredible sea views and a price that includes tea and toast for breakfast. 8-bed dorm £7.

St. Kevin's (☎ 61485), behind Kilronan Hostel. This pretty 40-bed hostel has clean rooms, high ceilings, and proximity to the pubs. Dorms £7.50.

St. Brendan's House (☎ 61149). An ivy-covered house across the street from the ocean. Apr.-Oct. £11, with continental breakfast £13; Nov.-Mar. £8, £10.

Beach View House (☎ 61141), 3 mi. west of Kilronan. A great outpost for hiking. Some rooms have inspiring views of Dún Aengus and framed versions of the Alps. Open May-Sept. Singles £23, doubles £34.

FOOD, PUBS, AND ENTERTAINMENT

Spar Market, past the hostel in Kilronan, seems to be the island's social center. (☎ 61203. Open M-Sa 9am-8pm, Su 10am-6pm.) The dinner at the **Mainistir House** (see above) is far and away the best deal for dinner on the island. Joel cooks up flavorful, mostly vegetarian buffets (8pm, call by 6pm. $8 for non-residents). The **Ould Pier,** up the hill from the town center, serves up great, cheap grub. Eat inside or outside on sturdy picnic benches adorned with fresh flowers. (☎ 61228. Fish and chips £4.95. Open July-Aug.) **Tigh Nan Phaidt,** in a thatched building at the turn-off to Dún Aengus, specializes in home-cooked bread with home-smoked fish. The chocolate cake is phenomenal! (☎ 61330. Smoked salmon sandwich £5, cake £2. Open daily July-Aug. 10am-9pm, Mar.-June and Sept.-Dec. 10am-5pm.) For wonderful organic (if more upscale) lunches in a historic setting, try **The Man of Aran Restaurant,** located just past Kilmurvey Beach to the right. (☎ 61301. Toasties £2. Lunch daily 12:30-3:30pm, dinners in the summer.)

Traditional musicians occasionally strum on the terrace at **Tí Joe Mac** (☎ 61248), overlooking the pier. West of the harbor on the main road, **Joe Watty's** offers food, music, and conversation to accompany thick pints. **The American Bar** (☎ 61303) attracts younger islanders and droves of tourists with music most summer nights. **Ragus,** performed at the Halla Ronain (down the street from the Aran Fisherman Restaurant), is an hour-long show of music, song, and dance that receives rave reviews. (Shows at 2:45, 5, and 9pm. £8, students £6.) On Friday, Saturday, and Sunday summer nights, the first steps of a *céilí* begin at midnight at the dance hall (cover £3). *Man of Aran* is still screened daily at the community center (£3).

SIGHTS

The sights themselves are crowded, but the paths between them are desolate and unmarked, especially since too many visitors do the minibus tour. Cycling or walking makes for a day-long, hugely rewarding excursion. The path leading from Dun Aran to Kilmurvy offers exhilarating views and bumpy, but fun, riding. The tourist office's £1.50 maps of the **Inis Mór Ways** correspond to yellow arrows that mark the trails, but the markings are frustratingly infrequent and can vanish in fog; it is best to invest in a Tim Robinson map for serious exploring. The island's most famous monument, dating from the first century BC, is magnificent **Dún Aengus,** 4 mi. west of the pier at Kilronan. The Center below guards the stone path leading up to the fort (£1, 40p for students). The fort's walls are 18 ft. thick and form a semi-circle around the sheer drop of Inishmore's northwest corner. One of the best-preserved prehistoric forts in Europe, Dún Aengus commands a sublime view of the ocean from its hill. Controversy continues as to whether it was built for defensive or ritual reasons. **Be very careful:** strong winds have blown tourists off the edge and to their deaths. Many visitors are fooled by the occasional appearance of an island on the horizon. The vision is so realistic that it appeared on maps until the 20th century. In ancient legend, there was an island named Hybrazil that appeared every seven years and was a ghostly mirror of other parts of the world.

A 30-minute path to the left of the fort offers tremendous views of the cliff from below. Another 10-minute walk from Dún Aengus, there is a small freshwater stream. If the wind and light are right, the droplets of water become suspended in the air in an upside-down waterfall, glinting like fireflies. A few minutes beyond the stream is a view of the **Worm Hole,** a saltwater lake filled from a limestone aquifer below the ground. The bases of the surrounding cliffs have been hollowed by mighty waves to look like pirate caves. If you follow the cliffs to the left of Dún Aengus for about a mile, you can climb down onto the tide pool filled rocks and walk back beneath the cliffs to the **Worm Hole** and the caves. The walk is thrilling at high tide, but is more accessible at low tide. The sound of the waves crashing under the rock is worth the 30-minute walk.

Two roads lead to the fort from Kilronan, an inland one and a quieter coastal one. Left off the main road a half-mile past Kilmurvey is **Dún Eoghanachta,** a huge circular fort with 16 ft. walls. To the right past Eoghanachta are the **Seven Churches.** Both are evidence of the island's earliest inhabitants. The island's best beach is at **Kilmurvey,** with a sandy stretch and cold, cold water. At the end of the road, past Kilmurvey, a view of lighthouses and crashing waves rewards the adventurer. The road along the shore skips the exhausting hills of the main road.

Uphill from the pier in Kilronan, the new, expertly designed **Aran Islands Heritage Centre** (Ionad Árann) beckons inquisitive tourists. (☎ 61355. Open daily Apr.-Oct.

10am-7pm. £2, students £1.50.) Soil and wildlife exhibits, old Aran clothes, a cliff rescue cart, and *curraghs* combine for a surprisingly fascinating introduction to the natural and human life of the island. The **Black Fort** (Dún Dúchathair), a mile south of Kilronan over eerie terrain, is larger than Dún Aengus, a millennium older, and the unappreciated beauty of the two.

INISHMAAN (INIS MEÁIN)

Seagulls circle the cliffs while goats chew their cud, but there's little human activity to observe in the limestone fields of Inishmaan (pop. 300). For those who find beauty in solitude, a walk along the rocky cliff top is bliss. With the rapid and dramatic changes on the other two islands over the last three years, Inishmaan remains a fortress, quietly avoiding the hordes of barbarians invading from the east via Doolin and Galway. The ferry runs to the island almost regularly, but it is difficult to find a budget bed for the night.

For **tourist information**, as well as a chance to buy a variety of local crafts, try the **Inishmaan Co-op** (☎ 73010). Take the turn-off for the knitwear factory, continue straight, and then make a right turn after the factory. The **post office** (☎ 73001) is in Inishmaan's tiny village, which spreads out along the road west of the pier and divides the island in half. **Mrs. Faherty** runs a B&B, signposted from the pier, and will fill you up with an enormous dinner. (☎ 73012. Open mid-Mar.-Nov. Dinner £12. Doubles £28.) **Tig Congaile**, on the right-hand side of the first steep hill from the pier, is a gorgeous B&B. (☎ 73085. £16.) Its restaurant concentrates on perfecting seafood. (Lunch under £5, dinner from £8.50. Open June-Sept. daily 9am-9pm.) The **An Dún Shop** (☎ 73067) sells some food at the entrance to Dún Chonchúir. **Padraic Faherty's** thatched pub is the center of life on the island, and serves a small selection of grub until 6:30pm.

Beyond the thoughts rolling around in your head, there's little to speak of or do on Inishmaan. All the same, the scenery's a feast for the eyes. The *Inishmaan Way* brochure (£1.50) describes a 5 mi. walking route to all of the island's sights. The thatched cottage where Synge wrote much of his Aran-inspired work from 1898 to 1902 is a mile into the island on the main road. Across the road and a bit farther down is **Dún Chonchúir** (Connor Fort), an impressive 7th-century ring fort. At the western end of the road is **Synge's Chair**, where the writer came to think and compose. The view of splashing waves and open seas is remarkable, but an even more dramatic landscape awaits a bit farther down the path where the coastline comes into view. To the left of the pier, the 8th-century **Cill Cheannannach** church left its remains on the shore. Islanders were buried here until the mid-20th century under simple stone slabs. A mile north of the pier is Inishmaan's safest, most sheltered beach, **Trá Leitreach**. Entering the **Knitwear factory** is uncannily like stepping into a Madison Ave. boutique. The company sells its sweaters internationally to all sorts of upscale clothiers, but visitors can get them here right off the sheep's back at nearly half the price; still, expect to pay at least £50 for an Aran sweater. (☎ 73009. Open M-Sa 10am-5pm, Su 10am-4pm.)

KEEPING ARAN IN STITCHES Handy Aran Island knitsters stitch up sweaters that ain't just pretty to look at: the islands' culture is woven right into these snugly woolen creations. **Blackberry stitch**, also known as the **Trinity stitch**, looks like large, raised bumps. It stands in for the Christian Trinity. A **Zig-Zag** pattern represents the rugged cliffs and winding paths of the islands. The **Plaited Cable stitch** hints at the interweave of family life, while the **Lobster Claw stitch**—strangely—tweaks the imagination to dream of Lobster Claws. The **Honeycomb stitch** denotes the sweetness that comes of hard work. **Moss stitch**, which resembles the Trinity stitch but has smaller bumps, symbolizes the wealth and fertility of mossy soil. A **Rope** design mimics the rope used by Aran fisherman, and the **Trellis stitch** is an abstraction of small Aran fields with stone walls. **Diamond stitch** spins out the end of this little yarn, as propitious icons of success and wealth.

INISHEER (INIS OÍRR)

The Arans have been described as "quietness without loneliness," but Inishmaan can get damn lonely, and Inishmore isn't always quiet. Inisheer (pop. 300), the smallest Aran, is a compromise that lives up to the famous phrase. Islanders and stray donkeys seem to be present in even proportions on this island that is less than 2 mi. in diameter.

Inisheer's **tourist information** is cheerfully given in English or Irish from the small wooden hut on the beach near the main pier. (☎ 75008. Open daily July-Aug. 10am-6pm.) **Rothair Inis Oírr** rents **bikes**. (☎ 75033. $5 per day, $25 per week.) The **post office** is farther up the island to the left of the pier, above the school, in the cream and turquoise house. (☎ 75001. Open M-F 9am-1pm and 2-5:30pm, Sa 9am-1pm.)

The **Brú Hostel (IHH)**, visible from the pier, is spacious with great views. Upper-level rooms have skylights for star-gazing. Call ahead in July and August. (☎ 75024. Continental breakfast $2, Irish breakfast $4. Laundry $4. 4- to 6-bed dorms $8; private rooms $11 per person.) A list of Inisheer's 19 **B&Bs** hangs on the window of the small tourist office. **Bríd Póil's B&B** is booked all summer six months in advance due to the reputation of its beautiful view and amazing gourmet meals. It is worthwhile to call in case there's been a last-minute cancellation. (☎ 75019. Meals $12. $16, with bath $17.) **Sharry's B&B**, behind the Brú Hostel, has views and high ceilings. (☎ 75024. $16.) The **Ionad Campála Campground** (☎ 75008) stretches its tarps near the beach for campers who don't mind chilly ocean winds. (Open May-Sept. Showers 50p. $2 per tent, $10 per week.)

Tigh Ruairí, an unmarked pub and shop in a white building just up the road, is your best bet for groceries on the island. (☎ 75002. Shop open July-Aug. daily 9am-8:30pm; Sept.-June M-Sa 9am-7:30pm, Su 10:45am-12:30pm.) **Marb Gané** serves coffee and treats by the pier. (☎ 75049. Open June-Sept. daily 10am-6pm.) 350 yd. to the right of the pier, ◙**Fisherman's Cottage** offers amazing, organic, mostly island-grown meals. (☎ 75053. Open daily 11am-4pm and 7-9:30pm. Soup and bread $2, dinners $10.) They also rent **kayaks** (July-Aug.; $5 per hr.), have **Internet access** ($6 per hr.), and offer "Food for Healing" courses in April-May and September, which include sea vegetables identification. **Tigh Ned's** pub is next to the hostel and caters to a younger crowd, while the pub at the **Ostan Hotel**, just up from the pier, is exceptionally crowded and dim. (☎ 75020. Food served daily 11am-9:30pm.)

You can see the sights of the island on foot or from a pony cart tour (☎ 75092. $5 for a 45min. tour). The **Inis Oírr Way** covers the island's major attractions on a 4 mi. path. The first stop is in town at **Cnoc Raithní**, a bronze-age tumulus (stone burial mound), which is 2000 years older than Christianity. Walking along the **An Trá** shore leads to the romantic overgrown graveyard of **St. Kevin's Church** (Teampall Chaomhain). This St. Kevin, patron saint of Inisheer, is believed to be a brother of St. Kevin of Glendalough (see p. 138). On June 14, islanders hold mass in the church's ruins in memory of St. Kevin; lately, a festival has been added. St. Kevin's nearby grave is said to have great healing powers. Below the church, a pristine, sandy beach stretches back to the edge of town. Farther east along the beach, a grassy track leads to **An Loch Mór**, a 16-acre inland lake full of wildfowl and ringed by wild leeks—the tall plants were used as a substitute for garlic by early islanders. The stone ring fort **Dún Formna** is above the lake. Continuing past the lake and back onto the seashore is the **Plassy wreck**, a ship that sank offshore and washed up on Inisheer in 1960. The wreck has been taken over by buttercups, crows' nests, and graffiti. The Inisheer lighthouse is nicely visible from the wreck. The walk back to the island's center leads through **Formna Village** and on out to **Cill na Seacht nInion**, a small monastery with a stone fort. The remains of the 14th-century **O'Brien Castle**, razed by Cromwell in 1652, sit atop a nearby knoll. On the west side of the island, **Tobar Einne**, St. Enda's Holy Well, is believed to have curative powers.

Counties Galway, Mayo, and Sligo

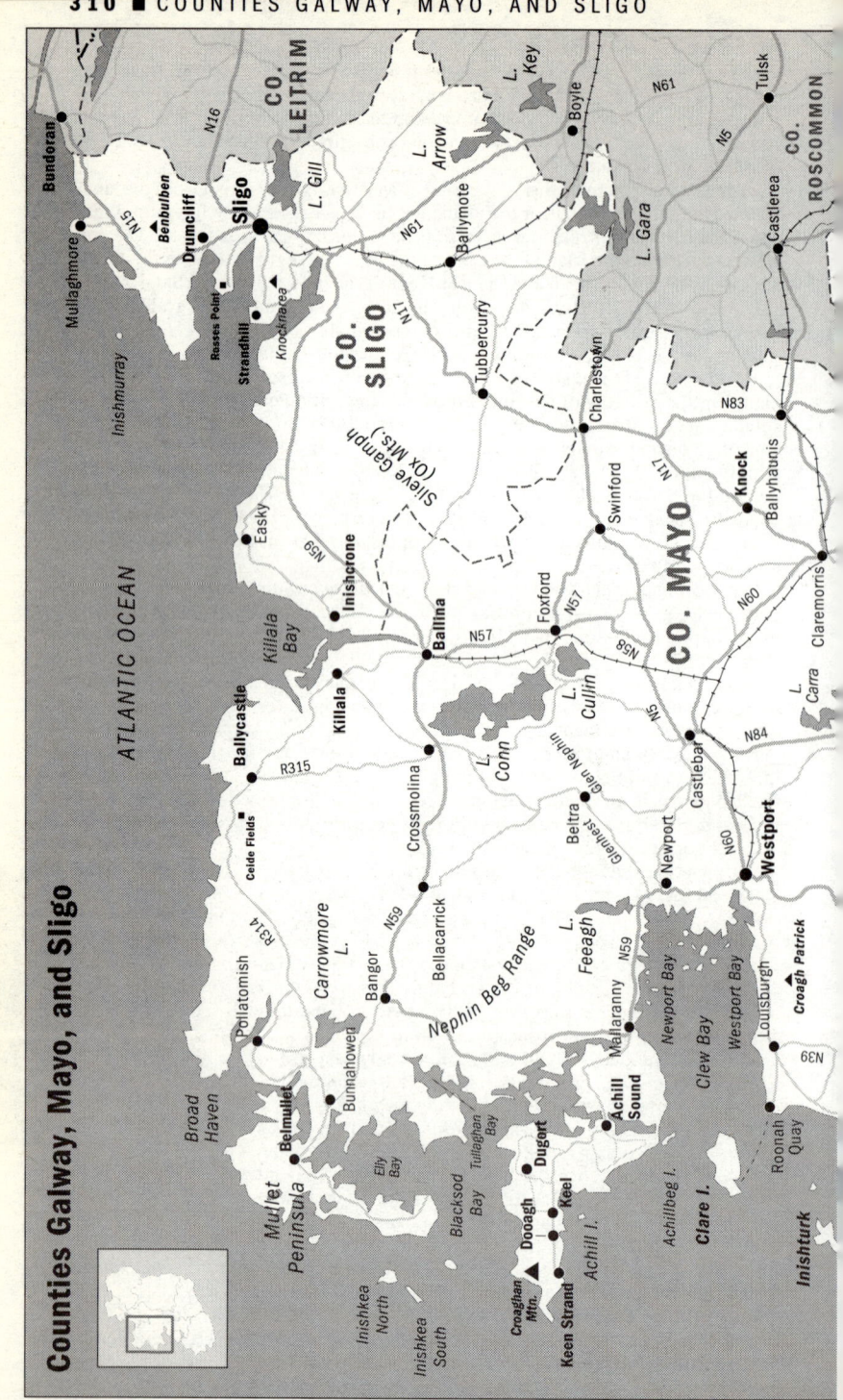

COUNTIES GALWAY, MAYO, AND SLIGO ■ 311

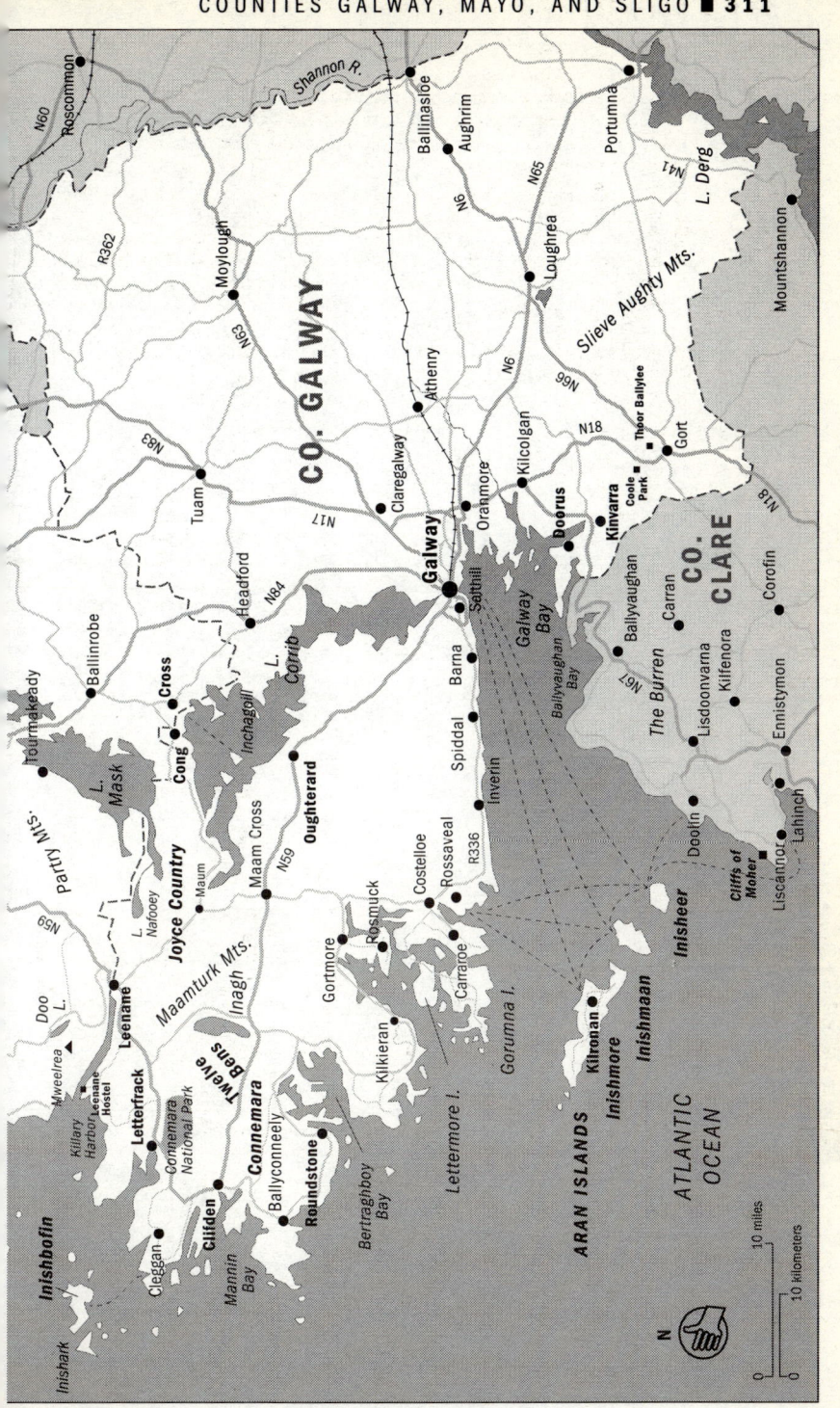

312 ■ GALWAY

Galway

♦ ACCOMMODATIONS
Archview Hostel, 4
Barnacle's Quay St. Hostel, 6
Celtic Tourist Hostel, 10
Corrib Villa, 7
The Galway Hostel, 11
Great Western House, 12
Kinlay House, 9
O'Connolly, 3
An Óige Galway Hostel, 1
Ruth Armstrong, 2
St. Martin's, 5
Woodquay Hostel, 8

COUNTY GALWAY

Small Co. Galway manages to contain a panorama of attractions in its 6000 sq. km. Galway City is the world headquarters of *craic*, especially during its many festivals. The area to the west of Galway, on the other hand, offers peaceful, rugged scenery for terrific hiking and biking opportunities. Clifden has a thriving nightlife, while Inishbofin is an intense dose of nothingness. Connemara is a largely Irish-speaking region lined with exquisite beaches. Cong, a popular hamlet just over the Mayo border, boasts grassy boglands and long-abandoned ruins.

GALWAY
☎091

In the past few years, Galway's reputation as Ireland's cultural capital has brought young Celtophiles flocking to Galway (pop. 60,000). Mix over 13,000 students at Galway's two major universities, a large transient population of twenty-something Europeans, and waves of international backpackers, and you have a small college town on *craic*.

Legacies of the 14 tribes who rebuilt and ruled Galway after a conflagration in 1490 mark the town. Later, the city became a commercial hub: Galway hookers, black boats with three sails, harvested the ocean for fish and trade, bringing in Spanish and English goods and exporting produce from fertile inland sections of the county. Today, Galway's energy is spent on its cultural endeavors: numerous theater companies and the promotion of the Irish language. Galway's arts, film, and horse-racing festivals follow one another in rapid succession during the summers, drawing still larger crowds. Sightseers find Galway a convenient base for trips along the Clare coast or to Connemara. Backpackers appreciate the disproportionate number of fine, if expensive, hostels. Pub-crawlers find inspiration in its wondrous variety of drinking establishments. Most of all, young people flock here in huge numbers for each other, making energetic, cosmopolitan Galway Europe's fastest-growing city.

■ GETTING THERE AND AWAY

Airport: Carnmore (☎ 755 569). 3 small Aer Lingus planes jet to **Dublin** daily.

Trains: Eyre Sq. (☎ 561 444). Open M-Sa 7:40am-6pm. Trains to **Dublin** (3hr.; M-F 5 per day, Sa-Su 3-4 per day; M-Th and Sa £15, F and Su £21) stop in **Athlone** (M-Th and Sa £7.50, F and Su £13.50); transfer at Athlone to all other lines.

Buses: Eyre Sq. (☎ 562 000). Open July-Aug. M-Sa 8:30am-7pm, Su 8:30am-6pm; Sept.-June M-Sa 8:30am-6pm, Su 8:30am-noon and 1:40-6pm. Private bus companies specialize in the run to **Dublin. P. Nestor Coaches** (☎ 797 144) leaves from Imperial Hotel, Eyre Sq. (M-Th, Su 2 per day, F 7 per day, Sa 5 per day; £5 single or day return, £8 open return). **Citylink** (☎ 564 163) leaves from Supermac's, Eyre Sq. (5 per day, last bus at 5:45pm; same prices as Nestor's). A west Clare **shuttle** to **Doolin, Lisdoonvarna,** and **Fanore** leaves various Galway hostels on request (June-Sept. 1 per day, £5). **Michael Nee Coaches** (☎ 51082) drives from Forester St. through **Clifden** to **Cleggan,** meeting the **Inishbofin** ferry (M-Sa 2-4 per day; £5 single, £7 return). **Bus Éireann** heads to **Belfast** (M-Sa 2-3 per day, Su 1 per day; £17), **Cork** (5 per day, £12), **Dublin** (M-Sa 8-9 per day, Su 7-8 per day; £8), and the **Cliffs of Moher** (May 24-Sept. 19 M-Sa 3-4 per day, Su 1-2 per day; £8.60) by way of **Ballyvaughan** (£5.90).

Ferries: Two companies ferry folks to the **Aran Islands;** both have ticket and information booths in the tourist office. **Island Ferries** (☎ 568 903) go from Rossaveal, west of Galway on the R336, to **Inishmore** (Apr.-Oct. 3 per day, May-Sept. 1 per day, 30min.), **Inisheer** (2 per day), and **Inishmaan** (1 per day; all routes £15 return for students). A bus runs to Rossaveal, leaving outside the tourist office 1½hr. before the ferry departure time. (£4, £2 discount at Mainistir House hostel on Inishmore). **O'Brian Shipping** (☎ 567 283) leaves from the Galway docks with possible connection to **Doolin** (daily June-Sept., Oct.-May 3 per week, £14 return, 1½hr.). See **Aran Islands,** p. 303.

314 ■ GALWAY

Car Rental: Budget Rent-a-Car, Eyre Sq. (☎ 566 376). Call for rates and restrictions.

Hitching: Dozens of hitchers wait on Dublin Rd. (N6) scouting rides to Dublin, Limerick, or Kinvara. Most catch bus #2, 5, or 6 from Eyre Sq. to this main thumb-stop. University Rd. leads drivers to Connemara via N59. *Let's Go* does not recommend hitchhiking.

▣ GETTING AROUND

Local Transportation: City buses (☎ 562 000) leave Eyre Sq. for all parts (every 20min., 70p). Buses go to each area of the city: #1 to **Salthill,** #2 to **Knocknacarra** (west) or **Renmare** (east), #3 to **Castlepark,** and #4 to **Newcastle** and **Rahoon.** Service M-Sa 8am-9pm, Su 11am-9pm. Commuter tickets £8 per week, £29 per month.

Taxis: Big O Taxis, 21 Upper Dominick St. (☎ 585 858). **Galway Taxis,** 7 Mainguard St. (☎ 561 111), around the corner from McSwiggan's Pub. 24hr. service. Taxis can usually be found around Eyre Sq. **Hackneys** are considerably cheaper than taxis due to differences in licensing and fixed-price service; they are run by **MGM** (☎ 757 888), **Claddagh** (☎ 589 000), and **Eyre Square** (☎ 569 444). There's a waiting station 3 doors down from the tourist office.

Bike Rental: Europa Cycles, Hunter Buildings, Earls Island (☎ 563 355), opposite the cathedral. £5 per day, £6 per 24hr., £25 per week; deposit £30. Open M-F 9am-6pm. **Celtic Cycles,** Queen St., Victoria Pl. (☎ 566 606), next to the Celtic Hostel. £7 per day, £30 per week; deposit £40 or ID; drop-off charge £12. Open daily 9am-6pm.

✦ ORIENTATION

Bus or rail to Galway will deposit you in **Eyre Sq.**, a central block of lawn and monuments with the train and bus station on its southeast side. To the northeast of the square along **Prospect Hill,** a string of B&Bs begs for business. The town's commercial zone spreads out to the south and west. West of the square, **Woodquay** is an area of quiet commercial and residential activity. Williamsgate St. descends southwest into the lively medieval area around **Shop St., High St., Cross St.,** and **Quay St.** Flashy pubs, restaurants, and shops dominate this area, which was recently pedestrianized. Fewer tourists venture over the bridges into the more bohemian **left bank** of the Corrib, where those in the know enjoy fantastic music in Galway's best pubs. Just south of the left bank is the **Claddagh,** Galway's original fishing village. A road stretches west past the quays to **Salthill,** a tacky beachfront resort with row houses and skyrocketing property values. To the north of the west bank are the university areas of **Newcastle** and **Shantallow,** quiet suburbs where students and families live. Galway's Regional Technical College is a mile east of the city center in suburban **Renmare,** which dozes peacefully by its bird sanctuary.

▣ PRACTICAL INFORMATION

TOURIST AND FINANCIAL SERVICES

Tourist Office: Victoria Pl. (☎ 563 081). A block southeast of Eyre Sq. The industrious staff and Aran Islands info booth make the pamphlet mania more exciting than ever. Go to the left for information, the right for purchasing small, touristy souvenirs. Open July-Aug. daily 8:30am-7:45pm; May-June and Sept. daily 8:30am-5:45pm; Oct.-Apr. M-F and Su 9am-5:45pm, Sa 9am-12:45pm. The **Salthill** office (☎ 520 500) is in an odd, round, metallic building visible from the main beach. Open daily 9am-5:45pm.

Travel Agency: usit, Mary St. (☎ 565 177). TravelSave stamps to reduce student bus fare £8. Open May-Sept. M-F 9:30am-5:30pm, Sa 10am-3pm; Oct.-Apr. M-F 9:30am-5:30pm, Sa 10am-1pm.

ACCOMMODATIONS ■ 315

Banks: Bank of Ireland, 19 Eyre Sq. (☎ 563 181). Open M-W and F 10am-4pm, Th 10am-5pm. **AIB,** Lynch's Castle, Shop St. (☎ 567 041). Exactly the same hours, but much more attractive. Both have **ATMs.**

LOCAL SERVICES

Camping Equipment: River Deep Mountain High, Middle St. (☎ 563 968). Open M-Th, Sa 9:30am-6pm, F 9:30am-7:30pm.

Bookstores: Eason, 33 Shop St. (☎ 562 284), has a huge selection of books and international periodicals, and art supplies upstairs. Open M-Th and Sa 9am-6:15pm, F 9am-8:45pm, Su 2-5:45pm. **Kenny's** (☎ 562 739), between High and Middle St., has an enormous collection of Irish interest books, an art gallery, and artsy postcards. Open M-Sa 9am-6pm. **Charlie Byrne's Bookshop,** Middle St. (☎ 561 776), has a massive stock of secondhand, discounted, remaindered books, and a friendly staff willing to give recommendations. Open July-Aug. M-Sa 9am-8pm, Su noon-6pm; Sept.-June M-Th and Sa 9am-5pm, F 9am-8pm.

Library: St. Augustine St. (☎ 561 666). Open Tu-Th 11am-8pm, M and F-Sa 11am-5pm. Overrun with small, loud children.

Bisexual, Gay, and Lesbian Information: P.O. Box 45 (☎ 566 134). Recorded information on meetings and events. Gay line Tu and Th 8-10pm. Lesbian line W 8-10pm. The *Gay Community News* is available at Charlie Byrne's Bookshop (above).

Laundry: The Bubbles Inn, 18 Mary St. (☎ 563 434). Wash and dry £4. Open M-Sa 9am-6:15pm. **Prospect Hill Launderette,** Prospect Hill (☎ 568 343). Wash and dry £4. Open M-Sa 8:30am-6pm; last wash 4:45pm.

Pharmacies: Flanagan's, Shop St. (☎ 562 924). Open M-Sa 9am-6pm. **McGoldrick's,** Upper Salthill (☎ 562 332). Open daily July-Aug. 9am-9pm, Sept.-June 9am-7pm.

EMERGENCY AND COMMUNICATIONS

Emergency: ☎ 999; no coins required. **Police** (*Garda*): Mill St. (☎ 563 161).

Counseling and Support: Samaritans, 14 Nun's Island (☎ 561 222). 24hr. phones. **Rape Crisis Centre,** 3 St. Augustine St. (☎ (850) 355 355). Limited hours.

Hospital: University College Hospital, Newcastle Rd. (☎ 524 222).

Post Office: Eglinton St. (☎ 562 051). Open M, W-Sa 9am-5:30pm, Tu 9:30am-5:30pm.

Internet Access: Cyberzone, the Old Malte Arcade, High St., (☎ 569 772). £5 per hr., £4 with student ID. Spacey murals to get you in the mood, free coffee when you log in. **Fun World,** Eyre Square. (☎ 561 415), above Supermac's. Log in to the bleeps of the arcade behind the row of computers along the wall. £3 per 30min., £4 per hr. Open M-Sa 10am-11pm, Su 11am-11pm.

ACCOMMODATIONS

In the last few years, the number of hostel beds in Galway has tripled to approach one thousand. Nevertheless, you'll need to call at least a day ahead in July and August and on weekends. Large, custom-built hostels gather around Eyre Sq. near the bus and train station. Smaller, friendlier ones clump a five-minute walk westward at Woodquay, or across the river around Dominick St. Rates are 10-20% higher in the summer.

HOSTELS

Barnacle's Quay Street Hostel (IHH), Quay St. (☎ 568 644). Shop St. becomes Quay St. Bright, spacious rooms and a peerless location in the city center make this hostel the place to be, especially for professional pub-crawlers. Excellent security. Challenging floorplans. Laundry £5. Big dorms £10-12; 8-bed dorms £7.50-9; 6-bed dorms £8-9.50; 4-bed dorms with bath £13.50; doubles with bath £35. Less in the off-season.

Woodquay Hostel, 23-24 Woodquay (☎ 562 618). Cute exterior, better inside. Loungers love the huge living room with potted plants and comfy couches. Marie's paintings of butterflies and flowers spark up the walls and bathrooms. The roomy candlelit dining area makes even the skimpiest of budget-conscious meals romantic. Clean and close to the pubs. Dorms £10; 4-bed suite £10; twins £12.50.

Great Western House (IHH), Eyre Sq. (☎ 561 150 or (800) 425 929), in a mammoth building across from the station. Somewhat impersonal, even with the pool room and sauna. Clean and modern with cheap full Irish breakfasts available. **Bureau de change.** Small breakfast included, full breakfast £2.50. Laundry £5. **Internet access** £2 per 20min. 24hr. reception. Wheelchair accessible. July-Aug. and bank holidays 8- to 12-bed dorms £10; 4- to 6-bed dorms with bath £12.50; singles £18; doubles with bath £32. Off-season £1.50-3 cheaper.

Archview Hostel, Dominick St. (☎ 586 661). The cheapest, most laid-back accommodations in town, in the heart of Galway's bohemian district. This place has seen some wear and tear over the years, but it's comfortable, and a short stumble home from your big night on Dominick St. Dorms £7, off-season £6. £30 a week for long-term stays.

Kinlay House (IHH), Merchants Rd. (☎ 565 244), across from the tourist office. Megalithic, and a bit sedate. Foosball table in the common room. Small breakfast included. Laundry £3.50. 24hr. **Internet access** £5 per hr. **Bureau de change.** Co-ed dorms. Wheelchair accessible. July-Sept. 8-bed dorms £10; 4-bed dorms £11.50, with bath £12.50; singles £20; doubles £29, £33 with bath; Oct.-June dorms 50p-£1 cheaper, private rooms £2 less.

The Galway Hostel, Eyre Sq. (☎ 566 959), across from the station. Burren Shale tiles lead up past the soft yellow walls to dorms with super-clean bathrooms. The kitchen fills fast in this 80-bed hostel. June-Sept. 14-bed dorms £8; 8-bed dorms £8.50; 4-bed £15; doubles £32; Sept.-May dorms £1 cheaper, doubles £2 less.

Corrib Villa (IHH), 4 Waterside (☎ 562 892), just past the courthouse, about 4 blocks down Eglinton St. from Eyre Sq. This Georgian townhouse has high ceilings and clean rooms and beds of varied comfort. Its interior is freshly painted in patriotic hues. Laundry £5. Dorms £8.50 per person.

An Óige Galway Hostel (☎ 527 411). Follow Dominick St. to the west and turn left onto St. Mary's Rd. When school lets out for the summer, St. Mary's school for boys, an imposing building surrounded by playing fields, puts bunks in its classrooms and gyms to form a 180-bed hostel. Open late June-Aug. Breakfast included. Close to Galway's best bars, but far from the station. Big dorms £9; 4-bed dorms £10; twins £11.

BED AND BREAKFASTS

St. Martin's, 2 Nuns' Island (☎ 568 286), on the west bank of the river at the end of Dominick St. (visible from the Bridge St. bridge). Gorgeous riverside location with a grassy lawn. Singles £20; doubles £36.

Mrs. E. O'Connolly, 24 Glenard Ave. (☎ 522 147), Salthill, off Dr. Mannix Rd. Bus #1 from Eyre Sq. Excellent B&B for super-cheap prices. £10 with continental breakfast, £12 with full Irish breakfast.

Mrs. Ruth Armstrong, 14 Glenard Ave. (☎ 522 069), close to Salthill. Full Irish breakfast and friendly chatter. £17 per person.

CAMPING

Salthill Caravan and Camping Park (☎ 523 972 or 522 479). Beautiful location on the bay, a half-mile west of Salthill. A good hour walk from Galway, along the shore. Open May-Oct. Crowded in summer. £3 per hiker or cyclist.

LONG-TERM STAYS

Galway has a large population of young, transient foreigners who visit, fall in love, find jobs, stay for a few months, and move on. Most share apartments in and around the city, where rents run from $30 to $50 per week. The best place to look is the *Galway Advertiser*. Apartment hunters line up outside the *Advertiser*'s office on Church St. (the small alley off Shop St. behind Eason) on Wednesdays at around 2pm; when the classified section is released at 3pm, they dash to the nearest phone box (one block up on Shop St.). An ideal time to start looking for jobs or apartments is the third week of May, when the university lets out. **Corrib Village** (☎ 527 112), in Newcastle, offers housing for the summer. Some hostels have cheap weekly rates ($30-35) in winter. Jobs aren't too hard to come by in Galway either. The Thursday morning *Galway Advertiser* is the place to look. Others find service jobs simply by asking. A four-month student visa or other work permit helps a great deal, although the situation isn't hopeless without them. The **Galway Chamber of Commerce** (☎ 563 536), on Merchant's Rd. near the docks, will put those seeking more permanent jobs in touch with recruiters.

FOOD

The large student population in Galway guarantees plenty of cheap, satisfying eats. The east bank has the greatest concentration of restaurants; the short blocks around Quay, High, and Shop St. are filled with good values, especially for lunches and early dinners. The **Supervalu**, in the Eyre Sq. mall, is a chef's playground. (☎ 567 833. Open M-W and Sa 9am-6:30pm, Th-F 9am-9pm.) **Evergreen Health Food,** 1 Mainguard St., has just the healthy stuff. (☎ 564 215. Open M-Sa 8:45am-6:30pm.) **Healthwise,** Abbeygate St., promises better living through conscientious consumption. (☎ 568 761. Open M-F 9:30am-6pm, Sa 9:30am-5:30pm.) On Saturday mornings, an **open market** sets up in front of St. Nicholas Church on Market St. with seafood, pastries, and fresh fruit. The crepes are a steal, $3 for a fresh egg, cheese and ham crepe. (Open 8am-1pm.)

- **Anton's** (☎ 582 067). A bit off the beaten path: a 3min. walk up Father Griffin Rd. over the bridge near the Spanish Arch. Amazing but cheap sandwiches make it worth the walk. Ham, tomato, and onion marmalade on foccacia bread, £2.50. Salad and bread £3; creative sandwiches £2- 2.50. Open Tu-Sa 11am-6pm.

- **Apostasy,** Dominick St. (☎ 561 478). A hip coffee shop with an unbelievable after-hours scene. New-age regulars fill the place pretending to talk art until 4am each morning. Pub crawlers halfheartedly try to sober up with cups of strong coffee. Garlic bread with olives and mozzarella £2.20. Cappuccino £1.20.

- **Da Tang,** Middle St. (☎ 561 443). Business men and hipsters alike crowd together in this busy Chinese noodle house. Pickled mustard mixes with shredded pork in a lovely broth (£6), tofu and veggies float in a yellow sauce (£5.50). Some of the best food in town. Take-away available. Open Su-Th noon-10pm, F-Sa noon-11pm.

- **The River God Cafe,** Quay St. (☎ 565 811). French and Asian flavors combine in subtle seafood curries and salmon steaks with seaweed pasta. The champagne sorbet makes bubbly heavenly. Lunch special, £5, dinners at least £10. Open noon-10pm.

- **Mocha Mania,** High St. (☎ 566 146). A bright, friendly, smoke-free coffee shop with good coffee. Lovely normandy apple tarts, tasty toasted panini. Espresso £1, desserts £2.50, panini £2.50-3. Open M-Sa 9:30am-6pm, Su noon-6pm.

- **The Home Plate,** Mary St. (☎ 561 475). Huge portions of yummy, vegetarian-friendly food makes tummies happy. The curry dishes can easily be split. Entrees £4-6, large sandwiches £2.50. Open M-Sa noon-9:30pm.

- **McDonagh's,** 22 Quay St. (☎ 565 809). Locals and tourists flock here for world-class fish & chips. Certificates, newspaper clippings, and magazine articles line the wall to prove its popularity. Cod fillet and chips to take away, £4.10. Restaurant open daily noon-11pm; take-away M-Sa noon-midnight, Su 5-11pm.

- **Pierre's,** Quay St. (☎ 566 066). 3-course meal £12. If you're going to break the bank (or at least a tenner) it ought to happen at this Quay St. favorite. Delicious lunches under £5; pre-theater special served 6-7pm, £8.90.

The Long Walk (☎ 561 114), next to the Spanish Arch and a lot more intriguing. The first floor of a medieval battlement is transformed into a relaxed cafe and wine bar with live jazz on most afternoons. Food served M-Sa 12:30-3pm and 6-10pm, Su 6-10pm.

Café Du Journal, Quay St. (☎ 568 428). Enter and instantly relax. Over-stuffed bookshelves and chilled-out regulars line the dark, multi-colored walls. Grab a newspaper, a powerful coffee, and a huge sandwich. Specials from £5. Open M-Sa 9am-10pm.

Fat Freddy's, Quay St. (☎ 567 279). Galway's youth give high marks to the large pies rolling down the pipe at this pizza joint, although the wait can be a drag. Large pizza £5.75. Students 10% off M-F 3-6pm. Open daily 9am-11:30pm.

◪ PUBS

Galway's pub scene is centuries old and still brilliantly creative. A swanky bar can be flanked by a dark, local haunt and a spinning pub, so shop around. Trad blazes across town nightly, but Dominick St. is best for impromptu sessions. Good and bad versions of rock, folk, country, and blues also rear their heads; some pubs have schedules posted in their windows. Very broadly speaking, Quay St. pubs cater more to tourists, while locals stick to Dominick St. pubs. Only big gigs have cover charges. For information, check *The List*, free and available at most pubs and newsstands. Thursday night is the big night out for most Galway pubsters.

DOMINICK STREET

◪ **Roisín Dubh** ("The Black Rose"), Dominick St. (☎ 586 540; www.RoisinDubh.net). Big-name Irish and international musicians light up the stage in this large, dark pub. Primarily rock, but folk, blues, and trad as well. Irish record labels, including the pub's own, promote new artists here, and music enthusiasts of all ages turn out in numbers. Occasional M and Tu cover £5-10.

◪ **The Crane,** 2 Sea Rd. (☎ 587 419), a bit beyond the Blue Note. Well known as the place to hear trad in Galway. Enter through the side door and hop up to the 2nd floor loft. 2 musicians quickly become 6, 6 become 10, 10 become 20. Trad "whenever."

La Graal, 38 Lower Dominick St. (☎ 567 614). A candlelit wine (only) bar and restaurant, La Graal is the center for the Latin community of Galway. A diverse crowd; gay-friendly. Exquisite staff. Salsa dancing Th. Open until 1:15am.

The Blue Note, William St. West (☎ 589 116). Sip expensive drinks on lush red couches while listening to guest DJs. With its finger firmly on the pulse of the European dance scene, the Blue Note throbs every night of the week with guest DJs.

Aras Na nGael, Dominick St. (☎ 526 509). A bar for Irish speakers, this club nonetheless welcomes all sorts (kind of). Come F or Sa night and absorb the rhythms of the Irish language as you quietly nurse your Guinness.

Taylor's, Dominick St. (☎ 589 385). A holdover from another era, Taylor's is overlooked by tourists seeking flashier new entertainment venues. The locals who proclaim it the best pint in town don't mind much. Trad several nights a week.

THE QUAY

◪ **The King's Head,** High St. (☎ 566 630). A locus for many pub-goers and a crawl in itself. Check out the modern club room on the 3rd floor. Huge stage area and funky lighting host live bands nightly. Several bars make the wait for a pint non-existent. Occasional trad. Lunchtime theater M-Sa 1-2pm, £2. Popular jazz brunch Su noon-1:45pm.

The Quays, Quay St. (☎ 568 347). Popular with the younger crowd and scamming yuppies. The massive, multi-floored interior was built with carved wood and stained glass from an old church. Worth a visit to see the interior. Cover bands electrify the equally impressive upstairs extension nightly 10pm-1:30am. £5 cover.

Seaghan Ua Neachtain (called **Knockton's**), Quay St. (☎ 568 820). One of the oldest and most genuine pubs in the county. An older crowd trades personal space for warmth and energy. Trad nightly. 21+.

Buskar Browne's/The Slate House (☎ 563 377), between Cross St. and Kirwin's Ln., is in an old nunnery. Get thee to this upscale, 20-something bar that packs a professional crowd onto wall-to-wall couches. Its fantastic 3rd floor "Hall of the Tribes" is the most spectacular lounge in Galway.

The Front Door, Cross St. (☎ 563 757). Beams of light criss-cross the dark interior of this deceivingly small pub. As it gets busier, more rooms open, moving up 3 stories and sprouting hydra-like appendages all over the block. Get lost with that special someone.

The Lisheen, 5 Bridge St. (☎ 563 804). Outstanding and ceaseless trad every night and Su mornings thrills tourists. Dancing too. A musicians' and pool-shooters' haven. 21.+

Padraig's, (☎ 563 696), at the docks. Opens daily at 7:30am for fishermen, and plain ol' die-hards. You know who you are.

EYRE SQUARE

The Hole in the Wall, Eyre Sq., This surprisingly large pub fills up fast with lots of singles and the occasional high-profile celebrity. An ideal meet-market with huge booths for intimate groups, 3 bars for mingling, and tables to dance on.

McSwiggin's, Eyre St. (☎ 568 917), near Eglinton St. A sprawling mess of small rooms and stairwells spanning 3 stories, McSwiggin's holds hundreds of tourists at a time. The *craic* is good, though, and so is the food.

Skeffington Arms (☎ 563 173). A splendidly decorated, multi-storied hotel with 6 different bars. A well-touristed pub crawl unto itself with a mixed crowd of young and old.

CLUBS

Between 11pm and midnight, the pubs empty out, and the tireless go dancing. Unfortunately, Galway's clubs lag slightly behind its pubs in the fun factor. On the other hand, those who arrive at the clubs between 11:30pm and 12:15am are legally assured of a free meal with their entrance fee. The place-to-be often rotates at disco-ball speed; a good strategy to find out what's hot is to simply follow the crowds as the pubs close.

GPO, Eglinton St., doesn't look good, but it draws a high-energy crowd nonetheless. Bank holiday Mondays are "Sheight Night"—dress your worst and listen to Abba's greatest hits. (☎ 563 073. 21+, cover £5). **Cuba,** on Prospect Hill, right past Eyre Sq., has great music and an energetic crowd. Cover varies. The more adventurous and mobile head out to the **Liquid Club,** King's Hill, in Salthill. Expect a provocative dance mix that should fuel your engine well into morning. Hackney service is the best way to get there and back. (☎ 522 715. Open Th-Su. Cover £6.)

TOURS

Half- or full-day group tours are often the best way to see the sights of Galway, the Burren, and Connemara if you don't have much time. Some offer excellent values, with lower prices than bus tickets. For hour-long tours in and around the city, hop on one of the many buses that line up outside the tourist office (most £5, students £4). Several lines depart from the tourist office once a day for both Connemara and the Burren (about £10, students £8), including **O'Neachtain Tours** (☎ 55388), **Gaeltacht Tours** (☎ 593 322), **Connemara Tours** (☎ 562 905), **Bus Éireann** (☎ 562 000), and **Healy Tours** (☎ 770 066). **Western Cultural and Heritage Tours** (☎ 521 699) leave from the tourist office at 2:30pm daily June through August. **Arch Heritage Tours** (☎ 844 133) explore the flora, fauna, and archaeology of the Burren. The **Corrib Princess** (☎ 592 447) sails from Galway's Woodquay on a tour of Lough Corrib to the north (1½hr., June-Aug. daily 2:30 and 4:30pm, £5).

SIGHTS

Present-day Galway is far more interesting than it was in days of yore, but those digging for interesting sights usually find enough to last at least an afternoon.

EYRE SQUARE. The park was rededicated to receive the official name John F. Kennedy Park. Around its grassy common, a small collection of monuments speak for various interests. A rusty sculpture celebrates the Galway Hooker. Another is a life-size portrait of the Irish-speaking poet Pádraig Ó'Cónaire. The sidewalk outside of the Great Southern Hotel on the square's east side hides two **foot-scrapers,** small cast iron implements once used by Galway's gentry to scrape the muck off their feet. On the south side of the square is the Eyre Square Shopping Center, a large indoor mall that encloses a major section of Galway's medieval town wall. The wall was originally built in the 13th century and stood unnoticed until the construction of the shopping development nine years ago.

CLADDAGH. Until the 1930s, this area was an Irish-speaking, thatched-cottage fishing village. Stone bungalows replaced the cottages, but a bit of the small-town appeal and atmosphere still persist. The famous Claddagh rings, traditionally used as wedding bands, are mass-produced today. The rings depict the thumb and forefingers of two hands holding up a crown-topped heart. The ring should be turned around upon marriage; once the point of the heart faces inward, the wearer's heart is no longer available. *(Across the river south of Dominick St.)*

NORA BARNACLE HOUSE. The home of James Joyce's life-long companion. The table where he composed a few lines to Nora draws the admiration of Joyce addicts. Also on display are their love letters. *(8 Bowling Green. ☎ 564 743. Open mid-May to mid-Sept. M-Sa 10am-1pm and 2-5pm. £1.)*

LYNCH'S CASTLE. The elegant 1320 mansion now houses the Allied Irish Bank. The Lynch family ruled Galway from the 13th to the 18th century. The bank's displays relate a dubious family legend. In the late 1400s, Lynch Jr. killed a Spaniard whom he suspected of liking his girlfriend. The son, sentenced to hang, was so beloved by the populace that no one would agree to be the hangman. Lynch Sr., the lord of the castle, was so determined to administer justice that he hanged his own son. The window behind St. Nicholas Church is supposedly the one from which Lynch Sr. lynched Lynch Jr. A skull and crossbones engraved in the glass remembers the deed. *(Exhibit room open M-W, F 10am-4pm, Th 10am-5pm. Free.)*

CHURCH OF ST. NICHOLAS. The church is replete with oddities from unpredictable sources. A stone marks the spot where Columbus supposedly stopped to pray before hitting the New World. Note the three-faced clock on the exterior; local folklore claims that the residents on the fourth side failed to pay their church taxes. Glorious stained glass and relics from the Connacht Rangers provide more distractions. *(Market St., behind the castle. Open May-Sept. daily 9am-5:45pm. Free. Unnecessary tour £1, students 50p.)*

CATHEDRAL OF OUR LADY ASSUMED INTO HEAVEN AND ST. NICHOLAS. The boring exterior of Galway's Catholic cathedral provides no hint of the controversy that assailed its eclectic design 25 years ago: the interior consists of enormous bare walls of Connemara stone decorated with elaborate mosaics. *(Beside the Salmon Weir Bridge at the intersection of Gaol and University Rd. Excellent tours M-F 9:30am-4:30pm. Organ practice M-F 3:30-5:30pm. Open Su for mass.)*

GALWAY CITY MUSEUM. Old photographs of the Claddagh, a knife-sharpener by a peat fire, and some fishy statistics are the main contents of this small museum. *(In the tower house next to the Spanish Arch. ☎ 567 641. Open May-Oct. daily 10am-1pm and 2:15-5:15pm; check at the tourist office for Nov.-Apr. opening times. £1, students 50p.)*

SALTHILL. From the Claddagh, the waterfront road leads west, where the coast alternates between pebbles and sand; when the ocean sunset turns red, it's time for some serious beach frolicking. Two casinos, a swimming pool, and an amusement park join the ugly new hotels that dominate the esplanade. The **Atlantaquiaria,** recently opened as the National Aquarium of Ireland, is worth a trip for mer-minded folk. (☎ 585 100. Open 10am-8pm.)

MENLO CASTLE. Depending on your energy level, hire a boat and drift, row, or zoom up Lough Corrib to visit the ruins of the seat of the Blake family. Frank Dolan's fleet of rowboats will take you away from the maddening crowd and up Galway's gorgeous stretch. *(13 Riverside, Woodquay.* ☎ *565 841. £3 per hr.)*

OTHER SITES. Across the University Rd. bridge from the cathedral is the **National University of Ireland at Galway,** founded 159 years ago during the Great Famine. Today the university enrolls some 6,000 students a year. By the river, the **Long Walk** makes a pleasant stroll, bringing you to the **Spanish Arch.** Built in 1584 as a defensive bastion for the port, this worn, one-story stone curve is revered by townspeople despite its unimpressive stature.

ARTS, THEATER, AND FILM

The *Advertiser* and *Galway Guide* (both free) provide listings of events, and are available at most pubs and newsagents.

SIAMSA NA GAILLIMHE. Dancers, singers, musicians, and actors routinely stun audiences with their showcase of traditional Irish art. *(The Galway Folk Theatre, at University College.* ☎ *755 479. Performances June 22-Aug. 28 M-F 8:45 pm. Tickets from £7.)*

THE GALWAY ARTS CENTRE. The center hosts rotating art and photography exhibits and frequent workshops on dance, writing, and painting. *(47 Dominick St.* ☎ *565 886. Open M-Sa 10am-5:30pm.)*

THE TOWN HALL THEATRE. This Courthouse Sq. theater hosts everything from the Druid Theatre Company's Irish-themed plays and original Irish films to international hit musicals. *(*☎ *569 777. Programming daily in summer; most performances 8pm. Tickets £5-15, student discounts most shows.)*

AN TAIBHDHEARC. (An TIVE-yark.) Founded in 1928 by a group of academics from Galway University, the mostly Irish-language theater has launched quite a few Irish actors into the limelight. Poetry readings, musicals, and other events alternate with full-blown plays. *(Middle St.* ☎ *562 024. 7 performances per year. Box office open M-F 10am-6pm, Sa 1-6pm. Tickets £6-9.)*

FESTIVALS AND EVENTS

Festivals rotate through Galway all year long, with the greatest concentration during the summer months. Reservations during these weeks are necessary.

GALWAY ARTS FESTIVAL. For two crazed weeks in mid-July, the largest arts festival in Ireland reels in famous trad musicians, rock groups, theater troupes, and filmmakers. The highlight of the festival is the Big Day Out, held on the first Saturday, when big-name pop groups come to town for a massive concert. (☎ *583 800.)*

GALWAY RACES. The gates go up at the end of July. Those attending the races celebrate horses, money, and stout, not necessarily in that order. The grandstand bar at the 23,000-seat-capacity Ballybrit track holds the world record for the longest bar in Europe, measuring over 70 yd. from end to end. The major social event is Ladies' Day, when those with the best hats and overall dress are officially recognized. Competition is notoriously stiff. *(*☎ *753 870. Race tickets £8-10 at the gate.)*

GALWAY INTERNATIONAL OYSTER FESTIVAL. Galway's last big festival of the year takes place in late September. Street theater, parades, and free concerts surround this 45-year-old Galway tradition, which culminates in the Guinness World Oyster Opening Championship. *(*☎ *566 490.)*

GALWAY POETRY AND LITERATURE FESTIVAL. Also known as the Cúirt, this festival gathers the very highest of the nation's brows in the last week of April. Past guests have included Nobel Prize winner and Caribbean poet Derek Walcott and reggae star Linton Johnston. (☎ 565 886.)

GALWAY FILM FLEADH. Ireland's biggest film festival, which features independent Irish and international filmmakers, screens its stuff in early July.

GALWAY HOOKER FESTIVAL AND TRADITIONAL BOAT REGATTA. Hookers can be seen in Galway all year round, but the fourth weekend in June, they race off to Portaferry, Northern Ireland (see p. 433). Fish nets, not fishnets, characterize these boating beauties with heavy, black hulls and billowing sails.

LOUGH CORRIB

Three hundred and sixty-five islands dot Lough Corrib, one for every day of the year. The eastern shores of Lough Corrib and Lough Mask stretch quietly into fertile farmland. The western shores slip into bog, quartzite scree ("scree" is landslide detritus, for those of us who are shaky on our geology), and the famously rough Connemara country. The island of Inchagoill, in the middle of the lough, contains the site of the second-oldest existing Christian monuments in Europe.

OUGHTERARD   ☎091

Little more than a small population center along the N59 between Galway and Clifden, Oughterard (OOK-ter-rard) sees most touring vehicles blink briefly in its direction before they head to bigger, better-known attractions. Still, Oughterard has a number of worthwhile outdoor activities: a relaxing canoe trip on Lough Corrib—the largest lake in Ireland—or a hike into the Maam Turk Mountains. The ruins on Inchagoill Island and Cong's *Quiet Man* mania are only a ferry ride away.

GETTING THERE AND PRACTICAL INFORMATION. Bus Éireann coaches on their way from **Galway** to **Clifden** stop in Oughterard (30min. to Galway, 1½hr. to Clifden; July-Aug. M-Sa 4-6 per day, Su 1-2 per day; Sept.-June 1 per day). **Hitchers** report easy going, at least in summer, between Galway and anywhere west or northwest. *Let's Go* does not recommend hitchhiking. An independent **tourist office** sells the useful *Oughterard Walking & Cycling Routes* handbook for £2. (☎ 552 808. Open May-Aug. M-F 9am-6pm, Sa-Su 10am-5pm; Sept.-Apr. M-F 9am-6pm.) The **Bank of Ireland**, Main St., has an **ATM**. (☎ 552 123. Open M-W and F 10am-4pm, Th 10am-5pm.) **Flaherty's Pharmacy**, sits on Main St. (☎ 552 348. Open M-Tu and Th-Sa 9:30am-1:45pm and 2:15-6pm, W 9:30am-1pm.) The **post office** is also on Main St. (☎ 552 201. Open M-F 9am-1pm and 2-5:30pm, Sa 9am-1pm.)

ACCOMMODATIONS, FOOD, AND PUBS. Cranrawer House (IHH), a 10-minute walk down Station Rd., is a beautiful hostel with superior facilities in a quiet spot. The owner is a professional angler and will guide day expeditions onto the lough. (☎ 552 388. Laundry £4.50. May-Sept. 8- to 10-bed dorms £7.50, 5-bed dorms with bath £8.50; private rooms with bath £9; Oct.-Apr. £6.50-8.50.) **Cregg Lodge B&B**, Station Rd., knows how to lodge. (☎ (095) 552 493. Open Apr.-Sept. £15 per person, with bath £17 per person.)

Keogh's Grocery, The Square, sells food, fishing tackle, and hardware. The photo of Bob Hope trying to buy some snacks is not for sale. (☎ 552 583. Open summer M-Sa 8am-10pm; winter M-Sa 8am-8pm, Su 9am-9pm.) Good pub grub and brilliant *craic* dock at **The Boat Inn**, The Square. (☎ 552 196. Irish stew £4.95. Food served 10:30am-10pm.) Thatched **Power's Bar**, a few doors down, is a local favorite. (☎ 552 712. Music F-Su.) Across the street, **Keogh's Bar** encourages people to eat, drink, and be merry. (☎ 552 222. Music Tu-Su in summer, F-Su off-season.)

Pack the Wallet Guide
and save 25% or more* on calls home to the U.S.

It's lightweight and carries heavy savings of 25% or more* over AT&T USA Direct and MCI WorldPhone rates. So take this YOU wallet guide and carry it wherever you go.

To save with YOU:
- Dial the access number of the country you're in (see reverse)
- Dial 04 or follow the English voice prompts
- Enter your credit card info for easy billing

YOU℠

Service provided by Sprint

*Based on AT&T USA Direct rates, Tariff 24.1.3.A, April 8, 2000 and MCI WorldPhone rates, Tariff 3.07341, May 1, 2000. 25% discount applies for calls less then 100 minutes. Promotion subject to change. Restrictions may apply. Copyright ©Sprint 2000. All rights reserved. All trademarks referenced herein are the property of their respective owners.

Hmm, call home or eat lunch?
With YOU℠ you can do both.

Nathan Lane for YOU℠.

No doubt, traveling on a budget is tough. So tear out this wallet guide and keep it with you during your travels. With YOU, calling home from overseas is affordable and easy.

If the wallet guide is missing, call collect 913-624-5336 or visit www.youcallhome.com for YOU country numbers.

Dialing instructions: Dial the access number for the country you're in. Dial 04 or follow the English prompts. Enter your credit card information to place your call.

Need help with access numbers while overseas? Call collect, 913-624-5336.

Country	Access Number	Country	Access Number	Country	Access Number
Australia ✔	1-800-551-110	Israel ✔	1-800-949-4102	Spain ✔	900-99-0013
Bahamas ✚	1-800-389-2111	Italy ✚ ✔	172-1877	Switzerland ✔	0800-899-777
Brazil ✔	000-8016	Japan ✚ ✔	00539-131	Taiwan ✔	0080-14-0877
China ✚ ▲ ✔	108-13	Mexico U ✔	001-800-877-8000	United Kingdom ✔	0800-890-877
France ✔	0800-99-0087	Netherlands ✚ ✔	0800-022-9119		
Germany ✚ ✔	0800-888-0013	New Zealand ▲ ✔	000-999		
Hong Kong ✔	800-96-1877	Philippines T ✔	105-16		
India ✔	000-137	Singapore ✔	8000-177-177	**YOU**℠
Ireland ✔	1-800-552-101	South Korea ✚ ✔	00729-16	*Service provided by Sprint*

✔ Call answered by automated Voice Response Unit.   ✚ Public phones may require coin or card.
▲ May not be available from all payphones.   U Use phones marked with "LADATEL" and no coin or card is required.
T If talk button is available, push it before talking.

🔍 **SIGHTS.** A mile south of town, a turn-off from N59 leads to 16th-century **Aughnanure Castle,** where a river, red with peat, curves around a fortified tower. (☎ 82214. Open daily mid-June to mid-Sept. 9:30am-6:30pm. £2, students £1.) The secret chamber, feasting hall, and murder hole are highlights of the quality tour. The view from the castle roof is tremendous. (Key available at the ticket booth.) Glann Rd. covers the 9 mi. from Oughterard to the infamous **Hill of Doon,** where the pre-Celtic Glann people annually sacrificed a virgin to the panther goddess Taryn. It is said that the practice continued in secret until the 1960s, when they ran out of virgins. The 16 mi. **Western Way Walk** begins where Glann Rd. ends and passes along the lake shore to Maam at the base of the Maam Turk mountain range.

Competitors from all over Ireland assemble in June for the **Currach Racing Championships.** The tourist office sells tickets for **Corrib Cruises,** with two to three boats running daily between Cong, Oughterard, Ashford Castle, and Inchagoill. (☎ 82644. £10 return, additional £3 per bike.) Equestrian hopefuls can start their careers by **pony trekking.** (☎ 55212. £15 per hr.)

🏞 **DAYTRIP FROM OUGHTERARD: INCHAGOILL.** 🏝**Inchagoill** (INCH-a-gill), reputed to mean "the Island of the Stranger," has been uninhabited since the 1950s. There is little to see on the island other than a few ancient monastic ruins and toppled gravestones. Yet, at the right time of day, Inchagoill's eerie beauty makes it as captivating as any of its more touristed island cousins. Two churches, about which very little is known, hide quietly down the right-hand path from the pier. **St. Patrick's Church,** built in the 5th century, is now only a stack of crumbling stone. The famous **Stone of Lugna,** supposedly the tombstone of St. Patrick's nephew and navigator, stands 3 ft. high among the stones surrounding the church. The inscription on the stone translates to mean "stone of Luguaedon the son of Menueh." It is the earliest known example of the Irish language written in Roman script, and the second-oldest known inscribed Christian monument in Europe (the oldest are the catacombs of Rome). **The Church of the Saint** dates back to the 12th century. On the south side of the island is a now-defunct coffee house built by the Guinnesses. The **Corrib Queen** (☎ (092) 46029), sails daily from Lisloughrea Quay on Quay Rd. in Cong (see p. 330), the Ashford Castle, and the Quay Road in Oughterard, and offers a brief but enlightening tour of the island (1½hr., June-Aug. 4 per day, £10 return.) Those interested in more extensive exploration should take a morning ferry out and return in the afternoon.

CONNEMARA

Connemara is composed of a lacy net of inlets and islands, a rough gang of inland mountains, and desolate stretches of bog. This thinly populated and geographically erratic western arm of Co. Galway harbors some of Ireland's most desolate yet breathtaking scenery. The jagged southern coastline of Connemara teems with safe beaches ideal for camping, sinuous estuaries, and tidal causeways connecting to rocky offshore islands. The relatively uninteresting developed strip from Galway to Rossaveal soon gives way to pretty fishing villages such as Roundstone and Kilkieran. Ireland's largest *gaeltacht* stretches along this coast; Connemara-based Irish-language radio, Radio na Gaeltachta, broadcasts from Costelloe. English-speaking Clifden, Connemara's largest town, also hosts its largest crowds. Ancient bogs spread between the coast and the rock-studded green slopes of the two major mountain ranges, the Twelve Bens and the Maamturks. Northeast of the Maamturks is Joyce Country, named for a long-settled Connemara clan. Tom Joyce, the original Welsh settler of the region, was said to be 7 ft. tall, and many of his descendents still tower high over the bog.

Cycling is a particularly rewarding way to absorb Connemara. The 60 mi. rides from Galway to Clifden via Cong or to Letterfrack are common routes, although the roads become a bit difficult toward the end. The seaside route through Inverin and Roundstone to Galway is another option, and each of the dozens of loops and backroads in north Connemara is as spectacular as the next. **Hiking** through the boglands and along the coastal routes is popular. The **Western Way** footpath offers dazzling views as it winds 31 mi. from Oughterard to Leenane through the Maamturks. **Buses** regularly service the main road from Galway to Westport, with stops in Clifden, Oughterard, Cong, and Leenane. N59 from Galway to Clifden is the main thoroughfare; R336, R340, and R341 make more elaborate coastal loops. **Hitchers** report that locals are likely to stop; *Let's Go* does not recommend hitchhiking. Watching Connemara fly by through the tinted windows of a **bus tour** (see **Galway**, p. 319), is better than missing it altogether.

SOUTH CONNEMARA

N59, the direct route from Galway to Clifden, passes through bare mountainous scenery, while the coastal route weaves in and out of the peninsulas and islands of South Connemara. A barren, boggy, lake-ridden frontier with few roads spans the large distance between the two highways. Drive-through territory runs straight along the Galway coast through the Irish-speaking suburbs of **Barna, Spiddal,** and **Inverin;** although Spiddal does have a small beach, far better ones await farther west. Boats leave for the Aran Islands from nearby **Rossaveal** (see **Aran Islands,** p. 303), west of which the landscape changes into a complicated mesh of intertwined estuaries, peninsulas, and islands. At low tide, bays become ponds and islands become peninsulas, and beaches open up for frolicking. The first turnoff after Rossaveal leads to **Carraroe,** an Irish-speaking hamlet notable for its coral sands.

At Gortmore, a detour through Rosmuck leads to **Padraig Pearse's Cottage,** which squats in a small hillock overlooking the northern mountains. Pearse and his brother spent their summers here learning Irish and dreaming of an Irish Republic (see **Easter Rising,** p. 16). The Republic-come-true declared the cottage a national monument. (☎ (091) 570 4292. Open mid-June to mid-Sept. daily 9:30am-6:30pm. £1, students 40p.) Farther along the coast, the little fishing village of **Roundstone** curves along a colorful harbor. From the bay, one can see a few striking Bens rising in the distance. **Errisbeg Mountain** overlooks Roundstone's main street, and the two-hour hike up culminates in a panoramic view of Connemara. **Roundstone Musical Instruments** (☎ (095) 35875) is the only full-time *bodhrán* maker in the world (see **Traditional Music,** p. 29); their instruments have been used by famous Irish musicians around the world, including the Chieftains. (Open daily M-Sa 9am-7pm, Su 9:30am-7pm.)Where there are musical instruments, there is music, and **An galún Taoscta** is where you're likely to find it. (W trad, Su lunch session.) Afterwards, bang your *bodhrán* in the direction of ◪**Wits End B&B.** (☎ (095) 35951. July-Aug. £19 with bath; lower prices in the off-season.) Roundstone hosts a yearly **music festival** in the second week of July.

Two miles along the coast from Roundstone, the beaches between Dog's Bay and Gorteen Bay fan out to a small knobby island. On a bog near Ballyconneely, the last town before Clifden, John Alcock and Arthur Brown landed the **first non-stop transatlantic flight** in 1919.

CLIFDEN (AN CLOCHÁN) ☎095

Clifden is called the capital of Connemara because of its size, not its cultural membership in the *gaeltacht*; this busy English-speaking town has more amenities and modernities than its old-world, Irish-speaking neighbors. Clifden's proximity to the scenic bogs and mountains of the region attracts crowds of tourists, who enjoy the frenzied pub scene that starts up in the town at nightfall. Two high spires overlook its central wad of hotels, pubs, and artsy shops. Clifden slumbers in the winter but explodes in the peak season as rental cars jockey for parking spaces, tour buses bring traffic to a standstill, and crowds of international visitors fill its five hostels. Yuppie shoppers check out the arts-and-crafts studios, and youths scope the liveliest pub scene this side of Galway.

CLIFDEN (AN CLOCHÁN) ■ 325

⌂ GETTING THERE AND GETTING AROUND

Buses: Bus Éireann rolls from the library on Market St. to **Westport** via **Leenane** (1½hr., late June-Aug. 1-2 per day), and **Galway** via **Oughterard** (2hr.; June-Aug. M-Sa 5 per day, Su 2 per day; Sept.-May 1 per day; £6.50). **Michael Nee** (☎ 51082) runs a private bus from the courthouse to **Galway** (June-Sept. 3 per day, £5), **Cleggan** (June-Sept. 1-2 per day, Oct.-May 2 per week; £3), and to other remote destinations in Connemara.

Taxi: Joyce's (☎ 21076 or 22082). £3 for the first mile, £1 for each mile after.

Bike Rental: Mannion's, Bridge St. (☎ 21160, after hours 21155). £7 per day, £40 per week; deposit £10. Open M-Sa 9:30am-6:30pm, Su 10am-1pm and 5-7pm.

Boat Rental: John Ryan, Sky Rd. (☎ 21069). Prices negotiable.

✱ ? ORIENTATION AND PRACTICAL INFORMATION

Market St. meets **Main St.** and **Church Hill** at **The Square.** The buildings on the south side of Market St. hide a surprising cliff drop. N59 makes a U-turn at Clifden; most traffic is from Galway, 1½ hours southeast, but the road continues northeast to Letterfrack and Connemara National Park. Hitchers usually wait at the Esso station on N59. *Let's Go* does not recommend hitching.

Tourist Office: Galway Rd. (☎ 21163). Info on all of Connemara. Open July-Aug. M-Sa 9:45am-5:45pm and Su noon-4pm; May-June and Sept. M-Sa 9:30am-5:30pm.

Banks: AIB, The Square (☎ 21129). Open M-Tu and Th-F 10am-12:30pm and 1:30-4pm, W 10am-12:30pm and 1:30-5pm. **ATM. Bank of Ireland,** Sea View (☎ 21111). Open M-F 10am-12:30pm and 1:30-5pm.

Laundry: The Shamrock Washeteria, The Square (☎ 21348). Wash and dry £4.50. Open M-Sa 9:30am-6pm.

Pharmacy: Clifden Pharmacy (☎ 21821). Open M-F 9:30am-6:30pm, Sa 9:30am-6pm.

Emergency: ☎ 999; no coins required. **Police** (*Garda*): ☎ 21021.

Hospital: ☎ 21301 or 21302.

Post Office: Main St. (☎ 21156). Open M-F 9:30am-5:30pm, Sa 9:30am-1:30pm.

Internet Access: Two Dog Cafe, Church Hill (☎ 22186). Cafe with interesting sandwiches (£4.35), periodic poetry readings, and computers upstairs. Open M-Sa 10:30am-7pm and Su 1-5pm.

⌂ ACCOMMODATIONS

B&Bs litter the streets; the going rate is £18-20 per person. Reservations are necessary in July and August.

The Clifden Town Hostel (IHH), Market St. (☎ 21076). Great facilities, spotless rooms, and a quiet atmosphere close to the pubs. Despite the modern decor, old stone walls remind you that the house is 180 years old. Beautiful views of the harbor from the upstairs kitchen. Sean has lived on this street his whole life and will cheerfully divulge its deepest secrets. Call ahead Dec.-Feb. to make sure it is open. Dorms £8; doubles £24; triples £30-33; quads £36; off-season private rooms £1-2 cheaper.

Brookside Hostel (IHH), Hulk St. (☎ 21812), head straight at the bottom of Market St. Clean, roomy dorms look over innocuous, fat sheep loitering in the backyard. Super-knowledgeable owner will painstakingly plot a hiking route for you. Laundry £4. Dorms £8; doubles £18.

Ard Rí Bay View, Market St. (☎ 21866), behind King's Garage. Small, comfortable hostel with nice views and a central location. July-Aug. dorms £5-6; private rooms £8.

Blue Hostel, Sea View (☎ 21835), Market St. This slightly tattered family home provides little elbow room, but prioritizes cleanliness. Comfy common room, with lots of travelers staying long-term. Free laundry. Dorms £6; private rooms £8.

WESTERN IRELAND

White Heather House, The Square (☎ 21655). Great location and panoramic views from most rooms, all with bath. Singles £20; doubles £36; triples £54.

Kingston House, Mrs. King, Bridge St. (☎ 21470). Friendly staff, huge breakfasts, and spiffy rooms with a partial view of the church. Singles £20; doubles £34-40.

Shanaheever Campsite, (☎ 21018), a little over 1 mi. outside Clifden on Westport Rd. The tranquility of this spot compensates for its distance from the pubs. Game room, hot showers, and kitchen. Laundry £4.50. £8 per 2-person tent, £3 per additional person.

FOOD

Finding a good restaurant or cafe in Clifden requires little effort; justifying the prices for a tight budget is more difficult. **O'Connor's SuperValu,** Market St., might be the best place to score some cheap eats. (Open M-F 9am-7pm, Su 10am-6pm.)

An Tulan, Westport Rd. (☎ 21942). Offers home-cooked meals at compassionate prices. Sandwiches from £1.20, entrees around £4. Open daily 10am-10:30pm.

Mitchell's Restaurant, The Square (☎ 21867). A cozy, candlelit restaurant with hearty plates for all palates. Burgers £5.95. Open daily noon-10:30pm, pricier after 6pm.

E.J. King's, The Square (☎ 21330). Crowded bar serves excellent food on exceptionally old wood furniture. Fish and chips £4.95. Food served daily noon-9pm. The official restaurant upstairs serves the same food at higher prices.

Derryclare Restaurant, The Square (☎ 21440). Hearty seafood dishes served on brightly checked table clothes. Mussels and chips £6.95. Pasta around £7. Open daily 8am-10:30pm.

Walsh's, The Square (☎ 21283). A busy bakery that looks tiny but actually has quite a large seating area. Soups, salads, and baps each around £2. Open Oct.-May M-Sa 8:30am-5:20pm, June-Sept. 8am-9pm.

PUBS

Malarkey's (☎ 21801), downstairs to the left on Church Hill. Pool table, candles, poetry readings, open mic nights and good impromptu music—revelers sit on the floor when the pool table and chairs fill up.

Mannion's, Market St. (☎ 21780). Bring your own instrument, or just pick up some spoons when you get there. Music nightly in summer, F-Sa in winter.

E.J. King's, The Square (☎ 21330). Dark but spacious wooden interior and live trad in the summer.

King's, The Square (☎ 21800). A quiet pub with an older (masculine), local crowd. The town's best pint by consensus.

Clifden House (☎ 21187), in Smuggler's Lodge at the bottom of Market St. The place to be for booty-shaking disco. Open June-Aug. Th-Su; off-season Sa. Cover £5.

SIGHTS

There are no cliffs in Clifden itself, but 10 mi. long Sky Rd. loops around the head of land to the west of town, and paves the way to some dizzying ones. It's best covered by bicycle, but involves several strenuous climbs. A mile down Sky Rd. stand the ruins of **Clifden Castle,** once home to Clifden's founder, John D'Arcy. Farther out, a peek at the bay reveals the spot where US pilots Alcock and Brown landed after crossing the ocean in a biplane. One of the nicer ways to acquaint yourself with Connemara is by hiking south to the Alcock and Brown monument, situated just off the Ballyconnelly road 3 mi. past Salt Lake and Lough Fadda.

Open yourself to the magic of the bog by joining the inspiring tours of a critically acclaimed archaeologist-raconteur from the **Connemara Walking Center** on Market St. The tours explore the history, folklore, geology, and archaeology of the region, and investigate bogs, mountains, and the Inishbofin and Omey islands. The center also sells wonderful maps and guidebooks. (☎ 21379. Open Mar.-Oct. M-Sa 10am-6pm. 1 full-day or 2 half-day tours daily Easter-Oct.; call for a schedule. £15-25.)

Clifden Town Hall erupts with performances of traditional music, dance, and song every Tuesday in July and August at 9pm. Clifden's artsy pretensions multiply in late September during the annual **Clifden Arts Week** (☎ 21295), featuring dozens of free concerts, poetry readings, and storytellings. On the third Thursday of August, attractive, talented contenders come to Clifden from miles around to compete for top awards at the **Connemara Pony Show.**

INISHBOFIN ISLAND ☎095

Inishbofin, the "island of the white cow," has gently sloping hills (flat enough for happy cycling) scattered with rugged rocks, an excellent hostel, and nearly deserted sandy beaches. Seven miles from the western tip of Connemara, the island of Inishbofin (pop. 200) keeps time according to the ferry, the tides, and the sun; visitors can easily adapt to their system. There's little to do on the island other than scramble up the craggy hills, sunbathe on the sand, commune with the seals, watch birds fishing among the coves, and sleep under a blanket of bright stars. The smattering of tourists suggests that the island isn't completely removed from the universe, but Inishbofin seems to be part of another world.

GETTING THERE AND PRACTICAL INFORMATION. Ferries leave for Inishbofin from **Cleggan,** a tiny village with stunning beaches 10 mi. northwest of Clifden. Two ferries serve the island. The **Island Discovery** is the larger, steadier, faster, and more expensive of the two. (☎ 44642. 30min.; July-Aug. 3 per day, Apr.-June and Sept.-Oct. 2 per day; £12 adult, £10 student, £6 children; tickets available at the pier or in Clifden). The **M.V. Dún Aengus** runs year-round. (Paddy O'Halloran, ☎ 45806. 45min.; July-Aug. 3 per day, Apr.-June and Sept.-Oct. 2 per day, Nov.-Apr. 1 per day; £10). Both ferries carry bikes for free. Tickets are most conveniently purchased on the ferry. Drivers can leave cars parked free of charge at the Cleggan Pier. Stock up at the **Spar** before you go, especially if you're taking a later ferry. (☎ 44750. Open daily 9am-10pm.) **Bike rental** is available at the Inishbofin pier (☎ 45833) for £5-7.50 per day. Four-legged contraptions can be hired from **Inishbofin Pony Trekking** (☎ 45853) for £15 per hr., but the island's steep hills and narrow roads are best explored on foot.

ACCOMMODATIONS, FOOD, AND PUBS. Kieran Day's excellent **Inishbofin Island Hostel (IHH)** is a 10-minute walk from the ferry landing; take a right at the pier and head up the hill. Visitors are blessed with a large conservatory and swell views. (☎ 45855. Sheets 50p. Laundry £4. Dorms £7.50; doubles £20. Camping £4 per person.) The **Emerald Cottage**, a 10-minute walk west from the pier, welcomes guests with home-baked goodies. (☎ 45865. Singles £17; doubles £30.) The very remote **Horseshoe Bay B&B** sets itself apart on the east end of the island. (☎ 45812. Doubles £30; triples £45.) There is no camping allowed on the beach or the adjacent dunes. Close to the pier, **Day's Pub** (☎ 45829) serves food from noon to 5pm. In back of the pub, **Olive's Bistro** delights wind-blown diners with huge, delicious servings. (Irish stew with fries and salad £7.50. Open nightly 7:30-9:30pm.) **Day's Shop** is behind the pub and sells picnic-applicable items. (☎ 45829. Open M-Sa 11:30am-1:30pm and 3-5pm, Su 11:30am-12:30pm.) The island's nightlife is surprisingly vibrant, with frequent trad performances in the summer. The smaller, more sedate **Murray's Pub,** a hotel-bar 15 minutes west of the pier, is the perfect place for conversation, slurred or otherwise.

SIGHTS. Days on Inishbofin are best spent meandering through the rocks and wildflowers of the island's four peninsulas. Paths are scarce; each peninsula usually warrants about a three-hour walk. Most items of historical interest are on the southeast peninsula. East of the hostel lie the ruins of a 15th-century **Augustinian Abbey,** built on the site of a monastery founded by St. Colman in 667. A well and a few gravestones remain from the 7th-century structure. East past the abbey, a conservation area encompasses long pristine beaches and a picturesque village. Swimming in the clear waters is safe, but please, no eroding the dunes. The most spectacular views of the island reward those who scramble up nearby **Knock Hill**. **Bishop's Rock,** a short distance off the mainland, becomes visible at low tide. Cromwell supposedly once tied a recalcitrant priest to the rock and forced his comrades to watch as the tide drowned him. On the other side of the island, to the west of the pier, is the imposing **Cromwellian fort,** which was built for defense but in practice used to hold prisoners before transporting them to the West Indies.

The ragged northeast peninsula is fantastic for bird watchers: gulls, cornets, shags, and a pair of peregrine falcons fish among the cliffs and coves. Nearby, gannets wet their nests. Inishbofin provides a perfect climate for vegetation hospitable to the corncrake, a bird that's near extinction everywhere other than in Seamus Heaney's poems; two pairs of corncrakes presently call Inishbofin home. Fish swim in the clear water of two massive blowholes, while small land masses called **The Stags** tower offshore. The tidal causeway that connects The Stags to the mainland during low tide is extremely dangerous—do not venture out onto it. **Trá Gheal** (meaning "Silvery Beach") stretches along the northwest peninsula, but swimming here is dangerous. Off to the west is Inishark, an island inhabited by sheep and gray seals; the seals are most visible during mating season in September and early October. Inspirational archaeologist Michael Gibbons, at **Connemara Walking Center** in Clifden, offers tours focusing on Inishbofin's history, archaeology, and ecology. Leo Hallissey's fantastic **Connemara Summer School** (☎ 41034), held during the first week in July, studies the island's archaeology and ecology.

INISHTURK ISLAND ☎098

Inishturk (pop. 90) is where Inishbofiners go to get away from the stress of modern life. A small, rounded peak rising 600 ft. out of the ocean between Inishbofin and Clare Island, Inishturk has more spectacular walks and views than either. You would never guess it now, but before the Famine, the island teemed with a population of nearly 800. Nowadays, Inishturk seems virtually undiscovered. Those attempting an expedition to Inishturk should treat it as such: bring adequate supplies and a good book. There are no budget restaurants on the island, but the three excellent B&Bs serve home-cooked meals of epic proportions. **Concannon's B&B** is just above a fish restaurant on the pier, and boasts enormous rooms with views. (☎ 45610. Dinner £12. Doubles £30, with bath £36.) **Paddy O'Toole's B&B,** about 1 mi. from the harbor on the west village road, comes with an in-house accordion player and occasional *ceilis* in the dining room. (☎ 45510. Dinner £12. Singles £18; doubles £30.) Guests at the Heanue's **Ocean View,** up the road from Concannon's, heartily applaud the fantastic meals and decadent rooms. (☎ 45520. Singles £17, with bath £19; doubles £32, with bath £36; off-season prices £2-3 less.) Above the pier to the left, the community center serves beer and light snacks, and hosts traditional dancing, singing, and music sessions. **John Heanue's Caher Star** discovers the island twice a day. (☎ 45541. Leaves from Cleggan Tu-Th, from Roonah F-M; £15 return.) Anything can happen in this brave new world, but nothing ever really does—that's part of its charm.

CLIFDEN TO WESTPORT

The area to the east and northeast of Clifden hunches up into high hills and then collapses into grass-curtained bogs occasionally interrupted by startling rocks. The landscape of Connemara National Park conceals a number of curiosities, including hare runs, orchids, and roseroot.

CONNEMARA NATIONAL PARK

Outside Letterfrack, Connemara National Park occupies 7¾ sq. mi. of mountainous countryside, which thousands of birds call home. The far-from-solid terrain of the park is composed of bogs thinly covered by a screen of grass and flowers. Be prepared to muddy your shoes and pants, and raise your pulse. Guides lead free two- to three-hour walks over hills and through the bogs (July-Aug. M, W, and F at 10:30am), tell about the history, breeding, and feeding of the Connemara ponies (M, W, and F 2pm), and offer several children's programs on Tuesdays and Thursdays. The ■Visitors Centre excels at explaining blanket bogs, raised bogs, turf, and heathland. The 25-minute slide show raises lichens and the battle against opportunistic rhododendrons to lofty heights. (☎ (095) 41054. Open daily June 10am-6:30pm; July-Aug. 9:30am-6:30pm; May and Sept. 10am-5:30pm. £2, students £1.)

The **Snuffaunboy Nature** and **Ellis Wood Trails** are easy 20-minute hikes. The Snuffaunboy features alpine views while the Ellis wood submerges walkers in an ancient forest; both teem with wildflowers. A guidebook mapping out 30-minute walks (50p) is available at the visitors center, where staff helps plan longer hikes. For the more adventurous, trails lead from the back of the **Ellis Wood Trail** and 10 minutes along the **Bog Road** onto ■**Diamond Hill,** a two-hour hike rewarding climbers with views of bog, harbor, and forest, or, depending on the weather, white mist. More experienced hikers often head for the **Twelve Bens** (*Na Benna Beola,* a.k.a. the Twelve Pins), a rugged range that reaches 2400 ft. heights and is not recommended for single or beginning hikers. There are no proper trails, but Jos Lynam's guidebook (£5) meticulously plots out 18 fantastic hikes through the Twelve Bens and the Maamturks. Hikers often base themselves at the **Ben Lettery Hostel (An Óige/HI),** which overlooks sheep and postcard-quality stretches of scenery in Ballinafad. The turn-off from N59 is 8 mi. east of Clifden. (☎ (095) 51136. June-Aug. £7.50; Easter-May and Sept. £6.50.) A hike from this remote but friendly hostel through the park to the Letterfrack hostel can be done in a day. A tour of all 12 Bens takes hardy walkers about 10 hours. **Biking** the 40 mi. loop through Clifden, Letterfrack, and Inagh valley is breathtaking, but only appropriate for fit bikers.

LETTERFRACK ☎095

Although it claims three pubs and a legendary hostel, Letterfrack, located at the crossroads of Connemara National Park, hasn't quite achieved town status. The **Galway-Clifden** bus (M-Sa; mid-June-Aug. 11 per week, Sept. to mid-June 4 per week) and the summertime **Clifden-Westport** bus (M and Th 2 per day, Tu-W and F-Sa 1 per day) stop at Letterfrack. Hitchers report medium-length waits on N59. *Let's Go* does not recommend hitchhiking.

Uphill from the intersection, the ■**Old Monastery Hostel** is one of Ireland's finest. Sturdy pine bunks, desks, and couches fill the spacious high-ceilinged rooms, a peat fire burns in the lounge, and framed photos of jazz greats hang in the cozy basement cafe. Dogs and cats curl together on the couches. Steve, the owner, cooks mostly organic vegetarian buffet dinners in the summer (buffet £7, plate £4, call by 5pm) and fresh scones and porridge for breakfast. (☎ 41132. Breakfast included. Laundry £4. **Bike rental** £6 per day. **Internet access** £3 per hr. 8-bed dorms £8; 6-bed dorms £9; 4-bed dorms £10.)

Great pub grub, exciting groceries, pints, and friendly locals are available at **Veldon's,** which fills at 10:30am and empties late, sometimes after a trad session. (☎ 41046. Shop open daily June-Aug. 9:30am-9pm, Sept.-May 9:30am-7pm.) **The Bard's Den** (☎ 41042), across the intersection, hopes for tourists with its skylight and large open fire. Photos of long-gone local characters dignify the walls of **Paddy Coyne's,** a few miles north of Letterfrack in Tully Cross. Jackie Coyne's Wednesday night lessons in the Irish broom dance dignify nothing at all, but they sure are fun.

Ocean's Alive is a new tourist magnet at Derryinver, 1½ mi. north of Letterfrack. Its touch-tank aquarium lets you fondle the crabs, but hands off the old fishing artifacts, life-sized fishermen, and potato spraying machine. In a cottage replica, the sunny coffee shop sells cheap eats (sandwiches £1-2), and hosts Sunday trad sessions in the afternoon or evening. (☎ 43473. Open May-Sept. 9:30am-7pm, Oct.-Apr. 10am-4:30pm. £3.50, students £2.50.) An hour-long cruise on the **Connemara Queen** runs from the center seven times daily in the summer, circling by seals and deserted islands, often with live music. John also offers fishing trips—catch mackerel off the back of the boat. ($8.50, students $6.50.) Letterfrack hosts two environmentally oriented festivals a year. During **Bog Week,** the last week in October, and **Sea Week,** the first week in May, world-famous environmentalists gather to discuss bog- and sea-related issues while musicians jam amongst the peat.

The road from Letterfrack to Leenane passes **Kylemore Abbey,** a castle dramatically set in the shadow of a rocky outcrop. Built in 1867 by an English industrialist, the castle has been occupied since 1920 by a group of Benedictine nuns, who cheerfully chat with interested tourists. There's more to see at the small neo-Gothic church a few hundred feet down from the abbey. A rocky path winds up above the castle to a ledge with a view of the lake that you'll be loath to leave. A statue with arms aloft marks the end of your 30min. climb. (☎ 41146. Abbey open Apr.-Oct. 9am-6pm, Nov.-Mar. 10am-4pm. $3, students $2.) The newly restored six-acre **Victorian Walled Garden** is worth a gander for those enamoured of banana plants and other horticultural anomalies in this hardly tropical country. (Open Easter-Nov. $3, students $2.50; garden and abbey $5, $4.)

LEENANE ☎095

Farther east along N59, **Killary Harbour,** Ireland's only fjord, breaks through the mountains to the wilderness outpost of Leenane (pop. 47). Wrapped in the skirts of the **Devilsmother Mountains,** this once populous region was reduced to a barren hinterland during the famine; today, the crumbled remnants of farms cover the surrounding hills. *The Field* was filmed here in 1989, and no one in town will ever forget it. The murder scene was shot at Aasleagh Falls. At **Leenane Cultural Centre,** on the Clifden-Westport Rd., spinning and weaving demonstrations reveal the final fate of wool. (☎ 42323. Open daily Apr.-Oct. 10am-7pm. $2, students $1.50.) The coffee shop in the Centre is your best bet for a cheap lunch in town. (Sandwiches and sweets $1.25-4.) **Killary Harbour Hostel (An Óige/HI)** perches on the very edge of the shore, 7 mi. west of Leenane. The turnoff is marked from N59. Follow the small, winding road for about 15 minutes and turn right up a very steep hill; the hostel is a five-minute drive along the road. This remote hostel has staked out an unbeatable waterfront location. The German philosopher Ludwig Wittgenstein stayed here for several months in 1947. Fluffy red-and-blue comforters and a fire in the common room keep travelers warm as they ponder unspeakables. (☎ 43417. Open Jan.-Nov. Dorms $7.50, off-season $6.50.) Bring food and supplies. If the *craic* has gotten a little much, retreat to **The Convent B&B,** on the northern side of town along N59. The dining room was once a chapel; the rooms connected to it come with great views of the bay. (☎ 42240. Singles $20-24; doubles $32.) Catching a lift from Leenane feels like winning the lottery, except for the money part. *Let's Go* does not see the incentive to hitchhike.

COUNTY MAYO

Co. Mayo fills northwestern Ireland with a large expanse of remarkable emptiness consisting of bog and beach. Towns and cities sporadically pop up out of nowhere: Westport is somewhat upscale and popular, Ballina is best known for its Moy fisheries, and old sea resorts such as Achill Island and Enniscrone line the seaboard. Mayo's 15 minutes of fame occurred in 1798, "The Year of the French," when General Humbert landed at Kilcummin. Combining French soldiers, Irish revolutionaries, and rural secret societies into an army, Humbert launched an attack, but the English retaliated and won at Ballina and Ballinamuck.

CONG ☎092

Just over the border from County Galway is princely little Cong (pop. 300). Bubbling streams and shady footpaths criss-cross the surrounding forests, at the edge of which crumbles a ruined abbey. Nearby, a majestic castle towers over the choppy waters of Lough Corrib. Cong was once the busy market center of a more densely populated region, and Cong's abbey was a tower of learning with 3000 students. In the past century, however, main roads were built to bypass the hamlet; were it not for two recent events, Cong might have slumbered into obscurity. In 1939, Ashford Castle was turned into a £300 per night luxury hotel, bringing the rich and famous to Cong from around the world. And, in 1951, John Wayne and Maureen O'Hara shot *The Quiet Man* here. Thousands of fans come each year to find the location of every shot, providing locals with amazement and profit.

GETTING THERE AND PRACTICAL INFORMATION. Buses leave for **Westport** from Ashford gates (Tu and Th), **Clifden** from Ryan's Hotel (M-Sa 1 per day), and **Galway** from both locations (M-Sa 1-2 per day; all are £6). Because of infrequent transportation, some travelers suggest that hitching from the nearby bus stop at Ballinrobe is a good option. *Let's Go* does not recommend hitchhiking. The town's **tourist office**, Abbey St., will point you toward Cong's wonders, listed in *The Cong Heritage Trail* (£1.50). *Cong: Walks, Sights, Stories* (£2.80) is—contrary to hitching—highly recommended and describes good hiking and biking routes. (☎ 46542. Open daily Mar.-Nov. 10am-6pm.) There are very nice **pay phones** across from the tourist office. **O'Connor's Garage,** Main St., **rents bikes.** (☎ 46008. Open daily 8am-9pm. £7 per day, students £5 per day; £30 per week; ID or £40 deposit.) Get your fix at **Daly's Pharmacy** on Abbey St. next to the tourist office. (☎ 46119. Open M-F 10am-6pm.) The **post office** is on Main St. (☎ 46001. Open M-Tu and Th-Sa 9am-1pm and 2-5:30pm, W 9am-1pm.)

ACCOMMODATIONS, FOOD, AND PUBS. The Quiet Man Hostel and the Cong Hostel, owned by the same gracious family, are perfect if you're in the mood for a bit of company. Both screen the "legendary" film nightly in mini-theaters, have a **bureau de change** and laundry service (£5), **rent bikes** (£6 per day, £4 per half-day), boats (£3 per hr.), guidebooks (£3 deposit), and lend fishing rods (free). **The Quiet Man Hostel (IHH),** Abbey St., across from Cong Abbey, is central, spotless, and sociable. For those who just can't shake Quiet Man fever, the rooms are all named after the film's characters. (☎ 46511, reservations 46089. Continental breakfast £2.75, Irish breakfast £4.50. Dorms £7.) **Cong Hostel (IHH),** Quay Rd., a mile down the Galway Rd., is clean and comfortable, with skylights in every room. The playground, picnic area, and game room are sure to keep you entertained. The camping area is tremendous, and sprouts its own little village every summer. (☎ 46089. Continental breakfast £2.75, full Irish breakfast £4.50. Showers 50p for campers. Dorms £7; doubles with bath £18. **Camping** with facilities £4.) The **Courtyard Hostel (IHH),** Cross St., provides peace of mind several miles off the beaten track, in the small village of Cross, east of Cong. Buses from Galway stop here, or call ahead for pick-up from Cong. This gem is worth the trek; stables have been beautifully transformed into dorms, and ducks and chickens roam the yard. (☎ 46203. **Bike rental** £5 per day. Dorms £7; doubles £16. **Camping** £3.) As usual, B&Bs are everywhere. Smothered in geraniums and ivy, **White House B&B,** Abbey St., across the street from Danagher's Hotel, offers TV and bath in every room. (☎ 46358. Singles £20 in summer, £16 Nov.-Apr.) As for **camping,** not even the ghosts can stop you from setting up a tent on **Inchagoill Island.**

Cooks can go crazy at **O'Connor's Supermarket,** Main St. (☎ 46008. Open daily 8am-9pm.) Just across the street from the White House B&B, young locals and Ashford Castle staffers down mammoth meals and countless pints at **Danagher's Hotel and Restaurant.** (☎ 46494. Roast of the day, vegetables, and potatoes £6. Live music.) **Lydon's** (☎ 46053), on Main St. across from the supermarket, has the most trad, starting around 10pm on weekends. **The Quiet Man Coffee Shop,** Main St., is obviously obsessed. A bright, cheery street-front counter rides in tandem with a dark dining room overlooking a river; both are freckled with black and white memorabilia from the film. (☎ 46034. Sandwich £2. Open mid-Mar. to Oct. daily 10am-6:30pm.) The nearest nightclub, **The Valkenburg,** is in Ballinrobe; a bus picks groups up outside Danagher's weekend nights at around 11:30pm and drops them back at 3am. (Cover £5, bus £3.)

> **WATER, WATER, EVERYWHERE** Clonbur, where Mount Gable rises up above the flatness, was the site of a 19th-century engineering disaster. The Dry Canal is a deep 4 mi. groove in the earth just east of Cong off the Galway road, near the Cong Hostel. Locks punctuate the useless canal as if water were flowing through it. While there is water a-plenty in Ireland, not even fairies could make it stay in the porous chalk bed. The canal-opening ceremony in the 1840s was a surprising failure, as water that was let into the canal from Lough Mask promptly vanished into the absorbent walls. The canal could have been sealed and made useful, but by the 1850s trains had already replaced canals as the most efficient means of commercial transport, leaving the canal as hapless as its engineers.

SIGHTS. The heirs to the Guinness fortune, Lord and Lady Ardilaun, lived in **Ashford Castle** from 1852 to 1939, a structure as impressive as the lake itself. Today, big-deal diplomatic visitors use government funds to spend nights here. *The Quiet Man* was shot on its grounds. The castle is closed to non-guests, but you can see the **gardens** for £3. Oscar Wilde once informed Lady Ardilaun that she could improve them by planting petunias in the shape of a pig, the family crest. A walk from the castle along Lough Corrib leads to a swimming beach, and, a few minutes further along the shore, a monument bearing Lady Ardilaun's alarming message to her lost Lord: "Nothing remains for me/ What does remain is nothing." The intricate criss-cross of paths that surround the castle are excellent for bicycling.

The sculpted head of its last abbot keeps watch over the ruins of the 12th-century **Royal Abbey of Cong,** near Danagher's Hotel in the village. (Always open. Free.) The last High King of a united Ireland, Ruairi ("Rory") O'Connor, retired to the abbey for his final 15 years of life, after multiple losses to Norman troops. Across the abbey grounds, a footbridge spans the **River Cong.** Past the **Monk's Fishing House** and to the right, the path leads to **Pigeon Hole, Teach Aille,** a 4000-year-old burial chamber, **Giant's Grave,** and **Ballymaglancy caves.** (Hostels lend out detailed cave maps.) Spelunkers have access to the caves, but **Kelly's Cave,** found on the road leading from Cong to the Cong Hostel, is locked; the key is held at The Quiet Man Coffee Shop. Safe spelunking requires a friend who knows when to expect you back, two flashlights, waterproof gear, and caution.

The Quiet Man Heritage Cottage, a replica of a set from the film, tries to make up for the fact that most of the film was actually shot on a Hollywood lot. "The Quiet Man will never die," the center's video promises. (☎ 46089. £2.50, students £2. Open daily 10am-6pm.) 2001 is the 50th anniversary of the making of *The Quiet Man*: be sure that Cong has something up its sleeve for this event (email paddyrock@esatclear.ie for information).

WESTPORT ☎098

One of the few planned towns in the country, Westport (pop. 4300) still looks marvelous in the Georgian-period costumes of her designer. In the summer, Westport doesn't know quite how to accessorize the droves of visitors that traipse through the tree-lined mall, central Octagon, and shop-encrusted Bridge Street. There's a range of activities to occupy tourists in town: savor its active pub life, drink tea at dapper cafes, shop for hand-woven scarves, and admire the fresh coats of paint on the newest rash of B&Bs. Book ahead in July and August and go to the pubs early if you want to beat the crowds—beds, pint glasses, and bar stools fill up faster than you can say "no vacancy."

GETTING THERE AND GETTING AROUND

Trains: Trains arrive at the **Altamont St. Station** (☎ 25253 or 25329 for inquiries), a 5min. walk up on North Mall. Open M-Sa 9:30am-6pm, Su 2:15-6pm. The train goes to **Dublin** via **Athlone** (M-Th and Sa 3 per day, F and Su 2 per day; £15).

WESTPORT ■ 333

Buses: For bus info, call the tourist office. Buses leave from the **Octagon** on Mill St. and travel to **Ballina** (1 hr.; M-Sa 1-3 per day, Su 1 per day; £6.70), **Castlebar** (20min., M-Sa 6 per day, £2.50), **Louisburgh** (40min., M-Sa 3 per day, £3.20), **Galway** (2 hr., M-F 6 per day, £8.80), and **Knock** (1hr.; M-Sa 3 per day, Su 1 per day; £8.80).

Taxis: Brendan McGing, Lower Peter St. (☎ 25529). 50p per mi.

Bike Rental: Breheny & Sons, Castlebar St. (☎ 25020). Bikes can be dropped off in Galway. £5 per day, £7 per 24hr., £35 per week; £30 deposit.

ORIENTATION AND PRACTICAL INFORMATION

The tiny **Carrowbeg River** runs through **Westport's Mall** with **Bridge St.** and **James St.** extending south. **Shop St.** connects **Bridge St.** to **James St.** on the other end. Westport House is on **Westport Quay,** a 45-minute walk west of town. The N60 passes through Clifden, Galway, and Sligo on its way to Westport. Hitchers proclaim it an easy route, but *Let's Go* still refuses to recommend hitchhiking.

Tourist Office: James St. (☎ 25711). Open Apr.-Oct. M-Sa 9am-12:45pm and 2-5:45pm, July-Aug. also Su 10am-6pm.

Travel Agency: Westport Travel, 4 Shop St. (☎ 25511). Student discounts; Western Union Money Transfer point. Open M-Sa 9:30am-6pm.

Banks: Bank of Ireland, North Mall (☎ 25522), and **AIB,** Shop St. (☎ 25466), have **ATMs** and are both open M-W and F 10am-4pm, Th 10am-5pm.

Laundry: Westport Washeteria, Mill St. (☎ 25261), near the clock tower. Full service £4, self-service £2.50, powder 40p. Open M-Tu, Th-Sa 9:30am-6pm, W 9:30am-1pm.

Pharmacy: O'Donnell's, Bridge St. (☎ 25163). Open M-Sa 9am-6:30pm. Rotating Su openings (12:30-2pm) are posted on the door.

Emergency: ☎ 999; no coins required. **Police** (*Garda*): Fair Green (☎ 25555).

Post Office: North Mall (☎ 25475). Open M and W-Sa 9am-noon and 2-5:30pm, Tu 9:30am-noon and 2-5:30pm.

Internet Access: Dunning's Cyberpub, The Octagon (☎ 25161). A Guinness with your email? £6 per hr. Open daily 9am-11:30pm.

ACCOMMODATIONS

Westport's hostels are exceptional. Its B&Bs are easily spotted on the Castlebar and Altamont Rd. off North Mall. Most charge £18-20.

The Granary Hostel (☎ 25903), 1 mi. from town on Louisburgh Rd., near the main entrance to Westport House. The converted granary includes a peace-garden and conservatory. Amenities are basic, but the lovingly placed stones and tree pushing through the wall of the conservatory give it natural decadence. Open Apr.-Oct. Dorms £6.

Old Mill Holiday Hostel (IHH), James St. (☎ 27045), between The Octagon and the tourist office. Character and comfort in a renovated mill and brewery. Kitchen and common room lockout 11pm-8am. Sheets £1. Laundry £3. **Bike rental** £4.50 per half-day, £7 per day. Dorms £8.

Slí na h-Óige (HYI), North Mall. (☎ 28751). Appropriately named "the way of the young," this small, family-run hostel has comfortable beds, frequent trad, and Gaelic lessons upon request. **Internet access** £1 per hr. Open June-Sept. Dorms £7.

Club Atlantic (IHH), Altamont St. (☎ 26644 or 26717), a 5min. walk up from the mall across from the train station. Popular with huge youth organizations, this massive 140-bed complex has recreational facilities, a shop, an elephantine kitchen, and an educational exhibition on Croagh Patrick. Dorms are quiet and comfortable. Camping space is beside a bubbling river and a forest. Use of the sauna and pool at the nearby Westport Hotel for £4. Sheets £1. Laundry £4. June-Sept. dorms £7.50; singles £13; doubles £20. Mid-Mar. to May and Oct. dorms £7; singles £10; doubles £17. **Camping** £4.

Dunning's Pub, The Octagon (☎ 25161). Centrally yet quietly located above a bustling pub and convenient Internet cafe. Guests lounge with their pints and pizzas at sidewalk tables out front, surveying all the action. £18 per person.

Altamont House, Altamont St. (☎ 25226). Enthusiastic guests wax poetic in the guest book. Roses peep in the windows wishing they could book a room—even though the garden is a modern Eden in itself. £17 per person, £19 with bath, £2-3 extra for singles.

FOOD

The **country market** by the Town Hall at The Octagon vends farm-fresh vegetables, eggs, baking, rugs, and crafts. (Open Th 9am-1pm.) Processed foods are abundant at the **SuperValu** supermarket on Shop St. (☎ 27000. Open M-Sa 8:30am-9pm, Su 10am-6pm.) Restaurants are generally crowded and expensive, catering to the mass of yuppie tourists; make reservations for tables after 6:30pm on weekends.

■ **McCormack's,** Bridge St. (☎ 25619). Locals praise this tea house's exemplary teas and pastries. Ravenous tourists devour huge sandwiches, salads, and hot dishes. Peruse local art while waiting for a table. Hot bacon bap £2.80, pasta salad £3.75. Open M-Tu and Th-Sa 10am-6pm.

The Reek, High St. (☎ 28955). Named after the local nickname for Croagh Patrick, this cafe and restaurant serves flavorful vegetarian-friendly dishes and delicious desserts. Vegetarian enchilada filled with spicy vegetables £6.95. Open daily 10am-10pm.

Sol Rio, Bridge St. (☎ 28944). Meat and fish dishes are expensive, but this bright Italian restaurant does affordable pasta dishes and creative pizzas. Pasta from £5; asparagus, mushroom, and tomato pizza £6.50. Open daily noon-3pm and 5:30-10pm.

The Urchin, Bridge St. (☎ 27532). A menu full of old favorites. Lunch is inexpensive (sandwiches about £3); dinner isn't, but does offer some good vegetarian options (spinach roulade £8.50). Open daily 10am-10pm; lunch served noon-3pm.

PUBS

Search Bridge St. (or browse the list below) to find a *craic* dealer that suits you. After your fill of pub fun, clubbing *craic* awaits at **Wits,** in the Westport Inn, Mill Street. Live bands and dancing start at 11pm. (Cover £6, Open F-Su. 21+). For a younger crowd, shimmy on over to the **Castlecourt Hotel,** Castlebar St. The guitars on the walls give an uninspired nod to the Hard Rock Cafe, but the computerized lighting effects are unique. (Cover £5. Open F-Su. 18+.)

■ **Matt Molloy's,** Bridge St. (☎ 26655). Owned by the flautist of the Chieftains. All the cool people, including his friends, go here. Officially, the trad sessions occur nightly at 9:30pm, but really any time of the day is deemed appropriate. Go early and don't flout the back room if you like yours sitting down.

Henehan's Bar, Bridge St. (☎ 25561). A run-down exterior hides a vibrant pub. The beer garden in the back is ripe for people-watching; 20-somethings fight 80-somethings for space at the bar. Music nightly in summer, on weekends in winter.

The Towers, The Quay (☎ 26534), 1 mi. from town center. Fishing nets and excellent grub hook customers; try beef in Guinness. Meals £5-10. Music F-Su in summer, F-Sa off-season.

O'Malley's Pub, Bridge St. (☎ 27308), across from Matt Molloy's. 20-somethings listen to yesterday's pop hits and sip Guinness at this smoky, dark pub. DJs F-Su.

Pete McCarthy's, Quay St. (☎ 27050), uphill from The Octagon. Old, dark, and smoky pub attracts regulars. Trad on weekends in summer.

SIGHTS

The current commercial uses of **Westport House** must be a bitter pill to swallow for its elite inhabitant, Lord Altamont, the 13th great-grandson of Grace O'Malley (see **Amazing Grace,** p. 125). The zoo and train ride may entertain children, but the carnival and terrifying **bog butter** in the museum are hardly worth the entrance fee. The grounds, on the other hand, are beautiful and free. To get there is a 45-minute stroll. Take James St. above The Octagon, bear right, and follow the signs to the Quay. (☎ 25430. Open May and early Sept. daily 2-5pm; June to late Aug. M-Sa 11:30am-6pm, Su 1:30-7; July to mid-Aug. M-Sa 10:30am-6pm, Su 2-6pm. May-June and Sept. £5, July-Aug. £6; £4 discount 2-6pm.) More interesting is the **Clew Bay Heritage Centre** at the end of the Quay. The narrow interior crams together a pair of James Connolly's gloves, a sash belonging to John MacBride, and a stunning original photograph of Maud Gonne. A genealogical service is also available. (☎ 26852. Open July-Sept. M-F 10am-5pm, Su 2-5pm; Oct.-June M-F noon-3pm. £1.) In late September, Westport celebrates its annual **Westport Arts Festival** (☎ 28833) with a week of free concerts, poetry readings, and plays.

DAYTRIP FROM WESTPORT

CROAGH PATRICK
Buses go to Murrisk (July-Aug. M-F 3 per day; Sept.-June M-Sa 2 per day), but a cab (☎ 27171) is cheaper for three people and more convenient. Murrisk is several miles west of Westport on R395 toward Louisburgh. Ballintubber Abbey (☎ (094) 30709) is about 6 mi. south of Castlebar on N84, and 22 mi. from Croagh Patrick.

Conical **Croagh Patrick** rises 2510 ft. over Clew Bay. The summit has been revered as a holy site for thousands of years. Perhaps because of its height, it was sacred to Lug, Sun God, God of Arts and Crafts, and one-time ruler of the Túatha de Danann (see **Legends and Folktales,** p. 23). St. Patrick worked it here in 441, praying and fasting for 40 days and nights, arguing with angels, and then banishing snakes from Ireland. The deeply religious climb Croagh Patrick barefoot on Lughnasa, **Lug's holy night** on the last Sunday in July. Others climb the mountain just for the exhilaration and the view. It takes about four hours total to climb and descend the mountain. Be warned that the ascent can be quite steep and the footing unsure. Well-shod climbers start their excursion from the 15th-century **Murrisk Abbey.** Pilgrims and hikers also set out for Croagh Patrick along the Tóchar Phádraiga path from **Ballintubber Abbey.** Founded in 1216 by King of Connacht Cathal O'Connor, the abbey still functions as a religious center.

NEAR WESTPORT: CLARE ISLAND ☎098

An isolated, scenic dot in the Atlantic, Clare Island (pop. 170) feels like a contemporary rural village that just happens to be out in the ocean. The school, church, and grocer are 1½ mi. straight along the harbor road. Grace O'Malley, known locally as Granuaile, ruled the 16th-century seas west of Ireland from her castle above the beach. Her notorious fleet swiftly and brutally exacted tolls from all ships entering and leaving Galway Bay (see **Amazing Grace,** p. 125). Granuaile died in 1603 and was supposedly laid to rest here under the ruins of the **Clare Island Abbey,** near the shop. Her descendants make sure that no new surnames make it onto the island. Hiking around the deserted island is fun when it's clear; a leaflet with five walks is available at the hotel or souvenir shop. You can search for buried treasure on the west coast of the island, where the cliffs of **Knockmore Mountain** (1550 ft.) rise from the sea. A two-hour walk runs along the east side of the island to the lighthouse. Ten minutes before the lighthouse, the **Ballytougheny Loom Shop and Demonstration Centre** is a short walk up a path to the left of the road. Weavers spin their own wool and dye it orange and yellow with lichens and onions. They sometimes let visitors take a hand at the spinning wheel. (☎ 25800. Open Apr.-Oct. M-Sa 11am-5pm, Su noon-4pm; Nov.-Mar., call ahead.) **Ozzy** runs off-road **tours** of the island out of his dockside souvenir shop (☎ 45120. 2hr., £5, 4-person min.).

To get on and off the island, Charlie O'Malley's **Ocean Star Ferry** (☎ 25045) and the **Clare Island Ferry** (☎ 26307) leave from **Roonah Point** (25min.; July-Aug. 5 per day, May-June and Sept. 3-5 per day; Oct.-Apr. call to schedule; £10 return; bikes free). Mini-buses leave from the Westport tourist office and cover the long stretch to **Roonah Point** several times a day (1 hr., £8 return). **O'Leary's Bike Hire** is near the harbor (£5 per day); if no one's there, knock at **Beachside B&B** (☎ 25640). Their clean rooms with bath and warm hospitality are yours for £16. Just past the beach, the **Sea Breeze B&B** (☎ 26746) offers similar comforts for the same price. **O'Malley's Cois Abhain** is 3 mi. from the harbor, but the proprietor will pick you up. She also whips up huge evening meals and packs lunches for island explorers. (☎ 26216. Packed lunch £3, dinner £12. Singles £18; doubles £30.)

Two miles along the west road, **O'Malley's Store** has food staples. (☎ 26987. Open daily 11am-6pm.) A little before **O'Malley's** is the **Wavecrest Coffee Shop,** which serves fabulous scones on tables overlooking the ocean. (☎ 26546. Open daily 11am-6pm, scones 80p, soup £1.80.) Clare's only pub, in the **Bay View Hotel** (☎ 26307), to the right along the coast from the harbor, pours pints until wee hours.

ACHILL ISLAND ☎ 098

Two decades ago, Achill (AK-ill) Island was Co. Mayo's most popular holiday refuge. Its popularity has inexplicably dwindled, but Ireland's biggest little island is still one of its most beautiful and personable. Ringed by glorious beaches and cliffs, Achill's interior consists of acres of bog and a few mountains. The town of Achill Sound, the gateway to the island, has the nicest hostel and the most amenities, while Keel has more promising nightlife. Connecting to Keel and forming a flat strip along Achill's longest beaches, the seaside resorts of Pollagh and Dooagh serve as brief stopovers for bikers, hillwalkers, and motorists. Dugort, in the north, is less busy, but its hostel, pub, and restaurant can sustain any backpacker. Achill's most potent vistas are farther west in Keem Bay and at Croaghaun Mountain, though the Atlantic Drive, with its secluded, rocky beaches and high cliffs also offers incredible views. During the first two weeks of August, the island hosts the **Scoil Acla** (☎ 45284), a festival of traditional music and art. The Achill Seafood Festival is held the second week in July.

Buses run infrequently over the bridge from Achill Sound, Dugort, Keel, and Dooagh to **Westport, Galway,** and **Cork** (summer M-Sa 5 per day, off-season M-Sa 2 per day), and to **Sligo, Enniskillen,** and **Belfast** (summer M-Sa 3 per day, off-season 2 per day). Hitchers report relative success during July and August, but cycling is more reliable and preferred by *Let's Go* (who does not recommend hitchhiking). The island's **tourist office** is next to Ted Lavelle's Esso station in Cashel, on the main road from Achill Sound to Keel. True island explorers will pay £3.35 for Bob Kingston's map and guide, but it's a freebie for the rest. (☎ 47353. Open daily 10am-5pm.) There is an **ATM** in Achill Sound, but there's no bank on the island, so change money on the mainland or suffer rates worthy of Grace O'Malley.

ACHILL SOUND

Achill Sound's convenient location at the island's entrance warrants the high concentration of shops and services in its center. Practicality isn't the only reason to stop in Achill Sound: an internationally famous stigmatic and faith healer sets up her House of Prayer here. She draws thousands to the attention-starved town each year. Townspeople are divided between utter skepticism and complete awe of her powers, but universally grateful for the business. About 6 mi. south of Achill Sound and left at the first crossroads, two sets of ruins stand near each other. The ancient **Church of Kildavnet** was founded by St. Dympna when she fled to Achill Island to escape her father's incestuous desires. The remains of **Kildavnet Castle,** really a fortified tower house dating from the 1500s, proudly crumble nearby. Grace O'Malley, the swaggering, seafaring pirate of medieval Ireland, once owned the castle. The spectacular Atlantic Drive, which roams along the craggy south coast past beautiful beaches to Dooagh, makes a fantastic bike ride.

The town has a **post office** with a **bureau de change** (☎ 45141; open M-F 9am-12:30pm and 1:30-5:30pm, Sa 9am-1pm), a **SuperValu supermarket** (open daily 9am-

7pm), an **ATM**, and a **pharmacy** (☎ 45248; open July-Aug. M-Sa 9:30am-6pm, Sept.-June Tu-Sa 9:30am-6pm). **Achill Sound Hotel** rents **bikes.** (☎ 45245. £6 per day, £30 per week; deposit £40. Open daily 9am-9pm.) **The Wild Haven Hostel,** a block left past the church, glows with polished floors and antique furniture. The sunny, conservatory doubles as a swanky dining room. (☎ 45392. Breakfast £3.50; candle-lit dinner £12.50. Sheets £1. Laundry £5. Lockout 11am-3:30pm, except on rainy days. Dorms £7.50; private rooms £10 per person. **Camping** £4.) The **Railway Hostel,** just before the bridge to town, is a simple affair in the old station (the last train arrived in the 1930s). The proprietors can be found at **Mace Supermarket** in town. They have the keys to the place, and a massive volume with all the info you could possibly need for any length stay. (☎ 45187. Sheets £1. Laundry £1.50. Dorms £7.50; doubles £18.) Opposite the Railway Hostel, **Alice's Harbour Bar** flaunts gorgeous views, a stonework homage to the deserted village, and a boat-shaped bar. (☎ 45138. Bar food £4-6. Served noon-6pm. Music on weekends.) The **Achill Folklife Center** offers lectures on subjects like "The Irish Ringfort," on Tuesday nights (☎ 43564. £5.)

KEEL

Keel is a pleasantly outdated resort at the bottom of a flat, wide valley. The sandy **Trawmore Strand** sweeps 3 mi. eastward, flanked by cliffs. Encouraged by a government tax scheme, hundreds of holiday developments have sprung up like dandelions across the valley in the past three years. Two miles north of Keel on the road looping back to Dugort, the self-explanatory **Deserted Village** is populated only by stone houses that were used until the late 1930s by cattle ranchers. Resist the temptation to crawl up and around the existing structures: not only are many of them dangerously unstable, but doing so will incur the wrath of the blood-thirsty archaeologists who rove the site in the summer months when the **Archaeological Summer School** hits town. (Call Theresa McDonald, ☎ (0506) 21627.)

    O'Malley's Island Sports center **rents bikes.** (☎ 43125. £7 per day, £40 per week. Open daily 9am-6pm.) The common areas of the **Wayfarer Hostel (IHH)** are almost as expansive as the views. (☎ 43266. Open mid-Mar. to mid-Oct. Sheets 50p. Laundry £2.50. Dorms £7.50; private rooms £10 per person.) The **Richview Hostel** is laid-back, friendly, and slightly disheveled. (☎ 43462. Dorms £7; private rooms £10.) Mrs. Joyce's **Marian Villa,** is a 20-room hotel/B&B with thoughtfully decorated rooms and a veranda that looks onto the sea. The panoramic breakfast buffet will keep you going all day, and then some. (☎ 43134. Singles £23; doubles £35.) **Roskeel House** has newly refurnished, spacious suites. Its sea views can be enjoyed a block behind the Annexe Inn. (☎ 43537. Open Easter-Oct. £18-25.) Cowering in the shadow of impressive cliffs, the **Keel Sandybanks Caravan and Camping Park** provides a sandy spot to pound your tent stakes. (☎ 43211. July-Aug. £6.50 per tent, late May-June and Sept. £5.)

    Spar market sells crisps and biscuits. (☎ 43125. Open M-Su 9am-9pm.) Although Keel has numerous chippers, nutritious food and sweaters are available at **Beehive Handcrafts and Coffee Shop.** Salads, sandwiches, and home-baked goodies delight; the apple-rhubarb pie is orgasmic. (☎ 43134. Open daily 10am-6:30pm.) **Calvey's,** next to Spar market, whips up hearty meals. (☎ 43158. Catch of the day £6. Open daily 10am-10pm.) Inspired drinking is encouraged at the very vinyl **Annexe Inn** (☎ 43268); music is applauded at nightly sessions during July and August, and Saturdays other months. On weekends, clubbers head to the **Achill Head Hotel** to rock out with the band. (☎ 43108. Su cover £5. 18+.) The **Shark's Head Bar** in the hotel, has a grinning shark head on the back wall, a remnant of the 365-pound Porbeagle shark caught off Achill Head in 1932 which still holds the record for the heaviest fish caught by an angler in Irish or British waters.

DOOAGH

Corrymore House, 2 mi. up the road from Keel in Dooagh (DOO-ah), was one of several Co. Mayo estates owned by Captain Boycott, whose mid-19th-century tenants went on an extended rent strike that verbed his surname. **The Pub** (☎ 43120), Main St., is managed by the beloved mistress of the house. Across from the pub is a monument to Don Allum, the first man to row across the Atlantic in both directions. A similarly grueling bike ride over the cliffs to the west of Dooagh leads to the blue-flag **Keem Bay** beach, the most beautiful spot on the island, wedged between the seas and great green walls of weed, rock, and sheep. Basking sharks, earth's second-largest fish, were once fished off Keem Bay, but bathers who don't look like plankton have nothing to fear. A river of amethyst runs through the Atlantic and comes up in **Croaghaun Mountain,** west of Keem Bay. Most of the accessible crystals have been plundered, but Frank Macnamara, an old local, still digs out the deeper veins with a pick and a shovel, and sells them from his store in Dooagh. The mountains, climbable from Keem Bay, provide bone-chilling views of the **Croaghaun Cliffs,** contenders in the Irish contest for the highest sea cliffs in Europe.

DUGORT

A right turn after Cashel leads to the northern part of the island, where Dugort, a tiny hamlet perched atop a sea cliff, has slept through the 20th century and will likely sleep through the 21st. Mist-shrouded **Slievemore Mountain** looms to its east. Curious Germans come here to see the former cottage of Heinrich Böll, which now serves as a retreat for artists-in-residence. His favorite pub, **The Valley House** (☎ 47204), serves pints to literary pilgrims, hostelers, and locals. Cemeteries and abandoned buildings west of Dugort are the result of a futile mid-1800s effort to convert the islanders to Protestantism by sending in Irish-speaking missionaries. On the other side of Slievemore Mountain lives **Giant's Grave,** a chambered tomb easily accessible from Dugort. Other megalithic tombs lurk nearby. The main tomb, a mile past McDowell's Hotel, up the main road past Keel, is signposted and the easiest to find. Boats leave for the **seal caves** from the pier at Dugort up the road from the Strand Hotel daily at 11am and 6pm. **McDowell's Hotel and Activity Centre** rents surfboards, kayaks, canoes, and other equipment and offers activity days and weeks for children. (☎ 43148. About £10 per hr., £9 a day for children.)

A soft pillow for your head awaits at **Valley House Hostel.** The 100-year-old house is a fading beauty, where sturdy bunks keep company with antique furniture, massive windows, and stately views. An in-house pub is the most luxurious amenity. (☎ 47204; www.valley-house.com. Open Easter-Oct. Dorms £7.) The brutal maiming of the woman who once owned the house was part of the inspiration for Synge's play *Playboy of the Western World* (see **Irish Literary Revival,** p. 26).

The road to the hostel turns left off the main road 2 mi. east of Dugort at the valley crossroads. Nearby, seafood specialist **Atoka Restaurant** feeds a whale of a portion to local fans. (☎ 47229. Entrees £6-12. Call ahead for hours.) Atoka also offers B&B. (£15 per person, with bath £16.) **Seal Caves Caravan and Camping Park** lies between Dugort Beach and Slievemore Mountain. Check in up the road at the blue house/shop. (☎ 43262. July-Aug. £3 per person, Apr.-June and Sept. £2.50.)

MULLET PENINSULA ☎ 097

Other than anglers ogling the 38 varieties of fish swimming off the west coast, few visitors make it out to the Mullet Peninsula. The blue-flag beaches are therefore empty, and outsiders are welcomed with genuine Irish hospitality. Cold Atlantic winds rip into the barren western half; soggy moorland covers the middle. Budget accommodations are scarce. Remote Belmullet, with the most amenities, occupies the isthmus between Broad Haven and Blacksod Bay. Irish is spoken farther down, where farms and small white cottages dot the bogland.

🗓 GETTING THERE AND PRACTICAL INFORMATION. An infrequent **bus** service runs the length of the peninsula from **Ballina** (M-Sa July-Aug. 2 per day, Sept.-June 1 per day; £7.50). The **Erris Tourist Information Centre,** is amazingly helpful. (☎ 81500. Call for hours and its new location.) **Lavelle's Bar** (☎ 81372) also provides solid, unofficial info. The **Bank of Ireland** has an **ATM.** (☎ 81311. Open M-W and F 10am-12:30pm and 1:30-4pm, Th 10am-12:30pm and 1:30-5pm.) **Belmullet Cycle Centre,** American St., rents bikes. (☎ (086) 237 7069. £7 per day. Open M-Sa

10:30am-6pm.) **Centra Supermarket** is on Main St. (Open M-Sa 9am-9:30pm.) The **post office** is at the end of Main St. (☎ 81032. Open M and W-Sa 9am-2pm and 3-5:30pm, Tu 9:30am-5:30pm).

▛▐▜▟ ACCOMMODATIONS, FOOD, AND PUBS. The relaxing **Kilcommon Lodge Hostel** is in Pollatomish, 10 mi. northeast of Belmullet. The rooms are clean, the common rooms cozy, and evening meals prepared with love. Bunnies, ducks, and other woodland characters are live lawn-ornaments. Owners advise on hiking routes. (☎ 84621. Dorms £7.50; private rooms £9 per person.) Just after the hostel, the new **Cuan na Farraige** dive center (☎ 87800) provides B&B (£18 per person), dinner, and water sports. **Mairín Murphy** runs Belmullet's nicest B&B from her turquoise house 350 yd. up the hill from Padden's; a studio apartment suite and meals available. (☎ 81195. Singles £23.50; doubles £34.) Half a block down from the square, the good ol' fashioned **Mill House B&B**, American St., near the bridge, has cute rooms and cheery conversation. (☎ 81181. Open June-Aug. Singles £25; doubles £38.) The **Western Strands Hotel**, Main St., is close to the pubs and provides breakfast and bath for all. (☎ 81096. Singles £25; doubles £40.)

The Appetizer sells sandwiches and desserts. (☎ 82222. Open daily 9am-3pm.) Belmullet's pub scene is purely *craic* and locals. **Lavelle's** provides expensive, hearty dinners and just-as-filling but half-as-expensive pub fare (☎ 81372. £4-6). At night, the crowds come to Lavelle's for Belmullet's best pints. Portraits of Mayo hurlers adorn the walls of **Lenehan's** (☎ 81098), the first and last stop on the old men's gossip circuit. **Clan Lir**, Main St., popular with the young, gets packed during football games. Knock if the doors are closed. Birdwatchers flock to the **Anchor Bar**, Barrack St., which records ornithological sightings; the nightclub out back opens on weekends. (☎ 81007. Cover £5.)

☎ SIGHTS. The **Ionad Deirbhle Heritage Centre**, in Aughleam at the end of the peninsula, explores items of local interest, including the history of the whaling industry and the Inishkey (*Inis Gé*) islands. (☎ 85728. Open Easter-Oct. 10am-6pm. £2.) **Josephine and Matt Geraghty** run boat trips to the islands, which were inhabited until a disastrous fishing accident in 1935. (☎ 85741. 1 per day in summer, 3 per week in winter. £12 per person; 6 person minimum.) Fly fishing abounds from both shore and boat in nearby **Cross Lake**; contact **George Geraghty** (☎ 81492). The **Belmullet Sea Angling Competition** (☎ 81076), in mid-July, awards £2 per pound for the heaviest halibut. The **Feille Iorras** peninsula-wide music festival (☎ 81147) is held the last weekend in July.

BALLINA ☎096

What Knock is to the Marian cult, Ballina (bah-lin-AH) is to the religion of bait and tackle. Hordes in olive-green waders invade the town each year during the salmon season (Feb.-Sept.). Ballina, however, has non-ichthyological attractions as well, including lovely vistas, river walks, and a raging weekend pub scene. Almost everyone in a 50 mi. radius, from sheep farmers to students, packs into town on Saturday nights. Former Irish President Mary Robinson grew up in Ballina and refined her political skills in the town's 40-odd pubs (see **Current Issues**, p. 20).

▛ GETTING THERE AND GETTING AROUND

Trains: Station Rd. (☎ 71818), near the bus station. Open M-F 7:30am-6pm, Sa 9am-1pm and 3:15-6pm. Service to **Dublin** via **Athlone** (M-Sa 3 per day, £15). From the station, go left, bear right and walk 4 blocks to reach the town center.

Buses: Station Rd. (☎ 71800 or 71825). Open M-Sa 9:30am-6pm. Buses to **Westport** (1½hr.; M-Sa 3 per day, Su 1 per day; £6.30), **Donegal** (M-Sa 3 per day, Su 1 per day; £10), **Sligo** (2hr., M-Sa 3-4 per day, £7.30), **Galway** (3hr.; M-Sa 9 per day, Su 5 per day; £9.70), **Athlone** (1 per day, £11), and **Dublin** via **Mullingar** (4hr., 3 per day, £8). From the bus station, turn right and take the first left; the city center is a 5min. walk.

Taxis: Mulherin Taxi Service, The Brook (☎ 22583 or 21783).

Bike Rental: Gerry's Cycle Centre, 6 Lord Edward St. (☎ 70455). £7 per day, £30 per week. Collection service available. Open M-Sa 9am-7pm.

ORIENTATION AND PRACTICAL INFORMATION

Ballina's commercial center is on the west bank of the **River Moy.** A bridge crosses over to the cathedral and tourist office on the east bank. The bridge connects to **Tone St.,** which turns into **Tolan St.** This strip intersects **Pearse St.** and **O'Rahilly St.,** which run parallel to the river, to form Ballina's center.

Tourist Office: Cathedral Rd. (☎ 70848), on the river by St. Muredach's Cathedral. Open Mar.-May and Sept. 10am-1pm and 2-5:30pm, June-Aug. 10am-5:30pm.

Banks: Bank of Ireland, Pearse St. (☎ 21144). Open M-W and F 10am-4pm, Th 10am-5pm. **Irish Permanent Building Society,** Pearse St. (☎ 22777). Open M-F 9:30am-5pm. Both have an **ATM.**

Bookstore: Keohane's, Arran St. (☎ 21475), stocks the best regional guidebooks. Open M-Sa 8am-6:30pm, Su 8:30am-2pm.

Laundry: Moy Laundrette, Clare St. (☎ 22358). Wash, dry, and conversation with Winnie £5. Open M-Sa 9am-6pm.

Pharmacy: S. Quinn and Sons, Pearse St. (☎ 21365). Open M-Sa 9am-6pm.

Emergency: ☎ 999; no coins required. **Police** (*Garda*): Walsh St. (☎ 21422).

Post Office: Casement St. (☎ 21498). Open M-Sa 9am-5:30pm.

Internet Access: Moy Valley Resources (☎ 70905), in the same building as the tourist office. Open M-Th 9am-1pm and 2-5:30pm, F 9am-1pm and 2-5pm. £6 per hr.

ACCOMMODATIONS

Much to the budget traveler's chagrin, there are no hostels in Ballina. However, dozens of nearly identical B&Bs line the main approach roads into town. The river, the lake, and sea fishing are just a cast away from Ms. Corrigan's **Greenhill,** on Cathedral Close behind the tourist office. Super-spacious, bright rooms look out onto rose gardens. (☎ 22767. Singles £23-25; doubles £38-34.) Two doors down, Breda Walsh's **Suncraft** is another good option. (☎ 21573. Doubles with bath £34.) **Hogan's American House,** a restful, family-run place with a dated but dignified interior, has a convenient location just up from the bus station. (☎ 70582. Breakfast £5. Singles £20; doubles £35.) **Belleek Camping and Caravan Park** is 2 mi. from Ballina toward Killala on R314, behind the Belleek Woods. (☎ 71533. Laundry and kitchen available. Open Mar.-Oct. £4 per person with tent.)

FOOD AND PUBS

Aspiring gourmets can prepare for a feast at the **Quinnsworth** supermarket on Market Rd. (☎ 21056. Open M-W 9am-7pm, Th-F 9am-9pm, Sa 9am-6pm.) Pubs and restaurants tend to go hand in hand in Ballina; get the same food for half the price by sitting in the pub. **Cafolla's,** just up from the bridge, is fast, cheap, and almost Italian. The milkshakes tingle tongues. (☎ 21029. Open M-Sa 10am-12:30pm.) **Tullio's,** Pearse St., exudes elegance and has pleasantly surprising prices. Gourmet pizzas, burgers, and pasta dishes around £5-7. (☎ 70815. Restaurant open daily noon-3pm and 6-10pm; bar food served noon-10pm.) **Duffy's,** Pearse St. (☎ 22576), is a local coffee and tea shop that provides cheap eats for £2-5.

Gaughan's has been pulling the best pint in town since 1936. No music or TV—just conversation, snugs, great grub, and homemade snuff. Jolly, musical drinkers are fixtures of **The Parting Glass** on Tolan St. (☎ 72714. Weekly trad sessions.)

Down by the river on Clare St., the **Murphy Bros.** (☎ 22702) serve pints to twenty-somethings amongst dark wood furnishings. They also dish out superb pub grub. The rest of the town's youngsters crowd the **Broken Jug** (☎ 72379) on O'Rahilly St., and **The Loft**, a dark, intimate cellar bar on Pearse St. (☎ 21881. Music Tu-F and Su.) **Doherty's**, by the bridge, revels in the angling lifestyle. (☎ 21150. Trad Th and Sa.) **An Bolg Bui** (☎ 22561) next door is Irish for "the yellow belly." The pub calls itself a "young fisherperson's pub" and sells tackle and licenses along with pints. Belleek Castle is an expensive hotel, but its **Armada Bar**, built from an actual 500-year-old Spanish wreck, is accessible and affordable. Downstairs, another bar occupies a medieval banquet hall. Of Ballina's four clubs, **Longneck's**, behind Murphy's, is the most popular. (☎ 22702. Cover £3-5. Open July-Aug. Tu-Su. 21+.) **The Pulse**, behind the Broken Jug, is a close and throbbing second. (Cover £3-5. Open W and F-Su.)

SIGHTS

The bird-rich **Belleek Woods** (bah-LEEK) around **Belleek Castle** are a fairytale forest with an astonishing bird-to-tree-to-stream ratio. To reach the Belleek Woods entrance, cross the lower bridge near the cathedral on Pearse St. and keep Ballina House on your right. At the back of the railway station is the **Dolmen of the Four Maols**, locally called "Table of the Giants." The dolmen, which dates back to 2000 BC, is said to be the burial site of four Maols who murdered Ceallach, a 7th-century bishop. They were hanged at Ardaree, then commemorated with a big rock. The lonely **Ox Mountains** east of Ballina are cyclable. Dirt and asphalt trails crisscross their way up the slopes. The 44 mi. **Ox Mountain Drive** traces the scenic perimeter of the mountains and is well sign-posted from Tobercurry (21 mi. south of Sligo on the N17). The **Western Way** footpath begins in the Ox mountains and winds its way past Ballina through Newport and Westport, ending up in Connemara. The **Sligo Way** meets the **Western Way**, continuing up toward Sligo. Tourist offices sell complete guides. Equestrian enthusiasts can ride at the **Archuan Lodge**, 5 mi. north of Ballina on the Sligo road. (☎ 45084. Pony trekking £15 per hr.)

The annual, week-long **Ballina Street Festival** (☎ 70905), has been swinging mid-July since 1964. All of Co. Mayo turns up for the festival's **Heritage Day**, when the streets are closed off and life reverts to the year 1910. All the flashier aspects of traditional Irish life are staged, including greasy pig contests.

NEAR BALLINA

N59 and N26 puncture Ballina; R297 off N59 northwest runs to Enniscrone, a quintessential Irish sea spot. Cute Killala, boggy Ballycastle, and the archaeological extravaganza of Ceide Fields are threaded onto R314 north. The remote and seemingly innocuous stone bridge, known as the **Musical Bridge**, fords the Owenmore River. Curious marks run the length of the stone walls on either side, and a pile of small stones sits on each end. To play a tune on the bridge, run full speed from end to end, dragging a stone across the top of the handrail.

ENNISCRONE (INISHCRONE) ☎ 096

Eight miles northeast of Ballina on scenic Quay Rd. (R297), the gorgeous Enniscrone Strand stretches along the east shore of Killala Bay. On sunny summer days Irish weekenders vie for towel space. Most days, however, the miles of sand are unpopulated. Zillions of new holiday homes sprawl around the town and behind the beach. Across from the beach, the family-run **Kilcullen's Bath House** simmers. Steam baths in cedar wood cabinets and cool seaweed baths relax even the most tense of travelers. (☎ 36238. Steam bath £10 per 30min. Seaweed bath £8, with steam bath. Massage £15. Towels supplied.) A tea room with views of the strand awaits post-soak. (Open daily July-Aug. 10am-10pm; May-June and Sept.-Oct. 10am-9pm; Nov.-Apr. 11am-8pm.) **Fishing** enthusiasts should contact John McDonagh (☎ 45332) for guidance and equipment. An unofficial **tourist office** hides off Pier Rd. (Open M-F 11am-7pm.)

Gowan House B&B, Pier Rd., is set just back from the sea. The big bedrooms are decorated in bright colors and finished off with Baltic Pine. (☎ 36396. Singles £25; doubles £38.) Maura O'Dowd's **Point View House,** Main St., serves a home-style dinner (£9) before sending you to a comfortable night's sleep. (☎ 36312. Doubles with bath £38.) **The Atlantic Caravan Park** puts some grass under your tent. (☎ 36132. Laundry facilities. £5 per tent.) **Walsh's Pub,** Main St. (☎ 36110), serves great pub grub all day and hosts weekly music sessions. **Harnett's Bar,** Main St., cooks good but pricey food amid matchbox-covered walls. (☎ 36137. Lamb £7. Food served 1-2:30pm and 6-8pm.)

BALLYCASTLE, CEIDE FIELDS, AND KILLALA

Ballycastle is a strip of houses, shops, and pubs bordered by rich farmland and holiday cottages on one side and bog on the other. By offering housing and studio space, the **Ballinglen Arts Foundation** has brought several prominent and emerging artists to Ballycastle. **Bus Éireann** has a service to **Killala** and **Ballina** (M-Sa 1 per day, £5). **Ulster Bank** opens its mini-office Tuesdays from 10am to noon.

Palatial digs, huge meals, and potpourri under the pillow grace **Mrs. Chambers' Suantai B&B,** on the Killala road. (☎ 43040. Singles £23; doubles £34; all with bath.) **Ceide House Restaurant,** has Mayo cuisine. (☎ 43105. Entrees £5-7. Open daily 9am-9pm.) They also offer comfortable lodgings in the center of town. (Singles £23; doubles £32.) **Mary's Bakery** whips up baked goods and scrumptious lunch specials. (☎ 43361. Open daily 10am-6pm.) **McNamee's Supermarket** sells peanut butter, jelly, and more. (☎ 43057. Open daily 9am-10pm.) Dark, low-ceilinged **Katie Mac's** wears its blackened floorboards and ancient walls with pride. (☎ 43031. Trad on weekends; sing-alongs known to happen.)

A small brochure from the tourist office (20p) outlines three walks around the area. One follows a bucolic path to the ocean, the **Dun Briste** seastack, and stoic **Downpatrick Head.** The multi-layered rock formation supposedly broke off from the mainland during a dispute between St. Patrick and a pagan king; St. Patrick used the geological disturbance to prove God's power. The **North Mayo Sculpture Trail** follows the R314 from Ballina to Belmullet. Fifteen modern sculptors have created site-specific installations of earth and stone to celebrate the rugged wilderness of north Mayo; brown "Tír Sáile" signs mark the trail.

Five miles west toward the Mullet Peninsula, the **Ceide** (KAYJ-uh) **Fields** are open to visitors through an **interpretive center,** which offers exhibits, films, and guided tours of the largest excavated neolithic landscape in the world. The center itself is particularly interesting: a tall, incongruous pyramid of peat and glass, constructed around a 5000-year-old Scotch pine that had been dug out of the bog. If all the muck gets you down, the 350-million-year-old **Ceide Cliffs** rise high nearby. (☎ 43325. Tours every hr., film every 30min. £2.50, students £1. Open daily June-Sept. 9:30am-6:30pm; mid-March to May and Oct. 10am-5pm; Nov. 10am-4:30pm.)

Eight miles south of Ballycastle along the Ballina road is **Killala,** a charming seaport best known as the site of the French Invasion of 1798 (see **Rebellion, Union, and Reaction,** p. 13). One thousand and sixty-seven French soldiers landed at Killala to join the United Irishmen under Wolfe Tone in a revolt against the British. Instead of finding a well-armed band of revolutionaries, the French found a smattering of poor, Irish-speaking peasants. Undeterred, they pressed on with the revolution, winning a significant victory at Castlebar before being soundly hammered by British forces at Ballnamuck.

KNOCK ☎ 094

At 8pm on August 21, 1879, St. Joseph, St. John, and the Virgin Mary appeared at Knock with a cross, a lamb, an altar, and a host of angels. The vision materialized before at least 15 witnesses, who stood in the rain for two hours watching the apparitions and chanting the Rosary. The Catholic hierarchy endorsed the miracle, and Knock quickly developed into a major pilgrimage site, with over 1½ million pilgrims visiting each year. The streets overflow with entrepreneurs hawking anything and everything emblazoned with the Knock label, while the churches fill with serious prayer.

GETTING THERE AND PRACTICAL INFORMATION.
Knock lies between Galway and Sligo on N17. The **Horan Cutríl Airport** (☎ 67222), 11 mi. north of town near Charlestown, is the subject of a tune by Christy Moore and attracts pilgrim cash with direct flights to the UK. **Bus Éireann** stops at Coleman's and Lennon's; buses depart for **Westport** (Su 1 per day, £9), **Sligo** (Su 3 per day, £7.70), and **Dublin** (2 per day, Su 1 per day; £10). Knock's **tourist office** is suitably central. (☎ 88193. Open daily May-Sept. 10am-5pm.) Inside the office is **Bank of Ireland.** (Open May-Oct. M and Th 10:15am-12:15pm; Nov.-Apr. M 10:15am-12:15pm.) The **shrine office**, across the street, sells Knock literature, official calendars, and the *Knock Pilgrim's Guide* (10p), which has prayers and a useful map. (☎ 88100. Open daily June-Oct. 9am-8:30pm; Nov. 10am-6pm.) The **post office** is in the Spar by the traffic circle. (☎ 88209. Open M 9am-1pm, Tu-Sa 9am-5:30pm.)

ACCOMMODATIONS, FOOD, AND PUBS.
"Hostels" in town are for the sick or elderly, but B&Bs line the roads into town. Mrs. Kelly's **Cara**, on Kiltamagh Rd., is particularly welcoming, if ascetic. (☎ 88315. Singles £19, doubles £32.) **Knock Caravan and Camping** is five minutes from the church on the Claremorris side. (☎ 88223. Laundry £3.50. July-Aug. £6 per tent, plus 50p per person; single backpacker £4; Mar.-June and Sept.-Oct. £5.50 per tent, 25p per person; single backpacker £3.50.) The **Knock International Hotel**, Main St. has clean, centrally located rooms; in July and August they're as scarce as atheists. (☎ 88466. Rooms from £15 per person; B&B from £16.) **Beirne's Restaurant,** on the main road offers a set three-course lunch and enough tables to seat bus loads of worshippers. (☎ 88161. £7.50. Lunch served noon-3pm. Open daily noon-6pm.) **Ard Mhuire's** is a split-level restaurant on Main St. that serves buffet-style food. (All entrees under £5. Open Apr.-Oct. 10am-7:30pm.)

SIGHTS.
Knock's religious sights cluster around the shrine built on the site of the Apparition. Numerous healings are believed to have occurred in the courtyard. The monumental **Church of Our Lady** holds 20,000 people for mass. (Services M-Sa 8, 9, 11am, noon, 3, and 7:30pm; Su 8, 9:30, 11am, noon, 3, and 7pm.) Free holy water is dispensed near the shrine. **The Knock Folk Museum,** to the right of the basilica, portrays rural 19th-century life. (☎ 88100. Open daily July-Aug. 10am-7pm; May-June and Sept.-Oct. 10am-6pm. £2, students £1.50.) The thatched cottage and the old photographs of Irish life are the best reasons to visit. Knock's biggest festival, the **Feast of Our Lady of Knock,** is on August 21.

NORTHWEST IRELAND

The farmland of the upper Shannon spans northward into Co. Sligo's mountains, lakes, and ancient monuments. A mere sliver of land connects Co. Sligo to Co. Donegal, the second-largest and most remote of the Republic's counties, with its most spectacular scenery. Donegal's *gaeltacht* is a storehouse of genuine, unadulterated Irish tradition. Hitchhikers report that the upper Shannon region is difficult to thumb through; drivers in Donegal provide the most rides in all of Ireland. Easy or hard, *Let's Go* does not recommend hitchhiking.

HIGHLIGHTS OF THE NORTHWEST: W.B. AND WILD BEACHES

Sligo (p. 344) is surrounded by **Benbulben, Drumcliff, Lough Gill,** and other sylvan, whimsical sites made famous by W.B. Yeats's poetry.

Begin your journey through **Slieve League Peninsula** (p. 364) at boisterous pubs in **Donegal Town** (p. 360). **Kilcar** (p. 365) and **Glencolmcille** (p. 367) provide a hearty night's rest before hiking on Europe's tallest sea cliffs on the peninsula's promontory.

Gweedore (p. 376) is Ireland's densest *gaeltacht,* and the setting of **Glenveagh National Park** (p. 381) and mythic **Bunbeg** (p. 377) and **Poison Glen** (p. 377).

Dunfanaghy (p. 381) offers spectacular coastal walks beside Muckish Mountain.

A trip up the **Inishowen Peninsula** (p. 386) leads past increasingly beautiful scenery culminating at **Malin Head** (p. 391), Ireland's northern-most and sunniest point.

COUNTY SLIGO

Since the beginning of the 20th century, Sligo has been a literary pilgrimage for William Butler Yeats fanatics. The poet divided his pre-adolescent time between London and Sligo; once he reached adulthood, he chose Sligo as his home, and set many of his poems around Sligo Bay. Fortunately, Yeats couldn't exhaust the county of its physical beauty, leaving that pleasure to today's visitors. After long days in the prosaic countryside, visitors return to Sligo town's pubs. It's easier and more exciting to spend the nights in town; everything else can be seen on daytrips.

SLIGO
☎071

The commercial center of the county does its dreary business during the day but goes wild at night with one of Ireland's most colorful pub scenes. Grey and relentless, the Garavogue River gurgles through the industrial and market center of Sligo Town (pop. 18,000). During business hours, traffic is locked in place in the downtown maze of one-way streets, while cargo ships come and go from the busy pier. Sligo's urban carnival is surrounded on all sides by a more impressive natural pageant. Two imposing hills, Knocknarea and Benbulben, loom like green bulls locked in a staring contest. W.B. Yeats spent long summer holidays here with his mother's family, who owned a mill over the Garavogue. Those early visits, and the exposure they provided to the superstitions of the local people, sparked Yeats's interest in the supernatural world. Most of Sligo boasts some connection to Yeats.

Northwest Ireland
ATLANTIC OCEAN
Malin Head
Glengad Head
Malin
Culdaff
Inishowen Head
Stroove
Greencastle
Ballyliffin
R238
Moville
Clonmany
Carndonagh
Farad Head
INISHOWEN PENINSULA
Lough Foyle
Rinmore Point
Lough Swilly
Portsalon
Limavady
A77
Downings
Buncrana
Tory Island
Horn Head
Sheep Haven
Muff
Carrigart
Rathmullen
Inch
CO. DERRY
Tory Sound
Dunfanaghy
Inch Island
Derry
A2
A6
Inishbofin
GWEEDORE
Creeslough
Milford
Grianán Aileach
Bloody Foreland
Falcarragh
N56
Rathmelton
N13
Errigal Mt.
Derryveagh Mts.
Glenveigh National Park
Derrybeg
A5
Gola I.
Bunbeg
Dunlewy
Letterkenny
Churchill
Owey I.
Crolly
N14
Lifford
Kincasslagh
Carrickfinn Airport
THE ROSSES
CO. DONEGAL
Burtonport
Stranorlar
N15
Dungloe
Aranmore Island
Crohy Head
Gweebarra Bay
CO. TYRONE
A505
Maas
Omagh
Glenties
Blue Stack Mts.
Dawros Head
Loughros Point
Ardara
Lough Eske
A32
Fintona
Lough Derg
Mountcharles
Donegal Town
Killybegs
Pettigoe
A35
Glencolmcille
Lower Lough Erne
Rossan Point
Carrick
Kilcar
A47
Rathlin O'Birne I.
St. John's Point
Beleek
A46
Ballyshannon
CO. FERMANAGH
Donegal Bay
Bundoran
Enniskillen
A4
Upper Lough Erne
Mullaghmore
Lough Melvin
Lough Allen
A509
Inishmurray
Lough Glencar
N16
Drumcliff
Manorhamilton
CO. CAVAN
0 10 miles
0 10 kilometers
Rosses Point
Lough Gill
Sligo Bay
Sligo
Strandhill
Dromahair
Knocknarea
CO. LEITRIM
Easky
Ballysadare
Lenadoon Point
N59
Collooney
Killala Bay
CO. SLIGO
Riverstown
Ox Mountains
Drumshanbo
N17
Ballymote
Lough Arrow
Lough Key
Carrick-on-Shannon
Boyle
Tobercurry
N4
N58
Ballina
N57
N61
N5
CO. MAYO
CO. ROSCOMMON

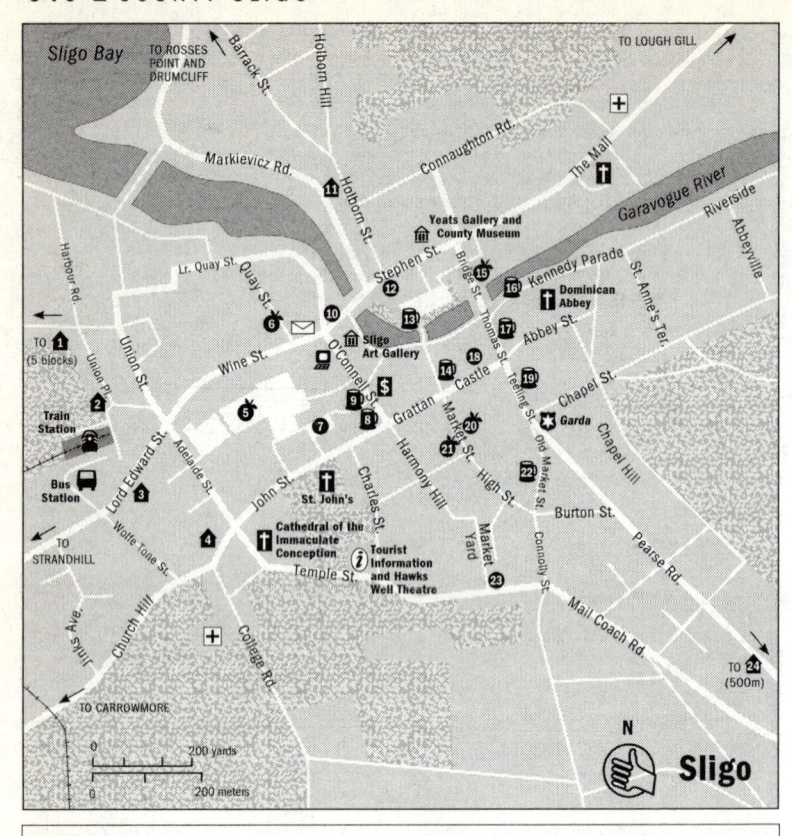

Sligo

ACCOMMODATIONS
Eden Hill Holiday Hostel (IHH), 24
Harbour House, 1
Railway Hostel, 2
Renaté House, 4
The White House Hostel (IHH), 11
Yeats County Hostel, 3

FOOD
Ho Wong, 20
Hy-Breasil, 15
Kate's Kitchen, 21
Lyon's Café, 6
Quinnsworth Supermarket, 5

PUBS AND CLUBS
The Belfry, 17
Equinox, 19
Garavogue, 13
Hargadon Bros., 8
McGarrigle's, 9
McLynn's, 22
Shoot the Crows, 14
Toff's, 16

SERVICES
Flanagan's Cycles, 23
Out & About Camping Supplies, 12
Pam's Laundrette, 7
Pharmacy, 18
The Winding Stair Booksore, 10

GETTING THERE AND GETTING AROUND

Airport: Sligo Airport, Strandhill Rd. (☎ 68280). Open daily 9:30am-5:30pm. To **Dublin** (50min.; M-F 3 per day, Sa-Su 2 per day).

Trains: McDiarmada Station, Lord Edward St. (☎ 69888). Open M-Sa 7am-6:30pm, Su 20min. before each departure. Trains to **Dublin** via **Carrick-on-Shannon** and **Mullingar** (3 per day, £13.50).

Buses: McDiarmada Station, Lord Edward St. (☎ 60066). Open M-F 9:15am-6pm, Sa 9:30am-5pm. Buses fan out to **Galway** (2½hr., 3-4 per day, £11), **Westport** (2½hr., 1-3 per day, £9.70), **Derry** (3hr., 3-6 per day, £10), **Dublin** (4hr., 4 per day, £9), and **Belfast** (4hr., 1-3 per day, £12.40).

Local Transportation: Frequent **buses** to Strandhill and Rosses Point (£1.65).

Taxis: Cab 55 (☎ 42333); **Finnegan's** (☎ 77777, 44444, or 41111). At least £3 in town, 50p per mi. outside.

Bike Rental: Flanagan's Cycles, Market Sq. (☎ 44477, after hours ☎ 62633), rents and repairs. Open M-Sa 9am-6pm, Su by prior arrangement. £7 per day, £30 per week; deposit £35.

ORIENTATION AND PRACTICAL INFORMATION

Trains and buses pull into McDiarmada station on **Lord Edward St.** To reach the main drag from the station, take a left and follow Lord Edward St. straight onto **Wine St.** then turn right at the post office onto **O'Connell St.** More shops, pubs, and eateries beckon from **Grattan St.,** left off O'Connell St.

TOURIST AND FINANCIAL SERVICES

Tourist Office: Temple St. (☎ 61201), at Charles St. From the station, turn left along Lord Edward St., then follow the signs right onto Adelaid St. and around the corner to Temple St. to find the Northwest regional office. Open June-Aug. M-Sa 9am-8pm, Su 10am-6pm; Oct.-May M-F 9am-5pm. The small **info booth** on O'Connell St. in Quinnsworth arcade can be helpful, and you won't have to fight the crowds. Open M-Tu 10am-7pm, W-F 10am-9pm, Sa 10am-6pm.

Bank: AIB, 49 O'Connell St. (☎ 41085). Get your greens at the **ATM.** Open M-W and F 10am-4pm, Th 10am-5pm.

LOCAL SERVICES

Luggage Storage: At the bus station. Open M-F 9:30am-1:30pm and 2:45-6pm. £1.50 per bag.

Bookstore: The Winding Stair, Hyde Bridge (☎ 41244). Fiction, Irish interest, used books, and a small cafe upstairs. Open daily 10am-6pm; Aug. also Su 1-6pm.

Newspapers: *The Sligo Guardian* has local news and useful listings.

Laundry: Pam's Laundrette, 9 Johnston Ct. (☎ 44861), off O'Connell St. Wash and dry from £6. Open M-Sa 9am-7pm.

Camping Supplies: Out & About, Stephen St. (☎ 44550). All your outdoor needs met indoors. Open M 2-6pm, Tu-Sa 9:30am-6pm.

Pharmacy: E. Horan, Castle St. (☎ 42560). Open M-Sa 9:30am-6pm. Local pharmacies post schedules of rotating Su openings.

EMERGENCY AND COMMUNICATIONS

Emergency: ☎ 999; no coins required. **Police** (*Garda*): Pearse Rd. (☎ 42031).

Crisis Line: Samaritans (24hr. ☎ 42011), **Rape Crisis Line** (☎ 1-800-750-780), M 10:30am-noon and 6:30-8:30pm, Tu-F 10:30am-midnight.

Hospital: On The Mall (☎ 42161).

Post Office: Wine St. (☎ 42646). Open M and W-Sa 9am-5:30pm, Tu 9:30am-5:30pm.

Internet Access: Cygo Internet Cafe, 19 O'Connell Street (☎ 40082). £5 per hr., students £4. Open M-Sa 10am-7pm.

ACCOMMODATIONS

There are plenty of hostels in Sligo, but they fill up quickly, especially while the Yeats International Summer School is in session in mid-August. If you're staying a few days with a group of people, getting a cottage can be cheaper. Contact the tourist office for more info. Over a dozen B&Bs cluster along Pearse Rd. on the south side of town; less refined ones are near the station.

Harbour House, Finisklin Rd. (☎ 71547). A 10min. walk from the bus station. The plain stone front hides a luxurious hostel. Big pine bunks have individual reading lights. Irish breakfast £3, continental £1.50. **Bike rental** £7. Dorms £10; private rooms £10.50 per person; singles £17.

Railway Hostel, 1 Union Place (☎ 44530). Sign-posted from the train station. From the main station entrance take three lefts, *et voilà*, you're there! An old rail station has been gracefully converted into nice digs. Plus, there's Socks the Friendly Hostel Dog. Limited kitchen utensils. Dorms £6.50; private rooms £8 per person.

The White House Hostel (IHH), Markievicz Rd. (☎ 45160). Take the first left off Wine St. after the bridge. The reception is in the brown house. A little run-down, but spacious dorms, some with river views, make this hostel a fine choice. Sheets 50p. Key deposit £2. Dorms £7.

Yeats County Hostel, 12 Lord Edward St. (☎ 46876), across from the bus station. Its location can make it crowded. Liam, the man in charge, was once butler to the Kennedy family. Spacious rooms, a private backyard, and an excellent location recommend this comfortable roost. Key deposit £5. Dorms and triples £7 per person; doubles £21.

Eden Hill Holiday Hostel (IHH), Pearse Rd. (☎ 43204). Entrance via Marymount or Ashbrook St., 10min. from town, at the opposite end from the train station. Cozy rooms and a Victorian sitting parlor in a grand but aging house. The funky paint jobs in the bathrooms make showering a joy. Huge backyard, and a common room with VCR. Laundry facilities. Dorms £7; private rooms £8.50 per person. **Camping** £4.

Renaté House, Upper Johns St. (☎ 62014). From the station, go straight 1 block and left ½ a block. Businesslike and spotless, with elegant leather, burgundy furnishings. Singles £23.50, with bath £25.50; doubles £34, with bath £38.

🔆 FOOD

"Faery vats/ Full of berries/ And reddest stolen cherries" are not to be found in Sligo today. **Quinnsworth Supermarket,** O'Connell St., sells neatly packaged berries as well as other assorted items. (☎ 62788. Open M-Tu 8:30am-7pm, W-F 8:30am-9pm, Sa 8:30am-7pm, Su 10am-6pm.) ■**Kate's Kitchen,** on Market Street, offers sophisticated pâtés and other deli delicacies. (☎ 43022. Frozen homemade soups are a steal at £1.20.) The demands of international visitors have induced culinary development here, pick up *Discover Sligo's Good Food* for new listings, free at most hostels and bookstores. Good restaurants and dinners are expensive; the best values tend to end around 6pm, so eat early or pay.

Hy-Breasil, Bridge St. (☎ 61180). Utopia of coffee and fresh-squeezed juice, just over the river. Local art on the walls. Juice £1.50. Open M-F 8:30am-6pm, Sa 10am-6pm.

Ho Wong, Market St. (☎ 45718). Cantonese and Szechuan take-out with an Irish-Asian flair. Dishes £4-7. Open daily 4-11pm.

Pepper Alley (☎ 70720), along the river, on the town side of the footbridge. Huge selection of cheap sandwiches for lunch, though many are heavy on the mayonnaise (£2-3). Open weekends for more upscale dinners. Open M-Sa 8am-6pm, Th-Sa 6-10pm.

Lyon's Cafe, Quay St. (☎ 42969). Tucked upstairs behind big windows, this cafe brews Bewley's coffee. Quiche with salad £4. Open M-Sa 9am-6pm; lunch served 12:30-2pm.

🎵 PUBS AND CLUBS

Over 70 pubs crowd Sligo's main streets, filling the town with live music during the summer. Events and venues are listed in *The Sligo Champion* (75p). Be forewarned that many Sligo pubs restrict to a 21+ crowd (a regulation reportedly relaxed for those of female persuasion).

■**Shoot the Crows,** Castle St. Small, murky joint where millennial hipsters and white-haired characters compete for bar stools. Dark fairy-folk dangle from the ceiling. Weird skulls and crazy murals look on in amusement. Music Tu and Th 9:30pm.

Garavogue (☎ 40100), across the river from the footbridge. Spacious, wooden interior, 20-something crowd, and palm trees combine in this new, modern pub.

Hargadon Bros., O'Connell St. (☎ 70933). A pub worth spending your day in. Open fires, old Guinness bottles, and *poitín* jugs in a maze of dark and intimate nooks. Perfect pints unfettered by the modern audio-visual distractions found elsewhere. Occasional Blues nights.

McGarrigle's, O'Connell St. (☎ 71193). 18th-century lanterns light the cave-dark interior. Upstairs is just as dark, with new-age murals, blaring techno, and young faces. Trad Th and Su.

McLynn's, Old Market St. (☎ 60743). The *International Pub Guide* ranks McLynn's as the best pub for music in Sligo; locals confirm that opinion. The owner is known to leap over the taps for a round of his own brand of guitar and vocals. A wood divider separates locals from tourists. Enter through the unmarked door on the left of the building and tear down social barriers. Music most weekends.

The Belfry (☎ 62150), off the bridge on Thomas St. Modern medieval castle decor, with a big bell and a bigger chandelier. 2 floors, 3 bars, and 30 Irish malt whiskeys make this the place for intrigue in Sligo.

Clubbers shake it at **Toff's,** on the river behind the Belfry. The well-lit, crowded dance floor reveals that local club-goers drink better than they dance. (☎ 62150. Disco Th-Sa. Cover £5, £1 off with card from the Belfry. 21+.) Up Teeling St., **Equinox** is darker with a younger crowd, with newfangled neon lights, zebra-patterned stools, and striped dance music. (Cover £5. Open W-Su.) Shake your dreads on Wine Street at **The Clarence Hotel's** reggae nights; the floor is small, but the music draws a funky crowd. (Cover £3-5. Reggae Th and F, chart Sa.)

👁 SIGHTS

Yeats praised peasants and aristocrats and disdained middle-class merchants and industrialists. Appropriately, most of the Yeatsian sights are at least a mile from the mercantile town center. In town, the 13th-century **Sligo Abbey,** Abbey St., is well preserved. (☎ 46406. Open daily in summer 9:30am-6:30pm; last admission 45min. before closing. If it's closed, ask for the key from Tommy McLaughlin, 6 Charlotte St. £1.50, students 60p.) The **Dominican Friary** boasts cloisters and ornate coupled pillars that, though old, can hardly be called ruins. A defaced monument stone, which bore the names of a mother and her child, graces the sacristy. Tradition claims that the mother's descendents, not wanting a public reminder of their forbearers' illegitimacy, hired a stonemason, Buddy Graffiti, to chisel the names away in secret. Next door, the 1874 **Cathedral of the Immaculate Conception,** John St., is best visited at dawn or dusk, when the sun streams through 69 magnificent stained-glass windows. Farther down John St., the **Cathedral of St. John the Baptist,** designed in 1730, has a brass tablet dedicated to Yeats's mother, Susan Mary. The 1878 **courthouse** on Teeling St. was built on the site of the previous one.

The Niland Gallery, Stephen St., but likely moving to the **Niland Center** on the Mall, houses one of the finest collections of modern Irish art, including a number of works by William's brother, Jack Yeats, and contemporaries Nora McGuinness and Michael Healy. Among the museum's other treasures are some first editions by the poet himself. The gems of the collection are a few illustrated broadside collaborations between father and son, and Countess Markievicz's prison apron. (Rotating exhibits. Open Tu-Sa 10am-noon and 2-5pm. Free.) On the corner of Stephen and Holborn street stands a statued, tall, thin, and poetic version of **Yeats.**

The **Sligo County Museum** preserves small reminders of Yeats, including pictures of his funeral. (Open Tu-Sa June-Sept. 10:30am-12:30pm and 2:30-4:50pm; Oct.-May 10:30am-12:30pm. Free.) The **Sligo Art Gallery,** Yeats Memorial Building, Hyde Bridge, rotates exhibitions of contemporary Irish art with an annual northwest Ireland exhibit in November. (☎ (071) 45847. Open daily 10am-5pm.)

🎵 ENTERTAINMENT

A monthly *Calendar of Events,* free from the tourist office, describes the festivals and goings-on in the Northwest region. **Hawk's Well Theatre,** Temple St., beneath the tourist office, presents modern and traditional dramas, ballets, and musicals. (☎ 61526 or 61518. Box office open M-Sa 9am-6pm. Shows £7-10, students £4.) The **Blue Raincoat Theatre Company,** Lower Quay St., is a traveling troupe covering a wide range of material in their Quay St. "factory space" 16 weeks a year. Look for flyers or call for show dates. (☎ 70381. Tickets £5-7.)

350 ■ COUNTY SLIGO

Lake Districts

The **Sligo Arts Festival** (☎ 69802) takes place during the first weekend in June. The final weekend focuses on world music. In the first two weeks of August, the internationally renowned **Yeats International Summer School** opens some of its poetry readings, lectures, and concerts to the public. International luminaries like Seamus Heaney are regular guests. (☎ 42693. For an application, contact the Yeats Society, Yeats Memorial Building, Douglas Hyde Bridge. Office open M-F 10am-1pm and 3-5pm.)

DAYTRIPS FROM SLIGO

Day-trippers from Sligo have a full volume of options: Lough Gill, Carrowmore, Strandhill, Rosses Point, and Drumcliff are all within a few miles. Small brown signs with quill and ink mark the Yeats trail, most easily navigated by car. Early risers can catch the **Bus Éireann** (☎ (071) 60066) coach tour, which drives from the station to **Glencar, Drumcliff,** and **Lough Gill** (3½hr., July-Sept. Tu and Th 9am, £6). **John Howe's** bus company (☎ (071) 42747) runs daily coach tours from the tourist office in July-Aug. through Yeats country (3½hr., £6.50) and **Lough Gill** (3hr., £5.50). **Peter Henry's Blue Lagoon** (☎ (071) 42530) rents out rowboats (£15 per day), and motorboats (£30 per day). The **Wild Rose Water-Bus** (☎ (071) 64266) tours Sligo, Parke's Castle, Innisfree, and Garavogue (3 per day, £4-5); a night lough cruise departs from Parke's Castle (F 9pm).

STRANDHILL PENINSULA, KNOCKNAREA MOUNTAIN, AND CARROWMORE

Bus Éireann leaves across the street from the Sligo bus station for Strandhill and the turn-off to Carrowmore (M-F 6 per day, Sa 3 per day; £1.65). R292 does a loop around the peninsula; the turn-off to Carrowmore is about 1 mi. west of Sligo on R292. Eliot's taxi (☎ (071) 69944) in Sligo runs all day and night, and will service the peninsula.

Best known for its two miles of dunes, windy Strandhill ducks under solemn Knocknarea at the southern edge of Sligo Bay. Surfing is fine for experts; swimming is dangerous for average mortals. At low tide, a causeway connects the beach to Coney Island, but don't get stuck—there ain't no rollercoaster out there. A fantastic assortment of passage graves spooks visitors 3 mi. southwest of Sligo, at **Carrowmore.** The site had over 100 tombs and stone circles before modern folks quarried and cleared many away. Of the 70 remaining, about 30 can still be visited, some dating back to 4840 BC. Excavation is ongoing, turning up one or two new formations each year. The small but interesting **interpretive center** explains their meaning. From Sligo, follow the signs west from John St. (☎ 61534. Open daily May-Sept. 9:30am-6:30pm. Tours available. £1.50, students 60p.)

The 1078 ft. **Knocknarea Mountain** faces **Benbulben** on the southwestern shore of Sligo Bay. Queen Mebdh, or Maeve, the villain of the *Táin bo Cuailnge* (see **Legends and Folktales,** p. 23), is reputedly interred in the 11 yd. high, 60 yd. wide cairn on the summit. Her notoriety is evident from the size of the cairn; she was buried standing up to face her enemies in Ulster. Decades ago, tourists started taking stones from the cairn as souvenirs; to preserve the legendary monument, local authorities created a "tradition" that anyone who brought a stone down the mountain would be cursed, while an unmarried man or woman who brought one up the mountain and placed it on the cairn would be married within a year. The stunning mountain also makes a cameo appearance in Yeats's "Red Hanrahan's Song about Ireland": "The wind has bundled up the clouds high over Knocknarea/ And thrown the thunder on the stones for all that Maeve can say."

The climb takes about 45 minutes, and the reward is a stunning view of the misty bay and heathered hills. Animal enthusiasts will delight in the bilingual sheep bleating insults at the less intelligent cows and tourists stumbling up the near-vertical path. Trails crisscross the forested park on Knocknarea's eastern slopes. There are several ways up. The main path is from the car park. From Carrowmore it's an hour's walk west; turn left, take a right at the church, then the first left to the sign Mebdh Meirach. From Strandhill (30min.), turn left from the hostel and keep to the left. Another path ascends from Strandhill, while a third begins in Glen Rd. a mile east of the car park.

LOUGH GILL

The forested 24 mi. road around Lough Gill, just southeast of Sligo, runs past woody nature trails, Yeatsian spots, an old castle, and several small towns. It's flat enough to make a wonderful bike ride from Sligo, but get an early start. Take Pearse Rd. and turn off to the left at the Lough Gill signs.

The first stop on the route is **Holywell**, a leafy, flower-strewn shrine with a well and waterfall. During the Penal Law years, secret masses were held at this site. If by chance the British military approached, the congregation would disband and pretend to be enjoying a football game. The main road itself reaches **Dooney Rock**, on the south shore of Lough Gill near Cottage Island. Here, Yeats's "Fiddler of Dooney" made "folk dance like a wave of the sea." Nature trails around the rock lead to views of Innisfree, a perfectly round island in the lake that a young Yeats wrote about. If you want to arise and go to Innisfree, John O'Connor (☎ (071) 64079) will **ferry** you out for £5; his house is next to the jetty 2½ mi. down the Inisfree turnoff from the main road.

The next town past the Inisfree turnoff along the same route is **Dromahair**, which still shelters **Creevelea Abbey**. Founded in 1508 as the Friary of Killanummery, its active days ended in 1650 when Oliver "Religious Freedom" Cromwell expelled monks from the confiscated monastery. It has been a burial site since 1721. Dromahair is the farther point of the Lough Gill route. From here, turn left onto R286 to head back to Sligo Town.

On the route back stands **Parke's Castle**, a recently renovated 17th-century castle. Built by Anglo Parkes in the 1620s to protect himself from dispossessed Irish landowners, the castle stands on the visible foundation of an earlier stronghold of the O'Rourke family, where its waterfront location enables a quick get-away across the lough. The manor house and turret walk are open for visitors; an excellent 20-minute video highlights all nearby attractions. (☎ (071) 64149. Open June-Sept. daily 9:30am-6:30pm, mid-Apr.-May Tu-Su 10am-5pm, Oct. daily 10am-5pm. Tours leave on the hr. £2, students £1.) Two miles from town, a left turn leads to Hazelwood, the park where Yeats walked "among long dappled grass" in "The Song of Wandering Aengus." Hazelwood's **sculpture trail** also makes a good walk.

DRUMCLIFF: YEATS, YEATS, YEATS

Buses from Sligo toward Derry stop at Drumcliff (10min.; in summer M-Sa 4 per day, Su 3 per day, in winter M-Sa 3 per day; £2.60 return). Hitching is reportedly painless, but Let's Go does not recommend it. Glencar lake is marked by a sign about 1 mi. north of Drumcliff on N15.

> Under Bare Ben Bulben's head
> In Drumcliffe churchyard Yeats is laid.
> An ancestor was rector there
> Long years ago, a church stands near,
> By the road an ancient cross.
> No marble, no conventional phrase;
> On limestone quarried near the spot
> By his command these words are cut:
>   Cast a cold eye
> On life, on death.
> Horseman pass by!

Yeats composed his grave's epitaph a year before his death in France in 1939. His wife George carried out his wish to be buried by Ben Bulben ("Bulben Peak") in 1948; she was later buried by his feet. The road Yeats refers to is the N15; the churchyard is 4 mi. northwest of Sligo. His grave is to the left of the church door. On Sunday evenings in the summer, the church sponsors concerts (☎ (071) 56629). A few miles northeast of Drumcliff, **Glencar Lake**, mentioned in Yeats's "The Stolen Child," is the subject of more literary excursions.

Farther north of Drumcliff, eerie **Benbulben**, rich in mythical associations, protrudes from the landscape like the keel of a foundered boat. In 574, St. Columcille founded a monastery on top, and it continued to be a major religious center until

> **SINK OR SIN** Stand by the shore of Lough Gill and listen carefully. What do you hear? The lapping of the waves? The wind rustling in trees? The soft peal of a pure silver bell sounding distantly from the bottom of the lake? No? That's because you're a sinner. When Sligo's Dominican Friary was wrecked during the Ulster rebellion of 1641, worshippers saved its bell and hid it in the bottom of Lough Gill. Legend insists that only those free from sin can still hear it.

the 16th century. The climb up the 1729 ft. peak is inevitably windy, and the summit can be downright gusty. However, if you can keep from being blown away, standing at the very point of Benbulben, where the land inexplicably drops 5000 ft., can be a watershed experience for even the most weathered of hikers. Marks from old turf cuttings on the way up give evidence of one of the mountainside's historic uses. Signs guide travelers to Benbulben from Drumcliff Rd. Ask at the gas station in Drumcliff for detailed directions to the trailheads.

Four miles west of Drumcliff is **Lissadell House,** where poet Eva Gore-Booth and her sister Constance Markievicz, second in command in the Easter Rising (see p. 16) and later the first woman elected to the Dáil, entertained Yeats and his circle. The gaunt house has lost some of its luster, and the carpets are wearing thin, but Constance's great-nephew still lives here and allows tours. Henry Gore-Booth was an Arctic explorer and avid hunter. The real trophy on display, a ferocious brown bear, was actually shot by the butler. Take the first left after Yeats Tavern Hostel on Drumcliff Rd. and follow the signs. (☎ (071) 63150. House open M-Sa June to mid-Sept. 10:30am-12:15pm and 2-4:15pm. £2.50. Grounds open year-round. Free.) Near Lissadell in the village of Carney, the excellent food and nightly entertainment at **Laura's Pub** (☎ (071) 63056) justify the prices.

ROSCOMMON AND LEITRIM

Rivers and lakes (and a significant number of fast-moving highways) meander through the untouristed counties Roscommon and Leitrim, which span a diamond-shaped area between Sligo and the middle of the island. Parke's Castle, Dromahair, and Crevelea Abbey are in Co. Leitrim, but are covered in Sligo (see p. 344). Carrick-on-Shannon is a relaxed town that nonetheless teems with pubs, while Boyle is an excellent festival hostess. Because of predominant fly-by, non-local car traffic, Roscommon and Leitrim don't always provide comfortable hitching venues. Even if granted the slowest of traffic flow, *Let's Go* would not recommend hitchhiking. Motor vehicle may be the *modus transportis* of choice in this region.

CARRICK-ON-SHANNON ☎078

Coursing slowly through the green hills of Leitrim on its way to the sea, the Shannon River pauses when it reaches the rows of white yachts moored at Carrick-on-Shannon's marina. Life is relaxed here in this proud seat of Ireland's least populated county. Anglers fish for pike during the day while merry drinkers fill the pubs with song in the evening. The few sights in town won't sustain an energetic visitor, but nearby parks and lakes make good daytrips. A bridge spans from Co. Roscommon over the Shannon and into town, leading to the clock tower and Main St.

GETTING THERE AND GETTING AROUND

Trains: The Elphin Road station (☎ 20036) is a 10min. walk southwest of town. Trains to **Sligo** (1hr., 3 per day, £6) and **Dublin** (2½hr., 3 per day, £12).

Buses: Buses leave from **Coffey's Pastry Case** (☎ (071) 60066) for **Boyle** (15min., 3 per day, £3.20), **Sligo** (1hr., 3 per day, £5), and **Dublin** (3hr., 3 per day, £8).

Taxis: P. Burke, Bridge St. (☎ 21343). 50p per mile.

354 ■ ROSCOMMON AND LEITRIM

Bike Rental: Geraghty's, Main St. (☎ 21316). Open daily 9am-9pm. £10 per day, £25 per week; deposit varies.

PRACTICAL INFORMATION

Tourist Office: (☎ 20170), on the Marina. Open July-Aug. M-Sa 9am-8pm, Su 9am-1pm and 2pm-5pm, Apr.-May, Sept. M-F 9am-1pm and 2pm-5pm.
Bank: AIB, Main St. (☎ 20055). **ATM.** Open M 10am-5pm, Tu-F 10am-4pm.
Laundromat: McGuire's Washeteria, Main St. (☎ 20339), in the insurance broker's building. Wash and dry £4.50. Open M-Sa 10am-1pm, 2pm-6pm.
Pharmacy: Cox's hocks bottles and boxes on Bridge St. (☎ 20158). Open M-Th 9:30am-6pm, F-Sa 9:30am-7pm.
Emergency: ☎ 999; no coins required. **Police** (*Garda*)**:** Shannon Lodge (☎ 20021).
St. Patrick's Hospital: Summerhill Rd. (☎ 20011 or 20287; nights 20091).
Post Office: St. George's Terr. (☎ 20020, Sa ☎ 20051). Open M-Sa 9am-5:30pm.
Internet Access: Upstairs at **Gartlan's,** Bridge St. (☎ 21735). £4.50 per hr. Open M-Sa 9:30am-5:30pm.

ACCOMMODATIONS. Sick animals and backpackers seek refuge at the **An Óige Hostel** (☎ 21848), upstairs from the local veterinary clinic on Bridge St. (Dorms £8.) B&Bs line the Dublin Rd., Station Rd., and the manicured lawns of St. Mary's Close. **The Four Season B&B,** Main St. (☎ 21333), has big, flowery rooms. (£18.) **Campers** can pitch tents for free on the riverbank by the bridge. (For more camping near Carrick-on-Shannon, see under **Sights,** below.)

FOOD AND PUBS. Chung's Chinese Restaurant, Main St., cooks up a storm. Order take-away and save big. (☎ 21888. Take-away about £5, sit-down £7. Open July-Aug. M-Th and Su 6-11pm, F-Sa 6pm-midnight; Sept.-June M and W-Th 6-11pm, F-Sa 6pm-midnight.) To eat in try **Coffey's Pastry Case,** Bridge St. without sampling the cake is a sin. (☎ 20929. Open M-Sa 8:30am-8:30pm, Su 10:30am-7pm.) **The Anchorage,** Bridge St. (☎ 20416), is the town's most popular and venerable pub. Move in with the locals of all ages in the splendidly furnished **Flynn's Corner Pub,** Main St. (☎ 20003), near the tiny town clock. **The Oarsmen,** Bridge St., with a beautiful raised wood bar, plays to the out-of-town crowd (that would be you). (☎ 21733. Rock Th and F.) **Ging's** (☎ 21054), just across the town bridge, boasts a beer garden on the River Shannon. A mile from the town center, **Rockin' Robbins** lives up to its claim to be the town's nearest nightclub. Minibuses (£1 one-way) leave from The Anchorage on weekends. (Open F-Su. Cover £3, students £2. 21 and over.) A more popular option is a booze-cruise down the Shannon; **Moon River Cruises** (☎ 21777) is a bargain at £5. Summer sailings at 2:30 and 4:30pm and weekend nights at 11pm leave from near the tourist office. For trad, try **Glancy's** across the river (Th-Su), **Cryan's** on Bridge St. (Tu and F-Su), or **Burke's** (Th).

SIGHTS AND CAMPING NEAR CARRICK-ON-SHANNON

At the intersection of Main and Bridge St., teeny tiny Costello Memorial Chapel is reputedly the second-smallest in the world, although no one in town seems to know what it's second to. Two coffins peer up at visitors through plexiglass. The Angling and Tourism Association (☎ 20489) gives the line on rentals, sites, and fishing-oriented accommodations. To go truly native, head to the 12,000-seat football pitch just outside town on a Sunday afternoon to watch Leitrim battle other counties in Gaelic football (see **Sports,** p. 33). (Tickets £3-5, £10 for playoff games; available at the field.) Pick up the *Leitrim Observer* at any newsagent for other local listings. Carrick has several craft workshops farther down Main St.

Four miles northwest of Carrick-on-Shannon on the road to Boyle, the **Lough Key Forest Park** bursts with rhododendrons in the springtime, but its 850 acres and 33 forested islands are worth exploring any time of the year. The park was once the center of the Rockingham Estate, which covered most of the surrounding area. Although the estate's classical mansion burned down in 1957, the stables, church, and icehouse still stand. Numerous signposts won't let you miss the round tower, fairy bridge, and wishing chair. (☎ (079) 62363. Park always open. Admission collected 10am-6pm. £2 per car.) The **Lough Key Campground** (☎ (079) 62212) is on the road to the lake. (£3 per person.) North of the lough lies the site of Ireland's most important pre-human battle, in which the Túatha De Danann defeated Ireland's indigenous demons, the Formorians (see **Legends and Folktales,** p. 23, and **How the Poison Glen Got its Name,** p. 376).

The Earls of Leitrim once roamed the **Lough Rynn Estate,** just outside Mohill, 15 mi. east of Carrick on N4 toward Dublin. Once a massive 90,000 acres, the estate has been whittled down to a mere 100. The century-old walled Victorian garden and turret house overlook 600 acres of lake. A pleasant weekend walking tour will guide you into the beautiful parklands, which include the country's oldest monkey-puzzle tree. On weekdays, a 50p guide will provide you with a map. (☎ (078) 31427. Open daily late Apr.-Aug. 10am-7pm. £1.50 per person, £3.50 per car. Tours £1. Last tour 4:30pm on weekends.) The **Lough Rynn Caravan Park** hosts campers beside the lough. (☎ (078) 31054. £2 per tent. Open May-Sept.)

STROKESTOWN

Fifteen miles south of **Carrick,** where R368 meets N5 from Longford, the 18th-century **Strokestown Park House** rises on Main St. This 27,000-acre family estate has been heavily restored. The family's history of outrages includes fighting as mercenaries for Oliver Cromwell, evicting 3006 tenants during the Famine, and subsidizing a number of coffin-ships, the infamous emigration boats. By 1847, the worst year of the Famine, the tenants had had enough and shot the landlord. The house has not been occupied since 1979, but a casual, unforced grandeur remains. The play room has a particularly eerie collection of 100 years of toys. (☎ (078) 33013. Tours £3, students £2.50. Gardens £2.50.) Following 10 years of restoration, the four-acre **Pleasure Garden,** an exact replica of the original, opened in 1998. **The Famine Museum,** in the old stables next to the house, sits in stark opposition to the wealth and privilege of the house. (Open daily Apr.-Oct. 11am-5:30pm. £3, students £2.50.) A detailed exhibit elaborates on the history of the Potato Famine and explores its connection with present-day social problems (see **Famine,** p. 14).

BOYLE ☎079

Squeezed on a river between the two lakes southeast of the Curlieu mountains, Boyle is an inevitable crossing point for anyone traveling in the northwest. Clans and troops used Boyle as a strategic base, and enterprising shopkeepers founded present-day Boyle to capitalize on its location. The modern explorer would do well to follow their example. Boyle offers convenient access to nearby mountains, lakes, and parks, as well as numerous interesting historical sites. In July, Boyle locals dust off their Stetsons and boots and party with a country western flair during their annual festival.

GETTING THERE AND GETTING AROUND. Trains (☎ 62027) run from Boyle to **Dublin** (3hr., 3 per day, £11.50), and **Sligo** (40min., 3 per day, £4.70). **Buses** stop outside the Royal Hostel on Bridge St. and roar out to **Dublin** (3½hr., 3 per day, £9) and **Sligo** (30min., 3 per day, £6.50). Find **Bike Rental** at **Sheerin Cycles,** Main St. (☎ 62010; Open M-Sa 9am-6pm. £6 a day).

PRACTICAL INFORMATION. Boyle's **Tourist Office** is on Main St., inside the main gates of King House. (☎ 62145. Open May-Sept. 10am-6pm.) **National Irish Bank,** at Bridge and Patrick St. has an **ATM.** (☎ 62058. Open M 10am-5pm, Tu-F 10am-4pm; closed 12:30-1:30pm.) Suds up your duds at **The Washing Well,** Main St. (☎ 62503. Wash and dry £4.50, including laundry detergent. Open M-Sa 9:30am-

356 ■ ROSCOMMON AND LEITRIM

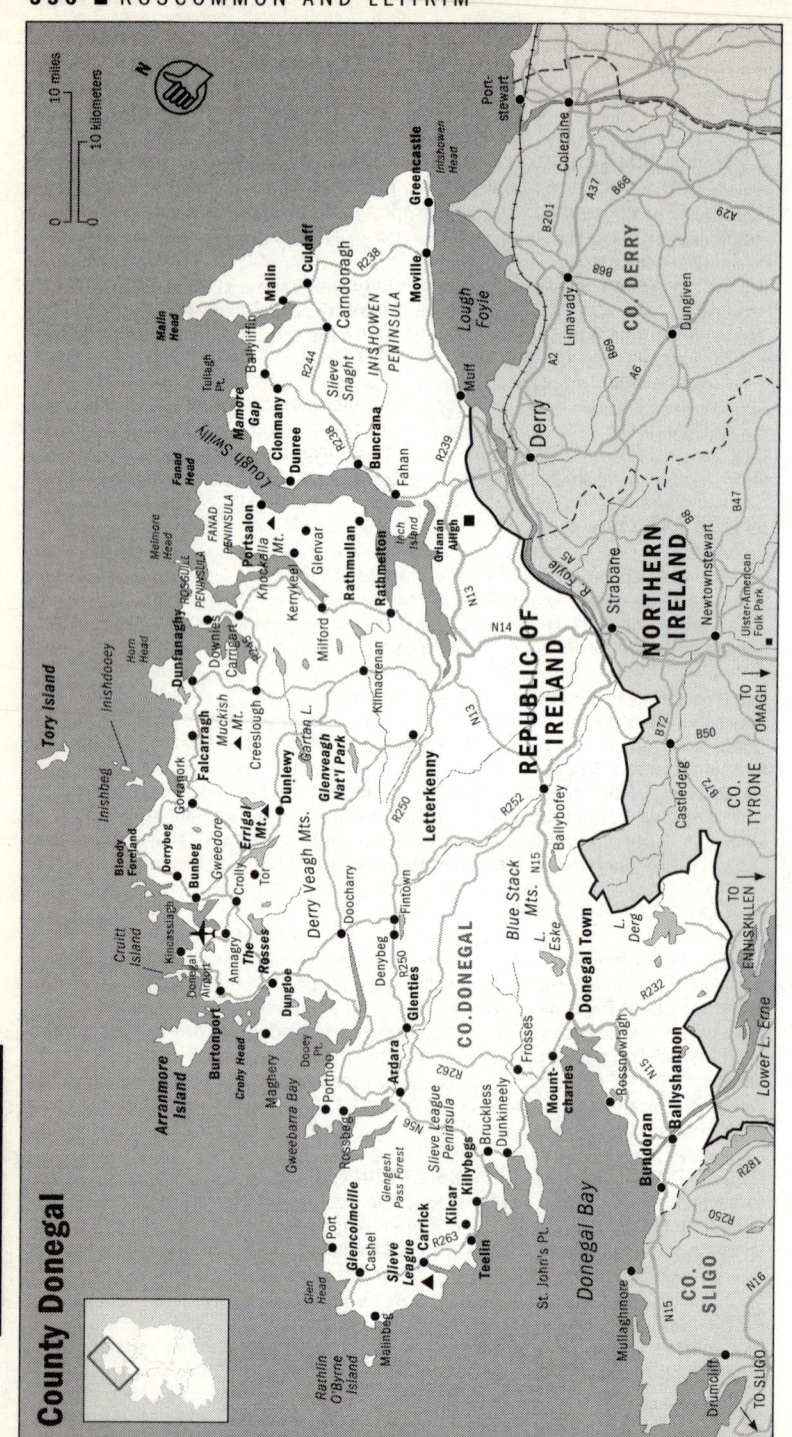

County Donegal

6:30pm.) **Ryan's pharmacy** is on Patrick and Main St. (☎ 62010. Open M-Sa 9am-6pm.) For **emergency** dial ☎ 999, no coins required. **Police** (*Garda*), are at Military Rd. (☎ 62030). The **Post Office** is on Carrick Rd. (☎ 62029 or 62028. Open M and W-F 9am-5:30pm, Tu 9:30am-5:20pm, Sa 9am-noon.)

ACCOMMODATIONS, FOOD, AND PUBS. The only hostels in the area are in nearby Carrick-on-Shannon. However, lavish beds can be procured in Boyle's B&Bs. Every visitor to the 170-year-old **Abbey House,** Abbeytown Rd. gets an uniquely decorated room. The sitting areas are decadent and have views of a bubbling stream. (☎ 62385. £16, with bath £20.) Cheery **Cesh Corran,** across from the Abbey, welcomes visitors with a turquoise hallway—rooms are bright and well-painted. (☎ 62247. £17 per person). **Lough Key Forest Caravan & Camping Park** and its laundry facilities are just a 5min. drive from Boyle on the Carrick road. (☎ 62212. Open Easter-Aug. £4 per person, £8 per tent.)

D.H. Burke, Main St., fulfills the duties of a supermarket. (☎ 62208. Open M-Th 9:30am-6pm, F 9:30am-8pm, Sa 9:30am-7pm.) **Una Bhan Restaurant** within the gates of the King House, is the place to go for breakfast and lunch. (☎ 63033. Salmon salad £3.95. Open M-Sa 9:30am-6:30pm.) **Chung's Chinese Restaurant,** Bridge St., has bunches of bean sprouts and a mean mushroom chicken for £5.10. (☎ 63123. Open Th-F 12:30-2:30pm, Sa-Su 5:30-11pm.) For perfect pints and rousing trad, everyone heads to **Kate Lavin's** (☎ 62855) on Patrick St.

SIGHTS AND ENTERTAINMENT. Off the A4, gothic arches curve over the green lawns of magnificent **Boyle Abbey** built in 1161 by Cistercian monks. (☎ 62604. Open mid-June to Oct. daily 9:30am-6:30pm. Guided tours on the hour. Key available from Mrs. Mitchell at the Abbey House B&B. £1, students 40p.) **King House,** Main St., recently reopened its Georgian doors and superb historical exhibits. Built by Sir Henry King around 1730 for entertaining VIPs, it served as a family home for 40 years and army barracks for 140. The house is now decked out with excellent interactive exhibits chronicling the history of the King family and the Connacht Rangers, as well as the reconstruction of the house. It also houses the Boyle Civic Art Collection. (☎ 63242. Open May-Sept. daily 10am-6pm, Apr. and Oct. Sa-Su 10am-6pm. £3, students £2.50. Last admission 5pm.) **Frybrook House,** a five-minute walk from the bridge, was built in 1752 and restored to its Georgian glory in 1994. The house is now a family home, but most of the furniture (ranging from horse-hair sofas to game-tables where the kill-of-the-day was displayed) is Georgian or Victorian; tours give a fabulous glimpse of the rich English lifestyle of these eras. (☎ 63513. Open daily June-Aug. 2-6pm. 1hr. tours £3, students £2.50.)

In the second week of July, the country-western tinged **Gala Festival** (☎ 62469) brings busking in the streets, soccer in the fields, and all-nighters in the pubs. The last week of July rings in the **Boyle Arts Festivals,** with a myriad of recitals, workshops, and exhibitions that leave art aficionados delirious. (☎ 64085. Tickets £2-5.)

COUNTY DONEGAL

Although its name means "fort of the foreigner," visitors are still likely to feel out of place in this most remote and least Anglicized of Ireland's "scenic" provinces. Among Ireland's counties, Donegal (DUN-ay-GAHL) is second to Cork in size and second to none in glorious wilderness. The landscape offers a sharp contrast to that of Northern Ireland and the South, replacing lush, smooth hillsides with jagged rock and bald, windy cliffs. Donegal escaped Ireland's widespread deforestation; vast wooded areas engulf many of Donegal's mountain chains, while the coastline alternates beautiful beaches with rocky drop-offs. The tallest sea-cliffs in Europe are near Slieve League. The remote Inishowen Peninsula provides excellent coastal driving and cycling. And, in between its larger pockets of civilization, distance from all things English has preserved the biggest *gaeltacht* in Ireland.

COUNTY DONEGAL

> **SESSION HOUSES** A "session house" is a Celtic tradition going back to the days of itinerant storytellers and musicians. These traveling bards would serve as one of the only sources of news for an area in olden days and were therefore held in high regard. In exchange for their services, session houses would provide the newsbearers with food to eat and a bed for the night. The session house tradition is still observed in Donegal—hence the county's reputation for truly stellar *craic* and trad.

Donegal's decent harbors and their remoteness from London made it a stronghold for Gaelic chieftains, especially the Northern Uí Néill (O'Neill), Ó Domhnaill (O'Donnell), and McSwain (McSweeney) clans, until the Flight of the Earls in 1607, when the English forcibly gained control of the region (see **Feudalism**, p. 9). After years of English occupation, during which few English actually lived in this barren "wasteland," Donegal was given to the Irish state in 1920, as its largely Catholic population would have put Northern Ireland's Protestant majority at risk. Today, cottage industries, fishing boats, and tweed factories occupy the locals' time by day, while a pure form of trad keeps them packed into the pubs at night. The tourist industry is just starting up in Donegal, but be assured that you'll encounter fewer camera-toting tourists here than anywhere else in the country.

GETTING THERE AND AROUND

Donegal has the public transportation to get you where you want to go, but only if you're willing to wait. No trains reach Donegal, and buses tend to hit smaller towns only once or twice per day, sometimes in the early morning or late at night. Some towns, including major towns like Letterkenny, Donegal Town, and Dungloe, rent bikes. Hitchers report very short waits and friendly drivers on the main roads, especially those north of Donegal Town. Byways are largely devoid of drivers. No matter what your position, *Let's Go* does not recommend hitchhiking.

When you hop on a bus, ask if **student, child,** or **senior fares** are available. **Bus Éireann** (Dublin ☎ (01) 836 6111; Letterkenny ☎ (074) 21309; Donegal ☎ (073) 21101; www.buseireann.ie) connects **Dublin** with **Letterkenny** (4hr., 5 per day) and **Donegal Town** (4¼hr., 5 per day), **Galway** with **Donegal Town** (4hr.) and **Letterkenny** (4¾hr.; M-Sa 5 per day, Su 3 per day), and some of the smaller villages in the southern half of the region. Private buses replace Bus Éireann on most of the major services in Donegal. Their prices are reasonable and their drivers more open to persuasion if you want to be let off on the doorstep of a remote hostel. The flexibility of their routes also means that the buses aren't always quite on time. **Lough Swilly Buses** (Derry ☎ (028) 7126 2017; Letterkenny ☎ (074) 22863) fan out over the northern area, connecting **Letterkenny, Derry,** the **Inishowen Peninsula,** the **Fanad Peninsula,** and western coastal villages as far south as **Dungloe. McGeehan's Bus Co.** (☎ (075) 46150) runs to and from Donegal and Dublin each day, passing through almost every intervening town (Donegal Town to Dublin 1-2 per day; route serves **Burtonport, Dungloe, Lettermacaward, Glenties, Glencolmcille, Carrick, Kilcar, Killybegs, Ardara, Ardaghey, Enniskillen,** and **Cavan**). Feda O'Donnell (☎ (075) 48114; Galway ☎ (091) 761 656; http://homepage.eircom.net/~fedaodonnell) runs up and down the Donegal coast, connecting northwest Ireland with **Galway** and **Sligo** (from **Donegal Town** via **Letterkenny** to **Dunfanaghy, Gweedore,** and **Crolly**; M-Th and Sa 2 per day, F and Su 3 per day; £10), and carries bikes for free. Bus prices on the main routes like Letterkenny-Dublin fluctuate due to competition and rising petrol prices.

BUNDORAN ☎072

At the mouth of the Dobhran River, Bundoran is the first stop in Donegal for visitors coming from Sligo or Leitrim. In 1777, Bundoran was the summer residence of Viscount Enniskillen, but it has since fallen into the hands of the masses. The resort's clear beaches, water sports, and horseback riding now attract a large crowd of vacationers from Northern Ireland. In recent years, tax break-fueled development has been rapid and haphazard—the population of the town swells from 2000 to 20,000 during the summer. The town is at least a mile long—just one long strip of gambling places, beach, and saloons, in fact. Nevertheless, it retains a pleasing beach-resort feel to it.

BALLYSHANNON ■ 359

🚍 GETTING THERE AND PRACTICAL INFORMATION. Bus Éireann (☎ 51101) leaves from the Main St. depot for **Dublin** (3 per day), **Galway** via **Sligo** (M-Sa 4 per day, Su 3 per day), and **Donegal** (7 per day). **Ulsterbus** runs to **Enniskillen** (summer M-Sa 7 per day, Su 3 per day; winter M-Sa 3 per day, Su 1 per day). **Feda O'Donnell** (☎ (075) 48356) serves **Galway** and **Letterkenny**. Heaping portions of information are available from the new **tourist office** just over the bridge on Main St. (☎ 41350. Open June M-Sa 9am-5pm, July-Aug. M-Sa 9am-8pm, Su 9am-5pm.) **AIB,** Main St., has an ATM. (Open M 10am-4:30pm, Tu-F 10am-3pm.) **Raleigh Rent-A-Bike** is on Main St. (☎ 41526. $6 per day, $30 per week. Open M-Sa 8:30am-6pm.)

🛏🍴 ACCOMMODATIONS, FOOD, AND PUBS. Every other house in Bundoran seems to be a B&B; the cheaper and quieter ones are farther down Main St., away from the bridge. **Homefield Hostel (IHH),** Bayview Ave., is off Main St.: head left up the hill between the Church of Ireland and the Bay View Guest House. One wing of the huge building connects to an Italian restaurant, while the other wing cradles a cyber-den and high-ceilinged parlor. (☎ 41288. Dorms $10; doubles $20, with bath $24.) A few steps down from the hostel is the **Bundoran Adventure Centre,** offering comfortable rooms and surf lessons. (☎ 42277. Free laundry. Curfew 3am. Twins $20-24.) **At Ceol-Na-Mwa B&B,** Tullanstrand, there's the beach out front and a horse pasture out back. Walk out Ballyshannon Rd. and turn left at the KFC to the end. (☎ 41287. Doubles $34.) **St. Edna's B&B,** West Main St., blesses visitors with impeccable rooms in a flower-draped home. (☎ 42096. Singles $21; doubles $34.)

The best restaurant in town is **La Sabbia,** a first-rate Italian bistro connected to the hostel. Cheap and impeccable food is served in a cool, cosmopolitan atmosphere. (☎ 42253. Gourmet pizzas and pasta dishes $6-7. Open M and W-Su 7-10pm.) **The Kitchen Bake,** Main St., housed in a renovated old church, serves lovely light sandwiches and lunch specials that are unique in a town of take-out. Sit upstairs for the best views. (☎ 41543. Entrees $3-5. Open M-W and F 11am-6pm, Sa 11am-6:30pm, Su 11am-7pm.) Bundoran is plum full of "saloons," but a few old-style pubs hold their ground. The **Ould Bridge Bar,** Main St., (☎ 42050) draws Bundoran's best trad players on weekends and a friendly, tipsy crowd nightly. Proof of wilder nights line the walls in the form of old Polaroids. **Brennan's,** Main St. (☎ 41810) has been in the same family for over 100 years and hasn't changed much.

📷 SIGHTS. The **Aughross Cliffs** ("headlands of the steeds") were once grazing grounds for war horses. A leisurely stroll past the Northern Hotel affords an impressive view of the mighty Atlantic waves to your left. Curious sights include the **Fairy Bridges,** the **Wishing Chair,** and the **Puffing Hole,** where water spouts up through a bed of rocks. Farther along are the golden beaches of **Tullan Strand,** a surfer's mecca. **Fitzgeralds Surfworld,** Main St. (☎ 41223), reports conditions, while **Donegal Surf Co.,** the Promenade, will rent you a wetsuit and board (☎ 41340; $6 per hr.). **The Homefield Hostel's Equestrian Centre** will have you galloping across the dunes and beaches. (☎ 41288. Open Apr.-Oct. Private lessons $15 per hr.) The annual **Bundoran Music Festival,** held over the October bank holiday weekend attracts big names in trad, show bands, and the occasional hypnotist.

BALLYSHANNON ☎072

Ballyshannon twiddles its thumbs by the River Erne, which splashes over the Falls of Assaroe (*Ess Ruaid*) just west of the bridge. The falls are one of Ireland's most ancient pagan holy sites, but there's little to see other than water and symbolism.

🚍 GETTING THERE AND PRACTICAL INFORMATION. Allingham's bridge connects the town's two halves and honors the Ballyshannon poet William Allingham who inspired Yeats to study the mythic traditions of Co. Sligo. Most of the town lies north of the river where **Main St.** splits halfway up a hill. This hill, named **Mullach na Sidh** ("hill of the fairies"), is believed to be the burial site of the legendary High King Hugh, who supposedly drowned in the Assaroe falls. Buses (☎ (074) 31008) leave the depot just beside the bridge for **Sligo** (1 hr.; M-Sa 11 per day, Su 5 per day; $5.70) and **Donegal Town** (25min.; M-Sa 10 per day, Su 3 per day; $3.40). If you need cash ASAP, the **AIB**, Castle St., has an **ATM**. (☎ 51169. Open M-W and F 10am-4pm, Th 10am-5pm.) The **post office** settles halfway up Castle St. (☎ 51111. Open M-F 9am-1pm and 2-5:30pm, Sa 9am-1pm.) **Internet access** is often a long wait at **The Engine Room** up on Market St. (☎ 52960. £2.50 per 30min. Open M-F 9am-6pm, Sa 11:30am-3:30pm.)

ACCOMMODATIONS, FOOD, AND PUBS. Duffy's Hostel (IHH) is a small bungalow-turned-hostel a five-minute walk from town on Donegal Rd. The friendly owners maintain a treasure trove second-hand bookshop out back, but the rooms are small and the toilets are a little dingy. (☎ 51535. Open Mar.-Oct. Dorms £7. Camping £4.) **Heavenly B&B** awaits you just up the stairs from Shannon's Corner Bistro at the top of Main St. Sunny, newly redecorated rooms are pristine. (☎ 51180. £16, with bath £17.) Downstairs, **Shannon's Corner Bistro** combines an airy, modern decor with seafood specialties in a crowded cafe. (Open prawn sandwich £4.25. Open M-Sa 8am-6pm.) The new **Mace Supermarket** offers loads of fruits, veggies, and supplies. (☎ 58144. Open M-Tu 8:30am-7pm, W and Sa 8:30am-7:30pm, Th-F 8:30am-8pm, and Su 9:30am-2pm.) Ten minutes down the Belleek Rd., the **Assaroe Lake Side Caravan & Camping Park** has a beautiful location and brand-new facilities. (☎ 52822. 2-person tent £8; 4- to 6-person tent £10.) **Finn McCool's**, Main St. (☎ 52677), is the most popular pub in town, reputedly with the best trad sessions in Donegal (M-Th 10pm). Get here early; the pub is tiny and Guinness bottles take up as much space as the people. **The Cellar**, Bundoran Rd. (☎ 51452), opens only on summer weekends, but great trad keeps the tourists coming.

SIGHTS. From the left fork of Main St., a left turn past the Imperial Hotel leads to **St. Anne's Church**, where William Allingham is buried with all the other Allinghams. Back by the river, a fish pass near the power station allows tourists to watch the ancient biological cycle of salmon and trout struggling upstream during spawning season, which is around June. Trying to distinguish the sun-god in salmon form is tricky (it is believed to swim past every night after dipping into the western ocean), but don't let that stop you from trying. The 12th-century **Cistercian Abbey of Assaroe** sits by the meandering river. From town, go up the left fork of Main St. past the Thatched Pub and take the second left. The Cistercians put a canal in the river, harnessing its hydraulic power for a water mill that still operates. A tiny path outside leads to the **Abbey Well**, blessed by St. Patrick. Pilgrims bless themselves with its water each year on August 15. To the right of the bridge and 120 yd. down the riverbank, a tiny cave harbors a **mass rock** used during Penal Days and two hollow stones that once held holy water. Things pick up during the first weekend in August, when the annual **Ballyshannon Music Festival** (☎ 51088) brings a mix of Irish folk and trad to town.

DONEGAL TOWN ☎073

Donegal takes its name from the Irish Dun na nGall, meaning "fortress of the foreigners." But the road sign as you enter Donegal Town reads "Gateway to North and Northwest Donegal," and that's exactly what the town should be used for. Most travelers use the town as a travel hub, taking advantage of its accommodations and bus routes to plan their wilderness excursions. Less practical reasons to spend the night here include decent trad sessions (but the ones in the county's smaller towns are often better), the peaceful setting on Donegal Bay, and the ruins of past kingdoms that still define the town's landscape.

GETTING THERE AND GETTING AROUND

Buses: Bus Éireann (☎ 21101; www.buseireann.ie) runs to **Sligo** (1hr.; M-Sa 7 per day, Su 3 per day), **Dublin** (4hr., 5 per day, £12) via **Ballyshannon** (25min., £4), and **Galway** (4hr.; M-Sa 5 per day, Su 3 per day; £10). **McGeehan Coaches** (☎ (075) 46150) go to **Dublin** via **Enniskillen** and **Cavan**; they also drive to **Killybegs, Ardara,**

DONEGAL TOWN ■ 361

Glenties, Glencolmcille, and **Dungloe** (2 per day). Both Bus Éireann and McGeehan stop outside the Abbey Hotel on The Diamond; timetables are posted in the lobby. **Feda O'Donnell** (☎ (075) 48114) leaves for **Galway** from the tourist office (M-Sa 9:45am and 5:15pm, additional times F and Su) and also goes to **Dunfanaghy** via **Crolly** and **Gweedore.**

Taxis: Rockhill Cabs (☎ (087) 248 6055), **Sean Quinn** (☎ 21507), or **Tems Cabs** (☎ 35119).

Bike Rental: The Bike Shop, Waterloo Pl. (☎ 22515), the 1st left off Killybegs Rd. from The Diamond. £7 per day, £45 per week; deposit £30; panniers £1 per day, £5 per week. Trip-planning advice. Locks, repair equipment included. Open M-Sa 10am-6pm.

ORIENTATION AND PRACTICAL INFORMATION

The center of town is **The Diamond,** a triangle bordered by Donegal's main shopping streets. At the top of the hill lies **Main Street,** which leads to **Killybegs Rd.**

Tourist Office: Quay St. (☎ 21148; www.donegaltown.ie). With your back facing the Abbey Hotel, turn right; the tourist office is just outside of The Diamond on Sligo Rd. Brochures galore on Co. Donegal, reservations for accommodations throughout the Republic, information on the North, and a free town map. One of a few tourist offices in the county; it's a wise stop before heading north. Open July-Aug. M-Sa 9am-8pm, Su 10am-4pm; Sept.-Oct. and Easter-June M-F 9am-5pm, Sa 10am-2pm.

Banks: AIB (☎ 21016), **Bank of Ireland** (☎ 21079), and **Ulster Bank** (☎ 21064) all on The Diamond. All open M-W and F 10am-4pm, Th 10am-5pm; all have **24hr. ATMs.**

Laundry: Derma's Launderette & Dry Cleaning, Mill Ct., The Diamond (☎ 22255). Wash and dry £6.50; powder 50p. Open M-Sa 9am-7pm.

Pharmacy: Begley's Chemist, The Diamond (☎ 21232). Open M-Sa 9:15am-6pm.

Emergency: ☎ 999; no coins required. **Police** (*Garda*): ☎ 21021.

Hospital: Donegal Hospital, Main St. (☎ 21074).

Post Office: Tirconaill St. (☎ 21007), past Donegal Castle and over the bridge. Open M-F 9am-1pm and 2-5:30pm, Sa 9am-1pm.

Internet Access: A cyber-cafe sits on the 2nd floor of **The Blueberry Tea Room** (see **Food,** below). £5 per hr., £3 for 15-30min. Open M-Sa 11am-11pm.

ACCOMMODATIONS

The Cliffview Hostel (and attached B&B) have agreed to house refugees and asylum-seekers for the next year, squeezing Donegal's already-cramped market for budget accommodation. Other hostels in the county may also be closing to the public; calling ahead is imperative, especially during the high season. The tourist office will provide you with a list of a plethora of Donegal Town B&B options.

Donegal Town Independent Hostel (IHH, IHO; ☎ 22805), ½ mi. out on Killybegs Rd. This family-run hostel makes siblings out of road-weary backpackers. Bright rooms, some with murals. Owners will pick up travelers in town if the hostel isn't too busy. Very popular and rather small, so make reservations. Separate showers for campers. Laundry £4. Dorms June-Aug. £7.50, Oct.-May £7; doubles £18. **Camping** £4 per person.

Ball Hill Youth Hostel (An Óige/HI; ☎/fax 21174), 3 mi. from town. Go 1½ mi. out of Donegal on the Killybegs Rd., turn left at the sign, and continue 1½ mi. toward the sea. Buses leaving from the Abbey Hotel (£1) often go as far as Killybegs Rd. Guests will be welcomed with a tour of the building and various semi-comic "shrines" surrounding it. The hostel's array of activities include horseback riding, swimming, day hikes, boat trips, bonfires with sing-songs, and relaxation with owners Kevin and Áine in the "uncommon" room. June-Aug. £7.50, Sept.-May £5; youth discounts.

Atlantic Guest House, Main St. (☎ 21187). Unbeatable location. Despite being on a busy street, this 16-room guest house offers the undisturbed privacy of a fancy hotel. Each room has plush carpets, TV, telephone, and sink. Singles £15, with bath £20.

FOOD

A good selection of cafes and take-aways occupy The Diamond and the streets nearby. For groceries, head to the **Supervalu**, minutes from The Diamond down Sligo Rd. (☎ 22977. Open M-W and Sa 9am-7pm, Th-F 9am-9pm.) **Simple Simon's**, The Diamond, sells fresh baked goods, local cheeses, and homeopathic remedies for the organic farmer in you. (☎ 22687. Open M-Sa 9am-6pm.)

Sam's Deli-Bar, Main St. (☎ 23174). The rare spot where you can just relax with a cup of tea and read the paper for hours. A colorful interior and abundance of baked goods. Big sandwiches around £2; entrees £4. Open July-Aug. M-Sa 9am-6pm, Sept.-June 9am-5:30pm.

The Blueberry Tea Room, Castle St. (☎ 22933), on the corner of The Diamond that leads to Killybegs Rd. Justifiably popular, with white porcelain geese and teapots. Sandwiches, daily specials, and all-day breakfast. Entrees around £5. Open M-Sa 9am-7pm. Houses a cyber-cafe upstairs (see **Practical Information,** above).

The Harbour Restaurant, Quay St. (☎ 21702), across from the tourist office. A family restaurant with a menu ranging from pizza (£4-8) to veggie lasagna (£5.25) to steaks (£10). Open M-Th 4-10:30pm, F-Su 11am-10:30pm.

The Coffee House and Deli Bar, The Diamond (☎ 21014), next to the Abbey Hotel. Try a sandwich (£2-2.50) or a satisfying 2-course "Plate of the Day" including veggies and potatoes (£5) in a homey atmosphere. Open June-Aug. 9am-7pm, Sept.-May 9am-6pm.

Donegal's Famous Chipper, Main St. (☎ 21428). The quintessential take-away. Any guesses on what's served here? Around £3.10 for the day's catch, plus any type of potatoes you want (as long as it's chips). Open daily 12:30-11:30pm.

PUBS AND CLUBS

Donegal puts on a good show at night, especially in the summertime. Almost every bar has live music on weekends, and many pubs host national acts during the Donegal Summer Festival in early July (see **Sights**).

The Schooner Bar and B&B, Upper Main St. (☎ 21671). The best trad and contemporary sessions in town happen here weekends. A great mix of hostelers and locals in a James Joyce Award-winning pub.

McGroarty's, The Diamond (☎ 21049), packs in the young and the young at heart for live bands on weekends. No cover.

The Coach House, Upper Main St. (☎ 22855). Spontaneous sing-alongs are known to break out at any point during the day in this wooden-beamed locals' hangout. Downstairs, the **Cellar Bar** opens its doors nightly at 9:30pm for trad and ballads. Confident musicians and singers are invited to join in. Cover £1.

The Voyage Bar, The Diamond (☎ 21201). This pub keeps its patrons happy, but ask the jovial proprietor about its name and a tear glints in his eye. "Everyone has a voyage to make in life." Live music on weekends.

Baby Joe's, Main St. (☎ 22322). Recently changed hands, name, and style. Lots of wrought iron and electric blue, and equally funky crowd. Live bands often on weekends.

Charlie's Star Bar, Main St. (☎ 21158), sparkles for young crowds with live rock, country, and blues. Music Th-Su in summer, F-Su in winter.

The Olde Castle Bar and Restaurant, Castle St. (☎ 21062). Old stone walls and corbel windows for that recently renovated medieval feel. An older crowd and excellent Guinness. Open in summer until 11:30pm, in winter until 11pm.

SIGHTS

During the daylight hours, tourists head to various ruins around town; most date from the 15th to 17th centuries.

> **STATION ISLAND.** Donegal's **Lough Derg** encircles **Station Island,** one of Ireland's most important pilgrimage sites. The Island witnesses a religious ordeal every summer, the subject of Seamus Heaney's long poem by the same name. The pilgrimage, which can be made in June or July, involves three days of fasting and circling the island barefoot. Fasting pilgrims may eat **Lough Derg soup,** an island delicacy of boiled water flavored with salt and pepper. Some scowl at a recent addition to the pilgrim's calendar—a special one-day retreat to the island that some pilgrims think is too easy as it does not require fasting or walking barefoot. Those hoping to descend should bring nothing but warm clothing and a repentant heart. For information, contact the Prior of St. Patrick's Purgatory (☎ (072) 61518; email lochderg@iol.ie).

DONEGAL CASTLE. Originally the seat of several chieftains, Irish-English conflicts tore Donegal apart in the 17th century. Evidence of this turmoil remains at Donegal Castle, the former residence of the O'Donnell clan, and, later, various English nobles. The recently refurbished ruins of the O'Donnell clan's castle of 1474 stand adjacent to the manor built by English rulers in 1623. Some of the refurbished rooms include displays detailing the history of the castle and the genealogy of the O'Donnells. *(Castle St.* ☎ *22405. Open Apr.-Sept. daily 9:30am-5:45pm. Guided tours on the hour. £3, seniors £2, students and children £1.25.)*

OLD ABBEY. The stones and doorways of the grand manor of Donegal Castle were taken from the ruins of the 15th-century Franciscan Friary, known as the Old Abbey, just a short walk from the tourist office along the south of town. The remains of the abbey—stairways and wall fragments—mingle with gravestones, evidence of the site's later incarnation as a cemetery. It was destroyed in 1601 when its gunpowder stores went off. Four of the disenfranchised monks went on to write the *Annals of the Four Masters,* the first narrative history of Ireland and the source of many extant myths. An **obelisk** built on The Diamond in 1937 pays homage to the four holy men, as does **St. Patrick's Church of the Four Masters,** a stolid Irish Romanesque church about a half mile up Main St. *(St. Patrick's open M-F 9am-5pm. Free.)*

DONEGAL CRAFT VILLAGE. Six craftspeople open their workshops to the public. The work of a potter, a batik artist, a jeweler, an *uilleann* pipe maker, a sculptor, and an ironsmith make great gift alternatives to the mass-produced leprechauns sold in stores. *(About a mile south of Donegal Town on Sligo Rd.* ☎ *22015. Open July-Aug. M-Sa 10am-6pm, Su noon-6pm; Sept.-June M-Sa 10am-6pm.)*

RAILWAY CENTRE. The Donegal Railway Heritage Centre features a few old train cars, an informative video on narrow-gauge railways, and a handmade model of Donegal's former rail system that took 40 years to build. If you're a railroad buff, it's worth a visit. *(A block past the post office on Tirconaill St.* ☎ *22655. Open June-Sept. M-Sa 9am-5:30pm and Su 2-5pm; Oct.-May M-F 10am-5pm. £1.50, students and children 75p.)*

FESTIVALS. The **Donegal Summer Festival,** held on the first weekend of July, brings to town such diverse activities as craft and antiques fairs, air-sea rescue display, clay-pigeon shoots, and the Bonny Baby show, as well as plenty of live bands and trad sessions. To join in on the three-day party, be sure to call ahead for a room, as the town doubles in size for the weekend.

DAYTRIP FROM DONEGAL TOWN

LOUGH ESKE
To go and return from the lough is an easy two-hour hike. Follow signs for "Harvey's Point" (marked from Killybegs Rd.). After about 3 mi. you will come to a stone building on your right with a gate and single stone pillar. Take a left after the gate to reach the Lough Eske Castle. If driving, follow signs from Mountcharles Rd. to Lough Eske and make a 15 mi. loop around the lake.

The most worthwhile of Donegal Town's sights actually lies a few miles outside of town at Lough Eske ("fish lake"), an idyllic pond set among a fringe of trees and ruins. The crumbling majesty of **Lough Eske Castle,** built in 1861, lies at the lough's side. Its slightly overgrown grounds and the seriously decrepit buildings provide a gorgeous site for a picnic or an afternoon ramble. Continue following the Lough Eske road and take the first path on your left after the castle to find a **Celtic high cross** (see **Early Christians and Vikings,** p. 8) surrounded by breathtaking gardens, which contain the burial site of the castle's former master.

SLIEVE LEAGUE PENINSULA ☎073

West of Donegal Town lies the Slieve League Peninsula, a jut of land that displays some of the most stunning scenery in Ireland. Its rugged, wild appearance shows little evidence of human habitation. The few villages on the peninsula all lie along busy N56, which leads from Donegal Town and turns into R63 as it approaches the peninsula's western tip. A good plan is to spend several days working your way up N56 on the way to Glencolmcille. Each bend in the road brings more views of windy fields of heather, lonely thatched cottages, and dramatic coastline. Ardara or Glenties make pleasant stops on the inland route back. Though most easily covered by car, the peninsula is a spectacular opportunity for cycling (expect to walk your bike on frequent, serious hills). Only a few buses go by the hostels on N56.

THE EASTERN PENINSULA

A handful of single-street villages lie along the coast road to the west of Donegal Town. Cyclists enjoy rewarding views and endure hilly terrain. Three miles down the road is the small town of **Mountcharles.** In July and August, there is a Saturday market at **The Tannery** on the coast road to Killybegs, featuring a craft shop with locally knit goods and a tea room. (☎ 35675. Open Mar.-Oct. daily 10am-6pm.) About 10 mi. past Mountcharles is tiny **Dunkineely,** surrounded by megalithic tombs, holy wells, and small streams; all are accessible by walks of 4 mi. or less round-trip. For information on these walks, continue another 1½ mi. to, or have the bus drop you in, the town of **Bruckless,** where **Gallagher's Farm Hostel (IHH)** sits about a quarter mile off the main road. Mr. Gallagher has turned his 17th-century barn into a wonderfully clean, well-outfitted hostel in the midst of pastoral farmscapes. Two kitchens (and a third for campers), a huge fireplace, and a ping-pong table may make your stay longer than expected. (☎ 37057. Laundry £3. **Bike rental** £6 per day. Dorms £8. **Camping** in a well-kept 3-acre field £4.50.) Between the hostel and Dunkineely, a turn-off leads to **St. John's Point,** which has fantastic views across the Sligo coastline.

KILLYBEGS

In Killybegs, you can gaze upon boats bobbing in the water, enjoy some of the day's catch over a pint at one of the late-licensed pubs, and savor the delicate aroma of fish wafting in the air at all times. The residents of Killybegs work hard and play hard: because of late licenses, last call isn't until 1am (which means no one leaves until 2am). Whether or not you've come to Co. Donegal to hear fiddling, a stop at the **Sail Inn,** at the far end of Main St. from the pier, is a must. It's renowned for serving above-average pub grub (2-course lunch specials £4). Renowned musicians are likely to turn up for frequent sessions. **The Harbour Bar** (☎ 31049), across from the pier, is notorious for its jolly late hours. **The Pier Bar,** on the other side of the car park, is where fishermen-maties hang out and consume pub grub during the day. (☎ 31045. Entrees £5, sandwiches under £3.) **Hughie's Bar,** a "small-world feel and a big-time bar" on the northern end of Main St., hops with impromptu music sessions most nights and a weekend disco. (☎ 31095. Open until 2am. Disco cover £3.)

The **Bus Éireann** (☎ 21101; www.buseireann.ie) route from **Donegal Town** to **Glencolmcille** stops in Killybegs and Kilcar (3 per day). **McGeehan Coaches** (☎ (075) 46150) also has service (at least 2 per day) to **Donegal Town** and **Dublin** from Dungloe, **Ardara, Glenties, Glencolmcille,** and several other towns on the peninsula. Killybegs has the only **banks** and **pharmacies** in the area. **Ulsterbank** is on the southern end of Main St. (Open M-W and F 10am-4pm, Th 10am-5pm.) **Bank of Ireland** is at the Kilcar end of town; their **ATM** accepts the widest range of foreign bank cards. (Open M-W and F 10am-4pm, Th 10am-5pm.) **McGee's Pharmacy,** Main St., sells a full cargo of medicines and toiletries. (☎ 31009. Open M-Sa 9:30am-6pm.) The **post office** sorts mail on Main St. (☎ 31060. Open M-F 9am-1pm and 2-5:30pm, Sa 9am-1pm.) If you tire of Killybegs' pub fare, **Kitty Kelly's,** halfway between Killybegs and Kilcar, has incredible seafood dishes (cajun mackerel £9.50) and innovative Italian fare. (☎ 31925. Open nightly 5-9:30pm.) For those staying overnight, Mrs. Tully puts up guests in her B&B, **Tullycullion House,** 1 mi. south off N56 (look for the boat-shaped signs), which has panoramic views of Killybegs Harbour and comfortable rooms. Unlike the area's myriad other B&Bs, Tullycullion has pet donkeys. (☎ 31842. £19 per person.)

KILCAR (CILL CHARTHAIGH)

A breathtaking 8 mi. past Killybegs along N56 is tiny Kilcar, the gateway to Donegal's *gaeltacht* and a commercial base for many Donegal tweed weavers. Many tweed sellers set up shop along Kilcar's main street, which is also the coast road that leads down to Killybegs, and up to Carrick in the direction of both of Kilcar's superlative budget accommodations.

GETTING THERE. The **Bus Éireann** (☎ 21101; www.buseireann.ie) route from **Donegal Town** to **Glencolmcille** stops in Killybegs and Kilcar (daily 3 per day). **McGeehan Coaches** (☎ (075) 46150) also has service (at least 2 per day) to **Donegal Town** and **Dublin** from **Dungloe, Ardara, Glenties, Glencolmcille,** and several other towns on the peninsula.

ACCOMMODATIONS. A 1½ mi. drive out on the coast road from Kilcar to Carrick and five minutes from the beach, Shaun at the ✦**Derrylahan Hostel (IHH)** welcomes guests like long-lost cousins—don't even think about refusing the initial cup of tea. This 200-year-old former church doubles as both a hostel and a working farm. The grocery shop stays well stocked. Call for pick-up from Kilcar or Carrick. Buses pass daily on the way to Killybegs and Glencolmcille. Calling ahead to book a bed in July and August is a good idea, but coming in the spring during lambing season is an even better one. (☎ 38079; email derrylahan@eircom.ie. Laundry £5. Dorms £7; private rooms £10. **Camping** £4, with separate showers and kitchen.) On the way to Derrylahan, just under 1 mi. from Kilcar, ✦**Dún Ulún House** is a luxurious alternative to hostel life at virtually the same price. Flowery beds, hardwood floors, and gorgeous views in the multi-bed rooms are turned into small dorms, if you're willing to share. Guests also have the option of self-catering (well-outfitted kitchen provided). The family leads walking tours of the Kilcar Way, plays occasional trad sessions, and will help you trace your Irish roots in the Slieve League Peninsula area. (☎ 38137. Laundry £5. Rooms with 3 or more beds £9.50 per person; doubles £25; B&B prices £16-20 per person. All with bath. Rooms in cottage across road £5 per person, with linens £6.50. **Camping** £3, with separate facilities.)

FOOD AND PUBS. Spar Market on Main St. sells groceries and fishing tackle. (Open M-Sa 9am-10pm, Su 9:30am-1pm and 7-10pm.) **The Rendezvous Coffee Shop,** fronted by a convenience store, serves sandwiches (£1.80) and lasagna for £4.50. (☎ 38344. Open M-Sa 10am-4pm.) Kilcar's best meal by far is at **Teach Barnai,** Main St. Ann and Michael Carr's restaurant has a rustic feel, and serves fare from lamb to *colcannon,* a traditional Irish vegetarian dish. (☎ 38160 or 38344. Entrees £8-13. Open nightly 6-10pm.) Just down the street, **John Joe's** (☎ 38015) hosts trad nightly. For pub life, the **Piper's Rest Pub & Restaurant,** Main St. has recently changed hands, stripping the stone walls of their musical instruments, so the *craic* has yet to be established. Expect a mixture of young and old folk inside. (☎ 38205. Soup and sandwich £3.80. Food served daily 11:30am-6pm.)

■ **SIGHTS. Studio Donegal** sells handwoven tweeds fresh off the loom. Visitors are invited to watch the cloth being woven, the yarn being spun, and the jackets being sewn. (☎ 38194. Watch for free. Open year-round M-F 9am-5:30pm, June-Sept. also Sa 9:30am-5pm.) Other companies' factory shops dot the streets. Still in the same building, on the same floor as Studio Donegal, is **Áistan Cill Cartha** (ASH-lahn kill KAR-ha). This community organization provides genealogical information, compendiums of residents' oral histories, and local history collections. By September 2000, they should have opened a **heritage center,** complete with craft shop, language classes, exhibitions, and computerized databases. (Open M-F 9am-4:30pm.) Locals (like your hostel or B&B proprietor) can give you directions to the prehistoric and natural wonders that surround Kilcar, including Megalithic tombs, old graveyards, and a Spanish church. If you're interested in **deep-sea fishing,** a local can also direct you to a boat; or, call Jim (☎ 38224). Kilcar's **International Sea Angling Festival** takes place the first weekend in August. (Contact Seamus McHugh, ☎ 38337.) It's directly followed by the **Kilcar Street Festival,** a week of sports competitions, music, dance, and tomfoolery. (Contact Kevin Lyons, ☎ 38433.)

CARRICK, TEELIN, AND SLIEVE LEAGUE MOUNTAIN

Slieve League claims the hotly contested title (in Ireland) of having the highest sea cliffs in Europe. Undoubtedly, the sheer face of its 2000 ft. drop into the Atlantic is spectacular. Most Slieve League hikers stay in Kilcar or Glencolmcille, from which they can comfortably drive, bike, or walk (about 6hr. return) to the mountain. From Kilcar, the coast road passes the tiny village of **Carrick.** For most of the year Carrick is but a brief stopping point for travelers seeking refreshment. The village scene is transformed during the last bank holiday weekend in October, when Carrick hosts the annual **Carrick Fleadh,** with barrels of creamy, foaming refreshment accompanied by trad. **Fishing** is rewarding around Teelin Bay, particularly in an area called **Salmon Leap.** (Remember that salmon fishing is illegal without a license.) The **Glen River** is best for trout. Tackle can be bought at the Spar Market in Kilcar. If you'd rather let someone else do the cooking, **Bialann na Sean Scoile** serves mountainous, reasonable portions in a diner resembling a high school gym. (The restaurant's name alone is a mouthful; just ask a local to point you in the right direction. ☎ 39477. Open daily 9am-10pm.) The Carrick area also offers several practical amenities for the local explorer. **Little Acorn Farm,** located off the main Kilcar-Carrick road approximately 1 mi. before Carrick, offers **horses** for guided trail rides for beginners to experienced riders. (☎ 39386; www.irish-marine.com/littleacorn. About £12 per hr.) About 1 mi. past Carrick is the even smaller village of **Teelin,** where Mrs. Maloney at **Teelin Bay House,** the third B&B on the road to Teelin, is famous for the care she bestows upon her guests. It's a bit of a hike, but the view just keeps getting better. Book ahead. (☎ 39043. Singles £15; doubles £26.)

In clear weather it'd be unconscionable *not* to visit **Slieve League,** a mountain set along a precipitous, beautiful coastline rimmed with 1000 ft. cliffs. To reach the mountain, turn left halfway down Carrick's main street and follow signs for Teelin. At the **Rusty Mackerel Pub** (☎ 39101), you can turn left for the inland route to Slieve League. Alternatively, a turn to the right (the most popular decision) leads along the sea cliffs on the way up to Bunglass. At the end of the road at Bunglass sits a carpark. From here, a cliff path heads west along the coast. It should take 1½ hours to walk from Carrick to the car park. About a half-hour along the path continuing from the car park, the mountain top narrows to 2 ft. On one side of this pass—called **One Man's Pass**—the cliffs drop 1800 ft. to the sea. On the other side, the cliffs drop a measly 1000 ft. to a rocky floor. There are no railings, and the phobic sometimes slide across the 30m pass on their behinds or hands and knees. The path then continues all the way along the cliffs to **Rossarrel Point,** near Glencolmcille. The entire Slieve League Way usually takes six to seven hours to walk. **Never go to Slieve League in poor weather.** Use extreme caution if you plan to cross the pass; it is not a necessary part of the hike across Slieve League. (You can still enjoy a steep climb by walking along the inland face of the mountain.) People have died here under poor conditions; several hikers have been blown off the pass by the strong winds. It's always a good idea to ask a local expert for advice. In non-ideal weather, the cliffs at Bunglass are a safer option.

GLENCOLMCILLE (GLEANN CHOLM CILLE)

The parish on the western top of the Slieve League peninsula, Glencolmcille (glen-kaul-um-KEEL), is the base of several tiny towns and huge natural wonders; its land consists of rolling hills and sandy coves that lie between two huge sea cliffs. Named after St. Columcille, who founded a monastery here, this Irish-speaking area and pilgrimage site centers around the street-long village of Cashel, which lies just off N56 on, unsurprisingly, Cashel St. The road leads past the village's several storefronts and down to the coast, where most of the area's accommodations and attractions are located. Buses of tourists head for the Folk Village (see **Sights**), but few venture beyond it to desolate, wind-battered cliffs. Though less dramatic than the mountain paths, N56 is the convenient route to most of Glencolmcille.

GETTING THERE AND PRACTICAL INFORMATION. McGeehan's buses leave from Biddy's Bar for **Carrick, Kilcar, Killybegs, Ardara, Glenties, Fintown,** and **Letterkenny** once a day, twice from July to mid-September. **Bus Éireann** (☎ 21101; www.buseireann.ie) leaves from the village corner to **Donegal Town,** stopping in Killybegs and Kilcar (3 per day). Glencolmcille's tiny **tourist office** is on Cashel St. (☎ 30116. Open July-Aug. M-Sa 9:30am-9pm, Su noon-6pm; Apr.-June and Sept. to mid-Nov. M-Sa 10am-6pm, Su 1-5pm.) A **bureau de change** can be found at the Folk Village and the **post office,** east of the village center. (Open M-F 7:30am-1pm and 2-5:30pm, Sa 9am-1pm.) The nearest banks and **ATMs** are in Killybegs and Ardara.

ACCOMMODATIONS, FOOD, AND PUBS. A trip to Donegal wouldn't be complete without a visit to Mary and her "favorite" son, Leo, at the ☒**Dooey Hostel (IHO),** the oldest independent hostel in Ireland. To get there, turn left at the end of the village and follow the signs uphill (¾ mi.). It's a hike, but the view is spectacular, and the hostel follows suit; it's built into the hillside overlooking the sea, and a wide spectrum of flowers grows out of the rocky face that is the hostel's corridor. The colorfulness of this atrium is matched only by that of its owners' personalities. (☎ 30130; fax 30339. Wheelchair accessible. Campers share hostelers' facilities. Dorms £7; doubles £14. **Camping** £4.) Mrs. Ann Ward's **Atlantic Scene,** the next house after the hostel, lives up to its name. The beds are soft, but you'll stay up just to admire the view longer. Brilliant breakfasts. (☎ 30186. Open May-Sept. £15 per person.) More B&Bs surround the Folk Village (see **Sights,** below).

The **Lace House Restaurant,** above the tourist office on Cashel St., is a chipper with a large menu of fried foods and small windows to admire the sea cliffs. (☎ 30444. Entrees £4-9. Open daily 9:30am-10pm.) **An Chistan** (AHN KEESHT-ahn, "the kitchen"), at the Foras Cultúir Uladh (see **Sights**), is especially affordable at lunch. (☎ 30213. Entrees £5-12. Open July-Aug. 9am-9:30pm, Sept.-June 11am-9:30pm.) The **teashop** in the Folk Village tempts with delicious sandwiches (£1.50) and Guinness cake (80p). **Byrne and Sons Food Store,** Cashel St., supplies the basics in solids, liquids, and printed matter. (Open M-Sa 9:30am-10pm, Su 9:30am-1pm and 7-9pm.) Cashel's pubs have a dark, dusty 1950s Ireland feel to them: imagine spare rooms with plastic-covered snugs and, for once, a minimal amount of wood paneling. Although the pubs are primarily a haven for locals, they develop an affinity for visitors during July and August. Most famous among them is the unassuming 120-year-old **Biddy's,** at the mouth of Carrick Rd. Since it's the favorite of the older crowd, you'll meet lots of Irish speakers. (☎ 30016. Trad at least 3 times a week during the summer.) **Roarty's** (☎ 30273), the next pub down Cashel St., welcomes guests with trad several times a week. Last on the road is **Glen Head Tavern** (☎ 30008), the largest and youngest of the three pubs. Practically the whole village could fit into its recently re-done lounge, which hosts legendary trad sessions.

SIGHTS. Glencolmcille's craft movement began in the 1950s under the direction of the omnipresent **Father James McDyer,** who was also responsible for getting electricity in Glencolmcille, founding the Folk Village, and building the local football field. Today, the town is renowned for its handmade products, particularly

> **ALONE IN THE HUSK OF MAN'S HOME** Many a poetic, brooding type has felt compelled to isolate him or herself in the far reaches of Co. Donegal. The valley next to Port has provided refuge to poet Dylan Thomas, as well as artist Rockwell Kent. Only two cottages stand in this valley, and no roads touch it. Dylan Thomas' self-imposed isolation was meant to cleanse the alcohol from his system, although the area's *poitín* smuggling foiled that plan. The locals are sure to break out into grins if you ask them about Rockwell Kent, who supposedly came to Port to hide from the American CIA, and never left his cottage after dark.

sweaters, which are on sale at numerous "jumper shops" on the roads surrounding the town. Close to town is the **Foras Cultúir Uladh** (FOHR-us KULT-er UH-lah; "The Ulster Cultural Institute"), which runs the Oideas Gael institute for the preservation of the Irish language and culture. The Foras offers regular courses on such varied pursuits as hill walking, painting, pottery, local archaeology, traditional music, and Gaelic. It also has frequently changing exhibitions on local history and concerts and performances on a regular basis. (☎ 30248. Open daily 9am-6pm.)

A bit past the village center is Father McDyer's **Folk Village Museum and Heritage Centre,** the town's attraction for non-hiking, non-Irish speaking tourists. The museum is housed in stone cottages with immaculately thatched roofs, which date from 1700, 1850, and 1900. The 1850s schoolhouse is open to the general public. The guided tours describe the furniture and tools from each of these eras in Irish history. A short nature trail from the village leads up a hill past various reconstructed remains, including a Mass rock, a sweat house, and a lime kiln. The **craft shop** stocks a good assortment of sweaters, books, and postcards and is possibly the only place in the world where you can buy rosary beads made from seaweed. The **sheebeen** (the old name for an illegal drinking establishment) sells homemade heather, fuchsia, and seaweed wines (free samples with tour) and whiskey marmalade. (☎ 30017. Open Easter-Sept. M-Sa 10am-6pm, Su noon-6pm. Tours July-Aug. every 30min., Apr.-June and Sept. every hr. £2; students, seniors, and children £1.25.) The beginning of July brings the two-day **Glencolmcille Folk Festival,** a lively and occasionally raucous celebration.

Fine beaches and cliffs make for excellent hiking in all directions. A 5 mi. walk southwest from Cashel leads to **Malinbeg,** a winsome hamlet at the edge of a sandy cove. This coastal area was once notorious for smuggling *poitín* through tunnels, some of which may still be in use. When a sunny day happens to grace Donegal, a trip to the **Silver Strand** will be well rewarded with stunning views of the gorgeous beach and surrounding rocky cliffs. From the strand, you can start the long-distance trek along the Slieve League coastline (see **Carrick, Teelin, and Slieve League,** p. 366). A sandy beach links the cliffs on the south and north sides of Glencolmcille. North of Glencolmcille, **Glen Head,** easily identifiable by the Martello tower at its peak, is an hour's walk from town through land laden with prehistoric ruins, including St. Colmcille's stations of the cross. The tourist office and hostel in town each have a map that shows the locations of major sites. A third walk from town begins at the Protestant church and climbs over a hill to the ruins of the ghostly "famine village" of **Port** in the valley on the other side (3hr. walk). Supposedly haunted by crying babies, this eerie village has been empty since its inhabitants emigrated during the Famine. The only current resident, according to local rumor, is an eccentric artist who lives by the isolated bay without electricity or water. The gargantuan **phallic rock** sticking out of the sea is just what it appears to be: the only part of the Devil still visible after St. Colmcille banished him into the ocean.

The road east from Glencolmcille to Ardara passes through the spectacular **Glengesh Pass.** Nine hundred feet above sea level, the road tackles the surrounding mountains with hairpin turns. Biking is common in these parts, but be warned that the steep and winding pass offers a challenging ride suitable to only the most intrepid cyclists. Hitching is a tough task along this unfrequented road, and *Let's Go* does not recommend hitchhiking.

ARDARA
☎ 075

The historic center of the Donegal tweed industry, Ardara (ar-DRAH) now attracts tweed-fiends with high credit limits. Ardara is one of the cheapest sources of locally knit and woven articles, but better deals can often be found at small "craft centres" in surrounding villages. Today, Ardara's Heritage Centre plays an important role in the movement to revive traditional hand-weaving techniques, silver-smithing, and a local arts consciousness. On the first weekend of June during the **Weavers' Fair,** weavers from all over Donegal congregate in Ardara to show their weft; musicians add further festivity to the weekend. For the less consumer-oriented, Ardara is a wonderful place to escape the congestion of Donegal Town, taking in the truly spectacular scenery along the Maghera Caves Rd.

GETTING THERE AND PRACTICAL INFORMATION. Bus Éireann (☎ 21101; www.buseireann.ie) stops in Ardara on its **Donegal-Dungloe** route (2 per day, via **Killybegs** and **Glenties**) in front of O'Donnell's. There is a **Spar market** on Main St. (☎ 41107. Open M-F 8:30am-8pm, Sa 8:30am-9pm, Su 8:30am-1pm.) **McGeehan's** (☎ 46150) halts on The Diamond at least twice a day in the summer as part of its **Dublin-Donegal Town-Dungloe** trip. The **Ardara Heritage Centre** has tourist information. (☎ 41704. Open Jan.-Nov. daily 9:30am-6pm.) **Ulster Bank,** The Diamond (☎ 41121) has a **24-hour ATM. Rent bikes** at **Don Byrne's,** past town on Killybegs Rd. (☎ 41156. Open M-W and F 10am-12:30pm and 1:30-4pm, Th 10am-12:30pm and 1:30-5pm.) The **Ardara Medical Hall,** Front St., next to the Heritage Centre, is just a **pharmacy.** (Open M-Sa 9am-1pm and 2-6pm.) The **post office** is opposite the Heritage Centre. (☎ 41101. Open M-F 9am-1pm and 2-5:30pm, Sa 9am-1pm.)

ACCOMMODATIONS. Ardara is one place where exceptional B&Bs make it not worth saving money at a hostel. One mile outside of town lies **The Green Gate (An Geata Glás),** simply one of the most idyllic places to stay in Ireland. Take the Donegal Rd. from town, turn right at the fork after 200m, and just keep going; or, call for a pickup in a 1950 Citroën. This little place is run by Paul Chatenoud, a Frenchman who traded his musical bookshop and apartment overlooking Notre Dame for a group of 200-year-old traditional cottages up a mountain (restored with his own hands, originally for the purpose of writing a book about "love, life, and death"). But The Green Gate offers more than just spectacular views of Donegal—you'll find Corsican lamp shades, a library complete with the works of Freud and Proust, hand-painted records of French operas, and breakfasts with homemade jams served in his own kitchen at any time of the day. You may end up staying a week. (£20. Book in advance.) If this is full, try the **Hollybrook B&B,** on Killybegs Rd. near the outskirts of town. The rooms are sunny and immaculate, but the owner's family is what makes this place special. Peter Oliver used to run Ardara's Central Bar, and his daughters have won national prizes in Irish step-dancing; one of them currently stars in Dublin's production of Riverdance. (☎ 41596. £17 per person.) The **Drumbarron Hostel (IHO)** offers clean, sunny rooms directly on The Diamond. Travelers can get keys at the house across the street from the hostel's side entrance. (☎ 41200. Dorms £7; doubles £16. Flexible curfew 1am.)

FOOD AND PUBS. L'Atlantique Restaurant, below Triona Design on Main St., serves some of the best French seafood you'll ever taste, in a relaxed dining room. Lobster is their speciality. Entrees are dear for budget travelers (£9-17), but you'd pay £70 for the same meal in Paris; the 4-course prix fixe menu is a great deal at £12.90. (☎ 41707. Open nightly 6:30-9:30pm. Reservations recommended.) On Main St., the **Nesbitt Arms Hotel** (☎ 41103) serves excellent, reasonable pub grub (£3-6, until 9pm), and the attached restaurant has snazzier fare. **Charlie's West End Cafe** lacks the trendy atmosphere its name suggests, but the service is quick and the prices are low—probably because Charlie's is frequented primarily by locals. (☎ 41656. Enormous lunch specials £3.75, sandwiches £1.50. Open M-Sa 10am-10:30pm, Su 2-10:30pm.) There are 13 pubs total in Ardara. Decked out in bright copper kettles and warm woolen mittens, **Nancy's Bar**, Front St., just might become one of your favorite things. Come for the seafood or the weekend trad sessions. (Steamed mussels £4.) **Central Bar**, Main St. (☎ 41311), has trad every single night June through September. Arrive early for breathing space. For a quieter pint, head two doors down to the **Corner Bar** (☎ 41726). It rumbles with trad twice a week.

SIGHTS. The **Ardara Heritage Centre**, The Diamond, tells the story of the centuries-old Donegal tweed industry and has also become somewhat of a craft village. Live weaving demonstrations show the full-bodied dexterity required of handloom weavers in creating the richly varied textiles that, these days, are sold in mass quantities throughout the world. Donegal tweeds incorporate dyes made from four natural ingredients: lichen, blackberries, heather, and soot. There is also a fantastic silversmith and a sculptor on site, whose works are available for purchase. (☎ 41704. Open daily Jan.-Nov. 9:30am-6pm. Free.) Next door in the same building, Yvonne has turned what was once a mere tea room into the **Ard Bia Coffee Shop**, which also serves as a local arts forum, exhibit hall, independent film club (screenings on W nights, with dinner beforehand), **Internet** cafe, and stage for drama classes, talks, and poetry readings. (☎ (087) 236 8648. Wonderful sandwiches and soups around £2. Open daily noon-8pm.)

Beautiful walks are there for the taking in the area surrounding Ardara. From town, head south toward Glencolmcille and turn right at the "Castle View" horse-riding sign toward **Loughros Point** (LOW-crus). At the next horse-riding sign, either turn right for a beautiful view of Ardara Bay, or continue straight to reach stupendous views of the sea at the Point (1hr. walk). One mile from town on Killybegs Rd., a sign points the way to the **Maghera Caves**, which once housed weapons during the Irish war for independence. The British eventually found the guns and killed their Irish rebel owners. After the turnoff, follow the signs several miles west on small roads, which are some of the most beautiful in Ireland. The six caves vary in size and depth; all require a flashlight. At low tide you can enter the Dark Cave, once the refuge of *poitín*-makers. The road that passes the caves continues across a mountain pass to Dungloe. Independent and guided **horse rides** start from **Castle View Ranch**, 2½ well-posted miles from Ardara off Loughros Point Rd. (☎ 41212. £10 per hr., £45 per day.)

Everyone needs at least one hand-knit sweater, and Ardara has four reasonable places to buy it. The **John Molloy Factory Shop** (☎ 41133), a half-mile out of town on Killybegs Rd., has tons to choose from, and if you ask nicely, they'll show you the factory floor in back. You'll gain a whole new respect for the art of knitting and weaving after the tour, dispelling previous notions of old women clustered together in rocking chairs. The town's other manufacturers are **Bonner's** (☎ 41303), Main St.; **Kennedy** (☎ 41106), near the top of the hill on Main St.; and **Triona Design**, at the entrance of town on Killybegs Rd.

GLENTIES ☎075

Glenties is best known for being a five-time winner of "Ireland's Tidiest Town" and—rather incongruously—for hosting one of the area's largest discos each Saturday. Dusting and dancing create a spirited beauty in this village; Brian Friel's play *Dancing at Lughnasa*, written about his aunts, captures Glenties beautifully. Several pleasant walks nearby also recommend the town. It makes a good stop along Bus Éireann or McGeehan's routes through northwest Donegal.

TRANSPORTATION AND PRACTICAL INFORMATION. Bus Éireann (☎ 21101; www.buseireann.ie) stops in front of the post office on its **Donegal-Dungloe** route (1-2 per day, via **Ardara, Carrick, Kilcar**, and **Glencolmcille**). McGeehan's (☎ 46150) also runs a summertime twice-daily **Letterkenny-Glencolmcille** bus (except Su) via almost all of the Slieve League Peninsula villages. In town, the **Bank of Ireland**, Main St., has one of the area's few **24-hour ATMs**. (Open M-W and F 10am-12:30pm and 1:30-4pm, Th 10am-12:30pm and 1:30-5pm). **Glentie's Medical Hall,**

Main St., provides pharmaceutical goodies. (Open M-Tu and Th-F 9:30am-1pm and 2-6pm, W 9:30am-1pm.) The **post office** is destined to appear on a postcard. (☎ 51101. Open M-F 9am-1pm and 2-5:30pm, Sa 9am-1pm.)

🏠🍴🍺 ACCOMMODATIONS, FOOD, AND PUBS. Campbell's Holiday Hostel (IHH), just around the bend at the far end of Main St. toward Ardara, provides cheap and clean rooms decorated in primary colors. The common space has a fireplace, satellite TV, and two fully equipped kitchens. (☎ 51491; email campbellq@eircom.net. Sheets £1. Wash and dry £3. Dorms July-Aug. £8, private rooms £10 per person; Sept.-June £6, £8. Wheelchair accessible.) The most convenient and best-priced B&Bs in the area are at the opposite end of Main St. **Andros B&B** has rooms and suites for up to four with plush carpeting. (☎ 51234. £17 per person, all with bath and TV.) Her daughter-in-law runs **Marguerite's B&B**, next door in a nearly identical house, although Marguerite's rooms have hardwood floors. (☎ 51699. £17 per person, all with bath.)

Thomas Beecht's **organic farm** (☎ 51286) is reached by heading down Main St. toward Columcille and turning left at its sign, located 2 mi. down Meenahall Rd. On Main St. there is a whole foods shop called **Good Earth** (☎ 51794; open M-Sa 9:30am-6pm), and a **Spar Market** (open M-Th 8am-8pm, F-Sa 8am-9pm and Su 8am-1:30pm). For a sit-down meal, the bar in the **Highlands Hotel** is a tasty option. (☎ 51111. 2-course lunch £4.50, chowder £3, sandwiches under £2.) The **Nighthawks Cafe**, Main St. (☎ 51389) bears little resemblance to an Edward Hopper painting; cheap burgers (£1.30-2) and house specials (£5) keep urban loneliness at bay.

Like everything else, the pubs in town are on Main St. **Paddy's Bar** draws youngish locals and hostelers with great music performances every night during the summer. (☎ 51158. Trad W.) At **John Joe's** (☎ 51333), on the opposite side of Main St., the older crowd's Irish tongue and live music bounces off the low ceilings at least twice a week. At the far end of town toward Dungloe, the **Limelight** is your typical small-town nightclub; one gets dressed up (and somewhat drunk) before going, and everyone in Donegal seems to come out of the woodwork to its four bars and disco. (☎ 51118. F alcohol-free for ages 14-18, cover £3; Sa 18+, £4. Su live music. Open nightly 10pm-2am.)

🔭 SIGHTS. Next to the hostel, **St. Connell's Museum and Heritage Centre** is a good starting point for exploration of the surrounding countryside. Its informed staff will introduce you to local history and nearby sites of interest. An assortment of exhibitions and videos mostly concern St. Connell and the remaining markers of his 6th-century missionary; it also has a "study room" for genealogy. (Open Apr.-Sept. M-Sa 10am-5:30pm. £2, students 50p.)

Good walks in the surrounding countryside are sign-posted from the crossroads next to the Heritage Centre, and the staff inside offer advice. Among the more satisfying walks is one that takes you to **Inniskeel Island**, 8 mi. past Glenties toward Dungloe; signs point the way from Narin Beach, where drivers can park. The island, where the ruins of **St. Connell's** 6th-century church lie, is accessible only when the tide is out; check the *Irish Independent* for times. An hour's walk brings you to **Lough Anney**, the reservoir for Glenties and Ardara; follow the directions to the organic farm (see **Food**, above), and the reservoir is a bit farther ahead to your right in the hills. A 2½ mi. walk along the **Owenrea River** leads to **Mullantayboyne**; follow the directions to the organic farm, but turn right off the main road at the Meenahalla sign. The river lies ahead on the right side of the road.

The 7th-12th of September brings the **Harvest Fair** to Glenties, an annual celebration of local agriculture, industry, and beer drinking. On the first weekend in October, fiddlers from all over the world descend upon Glenties for **Fiddler's Weekend**. Call the hostel for information on either.

THE DONEGAL GAELTACHT ☎ 075

In this part of Ireland, Irish culture—language, music, dance—is lived, not practiced. Most visitors, whether well-traveled backpackers, students of the Irish language, or the rare tour-bus passenger, come to Donegal with a purist's appetite for Irish culture and leave well satiated. The Donegal dialect of Irish is distinct from other dialects (like Connemara and Munster). The Donegal style of traditional music is bred most successfully around the *gaeltacht*. Buses run infrequently, so be sure to plan your schedule—or not, because you may decide to stay.

THE ROSSES

N56 bumps and bounces along the spectacularly beautiful midwest coast from Glenties to Dungloe. Expansive, sandy beaches are isolated by the eerie stillness of the Derryveagh Mountains. To the north and west of Burtonport lie the Rosses, a stretch of land that's largely untouched and a bog ecologist's paradise. Stony soil dotted with tiny ponds covers the glacially crumpled ground of this headland. The Rosses is referred to as the "broken" *gaeltacht*, for its Irish-speaking community also uses some English. The corruptive influence of the English language is hardly to be feared in these parts, for locals are likely to tell you that this is the "real" Donegal, where peat farming and salmon fishing keep the old customs alive.

DUNGLOE (AN CLOCHAN LIATH) AND CROHY HEAD

Dungloe (dun-LO), known locally as the capital of the Rosses, is a busy market town near spectacular Crohy Head where travelers stock up before hurrying on to the Gweedore and the mountains.

GETTING THERE AND PRACTICAL INFORMATION. Dungloe is a stopping point for **Bus Éireann** (☎ (073) 21101) on its way to Donegal Town thrice daily in July and August. The following private lines also service Dungloe: **McGeehan's** (☎ 46150) to **Dublin**, via **Glenties, Ardara, Donegal Town** and **Enniskillen**; **Swilly** (☎ 21380) to **Derry**, via **Burtonport, Annagry, Crolly, Bloody Foreland, Falcarragh** and **Letterkenny**; **Doherty's** (☎ 21105) to **Larne** via **Letterkenny** and **Derry**; **Jim O'Donnell** (☎ 48356) to **Belfast** via **Falcarragh, Dunfanaghy, Letterkenny** and **Derry**; and **Feda O'Donnell** (☎ 48214) to **Galway** (Su-M only) via **Glenties, Ardara, Killybegs, Donegal Town**, and **Sligo**. The Dungloe **tourist office**, on a well-marked side street off Main St. toward the shore, has free maps of the town, and it's a good idea to stop in here before heading into the Rosses and Gweedore since it's the last Bord Fáilte you'll find in the area. (☎ 21297. Open June-Sept. M-Sa 9am-6pm, Su 11am-5pm.) Main St. sports a **Bank of Ireland** with a **24-hour ATM**, and an **AIB** (☎ 21077 and ☎ 21179. Both open M-W and F 10am-12:30pm and 1:30-4pm, Th 10am-12:30pm and 1:30-5pm.) **Dennis Brennan** (☎ 22633) provides **taxi** services. Pharmaceuticals proliferate at **O'Donnell's Pharmacy**, Main St. (☎ 21386; open M-Sa 9am-6pm), like philatelists at the teeny **post office**, Quay Rd., off Main St. (☎ 21067; open M-F 9am-1pm and 2-5:30pm, Sa 9am-1pm).

ACCOMMODATIONS, FOOD, AND PUBS. Greene's Independent Holiday Hostel (IHH), Carnmore Rd., is right off Main St. away from the waterfront. Mr. Greene's basic hostel offers a well-upholstered common room and enormous kitchen. (☎ 21943. Curfew Tu-Th 1am, F-M 2am. **Bike rental** $5 per day. Laundry $3. 6- to 9-bed dorms $7; singles $8; doubles $18.) **Park House**, Carnmore Rd., across from the Supervalu, has huge, fluffy beds and an open kitchen. (☎ 21351. Singles $25; doubles $40. All with bath.) **Hillcrest B&B**, Barrack Brae, is at the top of the hill on the Burtonport end of town, about 100m past the end of Main St. It has views of the water and pretty rooms with bath (☎ 21484. $15 per person). There is also a two-bedroom flat, with bath and kitchen. ($40 per night.) **Dungloe Camping and Caravan Park** is right behind the hostel. (☎ 21943. $4 per tent with 1 person, $2 for each additional person; $2 per car.)

NEAR DUNGLOE: CROHY HEAD ■ 373

> **GAELTACHT PUBSPEAK** Irish can be a tricky tongue to traverse, especially in the loud confines of a pub, so *Let's Go* has assembled a course of conversation that may progress over an evening. When you enter a pub, you will most likely be greeted with a friendly "*Cen chaoi an bhfuil sibh?*" (ken QUEE on WILL shiv; "How's it going?") to which you would reply, "*Beidh mé go-brea ma tagann tu Guinness domsa!*" (BAY may GO-bra ma TA-gin to Guinness DUM-sa; "I'll be fine if you give me a Guinness!") As the night proceeds you may need to use the facilities. Just ask "*Cá bhfuil an leithreas le'dthoil?*" (ka WILL on le-RUSS le-the-HULL; "Where's the toilet?") And if you're deep in the *gaeltacht*, you'll likely hear "*Amach ansin*" (a-MOCK on-SHIN; "Outside"). If you survive that episode, and spot a young lass or lad, steel yourself and ask "*Ar mhaith leat a bheith ag damsha?*" (err WA lat a VE-egg DOWSA-a; "Would you like to dance?"). When the time is right, and you and Seamus/Molly are staring soulfully at each other through your pint glasses, you might slip in the subtle "*Ar maith leat, a beith ag dul a codladh liomsa?*" (err MA lat a VE-egg DULL-a COLL-ah LUM-sa; "Would you like to sleep with me?") If you receive a *bos* (slap) in the *aghaidh* (face), blame it on pronunciation. For more Irish vocabulary, see the **Glossary**, p. 494.

If you're cooking, stop by the **Cope Supermarket,** Main St. (Open M-Th and Sa 9am-6pm, F 9am-7pm.) **SuperValu** is about a half-mile down Carnmore Rd. (Open M-W and Sa 9am-7pm, Th-F 9am-8pm.) The posh **Riverside Bistro** has vegetarian entrees for just ₤6, but carnivores pay ₤10-13 for meat or fish. (☎ 21062. Open daily 12:30-3pm and 6-10pm.) Weekend trad sessions at **Beedy's,** Main St. (☎ 21219), bring in seasonal musicians from all over Donegal. During the week, a local crowd hangs out here. **Bridge Inn** hosts a disco on weekend nights. (☎ 21058. Cover ₤5.) When the nightclub isn't open, idle youngsters congregate at the **Atlantic Bar** (☎ 22166), across the street. At the other end of town, the **Tirconnail Bar,** Main St. (☎ 21479), has beautiful ocean views that inspire contemplative musing over slow pints.

◘ SIGHTS. Hundreds of party-lovers flock to Dungloe in the last week of July for the **Mary from Dungloe Festival,** named after a popular folk song about the tragic love affair between Mary and a callous American. The population swells to 80,000 during this 10-day celebration. The highlight of the festival, of course, is the selection of the annual Donegal ambassador, Mary from Dungloe, although most attendees would say that it's the three concerts that Daniel O'Donnell is guaranteed to perform during the week. For festival info and ticket bookings, call the **Festival Booking Office,** next to the tourist office. (☎ 21254. Open M-Sa 10am-6pm.)

NEAR DUNGLOE: CROHY HEAD

Crohy Head, the peninsula 6 mi. southwest of Dungloe, collects strangely shaped rock formations around a jagged coast. **Crohy Head Youth Hostel (An Óige/HI),** in an old coast guard station, offers stupendous views over the Atlantic. (☎ 21950. Easter-June ₤6.50, under 18 ₤5.50; July-Sept. ₤7.50, ₤6.50. Call ahead.) To reach the peninsula and the hostel from Dungloe, turn onto Quay Rd. toward Maghery halfway down Main St. and follow the bumpy road along the sea. The hostel is about a mile past the village of Maghery.

BURTONPORT (AILT AN CHORRÁIN)

About 5 mi. north of Dungloe, the fishing village of Burtonport is less a town than a few pubs clustered around a pier. The ferry to Arranmore Island docks here, and the village is also a good base for **fishing** and **boat trips** to the many uninhabited islands in the area. More salmon land here than in any other spot in Ireland or Britain. Intense sea angling competitions take place during July and August (call the Dungloe tourist office for details). The **Burtonport Festival** rouses up locals the week preceding the Mary from Dungloe Festival in July with a similar program of endemic trad, dance, and sport. **Sea anglers** are booked from the shop on Burtonport Pier; be sure to call ahead. (☎ 42077. Open daily 10am-5pm or so. Fishing trips

£20, rod rental £6.) The **post office** is at the start of town, about 200 yd. from the pier. (☎ 42001. Open M-F 9am-1pm and 2-5:30pm, Sa 9am-1pm.)

Of all the private bus companies in Northwest Donegal, only **Swilly** (☎ 21380) stops by Burtonport on its Derry-Letterkenny-Dungloe route. From Dungloe call for a pickup by the outstanding ■**Cois na Mara Hostel**, about a 10-minute walk from town on the main road. This former B&B has become a sort of guest house for hostelers, complete with high ceilings, specially made high bunk beds, and owner Tim's own delicious morning porridge. (☎ 42079. Breakfast included. Dorms £8; doubles £20.) The **Cope**, at the top of the town, is the largest **grocery** on either side of the water, so stock up before boarding the ferry to Arranmore Island. (☎ 42004. Open M-Sa 9am-6pm.) All Burtonport's pubs squat around the harbour, and most sport a maritime theme. Beside the harbor, the bar of **Skipper's Tavern** teems with nets, skippers' hats, and nautical knots. (☎ 42234. Trad most summer nights.) Nearby, the **Lobster Pot**, Main St., won the James Joyce award for authentic Irish pubs. The wall hangings include Irish soccer jerseys and Jaws's head bursting from the wall and clutching a nail-polished hand. (☎ 42012. Sandwiches £2, entrees £5-7. Restaurant open daily 6-10pm; bar open daily 1-10pm.) The **Harbour Bar and Takeaway**, next to the pier, has food and drink. (☎ 42321. Soup £1.20, entrees £3-4.) Across the street at **O'Donnell's Bar**, landlubbers can escape the salt air at Burtonport's oldest pub. (☎ 42255. Trad on weekends.) The town's best restaurant is **The Following Wind** (☎ 42204), on the pier above O'Donnell's. It features snacks from 11:30am-6:30pm, a la carte seafood and French cooking 6:30-10pm, and an excellent 4-course prix fixe menu for £12.90.

Five miles north of Burtonport on the Coast Road dwells the little village of **Kincasslagh**, birthplace of the sweetheart singer Daniel O'Donnell and the site of his **Viking House Hotel** (☎ 43295); the hotel, though beyond the means of the budget traveler, is a mecca for countless members of the blue-rinse gang on O'Donnell pilgrimages. A minor road heads west to **Cruit Island**, not really an island at all, but rather a peninsula with nice beaches and a host of thatched cottages. Farther north, the magnificent stretch of sand known as **Carrickfinn Strand** is marred only by the presence of tiny **Donegal Airport** (☎ 48284; flights to **Dublin** and other domestic airports, connections to international destinations).

ARRANMORE ISLAND (ÁRAINN MHÓR)

On **Arranmore Island** ("Arainn," "Aran," or "Arran" Island on some maps), a rocky, boulder-covered landscape makes for knee-scraping day-hikes and spooky midnight prowling. The ferry ride out is scenic, passing smaller, mostly abandoned rocky islands. About 600 people live in the sheltered southeast corner of the island, where most accommodations and amenities lie. The smaller population on the other side of the island speaks Irish and feels less influence from the mainland.

GETTING THERE AND PRACTICAL INFORMATION. The **Arranmore Ferry** office (☎ 20532) is open daily 8:30am-7:30pm and sends boats to Burtonport (20min.; July-Aug. M-Sa 8 per day, Su 7 per day, Sept.-June 4-6 per day; £6 return, students £5, seniors free with ID, children £3, bicycles £1.50). A tourist establishment of note is **Bonner's Ferryboat Restaurant**, which serves as a ferry booking office, **B&B**, and coffee shop. (☎ 20532. Open daily 8:30am-8:30pm.) Uphill behind Bonner's, the small **Tourist Information Centre** welcomes visitors and sells decorative maps of the island for £2. (Open M-Sa noon-6pm, Su 3-6pm.)

ACCOMMODATIONS, FOOD, AND PUBS. Along the shore to the left of the ferry port stretches a string of pubs and houses. The house closest to the ferry is the **Boat House**, where life-long residents offer clean rooms and expert advice on exploring the island. (☎ 20511. £18 per person.) Not far down the street lies the **Arranmore Hostel** (☎ 20114 or (087) 221 8014), a clean, modern building in an excellent seaside location. Call ahead to let the owners know when you're coming, as they're often absent during the day.

> **LET'S GO DOES NOT RECOMMEND HITCHHIKING (UNLESS IT'S WITH A FRIDGE...)** There's no shortage of Irish literature, extending from the stories of Cúchulainn in the 8th century to James Joyce's *Ulysses* in the 20th. And then there's Tony Hawks, author of the 1998 book *Round Ireland With a Fridge*. Here's the basic premise: during a night of Guinness-induced revelry, a friend bets Tony £100 that he cannot hitchhike the circumference of Ireland, in one month, with a fridge. From this wager, the author embarks on his circuit and is discovered by the Irish media, who elevated him to folk-hero status. Dubbed "Fridge Man," he meets kings (of Tory Island), nuns (who bless him), spoons players, and wacky locals who take his dorm fridge (which he uses as a suitcase) horse-riding and surfing. Oh, and he drinks a lot. He's since written another book, *Playing the Moldovans at Tennis*, also the product of a Guinness-y gamble. So while we at *Let's Go* do not recommend hitchhiking, we must begrudgingly admit that undertaking this activity with a refrigerated appliance may make you famous and a folk-hero; perhaps a new Finn "McCool"!

One of the island's greatest traditions is its great summer nightlife. With 24-hour licenses to serve fishermen returning from sea, some pubs serve "refreshments" into the morning. Accordingly, the list of pubs is a long one for such a small island. To the left of the ferry dock as you step off the boat is **Phil Bàn's**. The ocean laps against its foundation at high tide, but it's well-established on the island, as is the attached grocery store. (☎ 20908. Open M-Sa 9am-6pm, Su noon-2pm and 4-5pm.) **Pally's** (☎ 20584) is a mile past the ferry dock; turn left off the main road toward the sea, and turn left at the sign. Make sure to take the advice of the enormous signpost that reads "have a jar at Pally's Bar." **Neily's** (☎ 20509), a half-mile more down the main road, is a local watering hole. **O'Donnell's** (☎ 20918) offers sessions most weekends during the summer and a terrific view of the bay. Just above the ferry docks, **Early's Bar** (☎ 20515) is where famous crooner Daniel O'Donnell earned his first gig, but the tiny space wouldn't fit an umpteenth of O'Donnell's present following. As a token of thanks to Arranmore's early support, O'Donnell gives an annual concert on the island and brings teary-eyed hordes with him.

SIGHTS. Four priceless pearls were a gift to Red Hugh O'Donnell from Philip II for Red Hugh's help in saving Spanish sailors when Armada ships went down off the coast. The pearls were last seen on Arranmore Island in 1905, and people are still searching. Locals can also tell you a less romantic version of the story: hungry Spanish sailors exchanged the pearls for food, tobacco, and booze. The last inheritor put them in Lloyd's Bank in London, where they sit today in their not-so-priceless splendor. The pearls make a great story, but more impressive are the island's landscape and hiking opportunities. **The Arranmore Way**, a well-marked footpath, runs the circumference of the island and will lead you along three possible paths; the longest trail goes to the lighthouse at the far tip of the island, high above impressive cliffs and rushing water. A map of trails (£2) is available from the tourist center. A full perambulation of Arranmore Way takes a good six hours.

RANNAFAST

In the heart of the Donegal *gaeltacht*, the village of **Annagry** (*Anagaire*) marks the beginning of the **Rannafast** area, famous for its storytelling tradition. *Seanachies*, or storytellers, prolong the life of the Irish language and narrative tradition. In the summer, Annagry hosts total-immersion Irish-language camps that draw teenagers from all over the Republic. About 500 yd. south of the village, on top of a hill to the left of the road, is **Teàc Jack's** pub and restaurant. Local musicians congregate here on weekend nights in the summer. (☎ 48113. Soup and bread £1.30, sandwich £1.20, entrees £2-4.) About 3 mi. farther down the road is the (some would say) kitschy **Leo's Tavern** (☎ 48143). Leo is the father of multi-layered voice guru Enya and the family group Clannad, whose silver, gold, and platinum records decorate the walls. Leo plays his enormous electric piano-accordion on stage and leads a sing-along for daytime tour groups and nightly audiences, while his son Bartely runs the pub. On Wednesday nights in July and August a large company of musicians gather at Leo's for trad sessions. (Trad on unpredictable nights in off-season.) For a more predictable music experience, head to **Teàc Tessie,** across the street, where locals gather for fine trad on Sunday nights.

GWEEDORE (GAOTH DOBHAIR)

Gweedore, the Irish-speaking coastal region northeast of the Rosses, is one of the most remote and wonderful parts of Ireland. Quilted with sheep and stone fences, the ragged, grassy mountains welcome walking enthusiasts. Cyclists are enthralled with the challenging but quiet roads. Crolly is the gateway to this, the most beautiful part of Donegal. Beyond Crolly, the road leads to exquisite beaches and the legendary Poison Glen. Errigal Mountain's sheer face and Bloody Foreland's oceanfront appear otherworldly; Tory Island *is* a world apart from Ireland, with its own elected king and freedom from Irish taxes, as well as a demonic past.

CROLLY (CROITHLI) AND TOR

The N56 intersects with the coastal road at a small bridge. The coastal road twists and bends along the jagged edges where Donegal meets the sea, leading you through spectacular scenery dotted with small Irish-speaking villages. Smart travelers stop at **Crolly,** just past the bridge at N56, for a pint or groceries. Several buses stop in front of Paddy Oig's pub. **Feda O'Donnell** (☎ 48114) provides a daily coach service to and from **Galway** and **Donegal Town** via **Letterkenny; Swilly** (Dungloe ☎ 21380, Derry ☎ 7126 2017) passes on its **Dungloe-Derry** route; **John McGinley Coaches** (☎ (074) 35201) makes Crolly its starting point for a **Dublin** journey; and **O'Donnell Trans-Ulster Express** (☎ 48356) goes by on its way to **Belfast.** The postmistress at the Crolly **post office** is a good source of information on the area and can point you toward accommodations. (☎ 48120. Open M-F 9am-5:30pm, Sa 9am-1pm.) The **Crolly Filling Station,** next to the post office, provides everything from groceries and gasoline to bike repairs and **car rental.** (Open M-Sa 9am-11pm, Su 9am-10pm.)

Paddy Oig's pub (☎ 31306) has everything a body could need: camping, pub grub (sandwiches £1.40), and Tuesday and Thursday night trad sessions in the summer. **Coillín Darach Caravan & Camping Park,** just behind the pub, has modern facilities, a small store with the basic commodities (open daily 9am-10pm), and the odd tennis court. (☎ 32000. Electricity £1. Laundry £2. July-Aug. £7 tent, Sept.-June £5.)

Just past Paddy Oig's, a weather-beaten sign will point you toward **Screagan an Iolair Hill Hostel** (SCRAG an UH-ler), which lies 4 mi. up a mountain road to **Tor** in **Glenveagh National Park.** Turn left off the coastal road at the sign and follow Tor

HOW POISON GLEN GOT ITS NAME
According to the Ulster Cycle of Irish mythology, the coast of Donegal was originally inhabited by the Fomorian race of evil-tempered devils. The leader of the Fomorians was the giant Balor, a demon famed for his single "evil eye" that would turn the beholder to dust when the eyelid was lifted by two assistants tugging on its chains. Balor ruled the country from his fort on Tory Island until the fateful day when the young Lugh (later to be the god of light) challenged him to battle. Balor accepted the challenge and met Lugh at Dún Lughaidh ("Lugh's Fort," pronounced Dun-LEW-y). Intelligent Lugh took aim for Balor's eye before the eyelid was lifted, then closed his own eyes and let his arrow fly; it struck Balor directly in the Evil Eye and killed him. The poison from Balor's eye supposedly spread across the ground of the battle site, making it unfit for even animals to graze on. The poisonous plant that today covers the valley is called "spurge" (Latin name *euphorbia*), although where that name comes from is anyone's guess. Another theory states that Poison Glen is a mistranslation of the Irish for "Beautiful Glen."

Road past breathtaking scenery and climbs; when you pass Lough Keel, the road divides. Hostel-seekers should continue straight ahead to reach one of the best hostels in Ireland, with a great book collection, ever-changing views of the surrounding crags, and a "meditation room." The hostel is remote, but most visitors come here for at least several days; kind owners Eamon and Mireilla will share a wealth of information on local hikes and points of interest, and the stellar common room stores a fine library of pamphlets and books on regional events, sites, and transportation. (☎ 48593. Open all year, but call ahead Nov.-Feb. Laundry $3. Dorms $7.50; private rooms $9.)

Tor Rd. continues past **Ashardan Waterfall** and **Lake**, and finally into **Glen Tor**. Crolly and the hostel nearby make a good base for exploring the pristine heath lands of the **Derryveagh Mountains,** inhabited by red deer. Trails for hikers of varying abilities, clearly shown on the *Ordnance Survey Discovery Series I*, begin at the hostel in Tor. As the trails are often hard to follow, hikers should always inform the hostel warden of their plans.

ERRIGAL MOUNTAIN AND DUNLEWY (DUN LUICHE SNACHT)

One mile north of Crolly, N56 and the coastal road diverge. N56 turns inland and reaches R251 after about 5 mi. This road leads east through **Dunlewy** past the foot of conical **Errigal Mountain,** Ireland's second highest mountain, and eventually to Glenveagh National Park. The drive is studded with stunning views. A mile from the foot of Errigal Mountain in Dunlewy village, the spruce-sheltered 46-bed **Errigal Youth Hostel (An Óige/HI)** is a clean, no frills, hiker's haven with a warm proprietress. (☎ 31180. Dorms June-Sept. $7.50, Oct.-May $6.50.) A few minutes up the road is a turn-off to **Dunlewy Lake** and the **Poison Glen** (see **How Poison Glen Got Its Name,** above). Within the wooded area of the glen is the former manor of the English aristocracy. In an open spot next to the lake stands their abandoned church; its decaying, roofless exterior makes a spooky addition to the myth-laden glen. If you continue along the paved road around a few curves, you will eventually reach an unmarked car park that signals the beginning of the trail up the side of Errigal Mountain (2466 ft.). You must follow this trail in order to scramble through the loose scree to the summit. Expect the climb to take two to three hours total. A dangerous, narrow ridge must be traversed to reach the summit. Be sure to keep an eye on the clouds—they've been known to congregate suddenly around the mountaintop. The summit is the smallest in Ireland, and the sheer face of the mountain could shorten your journey from one hour to one minute.

Back at the bottom, just before the hostel, the **Ionad Cois Locha Dunlewey,** or **Dunlewey Lakeside Centre,** offers boat tours, weaving demos, a craft shop, roaming local animals, enough info on the area to count as a tourist office, and a fire-warmed cafe. (☎ 31699. Open Easter-Oct. M-Sa 10:30am-6pm, Su 11am-7pm. Boat trips $3, students $2.50. Thatched weaving cottage town $3, students $2.50. Combined ticket $5, students $4.) The center also offers a series of trad concerts during the summer (tickets $5-10, usually $10) and music workshops all year.

BUNBEG (AN BUN BEAG) AND BLOODY FORELAND

Where N56 moves inland, R257 continues along the coast to **Bunbeg**. The coastal road traverses a strip of continuously stunning scenery; this stretch is perfect for cyclists, since there's little traffic. Hitchers tend to stay on N56, where cars are more common. *Let's Go* does not recommend hitchhiking. Bunbeg Harbour, the smallest enclosed harbor in Ireland, was a main exit and entry point at the height of Britain's imperialism. Relics from that period line the harbor: military barracks, grain stones, and look-out towers. Bunbeg's harbor is one of two docking places for **Donegal Coastal Cruises** (a.k.a. **Turasmara**), the ferry service for Tory Island; in the summer, it makes a morning trip daily, weather permitting. (☎ 31991. $15 return, students $13.) Halfway from the town to the harbor, a single stone pillar marks a rough path that leads to the banks of the Clady River, where salmon fishermen do their craft. The **Bunbeg House** (☎ 31305), on the waterfront, serves sandwiches ($2.50) and seafood (from $5).

If you continue past the Bunbeg turnoff, you will immediately see the irresistible ◼Hudi Beag's pub (☎ 31016). On Monday nights, only the truly unmusically inclined could walk past the intense session taking place within this pub. A stone's throw away is **An Chisteanach** (an KEESH-nach), a cozy sit-down deli with stomach-stretching portions for about £5. (Open M-Sa 8:30am-7pm.)

On the streets of nearby **Derrybeg** are several banks, but only the **AIB** has both a **bureau de change** and an **ATM**. (Open M-W and F 10am-12:30pm and 1:30-4pm, Th until 5pm.) **Teach Thomais** (☎ 31054), the oldest shop in the parish, sells a collection of English and Gaelic books and crafts (if the shop's locked, knock at the kitchen door to its right). **Gweedore Chemists** (☎ 31254) is housed in a green building across the street from Hudi Beag's. The **post office** is also on the main street. (Open M-F 9am-1pm and 2-5:30pm.)

About 7 mi. north of Bunbeg, **Bloody Foreland**, a short length of rough scarlet rock, juts into the sea. At sunset, the sea reflects the deep red hue of the sky and rocks. An old legend holds that the sea is colored with the blood of sailors who perished in the wrecks of Spanish galleons. Farther west, the headland at **Magheraroarty** offers miles of unspoiled beaches. A holy well remains full of fresh water despite tidal rushes twice a day. **Ferries** to Tory Island (☎ (074) 35061) travel more frequently from Magheroarty, but the pier is much more isolated than Bunbeg's.

TORY ISLAND

Visible from the Bloody Foreland, barren Tory Island, named for its *tors* (hills), sits 8 mi. off the coast. The weather-beaten cottages and people of Tory fulfill many visitors' imaginative visions of what old Ireland looked like, but that characterization underestimates the weirdness of Tory's landscape and people. The island has a mythical status as the home of the demonic Fomorians. The Fomorians were the original Tory Island pirates who regularly invaded the mainland under the leadership of Balor of the Evil Eye (see **How the Poison Glen Got Its Name**, p. 376). Its age-old reputation as a haven for pirates prompted people to equate the word "Tory" with "pirate" or "rascal." The use of "Tory" to mean "Conservative" derives from this Irish slang. (A Whig was originally a Scottish horse thief.) Tory's pirateering reputation was accurate as recently as last century, when the island thrived off its *poitín* production—the inaccessibility of the island thwarted British efforts to control its trade. The present-day island is completely exhausted of turf, all six layers of which were burned in *poitín* production, and its soil appears more sandy and grassy than that on the mainland. Only one tree survives in the harsh conditions of the small island's sea-exposed area. The eastern end of the island breaks apart into a series of jagged sea cliffs.

This small Irish-speaking community has managed to maintain a strong sense of independence. Islanders refer to the mainland as "the country," and still elect a **"Rí na nOileán"** (king of the island) to a lifetime position, which mainly involves serving as the island's PR man—he'll greet you when you get off the boat and can tell stories of the island's past. Many of the island's unusual traditions remain intact, including the superstition that deters fishermen from rescuing drowning boatsmen. Another tradition claims that a stone on one of the island's hills has the power to fulfill wishes. This stone sits on the east end of the island on an unapproachable perch; if you throw three stones onto it, your wish will come true. In addition to the wishing stone, the island offers a cursing stone. The location of the latter has been concealed by local elders to prevent its misuse. The cursing stone has been credited with the 1884 shipwreck of a Dublin gunboat coming to collect taxes. The islanders still pay no taxes.

Club Thoraighe (☎ (074) 65121) features Tory Island trad, which beats out a slightly stronger rhythmic emphasis than the mainland music, and *ceilis*, with mandatory attendance for all islanders. The island's 160 people support a surprising number of businesses, all located along a quarter of a mile stretch of the island's one street: store, hotel and restaurant, craft shop, chipper, and **Gailearai Dixon** (Dixon Gallery). The gallery showcases the work of the Tory Primitives, a group of local artists promoted by Derrick Hall of Glebe Gallery fame (see p. 380).

SAINT—OR PIED PIPER?
Saint Columcille (also known as Columba) landed on Tory Island 1400 years ago. Since that time, nary a rat has been seen on the isle. Locals say the land remains vermin-free because Columcille blessed its clay, banishing the rodents. Today, rat-plagued individuals journey here from hither and yon to collect a lump of Tory's holy clay. The owner of a house a bit past the gallery dispenses the mud, always free of charge, since you can't sell Saintliness.

The "primitive" moniker derives from the fact that the first Tory artist, James Dixon, began painting with the materials available to him: house paint and a brush made from his donkey's tail. Their work usually depicts the natural scenery of the island in color-drenched pigments, evoking the living fury of the sea around Tory or the shadowy ruins of the island's medieval religious past. The island's interesting historical sights include the ruins of the **monastery** that St. Colmcille founded in the 6th century and the **Tau Cross** close to the town center.

The only way to get out to the island is via the **ferry**, also known as **Donegal Coastal Cruises** or **Turasmara** (☎ 31320 or 31340). The ferry runs boats from **Bunbeg** (☎ 31991; 1½hr., June-Aug. 1 per day, fewer Oct.-May), **Magheroarty** (☎ (074) 35061; 40min., June-Aug. 2 per day), and **Portnablagh** (departs July-Aug. W 2pm). All crossings are £15 return (students £13; bicycles free). Be sure to call ahead to check departure times as they depend on tides and weather; storms have stranded travelers here for days in summer or even weeks in winter.

FINTOWN (BAILE NA FINNE) AND DENYBEG
Two tiny villages provide further accommodations for travelers meandering about the Donegal *gaeltacht*. Barely living up to its second syllable, **Fintown** is a miniscule settlement within easy reach of good hiking and fishing. At **Glenleighan House (IHO)**, Bríd (Breege) McGill welcomes guests with open arms. (☎ 46141. 4-bed dorms £6; private rooms £7; B&B doubles £24, with bath £30.) To get there, take the R250 from Glenties. Near the intersection with R250, you'll see a phone booth on the right. Turn left there, and the hostel is the third house on the left. Located about 1 mi. off the main road in **Denybeg**, toward the coast, **Backpacker's Hostel** offers guests beds, views of the beach, and the sound of sheep bleating under your window. (☎ 32244. 8-bed dorms £7, private rooms £10 each.)

GLENVEAGH NATIONAL PARK
On the eastern side of the Derryveagh Mountains, **Glenveagh National Park** is 37 sq. mi. of forest glens, bogs, and mountains. One of the largest herds of red deer in Europe roams the park; deer-watching is best done at dusk and in the winter months after October, when the deer come down to the valley to forage. Despite Glenveagh's being the second most popular national park in Ireland, you probably won't be aware of any other human presence within the enormous pristine area—make sure to hold on to the free map handed out at the visitors center. The hostels in **Crolly** (p. 376) and **Dunlewy** (p. 377) are most convenient to the park, though many choose also to daytrip out from Letterkenny via **Bus Éireann's** "Hills of Donegal" Tour. (Letterkenny ☎ (074) 21309. £6 return, whole tour £13. Park ☎ (074) 37090 or 37262. Open Mar.-Nov. daily 10am-6:30pm. £2, students £1, seniors £1.50.)

Summertime tourists can take the free minibus from the park's entrance to **Glenveagh Castle**, 2½ mi. away (every 10-15min., last trip 1½hr. before closing. The castle was built in 1870 by the founder of the Glenveagh Estate, John Adair, shortly after he was married. Despite its relative youth, Glenveagh Castle looks like a medieval keep with its thick walls, battle-ready rampart, turrets, and round tower. Adair had a nasty reputation that doesn't suit the beauty of the land; in the cold April of 1861, he evicted 244 tenants on trumped-up charges. Many of them decided to emigrate to Australia, while others were forced into the workhouse. (Castle's hours same as park. Last tour 1¼hr. before closing. £2, students and children £1, seniors £1.50.) The surrounding **gardens** brighten up the bleak aspect of

Adair's lonely castle; they are the design of a later owner, the American Henry McIlhenry. (Tours of the garden leave from Castle Courtyard July-Aug. Tu and Th 2pm.) He planted the gardens around the estate and left it to the government at his death. The areas around the castle are posh and highly cultivated; plots farther away are named after the area of the world to which their species belong (the Dutch garden, for example) and appear almost unkept. Marked nature trails begin at the castle. A mile up the incline behind the castle is **View Point,** which provides a glimpse of the park's vast expanse. Park rangers lead guided nature walks and more strenuous hill walks. (Call for information or to schedule a walk.) The **visitors center** has more information about these or self-guided hikes. (Open Mar.-Nov. Same hours as park.) The center can also prepare you for your hike with a 10-minute video on the park's wildlife and history, several exhibits, and a meal at its cafeteria-style **restaurant.** (Most entrees £4-5.)

Five miles away from the visitors center in Churchill is the **Glebe Gallery,** the display space of artist Derek Hill. He sponsored the Tory Island school of painters, and their work makes up the majority of the gallery's collection, supplemented by the work by mainland Donegal artists, and several pieces by internationally renowned European masters, including Picasso. (☎ (074) 37071. Open Easter week and late-May to late-Sept. Sa-Th 11am-6:30pm, last tour 5:30pm. £2, students £1. "3-in-1" ticket £3, students and children £1.50; good for Glenveagh Park, Glebe Gallery and the Letterkenny Newmills Corn and Flax Museum.) On the other side of the lake at **Glebe House,** a centuries-old family home, the newly opened **St. Colmcille Heritage Centre** has a permanent display on the life of the saint who brought Christianity to Donegal. (Hours and admission same as the Glebe Gallery.) Nearby is St. Colmcille's **Bed of Loneliness,** an enormous horizontal stone slab on which the saint spent the night before entering exile. Many emigrants have since lain on the stone overnight to stave off future loneliness.

FALCARRAGH (AN FÁL CARRACH) ☎074

Northeast of the Bloody Foreland, white beaches stretch along the coast. Inland a bit, in the midst of a continuously irregular area of rocky hills and fertile valleys, sits Falcarragh. This Irish-speaking town is remarkably busy, considering its language preference. It's a colorful rest stop for those heading to beach beyond Dunfanaghy. While *Let's Go* does not recommend **hitching,** it is reportedly easy here.

Falcarragh provides many of the region's basic services. The **Bank of Ireland** provides an **ATM.** (☎ 35484. Open M,W, and F 10am-12:30pm and 1:30-4pm, Th 10am-12:30pm and 1:30-5pm.) **Flynn's Pharmacy** has medical goods and more. (☎ 35778. Open M-Sa 9:30am-6pm.) **McGinley's** supermarket provides the usual fare. (☎ 35126. Open daily 9:30am-10pm.) Falcarragh's **post office,** Main St., delivers mail. (☎ 35110. Open M-F 9am-1pm and 2-5:30pm, Sa 9am-1pm.)

The **Shamrock Lodge Hostel (IHH),** above the pub on Main St., was recently gutted by a fire, though it plans to reopen soon. Call ahead. (☎ 35859. Dorms £7; doubles £20.) Next to the post office, Patricia McGroddy's **Loistin Oiche** offers bed and breakfast in a modern abode with mountain views. (☎ 35145. £15.) You can eat huge portions in sun-kissed wooden booths at **John's Restaurant** at the top of Main St. (Steaks £9-10, seafood and salads £5-6, sandwiches £1.50. Open M-Sa 10am-9pm, Su noon-9pm.) Alternatively, head to **Mighty Mac's,** next to the post office, for cheaper fare in a "take-away/cafe." (☎ 65386. Burgers £1.20. Open daily 9am-1:30am.) The **Gweedore Bar,** Main St., curries the local businessmen's favor with a reasonable lunch menu. (☎ 35293. Lunch specials £3.75, served 12:30-2:30pm.)

Falcarragh lives pub life to the fullest. The **Shamrock Lodge,** or **Lóistín na Seamróige,** in the center of town, is by far the most distinctive. It buzzes with human activity well into the night. The "young room," as owner Mary calls it, has a jukebox, pool table, and comfy leather seats; old folks congregate in the poster-bedecked front bar. Trad sessions here display the local talent—and remember that most of Ireland's best trad bands have come out of Northern Donegal. (W and Sa trad, F rhythm and blues.) On Ballyconnell Rd., just off Main St. at the northern end of town, **The Loft Bar** (☎ 35992) presents a collection of old mugs and flowery upholstery in a cave-dark space, with folk music on summer weekends. The **Anchor Bar** offers lively trad on Wednesday nights.

About three miles outside of Falcarragh, colossal sand dunes squat on the beaches of **Back Strand** and **Ballyness**. To reach them follow the signs for "Trà," meaning beach, from the southern end of town. The **New Lake**—so called because it was formed in 1912 after a massive storm blocked up this former estuary—features a world-famous ecosystem and lots of frisky otters.

DUNFANAGHY

Seven miles north of Falcarragh, Dunfanaghy still has an Anglo-Irish feel from its days as the administrative center of the region. Today it's home to one of Donegal's finest hostels, the ▓**Corcreggan Mill Hostel and B&B (IHH)**. Nearly six miles north of Falcarragh and 1½ miles south of Dunfanaghy, Corcreggan sits by the side of the road in a complex that consists of a kiln house, a railway car, and an organic garden/restaurant. Owner Brendan has converted an old wooden railway car into comfortable 4-bed dorms and private doubles with mahogany floors and walls. The railway car is sheltered underneath the roof of a house and has exceedingly comfortable common rooms laden with fascinating railroad memorabilia and furniture. In addition, 10-bed dorms and doubles are available in the former kiln house. Three kitchens—two for hostelers, one for campers—have been redone using recycled materials to keep the traditional atmosphere. Almost every bus, from Swilly to the private coaches, stops right at the door. (☎ (074) 36409. Kiln house dorms £7 in summer, off-season £6; loft doubles £18, £16. Railway dorms £9 in summer, off-season £8; doubles £22, £20. **Camping** £4.) Hostelers team up at night to hire a local minibus to travel to and from the pubs (about £2 per person).

Danny Collins's bar stays open from 10:30am until whenever the *Garda* come to shut it down. (☎ 36205. Food served 1-6pm. Soup £1.50, meat and vegetarian entrees £4-6.) Across the street, the Carrig Rua Hotel houses the **Red Rock Cafe**, which offers substantial, well-made lunches for £5. (Lunch served 12:30-2:30pm.) The **Village Shop** sells groceries. (Open 9am-11pm.)

The **Dunfanaghy Workhouse Heritage Centre** has created an excellent exhibit on the effects of famine in northwest Donegal, including a series of life-size dioramas following the life of a local woman named Hannah (1834?-1926), who survived the Famine and at one point lived in the workhouse. This former poorhouse has undergone a miraculous transformation from the days of the Famine, when it gave minimal shelter and rations to the destitute under prison-like conditions. A small coffee house and a craft shop are attached. (☎ 36540. Open Mar.-Oct. M-F 10am-5pm, Sa-Su noon-5pm. £2.50, children £1.25.)

Between Dunfanaghy and Falcarragh is a maze of small roads and boggy hills. One can easily walk, cycle, drive, or hitch to any of the natural attractions within a 5 mi. radius of either town. **Horn Head**, sign-posted on the way into Dunfanaghy, invites long rambles around its pristine beaches, megalithic tombs, and gorse-covered hills. Those tireless hikers who make the 3½-hour trek to the far north tip of Horn Head from Dunfanaghy will experience some of the most spectacularly high sea cliffs in Ireland. **Ards Forest**, a couple of miles past Dunfanaghy, features a number of nature trails ranging from 1½ to 8 mi. Adjacent to the forest are pristine beaches accessible only on foot. (Open daily July-Aug. 10:30am-9pm, Easter-June and Sept. Sa-Su 10:30am-4pm.) **Marble Hill Windsurfing** lets you experience the water's strength firsthand. (☎36231. Instruction session £20; board hire £8 per hr., £12 per 2hr.) Those interested in cycling to Horn Head or the area's other sights may **rent bikes** from the **Cyclists' Touring Club**, Main St. (☎ 36470 in advance. £7 for the first day, £5 each day afterwards.) Turning your back to the sea anywhere in Dunfanaghy will bring the expanse of the Muckish Mountain into view.

FANAD PENINSULA ☎ 074

The Fanad Peninsula juts into the Atlantic between Lough Swilly and Mulroy Bay. Lush greenery makes a striking complement to the peninsula's sandy beaches. The eastern edge, outlined by the villages of **Rathmelton, Rathmullan,** and **Portsalon,** is by far the nicest part of the peninsula, with colorful old houses and sweeping views across Lough Swilly. Rathmelton and **Milford** (on the western edge of the Lough) offer the most services and nightlife. The pretty **Knockalla Mountains** are easy to climb. The few who get to the far reaches of the peninsula will find their efforts rewarded with a bounty of beaches. The peninsula favors drivers, with beautiful views from remote roads. The Swilly bus only runs as far as Portsalon once per day; without a car, you had better plan on spending the night there or you may end up hitching back. *Let's Go* does not recommend hitchhiking. The broad, relatively flat stretches of road from Rathmelton to Rathmullan are kind to cyclists; after that, sharp inclines become frequent as the road narrows and grows unkempt.

RATHMELTON

A river flanked by stone walls and trees runs through the venerable, 17th-century town of Rathmelton (ra-MEL-ton) at the mouth of the Leannan Estuary, the eastern gateway to the peninsula.

ORIENTATION AND PRACTICAL INFORMATION.
The **Mall** runs along the river and contains most of the town's handful of goods and services. The **National Irish Bank,** The Mall, has a **bureau de change** but no ATM. (☎ 51028. Open M-W and F 10am-12:30pm and 1:30-3pm, Th 10am-12:30pm and 1:30-5pm.) **Bridge Launderette,** The Mall, takes its name from its location. (☎ 51333. Laundry £4.50. Open M-Sa 9am-6pm.) **O'Donnell's Pharmacy** is also on The Mall. (☎ 51080. Open M-Tu and Th-Sa 9am-1pm and 2-6pm, W 9am-1pm.) **Rent bikes** at **Ramelton Exhaust Centre,** Shore Rd. (☎ 51154. Open M-Sa 9:30am-6pm.) The **post office** resides on Castle St., off The Mall. (☎ 51001. Open M-F 9am-5:30pm, Sa 9am-1pm.)

ACCOMMODATIONS, FOOD, AND PUBS.
Just off The Mall and right along the Swilly bus route, **Crammond House,** Market Sq., has expansive rooms with high ceilings in a 1760s townhouse. (☎ 51055. Open Easter-Oct. £17, with bath £19.) Just around the corner, **Lennon Lodge** is a hostel/B&B that houses guests in tidy 2- to 5-bed rooms. (☎ 51228. Breakfast £3. £10 per person, with bath £12.) If both are full, signs in the center of town point to myriad other B&Bs.

Whoriskey's/Spar Supermarket sells DIY meals. (☎ 51006. Open M-Sa 8:30am-10pm, Su 8:30am-9pm.) Rathmelton's eateries offer sandwiches and fine dining, but little middle ground. **The Fish House Craft Gallery,** where salmon were once smoked in the town's fishing heyday, now sells tea and sandwiches along with sweaters and local pottery. (☎ 51316. Open May-Sept. daily 10am-7pm.) Take your sandwich outside and you can dine with the swans along the river. For affordable feasts in a more refined, candlelit setting, cross the street to the posh but reasonably priced **Mirabeau Steak House** on The Mall. (☎ 51138. Steak from £9, fish from £7.) At the top of town on the road to Milford, well-established **Bridge Bar** (☎ 51119) knows how to please its customers with music at least three nights a week. **Conway's** (☎ 51297), an old thatched cottage at the bottom of the hill down Church St., pours proper pints.

SIGHTS.
To discover the area's heritage, turn off The Mall and go uphill past Market Sq.; a right at Mary's Bar after Crammond House will bring you to Back Lane and the old **Presbyterian Meetinghouse.** Francis Makemie, who founded the first American Presbytery in 1706, grew up in Rathmelton and worshiped here. The building now houses the town library and the paper-pushing **Donegal Ancestry Centre.** The center, part of Irish Genealogical Project Centres, will help you trace your Donegal ancestors for a fee. (☎ 51266. Open M-Th 9am-4:30pm, F 9am-4pm.) Crowds flock to the **Lennon Festival** in mid-July for a carnival and parade.

RATHMULLAN

Five miles north along the main coastal road, the coastal town of Rathmullan boasts historical, mythical, and logistical significance. In 1607, the last powerful Gaelic chieftains, Hugh O'Neill and Red Hugh O'Donnell, fled from Ireland after suffering numerous defeats to British invaders. They and 99 of their retinue set sail from Rathmullan for Spain to gather military support from the Catholic King Phillip II. Their ship blew off course, and they landed in France. Eventually, they died in Rome while still soliciting foreign aid. Their departure is known as the Flight of the Earls (see **Feudalism,** p. 9). In more recent Anglo-Irish struggles, Wolfe Tone, the famous champion of Irish independence, was arrested in Rathmullan in 1798 (see **Rebellion, Reunion, Reaction,** p. 13). The town's tales are very much alive and present at the **"Flight of the Earls" Heritage Centre,** at the town center. A helpful staff uses artwork, literature, and wax models to recount Rathmullan's history in detail. The building, a particularly foreboding Martello tower, is a historic monument of the British Admiralty. (☎ 58229. Open Apr.-Sept. M-Sa 10am-12:30pm and 1:30-5pm, Su noon-1pm and 2-5pm. £1.50, students and seniors £1, children 75p.) Around the corner, the remains of the **Rathmullan Priory,** a 14th-century Carmelite monastery, lie shrouded in ivy.

Tourist information is gladly dispensed at the Heritage Centre (see above). **Mace Supermarket,** on the coast road into town, supplies basic gastronomic needs. (☎ 58148. Open daily 8am-10pm.) Quiet **Pier Hotel** has multiple personalities: its **B&B** offers very clean, sunny rooms in an old Georgian home (☎ 58178; £15, with bath £27.50); it serves pub grub (entrees £4-5; food served 12:30-9:30pm), and it's a popular **pub,** with a good mixture of young and old around the simple bar (midweek trad sessions, and live contemporary music F-Sa). Next door to the Heritage Centre, the **Beachcomber Bar** (☎ 58125) offers beach access. One wall is taken up by a gigantic view of the water, and a sandy beer garden opens out back in the summer.

THE NORTHERN AND WESTERN PENINSULA

North of Rathmullan, the road narrows and winds and dips to accommodate the increasingly wild landscape. These remote roads are discouraging to pedestrians and all but the most fit bikers, and hitchhiking is nearly impossible; *Let's Go* does not recommend hitchhiking. As the road continues, it hits a series of clustered buildings, called "towns" only because each has a church and a post office. A little over halfway from Rathmullan to Portsalon, a sign-posted lane leads from the main road to remote **Bunnaton House Hostel (IHO),** Glenvar, high on a hill above the lough. The hostel lodges in the Captain's Quarters of a former Coast Guard Station, built in 1813. (☎ 50122. Breakfast £3-4.50. Dorms £7.50; private rooms £10.) Continuing north, the main road becomes both mind-bogglingly steep and breathtakingly beautiful. Just before Portsalon, the road crests a hill, where **Knockalla Strand** (rated the second best in the world by a British "beach expert") and the tip of the northern peninsula suddenly appear. **Camping** facilities are available next to Knockalla Strand at the **Knockalla Holiday Centre,** 3 mi. south of Portsalon. (☎ 59108. Open Mar.-Sept. £8 per 2-person tent, £11 per 3- to 4-person tent.)

Portsalon (port-SAL-un), on the descent, consists of three shops and a series of homes along the water. It was once a resort town, but the resort hotel burned down three years ago, leaving just a beach that needs nothing to recommend it. The **Portsalon House B&B,** next to the post office on the main road, has wonderful rooms perfumed by the rosebushes outside, but may be closing; call in advance. (☎ 59395. £20 per person.) About one hour north of Portsalon by bike, the **Great Arch of Doaghbeg** keeps the **Fanad Lighthouse** company. The arch, a mass of rock over 80 ft. wide detached from seaside cliffs, is visible from above, though not from the main road. It is best reached through the six-acre **Ballydaheen Gardens,** a seaside array of Japanese and English gardens that blends into the natural landscape amazingly well. (Open May-Sept. M, Th, and Sa 10am-3pm. £3, children £1.) From Fanad Head, the route down the western side of the peninsula winds in and out of the inlets of **Mulroy Bay.** Mrs. Borland's **Avalon Farmhouse,** on Main St. in tiny

Tamney—also reachable by a road that cuts across the peninsula from Portsalon—has homemade jam and attractive decor. (☎ 59031. Open Easter-Sept. £17, with bath £19.) In **Kerrykeel,** farther south at the foot of the Knockalla Hills, lies **Rockhill Park** (☎ 50012). About 1½ mi. out of Kerrykeel along Glenvar Rd. is a signpost to the **Gortnavern Dolmen,** a spectacular megalithic tomb.

LETTERKENNY (LEITIR CEANNAN) ☎074

Letterkenny is Donegal's commercial and ecclesiastic center, but that's not saying much. The "white-streaked hill face" (Leitir Ceannan) has a bus station, a movie theater, a couple of great bars, Internet access, and one traffic light, but not much more to recommend it. A series of roundabouts and a crowded Main St. make downtown a honking, trafficked stew, and the town's geography is not conducive to long stays; the tourist office lies well outside of town, as does the area's only hostel and almost all B&Bs. Most tourists arrive in Letterkenny just to make bus connections to the rest of Donegal, the Republic, and Northern Ireland.

GETTING THERE AND GETTING AROUND

Buses: The **Bus Éireann Station** (☎ 22863) lies on a roundabout at the junction of Port (Derry) and Pearse Rd. in front of the Letterkenny Shopping Center. **Bus Éireann** (☎ 21309) runs a "Hills of Donegal" tour, including **Dungloe, Glenveigh National Park,** and **Gweedore** (M-Sa 11am, £10), and regular service to **Derry** (40min.; M-Sa 12 per day, Su 3 per day; £5), **Sligo** (2hr., 3 per day, £9.50), **Donegal Town** (50min., £5.50) on the way to **Galway** (5hr., 3 per day, £12.50), and **Dublin** (5hr., 4 per day, £11). **Feda O'Donnell Coaches** (☎ (075) 48114 or (091) 761 656) drives to **Galway** (£10) via **Donegal Town** (M-Th and Sa 2 per day, F and Su 3 per day; £5) and to **Crolly** (£5) via **Dunfanaghy** (2 per day, more F and Su). **Lough Swilly Buses** (☎ 22863) head north toward the **Fanad Peninsula** (M-Sa 2 per day, £6) to **Derry** (M-Sa 9 per day, £5), and south to **Dungloe** (M-Sa 3 per day, £8). **John McGinley Coaches** (☎ 35201) sends a bus twice a day to **Gweedore** via **Dunfanaghy** and to **Dublin** (£11). **McGeehan's Bus** (☎ (075) 46150) goes twice a day to **Killybegs** (£8) and **Glencolmcille** (£10). **Northwest Busways** (☎ (077) 82619) sends buses around Inishowen (M-F 4 per day, Sa 3 per day), making stops in **Buncrana** (£4.50), **Carndonagh** (£5), and **Moville** (£5.50). **Doherty's Travel** (☎ (075) 21105) has buses that leave for **Dungloe** and **Burtonport** from Dunnes at 5pm daily (£6).

Bike Rental: Church St. Cycles (☎ 26204), by the cathedral. £40 per week; deposit £40. Open M-Sa 10am-6pm. **Starlight Garage** (☎ 22248). £7 per day, £35 per week; deposit £10. Open M-Sa 9am-6pm.

PRACTICAL INFORMATION

Tourist Offices: Bord Fáilte (☎ 21160), ¾ mi. past the bus station and out of town on Port (Derry) Rd. Info on Co. Donegal and accommodations bookings. Open July-Aug. M-Sa 9am-7pm, Su 10am-2pm; Sept.-June M-F 9am-5pm. **Chamber of Commerce Visitors Information Centre,** 40 Port Rd. (☎ 24866), is closer with a slightly smaller selection of info on Letterkenny and the rest of Co. Donegal. Open M-F 9am-5pm.

Banks: AIB, 61 Upper Main St. (☎ 22877 or 22807). **Bank of Ireland,** Lower Main St. (☎ 22122). **Ulster Bank,** Main St. (☎ 24016). All are open M-W and F 10am-4pm, Th 10am-5pm. AIB and Bank of Ireland both have **24hr. ATMs.**

Laundry: Duds n' Suds, Pearse Rd. (☎ 28303). Open June-Sept. M-Sa 8am-7pm, Oct.-May M-Sa 8am-9pm. Wash and dry about £5.

Hospital: Letterkenny General (☎ 25888), off High Rd. past the roundabout, north of town.

Pharmacy: Magee's Pharmacy, Main St. (☎ 21409 or 21419). Open M-W 9am-6:30pm, Th-F 9am-8pm, Sa 9am-6:30pm.

LETTERKENNY (LEITIR CEANNAN) ■ 385

Counseling and Support: Samaritans, 20 Port Rd. (24hr. phone-line ☎ 27200). Drop in for one-on-one counseling Th-Su 7-10pm. **Letterkenny Women's Refuge,** Pearse Rd. (☎ 26267). Open M-F 9am-5pm. **Letterkenny's Women's Centre,** Port Rd. (☎ 24985). Open M-F 9am-1pm and 2-5pm.

Post Office: Halfway down Main St. (☎ 22287). Open M and W-F 9am-5:30pm, Tu 9:30am-5pm, Sa 9am-5:30pm.

Internet Access: Cyberworld, Main St. (☎ 20440), in the Courtyard Shopping Centre. £5 per hr., students £3.50. Open M-Sa 10:30am-9:30pm, Su 1-7:30pm. **Letterkenny Central Library and Arts Center,** Main St. (☎ 24950 or 21968). Open M, W, and F 10:30am-5:30pm; Tu and Th 10:30am-8pm; Su 10:30am-1pm.

ACCOMMODATIONS

The Arch Hostel (IHO), Upper Corkey (☎ 57255). This hostel is located 6 mi. out of town in Pluck; take the Derry (Port) Rd. from the roundabout near the bus station. Continue straight at the next roundabout onto the divided carriageway. At the first break in the median, turn right across the way and then head left, following the signs for Pluck. Stay on the same road until it passes under an archway, then fork right. The hostel is on the right. Better yet, call from town for pick-up. The Gallagher family welcomes hostelers to the 6 beds in a refinished loft above their stable. Open May-Oct. £7.50 per person.

White Gables, Mrs. McConnellogue, Lower Dromore (☎ 22583). Lower Dromore is the 3rd exit from the roundabout 3 mi. out on Derry Rd.; the house is ½ mi. along Lower Dromore, around a bend. Call for pick-up from town. Clean and cheery rooms. The upstairs balcony has great views of Letterkenny's green fields. £16, with bath £17.

Riverview B&B (☎ 24907), off Derry Rd. 2 mi. past Letterkenny. Turn left after the Clan Ree Hotel; signs point the way. Huge rooms with views of the quiet countryside. Full-sized snooker table. £16, with bath £18.

FOOD

Letterkenny offers a fair share of cheap meals in pleasant—even quirky—cafe settings. **Tesco,** in the Letterkenny Shopping Centre behind the bus station, has all you could ask for in a grocery store. (Open M-W 9am-7pm, Th-F 9am-9pm, Sa 9am-6pm, Su noon-6pm.) **SuperValu,** on the lower level of the Courtyard Shopping Centre, is well-stocked and central. (☎ 27053. Open M-W and Sa 8:45am-6:15pm, Th-F 8:45am-9pm.) **The Natural Way,** 55 Port Rd., sells wholefood and herbal remedies. (☎ 25738. Open M-Sa 9am-6pm, F 9am-8pm.)

Galfees, in two locations: 63 Main St. (☎ 28535), near the High Rd. fork, and in the basement of the Courtyard Shopping Centre (☎ 27173). The stand-alone one is the nicer of the 2. Bistro upstairs 6-9:30pm. Open M-Sa 9am-10pm, Su noon-7pm. In the Courtyard Centre, Irish illustrations and wood walls transcend the shopping mall. Most evening entrees £4-5. Open 8:30am-7:30pm, cheaper evening menu served from 5pm.

Cafe Rico, 3-4 Oliver-Plunkett Rd. (☎ 29808), at the end of Main St. across from the library. Full breakfasts and sandwiches (£2-4) in a coffee shop decked in wrought-iron lamps and tile prints. Open M-F 8:30am-5:30pm, Sa until 6pm, Su 11am-4pm.

Pat's Too, Main St. (☎ 21761). Hearty take-away meals for the budgeteer. Sit-in option in its tiled interior. Always crowded at night. 9 in. pizza about £4, kebab special £3.75. Delivery available. Open M-Th 1pm-12:30am, F and Su 1pm-1am, Sa 1pm-3:30am.

PUBS

Cottage Bar, 42 Main St. (☎ 21338). A kettle on the hearth, animated conversation around the bar, and nuns drinking Guinness in the corner. Trad Tu and Th.

McClafferty's, 54 Main St. (☎ 21581). Daytime patrons are an older, contemplative set; at night they're younger. Modern ballads and rock Su.

McGinley's, 25 Main St. (☎ 21106). Hugely popular student bar in the chapel-like upstairs; slightly older crowd on the Victorian ground floor. Live rock and blues W-Su.

The Old Orchard Inn, High Rd. (☎ 21615). A 5min. walk past Manse Hostel in a secluded parking lot. The 3 floors of logwood furniture and leafery are always packed. The cellar bar on the bottom floor hosts occasional trad; the disco on the top floor is a local magnet. Disco open W and F-Sa until 2am. Cover £4-5.

SIGHTS

Neo-Gothic **St. Eunan's Cathedral,** perched high above town on Church Ln., looks like the heavenly kingdom when it's floodlit at night. Church Ln. is on your right up Main St. away from the bus station. Proposed as a "resurrection of the fallen shrines of Donegal," the cathedral's construction took 11 years—all years of economic hardship and depression. The story of St. Columb is beautifully carved in the arch at the junction of the nave and transcript. (Open daily 8am-5pm, except during Su masses at 8, 9, 10, 11:15am, and 12:30pm. Free.) Opposite, the smaller **Parish Church of Conwal** (Church of Ireland) shelters a number of tombstones, some of which date from circa 1600. (Su services 8 and 10:30am.)

Renovated during the summer of 1999, the **Donegal County Museum,** High Rd., displays exhibits of anything and everything having to do with Co. Donegal. (☎ 24613. Open M-F 10am-12:30pm and 1-4:30pm, Sa 1-4:30pm. Free.)

INISHOWEN PENINSULA ☎ 077

It would be a shame to leave Ireland without seeing the Inishowen Peninsula, an untouristed mosaic of pristine mountains, forests, meadows, and white sand beaches that reaches farther north than "the North." The peninsula is dotted with villages and two towns, Buncrana and Carndonagh. The winding road that connects them affords views of continually sublime scenery. It takes three to five days to see the entire peninsula properly without a car, and even with a car one would hardly want to spend less time.

The nearest commercial center to Inishowen is Derry, whose residents often vacation here. **Lough Swilly** (Derry head office ☎ (028) 7126 2017; Buncrana depot ☎ (077) 61340) runs buses from Derry to points on the Inishowen: **Buncrana** (35min.; M-F 10 per day, Sa 12 per day, Su 3 per day); **Moville** and **Greencastle** (50min.; M-F 5 per day, Sa 6 per day); **Carndonagh** (55min.; M-F 6 per day, Sa 4 per day); **Malin** (1hr.; M, W, and F 2 per day, Sa 3 per day); and **Malin Head** (1½hr.; M, W, and F 2 per day, Sa 3 per day). Swilly also connects **Buncrana** directly to **Carndonagh** (50min., M-Sa 3 per day). Swilly Buses offers an eight-day "Runabout Ticket" (£20, students £15) and student rates on all individual trips; their return fares are considerably cheaper than two one-way tickets. **Northwest Buses** (Moville office ☎ 82619) runs from **Moville** through **Culdaff, Carndonagh, Ballyliffin, Clonmany, Buncrana, Fahan,** and on to **Letterkenny** (M-Sa 2 per day); from **Shrove** to **Derry** via **Moville** (1hr., M-Sa 2 per day); from **Buncrana** to **Derry** (M-Sa 5 per day); and from **Malin Head** to **Derry** via **Culdaff** and **Muff** (M-Sa 1 per day). The last bus of the day will also stop in Malin Head if you request so in Derry.

Inishowen's unusual inland landscape is outdone only by its striking northern and western shores. The clearly posted **Inish Eoghain 100** road takes exactly 100 mi. to navigate the peninsula's perimeter. Drivers will find this the best route for seeing Inishowen. *Let's Go* does not recommend hitchhiking, but hitchers report having an easy time on this road. Cycling can be difficult in places, particularly near the Gap of Mamore, due to ferocious northwesterly winds and hilly terrain. Cyclists may resort to using the roads that crisscross the peninsula to shorten long distances between sights. The map published by the Inishowen Tourism Society, available at the Carndonagh tourist office, is the most comprehensive.

GRIANÁN AILIGH

Ten miles south of Buncrana at the bottom of the peninsula and 3 mi. west of Derry (see **Derry**, p. 465), the hilltop ringfort Grianán Ailigh (GREEN-in ALL-ya) is an excellent place to start or finish your tour of Inishowen. This site has been a cultural center for at least 4000 years: first as a Druidic temple at the grave site of Aedh, the son of The Dagda, divine king of the Túatha De Dannan of pre-Christian Ireland; then as a seat of power for the northern branch of the Uí Néill clan, who ruled Ulster and moved here after their chieftain married Princess Aileach of Scotland; and finally as a Mass rock where Catholics worshipped in secret during the time of the Penal Laws (see **Protestant Ascendancy**, p. 11). Much of the present stone structure is a 19th-century reconstruction, but the bottom section of the circular wall is original. Beyond the fort, a cross marks the site of a healing well holy since pre-Christian times and supposedly blessed by St. Patrick.

The fort figures into many legends and tales, including the naming of Inishowen (the Island of Owen). Owen was the son of **Niall of the Nine Hostages**, the semi-legendary ancestor of the Uí Néill (O'Neill) clan. One story claims that Niall slept with an old hag to gain sovereignty over Ireland. Once in charge, he captured young St. Patrick and brought him to Ireland as a slave. Having escaped captivity and begun his missionary work, St. Patrick baptized Niall's son Owen at this very same hillfort, consecrating the Uí Néill fortress as a Christian holy site. The prominence of Grianán Ailigh as the home of rulers ended in the 11th century when Donal McLaughlin, the Prince of Inishowen, was defeated by Brian Ború's grandson, Murtagh O'Brien. Each of O'Brien's men was ordered to carry away one stone from the royal palace of Aileach so that it could never be an outsider's seat of power. The symbolic identity of the fort survived past its physical destruction, and after the Flight of the Earls in 1607 (see **Feudalism,** p. 9, and **Rathmullan,** p. 383), Red Hugh O'Neill swore he'd return to Grianán Ailigh as high ruler of Ireland. Legend has it that Red Hugh's soldiers still lie slumbering in a cave near the fort, each with one hand on the hilt of his sword and the other on the reins of his also-sleeping horse. When the new ruler of Ireland lands on the island, they will awake. Shh.

To reach the fort from Derry, turn off Derry Rd. at Bridgend onto N13, which leads to Letterkenny. From Letterkenny, follow N13 past the turnoff for R265 and R237. Signs before Burt point the way. Two miles down N13 from Bridgend is the Catholic **Burt Circular Chapel,** a modern-day replica of the ancient fort. Just past the Circular Chapel on the N13 is the **Grianán Ailigh Heritage Center,** inside a former Church of Ireland. The center can prepare you for the 2 mi. journey with informative displays and stomach-bending meals. (☎ 68000. Open 10am-10pm. £1.50; students, seniors, and children £1. Lunch specials £4-5; served noon-3pm.) Grianán Ailigh is on top of the hill, on a path behind the Circular Chapel. The 300- year-old **Burt Woods** are next to the fort. No public transport comes near the fort, so the carless will have to cycle or walk. Travelers who choose to hitch say drivers are particularly nice on the 2 mi. incline; hill or no hill, *Let's Go* does not recommend hitching. A 2½ mi. route begins at the Burt Circular Chapel, offering cyclists a gentler alternative. (Directions available at the tourist office.) A pleasant 9 mi. shortcut returns to Buncrana; take the first left after Burt Circular Chapel heading towards Bridgend.

BUNCRANA

Long Slieve Snaght looms over Buncrana, north of Fahan. While not terribly exciting in itself, the town is Inishowen's most common entry point, offering beds and conveniences to peninsular explorers.

▶ PRACTICAL INFORMATION. A temporary **tourist office** resides in the Chamber of Commerce building on St. Oran's Rd. To get there, proceed down Main St. away from the bus depot. Halfway down the hill, turn right on St. Oran's Rd.; the tourist office is one block away on the right. It offers maps and brochures for Buncrana and the entire peninsula and books accommodations. (☎ 20020. Open June-Aug. M-F 9am-5pm, Sa 9am-1pm.) **AIB,** 8 Market Sq. (☎ 61087; open M-W and F 10am-12:30pm and 1:30-4pm, Th 10am-12:30pm and 1:30-5pm), and **Bank of Ireland,** Main St. (☎ 61795; open M-W and F 10am-4pm, Th 10am-5pm), both have **24-hour ATMs. Valu-Clean,** Lower Main St., removes clothes' odoriferous emanations. (☎ 62570. Laundry £4.50. Open M-Sa 9am-6pm.) **E. Tierney Chemist's,** Lower Main St., is the local pharmacy. (☎ 62412. Open M-F 9:30am-6:30pm, Sa 9:30am-6pm.) For **police** (*Garda*), ☎ 61555, and in an **emergency,** ☎ 999. The **post office,** Main St., is also a newsagent. (☎ 61010. Open M-F 9am-1:15pm and 2:15-5:30pm, Sa 9am-1pm.)

▶ ACCOMMODATIONS, FOOD, AND PUBS. Waterfront House, Swilly Terr., has huge, comfortable rooms, a great view of Swilly Lough, and an inexhaustibly hospitable owner. To get there, take Derry Rd. toward the town center, turn onto Swilly Rd. just before the shorefront, then turn left onto Swilly Terr. All rooms have baths; a kitchen, coffee, and tea are always accessible. (☎ 61222. £16 per person.) **O'Donnell's Supermarket,** past the bus depot away from the waterfront, sells staples behind a stunning storefront with two cheery murals. (☎ 61719. Open daily 7am-10:30pm.) Banks, bars, and bikes bump elbows on Main St. In the middle of Main St., the **Town Clock Restaurant** covers the middle ground, with local favorites from toasties to kebabs. (☎ 63279. Most dishes £4. Open daily 9am-9pm.) The **West End Bar,** Upper Main St., has a copper bar that shines like a lucky penny. (☎ 61564. Live music some Sa nights.) **O'Flaitbeartais** (o-FLAH-her-tees), Main St. (☎ 61305), has a hunting aesthetic, but locals of all trades flock here nightly.

▶ SIGHTS. The town's most widely promoted attraction—aside from its shore—is the community owned and operated **Tullyarvan Mill,** half a mile north of town on Dunree Rd. (a continuation of Main St.). This renovated corn mill presents a mixture of exhibitions on textile history, tracing Buncrana's transition from handweaving in 1739 to Fruit-of-the-Looming in 1999. The mill also houses a craft shop and coffee shop. (☎ 61269. Open year-round M-F 10am-5pm, June-Sept. also Sa-Su 2-5pm.) Two castles overlook peaceful, pretty **Swan Park:** the stately Queen Anne-era **Buncrana Castle,** in which Wolfe Tone was imprisoned after the French "invasion" of 1798 failed (see **Rebellion, Union, and Reaction,** p. 13); and the 1430 **O'Doherty Keep,** a not quite Arthurian castle that looks more like a derelict mansion. Both are closed to the public. To reach the park, walk up Main St. toward the shorefront. Follow Castle Ave. from the roundabout next to the West End Bar and Cinema. The park is beyond the Castle Bridge, which arcs 100 yd. to the right. A **coastal walk** begins at Castle Bridge, goes past the keep, turns left at the castle, and then ascends the hill. **Ned's Point Fort,** also along the coast, was built in 1812 but is surprisingly (but not pleasantly) modern-looking. The path passes Porthaw Bay and culminates in sandy **Sragill Strand. Friar Hegarty's Rock,** beyond the beach, witnessed the friar's murder during the Penal Times (see **Protestant Ascendancy,** p. 11).

WEST INISHOWEN
From Buncrana, the Inish Eoghain 100 runs through Dunree Head and the Mamore Gap, while R238 cuts through the interior directly to Clonmany and Ballyliffin.

DUNREE HEAD AND THE MAMORE GAP
Fort Dunree and the Mamore Gap were the last area of the Republic occupied by the British, who passed the fort to the Irish army in 1938. **Dunree Head** pokes out into Lough Swilly 6 mi. northwest of Buncrana. Salt-and-peppered peaks rise up against the ocean buffered by the occasional bend of sandy, smooth beach. At the tip of the head, **Fort Dunree** hides in the jagged sea cliffs. Today the fort holds a military museum and is a superb vantage point for admiring the sea-carved landscape of the Inishowen and Fanad peninsulas. An example of the Guns of Dunree, one of six built during the 1798 Presbyterian Uprising to defend Lough Swilly against hypothetical Napoleonic invaders, is among the museum's displayed weaponry. The museum's exhibits also include copies of German Intelligence maps of the Inishowen Peninsula from World War II. The fort's location overlooking Lough Swilly is a boon for birdwatchers. (Open June-Sept. M-Sa 10am-6pm, Su 1-6pm. Fort and walks £2; students, seniors, and children £1.)

Farther north along Inish Eoghain 100 toward Clonmany, a sign points left up a hill to the edge of the **Mamore Gap.** This breathtaking pass teeters 800 ft. above sea level between Mamore Hill and Urris. Otherworldly views over the mountains to the Atlantic can be seen from the pass's eastern face. The steep road through proves difficult but worthwhile for hikers and cyclists. It's only a 30-minute climb uphill; most bikers will be forced to walk. It's easier to drive, although the hairpin turns over the sea are sometimes frightening. Queen Mebdh of Connacht, Cú Chulainn's archenemy in the Táin (see **Legends and Folktales,** p. 23), is supposedly buried here (and at Knocknarea, Co. Sligo, and a few other places).

The road descends from the gap onto wave-scoured northern beaches. The Inish Eoghain 100 proceeds to **Urris, Lenan Head,** and inviting **Lenan Strand.** Once known for its prodigious (even for Donegal) *poitín* production, Urris was the last area in Inishowen to relinquish spoken Irish. The subdivided flat-bed farms along the road reveal the continued influence of Famine-era farming practices. Heading north, the road passes over Dunaff Head, through Rockstown Harbour and ends in an outstanding beach.

CLONMANY, BALLYLIFFIN, AND DOAGH ISLAND
North of the Gap, two tiny villages, **Clonmany** and **Ballyliffin,** are separated by 1 mi. Their combined forces make a restful spot to spend the night on a leisurely exploration of the Inishowen peninsula: Clonmany provides the pubs and food, while Ballyliffin has plenty of accommodations and long stretches of sandy beach tackled by crystal-clear ocean water.

In Clonmany, grab a big bite to eat at the **Glashady Bistro,** Main St., which has a friendly staff and home-cooked meals. (☎ 76915. Full entrees £3-4. Open daily 9am-midnight.) More country music and occasional trad fills the weekend air in and around **McFeeley's** (☎ 76122), across the street at Corner House. Both pubs are saturated with trad during the **Clonmany Festival** in the first full week of August.

Ballyliffin's highlights are a famous golf course and three long miles of golden sands on Pollen Strand. Grassy dunes connect Ballyliffin with **Doagh Island,** where **Carricksbrahy Castle,** a former seat of the MacFaul and O'Donnell clans, now exists in wave-crashed ruins at the end of a 2½ mi. beach walk. The golf links have attracted the likes of golf pro Nick Faldo, who described them as the most natural he had ever seen. Many who play here, including Mr. Faldo, stay at the incredible ◪**Rossaor House,** near the entrance of town. Though dearer than other B&Bs, Rossaor pampers guests with a landscaped garden, fantastic views of the Strand and Malin Head, and smoked salmon scrambled egg breakfasts. (☎ 76498; email Rossaor@gofree.indigo.ie. Singles £27; doubles £45.) Alternatively, wanderers can stay in spacious, well-furnished rooms at the **Castlelawn House,** just behind the Strand Hotel. (☎ 76600; singles £20, doubles with bath £38), or next door at **Carrickabraghey House,** owned by the sister of Castlelawn's proprietress. (☎ 76977. Same rates, lessening any sibling rivalry.)

Doagh Visitors Centre can be reached by turning left off the road from Ballyliffin to Cardonagh, well-signposted along the only road on the land strip. The center is a well-meaning reconstruction of famine life, with sod houses and a display of the local plants used for sustenance and medicinal purposes. Check out the bogbine, a plant that grows in mossy wetland areas; its juice is still used as a last-resort cure for acne. (☎ 76493. Open daily 10am-5pm. £3; students, seniors, and children £2.)

NORTH INISHOWEN

From the southeastern coast, R240 cuts straight up the middle of the peninsula to commercial Carndonagh, a good stop for amenities. North of Carndonagh, R238 veers east to Culdaff. Going north on R242 leads to Malin Head, the northernmost tip of the island.

CARNDONAGH

Two miles south of Trawbreaga Bay, "Carn" is Inishowen's main market town, where the peninsula's farmers swarm on alternate Mondays to sell sheep and cattle. Northern explorers conveniently hit all the necessary commodities and services in this busy hub of the northern peninsula. Predictably, commercial Carn has but one sight to offer, the old Church of Ireland that hulks half a mile down Bridge St. Outside its walls, **Donagh Cross,** a 7th-century Celtic cross, is all that remains of the monastery founded by St. Patrick when he brought Christianity to the peninsula. Two shorter pillars flank the cross. One depicts David playing his harp; the other stands in the graveyard of the church and displays Christ's crucifixion. The church's bell supposedly came from the Spanish Armada ship *Trinidad de Valoencera,* which went down in Kinnagoe Bay.

Inishowen Tourism, Chapel St., just off The Diamond, is non-Bord Fáilte and remarkably helpful with info on the entire peninsula and accommodations bookings. (☎ 74933. Open June-Aug. M-F 9:30am-7pm, Sa 10am-6pm, Su noon-6pm; Sept.-May M-F 9:30am-5:30pm.) **AIB,** The Diamond, is the only bank in town with a **24-hour ATM.** (☎ 74388. Open M 10am-12:30pm and 1:30-5pm, Tu-F 10am-12:30pm and 1:30-4pm.) **Carn Cabs,** The Diamond (☎ 74580), provides taxis for late-night jaunts. **McCallion's Cycle Hire,** 3 mi. from town on Ballyliffen Rd., will collect and deliver cycles anywhere on the peninsula. (☎ 74084. £6 per day, £25 per week.) **ValuClean,** Bridge St., washes and dries for £4.80. (☎ 74150. Open M-Sa 9am-6pm.) **McAteer's,** The Diamond, is the local pharmacy. (☎ 74120. Open M-Sa 10am-6pm.) **G&S Supersave,** in the Carnfair Shopping Centre on Bridge St., sells a full array of foods. (☎ 74124. Open M-Sa 9am-9pm, Su 11am-9pm.) Also in the Carnfair Shopping Centre is **The Book Shop,** which offers used books to read on the beach and a huge selection for Irish history enthusiasts. (☎ 74389. Open Su-Tu and Th-F 2-7pm, Sa 11am-7pm.) For **police** (*Garda*), ☎ 74109. The **post office** meters mail on Bridge St. (☎ 74101. Open M-F 9:30am-1:30pm and 2:30-5:30pm, Sa 9:30am-1pm.)

Less than a quarter mile from The Diamond, Chapel St. turns into Millbrae when it hits **Dunshenny House,** where dainty flowered wallpaper sets the mood. (☎ 74292. Singles £20; doubles £35; all with bath and full breakfast included. Book in advance.) Just down Chapel St. from the church, the house of **Oregon B&B** has stood since 1911. Except for the addition of a few modern fixtures, it hasn't changed much over the years, and is full of character. (☎ 74113. £15 per person.) **The Coffee Shop,** The Diamond, is a hugely popular spot where the owner is sure to give a proper welcome to new faces in Carndonagh. (☎ 74177. Sandwiches £1.30. Open M-Sa 9am-5pm.) The **Bridge St. Cafe** sells cheap eats and is open late. (☎ 74528. M-Th 10am-12:30pm, F-Sa 10am-1am, Su 5pm-1am.) **The Quiet Lady,** Main Rd., gets noisy at night when she plays modern beats for a dancing local crowd. During the day she offers quiet but filling two-course meals, including roasted meats and vegetables for about £4. (☎ 74777. Live music W and Sa-Su. DJ F.) Tiny **Bradley's Bar,** Bridge St. (☎ 74526), is best known as the local "men's pub." Queen Victoria supposedly used the toilet in the men's room, although the place shows no hint of having been graced by her requisite royal frills.

CULDAFF

The area around Culdaff on the eastern side of the peninsula holds a variety of ancient monuments. The "Bronze Age triangle" above the Bocan Parochial House, 1 mi. from Culdaff toward Moville, includes the **Bocan Stone Circle,** the **Temple of Deen,** and **Kindroyhead,** where there is evidence of a prehistoric field and fort system. A 4 yd. tall **high cross** stands next to the **Cloncha Church,** which is signposted 1½ mi. from Culdaff toward Moville. Culdaff hosts the annual **Charles Macklin Festival** (☎ 79104) in the second weekend in October, with performances of the 17th-century playwright's plays, poetry competitions, and a slew of trad sessions. **Culdaff Strand,** an outstanding stretch of beach best seen at daybreak or dusk, is a short walk from McGrory's.

The brand-spanking-new ■**Pines Hostel,** Bunagee Rd., houses guests in a spiffy owner-built house with a hearth-warmed common room. (☎ 79060. Sheets £1. Dorms £7.50; doubles £20.) Anyone on a trad pilgrimage should stop in at ■**McGrory's,** where sessions sometimes last until dawn and the fresh food attracts half the town at dinner time. (☎ 79104. Meat and vegetarian entrees £5-8.) Attached to McGrory's is possibly the best live music venue in the northwest, **Mac's Backroom Bar.** Chummy owners Neil and John McGrory play regularly in sessions. Wednesday nights are the wildly popular "country jam" (£4), where you're likely to hear tongue-in-cheek covers of anything from Al Green to Prince. (Trad Tu and Sa, in summer Th as well. Cover £5 on Sa.)

MALIN HEAD

Inishowen's most popular attraction is Malin Head, the northernmost tip of Ireland. Aside from its latitude, the stretch is remarkable for its rocky, wave-tattered coast and sky-high sand dunes. Inish Eoghain 100 continues east from Cardonagh to Malin Head, passing through the tiny, tidy town of Malin on its way. Five miles from Culdaff, R242 coincides with the Inish Eoghain 100 and winds toward Lagg, where the five standing rocks of **Five Fingers Strand** jut into the ocean. The water looks tempting but is icy cold and dangerous for swimming. The sand dunes here are reputedly the highest in Europe, towering over 100 ft. high in some places. Turn left above the little white church (near the Inish Eoghain 100 signs) to get to this worthwhile detour. High above the beach, **Knockamany Bens** provide fantastic views of the whole peninsula and even Tory Island on a clear day. Meteorologists have repeatedly recorded Malin Head as the **sunniest spot in Ireland.**

The scattered town of **Malin Head** includes **Bamba's Crown,** the northernmost point in Ireland, a tooth of dark rock rising up from the ocean spray. Until the 19th century, Malin Head was the site of an annual pilgrimage in which young men and women "frisked and played in the water all stark naked" to celebrate the sea god's affair with the goddess of the land (see **The Wee of all Flesh,** p. 393). On a clear day, the Head offers a view of Scotland, and perhaps an opportunity to hear the call of the corncrake, a nearly extinct bird. A Lloyd's of London signal tower, built in 1805 by the British Admiralty to catalog the ships sailing to and from North America, still stands sentry over the point. Written in white-washed stones on a nearby lower cliff and readable from thousands of feet above, "S. S. EIRE" (*Saor Stát Éire*; "Irish Free State") identified Ireland as neutral territory to Nazi would-be bombers. People have removed many of the stones to spell out their own names nearby. A path to the left of the carpark skirts the cliff face and leads to **Hell's Hole,** a 250 ft. chasm that roars with the incoming tide. Farther down the coast arcs around the naturally formed **Devil's Bridge.** The bridge is no longer safe to walk on, so the Devil is stuck down in the hole. The raised beaches around Malin Head (the result of glaciers' passage through the region millions of years ago) are covered with semi-precious stones; walkers sifting through the sands may find jasper, quartz, small opals, or amethysts. The **Atlantic Circle** is a 5 mi. circuit of the Inish Eoghain 100 that tours the tip of the peninsula.

The area around Malin Head teems with affordable accommodation. To reach the **Sandrock Holiday Hostel (IHO/IHH),** Port Ronan Pier, take the left fork off the Inish Eoghain 100, just before the Crossroads Inn (also a bus stop). This hostel is right on the water with huge views and potential glimpses of seals, dolphins, and puffins. (☎ 70289; www.carndonagh.com/sandrock. Sheets £1. Wash £3, dry £1.50. 10-bed dorms £7.) **Rent bikes** at **McCallion's Cycle Hire** in Carn. (☎ 74084. £6 per day.) On the Inish Eoghain 100, after the phone booth and across from the post office, the **Malin Head Hostel (IHO/IHH)** welcomes guests with an open fire, reflexology, aromatherapy, homemade elderflower cordial, and carraigan moss jam (made from a local seaweed). The rooms are impeccably clean, and Mary's garden yields fresh, cheap veggies for hostelers' consumption. (☎ 70309. Wash £2, dry £1.50. **Bike rental** £6 per day. 5-bed dorms £7; twins and doubles £20.) Half a mile south of the Crossroads Inn, across the street from the phone box, Mrs. Doyle at **Barraicín** keeps a friendly, comfortable B&B and tends a beautiful garden. A bulletin board with maps and photos of local sights helps plan the day's agenda. If you're traveling by bus, get off at Malin Head's only phone booth, which stands a bit before the post office. (☎ 70184. Singles £18; doubles £30, with bath £32.) Five miles past Malin on the way into Malin Head, the **Druin Doo B&B,** has a wonderful loft for weary travelers. (☎ 70287. £16 per person.)

All of Malin Head's pubs have licensed fisherman's late hours and sell groceries. Trad sessions, fishing tackle, and revitalizing brew are all sold at **Farren's,** Ireland's northernmost pub. (Music nightly July-Aug.) **Seaview Tavern and Restaurant** (☎ 70117), commonly referred to as "Vera Dock's," pours your pint in its 12 ft. by 12 ft. space beneath shelves full of corn flakes and motor oil. It opens at 8am and closes (supposedly) at 1am. The restaurant next door serves tasty local seafood. (£5-9. Open daily 9am-10pm.) **The Cottage,** located along the Atlantic Circle near Bamba's Crown, provides tea, scones, crafts, and the closest thing to a tourist trap at Malin Head. (☎ 70257. Open June-Aug. daily 11am-6pm. Sessions 9:30pm F mid-July to mid-Aug. £2; bring in your own alcohol.) Back toward Malin along R242, **Bree Inn** delivers heaping plates of food in front of an open fire. (☎ 70161. Food served daily Easter-Aug. noon-10pm, Sept.-Easter 4-10pm.)

EAST INISHOWEN

Though overshadowed by its northern neighbor Malin Head, **Inishowen Head** draws beach-bathers to the natural beauty of Shroove Strand. The most northern beaches, which look over Lough Foyle, gather small crowds on the handful of hot days in an Irish summer. A delightful "shore walk" runs about 6 mi. between the small thumb of Inishowen Head and Moville. Any local can direct you to **Port a**

THE WEE OF ALL FLESH Just past Bree along the right-hand fork of R242 is the "Wee House of Malin" *(Teach na Maiohann)*. This unassuming collection of cave, well, and ruined stone church in a seaside cove exemplifies the melding of pagan and Christian ritual. The well was once the site of Druidic festivals, but after its blessing by medieval St. Muirdhealach, it became the object of devout Christians' annual pilgrimages on August 15. The pilgrims' behavior, however, might not accord with usual expectations: a 17th-century observer commented that upon reaching the well, male and female bathers would wash the sins off each others' naked flesh. The famed "wee house" (actually a cave behind the church) was said to fit an infinite number of people inside. In reality, the cave contains a copper mine; experts speculate that this ancient story developed from the ease with which copper was removed and the cave expanded. The young people of Malin Head still celebrate August 15, but in these more modest days they call it "Sports Day" and participate in only fully clothed athletic events in broad daylight.

Doris, a delightful little cove accessible only at low tide, and littered with semi-precious Shroove pebbles. **Tunn's Bank,** a huge sandbank a few hundred yards offshore, is reputedly the resting place of *Manannan McLir*, the Irish sea god whose children were turned into swans.

MOVILLE AND GREENCASTLE

Small Moville is located at the intersection of R239 (from Derry) and R238 (from Culdaff). Smaller Greencastle hides 3 mi. north along R239.

Inishowen Adventures, at the Moville Boat Club on Front Shore, offers **sailing, windsurfing,** and **snorkeling.** (☎ 82460. Open from 2pm F-Su or by appointment; instruction available.) An **AIB** with a **24-hour ATM** is on Main St. (☎ 82050. Open M-W, and F 10am-12:30pm and 1:30-4pm, Th 10am-12:30pm and 1:30-5pm.) **Ulster Bank,** Main St., also has a 24-hour ATM. **Hannon's Pharmacy,** Main St., cures ills. (☎ 82649. Open M-Sa 9:30am-6pm.) The **post office** is on Malin Rd., which intersects Main St. (☎ 82016. Open M-F 9am-1pm and 2-5:30pm, Sa 9am-1pm.)

Moville's only hostel, the **Moville Holiday Hostel (IHH)** on Malin Rd. is, for the time being, closed to the public and instead has signed an agreement to house refugees and asylum-seekers. (☎ 82378. Don't bother asking for asylum for a night—trust us, it won't work.) Instead, try Mrs. McGuinness's **Dunroman B&B,** off Derry Rd. across from the football field, where breakfast is served in a sunny conservatory overlooking the River Foyle. Green plants and murals painted by the eldest daughter complete the splendid setting. (☎ 82234. £17.50, with bath £18.50.) **Mace Grocery,** Main St., will sell you all the groceries you require. (☎ 82045. Open daily 7am-9pm.) The local budget traveler's haven is at the **Barron's Cafe,** Main St., which serves heaps of food cooked in the kitchen of the family house behind the storefront. (☎ 82472. All-day breakfast £3.85, burgers around £2, entrees £4-6. Open daily 9:30am-9:30pm.) There is also a plethora of chippers and tea shops scattered along the streets leading to the shore. Fishermen and bikers keep company at the **Hair o' the Dog Saloon,** at the Lower Pier behind Main St. Not so common pub grub includes juicy, American-style hamburgers on homemade kaiser buns for £2-4, and pizza for £3-5. (☎ 82600. Live music weekends. Food is served noon-9pm.) Patrons are welcome to bring along their tent or caravan and **camp** the night overlooking the lough. **Terry's Tavern,** on Main St., gathers an older local crowd in its front rooms, and a younger set in the back room. (☎ 82183. Open M-F 5pm-1am, Sa-Su 2pm-1:30am.) Thirteen other pubs also grace the streets of tiny Moville, making for a pleasant pub crawl.

From Inishowen Head, the road leads south to **Greencastle,** a village that throws some spice (or sea salt, at least) into the one-street Irish-village mix. Institutions associated with a sophisticated fishing industry line its coast, including fishermen's schools, a net-weaving factory, a maritime museum, and a fish factory. Greencastle's **castle,** built by the Red Earl of Ulster, is now an ivy-covered ruin.

The Irish government maintains a center for training professional fishing boats next to the ruins. Relics of life on the seas are in the spotlight at the **Greencastle Maritime Museum** on the shorefront. Housed in an old coast guard station, the museum's impressive collection includes a traditional but newly built Fanad *curragh*, an Armada room, a 19th-century rocket cart for rescuing passengers of wrecked ships, ship models, and photographs. (☎ 81363. Open June-Sept. M-Sa 10am-6pm, Su noon-6pm, by appointment during the rest of the year. £2; students, seniors, and children £1.)

In a secluded mansion overlooking Lough Foyle, Mrs. Anna Wright warmly welcomes guests to the high-ceilinged, aristocratic **Manor House** (☎ 81010). From Main St., head out of town in the direction of the castle. Turn right at the first road after the town, following the sign to the castle and the fort. Pass both and fork right at the bottom of the hill, following the signs to the B&B. Also on the road from Derry is the **Brooklyn Cottage,** a modest whitewashed house with all the conveniences of a modern urban apartment. You'll further appreciate its view of Lough Foyle after a conversation with its owner, Peter Smith, chairman of the Maritime Museum. (☎ 81087. Open Mar.-Nov. Singles £20; doubles £36; all with bath and TV.) In a spic 'n' span kitchen behind an inviting neo-Georgian storefront, **Seamy's Fish and Chips** does justice to the work of Greencastle's fishermen. (☎ 81379. All meals under £3. Open M-F noon-1am, Sa-Su 2pm-1am.) Next door at **Kealey's Bar** (☎ 81105), not to be confused with Kealey's down the street, stacked gleaming bottles line the walls. While Kealey's has enough liquor to keep a trawler's worth of fishermen happy, there's only enough seating for Greencastle's tiny population. The **Greencastle Fort,** next to the castle, was once a Napoleonic sea fort that housed 160 redcoats and 30 bluecoats to man nine cannons, and it has served the likes of Kaiser Wilhelm and the emperor of Japan. Today it protects an inn and a pub with affordable grub. (☎ 81044. Meals £6-8; served daily in summer noon-9:30pm. Spontaneous trad sessions most summer weekend nights.) **The Drunken Duck** (☎ 81362), 3 mi. north of Greencastle, is a friendly pub so-called because of a local woman whose beer leaked into her ducks' feeding troughs.

NORTHERN IRELAND

Northern Ireland's natural beauty includes the Glens of Antrim's pockets of green; Giant's Causeway, one of the world's strangest geological sights; and the Fermanagh Lake District. The cease-fires of recent years have allowed Belfast and Derry to develop into hip, pub-loving destinations for travelers and students. Pub culture, urban neighborhoods, and tiny villages show everyday life in a divided society of mostly peaceful citizens.

The predominantly calm tenor of life in the North has been overshadowed overseas by media headlines concerning politics and bombs. Although the North maintains a strong education system and a progressive health insurance policy, unemployment and poor housing are pressing problems. Some writers describe the North's conflicts in terms of class. According to these essayists, the moderate middle class wants peace, but the working classes have less to lose and therefore have historically supported the reactionary extremists. Violent fringe groups on both sides are less visible than the huge division in civil society that sends Protestants and Catholics to separate neighborhoods, separate stores, separate pubs, and often separate schools, with separate, though similar, traditional songs and slang. Oftentimes the split is hard for an outsider to discern, especially in rural vacation spots. On the other hand, it would be near impossible for a visitor to leave Northern Ireland without seeing street curbs in both cities and villages painted the official colors of their residents' sectarian identity. The widespread support of the 1998 Peace Agreement and the reinstatement of Home Rule in 2000 raises hopes for a resolution to the struggles that have divided the island for centuries, but a lasting peace still hangs in the balance.

HIGHLIGHTS OF NORTHERN IRELAND

Take in **Belfast's** fascinating political murals (p. 406), the Golden Mile, Donegall Square, and Docklands on a black cab tour.

The **Glens of Antrim** (p. 448) harbor tiny villages between glorious mountains, forests, and lush valleys; the **Ulster Way** walking trail snakes along the nearby coast.

60 million-year-old volcanic rock formations at **Giant's Causeway** (p. 459) are the stuff of Irish myth and legend. Sip whiskey at nearby **Bushmills** (p. 460) distillery.

Derry's (p. 465) Tower Museum, St. Columb's Cathedral, Bloody Sunday Centre, and the murals of the Bogside neighborhood illuminate this city's complex past.

The **Ulster Way** weaves a hiking path through 560 mi. of Northern Ireland, passing through the spectacular and under-explored **Sperrin Mountains** (p. 481).

Dreamily absorb seaviews and castle ruins in **Downhill**, Co. Derry (p. 464).

ESSENTIALS

MONEY

Legal tender in Northern Ireland is the British pound. Northern Ireland has its own bank notes, which are identical in value to English and Scottish notes of the same denominations but not accepted outside Northern Ireland. Both English and Scottish notes, however, are accepted in the North. The Republic of Ireland's pounds

396 ■ ESSENTIALS

Northern Ireland

[Map of Northern Ireland showing counties, towns, and surrounding geography including the Atlantic Ocean, North Channel, Scotland, and Irish Sea.]

CURRENCY

THE BRITISH POUND	UK£1
AUS$1 = £0.30	= AUS$2.57
CDN$1 = £0.44	= CDN$2.25
EUR€1 = £0.60	= EUR€1.67
IR£1 = UK£0.76	= IR£1.31
NZ$1 = £0.30	= NZ$3.32
SAR1 = £0.09	= SAR10.55
US$1 = £0.66	= US$1.51

! The information in this book was researched in the summer of 2000. Inflation and the Invisible Hand may raise or lower the listed prices by as much as 20%. Up-to-date exchange rate information can be found at http://finance.yahoo.com/m3?u.

are generally not accepted in the North, with the exception of some border towns which will calculate the exchange rate and add an additional surcharge. UK coins now come in logical denominations of 1p, 2p, 5p, 10p, 20p, 50p, and £1. Most banks are closed on Saturday, Sunday, and all public holidays. On "bank holidays," occurring several times a year in both countries (see p. 494), most businesses shut down. Usual weekday bank hours in Northern Ireland are Monday to Friday 9:30am to 4:30pm.

For more comprehensive travel information, see **Essentials,** p. 40.

> Northern Ireland is reached by using the UK **country code 44;** from the Republic dial **048**. The **phone code** for every town in the North is **028**.

SAFETY AND SECURITY

Although sectarian violence is dramatically less common than in the height of the Troubles (see p. 399), some neighborhoods and towns still experience turmoil during sensitive political times. It's best to remain alert and cautious while traveling in Northern Ireland during **Marching Season,** from July 4 to 12 (**Orange Day;** see p. 397). The twelfth of August, when the Apprentice Boys march in Derry (see p. 13), is also a testy period during which urban areas should be avoided or traversed with much circumspection. The most common form of violence is property damage, and tourists are unlikely targets (beware of leaving your car unsupervised, however, if it bears a Republic of Ireland license plate). In general, if you are traveling in Northern Ireland during Marching Season, be prepared for possible transport delays (such as a few regular bus routes canceled), and for some shops and services to be closed. Vacation areas like the Glens and the Causeway Coast are less affected by the parades. In general, use common sense in conversation, and, as in dealing with any issues of a culture not your own, be respectful of locals' religious and political perspectives. Overall, Northern Ireland has one of the lowest tourist-related crime rates in the world.

Border checkpoints have been removed, and armed soldiers and vehicles are less visible in Belfast and Derry. Do not take **photographs** of soldiers, military installations, or vehicles; your film will be confiscated and you may be detained for questioning. Taking pictures of political murals is not a crime, although many people feel uncomfortable doing so in residential neighborhoods. Unattended luggage is always considered suspicious and worthy of confiscation. It is still generally unsafe to hitch in Northern Ireland. *Let's Go* never recommends hitchhiking.

HISTORY AND POLITICS

Northern Ireland is a region that lacks a collective cultural identity. Its citizens still recognize themselves by their political allegiances rather than geographic lines—as Unionists and Nationalists. The 950,000 Protestants are generally Unionists, who want the six counties of Northern Ireland to remain in the UK; the 650,000 Catholics tend to identify with the Republic of Ireland, not Britain, and many are Nationalists, who want the six counties to be part of the Republic. Extremists bring violence into the argument; they are referred to as Loyalists and Republicans, respectively. The conflict between them has seemed intractable. In December 1999, the world felt a tentative optimism descend upon the North after the reinstatement of Home Rule, but persistent internal roadblocks have proven that dreams of a unified North still lie off in the distance.

For more information about the geographic region of Northern Ireland before the formation of the Republic, see **Life and Times,** p. 7.

BRITISH RULE AND THE DIVISION OF IRELAND

The 17th century's **Ulster Plantation** systematically set up English and Scottish settlers on what had been Gaelic-Irish land and gave Derry to the City of London—hence the name "Londonderry" (see p. 10). Protestants fleeing France in the late 17th century sought refuge in Ulster, bringing commercial skills to the small linen manufacturing industry. Over the following two centuries, merchants and working-class immigrants from nearby Scotland settled in northeast Ulster. Institutionalized religious discrimination that limited Catholic access to land ownership and

398 ■ HISTORY AND POLITICS

1609
English and Scottish settlers set up the Ulster Plantation in Counties Donegal, Derry, Tyrone, Armagh, Cavan, and Fermanagh.

1613
Derry incorporated as Londonderry on March 29.

1641
An uprising (ostensibly for Charles I) begins in Ulster, spreads south, and massacres thousands of Protestants.

1689
Jacobites (followers of James II) lay siege to Protestant Derry. Thousands die of starvation and disease.

1717
Beginning of mass migration of Ulster-Scots to the American colonies.

1795
Protestant Orange Order founded in Armagh.

1798
United Irishmen rebellion begins.

1801
Act of Union creates "United Kingdom of Great Britain and Ireland" and "United Church of England and Ireland."

other basic rights made it profitable for Scottish Protestants to settle here. The British developed an industrial economy in Counties Antrim and Down while the rest of the island remained agricultural. By the end of the 19th century, Belfast was a booming industrial center with thriving textile and shipbuilding industries, but most refused to hire Catholic workers.

As the Republican movement gained fervor in the South in the late 19th century, the picture looked much different in the Northeast. The Ulster Plantation and Scottish settlement, over the course of 300 years, had created a working- and middle-class population in Ulster who identified with the British Empire and did not support Irish Home Rule. The **Orange Order**, named after King William of Orange, who had won victories over Catholic James II in the 1690s (see p. 11), organized the Ulster Protestants in local lodges, with ritualistic behaviors resembling those of the masonic order. They ordained July 12th as an annual holiday on which to hold parades to celebrate William's defeat of James at the Battle of the Boyne. The Order's constituency continued to grow long after the Act of Union in 1801 (see p. 13) made its original mission obsolete. In the 1830s, the government attempted to dissolve the Order. It quietly gained momentum, however, culminating in its explosive opposition to the first Home Rule Bill in 1886 (see p. 15).

Lawyer and politician **Edward Carson** and his ally **James Craig** translated Ulster Unionism into terms the British elite understood. When Home Rule looked likely in 1911, Carson held a mass meeting, and Unionists signed the Ulster Covenant of Resistance to Home Rule (1912). In 1914, when Home Rule appeared imminent, the Unionist **Ulster Volunteer Force** (**UVF**; see p. 15) armed itself by smuggling guns in through Larne—an act that prompted fearful Nationalists to smuggle their own guns in through Howth. World War I gave Unionists more time to organize and gave British leaders time to see that the imposition of Home Rule on all of Ulster would mean havoc: the UVF intended to fight the **Irish Republican Army** (**IRA**; see p. 17) who in turn would fight the police. The **1920 Government of Ireland Act** created two parliaments for North and South. The Act of Union went nowhere in the south and was quickly superseded by the Anglo-Irish Treaty and Civil War (see p. 17), but the measure—intended as a temporary one—became the basis of Northern Ireland's government until 1973. The new Parliament met at **Stormont**, near Belfast.

The new statelet included only six of the nine counties in the province of Ulster, excluding Donegal, Monaghan, and Cavan, which had Catholic majorities. This arrangement suited the one million Protestants in the six counties, yet it threatened the several hundred thousand Protestant Unionists living elsewhere on the island and the half-million Catholic Nationalists living within the new Ulster. Carson and Craig had approved these odd borders, hoping to create the largest possible area with a permanent Protestant majority. Craig, as the North's first Prime Minister, his successor **Sir Basil Brooke**, and most of their Cabinet ministers thought in terms of, as Brooke put it, of "a Protestant state for a Protestant people." Orange lodges and other strongly Protestant groups continued to control politics, and the Catholic minority boycotted elections. Anti-Catholic discrimination was widespread. The **Royal Ulster Constabulary** (**RUC**), the new and Protestant police force in the North, filled its ranks with part-time policemen called Bs and **B-Specials**, a major source of Catholic casualties. The IRA continued sporadic campaigns in the North through the 20s and 30s with little result. In the Irish State, the IRA was gradually suppressed.

The 1930s sent the Northern economy into the dumps, requiring more and more British subsidies, while the Stormont Cabinet aged and withered. **World War II** gave Unionists a chance to show their loyalty. The Republic of Ireland stayed neutral and stayed out, but the North welcomed Allied troops, ships, and airforce bases. The need to build and repair warships raised employment in Belfast and allowed Catholics to enter the industrial workforce for the first time. The Luftwaffe firebombed Belfast toward the end of the war, making it one of the UK's most damaged cities. In May 1945, Churchill thanked the North and attacked Éire's neutrality in a famous speech.

Over the following two decades, a grateful British Parliament poured money into Northern Ireland. The North's standard of living stayed higher than the Republic's, but discrimination and joblessness persisted. The government at Stormont neglected to institute social reform, and parliamentary districts were painfully and unequally drawn to favor Protestants. Large towns were segregated by religion, perpetuating the cultural separation. After a brief, unsuccessful try at school desegregation, Stormont ended up granting subsidies to Catholic schools. As the Republic gained a sure footing, violence receded on the island and, barring the occasional border skirmish, the IRA was seen as finished by 1962 when the *New York Times* bid it a formal, eulogy-like farewell. **Capt. Terence O'Neill**, who became the third Stormont Prime Minister in 1963, tried to enlarge the economy and soften discrimination, meeting in 1965 with the Republic's Prime Minister, Sean Lemass. O'Neill may have epitomized the liberal Unionist attitude when he said, "If you treat Roman Catholics with due kindness and consideration, they will live like Protestants."

THE TROUBLES

The economy grew, but the bigotry festered, as did the Nationalist community's resentment at being left unemployed and unrepresented. The American civil rights movement inspired the 1967 founding of the **Northern Ireland Civil Rights Association (NICRA)**, which worked to end anti-Catholic discrimination in public housing. NICRA leaders tried to distance the movement from constitutional concerns, although many of their followers didn't get the message: the Republican song "A Nation Once Again" often drowned out "We Shall Overcome" in demonstrations. Protestant extremists included the acerbic **Dr. Ian Paisley**, whose **Ulster Protestant Volunteers (UPV)** overlapped in membership with the illegal, resurrected, paramilitary UVF. The first NICRA march was raucous but nonviolent. The second, in Derry in 1968, was a bloody mess disrupted by Unionists and then by the RUC's water cannons. This incident is thought of as the inception of the Troubles.

Catholic **John Hume** and Protestant **Ivan Cooper** formed a new civil rights committee in Derry but were overshadowed by Bernadette Devlin's student-led, radical **People's Democracy (PD)**. The PD encouraged, and NICRA opposed, a four-day peaceful march from Belfast to Derry starting on New Year's Day, 1969.

1845
Great Irish Famine begins.

1870
Filibustering Isaac Butt seats himself as head of the new Home Rule League.

1886
First Home Rule Bill, attempting to return autonomy to Ireland, defeated.

1892
Ulster Convention at Belfast opposes Home Rule Parliament.

1893
2nd Home Rule Bill finds defeat in British House of Lords.

1905
Sinn Féin and Ulster Unionist Council both formed.

1912
Over 500,000 Protestants in the North sign a pledge to oppose Home Rule by all means necessary.

1914
Home Rule Bill passed by England but suspended because of WWI.

1916
Easter Rising.

1920
IRA kills 14 British secret agents. British soldiers retaliate, killing 12.

1920
Government of Ireland Act partitions country into North and Republic.

NORTHERN IRELAND

1939
The North joins WWII while the Republic remains neutral.

1967
Northern Ireland Civil Rights Association (NICRA) founded.

October 1968
Derry riots over the NICRA's march; unofficial start to the Troubles.

January 1969
People's Democracy student-led march meets violent RUC opposition in Derry. RUC banned from Bogside, known as "Free Derry."

July 1969
Further riots break out during Marching Season.

August 1969
British Army arrives to maintain order.

1970
IRA divides, with the more violent Provos taking charge.

August 1970
Moderate Social Democratic and Labor Party (SDLP) founded.

January 1972
"Bloody Sunday" in Derry. 14 Catholics killed. British embassy in Dublin burned down in retaliation.

Paisleyite harassment along the way was nothing compared to the RUC's physical assault on Derry's Catholic Bogside once the marchers arrived. After that, Derry authorities agreed to keep the RUC out of the Bogside, and this area became **Free Derry.** O'Neill, granting more civil rights concessions in hopes of calming everyone down, was deserted by more of his hard-line Unionist allies. On August 12, 1969, Catholics based in Free Derry threw rocks at the annual Apprentice Boys parade along the city walls. The RUC attacked the Bogside residents, and a two-day siege ensued. Free Derry retained its independence, but the violence showed that the RUC could not maintain order alone. The British Army arrived—and hasn't left yet.

O'Neill resigned in 1969. Between 1970 and 1972, Stormont leaders alternated concessions and crackdowns to little effect. The rejuvenated IRA split in two, with the Socialist "Official" faction practically fading into insignificance as the new **Provisional IRA, or Provos** (the IRA we primarily hear about today), took over with less ideology and more arms. British troops became the IRA's main target. In 1970, John Hume founded the **Social Democratic and Labor Party (SDLP),** with the intention of bringing about social change through the support of both Catholics and Protestants; by 1973, it had become the moderate political voice of Northern Catholics. British policies of **internment without trial** outraged Catholics and led the SDLP to withdraw from government. The pattern was clear: any concessions to the Catholic community might provoke Protestant violence, while anything that seemed to favor the Unionists risked an explosive IRA response.

On January 30, 1972, British troops fired into a crowd of nonviolent protesters in Derry; the famous event, called **Bloody Sunday,** and the ensuing reluctance of the British government to investigate, increased Catholic outrage. Fourteen Catholics were killed: the soldiers claimed they had not fired the first shot, while Catholics said the soldiers shot at the backs of unarmed, fleeing marchers. Only in 1999 did official re-examination of the event begin. On February 2, 1972, the British embassy in Dublin was burned down. Soon thereafter, the IRA bombed a British army barracks. After further bombings in 1973, Stormont was dissolved and replaced by the **Sunningdale executive,** which split power between Catholics and Protestants. This policy was immediately crippled by a massive Unionist work stoppage, and a policy of **direct British rule** from Westminster began. A referendum that year, asking if voters wanted Northern Ireland to remain part of the United Kingdom, showed that voters supported the Union at a rate of 90 to 1—Catholics had boycotted the polls. The verdict didn't stop the violence, which brought an average of 275 deaths per year between 1970 and 1976.

In 1978, 300 Nationalist prisoners in the Maze Prison in Northern Ireland began a campaign to have their special category as political prisoners restored. The campaign's climax was the 10-man H-Block **hunger strike** of 1981. The leader, **Bobby Sands,** was the first to go on hunger strike. He was elected to Parliament from a Catholic district in Tyrone and Fermanagh even as he starved to death. Sands died after 66 days and became a martyr; his face is still seen on murals in the Falls section of Belfast (see p. 423). The remaining prisoners officially ended the strike on October 3.

Sands's election was no anomaly. The hunger strikes galvanized Nationalists, and support for **Sinn Féin,** the political arm of the IRA, surged in the early 80s. British Prime Minister Margaret Thatcher and Taoiseach Garret FitzGerald signed the **Anglo-Irish Agreement** at Hillsborough Castle in November 1985. The Agreement granted the Republic of Ireland a "consultative role" but no legal authority in the governance of Northern Ireland. It improved relations between London and Dublin but infuriated extremists on both sides. Protestant paramilitaries began to attack the British Army, while the IRA continued its bombing campaigns in England. In 1991 and 1992, the Brooke Initiative led to the first multi-party talks in the North in over a decade, but they did not include Sinn Féin. In December 1993, the **Downing Street Declaration,** issued by Prime Minister John Major and Taoiseach Albert Reynolds, invited the IRA to participate in talks if they refrained from violence for three months.

THE 1994 CEASEFIRE

On August 31, 1994, the IRA announced a complete cessation of violence. While Loyalist guerillas cooperated by announcing their own ceasefire, Unionist leaders bickered over the meaning of the IRA's statement; in their opinion, it did not go far enough—only the IRA's disarmament could signify a commitment to peace. Nonetheless, **Gerry Adams,** Sinn Féin's leader, defended the statement and called for direct talks with the British government. The peace held for over a year.

In February 1995, John Major and Irish Prime Minister John Bruton issued the **joint framework** proposal. The document suggested the possibility of a new Northern Ireland Assembly that would include the "harmonizing powers" of the Irish and British governments and the right of the people of Northern Ireland to choose their own destiny. Subsequently, the British government began talks with both Loyalists and, for the first time, Sinn Féin. Disarmament was the most prominent problem in the 1995 talks—both Republican and Loyalist groups refused to give up their weapons.

A flurry of tragic events left the future of Northern Ireland as tenuous as ever. The IRA ended their ceasefire on February 9, 1996, with the bombing of an office building in London's Docklands. Despite this setback, the stalled peace talks, to be chaired by US diplomat **George Mitchell,** were slated for June 10, 1996. Ian Paisley, now leader of the extreme **Democratic Unionist Party (DUP),** objected to Mitchell's appointment, calling it a "dastardly deed," but did not boycott the talks. The talks proceeded sluggishly and precariously. Sinn Féin did not participate in these talks because it did not agree to the **Mitchell Principles,** which included the total disarmament of all paramilitary organizations. Despite this exclusion, Sinn Féin's popularity grew in Northern Ireland: in the May elections, they gathered 15% of the vote. The credibility of Sinn Féin was seriously jeopardized on June 15, 1996, when a blast in a Manchester shopping district injured more than 200 people.

As the peace process continued, the Orangemen's July and August marches grew more contentious. Parades through Catholic neighborhoods incited violence on the part of both residents and marchers. The government created a **Parades Commission** to oversee the rerouting of parades and encourage

---

May 28, 1974
Direct British rule from Westminster begins after failed power-sharing experiment.

1970-1976
Strife brings an average of 275 deaths per year.

March 1981
Bobby Sands leads Nationalist prisoners in hunger strike.

November 1985
Anglo-Irish Agreement signed; grants Republic a "consultative role" without legal authority in governance of North.

March 1993
IRA bomb in Warrington kills 2 children and provokes public outcry.

August 1994
IRA announces a ceasefire, but refuses to disarm.

January 1995
British army ends daytime patrols in Belfast.

February 1995
"Joint framework" proposal opens up talks with Sinn Féin, IRA's political arm.

January 1996
US diplomat George Mitchell proposes surrender of all guerilla weaponry.

February 1996
IRA breaks ceasefire with London office bombing.

NORTHERN IRELAND

July 1996
4-day clash between Catholics and Protestants in Portadown.

May 1997
Tony Blair elected Prime Minister of Britain. Sinn Féin-Sinn Féin wins more seats in Parliament but refuses to swear allegiance to Queen.

July 1997
Portadown riots after Marching Season; Orange Order cancels and re-routes several parades.

July 1997
IRA announces a 2nd ceasefire.

1998
Peace process delayed by violent outbursts from extremist groups.

January 1998
Tony Blair announces an independent judicial inquiry into the 1972 Bloody Sunday massacre.

April 11, 1998
Northern Ireland Peace Agreement drafted. A May 22 landslide vote confirms that even a majority of Protestants approve. 108-member Northern Ireland assembly assigned governing responsibilities.

the participation of both sides in negotiations. Protestants see the Commission's decisions as infringing on their rights to practice their culture. Catholics argue that the marches are a form of harassment and intimidation from which they deserve protection. Violence flared around **Orange Day, 1996,** when the Parades Commission banned an Orange Order march through the Catholic Garvaghy Rd. in Portadown, a staunchly Protestant town. Unionists reacted by throwing petrol bombs, bricks, and bottles at police, who answered with plastic bullets. After four days of violence, police allowed the marchers to go through, but this time Catholics responded with a hail of debris. Nightly rioting by both sides also took place in Belfast, where RUC policemen were wounded, and in Derry, where Catholic Dermot McShane died after being run over by a jeep.

On October 7, the IRA bombed British army headquarters in Belfast, killing one soldier and injuring 30 in Northern Ireland's first bombing in two years. In early 1997, the IRA tried to make the North an issue in the upcoming British elections by making several bomb threats, including one that postponed the Grand National horse race. No one was injured, but public ire was aroused and John Major condemned Sinn Féin.

In May of 1997, the Labour party swept the British elections and **Tony Blair** became Prime Minister, bringing hope for peaceful change. Sinn Féin made its most impressive showing yet: Gerry Adams and member Martin McGuinness won seats in Parliament but were barred from taking their seats by their refusal to swear allegiance to the Queen. Despite this act, the government ended its ban on talks with Sinn Féin. Sinn Féin, however, refused to join the talks. Hopes for a ceasefire were dashed when the car of a prominent Irish republican was bombed; in retaliation, the IRA shot two members of the RUC.

GOOD FRIDAY AGREEMENT

The British government's Northern Ireland Secretary Mo Mowlam had a rough introduction to her new job: marching season in 1997 was the most violent in recent years. The Orange Order held a large march through Portadown a week before Orange Day. More than 80 people were hurt in the ensuing rioting and looting, and Mowlam came under scrutiny for allowing the parade to go on without considering the consequences. On July 10, the Orange Order called off and re-routed a number of contentious parades, offering hope for peace. The marches that were held were mostly peaceful; police fired plastic bullets at rioters in Derry and Belfast, but there were no casualties. On July 19, the IRA announced an "unequivocal" ceasefire to start the following day.

In September 1997, Sinn Féin joined the peace talks. Members of the **Ulster Unionist Party (UUP),** the voice of moderate Protestants, joined shortly thereafter and were attacked by Ian Paisley and the DUP for sitting with terrorists. **David Trimble,** leader of the UUP, assured Protestants that he would not negotiate directly with Sinn Féin. Co-founders of the recently formed, religiously mixed **Northern Ireland Women's Coalition,** Catholic Monica McWilliams and Protestant Pearl Sagar brought a human rights agenda and a commitment to peace to the talks, where they were subjects of derision by Ian Paisley.

Some groups still opposed the peace process. In January 1998, another 12 people were killed by sectarian violence, mostly committed by extremist Loyalists against Catholic civilians. After two Protestants were killed by Catholic extremists in early February, Unionist leaders charged Sinn Féin with breaking its pledge to support only peaceful actions toward political change and tried to oust party leaders from the talks. Mitchell, Mowlam, Blair, and Irish Prime Minister Bertie Ahern continued to push for progress, holding the group to a strict deadline in April. Mowlam made the unprecedented move of visiting Republican and Loyalist prisoners in the maximum-security Maze prison to encourage their participation in the peace process.

After an interminable week of negotiations, the delegates approved a draft of the **1998 Northern Ireland Peace Agreement** in the early morning after April 10, Good Friday. The Agreement emphasized that change in Northern Ireland could come only with the consent of the majority of its people. It declared that the "birthright" of the people is the right to choose whether to identify personally as Irish, British, or both; even as the status of Northern Ireland changes, the Agreement says, residents retain the right to hold Irish or British citizenship.

On Friday, May 22, in the first island-wide vote since 1918, residents of both the North and the Republic voted the Agreement into law. A resounding 71% of the North and 94% of the Republic voted yes to the Agreement, meaning that a majority of Protestants voted in favor of the Peace Agreement, which divided governing responsibilities of Northern Ireland into three strands. The main body, a new 108-member **Northern Ireland Assembly**, assigns committee posts and chairs proportionately to the parties' representation. Catholics see this body as an opportunity for reclaiming the political power they were long denied. On June 25, the UUP and the SDLP won the most seats, and Sinn Féin garnered more support than ever before, winning 18 assembly seats and two in the executive. David Trimble of the UUP and Seamus Mallon of the SDLP were elected First Minister and Deputy First Minister, respectively, by the assembly. The second strand, a **North-South Ministerial Council**, serves as the cross-border authority. At least 12 possible areas of focus were under consideration by them in 1998, including social welfare issues such as education, transportation, urban planning, tourism, and EU programs. The final strand, the **British-Irish Council**, approaches issues similar to those considered by the North-South Council, but operates on a broader scale, concerning itself with the entire British Isles.

While most felt that Northern Ireland was finally on the verge of lasting peace, a few controversial issues remained unresolved. Sinn Féin called for disbanding the still very largely Protestant RUC, which was cited in an April 1998 United Nations report for its systematic intimidation and harassment of lawyers representing those accused of paramilitary crimes. Blair declared that the RUC would continue to exist, but in June appointed Chris Patten, the former governor of Hong Kong, to head a small one-year commission to review the RUC's recruiting, hiring, training practices, culture, and symbols.

The 1998 marching season brought challenges and tragedy to the newly arrived peace. In the end of May, just a week after the Agreement was voted in, a march by the Junior Orange Order

June 1998
David Trimble and Seamus Mallon elected First Minister and Deputy First Minister, respectively.

June 1998
Tony Blair retains RUC, but appoints Chris Patten to review RUC record.

July 1998
Marching season disrupts the newfound peace.

August 15, 1998
Bombing in Omagh by "Real IRA" splinter group leaves 29 dead and 382 injured.

October 1998
Hume and Trimble receive Nobel Peace Prize.

1999
Northern Ireland Assembly fails to establish itself as politicians battle over disarmament and the release of political prisoners.

December 1999
London signs devolution bill; returns home rule to Northern Ireland. A power-sharing 12-member cabinet is formed.

January 2000
Trimble gives IRA an ultimatum to disarm. The IRA refuses.

February 2000
Inability to resolve disarmament issue leads Britain to suspend power-sharing experiment after 11 weeks.

NORTHERN IRELAND

May 29, 2000
Britain restores power-sharing after IRA promises to disarm.

June 2000
IRA weapon caches are inspected for the first time.

June 30, 2000
Taoiseach Ahern wins an 84-80 "no-confidence" vote. He defends his party's role in the peace process and his questioned appointment of a disgraced former judge to a high financial post.

July 2000
Marching season concludes after 10 days of widespread riots, protests over marching routes, and at least one casualty. Belfast and Portadown are barricaded and shut down by the Orange Order.

July 28, 2000
Final political prisoners are released from Maze Prison near Belfast to both heroic welcomes and bitter disgust. The historic prison is scheduled to close by the end of the year.

Summer 2000
Royal Ulster Constabulary overhaul urged on by Catholics and opposed by Protestants.

provoked violence on Garvaghy Rd., the Catholic zone in largely Protestant Portadown, where violence had erupted in 1996. In light of this disturbance, the Parades Commission hesitated in granting the Orange Day marching permits. On June 15, the Parades Commission rerouted the Tour of the North, banning it from entering the Catholic Cliftonville Rd.-Antrim Rd. areas in Belfast. Aside from two short stand-offs with the RUC, the parade proceeded without conflict. The day after the assembly elections, however, violence broke out between Nationalists and policemen at a parade in West Belfast. The beginning of July saw a wave of violence that included hundreds of bombings and attacks on security forces as well as a slew of arson attacks on Catholic churches.

Other parades passed peacefully, but a stand-off began over the fate of the **Drumcree** parade. The parade, which occurs July 4, was not given permission to march down the Catholic section of Garvaghy Rd. in Portadown. Angered by the decision but encouraged by a history of indecision by the British government, thousands of people participated in a week-long standoff with the RUC that affected the whole country. Rioting occurred there and elsewhere, and Protestant marchers were angered by what they saw as the disloyalty of their own police force. Neither the Orangemen nor the Parade Commission would budge, and the country looked with anxiety toward climactic Orange Day, July 12. On July 11, however, a Catholic home in almost entirely Protestant Ballymoney was firebombed in the middle of the night by local hooligans, and three young boys, Richard, Mark, and Jason Quinn, were killed. Marches still took place the following day; but instead of rioting against the Orangeman who passed though their neighborhoods, Catholics looked on at the marches in silence, holding black balloons and carrying signs that read "for shame." The seemingly intractable Drumcree stand-off gradually lost it numbers, and the Church of Ireland publicly called for its end. Although some tried to distance the boys' deaths from the events at Drumcree, the murders led to a reassessment of the Orange Order and to a new sobriety about the peace process.

On August 15, 1998, a bombing in the religiously mixed town of **Omagh**, Co. Tyrone, left 29 dead and 382 injured. A tiny splinter group calling itself the "Real IRA" claimed responsibility for the attack. The terrorists' obvious motive for one of the worst atrocities of the Troubles was to undermine the Agreement. Sinn Féin's Gerry Adams unreservedly condemned the attack. However, the terrible act only underlined the fact that the majority of people in Northern Ireland, both Catholic and Protestant, had voted in favor of the agreement.

In October of 1998, Catholic John Hume and Protestant David Trimble received the Nobel Peace Prize for their participation in the peace process. The coming year, however, evidenced the failure to form the Northern Ireland Assembly, the fundamental premise of the Agreement. Two major provisions of the pact became the source of irreconcilable difference between Catholic and Protestant politicians: the gradual decommissioning of all paramilitary groups' arms, and the early release of political prisoners. Tensions rose out of the **Northern Ireland (Sentences) Bill,** voted against by members of the UUP, the DUP, and the British Conservative Party, splitting the UK Parliament for the first time during the talks. The bill would release all political prisoners, including those convicted of murder, by May 2000; dissenters feared that the bill did not sufficiently link the release of prisoners to their organizations' full disarmament. The last of the prisoners were released in July (see below). Of greatest concern for most Unionists was the issue of decommissioning: the military wings of political parties, most notably Sinn Féin, were expected to disarm themselves in time for the June elections. Difficulties arose from the Agreement's lack of a time frame for decommissioning. During the summer of 1999, the deadline for the Assembly's inauguration was pushed farther back as Unionists refused to take seats with Sinn Féin; Blair, Mowland, and Ahern spent long nights attempting to negotiate between sides. In July of 1999, Prime Minister Trimble failed to appear on the day that he was due to appoint the newly elected Assembly. Many interpreted Trimble's behavior as following the prerogatives of his own Unionist political party, rather than the democratic will of the voters who approved the Peace Agreement. Trimble's nationalist Deputy Prime-Minister Seamus Mallon resigned the following day.

The 1999 marching season started well, with little trouble around the twelfth of July. Violence began on August 12 as the Apprentice Boys marched through Derry and Belfast. Catholics in Belfast staged a sit-down protest in the path of the marchers, only to be forcefully removed by the RUC. In Derry, the streets fell prey to petrol bombs and riot gear.

DIRECT RULE AND CURRENT EVENTS

In December 1999, London signed the devolution bill and returned home rule to Northern Ireland after 27 years of British rule. A power-sharing 12-member cabinet and government was formed under the leadership of Trimble and Mallon, but the IRA's hidden weapon caches remained a central conflict and threatened the collapse of the new assembly, made up of four parties: the Democratic Unionist Party, the UUP, the Labor Party, and the controversial inclusion of Sinn Féin.

In late January 2000, Trimble gave the IRA an ultimatum to put its weapons "beyond use," a euphemism for disarmament, and predicted a return to British rule if his demands were not met. The February peace talks were hamstrung by the IRA's unwillingness to comply, and further complications arose when the dissident IRA Continuity group bombed a rural hotel in Irvinestown on February 6 in protest of the IRA's 1997 truce. Every Irish political group, including Sinn Féin, condemned the attack. Though the blast injured no one, it was an unwelcome reminder of the past during the stalled peace talks. Soon after, Britain suspended the power-sharing experiment just 11 weeks after its implementation and reintroduced direct British rule.

On midnight of May 29, 2000, Britain restored the power-sharing scheme after the IRA promised to begin disarmament. In June, two ambassadors inspected the secret weapon caches. The monumental advances did little to dispel conflict throughout the rest of the summer. "Teflon" Taoiseach Bertie Ahern scraped out an 84-80 "no-confidence" victory against the opposition Labor party on June 30, defending his Fianna Fail-led government's role in the peace process, as well as the dubious appointment of a disgraced former judge to a high-ranking European Union job. Marching season was, again, a violent, widespread affair, although Tony Blair and Ahern expressed satisfaction over its containment by security. Reacting against the prevention of a march by the Parades Commission through a Catholic section of Portadown, the Orange Order shut down both Belfast and Portadown, barricading streets and rioting with police. The marching season concluded after 10 successive days of violence and at least one casualty. Soon after, On July 28, the last of political prisoners in Maze Prison, near Belfast, walked free under the highly criticized provisions of the 1998 accord. The jail, an intimidating symbol of conflict, is to be closed and possibly used as a museum or monument. While supporters gave the prisoners heroes' welcomes, other civilians and relatives of the deceased found the early release of convicted murderers, often given life sentences, appalling. Many men expressed remorse for the past and stated that their war was over, but others refused to apologize. Though this provides the North with new hope, party disputes are inevitable. More debates remain unresolved, such as the overhaul of the RUC, urged on by Catholics and opposed by Protestants. This promises to be one of many political jousts—Protestant hard-liners have vowed to remove Sinn Féin from the government, while the DUP plans to lock horns with the UUP. The UUP, the Labor Party, and Sinn Féin appear enthusiastic about the peace process in the face of these problems. Much like Stephen Dedalus, Northern Ireland is still trying to awake from its nightmarish history.

BELFAST

Despite Belfast's reputation as a terrorist-riddled metropolis, the city feels more neighborly than most international and even Irish visitors expect. The second-largest city on the island, Belfast (pop. 330,000) is the center of the North's cultural, commercial, and political activity; for several hundred years it has been a cosmopolitan and booming center of mercantile activity, in brazen contrast to the rest of the island (until the "Celtic Tiger" began its own boom over the last decade). Renowned writers and the annual arts festival maintain Belfast's reputation as a thriving artistic center. Such luminaries as poet and Nobel Prize winner Seamus Heaney and poet Paul Muldoon recently haunted the halls of Belfast's esteemed Queen's College, giving birth to a modern, distinctive Northern Irish literary *esprit* that grapples with—and transcends—the difficult politics of the area. The Belfast bar scene, a mix of Irish-British pub culture and international trends, entertains locals, foreigners, and a student population that is as lively as any in the world.

Belfast was founded as the capital of the "Scots-Irish" Presbyterian settlement in the 17th century, and was William of Orange's base during his battles against King James II in 1690 (see **The Protestant Ascendancy**, p. 11). In the 19th century, Belfast became the most industrial part of Ireland, with world-famous factories and shipyards. By 1900, Belfast had gathered enough slums, smoke, flax mills, Victorian architecture, and social theorists to look more British than Irish. The ship-building industry regularly drew Scottish laborers across the channel for jobs, securing the region's allegiance to the UK. During the Troubles (see p. 399), armed British soldiers patrolled the streets, frequent military checkpoints slowed auto and pedestrian traffic, and stores advertised "Bomb Damage Sales."

Those days are over, and due to extensive renovations of Belfast's downtown commercial district, the unobservant traveler could remain oblivious to the city's prior history. The famous sectarian murals of West Belfast are perhaps the most informative source on the effects of the Troubles on the city. During July 5-12, "Marching Season" (also known by some locals as "the silly season"), these murals seem to leap off the walls. This is the week when the "Orangemen," Protestants celebrating William of Orange's victory over Catholic King James II, parade Northern Ireland's streets wearing orange sashes and bowler hats. These marches are usually met with Nationalist (see **Glossary**, p. 495) protests, and violence can ensue. If you are in Belfast during this week, exercise common sense, and expect delays in transportation and availability of services. But be most wary of excessive trepidation; this can actually be one of the most educational times of the year to travel in Northern Ireland.

■ GETTING THERE AND AWAY

Airports: Belfast International Airport (☎ 9442 2888) in Aldergrove. **Aer Lingus** (☎ (0845) 973 7747), **British Airways** (☎ (0845) 722 2111), **Jersey European** (☎ 9045 7200), **British Midland** (☎ 9024 1188), and **Sabena** (☎ 9448 4823) land here. **Airbus** (☎ 9033 3000) runs to Belfast's Europa and Laganside bus stations in the city center (M-Sa every 30min. 5:45am-10:30pm, Su about every hr. 7:10am-8:45pm; £5, £8 return). **Belfast City Airport** (☎ 9045 7745), at the harbor, is the destination of **Manx Airlines** (☎ (0845) 7256 256) and **Jersey European. Trains** run from the City Airport **(Sydenham Halt)** to Central Station (M-Sa 25-33 per day, Su 12 per day; £1).

Trains: All trains arrive at Belfast's **Central Station**, East Bridge St. (☎ 9089 9400; inquiries M-Sa 7:30am-6pm, Su 9:30am-6:30pm). Some also stop at **Botanic Station** (☎ 9089 9400) on Botanic Ave. in the center of the University area, or the **Great Victoria Station** (☎ 9043 4424; open M-Sa 7:30am-6:30pm), next to the Europa Hotel. To: **Derry** (2½hr.; M-F 7 per day, Sa 6 per day, Su 3 per day; £6.70); **Dublin** (2hr.; M-F 8 per day, Sa 8 per day, Su 5 per day; £17); **Bangor** (33min.; M-F 39 per day, Sa 25 per day, Su 9 per day; £3); and **Larne** (M-F 21 per day, Sa 16 per day, Su 6 per day; £3). To get to Donegall Sq. from Central Station, turn left and walk down East Bridge St. Turn right on Victoria St. then left after 2 blocks onto May St., which runs into Donegall Sq. South. A better option for those encumbered with luggage is the **Centrelink** bus service, free with rail tickets (see **Local Transportation,** below).

Buses: There are 2 main stations in Belfast. Buses traveling to and from the west, north coast, and the Republic operate out of the **Europa Station** off Great Victoria St. behind the Europa Hotel (☎ 9032 0011; inquiries M-Sa 7:30am-6:30pm, Su 12:30-5:30pm). Buses to **Dublin** (3hr.; M-Sa 7 per day, Su 4 per day; £10.50) and **Derry** (1hr.40min.; M-Sa 19 per day, Su 6 per day; £6.50). Call for other route info. Buses to and from Northern Ireland's east coast operate out of **Laganside Station** off Donegall Quay (☎ 9033 3000; inquiries M-Sa 8:30am-5:45pm). If on foot, take a left when you exit the terminal onto Queen's Square and walk past the clock tower. Queen's Square becomes High St. and runs into Donegall Pl.; a left here will get you to City Hall and Donegall Sq. (at the end of the street). The **Centrelink** bus connects both stations with the city center and the hostels and B&Bs near Queen's University (see **Local Transportation,** below).

Ferries: To reach the city center from the **Belfast SeaCat terminal** (☎ (08705) 523 523; www.seacat.co.uk), off Donegall Quay, you have 2 options. Late at night or early in the morning, a **taxi** is your best bet; the docks can be somewhat unsafe at these times. If on foot, take a left when you exit the terminal onto Donegall Quay. Turn right onto Albert Sq. about 2 blocks down at the Customs House (a large Victorian stone building). After 2 more short blocks, turn left on Victoria St. (not Great Victoria St.). Turn right again at the clock tower onto High St., which runs into Donegall Pl. Here, a left will lead you to the City Hall and Donegall Sq. (at the end of the street), where you can catch a **Centrelink** bus (see **Local Transportation,** below). SeaCat departs twice or less daily for **Troon** in Scotland (2½hr.); **Heysham** in England (3¾hr.); and the **Isle of Man.** Fares £10-30 without car, cheapest if booked 4 weeks in advance. **Norse Irish Ferries** (☎ 9077 9090) run to **Liverpool** in England. **P&O Ferries** in **Larne** (☎ 0870 2424 777) run to **Cairnryan** in Scotland, and to **Fleetwood**. For information on ferries and hovercraft to Belfast from **England** and **Scotland,** see **By Ferry,** p. 59.

Car Rental: McCausland's, 21-31 Grosvenor Rd. (☎ 9033 3777; fax 9024 1255), is Northern Ireland's largest car rental company. Ford Fiesta or VW Polo £20 per day, £95 per week, discounted rates for longer rentals. Ages 21-70. Open M-Th 8:30am-6:30pm, F 8:30am-7:30pm, Sa 8:30am-5pm, Su 8:30am-1pm. 24hr. car return at all offices. Other offices at **Belfast International Airport** (☎ 9442 2022) and **Belfast City Airport** (☎ 9045 4141). **Budget,** 96-102 Great Victoria St. (☎ 9023 0700). Ages 23-70. Open M-F 9am-5pm, Sa 9am-noon. **Belfast International Airport Office** (☎ 9442 3332). Open daily 7:30am-11:30pm; **Belfast City Airport Office** (☎ 9045 1111). Open M-Sa 8am-9:30pm, Su 10am-9:30pm.

Hitching: Notoriously hard in and out of Belfast—most people take the bus out as far as Bangor or Larne before they stick out a thumb. *Let's Go* does not recommend using your thumb or any other part of your body for this activity.

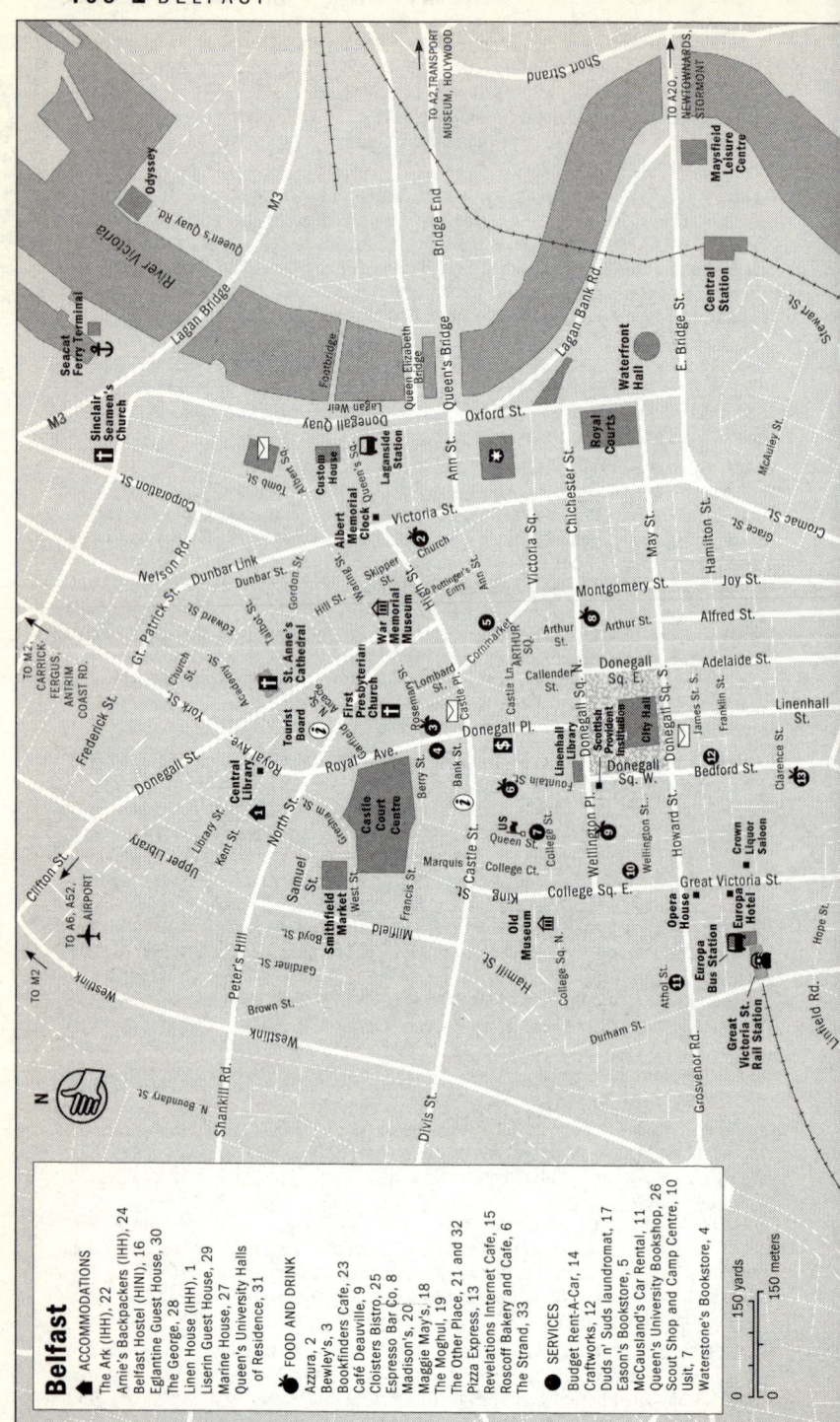

Belfast

ACCOMMODATIONS
The Ark (IHH), 22
Arnie's Backpackers (IHH), 24
Belfast Hostel (HINI), 16
Eglantine Guest House, 30
The George, 28
Linen House (IHH), 1
Liserin Guest House, 29
Marine House, 27
Queen's University Halls of Residence, 31

FOOD AND DRINK
Azzura, 2
Bewley's, 3
Bookfinders Cafe, 23
Café Deauville, 9
Cloisters Bistro, 25
Espresso Bar Co, 8
Madison's, 20
Maggie May's, 19
The Moghul, 19
The Other Place, 21 and 32
Pizza Express, 13
Revelations Internet Cafe, 15
Roscoff Bakery and Cafe, 6
The Strand, 33

SERVICES
Budget Rent-A-Car, 14
Craftworks, 12
Duds n' Suds laundromat, 17
Eason's Bookstore, 5
McCausland's Car Rental, 11
Queen's University Bookshop, 26
Scout Shop and Camp Centre, 10
Usit, 7
Waterstone's Bookstore, 4

BELFAST ■ 409

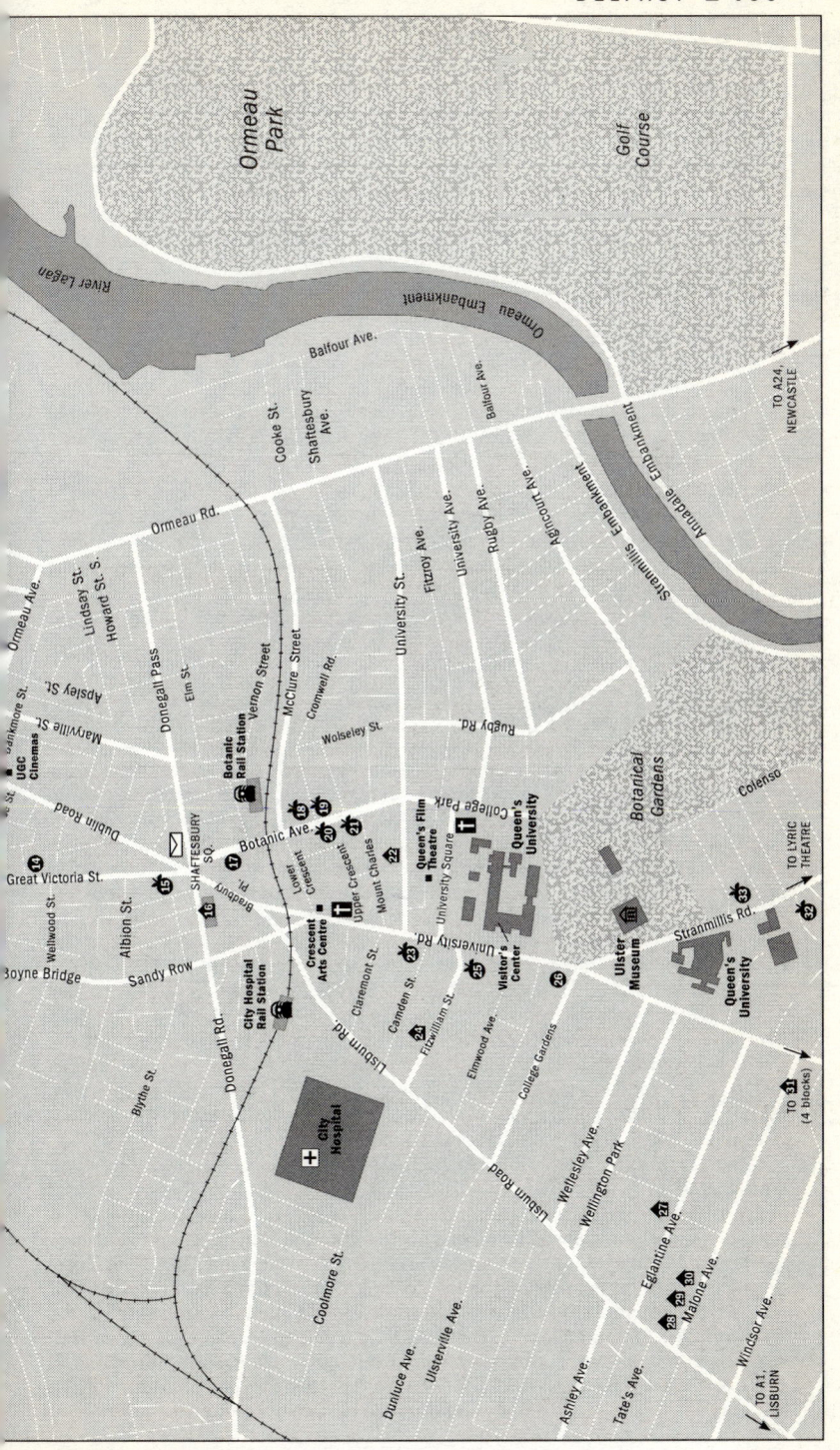

GETTING AROUND

Local Transportation: The red **Citybus Network** (24hr. recorded info ☎ 9024 6485), is supplemented by **Ulsterbus's** "blue buses" to the suburbs. Travel within the city center 50p, seniors and children under 16 free. Citybuses going south and west leave from Donegall Sq. East; those going north and east leave from Donegall Sq. West (80p). Money-saving 4-journey tickets £2.70, seniors and children £1.35. 7-day **"gold cards"** allow unlimited travel in the city (£11.50). 7-day **"silver cards"** permit unlimited travel in either North Belfast, West/South Belfast, or East Belfast (£7.50). All transport cards and tickets can be bought from the kiosks in Donegall Sq. West (open M-Sa 8am-6pm) and around the city. The **Centrelink** bus connects all the major areas of Belfast in the course of its cloverleaf-shaped route: Donegall Sq., Castlecourt Shopping Centre, Europa and Laganside Bus Stations, Central train station, and Shaftesbury Sq. The buses can be caught at any of 24 designated stops (every 12min.; M-F 7:25am-9:15pm, Sa 8:36am-9:15pm; 50p, free with bus or rail ticket). Late **Nightlink** buses shuttle the tipsy from Donegall Square West to various small towns outside of Belfast 1am and 2:30am F-Sa. (£3, payable on board or at the Donegall Sq. W. kiosk.)

Taxis: 24hr. metered cabs abound: **Value Cabs** (☎ 9023 0000); **City Cab** (☎ 9024 2000; wheelchair accessible), **Fon a Cab** (☎ 9023 3333), and **Abjet Cabs** (☎ 9032 0000). Residents of West and North Belfast utilize the huge **black cabs** you'll see in the city center; some are metered, but some follow set routes, collecting and discharging passengers along the way (under £1 charge).

Bike Rental: McConvey Cycles, 10 Pottingers Entry (☎ 9033 0322) and 467 Ormeau Rd. (☎ 9049 1163). Locks supplied. Open M-Sa 9am-5:30pm. £7 per day, £40 per week; deposit £30; panniers £5 per week.

ORIENTATION

Buses arrive at the Europa bus station on **Great Victoria St.** near several landmarks: the Europa hotel, the Crown Liquor Saloon, and the Opera House. To the northeast is the **City Hall** in **Donegall Sq.** A busy shopping district extends north for four blocks between City Hall and the enormous Castlecourt Shopping Centre. Donegall Pl. becomes **Royal Ave.,** and runs from Donegall Square through the shopping area. In the eastern part of the shopping district is the **Cornmarket** area, where several centuries of characteristically Belfast architecture and the pubs of the narrow **entries** hold their ground amongst modern establishments. South of the bus station, Great Victoria St. meets **Dublin Rd.** at **Shaftesbury Sq.** The stretch of Great Victoria St. between the bus station and Shaftesbury Sq. is known as the **Golden Mile** for its highbrow establishments and Victorian architecture. **Botanic Ave.** and **Bradbury Pl.** (which becomes **University Rd.**) extend south from Shaftesbury Sq. into the **Queen's University** area, where cafes, student pubs, and budget accommodations await. In this southern area, the busiest neighborhoods center around **Stranmillis, Malone,** and **Lisburn Rd.** The city center, Golden Mile, and the university area are quite safe; Belfast is generally safer than most American or European cities.

Divided from the rest of Belfast by the Westlink Motorway, working class **West Belfast** is more politically volatile than the city center. There remains a sharp division between sectarian neighborhoods. The Protestant neighborhood stretches along **Shankill Rd.,** just north of the Catholic neighborhood, centered around **Falls Rd.** The two are separated by the **peace line.** The **River Lagan** divides industrial **East Belfast** from the rest of the city. The shipyards and docks that brought Belfast fame and fortune extend north on both sides of the river as it grows into **Belfast Lough.** During the week, the area north of City Hall essentially becomes deserted after 6pm. Although muggings are infrequent in Belfast, it's wise to use taxis after dark, particularly near the clubs and pubs of the northeast area. West Belfast's murals are best seen by day.

PRACTICAL INFORMATION ■ 411

M1 and M2 motorways join to form a backwards "C" through Belfast. A1 branches off from M1 around **Lisburn** and heads south to Newry, where it changes to N1 before continuing through **Dundalk** and **Drogheda** to **Dublin**. M2 merges into A6 then heads northwest to **Derry. Larne** is connected to Belfast by the A8.

🛈 PRACTICAL INFORMATION

TOURIST AND FINANCIAL SERVICES

Tourist Office: 59 North St., St. Anne's Court (☎ 9024 6609). Supplies a great booklet on Belfast, the usual info on the surrounding areas, and an excellent map of the city with bus schedules (free). Formulate specific questions for the harried staff. 24hr. computerized info kiosk outside. Open July-Aug. M-F 9am-7pm, Sa 9am-5:15pm, Su noon-4pm; Sept.-June M 9:30am-5:15pm, Tu-Sa 9am-5:15pm.

Irish Tourist Board (Bord Fáilte), 53 Castle St. (☎ 9032 7888). Provides info on the Republic and makes reservations for accommodations "south of the border." Open June-Aug. M-F 9am-5pm, Sa 9am-12:30pm; Sept.-May M-F 9am-5pm.

Irish Cultural Centre: Culturlann McAdam O Fiaich, 216 Falls Rd. (☎ 9096 4180). Arts center celebrating the Irish language, including performances with simultaneous English translation. Satellite tourist information office located here. Open M-Sa 9am-5pm.

Travel Agency: usit, College St., 13b The Fountain Centre (☎ 9032 7111), near Royal Ave. Sells ISICs, European Youth Cards, **TravelSave** stamps (£6), and virtually every kind of bus or rail pass imaginable. Books ferries and planes, and compiles round-the-world itineraries. Open M and W-F 9:30am-5:30pm, Tu 10am-5:30pm, Sa 10am-1pm. **Additional office** at Queen's University Student Union (☎ 9024 1830). Open M-Tu and Th-F 9:30am-5:30pm, W 10am-5:30pm.

Hostelling International Northern Ireland (HINI): 22 Donegall Rd. (☎ 9032 4733). Books HINI hostels free, international hostels for £2.80. Sells HI membership cards to NI residents (£10, under 18 £6). Open M-F 9am-5pm.

Consulates: US Consulate General, Queens House, Queen St. (☎ 9032 8239). Open M-F 1-4pm. **Canada, Australia, Republic of Ireland, South Africa,** and **New Zealand** not represented.

Banks: Banks and **ATMs** are a dime a dozen in Belfast, virtually one on every corner. The major offices are: **Ulster Bank,** 47 Donegall Pl. (☎ 9027 6000); **First Trust,** 1-15 Donegall Sq. North (☎ 9031 0909); **Bank of Ireland,** 54 Donegal Pl. (☎ 9023 4334); and **Northern Bank,** 14 Donegall Sq. West (☎ 9024 5277). Most banks open M-F 9am-4:30pm.

Currency Exchange: Thomas Cook, 22-24 Lombard St. (☎ 9088 3800). Cashes Thomas Cook traveler's checks with no commission, others with 2% commission. Open May-Oct. M-Tu and Th 5:30am-10pm, W 5:30am-11pm, F-Su 5:30am-midnight; Nov.-Apr. daily 5:45am-8pm. **Belfast International Airport office** (☎ 9444 7500). Open May-Oct. daily M 5:30am-midnight; Nov.-Apr. Sa-Th 5:30am-9pm. Most banks, the HINI on Donegall Rd., and post offices provide bureaux de change and travelers check cashing services for a small fee.

LOCAL SERVICES

Luggage Storage: For security reasons there is no luggage storage at airports, bus stations, or train stations. All 4 **hostels** will hold bags during the day for those staying there, and **the Ark** will also hold bags during extended trips if you've stayed there (see **Accommodations,** below).

Bookstore: Waterstone's, 44-46 Fountain St. (☎ 9024 0159), has a huge selection of everything from chess to chemistry. Open M-W and F-Sa 9am-5:30pm, Th 9am-9pm, Su 1-5pm. **Eason's,** Royal Ave., Castlecourt Shopping Centre (☎ 9023 5070). Large Irish section; lots of travel guides. Open M-W and F-Sa 9am-6pm, Th 9am-9pm, Su 1-6pm. **Queen's University Bookshop,** 91 University Rd. (☎ 9066 6302), offers Irish history textbooks and a renowned collection of Beat generation authors and manuscripts. Open

M-F 9am-5:30pm, Sa 9am-5pm. There are dozens of 2nd-hand bookstores around; a quick walk in the university area is sure to turn up several.

Libraries: Belfast Central Library, 122 Royal Ave. (☎ 9024 3233). Open M and Th 9:30am-8pm, Tu-W and F 9:30am-5:30pm, Sa 9:30am-1pm. Free email 30min. per day. **Linen Hall Library,** 17 Donegall Sq. North (☎ 9032 1707). See **Sights,** p. 419. Extensive genealogy and information on the Troubles. Free Irish language courses Sept.-May. Bring a photo ID for visitor's pass. Open M-F 9:30am-5:30pm, Sa 9:30am-4pm.

Public Record Office: 66 Balmoral Ave. (☎ 9066 1621). For those hoping to track down long-lost relatives. Open M-F 9:15am-4:15pm.

Women's Resources: Ardoyne Women's Group, Butler St. (☎ 9074 3536).

Bisexual, Gay, and Lesbian Information: Rainbow Project N.I., 33 Church Ln. (☎ 9031 9030). Open M-F 10am-4pm. **Lesbian Line** (☎ 9023 8668). Open Th 7:30-10pm.

Counseling and Support: Samaritans (☎ 9066 4422). 24hr. line for depression. **Rape Crisis Centre,** 29 Donegall St. (☎ 9024 9696). Open M-F 10am-6pm, Sa 11am-5pm. **Contact Youth,** 2A Ribble St. offers a counseling hotline M-F 10am-midnight (☎ 9045 7848) and one-on-one counseling appointments. Toll-free number available M-F 4-9pm and varied weekend hours (☎ 0808 808 8000).

Disability Resources: Disability Action (☎ 9049 1011). Open M-F 9am-5pm.

Laundry: The Laundry Room (Duds n' Suds), Botanic Ave. (☎ 9024 3956). TV for the wait. Wash £1.95, dry £1.95; £1.80 each for students and seniors. Open M-F 8am-9pm, Sa 8am-6pm, Su noon-6pm. Last load 1½hr. before closing. **HINI,** 22 Donegall Rd. £3 for powder, wash, and dry (see **Hostels,** p. 412). **Student's Union,** Queen's University, University Rd. Wash £1, dry 20p per 5min. Open M-F 9am-9pm, Sa 10am-9pm, Su 2-9pm. Students only.

Camping Equipment: The Scout Shop and Camp Centre, 12-14 College Sq. East (☎ 9032 0580). Ring bell for entry. Vast selection. Open M-Sa 9am-5pm. **Graham Tiso of Scotland,** 12-14 Cornmarket (☎ 9023 1230), offers 3 floors of everything you could possibly need to survive in the great outdoors. Also has notice boards and flyers for people trying to coordinate hiking, climbing, and water-related trips. Open M-Tu and F-Sa 9:15am-5:30pm, W 10am-5:30pm, Th 9:15am-8:30pm.

Pharmacy: Boot's, 35-47 Donegall Pl. (☎ 9024 2332), next to the Europa Bus Station. Open M-W and F-Sa 8:30am-6pm, Th 8:30am-9pm, Su 1-5pm.

EMERGENCY AND COMMUNICATIONS

Emergency: ☎ 999; no coins required. **Police:** 65 Knock Rd. (☎ 9065 0222).

Hospitals: Belfast City Hospital, 9 Lisburn Rd. (☎ 9032 9241). From Shaftesbury Sq. follow Bradbury Pl. and take a right at the fork. **Royal Victoria Hospital,** 12 Grosvenor Rd. (☎ 9024 0503). From Donegall Sq., take Howard St. west to Grosvenor Rd.

Post Office: Central Post Office, 25 Castle Pl. (☎ 9032 3740). Open M-Sa 9am-5:30pm. **Poste Restante** mail comes here. **Postal code:** BT1 1NB. 2 **branch offices** are: **Botanic Garden,** 95 University Rd. (☎ 9038 1309), across from the university **(postal code:** BT7 1NG), and **Shaftesbury Square,** 7-9 Shaftesbury Sq. (☎ 9032 6177; **postal code:** BT2 7DA). Both open M-F 8:45am-5:30pm, Sa 10am-12:30pm.

Internet Access: The **Belfast Central Library** (see **Local Services,** above) allows 30min. of free email per day; £2 per hr. for web access. **Revelations Internet Cafe,** 27 Shaftesbury Sq. £4 per hr., students and hostelers £3 per hr. Open M-F 10am-10pm, Sa 10am-6pm, Su 11am-7pm. Some accommodations also have net access.

ACCOMMODATIONS

Despite a competitive hostel market, Belfast's rapidly growing tourism and rising rents have shrunk the number of available cheap digs. Nearly all are located near Queen's University, south of the city center; convenient to pubs and restaurants, this area is by far the best place to stay in the city. If you have a lot of baggage you may want to catch a **Centrelink** bus to Shaftesbury Sq., or **Citybus** #59, 69, 70, 71, 84, or 85 from Donegall Sq. East to areas in the south. A walk to these accommodations takes 10 to 20 minutes from the bus or train station. Hostels and B&Bs are busy in the summer; reservations are recommended.

HOSTELS AND UNIVERSITY HOUSING

The Ark (IHH), 18 University St. (☎ 9032 9626). A 10min. walk from Europa bus station on Great Victoria St. Take a right and head away from the Europa Hotel; at Shaftesbury Sq., take the right fork on Bradbury Pl. then fork left onto University Rd. University St. is the 4th left off University Rd. Has an amazing sense of community; perfect strangers gather for meals and the occasional *Simpsons* episode. Owner John leads informative, if somewhat talky, tours of Belfast (£8), in addition to Giant's Causeway excursions (single-day £15). The lovely staff members must love to clean—this place is immaculate. Weekend luggage storage. **Internet access** £2 per 30min. Laundry £4. 2am curfew. 6-bed dorms £6.50; 4-bed dorms £7.50; doubles £28.

Arnie's Backpackers (IHH), 63 Fitzwilliam St. (☎ 9024 2867). Follow the directions to the Ark above; Fitzwilliam St. is on your right across from the university. Relaxed, friendly atmosphere. Amusing triple-bunked beds in some rooms are, if nothing else, conversation starters. If people bore you, peruse the library of travel info including bus and train timetables, or find companionship in Rosy and Snowy, the Jack Russell proprietors. Key deposit £2. Luggage storage during the day. 4- to 6-bed dorms £7.50.

Belfast Hostel (HINI), 22 Donegall Rd. (☎ 9031 5435; www.hini.org.uk), off Shaftesbury Sq. Clean, modern rooms with 2 to 6 beds, some with bath. Located near Sandy Row, a Loyalist area that has seen violence during the July marching season. Books city and Causeway tours. Breakfast £2. Laundry £3. No kitchen. 24hr. reception. Book ahead for weekends. Wheelchair accessible. Dorms £8-10.

The Linen House Youth Hostel (IHH), 18-20 Kent St. (☎ 9058 6400; email info@belfasthostel.com; www.belfasthostel.com) in West Belfast. From Europa Bus Station turn left on Great Victoria St. for 2 blocks, then right onto Howard St. for 2 more. Across from the main entrance to City Hall, turn left onto Donegall Place, which becomes Royal Ave. Take a left onto Kent St. just before the Belfast Library. This converted 19th-century linen factory now houses scores of weary travelers (about 160 beds total). A new basement common room tries to make up for any impersonality. Downtown location is a good or bad thing, depending on the time of night and year. Books black cab (£8) and Causeway tours (£15). 24hr. secure parking. **Internet access** £3 per hr. Laundry £3. No curfew. 18-bed dorms £6.50; 6- to 10-bed dorms £7.50; 8-bed dorms with bathroom £8.50; singles £12; doubles £28.

Queen's University Accommodations, 78 Malone Rd. (☎ 9038 1608). Bus #71 from Donegall Sq. East or a 25min. walk from Europa. University Rd. runs into Malone Rd.; the residence halls are on your left. An undecorated, institutional dorm provides spacious singles or twin rooms with sinks and desks. Strong, reliable showers. Open mid-June to mid-Sept. and Christmas and Easter vacations. Singles and doubles £8 per person for UK students, £9.40 for international students, £11.75 for non-students.

BED AND BREAKFASTS

B&Bs occupy every other house between Malone and Lisburn Rd., just south of Queen's University. They tend to be surprisingly similar in price, quality, and decor, and their competitive standards work in the traveler's favor. Calling ahead is generally a good idea; most owners, however, will refer you to other accommodations if necessary.

Marine House, 30 Eglantine Ave. (☎ 9066 2828). This mansion defies the stereotypes of B&B architecture and overcomes the alienating hotel-like implications of its size. Hospitality and housekeeping standards as high as the ceilings. Singles £22; doubles £40, with bath £45; triples £57.

The George, 9 Eglantine Ave. (☎ 9068 3212). Immaculately clean rooms, all with shower and TV. More stained-glass windows than your average Victorian row-house, and saloon-appropriate leather couches in the common room. Bring cash; no credit cards accepted. Singles £22; doubles £44.

Botanic Lodge, 87 Botanic Ave. (☎ 9032 7682), on the corner of Mt. Charles Ave. B&B comfort with as short a walk to the city center as possible. Singles £22; doubles £40.

Liserin Guest House, 17 Eglantine Ave. (☎ 9066 0769). Comfy beds and a huge velvet-covered lounge make the Liserin an inviting abode. Watch TV while taking a shower; they're both in the room. Top-floor rooms have skylights. Coffee, tea, and biscuits available all day in the dining room. Singles £22; doubles £40; triples £60.

Eglantine Guest House, 21 Eglantine Ave. (☎ 9066 7585). The owner is the sister of the Liserin's proprietor, and treats her guests with equal hospitality. Small but comfortable rooms. Singles £22; doubles £38; triples £57.

Avenue Guest House, 23 Eglantine Ave. (☎ 9066 5904; email stephen.kelly6@ntl-world.com). Though pricier than some of its neighbors, this B&B justifies the cost with fluffy beds, a modem decor, and plentiful accoutrements. All rooms with bath. Singles £35; doubles £45.

FOOD

Belfast's eateries assume a cosmopolitan character, with flavors from around the globe. Dublin Rd., Botanic Rd., and the Golden Mile have the highest concentration of restaurants. Bakeries and cafes dot the shopping areas; nearly all close by 5:30pm. On Thursdays, however, most of the city center stays open until 8:45pm. Most convenience stores offer a full supply of groceries, although their prices are high. **Tesco Supermarket** at 2 Royal Ave. (☎ 9032 3270) and 369 Lisburn Rd. (☎ 9066 3531) sells slightly cheaper food. (Open M-W and Sa 8am-7pm, Th 8am-9pm, F 8am-8pm, Su 1-5pm.) The **Spar Market** at the top of Botanic Rd. is open 24 hours; order your food through a service window at night. For fruits and vegetables, plunder the lively **St. George's Market,** East Bridge St., in the enormous warehouse between May and Oxford St. (Open Tu and F 6am-3pm.). Try **Canterbury Dyke's,** 66-68 Botanic Ave. for healthy foods or more fruit and veggies. (Open M-F 7:30am-7pm, Sa-Su 8am-6:30pm.) **The Nutmeg,** 9A Lombard St. (☎ 9024 9984), also supplies healthy foods, baked goods, and raw ingredients. (Open M-Sa 9:30am-5:30pm.) **Lower Lisburn Rd.,** which runs parallel to University Rd., has a good selection of inexpensive bakeries and fruit stands.

QUEEN'S UNIVERSITY AREA

If students learn how to do one thing, it's eat—Botanic Ave. is strewn with cafes, take-aways, and full-fledged restaurants.

■ **The Other Place,** 79 Botanic Ave. (☎ 9020 7200), 133 Stranmillis Rd. (☎ 9020 7100), and 537 Lisburn Rd. (☎ 9029 7300). Stomping grounds for the backpacker's unicorn, the mythic 99p breakfast. (Served 8-10am.) Features an array of ethnic foods, from Thai to Cajun, accompanied by an eclectic soundtrack. Open daily 8am-11pm.

Bookfinders, 47 University Rd. (☎ 9032 8269). Smoky bookstore/cafe with mismatched dishes and retro counter-culture paraphernalia. Art gallery upstairs, for the more visually oriented. Soup and bread £1.75. Sandwiches £2.20-2.50. Open M-Sa 10am-5:30pm.

Maggie May's Belfast Cafe, 50 Botanic Ave. (☎ 9032 2622). Walls covered with brown newsprint depicting the Belfast of yesteryear. Relax with a cup of tea and a free newspaper; order food when you feel like it. Sandwiches £2-3. 3-course meals £4-6. Open M-Sa 8am-10:30pm, Su 10am-10:30pm.

The Moghul, 62A Botanic Ave. (☎ 9032 6677), overlooking the street from 2nd floor corner windows. Outstanding traditional Indian lunch buffet M-F noon-2pm (£4.95). Open for dinner M-Th 5-11:30pm, F-Sa 5-11:45pm, Su 5-10:30pm.

Giraffe, 54-56 Stranmillis Rd. (☎ 9066 1074), near the Ulster Museum. Living up to the place's namesake, tall, long-necked twenty-somethings come here to graze by candlelight. Interesting hanging wall sculptures of hands and legs. Pizza and pastas £5-8. Open daily 9:30am-10:30pm.

Cafe Clementine, 245 Lisburn Rd. (☎ 9038 2211), 3 blocks south of Eglantine St. Young hotspot with a saffron hue. Sandwiches on croissants or baguettes around £4, entrees £5-7. Open Su-Tu 9am-4:30pm, W-F 9:30am-10pm, Sa 9:30am-10pm.

Esperanto, 35 Botanic Ave. (☎ 9059 1222) and 158 Lisburn Rd. (☎ 9059 0888). It's difficult to label their cuisine—they serve everything under the sun, from burgers to kebabs and a separate vegetarian menu. Meals lean towards Mediterranean, averaging around £3. Botanic open daily 11am-late, Lisburn 4:30pm-late.

Cloisters Bistro, 1 Elmwood Ave. (☎ 9032 4803), in the Queen's University Student Union. Cafeteria-style food served in—drum roll, please—a cafeteria. Fill up with the young scholars for under £3. Open in summer M-Th 11am-4:30pm, F 11am-3pm; during the school year M-F 8:30am-6:30pm.

THE GOLDEN MILE AND DUBLIN ROAD

We at *Let's Go* always try to score you a classy meal, but when late-nite Guinness-induced munchies strike, Dublin Rd. is the place to go. Besides the establishments listed below, it has the highest density of take-aways in Belfast, ranging from Chinese to Mediterranean fare. Embrace Man's eternal search for cheap fast-food.

Pizza Express, 25-27 Bedford St. (☎ 9032 9050). It sounds like your typical franchise, but the grandeur of its spiral staircase and Tuscan decor belie its mundane name. Plus, it's one of the few places in town that actually serves real pizza. 1- to 2-person pies £4-6. Open M-Sa noon-11:30pm.

Feasts, 39 Dublin Rd. (☎ 9033 2787). Pleasant street-side cafe, serving Irish and international farmhouse cheeses in sandwiches (£3) and other dishes. Makes their own pasta on the premises (£5). Open M-F 9am-7pm, Sa 10am-6pm.

Spuds, 23 Bradbury Pl. (☎ 9033 1541). Meat and potatoes—in fast-food form. Get your spud stuffed with anything from bacon and cheese to chicken curry (most around £2). Open M-W 9am-2am, Th-Sa 9am-3am, Su 9am-1am.

Revelations Internet Cafe, 27 Shaftesbury Sq. (☎ 9032 0337). Is eating and surfing the web simultaneously a revelation? **Internet access** £4 per hr., students and hostelers £3 per hr. Sandwiches £2-3; lots of veggie options. Open M-F 10am-10pm, Sa 10am-6pm, Su 11am-7pm.

NORTH OF DONEGALL SQUARE

Lots of great places for lunch reside in the shopping district north of City Hall, but good luck finding a meal here after 5:30pm. You're better off walking along the Golden Mile, south of Donegall Square.

■ **Azzura,** 8 Church Ln. (☎ 9024 3503). This tiny cafe dishes out pizzas and gourmet sandwiches for £2-3, and mountains of pasta for about £4. Open M-Sa 9am-5pm.

Caffe Casa, 12-14 College St. (☎ 9031 9900). Claims to serve the best coffee in Belfast, in a swank wood-and-metallic setting that feels like an art gallery. Popular with the young crowd. Sandwiches (£3), entrees (£4), and sumptuous desserts. Open M-Sa 8am-5:30pm, Th 8am-7:30pm.

Espresso Bar Company, 11 Chichester St. (☎ 9043 9400). Ultra-modern take on a Tuscan countryside cafe, with an upscale and innovative menu. Wild boar foccaccia £3.95; char-grilled steak bocata £5. Wine and beer available. Open M-F 7:30am-4:30pm, Sa 8:30am-5:30pm.

Bewley's, Rosemary St. (☎ 9023 4955), just inside of the Donegall Arcade. For those missing Dublin, this Bewley's is a good replica of the original Japanese tea room (see p. 102). Newspapers and magazines upstairs. Sandwiches £2.25; entrees £4.75. Open M-Sa 8am-5:30pm.

Roscoff Bakery & Cafe, 27-29 Fountain St. (☎ 9031 5090). This fast-food cousin of the world-famous Roscoff's Restaurant serves more affordable treats. Soup £2.40, sandwich £2.50. Divine breads. Open M-W and F-Sa 7:30am-5:30pm, Th 7:30am-8:30pm.

Cafe Deauville, 58 Wellington Pl. (☎ 9023 4303), at the corner of College Sq. Cafe with a diner feel. Breakfast or lunch £2-3. Open M-F 8am-4:30pm, Sa 10am-3pm.

416 ■ BELFAST

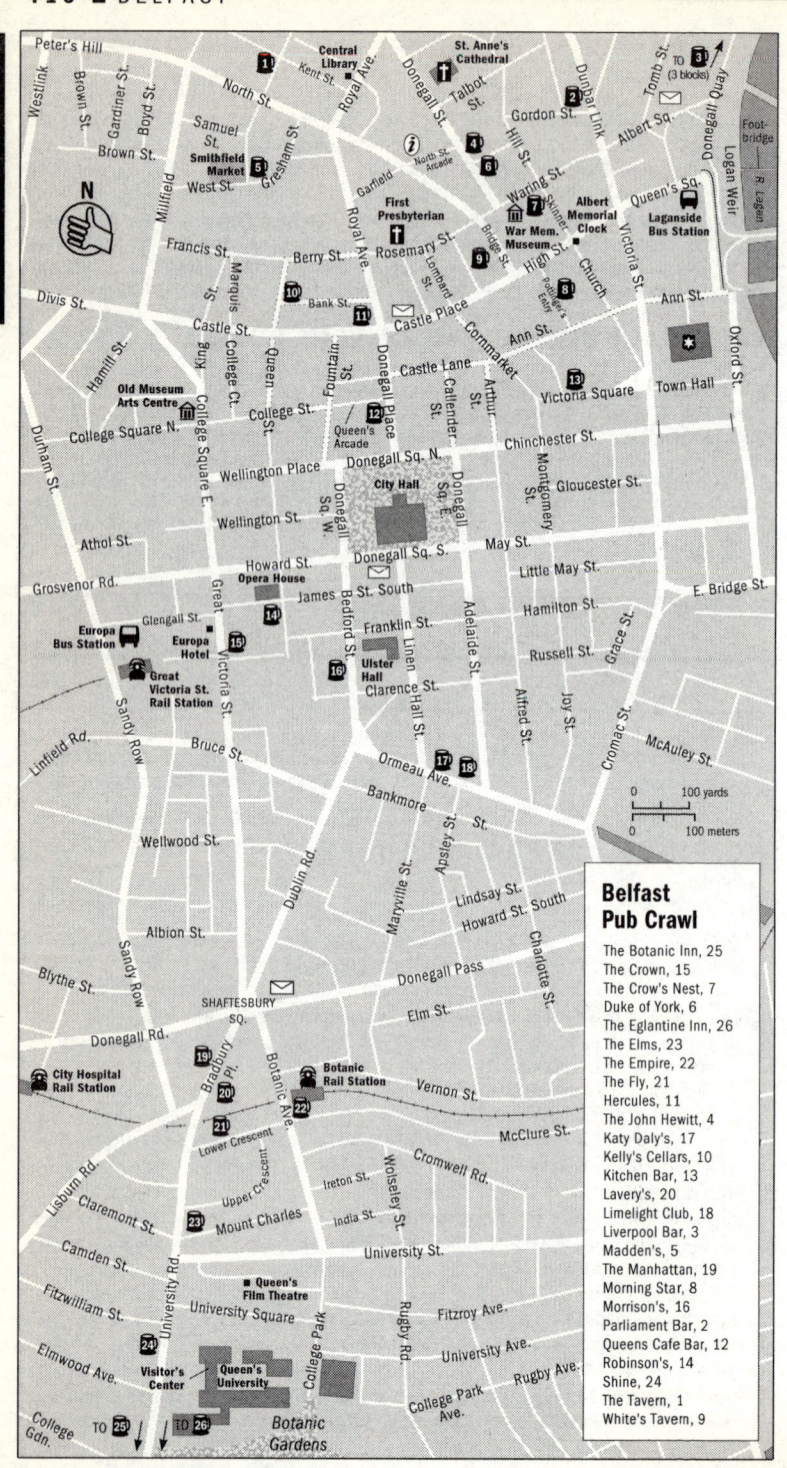

Belfast Pub Crawl

The Botanic Inn, 25
The Crown, 15
The Crow's Nest, 7
Duke of York, 6
The Eglantine Inn, 26
The Elms, 23
The Empire, 22
The Fly, 21
Hercules, 11
The John Hewitt, 4
Katy Daly's, 17
Kelly's Cellars, 10
Kitchen Bar, 13
Lavery's, 20
Limelight Club, 18
Liverpool Bar, 3
Madden's, 5
The Manhattan, 19
Morning Star, 8
Morrison's, 16
Parliament Bar, 2
Queens Cafe Bar, 12
Robinson's, 14
Shine, 24
The Tavern, 1
White's Tavern, 9

FOOD ■ 417

PUBS AND CLUBS

Pubs were prime targets for sectarian violence at the height of the Troubles in the 60s and 70s. As a result, most of the popular pubs in Belfast are new or restored. The *Bushmills Irish Pub Guide*, by Sybil Taylor, relates the history of Belfast's pubs (£7.95; available at local book stores). For information on the city's nightlife, most club-kids consult *The List*, a biweekly newsletter available at the tourist office, hostels, and certain restaurants around town. Ask the staff at the Queen's University Student Union or the staff at the hostels about the latest night spots. Once again, *Let's Go* proudly presents the Belfast Pub Crawl and Pub Crawl Map. Since the city center closes early and can feel pretty deserted late at night, we recommend beginning early in Cornmarket's historic entries, visiting the traditional downtown, then partying until closing time in the university area.

CORNMARKET

Morning Star Pub, 17-19 Pottinger's Entry (☎ 9032 3976), between Ann and High St. Look for the Victorian wrought-iron bracket hanging above the entry. Excellent U-shaped bar with wooden snugs for closer chats. Pile a plate high at the daily buffet (11:30am-3pm). Open M-Sa 11:30a-1am.

White's Tavern, 2-4 Winecellar Entry (☎ 9024 3080), off Lombard and Bridge St. Belfast's oldest tavern, serving drinks since 1630. An excellent stop for an afternoon pint. W is gay night. Open daily noon-1am, W until 2:30am.

NORTH OF DONEGALL SQUARE

Queen's Cafe Bar, 4 Queen's Arcade (☎ 9032 1347), off Fountain St. Friendly, low-pressure atmosphere in a glitzy shopping arcade off Donegall Pl. Mixed, gay-friendly crowd.

Hercules Bar, 61-63 Castle St. (☎ 9032 4587). A working man's pub that pulls in the best musicians the local soil produces. Trad jam sessions F-Sa, blues and jazz other nights. Owners will direct you to other good live music venues. Open until 1am on weekends. No cover.

Kelly's Cellars, 30 Bank St. (☎ 9032 4835), off Royal Ave. just after the Fountain St. pedestrian area. The oldest pub in Belfast that hasn't been renovated, and it doesn't need to be. Become a regular. Trad F and Sa afternoons and Sa nights; occasional live bands, including folk and rock. No cover.

Madden's, 74 Berry St. (☎ 9024 4114). Old wooden bar with musical instruments on the walls. Attracts good-sized crowds with its traditional Irish bands (Th-Sa) and traditional blues and folk (Su). £2-3 cover for live bands.

THE GOLDEN MILE AND THE DUBLIN ROAD
PUBS

Lavery's, 12 Bradbury Pl. (☎ 9087 1106). 3 floors of unpretentious socializing: unlike nightclubs, you don't have to dress up to get noticed (some do anyway). Live music W nights in the 1st-floor back bar, DJs on weekends (no cover); disco in the 2nd-floor Gin Palace (£1 cover); 3rd floor "Heaven" club (£5 cover). Open until 1am.

Robinson's, 38-40 Great Victoria St. (☎ 9024 7447), has 4 floors of theme bars, but is most renowned for **Fibber McGees** in the back, which hosts incredible trad sessions Tu-Sa twice daily (no cover). Non-trad F evening and Sa afternoons. Decent nightclub on top 2 floors Th-Sa (cover £5-7).

Morrisons, 21 Bedford St. (☎ 9024 8458). Painstakingly reconstructed "traditional" atmosphere, modeled after a bar of the same name in the Republic. Strike up a conversation at the bar, then retreat to large wooden snugs. Live bands F and Sa (cover around £4), closed Su.

Crown Liquor Saloon, 46 Great Victoria St. (☎ 9024 9476). This, the only National Trust-owned pub, has been bombed 32 times, but you'd never know it; the stained glass, gas lamps, and Victorian snugs seem original. It's more to impress tourists, though, as the locals go elsewhere.

CLUBS

The Fly, 5-6 Lower Crescent (☎ 9023 5666). Look for the big torches. Extremely popular, with an entomological decor geared towards its namesake. 1st-floor bar for the pints, 2nd-floor bar for mingling, and an Absolut lounge on the 3rd. No cover.

The Manhattan, 23-31 Bradbury Pl. (☎ 9023 3131). Huge 3-story dance club that's packed with a younger crowd clad in Brit-pop fashions. Dress to impress. Events are sporadic, but F is often 70s night. No cover for 1st-floor bar; nightclub cover £4-6.

Katy Daly's and **The Limelight,** 17 Ormeau Ave. (☎ 9032 5942). High-ceilinged, wood-paneled, antique pub, with strobe-filled nightclub next door. Tu disco, F funk, Sa "helter skelter." Cover £3. Has a knack for hiring bands before their time, but don't come with a sore throat—it's LOUD.

QUEEN'S UNIVERSITY AREA

The Botanic Inn (the "**Bot**"), 23 Malone Rd. (☎ 9066 0460). Huge and hugely popular student bar. Pub grub daily £4-5, Su carvey meal £4.50, students £3.50. Trad on Tu, no cover. Th-Sa 60s-80s music. Cover £2. 21+. Open until 1am.

The Eglantine Inn (the "**Egg**"), 32 Malone Rd. (☎ 9038 1994). Almost an official extra-curricular, this pub keeps students from their studies. Satisfies their munchies, too; entrees £2-6, served noon-8pm. Live music M-Tu, shake your bootie W-Sa; both free. Open until 1am.

The Empire, 42 Botanic Ave. (☎ 9024 9276). This 120-year-old building was once a church, but its 2 stories have been entirely revamped to resemble Belfast's Victorian music halls. More like a sports bar, though, and just as dark. Sept.-June comedy Tu, live bands Th-Su. Cover £3.

Shine, Queen's University Student Union (☎ 9032 4803). A convenient, expensive spot to play hooky. Live DJs make the Union the place to learn about cutting edge trends in youth culture. Cover £7-12.

NORTH BELFAST

Given that the city center clears out after 6pm, pubs in this area should be your starting point. After dark, one should take a cab to the pubs near the dock lands.

◼ The John Hewitt, 51 Lower Donegall St. (☎ 9023 3768). A spanking new pub suited for business lunches and named after the late Ulster poet. It's run by the Unemployment Youth Resource Centre, to which half the profits go, so drink up. Really great food, too. Live music W and Su nights (open until 2am) and Sa afternoons.

The Duke of York, 11 Commercial Ctr. (☎ 9024 1062). How to describe the Duke? "Better than sitting at home and watching TV," according to one devoted patron. The collection of beer advertisements shows discriminating aesthetic taste. Sa disco upstairs, live bands downstairs. £4 cover.

The Liverpool Bar, Donegall Quay (☎ 9032 4796), opposite the SeaCat terminal. This 150-year-old building has also been a lodging house and a brothel. Today it boasts some of the best trad in the city. Music M, W, F, and Su. Occasional cover.

The Front Page, 9 Ballymoney St. (☎ 9032 4924). The tiny box of a building sits alone among vast and vacant docks, but it's the center of the universe to the locals who pack it nightly. Live music on weekends ranges from fine to amazing.

GAY AND LESBIAN NIGHTLIFE

On Wednesday nights, **White's Tavern,** the oldest pub in Belfast, becomes one of the most progressive (see **Cornmarket,** above), and **Queen's Cafe Bar** always attracts a mixed crowd, gay and straight (see **North of Donegall Square,** above).

The Kremlin, 96 Donegall St. (☎ 9080 9700). Look for the imposing statue of Stalin above the entrance. Belfast's newest and hottest gay nightspot with too many different venues to list, from foam parties to internationally renowned drag queens. Mixed crowd, but mostly men. Theme night F; "Kink" night once a month. Tight security. Open M-Sa 7:30pm-late, Su 5pm-late. Cover varies, but free Su, M, W, and before 9pm.

The Crow's Nest, 26 Skipper St. (☎ 9027 9920), off High St. 1 block west of the Albert Memorial Clock. Proud to be loud, with discos Th-Sa. Mixed crowd, more in terms of age than sex; a mostly male crowd. Sa night karaoke upstairs with Miss May, the local drag act. F-Sa £2 cover.

Parliament Bar, 2-6 Dunbar St. (☎ 9023 4520), corner of Dunbar and Talbot St.; Talbot is off Donegall St. Like something out of *Police Academy*. Once the premier gay bar of Northern Ireland, its patrons have gone elsewhere; recent retro-style refurbishing hopes to lure them back. Disco W and F-Sa; cover £2-7. Live bands Su. Bingo on Tu.

SIGHTS

TOURS

BLACK CAB TOURS. If you do only one thing in this city, take a taxi tour of West Belfast. Cab tours provide a fascinating, if potentially biased, commentary that highlights the murals, paraphernalia, and sights on both sides of the Peace Line. Almost every hostel books these tours, some their own (such as **The Ark,** p. 413) but most with their favored **black cab** operators, which can be hit-or-miss depending on the driver, usually for about £7. Michael Johnston of **Black Taxi Tours** has made a name for himself by giving witty, objective presentations. (☎ 9064 2264; www.belfasttours.com. £7.50 per person.)

CITYBUS. Citybus provides several tours that hit the city's major sights, both glitzy and gritty. The **Belfast City Tour** introduces visitors to the landmarks of downtown Belfast. *(M-Sa 1:30pm, £6.)* **Belfast: A Living History** is their answer to the numerous black cab tours of West Belfast. *(Tu, Th, and Su 1pm; £9, students £8, seniors and children £6.)* They also offer a hop-on-hop-off **City Hopper Tour** for those who move at their own pace. *(Tu-Sa every hour; £5, £2.50 seniors and children.* ☎ 9045 9484. *All tours leaves from Castle Place, in front of the post office.)*

DONEGALL SQUARE

BELFAST CITY HALL. The administrative and geographic center of Belfast is distanced from the crowded downtown streets by a grassy square. Its green copper dome (173 ft.) is visible from any point in the city. After Queen Victoria granted Belfast's cityhood in 1888, this symbol of civic pride was built on the site of demolished linen warehouses. Neoclassical marble columns and arches figure prominently in A. Brunwell Thomas's 1906 design. Inside, a grand marble staircase ascends to the second floor. Portraits of the city's lord mayors somberly line the halls, and glass and marble shimmer in three elaborate reception rooms. The **City Council's** oak-paneled chambers, used only once a month, are deceptively austere considering the Council's reputation for rowdy meetings that sometimes devolve into fist fights. If you want to see the council in action, a councillor can sign you into the otherwise inaccessible debates with 48-hour notice. Directly in front of the main entrance, an enormous marble **Queen Victoria statue** stares down at visitors with a formidable grimace, while bronze figures representing shipbuilding and spinning writhe at her feet. A more sympathetic sculpted figure of womanhood stands on the eastern side of the garden, commemorating the fate of the *Titanic* and its passengers. An inconspicuous pale gray stone column commemorates the 1942 arrival of the U.S. Expeditionary Force, whose soldiers were stationed here to defend the North from Germany; it was rededicated after President Clinton's visit to Belfast in 1996. The interior of City Hall is accessible only by guided tour. (☎ 9032 0202, ext. 2346. *1hr. tours June-Sept. M-F 10:30am, 11:30am, and 2:30pm; Sa 2:30pm. Oct.-May M-Sa 2:30pm. Free.)*

OTHER SIGHTS. One of Belfast's oldest establishments is the **Linen Hall Library.** The library was originally located across the street in the linen hall that became present-day City Hall; it was moved to its present location in 1894. The red hand of Ulster decorates the top of its street entrance. The library contains a famous collection of political documents relating to Northern Ireland. Devoted librarians scramble for every Christmas card, poster, hand bill, and newspaper article related to the Troubles that they can get their hands on. *(17 Donegall Sq. North.* ☎ *9032 1707. Open M-F 9:30am-5:30pm, Sa 9:30am-4pm.)* Nearby, the **Scottish Provident Institution,** built in 1902, displays a decadent facade that glorifies virtually every profession that has contributed to industrial Belfast. *(Across the street from City Hall, on the corner of Donegall Sq. North and East Bedford St.)* For a taste of Irish craftsmanship, head to **Craftworks.** Collections include leather goods, handwoven throws, knitwear, ceramics and unique jewelry. *(Bedford St.* ☎ *9024 4465. Open M-W and F-Sa 9:30am-5:30pm, Th until 8:30pm.)*

CORNMARKET AND ST. ANNE'S CATHEDRAL

Just north of the city center, a shopping district envelops eight blocks around Castle St. and Royal Ave. This area, known as Cornmarket after one of its original commodities, has been a marketplace since Belfast's early days. In the 17th century, it was surrounded by city walls. A McDonald's stands on the site of the old city castle (hence Castle St.). Although the Cornmarket area is dominated by modern buildings, relics of old Belfast remain in the tiny alleys, or **entries,** that connect some of the major streets. A drink at any of the pubs along these alleys will have your imagination swimming in nostalgic reverie.

ST. ANNE'S CATHEDRAL. Belfast's newspapers all set up shop around St. Anne's, also known as the **Belfast Cathedral.** This Church of Ireland cathedral was begun in 1899. To keep from disturbing regular worship, it was built around a smaller church already on the site. Upon completion of the cathedral's exterior, builders extracted the earlier church brick by brick. Each of the cathedral's 10 interior pillars name somebody's idea of Belfast's 10 fields of professionalism: Science, Industry, Healing, Agriculture, Music, Theology, Shipbuilding, Freemasonry, Art, and Womanhood (a nice enough profession, but the pay is lousy). In a small enclave called the Chapel of Peace, the cathedral asks visitors to pray for international peace between 1 and 2pm. *(Donegall St., located near the Tourist Office, a few blocks from the city center. Open daily 9am-5pm. Su services: communion 10am, Eucharist 11am, evensong 3:30pm.)*

ENTRIES. Between Ann and High St. runs **Pottinger's Entry,** which contains the **Morning Star Pub** (see **Pubs,** p. 417) in all its old-world splendor. *(Open M-Sa 11:30am-1am.)* **Joy's Entry,** farther down Ann St., is the alley where the *Belfast News Letter* was printed for over 100 years. The only establishment still in the entry, Globe Tavern, is disappointingly modern inside. Off Lombard and Bridge St., **Winecellar Entry** is the site of Belfast's oldest pub, **White's Tavern** (see **Pubs,** p. 417), serving drinks since 1630. *(Open daily noon-1am, W until 2:30am.)*

OTHER SIGHTS. The city's oldest public building, **The Old Stock Exchange,** sits on the corner of North and Waring St. Tireless Charles Lanyon designed a new facade for the building in 1845 when the original was deemed not grand enough. The **First Presbyterian Church of Belfast,** the city's oldest church, still stands just a block to the west, on Rosemary St. *(Open W 10:30am-12:30pm.)*

THE DOCKS AND EAST BELFAST

Although the docks area was once the activity hub of old Belfast, continued commercial development has made the area more suitable for industrial machinery than people. Reminders of the city's ship-building glory days, however, remain in the East Belfast shipyards, surrounded by former employee housing. The most famous of the shipyards is Harland & Wolff, whose most famous creation was, unfortunately, the *Titanic.* The shipyards figure in numerous poems and novels set in Belfast, notably at the end of Paul Muldoon's "7, Middagh St." Today, the twin cranes nicknamed **Samson and Goliath** tower over the Harland & Wolff shipyard and are visible from all points across the river.

LAGAN LOOKOUT AND LAGAN WEIR. The £14-million weir was built to eliminate the Lagan's drastic tides, which used to expose stinking mud flats during ebb. The Lookout offers an interesting room full of displays on the history of Belfast, and the purpose and mechanism of the weir. Both structures are part of a huge development project that includes the **Laganside Trail** along the far side of the river and **Waterfront Hall,** a recently opened concert hall with an uncanny resemblance to a sponge cake. *(Donegall Quay, across from the Laganside bus station.* ☎ *9031 5444. Lookout open Apr.-Sept. M-F 11am-5pm, Sa noon-5pm, Su 2-5pm; Oct.-Feb. Tu-F 11am-3:30pm, Sa 1-4:30pm, Su 2-4:30pm. £1.50, children 75p, concession £1.)*

SINCLAIR SEAMEN'S CHURCH. The Presbyterian minister delivers his sermons from a pulpit carved in the shape of a ship's prow, collections are taken in miniature lifeboats, and an organ with port and starboard lights taken from a Guinness barge carries the tune. The exterior was designed by prolific Charles Lanyon, who also designed the Custom House, the Queen's campus, and almost every other notable 19th-century building in Belfast—except the Albert Memorial Clock Tower, and boy, was he angry about that. *(Corporation St., just down the street from the SeaCat terminal. Su services 11:30am and 7pm. Tours W 2-4pm.)*

ODYSSEY. Scheduled to open November 2000 is Odyssey, an enormous indoor entertainment and shopping complex. Supposedly, it will include a 10,000-seat indoor arena, a 14-screen multiplex cinema and IMAX theatre, and a Pavilion of restaurants, bars, and shops. Time will tell if it manages to draw Belfasters to the industrial docks. *(Queen's Quay.* ☎ *9045 1055.)*

OTHER SIGHTS. The stately **Custom House,** built by Charles Lanyon in 1857, stands between Queen Sq. and Albert Sq. on the approach to the river from the clock tower. Designed in an imaginative E-shape, it rests on an elaborate pediment of Britannia, Neptune, and Mercury, the god of trade. Belfast also has its own version of the leaning tower of Pisa and Big Ben in one: the **Albert Memorial Clock Tower.** Designed in 1865 by W. J. Barre, the 115 ft. tower leans precariously at the entrance to the docks area, where Oxford St. runs beside the Lagan. The name refers to Prince Albert, Queen Victoria's consort.

THE GOLDEN MILE

"The Golden Mile" refers to a strip along Great Victoria St. containing many of the jewels in the crown of Belfast's establishment.

GRAND OPERA HOUSE. Belfast's pride and joy, the opera house was cyclically bombed by the IRA, restored to its original splendor at enormous cost, and then bombed again. Ask at the stage door on Glengall St. if there's a rehearsal going on; if not, they'll give you a tour. *(☎ 9024 0411. Booking office open M-Sa 9:45am-5:30pm.)* **The Grand Opera House Ticket Shop** sells tickets for performances including musicals, operas, ballets, and concerts. *(2-4 Great Victoria St.* ☎ *9024 1919, 24hr. info line* ☎ *9024 9129. Open M-W 8:30am-8pm, Th 8:30am-9pm, F 8:30am-6:30pm, Sa 8:30am-5:30pm.)*

THE CROWN LIQUOR SALOON. The National Trust has restored this highly frequented pub to make it a showcase of carved wood, gilded ceilings, and stained glass. Box-like snugs fit groups of two to 10 comfortably. One used to order another round by hitting the buzzer in the booth, but now you have to stumble to the bar (see **Pubs,** p. 417).

EUROPA HOTEL. Damaged by 32 bombs in its history, the Europa has the dubious distinction of being "Europe's most bombed hotel." In March of 1993, the hotel installed shatterproof windows, which seem to have deterred would-be bombers.

QUEEN'S UNIVERSITY AREA

QUEEN'S UNIVERSITY BELFAST. Charles Lanyon designed the Tudor-revival brick campus in 1849, modeling it after Magdalen College, Oxford. The **Visitors Centre**, in the Lanyon Room to the left of the main entrance, offers Queen's-related exhibits and merchandise. *(University Road. Visitors Centre ☎ 9033 5252. Open May.-Sept. M-Sa 10am-4pm, Oct-Mar. M-F 10am-4pm.)*

BOTANIC GARDENS. Birds do it; bees do it; and on warm days, the majority of the student population does it. You, too, can bask in Belfast's occasional sun behind the university. Meticulously groomed, the gardens offer a welcome green respite from the traffic-laden city streets. Inside the gardens lie two 19th-century greenhouses, the toasty **Tropical Ravine House** and the more temperate Lanyon-designed **Palm House.** Don't forget to stop and smell the rose gardens, featuring Europe's most fragrant bloomers. *(☎ 9032 4902. Open daily 8am-dusk. Tropical House and Palm House open Apr.-Sept. M-F 10am-noon and 1-5pm, Sa-Su 2-5pm; Oct.-Mar. M-F 10am-noon and 1-4pm, Sa-Su 2-4pm. Free.)*

ULSTER MUSEUM. This national-caliber museum has developed a variety of exhibits to fill its huge display halls. Irish and modern art, local history, antiquities, and the Mummy of Takabuti are all subjects for investigation. The treasure salvaged from the *Girone*, a Spanish Armada ship that sank off the Causeway Coast in 1588, is also on display here, as well as steam engines to rival those of the Transport Museum (see p. 437). *(In the Botanic Gardens, off Stranmillis Rd. ☎ 9038 3000 or 9038 1251. Open M-F 10am-5pm, Sa 1-5pm, Su 2-5pm. Free, except for some traveling exhibitions.)*

SOUTH BELFAST

Riverside trails, ancient ruins, and idyllic parks south of Belfast make it hard to believe that you're only a few minutes from the city center. The area can be reached by buses #70 and 71 from Donegall Sq. East. The **Belfast Parks Department** (☎ 9032 0202) provides maps.

SIR THOMAS AND LADY DIXON PARK. The most stunning of the parks, Upper Malone Rd., boasts over 20,000 rose bushes. The gardens were founded in 1836 and include the stud China roses, imported between 1792 and 1824, which provided the foundation for present-day British roses.

OTHER SIGHTS. Four miles north along the tow path near Shaw's Bridge lies Giant's Ring, a 4500-year-old earthen ring with a dolmen in the middle. Little is known about the 600 ft.-wide circle, but experts speculate that it was built for the same reasons as England's Stonehenge. *(Always open. Free.)*

NORTH BELFAST

BELFAST ZOO. Underwater viewing of sea lions and penguins; also keeps spectacled bears, marmosets, gorillas, and red panda. No sheep. This place is a zoo in more ways than one—it can get pretty crowded in the summer. *(4 mi. north of the city on Antrim Rd; take Citybuses 9 or 45-51. ☎ 9077 6277. Open daily Apr.-Sept. 10am-5pm, Oct-Mar. 10am-2:30pm. £5.10, children £2.55.)*

BELFAST CASTLE. In 1934, the Earl of Shaftesbury presented this relatively new building to the city. The castle sits on top of cave hill, long the seat of Ulster rulers. The ancient King Matudan had his McArt's Fort here, where the more modern United Irishmen plotted rebellion in 1795. The summit is nicknamed "Napoleon's Nose." Marked trails lead north from the fort to five caves in the area, thought by historians to be ancient mines; only the lowest is accessible. *(Open M-Sa 9am-10:30pm, Su 9am-6pm. Free.)*

WEST BELFAST AND THE MURALS

Separated from the rest of the city by the Westlink motorway, the neighborhoods of West Belfast have historically been at the heart of the political tensions in the North. The Catholic area (centered on **Falls Rd.**) and the Protestant neighborhood (centered on the **Shankill**) are grimly separated by the **peace line**, a gray and seemingly impenetrable wall; it is, in fact, a 20 ft.-high, graffitied, corrugated iron sheet that reaching arms from nearby houses can touch. Along the wall, abandoned houses with blocked-up or broken windows point to a troubled past and an uncertain future. These two neighborhoods embody both the raw sentiment that drives the Northern Irish conflict and the casual calm with which those closest to the Troubles approach daily life. The most dominant feature of the neighborhoods is their family community. West Belfast is not a center of consumer tourism or a "sight" in the traditional sense. The streets display political murals, which you will soon come across as you wander among the houses. While it is tacky to gawk at and photograph murals, residents often appreciate it since the walls are partly intended as propaganda. The murals in the Falls and Shankill change constantly, so the sections below describe only a few. We provide a glossary of some common symbols (see **A Primer of Symbols**, p. 425). Do not take photographs of any **military installations**. It is illegal, and your film may be confiscated.

It is best to visit the Falls and Shankill during the day, when the murals can be seen. The Protestant Orangemen's marching season, around July 12, is a risky time to visit the area, since the parades are underscored by mutual antagonisms that can lead to political violence (see **History and Politics**, p. 397). To see both the Falls and Shankill, the best plan is to visit one then return to the city center before heading to the other, as the area around the peace line is still desolate. The most popular transport to Belfast's sectarian neighborhoods is offered by **black cabs**, community shuttles that whisk residents to the city center, picking up and dropping off passengers along their set routes. For the standard fare (60p), you can ask to be let off anywhere along the route. Select black cabs can also reasonably be hired by groups for **tours** of the Falls or Shankill (see **Tours**, p. 419).

THE FALLS. This Catholic neighborhood is much larger than Shankill and houses a younger, rapidly multiplying population. On **Divis St.**, a high-rise apartment building marks the site of the **Divis Tower**, an ill-fated housing development built by optimistic social planners in the 1960s. This project soon became an IRA stronghold and saw some of the worst of Belfast's Troubles in the 1970s. The British army still occupies the top three floors, and Shankill residents refer to it as "Little Beirut."

Continuing west, Divis St. turns into the **Falls Rd.** The **Sinn Féin** office is easily spotted: one side of it is covered with an enormous portrait of Bobby Sands (see **The Troubles**, p. 399) and an advertisement for the Sinn Féin newspaper, *An Phoblacht*. Continuing down the Falls you will see a number of murals characterized by Celtic art and the Irish language. They display scenes of traditional music and dance, or grimmer portraits of Famine victims. One particularly moving mural, on the corner of the Falls and RPG Ave., shows the 10 hunger strikers who died in 1981-82 above a quote from Bobby Sands: "Our revenge will be the laughter of our children." Murals in the Falls, unlike those of the Shankill, are becoming less militant in nature, though there are a few left in the Lower Falls that refer to specific

---

"THE RAPE OF THE FALLS" The area stretching from Divis Tower to Cavendish Sq. is known as the **Lower Falls**. This area was sealed off by the British Army for 35 hours in July, 1970, in an episode known as the **Rape of the Falls**. Soldiers, acting on a tip that arms were hidden in some of the houses, searched homes at random while residents were forbidden to leave the area, even for milk or bread. It is estimated that before this event, there were only 50 Republicans in the area. After the incident, however, over 2000 people turned to the IRA. Many regard this raid as the biggest tactical mistake ever made by the British army in Northern Ireland.

acts of violence. One shows women banging bin lids on the ground to warn neighbors of British paratroopers. The grim slogan reads: "25 years of resistance—25 more if needs be." Other political graffiti, concerning Sinn Féin, the RUC, and Protestant paramilitary groups, is everywhere.

The Falls Rd. soon splits into **Andersontown Rd.** and **Glen Rd.**, the site of Ireland's only urban *gaeltacht*. On the left are the Celtic crosses of **Milltown Cemetery**, the resting place of many Republican dead. Inside the entrance, a memorial to Republican casualties is bordered by a low green fence on the right. The grave of Bobby Sands rests here. Another mile along the Andersontown Rd. lies the road's namesake—a housing project (formerly a wealthy Catholic neighborhood)—and more murals. The Springfield Rd. RUC station is the most-attacked police station in Ireland and the UK; its charred defenses are formidable, as are the directional video cameras and microphones that deck its eight-story radio tower.

SHANKILL. North St., to the left of the tourist office, turns into **Shankill Rd.** as it crosses the **Westlink** and then arrives in Protestant Shankill, once a thriving shopping district. Current housing preferences (younger, middle-class Protestants have moved elsewhere) have led to a generational gap between the residents of Shankill and the Falls. Turning left (coming from the direction of North St.) onto most side roads leads to the **peace line**. At Canmore St., a mural on the left depicts the Apprentice Boys "Shutting the Gates of Derry—1688" as the Catholic invaders try to get through (see **Rebellion, Reunion, Reaction,** p. 13). A little farther, also on the left and across a small park, a big, faded mural labeled "UVF—then and now" depicts a modern, black-garbed Protestant paramilitary man and a historical "B-Specials" soldier side-by-side (see **British rule and the Division of Ireland,** p. 397). The densely decorated **Orange Hall** sits on the left at Brookmount St. McClean's Wallpaper, on the right, was formerly Fizzel's Fish Shop, where 10 people died in an October 1993 bomb attack. The side streets on the right guide you to the **Shankill Estate** and more murals. Through the estate, **Crumlin Road** heads back to the city center past an army base, the courthouse, and the jail, which are on opposite sides of the road but linked by a tunnel. The oldest Loyalist murals are found here.

SANDY ROW AND NEWTOWNARDS RD. The Shankill area is shrinking as middle-class Protestants leave it, but a growing Protestant population lives on **Sandy Row.** This stretch is a turn off **Donegall Rd.** at **Shaftesbury Sq.** An orange Arch topped with King William marks its start. Nearby murals show the Red Hand of Ulster, a bulldog, and King William crossing the Boyne.

While murals in the Falls and Shankill are often defaced or damaged, better-preserved and more elaborate murals adorn the secure Protestant enclave of **East Belfast**, across the Lagan. A number line **Newtownards Rd.** One mural likens the UVF to the ancient hero, Cúchulainn—Ulster's defender. In so doing, it unintentionally illustrates the overlap in the two sides' cultural authorship.

ARTS AND ENTERTAINMENT

Belfast's many cultural events and performances are covered in the monthly *Arts Council Artslink*, which is free at the tourist office. Daily listings appear in the daily *Belfast Telegraph* (which also has a Friday arts supplement) as well as in Thursday's issue of the *Irish News*. For more extensive information on pub entertainment, pick up the free, biweekly, two-page news bulletin *The List*, available at the tourist office, hostels, and many pubs. The **Crescent Arts Centre**, 2 University Rd., supplies general arts info, but mostly specific news about their own exhibits and concerts, which take place September through May. They also host eight-week courses in yoga, trapeze, writing, trad, ballet, and drawing. (☎ 9024 2338. Open M-Sa 9:30am-5pm.) **Fenderesky Gallery,** 2 University Rd., inside the Crescent Arts Centre building, hosts contemporary shows all year. (☎ 9023 5245. Open Tu-Sa 11:30am-5pm.) The **Old Museum**, 7 College Sq. North, is Belfast's largest venue for new contemporary artwork. (☎ 9023 5053; 9023 3332 for tickets. Open M-Sa 9am-5:30pm. Free.) Besides art exhibits, it features a variety of dance, theater, and

A PRIMER OF SYMBOLS IN THE MURALS OF WEST BELFAST

PROTESTANT MURALS

Blue, White, and Red: The colors of the British flag; often painted on curbs, signposts, etc., to demarcate Unionist murals and neighborhoods.

The Red Hand: The symbol of Ulster (found on Ulster's crest), usually used by Unionists to emphasize the separateness of Ulster from the rest of Ireland. Symbolizes the hand of the first Norse King, which he supposedly cut off and threw on a Northern beach to establish his primacy.

King Billy/William of Orange: Sometimes depicted on a white horse, crossing the Boyne to defeat the Catholic King James II at the 1690 Battle of the Boyne. The Orange Order was later founded in his honor.

The Apprentice Boys: A group of young men who shut the gates of Derry to keep out the troops of James II, beginning the great siege of 1689. They have become Protestant folk heroes, inspiring a sect of the Orange order in their name. The slogan **"No Surrender,"** also from the siege, has been appropriated by radical Unionists, most notably Rev. Ian Paisley (see **The Troubles,** p. 399).

Lundy: The Derry leader who advocated surrender during the siege; now a term for anyone who wants to give in to Catholic demands.

Taig: Phonetic spelling of the Irish given name Teague; Protestant slang for a Catholic.

Scottish Flag: Blue with a white cross; recalls the Scottish-Presbyterian roots of many Protestants whose ancestors were part of the Ulster Plantation (see **Plantation and Cromwell,** p. 10).

CATHOLIC MURALS

Orange and Green: Colors of the Irish Republic's flag; often painted on curbs and signposts in Republican neighborhoods.

Landscapes: Usually imply Republican territorial claims to the North.

The Irish Volunteers: Republican tie to the earlier (nonsectarian) Nationalists.

Saiorsche: "Freedom"; the most common Irish term found on murals.

Éireann go bráth: "Ireland forever"; a popular IRA slogan.

Tiocfaidh ár lá: (CHOCK-ee-ar-LA) "Our day will come."

Slan Abnaile: (slang NA-fail) "Leave our streets"; directed at the primarily Protestant RUC police force.

Phoenix: Symbolizes united Ireland rising from the ashes of British persecution.

Lug: Celtic god, seen as the protector of the "native Irish" (Catholics).

Green ribbon: IRA symbol for "free POWs."

Bulldog: Britain.

Bowler Hats: A symbol for Orangemen.

live music performances as well as workshops. (Most performance tickets around £7, students and concessions £4.) A word of warning to summer travelers: July and August are slow months for Belfast arts; around July 12 the whole city shuts down.

THEATER

Belfast's theater season runs from September to June. The truly **Grand Opera House,** 2-4 Great Victoria St. (☎ 9024 0411), shows off a mix of opera, ballet, musicals, and drama. Tickets for most shows can be purchased either by phone or in person at the box office, 2-4 Great Victoria St. (☎ 9024 1919 for reservations; 24hr. info line ☎ 9024 9129. Open M-W 8:30am-8pm, Th 8:30am-9pm, F 8:30am-6:30pm, Sa 8:30am-5:30pm. Tickets £8 and up. 50% student rush tickets available after noon for M-Th performances. Wheelchair accessible.) **The Lyric Theatre,** 55 Ridgeway St., mixes Irish plays with international theater. (☎ 9038 1081. Box office open M-Sa 9:30am-7pm. Tickets M-Th about £8.50., F-Su £12.50; students £6, except Sa.) **The Group Theatre,** Bedford St., produces comedies and farces in the Ulster Hall from September to May. (☎ 9032 9685. Box office open M-F noon-3pm. Tickets £2-6.) The **Old Museum Art Centre,** 1 College Sq. North, presents avant-garde contemporary works. (☎ 9023 3332 for tickets. Tickets usually £6, students and seniors £3.)

MUSIC

Ulster Hall, Bedford St. (☎ 9032 3900), brings Belfast everything from classical to pop. Try the independent box offices for tickets: **Our Price** (☎ 9031 3131) or the **Ticket Shop** at Virgin (☎ 9032 3744). **The Grand Opera House** (see **Theater**) resounds with classical vocal music. **Waterfront Hall,** 2 Lanyon Pl., is Belfast's newest concert center, hosting a series of performances throughout the year. (☎ 9033 4400. Tickets £10-35, average £12; student discounts available.) The **Ulster Orchestra** plays concerts at Waterfront Hall and Ulster Hall. (☎ 9023 3240. Tickets £5-23.)

FILM

There are two major movie theaters in Belfast. Commercial films are shown at **UGC Cinemas,** 14 Dublin Rd.; most movies come here three to seven months after their US release. (☎ 9024 5700 for 24hr. info; ☎ (0541) 555 176 for credit card bookings. £4.40, £3.20 before 5pm; students and seniors £3.20, children £2.90, discounts available Su-F only; £3.20 all day Tu and daily before 5pm. **Queen's Film Theatre,** in a back alley off Botanic Ave., draws a more artsy crowd. (☎ 9024 4857. £2-3.80. "Meal and movie" discounts for certain restaurants.)

■ FESTIVALS

QUEENS UNIVERSITY BELFAST FESTIVAL. Belfast reigns supreme in the art world for three weeks each November during the university's annual festival. Over 300 separate performances of opera, ballet, film, and comedy invade venues across the city, drawing groups of international acclaim. Tickets for the most popular events sell out months ahead of time, although there's almost always something to see without planning ahead. (☎ 9066 7687. For advance tickets and schedules, write to: Mailing List, Festival House, 25 College Gardens, Belfast BT9 6BS. Tickets sold by mail and phone from September 15 through the festival's end. Prices range from £2.50 to £25.)

WEST BELFAST ARTS FESTIVAL. This week-long series of events is the high point of Falls residents' year. The nationalist festival celebrates Irish traditional culture, hosting both big name trad groups and indebted rockers. It will convince you, if nothing else can, that West Belfast is more proud and friendly than most neighborhoods. (Second week of August. ☎ 9031 3440; www.feileanphobail.ie.)

■ DAYTRIPS FROM BELFAST

ULSTER FOLK MUSEUM AND TRANSPORT AND RAILWAY MUSEUMS

In Holywood, the Ulster Folk Museum and Transport Museum stretches over 176 acres. To reach it, take the Bangor Rd. 7 mi. east of Belfast on A2. Both buses and trains stop here on their way to Bangor. ☎ 9042 8428. Open July-Aug. M-Sa 10:30am-6pm, Su noon-6pm; Apr.-June and Sept. M-F 9:30am-5pm, Sa 10:30am-6pm, Su noon-6pm; Oct.-Mar. M-F 9:30am-4pm, Sa-Su 12:30-4:30pm. £4, students and seniors £2.50. Partially wheelchair accessible.

Half a day is just long enough to see the museums here, although spending fewer than two hours would be foolish. Established by Act of Parliament in the 1950s, the ■**Folk Museum** aims to preserve the way of life of Ulster's farmers, weavers, and craftspeople. The Folk Museum contains over 30 buildings from the past three centuries and all nine Ulster counties, including Monaghan, Cavan, and Donegal in the Republic. All but two of the buildings are transplanted originals, painstakingly moved and reconstructed stone by stone. All have been successfully placed in the museum's natural landscape to create an amazing air of authenticity. While attendants unobtrusively stand nearby to answer questions, there are no cheesy historical scenes or written explanations to interrupt the visitor's own imaginative role-play. The printer's shop on "Main Street" contains a working original 1844 newspaper press from the *Armagh Guardian*—ask the attendant for a demonstration. The museum also hosts special events, including trad music, dance performances and workshops, storytelling festivals, and textile exhibitions.

The Transport Museum and the Railway Museum are across the road from the Folk Museum. Inside the **Transport Museum,** horse-drawn coaches, cars, bicycles, and trains display the history of moving vehicles. Their motorcycle exhibition is extensive, following the evolution of the genre from the ABC Skootamota, a 1919 gem, to Harley mania with a life-size 1950s diner installation. A *Titanic* exhibit that includes original blueprints traces the Belfast-built ship and its fate. The hangar-shaped **Railway Museum** stuffs in 25 old railway engines, including the largest locomotive built in Ireland.

DOWN AND ARMAGH

Locals flock to this sleepy but scenic area to take advantage of the seaside. The coast of Down and the Ards Peninsula is covered with fishing villages, holiday resorts, and 17th-century ruins. The Mourne Mountains, almost directly south of Belfast and just a *lough* away from the Irish Republic, rise above the town of Newcastle, the largest seaside resort in Down. An inland county surrounded by rivers and lakes, Armagh is set on the rolling hills of Northern Ireland's Drumlin Belt. The best time to visit Co. Armagh is during apple blossom season in May, when the countryside, known as the "Orchard of Ireland," is covered in pink. Armagh town is an ecclesiastical center of great historical interest; traces of human habitation at Navan Fort date back to 5500 BC. Co. Armagh's other population centers, Craigavon and Portadown, near Lough Neagh, are industrial centers of less interest to tourists, although Craigavon does host the Lough Neagh Discovery Centre, a base from which to explore acres of feathered friends and wooded park land (see **Lough Neagh and Oxford Island,** p. 447). The Ring of Gullion in South Armagh is a circle of hills containing Slieve Gullion and some astounding volcanic rock formations. Much of the area is privately owned, but visitors can enjoy its amenities at **Slieve Gullion Forest Park,** which has trails up the mountain as well as an 8 mi. road for cars or bikes. Call the Slieve Gullion tourist office (☎ (01693) 848 084) for info.

BANGOR

Bangor found a place on early medieval maps of Ireland with its famous Abbey, a center of missionary activity, but this pious era in Bangor's history ended in the 9th century with the Viking raids. By the Victorian era, Bangor had become eminent again, this time as *the* seaside resort for Belfast residents. Today, Bangor caters to families and older vacationers during the week, while its outstanding nightlife draws busloads of twenty-somethings on the weekends. Its location makes it an inevitable (and enjoyable) stop on the way down the Ards Peninsula.

GETTING THERE AND AWAY

Trains: Abbey St. (☎ 270 141), at the south end of town. To **Belfast** (30min.; M-F 38 per day, Sa 26 per day, Su 9 per day; £2.70).

Buses: Abbey St. (☎ 271 143), next to the train station. To **Belfast** (45min.; M-Sa 33 per day, Su 8 per day; £2.60) and all **Ards Peninsula** towns, including **Donaghadee** (23min.; M-F 19 per day, Sa 15 per day, Su 5 per day; £1.60).

428 ■ DOWN AND ARMAGH

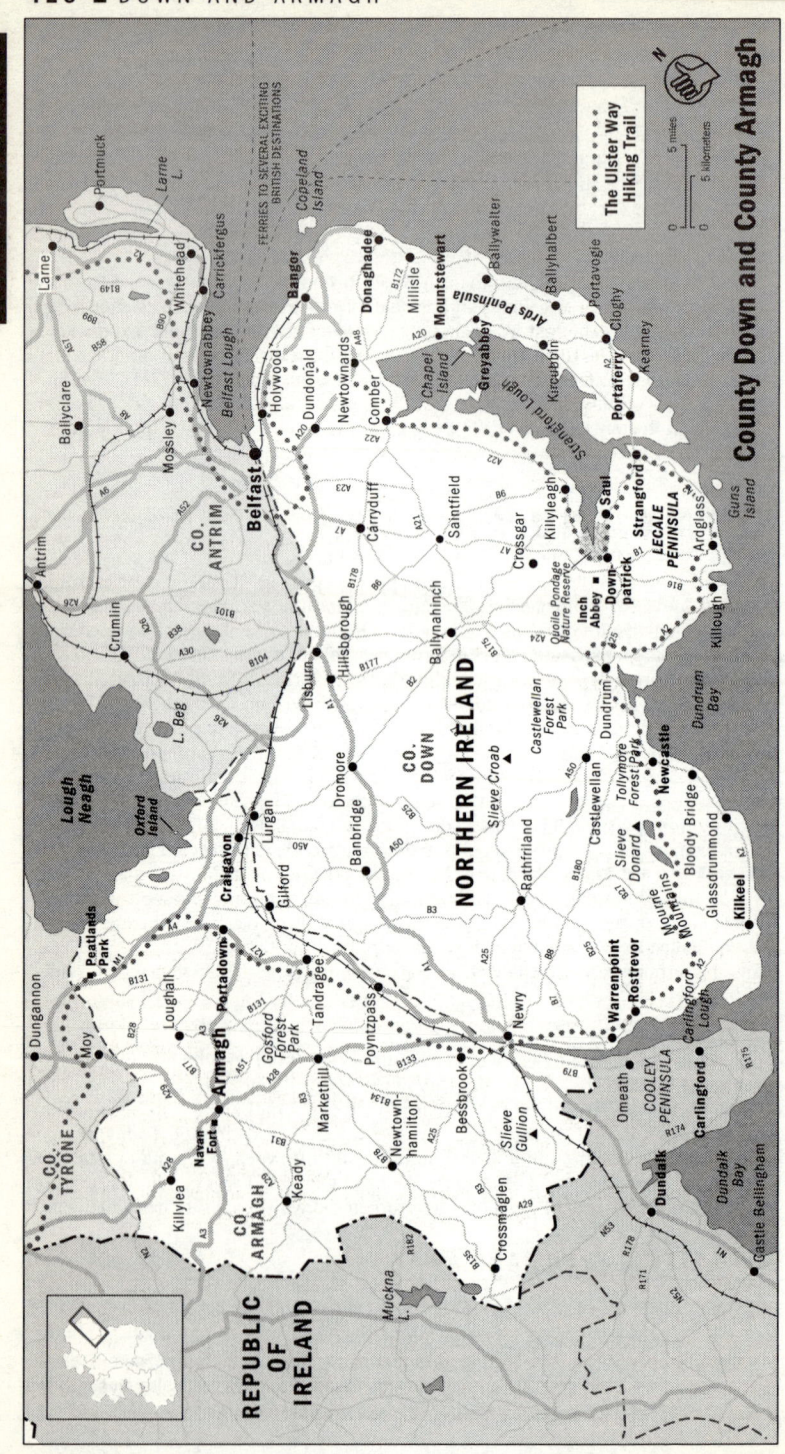

ORIENTATION AND PRACTICAL INFORMATION

The road from Belfast runs South-North through town, changing names several times along the way to **Abbey St., Main St., Quay St.,** and finally **Seacliff Rd.** at the waterfront. The train and bus stations are next to each other at the end of Abbey St. From there, Main St. intersects three important roads: **Castle Park Ave.,** which becomes the restaurant-filled **Dufferin Ave.** (and further inland **Princetown Rd.**) as it crosses Main St.; **Hamilton Rd.,** which becomes **Central Ave.** as it leads to Crawfordsburn; and pub-intensive **High St.,** which crosses Quay St. to lead to the marina and the B&Bs of **Queens Parade.**

Tourist Office: Tower House, 34 Quay St. (☎ 9127 0069; fax 9127 4466). Great brochures on the Down coast. Will book accommodations. Open July-Aug. M 10am-7pm, Tu-F 9am-7pm, Sa 10am-7pm, Su noon-6pm; Sept. and June M until 5pm, Sa until 4pm, Su 1-5pm; off-season same hours as Sept. and June but closed Su.

Banks: First Trust, 85 Main St. (☎ 9127 0628). Open M-Tu and Th-F 9:30am-4:30pm, W 10am-4:30pm. **Northern Bank,** 77 Main St. (☎ 9127 1211). Open M 10am-5pm, Tu-F 10am-3:30pm. **Ulster Bank,** Main St. (☎ 9127 0924). Open M-F 9:30am-4:30pm. All have 24hr. **ATMs.**

Pharmacy: Boots Pharmacy, 79-83 Main St. (☎ 9127 1134). Open M-Sa 9am-5:30pm.

Emergency: ☎ 999; no coins required. **Police:** Castle Park Ave. (☎ 9145 4444).

Counseling and Support: Samaritans, 92 Dufferin Ave. (☎ 9146 4646). Open 24hr.

Internet Access: The Bangor Library, corner of Hamilton and Prospect Rds., has web access. Open M-W 10am-8pm, F 10am-5pm, Sa 10am-1pm and 2-5pm. Inconveniently across town is **Insomnia,** 59 Balloo Drive (☎ 9146 3676). Open M-Sa 10am-8pm.

Post Office: 143 Main St. (☎ 9146 3000), on the corner with Dufferin Ave. Open M-Sa 9am-5:30pm. **Postal Code:** BT20.

ACCOMMODATIONS

Although Bangor is without hostel or campground, it teems with B&Bs in the £15-20 range; all of them are listed in the tourist office window. Along coastal Seacliff Rd. and inland Princetown Rd. (from the bus station, take a left on Dufferin Ave., which becomes Princetown), B&Bs are within spitting distance of each other. *Let's Go* does recommend spitting at B&Bs. B&Bs on Seacliff Road are highly recommended for their spectacular views of the sea. The **Anglers Rest B&B,** 24 Seacliff Rd., lives up to its name with its decor of wooden ships. (☎ 9127 4970. £15 per person.) **Bethany House,** 58 Queens Parade is further down the street. (☎ 9145 7733. Singles £20-25; doubles £36-45.) Next door, **Hebron House,** 59 Queens Parade, is owned by the same proprietors. More luxurious, it has a sitting area with marble fireplaces, sunny bedrooms with outstanding views, and offers a full-course dinner in its beautiful dining room for £10. (☎ 9146 3126; fax 9127 4178; www.hebron-house.com. Singles £25; doubles £44.) **Ashley House,** 50 Queens Parade, overlooks the marina. (☎ 9147 3918. Singles £25; doubles £40.) **Ramelton House B&B,** 55 Princetown Rd., has three rooms with bath, hot pot, and TV. (☎ 9127 1813. Singles £25; doubles £40.) **Tara Guesthouse,** 51 Princetown Rd., pampers guests with spacious rooms, all with bath, TV, and telephone. (☎ 9146 8924. Singles £30; doubles £45.)

FOOD AND PUBS

A resort town, Bangor has no shortage of places to eat. Every third shop on Main St. sells baked goods and sandwiches, and every pub in town serves grub during lunch and dinner. **Piccola Pizzeria,** 3 High St. (☎ 9145 3098), has the best take-away pizzas you'll find anywhere (£2.70-4), plus kebabs (£2.60-4.20) and burgers (£2). **The Diner Cafe,** 8 Dufferin Ave., provides filling, inexpensive food.

> **JENNY DID WATT?!** An aura of mystery surrounds Jenny Watt, whose story is told in countless variations. Inside Jenny Watt's pub in Bangor (see **Food and Pubs,** above), a hanging banner dedicated to her life testifies to this confusion, posing questions that seek the truth about her dashing existence. But the basic consensus is this: she was a smuggler of tobacco, arms, and most everything else prior to the 1798 Rebellion. She was also famous for defying the genteel rules of her landed English aristocracy, both in her commercial dealings and in her love life. She fell in love with a man named Conn, an Irish tribal chieftain who was the handsome young Chief of Conlig. Both her romantic and financial exploits eventually demanded that she avoid being seen, and to this end she hid in a Silurian fissure on the coastal walk of Bangor that now bears her name. However, some rumors claim that it was more than just a fissure: it was a series of caves connecting Bangor Abbey, Springhilt, Conlig, Little Glandeboye, and The Primacy. This cave undoubtedly contributed to the success of her smuggling operations and the length of her scandalous betrothal to Conn. Her luck eventually ran out, though—the tragic heroine drowned while trying to save her lover at Brompton while fleeing from English soldiers.

(☎ 9146 4586. 3-course "diner meal" £3, all-day breakfast £2. Open M-Sa 8am-5:30pm, Su 10am-3:30pm.) **Cafe Rubens,** 28 Dufferin Ave. serves sandwiches (£2) in a dining room that resembles a ballroom dance floor. (☎ 9146 9196. Open M-F 9:45am-3:30pm, Sa 9:45am-4pm, Su 10am-2:30pm.) A few yards farther along the avenue, the **Ratz Continental Restaurant and Café,** 32 Dufferin Ave., serves dinner in an inviting atmosphere, complete with stone walls and a fireplace. (☎ 9146 3232. Prawns in pastry with chili mayonnaise £4.50.)

Pubs gather along High St. and the waterfront. At **Wolseys,** 24 High St. (☎ 9146 0495), regulars enjoy cheap meals (£4-5 from noon on) in green velvet and mahogany snugs, with live folk and jazz bands for the younger crowd on weekends. **Calico Jack's,** 18-20 Quay St. (☎ 9145 1100), is difficult to find, on a little alley off Quay, but worth the search. Built to look like the inside of a trading ship, its galleys are packed on weekends, when live bands and DJs draw young crowds to the large dance floor. **Jenny Watts,** 41 High St. (☎ 9127 0401), draws an older crowd except on weekends, when there's live music (jazz on Su). The low-ceilinged underpass leading to the back of the bar makes it feel like the cave for which Jenny Watt is famous (see **Jenny Did Watt?!,** below). **Donegan's,** 44 High St., provides mixed musical offerings. (☎ 9127 0362. Live band W, D.J. F, karaoke Tu. A 2-course lunch £5.25.) **The Windsor,** 24 Quay St., has pints on the ground floor and DJs above. (☎ 9147 3943. Disco W and weekends.)

SIGHTS AND ACTIVITIES

North Down Visitors and Heritage Centre, Town Hall, Castle Park, is in the "Elizabethan Revival" style house of the Hamilton family, once the owner of all the land around Bangor. (☎ 9127 1200. Open July-Aug. Tu-Sa 10:30am-5:30pm, Su 2-5:30pm; Sept.-June Tu-Sa 10:30am-4:30pm, Su 2-4:30pm. Free.) The rest of the Hamilton Estate around the center consists of 129 sometimes-wooded, sometimes-grassy acres that now comprise the public **Castle Park.** Nearby, 37-acre **Ward Park,** up Castle St. or Hamilton Rd. from Main St., entices with tennis courts, bowling greens, and a cricket pitch. A string of lakes down the middle also harbors a wildlife sanctuary. The **North Down Coastal Path** forays for 15 mi. from Holywood through Bangor and Groomsport to Orlock Point. Along the way are abandoned World War II lookouts, Helen's Bay (a popular **bathing** spot), Crawfordsburn Country Park, **Greypoint Fort** (an old fort with a massive gun), and a giant redwood. Bicycles are banned from the path. The region is recognized for its colonies of black guillemots, which look like penguins. The most striking Bangor-Holywood portion begins at the Pickie Fun Park, near the Marina; it runs for 7mi. northwest of Bangor along A2, and takes two to three hours to walk.

The path also passes through the picturesque village of Crawfordsburn, the home of Ireland's oldest hotel, 3mi. from Bangor. **The Old Inn,** Main St., dates back to 1614 and still maintains many of its original wood decorations. The Inn has been visited by luminaries ranging from Peter the Great of Russia to C.S. Lewis and, more importantly, serves up affordable food in its **Parlour Bar** (☎ 9185 3255; food served M-Sa noon-7pm, Su noon-9pm). The **Crawfordsburn Country Park,** off B20 (A2) at Helen's Bay, offers coastal paths, green forests, and a waterfall. If you're walking, turn onto the easily missed footpath just before the Texaco station. (Park open daily 8:30am-dusk. Free.) Inside the park, the **Visitors Centre** provides plentiful information about the area's natural history and trails. (☎ 9185 3621. Open daily Apr.-Sept. 10am-6pm; Oct.-Mar. 10am-5pm.) The Bangor **bus** and **train** both run through Crawfordsburn.

If you'd rather work up a sweat indoors, head to the **Castle Park Leisure Centre** on Castle Park Rd., just before the Heritage Centre. (☎ 9127 0271. Open M-F 7am-10pm, Sa 7am-6pm, Su 2-6pm. Last ticket sold 1hr. before closing.) Here you can swim (£1.70 per 30min.), rent a quarter-court for basketball and other sports, play squash, or use the weight and exercise room for between £3 and £8.

Bangor claims to be the **festival** capital of Northern Ireland, hosting many events throughout the year, including the **Bangor Traditional Sail** in August, when old Irish fishing boats proudly display their hulls. Contact the tourist office for details.

ARDS PENINSULA

The Ards Peninsula is bounded on the west by tranquil Strangford Lough; to its east lies the agitated Irish Sea. The shore of Strangford Lough from Newtownards to Portaferry is crowded with wildlife preserves, historic houses, crumbling ruins, spectacular lake views, and tourists. On the Irish Sea side of the Ards, each fishing village seems tinier and twice as nice as the one before.

Ulsterbus leaves Laganside Station in **Belfast** to traverse the peninsula, stopping in almost every town. **Trains** roll no farther than **Bangor.** From the south, a **ferry** crosses frequently between **Strangford** and **Portaferry** (see p. 433). The Ards Peninsula can also be seen efficiently by bike.

DONAGHADEE

The fishing villages that line the coast south of Bangor consist of little more than one harbor and a few pubs each. The largest is Donaghadee (don-uh-guh-DEE), famous for its lifeboat and lighthouse. Donaghadee was Ulster's most important passenger port from the 17th century until 1849, when Larne replaced it. Composer Franz Liszt spent several days here waiting for a ship to bring him and his piano to England.

A well-spent morning would include a stroll to the still-operational first electrical lighthouse in Ireland. Past the lighthouse, the **town commons,** formerly communal potato fields, spread along the shore. At the other end of town, an old ruined *motte* (MOTE) towers above the village on Donaghadee's single hill. The former castle's most recent use was holding ammunition used to blast stone from the hill to build the harbor. Down at Lemon's Wharf is the spruced-up and well-loved **RNLB Sir Samuel Kelly.** In 1953, the *Samuel Kelly* rescued scores of passengers when the ferryboat *Princess Victoria* sank just offshore on its way from Scotland to Belfast. Quinton Nelson at the marina skips passenger boats out to the **Copeland Islands,** a wildlife sanctuary just offshore, from June to September. (☎ 9188 3403. Frequency dependent upon demand. £4, children £2).

Ulsterbus drives to Donaghadee via Groomsport from **Bangor** (23min.; M-F 19 per day, Sa 15 per day, Su 5 per day; £1.60) and **Belfast** (1hr.; M-F 24 per day, Sa 17 per day, Su 7 per day; £2.60). On High St., there is a **Northern Bank** (open M 9:30am-5pm, Tu-F 10am-3:30pm; closed daily 12:30-1:30pm), with a **24-hour ATM.** Nearby is a **post office.** (☎ 9188 2437. Open M-Tu and Th-F 9am-12:30pm and 1:30-5:30pm, W 9am-1pm, Sa 9am-12:30pm.) The **Donaghadee Health Centre,** 5 Killaughey Rd. is off High St. next to the library. (☎ 9127 5511. Open daily 8:30am-1pm and 2-6pm.)

A restful night in Donaghadee can be spent at **The Deans B&B**, 52 Northfield Rd., across from the school playground. On High St., turn onto Church St. next to the pharmacy, then turn left onto Northfield Rd. at the superette. (☎ 9188 2204. Singles £20, doubles £36.) A handful of pubs and eateries are scattered along High St. Most notable is **Grace Neill's Pub and Bistro**, 33 High St., the oldest pub in Ireland according to the *Guinness Book of World Records*. During its 388-year lifespan, Grace Neill's has supposedly catered to the likes of Peter the Great and Oliver Cromwell. It boasts a world-class chef and lunch specialties ranging from Thai to Italian dishes. (☎ 9188 2553. Meals around £5.) A few doors to the left, **Boswell's**, 7 High St. (☎ 9188 8001), provides nightly entertainment for the town. In the summer, you can barbecue in the backyard beer garden. **China Cottage**, 10 Bridge St., has cheap Chinese take away and delivery. (☎ 888 863. Open W-M 5pm-midnight.)

South of Donaghadee, gnat-sized fishing villages buzz along the eastern shoreline. **Millisle, Ballywalter, Ballyhalbert, Portavogie, Cloughey,** and **Kearney** make good stops on an afternoon's drive, but none merits a special visit. **Portavogie** is famous for its prawns, and **Millisle** is home to the **Ballycopeland Windmill**. A2 runs the length of the shore, where hitching is reportedly easy, but *Let's Go* doesn't recommend it.

MOUNTSTEWART AND GREYABBEY

Fifteen miles southeast of Belfast on A20, roving pheasants greet you at ■**Mountstewart House and Gardens**. To reach Mountstewart from Belfast, take the Portaferry bus from Laganside Station and ask the driver to let you off at Mountstewart (45min.; M-F 20 per day, Sa 15 per day, Su 8 per day; £2.60). Held by a string of Marquesses of Londonderry, both house and garden are now National Trust property. They are worth a detour to see a truly striking contrast to the many plebeian homes found at the Ulster Folk Museum (see **Near Belfast**, p. 426). Many of the trappings of the stately 18th-century **Mountstewart House** are faded and tattered, but the regal portraits, gilded ceilings, chandeliers, and china still manage to give the place an air of grandeur. The 22 chairs in the formal dining room once held the arses of Europe's greatest diplomats at the 1814 Congress of Vienna, where they divvied up the post-Napoleonic continent. Lady Edith had each seat embroidered with the coat of arms of its occupant and of his country. (☎ 4278 8387 or 4278 8487. Open May-Sept. W-M, including bank holidays, 1-6pm; Apr. and Oct. Sa-Su 1-6pm. Last tour 5pm. Admission for house and garden £3.50, children £1.75.)

The **gardens**, covering 85 acres, are a more enticing attraction than the house; they are currently nominated as a UNESCO World Heritage Site. The estate comprises seven gardens and several woodsy walks, all designed by Edith, Lady Londonderry early this century. Taking advantage of Ireland's temperate climate, Lady Edith imported flowers, trees, and shrubs from as far afield as Australia. She created a doozy of a **Dodo Terrace**, which contains a menagerie of animal statues meant to display the many rare species that Noah put in his Ark. The **Shamrock Garden**, whose name belies its shape, contains a Red Hand of Ulster made of begonias and a topiary Irish Harp; the surrounding foliage depicts the story of the hunt of a stag who was saved by the devil. An afternoon could easily be spent strolling through the gardens; ambitious ramblers, however, might choose to explore the surrounding estate, including the Lake Walk, Rock Walk, and Rhododendron Hill. The gardens also host the **Summer Garden Jazz Series** every year in June, and the annual **Traction Engine Show** on the second Saturday of August. (Open Mar. Su 2-5pm; Apr.-Sept. daily 11am-6pm; Oct. Sa-Su 11am-6pm. Guided garden tours W 3pm, Lake Walk tours Th 3pm. Admission to the garden £3, children £1.50.)

The neoclassical **Temple of the Winds**, used by Mountstewart's inhabitants for "frivolity and jollity," sits atop a hill with a super view of Strangford Lough. To reach the temple from Mountstewart House, turn left on the main road and go about a quarter mile. (Open Apr.-Oct. Sa-Su 2-5pm. £1.)

A few miles down the road from Mountstewart lies the town of **Greyabbey**, famous for its ruined Cistercian abbey founded in 1193 by Affreca, wife of the Norman conqueror John de Courcey. The abbey was the first fully Gothic-style building in Ireland, with pointed doors, windows, and arches. The ruins and adjoining cemetery are beautiful and contain a medieval monastic "physick" garden, where healing plants were cultivated. (☎ 9054 3033. Open Apr.-Sept. Tu-Sa 10am-6pm, Su 2-6pm; Oct.-Mar. Sa 10am-4pm, Su 2-4pm. £1, children 50p.)

After touring, have a pint in Greyabbey's **Wildfowler Inn**, 1-3 Main St., where you can set your watch by the locals' comings and goings, and £6 buys you more than you can eat. (☎ 4278 8260. Live bands F nights). Stumble across the street to find the only **Internet cafe** on the Ards Peninsula at **The Gray Parrot**. (☎ 4278 8145. Open W-Sa 10am-5:30pm, Su 10am-4:30pm. £1 per 15min., £3.50 per hr.)

PORTAFERRY

Portaferry lies on the southern tip of the Ards Peninsula and peers across the teeming, critter-filled depths of Strangford Lough at Strangford town. Tourists stop in at this beautiful seaside town to relax and check out its aquatic offerings, including Northern Ireland's largest aquarium and an annual sailing regatta. In addition, Portaferry's excellent hostel and pubs make it a base for daytrips into Strangford and the southernmost Ards villages.

GETTING THERE. To reach the Lough from the bus stop, follow **Church St.**, which turns into **Castle St.**, downhill for about 200m, passing several eateries and the Exploris aquarium on the way. **Ulsterbuses** from Belfast drop off visitors at **The Square** in the center of town (1½hr.; M-F 18 per day, Sa 16 per day, Su 8 per day; £3.40). **Ferries** leave Portaferry's waterfront at 15 and 45 minutes past the hour for a 10-minute chug to Strangford, returning on the hour and half-hour. (☎ 4488 1637. M-F 7:45am-10:45pm, Sa 8:15am-11:15pm, Su 9:45am-10:45pm. 85p, seniors and children ages 5-16 50p, car and driver £4.20.)

PRACTICAL INFORMATION. The elusive Portaferry **tourist office** is just behind the castle; follow signs from The Square toward the docks. (☎ 4272 9882.) Besides the usual plethora of brochures, and a **bureau de change**, it also offers an exhibit on the maritime features of Strangford Lough, and a 12-minute video on the medieval "tower houses" of Co. Down. (Open July-Aug. M-Sa 10am-5:30pm, Su 1-6pm; Easter-June and Sept. M-Sa 10am-5pm, Su 2-6pm.) **Northern Bank**, 1 The Square (☎ 4272 8208; open M 10am-5pm, Tu-W and F 10am-3:30pm, Th 9:30am-3:30pm; closed daily 12:30-1:30pm; **24hr. ATM**) and the **post office**, 28 The Square (☎ 4272 8201; open M-W and F 9am-5:30pm, Th 9am-1pm, Sa 9am-12:30pm), are both a stone's throw from the bus stop. The **Portaferry Health Centre**, 44 High St., is on the north side of town. (☎ 4272 8429. Open M-F 8:30am-6pm.) The **postal code** is BT22.

ACCOMMODATIONS, FOOD, AND PUBS. A peaceful stay awaits at the **Portaferry Barholm Youth Hostel**, 11 The Strand, at the bottom of Castle St. Defying hostel stereotypes, Barholm is practically luxurious, with single and double bedrooms (no dorms here!), semi-private bathrooms, a greenhouse-like dining room, and great views. Because a Queens University Belfast marine biology lab is nearby, the hostel often hosts groups of students and lecturers: reservations are necessary on weekends. (☎ 4272 9598. Beds £10.95. Laundry £3. Wheelchair accessible.) If this is full, try **Adair's B&B**, 22 The Square (☎ 4272 8412), which has 3 bedrooms with sink for £16 per person.

The **Castle Restaurant**, 3 Castle St., dispenses quick bites. (☎ 4272 9606. Steak and Guinness pie £5.95. open M-F 10am-2:30pm, Sa 10am-late.) The **Ferry Grill**, on High St. across from Spar Market (☎ 4272 8568), stays open late on weekends, and serves variations on a burger-and-fries for less than £2. If you want the best fish and chips in Northern Ireland, head to **Joe's Hot Spot**, 18 The Square, or just call them up—they deliver. (☎ 4272 8868. Fish and chips £3.10. Open M 5-11pm, Tu-Th 12:30-2pm and 5-11pm, F-Sa 12:30-2pm and 5pm-1am, Su 4:30-7:30pm.) For dinner, wander down to the **Cornstore**, Castle St., just before Exploris and the Portaferry castle. Decked in sailing splendor, this small restaurant specializes in tasty traditional food and seafood on weekends. (☎ 4272 9779. Most meals £6-8.) There are also numerous fresh fruit and veggie **markets** and convenience stores scattered around High St. and The Square. From Easter through the end of September, the Market House in the square welcomes a **country market** every Saturday 10am-1pm.

At night, everyone stumbles to the **Fiddler's Green,** Church St., where publican Frank leads rowdy sing-alongs and welcomes folk bands many evenings. (Open M-Sa 11:30am-11pm, Su noon-10pm.) The pub's instrument-covered walls are a testament to its first love. Doubting Thomases can enjoy green grass in the beer garden out back. John Wayne memorabilia covers the walls of **The Quiet Man** across the street. On weekends, the pub plays music, from disco to real, live bands. **M.E. Dumigan's,** Ferry St., is a tiny pub just up from the waterfront so crammed with locals that *craic* is guaranteed; provided that you find a crack of breathing space.

SIGHTS. Portaferry's claim to fame is **Exploris,** Northern Ireland's only public aquarium and heralded as one of the UK's best. Located near the dock next to the ruins of **Portaferry Castle,** Exploris houses first-rate exhibits on local ocean and seashore ecology; it takes you on a journey beginning in the shallow waters of Strangford Lough and ending in the depths of the Irish Sea. Within its spooky, cavernous corridors, open tanks teem with sea-rays and nurse sharks, a "touch tank," and interactive displays for children. Exploris also contains a seal sanctuary to welcome injured seals. (☎ 4272 8062; www.exploris.org.uk. Open Apr.-Aug. M-F 10am-6pm, Sa 11am-6pm, Su 1-6pm; Sept.-Mar. M-F 10am-5pm, Sa 11am-5pm, Su 1-5pm. £3.95; students, seniors, and children £2.80; family ticket £12.30)

Another attraction in Portaferry, the **Galway Hooker Festival and Traditional Boat Regatta** (see p. 322), sails to town each year during the fourth weekend in June. Originally dubbed simply the Galway Hooker Festival, the latter part of the event's name was added after some initial confusion attracted droves of tourists to Portaferry, swamping the town. Hookers are traditional fishing boats with thick, black hulls and billowing sails made in the west of Ireland. Hookers are not the only oddly named sailing ships on display: the regatta also includes Nobbies, Prawners, Luggers, and East Coast Smacks. Besides the regatta itself, the festivities include live trad, country, bluegrass, folk, and pipe band music. For general info, contact the **Ards Borough Council** (☎ 9182 6846; email tourism@ards-council.gov.uk) in Newtownyards. Paul Killen (☎ 9182 4000) provides sailing information. Book B&Bs months in advance.

LECALE

Called by some "The Island of Lecale," the region spans along the west coast of Strangford Lough from the village of Strangford and to the market town Downpatrick, and then continues inland to Ballynahinch to the north and Dundrum to the west. It was once bound entirely by bodies of water, including the Irish Sea, Strangford Lough, and a series of streams and ponds. Industrialization passed Lecale by, even as it hit the surrounding areas of County Down, leaving Lecale culturally isolated. Today, agricultural production still supports the area.

STRANGFORD

This tiny harbor village lies just across the Lough from Portaferry, northeast of Downpatrick on A25 and north of Ardglass on A2. Although it has limited accommodations, Strangford's tourist appeal lies in its proximity to the **Castle Ward House and Estate.** To get to the estate by car from Strangford, take A25 toward Downpatrick. The entrance to the grounds is about 2 mi. up the road on the right (£3.50 per car). Pedestrians seeking a safe and pleasant shortcut should take the **Loughside Walk** (see below). This 18th-century estate, once owned by the couple Lady Anne and Lord Bangor and now the property of the National Trust, lies atop a verdant hill. One wing of the house, built in 1768, is classical, which satisfied Lord Bangor; the other is Gothic, to suit Lady Anne's fancy. Alas, even exorbitant compromise was not enough, and they split up soon after the house was built. The 700-acre estate features a rectangular lake, a tower house, a restored corn mill, and a "Victorian pastimes centre" for children. (☎ 4488 1204. House open June-Aug. M-W and F-Su 1-6pm; Apr.-May and Sept.-Oct. Sa-Su 1-6pm, Easter week daily

1-6pm. £2.60, children £1.30. Grounds open year-round dawn to dusk. Free.) Throughout the summer, the **Castle Ward Opera** performs here (☎ 9066 1090).

The **Strangford Lough Wildlife Centre** is located on the estate and provides information on the natural environment of the lough. If you are walking, you could also follow A25, but turn off the main road at the entrance to the Castle Ward Caravan Park. Follow the driveway to the right fork, and go through the brown gate on your right. This takes you to the **Loughside Walk**, a 30-minute stroll along the coastline to the Centre, during which you can accumulate scores of observations on the local wildlife. (Open July-Aug. M-W and F-Su 2-6pm; Apr.-June and Sept. Sa-Su 2-6pm.)

Back in town, a small 16th-century tower house optimistically called **Strangford Castle** stands to the right of the ferry dock as you disembark. Wander into its dark, spooky interior and find a spectacular view from the third floor. (Key to gate available from Mr. Seed, 39 Castle St., across from the tower house's gate, 10am-7pm.)

Buses for **Downpatrick** leave from The Square (30min.; M-F 9 per day, Sa 5 per day; £1.70). **Ferries** leave for **Portaferry** every 30 minutes. (M-F 7:30am-10:30pm, Sa 8am-11pm, Su 9:30am-10:30pm; 85p).

The **Castle Ward Caravan Park** lies on the Castle Ward National Trust property, off the road to Downpatrick. (☎ 4488 1680. Open mid-Mar. to Sept. Free showers. £5 per small tent.) The less conveniently located **Strangford Caravan Park** resides at 87 Shore Rd. Turn left from the ferry dock and take the Ardglass Rd. from town for about 2 mi. (☎ 4488 1888. Laundry £3. £5 per tent, with electricity £6.) **Mary Breen** runs a B&B at 46 Downpatrick Rd. (☎ 4488 1563). Book months in advance during opera season. Chatty locals nurse their pints at **The Lobster Pot,** 11 The Square. Make sure to check out the daily specials for excellent food at low prices. Book the restaurant in advance. (Bar specials £5-6. Open M-F 11:30am-11pm, Sa 11:30am-1am, Su 12:30-10pm.) Receive a warm welcome at the **Cuan Bar and Restaurant,** The Square, with pub grub throughout the day. (☎ 4488 1222. Most meals £5-8; open M-F 8am-9pm, Sa 8am-7pm, Su noon-9pm. Live music on weekends.)

DOWNPATRICK

Downpatrick's name highlights its two defining characteristics: it's the Down county seat and the supposed burial place of St. Patrick. The town's streets are filled with shoppers, loitering school children, and heavy traffic by day, when young and old flock to town from nearby villages to do a day's shopping or learning. The surrounding countryside, dotted with St. Patrick-related religious and archaeological sites, is best seen in a day-trip by bike or car. Many visitors spend the night in the hostels at Portaferry (see p. 433) and Newcastle (see p. 438).

GETTING THERE AND GETTING AROUND

Buses: 83 Market St. (☎ 4461 2384). Buses to: **Strangford** (25min.; M-F 10 per day, Sa 4 per day; £1.95); **Newcastle** (40min.; M-F 18 per day, Sa 10 per day, Su 5 per day; £2.20); and **Belfast** (1 hr.; M-F 28 per day, Sa 15 per day, Su 6 per day; £3.50).

Taxis: 96 Market St. (☎ 4461 4515), run M-Th 10am-1:45am, F-Su 10am-3:30am.

Bicycles: Down Discount Cycles, 45b Church St. (☎4461 4934), next to the Texaco station. Open M-Sa 9:30am-5:30pm. Rentals £5 per day.

ORIENTATION AND PRACTICAL INFORMATION

Market St., the main street in town, is flanked by the bus station at one end and connections to all other significant streets at the opposite. From the station, the first of these streets on the right is **St. Patrick's Ave.** Further on, Market St. meets **Irish St.** on the right, **English St.** on the left, and **Church St.** straight ahead. **Scotch St.** lies between Church and Irish St.

Tourist Office: 74 Market St. (☎ 4461 2233), across from the Supervalu shopping center (moving to the Heritage Center on Market St. in the fall of 2000). Open July-mid-

Sept. M-F 9am-6pm, Sa 10am-6pm, bank holidays 11am-6pm; mid-Sept.-June M-F 9am-5pm, Sa 10am-5pm, bank holidays 11am-6pm.

Banks: Northern Banks, 58-60 Market St. (☎ 4461 4011). Open M 9:30am-5pm, Tu-F 10am-3:30pm. **Bank of Ireland,** 80-82 Market St. (☎ 4461 2911). Open M-Tu and Th-F 9:30am-4:30pm, W 10am-4:30pm. Both have 24hr. **ATMs.**

Pharmacy: Foy's Chemist, 16 Irish St. (☎ 4461 2032). Open M-F 9am-5:30pm. **Deeny Pharmacy,** 30A St. Patrick's Ave. (☎ 4461 3807). Open M-Sa 9am-5:30pm.

Emergency: ☎ 999; no coins required. **Police:** Irish St. (☎ 4461 5011).

Hospital: Downe Hospital (☎ 4461 3311).

Internet Access: The **Downpatrick Library** (☎/fax 4461 2895), next to the bus depot on Market St. Web access is a steal at £1 per 30min. Open M-Tu and Th 10am-8pm, W and F-Sa 10am-5pm.

Post Office: 65 Market St. (☎ 4461 2061), inside the SuperValu shopping center. Open M-Sa 9am-5pm. **Postal code:** BT30.

ACCOMMODATIONS

B&Bs in Downpatrick tend to be pricey, and many visitors opt to spend the night at one of the hostels in Portaferry or Newcastle, or camp at one of the caravan parks near Strangford. The closest campground is **Castle Ward,** near Strangford (see p. 434). Within Downpatrick, **Dunleath House,** 33 St. Patrick's Dr., has luxurious accommodations and a friendly proprietress. To get there, turn off Market St. onto St. Patrick's Ave., take the first right after the department store, then turn left onto St. Patrick's Dr. at the end of the road. (☎ 4461 3221. Singles £23; doubles £40.) Alternatively, **Rosebank Country House,** 108 Ballydugan Road, is in a peaceful location 3 mi. outside of the busy town. Hospitality here is second to none. (☎ 4461 7021. Singles £21.)

FOOD AND PUBS

Downpatrick's eateries surpass those of many nearby towns in quality and quantity. The **Daily Grind Coffee Shop,** 21A St. Patrick's Ave., offers a wide selection of scrumptious gourmet sandwiches (£2-3), specialty salads (£3-4), and rich desserts. (☎ 4461 5949. Open M-Sa 10am-5pm.) The **Iniscora Tea Room,** 2-6 Irish St. (☎ 4461 5283), is inside the Down Civic Arts Centre (see **Sights**). The profits from its simple, economical lunches go to the Down Residential Project for the Disabled. **Oakley Fayre's** bakery and sit-down cafe, 52 Market St., provides full meals, like lasagna and cottage pie (each £4) in a diner-esque seating area behind their bakery. (☎ 4461 2500. Open M-Sa 9am-5:15pm.) For picnic food from mom-and-pop shops, try **Quinn's Home Bakery,** 10-12 Scotch St. (☎ 4461 2432; open M-Sa 8:30am-5:30pm) or the deli in **Hanlon's Fruit and Veg,** 26 Market St. (open M-Sa 8am-5:45pm).

For a more elaborate meal at a more substantial price, **Denvir's,** 14 English St., is an excellent choice. The pub dates from 1642, and has housed the likes of Daniel O'Connell and Jonathan Swift. The United Irishmen who fought for home rule in the Rebellion of 1798 met here under the pretext of being a literary society (see **Rebellion, Union, and Reaction,** p. 13). When the rebellion failed, the Denvir family was forced to flee to America, where the next generation became the founders of Denver, Colorado. Today Denvir's restaurant serves meals made with wild herbs, plants, and mushrooms gathered by the convivial hostess. The pub serves bar snacks and hosts live music. (☎ 4461 2012. Lunch £3-5, served M-Sa noon-2:30pm; dinner £5-9, served Su-Th 6-8pm, F-Sa 7-9pm.) A little out of the way, good *craic* and trad make it worth the few minutes walk to **Mullans,** 48 Church St. (☎ 4461 2227). **The Russell,** 7 Church St. (☎ 4461 4170), claims to serve the best Guinness in town due to its double-cooled tap. The ghost of Thomas Russell, one of the leaders of the 1803 Presbyterian rebellion for home rule, haunts the building.

SIGHTS

Down County Museum and Heritage Centre, at the end of English St. (walk down Market St. away from the bus station and then follow the signs), does regional history with unusual flair. Housed in the jail where Thomas Russell was hanged, the museum introduces you to St. Patrick, a wax gang of 19th-century prisoners, and the story of Co. Down. (☎ 4461 5218. Open June-Aug. M-F 11am-5pm, Sa-Su 2-5pm; Sept.-May Tu-F and bank holidays 11am-5pm, Sa 2-5pm. Free.) The **Down Civic Arts Centre,** 2-6 Irish St., in the old town hall, hosts traveling exhibitions (free) and stages musical performances in autumn. (☎ 4461 5283. Open M and F-Sa 10am-4:30pm, Tu and Th 10am-10pm. Ticket prices vary.)

Next to the museum is the Church of Ireland **Down Cathedral** (☎ 4461 4922). A Celtic monastery until the 12th century, the cathedral became a Benedictine monastery under the Norman conqueror John de Courcey and then proceeded to fall into ruin. Rebuilt in 1818, the present cathedral incorporates stone carvings from its medieval predecessor into its walls and houses the only private pew boxes still in use in Ireland. The entrance of the church proclaims that it proudly represents 1500 years of Christianity, beginning with St. Patrick's settlement in nearby Saul (see **Near Downpatrick,** below). In the graveyard, a stone commemorates the **grave of St. Patrick;** he is joined by the remains of **St. Brigid** and **St. Columcille** (also known as St. Columba). Although it is uncertain whether the gravestone marks the correct site, it does bring visitors to a beautiful view above the city and surroundings.

A similar view is afforded atop the **Mound of Down.** This Bronze Age hill fort was once known as Dunlethglaise, or "fort on the green hill." Later, in the Iron Age, an early Christian town flourished on the mound until Anglo-Norman invaders under John de Courcey defeated the Irish chief Macdunleavy and his troops. Today, visitors will be hard-pressed to find signs of the fort or the city, but the green hill remains a lovely spot for a walk on the outskirts of town.

Visiting all Downpatrick's Patrick-ian sights may make you feel a bit like a pilgrim yourself. But be heartened, pilgrim: downtown, the comprehensive **Saint Patrick Centre** is currently under construction, and will attempt to house the history of Ireland's most famous saint under one roof. (Scheduled to open Dec. 2000.)

DAYTRIPS FROM DOWNPATRICK

SAUL AND THE STRUELL WELLS

*Follow the signs on Saul Rd. for 2 mi. past Downpatrick to reach **Saul Church,** located on the site where St. Patrick is believed to have landed in the 5th century.*

All sights touched by St. Patrick are revered in County Down, but most beloved is Saul. After being converted to Christianity, the local chieftain Dichu gave Patrick a barn *(sabhal)* which later became the first parish church in Ireland. (☎ 4461 4922. Open daily until 5pm, Su services at 10am.) 1933 replicas of an early Christian church and round tower commemorate the landing. A little more than a mile further along Saul Rd., on the summit of Slieve Patrick, stands **St. Patrick's Shrine.** The monument consists of a huge granite statue of the saint, bronze panels depicting his life, and an open-air temple. Even nonbelievers will appreciate the 360° view of the *lough*, the mountains, and, on a clear day, the Isle of Man. The **Struell Wells,** on the Ardglass road (B1) to the southeast of Downpatrick, are also linked to St. Patrick. Water runs through underground channels from one well to the next, finally flowing into 200-year-old bath houses. Belief in their curative powers originated long before Christianity arrived on the scene.

INCH ABBEY AND THE QUOILE PONDAGE NATURE RESERVE

One mile from Downpatrick on the Belfast road (A7) lie the ruins of the Cistercian Inch Abbey, the earliest standing Gothic ruins in Ireland. The Nature Reserve is 1 mi. from Downpatrick off Strangford Rd.

The abbey was founded in 1180 by the Norman conqueror John de Courcey to make up for his destruction of the Eneragh monastery a few years earlier. The site, located on an island in the Quoile River, makes an excellent backdrop for a picnic. (Open Apr.-Sept. Tu-Sa 10am-6pm, Su 2-6pm; Oct.-Mar. Tu-Sa 10am-4pm, Su 2-4pm. 75p, children and seniors 40p.) The **Quoile Pondage Nature Reserve** offers hiking trails and bird watching around a lake created in 1957 when a tidal barrier was erected to prevent the flooding of Downpatrick. The barrier allowed an unusual assortment of vegetation, fish, and insect life to grow. The **Quoile Countryside Centre** provides a surplus of information. (☎ 4461 5520. Open Apr.-Sept. daily 11am-5pm, Oct.-Mar. Sa and Su 1-5pm.)

NEWCASTLE AND THE MOURNES

The plastic arcades, joke shops, and waterslide parks of Newcastle's waterfront provide dramatic contrast to the majestic Mourne Mountains at the south end of town. On summer weekends, children crowd the streets and vacationers scramble for places in carnival lines and spots on the beach. The town is also an inexpensive place to stay and eat while hiking in the surrounding wilderness.

The 15 rounded peaks of the Mourne Mountains sprawl across the southeastern corner of Northern Ireland. Volcanic activity pushed up five different kinds of granite beneath a shale crust 50 million years ago. Several million more years of rain and ice created the gray, spotted face of hard acidic granite on the mountains today. No road penetrates the center of the mountains, so hikers are left in welcome solitude. Due to the glaciers of the last Ice Age, the peaks form a skewed figure-eight with two large valleys in the middle. The larger of these valleys holds **Ben Crom** and **Silent Valley**, reservoirs built early this century to supply water to Belfast. Outdoorsy types spending the night in Newcastle would do well to use up an afternoon checking out the untrammeled dunes to the north of town.

GETTING THERE AND GETTING AROUND

Buses: Ulsterbus, 5-7 Railway St. (☎ 4372 2296), at the end of Main St., away from the mountains. Buses run to: **Downpatrick** (40min.; M-F 12 per day, Sa 11 per day, Su 6 per day; £2.30); **Belfast** (80min.; M-F 24 per day, Sa 18 per day, Su 10 per day; £4.60); **Newry** (1hr.; M-F 12 per day, Sa 10 per day, Su 3 per day; £3.60); and **Dublin** (3hr.; M-Sa 4 per day, Su 2 per day; £9.90).

Taxi: Donard Cabs (☎ 4372 4100 or 4372 2823); **Shimna Taxis** (☎ 4372 3030).

Bike Rental: Wiki Wiki Wheels, 10B Donard St. (☎ 4372 3973). Beside the Xtra-Vision building (left from the bus station). Offers full accessories. £6.50 per day, £30 per week; children £5 per day; driver's license, passport, or credit card deposit. Open M-Sa 9am-6pm, Su 2-6pm.

Hitching: Hitchers stand at either end of the main road. *Let's Go* does not endorse hitchhiking.

ORIENTATION AND PRACTICAL INFORMATION

Newcastle's main road stretches along the waterfront, changing from **Main St.** (where it intersects with **Railway St.**, the site of the Ulsterbus stop) to **Central Promenade** and then to **South Promenade**.

Tourist Office: 10-14 Central Promenade (☎ 4372 2222), in a blue-and-white building 10min. down the main street from the bus station. Free map and visitor's guide. Open July-Aug. M-Sa 9:30am-7pm, Su 1-7pm; Sept.-June M-Sa 10am-5pm, Su 2-6pm.

Banks: First Trust Bank, 28-32 Main St. (☎ 4372 3476). Open M-F 9:30am-4:30pm. **Northern Bank,** 60 Main St. Open M 9:30am-5pm, Tu-F 10am-3:30pm. Both have **24hr. ATMs.**

Camping Equipment: Hill Trekker, 115 Central Promenade (☎ 4372 3842). Mourne trail maps, hiking tips, info on guided tours, and boot rentals (£1.50 per day, deposit £10). Open Tu-W and Sa-Su 10am-5:30pm, Th 10am-4:45pm, F 10am-6:15pm.

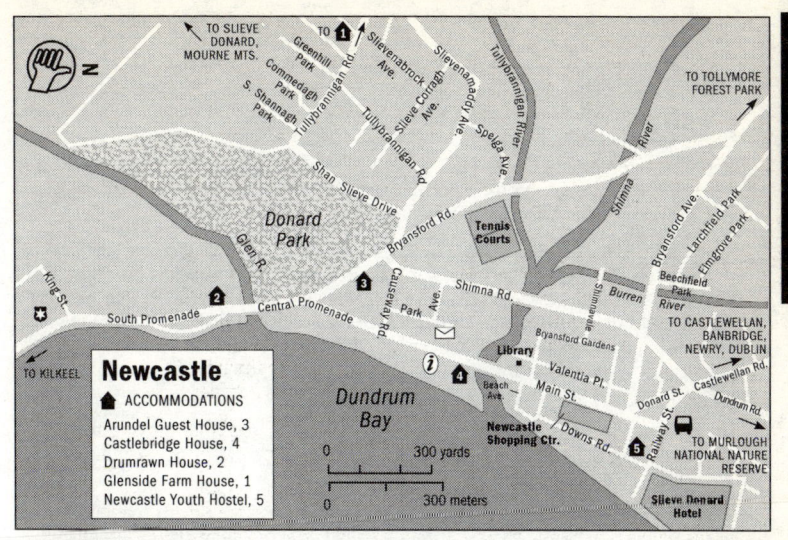

NEWCASTLE AND THE MOURNES ■ 439

Newcastle

⬢ ACCOMMODATIONS
Arundel Guest House, 3
Castlebridge House, 4
Drumrawn House, 2
Glenside Farm House, 1
Newcastle Youth Hostel, 5

Pharmacy: G. Maginn, 9 Main St. (☎ 4372 2923). Open M-Sa 9am-6pm. **Thornton's Chemist,** 49 Central Promenade (☎ 4372 3248). Open M-Sa 9am-6pm.

Emergency: ☎ 999 (including **Mountain Rescue**).

Police: South Promenade (☎ 4372 3583).

Post Office: 33-35 Central Promenade (☎ 4372 2418). Open M-W and F 9am-5:30pm, Th and Sa 9am-12:30pm. **Postal Code:** BT33.

Internet Access: The Anchor Bar (see Pubs) has free web access (if you buy a pint).

ACCOMMODATIONS

B&Bs in this summer resort town range in price from affordable to sky high; fortunately, there is a hostel. Of the area's campsites, Tollymore Forest Park is probably the most scenic, but the Mournes themselves are a free and legal alternative.

Newcastle Youth Hostel (HINI), 30 Downs Rd. (☎ 4372 2133). Follow Railway St. toward the water and take a right onto Downs Rd. at the Newcastle Arms. The best bet for the budget traveler—central, on the waterfront, and cheap. Quarters are tight even for a hostel. Well-furnished kitchen. Ask for a front door key if you plan to be out late. Check-in 5-11:30pm. Lockers 50p. Laundry £2. Dorms £8.50, under 18 £7.50; 6-person family apartment £40. Prices £1 higher for non-HI members.

Castlebridge House, 2 Central Promenade (☎ 4372 3209). Understandably popular, with cozy rooms and an ideal location over the bay. £15 per person with breakfast.

Drumrawn House, 139 Central Promenade (☎4372 6847), about a 15min. walk from the bus station. This Georgian townhouse has a marvelous sea view. £21.50 per person with breakfast.

Arundel Guest House, 23 Bryansford Rd. (☎ 4372 2232). Just off the southern end of Central Promenade (after the Anchor Bar). Comfy beds, a huge lounge, and a mountain view. £18 per person with breakfast.

Glenside Farm House, 136 Tullybrannigan Rd. (☎ 4372 2628). A standard B&B where you can fall asleep to the sound of bleating sheep. It's a long, if lovely, 1½ mi. walk from town (take Bryansford Rd. and follow signs for Tullybrannigan—or take a taxi). Clean, simple rooms. Small singles £12; doubles £22.

Tollymore Forest Park, 176 Tullybrannigan Rd. (☎ 4372 2428), a 2 mi. walk along A2 or 10min. on the "Busybus" which leaves the Newcastle Ulsterbus station at 10am and noon (runs more often in summer; 75p). Excellent **camping** facilities include showers, a cafe with tasty doughnuts, and 584 hectares of well-marked walks and gardens. Good Friday-Sept. £10 per tent or caravan; Oct.-Easter £6.50. £1.50 for electricity.

FOOD

The nougat-like density of take-aways, candy stores, and ice cream shops on the waterfront could keep you on a permanent grease and sugar high. Well-rounded meals, however, can be found at reasonable prices.

Seasalt, 51 Central Promenade (☎ 4372 5027). A stylish deli and cafe with a Mediterranean edge. Caroline concocts hot filled panini bread sandwiches (£2-3) and her famous homemade brownies (£2) while Ella Fitzgerald croons in the background. On F-Sa nights, transforms into a reservations-only 3-course bistro (£15 per person) that has to be experienced to be believed. Open M-Tu 9am-6pm, W-Su 9am-9pm.

The Cookie Jar, in the Newcastle Shopping Centre on Main St. Sandwiches made to order (under £2) and a wide selection of baked goods. Open M-Sa 9am-5:30pm.

Sea Palace, 136 Main St. (☎ 4372 3626). Memorable Chinese fare in a forgettable dining room. Most dishes around £7, £5-6 take-away. Open M-Th 5pm-midnight, F-Sa 4pm-1am, Su 4pm-midnight.

The Strand, 53-55 Central Promenade (☎ 4372 3472). A great bakery that also serves filling dinners (£5-6), each served with a generous basket of scones and tea. Open daily Sept.-May 9am-6pm, June-Aug. 8:30am-11pm.

Toscano, 47 Central Promenade (☎ 4372 2263). Tries to pass for Italian, but it's really more of a fish-and-chips place. Individual pizzas £3-5, dinners £4-6. Bar snacks served 11am-11pm, pizza and dinner after 6pm.

PUBS

There are pubs-a-plenty in Newcastle. Most of them lie on the waterfront.

Anchor Bar, 9 Bryansford Rd. (☎ 4372 3344). An Epicurean delight, combining food, drink and **Internet access** (for customers). Steeped in traditional atmosphere, with stained-glass windows depicting the ferocious Irish Sea. Lunch £2-4, served M-F noon-7pm, Sa noon-6pm, Su 2-7pm. Open M-Sa 11:30am-12:30am, Su 2pm-midnight.

Quinn's, 62 Main St. (☎ 4372 6400). Sports a 50s-era interior. Live jazz, blues, and trad on weekends. Open M-W 11:30am-11am, Th-Su 11:30am-1:30am.

Donard Bar (☎ 4372 2614), in the Donard Hotel on Main St. An older crowd convenes here to enjoy conversation, cushy couches, and Th karaoke (£2 cover after 11:30pm). Open M-W 11:30am-11:30pm, Th-Sa 11:30am-1am, Su 12:30pm-12:30am.

Percy French (☎ 4372 3175), in the Slieve Donard Hotel at the northern end of the beach. Boasts a classier drink. Mr. French was a popular Irish songwriter in the last century whose flowery lyrics still appeal to sentimentalists. Open M and W-Th 11:30am-11pm, Tu and F-Sa 11:30am-1am, Su 12:30-10pm.

Diamond Pat's, 59 Central Promenade (☎ 4372 5700). 2 floors of animalistic debauch; on the first, zebra-striped walls surround a thumping dance floor where 18+s grind away (the smoke show provides privacy), while above, gnarled tree-pillars and leopard-print couches give the lounge a jungle theme. Don't expect to get much talking done; people come here to pounce on each other. Open F -Sa nights 9pm-1am.

THE MOURNE MOUNTAINS

Before heading for the hills, stop at the **Mourne Countryside Centre**, in Newcastle, 91 Central Promenade (☎ 4372 4059), and the **Mourne Heritage Trust**, just two doors down. A friendly and knowledgeable staff leads hikes and offers a broad selection of guides and maps of the mountains. Those planning short excursions can purchase *Mourne Mountain Walks* (£6), which describes 10 one-day hikes. Those

NEWCASTLE AND THE MOURNES ■ 441

planning to stay in the Mournes overnight should buy the *Mourne Country Outdoor Pursuits Map* (£4.25), a detailed topographical map. (Open year-round M-F 9am-5pm.) If the center is closed, ask for maps at the Newcastle tourist office and advice at Hill Trekker (see **Practical Information,** above). Seasoned hikers looking for company might want to join the **Mourne Rambling Group** (☎ 4372 4315), which sends groups into the Mournes each Sunday. Shuttle buses run between Silent Valley and Ben Crom Reservoirs (June Sa-Su 1 per day, July-Aug. 3 daily; £2.15).

The **Mourne Wall,** built between 1904 and 1923, encircles 12 of the mountains just below their peaks. Following the length of the 22 mi. wall takes a strenuous eight hours; many people break it up with a night under the stars. The Mourne's highest peak, **Slieve Donard** (850m), towers above Newcastle. The trail to it is wide and well-maintained, and paved in many places with flags and cobblestones (5hr. return). The record for running up and down is fabled to be 98 minutes. **Donard Park** provides the most direct access to the Mournes from Newcastle; it's convenient to both Slieve Donard and nearby **Slieve Commedagh** ("the mountain of watching"). The park lies on the corner of Central Promenade and Bryansford Rd. Follow the dirt path at the back of the carpark carefully (it crosses 2 bridges). It eventually joins the Glen River Path for about 1½ mi. to reach the Mourne Wall. At the wall, turn left for Slieve Donard, right for Slieve Commedagh. Those seeking a more remote trek might try **Slieve Bernagh** (739m) or **Slieve Binnian** (747m), most easily accessed from **Hare's Gap** and **Silent Valley,** respectively. The two craggy peaks, both with tremendous views, can be combined into a half-day, 12 mi. hike. A comprehensive walk will combine highlands, lowlands, mountains, and the coastal area to the south of town, or rolling farmland to the north. Most of the land in and around the Mournes is privately owned. Visitors should bear this in mind and treat the environs with respect (close those sheep gates!).

Wilderness **camping** is legal and popular. Common spots include the **Annalong Valley,** the shores of **Lough Shannagh,** and near the **Trassey River. Hare's Gap** and the shore of **Blue Lough** at the foot of Slievelamagan are also good places to pitch a tent. While camping around the Mourne Wall is allowed, camping in the forest itself is strictly prohibited because of the risk of forest fires. Remember to bring warm clothing since the mountains get cold and windy at night and Irish weather conditions are known to change suddenly. A local volunteer **Mountain Rescue** team (☎ 999) is available in case of emergencies.

◪ NEARBY FOREST PARKS

Three parks managed by the Department of Agriculture are just a hop, skip, and a jump from Newcastle. **Tollymore Forest Park** lies just 2 mi. west of town at 176 Tullybrannigan Rd. Within the park, ancient stone bridges, rushing waters, and very well-marked trails delight all ages. The Shimna River cuts the park in half from east to west. Four main trails, ranging from 1-8 mi. in length, afford glimpses of diverse wildlife including deer, foxes, badgers, and, if you're particularly quiet and good, otters. The "Rivers Trail" hike (3 mi.) encompasses most of the park and is highly recommended, as is the hike (3½ mi.) to the viewpoint. (☎ 4372 2428. Open daily 10am-10pm. £2, under 17 50p; £3.50 car.) The park is amply equipped with a campground (see p. 439), visitors center, cafe, and impressive outdoor arboretum. If you're not up for the rambling walk to Tollymore, take one of Ulsterbus's "Tollymore" shuttles from the Newcastle bus station (15min.; departs 10am, noon, and 4:30pm year-round, more frequently in July and Aug.; 75p).

Castlewellan Forest Park spreads itself out in the hills just north and east of the Mournes. Its entrance is at the top of the main street in Castlewellan. From the Newcastle bus station take Castlewellan Rd. into town. Turn left on Main St. at the roundabout and continue for 400m. (☎ 4377 8664. Open daily 10am-sunset. £3.50 per car. Call M-F 8:30am-4:30pm for info and site booking. **Camping** Easter-Sept. £10 per large tent, £6.50 small tent; Oct.-Easter £6.50; additional £1.50 for electricity.) The campground is opposite the library. The park contains easily accessible attractions: a Scottish baronial castle (now a Christian Conference Centre, not open to the public), an impressive **Sculpture Trail** (with sculptures made of natural materials), and the North's **National Arboretum.** The park's lake overflows with trout; single-day or seasonal fishing permits are available from the ranger station April to mid-October. Buses run from Newcastle to Castlewellan (10min.; M-F 26 per day, Sa 20 per day, Su 6 per day; 95p).

At the opposite end of town you'll find the **Murlough National Nature Reserve,** on Dundrum Rd. (A24) to Belfast. Home to sand dunes, heath, and woodlands, Murlough boasts marvelous swimming, as well as seal-watching during the fall moulting season. Plenty of critters can be observed throughout the year, including badgers, foxes, skylark, meadow pipits, and the endangered European insect species of marsh fritillary. To get there, take the Downpatrick or Belfast bus from Newcastle and get off at Murlough. (☎ 4375 1467. Beach and walks open in daytime. £2 per car in high season; free other times.)

WARRENPOINT

A few miles down the coast from Newcastle, on the north side of Carlingford Lough, is the harbor town of Warrenpoint. It first gained fame as a resort town in the 1800s, when having just a pretty beach was enough to satisfy tourists. Today, nearby Rostrevor is a large part of Warrenpoint's appeal. Rostrevor draws annual crowds to the area for the Fiddler's Green Festival, making Warrenpoint a hospitable source of accommodations. During the rest of the year, you can sit on the sea wall for hours and watch colorful spinnakers float across the water against the backdrop of the Mourne Mountains.

ORIENTATION AND PRACTICAL INFORMATION. The bus drop-off is in **The Square,** with **Church St.** to the left and the waterfront to the right as you leave the station; **ferries** land at the other end of the waterfront. **Ulster Bank,** 2 Charlotte St., **Northern Bank** on Queen St., and **First Trust** at The Square all have **24hr. ATMs.** The **Red Star Passenger Ferry** (☎ 4177 3070), runs a sporadic service across the *lough* to Omeath, a town in the Republic (May-Aug., weather and tides permitting; £2 return). **Rent bicycles** at **Stewart's Cycles,** 14 Havelock Pl., beside the Surgery Clinic on Marine Parade. (☎ 4177 3565. Also does repairs. £6 per day, £25 per week. Open M-Tu and Th-F 2-6pm.) **Ace Taxis** (☎ 4175 2666) will pick you up at any hour. **Walsh's Pharmacy,** is at 25 Church St. (☎ 4175 3661. Open M-Sa 9am-6pm, W 9am-6pm.) In an **emergency** dial ☎ 999, no coins required. The **post office** sits at 9 Church St. (☎ 4175 2225. Open M-Tu and Th 8:30am-5:30pm, W 8:30am-1pm, F 9am-5:30pm, Sa 9am-12:30pm.) The local **postal code** is BT34.

ACCOMMODATIONS, FOOD, AND PUBS. If you want a single and insist on luxury close to town, stay at the **Whistledown Inn,** 6 Seaview. This B&B is directly on the waterfront at the end of Church St., on the second floor of an enormous Victorian townhouse. (☎ 4175 2697. £25 per person.) **The Mournes,** 16 Seaview, offers basic rooms with hot pot and TV. (£20 per person.)

Warrenpoint has eateries a plenty, and most have a take-out option ideal for beach picnics. **Diamonds Restaurant,** The Square, is always packed with locals devouring burgers, pasta, seafood, and desserts. (☎ 4175 2053. All £2-5. Open M-Th 10am-7:30pm, F-Su noon-10pm.) The **Genoa Cafe,** next door, boasts about having served fish and chips to Warrenpoint since 1910. Today the restaurant sports a thoroughly modern decor, but the fish and chips (£2.25) are deep-fried in tradition. (☎ 4175 3688. Open daily noon-11pm.) Opened in 1854, **Bennetts,** 21 Church St., is a local favorite for lunch (☎ 4175 2314. Under £4, served daily 12:30-3pm; dinner and bar snacks 5-9:30pm.) For a quick bite, try the **Central Cafe,** 32 Church St., the closest you'll get to a diner atmosphere. (☎ 4175 2693. Sandwiches £1.50. Open daily 9:30am-6pm.)

Pubs fill in the gaps between restaurants around The Square. **Jack Ryan's** offers live music Thursday to Sunday, and pub grub. (☎ 4175 2001. Most dishes £4-5; served 12:30-2:30pm, till 8:30pm on weekends.) At **Cearnógs** ("the square"), 14 The Square, young crowds pour in on weekends for good *craic.* Live music Th-Su nights. (☎ 4177 4077. Open daily 11:30-1am.)

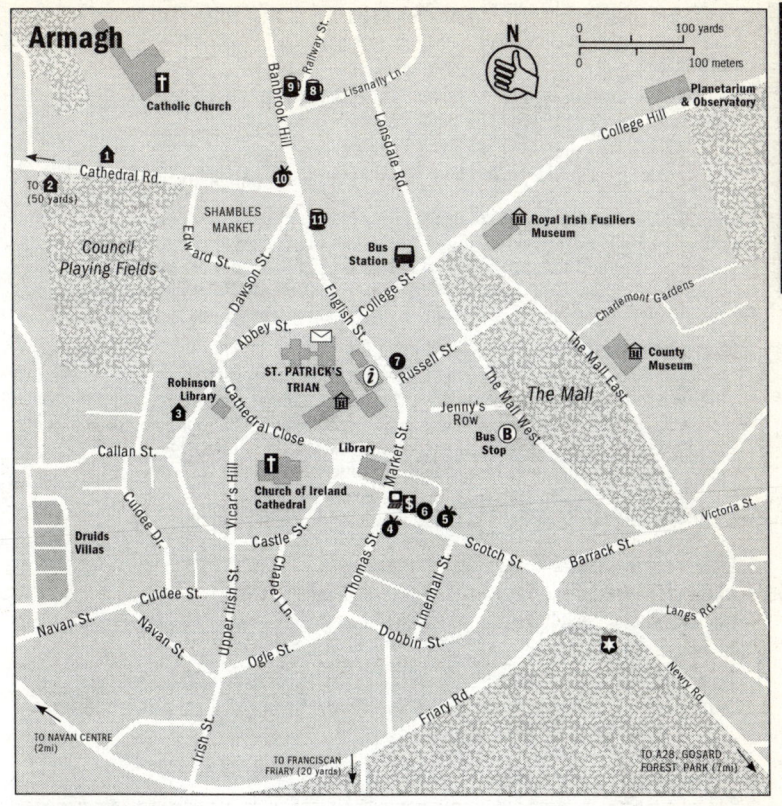

ROSTREVOR

The village of Rostrevor lies 3 mi. from Warrenpoint along A2, and hosts several lively festivals during the summer. Thousands of people gather here mid-August to witness the **Maiden of the Mournes Festival;** maidens from Ireland, Europe, and some parts of the US gather to display their personalities and talents. This event is preceded by the **Fiddler's Green Festival.** During this late-July extravaganza, fans (and performers) of traditional Irish music, storytelling, and art gather to share good *craic*. (Contact Tommy or Sam Sands, ☎ 38577.) Rostrevor is also known for **Kilbroney Park** which contains Rostrevor Forest, one of the few remaining virgin Irish Oak forests in Ireland, as well as the usual assortment of wildlife, wild walks, and wild picnic facilities. (Open daily dawn-dusk. Free.)

ARMAGH

The pagan worshippers who built huge ceremonial mounds at Navan Fort named their city Ard Macha (Macha's Height) after the legendary Queen Macha. According to tradition, St. Patrick came to Armagh (arm-AH) in the 5th century to convert the pagan hot-spot. Since then, Armagh has become Ireland's ecclesiastical capital for both the Catholic Church and the Church of Ireland, amassing cathedrals and monuments along its tree-lined streets.

GETTING THERE AND GETTING AROUND

Buses: Buses stop at the station on Lonsdale Rd. To **Belfast** (1hr.; M-F 20 per day, Sa 15 per day, Su 8 per day; £5) and **Enniskillen** (2hr., M-Sa 3 per day, £5.50).

444 ■ ARMAGH

Local Transportation: Intercity **buses** (☎ 3752 2266) stop at The Mall West. Two refurbished 40s-style **coaches** cart tourists from sight to sight in summer. Schedules available at the tourist office.

Bike Rental: Brown's Bikes, 21A Scotch St. (☎ 3752 2782). £7 per day, £30 per week. Helmets £1 per day. Open M-Sa 9am-5:30pm.

ORIENTATION AND PRACTICAL INFORMATION

English St., Thomas St., and **Scotch St.** comprise Armagh's city center. Just to the east lies **The Mall,** a former race course that was converted into a grassy park when betting was deemed inappropriate to the city's sanctity. Just west of the city center, two cathedrals sit on neighboring hills: the Catholic Cathedral lifts two neo-Gothic spires, while a medieval-looking tower represents the Church of Ireland.

Tourist Office: Old Bank Building, 40 English St. (☎ 3752 1800). From the bus stop, facing The Mall, turn left, walk past The Mall, and turn left up the hill onto College St. The tourist office is 15 yd. down the 1st street on the left. Pick up the *Armagh Visitor Magazine* (free), with a map of all the major sites. Open M-Sa 9am-5pm, Su 1-5pm.

Bank: Northern Bank, 78 Scotch St. (☎ 3752 2004). Open M 9:30am-5pm, Tu-F 10am-3:30pm. **ATM.**

Pharmacy: J.W. Gray, corner of Russell and English St. Open M-Sa 9am-6pm. Rotating Su schedule.

Emergency: ☎ 999; no coins required. **Police:** Newry Rd. (☎ 3752 3311).

Hospital: Tower Hill (☎ 3752 2341), off College Hill.

Internet Access: Armagh Computer World, 43 Scotch St. (☎ 3751 0002). Open M-Sa 9am-6pm. £3 per 30min.

Post Office: 31 Upper English St. (☎ 3751 0313). *Poste Restante* mail held across the street at 46 Upper English St. (☎ 3752 2856). Open M-F 9am-5:30pm, Sa 9am-12:30pm. **Postal code:** BT617AA.

ACCOMMODATIONS

Armagh's **hostel (HINI),** behind the old health clinic, is sparkling clean and huge, with tremendous reinforcements surrounding the building and parking lot. From the tourist office, turn left twice and follow Abbey St. for two blocks. Walk through the parking lot; the entrance to the hostel is tucked in a small alley. All rooms are with bath, and some have TV. Dinner and breakfast are available. (☎ 3751 1800. Reception 8-11am and 5-11pm. Main doors and gate closes at 9pm. Laundry £3. 6- and 4-bed dorms £10.75; doubles £11.50; £1 off for members.) The **Padua Guest House,** 63 Cathedral Rd., is just past the Catholic Cathedral. Mrs. O'Hagen and her large doll collection greet guests with a cup of tea. (☎ 3752 2039. Doubles £32.) Make a right on Desart Rd., and turn left 50 yd. down to reach **Desart Guest House,** 99 Cathedral Rd. It's a formidable mansion, but the rooms are sunny, clean, and plush. (☎ 3752 2387. Singles £20; doubles £30.)

Gosfard Forest Park, off A28, offers **camping** 7 mi. southeast of Armagh. Take the #40 bus to Market Hill. (☎ 3755 1277; ranger ☎ 3755 2169. Easter-Sept. £8.50 per 2-person tent, Oct.-Easter £5.50.)

FOOD AND PUBS

On weekdays it can be hard to find a restaurant in Armagh that stays open after 6pm. The city's few eateries are scattered across English and Scotch St. Your best bet may be to pick up groceries at **Emerson's** on Scotch St. (☎ 3752 2846. Open M-W 8:45am-5:30pm, Th-F 9am-9pm, Sa 8:45am-6pm.) The **Basement Cafe** sits under the Armagh Film House on English St. next to the library, and serves cheap meals to cool cats. (☎ 3752 4311. Sandwiches £1.85. Open M-Sa 9am-5:30pm.) **Hong Kong**

Chef, English St., serves up tasty Chinese take-out and is open later than most other options. (☎ 01 8615 11047. Curry chicken £3.70. Open Su and Tu-W 5pm-midnight, Th noon-2pm and 5pm-midnight, F-Sa noon-2pm and 5pm-1am.) The **Rainbow Restaurant**, 13 Upper English St., serves standard lunch fare buffet style. (☎ 3752 5391. 4-course lunch special £3.50; lunch served noon-2pm. Open M-Sa 8:30am-5:30pm.) **Our Ma's Cafe**, 2 Lower English St., is clever, cheap, and delicious. (☎ 3751 1289. 3-course lunch £3.75. Open M-Sa 9am-5:30pm, Su 9am-3:30pm.) When the fruits fall from Armagh's apple trees, **Johnston's Bakery**, 9 Scotch St., turns them into delicious treats. (☎ 3752 2995. Apple turnovers 30p. Open M-Sa 9am-6pm.) **The Station Bar**, 3 Lower English St. (☎ 3752 3731), looks like a dive, but is one of the most popular pubs in town, with trad two nights a week in winter and good conversation year-round. **Harry Hoots**, Railway St. (☎ 522 103), sounds and is fun. **The Northern Bar** (☎ 3752 7315), across the street, provides live entertainment and dancing three nights a week at 9:30pm.

SIGHTS

CHURCHES. Armagh's twin cathedrals preside impressively over the city. The **Church of Ireland Cathedral of St. Patrick** is a 19th-century restoration of a 13th-century structure that enlarged upon the 5th-century original attributed to Patrick himself. The cathedral is the final resting place of the great Irish King Brian Ború (see **Early Christians and Vikings**, p. 8). It also contains an Iron Age sculpture of a king with a prosthetic arm. (☎ 3752 3142. Open daily Apr.-Sept. 10:30am-5pm; Oct.-Mar. 10:30am-4pm. Tours June-Aug. M-Sa 11:30am and 2:30pm. Free.) Across town, the **Catholic Church of St. Patrick** raises its spires from Cathedral Rd. Opened in 1873, the cathedral's imposing exterior and exquisite mosaic interior are marred only by the ultramodern granite sanctuary, which appears to be a combination of pagan and Martian design. Dark water stains on lower sections of the cathedral walls are legacies of the Famine, when work on the cathedral halted and the half-completed building was left exposed to the elements. (Open daily 9am-6pm. Free.)

BO KNOWS GLYCEROPHOSPHATE Buckfast tonic wines, produced by the Benedictine monks of the Buckfast Abbey, are sold in two places: Devon and Co. Armagh. While the government warning on the orange label informs the would-be drinker that "Tonic wine does not imply health-giving or medicinal properties," "Bo," as it is popularly termed, has gained near-mythic stature with a certain section of the Armagh community. Though some might pass it off as Bacchus's gift to the wino, those who make the drink a part of their lives know better. Swearing that it's an experience as much like drunkenness as Budweiser is like Guinness, aficionados advise restrained consumption for first-time Buckfast drinkers. Evidence of its effects appears on Sunday mornings, when broken green Buckfast bottles are strewn across Armagh's streets. It's made of, among other things, .009% vanillin, .05% caffeine, .65% sodium glycerophosphate (to keep the drinker very regular), and 15% alcohol. At £5 for .75 liters, it's dirt cheap.

ARMAGH LORE. In the center of town, **St. Patrick's Trian** shares a building with the tourist office. Most of the exhibits emphasize St. Patrick's role in Armagh, although his link to the town is historically ambiguous. The **Armagh Story** is a walk-through display and audio-visual presentation in which plaster Vikings, priests, and pagan warriors relate the lengthy history of the town. A smaller, fanciful display geared for children recreates **Swift's Land of Lilliput**. (☎ 3752 1801. Open July-Aug. M-Sa 10am-5:30pm, Su 1-6pm; Sept.-June M-Sa 10am-5pm, Su 2-5pm. £3.50, students £3.)

STARS AND PLANETS. Up College Hill north of The Mall is the **Armagh Observatory**, founded in 1790 by Archbishop Robinson (see below). Would-be astronomers can observe the modern weather station and a refractory telescope dating from 1885. The **Robinson Dome** provides self-guided tours. (☎ 3752 2928.) More celestial wonders await in the **Planetarium,** College Hill, where a 3cm chunk of Mars is on display. (☎ 523 689. *45min. shows 3-5 times daily July-Aug.; 1 per day M-F, Apr.-June. Seating limited; booking ahead is strongly recommended. £3.50, students £2.50.)*

PALACE DEMESNE. On Friary Rd., south of the town center, the ruins of the 13th-century **Franciscan Friary,** the longest-standing friary in Ireland, occupy a peaceful green corner of the **Palace Demesne.** The palace and its chapel and stables were built by the 18th-century Archbishop of Armagh, Richard Robinson, in an effort to rebuild the entire city. Although the palace itself is closed to the public, the **Palace Stables Heritage Centre** puts on a slick multi-media show about "A Day in the Life" of the closed palace. *(☎ 3752 9629. Open Apr.-Sept. M-Sa 10am-7pm, Su 1-7pm; Oct.-Mar. M-Sa 10am-5pm, Su 2-5pm. £2.80, students £2.20.)*

OTHER SIGHTS AND ODDITIES. At the **Armagh County Museum,** on the east side of The Mall, undiscriminating historians have crammed a panoply of 18th-century objects—old wedding dresses, pictures, stuffed birds, jewelry, and militia uniforms—into huge wooden cabinets. *(☎ 3752 3070. Open M-Sa 10am-5pm. Free.)* The **Royal Irish Fusiliers Museum,** The Mall East, houses the treasure of over 150 years of the business of war. *(☎ 522 911. Open M-F 10am-12:30pm and 1:30-4pm. £1.50, students £1.)* Peek at a first edition of ▨*Gulliver's Travels,* covered with Swift's own scrawled comments, at the **Armagh Public Library,** built on Abbey St. in 1771. *(☎ 3752 3142. Open M-F 10am-12:30pm and 2-4pm.)* One might prefer to spend a nice day at **Gosford Forest Park,** 7 mi. southeast of Armagh, which includes a castle, an old walled garden, poultry sheds, and miles of nature trails. *(Open daily 10am-sunset. £2 per car, £1 per person.)*

FESTIVALS. Armagh holds an annual **Comhaltas Ceoltori Traditional Music Festival** around the first week of June and an arts festival in October. In mid-August, the Ulster **Road Bowls Finals** (for more on road bowls, see **Bowl Movement,** p. 229) are held throughout Armagh. In this popular local game, contestants compete to see who can throw an 8 oz. solid ball 4km in the fewest throws. Negotiating the bumps and turns in the road can be difficult, injecting an element of brain into this contest of brawn. **The Apple Blossom Festival** *(☎ 3752 9600),* in the second week of May, brings a number of events to the city and culminates in a lavish May Ball. On March 17, people come from far and near for the feast of the city's patron on **St. Patrick's Day.**

DAYTRIPS FROM ARMAGH

NAVAN FORT (EMAIN MACHA)
The Navan Centre is on Killylea Rd. (A28), 2 mi. west of Armagh; the fort is a 10-minute walk from the center. ☎ *(01861) 525 550. Open M-Sa 10am-6pm. £3.95, students £3. Fort always open. Free.*

On the outskirts of Armagh, the mysterious Navan Fort, also called Emain Macha (AHM-win maka), was the capital of the Kings of Ulster for 800 years. It may look like a grassy mound of dirt but with a little imagination and a lot of historical knowledge, you might see extensive defensive fortifications and elaborate religious paraphernalia on the site. Where the mound now stands, a huge wooden structure 40 yd. in diameter was constructed in 94 BC, filled with stones, promptly burnt to the ground in a religious rite, and covered with soil. In legend, Queen Macha founded the fort, although it is also associated with St. Patrick, who probably chose Ard Macha as a base for Christianity because of its proximity to this pagan stronghold. ▨**Navan Centre,** built deep into a nearby hill, presents a fascinating hour-long program of films and interactive exhibits on the archaeological evidence of the hills and their associated legends.

PEATLANDS PARK
☎ *(38) 851 102. Park open daily Easter-Sept. 9am-9pm; Oct.-Easter 9am-5pm. Visitors center open June-Sept. 1st daily 2-6pm. Both free; railroad £1, seniors and children 50p.*

Just off M1, 10 mi. north of Armagh, **Peatlands Park** contains nature reserves, an interpretive center with interactive displays on the natural and human history of peat bogs, and a small railroad that was originally used to carry turf out of the bogs. Turf-cutting demonstrations take place on busy days.

LOUGH NEAGH AND OXFORD ISLAND

Birdwatching, water-skiing, and various aquatic activities are just about the only amusements in the towns around Lough Neagh; its shores are best seen by car as daytrips from Belfast or Armagh. Route A3 runs northeast from Armagh to Craigavon and Lurgan.

A giant once scooped a heap of prime Ulster real estate out of the ground and hurled it into the Irish sea, creating the Isle of Man and Lough Neagh. The UK's largest lake sits smack in the center of Northern Ireland, touching five of the North's six counties. Though not yet appreciated in Ireland, the Lough Neagh eel is considered a great delicacy on the continent. On the southeast shore of the Lough, the **Lough Neagh Discovery Centre,** Oxford Island National Nature Reserve, Craigavon, contains acres of wooded parkland for exploration, with or without a guided tour. The lakeshore hosts hundreds of bird species. Audio-visual displays inside the center detail the lake's ecosystem and wildlife. Boat rides to the islands run June to August. (☎ (38) 322 205. Open Apr.-Sept. daily 10am-7pm; Oct.-Mar. W-Su 10am-5pm. Last admission 1hr. before closing. Audio-visual displays £1.50, seniors and children £1.) The **Kinnego Caravan Park,** Kinnego Marina, Lurgan, greets campers. (☎ (38) 327 573. £6 per 2-person tent.)

ANTRIM AND DERRY

A coastal road skirts the northern edge of Co. Antrim and Derry, traveling across a long distance of rapidly changing geological, commercial, and cultural phenomena. As the road meanders west from Belfast, stodgy and industrial Larne gives way to lovely little seaside towns. The nine wooded glens of Antrim, stomping grounds of the Ancient Ulaid dynasty, squat in valleys between tame mountains. Near the midpoint of the island's northern coast, fantastic Giant's Causeway spills out into the ocean. This moderately trafficked middle section of the coast road is a cyclist's paradise. Industrialization resumes past the Causeway when the road hits the carnival lights of Portrush and Portstewart. The road finally arrives at Derry, the North's second largest city, where a turbulent history and recent redevelopment projects contribute to a fascinating cityscape.

LARNE

The **ferries** that depart for Scotland from the harbor are the only worthwhile reason to pass through industrial Larne. This route is less frequented since the creation of the more convenient Hoverspeed SeaCat service to Belfast (see **By Ferry,** p. 59). **P&O Ferries** (☎ (0990) 980777) operates passages from Larne to Cairnryan, Scotland. Travelers should book ahead and arrive 45 minutes early, as there are always standby passengers waiting for your seat. The center of Larne Town is 15 minutes inland from the harbor.

GETTING THERE AND ORIENTATION. To reach Larne Town from the Larne Harbour **ferry terminal,** take the first right outside of the ferry port. As the road curves left, it becomes **Curran Rd.** and then **Main St.** The **bus station** is just south of town, on the other side of the A8 overpass to Belfast; the **train station** lies adjacent to a roundabout, down the street from the tourist office on Narrow Gauge Rd. **Trains** chug from Central Station in **Belfast** to Larne Town and Larne Harbour (Belfast office ☎ 9089 9400, Larne office ☎ 2826 0604. 50min.; M-F 20 per day, Sa 16 per day, Su 6 per day; £3.20.) **Buses** leave frequently from Station Rd. for Laganside Station in **Belfast.** (☎ 2827 2345. 1½hr., express 50min.; M-F 14 per day, Sa 15 per day, Su 2 per day.) Those departing on a ferry from Larne should ensure that their train or bus terminates in Larne Harbour rather than in Larne Town, a 15-minute walk away.

🛈 PRACTICAL INFORMATION. The **tourist office**, Narrow Gauge Rd., has loads of info, a free town map, and **email access.** If you're just off the boat, the 20-minute video overview of the sights of Northern Ireland is worth a view. The staff books accommodations in the North, the Republic, and Scotland. (☎/fax 2826 0088. Open July-Aug. M-F 9am-6pm, Sa 9am-5pm; Sept.-Easter M-F 9am-5pm; Easter-June M-Sa 9am-5pm. 24hr. computerized info kiosk on exterior.) **Northern Bank,** 19 Main St., has a 24-hour ATM. (☎ 2827 6311. Open M 9:30am-5pm, Tu-F 10am-3:30pm, Sa 9:30am-12:30pm.) **Ulsterbank,** 9 Upper Cross St., also has a 24-hour ATM. (☎ 2827 5757. Open M-F 9:30am-4:30pm.) Larne's **post office,** 98 Main St., feels an affinity for **postal code** BT40. (☎ 2826 0489. Open M-F 9am-5:30pm, Sa 9am-12:30pm.)

🏠🍴🍺 ACCOMMODATIONS, FOOD, AND PUBS. Larne's not really the sort of town that people want to languish in. But if you're too weary to move on, there's no shortage of beds. B&Bs most convenient to both the harbor and the bus and train stations and adjacent streets are along Curran Rd. The clean rooms in Mrs. McKane's **Killyneedan,** 52 Bay Rd., are stocked with TVs, hotpots, and decorative mugs. (☎ 2827 4943. £15; with bath £16.) Bay Rd. intersects Curran Rd. just before the ferry terminal. **The Curran Caravan Park,** 131 Curran Rd., midway between the harbor and town, has congested caravan and tent grounds. Be sure to pause reflectively before Larne's Ulster-American Memorial Statue just outside the park gates. (☎ 2827 5505. £4.50 per 2-person tent, £1.50 per extra person.)

The giant **Co-op Superstore,** Station Rd., next to the bus station, has an enormous selection. (☎ 2826 0737. Open M-W 9am-9:15pm, Th-F 9am-10:15pm, Sa 9am-8pm, Su 1-6pm.) The main street of town is littered with cheap sandwich shops, all basically equivalent in value and quality. **Caffe Spice,** 7 Dunluce St., is especially popular with the younger crowd. (☎ 2826 9633. Open M-W 10am-5pm, Th-Sa 10am-10pm.) **Chekker's Wine Bar,** 33 Lower Cross St., serves a broad selection of bistro food in a take-your-time atmosphere. (☎ 2827 5305. Most meals £5; food served daily noon-9pm.) The cozy, lamp-lit **Bailie,** 111-113 Main St., serves congratulatory pints to brave sea travelers. (☎ 2827 3947. Entrees £4-5; food served 12:30-8pm.)

GLENS OF ANTRIM

North of Larne, nine lush green valleys, or "glens," slither from the hills and high moors of Co. Antrim down to the seashore. The villages along the coast provide beds and basic sustenance for glen-wanderers, as well as a glimpse into the cultural traditions of rural Northern Ireland. A2 connects the small towns at the foot of each glen. The glens and the mountains and waterfalls within them can best be seen by making daytrips inland from one of the coastal villages. The area's only hostel is in Cushendall (see p. 450).

Two **Ulsterbus** routes serve the area year-round (Belfast ☎ 9032 0011, Larne ☎ 2827 2345). Bus #162 from **Belfast** stops in **Larne, Ballygally, Glenarm,** and **Carnlough** (M-F 7 per day, Sa 6 per day, Su 3 per day) and sometimes continues to **Waterfoot, Cushendall,** and **Cushendun** (M-F 5 per day, Sa 3 per day). Bus #150 runs between **Ballymena** and **Glenariff** (M-Sa 4 per day) then **Waterfoot, Cushendall,** and **Cushendun** (M-F 5 per day, Sa 3 per day). #150 also connects to **Belfast** via **Cushendun, Cushendall, Waterfoot,** and **Glenariff** (M-Sa 3 per day). The Antrim Coaster (#252) just began running year-round, following the coast road from **Belfast** to **Coleraine,** stopping at every town along the way (daily 2 per day). Cycling is fabulous. The coast road from Ballygally to Cushendun is both scenic and flat; once the road leaves Cushendun, however, it becomes hilly enough to make even motorists groan. The Cushendall hostel **rents bikes.** Hitching is difficult, and the winding, narrow road between the cliffs and the sea wall make drivers feel less guilty about not stopping. Crossroads are the best places to try one's luck, but *Let's Go* sees hitchhiking as the wrong path to follow in life.

GLENARM

Six flat, winding, coastal miles lead through gradually less polluted and populated skylines to arrive at pristine Glenarm. Glenarm ("glen of the army") was once the chief dwelling place of the MacDonnell clan. The village is comprised of several centuries-old houses, a couple of pubs, and a wealth of short walks. The **madman's window** appears on the right just before you enter town. The natural formation earned its name when an artist jumped to his death from it. A huge arch at the top of Altmore St. is the entrance to **Glenarm Forest,** where trails trace the river's path for miles. (Open daily 9am to dusk.) **Glenarm Castle,** nestled just off the main street behind the trees north of the river, is the current residence of the 13th Earl of Antrim. Its 17th-century gate is visible from Castle St. and open to the public annually on July 14 and 15; the castle's gardens are open year-round and entered by way of the left fork off the Ballymena road past town towards Cushendall. The town also boasts both a heritage trail and a walk along a former water-duct; brochures on both are available at the tourist office or from B&B proprietors. The **Ulster Way** trail passes through town, if you're up for the hike. The **Glenarm Festival** brings this sleepy town to life during the first week of July with events ranging from an eating competition to the multi-categoried Best Garden/Basket/Windowbox/Tub Contest.

The **tourist office,** in the town council building beside the bridge, provides friendly advice on the attractions of the area. (☎ 2884 1087. Open M 1-5pm, Tu and Th-F 9:30am-5pm, Sa 1-4pm, Su 1-6pm.) Glenarm's **post office** is halfway down Toberwine St. (☎ 2884 1218. Open M-Tu and Th-F 9am-1pm and 2-5:30pm, W and Sa 9am-12:30pm.) The **postal code** is BT44.

The period furniture and exposed wooden beams at **Nine Glens B&B,** 18 Toberwine St., have aged as well as Glenarm itself. The bedrooms, however, are completely modern. Fresh fruit and tea available all day. (☎ 2884 1590. £15 with bath.) **Margaret's B&B,** 10 Altmore St., provides comfortable rooms with 50s decor. (☎ 2884 1307. £14 per person.) The **Spar Market,** 4 Toberwine St., fulfills picnic needs. (☎ 2884 1219. Open M-Tu and Th-Sa 9am-6pm, W 9am-5pm.) **Poacher's Pocket,** 1 New Rd., serves meaty plates. (☎ 2884 1221. Entrees £6-7, burgers £3.50; food served daily noon-8pm.) **The Coast Road Inn,** 3-5 Toberwine St., draws a more mature clientele. (☎ 2884 1207. Lunch served Th-M.) The **Bridge End Tavern,** 1-3 Toberwine St. (☎ 2884 1252), is nothing fancy, just drinks and good company.

WATERFOOT AND GLENARIFF

Nine miles farther up the coast, the village of Waterfoot guards Antrim's broadest glen, Glenariff, often deemed the most beautiful of the nine. Thackeray dubbed Glenariff "Switzerland in miniature," presumably because of its steep and rugged landscape; numbered bank accounts and trilingual skiers are rare. The glen is contained within the very large **Glenariff Forest Park,** 4 mi. south of the village along Glenariff Rd. (A43 toward Ballymena). The **bus** between **Cushendun** and **Ballymena** (#150) stops at the official park entrance (M-F 5 per day, Sa 3 per day). If you're walking from Waterfoot, however, you can enter the park 1½ mi. downhill of the official entrance by taking the road that branches left toward the Manor Lodge Restaurant. Cars can park in either the official car park or the Manor Lodge's parking lot, but you'll have to pay pedestrian admission charges if you enter Glenariff from Manor Lodge. (☎ 2175 8769 or 2175 8232. Open daily 10am-8pm. £3 per car or £1.50 per adult pedestrian, 50p per child pedestrian.)

Once inside the park, you are confronted with a wealth of trails ranging from a ½ mi. to 5 mi. round-trip; all trails pass the Glenariff and Inver Rivers and the three waterfalls that supply them. The most stunning walk is the **Waterfall Trail,** marked by blue triangles: it follows the cascading, fern-lined Glenariff River from the park entrance to the Manor Lodge (1 mi. from entrance to lodge, 3 mi. round-trip). Other trails lead to more subtle and less frequented beauty. All of the walks officially begin and end at the car park, where you will also find the **Glenariff Tea House.** This bay-windowed restaurant offers fresh snacks (sandwiches £1.75), exotically seasoned meals (£5-6), and free **maps** of the park's trails. (☎ 2565 8769. Open daily Easter-Sept. 11am-6pm.) The entrance to the **Moyle Way,** a 17 mi. hike from Glenariff to Ballycastle, is directly across from the official park entrance. Ask a ranger for details.

Glenariff Forest Park Camping, 98 Glenariff Rd., encourages travelers to pitch a tent. (☎ 2175 8232. Tents £10, off-season £7.) In Waterfoot, closer to the comfort of civilization, **Lurig View B&B,** 4 Lurig View, Glen Rd., off Garron Rd. about a half-mile past town on the waterfront, provides big, comfy beds and tasty, enormous breakfasts. (☎ 2177 1618. £16, off-season £15.)

Waterfoot is a one-street town, with two charismatic pubs. **The Mariners' Bar,** 7 Main St. (☎ 2177 1330), has live music of various sorts on Friday and Saturday nights. Across the street, **The Saffron Bar,** 4-6 Main St. (☎ 2177 2906), named after the Co. Antrim colors, has indoor and outdoor *craic* with a bar and a beer garden. **The Cellar Bar,** downstairs, has live music ranging from country to trad on weekends. **Angela's Restaurant and Bakery,** 32 Main St., run out of a family home, serves home-cooked meals with cheeky names like Knickerbocker Glory. (Most meals £4-5.) The back patio has grand views of Lurigethan Hill, to the left, and Garron Point, to the right. (☎ 2177 1700. Open M-Tu 10am-5pm, W-Su until midnight, takeaway 6pm-midnight.) Stock up at **Kearney's Costcutter,** 21 Main St., before your hike through Glenariff. (☎ 2177 1213. Open M-Sa 8am-10:30pm, Su 8am-9pm.)

The road from Waterfoot to Cushendall may scarcely be a mile, but it's jampacked. The **coastal caves** that line the Coast Rd. have served as everything from a school to a blacksmith's shop. Their most famous inhabitant was "Nanny of the Caves," a 19th-century *poitín* brewer who lived in her two-compartment cavehome for 50 years. The lucrative business kept Nun Marry, as she was legally known, alive to the ripe old age of 100. Just beyond the caves is the unmistakable **Red Arch,** carved out of sandstone by wind and water. On top of the arch lie the ruined walls of Red Bay Castle, built by Scottish exiles in the 13th century and currently being renovated. The arch's underside has been reinforced with concrete.

CUSHENDALL

Cushendall is nicknamed the capital of the Glens, most likely because its village center consists of *four* streets instead of just one. The additional storefronts house a surplus of goods, services, and pubs. Moors and hills border the town. Cushendall is the closest human settlement to three of the nine glens: Glenballyeamon, Glenaan, and Glencorp.

GETTING THERE AND GETTING AROUND

Buses: Ulsterbus (☎ 9033 3000) #150 runs to **Belfast** via **Ballymena, Waterfoot,** and **Glenariff** (M-F 5 per day, Sa 3 per day). Ulsterbus #162 goes to **Larne** via **Waterfoot, Glenarm,** and **Ballygally** (M-F 5 per day, Sa-Su 1 per day). The **Antrim Coaster** (#252) runs through Cushendall toward **Portrush, Larne,** and **Belfast** (2 per day).

Bike Rental: Ardclinis Activity Centre, 11 High St. (☎ 2177 1340). Mountain bikes £10 per day; deposit £50. Wet-suits £5 per day. They also provide advice on hill-walking, canoeing, and gorge-walking.

ORIENTATION AND PRACTICAL INFORMATION

The busiest section of Cushendall is its crossroads. From the center of town, **Mill St.** turns into **Chapel Rd.** and heads toward Ballycastle; **Shore Rd.** extends in the other direction toward Glenarm and Larne. **Hill St.** leads uphill from **Bridge Rd.,** a section of the **Coast Rd.** that continues towards the sea at Waterfoot.

Tourist Office: 25 Mill St. (☎ 2177 1180), near the bus stop at the Cushendun end of town, has a wealth of info. Open July-Sept. M-F 10am-1pm and 2-5:30pm, Sa 10am-1pm; Oct. to mid.-Dec. and Feb.-June Tu-Sa 10am-1pm.

Banks: Northern Bank, 5 Shore St. (☎ 2177 1243). Open M 9:30am-12:30pm and 1:30-5pm, Tu-F 10am-12:30pm and 1:30-3:30pm. **24hr. ATM.**

WORLDWIDE CALLING MADE EASY

The MCI WorldCom Card, designed specifically to keep you in touch with the people that matter the most to you.

MCI WORLDCOM — WORLDPHONE
1·800·888·8000
J. L. SMITH

www.wcom.com/worldphone

Please tear off this card and keep it in your wallet as a reference guide for convenient U.S. and worldwide calling with the MCI WorldCom Card.

HOW TO MAKE CALLS USING YOUR MCI WORLDCOM CARD

> **When calling from the U.S., Puerto Rico, the U.S. Virgin Islands or Canada** to virtually anywhere in the world:
1. Dial 1-800-888-8000
2. Enter your card number + PIN, listen for the dial tone
3. Dial the number you are calling :
   Domestic Calls: Area Code + Phone number
   International Calls:
   011+ Country Code + City Code + Phone Number

> **When calling from outside the U.S.,** use WorldPhone from over 125 countries and places worldwide:
1. Dial the WorldPhone toll-free access number of the country you are calling from.
2. Follow the voice instructions or hold for a WorldPhone operator to complete the call.

> **For calls from your hotel:**
1. Obtain an outside line.
2. Follow the instructions above on how to place a call.
   Note: If your hotel blocks the use of your MCI WorldCom Card, you may have to use an alternative location to place your call.

RECEIVING INTERNATIONAL COLLECT CALLS*

Have family and friends call you collect at home using WorldPhone Service and pay the same low rate as if you called them.
1. Provide them with the WorldPhone access number for the country they are calling from (In the U.S., 1-800-888-8000; for international access numbers see reverse side).
2. Have them dial that access number, wait for an operator, and ask to call you collect at your home number.

* For U.S. based customers only.

START USING YOUR MCI WORLDCOM CARD TODAY. MCI WORLDCOM STEPSAVERS℠

Get the same low rate per country as on calls from home, when you:
1. **Receive international collect calls to your home** using WorldPhone access numbers
2. **Make international calls with your MCI WorldCom Card** from the U.S.*
3. **Call back to anywhere in the U.S. from Abroad** using your MCI WorldCom Card and WorldPhone access numbers.

* An additional charge applies to calls from U.S. pay phones.

WorldPhone Overseas Laptop Connection Tips —
Visit our website, www.wcom.com/worldphone, to learn how to access the Internet and email via your laptop when traveling abroad using the MCI WorldCom Card and WorldPhone access numbers.

Travelers Assist® — When you are overseas, get emergency interpretation assistance and local medical, legal, and entertainment referrals. Simply dial the country's toll-free access number.

Planning a Trip? — Call the WorldPhone customer service hotline at 1-800-736-1828 for new and updated country access availability or visit our website:

www.wcom.com/worldphone

MCI WorldCom Worldphone Access Numbers

Easy Worldwide Calling

MCI WORLDCOM™

The MCI WorldCom Card.
The easy way to call when traveling worldwide.

1·800·888·8000
J. L. SMITH

The MCI WorldCom Card gives you...
- Access to the US and other countries worldwide.
- Customer Service 24 hours a day
- Operators who speak your language
- Great MCI WorldCom rates and no sign-up fees

For more information or to apply for a Card call:
1-800-955-0925

Outside the U.S., call MCI WorldCom collect (reverse charge) at:
1-712-943-6839

© 2000, MCI WORLDCOM, Inc. MCI WorldCom, its logo, as well as the names of MCI WorldCom's other products and services referred to herein are proprietary marks of MCI WorldCom, Inc. All rights reserved.

COUNTRY	WORLDPHONE TOLL-FREE ACCESS #
Argentina (CC)	
Using Telefonica	0800-222-6249
Using Telecom	0800-555-1002
Australia (CC) ♦	
Using OPTUS	1-800-551-111
Using TELSTRA	1-800-881-100
Austria (CC) ♦	0800-200-235
Bahamas (CC) +	1-800-888-8000
Belgium (CC) ♦	0800-10012
Bermuda (CC) +	1-800-888-8000
Bolivia (CC) ♦	0-800-2222
Brazil (CC)	000-8012
British Virgin Islands +	1-800-888-8000
Canada (CC)	1-800-888-8000
Cayman Islands +	1-800-888-8000
Chile (CC)	
Using CTC	800-207-300
Using ENTEL	800-360-180
China ♦	108-12
Mandarin Speaking Operator	108-17
Colombia (CC) ♦	980-9-16-0001
Collect Access in Spanish	980-9-16-1111
Costa Rica +	0800-012-2222
Czech Republic (CC) ♦	00-42-000112
Denmark (CC) ♦	8001-0022
Dominica+	1-800-888-8000
Dominican Republic (CC) +	
Collect Access	1-800-888-8000
Collect Access in Spanish	1121

COUNTRY	ACCESS #
Ecuador (CC) +	999-170
El Salvador (CC)	800-1767
Finland (CC) ♦	08001-102-80
France (CC) ♦	0-800-99-0019
French Guiana (CC)	0-800-99-0019
Germany (CC)	0800-888-8000
Greece (CC) ♦	00-800-1211
Guam (CC)	1-800-888-8000
Guatemala (CC) ♦	99-99-189
Haiti +	
Collect Access	193
Collect access in Creole	190
Honduras +	8000-122
Hong Kong (CC)	800-96-1121
Hungary (CC) ♦	06⁺-800-01411
India (CC) ♦	000-127
Collect access	000-126
Ireland (CC)	1-800-55-1001
Israel (CC)	1-800-920-2727
Italy (CC) ♦	172-1022
Jamaica +	
Collect Access	1-800-888-8000
From pay phones	#2
Japan (CC) ♦	
Using KDD	00539-121 ▶
Using IDC	0066-55-121
Using JT	0044-11-121

COUNTRY	ACCESS #
Korea (CC)	
To call using KT	00729-14
Using DACOM	00309-12
Phone Booths +	
Press red button ,03,then*	
Military Bases	550-2255
Luxembourg (CC)	8002-0112
Malaysia (CC) ♦	1-800-80-0012
Mexico (CC)	01-800-021-8000
Monaco (CC) ♦	800-90-019
Netherlands (CC) ♦	0800-022-91-22
New Zealand (CC)	000-912
Nicaragua (CC)	166
Norway (CC) ♦	800-19912
Panama	00800-001-0108
Philippines (CC) ♦	
Using PLDT	105-14
Filipino speaking operator	105-15
Using Bayantel	1237-14
Using Bayantel (Filipino)	1237-77
Using ETPI (English)	1066-14
Poland (CC) ♦	800-111-21-22
Portugal (CC) +	800-800-123
Romania (CC) ♦	01-800-1800
Russia (CC) ♦ +	
Russian speaking operator	
	747-3320
Using Rostelcom	747-3322
Using Sovintel	960-2222
Saudi Arabia (CC)	1-800-11

COUNTRY	WORLDPHONE TOLL-FREE ACCESS #
Singapore (CC)	8000-112-112
Slovak Republic (CC)	08000-00112
South Africa (CC)	0800-99-0011
Spain (CC)	900-99-0014
St. Lucia +	1-800-888-8000
Sweden (CC) ♦	020-795-922
Switzerland (CC) ♦	0800-89-0222
Taiwan (CC) ♦	0080-13-4567
Thailand (CC)	001-999-1-2001
Turkey (CC) ♦	00-8001-1177
United Kingdom (CC)	
Using BT	0800-89-0222
Using C&W	0500-89-0222
Venezuela (CC) ♦ +	800-1114-0
Vietnam + ●	1201-1022

KEY
Note: Automation available from most locations. Countries where automation is not yet available are shown in *Italic*
(CC) Country-to-country calling available.
+ Limited availability.
★ Not available from public pay phones.
♦ Public phones may require deposit of coin or phone card for dial tone.
● Local service fee in U.S. currency required to complete call.
▶ Regulation does not permit Intra-Japan Calls.
* Wait for second dial tone.
■ Local surcharge may apply.
Hint: For Puerto Rico and Caribbean Islands not listed above, you can use 1-800-888-8000 as the WorldPhone access number.

©2000 MCI WORLDCOM, Inc. All Rights Reserved. The names, logos, and taglines identifying MCI WorldCom's products and services are proprietary marks of MCI WORLDCOM, Inc. or its subsidiaries.

CUSHENDALL ■ 451

Camping Equipment: O'Neill's Country Sports, 25 Mill St. (☎ 2177 2009). Fishing tackle, tents, and maps. Open Easter-Oct. M and W-Sa 9:30am-6pm, Tu 9:30am-1pm, Su 12:30-4:30pm; Oct.-Mar. M-Sa 9:30am-6pm.

Pharmacy: Numark Pharmacist, 8 Mill St. (☎ 2177 1523). Open M-Sa 9am-6pm.

Post Office: Mill St. (☎ 2177 1201). Open M and W-F 9am-1pm and 2-5:30pm, Tu and Sa 9am-12:30pm. **Postal code:** BT44.

ACCOMMODATIONS

B&Bs occupy every other house on Kilnadore Rd. From Coast Rd., turn right at the RUC station.

Cushendall Youth Hostel (HINI), 42 Layde Rd. (☎ 2177 1344). May be closing in the near future; call ahead to confirm its existence. ½ mi. from town. Layde Rd. is the left-hand (uphill) fork off Shore Rd. A recent architectural tune-up generated a gargantuan kitchen and dining area. Continental breakfast £2. Laundry £2. **Bike rental** £6 per day, £4 per half-day. Reception 7:30-10:30am and 5-11pm. 11:30pm curfew. 10- to 14-bed dorms £8.50, under 18 £7.50, non-HI members £1 more.

Glendale, Mrs. Mary O'Neill's, 46 Coast Rd. (☎ 2177 1495). Coming from Bridge St., turn left at the Spar. It's hard to imagine a warmer welcome. Rooms are huge and as soothing to the weary traveler as is the proprietress's colorful company. Tea, coffee, biscuits, and bath in each room. £16 per person.

Cushendall Caravan Park, 62 Coast Rd. (☎ 2177 1699), adjacent to Red Bay Boat yard. Free showers but no kitchen. Wash £1, dry £1.50 per 15min. 2-person tent £5; family tent £8.50.

Glenville Caravan Park, 22 Layde Rd. (☎ 2177 1520), 1 mi. out of town. Showers, toilets, and a splendid view of the ocean. £4 per tent.

FOOD AND PUBS

Spar Market, 2 Coast Rd., just past Bridge Rd., has a plentiful fruit and veggie selection. (☎ 2177 1763. Open daily 7:30am-10pm.)

Harry's, 10-12 Mill St. (☎ 2177 2022). Bar snacks break the boundaries of their nomenclature with everything from orange to cointreau sauces on their meats; vegetarian entrees on request. Bar snacks around £5, restaurant meals £2-3 more; food served daily noon-9:30pm.

Gillan's Home Bakery and Coffee Shop, 6 Mill St. (☎ 2177 1404). Vinyl booths lend a diner atmosphere to this excellent bakery. Most meals around £2. Open M and W-Sa 9am-6pm, Tu 9am-3pm.

The Restaurant Formerly Known as The Half Door, 6 Bridge St. (☎ 2177 1300). New management has turned this eatery into a take-away fish and chip shop (£3.10). Also serves pizzas with inexplicable North American names. (Ham + pineapple = "The New Yorker.") Medium £4; toppings 50-70p. Open daily from 5pm until the pubs close.

Joe McCollam's (Johnny Joe's), 23 Mill St. (☎ 2177 1876). One of the best pubs on the island. Features impromptu ballads, fiddling, and slurred limericks. Exciting most nights of the week, but musicians are guaranteed to gather F-Su nights.

Lurig Inn, 5 Bridge St. (☎ 2177 1527), in an inconspicuous off-white building across the street from the Half Door. Rough and ready. Karaoke every Su.

SIGHTS

The sandstone **Curfew Tower** in the center of town on the corner of Mill and High St. was built in 1817 by the eccentric, slightly paranoid Francis Turley. While in China, this Cushendall landlord made a fortune which, upon return, he eagerly wanted to protect. He built the Curfew Tower with features that include openings for pouring boiling oil onto non-existent attackers, and a bell rung every night at "quiet time" for the town (hence the tower's name). Today it is privately owned and closed to the public. The extensive remnants of **Layde Church,** a medieval friary, lie a quarter-mile past the hostel along Layde Rd. The church was established in 1306, at which time it was valued at 20 shillings for tax purposes. Today its ruins are noteworthy for their surrounding graveyard and spectacular seaviews. (Always open. Free.) Pretty cliffside walks begin at its carpark. The graveyard includes **Cross Na Nagan,** a pagan holestone used for marriage ceremonies and Christianized into a Celtic cross by four strokes carved into the hole. **Tieveragh Hill,** a half-mile up High St., is known locally as Fairy Hill, with a gate that leads to the Otherworld inhabited by ancient "little people." Locals still refuse to cut the hedgerows in which the little people supposedly dwell. **Lurigethan Hill** (1153 ft.) would soar above town if its summit weren't flattened on the way up. A climb to the top rewards with up-close access to a virtually intact Iron Age promontory fort. Locals race up the hill for a "Lurigethan Run" during the annual **Cushendall Festival,** a 10-day affair starting the second Friday of August.

Ossian's Grave rests a few miles away on the lower slopes of **Tievebulliagh Mountain.** Actually a neolithic burial cairn dating from around 4000 BC, it is linked by tradition with the Ulster warrior-bard Ossian who was supposedly buried here in about AD 300. Ossian, while relaying his family's adventures to St. Patrick, allegedly tried to convince the saint that Christianity was far too restrictive for the boisterous Gaels. Young Yeats's first long poem is based on this episode. A2 leads north from Cushendall toward Ballymoney to the lower slopes of Tievebulliagh, where a sign points the way to the grave. The steep walk up the southern slope of **Glenaan** rewards with views of the lush valley.

The Glens of Antrim **Rambling Club** has a series of short and long walks planned throughout the year. Contact the chairman (Liam Murphy, ☎ 2565 6079) or the Cushendall tourist office for details. In the third week of July, the annual **Guinness Relay** pits neighbor against neighbor in a race across the Dunn Bridge (all of 100 ft.) with a tray of Guinness.

NEAR CUSHENDALL

CUSHENDUN

In 1954, the National Trust bought the miniscule, picturesque seaside village of Cushendun, 5 mi. north of Cushendall on A2. Since then, Big Brother has protected the town's "olde," squeaky-clean image. This white-washed and black-shuttered set of buildings lies by a vast beach perforated by wonderful, murky **caves** carved within red sea cliffs. The largest cave, located just past the Bay Hotel, serves as the only entrance to **Cave House,** which was built in 1820 and is currently occupied by the Mercy religious order and closed to the public. From behind the hotel, an excruciatingly steep path leads to the cliff top. Other, less painful walks meander around historical monuments in the town and nearby **Glendun** (free map of walks available at the Cushendun Tea Room), a preserved village that is a fine example of Cornish architecture. The relatively unimpressive "Maud Cottages" that line the main street were built by Lord Cushendun for his wife in 1925. Tourist information postings in town warn you against mistaking them for almshouses.

Buses pause at Cushendun's one grocery shop on the coast road on their way to **Waterfoot** via **Cushendall** (June-Sept. M-F 9 per day, Sa 5 per day, Su 3 per day; Oct.-May M-F 7 per day, Sa 3 per day, Su 1 per day) and to **Portrush** (June-Sept. M-F 2 per day, Sa 2 per day, Su 2 per day; Oct.-May M-F 3 per day, Sa 2 per day).

The town's most popular attraction is also its only real pub. **Mary McBride's,** 2 Main St. (☎ 2176 1511), used to be the *Guinness Book of World Records*'s "**smallest bar in Europe.**" Today the original bar is still there, but it has been vigorously expanded to create a lounge. Cushendun's characters leave the smallest bar only when trad musicians arrive and start a session in the lounge, usually on Thursday nights in the summer. McBride's also offers pub grub. (Steak and Guinness pie £5; food served daily noon-9pm.) **Cushendun Tea Room,** across the street, serves less exciting and less expensive food. It also passes out some tourist brochures on the town's sights, but you're best off consulting the Cushendall Tourist Office for such information before you hit Cushendun itself. (☎ 2176 1506. Burgers and sandwiches £1.70-2.50, full entrees around £4.50. Open July-Aug. daily 11am-6pm; Sept.-June weekends only, noon-6:30pm.) One mile toward Cushendall, **Sleepy Hollow B&B,** 107 Knocknacarry Rd., is to your right off the coast road and has flowery, well-kept rooms and a sweet proprietress. (☎ 2176 1513. Singles £20; doubles £36; all with bath.) **Camping** at **Cushendun Caravan Site,** 14 Glendun Rd. 50 yd. from the end of the beach, is cheap, with a TV/game room and showers but no kitchen. (☎ 2176 1254. Laundry £2. Open Mar.-Sept. £5.50 per small tent.)

CAUSEWAY COAST

Past Cushendun, the northern coast shifts from lyrical to dramatic mode. Six-hundred-foot sea-battered cliffs tower over white wave-lapped beaches and then give way to spectacular Giant's Causeway, for which the region is named. Lying among colossally beautiful scenery, the Causeway itself is a spillage of 40,000 black and red hexagonal stone columns formed by volcanic eruptions 65 million years ago. Thousands of visitors swarm the site today, but few venture beyond the Visitors Center to miles of stunning coastline.

A2, which is suitable for cycling, is the major thoroughfare between the main towns along the Causeway. **Ulsterbus** #172 runs between **Ballycastle** and **Portrush** along the coast (1hr.; M-F 7 per day, Sa 5 per day, Su 4 per day; £3.50) and makes frequent connections to **Portstewart.** In good summer weather, the open-topped orange **Bushmills Bus** outlines the coast between **Coleraine,** 5 mi. south of Portrush, and **Giant's Causeway.** (Coleraine bus station, ☎ 7043 3334. July-Aug. 5 per day). The #252 Antrim Coaster bus runs up the coast from **Belfast** to **Portstewart** via just about every town in *Let's Go.* (Belfast Laganside Bus Station, ☎ 9033 3000. 2 per day). Ulsterbus also runs package **tours** in the area that leave from **Belfast, Portrush,** and **Portstewart** (£3-9). Those hitching along A2 or the marginally quicker inland roads find that the lack of cars and high ratio of tourists slows them down. *Let's Go* does not recommend hitchhiking.

CUSHENDUN TO BALLYCASTLE

There are two popular ways to travel this stretch of land, and both have their merit. The quick route follows the relatively straight A2. The other is twisty and more scenic, beginning just outside of Cushendall. It passes the relatively unexplored **Murlough Bay,** protected by the National Trust, where a stunning landscape hides the remains of the medieval church of **Drumnakill,** once a pagan holy site. Farther west is **Torr Head,** a long peninsula that is the closest Ireland physically gets to Scotland. The road then bumps and grinds on to **Fair Head,** 7 mi. north of Cushendun and 3 mi. south of Ballycastle. This headland of heather-covered rocks attracts international hikers and winds past lakes, including **Lough na Cranagh.** In the middle of this lake sits a *crannog,* a man-made island built by Bronze Age Celts as a well-fortified yet recreationally equipped dwelling-place for elite chiefs.

Bikes should be left at the hostel: the hills are so horrific that cyclists will spend more time walking than wheeling, and it's only a 1½-hour hike from Ballycastle. Although drivers should head straight for this splendid stretch of road, they seldom do. The lack of autos translates into poor hitching conditions, though *Let's Go* believes that's always the case. Taking A2 straight from Cushendun to Ballycastle also has its advantages. It is more manageable for cyclists, with one long climb, but an even longer descent from a boggy plain. A2, the official bus route, also leads past its own set of attractions.

A few miles northeast of Cushendun, a high hollow contains a vanishing lake, called **Loughareema,** that in the summer can appear and disappear into the bog in less than a day. When the lake is full, it has fish in it, but where do they go when it empties? Answer: into the caverns beneath the porous limestone on which the

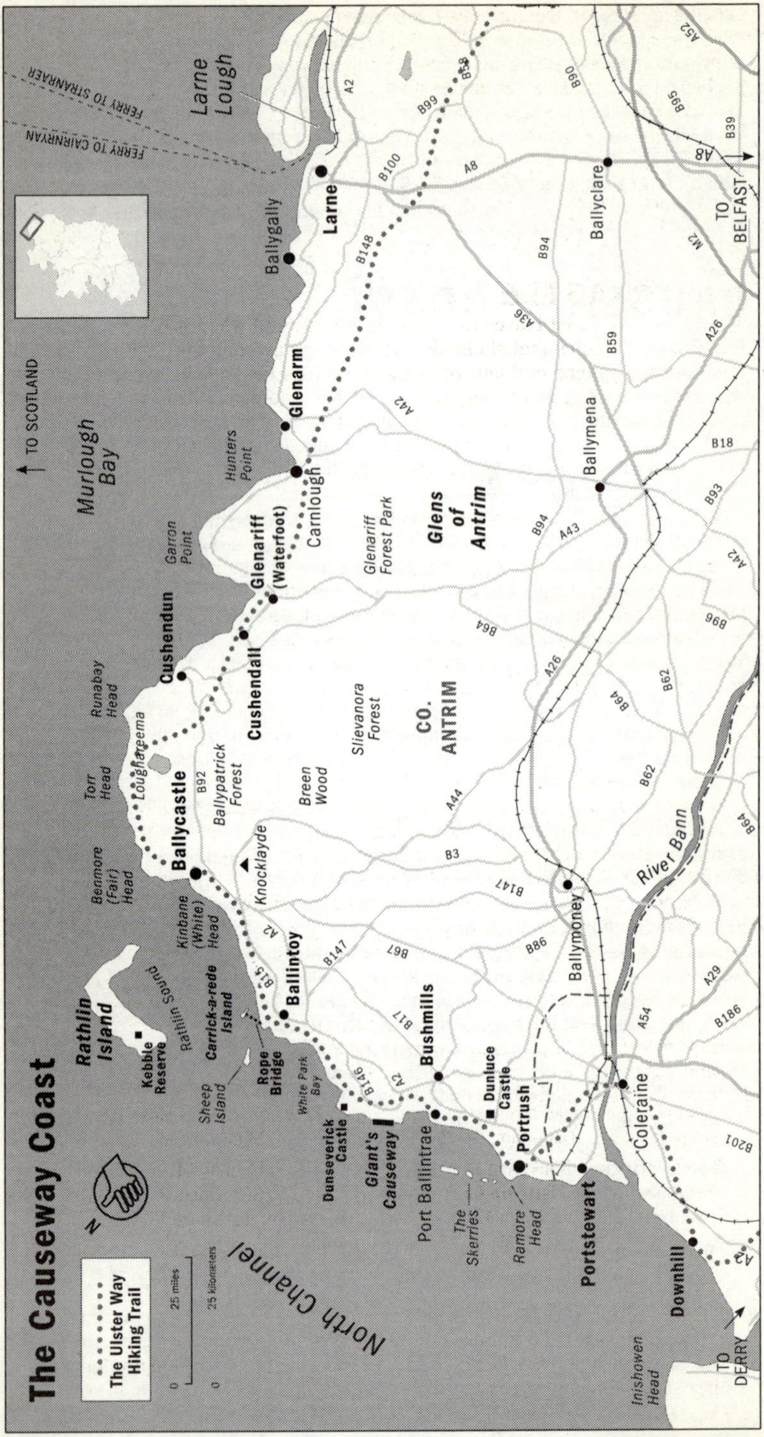
The Causeway Coast
N
The Ulster Way Hiking Trail
0
25 miles
0
25 kilometers
North Channel
Murlough Bay
TO SCOTLAND
FERRY TO STRANRAER
FERRY TO CAIRNRYAN
Larne Lough
Rathlin Island
Kebble Reserve
Rathlin Sound
Carrick-a-rede Island
Rope Bridge
Sheep Island
White Park Bay
Dunseverick Castle
Giant's Causeway
Port Ballintrae
The Skerries
Ramore Head
Portstewart
Portrush
Dunluce Castle
Bushmills
Ballintoy
Kinbane (White) Head
Benmore (Fair) Head
Ballycastle
Torr Head
Loughareema
Runabay Head
Cushendun
Cushendall
Glenariff (Waterfoot)
Garron Point
Carnlough
Hunters Point
Glenarm
Ballygally
Larne
Ballypatrick Forest
Knocklayde
Breen Wood
Slievanora Forest
CO. ANTRIM
Glenariff Forest Park
Glens of Antrim
Ballymena
Ballyclare
TO BELFAST
Ballymoney
River Bann
Coleraine
Downhill
Inishowen Head
TO DERRY
A2
A8
A26
A29
A36
A42
A43
A44
A52
A54
M2
B3
B15
B17
B18
B39
B58
B59
B62
B64
B67
B86
B90
B92
B93
B94
B95
B96
B99
B100
B146
B147
B148
B186
B201

lake lies. The lake stays full only when silt is blocking the pores. The lake is more commonly called Fairy Lough, but there's no scientific explanation for that. Farther along, part of the high plain has been drained and planted with evergreens. The result is secluded **Ballypatrick Forest,** which includes a forest drive and several pleasant, pine-scented walks. **Camping** is allowed with a permit from the ranger or the **Forest Office,** 155 Cushendall Rd., 2 mi. toward Ballycastle on A2. (☎ 2076 2301 or 2563 1860. Tents £5. Basic facilities. Park open daily 10am to sunset.) Just before Ballycastle is **Ballycastle Forest,** significant for harboring **Knocklayde Mountain** (1695 ft.) in its midst. The mountain is eminently climbable. Its base is approximately 1 mi. into the forest.

BALLYCASTLE

The Causeway Coast leaves the sleepy Glens behind when it hits Ballycastle, a bubbly seaside town that shelters Giant's Causeway-bound tourists. Warm summer weekends bring carloads of locals to its beaches; music-lovers flock to its pubs every summer weekend. Although Ballycastle means "town of the castle," don't look for one here: the castle met its demise in 1856.

GETTING THERE AND GETTING AROUND

Buses: Stop at the Marine Hotel at the end of Quay Rd. **Ulsterbus** #172 rides to **Portrush** (1hr; M-F 7 per day, Sa 5 per day, Su 4 per day; £3.50), #171 to **Coleraine** via **Ballymoney** (M-F 5 per day, Sa 4 per day; £3.80), #162A to **Cushendall** via **Cushendun** (50min., M-F 1 per day, £3), and #131 to **Belfast** via **Ballymena** (3hr.; M-F 6 per day, Sa 5 per day; £6.10). The #252 **Antrim Coaster** runs through the **Glens of Antrim** and **Larne** to **Belfast** (full trip 3½-4hr., 2 per day).

Ferries: Argyll and Antrim Steam Packet Co. (☎ (08705) 523 523) runs ferries between **Campbeltown, Scotland** (on the Kintryre Peninsula) and Ballycastle (3hr.; July-Oct. 19 2 per day in each direction; £20-25, cars and caravans accepted, vehicles and driver £80-105). See **Rathlin Island,** p. 457 for info on the service to it.

Bike Rental: Cushleake B&B, Quay Rd. (☎ 2076 3798). £6 per day.

Taxis: Delargy's Taxis (☎ 2076 2822) or **Styler's Taxis** (☎ 2076 3697).

ORIENTATION AND PRACTICAL INFORMATION

Ballycastle's main street runs perpendicular to the waterfront. It starts at the ocean as **Quay Rd.,** becomes **Ann St.,** and then turns into **Castle St.** as its passes **The Diamond.** Most restaurants and shops are found along Ann and Castle St. As Quay Rd. meets the water, the road takes a sharp left onto **North St.,** where more stores and food await; a right from Quay puts you on **Mary Rd.,** where the tourist office rests. A park sits on the harbor; facing the water, the ferry service is on the right, and the town's beach is on the left. B&Bs nest on Quay Rd.

Tourist Office: Sheskburn House, 7 Mary St. (☎ 2076 2024). Information on the entire Antrim coast. Books accommodations. 24hr. computerized info kiosk outside. Open July-Aug. M-F 9:30am-7pm, Sa 10am-6pm, Su 2-6pm; Sept.-June M-F 9:30am-5pm.

Banks: First Trust Bank, Ann St. (☎ 2076 3326). Open M-Tu and Th-F 9:30am-4:30pm, W 10am-4:30pm. **Northern Bank,** Ann St. (☎ 2076 2238). Open M 9:30am-12:30pm and 1:30-5pm, Tu-F 10am-12:30pm and 1:30-3:30pm. Both have **ATMs.**

Pharmacy: McMichael's, 10 Ann St. (☎ 2076 3342). Open M-Sa 9am-1pm and 2-6pm.

Emergency: ☎ 999. **Police:** Ramoan Rd. (☎ 2076 2312 or 2076 3125).

Hospital: Dalriada Hospital, Coleraine Rd. (☎ 2076 2666).

Internet Access: The town **library,** on the corner of Castle and Leyland St., charges £2.50 per hr., but is **free** for members (sign up for a card). Open M-Tu and Th-Sa 10am-1pm and 2-5:30pm, Tu and Th 6-8pm.

Post Office: 3 Ann St. (☎ 2076 2519). Open M-Tu and Th-F 9am-1pm and 2-5:30pm, W 9am-1pm, Sa 9am-12:30pm. **Postal code:** BT54.

ACCOMMODATIONS

Watch out for the Ould Lammas Fair on the last Monday and Tuesday in August. B&Bs fill almost a year in advance, and hostel beds fill weeks before the big event.

Castle Hostel (IHH), 62 Quay Rd. (☎ 2076 2337), slightly out of town next to the Marine Hotel. 40-bed hostel with a relaxed and welcoming atmosphere. Wash £1. Dorms £7; private rooms £8.50 per person.

Cúchulainn House, 56 Quay Rd. (☎ 2076 2252). Breakfast on fresh fruit and local baked goods. Mrs. McMahon outdoes herself with home-made pamphlets on the Ulster myth cycle and immaculate rooms. Singles £16.50; doubles with bath £39.

Fragrens, 34 Quay Rd. (☎ 2076 2168). Mrs. Greene offers a fruit bowl at breakfast in her 17th-century home, one of Ballycastle's oldest. £15, with bath £17.

Hilsea, 28 North St. (☎ 2076 2385). A large guest house offering bright rooms decorated with watercolors; some have beautiful views of gorgeous Fair Head. Snack on tea and scones in the dining room. Singles £17.50; doubles £35, with bath £37.

FOOD AND PUBS

Brady's Supermarket, 54 Castle St., is a 10-minute walk from the hostels. (☎ 2076 2268. Open daily 8am-10pm.) **Herald's,** 22 Ann St., serves huge portions at cheap prices. The kind staff is the icing on the cake. (☎ 2076 9064. Entrees £2-3. Open daily 8am-9pm.) **Wysner's,** 16 Ann St., sets its sights on healthy meals. (☎ 2076 2372. Lunch around £5, dinner special £8-9. Open M-Tu and Th-F 9am-5pm, plus 7-9pm F-Sa.) **Donnelly's Home Bakery and Restaurant,** 28 Ann St., offers a selection of soups, pizza, quiche, and pies for under £4. (☎ 2076 2326. Open M-Sa 9am-6pm.) **The Strand Restaurant,** 9 North St., next to the sea, has a large menu that specializes in fresh-cooked produce. (☎ 2076 2349. Cold platters £4.25, burgers £4. Open daily July-Aug. 11am-10pm, Sept.-June 11am-9pm.) At the other end of the food spectrum is **Flash-in-the-Pan,** 74 Castle St.; it won Fish and Chip Shop of the Year Award in 1995. (☎ 2076 2251. Meals £3. Open Su-Th 11am-midnight, F-Sa 11am-1am.)

Trad is in vogue year-round in Ballycastle, but summer nights promise several venues nightly. Tourists head for tiny, fire-warmed **House of McDonnell,** 71 Castle St. (☎ 2076 2975), for trad on Fridays; it also features folk on Saturday and spontaneous trad other days of the week. Guinness guzzlers fill the **Boyd Arms,** 4 The Diamond (☎ 2076 2364), to enjoy trad on Friday nights. **McCarroll's Bar,** a.k.a. "Pat's," 7 Ann St. (☎ 2076 2123), is the place to be on Thursdays, when it hosts terrific traditional reels and jigs. The trad-bursting **Central Bar,** 12 Ann St., has an ebullient owner who can't contain the crowds. (☎ 2076 3877. Music W.) **The Harbour Bar,** 6 North St. (☎ 2076 2387), is the least self-conscious of pubs; locals come here for strong drinks and *craic*.

SIGHTS

BOYD CHURCH. Just off The Diamond, the Holy Trinity Church of Ireland—better known as the Boyd Church—raises an octagonal spire over its plain interior. This edifice, like most of Ballycastle, was built by the 18th-century landlord Hugh Boyd, who industrialized the area and created the town center, including Quay Rd., Ann Rd. (named after his wife), and the docks where the tennis courts now are. Most of his improvements fell to ruin when his grandsons took over in the days when industry-derived incomes fell out of fashion.

BONAMARGY FRIARY. Perhaps the town's most impressive sight is the 15th-century Bonamargy Friary, which stands relatively intact in the middle of the golf course a half-mile out of town on Cushendall Rd. You can clamber around some of the rooms in the priory and read the fascinating gravestones surrounding the church. The cemetery's most notable resident is "the black nun," a 17th-century recluse who had her grave placed where people would step on her, as a posthumous self-punishment for having turned away her unmarried pregnant sister.

FISHING. Those who want to get up close and personal with the Irish Sea should contact **Moyle Outdoor Pursuits** for fishing and sightseeing tours. (☎ 2076 9521.) If you're lacking in sea legs, you could just fish off the pier, where pollock, mackerel, colefish, plaice, and cod abound. The Town Council sells fishing licenses in the same building as the tourist office. (£11, 8-day £23.50. Open M-F 9:30am-1pm and 2-5pm.) Otherwise, you can always throw on your toggins and swim by the beach.

FESTIVALS. The ■**Ould Lammas Fair,** Northern Ireland's oldest and most famous fair, has taken place in Ballycastle in the last week of August for 412 years. Originally a week-long fiesta, the festival is now crammed into two frenzied days. Continuing the traditions of the ancient Celtic harvest festival, the fair jams Ballycastle's streets with vendors selling cows, sheep, crafts, and baked goods. Trad musicians have the pubs packed. *Dulse* (nutritious seaweed dried on local roofs, reputedly good for the brain) and *yellow-man* (sticky toffee made from a secret recipe) are two curiosities that originated with the fair.

■ DAYTRIP FROM BALLYCASTLE

RATHLIN ISLAND

Caledonian MacBrayne runs a ferry service from Ballycastle to Rathlin Island. In the summer, the ferry runs to the island four times daily from the pier at Ballycastle, up the hill from Quay Rd. on North St. ☎ 2076 9299. 45min.; June-Sept. 4 per day, Oct.-May 2 per day; £8 return. The small MacBrayne office at the Ballycastle pier (☎ 2076 2024), open before each departure, sells tickets; you can also buy them on board.

Just off the coast at Ballycastle, bumpy, boomerang-shaped Rathlin Island ("Fort of the Sea") is the ultimate in escapism for 20,000 puffins, the odd golden eagle, 100 human beings, and four daily ferries of tourists. Its windy surface supports few trees, but it's an ecological paradise of orchids, purple heather, and seabirds. The contrast between the white chalk and black basalt cliffs that encircle the island caused the novelist Charles Kingsley to compare Rathlin to a "drowned magpie." Before the Famine ravaged Ireland, more than 1000 people inhabited the island; in just 20 years, the population dwindled to half of that. Most of Rathlin's emigrants set sail for America and created their own community in Maine. Despite the fact that electricity only arrived in Rathlin in 1992, the island has a unique place in the history of science and technology; in 1898, the Italian scientist Marconi sent the first wireless telegraph message from Rathlin to Ballycastle.

Rathlin makes a beautiful daytrip, but be warned that there is absolutely nothing to do on the island in bad weather. A leaflet available at the Ballycastle tourist office contains a decent map and description of the island's walks and sights. For a more complete presentation of the island's intricately intertwined history and myths, visit the island's own **Boat House Heritage Center,** a.k.a. the Rathlin Island Visitors Centre at the opposite end of the harbor from the ferry. It's a tourist office-cum-museum, showcasing a wealth of photographs and documents that relay Rathlin's history, including pamphlets on the birds of Rathlin and the lighthouses for a few pence. (☎ 2076 3951. Open May-Aug. daily 11:30am-4:30pm, other months by arrangement. Admission 50p, children free.)

One main **minibus** service (Gusty McCurdy, ☎ 2076 3909) leaves from the ferry docks to drive to the **Kebble Bird Sanctuary** at the western tip of the island, 4½ mi. from the harbor (20min., every 45min., $2 each way). The **lighthouse** is the best place to view birds, but it's accessible only with the warden's supervision; call in advance (☎ 2076 3948). Peak bird-watching season lasts from May to mid-July.

The minibus will also make trips to **Rue Point**, 2½ mi. from the harbor ($3 return). Here, visitors marvel at the crumbled remains of **Smuggler's House**, with wall cavities that hid contraband in the days when pirates and smugglers fueled Rathlin's economy. Ironically, the official tax house is just yards away. The feud between the hated coast guards and Rathlin residents reached boiling point when the former filled in the smuggler-frequented harbor at Usher Point, at the south end of the island. **Fair Head,** where seals frolic, looms a few miles away from Rue Point.

If you need a break from civilization, spend the night at tiny **Soerneog View Hostel** (SIR-nock). Take a right from the dock and turn left at the side road before the pub. At the top of the road, turn right; the hostel is a quarter-mile ahead on the left. Call ahead for pick-up. This tiny hostel has six beds, so be sure to call from the mainland to make sure there's one left for you. Most importantly, bring groceries with you. (☎ 2076 3954. Laundry £2. **Bike rental** £7 per day. Dorms £8.) **McCuaig's Bar** sometimes allows free **camping** on its grounds. The bar is the single entetainment center for the entire island, and a food source. (☎ 2076 3974. Sandwiches and toasties £1.60-2, burgers £1.90, a limited selection of entrees around £5. Served 9am-9pm.) The head of Duncan, Rathlin's last Highland bull who went crazy and had to be shot in 1880, is the showpiece of the pub's otherwise plain interior.

BALLINTOY AND CARRICK-A-REDE ISLAND

Five miles west of Ballycastle on route B15, the modest village of Ballintoy consists of a church, a tiny harbor, several pubs, a hostel, and a fisherman's bridge that's one of the most frequented tourist destinations in Northern Ireland. Two remarkable islands put Ballintoy's name on the map: Sheep Island and Carrick-a-rede Island, both of which are so small in size that they might more aptly be described as giant grass-covered rocks. Visible from Ballintoy village, Sheep Island is home to puffins, razor bills, shag, kittiwakes, and the largest cormorant colony in Ireland. The miniscule island was once used to graze sheep—11 sheep, to be exact. Ten were thought to be too few (they would get fat) and 12 too many (they would starve). Smaller and better-known Carrick-a-rede Island lies offshore to the east of Ballintoy. Meaning "rock in the road," Carrick-a-rede presents a barrier to migrating salmon returning to their home rivers. Fishermen have set up their nets for over 250 years at the point off the island by which salmon have to pass in their migration westward. To reach the nets, the fishermen annually string a rope bridge between the mainland and the island, where it hangs from April to September. Crossing the shaky, 48 in. wide, 67 ft. long bridge over the dizzying 100 ft. drop to rocks and sea below is now the business of thousands of tourists every year. Be **extremely careful** in windy weather, and do not cross more than two at a time. Wardens are on site during opening hours to ensure visitors' safety, and the bridge is certainly a lot safer than the days when it only had one handrail to cling to. A sign a half-mile east of Ballintoy marks the turn-off for the bridge from the coast road; the car park is a quarter-mile farther, and the bridge is three-quarters of a mile past the car park.

The walk out to the bridge takes you along the heights of the Larrybane sea cliffs. You'll likely notice at least one of several species of unusual birds, including cliff-nesting, black-and-white razor bills, brown-and-white-bellied guillemots, and lots of mundane gulls. Tiny Carrick-a-rede is as generous to birdwatchers as it is to salmon fishermen. Ask the wardens for the National Trust's leaflet on the site, which provides a map of the area's geological notables. A fishing hut totters on the east side of the island, from which salmon nets stretch out into the sea. On a clear day, you can see the Hebrides. The **tea room** by the parking lot sells snacks, posts information on the site, and offers a bit of local advice. For 50p, they'll give you a certificate stating that you successfully crossed the bridge; you can save your money and use ours instead (see **I am a certified Hero,** below). Free **camping** can be arranged with the wardens. (☎ 2076 2178. Cliff walks always open. Tea room open July-Aug. daily noon-6pm. £2.50 per car, £1 per motorcycle, others free.)

Quiet Ballintoy provides beds and grub to Carrick-a-rede's thrill-seekers. The aptly titled **Sheep Island View Hostel (IHH),** 42A Main St., has one of the biggest

> **I AM A CERTIFIED HERO**
>
> I, _____, Let's Go: Ireland 2001 reader, am hereby to be referred to as a hero because I crossed the treacherous rope-bridge to Carrick-a-rede Island. Possession of this certificate entitles me to hero-worship.
>
> Witness: _____
>
> Date: _____

kitchens you'll ever see. (☎ 2076 9391; fax 2076 9994; email sheepisland@hotmail.com. Continental breakfast £2.50; Ulster fry £4. Wash £1, dry £1. Barbecue facilities available. Wheelchair accessible. Dorms with bath £9.) The two surrounding **camping** greens are as pristine as the hostel, with separate facilities and views of Sheep's Island. (£3 per person.) Call the hostel for pick-up from anywhere between Ballycastle and Portrush. A shop at the entrance to the hostel provides basic groceries. (Open daily 8:30am-9pm.) In town, the frosted-glass-windowed **Fullerton Arms** (☎ 2076 9613) and the come-as-you-are **Carrick-a-rede** (☎ 2076 2241) compete from across the street for locals' business. Fullerton offers standard pub grub daily from 12:30 to 8:30pm in the £5-6 range, while Carrick's is slightly cheaper (most meals £3.50-5.50), but both have music almost every summer night.

Three miles west along the coast road from Ballintoy is **Whitepark Bay Youth Hostel (HINI)**. Its out-of-the-way setting, overlooking one of the most famous—though unswimmable—beaches on the Antrim Coast is either a blessing or a bane, depending on whether or not you have a car. The Portrush-Ballycastle bus (#172) or the Antrim Coaster (#252) will drop you off 200 yd. from the hostel, but there are no shops or pubs for miles around. Once there, few of the visitors spend their precious time complaining and save their energy for the beach. Impeccably clean, this hostel is the HINI of the 21st century. A restaurant sells the most basic food stuffs. (☎ 2073 1745. **Bike rental** £6 per day. Breakfast £2.50, dinner £4.50. Oct.-Mar. lockout 11am-5pm. 4-bed dorms £9.75; twin room £11.75.) There is a splendid 1 mi. **nature trail** along the bay.

GIANT'S CAUSEWAY

Advertised as the eighth natural wonder of the world, Giant's Causeway is Northern Ireland's most famous sight. Be warned that 2000 visitors arrive each day in July and August. A spillage of 40,000 hexagonal columns of basalt form a 60-million-year-old honeycomb path from the foot of the cliffs far into the sea. Geologists have decided that the Causeway resulted from an unusually steady cooling of lava that stimulated crystallization.

The Causeway is always open and free to pedestrians. Ulsterbuses #172 to Portrush, the #252 Antrim Coaster, the "Causeway Rambler," and the open-topped Bushmills Bus all dump visitors throughout the day at the **Giant's Causeway Visitors Centre**, in the shop next to the carpark. Besides offering the usual tourist information, a **bureau de change**, and a **post office**, it sells an excellent leaflet of walks (75p) that will guide you the 8 mi. back to Whitepark Bay or along several shorter circular walks. Every 15 minutes, it runs Causeway Coaster minibuses the half-mile to the columns (60p, £1 return). An audio-visual show (£1) informs about the facts and fictions of the Causeway. (☎ 2073 1855. Centre open daily June 10am-6pm; July-Aug. 10am-7pm; Mar.-May and Sept. 10am-5pm; Nov.-Feb. 10am-4:30pm. Parking £3 per car.) A tea room offers refreshment in the Centre. (Tea room closes 30min. before the Visitors Centre.)

Many paths loop to and from the Causeway. Two begin at the Visitors Centre, one passing along the high cliffs and another along the low coast close to the Causeway. The paths meet after 1 mi., and you can return by the road not taken. Taking the low road provides more instant gratification, while the high road affords spectacular sea views. The low road also allows something of a downhill

THE REAL MCCOOL

Irish legend states that the warrior giant Finn McCool fell in love with a female giant named Una on Staffa Island, off the Scottish coast. The devoted lover built the Causeway to bring her across to Ulster, which explains the existence of similar beehive-esque rock formations on Staffa. The Scottish giant Benandonner followed them to Ireland to defeat Finn and take Una back home with him. When McCool realized how big his Scottish rival was, he realized the folly of his physical confidence and decided to rely on the strength of his wit. The wily Irishman, with the help of his wife Una, disguised himself as an infant. When the Scottish giant saw the size of this Irish "baby," he was terrified by the anticipated proportions of the father. Benandonner quickly fled back to Scotland, destroying the Causeway on his return trip in order to ensure that the huge father McCool would never be able to cross the sea to challenge him.

walk for a portion of the trail. At the end of this walk, 4½ mi. east of the Causeway's center, you will see the scanty though overwhelmingly romantic ruins of **Dunseverick Castle,** the Iron Age fort of Sobhairce, high above you on a sea cliff. Bus #172 and the #252 Antrim Coaster stop in front of the castle, from where it's 4½ mi. farther to Ballintoy. The well-tended track winds through naturally sculpted amphitheaters and inlets studded with creatively named formations (such as the "organ"). Although not essential, the center's trail leaflet contains a helpful map and basic geological descriptions.

BUSHMILLS

The ardently Protestant town of Bushmills, 2 mi. west of Giant's Causeway, has been the home of **Bushmills Irish Whiskey** since 1608, making it the oldest functioning whiskey producer in the world. The Bushmills distill their whiskey three times, a process that your tour guide happily expounds upon. Irish monks invented whiskey in the 6th century and called it *uisce beatha* (is-CAH BAHN-a), "water of life." Travelers have been stopping at Bushmills for some stimulation since ancient days when it was on the route from the castles of Dunluce and Dunseverick to Tara. When the distillery is operating, you get to see whiskey being made. Production stops for three weeks in July for maintenance, but (less interesting) tours are still held; around Christmas, neither distilling nor tours occur. (☎ 2073 1521. Open M-Sa 9:30am-5:30pm; last tour 4pm. Tours, with free sample Apr.-Oct. when enough people accumulate; Nov.-Mar. M-F at 10:30, 11:30am, 1:30, 2:30, and 3:30pm. $3.50, students and seniors $3.) A not-yet-open **Electric Tramway line,** the first of a few hydroelectric-powered tram rails, will eventually run from Bushmills to the Causeway visitors center via Portrush; for now, the Causeway Rambler bus and the open-topped Bushmills bus will have to suffice.

PORTRUSH

By day, the merry-go-rounds, water slides, and arcades of Portrush go full-throttle as bushels of Northern vacationers roam the streets and its two beaches. By night, young mobs party at nightclubs along the chilly sea front. Giant's Causeway and Portstewart are within easy cycling distance.

GETTING THERE AND GETTING AROUND

Trains: Eglinton St. (☎ 7082 2395), in the center of town. Trains to **Belfast** (2hr.; M-F 8 per day, Sa 8 per day, Su 3 per day; £5.30) and **Derry** (1hr.; M-F 7 per day, Sa 6 per day, Su 4 per day; £5.10).

Buses: Leave from Dunluce Ave. Ulsterbus #140 runs to **Coleraine** via **Portstewart** (30min.; M-F 23 per day, Sa 18 per day, Su 9 per day; £1). Ulsterbus #172 (M-F 6 per day, Sa 5 per day, Su 2 per day) runs along the coast to **Bushmills** (20min.), **Giant's Causeway** (25min.), **Ballintoy** (40min.), and **Ballycastle** (1hr.). The open-topped Bushmills Bus (#177) goes to **Portstewart, Bushmills,** and **Giant's Causeway** in good weather (summer only, daily 5 per day). The Ulsterbus **Portrush Puffer** runs circles around the town (July-Aug. M-Sa 11am-7pm, Su 2-7pm; £1.40).

Taxis: ☎ 7082 3421, 7082 2223, or 7082 4446.

Bike Rental: Thompson Cycles, 77B Lower Main St. (☎ 7082 9606). £7 per day, deposit required. Open daily 9am-6pm; bikes can be returned after closing via the Portrush Hostel. **Woodie's Surf-Skate-Snow** (see **Surfing Equipment,** below).

PRACTICAL INFORMATION

Tourist Office: Dunluce Centre (☎ 7082 3333), off Sandhill Dr., just south of the town center. Brochures galore, **bureau de change,** and accommodation bookings. Ulsterbus representative on hand to arrange day tours. Open mid-June to Aug. daily 9am-7pm; Apr.-June and Sept. M-F 9am-5pm, Sa-Su noon-5pm; Mar. and Oct. Sa-Su noon-5pm.

Banks: First Trust, 25 Eglinton St. (☎ 7082 2726). Open M-Tu and Th-F 9:30am-4:30pm, W 10am-4:30pm. **Northern Bank,** 60 Main St. (☎ 7082 2327). Open M 9:30am-5pm, Tu-F 10am-3:30pm; closed daily 12:30-1:30pm except July-Aug. **Bureau de change. Ulster Bank,** 33 Eglinton St. (☎ 7082 3730). Open M-F 9:30am-12:30pm and 1:30-4:30pm. All have **24hr. ATMs.**

Surfing Equipment: Troggs Surf Shop, 88 Main St. (☎ 7082 5476). Surfboards £5 per day, bodyboards £3 per day, wet-suits £5 per day; deposit credit card or driver's license. 2hr. lesson with equipment £15. Open daily July-Aug. 10am-10pm; Sept.-June 10am-6pm. **Woodie's Surf-Skate-Snow,** 102 Main St. (☎ 7082 3273). Surfboards £5 per day, wet-suits £4 per day; deposit credit card. Bicycle rental £7 per day. Open daily July-Aug. 10am-6pm; Sept.-June 11am-6pm.

Pharmacy: Heron Chemist, 5-9 Main St. (☎ 7082 2324). Open July-Aug. daily 9am-10pm; Sept.-June M-Sa 9am-6pm, Su 2-6pm.

Emergency: ☎ 999; no coins required. **Police:** ☎ 7082 2721.

Post Office: 23 Eglinton St. (☎ 7082 3700). Open M-Tu and Th-F 9am-12:30pm and 1:30-5:30pm, W 9am-1pm, Sa 9am-12:30pm. **Postal code:** BT56.

ACCOMMODATIONS

Portrush is a convenient place to begin or end a tour of Giant's Causeway, since most buses that serve the Causeway stop here. When the university at Coleraine sets students free for the summer, plenty of student housing becomes holiday digs. Almost every other townhouse along Mark St., Kerr St., and Raymore Ave. is a B&B. Most are indistinguishable in character and price (£15-20 per person).

Portrush Hostel (Macools), 5 Causeway View Terr. (☎ 7082

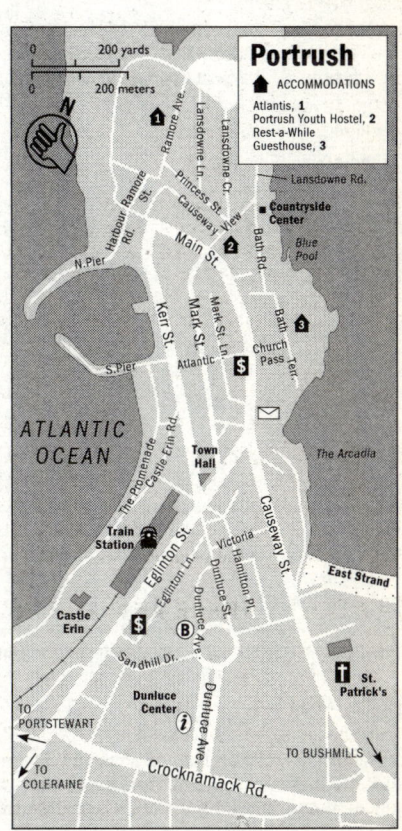

4845). One of the only good things in Portrush besides the nightlife. A 10min. walk from the bus stop; turn left onto Dunluce St. and follow it toward the harbor. When you come to a 3-pronged fork, take the middle road, which is Mark St. The hostel is a few yards past the intersection of Mark St. and Main St., on Causeway View Terr. From the train station, Mark St. is the 2nd left after turning left out of the station. Relax in the homey common room, filled with surveyor's maps of the area's hiking trails. Avid hikers, the proprietors provide a series of walking guides, in multiple languages. Free tea and coffee. Laundry £3. Bicycles £5 per day. **Internet access** £4 per hr. Dorms £7.

A-Rest-a-While Guesthouse, 6 Bath Terr. (☎ 7082 2827). Mismatched neo-Victorian decorations endear guests to this huge B&B. Some rooms overlook the beach. £15.

Atlantis, 10 Ramore Ave. (☎ 7082 4583). An ocean view. Free tea and coffee. Evening meal £5. Singles £16; doubles £30, with bath £35.

FOOD

The proliferation of fast food in Portrush may overwhelm, but a few good restaurants hide amid the neon. If you're not up to the search, stock up on groceries at **Mace,** 58 Main St. (Open daily 9am-10pm.)

The Singing Kettle, 3-5 Atlantic Ave. (☎ 7082 4254). Soothing, lace-curtained relief for weary travelers. While in any other town it might seem boring, such wholesomeness is appreciated in Portrush. Vegetarian options. All-day dinner £4-5; slightly more exotic evening meals £6-9, served after 5pm. Open daily July-Aug. 10:30am-10pm, Sept.-June 11am-5pm.

Donovan's, Main St. (☎ 7082 2063), looks and sounds like a trad pub but doesn't taste like pub grub. Irish meals are made zesty by worldly seasonings. Most lunches £5-8. Dinners £8-11. Music nightly. Open M-Sa noon-2:30pm and 5-10pm, Su noon-9:30pm.

Don Giovanni's, 9-13 Causeway St. (☎ 7082 5516). Authentic Italian food and owners. Impeccable interior. Pizza £4-7, pasta £6-7. Open daily 5:30-11pm.

The Alamo, Eglinton St. (☎ 7082 2000). Celebrate Ulster-American imperialism with American-style pizza. Free delivery. 10 in. pizza £2.75-5. Open M-Th 5pm-2am, F-Sa 5pm-3am, Su 5pm-1am.

PUBS AND ENTERTAINMENT

The **Harbour Bar,** 5 Harbour Rd. (☎ 7082 2430), wants to be a sailors' pub. The hippest complex in town swallows up one whole corner block in the Londonderry Hotel on Main St. with the **Atlantic Bar** and the **Front Bar** (☎ 7082 3693). At the Front Bar, DJs and live bands do their thing while customers sample 35 different flavors of vodka. **Shunter's,** in the railway station, powers its engines with live music most summer nights. (Cover £1-5.) Partiers head to techno-heavy **Traks Nightclub** (☎ 7082 2112) at the railway station. Facing the Harbor, **Rogues,** 54 Kerr St., is another wiggle-silly night spot. (☎ 7082 2946. Cover varies.) Finish your evening (or begin your morning) at a Portrush institution: **Beetles Bar and Disco** (everyone calls it **Kelly's;** ☎ 7082 3539), just outside Portrush on Bushmills Rd. Kelly's has 11 bars and four discos, including **Lush!** (☎ 7082 2027), voted one of the top-ten UK clubs by *DJ Magazine.* Excessive and occasionally tacky, the club has a niche for every imaginable type of teenager.

Higher art forms reach this non-stop party when Northern Irish theater companies travel to Portrush to perform on the **Summer Theatre** stage (☎ 7082 2500).

SIGHTS

DUNLUCE CENTRE. The most widely advertised attraction in Portrush is the kiddie-ride of a heritage site, **Dunluce Centre,** Dunluce Arcade. Technologically vivid displays about anything from zoo creatures to mythical heroes keep kids wide awake. Moving seats in the Turbo Tours theater make wide-screen "adventure" films that much more real. For 50p you can climb a squat tower to look at the view. (☎ 7082 4444. Open July-Aug. daily 10am-7pm; Sept. daily noon-5pm; April Sa-Su noon-5pm; May-June daily noon-5pm. Turbo Tours £2.50, Myths and Legends £2.50; whole center £5.)

PORTRUSH COUNTRYSIDE CENTRE. In refreshing contrast to the Dunluce Centre, the understated Portrush Countryside Centre, 8 Bath Rd., next to East Strand, is small but enthusiastically attended. The assortment of displays includes wildlife exhibits, a tide pool with sea urchins and starfish, a fossil and crystal exhibit, and a display of a sea-wreck. A viewing platform outside can help identify the many land masses in the distance. A governmentally protected fossil bed sits outside. (☎ 7082 3600. Open June-Sept. W-M noon-8pm. Viewing platform always open. Free.)

DUNLUCE CASTLE AND BEACHES. Luckily, it is not difficult to escape Portrush's amusement-park atmosphere. The **East Strand Beach** stretches out for 1½ mi. toward Giant's Causeway. At the far end of the beach is a car park; from here, it is another 1½ mi. along the main road to **Dunluce Castle,** a surprisingly intact 16th-century fort. The castle has been partially restored and houses an information center, complete with a 15-minute video. A walk around the peripheral castle grounds is almost as interesting, and it's free. The castle was built close to the cliff's edge; so close, in fact, that one day the kitchen fell into the sea. (Open Apr.-Oct. Tu-Sa 10am-7pm, Su 2-7pm, plus June-July Su 11am-8pm; Nov.-Mar. Tu-Sa 10am-4pm, Su 2-4pm. Last admission 30min. before closing. £1.50, students and seniors 75p.) Near the edge of the castle, the mouth of a **sea cave** stretches down to the water. Getting down can be quite slippery, but the adventurous are rewarded with outstanding cavernous sea views. The best surfing on the North Antrim coast is at **Portballintree Beach,** where the waves majestically soar almost as high as the nearby castle. Inside Portrush proper are a series of short walks on **Ramore Head,** next to the harbor.

PORTSTEWART

Although it's as crowded as its neighbor Portrush, Portstewart feels more like a friendly small town. A friendly rivalry between the two manifests itself in the different characteristics of their beach bathers: while Portrush's techno beat draws in swarms of young slicksters, Portstewart is geared towards backbiting family-types. A good beach and an oceanfront lined with ice cream parlors are the main attractions for the locals that swarm Portstewart.

GETTING THERE AND PRACTICAL INFORMATION. Buses stop in the middle of **The Promenade.** Ulsterbus #140 makes a triangular route connecting Portstewart, Portrush, and Coleraine (M-F 28 per day, Sa 21 per day, Su 9 per day). Portstewart's tiny **tourist office,** in the library behind Town Hall, is in the red brick building that sits on the crescent at the far end of The Promenade. The library also provides **Internet access** for £2.50 per hour and free to members. (☎ 7083 2286. Open July-Aug. M-Sa 10am-1pm and 1:30-4:30pm.) **First Trust,** 13 The Promenade, offers financial services inside and out with a **24-hour ATM.** (☎ 7083 3273. Open M-Tu and Th-F 9:30am-4:30pm, W 10am-4:30pm.) **McElhone's Numark Pharmacy,** 22A The Promenade, distributes prescriptions and advice. (☎ 7083 2014. Open M-Sa 9am-5:30pm.) The **post office,** 90 The Promenade, does the usual. (☎ 7083 2001. Open M-Tu and Th-F 9am-1pm and 2-5:30pm, W 9am-1pm, Sa 9am-12:30pm.) The **postal code** is BT55.

ACCOMMODATIONS, FOOD, AND PUBS. The Victoria Terr. area, on the left as you head out of town on the Portrush Rd., has beds galore. From the bus stop, face the sea, turn right, and follow Main St. around the corner. Victoria Terr. juts out to the left. **Rick's Causeway Coast Independent Hostel (IHH),** 4 Victoria Terr., is friendly and comfortable. The walls are lined with maps and stunning mountain photographs. The staff will take as good care of you as they do of the healthy plants that make something of a conservatory out of the common room. (☎ 7083 3789. Barbecue available for use. Laundry £2, free if you stay for more than one night. £2 key deposit. Dorms £7; doubles and twins £17.) **Wanderin' Heights,** 12 High Rd., near Victoria Terr., provides B&B amidst yellow-print wallpaper. (☎ 7083 3250. Depending on view, rooms £20-25, £16-20 off-season, all with bath.)

Portstewart cultivates both good cooks and a tradition of superb ice cream. **Mace Supermarket,** on The Promenade, has an impressive selection of groceries and cheeses. (☎ 7083 3203. Open M-Su 8am-midnight.) **Good Food and Company,** 44 The Promenade, serves sandwiches (£1.50-1.70), breads, and baked goods. (☎ 7083 6386. Open M-Sa 9am-10pm; Sept.-June M-Sa 9am-6pm.) **Ashiana Indian Kitchen,** 12 The Diamond, has take-away options, which come with rice or bread and are slightly cheaper than eating at the restaurant. (☎ 834 455. Entrees around £7. Open daily 5-11pm, take-away open M-F and Su 5pm-midnight, Sa 5pm-2am.) The more adventurous diner might try the **Montagu Arms** (☎ 7093 4146), on The Promenade, which offers a 10 oz. sirloin steak with chips and sautéed onions for £6.35 from 5-7pm. The really early bird can enjoy a two-course lunch for £5 from 12:30 to 2:30pm. **Morelli's Sundae Garden,** the dance-club look alike on The Promenade, is infamous for its superbly sugary concoctions. (☎ 7083 2150. Sundaes about £3. Open July-Aug. daily 9am-11pm; hours vary during the rest of the year.) Most of the town, and all of its students, head for the **Anchor Pub,** 87 The Promenade, to put back some pints by the fire while studying the intricate handiwork of the framed sailor's knots on the walls. (☎ 7083 2003. Disco upstairs Tu and Th-Sa. Cover £3 or free.) **Skipper's Wine Bar,** next door in the Anchorage Inn, serves upscale pub grub in the shinier version of the Anchor Pub. (☎ 7083 4401. Lunch about £5, bigger dinner portions for about £6-8; food served noon-2:30pm and 5-9:30pm.) Across the street, **Stafford's,** 28 The Promenade, dark green and mahogany bar draws a mixed crowd, while its upstairs nightclub, **Chaines,** packs in dancing youngsters. (☎ 7083 6000. Disco M-Tu, Th-Sa. Cover £3 on Sa.)

■ SIGHTS. Beachcombers have a full day ahead of them on the 6½ mi. coastal path that leads from **Portstewart Strand** on the west side of town east toward Portrush. The path takes you past sea cliffs, blow holes, an ancient hermit's house, and plenty of other odd sights that a free map from the tourist office will help you recognize. Portstewart Strand, half a mile west of town, is owned and preserved in all its beauty by the National Trust. (Visitors facilities open daily May-Aug. 10am-6pm. £2.50 per car.) The **Port-na-happle rock pool,** located between town and the beach, is ideal for bathing. A small but dedicated group of surfers call these waters home. For those who dare to try out the Irish waves, there are two surf shops in town. **Troggs,** 20 The Diamond, rents wet-suits, surfboards, bodyboards, and wild things. (☎ 7083 3361. Equipment £3-10 per day. Open July-Aug. daily 10am-7pm; Apr.-June Sa-Su 10am-6pm.) **Ocean Warriors,** located at both 80 The Promenade and on the Strand, rents wet-suits and bodyboards, each £2 per hour or £5 per day. (☎ 7083 6500. Open daily 10am-6pm.) According to locals, the best waves hit the shore from September to March and reach 5 to 6 ft. The **Flowerfield Arts Center,** 185 Coleraine Rd., shelters traveling art exhibitions and holds frequent lectures on subjects ranging from local history and folklore to the royal family. (☎ 7083 3959. Open M-F 10am-1pm and 2-5pm.)

DOWNHILL

Farther out along the A2 coast road toward Derry is Downhill, home to a pub, a beach, and the still glorious remnants of a royal estate. Downhill is very difficult to reach, but is one of the most beautiful areas in Northern Ireland; it's worth spending a couple of days here just to relax by the pristine coastline. Such a pursuit is easily accomplished at the **■Downhill Hostel.** The hostel has a beach out front, is backed by cliffs, and is bordered by a rocky stream. High bunks, hand-sewn quilts, and a luxurious shower provide more reason to stay longer than planned. (☎ 7084 9077. Laundry £3.50. Dorms £7; private rooms £9 per person.) The closest food source other than Downhill's pub is the grocery store 2 mi. away in Castlerock, so do your shopping before you arrive. **Bus** #134 from Coleraine to Limavady swings by (7-8 per day); ask the driver to stop at the hostel and it's a two-minute walk straight ahead. The **train** stops 2 mi. from Downhill at Castlerock on its way from Belfast to Derry; from there, call the hostel for free pick-up.

The land between Castlerock and Downhill once belonged to the Earl Bishop Frederick Hervey, Earl of Bristol and Derry, who will long be remembered as one of the wackiest members of British aristocracy ever to tamper with the Irish landscape. Challenging the coast's stoic, irreproachable sea cliffs with the heavy hand of human decadence, he built **Downhill Castle** in the late 18th century. His house was once one of Europe's greatest treasure troves, but it suffered from a disastrous fire and was completely abandoned after World War II. The residence was later bought by an American businessman who gutted it and sold the windows, chandeliers, furnishings, and even the roof abroad, leaving behind only the stone shell of the former palace. On the cliffs in front of the castle, **Musenden Temple** all but teeters before a precipitous drop to the sea. This circular library was based on the Temples of Vesta in Italy and was named after the niece with whom locals speculated the Earl Bishop had an affair. Behind the castle sit the remains of another of Hervey's architectural frivolities, the mausoleum he built for his brother. Ignoring warnings that the windy cliff top would not long support a structure, he erected a monument twice the height of the one that now stands. A second tier and the statue atop it both toppled in a windstorm. The decapitated statue now stands in the National Trust-administered gardens farther inland on the property. (Temple open July-Aug. daily noon-6pm; Apr.-June and Sept. Sa-Su noon-6pm. Grounds open year-round. Free.) Hervey's estate peers down at **Downhill Beach,** one of the most gorgeous on the Northern coast.

DERRY (LONDONDERRY)

Derry competes with Dublin for the most long-lasting contributions to Irish political history. The past is remarkably present in the landmarks and districts that comprise Derry's physical appearance, from the administrative centers within its city walls to the murals of the Bogside neighborhood that sits outside them.

Derry has been a center of culture and politics for thousands of years. Once a Celtic holy place, the arrival of Christianity converted it into a monastic center in the 6th century. Derry became a major commercial port under the Ulster Plantation of the 17th century (see p. 10); under the English feudal system, the city became the outpost of London's authority, who renamed it Londonderry. (Phone books and other such bureaucratic traps use this official title, but most Northerners refer to the city as Derry.) The past three centuries of Derry's history have given rise to the iconography used by both sides of the sectarian conflict. The city's troubled history spans from the siege of Derry in 1689, when the now-legendary Apprentice Boys closed the city gates on the advancing armies of the Catholic King James II (see p. 11), to the civil rights turmoil of the 1960s, when protests against religious discrimination against Catholics exploded into violence publicized worldwide. In 1972, the Troubles reached their pinnacle on Bloody Sunday, a tragic public massacre in which British soldiers shot into a crowd of peaceful protesters. None of the soldiers was ever convicted or punished, and the nationalist population is still seeking redress from the British government for the event (see **The Troubles,** p. 399). Hearings into the Bloody Sunday Massacre were recently reopened, and will be held in Derry's Guildhall over the next few years.

Modern Derry is in the middle of a determined and largely successful effort to cast off the legacy of the Troubles. While the political turmoil that lasted until the mid-1980s flattened parts of the city, today the city's skyline displays both medieval and modern architectural feats. And, despite occasional unrest in the staunchly sectarian areas of the city, it seems that many Derry residents believe consensus is possible. Construction and commerce are booming, and most parts of the city, especially the downtown, show evidence of Derry's rapid development. The city council is starting new programs to promote peace, improve morale, and

Derry

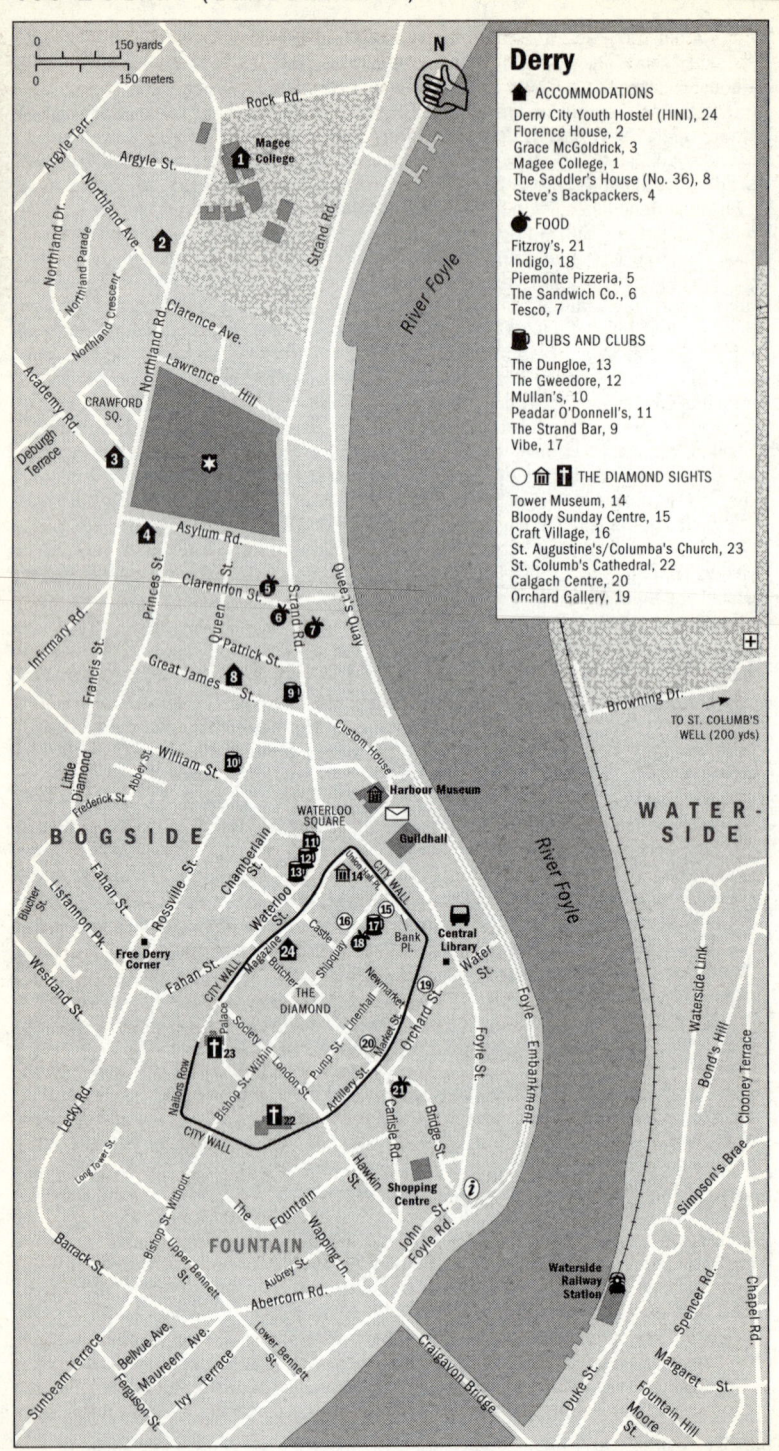

ACCOMMODATIONS
Derry City Youth Hostel (HINI), 24
Florence House, 2
Grace McGoldrick, 3
Magee College, 1
The Saddler's House (No. 36), 8
Steve's Backpackers, 4

FOOD
Fitzroy's, 21
Indigo, 18
Piemonte Pizzeria, 5
The Sandwich Co., 6
Tesco, 7

PUBS AND CLUBS
The Dungloe, 13
The Gweedore, 12
Mullan's, 10
Peadar O'Donnell's, 11
The Strand Bar, 9
Vibe, 17

THE DIAMOND SIGHTS
Tower Museum, 14
Bloody Sunday Centre, 15
Craft Village, 16
St. Augustine's/Columba's Church, 23
St. Columb's Cathedral, 22
Calgach Centre, 20
Orchard Gallery, 19

attract more tourists. Derry's controversial history and its depiction in murals make for fascinating sights, as do less contentious aspects of the city, including its brilliant music scene, thriving artistic community, and irrepressible pub life.

GETTING THERE AND AROUND

Airport: Eglinton/Derry Airport, Eglinton (☎ 7181 0784). 7 mi. from Derry. Flights to points within the British Isles.

Trains: Duke St., Waterside (☎ 7134 2228), on the east bank. A free **Rail-Link bus** connects the bus station to the train station. Trains from Derry go east to **Belfast** via **Castlerock, Coleraine, Ballymoney, Ballymena**, and **Lisburn** (2½hr.; M-F 7 per day, Sa 6 per day, Su 4 per day; £7). Connections may be made from Coleraine to **Portrush**.

Buses: Most stop on Foyle St. between the walled city and the river. **Ulsterbus** (☎ 7126 2261) serves all destinations in the North and some in the Republic. #212 to **Belfast** (1½-3hr.; M-Sa 15 per day, Su 8 per day; £7.50), #273-4 to **Omagh** (M-Sa 13 per day, Su 8 per day; £4.90), #274 to **Dublin** (M-Sa 5 per day, Su 3 per day; £11). **Lough Swilly** bus service (☎ 7126 2017) heads to **Letterkenny** and northwest Donegal, the **Fanad Peninsula**, and the **Inishowen Peninsula**. Buses to **Malin Head** (1½hr.; M-F 2 per day, Sa 3 per day; £6), **Letterkenny** (1hr., M-Sa 11 per day, £4.20), **Buncrana** (35min.; M-F 10 per day, Sa 12 per day, Su 3 per day; £2.60). **Northwest Busways** (☎ (077) 82619 in the Republic) heads to **Inishowen** from Patrick St. opposite the Multiplex Cinema; to **Malin Head** (2 per day, £4.20) and **Carndonagh** (M-Sa 3 per day, £3.20), and to **Buncrana** (4 per day, £2.50).

Taxi: City Cabs, William St. (☎ 7126 4466). **Foyle Taxis**, 10a Newmarket St. (☎ 7126 3905 or 7137 0007).

Car Rental: Ford Rent-a-Car, Desmond Motors Ltd., 173 Strand Rd. (☎ 7136 0420). 25+. Open July-Aug. M-F 9am-5:30pm, Sa 9am-4pm; Sept.-June M-F 9am-5:30pm, Sa 9am-1pm.

Bike Rental: Rent-A-Bike, 245 Lone Moor Rd. (☎ 7128 7128). Sells a range of accessories and offers a pick-up service. £9 per day, £35 per week; deposit passport or £50.

ORIENTATION

Derry straddles the **River Foyle** just east of the border of Co. Donegal in the Republic. The **city center** and the **university area** both lie on the Foyle's western banks. The old city within the medieval walls is now Derry's downtown with a pedestrianised shopping district around Waterloo St. In the center of the old city lies The Diamond, from which radiate four main streets: **Shipquay St.** to the northeast, **Butcher St.** to the northwest, **Bishop St.** to the southwest, and **Ferryquay** to the southeast. **Magee University** is to the north on **Strand Rd.** The famous Catholic **Bogside** neighborhood that became Free Derry in the 70s (see **The Troubles**, p. 399) is west of the city walls. On the south side of the walls is the tiny Protestant enclave of the **Fountain**. The residential areas of the Foyle's western bank are primarily Catholic, while most of Derry's Protestant population lives on the eastern bank, where the housing estates commonly known as the **Waterside** are located. The train station is on the east side of the river and can be reached from the city center by way of the **Craigavon Bridge**, or via a free shuttle at the bus station.

PRACTICAL INFORMATION

TOURIST AND FINANCIAL SERVICES

Tourist Office: 44 Foyle St. (☎ 7126 7284), inside the Derry Visitor and Convention Bureau. Be sure to ask for the truly useful *Derry Tourist Guide*, *Visitor's Guide*, and free maps of the town. 24hr. computerized info kiosk. Books accommodations throughout the island. **Bord Fáilte** (☎ 7136 9501) keeps a desk here, too. Open July-Sept. M-F

9am-7pm, Sa 10am-6pm, Su 10am-5pm; Oct.-Easter M-F 9am-5pm; Easter-June M-F 9am-5pm, Sa 10am-5pm.

Budget Travel: usit, 4 Shipquay Pl. (☎ 7137 1888; www.usitnow.com). ISICs, Travel-Save stamps, and the like. Sells bus and plane tickets and rail passes. Books accommodations world-wide. Open M-F 9:30am-5:30pm, Sa 10am-1pm.

Banks: First Trust, Shipquay St. (☎ 7136 3921). Open M-Tu and Th-F 9:30am-4:30pm, W 10am-4:30pm. **Bank of Ireland,** Strand Rd. (☎ 7126 4141). Open M-F 9:30am-4:30pm. **Northern Bank,** Guildhall Sq. (☎ 7126 5333). Open M-W and F 9:30am-3:30pm, Th 9:30am-5pm, Sa 9:30am-12:30pm. **Ulster Bank,** Guildhall Sq. (☎ 7126 1882). Open M-F 9:30am-4:30pm. All have **24hr. ATMs.**

LOCAL SERVICES

Laundry: Duds 'n' Suds, 141 Strand Rd. (☎ 7126 6006). Pool table and TV. Wash and dry £3.60. Open M-F 8am-9pm, Sa 8am-6pm. Last wash 1½hr. before closing.

Women's Center: 32 Great James St. (☎ 7126 7672). Girls' Club. Open M-Th 9:30am-5pm, F 9am-2pm.

Gay, Lesbian, and Bisexual Information: 37 Clarendon St. (☎ 7126 4400). Information for the whole of the North. Open Th 7:30-10pm.

Disability Resources: Foyle Disability Action, 52-58 Strand Rd. (☎ 7136 0811), serves the physically or mentally disabled. Open M-F 9am-1pm and 2-5pm. **P.H.A.B.,** 6 Pump St. (☎ 7137 1030), gives advice. Open M-F 9am-5pm.

Pharmacy: Boots, 3a-b Strand Rd. (☎ 7126 4502). Open M-Th 9am-5:30pm, F 9am-9pm, Sa 9am-6pm.

EMERGENCY AND COMMUNICATIONS

Emergency: ☎ 999; no coins required. **Police:** Strand Rd. (☎ 7136 7337).

Hospital: Altnagelvin Hospital, Glenshane Rd. (☎ 7134 5171).

Counseling and Support: Samaritans, 16 Clarendon St. (☎ 7126 5511). Open daily 10am-10pm. 24hr. phone service.

Post Office: 3 Custom House St. (☎ 7136 2563). Open M 8:30am-5:30pm, Tu-F 9am-5:30pm, Sa 9am-12:30pm. **Postal code:** BT48. Unless addressed to 3 Custom House St., *Poste Restante* letters will go to the Postal Sorting Office (☎ 7136 2577) on the corner of Great James and Little James St.

Internet Access: Central Library, Foyle St. (☎ 7127 2300). Free until 1pm, £2.50 per hr. after. Open Tu-W and F 9:15am-5:30pm, M and Th 9:15am-8pm, Sa 9:15am-5pm.

ACCOMMODATIONS

Derry is home to two hostels, but budget travelers do well to indulge in beautiful and well-priced B&Bs. Most accommodations are just outside the city walls.

Steve's Backpackers, 4 Asylum Rd. (☎ 7137 7989 or 7137 0011). Down Strand Rd. 7min. from the city center; Asylum Rd. is on the left just before the RUC station. Welcome to the Derry Vortex; once you stay, you'll have a hard time leaving (the 5th night is free). This relaxed 16-bed hostel offers maps and earfuls of advice on Derry's history and nightlife. Laundry £3. **Internet access** £3 per hr. 6pm-8am, £4 per hr. 8am-6pm. £2 key deposit. Dorms £7.50.

Derry City Youth Hostel (HINI), Magazine St. (☎ 7128 4100). A sky-high mural on the side of the building identifies this large and institutional hostel located within the city walls. 24hr. access with night watchman. Lockers available; bring your own lock. Wheelchair accessible. Breakfasts £1.50-2.50. Towels 50p. Laundry £3.50. Check-out 10am. 8- to 10-bed dorms £7.50; 3- to 10-bed dorms with bath £8.50; B&B with bath £15.

Magee College (☎ 7137 5255), on corner of Rock and Northland Rd. Walk ¼ mi. up Strand Rd. and turn left onto Rock Rd; Magee College is at the top of the hill on the left. The Housing Office is on the ground floor of Woodburn House, a red brick building just after the main building. Available during Easter week and mid-May to Sept. Mandatory reservations M-F 9am-5pm. Ask for dishes and linens. Free laundry. Wheelchair accessible. Singles in 5-bedroom flats £14.10, students £11.50.

The Saddler's House (No. 36), 36 Great James St. (☎ 7126 9691). Friendly, historically knowledgeable owners make their Victorian house into your ultimate comfort zone. French press coffee, fresh fruit and cheese, and homemade jam at breakfast. The same couple also runs **The Merchant's House,** an award-winning, restored Georgian townhouse at 16 Queen St. Both houses £20, with bath £25.

Florence House, 16 Northland Rd. (☎ 7126 8093; email ray@mcginley.in2home.co.uk). Large, sunny bedrooms in a Georgian house that looks onto the university. Home to 2 grand pianos, 3 uprights, and an astonishingly musical family. £17 per person.

Grace McGoldrick, 10 Crawford Sq. (☎ 7126 5000), off Northland Rd., near Strand Rd. and the university. A 5min. walk to city center. Soothing rooms with high ceilings. Singles £20; doubles £35; all with bath.

FOOD

Excellent take-aways and cafes abound in Derry, but restaurants, mostly located around the walled city, tend to be expensive. **Tesco** supermarket, in the Quayside Shopping Center, is a few minutes' walk from the walled city along Strand Rd. (Open M-Sa 8:30am-9pm, Su 1-6pm.) Various convenience stores with later hours are scattered around Strand Rd. and Williams St.

Rhubarb and Custard, Custom House St. (☎ 7137 7977), near the Guildhall. This colorfully rustic cafe sells sandwiches (£2) and a filling 2-course lunch special (£3). Lots of vegetarian options. Open M-Sa 9am-5pm.

Cappuccinos, 31 Foyle St. (☎ 7137 0059). Green paisley wallpaper makes you wax nostalgic for grandma's house. Excellent for breakfast (£2.95 special, served till noon). Open M-Sa 8am-6pm.

Indigo, 27 Shipquay St. (☎ 7127 1011), serves flavorful, international foods in a stylish interior. Entrees £7-9, Su-W 2-course for 2 £15. Open daily 11am-11pm.

Fitzroy's, 2-4 Bridge St. (☎ 7126 6211), next to Bishops' Gate. Cafe culture and filling meals ranging from a simple chicken breast to mussels cooked in champagne. Most day meals around £5, dinners £7-12. Open M-W 9:30am-10pm, Th-F 9:30am-11pm, Sa 9am-11pm, Su noon-9pm.

The Sandwich Co., The Diamond (☎ 7137 2500) and 61 Strand Rd. (☎ 7126 6771), corner of Ferryquay and Bishop St. Big baguettes stuffed with a wide range of tasty fillings. Sandwiches £1.50-2.50. Open M-Th 8am-5:15pm, F 8am-5:30pm, Sa 8am-5pm.

Piemonte Pizzeria (☎ 7126 6828), at the corner of Clarendon St. and Strand Rd. Pizza to please all palates. Lots of happy families and favorably impressed dates. Individual pizzas £4-6. The take-away next door is 50p-£1 cheaper and open 30min. later. Restaurant open Su-Th 5-11:30pm, F-Sa 5pm-midnight.

Boston Tea Party, 13-15 Craft Village (☎ 7126 9667), off Shipquay St. Delicious cakes and incredibly inexpensive food. Outside seating is a relief in the anti-urban but cramped setting of the craft village. Full meal £2-3. Open daily 9am-5:30pm.

PUBS AND CLUBS

Plenty of pubs lie within spitting distance of each other, and pub crawls are a mode of transport after nightfall. Trad and rock can be found any night of the week, and all age groups keep the pubs lively until the 1am closing time. Many bars have cheap drink promotions during the week.

Peadar O'Donnell's, 53 Waterloo St. (☎ 7137 2318). Named for the famous Donegal Socialist who organized the Irish Transport and General Workers Union and took an active role in the 1921 Irish Civil War. Banners and sashes of all nationalities and orders cover the ceiling, while *craic* covers the ground level. Live trad nightly.

The Gweedore, 59-61 Waterloo St. (☎ 7126 3513). The back door has connected to Peadar's since Famine times. Hosts rock, bluegrass, and funk venues nightly.

Mullan's, corner of William and Rossville St. An incredible pub with idiosyncratically lavish decor, from stained glass ceilings and bronzed lion statues to plasma flat-screen TVs. Hosts excellent jazz many nights of the week.

The Townsman, 33 Shipquay St. (☎ 7126 0820). Attracts a young and colorful crowd to its surreal decorative scheme. 20 purple pool tables and an open ceiling (in nice weather) over the bar. DJs nightly. Weekend cover £5-6.

Vibe, 33 Shipquay St. (☎ 7126 6017). The Townsman's sweaty cousin where big-name DJs drop in the last Sunday of every month. Dry ice and an alternative music room. Live bands M, 2 DJs Th-Su. Cover £2-10; usually around £2 until 11pm, £4 after.

The Strand Bar, 35-38 Strand Rd. (☎ 7126 0494). 4 floors of decadently decorated space. The downstairs has live Irish music Tu-Th; the middle bar plays 70s and 80s; and the top floor is a nightclub with theme nights and promotions (cover £3-6).

The Dungloe (dun-LO), 41-43 Waterloo St. (☎ 7126 7716). 3 huge floors with a 1950s feel. Live music weekly every Tu-Sa at 11pm, including trad, blues, and rock in the upstairs lounge.

SIGHTS

HISTORY

Derry began as a Celtic holy place and later became the site of a monastery founded by St. Columcille in the 6th century. The city itself was built at the beginning of the 17th century as the crowning achievement of the Ulster Plantations (see **Plantation and Cromwell,** p. 10). After the "Flight of the Earls" in 1607 (see **Rathmullan,** p. 383), much of Ulster was left without local leaders. The English seized the moment to take land from native Catholic residents for redistribution to Protestant settlers from England and Scotland. Derry itself was granted to the London guilds and renamed on the maps as "Londonderry" to assert its new Anglo-Irish identity. The displaced local Catholics rebelled several times with no success, while sectarian antagonism grew. When King James II approached the city in 1689 with several thousand French troops behind him, the Protestant inhabitants of the city rallied around the cause of his opponent, King William of Orange; the ensuing **Siege of Derry** lasted 105 days (see **The Protestant Ascendancy,** p. 11). The siege created Loyalist heroes in the **Apprentice Boys,** who closed the city gates on James. They did so against the will of **Robert Lundy,** the city leader who advocated surrender during the siege and has been hated by Loyalists ever since. His effigy is still burnt annually at the **August 12th** ceremony commemorating the event, when hundreds of present-day Apprentice Boys gather from around the world and march around the city's walls.

Always a major port, Derry became an industrial center by the 19th century. The city was also the main emigration point in Ireland, and massive numbers of Ulster-Irish Catholics as well as Presbyterians fled the area's religious discrimination. Around the time of the Famine, many Catholics gave up on emigration and formed the **Bogside** neighborhood outside the city walls. The creation of the Republic made Derry a border city, and a Catholic majority made it a headache for Unionist leaders; it became the locus of some of the most blatant civil rights violations, including gerrymandering and religious discrimination. The civil rights marches that sparked the Troubles originated here in 1968. The following became powerful logos for Catholics in Derry and Nationalists everywhere. **Free Derry,** the western, Catholic part of the city, controlled by the IRA and a "no-go area" for the army from 1969 to 1972; **Bloody Sunday,** January 30, 1972, when British troops fired on demonstrators and killed 14 (see p. 400); and **Operation Motorman,** the July 1972 army effort to penetrate the "no-go" area and arrest IRA leaders. Although the Derry landscape was once razed by years of bombings, today the city has been rebuilt and looks sparklingly new. Violence still erupts occasionally in Derry during the marching season and other contentious sectarian events, but, on the whole, recent years have seen the relatively peaceful coexistence of Derry's Catholic and Protestant populations. Moves to mix religions in the Derry school system may someday unify civil society.

TOURS

Walking tours provide an introduction to the city's history-laden geography. These tours let you walk on top of the city walls in order to show how what lies within them has shaped what lies without.

DERRY VISITOR AND CONVENTION BUREAU GUIDED WALKING TOURS. The tourist office sponsors several well-prepared guided walks. *(Leave from the tourist office. ☎ 7126 7284. July-Oct. M-F 11:15am and 3:15pm, Nov.-June M-F 2:30pm. £3.25; students, seniors, and children £2.)*

NORTHERN IRELAND TOURS AND GUIDES LIMITED. Stephen McPhilemy intelligently describes Derry's history with vim and vigor. *(Tours depart from the tourist office. ☎ 7128 9051. May-Sept. daily at 2:30pm. Call to schedule other times. £3.)*

FOYLE CIVIC BUS TOURS. This Ulsterbus tour suits non-walkers and makes six stops, including the university, Guildhall, and St. Eugene's Cathedral. *(Leaves from the Foyle St. bus depot. ☎ 7126 7284. July-Aug. Tu 2pm. £3.)*

THE OLD CITY

THE WALLS. Derry's city walls, 18 ft. high and 20 ft. thick, were erected between 1614 and 1619. They have never been breached, hence Derry's nickname "the Maiden City." A walk along the top of this mile-long perimeter takes about 20 minutes and affords a far-reaching view of Derry from its self-contained early days to its present urban sprawl. Seven **cannons** perch along the northeast wall between Magazine and Shipquay Gates. They were donated by Queen Elizabeth I and the London Guilds who "acquired" the city during the Ulster Plantation. A plaque on the outside of this section of wall marks the water level in the days when the Foyle ran right along the walls (it's now 300 ft. away). The stone tower along the southeast wall past New Gate was built to protect **St. Columb's Cathedral,** the symbolic focus of the city's Protestant defenders. Stuck in the center of the southwest wall, **Bishop's Gate** was remodeled in 1789 into an ornate triumphal gate in honor of William of Orange, the Protestant victor of the battles of 1689. The northwest wall supports **Roaring Meg,** a massive cannon donated by London fishmongers in 1642 and used in the 1689 siege. The sound of the cannon alone was rumored to strike fear into the hearts of enemies. The huge marble platform that now stands here was built to hold a marble statue of the Rev. George Walker, joint-governor of Derry during the siege. The first statue placed here, blown up in 1973, showed him waving a fist in the direction of the site of the Battle of the Boyne and the Bogside. Its replacement was ready in 1992, but hours before its unveiling, an anonymous phone call threatened to blow the new one up if it overlooked the Bogside. The authorities backed down, and the quite defaced marble Rev. Walker II now stands in a churchyard within the city walls.

MEMORIAL HALL. The Apprentice Boys have had their headquarters here for centuries. Inside, there is supposedly a museum's worth of historical items dating back to the Apprentices who shut the 1689 city gates. Admission is strictly regulated and highly unlikely. Membership today is open only to Protestant men, although they allow women in to cook and clean. *(Between Royal Bastion and Butcher's Gate. Closed to non-members.)*

ST. COLUMB'S CATHEDRAL. The tall spire of the cathedral in the southwest corner of the walled city is visible from almost anywhere in Derry. Built between 1628 and 1633, St. Columb's Cathedral was the first Protestant cathedral in Britain or Ireland (all the older ones were confiscated Catholic cathedrals). The original spire of wood coated with lead was in disrepair at the time of the Great Siege, so the city's defenders removed its lead and smelted it into bullets and cannonballs. Today's steeple is the church's third. The interior is fashioned of roughly hewn stone and holds an exquisite Killybegs altar carpet, a bishop's chair dating from 1630, and 214 hand-carved Derry-oak pews, of which no two are the same. The entrance room of the church displays a large mortar ball on a stand. Look in the top and you'll notice a deep well in the ball. During the siege of Derry, hundreds of such mortars were packed with gun power and fired upon the city, exploding on impact. This one, however, was packed with the surrender note from King James's forces, and fired onto church grounds. Given the infrequency with which those under siege inspected the cannon balls that fell on their city, it probably took a considerable amount of time before the note was discovered. Like many Protestant churches in the North, St. Columb's is bedecked with war banners, including flags from a Napoleonic battle, the Crimean War, the first and second World Wars, and the two yellow flags captured from the French at the Great Siege. A tiny, museum-like **chapterhouse** at the back of the church displays the original locks and keys of the four main city gates, part of Macaulay's *History of England*, and relics from the 1689 siege. The tombstones flat on the ground in the graveyard outside were leveled during the siege to protect the graves from Jacobite cannonballs. *(Off Bishop St. in the southwest corner of the city.* ☎ *7126 7313. Open Apr.-Oct. M-Sa 9am-5pm, Nov.-Mar. M-Sa 9am-4pm. £1 donation suggested for cathedral; chapterhouse 50p.)*

GUILDHALL. This neo-Gothic building was formerly home to the City Council. First built in 1887, wrecked by fire in 1908, and destroyed by bombs in 1972, today's structure contains replicas of the original stained-glass windows. Among the bountiful rarities is the mayor's chain of office, which was officially presented to the city by William of Orange. Upstairs, the hall houses an enormous organ with over three thousand pipes. The ghost of Sam Mackay, a former superintendent, now haunts the Guildhall. The hall also sponsors various concerts, plays, and exhibitions throughout the year. *(Shipquay Gate.* ☎ *7137 7335. Free tours every hr. on the hr. 9:30am-4:30pm. Open M-F 8:30am-5:30pm.)*

TOWER MUSEUM. Engaging walk-through dioramas and audiovisual displays relay Derry's long history. A series of short videos illustrate Derry's economic, political, and cultural past. The whole museum deserves at least two hours. *(Union Hall Place, just inside Magazine Gate.* ☎ *7137 2411. Open July-Aug. M-Sa 10am-5pm, Su 2-5pm; Sept.-June Tu-Sa 10am-5pm. Last entrance 4:30pm. £3.75, students and seniors £1.25.)*

OTHER SIGHTS. Maritime buffs should head to the **Harbour Museum,** which features paintings and artifacts related to Derry's harbor history. *(Guildhall St.* ☎ *7137 7331. Open M-F 10am-1pm and 2-4:30pm. Free.)* The **Calgach Center,** 4-22 Butcher St., helps trace Donegal and Derry roots with an extensive heritage library and a helpful genealogy center. *(*☎ *7137 3177. Open M-F 9am-5pm. Free admission. Database search usually over £20.)* Also in the center is **The Fifth Province,** a flashy multimedia display of the history of Celtic Ulster. *(Open M-F 9:30am-4pm. £3, students and seniors £1.)* The **Derry Craft Village,** Shipquay St., was built from cast-away build-

> **I'M TOO SEXY...** In the last century, the opulent homes of the local statesmen and merchants were located within Derry's city walls. In those days, the wealthy wives of the city would order their fashionable dresses from London. When the dresses arrived, the ladies donned their new garb and met to stroll about all day long on the city walls in their new frilly frocks. The poverty-stricken residents of the Bogside looked up at the ladies on the wall above their neighborhood and were enraged at the decadent lifestyle on display. On one occasion, several Bogside residents took it upon themselves to write a letter of complaint to the London papers about the parading "cats". The press in London were so amused by the nickname for Derry's finest ladies that it stuck, and the phrase "cat walk" fell into common usage.

ing materials by entrepreneurial youth in an abandoned lot in the Bogside. The village encompasses a pleasant courtyard surrounded by cafes, kitschy craft shops, and **Bridie's Cottage,** the summertime host to Derry's award-winning **Teach Ceoil (Music House).** In summer, the Cottage offers lunchtime performances of Irish music, reading, and dance and "Irish suppers" (includes supper, *ceili* dancing, and trad sessions). Stop by **The Irish Shop** in the Craft Village for information. *(Open July 10-Sept. 30, M-Sa 9am-5:30pm. Lunchtime performances M-F 1-2pm; free. Irish supper Th only 8:30pm; £6.)*

OUTSIDE THE WALLS
Much has been preserved in the "walled city" of Derry, providing visitors with a sense of the city as it stood during the days of the Great Siege. Everything outside the walls, on the other hand, hails a new age of onrushing modernity with multiple commercial, political, and religious interests.

ST. COLUMBA'S CHURCH. Its builders intended to construct the edifice on the site of St. Columba's first monastery. Recent scholarship, however, suggests that it is on the site of the holyman's visions of Christ. Current thought places St. Columba's first monastery at the site where St. Augustine's Church now stands, on Palace St., inside the walled city. Even so, St. Columba's Church, which houses a rough copy of the Book of Kells, is worth a visit. *(☎ 7126 2301. Church open daily July-Aug. 9am-9pm, Sept.-June 9am-8:30pm. Free.)*

MAGEE COLLEGE. The university has changed its affiliation several times: originally a member of the Royal University of Ireland in 1879, by 1909 it had become part of Trinity College Dublin. It has been part of the University of Ulster since 1984. The neo-Gothic building shines among its clumsy neighbors. *(10min. east of city center. ☎ 7137 1371.)*

WORKHOUSE MUSEUM. This original building displays the history of its use during the Famine. *(Glendermot Rd. ☎ 7131 8328. Open M-Sa 10am-4:30pm.)*

RESIDENTIAL NEIGHBORHOODS AND MURALS
Near the city walls, Derry's residential neighborhoods, both Catholic and Protestant, display brilliant murals; most pay tribute to past historical events, such as the civil rights movements of the 1970s, and are less immediately inflammatory than some of those in Belfast. Many of the murals can be seen from the viewpoints on the city wall. For a key to their iconography, see p. 425.

WATERSIDE AND THE FOUNTAIN ESTATE. These two neighborhoods are home to Derry's Protestant population. The Waterside is nearly split in its percentage of Catholics and Protestants, but the Fountain is almost entirely Protestant. The Fountain is reached from the walled city by exiting through the left side of Bishop's Gate; it is contained by Bishop, Upper Bennett, Abercorn, and Hawkin St. This small area of only 600 residents holds the more interesting Protestant murals. The few Loyalist murals in the Waterside lie along Bond and Irish St.

THE BOGSIDE. This famous Catholic neighborhood is easily recognizable. A huge wall just west of the city walls at the junction of Fahan St. and Rossville Sq. declares "You Are Now Entering Free Derry." It was originally painted in 1969 on the end of a row-house; the houses of the block have since been knocked down, but this end-wall remains with a frequently repainted but never reworded message. This powerful mural is surrounded by other, equally striking, nationalist artistic creations, and the spot is referred to as **Free Derry Corner.** Nearby, a stone monument commemorates the 14 protesters shot dead on Bloody Sunday. In both Belfast and Derry, peace groups have recently organized children of all religions to paint large non-sectarian murals. "The Auld Days," at the junction of William and Rossville St. across from Pilot's Row Community Centre in the Bogside, is one of several such works. Another piece of public art, a sculpture at the city-side end of Craigavon Bridge, shows two men reaching out to each other across a divide.

474 ■ DERRY (LONDONDERRY)

Counties Tyrone & Fermanagh

♪ ARTS AND ENTERTAINMENT

Derry has a full-blooded arts scene. **Orchard Gallery,** Orchard St., is one of the best spots on the island for viewing well-conceived exhibitions of contemporary Irish and international artists' works. (☎ 7126 9675. Open Tu-Sa 10am-6pm. Free.) The **Foyle Arts Centre,** on Lawrence Hill off Strand Rd., offers classes in a broad range of arts, including music, drama, and dance; they also have a darkroom and occasional exhibitions and concerts. (☎ 7126 6657. Open M-Th 9am-10pm, F-Sa 9am-6pm.) The **Rialto Entertainment Center,** 5 Market St., looks like a tacky multiplex but is actually Derry's most prestigious and largest venue for plays, concerts, and musicals, as well as the occasional photography show. (Box office ☎ 7126 0516. Box office open M-Sa 9:30am-5pm. Tickets £2-20, student rates available.) **The Playhouse,** 5-7 Artillery St., specializes in the work of young playwrights and performers. (☎ 7126 8027. Tickets £3-7.) **St. Columb's Hall,** Orchard St., houses the **Orchard Cinema,** an intimate theater that screens a mix of art house, cult, classic, and foreign films. (☎ 7126 7789. Tickets £3.50, students £2.50.) The **Guildhall** (☎ 7137 7335) combines government and artistic functions to produce a range of shows, including jazz concerts and dance championships. Checking the local paper is ultimately the most successful means of scoping out the local arts scenes.

Feís Doirecdmcill, during Easter week, is a festival of Irish dancing, verse speaking, and music in the Guildhall with three sessions daily (£1 each). In late February, **Feís Londonderry,** also held in the Guildhall, features Irish music and a drama competition; three daily sessions cost £1 each.

FERMANAGH

Fermanagh is Northern Ireland's lake district; Upper and Lower Lough Erne extend on either side of Enniskillen, connecting to the Shannon River through a canal to the south. The northern section of Lower Lough extends to Donegal, while the Upper Lough, a labyrinth of connected pools and rivers concealed by trees, extends south into Co. Cavan. Islands surface in both lakes. Vacationers, mostly Northerners, crowd the caravan parks and the walking paths in July and August. Hiking, biking, boating, canoeing, and orienteering provide the area's excursions. The well-marked **Kingfisher Bike Trail** (☎ 6632 0121), inaugurated in 1998, connects the towns in the lake district, circling from Belleek through Enniskillen, Belturbet, Leitrim, and back up through Belcoo and Kittycloguer. A free tourist office pamphlet outlines several itineraries. Serious hikers might consider tackling the Fermanagh stretch of the Ulster Way. These 23 mi. of forested paths are marked by wooden posts with yellow arrows and stenciled hikers. Leading from Belcoo to Lough Navar, the path is neither smooth nor level, so bicyclists should think again. Take a detailed map; food and transport are scarce. The tourist office's Ulster Way pamphlet and the Fermanagh section of *The Ulster Way* (both 75p) contain detailed descriptions of the route, its sights, and its history.

A week of boating on the **Shannon-Erne Waterway** is another option to consider. The original Shannon-Erne link was built in 1846, abandoned in 1869 in favor of the steam engine, and restored for tourism in 1994 as the longest navigable inland waterway in Europe. Boats cost £15-40 per person per night on a two- to eight-person boat; most marinas on the lakes are free, there are kitchenettes on the boats, and no experience is necessary. **Aghinver** (☎ 6663 1400), **Belleek Charter Cruising** (☎ 6665 8027), **Carrybridge** (☎ 6638 7034), and **Erne Marine** (☎ 6634 8267) rent boats by the week; prices range from £380-675 per week for a two- to four-person boat to £700-1450 per week for an eight-person boat. Services are available along the way.

ENNISKILLEN

Busy Enniskillen (pop. 14,000) lies on an island between Upper and Lower Lough Erne, connected to the mainland by five traffic-choked bridges. A lively city in the midst of a large but declining farming district, Enniskillen's shops and services make it a good base for exploring the Lake District. The town will never forget the IRA bombing on Remembrance Day, 1987, that killed 11 people and injured 61.

GETTING THERE AND GETTING AROUND

Buses: Wellington Rd. (☎ 6632 2633), across from the tourist office. Open M-Sa 8:45am-5:30pm. Service to **Sligo** (1hr., M-Sa 3 per day, £7.30); **Belfast** (2½hr.; M-F 10 per day, Sa 8 per day, Su 5 per day; £6.50); **Derry** (3hr.; M-F 7 per day, Sa 4 per day, Su 3 per day; £6.30); **Dublin** (3hr.; M-Sa 4 per day, Sa 5 per day, Su 3 per day; £9.70), and **Galway** (5hr., M-Sa 1 per day, £13).

Taxis: Call-a-Cab (☎ 6632 4848).

Bike Rental: Inquire at the tourist office.

ORIENTATION AND PRACTICAL INFORMATION

Enniskillen's main streets run laterally across the island: **Queen Elizabeth Rd.** to the north, the five segments that compose the island's main street in the middle tiers, and **Wellington Rd.** to the south.

Tourist Office: Fermanagh Tourist Information Centre, Wellington Rd. (☎ 6632 3110), across from the bus station. Free giant maps. Open July-Aug. M-F 9am-7pm, Sa 10am-6pm, Su 11am-5pm; May-June and Sept. M-F 9am-5:30pm, Sa 10am-6pm, Su 11am-5pm; Oct.-Mar. M-F 9am-5pm; Apr. M-F 9am-5pm, Sa 10am-6pm, Su 11am-5pm.

Banks: First Trust Savings Bank, 8 East Bridge St. (☎ 6632 2464). Open M-F 9:30am-4:30pm. **Halifax Building Society,** 20 High St. (☎ 327 072). Open M-F 9am-5pm, Sa 9am-noon. Both have **ATMs.**

Luggage Storage: Ulsterbus Parcel-link (☎ 6632 2633), at the bus station. 50p per bag. Open daily 9am-5:30pm. Closed on bank holidays.

Laundry: Paragon Cleaners, 12 East Bridge St. (☎ 6632 5230). £5-7 per load. Open daily 9am-1pm and 1:30-5:30pm.

Pharmacy: P.F. McGovern, High St. (☎ 6632 2393), passes out pills. Open M-Sa 9am-5:30pm. Rotating Su hours.

Emergency: ☎ 999; no coins required. **Police:** Queen St. (☎ 6632 2823).

Hospital: Erne Hospital, Cornagrade (☎ 6632 4711).

Post Office: East Bridge St. (☎ 6632 4525). Open M-F 9am-5:30pm, Sa 9am-12:30pm. **Postal code:** BT747BW.

ACCOMMODATIONS

Backpackers choose between the pseudo-island a stone's throw from the downtown and the solace of a renovated stable in a country park 11 mi. from town. Have the foresight to call ahead to either and all else.

Lakeland Canoe Centre, Castle Island (☎ 6632 4250, evenings ☎ 6632 2411). Walk down from the tourist office to the river, ring the bell for a ferry, and be prepared to wait. Last ferry crossing at midnight. The hostel is on 3 interlocking pagodas on the island. Popular with youth groups. **Canoe rentals** £8 per hr. **Camping** £4 per person, includes ferry fee and use of hostel facilities. Dorms £9; B&B £11.

Castle Archdale Youth Hostel (HINI; ☎ 6862 8118), 11 mi. from town. Take the Pettigoe bus to Lisarrick, head 1 mi. left down Kesh-Enniskillen Rd., turn right into the park at a small church, and walk 1 mi. The hostel occupies the stables of a now demolished but once stately home. The park's extensive grounds have a marina, tea room, deer pen, bog garden, and miles of forested nature walks. Peacocks roam the yard. Open Mar.-Oct. Dorms £8.50. **Camping** (☎ 6862 1333) at the caravan park down the hill. £6 per 2-person tent; £10 per 4-person tent.

Rossole House, 85 Sligo Rd. (☎ 6632 3462). An expensive, spiffy option. Located in a gorgeous stone Georgian house on Rossole Lough. Singles £22; doubles £36.

Abbeyville, 1 Willoughby Ct. (☎ 6632 7033). A well-marked 10min. walk down the A46 Belleek Rd. Mrs. McMahon's flowery rooms are stocked with tourist info. Singles £25; doubles £36.

FOOD AND PUBS

The best budget option for eats in Enniskillen may be to scavenge through the many groceries that line the main street. Pub grub is a close second.

Kamal Mahal, Water St. (☎ 6632 5045). Bowls of rice round out already large portions of awe-inspiring Indian food. Lunch buffet £4.95, noon-3pm. Take-away or sit-down. Open daily noon-midnight.

Franco's, Queen Elizabeth Rd. (☎ 6632 4424). Cozy nooks, wooden tables, and red napkins hide behind the wall of plants that fronts this popular bistro. Pizza from £5.65, pasta from £6.65. Open daily noon-late.

The Crowe's Nest, High St. (☎ 6632 5252). Gas masks, swords, and other digestive aids are exhibited around this central pub-and-grill that serves a number of health-conscious meals. Huge all-day breakfast £4. Lasagna £5. Live music nightly 10pm ranges from country to trad. Nightclub out back on weekends. Cover £3-5.

Bush Bar, 26 Townhall St. (☎ 6632 5210). The middle room glows with orange light bulbs while the back room has a clubby atmosphere. Trad M 9:30pm.

Blakes of the Hollow, 6 Church St. (☎ 6632 2143). Reads "William Blake" out front. So old and red they put it on a postcard. Brightly lit for golden youths. Tu and Th trad.

👁 SIGHTS

Enniskillen Castle was home in the 15th century to the fearsome Gaelic Maguire chieftains and became Elizabethan barracks in the middle ages; these days it houses two separate museums. The **Heritage Centre** presents a comprehensive look at rural Fermanagh, beginning with a pottery display and culminating in a large-scale tableau of an 1830s kitchen. The **Museum of the Royal Inniskilling Fusiliers and Dragoons** is a military buff's playground. (☎ 6632 5000. Open M 2-5pm, Tu-F 10am-5pm; May-Aug. also Sa 2-5pm; July-Aug. also Su 2-5pm. £2, students £1.50.) The **Buttermarket,** on Down St., has been turned into a craft center filled with shops and display rooms for weavers, painters, potters, and spinners. (☎ 6632 4499. Open M-Sa 9:30am-5:30pm.)

A mile and a half south of Enniskillen on A4, **Castle Coole** rears up in neoclassical hauteur. The National Trust spent £7 million restoring it for tourists. The acres of landscaped grounds are covered by buttercups, wild daisies, and the occasional golf ball. Don't miss the addition of the servant's tunnel tour on how the other nine-tenths lived. The castle grounds are 10 minutes along on Dublin Rd.; the castle itself appears at the end of a 20 minutes hike up the driveway. (☎ 6632 2690. Open May-Aug. F-W 1-6pm, Apr. and Sept. Sa-Su 1-6pm. Last tour 5:15pm. Tours £2.80. Parking £2.) Diagonally across the street from the castle entrance, the **Ardhowen Theatre** poses by the lake shore, satisfying dance, drama, music, and film enthusiasts. (☎ 6532 5440. Box office open M-Sa 10am-4:30pm, and until 8:30pm performance nights. Tickets £5-8.)

🎒 DAYTRIPS FROM ENNISKILLEN

Ten miles southwest of Enniskillen, Florence Court and the Marble Arch Caves can be combined into a single daytrip.

FLORENCE COURT AND FLORENCE COURT FOREST PARK

To reach the estate, take Sligo Rd. out of Enniskillen, then turn left onto the A32 (Swanlinbar Rd.) and follow the signs. ☎ 6634 8249. Estate open year-round 10am to 1hr. before dusk. Florence Court open June-Aug. W-M noon-6pm; Apr.-May and Sept. Sa-Su noon-6pm; last tour 5:15pm. £2.80.

Florence Court is an 18th-century Georgian mansion. The building is surrounded by the Florence Court Forest Park, which includes an impressive walled garden. The Rococo Court once housed the Earls of Enniskillen; the third Earl left behind his fossil collection for visitors' delectation. Aside from this remnant, however, few of the original contents of the house remain.

MARBLE ARCH CAVES

Take the Sligo bus to Belcoo and follow the signposts for 3 mi.; this route uses backroads that make it a fairly difficult hitch, as does Let's Go's stern disapproval of hitchhiking. ☎ 6634 8855. Open daily July-Aug. 10am-5pm, Mar.-Sept. 10am-4:30pm. Tours every 15min. £5, students £3. Spelunkers should book a day ahead in summer.

Four miles farther on the road from Florence Court to Belcoo are the Marble Arch Caves, a subterranean labyrinth of hidden rivers and weirdly sculpted limestone. An underground boat trip begins the one hour, 15-minute tour, which leads to impressive creations sculpted by nature's weird hand over thousands of years. The reflections of stalactites in the river are not to be missed.

LOWER LOUGH ERNE: BELLEEK

Tiny Belleek, 25 mi. from Enniskillen on A46 at the northern tip of Lower Lough Erne, is famous for its delicate, lace-like china. Tours of the **Belleek Pottery Factory** feature the tradesmen in action. The visitors center has new goods for sale and old goods for show, such as "Crouching Venus." Nothing's at discount prices, however, since all flawed pieces are destroyed. (☎ 6865 8501. Open Mar.-Oct. Sa 10am-6pm, Su 2-6pm; Nov.-Feb. M-F 9am-6pm. 3 tours per hr. £2.) **ExplorErne,** also in Belleek, provides tourist info and chronicles the history and heritage of the Lough Erne region. (☎ 6865 8866. Open daily mid-Mar. to Oct. 10am-6pm. £1.)

DEVENISH ISLAND

The ruins on tiny Devenish Island are a worthwhile destination for those interested in Irish medieval history and archaeology. St. Molaise founded a monastic center here in the 6th century. Viking raids and later Plantation reforms hurt monastic life; by the 17th century, the whole congregation moved to Monea, on the mainland. Today all that remain are **St. Molaise's House,** an oratory; an 81 ft. round tower dating from the 12th century; and a 15th-century Augustinian priory. The round tower is completely intact—you can even climb to the top. **MV Kestrel** tours cruise to Devenish Island and Lower Lough Erne from the Round 'O' Jetty in Brook Park, just down A46 (Belleek Rd.) from Enniskillen. (☎ 6632 2882. May-June 1 per week, July-Aug. 1-2 per day, Sept. 3 per week. £4-5.) If you want to see only the island, the **Devenish Ferry** leaves from Trory Point, 4 mi. from Enniskillen on Irvinestown Rd. or a mile walk to the left from the Trory ferry bus stop on the Pettigoe route (Apr.-Sept. Tu-Sa 10am-7pm, Su 2-7pm; £2.25, includes ticket to small museum on island). Dress warmly, as strong winds howl across the lake.

For more monastic ruins, try **Boa Island** and **White Island,** a few miles from Devenish. The dashing duo are also of interest for their many brilliant examples of both pagan and Christian carvings. You can drive across Boa Island on the Kesh-Belleek Rd., and a ferry service based at the **Castle Archdale Marina** runs an hourly boat to White Island. (☎ 6663 1850. July-Aug. daily 11am-6pm on the hr., Easter-June and Sept. on weekends. £3.)

BELTURBET ☎049

The sleepy village of Belturbet, Co. Cavan in the Republic (20 mi. south of Enniskillen on A509), sits on a hill that overlooks the River Erne. Much to the town's surprise, recreational anglers and Shannon-Erne boaters recently put Belturbet on the tourist map, so the town went ahead and opened a **tourist office** on Bridge St. (☎ 22044. Open daily 10am-8pm.) A pleasant walk meanders down the river and across **Turbet Island,** where a 12th-century Norman fortification deteriorates gracefully. West of Belturbet, the ■**Sandville House Hostel** offers nature-lovers splendid rambles and quiet-lovers a feast of solitude. Lose yourself in a morning of canoeing through the thousand fingers of the Upper Erne; find yourself in the evening by the roaring fireplace of the converted barn. Call from Belturbet or Ballyconnell for pick-up by one of the friendly staff. (☎ 22591. Open Mar.-Nov. **Canoe rental** £5 per day. Dorms £7.50.) **Bus** service to Belturbet is relatively frequent. (To **Cavan** and **Enniskillen** 4-5 per day, 20min.) **Mrs. McGreevy's Erne View House,** Bridge St., provides a quiet night's sleep. (☎ 22289. Singles £18-20; doubles £22-26.) Stop in at **The Seven Horseshoes,** Main St. (☎ 22166), for a pint of the blonde in the black skirt among wagon-wheel chandeliers, furry hides, and stuffed pheasants. A few drinks at **The Mad Ass** (☎ 22595) and you'll bet yours on just about anything. Belturbet rouses itself a bit the first week of August during the **Festival of the Erne** (☎ 22044), when women seek the title "Huzzar Lady of the Erne," and men compete to see which man can pull the largest fish out of the water.

TYRONE

What lakes are to Fermanagh, trees are to Tyrone. In a country where trees are as rare as sunshine, Tyrone has something to boast about. This forested expanse of parks and mountains stretches from Lough Neagh to Donegal. Omagh is a quiet, pretty town with a fantastic—though remote—hostel. The tourist-hungry Ulster History Park and Ulster American Folk park provide distraction nearby. The Gortin Glen Forest park is just 8 mi. from Omagh, and quiet Gortin provides a base for hikes into the surrounding countryside.

OMAGH

On August 15, 1998, a bomb ripped through Omagh's busy downtown area, killing 29 innocent people and injuring hundreds more. Later, "The Real IRA," a splinter group of the Provisional IRA, took responsibility for the act. The bombing cast a tragic spotlight on the formerly obscure town. Yet the grotesquely violent act did not quash the friendliness of this resilient market town. Omagh is a short drive away from two major tourist attractions: the elaborate Ulster American Folk Park and the informative Ulster History Park. It sits in view of a mist-shrouded mountain range with a pine-scented forest spread across it. In the town itself, Georgian townhouses slope up the main street and abut a classical courthouse.

GETTING THERE AND GETTING AROUND

Buses: Ulsterbus runs from the station on Mountjoy Rd. (☎ 8224 2711) to **Derry** (1hr.; M-Sa 11 per day, Su 4 per day; £4.50), **Belfast** (2hr.; M-Sa 8-9 per day, Su 4 per day; £5.90), **Dublin** (3hr.; M-Sa 6 per day, Su 4 per day; £9.50), and **Enniskillen** (1hr., 1 per day, £4.20). **Luggage storage** 50p. Open M-F 9am-5:45pm.

Taxis: ☎ 8210 5050. At the bus depot, with 2 drivers per cab for evening company. £4 to hostel, £6 to Folk Park (see **Sights**, below).

ORIENTATION AND PRACTICAL INFORMATION

Omagh clusters around the south side of the **River Strule.** Cross the bridge from the bus depot to get downtown; to the right of the bridge, **High St.** splits into **John St.** and **George St.,** which are lined with pubs.

Tourist office: ☎ 8224 7831. Town maps and warm welcomes are free, but that detailed geological survey of the Sperrin Mountains with all the hiking trails and roads marked on it in all sorts of colors will cost you (£5.99). Open Apr.-Sept. M-Sa 9am-5pm, Oct.-Mar. M-F 9am-5pm.

Banks: First Trust (☎ 8224 7133) has an **ATM.** Open M-Tu and Th-F 9:30am-4:30pm, W 10am-4:30pm.

Pharmacy: Boots, 47 High St. (☎ 8224 5455). Open M-Sa 9am-5:30pm.

Hospital: Tyrone County ER (☎ 8224 5211).

Internet Access: At the **Public Library,** 1 Spillars Place (☎ 8224 4821). Walk down Market St. and turn onto Dublin Rd.; the library is in a brown building. £2.50 per hr., free M-F until 1pm. Open M, W, and F 9:15am-5:30pm, Tu and Th 9:15am-8pm, Sa 9:15am-1pm and 2-5pm.

Post office: 7 High St. (☎ 8224 2970). Open M-F 9am-5:30pm, Sa 10am-12:30pm. **Postal code:** BT78 1AB.

ACCOMMODATIONS

Commune with the sheep at the **Glenhordial Hostel,** 9a Waterworks Rd. The white building peers down on the distant lights of Omagh through a thick veil of boxed, potted, and hung flowers. The attached conservatory provides the perfect setting for an early evening chat. Call the owners for pick-up or directions for the 45-minute walk. (☎ 8224 1973. Laundry £1.50. Dorms £7.) A 10-minute walk from town, the **4 Winds,** 63 Dromore Rd., defines comfortable accommodation. Mr. Thomas, a former professional chef, provides tea, coffee, a filling Irish breakfast, and packs lunches on request. Call for pick-up or directions. (☎ 8224 3554. Singles £20;

doubles £32-36.) Pitch a tent 8 mi. (or 15min. by bus) north of Omagh a little before Gortin; **Glen Caravan and Camping Park,** Gortin Rd., provides plots in the forest. (☎ 8164 8108. £4 per 2-person tent.)

FOOD AND PUBS

The best food in Omagh is found in the pubs; **McElroy's,** Castle St. serves up sandwiches, spicy chicken nuggets, and seafood at reasonable prices. (☎ 8224 4441. Club sandwich £2.75.) Watch huge, made-to-order sandwiches materialize before your eyes at **Central Perk,** Dublin Rd. Fresh coats of bright paint and a stellar coffee menu attract friends and enemies to this hip little sandwich cafe. (☎ 8224 6236. Sandwiches £1.25-2.50. Open M-Sa 9am-5pm.) **Grant's,** 29 George St., serves a wide range of pastas, steaks, and seafood to earn scrumptious success. Dinner is pricey, while lunch fits most budgets. (☎ 8225 0900. Entrees about £5. Open M-Th noon-10pm, F-Sa noon-10:30pm, Su 5-10pm.) High atop High St., **Chinese Castle** dishes out affordable, yummy food. Takeaway dishes are £5-6; eating in will cost a wee bit more. (☎ 8224 5208. M-Sa noon-2pm and 5-11:45pm, Su 5-11:45pm.) **Sally O'Brien's,** down the street, started as a tea merchant back in the 1880s but has since moved on to stronger brews. The old tea boxes are still on display. On weekend nights, clubbers swarm the disco upstairs. (☎ 8224 2521. Cover £3-5.) They drift to **McElroy's,** on Saturday nights, to join the suits of armor and a wooden tiger on the dance floor. (☎ 8224 4441. Cover £4-6.)

SIGHTS

Five miles north of Omagh on Strabane Rd., the **Ulster American Folk Park** eagerly chronicles the experiences of the two million folk who emigrated from Ulster in the 18th and 19th centuries. Full-scale tableaux of a famine cottage, a New York City Irish tenement, and a non-cuddly bear are included in the indoor museum's exhibits. Most of the outdoor buildings are originals, including the dockside brick buildings and the 100 ft. brig in the Ship and Dockside Gallery. Live 19th-century people are on display in the 19th-century Ulster town, American seaside town, and Pennsylvania back-country village, where they answer questions, pose for pictures, and ply their trades. July 4th celebrations, farming demonstrations, craft workshops, and historical reenactments are among the frequent special events. Admission includes access to the **Emigration Database,** an extensive collection of books about Irish-Americana and emigration. (☎ 8224 3292. Park open Apr.-Sept. M-Sa 10:30am-6pm, Su 11am-6:30pm. Oct.-Mar. M-F 10:30am-5pm. Last admission 1½hr. before closing. £4, students £2.50. Database open M-F 9:30am-4:30pm. Wheelchair accessible.) The bus from Omagh to Strabane can leave you at the park (M-Sa 5-7 per day, Su 2 per day; £1.20).

The **Ulster History Park,** 7 mi. out of town on Gortin Rd., is a sort of theme park for historical Irish structures. The many replicas include a dolmen, an early monastery, a *crannog*, and a Plantation settlement (see **Plantation and Cromwell,** p. 10). An indoor museum shows you the way. Special events, such as the St. Patrick's Day festivities and early August craft fair, mark the calendar. (☎ 8164 8188. Open Apr.-Sept. 10:30am-5:30pm, June-Aug. until 6:30pm; Oct.-Mar. M-F 10:30am-5pm. Last admission 1hr. before closing. £3.75, students £2.50; joint ticket with folk park £6, £4.) The Gortin bus will stop here (M-Sa 5 per day, £1.30). The deer-infested, "purely coniferous" **Gortin Glen Forest Park** is just a three-minute walk left from the History Park. Nature trails and breathtaking views abound. (Open daily 10am-sunset. Cars £3.) Archaeology enthusiasts should check out Ireland's answer to Stonehenge; situated on the A505 between Omagh and Cookstown, **An Creagán** overflows with 44 well-preserved monuments dating from the Neolithic Period. (☎ 8076 1112. Open Apr.-Sept. daily 11am-6:30pm; Oct-Mar. M-F 11am-4:30pm. £2, students £1.50.) During the first weekend in May, born-again Celts descend on **Creggan** to re-enact the ancient **Bealtaine Festival,** a seasonal rite at which ancient livestock paraded through rings of fire.

NEAR OMAGH

GORTIN

Ten miles north of Omagh on B48, Gortin is a one-street, two-hostel town, a stone's throw from the **Ulster Way** walking trail and the **Gortin Forest Park** (see above, in Omagh **Sights**). Even with its central location, on the edge of the **Sperrin Mountains,** Gortin feels largely undiscovered. The Troubles have inhibited much development of tourism in this area, and it is only in the past five years that the blossomings of an industry have begun to appear. Enter the twin flowers of Gortin: the town's two hostels make an excellent base for a budget traveler to revel in the surrounding natural offerings. Several short walks surround the town: the **Gortin Burn Walk** is a gentle, 2 mi. walk along a twisting river toward the forest park. (It starts up a gravel road a few buildings before the post office.) Una McKenna **guides walks** of the Sperrins and surrounding areas. (☎ 8164 8157, call for details.)

Bus service from Omagh to Gortin is as regular as bowels on oatbran (30min., 4 per day, £2). The **Ulster Bank** has a **24-hour ATM.** (Open M-F 9:30am-12:30pm and 1:30-4:30pm.) The **Post office** and **pharmacy** are at the end of the main street.

The **Gortin Hostel,** located in a renovated schoolhouse, sits on the Omagh road (B48). The beds are comfortable in lofty rooms. The comfy chairs are perfect for sitting beside the fire; wood is in a shed behind the building. (☎ 01 6626 48083. **Bike rental** £6 per day for hostelers, £9 per day for others. Dorms £6.) The **Gortin Tourist Accommodation,** down main street, is more modern and is child-friendly with family room and a play center out back. (☎ 8164 8346. £7.50.) The **Badoney Tavern** (☎ 8164 8157) offers tasty meals (Irish stew, £3.50), great late-night conversation, pints, and **tourist information**—talk to Peter for the scoop on Gortin. **McSwiggen's** sells groceries. (☎ 8164 8270. Open M-F 8am-9pm, Sa 8am-10:30pm, Su 9am-8pm.) **Glenview,** down the street, fries up cheap take-away. (☎ 01 6626 48705. Cheeseburger £1.75. Open Su-Th 5-11:30pm, F-Sa 5pm-1:30am.)

SPERRIN MOUNTAINS

A little more than 20 mi. northeast of Omagh sprout the petite but striking Sperrin Mountains. Fortunately for nature, but not for tourists, only narrow and poorly marked roads make their way into the area. Walkers and cyclists can pick up the **Ulster Way** 3½ mi. east of Sperrin (see **By Foot,** p. 65). This section of the trail is over 25 mi. long: it weaves through the heart of the mountains and then meets A6 4 mi.

ISN'T IT GOOD, IRISH WOOD Drafty hostels can become cozy paradises with a roaring fire and a cup of tea. However, travelers all too often have had little experience with fires and, without the help of a firestarter, throw a log in the fireplace, light a couple of wads of newspaper, then pray to St. Patrick that the fire won't sputter out. Avoid this temptation and become the envy of every hosteler. First, gather all wood before lighting a match. Make sure to have a substantial lower layer of small pieces of flammable wood (an inch wide, a few inches long) as well as a few logs positioned on top, tee-pee style, ready to catch the lower flames. If no smaller pieces of wood exist, use a knife to scrape wood from the larger log. Twist paper into compact rolls, and place in fireplace under your airy wooden edifice. Blow gently on wood if log fails to ignite immediately. Once logs do flame up, place a few more on the fire, blow gently and close door. Dry more firewood for future use by stacking logs near your now-roaring, toasty fire.

south of Dungiven. Omagh's **tourist office** (see p. 479) sells the *Ordnance Geological Map* (£4), *The Ulster Way: Accommodation for Walkers* (30p), and *The Ulster Way* (£1); the latter details the best trails through the mountains (5 trails 10-36 mi. long). The **Sperrin Heritage Centre,** on the Plumbridge-Draperstown Rd. 1 mi. east of Cranagh, presents a state-of-the-art multimedia presentation featuring story-telling ghost bartenders, glaciation, bootlegging in the Poteen Mountains, and the discovery of gold. Try your own luck with a pan for 65p. (☎ 8164 8142. Open May-Oct. M-F 11am-6pm, Sa 11:30am-6pm, Su 2-7pm. £1.80.)

Just north of the Sperrins in **Dungiven** on A6, the **Flax Mill Hostel (IHH),** charms visitors with gas lamps, a sit-down bath, and beds covered with homemade quilts. Visitors should take advantage of the cheap, wholesome organic food available on site: the owners grow their own vegetables, make their own breads and jams, and collect eggs from their free-range chickens. Owner Herman provides history lessons and hill-walking routes. Call for pick-up, or take Derry Rd. from Dungiven, turn right after the bridge toward Limavady, and follow the signs for 2 mi. (☎ (015047) 42655. Continental breakfast £2. Dorms £6. **Camping** £3.)

LONDON

Cheap flights to Ireland often involve stop-overs in London. Long-term visitors to Ireland might take advantage of the inexpensive tickets to London from Dublin and Belfast. The center of flashy young Britpop culture, London also has Big Ben, Buckingham Palace, and the Tower of London looming in the background. Its arts scene shines, and its shops and clubs are world renowned (though beware that London's pubs close at 11pm). In between the hostel, the airport, and the ferry, you should find time to experience a dab of London's pulsing urbanity. See the currency chart in Northern Ireland, p. 396, for exchange rates. For a smashing little book packed with first-rate information on this city, grab a copy of *Let's Go: London 2001*, or its trusty glossy, mappy sidekick, *Let's Go Map Guide: London*.

GETTING THERE AND AROUND

Airports: Heathrow Airport (☎ 8759 4321; www.baa.co.uk) is the world's busiest airport. The **Heathrow Express** (www.heathrowexpress.com) travels between Heathrow and **Paddington Station** every 15min. (5:10am-11:40pm, £10); the express train departs from Heathrow terminals #1, 2, 3, and 4. London Transport's **Airbus** ☎ (07805) 757 747) zips from Heathrow to central London (1hr., £7). From **Gatwick Airport** (☎ (01293) 535 353), take the **BR Gatwick Express** (☎ (0990) 301 530) train to **Victoria Station** (35min.; every 15min. daily 5am-midnight, every 30min. midnight-5am; £8.50). **National Express** (☎ (08705) 808 080) buses run from Victoria Station to Gatwick (1hr., departs every hr. 5:05am-8:20pm, £8.50). **Taxis** take twice as long and cost 5 times as much.

Public Transportation: London is divided into 6 concentric transport zones; fares depend on the distance of the journey and the number of zones crossed. Call the **24hr. help line** (☎ 7222 1234) for help planning subway and bus travel. The **Underground** (or **Tube**) is fast, efficient, and crowded. Open 6am-approx. midnight. Buy your ticket before you board and pass it through automatic gates at both ends of your journey. Buying a **Travelcard** allows unlimited trips within the Zones for which it's valid. Travelcards can be used on the Underground, regular buses, British Rail (Network SouthEast), and the Docklands Light Railway. Available in 1-day, 1-week, and 1-month increments from any station; some restrictions apply. The **bus** network is divided into 4 zones. In and around central London, one-way fares range from 50p to £1.20, depending on the number of zones you cross. **Night buses** (the "N" routes) run frequently throughout London 11:30pm-6am. All pass through Trafalgar Sq. Pick up free maps and guides at **London Transport's Information Centres** (look for the lower-case "i" logo on signs) at the following Tube stations: Euston, Victoria, King's Cross, Liverpool St., Oxford Circus, Piccadilly, St. James's Park, and at Heathrow Terminals 1, 2, and 4.

Taxis: A light signifies that they're empty. Fares are steep, and 10% tip is standard.

ORIENTATION

London is divided into boroughs, postal code areas, and districts. Both the borough name and postal code prefix appear at the bottom of most street signs. **Central London**, on the north side of the Thames and roughly bounded by the Underground's Circle Line, contains most of the major sights. Within central London, the vaguely defined **West End** incorporates Mayfair, the shopping streets around Oxford Circus, the theaters and tourist traps of Piccadilly Circus and Leicester Sq., Soho, chic Covent Garden, and **Trafalgar Square**. East of the West End lies **Holborn**, center of legal activity, and **Fleet Street**.

The City (on the Tube map, this area looks like a bottleneck) is London's financial district. Farther east lies the ethnically diverse and working-class **East End**, the

483

484 ■ CENTRAL LONDON

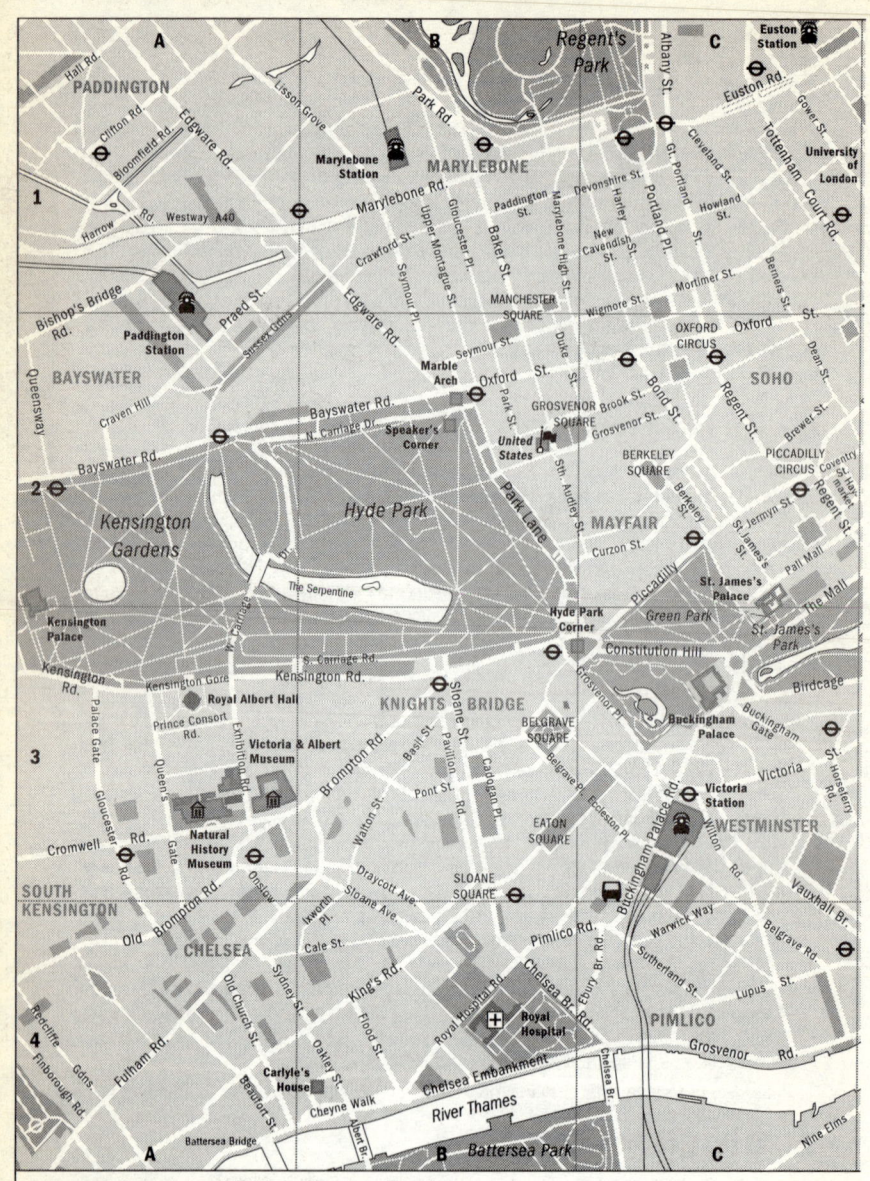

Central London: Major Street Finder

Albert Embankment **D4**	Berkeley St **C2**	Buckingham Palace Rd **C3**	Clerkenwell Rd **E1**
Aldersgate **E1**	Birdcage Walk **C3**	Cannon St **F2**	Constitution Hill **C3**
Aldwych **D2**	Bishops Br. Rd **A1**	Chancery Ln **D1**	Cornhill/Leadenhall St **F2**
Audley(N&S) **B2**	Bishopsgate **F1**	Charing Cross Rd **D2**	Coventry/Cranbourne **D2**
Baker St **B1**	Blackfriars Rd **E2**	Charterhouse St **E1**	Craven Hill Rd/Praed St **A2**
Bayswater Rd **A2**	Bloomsbury Way **D1**	Cheapside **E2**	Cromwell Rd **A3**
Beech St/Chiswell St **E1**	Bond St (New&Old) **C2**	Chelsea Br. Rd **B4**	Curzon St **C2**
Belgrave Pl **B3**	Bow St/Lancaster Pl **D2**	Chelsea Embankment **B4**	Drury Ln **D2**
Beaufort **A4**	Brompton Rd **B3**	Cheyne Walk **B4**	Eastcheap/Great Tower **F2**
Belgrave Rd **C4**	Buckingham Gate **C3**	City Rd **F1**	Eccleston Pl **C3**

CENTRAL LONDON ■ 485

Gower St **C1**
Grace Church St **F2**
Gray's Inn Rd **D1**
Gt Portland St **C1**
Gt Russell St **D1**
Grosvenor Pl **C3**
Grosvenor Rd **C4**
Grosvenor St (Upr) **C2**
Haymarket **C2**
Holborn/High/Viaduct **D1**
Horseferry Rd **C3**
Jermyn St **C2**
Kensington High St/Rd **A3**
King's Cross Rd **D1**
King's Rd **B4**
Kingsway **D2**
Knightsbridge **B3**
Lambeth Palace Rd **D3**
Lisson Grove **A1**
Lombard St **F2**
London Wall **E1**
Long Acre/Grt Queen **D2**
Long Ln **E1**
Ludgate Hill **E2**
Marylebone High St **B1**
Marylebone Rd **B1**
Millbank **D4**
Montague Pl **D1**
Moorgate **F1**
New Bridge St **E2**
New Cavendish **C1**
Newgate St **E1**
Nine Elms Ln **C4**
Oakley St **B4**
Old St **F1**
Old Brompton Rd **A4**
Onslow Sq/St **A3**

Oxford St/New Oxford **C2**
Paddington St **B1**
Pall Mall **C2**
Park Ln **B2**
Park Rd **B1**
Park St **B2**
Piccadilly **C2**
Pont St **B3**
Portland Pl **C1**
Queen St **E2**
Queen Victoria St **E1**
Queen's Gate **A3**
Queensway **A2**
Redcliffe Gdns **A4**
Regent St **C2**
Royal Hospital Rd **B4**
St. James's St **C2**
Seymour Pl **A1**
Seymour St **A2**
Shaftesbury Ave **C2**
Sloane/Lwr Sloane **B3**
Southampton Row **D1**
Southwark Bridge Rd **E2**
Southwark Rd **E2**
St. Margarets/Abingdon **D3**
Stamford St **E2**
Strand **D2**
Sydney St **A4**
Thames St(Upr&Lwr) **F2**
The Mall **C2**
Theobald's Rd **D1**
Threadneedle St **F2**
Tottenham Ct Rd **C1**
Vauxhall Br. Rd **C4**
Victoria Embankment **D2**
Victoria St **C3**
Warwick Way **C4**

Waterloo Rd **E1**
Westway A40 **A1**
Whitehall **D2**
Wigmore/Mortimer **C1**
Woburn Pl **D1**
York Rd **D3**

RAILWAY STATIONS
Blackfriars **E2**
Cannon St **F2**
Charing Cross **D2**
Euston **C1**
Holborn Viaduct **E1**
King's Cross **D1**
Liverpool St **F1**
London Bridge **F2**
Marylebone **B1**
Paddington **A2**
St Pancras **D1**
Victoria **C3**
Waterloo East **E3**
Waterloo **D3**

BRIDGES
Albert **B4**
Battersea **A4**
Blackfriars **E2**
Chelsea **C4**
Hungerford Footbridge **D2**
Lambeth **D3**
London Bridge **F2**
Southwark **E2**
Tower Bridge **F2**
Waterloo **D2**
Westminster **D3**

Edgware Rd **A1**
Euston Rd **C1**
Exhibition Rd **A3**
Farringdon Rd **E1**
Fenchurch/Aldgate **F2**
Fleet St **E2**
Fulham Rd **A4**
Gloucester Pl **B1**
Gloucester Rd **A3**
Goswell Rd **E1**

Docklands, and **Greenwich,** famous not only as the boundary between hemispheres but also as the site of the **Millennium Dome.** Back west along the river and the southern part of the Circle Line is the district of **Westminster,** the political and ecclesiastical center of England. In the southwest corner of the Circle Line, below the expanse of **Hyde Park,** are gracious **Chelsea,** embassy-laden **Belgravia,** and posh **Kensington.** Around the northwest corner of the Circle Line, tidy terraces border **Regent's Park;** nearby are **Paddington** and **Notting Hill Gate,** home to large Indian and West Indian communities. The Circle Line's northeast corner leads to **Bloomsbury,** which harbors the British Museum.

Trying to reach a **specific destination** in London can be frustrating. Numbers often go up one side of a street and down the other. **Postal code prefixes,** which often appear on London street signs and in street addresses, may help you find your way. The letters stand for compass directions, with reference to the central district (itself divided into WC and EC, for West Central and East Central). A **good map** is key. Visitors staying longer ought to buy a London street index such as *London A to Z* (from £2).

For the most part, London is a tourist-friendly city. It's hard to wander unwittingly into unnerving neighborhoods; these areas, in parts of Hackney, Tottenham, and South London, lie well away from central London. The areas around King's Cross/St. Pancras and Notting Hill Gate Tube stations are a bit seedy at night.

🛈 PRACTICAL INFORMATION

TOURIST AND LOCAL SERVICES

London Tourist Board Information Centre, Victoria Station Forecourt, SW1 (recorded message ☎ (0839) 123 432; 39-49p per min.). Tube: Victoria. Offers information on London and England and an accommodations service (☎ 7932 2020; fax 7932 2021) £5 booking fee, plus 15% refundable deposit; MC, V. Open Apr.-Nov. daily 8am-7pm; Dec.-Mar. M-Sa 8am-7pm, Su 8am-5pm. Additional tourist offices located at: **Heathrow Airport** (open daily Apr.-Nov. 9am-6pm; Dec.-Mar. 9am-5pm); **Liverpool St. Underground Station** (open M 8:15am-7pm, Tu-Sa 8:15am-6pm, Su 8:30am-4:45pm); and **Selfridges.**

Embassies and High Commissions: Australian High Commission, Australia House, The Strand, WC2 (☎ 7379 4334; www.australia.org.uk). Tube: Temple. Open M-F 9:30am-3:30pm. **Canadian High Commission,** MacDonald House, 1 Grosvenor Sq., W1 (☎ 7258 6600). Tube: Bond St. or Oxford Circus. **Irish Embassy,** 17 Grosvenor Pl., SW1 (☎ 7235 2171). Tube: Hyde Park Corner. Consular services at **Montpelier House,** 106 Brompton Rd., Knightsbridge (☎ 7225 7700). Open M-F 9:30am-4:30pm. **New Zealand High Commission,** New Zealand House, 80 Haymarket, SW1 (☎ 7930 8422). Tube: Charing Cross. Open M-F 10am-noon and 2-4pm. **South African High Commission,** South Africa House, Trafalgar Sq., WC2 (☎ 7451 7299). Tube: Charing Cross. Consular services M-F 8:45am-12:45pm. **United States Embassy,** 24 Grosvenor Sq., W1 (☎ 7499 9900). Tube: Bond St. Phones answered 24hr.

Gay, Lesbian, and Bisexual Information: London Lesbian and Gay Switchboard (☎ 7837 7324). 24hr. advice and support service.

Disability Resources: RADAR, 12 City Forum, 250 City Rd., EC1V 8AF (☎ 7250 3222). Open M-F 10am-4pm.

Pharmacies: Police stations keep lists of emergency doctors and pharmacists. Listings under "Chemists" in the Yellow Pages. **Bliss Chemists,** 5 Marble Arch, W1 (☎ 7723 6116), at Marble Arch. Open daily 9am-midnight. Branches throughout London.

EMERGENCY AND COMMUNICATIONS

Emergency: ☎ 999; no coins required.

Counseling and Support: Samaritans, 46 Marshall St., W1 (☎ 7734 2800). Tube: Oxford Circus. 24hr. crisis line listens to callers with suicidal depression and other problems. **Women's Aid,** 52-54 Featherstone St., EC1 (☎ 7392 2092). 24hr. hotline and emergency shelter for victims of domestic and sexual abuse. **Alcoholics Anonymous** (☎ 7352 3001). **National AIDS Helpline,** (☎ (0800) 567 123). 24hr.

Hospitals: In an emergency, you can be treated at no charge in the A&E ward of a hospital. The following have 24hr. walk-in A&E (also known as casualty) departments: **Royal London Hospital,** Whitechapel (☎ 7377 7000; Tube: Whitechapel); **Royal Free Hospital,** Pond St., NW3 (☎ 7794 0500; Tube: Belsize Park); **Charing Cross Hospital,** Fulham Palace Rd. (entrance St. Dunstan's Rd.), W6 (☎ 8846 1234; Tube: Baron's Ct. or Hammersmith); **St. Thomas's Hospital,** Lambeth Palace Rd., SE1 (☎ 7928 9292; Tube: Westminster); **University College Hospital,** Gower St. (entrance on Grafton Way), WC1 (☎ 7387 9300; Tube: Euston or Warren St.).

Royal Mail (www.royalmail.co.uk). Delivers twice a day M-F, once Sa. Rates within the UK: 1st class letter (next business day) 27p, 2nd class letter (3 business days), 19p. Airmail letters 36p within Europe, 45p inter-continental. Offices all over London.

Internet Access: easyEverything, 9-13 Wilson Rd., W1 (☎ 7482 9502; www.easyeverything.com). Tube: Victoria. Also at numerous other branches.

ACCOMMODATIONS

Reserve rooms in advance for summer—landing in London without reservations is like landing on a bicycle that has no seat. B&Bs are a bargain for groups of two or more, but hostels are the cheapest (and most social) option for small groups.

YHA/HI HOSTELS

YHA City of London, 36 Carter Ln., EC4 (☎ 7236 4965; fax 7236 7681). Tube: St. Paul's. Luggage storage, currency exchange, laundry facilities (£1.50 for washers), **Internet access** (£5 per hr.), and theater box office. 24hr. security. Reception 7am-11pm. Dorms £20.50, under 18 £18.70; 5- to 8-bed dorms £22.95, under 18 £19.70; 3- to 4-bed dorms £20.80, under 18 £24.10; singles £26.80, £23.30; doubles and twins (some with TV) £52.10, £44.60. Private rooms £50-135, families £40-120. MC, V.

Finsbury Residences (City University), 15 Bastwick St., (☎ 7477 8811; fax 7477 8810; www.city.ac.uk/ems). Tube: Barbican. Breakfast. Licensed bar, lounge, TV room and laundry. Rooms include phone, desk, basin, and closet. Available around Easter and summer. Max. stay 3 weeks. Singles £21.

International Student House, 229 Great Portland St. (☎ 7631 8300 or 7631 8310; fax 7631 8315; email accom@ish.org.uk; www.ish.org.uk). Tube: Great Portland St. Lockable cupboards in dorms, laundry, and **Internet access.** No curfew. Reserve at least 1 month ahead, earlier during academic year. Dorms £10; singles £30, with bath and phone £32.50; twins £44, with bath and phone £50; triples £52.50. MC, V.

YHA King's Cross/St. Pancras, 79-81 Euston Rd. (☎ 7388 9998; fax 7388 6766; stpancras@yha.org.uk). Tube: King's Cross/St. Pancras. Convenient location and comfortable beds. Dorm £23, under 18 £19.70; 2-bed family rooms £40; 4-bed £80; 5-bed £100; premium double £53; premium quad £100. MC, V.

PRIVATE HOSTELS

Ashlee House, 261-65 Gray's Inn Rd. (☎ 7833 9400; fax 7833 6777; info@ashleehouse.co.uk; www.ashleehouse.co.uk). Tube: King's Cross. Clean, bright rooms; be careful near King's Cross. No hot water noon-6pm. Generous breakfast (served M-F 7:30-9.30am, Sa-Su 8-10am). 24hr. reception. Check-out 10am. Summer prices Apr. 1-Oct. 31. Dorms £15, Apr.-Oct. £13; 4- and 6-bed rooms £19, 17; doubles £48, 44.

Astor's Museum Inn, 27 Montague St. (☎ 7580 5360; fax 7636 7948; astorhostels@msn.com; www.astorhostels.com). Tube: Russell Sq. Across the street from the British Museum. Coed dorms almost inevitable. Kitchen, cable TV. Continental breakfast. Linens provided. 24hr. reception. No curfew. Book 1 month ahead. 4-10 bed dorms £14-£16; doubles £40; triples £51. Discounts available Oct.-Mar., including a weekly dorm rate of £70. MC, V. No surcharge if greater than £30.

BED AND BREAKFASTS
WESTMINSTER

■ **Melbourne House,** 79 Belgrave Rd., SW1 (☎ 7828 3516), past Warwick Sq. Tube: Pimlico. Sparkling rooms with TV, phone, and hot pot. Singles £30-50; doubles or twins with bath £70-75; triples £90-95; quads £110. Winter discounts. Irish breakfast with cereal option (7:30-8:45am). Book ahead with credit card.

■ **Luna and Simone Hotel,** 47-49 Belgrave Rd., SW1 (☎ 7834 5897), past Warwick St. Tube: Victoria or Pimlico. Immaculate and well maintained. Singles £28-34; doubles £48-55, with bath £50-70; triples with shower £90. 10% discount for long-term stays. Winter discount. Luggage storage.

EARL'S COURT

The area feeds on the tourist trade and has a vibrant gay and lesbian population. Rooms tend to be dirt cheap, but ask to see a room to make sure the "dirt" isn't literal. Beware of overeager guides willing to lead you from the station to a hostel.

Philbeach Hotel, 30-31 Philbeach Gdns. (☎ 7373 1244; fax 7244 0149; www.philbeachhotel.freesere.). The largest gay B&B in England. **Internet access.** Continental breakfast included. Book 1 week ahead. Budget single £30, else £35-50, with shower £50-60; doubles £65, with bath £85; triple £75, £90; MC, V, AmEx, DC.

Mowbray Court Hotel, 28-32 Penywern Rd., SW5 (☎ 7373 8285 or 7370 3690; email mowbraycrthot@hotmail.com). Relatively expensive, but helpful staff is a rarity in London; wake-up calls, tour arrangements, taxicabs, theater bookings, and dry cleaning are all available. Singles £45-52; doubles £56-67; triples £67-80. Continental breakfast.

Beaver Hotel, 57-59 Philbeach Gdns. (☎ 7373 4553; fax 7373 4555). Immaculate. Wheelchair accessible. Parking £5. Singles £38, with bath £55; doubles £45, with bath £80; triples with bath £90. English breakfast served in lovely room 7:30-9:30am. Reserve several weeks ahead. MC, V, AmEx, DC.

BLOOMSBURY

Brimming with accommodations, Bloomsbury is near the British Museum and convenient to most major sights.

■ **Arosfa Hotel,** 83 Gower St. (☎/fax 7636 2115). Tube: Tottenham Court Rd. The name is Welsh for "place to rest," and it lives up to its name admirably by offering spacious rooms, immaculate facilities, and furnishings. All rooms with TV and sink. No smoking. Full English breakfast included. Singles £35; doubles £48, with bath £63; triples £65, £76; quad with bath £88. MC, V with 2% surcharge.

■ **Euro Hotel,** 51-53 Cartwright Gdns., WC1 (☎ 7387 4321; fax 7383 5044; reception@eurohotel.co.uk; www.eurohotel.co.uk). Tube: Russell Sq. Large, high-ceilinged rooms. Sparkling, spacious bathroom facilities. Free email. Full English breakfast included. Singles £46, with bath £68; doubles £65, £85; triples £79, £99; quads £88, £108. Under 13 sharing with adults £10. AmEx, MC, V.

Passfield Hall, 1-7 Endsleigh Pl., WC1 (☎ 7387 3584; fax 7387 0419; www.lse.ac.uk/vacations). Tube: Euston. Rooms vary in size; all have desks and phones (incoming calls only). English breakfast included. Laundry and kitchen facilities. Singles £25; doubles £44, triples £57. MC, V.

John Adams Hall, 15-23 Endsleigh St., WC1 (☎ 7387 4086; fax 7383 0164; jah@ioe.ac.uk; www.ioe.ac.uk). Tube: Euston Sq. An elegant if somewhat old-looking Georgian building with small, wrought-iron balconies. Singles are small and simple. TV lounge, pianos. Laundry facilities. English breakfast included. Open July-Sept. and Easter. Singles £24, doubles £42, triples £59. Discounts for students, stays of 6 nights or more, and in the off-season. MC, V.

Connaught Hall, 36-45 Tavistock Sq., WC1 (☎ 7685 2800; fax 7383 4109). Tube: Euston Sq. or Russell Sq. Quiet atmosphere, overlooking a garden. Rooms have sinks and desks. Reading rooms and laundry. English breakfast included. Wheelchair accessible. Open Easter and July-Aug. Singles £22.50; doubles £40. No credit cards.

KENSINGTON, KNIGHTSBRIDGE, AND HYDE PARK

Accommodations are a little more expensive here but close to the major sights.

Abbey House Hotel, 11 Vicarage Gate. (☎ 7727 2594) Tube: High St. Kensington. The hotel achieves a level of comfort unrivaled at these prices. English breakfast. Reception 8:30am-10pm. Book far ahead. Singles £43; doubles £68; triples £85; quads £95; quints £105. Weekly rates in winter only. No credit cards.

Vicarage Hotel, 10 Vicarage Gate. (☎ 7229 4030; fax 7792 5989; reception@london-vicaragehotel.com; londonvicaragehotel.com). Tube: High St. Kensington. Clean, comfortable. Singles £45; doubles£74-98; triples £90; family rooms £98. No credit cards.

Swiss House Hotel, 171 Old Brompton Rd. (☎ 7373 2769; fax 7373 4783; recep@swiss-hh.demon.co.uk). Tube: Gloucester Rd. Gorgeous B&B. All rooms have showers. Breakfast. Reception open M-F 7:30am-11pm, Sa-Su 8am-11pm. Singles £46-65; doubles/twins £80-90; triples £104; quads £118. AmEx, MC, V, DC.

FOOD

London presents a tantalizing range of foreign and English specialties. Indian, Lebanese, Greek, Chinese, Thai, Italian, West Indian, and African food is inexpensive and readily available. If you eat but one meal in London, let it be Indian—London's Indian food is rivaled only by that of the native land.

Yo!Sushi, 52 Poland St. (☎ 7287 0443). Tube: Oxford Circus. Delicious noodles served on conveyor belts (£1.50-3.50). Open daily noon-midnight. AmEx, MC, V.

Belgo Centraal, 50 Earlham St. WC2. (☎ 7813 2233) 2nd branch, **Belgo Noord,** now open in Camden Town on 72 Chalk Farm Rd., NW1. Waiters in monk's cowls and 21st century beerhall decor. Wild boar sausage, Belgian mash, and a beer from £5 daily noon-5pm. Open M-Sa noon-11:30pm, Su noon-10:30pm. Wheelchair accessible.

World Food Café, 14-15 Neal's Yard (☎ 7379 0298). Features a worldwide array of *meze*, light meals, and appetizing platters (£6-8). Open M-Sa noon-5pm.

Don Zoko, 15 Kingley St. (☎ 7734 1974). Tube: Oxford Circus. Made-as-you-order sushi is some of London's best. *Don Zoko* means "rock bottom," and its prices are just that. Sushi £2-4. Open M-F noon-2:30pm and 6-10:30pm; Sa-Su 6-10:30pm. AmEx, MC, V.

Lok Ho Fook, 4-5 Gerrard St. (☎ 7437 2001). Tube: Leicester Sq. Busy place with good prices and a welcoming atmosphere. Extensive selection of seafood, noodles, and vegetarian dishes (£4-8). Dim sum (£1.40-1.60). Open daily noon-11:45pm. AmEx, DC, MC, V.

The Stockpot, 18 Old Compton St., W1. Tube: Leicester Sq. or Piccadilly Circus. The cheapest place in Soho to soak up style. Open M-Tu 11:30am-11:30pm, W-Sa 11:30am-11:45pm, Su noon-11pm. Also at 40 Panton St.

Sofra, 18 Shepherd St. (☎ 7493 3320). Tube: Green Park/Hyde Park Corner. The house specialty, mixed *meze*, goes for £5.45, while other main courses will run you around £7.45-8.95. Open noon-midnight. Other **branches** at 36 Tavistock St. (☎ 7240 3773) and 1 St. Christopher's Pl. (☎ 7224 4080; Tube: Bond St.).

BLOOMSBURY AND NORTH LONDON

Wagamama, 4a Streatham St., WC1. Tube: Tottenham Ct. Rd. Fast food: waitstaff takes your orders on hand-held electronic radios that transmit directly to the kitchen. Noodles £4.50-5.70. Open M-Sa noon-11pm, Su 12:30-10pm.

Diwana Bhel Poori House, 121 Drummond St. (☎ 7387 5556). Tube: Warren St. The specialty is *thali* (an assortment of vegetables, rices, sauces, breads, and desserts; £4.50-6.20). The "Chef's Special" is served on weekdays with rice for £4.80. Open daily noon-11:30pm. AmEx, MC, V.

Tartuf, 88 Upper St. (☎ 7288 0954). A convivial Alsatian place that serves excellent *tartes flambées* (£4.90-6.10), rather like pizzas on very thin crusts, except much tastier. All-you-can-eat tartes £8.90. Before 3pm, the £4.90 "lunch express" gets you a savory *tarte* and a sweet one. Open M-F noon-2:30pm and 5:45-11:30pm, Sa noon-11:30pm, Su noon-11pm.

NOTTING HILL

The Grain Shop, 269a Portobello Rd., W11. Tube: Ladbroke Grove. A large array of tasty take-away foods and a long line of customers. Organic whole grain breads baked daily (80p-£1.40 per loaf). Groceries also available, many organic. Open M-Sa 9:30am-6pm.

PUBS

The character of London's 700 pubs varies widely from one neighborhood to the next. For the best prices head to the East End. Stylish, lively pubs cluster around the fringes of the West End. Don't be afraid to leave a good pub—doing a pub crawl lets you experience the diversity of a neighborhood's nightlife.

Freud, 198 Shaftesbury Ave. A beer here (£2-3) is cheaper than an hour on the couch. Open M-Sa 11am-11pm, Su noon-10:30pm. No credit cards.

Black Friar, 174 Queen Victoria St. (☎ 7236 5650). Tube: Blackfriars. A pub of fascinating historical interest. Carlsberg £2.35, Tetley's £2.15. Lunch served 11:30am-2:30pm. Open M-F 11:30am-11pm, Sa noon-5pm, Su noon-4:30pm.

Pharmacy, 150 Notting Hill Gate (☎ 7221 2442). Tube: Notting Hill Gate. An intriguing place for a cocktail. Open M-Th noon-3pm and 6pm-1am, F-Sa noon-3pm and 6pm-2am, Su 6-10:30pm. AmEx, MC, V.

Crown and Anchor, 22 Neal St. (☎ 7836 5649). One of Covent Garden's most popular pubs. A young mix of the down-and-out and the up-and-coming perches on kegs or sits on the cobblestones outside. Open M-Sa 11am-11pm, Su noon-10:30pm. MC, V.

Shoreditch Electricity Showrooms, 39a Hoxton Sq. (☎ 7739 6934). Tube: Old St. If you wanted to know where the super-cool go, this is the answer. Cocktails £6, beers £2.30 and up. Open Tu, W noon-11pm, Th noon-midnight, F-Sa noon-1am, Su noon-10:30pm. MC, V.

SIGHTS

The **Original London Sightseeing Tour** provides a convenient overview of London's attractions from a double-decker bus. (☎ 8877 1722. Tours daily in summer 9am-7pm; in winter 9:30am-5:30pm. £12, under 16 £6.) Two-hour tours depart from Baker St., Haymarket (near Piccadilly Circus), Marble Arch, Embankment, and near Victoria Station. Walking tours can fill in the specifics of London that bus tours run right over. Among the best is **The Original London Walks,** two-hour tours led by well-regarded guides. (☎ 7624 3978. £5, students £4.)

MAYFAIR TO PARLIAMENT

Begin a day wandering **Piccadilly Circus** and its towering neon bluffs. (Tube: Piccadilly Circus). North are the tiny shops of Regent St. and the renovated seediness of **Soho,** where a sidewalk cafe culture has replaced pornography. Outdoor cafes, upscale shops, and slick crowds huddle in **Covent Garden,** to the northeast. Paths across **Green Park** lead to **Buckingham Palace,** now partially open to tourists. (☎ 7799 2331; www.royal.gov.uk. Tube: Victoria, Green Park, and St. James's Park. Call for details of guided tours. Open daily Aug.-Sept. £10.50, seniors £8, under 17 £5.) The **Changing of the Guard** occurs daily (Apr. to late Aug.) or every other day (Sept.-Mar.) at 11:30am, unless it's raining. Arrive early or you won't see a thing.

The Mall, a wide processional, leads from the palace to **Admiralty Arch** and **Trafalgar Square.** Political Britain branches off **Whitehall,** just south of Trafalgar. The Prime Minister resides off Whitehall at **10 Downing Street,** now closed to tourists.

Whitehall ends by the sprawling **Houses of Parliament** (Tube: Westminster). Access to the House of Commons and the House of Lords is extremely restricted; queue up outside when they are in session in order to sit in the upper galleries of the Lords or Commons. You can hear **Big Ben** but not see him; Big Ben is neither the tower nor the clock, but the 14-ton bell, cast when a similarly proportioned Sir Benjamin Hall served as Commissioner of Works. Church and state tie the knot in **Westminster Abbey,** coronation chamber to English monarchs since 1066 and the site of **Poet's Corner,** the **Grave of the Unknown Warrior,** the **Stone of Scone,** and the elegantly perpendicular **Chapel of Henry VII.** (☎ 7222 7110. Abbey open M-F 9am-4:45pm, Sa 9am-2:45pm. Last admission 3:45pm, some W until 7:45pm. £5, concessions £3, ages 11-18 £2. Tours £3. Photography permitted W evenings only.)

HYDE PARK AND KENSINGTON TO CHELSEA

Hyde Park shows its best face on Sundays, when soapbox orators take freedom of speech to the limit at **Speaker's Corner.** (Tube: Marble Arch, *not* Hyde Park Corner.) To the west lies **Kensington Palace.** Hourly tours of the palace visit collections of regal memorabilia, including Court dresses. (1½hr. tours May-Sept. M-Sa 10am-5pm; £8.50, students £6.70.) Up Brompton Rd. near Knightsbridge, **Harrods** (Tube: Knightsbridge) vends under their humble motto, *Omnia Omnibus Ubique*—*"All things for all people, everywhere."* (Open M-Tu and Sa 10am-6pm, W-F 10am-7pm.)

REGENT'S PARK TO FLEET STREET

Take a break from the city and picnic in the expanse of **Regent's Park,** northeast of Hyde Park across Marylebone. (Tube: Regent's Park.) **Camden Town** (Tube: Camden Town), bordering the park to the northeast, sports rollicking street markets. **Bloomsbury**—eccentric and erudite—is known for its literary and scholarly connections, including the **British Museum.**

CITY OF LONDON AND THE EAST END

Once upon a time, "London" meant the square-mile enclave of the **City of London.** The **Tower of London,** the grandest fortress in medieval Europe, was the palace and prison of English monarchs for over 500 years. Inside, the **Crown Jewels** include the Stars of Africa, cut from the enormous Cullinan Diamond, which was mailed third-class from the Transvaal in an unmarked brown paper package. In 1483, the "Princes in the Tower" (Edward V and his brother) were murdered in the **Bloody Tower** in one of the great unsolved mysteries of British royal history. (Tube: Tower Hill. Open M-Sa 9am-5pm, Su 10am-5pm; last ticket sold at 4pm. £11, concessions £8.50.) Next to the tower is **Tower Bridge,** one of London's best-known landmarks. In the German Blitz in 1940, **St. Paul's Cathedral** stood firm in a sea of fire. (Tube: St. Paul's. Open M-Sa 8:30am-4pm. Ambulatory and galleries open M-Sa 8:45am-4:15pm. Cathedral, ambulatory, crypt, and galleries £5, students £4.)

The **East End** is a relatively poor section of London with a history of racial conflict. During the Industrial Revolution a wave of Jewish immigrants fleeing persecution in Eastern Europe settled around **Whitechapel.** Notable remnants of the former East End community include the city's oldest standing synagogue, **Bevis Marks Synagogue,** Bevis Marks and Heneage Ln., EC3. (☎ 7626 1274; Tube: Aldgate.) At the heart of the East End's Bangladeshi community is **Brick Lane** (Tube: Aldgate East), a street lined with restaurants and groceries. To reach Brick Lane, head left up Whitechapel as you exit the Tube station; turn left onto Osbourne St., which turns into Brick Lane.

THE SOUTH AND OUTSKIRTS

Lesser-known but equally rewarding treasures lie south of the river, the area currently experiencing a cultural and economic renewal. Not for the squeamish, **London Dungeon** lurks beneath the London Bridge with exhibits on execution, torture, and plague. (Open daily Apr.-Sept. 10am-6:30pm, last entrance 5:30pm; Nov.-Feb.

10am-5:30pm, last entrance 4:30pm. £9.50, students £7.95.) West along the riverbank, a reconstruction of **Shakespeare's Globe Theatre** is used for performances. (☎ 7902 1400. 1hr. tours available May-Sept. May-Sept. daily 9am-12:30pm; Oct.-Apr. daily 10am-5pm. £7.50, concessions £6.)

🏛 MUSEUMS

British Museum, Great Russell St., WC1 (info ☎ 7323 8299). Tube: Tottenham Ct. Rd. or Holborn. Close to a complete record of the rise and ruin of world cultures. Among the plunder on display are the **Rosetta Stone** (whose inscriptions allowed French scholar Champollion to decipher hieroglyphics) and the Elgin Marbles. Open M-Sa 10am-5pm, Su noon-6pm. Free, suggested donation £2.

National Gallery, Trafalgar Sq., WC2 (☎ 7747 2885, recorded info 7747 2885). Tube: Charing Cross, Leicester Sq., Embankment, or Piccadilly Circus. One of the world's best collections of Western paintings. The Micro Gallery can print out a free personalized tour. Open M-Sa 10am-5pm, W 10am-8pm, Su noon-6pm. Free.

National Portrait Gallery, St. Martin's Pl., WC2, opposite St.-Martin's-in-the-Fields. Tube: Charing Cross or Leicester Sq. Mugs from Queen Elizabeth II to John Lennon. Doubles as *Who's Who in Britain.* Open M-W 10am-6pm, Th-F 10am-9pm, Su noon-6pm. Free.

Tate Modern, Sumner St., Bankside (☎ 7887 8000; www.tate.org.uk) Tube: Southwark. Highlights of modern art. Open Su-Th 10am-6pm, F-Sa 10pm-10pm. Free; admission charged to some exhibitions.

Tate Britain, Millbank, SW1 (☎ 7887 8008) Tube: Pimlico. The Tate Gallery opened in 1897 to display British art. In time, the museum collection expanded to include modern art from all over the world. Open daily 10am-5:50pm. Free.

Victoria and Albert Museum, Cromwell Rd. (☎ 7942 2000; www.vam.ac.uk). Tube: South Kensington. The V&A is one of the most enchanting museums in London and one of the finest museums of decorative arts and design in the world. Wheelchair users should use the side entrance on Exhibition Rd. and call ahead (☎ 7942 2000). Open M-Su 10am-5:45pm plus W 6:30-9:30pm. £5, seniors £3; free for students, disabled, and under 15; free for everyone 4:30-5:45pm.

THEATER

London theater is unrivalled. Seats are expensive, but student and senior standby (with an "S," "concessions," or "concs" in listings) puts even the best seats within reach—£7-10 just before curtain (come 2hr. early with ID). **Day seats** are cheap to all; queue up earlier (9-10am the day of performance). The **Leicester Square Ticket Booth** sells half-price tickets on the day of major plays. (Open M-Sa noon-6:30pm, Su noon-3pm.) Standby tickets for the **Royal National Theatre** (☎ 7452 3400; Tube: Waterloo), on the South Bank Centre, sell two hours beforehand. (£10-14; students £7.50, 45min. before.) The **Barbican Theatre** (24hr. info ☎ 7382 7272, reservations 7638 8891; Tube: Barbican or Moorgate), London home of the Royal Shakespeare Company, has student and senior standbys for £6 from 9am on the performance day. For a mere £5, you can stand as a groundling and watch Shakespearean productions in the meticulously reconstructed **Shakespeare's Globe Theatre,** New Globe Walk, Bankside SE1. (☎ 7401 9919 for tickets. Tube: London Bridge. Box office open M-Sa 10am-8pm.)

CLUBS

London pounds to 100% groovy Liverpool tunes, Manchester rave, soul and house. Check listings in *Time Out* for the latest.

The Aquarium, 256 Old St., EC1 (☎ 7251 6136). Tube: Old Street. Ultra-trendy club comes complete with swimming pool for club kids to take a dip in. Caters to a 20-something crowd. Open Th 9am-3pm, F (garage) 10pm-4am, Sa (house) 10am-5pm. £5-15.

Ministry of Sound, 103 Gaunt St., SE1 (☎ 7378 6528; www.ministryofsound.co.uk). Tube: Elephant and Castle. Take the exit for South Bank University. The granddaddy of all serious clubbing. Open F 10:30pm-6:30am, Sa midnight-9am. Cover £10-15.

Notting Hill Arts Club, 21 Notting Hill Gate, W11 (☎ 7460 4459). Tube: Notting Hill Gate. Hard beats fill the basement dance floor. Soul, Latin, jazz, house. £3-5. Open M-Sa 5pm-1am, Su 4-11pm. £3-5 M-Sa after 8pm, Su after 7pm

The Fridge, Town Hall Parade, Brixton Hill, SW2. Tube: Brixton. Night bus #N2. A serious dance dive with a stylish crowd. Saturday's "Love Muscle" one-nighter, packs in a beautiful and shocking mixed-gay clientele. Open F-Sa 10pm-6am. Cover £10, with flyer £8.

Nu Bar, 196 Essex Rd., N1 (☎ 7354 8886). Tube: Angel or Highbury & Islington. Loads of couches make for a great lounging space. DJs spin music every night from the booth above the bar. Open M-Th 4-11pm, F noon-11pm, Sa 11am-11pm, Su noon-10:30pm.

The Office, 3-5 Rathbone Pl. (☎ 7636 1598). Tube: Tottenham Court Rd. By day it's a restaurant/bar, by night a 300-capacity club that pulls in a twenty-something crowd. Cover £4-9 on Th-Sa nights. Open daily noon-3am, some Su from 6:30am.

GAY, LESBIAN, AND BISEXUAL LONDON

London has a very visible gay scene, covering everything from the flamboyant to the mainstream. Gay newspapers include *Capital Gay* (free, caters to men), *Pink Paper*, and *Shebang* (for women). *Gay Times* (£3) is the British counterpart to the *Advocate*; *Diva* (£2) is a monthly lesbian mag.

The Candy Bar, 4 Carlisle St., W1 (☎ 7494 4041). Tube: Tottenham Ct. Rd. Three floors of women (men welcome as guests) at London's first and the UK's original 7 days a week lesbian bar. Bar open M-Th 5pm-midnight, F 5pm-2am, Sa 11am-11pm, Su 5-10:30pm. Club open M-Th 8pm-midnight, F-Sa 8pm-2am, Su 7-11pm.

The Black Cap, 171 Camden High St., NW1 (☎ 7428 2721). Tube: Camden Town. North London's best-known drag bar. Live shows every night attract a mixed male and female crowd. When the shows aren't on. Open M-Th 9pm-2am, F-Sa 9pm-3am, Su noon-3pm and 7pm-midnight. Tu-Sa £2-4, free before 11pm.

The Box, Seven Dials, 32-34 Monmouth St., WC2 (☎ 7240 5828). Tube: Covent Garden or Leicester Sq. Intimate and stylish gay/mixed bar and brasserie. Open M-Sa 11am-11pm, Su 7-10:30pm. MC, V.

Freedom, 60-66 Wardour St., W1 (☎ 7734 0071). Tube: Piccadilly Circus. A very trendy (look the part!) cafe-bar that draws in a mixed crowd for cocktails. DJs and dancing space below.

Heaven, Under The Arches, Craven St., WC2 (☎ 7930 2020; www.heaven-london.com). Tube: Charing Cross or Embankment. Biggest gay club in Europe. Open M, W, F-Sa, some Tu and Th 10pm-5am. £1-12. AmEx, MC, V.

APPENDIX

AVERAGE TEMPERATURE AND RAINFALL

Avg. Temp. (lo/hi), Precipitation	January			April			July			October		
	°C	°F	mm	°C	°F	mm	°C	°F	mm	°C	°F	mm
Dublin	2/7	37/46	63	5/11	41/52	48	12/18	54/66	66	7/12	46/55	73
Cork	3/7	38/46	124	4/11	40/52	66	11/18	53/65	68	7/12	46/65	106
Belfast	4/7	40/45	83	6/10	44/51	51	13/17	56/63	79	8/11	47/52	85
London	2/7	36/45	60	5/12	41/55	43	13/22	56/72	45	7/14	46/58	78

TELEPHONE CODES

CITY CODES	
Dublin	01
Belfast	028
Cork	021
Galway	091
Killarney	064
Letterkenny	074
London	020
Limerick	061
Sligo	071
Waterford	051

COUNTRY CODES	
Australia	61
Canada	1
Ireland	353
New Zealand	64
Northern Ireland from the Republic	048
South Africa	27
U.K.	44
U.S.	1

TIME ZONES

Ireland and the UK are on Greenwich Mean Time (GMT), which sets its clock: one hour earlier than (most of) continental Europe; five hours later than New York, New York (EST); six hours later than Hibbing, Minnesota (CST); seven hours later than Phoenix, Arizona (MST); eight hours later than Los Angeles, California (PST); 10 hours later than Hawaii; eight, 9½, and 10 hours earlier than Australia; and 12 hours earlier than Auckland, New Zealand.

GLOSSARY

For a brief history of the Irish language, see **History of the Irish Language**, p. 22. The following bits of Irish are either used often in Irish English or are common in Irish place names. Spelling conventions do not always match English pronunciations: for example, "mh" sounds like "v," "dh" sounds like "g," and "ai" sounds like "ie."

IRISH	PRONUNCIATION	(AMERICAN) ENGLISH
		Useful Phrases
Ba mháich liom point.	ba WHY-lum pee-yunt	I would like a pint.
Cann eille led' thoil.	cahn EYE-leh led-TOIL	Another one, please.
Conas tá tú?	CUNN-us taw too	How are you?
dia dhuit	JEE-a dich	good day, hello
dia's muire dhuit	Jee-as MWUR-a dich	reply to "good day"
fáilte	FAHL-tshuh	welcome
go raibh maith agat	guh roh moh UG-ut	thank you

GLOSSARY 495

IRISH	PRONUNCIATION	(AMERICAN) ENGLISH
mór	more	big, great
ní hea	nee hah	no (sort of; it's tricky)
oíche mhaith dhuit	EE-ha woh dich	good night
sea	shah	yes (sort of; it's tricky)
sláinte	SLAWN-che	cheers, to your health
slán agat	slawn UG-ut	goodbye
Tá mé i mo idirgalacht-ach bhithiúnach.	ta-MAY imah va-HOO-nock idder gah-lachtach	I am an inter-galactic space criminal.
Tá sé fluic.	tah SHAY fluck	It's raining.
Tá sé trim!	tah SHAY trim!	It's not raining!
tóg é go bog é	TOG-ah BUG-ay	take it easy
tuigim	tiggum	I understand
	Geography	
An Lár	on lahr	city center
Baile Átha Cliath	BALL-yah AW-hah CLEE-ah	Dublin
drumlin		small hill
Éire	AIR-uh	Ireland; official name of the Republic of Ireland
gaeltacht	GAYL-tokt	a district where Irish is the everyday language
inch, innis		island
slieve or sliabh	shleev	mountain
sraid	shrawd	street
strand		beach
trá	thraw	beach
	Sightseeing	
Bord Fáilte	Bored FAHL-tshuh	Irish Tourist Board
concession		discount on admission for seniors and students
dolmen		chamber formed by huge stones
dún	doon	fort
gaol	jail	jail
kil	kill	church; monk's cell
queue up, "Q"		waiting line
rath	rath or rah	earthen fort
tumulus		stone burial mound
way out		exit
	Politics	
Dáil	DOY-il	House of Representatives in the Republic
dole, on the dole		welfare or unemployment benefits
DUP		Democratic Unionist Party; right-wing N.I. party led by Ian Paisley
Fianna Fáil	FEE-in-ah foil	"Soldiers of Destiny," political party in Éire
Fine Gael	FINN-eh gayl	"Family of Ireland," political party in Éire
INLA		Irish National Liberation Army, an IRA splinter group
IRA (Provisional IRA)		Irish Republican Army; a Nationalist paramilitary group
Loyalist		pro-British (see Unionists)
Nationalists		those who want Northern Ireland and the Republic united (see Republicans)
Oireachtas	OR-uch-tus	both houses of the Irish Parliament
Orangemen		a widespread Protestant Unionist secret order
Provos		slang for the Provisional IRA

APPENDIX

496 ■ APPENDIX

IRISH	PRONUNCIATION	(AMERICAN) ENGLISH
Real IRA		small splinter group responsible for the 1998 Omagh bombing
Republicans		Northern Irish who identify with the Republic (see Nationalists)
SDLP		Social Democratic and Labor Party; moderate Nationalist Party in the North
Seanad	SHAN-ud	Irish Senate
Sinn Féin	shin fayn	"Ourselves Alone," Northern political party affiliated with the IRA
Taoiseach	TEE-shukh	Irish Prime Minister
teachta dála (TD)	TAKH-ta DAH-lah	member of Irish parliament
the Troubles		the period of violence in the North, starting in 1969
UDA		Ulster Defence Association, a Unionist paramilitary group
UDR		Ulster Defence Regiment, the British Army unit in the North
UFF		Ulster Freedom Fighters (synonymous with UDA)
Unionists		those who want Northern Ireland to remain part of the UK (see loyalists)
UUP		Ulster Unionist Party, the largest political party in the North
UVF		Ulster Volunteer Force, Unionist paramilitary group

Pubs & Music

bodhrán	BOUR-ohn	traditional drum
brilliant		great, "awesome"
busker		street musician
céilí	KAY-lee	Irish dance
to chat up		to hit on
concertina		small, round-button accordian
craic	krak	good cheer, good pub conversation, a good time
faders		party poopers who go to bed early
fag		cigarette
feis	fesh	an assembly or Irish festival
fleadh	flah	a musical festival
knakered		drunk, exhausted
off-license		retail liquor store
pissed		drunk
poitín	po-CHEEN	moonshine; sometimes toxic homemade liquor
pub grub		quality bar food
publican		barkeep
to slag		to tease and ridicule
to snog		to kiss
snug		enclosed booth within a pub
to take the piss out		to make fun of
trad		traditional Irish music
uilleann pipes	ILL-in	"elbow pipes", a form of bagpipes
táim	thaw im	I am...
súgach	SOO-gakh	tipsy
ar meisce	uhr MEH-shka	drunk
ar dearg mheisce	uhr jar-eg VEH-shka	very drunk
ólta	OLE-ta	quite drunk
caoch ólta	KWEE-ukh OLE-ta	"blind drunk"

Literature

IRISH	PRONUNCIATION	(AMERICAN) ENGLISH
aisling	ASH-ling	vision or dream, or a poem or a story about one
Ar aghaidh linn: Éire	uhr EYE linn: AIR-ah	Let's Go: Ireland
ogham	Oh-um	early Irish, written on stones
seanachaí	SHAHN-ukh-ee	storyteller
Sports		
football		Gaelic football in the Republic, soccer in the North
GAA		Gaelic Athletic Association; organizes Gaelic sports
iománaíocht	umauneeakht	hurling
peil	pell	football
snooker		a board game like pool
Food		
bangers and mash		sausage and mashed potatoes
bap		a soft round bun
bill		check (in restaurants)
biscuit		cookie
candy-floss		cotton candy
carvey		meal of meat, potatoes, and carrots/vegetables
chips		french fries
chipper		fish and chips vendor
crisps		potato chips
rashers		Irish bacon
take-away		take-out, "to go"
Accommodations and Daily Life		
bedsit		one-room apartment, sometimes with kitchen
biro		ball point pen
caravan		RV, trailer
dust bin		trash can
ensuite		with bathroom attached
fir	fear	men
first floor		first floor up from the ground floor (second floor)
flat		apartment
ground floor		first floor
half-ten, half-nine, etc.		ten-thirty, nine-thirty, etc.
hoover		vacuum cleaner
lavatory, lav		bathroom
lei thras	LEH-hrass	toilets
to let		to rent
loo		bathroom
mná	min-AW	women
pram		baby carriage
self-catering		accommodation with kitchen facilities
teach		house
torch	chock	flashlight
siopa	SHUP-ah	shop
Money		
cheap		inexpensive (not shoddy)
dear		expensive

IRISH	PRONUNCIATION	(AMERICAN) ENGLISH
fiver		£5 note
punt		Irish pound
sterling		British pound
tenner		£10 note
Clothing		
nappies		diapers
pants		underwear
trainers		sneakers
Transport		
coach		bus (long distance)
hire		rental
left luggage		luggage storage
a lift		a ride
lorry		truck
motorway		highway
petrol		gasoline
return ticket		round-trip ticket
roundabout		rotary road interchange
self-drive		car rental
single ticket		one-way ticket
Civic and Cultural		
chemist		pharmacist
garda, Garda Síochána	GAR-da SHE-och-ANA	police
OAP		old age pensioner, "senior citizen"
Oifig an Phoist	UFF-ig un fwisht	post office
quay	key	a waterside street
redundancies		job layoffs
RTÉ		Radio Telefís Éireann, the Republic's broadcasting authority
RUC		Royal Ulster Constabulary, the police force of Northern Ireland

MEASUREMENTS

MEASUREMENT CONVERSIONS	
1 inch (in.) = 2.5 centimeters (cm)	1 centimeter (cm) = 0.39 in.
1 foot (ft.) = 0.30 m	1 meter (m) = 3.28 ft.
1 yard (yd.) = 0.914m	1 meter (m) = 1.09 yd.
1 mile = 1.61km	1 kilometer (km) = 0.62 mi.
1 ounce (oz.) = 28.35g	1 gram (g) = 0.035 oz.
1 pound (lb.) = 0.454kg	1 kilogram (kg) = 2.202 lb.
1 fluid ounce (fl. oz.) = 29.57ml	1 milliliter (ml) = 0.034 fl. oz.
1 gallon (gal.) = 3.785L	1 liter (L) = 0.264 gal.
1 acre (ac.) = 0.405ha	1 hectare (ha) = 2.47 ac.
1 square mile (sq. mi.) = 2.59km^2	1 square kilometer (km^2) = 0.386 sq. mi.

ABOUT LET'S GO

FORTY YEARS OF WISDOM

As a new millennium arrives, *Let's Go: Europe*, now in its 41st edition and translated into seven languages, reigns as the world's bestselling international travel guide. For over four decades, travelers criss-crossing the Continent have relied on *Let's Go* for inside information on the hippest backstreet cafes, the most pristine secluded beaches, and the best routes from border to border. In the last 20 years, our rugged researchers have stretched the frontiers of backpacking and expanded our coverage into Asia, Africa, Australia, and the Americas. This year, we've introduced a new city guide series with titles to San Francisco and our hometown, Boston. Now, our seven city guides feature sharp photos, more maps, and an overall more user-friendly design. We've also returned to our roots with the inaugural edition of *Let's Go: Western Europe*.

It all started in 1960 when a handful of well-traveled students at Harvard University handed out a 20-page mimeographed pamphlet offering a collection of their tips on budget travel to passengers on student charter flights to Europe. The following year, in response to the instant popularity of the first volume, students traveling to Europe researched the first full-fledged edition of *Let's Go: Europe*, a pocket-sized book featuring honest, practical advice, witty writing, and a decidedly youthful slant on the world. Throughout the 60s and 70s, our guides reflected the times. In 1969 we taught travelers how to get from Paris to Prague on "no dollars a day" by singing in the street. In the 80s and 90s, we looked beyond Europe and North America and set off to all corners of the earth. Meanwhile, we focused in on the world's most exciting urban areas to produce in-depth, fold-out map guides. Our new guides bring the total number of titles to 51, each infused with the spirit of adventure and voice of opinion that travelers around the world have come to count on. But some things never change: our guides are still researched, written, and produced entirely by students who know first-hand how to see the world on the cheap.

HOW WE DO IT

Each guide is completely revised and thoroughly updated every year by a well-traveled set of nearly 300 students. Every spring, we recruit over 200 researchers and 90 editors to overhaul every book. After several months of training, researcher-writers hit the road for seven weeks of exploration, from Anchorage to Adelaide, Estonia to El Salvador, Iceland to Indonesia. Hired for their rare combination of budget travel sense, writing ability, stamina, and courage, these adventurous travelers know that train strikes, stolen luggage, food poisoning, and marriage proposals are all part of a day's work. Back at our offices, editors work from spring to fall, massaging copy written on Himalayan bus rides into witty, informative prose. A student staff of typesetters, cartographers, publicists, and managers keeps our lively team together. In September, the collected efforts of the summer are delivered to our printer, who turns them into books in record time, so that you have the most up-to-date information available for your vacation. Even as you read this, work on next year's editions is well underway.

WHY WE DO IT

We don't think of budget travel as the last recourse of the destitute; we believe that it's the only way to travel. Living cheaply and simply brings you closer to the people and places you've been saving up to visit. Our books will ease your anxieties and answer your questions about the basics—so you can get off the beaten track and explore. Once you learn the ropes, we encourage you to put *Let's Go* down now and then to strike out on your own. You know as well as we that the best discoveries are often those you make yourself. When you find something worth sharing, please drop us a line. We're Let's Go Publications, 67 Mount Auburn St., Cambridge, MA 02138, USA (email: feedback@letsgo.com). For more info, visit our website, www.letsgo.com.

Liberty, Justice, and Globe-trotting for all.

Sip espresso in Paris. Cheer the bulls in Barcelona. Learn the waltz in Saltzburg. 85 years after the Wright brothers discovered flying was easier than walking, wings are available to all. When you Name Your Own Price[SM] on airline tickets at priceline.com, the world becomes your playground, the skies your road-less-traveled. You can save up to 40% or more, and you'll fly on top-quality, time-trusted airlines to the destinations of your dreams. You no longer need a trust fund to travel the globe, just a passion for adventure! So next time you need an escape, log onto priceline.com for your passport to the skies.

priceline.com[SM]
Name Your Own Price[SM]

INDEX

A

Abbey Theatre 119
Abbeystrewery Cemetery 235
abortion 53
accommodations 55
  Bed and Breakfasts 69
  dorms 69
  home exchange 69
  hostels 67
Achill Island 336–338
Achill Sound 336
Act of Union 13
Adams, Gerry 20
Adare 283
Aer Lingus. See airlines
Ahakista 242
Ahern, Bertie 403, 405
AIDS 52, 53
airlines
  Aer Lingus 57, 313
  British Airways 58
  British Midland Airways 58
  Ryanair 58, 213
airplane travel
  charter flights 58
  courier flights 59
  fares 55
  standby 59
airports
  Belfast City 406
  Belfast International 406
  Cork 213
  Donegal 374
  Dublin 92
  Eglinton/Derry Airport 467
  Galway 313
  Gatwick 483
  Heathrow 483
  Kerry 271
  Shannon 286
  Sligo 346
Alcock, John 324
alcohol 48
All Ireland
  Championships 34
Allihies 246
Altan 29
alternatives to tourism 55

American Express 45, 47, 48
  Killarney 252
An Óige 59, 68
  Dublin 92
Anglo-Irish Agreement (1985) 19, 401
Anglo-Irish Treaty (1921) 17
Annagry 375
Annals of the Four Masters 363
Co. Antrim 447–464
Antrim Coaster 453
Apocalypse 145
appendix 494–498
Apprentice Boys 424, 425, 465, 470, 471
Aran Island. See Arranmore Island
Oileáin Árann (Aran Islands) 303–309
Ardara 369
Ardgroom 247
Ardmore 204
Ards Forest 381
Ards Peninsula 431–434
Arklow 137
Co. Armagh 427–447
Armagh 443–446
Arranmore Island 374
Arthurstown 199
Ascendancy, Protestant 11
Ashardan Waterfall 377
Ashford 142
Athlone 163
ATM cards 47
au pair 80
Aughinish Peninsula 302
Avery, Joe 459
Avoca 137
Avondale House 136

B

Ballacolla 167
Ballina, Co. Limerick 284
Ballina, Co. Mayo 339
Ballinafad 329
Ballingeary 229
Ballinrobe 331
Ballinskelligs 262
Ballinspittle 231

Ballintoy 458
Ballycastle, Co. Antrim 455–457
Ballycastle, Co. Mayo 342
Ballyconneely 324
Ballydehob 239
Ballyferriter 270
Ballyhack 199
Ballyhalbert 432
Ballylickey 241
Ballyliffin 389
Ballynahoun 165
Ballyness 381
Ballyshannon 359
Ballyvaughan 300
Ballywalter 432
Balor 376
Baltimore 235–237
Banba's Crown 391
Bandon 232
Bangor 427–431
Bansha 182
Bantry 241–242
Bantry Bay 242
bargaining 48
Barna 324
Barnacle, Nora 320
Battle of Kinsale 230
Battle of the Boyne 11, 155
Beal Ború 285
Beamish 36, 219
Beara Peninsula 240–247
bears 300
Beckett, Samuel 28, 109, 116, 129
Bed and Breakfasts 69
Beginish 269
Behan, Brendan 116
Belfast 406–426
  Albert Memorial Clock Tower 421
  Belfast Castle 422
  Botanic Gardens 422
  City Hall 419
  Cornmarket 410, 417, 420
  Crown Liquor Saloon 421
  Divis Tower 423
  the docks 420

501

Donegall Square 419
East Belfast 420
The Falls 423
Giant's Ring 422
The Golden Mile 421
Grand Opera House 421, 425
Linen Hall Library 412, 420
Milltown Cemetery 424
murals 423
North Belfast 422
Orange Hall 424
peace line 423
Pub Crawl 417
Queen's University 410, 424
Sandy Row 424
Shankill 424
South Belfast 422
West Belfast 410, 423, 424
Belleek 477
Belleek Woods 341
Bellharbor 300
Belmullet 338
Belturbet 478
Belvedere House 163
Belvedere Trail 163
Benbulben 344, 352
Bere Island 245
Berkeley, Bishop George 11
bicycles 64
Big Ben 491
Birr 166
blaa 35, 208
Black and Tans 17
Black Fort (Dún Dúchathair) 308
black pudding 218
Blackrock 127, 157
Blair, Tony 402
Blarney 223–225
Blarney Stone 223
Blasket Islands 269
Blessington 143
blood sacrifice 16
Bloody Foreland 377, 378
Bloody Sunday 400, 465, 470, 473
Bloomsday 120
Blues Festival 190
bodhrán 36, 324
bogs 70
Boland, Eavan 28
Böll, Heinrich 338
Bolus Head 262

Book of Durrow 8, 109
Book of Invasions 24, 241
Book of Kells 8, 109, 151, 152
Book of Lismore 186
Book of the Dun Cow 165
Boole, George 222
Bord Fáilte 43
border checkpoints 397
Ború, Brian 285, 445
Boyd, Hugh 456
Boyle 355–357
Boyle, Robert 186
Boyne valley 148
Brandon 265
Brannon, Josh 375
Bray 130–131
Bray Head 261
breatheamh 23
breweries
  Guinness 114
  Smithwicks 175
Brian Ború 387
British Midland Airways. See airlines
British Museum 491, 492
British rule and the Division of Ireland 397
Brooke, Sir Basil 398
Brown, Arthur 324
Brú na Bóinne 148
Bruckless 364
Bruton, John 20
B-Specials 399, 424
Buckfast tonic 445
Buckingham Palace 490
Bull, Duncan the 458
Bunbeg 377
Buncrana 388
Bundoran 358
Bunratty 284
Burke, Edmund 11, 109
Burncourt 182
Burns, Monty 264
The Burren 298–302, 319
Burtonport 373
Bus Éireann 60, 61
Buses 60, 61
Bushmills Irish Whiskey 36, 460
Butt, Isaac 14
butter
  preserved bog 221
  terrifying preserved bog 335

C

Caha Mountains 241

Cáherconree 271
Caherdaniel 263
Cahersiveen 259
Cahir 181
calling cards 73
camogie. See sports
camping 70
Cape Clear Island 235, 237
Co. Carlow 170–178
Carlingford 158
Carlow 177–178
Carndonagh 390
Carney 353
Carraroe 324
Carrick 366
Carrick-a-rede Island 458
Carrick-on-Shannon 353–355
Carrigaholt 293
Carron 299, 300
Carrowkeel 384
Carrowmore 351
cars 62
  rental 63
Carson, Edward 398
Casement, Roger 16
cash cards 47
Cashel, Co. Donegal 367
Cashel, Co. Mayo 338
Cashel, Co. Tipperary 179
Castlebar 335
Castleblayney 160
Castlegregory 271
Castlepollard 162
Castletownbere 244–245
Castletownshend 233, 234
Catholic Church 18
"Cattle Raid of Cooley" 24, 157
Causeway Coast 453–464
Co. Cavan 153, 398, 427, 475, 478
ceasefire (1997) 402
Ceide Cliffs 342
Ceide Fields 342
céilí 30
Celbridge 145
Celtic crosses 8
changing money 44
Chapeltown 261
Chaplin, Charlie 262
Charles I 10
Charlestown 343
charter flights 58
Chieftains 29
children and travel 78
Christ Church Cathedral

INDEX ■ 503

113
Church of Ireland
 (Protestant) 10, 15, 25
Churchill, Winston 399
Cill Rónáin 306
cinema. See film
Cirrus 48
Citicorp 47
civil war 17
Clancy, Tom 102
Clancy, Willie 294
Clannad, 376
Co. Clare 277, 284–303
Clare Coast 289–299
Clare Island 335
Clifden 324
Cliffs of Moher 295, 299
climate 2, 494
Cloghane 265
Clogheen 185
Clonakilty 232–233
Clonbur 332
Clonmacnois 165
Clonmany 389
Clonmel 182
Cloughey 432
Cobh 226–227
coddle 35
Collins, Michael 17, 137, 232
Collinstown 163
Columbus, Christopher 320
Columcille 371
Comeragh Mountains 185
Conchobar, King of Ulster 24
Confederation of Kilkenny 10
Cong 330–332
Connacht 1
The Connemara 319, 323–330
Connemara gaeltacht 323
Connemara National Park 328
Connolly, James 15, 111, 335
consulates 40
contraceptives 53
converting currency 44
Cooley Peninsula 157–159
Cooper, Ivan 399
Copeland Islands 431
Co. Cork 211–247
Cork 213–223
 accommodations 217
 entertainment 222
 food 218

getting there 213
music and clubs 220
Old City 220
orientation and practical information 216
pubs 219
sights 220
Cork-Swansea Ferries 60
Corofin 289
Cosgrave. W.T. 18
Costelloe 323
Council Travel 57
courier flights 59
Covent Garden 490
craic 36, 496
Craig, James 398
Craigavon 427
Crawfordsburn 431
credit cards 47
Croaghaun Cliffs 338
Croaghaun Mountain 336, 338
Crohy Head 372, 373
Croke Park 119
Crolly 376
Cromane Beach 259
Cromwell, Oliver 10
 and his drunken soldiers 189
 being devious 200
 drowning priests 328
 eating and drinking 432
 his mercenaries 355
 kicking out monks 352
 philosophical contemplation 298
 pyromaniac 256
 rejected for Good Landlord award 213
 stealing things 151
 turns up in Ireland 11
 victory over Munster 256
Crookedwood 163
Crookhaven 240
crubeen 35
Cruit Island 374
Cúchulainn 24
Culdaff 391
Cultra 426
The Curragh 147
currency exchange 44
Current Issues 20
Cushendall 450
Cushendun 452, 453
customs 44
cwms 185
cycling 64

D

Dáil 18, 111
Dancing at Lughnasa 370
DART 84
de Clare, Richard. See Strongbow
de Courcy, John 438
de Gaulle, Charles 264
de Valera, Éamon 17, 114
The de Valera Era 18
Defenders 12
Deputy Prime Minister 18
Co. Derry 447, 465–474
Derry 465–474
 Bogside 467
 Fountain 467
 Magee College 473
 pubs and clubs 469
 Tower Museum 472
 Waterside 467, 473
Derrybeg 378
Derryinver 329
Derrynane House 263
Derrynane National Park 263
Derryveagh Mountains 377, 379
Desmond Castle 231, 283
Devenish Island 477, 478
devil
 his penis 368
 stuck 392
 sounds gross, doesn't it?
Devil's Bridge 392
Devilsmother Mountains 330
Dichu 437
dietary concerns 78
Dingle 265–268
Dingle Bay 265
Dingle Ocean World 268
Dingle Peninsula 265–276
disabilities 77
disabled travelers 77
diseases 52
distilleries
 Bushmills 460
 Jameson 225
divorce 21
Doagh Island 389
Dodo Terrace 432
Dog's Bay 324
Dolmen of the Four Maols 341
dolphins 265
Don Quixote 180
Donaghadee 431

504 ■ INDEX

Co. Donegal 357–393
Donegal gaeltacht 372–379
Donegal Town 360–363
Dooagh 336, 337
Doolin 296
Doorus Peninsula 302
dorms 69
Co. Down 427–443
Downhill 464
Downing Street Declaration 401
Downpatrick 435
Downpatrick Head 342
Dowth 148
Doyle, Roddy 28
driving permits 63
Drogheda 153
drugs 48
Co. Dublin 82–127
Dublin 84–123
  Abbey Theatre 119
  Bloomsday 120
  Casino Marino 118
  Christ Church Cathedral 113
  cinema 120
  Croke Park 119
  Custom House 117
  Garden of Remembrance 116
  General Post Office 116
  Grafton Street 102, 110
  Guinness brewery 114
  Kilmainham Gaol 114
  Merrion Square 111
  National Concert Hall 119
  North Side 91, 115
  O'Connell St. 98
  Phoenix Park 91, 94
  Pub Crawl 102
  St. Patrick's Cathedral 114
  St. Stephen's Green 91
  South Side 91, 109
  Temple Bar 91, 100, 113
  Theatre Festival 121
  Trinity College 91, 109
  Trinity College Walking Tour 108
  Writers' Museum 116
  Zoo 118
Dugort 338
dulse 457
Dún Aengus (Dún Aonghasa) 307
Dún An Óir 270
Dún Briste 342
Dún Dúchathair 308
Dún Laoghaire 127–131
Dunaff Head 389
Dunbrody Abbey 199
Duncannon 200
Dundalk 156
Dunfanaghy 381
Dungarvan 203
Dungloe 372
Dunkineely 364
Dunlewy 377
Dunmanway 229
Dunmore Cave 176
Dunmore East 201
Dunquin 268
Dunree Head 389
Dursey Island 246

E

Earls of Kildare 9
East Inishowen 392–394
East Munster Way 184
Easter Rising 16, 114
Eastern Ireland 133–169
electronic banking 47
Elizabeth I 12, 36, 270, 471
email 75
Emain Macha 24, 446
embassies 40
  foreign in Ireland 40
  in the UK 40
  London 486
the Emergency 18
Emmett, Robert 109
Ennis 286–289
Enniscorthy 188–190
Enniscrone 341
Enniskerry 142
Enniskillen 475
entrance requirements 41
environmentally responsible tourism 72
Enya 375
Errigal Mountain 377
Errisbeg Mountain 324
Eurailpass 62
Eurolines 60
European Union 19
exchange 44
Exploris Aquarium 434
Eyeries 247

F

Fair Head 453, 458
Falcarragh 380
Falls Road 423
the Famine 14
  murals depicting 423
Fanad Peninsula 382–384
Fanore 301
Far and Away 265, 268
Father Murphy 190
FedEx 48, 73
Fenians 15
Co. Fermanagh ??–477, 477–??
ferries 59
  Ballycastle 455
  Belfast 407
  Cork-Swansea 60
  Larne 447
festivals and holidays 37
feudalism 9
Fianna Fáil 18
Fiddler's Green Festival 443
The Field 330
Field Day movement 29
fili 23
film 33
  festivals 32
financial matters 44
finding your mate
  Johnston's Hostel 301
  Lisdoonvarna Match Making Festival 298
  Mullingar International Bachelor Competition 162
  Rose of Tralee Festival 276
Fine Gael 18
Fir Bolg 24
first
  electrical lighthouse in Ireland 431
  indoor barbeque in Ireland 259
  nonstop transatlantic flight 324
  Protestant Cathedral in British Isles 471
fishing spots 160, 162, 163, 182, 285, 286, 322, 341, 353, 366, 373, 457, 478
FitzGerald, Garret 19, 401
FitzGerald, Thomas 10
fjords, pining for 330
Flaherty, Robert 305
fleadh 30, 496
Flight of the Earls 383, 388
Florence Court 477
food

blaa 35, 208
black pudding 35, 218, 233
colcannon 34
crubeen 35
dulse 457
potatoes 34
yellow-man 457
Food and Drink 34
Fore Trail 162
forest parks
  Castlewellan 442
  Connemara National Park 328
  Crawfordsburn 431
  Curraghchase 283
  Glenariff 449
  Glenarm 449
  Glengarriff 243
  Lough Key 354
  Tollymore 441
Formorians 376
Forty Foot Men's Bathing Place 129
Fota Island 227
Free Derry 400, 470, 473
French, Percy 440

G

Gaelic Athletic Association (GAA) 15, 33
Gaelic football. See sports
Gaelic League 15
gaeltachta
  Connemara 323
  Donegal 372
  Glen Rd., Belfast 424
  pub language 373
Galty Mountains 182
Galtymore, 182
Co. Galway 313–330
Galway 313–321
  Newcastle 314
  The Claddagh 320
  Galway Hooker Festival and Traditional Boat Regatta 434
  Renmare 314
  Salthill 316, 320
  Shantallo 314
Gap of Dunloe 257
Garda Siochana 17
Garden of Remembrance 116
Garinish Island 243–244
Garron Point 450
gay and lesbian rights 21
gay travelers 77

genealogy
  Áistan Cill Cartha, Kilcar 366
  Ancestor Research Centre, Monaghan 159
  Calgach Centre, Derry 472
  Cashel, Co. Tipperary 180
  Clare Heritage Centre 289, 293
  Clew Bay Heritage Centre, Westport 335
  Donegal Ancestry Centre 382
  Dun Ulun House, Slieve League 365
  Emigration Database, Omagh 480
  Family Heritage Center, Wicklow 136
  Linen Hall Library, Belfast 412
  National Library, Dublin 112
  Public Record Office, Belfast 412
  St. Connell's Museum and Heritage Centre, Glenties 371
General Delivery 72
Getting Around 60–66
  safety 50
giant babies 460
giant lobster clutching a Guinness 262
Giant's Causeway 459
giardia 52
Glandore 233
Glen Head 368
Glen of Aherlow 182
Glen Tor 376
Glenariff 449
Glenariff Forest Park 449
Glenarm 448
Glenarm Forest 449
Glencolmcille 367–368
Glendalough 138
Glengarriff 243
Glengarriff and Garinish Island 243–244
Glengesh Pass 368
Glens of Antrim 448–453
  Glenaan 452
  Glenariff 449
  Glenarm 448
Glenties 370
Glenvar 383
Glenveagh National Park 376, 379
Glorious Revolution 11
glossary 494
GO25 card 43
Gogarty, Oliver St. John 128
Goleen 240
golf 295, 390
Gonne, Maud 125
Good Friday Agreement 402, 403
Gort 302
Gorteen 324
Gortin Glen Forest Park 480
Gortmore 324
Gougane Barra Forest 229
Government of Ireland Act 17, 398
Graigue 185
Granuaile. *See* O'Malley, Grace
grave of the black nun 457
Great Blasket 269
Greencastle 393
Gregory, Lady Augusta 27, 111, 119, 302, 303
Grey Abbey 432
Grianán Ailigh 387
Guinness 36
  brewery 114
  Jazz Festival 223
  nuns drinking 385
  Roaring 1920s Festival 254
Guinness, Arthur 114
Gweedore 376–379

H

Hackettstown. 142
Hall, Derrick 378
harp 30
health 51
  AIDS 53
  sexually transmitted diseases 52
  women 53
Heaney, Seamus 29, 165
hedge schools 12
Hell's Hole 392
Henry II 9
Henry VIII 10
high crosses 8
hiking
  see also forest parks 254
  see also trails 65
hiking equipment 70
Hill of Tara 149
Hill, Derek 380

INDEX

HINI (Hostelling International Northern Ireland) 68, 411
history 7–22
  Northern Ireland 397–406
hitching 66
HIV 52
holidays and festivals 37
Holywood 430
home exchange 69
Home Rule 398
Hook Head 200
The Hook Peninsula 198–200
hookers 320
Hopkins, Gerard Manley 112
Horn Head 381
Hostelling International (HI) 67
hostels 67
Hoverspeed SeaCat 60
Howth 124
Hume, John 399
hunger strikes 400
Hungry Hill 245
hurling. See sports
Hyde, Douglas 22

I

Iarnród Éireann (Irish Rail) 62
identification 42
IHH (Independent Holiday Hostels) 68
Inchagoill 323
Inchydoney Beach 233
Independence and Civil War 17
Independent Holiday Hostels (IHH) 68
Inishark 328
Inishbofin 327
Inisheer (Inis Oírr) 309
Inishmaan 308
Inishmaan (Inis Meáin) 308
Inishmore (Inis Mór) 305, 308
Inishnabro 269
Inishowen Head 392
Inishowen Peninsula 386–393
Inishtooskert 269
Inishturk 328
Inishvickillane 269
Inniskeel Island 371

insurance 53
International Student Identity Card (ISIC) 42
International Teacher Identity Card 43
International Youth Discount Travel Card 43
Internet 75
Inverin 305, 324
IRA. See Irish Republican Army
Irish Civil War 17, 117, 211, 242
Irish coffee 36
Irish dancing 30
Irish Derby 147
Irish Ferries 60
Irish film 32
Irish Jewish Museum 112
Irish Literary Revival 26
Irish music 29
Irish National Heritage Park 194
Irish pubs 36
Irish Rail 62
Irish Republican Army (IRA) 17, 20, 398, 401, 405
Irish Republican Brotherhood. See Fenians
Irish Supremacy Act 10
Irish Tourist Board. See Bord Fáilte
Irish Volunteers 16
ISIC 43, 59, 62, 92
ITIC card 43
Iveragh Peninsula 257

J

James II 11, 12, 230, 465, 470
James Joyce 128
Jameson Irish Whiskey 36, 225
Jealous Wall 163
Jerpoint Abbey 176
Jordan, Neil 32
Joyce, James 27, 107, 111, 112, 116, 120
  see also Ulysses

K

Kavanaugh, Patrick 28, 116
Kearney 432
Kearney, Kate 257
Keel 337
Keem Bay 336
Kells, Book of 151

Kenmare 248–250
Kent, Rockwell 368
Co. Kerry 248–276
Kerry the Kingdom 274
Kerrykeel 384
Kilbeggan 163
Kilbroney Park 443
Kilcar 365
Co. Kildare 144–147
Kildare 145–147
Kilfenora 299
Kilkee 292
Co. Kilkenny 170–177
Kilkenny 170–176
Kilkieran 323
Killala 342
Killala Bay 341
Killaloe 284
Killarney 250–254
Killarney National Park 254–257
Killary Harbour 330
Killimer 276
Killiney 127
Killnaboy 300
Killorglin 258
Killybegs 364
Kilmainham Gaol 17, 114
Kilmore Quay 196
Kilmurvy 306
Kilrane 195
Kilronan 306
Kilrush 289
Kincasslagh 374
Kinnitty 167
Kinsale 230–232
Kinvara 301
Knightstown 260
Knock 342
Knock Hill 328
Knockalla Mountains 382
Knockamany Bens 391
Knockgarra 302
Knockmealdown Gap 185
Knockmealdown Mountains 185
Knockmealdown Peak 185
Knockmore Mountain 335
Knocknarea 344
Knocknarea Mountain 351
Knowth 148
kosher 79
Kramer, Cosmo 241

L

Lahinch 294
lakes and reservoirs
  Bay Loch 185

INDEX ■ 507

Belfast Lough 410
Ben Crom 438, 441
Coole Lake 303
Dunlewey Lake 377
Lake
 Eekenhoolikeaghaun 244
Lough Anney 371
Lough Avaul 244
Lough Corrib 319, 322, 330
Lough Derg, Co. Donegal 284, 363
Lough Ennell 163
Lough Erne 478
Lough Eske 363
Lough Gill 352
Lough Hyne 236
Lough Keel 377
Lough Key 355
Lough Leane 256
Lough Mask 322, 332
Lough Muckno 160
Lough na Cranagh 453
Lough Neagh 427, 447
Lough Rynn 355
Lough Swilly 382
Loughareema 453
Silent Valley 438, 441
Strangford Lough 431, 432
Lakes of Killarney 254
 Meeting of the Waters 256
Land League 15
language 494
Lanyon, Charles 421
Co. Laois 161
Laragh 139
largest
 cormorant colony in Ireland 458
 egg in the world 118
 operating windmill in Britain or Ireland 275
 waterfall in Ireland 131
Larkin, James 15, 115
Larne 447
Lauragh 244
Leannan Estuary 382
Lecale 434–438
Leenane 330
Leinster 1
Co. Leitrim 353–355
Lemass, Sean 399
Lenan Head 389
Leprechaun of Slieve Foy 159, 430

leprechauns 25, 159, 452
lesbian travelers 77
Letterfrack 329
Letterkenny 384–386
Lewis, C.S. 431
life and times 7–23
Co. Limerick 277–285
Limerick 277–283
Liscannor 295
Lisdoonvarna 299, 300
Lismore 185
Liss Ard Experience 235
Listowel 276
Liszt, Franz 431
literature 23–29
little people 452
Locke's Distillery 163
London 483–493
London Tourist Board Information Centre 486
Londonderry. See Derry City
Co. Longford 161
lost passports 41
Lough Corrib 322
Lough Derg 284
 soup 363
Loughcrew Cairns 162
Loughros Point 370
Louisburgh 335
Co. Louth 153–159
Lugh 376
Lullymore 147
Lurigethan Hill 450, 452
Lusitania 226, 230, 232, 238
Lyme disease 52

M

Maam 323
Maamturks 322, 323, 329
Macgillycuddy's Reeks 255
Queen Macha 25, 446
MacNeice, Louis 29
Macroom 229
madman's window 449
Maghera Caves 370
Magheraroarty 378
Maharees Peninsula 271
mail 72
Major, John 401
Makemie, Francis 382
Malahide 126
Malin Head 391–392
Malinbeg 368
Mamore Gap 389
Man of Aran 305
Manannan McLir 393
mangonel 282

Marble Arch Caves 477
marching season 403, 423
Martello towers 13
MasterCard 47
Maundy Money 110
Maynooth 144
Co. Mayo 330–343
Maze Prison 405
McCool, Finn 460
McCormack, John 165
McCourt, Frank 29
McDyer, Father James 367
McShane, Dermot 402
measurements 498
Co. Meath 147–153
Queen Mebdh of Connacht 24, 389
media 33
medical assistance 51
Meenahalla 371
Mellifont Abbey 156
Midleton 225
Milford 382
Millisle 432
Milltown Cemetary, Belfast 424
Milltown Malbay 294
Minority Travelers 78
Mitchel, John 14
Mitchell principles 401
Mitchell, George 401
Mitchelstown Caves 182
Mizen Head 240
Mizen Head Peninsula 238–240
Model Mugging 50
Modern Writers in Northern Ireland 29
Co. Monaghan 153, 159–161
Monasterboice 156
monastic cities 8
money 44
Monkstown 127
Moore, Christy 31, 343
Moore, Thomas 25, 109
mopeds 64
Morrison, Van 31
motorcycles 64
mountains
 Croagh Patrick 335
 Ox 341
Mountcharles 364
Mountrath 167
Mountstewart 432
Mourne Mountains 427, 438, 440
Mourne Wall 441

508 ■ INDEX

Moville 393
Mowlam, Mo 402
Muckish Mountain 381
Muckross House 256
Muldoon, Paul 421
Mullantayboyne 371
Mullet Peninsula 338
Mullingar 161
Mulroy Bay 382, 383
Multyfarnham 162
Munster 1
Murlough 442
Murlough Bay 453
Murphy's 36, 219
Murrisk 335
music
 rock, punk, and pop 31
 trad 29
Musical Bridge 341

N

National 1798 Visitor Centre 189
National Concert Hall 119
Nationalists 397
Natterjack toad 271
Navan Fort 446
New Lake 381
New Ross 197
New Year's Day 1969 399
Newcastle 185, 438
Newgrange 148
Newtownards 431
North Inishowen 390–392
North Mayo Sculpture Trail 342
Northern Beara Peninsula 246–247
Northern Ireland 395–482
 NI (Sentences) Bill 404
 NI Civil Rights Association (NICRA) 399
 NI Council on Disability 412
 NI no-confidence vote 405
 NI Peace Agreement (1998) 403
 NI Railways 62
 NI Tourist Board 43
 NI Women's Coalition 402
Northern Ireland
 NI Tourist Board
  Dublin 92
Northwest Ireland 344–393
nudity
 co-ed pilgrims 393
Nun Marry 450
nuns drinking Guinness 385

O

O'Casey, Sean 27, 107, 116
O'Connell, Daniel 113, 13, 115, 263, 288, 436
O'Connor, Rory 17, 117
O'Connor, Ruairi 332
O'Donnell, Daniel 373, 375
O'Donnell, Red Hugh 383
O'Driscoll clan 236
Co. Offaly 161, 165–168
ogham stones 8, 257, 265
O'Hara, Maureen 331
Oileán Chléir 237
Oldbridge 155
oldest
 church in Belfast 420
 functioning whiskey producer in the world 460
 harp in Ireland 110
 pub in Ireland 417, 432
Omagh 479–481
O'Malley, Grace 125, 334, 335, 336
Omeath 442
One Man's Pass 366
O'Neill clan 9, 387
O'Neill, Capt. Terence 399
O'Neill, Hugh 230, 383
O'Neill, Owen Roe 10
Operation Motorman 470
Orange Day (July 12) 397
Orange Hall 424
Orange Order 398
O'Shea, Kitty 136
Ossian's Grave 452
otters 381
Otto the bus driver 151
Oughterard 322
Ould Lammas Fair 457
outdoors 70
Oxford Island 447

P

packing 53
Paddy's 36
Paisley, Rev. Ian 399
parks. See forest parks.
Parnell, Charles Stewart 15, 115, 118, 136
Parnell's Cultural Nationalism 15
passage graves 7
passports 41
 lost 41
Peace Corps 81
peace line 423
Pearse, Padraig 16, 116, 324
Peatland World 147
Peatlands Park 447
Penal Laws 11
People's Democracy (PD) 399
Peter the Great 431, 432
Phoenix Park 91, 94
Phoenix Park Murders 15
Piccadilly Circus 490
pickpockets 51
Plantation 10
Poison Glen 376, 377
poitín 37
Pollatomish 339
Port 368
Portadown 402, 405, 427
Portaferry 433
Portavogie 432
Portlaoise 168
Portmagee 260
Portnablagh 379
Portrush 460–463
Portsalon 383
Portstewart 463
Poste Restante 72
Powers and Sons Irish Whiskey 36
Powerscourt Estate 131
Powerscourt Waterfall 131
Poynings' Law 10
Presbyterian Rebellion of 1803 436
President of Ireland 18
PRIDE 122
prostitution 284
Protestant Ascendancy 11
Provisional IRA 400
Provos 400
pub grub 34
pubs 34, 49
 northernmost in Ireland 392
 westernmost in Europe 269

Q

Queen Macha 443
Queen's University Belfast 410, 424
 study abroad 80
The Quiet Man 331

R

Raleigh Rent-A-Bike 65, 90, 291
Raleigh, Sir Walter 186, 228
Ramelton 382
Rannafast 375
The Rape of the Falls 423
Rathdrum 137
Rathlin Island 457
Rathmullan 383
Rebellion of 1798 436
Red Arch 450
Reenard Point 260
Regent's Park 491
Rerrin Village 245
Retail Export Scheme 49
Reynolds, Albert 20, 401
Ring of Gullion 427
Ring of Kerry 257–264
rivers
  Abbey 280
  Blackwater 185
  Boyne 150, 153
  Carrowbeg 333
  Cong 332
  Fergus 289
  Glenariff 449
  Inagh 295
  Inver 449
  Kenmare 257
  Lagan 410, 421
  Liffey 91
  Owenmore 341
  Owenrea 371
  Quoile 438
  Shannon 280, 353
  Strule 479
  Suir 182
road bowling 230
Roaring Meg 471
Robinson, Mary 21
Rock of Dunamase 168
Roonah Point 335
Roscommon 353
Roscrea 168
Roses of Tralee 275
Rosmuc 324
Ross Castle 256
Rossaveal 324
The Rosses 372–376
Rosslare Harbour 194–196
Rostrevor 443
round towers 8
Roundstone 323, 324
Roundstone Musical Instruments 324
Royal Dublin Horse Show 120
Royal Mail 487
Royal Ulster Constabulary (RUC) 398
Rue Point 458
Rushdie, Salman 125
Russborough House 143
Russell, Thomas 436
RVs 71
Ryan's Daughter 265, 268

S

St. Adjutor 193
St. Bride's Head 136
St. Brigid 145, 437
St. Canice 175
St. Colman 327
St. Columcille 437
St. Columba. See St. Columcille
St. Columcille 151, 352, 367, 368, 379, 380, 470
St. Connell 371
St. Declan 205
St. Dympna 336
St. Eunan 386
St. Fechin 162
St. Finian the Leper 256
St. John's Point 364
St. Kevin of Glendalough 137
St. Kevin of Inisheer 309
St. Louis 160
St. Macartan 160
St. Multose 232
St. Nessan 125
St. Oliver Plunkett 155, 162
St. Patrick 114, 136, 149, 335, 387, 437, 443, 445, 446, 452
  shrine 437
  burial 437
  preparing to banish snakes 335
  proving God 342
St. Patrick's Cathedral 114
St. Patrick's Day, Dublin 121
St. Patrick's Rock 180
St. Patrick's Vale 442
St. Stephen's Green 91
Saltee Islands 196, 197
Salthill 314, 316, 320
Samuel Kelly 431
Sands, Bobby 400, 423
Sandy Row 424
Saul 437
Sayers, Peig 26
Scattery Island 291
Schull 239–240
Schull Planetarium 240
Scotland 397
seals 458
seanachaí 36
Seanad 18, 111
security
  Northern Ireland 397
Seinfeld, Jerry 154
self-defense 50
Selskar Abbey 193
senior travelers 76
session houses 358
sexually transmitted diseases 52
Shandon and Emmet Place 221
Shankill 424
Shannon Airport 286
Shannon-Erne Waterway 475
Shaw, George Bernard 26, 111, 116, 130
Sheep Island 458
Sheep's Head 242
Sherkin Island 235, 237
Shillelagh 142
Shroove Strand 392
Siamsa Tíre Theatre 275
Sinn Féin 16, 17, 401
Sixmilebridge 285
The Skellig Rocks 261
Skibbereen 234–235
Slea Head 268
Slí Charman 187
Slieve Bloom Mountains 167
Slieve Donard 441
Slieve Foy 158
Slieve Gullion 427
Slieve Leage 366
Slieve League Peninsula 364–366
Slieve Mish Mountains 271
Slieve Miskish Mountains 241
Slieve Patrick 437
Slievemore Mountain 338
Co. Sligo 344–353
Sligo 344–351
Sligo Bay 344
sliothar 34
The Slobs 194
smallest
  bar in Europe 452

book in the world 180
  enclosed harbor in Ireland 377
snakes
  nope 335
  uh-uh 70
Sneem 264
Social Democratic and Labor Party (SDLP) 400
sodium glycerophosphate 445
solo travel 76
South Connemara 324
Southeast Ireland 170–210
Southwest Ireland 211–276
spas
  Kilcullen's Bath House 341
speed limits 63
Sperrin Mountains 481
Spiddal 324
sports 33
  camogie 15, 120
  Croke Park 119
  dog racing 120
  Dublin 120
  football 33
  Gaelic football 15, 34, 120, 222, 274
  horse racing 120
  hurling 15, 120, 222
  Irish Derby 147
  rugby 120
  soccer 222
St. Aiden's Cathedral 190
STA Travel 57, 62
Staigue Fort 263
Station Island 363
Statutes of Kilkenny 9
Stena Line 60
Stephens, James 14
Stoker, Bram 112
stone circles 7
Stormont 398
Stradbally 271
Strandhill Peninsula 351
Strangford 434
Strawberry Fair 190
Strokestown 355
Strongbow 9, 113
Struell Wells 437
studying abroad 79
Sugarloaf Hill 185
sunniest spot in Ireland 391
Swift, Jonathan 11, 25, 109, 114, 116, 163, 233, 436, 445, 446
  park 163
Synge, John Millington 27, 119, 305, 308, 338

T

Table of the Giants 341
Táin bo Cuailnge 24
Tamney 384
Tánaiste 18
Taoiseach 18
Tarbert 289
Tate Gallery
  Britain 492
  Modern 492
taxes 49, 50
Tearaght 269
Teelin 366
telephone codes 37
Temple Bar 91, 100, 113
terrorism 49
Thatcher, Margaret 401
The 1994 Ceasefire 401
Theatre Royal 194
theft 51
Thomas, Dylan 368
Thomastown 176
Thoor Ballylee 302, 303
ticks 52
Tievebulliagh Mountain 452
Tieveragh Hill 452
time zones 494
tin whistle 30
Tinahely 142
Co. Tipperary 168, 178–185
Tipperary Town 178
tipping 49
Titanic 226
  blueprints 427
  building of 420
  Leo 227, 283, 367
  sculpture commemorating 419
Tobercurry 341
Tor 376
Torr Head 453
Tory Island 378
Tower House 302
Tower of London 491
trad 29
traditional music. See trad
Trafalgar Square 490
trails
  Beara Way 241
  Belvedere Trail 163
  Dingle Way 265
  Fore Trail 162
  Inishmaan Way 308
  Kerry Way 255
  Killarney National Park 254
  Kingfisher Bike Trail 475
  Lough Derg Way 284
  Moyle Way 449
  Munster Way 183
  Slí Charman 187
  Ulster Way 449, 482
  Waterfall Trail 449
  Western Way 324
  Wicklow Way 141
trains 62
Tralee 271–276
Tramore 201
transportation
  bicycles 64
  cars 62
  mopeds and motorcycles 64
travel agencies 55
traveler's checks 45
  lost or stolen 45
traveling safely 50
TravelSave stamps 43, 62, 216, 280, 314, 411, 468
Treaty of Limerick 11
Trim 150, 151
Trimble, David 402
Trinity College Dublin 11, 12, 79, 91, 109
Trinity College University Philosophical Society 110
Trinity College Walking Tour 108
The Troubles 399
Túatha de Danann 24
Tully Cross 329
Turrell, James 235
Twelve Bens 323, 329
Co. Tyrone 479–482
Tyrone 478

U

U2 274
Uí Néill (O'Neill) clan 9
uilleann 30
Ulaid of Ulster 24, 447
Ulster 1, 397
Ulster American Folk Park 480
Ulster Cycle 24, 376
Ulster Folk & Transport Museum 426
Ulster History Park 480

INDEX ■ 511

Ulster Plantation 397
Ulster Protestant Volunteers (UPV) 399
Ulster Unionist Party (UUP) 402
Ulster Volunteer Force (UVF) 16, 398
Ulster Way 65, 449
Ulsterbus 61
Ulysses 28, 120, 125, 128
  map of Dublin 107
  primer 129
Union Hall 233
Unionists 397
United Irishmen 13, 129
University College Cork 222
University College Dublin 79
University College Galway 79
Urris 389
US Consulate General Northern Ireland 411

V
Valentia Island 260
valuables, protecting 50
vanishing lakes
  Carron 299
  Loughareema 453
vegetarians 79
Ventry 269
Victoria 391
  consort of 421
Vikings 9
Vinegar Hill 13, 188, 189
Visa 47
Volunteer 81

W
War of Independence 213
Warrenpoint 442
waterfalls
  Powers Court 138
Waterfoot 449
Co. Waterford 187, 200-210
Waterford 205
Waterford 205-210
Waterford Harbour 198
Waterville 262
Wayne, Gregory 72
Wayne, John 331, 434
weather 2, 494
West Belfast 410
West Cork 228-240
West Inishowen 389-390
West Waterford Vineyards 186
Western Cork City 222
Western Ireland 277-343
Western Union 48
Western Wicklow 143
Westgate Heritage Centre 193
Co. Westmeath 161-165
Westminster Abbey 491
Westport 332-335
Co. Wexford 187-200
Wexford Arts Centre 193
Wexford City 190-194
Wexford County Museum 189
Wexford Festival Opera 194
wheelchair accessible hostels
  Avalon House, Dublin 95
  Barnacle's Viking House, Waterford 207
  Broad St. Hostel, Limerick 281
  Campbells, Ardara 371
  Carraig Donn, Wexford 192
  Castlepark Marina Centre, Kinsale 231
  Clonakilty Hostel, Clonakilty 232
  Collis-Sandes House 273
  Corofin Village Hostel and Camping Park, Corofin 289
  Dooey Hostel, Glencolmcille 367
  Dublin International Youth Hostel, Dublin 96
  Dungarvan Holiday Hostel 203
  Farren House, Ballacolla 167
  Glendaloch Hostel, Glendalough 139
  Great Western House, Galway 316
  Jacobs Inn, Dublin 95
  Kilrush Creek Lodge 291
  Kinlay House, Galway 316
  Lough Ree Lodge, Athlone 164
  Luane Valley Farm Hostel, Killorglin 258
  Magee College, Derry 469
  Maria's Schoolhouse, Union Hall 233
Oakgrove Manor 468
Old Presbytery Hostel, Rathdrum 137
Peacock Farms, Killarney 253
Platform 1, Enniscorthy 188
Portaferry Barholm Youth Hostel 433
Sheep Island View Hostel, Ballintoy 459
Westward Court, Tralee 273
YHANI, Belfast 413
Whiddy Island 242
whiskey
  a guide to 226
  Bushmills 460
  Irish 36
whisky 36, 226
Whitepark Bay 459
Co. Wicklow 133-145
Wicklow 141
Wicklow Coast 133-138
Wicklow Mountains 138-143
Wicklow town 135
Wicklow Way 65, 141
Wilde, Oscar 26, 109, 116
  quotes and apocryphy 332
wilderness 72
William of Orange 11, 398, 425, 470, 471, 472
wishes
  fulfilling 378
witchcraft 130
Wolfe Tone, Theobald 13, 342, 383
women travelers 75
  health 53
work 80
World Wide Web 81
Wyndham Land Purchase Act 15

Y
Yeats, William Butler 14, 27, 116, 119, 125, 302, 305, 344, 352, 452
yellow-man 457
Youghal 227

Z
There is nothing starting with Z in this book.

www.lowealpine.com

If I had my life to live over again,

I would relax. I would limber up. I would take more chances.

I would take more trips.

I would climb more mountains, swim more rivers, and watch more sunsets.

I would go places and do things and travel lighter than I have.

I would ride more merry-go-rounds.

Excerpt from Nadine Stair, 85 years old / photo> John Norris

Lowe alpine

technical packs & apparel

Find Yourself. Somewhere Else.

Don't just land there, do something. Away.com is the Internet's preferred address for those who like their travel with a little something extra. Our team of travel enthusiasts and experts can help you design your ultimate adventure, nature or cultural escape. Make Away.com your destination for extraordinary travel. Then find yourself. Somewhere else.

away.com
1.877.769.2929

Will you have enough stories to tell your grandchildren?

Yahoo! Travel

Do You Yahoo!?

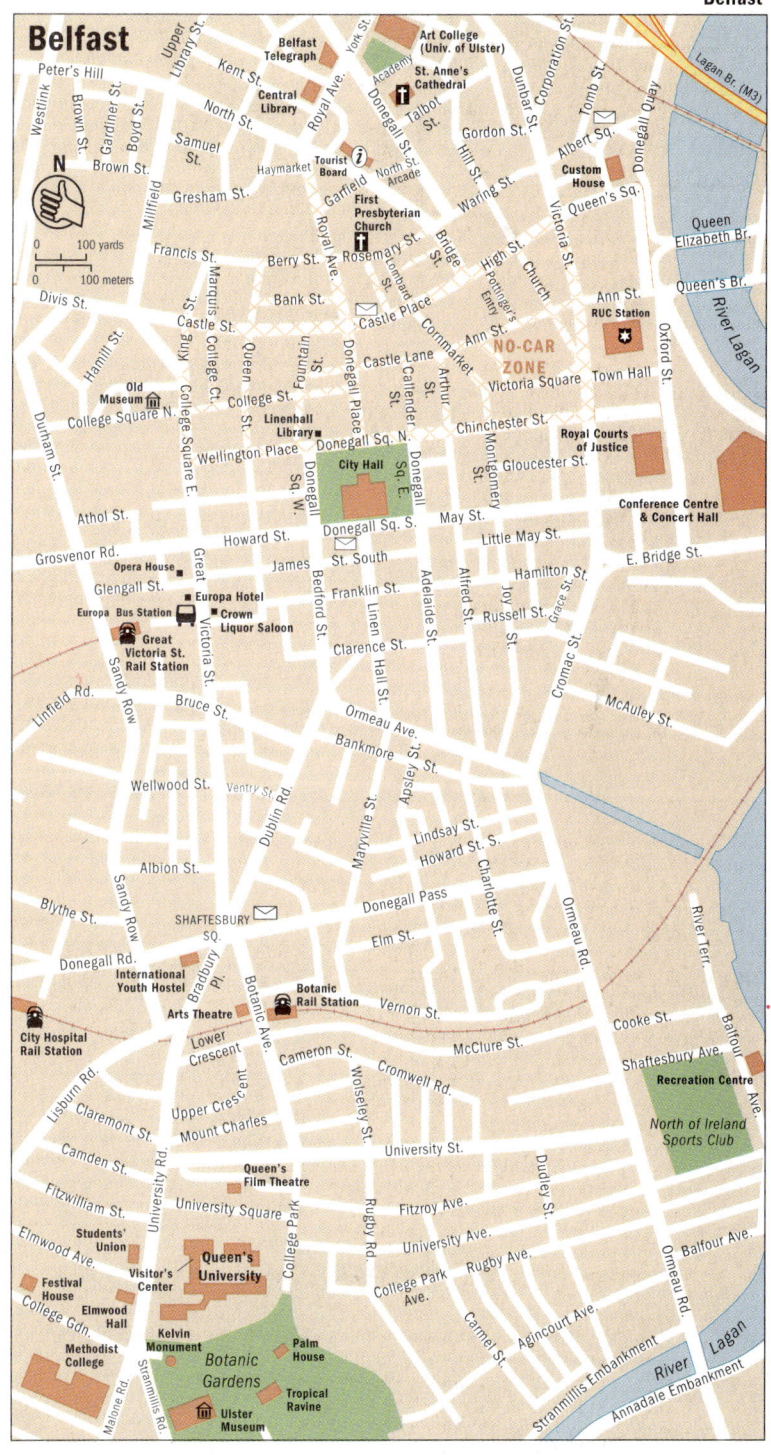

Belfast

Dublin

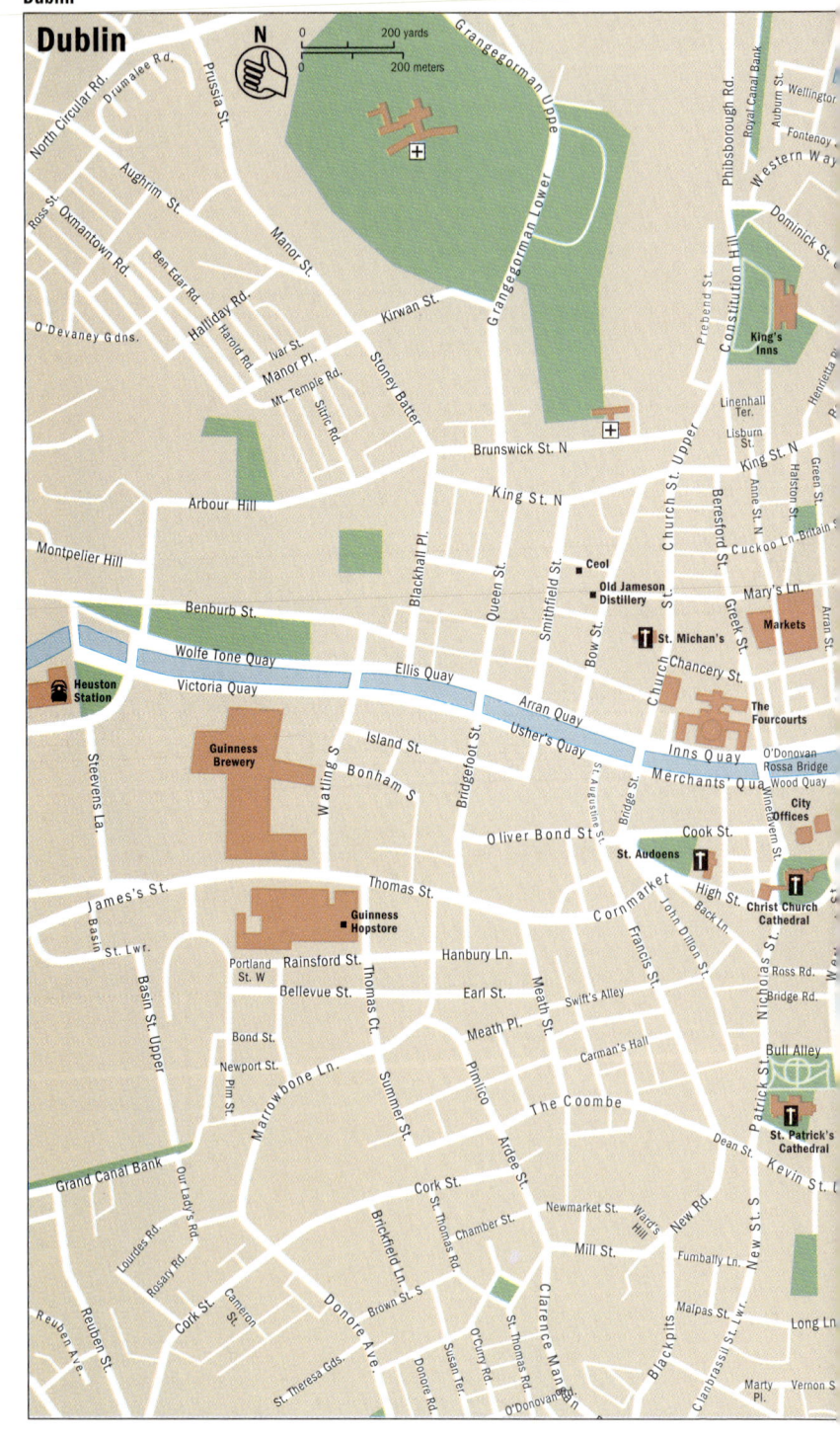

Dublin

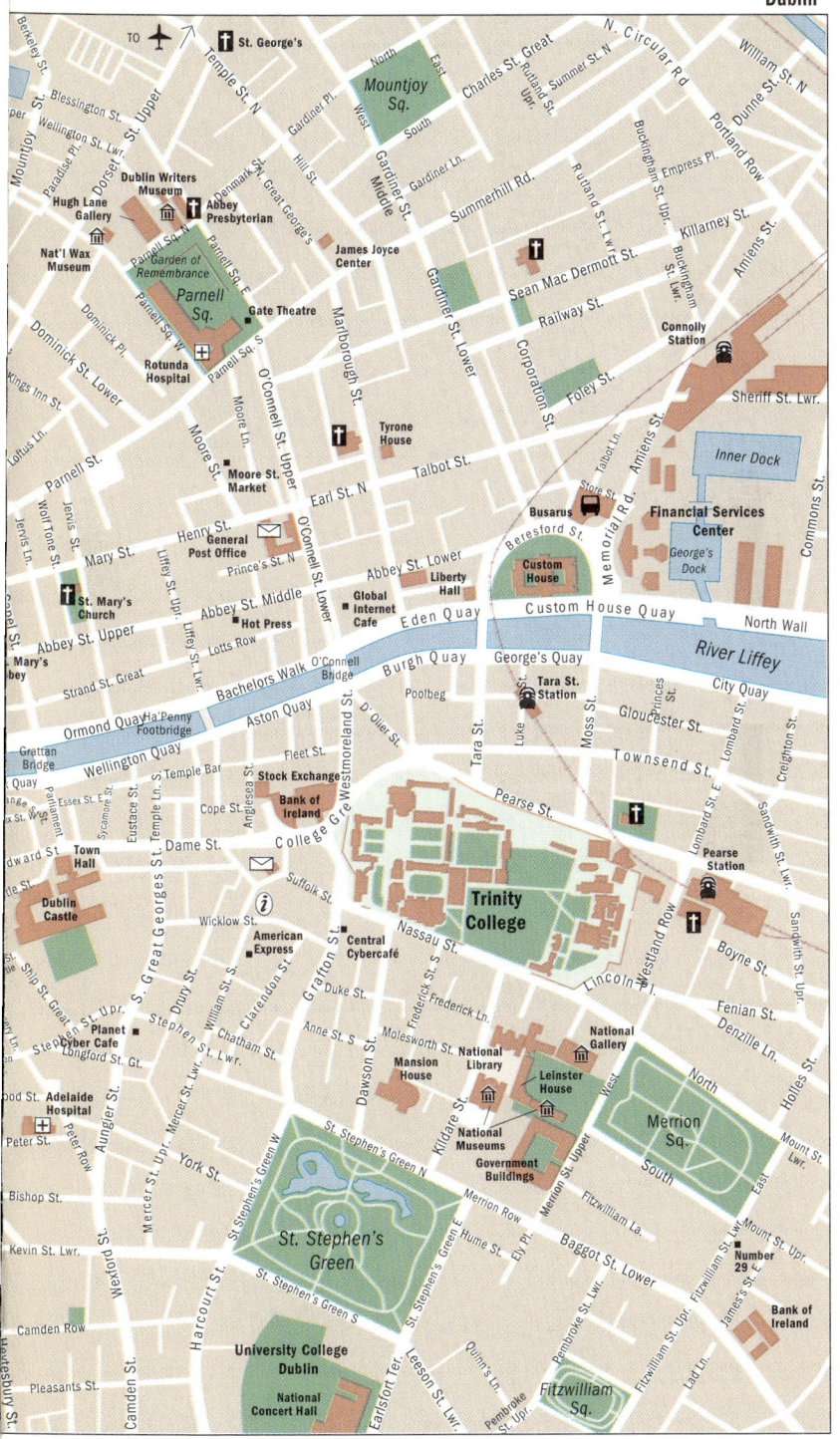

Cork and Galway

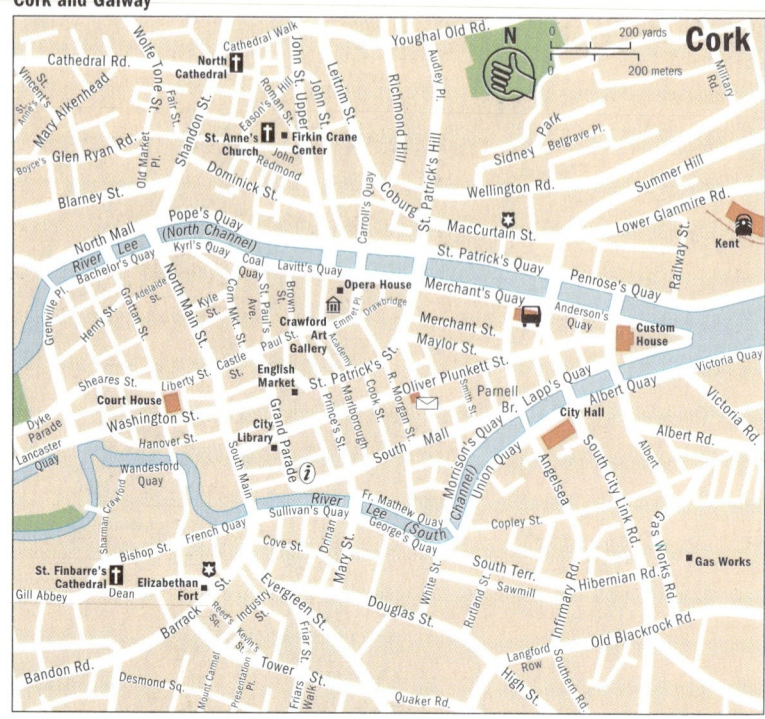

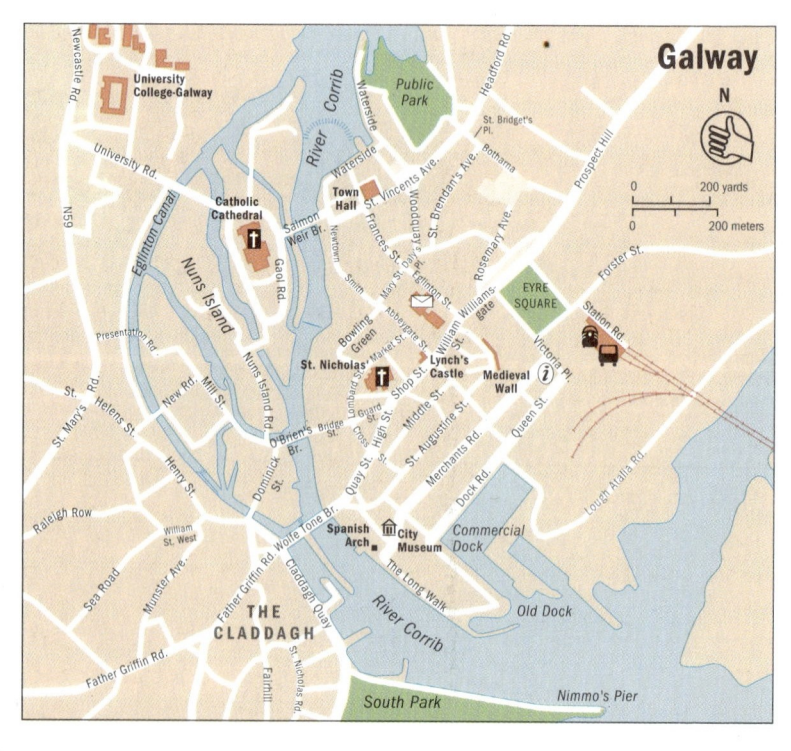